The Definitive History of World Championship Boxing
Junior Welterweight to Middleweight
By Barry J. Hugman

Published by G2 Entertainment Ltd
© Barry J. Hugman 2016

G2 entertainment

Author: Barry J. Hugman
http://tiny.cc/2r16gy
Editor: Sean Willis
Cover Design: Paul Briggs (twocan.co.uk)
Publishers: Edward Adams and Jules Gammond
Printed in the UK & USA

Contents

Acknowledgements

I dedicate this work to my Mother and Father who gave me an excellent start in life. It was this that enabled me to pursue my dreams, one of them being boxing, both inside and outside the ring.

After working on this project since the late 1980s and having quickly realised that listings of world title fights did not add up in many cases, I have decided to go into print and set the record straight. It has been a mammoth task, and one which I couldn't have achieved on my own.

Once I had analysed the work of Harold Alderman MBE, who has made a 60-year study of British boxing and had recorded much of what he found, I realised that this was the missing piece of the jigsaw. Harold is *the* foremost expert on English championship boxing which took place between 1870 and 1909. He is also a walking mine of boxing information, having been involved in the sport for as long as he can remember. As a young schoolboy boxer he had aspirations of eventually turning pro, but unfortunately poor eyesight meant that he had to give the game up. A longstanding member of London Ex-Boxers' Association and other ex-boxers' associations, as well as being a member of the American-based International Boxing Records Organisation, over the years he has also helped family members with information relating to their boxing fathers.

I first met Sean Willis, a passionate editor of sports books as well as occasional author, towards the end of 2015 at which point I shared the outline of this labour of love with him. He embraced my vision and has worked alongside myself, tirelessly and enthusiastically for many months in editing this unique and comprehensive boxing tome, without once throwing the towel in.

Tracy Callis, of the International Boxing Record Organisation, has helped no end with information on the heavyweight and middleweight divisions, especially 'black titles', and is a hugely valued researcher.

Luckett Davis, who is recognised as one of the leading record compilers and co-ordinators in America, gave me much help in having a greater understanding of how boxing was in the early days in America providing key data prior to my many visits to American libraries in the 1990s.

John Sheppard, of BoxRec (boxrec.com), also deserves a big thank you for setting up a website totally immersed in boxers' records, both past and present. With it expanding by the minute it has become the largest boxing website in the world and is used by all involved in the sport as well as those who have an interest. In short, anyone who reads this must make a point of visiting it.

Other people who have helped in no small way include those listed below:

Mike Attree	Charles Johnston	David Roake
Paul Baumgartner	Ove Jonassen	Hy Rosenberg
Joseph Brower	Ric Kilmer	John Sheppard
Les Clark	Jack Kincaid	Ron Silverberg
Mike Delisa	Joe Koizumi	Kevin Smith
Mike Featherstone	Tim Leone	Bob Soderman
Christer Franzen	Ruth Lewis	Mike Sweeney
Tony Gee	Arne Leyenberg	Matt Tegan
Herb Goldman	Andrew Lindsay	Miles Templeton
Jose Luis Gomez Camarillo	Bill Matthews	Daniel Van de Wiele
Elio Guzman	Derek O'Dell	Bob Yalen
Peter Hatton	Perry Palumbo	Robert Young
John Hogg	Jeffrey Pamungkas	Paul Zabala
Jennifer Hugman	Gary Phillips	
Raymond Hugman	John Redfern	

Jean Adkins & Sherie Brown (Massillon Public Library)
Mary Beveridge (Missouri Valley Special Collections)
Don Bonsteel (Enoch Pratt Free Library, Baltimore)
Mary Piero Carey (Stark County District Library, Canton, Ohio)
Linda Chapman (Allen County Public Library, Indiana)
Janice Collins (West Palm Beach Public Library)
Marc D'Houre/Wim De Troyer (Bibliotheque Royal de Belgique)
Debra Dixon (San Diego LB, California)
Terri Dood (Bozeman Public Library)
Anna Fahey-Flynn and Patricia Feeley (Boston Public Library)
Wendy Flourno (Library of Michigan)
Natalie Fritz (Clark County Historical Society)
Ellen Gamache, Katie Quinn, Virginia Marcellus (Albany Public Library)
Michael Gillman (Sacramento Public Library)
Varney Greene (Buffalo & Erie County Public Library)
Cathy Hackett (Clark County Public Library, Springfield, Ohio)
Richard Hill (State Library of Pennsylvania)
Lynn Humphries (Sheffield Central Library, UK)
Judy James (Akron Public Library)
Cara Janowski (New York State Library)
Paula Kepich (Carnegie Library)
June Kofi (Brooklyn Public Library)
Katherine LaBarbera & Gayle Camarda (St Louis Public Library)
Ronald Lee (Tennessee State Library)
Lauren Leeman (State Historical Society of Missouri)
Bonnie Linck & Marcia Matika (Connecticut State Library)
Margot McCain (Portland Public Library)
Sara McKinley (Muncie Public Library)
Bill Markley (Georgia Historical Society)
Janet Meek (Indiana State Library)
Michelle Mellor (Youngstown Public Library)
David Mook (Sioux City Public Library)
Karen Myers (Mullins Library)
Phil Panum (Denver Public Library)
Gloriane Peck (Library of Michigan)
Ann Poulos & Mark Sweberg (Providence Public Library)
Janice Prater (Denver Public Library)
Marianne Reynolds & Arlene Belletire (Cincinnati Public Library)
Hope Rider (Arkansas State Library)
Jeanne Sanchez (Wyoming State Public Library)
John Sheppard (BoxRec.com)
Dr Skelton-Foord & Brian Hough (British Newspaper Library)
David Smith (New York Public Library)
Hampton Smith (Minnesota Historical Society)
Sarah Striner, Georgie Higley & Frank Carroll (Library of Congress, Washington DC)
Louise Talbott (Akron-Summit County Public Library)
Pat Watson (New Britain Public Library)
Melissa Williams & Sally Freaney (Public Library of Youngstown & Mahoning County)
Melissa Whitesell (Terre Haute Public Library)
Julie Zachau (Superior Public Library)

Introduction

Having spent many years researching the history of world championship boxing from the start of gloves (1871 to date), I am delighted to present my extensive findings in the shape of these four volumes.

The Definitive History of World Championship Boxing - Mini Fly to Bantam.
The Definitive History of World Championship Boxing - Junior Feather to Light.
The Definitive History of World Championship Boxing - Junior Welter to Middle.
The Definitive History of World Championship Boxing - Super Middle to Heavy.

This work came about due to limited information on world title fights being available when I was growing up, it becoming clearer to me each year that the record books of the day were merely scratching the surface. After discovering that boxing with gloves had started in Britain I could not understand why the majority of fights happened in America according to the record books, especially as some of the great fighters of the 1880s fighting in America were born in Britain, such as Nonpareil Jack Dempsey and Jack McAuliffe. I was already convinced that many of the contests recorded in the listings prior to the early 1900s were American title bouts only. Thus I began my research.

Years later, as the editor of the British Boxing Board of Control (BBBoC) British Boxing Yearbook, I was introduced to Harold Alderman MBE who told me that, starting in the 1960s, he had documented all of the contests of note that had taken place in Britain since the early 1870s. I had already done much research of my own on boxing in Britain, Europe, the Commonwealth and America, visiting many libraries around the world, and Harold's input was the missing link. Once the British (then known as the English) championship contests, winners and claimants at every two pounds had been built in everything came together.

Wherever possible, all of the leading fighters down the years since the early 1870s have had their known records analysed and cross referenced against thousands of newspapers and magazines in order to find the weight that their prime contests were made at. This exercise also led to many more claimants and contests being discovered.

There is a fight summary for all of the championship contests that are listed within these pages. All are shown in chronological order within their respective weight divisions by date, weight, result, scheduled rounds, venue, recognition, referee (if known) and scorecards. In the days leading up to 'modern day' boxing, when there were fewer recognised weight divisions and therefore a wider range of weights within each division, I have detailed the stipulated fight weight (shown in brackets) after the fight date. Therefore there are many 'claimants' at varying weights within each division at any given time. From thereon in use 'Recognition' to follow the body in question's champions, as well as relative information. Because the term 'Junior' was the original name used to determine recently added weight divisions, I have continued in that vein rather than using the term 'Super'.

Historical Background

After going from 'bare-knuckle fighting' under London Prize Ring Rules to 'boxing with gloves' under Marquess of Queensberry Rules (MoQ Rules), the sport of boxing gradually found its way to North America and Australia by the 1880s. The Marquess of Queensberry Rules had been established in 1867, whilst London Prize Ring Rules were developed in 1838 by the London-based Pugilistic Society, being revised in 1853 and 1866. They had replaced the Broughton's Rules of 1743.

While hard and skin-tight gloves were more often than not used in America prior to the 1890s, in Britain it was far more acceptable, especially in clubs, to use gloves weighing no less than two ounces and up to eight ounces right from the beginning. Bare-knuckle fights are not covered within these pages.

Some of the men who were classified as champions in the days before proper regulation are now viewed as 'claimants', unless stated otherwise, as they were not officially recognised and gained their reputation purely through newspaper support. You only have to view the number of men claiming a title at the same weight at the same time to see the chaos. Even in America it was difficult to decide on a champion, and much of what has been printed in the following years has been selective to make things look black and white. On top of that the main men in Britain, who rarely met their American counterparts due to the amount of travelling required, had as much right to claim the British version of the world title if the fights could not be made. Because of this I have shown many of the English championship winners and claimants as having a share of the world title prior to the National Sporting Club (NSC) introducing the eight named weight divisions on 11 February 1909. With the English championships being phased out from that date, from thereon in only men recognised throughout Britain as having a strong claim to the world title are recorded.

In the early part of the 20th Century in much of America, when no-decision and short distance bouts kept boxing alive due to those of endurance being banned, because it was impossible to know whether a title claimant was contractually protected or not I have gone with the weights shown in the press. In those days contractual conditions would barely have mattered if a claimant was beaten inside the distance. A good example of this came when George Chip claimed the American version of the world middleweight title in 1913 after twice stopping Frank Klaus in six-round no-decision contests, despite neither man weighing inside the generally accepted American middleweight limit of 158lbs.

At the start of gloved fighting although certain named weight classes were already recognised, such as bantam, feather, light, middle and heavy, men in Britain generally claimed what was then known as the English title at every two pounds within those loosely defined weight bands. Welter (1887) was the next to arrive followed by light heavy (1899) and fly (1909), prior to junior light (1921), junior welter (1923), junior middle (1962), junior fly (1975), junior feather (1976), cruiser (1979), junior bantam (1980), super middle (1984) and mini fly (1987) becoming established at later dates.

Because there were many variations in the weight limits between Britain and America in the early days, I have gone with what was generally perceived by those running the sport in Britain at the start of boxing - bantam (116lbs), Feather (126lbs), Light (140lbs), Middle (166lbs) and Heavy (166lbs+). The middleweight limit of 166lbs includes those fighting at catchweights between 160 and 166lbs who were too small for the heavyweights. With the advent of new weight classes, and in certain cases where great fighters moved up in weight and were seen by the majority of the press to have taken their named title with them, as in the case of Young Corbett at featherweight, I have massaged the weight divisions accordingly until we enter the modern era.

In hastening the demise of the every two-pounds English championships, on 11 February 1909 the NSC in London stipulated that there should be eight named weight classes governing British boxing - Fly (112lbs), Bantam (118lbs), Feather (126lbs), Light (135lbs), Welter (147lbs), Middle (160lbs), Light heavy (175lbs) and Heavy (175lbs+). With fights held in Britain, the British Empire and Europe, I have gone with those weights from that date. For the same period, and falling in line with those running boxing in America, I have taken the American weight classes to be 116lbs for Bantam, 122lbs for Feather, 133lbs for Light, 142/145lbs for Welter and 158lbs for Middle. By 1920 all the weight class limits had been standardised and are reflected as such within the listings.

With regard to weights in the days before tighter regulation, without contractual knowledge I have gone with what was reported in newspapers. In many cases I discovered that fighters weighed-in according to contract and that the weights announced were those at ringside, which would, in most cases, have been heavier. This has made it extremely difficult to ascertain whether title claims were on the line or not. However, when in doubt I have built those fights into the text. In America at the early part of the 20th Century, especially in New York, weights reported were nearly always those taken at ringside immediately prior to the fight. I have ignored those weights if contracts called for a stipulated weigh-in time.

Fight Summary and General Text

Reports on all selected fights are given, using at least two different newspapers in order to eradicate inaccuracies. I have used many miscellaneous worldwide newspapers since 1871, including Britain's *Sporting Life* and *Mirror of Life*, and more recently *Boxing News* and *The Ring* magazine. The internet's *YouTube* was more than useful when trying to find better information, even for some fights that took place years ago. Using a précis format I have tried to give one a general idea of how any fight in question went in general, as well as mentioning cut eyes, knockdowns and stance, if a southpaw. I have also tried to produce it in a way that fight fans readily understand.

All title fights involving 'second tier' (called 'regular' champions by commissions who have got a 'super' champion in place) and 'interim' champions are shown within the text. For my purposes, 'super' champions take precedence over 'second tier' champions for obvious reasons. Details regarding those handed 'emeritus' status, which is a lifetime award issued by the WBC to top-class champions who are retiring or cannot defend their title for whatever reason, are also shown in the text. If such a champion returns to the ring he may request an immediate challenge to a WBC world champion without first boxing in an elimination contest. The WBA's term 'champion in recess' effectively serves the same purpose. Where an 'interim' champion moves on to contest the main title the 'interim' title is automatically declared vacant.

If the IBF, WBA, WBC or WBO fail to accept a title fight for whatever reason but continue to recognise the champion involved, I have left the general status intact while making note of their reasoning within the text. This tends to happen when a challenger is not seen as a worthy opponent. If a title changes hands under these circumstances the body concerned would either recognise the winner or declare their portion of the title vacant.

Fights of less than ten rounds duration, including no-decision affairs, are not included as championship contests, other than when a title claim changed hands. They are, however, shown within the text where a risk is involved, which would have come about when a claimant allowed his opponent to make the weight that he was claiming a title at, whether he did so or not. Also shown in the text, are 'black title' fights, politics, fights leading to championship bouts where applicable, eliminators, and information for all champions who forfeited or relinquished their titles or claims.

The term 'modern day boxing' used within these pages relates to when weights in all weight divisions other than heavyweight were standardised, ie 1920. Regarding the heavyweight division, I have taken the Jack Johnson v Tommy Burns fight in 1908 to be the first of the modern era, as it was the first time a black man fought for what was generally recognised by the great majority as the World title.

'Black title' bouts are shown specifically because of the 'Colour Bar' being in place in America at the start of boxing. Not only did many States ban mixed matches, but many 'white champions' used it as an excuse to avoid meeting top black fighters. However, despite black champions and their 'title fights' not being officially recognised in the United States I have included instances of fights and boxers that warrant mention on the grounds of the undoubted abilities of the black boxers concerned, who were never given the chance to officially prove their skills and prowess in the ring against white opponents. A great number of black men suffered, which was exacerbated during and after Jack Johnson's title reign, and it was not until Joe Louis became heavyweight champion that things began to settle down and laws changed. Even in the 1940s there were 'black title' fights, but these champions were not ignored as in the past.

English championship tournaments, normally contested between three and six rounds, along with other tournaments where a title claim emanated from the winner are spelt out within the text. It was boxing in this format that allowed matches to take place in Britain prior to the 1900s when finish fights were deemed to be illegal. Many of these tournaments were governed by Amateur Boxing Association (ABA) rules, and because there were so many contests involved I have selected those that backed up leading fighters' claims.

Additional contests and other data, including dates by day/month, that have been built into the text of a title fight belong to the same year and the same weight unless stated otherwise.

Also built into the text are all the top-five rated fighters according to *The Ring* magazine rankings between May 1928 and March 1989 who do not show up in championship contests. I have not gone beyond that date due to there being four world organisations in operation from that time onwards, thus giving more opportunities to fighters.

Because I have built all ongoing information appertaining to the champion and body/bodies concerned into the text, follow the applicable 'Recognition' for continuity.

Weights

The weight at which fights were contracted at fall into two categories within these pages, those that were contested prior to what I classify modern day boxing and those that followed. Within each weight division the weight that the contest was made at is shown in brackets immediately following the date, and when the modern day era is reached there is an explanatory note.

Individual weights for both fighters are given, if published, and are shown (in pounds) alongside the fighter's name. Where the figure is the same as the limit it could be that the men in question came in exactly on the weight or that the officials declared that both men were inside, but failed to announce the exact individual weights. Also, on occasion, the weights were reported in the press to the nearest pound and that is what we have shown.

In the no-decision era of boxing in America many of the weights reported were those taken at ringside immediately prior to the contest taking place, but in some cases those weights have been ignored if contractual conditions called for an earlier weigh-in that both fighters adhered to. Where known weighing-in times are reported.

Results

Here are the abbreviations used within these pages to describe results of contests:

CO - Count Out. Often given as a knockout, it involves a fighter being counted over up to 'ten' seconds before getting into a standing position. Over the years many record books have listed stoppages, retirements and knockouts under the heading of KO. All results within these pages are broken down separately.

DISQ - Disqualification.

DREW - In the early days of boxing, especially in America, it was agreed in some fights that if both men were still standing at the end of the contest a draw should be given, regardless. Draws were also given on occasion after the police stopped a contest. In more recent times draws have given either by a sole arbiter or by three judges, which is the current situation.

NC - No Contest. It includes contests that were stopped due to neither man giving of his best, police interference, and if both men are fighting outside the rules. Such a decision can also be made at a later stage if a fighter fails a drugs test, etc.

ND - No Decision. For the first 30 odd years of the 1900s many States in America allowed no-decision contests to take place, enabling boxing to carry on by bending the rules after government officials had decided that only exhibition bouts were legal. Although a referee was in place to make sure that the rules were not broken, he could not give a decision apart from counting out, disqualifying, or stopping a fighter from carrying on. For betting purposes, one of the ways of getting around the situation when a fight went the full distance was by allowing pressmen representing three named local newspapers to give a decision that would be reported the next day. For example, nd-w pts 10 would determine a press win for one of the fighters if at least two of the selected papers had him winning. Because this was not a perfect system as one does not know which three papers were selected at the time, I have gone with three different local newspaper reports. This, at least, gives one an idea of who was the better man on the night even if it does not always agree with what others might have recorded.

PTS - Points. Fights can won on points unanimously (all three judges in favour of one man), by a majority (two judges for one man and the other calling a draw) or on a split decision (two judges for one man and one against).

RSC - Referee Stopped Contest. Sometimes recorded elsewhere as referee stopped fight, the term also includes a situation where one of the fighters is probably going to be counted out but the referee discards or discontinues the count as to allow treatment to be given. Unfortunately, many stoppages came about when a fighter's injuries were too bad for him to continue even if he was ahead on points at the time. This has been partly rectified by the use of technical decisions. Another way a fighter can be stopped from continuing is if he is knocked down three times in a round and the 'Three Knockdown' rule is in place.

RTD - Retired. A retirement is recorded when the decision is made by his corner rather than by the referee, during the interval between rounds. Retirements also used to take place if the corner threw the towel or sponge into the ring while the contest was ongoing, but more recently stoppages in mid-round can only be made by the referee. Because it is too difficult to know which countries/states allowed mid-round retirements to take place I have gone with the term 'referee stopped contest' (rsc) from 1920 onwards after the New York State Athletic Commission (NY/NYSAC) was restructured and the National Boxing Association (NBA) was formed. If a towel was thrown in prior to the stoppage it will be reported in the text.

TDEC - Technical Decision. Where a contest goes beyond four rounds - previously three and six, dependent on the body - and is stopped due to an accidental injury to one of the fighters.

TDRAW - Technical Draw. The term denotes that a contest has been stopped due to an accidental injury in a round deemed to be too early in the contest to go to the scorecards. At present all the main bodies agree on it being prior to the fifth round.

Scheduled Rounds

Shown after the result in brackets, it includes all fights that were contested above ten rounds and those where a claimant lost his title claim in a six or eight round no-decision contest. When the scheduled rounds become standardised across the world of boxing in the late 1980s the brackets disappear. At the beginning of boxing many contests were made to a finish, and are shown as such, but as boxing progressed the rounds decreased in line with common sense and safety. In the early part of the 20th Century it was commonplace to have 45 rounds for a championship fight, but gradually 20 rounds, then 15, and now 12 became the standard.

Venues

In earlier times many fights were not reported locally due to the fact that they were illegal, and because of this we have limited details. However, where known, the venues are spelt out in English. This has been standardised because a high percentage of foreign venues are more often than not reported in English.

AC - Athletic Club
SC - Sporting Club

Recognition

Prior to boxers receiving general recognition from established bodies within the sport, those shown within these pages without it should be seen as claimants. Things really got going in America when the New York State Athletic Commission (NY/NYSAC) legalised boxing in New York with the passing of Walker Law in 1920 and the National Boxing Association (NBA) was set up in 1921, the latter body being formed to protect States who were not aligned to the NYSAC or were not independent, such as California. In Europe the International Boxing Union (IBU) had been formed in 1911 to bond European nations together, while after the Great War those involved in boxing in Britain had a working agreement that would eventually see all parties concerned signing up to form the British Boxing Board of Control (BBBoC) in 1929. Although there was an on-off relationship between the IBU and the BBBoC during the early days, in 1946 all countries in Europe, including Britain, became members of the newly formed European Boxing Union (EBU). Recognition from Great Britain alone is shown as GB, while Hawaiian recognition comes under Territorial Boxing Commission (TBC).

Despite there being several attempts to create a workable World Boxing Commission it never properly came to fruition due to the stance taken by the NYSAC, who deemed that they were only empowered to deal with boxing in New York. Eventually, after many attempts to set up one body the NBA reorganised themselves in August 1962 and were renamed as the World Boxing Association (WBA), while in February 1963 the World Boxing Council (WBC) was formed, with the NYSAC still isolating themselves. In 1983 a breakaway group from the WBA set themselves up, initially as the United States Boxing Association/International (USBA/I) and then as the International Boxing Federation (IBF). Then, in 1989, the World Boxing Organisation (WBO) was formed by another group of disaffected former WBA members. Although there are several other organisations purporting to be world bodies, the above mentioned groups are the only ones given credit within these pages other than *The Ring* magazine champions since December 2001. Men holding *The Ring* Championship Belt should be considered as the most worthy of champions, whilst men shown with World recognition are those who are supported by all the main bodies.

Scorecards

Where known, scores listed only apply to fights going the full distance or those that require a technical decision. Many early contests and some more recently used a referee only to decide a winner. Not only that, but they did not make their scorecards available to the outside world. Prior to the current 'ten-point must' ruling, other scoring methods that have also been used at various times include the 'five-point must', the 'one-point' system, and by rounds. The 'five-point must' ruling allowed for the winning fighter to be given five points and the loser four or less, while the 'one-point' system saw the winning fighter awarded one or more points and the losing fighter zero. The most simple way of scoring was the one in which the round was awarded to the winning fighter. More recently, judges have used the 'ten-point' must system, which assigns ten points to the winner of each round, whilst the loser receives nine. When a fighter is knocked down (or in some cases outclassed) he will receive eight points or seven if he is floored twice. On occasion both men can receive ten points if they are deemed equal, and if and when both are knocked down the same amount of times during the round the knockdowns are disregarded. At the end of the contest, the boxer with the most accumulated points is the winner as long as two of the three judges are in agreement.

Boxers' Index

At the end of each weight division is an alphabetical listing of boxers mentioned within that section. Boxers belonging to a different weight division are shown elsewhere. They are all shown by: country of birth (where known)/Domicile. Other than some of those boxing in America prior to the modern era birthplace and domicile are the same unless stated. If the names of countries have changed, the modern adaptation is used. Although Hawaii and Alaska became American States in 1959 they are shown among the listings as separate countries. Out of interest, Ireland was part of the United Kingdom until 1922. Also, where two fighters' names are the same, I have shown career dates in order to distinguish them. If by chance a boxer is not in the specific index you are looking at he will certainly be found in one of the other weight indexes.

Junior Welterweight Division

This division, contested by men at 135 to 140lbs who are sometimes called super lightweights or light welterweights, first came into prominence in 1922 when Pinky Mitchell was proclaimed world champion on 15 November after the result of a 'poll' taken by a weekly boxing magazine in Minneapolis called the *Boxing Blade*. There had been 20 names in the hat and 766,000 casting votes, many of them coming from outside America, but it was Mitchell who led the way with 100,800 to Harvey Thorpe's 60,400.

Following that, on 16 November 1922 it was announced that the publisher would be awarding Mitchell a diamond-studded belt emblematic of the junior welterweight championship of the world that he would be asked to defend every six months against a selected opponent in the name of the National Boxing Association (NBA).

Unfortunately, the NBA - which had been formed on 10 January 1921 when Arkansas, Connecticut, Kentucky, Louisiana, Maine, Maryland, Michigan, Minnesota, Montana, New Jersey, Ohio, Oregon, Pennsylvania, Rhode Island, Wisconsin and Toronto came together as a group - failed to reach agreement among its membership at their convention in January 1923, as to whether they should even support a 140lbs weight class let alone recognise Mitchell as its champion. This decision left Wisconsin in the invidious position of operating the championship without the support of the NBA, and although threatening to withdraw from the Association it made no difference.

Weight Band
135lbs to 140lbs

Junior Welterweight World Championship Fights:

30 January 1923. Pinky Mitchell nd-w pts 10 Bud Logan.
Venue: The Auditorium, Milwaukee, Wisconsin, USA. **Recognition:** Wisconsin.
Fight Summary: For his first defence Mitchell (139¾) took on the unsophisticated Logan (137¼), showing his worth when pumping the left into the latter's face with much regularity, while also getting accurate rights off without response. Nearly six foot tall, with Mitchell's height and reach being too much of a factor for Logan to handle, only in one round, the ninth, did Logan bother the champion, a right to the head landing heavily. Being a no-decision contest, due to fights to a decision being illegal in Wisconsin at the time, the general consensus among the press was that Mitchell had won every round against the floundering, wild-swinging Logan.

13 February 1923. Pinky Mitchell nd-w pts 10 Johnny Tillman.
Venue: The Auditorium, Milwaukee, Wisconsin, USA. **Recognition:** Wisconsin. **Referee:** George Duffy.
Fight Summary: In what was a sensational fight, full of furious action, Mitchell (140) was down in the second from an overarm right before having to fight for his life to retain the title, his body attacks taking the steam out of Tillman (139) in the latter rounds. On occasion neither man heard the bell, the sixth session seeing both on the floor after landing simultaneously. Despite all that had gone before the tenth turned into the most exciting round, as Mitchell, on the verge of landing a kayo, was dropped by a terrific left to the jaw before surprising everybody, including Tillman, when getting to his feet immediately to retain his honours.

13 April 1923. Pinky Mitchell nd-w pts 10 Harvey Thorpe.
Venue: The Auditorium, Milwaukee, Wisconsin, USA. **Recognition:** Wisconsin.
Fight Summary: Regardless of the fact that Mitchell's crown was up for grabs at no stage did Thorpe (140) ever look like he was interested, the fight developing into farce as the latter rushed to cover at every opportunity while using all manner of 'wrestling' holds you could think of in order keep out of trouble. A veteran of more than 300 ring battles, from the moment Thorpe tasted Mitchell's right hand it was all about survival. Although he occasionally attempted to take the fight to Mitchell (140) he was soon back in defensive mode, the press verdict being a formality.

18 May 1923. Pinky Mitchell nd-w co 5 (12) Tim Droney.
Venue: The Armoury, Louisville, Kentucky, USA. **Recognition:** Kentucky/Wisconsin. **Referee:** Tommy Devlin.
Fight Summary: The challenger certainly came to fight, but following an even first round Mitchell (139½) dropped him for 'three' with a right cross. Not to be put off, Droney (139) continued to bore in, both men swapping solid punches through to the end of the fourth. The pattern continued in the fifth, each giving and taking in equal measures before Droney took a count of 'nine' after being nailed by a short, vicious right to the jaw. Although he got to his feet, Droney, groggy and unstable, was quickly set upon before a solid jab to the head sent him to the canvas where he was counted out.

Next time out, on 29 May, Mitchell was stopped in the tenth and final round of a no-decision affair against the lightweight champion, Benny Leonard, at the Dexter Park Pavilion, Chicago, Illinois. Despite it being reported by some of the press that Leonard had failed to weigh in, his manager, Billy Gibson, still tried to claim the title for his charge, stating that he had made the scales at 137lbs. In response, the Wisconsin Boxing Commission announced that no specific weight was articled in the contract and that the referee had not ascertained as to whether Mitchell could have made it through the remaining few seconds before bringing the fight to a conclusion. Thus, with the support of Wisconsin, Mitchell continued as champion.

Not contested over the championship distance, on 9 July at the Phillies Ballpark, Philadelphia, Pennsylvania, Mitchell (139lbs) was adjudged to have lost the eight-round press decision to Nate Goldman (140lbs).

Following that, three ten-round fights where Mitchell allowed the opposition to make less than 140lbs while he came in above the weight, came against Goldman 137¾ (nd-w disq 4 at the Auditorium, Milwaukee, Wisconsin on 14 December), Lew Tendler 138¾ (nd-l pts 10 at the Auditorium, Milwaukee on 18 February 1924) and Al Van Ryan 140 (nd-w pts 10 at Mizzou Park, Sioux City, Iowa on 10 June 1924).

Although the NBA finally announced that they recognised Mitchell as champion at their Convention in October 1924, by the following October they had changed their minds, even stating that they had never recognised the weight class.

According to the 1987 *Ring Record Book* Mitchell supposedly lost his title to Red Herring by a sixth-round disqualification at The Arena Gardens, Detroit, Michigan on 27 March 1925 in a ten-round no-decision contest, but research into that contest proves the fight was made at 145lbs, some five pounds above the weight class. Herring (139lbs), who was knocked out on the 'break', tried to claim the belt but was overruled by W. J. Hedding, Chairman of the Wisconsin Boxing Commission, who stated that a title could only change hands if all contractual conditions had been met, which had not been the case.

Even though Herring carried on claiming the title, being named as the holder in the October 1925 edition of *The Ring* magazine, no official support was forthcoming, and after being outpointed over ten rounds by Mushy Callahan at the Vernon Arena, Los Angeles, California on 18 August 1925 he was not even considered.

Subsequently, Mitchell continued to participate in further no-decision contests at weights in excess of 140lbs. One such bout, against Russie LeRoy at The Auditorium, Fargo, North Dakota on 14 January 1926, saw him make an estimated 149lbs against his opponent's 140. The day before it was reported in the *Bismarck Tribune* that LeRoy would come in under 140lbs at the 3pm weigh-in to ensure that if he won inside the distance the title would be his. In the event he failed, being knocked down twice in an extremely close contest which saw the press side with Mitchell.

Dismayed that Mitchell was not taking the title seriously, on 23 August 1926 the Wisconsin Boxing Commission ordered him to make a defence by 1 October against any one from Ace Hudkins, Andy DiVodi, Spug Myers, LeRoy or Callahan.

21 September 1926. Mushy Callahan w pts 10 Pinky Mitchell.
Venue: Vernon Arena, Los Angeles, California, USA. **Recognition:** California. **Referee:** Duke Kenworthy.

Fight Summary: Making his first defence outside of a no-decision contest, as much as Mitchell (140) tried he was outfought, outboxed and outsmarted by a tough challenger whose main aim was to batter his rival from his championship with strong right-arm punches. Trained to the minute, Callahan (140) showed a good defence, rarely wasted a punch, had Mitchell down in the eighth from a left-right to the jaw, and was well worth the referee's decision.

14 March 1927. Mushy Callahan w co 2 (12) Andy DiVodi.
Venue: Madison Square Garden, Manhattan, NYC, New York, USA. **Recognition:** California. **Referee:** Jim Crowley.
Fight Summary: Despite Tex Rickard promising the winner a $2,000 diamond studded belt and promoting the fight in New York, the New York State Athletic Commission (NYSAC) continued to state that they did not recognise any champions within the 140lbs weight class. Regardless of the NYSAC position, DiVodi (139½), who was unbeaten in 38 bouts, was more than happy to get a crack at Callahan (138½) on home turf. Although forcing the action from the opening bell, with DiVodi continually walking into punches he was punished when a long left floored him in the first round. Even then he appeared to be confident of winning until a solid left hook to the body in the second, followed by a right to the jaw, saw him fall into a clinch. The damage done was there for all to see, and as Callahan stepped back DiVodi slumped to the floor to be counted out on the 2.13 mark.

31 May 1927. Mushy Callahan w pts 10 Spug Myers.
Venue: Wrigley Field, Chicago, Illinois, USA. **Recognition:** California/Illinois. **Referee:** Jim Gardner.
Fight Summary: Successfully defending his title by a unanimous decision, Callahan (139½) was the master at long range, sending in solid lefts to the body and rights to the jaw in every round, while Myers (137½), badly cut over the left eye in the third, had the better of it when at close quarters. The challenger had a good fifth round, shared the next three, and even though tearing in for the last two sessions with long left and right swings he was unable to turn it his way.

Known as 'The Jewel of the Ghetto', Ruby Goldstein topped Tex Rickard's ratings at the end of the year despite having suffered bad defeats at the hands of Ace Hudkins, Billy Alger and Sid Terris. Rickard obviously thought highly of him but he never did get a crack at the title, and following a second-round kayo defeat inflicted on him by a rampant Jimmy McLarnin in December 1929 he faded from the scene. He later became one of America's leading referees.

28 May 1929. Mushy Callahan w rsc 3 (10) Fred Mahan.
Venue: Olympic Auditorium, Los Angeles, California, USA. **Recognition:** California. **Referee:** Jack Kennedy.
Fight Summary: In what was a tempestuous skirmish Callahan (139¼) touched down in both the first and second rounds before flooring Mahan (140), a deaf mute, twice in the second to put himself well on the way to retaining his title. The referee halted the contest on the towel being thrown in by Mahan's corner after their man had been flattened and left senseless by a right-hand uppercut in the third session.

Although the NBA finally recognised the weight division with Callahan as champion, at their Convention in November, on 31 December the NYSAC abolished the junior weight classes on the grounds that they were riddled with 'unsatisfactory' title bouts. A few days later, on 4 January 1930, Edward Foster, the Chairman of the NBA Championship Committee, recommended that the NBA should do likewise, but despite giving lukewarm support to the weight class the Association took no action to abandon it for close on two years.

Early in 1930 it was also reported that an American, Jeff Dickson, who was promoting in Europe but not licensed by the British Boxing Board of Control (BBBoC), was to match Jack Kid Berg against Callahan for the title at the Royal Albert Hall, Kensington, London on 18 February. Although announced as a title bout, with the weight class not being recognised in Britain at the time it failed to gain much support, despite Berg, who had been campaigning in America since May 1928, having wins over Bruce Flowers, Herman Perlick, Spug Myers, Tony Canzoneri and Callahan under his belt.

Before the 'rebel' promotion took place, *Boxing News* reported that the NBA had stripped Callahan on 4 February for not having defended the title against someone of their choice earlier. However, that edict was quickly rescinded, and despite a strong protest by Lord Lonsdale, sitting at ringside, the fight got underway, supported by the NBA, in front of less than 2,000 fans.

18 February 1930. Jack Kid Berg w rtd 10 (15) Mushy Callahan.
Venue: Royal Albert Hall, Kensington, London, England. **Recognition:** NBA. **Referee:** Ted Broadribb.
Fight Summary: The title changed hands after Berg (137¼) forced Callahan (137¾) to retire in his corner at the end of the tenth round after the American had been saved by the bell in the ninth and suffered a broken nose as well as receiving cuts over both eyes. Right from the start Berg had shown his mastery, shooting in jabs while swinging and hooking with great speed, which forced the champion to defend throughout. All-in at the end of the ninth Callahan made a supreme effort in the tenth, but after being subjected to a hail of blows from every angle it was time to call it a day. A few days later, the BBBoC invited the promoter, Jeff Dickson, to form a British promotional company, which he did with Ted Broadribb, while Berg decided to go back to America to defend his new title where the big money was.

4 April 1930. Jack Kid Berg w pts 10 Joe Glick.
Venue: Madison Square Garden, Manhattan, NYC, New York, USA. **Recognition:** NBA. **Referee:** Jack Dorman.
Fight Summary: Even though it was unable to be billed as a championship fight in New York, the *New York Times* reported it to be a defence of Berg's NBA crown in a match made at 140lbs. Berg always considered his title to be on the line when his opponent made the weight, being supported by *The Ring* magazine to that end. In a bitterly waged fight that was ceaseless and tireless all the way, Berg (139¼) started by swarming all over the rugged Glick (137¼) in an effort to negate the latter's punches. Interestingly, when Berg was put down by a left-right combination in the third he was up before a count could commence. Having cut Glick over the left eye in the fourth, Berg continued relentlessly through to the eighth when he was hurt by a low blow. After telling the referee that he did not want to win on a foul Berg took another 'low one' to the body, this time on the blind side of the third man, and was forced to take a count of 'seven' before getting up to chase Glick all over the ring. From then on Berg fought with increased fury, despite being jarred by right-hand smashes every now and again, to land the unanimous decision - reckoned to be by eight rounds to two.

29 May 1930. Jack Kid Berg w rsc 4 (10) Al Delmont.
Venue: Dreamland Park, Newark, New Jersey, USA. **Recognition:** NBA. **Referee:** Gene Roman.
Fight Summary: Recognised as a championship fight by the New Jersey Boxing Commission, this was the first time that Berg (139) had defended his title claim on NBA territory, Delmont (136) being pretty much outclassed. Although Delmont had held the champion in an even first round he was dropped for a count of 'nine' in the second, and following an uneventful third it was obvious that Berg was looking to finish the job in the fourth. That was precisely what happened when Berg put his rival down twice before the referee brought matters to a halt after Delmont's corner threw the towel in with just five seconds of the session remaining.

11 June 1930. Jack Kid Berg w pts 10 Herman Perlick.
Venue: Queensboro Stadium, Queens, NYC, New York, USA. **Recognition:** NBA. **Referee:** Johnny McAvoy.
Fight Summary: Although not supported as a title bout by the New York authority, as far as Berg was concerned he was the NBA champion and had a right to defend the title where he wanted as long as he adhered to the every-six-month defence ruling against worthy opposition. Made at 140lbs, this was another humdinger for Berg (138¼) as he came under more pressure than he had been forced to endure during his sojourn in the USA when faced by Perlick (138½), the twin brother of Henry, who was also a more than useful fighter. Perlick started strongly, going punch for punch to gain a good lead in the early rounds before Berg began to make up lost ground in the middle sessions. Belabouring Perlick with an assortment of body blows Berg got stronger as the fight progressed, being good value for his points win.

Another contest that saw both Berg (135) and his opponent weighing in below 140lbs came at the Polo Grounds, Manhattan, NYC, against Kid Chocolate (124) on 7 August. However, with both men inside the lightweight limit this was considered to be an eliminator for the 135lbs title. Berg won on points over ten rounds.

15

3 September 1930. Jack Kid Berg w pts 10 Buster Brown.
Venue: Dreamland Park, Newark, New Jersey, USA. **Recognition:** NBA. **Referee:** John Healey.
Fight Summary: Contested on NBA territory, Berg (136) won this defence as he pleased over the undeniably tough Brown (134), who was rugged enough but lacked the champion's work-rate. There were no knockdowns, but Berg was a clear winner on referee's card.

18 September 1930. Jack Kid Berg w pts 10 Joe Glick.
Venue: Queensboro Stadium, Queens, NYC, New York, USA. **Recognition:** NBA. **Referee:** Arthur Donovan.
Fight Summary: This was yet another New York 'defence' for Berg, who had been confirmed as the NBA champion at their convention held a few days earlier, on 15 September. The NBA also ruled that if any champion defended titles in New York, California, Massachusetts or Pennsylvania after 1 January 1931 they would be barred from fighting in member States, but with Rhode Island and seven other States railing against the judgement it never came into being. As ever, Berg (136) just got on with defending the title wherever the money was. Starting like a train he sailed into Glick (139) from the opening bell with a two-fisted attack, and although the latter met the champion's rushes on even ground in the first round the American soon began to be overwhelmed by his old rival. Pushed back round after round, Glick often held on for dear life at times after being hit by an assortment of solid blows, but ultimately unable to cope with Berg's stamina he went down on points.

10 October 1930. Jack Kid Berg w pts 10 Billy Petrolle.
Venue: Madison Square Garden, Manhattan, NYC, New York, USA. **Recognition:** NBA. **Referee:** Arthur Donovan.
Fight Summary: Recognised by the NBA but not by the NYSAC, who once again failed to give the fight world title status, it was another defence at 140lbs for a champion more than happy to put his crown up for grabs against a dangerous rival in Petrolle (137). Petrolle made a good start, shaking Berg (135¼) up early in the first until the latter came storming back. Although Berg was pounded to the body in the second with wicked left hooks he kept pressing Petrolle, catching him with some cracking rights to the jaw in the third before the challenger took the fourth with a punishing body attack. It was first one man then the other, Berg coming on strong in the fifth after Petrolle had a point deducted for low blows. Despite Berg having a good sixth Petrolle took the seventh with lusty body punches, but over the remaining three sessions the champion picked it up while virtually ignoring the volume of punches coming his way. When the decision was announced in Berg's favour it was not stated whether it was unanimous or otherwise, but for certain it had been a hard, gruelling affair.

23 January 1931. Jack Kid Berg w pts 10 Goldie Hess.
Venue: The Stadium, Chicago, Illinois, USA. **Recognition:** NBA. **Referee:** Tommy Thomas.
Fight Summary: Shooting in left hands at rapier-like speed and travelling 30 minutes without a pause, Berg (138¼) made a successful defence of his title by a unanimous decision. Hess (137¾), unable to fight at distance and swamped with blows from every conceivable angle, had his first success in the eighth, but having called upon all of his reserves he was almost done for as Berg continued to throw a terrific amount of leather thereafter. Somehow he survived the remaining six minutes to make it to the final bell, but he only just got there.

30 January 1931. Jack Kid Berg w pts 10 Herman Perlick.
Venue: Madison Square Garden, Manhattan, NYC, New York, USA. **Recognition:** NBA. **Referee:** Johnny McAvoy.
Fight Summary: Berg (138½) was the first man to test the water when he met Perlick (139) in a New York return, and after making a good start he was rocked by lefts and rights to the head in the second before regaining control. From the third round Perlick went on the back foot for the rest of the fight, holding on tight, running, or flashing his right hand weakly in a vain attempt to hold Berg off. The champion's burning pace and furious attacks were just too much for the American, who went down unanimously by nine rounds to one.

10 April 1931. Jack Kid Berg w pts 10 Billy Wallace.
Venue: Olympia, Detroit, Michigan, USA. **Recognition:** NBA. **Referee:** Elmer McClelland.
Fight Summary: Making another defence Berg (138) kept Wallace (137) on the defensive throughout, landing two for every blow his rival landed, despite many of them lacking real sting. With the exception of a hard right to Wallace's head in the opening round there was little damage done, with most of the action being at close quarters, and at the final bell Berg was a popular winner when handed the unanimous decision.

24 April 1931. Tony Canzoneri w co 3 (10) Jack Kid Berg.
Venue: The Stadium, Chicago, Illinois, USA. **Recognition:** NBA. **Referee:** Phil Collins.
Fight Summary: After a fairly even couple of rounds as both men warmed to the task, Berg (134¼) decided to give it a go in the third, landing to head and body to drive Canzoneri (132) before him until he walked into a countering right cross. Falling flat on his face, the challenger made every effort to rise but was counted out on the 2.23 mark. Rather belatedly, the NBA had presented Berg with their Championship Belt on 21 April, just three days earlier.

Although this contest really belongs to the lightweight class in their wisdom the Chicago Boxing Commission and the NBA contentiously decided that Canzoneri had also won the Englishman's 140lbs title. Following the fight Berg claimed he had been contracted to contest the lightweight title only, and that his junior welterweight crown was safe because different titles at different weights could not be at stake during the same bout. That did not wear with the Illinois Boxing Commission and the NBA, even though Berg had been forced to come inside 135lbs in order to challenge Canzoneri.

Regardless of the fact that he was not recognised by any of the official bodies, Berg, who had continued support from *The Ring* magazine, styled himself as champion in contests against Tony Herrera, Ray Kiser and Tony Lambert. All three men were beaten - Herrera 138½ (w pts 10 at Madison Square Garden, Manhattan, NYC, New York on 8 May), Kiser 138½ (w pts 10 at the Mayers Bowl, Pittsburgh, Pennsylvania on 18 May) and Lambert 139 (w rsc 8 at Dreamland Park, Newark, New Jersey on 22 June).

25 June 1931. Tony Canzoneri w pts 10 Herman Perlick.
Venue: White City Stadium, New Haven, Connecticut, USA. **Recognition:** NBA. **Referee:** Billy Conway.
Scorecard: 9-1.
Fight Summary: Both men started at a fast clip, but it was the champion, displaying lightning right hands from all angles to offset the Perlick (140) left jab, who went clear round after round. In the penultimate session, Canzoneri (134), who had been stung by a right hander to the chin, ripped into Perlick who met him punch for punch which lasted until the final bell and the referee's decision. It had been an exciting contest that was full of heavy slugging, with Canzoneri protected from losing his lightweight crown after Perlick was contracted to come in above 135lbs.

Supported by *The Ring* magazine as their champion, Jack Kid Berg took on the 139lbs Teddy Watson (w co 7 at the Baseball Park, Jersey City, New Jersey on 24 July) in a match made at 140lbs.

13 July 1931. Tony Canzoneri w pts 10 Cecil Payne.
Venue: Wrigley Field, Los Angeles, California, USA. **Recognition:** California/NBA. **Referee:** Abe Roth.
Fight Summary: Although not a member of the NBA the Californian Boxing Commission were happy enough to recognise this one as a title fight, but in order to protect Canzoneri's lightweight title the terms of the contract called for the challenger, normally a 133lbs man, to come in at 136lbs. Watched by an 18,000 strong crowd, Payne (136) took a merciless beating, being almost counted over after taking heavy right hands from Canzoneri (136) in the first (when he was downed but got up before the referee could start counting) and eighth rounds, and was unable to escape the champion's hooks and jabs. At the final bell the referee had no doubt about who had won, immediately holding up Canzoneri's arm.

Meanwhile, Jack Kid Berg continued to defend 'The Ring magazine' recognised title when beating the 138lbs Jimmy McNamara on points over ten rounds at Queensboro Stadium, Queens, NYC, New York on 4 August.

10 September 1931. Tony Canzoneri w pts 15 Jack Kid Berg.
Venue: Polo Grounds, Manhattan, NYC, New York, USA. **Recognition:** NBA. **Referee:** Patsy Haley.
Fight Summary: Down from a Canzoneri (131¾) left hook to the jaw after less than two minutes of fighting Berg (134½) was not expected to last much longer, but despite shipping heavy punishment, mainly to the body, throughout and being twice hit low he bravely remained on his feet to hear the final bell and the unanimous decision that went against him. While the fight had proved that Berg did not have the power to disturb the champion, the low blow delivered in the eighth round appreciably slowed him down, and in any State other than

New York, which carried the No-Foul Rule, Canzoneri would have been disqualified. Billed for the world lightweight title, this one was also recognised by the NBA as involving Canzoneri's junior welterweight crown.

29 October 1931. Tony Canzoneri w pts 10 Philly Griffin.
Venue: The Armoury, Newark, New Jersey, USA. **Recognition:** NBA. **Referee:** John Healy.
Fight Summary: Canzoneri (132) was never in danger of losing his title to Griffin (138¾), holding his rival off with long lefts to the body and doing very much as he pleased as he easily evaded the right-hand counters coming his way. Only in the last three rounds did he open up with savage attacks that saw Griffin holding on at every opportunity. The referee's decision was a formality.

Back in England, Jack Kid Berg defeated France's Marius Baudry (w rsc 5 at the Royal Albert Hall, Kensington, London on 14 December) in a fight promoted by Jeff Dickson and billed for the junior welter title despite not being supported by the BBBoC.

20 November 1931. Tony Canzoneri w pts 15 Kid Chocolate.
Venue: Madison Square Garden, Manhattan, NYC, New York, USA. **Recognition:** NBA. **Referee:** Willie Lewis.
Fight Summary: Billed for the world lightweight championship, the NBA also recognised it as involving their junior welterweight title even though it was contested in New York. Despite the determined efforts of the challenger, Canzoneri (132) came through to win the split decision in what had been a fiercely contested affair and one that could have gone either way. Performing at his very best Chocolate (127½) outboxed the champion for much of the time, his right-hand uppercuts catching Canzoneri as he came in and his silky skills a treat to watch. However, it was the latter's aggression, gameness and drive that gained him the decision.

18 January 1932. Johnny Jadick w pts 10 Tony Canzoneri.
Venue: The Arena, Philadelphia, Pennsylvania, USA. **Recognition:** NBA/Pennsylvania. **Referee:** Leo Houck.
Scorecards: 5-4-1, 5-4-1, 4-3-3.
Fight Summary: As in the case of California, the Pennsylvanian Boxing Commission was not affiliated to the NBA but were happy to recognise Canzoneri v Jadick for the title. Down in the first, Jadick (136½), obviously cautious, came back with the jab, and although occasionally opening up relied on that punch to win him the fight. Canzoneri (132½) was the heavier puncher but was unable to sustain a steady work-rate. Despite flailing away wildly with both hands he did not land enough quality punches to retain the title, Jadick fully deserving the unanimous verdict.

In another so-called 'title defence', Jack Kid Berg drew over ten rounds with Sammy Fuller (136½), on 1 April at Madison Square Garden, Manhattan, NYC, New York. Berg finally lost *The Ring* magazine's championship recognition on 20 May after being outpointed over 12 rounds by Fuller (138lbs) at the same venue.

18 July 1932. Johnny Jadick w pts 10 Tony Canzoneri.
Venue: Baker Bowl, Philadelphia, Pennsylvania, USA. **Recognition:** NBA/Pennsylvania. **Referee:** Joe McGuigan.
Scorecards: 6-3-1, 5-3-2, 2-7-1.
Fight Summary: Although not a member State of the NBA, as in their first contest the Pennsylvanian Boxing Commission were more than happy to accommodate the return as a title fight, and once again it was very close. This time round Canzoneri (133) looked to counter Jadick (135¼), who proved a shade too smart for that tactic, and despite landing the heavier punches the former champion missed his opportunity. In the final round Jadick was floored by a left hook to the jaw, but was up immediately to finish the course, worn out and bloodied but still champion. Canzoneri finished with a bad cut on the right eye, testament to Jadick's probing jabs.

During the month of August, the New Orleans promoter, Martin Burke, set up a four-man eliminating series over ten rounds at The Coliseum in order to find Jadick's next challenger. The tournament got underway on 15 August with Battling Shaw outpointing Ray Kiser, and was followed by Joe Ghnouly outscoring Davey Abad on 22 August. The final saw Shaw outpoint Ghnouly on 29 August.

On 20 September, the NBA decided not to recognise the 'junior' divisions in future, although States such as Pennsylvania, California. Illinois and Louisiana, plus Washington, Florida, Missouri and Ohio were happy to support their own champions or contests taking place on home territory.

A short while later, on 6 December, Sammy Fuller made a *Ring* magazine defence when he gained a ten-round points win over the 135lbs Billy Wallace at the Public Auditorium, Cleveland, Ohio.

Regardless of the fact that Jadick had signed to defend his title against Shaw in New Orleans on 20 February 1933 and Wesley Ramey in Grand Rapids five days later, it was reported in several papers on 7 February that he had given up his junior title to campaign at lightweight. While the contest against Ramey would be cancelled on 18 February due to poor ticket sales, Jadick would be putting his title on the line against the hard-hitting Shaw, who had won just two of five contests since beating Ghnouly.

20 February 1933. Battling Shaw w pts 10 Johnny Jadick.
Venue: The Coliseum, New Orleans, Louisiana, USA. **Recognition:** Louisiana. **Referee:** Jimmy Moran.
Scorecards: 4-3-3, 4-3-3, 4-4-2.
Fight Summary: Starting well with a great long left jab, Jadick (135) took the fight to Shaw (136) before being forced to defend more and more as the challenger worked at close quarters using effective overarm rights. Although Jadick was cut on the left eye in the sixth and shaken up in the tenth he fought back well, the decision being close enough to have gone either way.

In another so-called title defence, despite his defeat at the hands of Sammy Fuller, Jack Kid Berg was outscored over ten rounds at the Royal Albert Hall, Kensington, London, England on 27 April by Cleto Locatelli. Billed by promoter, Jeff Dickson, as a championship defence for the Englishman, it was not supported by the BBBoC. The title was never mentioned again, even as far as Locatelli was concerned.

21 May 1933. Tony Canzoneri w pts 10 Battling Shaw.
Venue: Heinemann Park, New Orleans, Louisiana, USA. **Recognition:** Louisiana. **Referee:** Jimmy Moran.
Fight Summary: Making his first defence, Shaw (136½) was no match for Canzoneri (133) who scored knockdowns in the seventh and eighth rounds to walk off with the unanimous decision. Although Shaw gave Canzoneri a stubborn battle for the first five rounds, after that it was an uphill struggle which he did well to survive.

23 June 1933. Barney Ross w pts 10 Tony Canzoneri.
Venue: The Stadium, Chicago, Illinois, USA. **Recognition:** Illinois. **Referee:** Tommy Gilmore.
Scorecards: 52-48, 53-47, 50-50.
Fight Summary: Despite being outsmarted by Canzoneri (133½) over the first six rounds, and despite carrying two cut eyes coming into the seventh, Ross (134¾) came through admirably to gain a majority decision in what for him was an uphill struggle. Having got off to a good start the champion had peppered Ross with an array of lefts and rights in a seemingly never-ending display of aggression, but gradually the tide turned as the latter stuck to his guns to lash in two-fisted attacks which ultimately cut back the deficit according to the judges. Billed for the world lightweight championship, with the result the Illinois Boxing Commission stated that Ross had also won Canzoneri's junior welterweight title.

26 July 1933. Barney Ross w rsc 6 (12) Johnny Farr.
Venue: Convention Hall, Kansas City, Missouri, USA. **Recognition:** Illinois/Missouri. **Referee:** Walter Bates.
Fight Summary: Defending his newly won crown for the first time, Ross (134¾) used Farr (136½) as a punch-bag to win almost without reply. It was Ross all the way as he sent in punishing blows from the start, closing Farr's right eye as early as the first round and thereafter hitting his man very much as he pleased. At the end of the sixth it came as no surprise when the doctor ordered the referee to call a halt after his examination of Farr had disclosed a broken nose to go with severe facial injuries.

12 September 1933. Barney Ross w pts 15 Tony Canzoneri.
Venue: Polo Grounds, Manhattan, NYC, New York, USA. **Recognition:** Illinois/Missouri. **Referee:** Arthur Donovan.

Scorecards: 9-2-4, 8-4-3, 7-8.

Fight Summary: Although billed for the world lightweight championship, it was recognised by Illinois and Missouri as also involving Ross' junior welterweight title. As in their previous encounter this was again close. Reporting on the fight, Nat Fleischer, of *The Ring* magazine, felt that had Canzoneri (133¼) stuck to his boxing instead of going right-hand crazy it would probably have brought him the decision, which again was a split one. However, the left hand of Ross (135) was superb, whether it was the jab or the hook, and it stopped the challenger in his tracks, thus paving the way for victory in a fight that was always going to be closely contested.

17 November 1933. Barney Ross w pts 10 Sammy Fuller.
Venue: The Stadium, Chicago, Illinois, USA. **Recognition:** Illinois/Missouri. **Referee:** Joe McNamara.
Scorecards: 51-49, 53-47, 50-50.
Fight Summary: Even though Ross (135½) appeared to win seven of the ten rounds he boxed with some caution in taking no unnecessary risks, and the majority decision rendered in his favour showed it to be much closer than it seemed. However, despite one judge voting for him, the hard-punching Fuller (139), a man with a lesser title claim, was also a disappointment. And, apart from the fourth round when he fought furiously, he often appeared slow and plodding as his powerful punches failed to hit the target. On reflection, it was difficult to analyse why Ross, who threw a lot of left hooks early on, did not open up more as it was not until the tenth that he really shook Fuller with blows to head and body. Afterwards, Ross claimed that he had looked bad because Fuller refused to lead. With the result, Fuller finally lost his claim to be recognised as the rightful titleholder.

7 February 1934. Barney Ross w pts 12 Pete Nebo.
Venue: Convention Hall, Kansas City, Missouri, USA. **Recognition:** Illinois/Missouri.
Fight Summary: The champion showered Nebo (139) with leather throughout, winning ten of the 12 contested rounds to fully deserve the unanimous decision. Not undaunted, Nebo bothered Ross (135½) constantly with left hands, many of the rounds being closely fought as he tried to force his way in using a crouching, weaving style. Winning the fourth and 11th sessions with forceful attacks while getting in smashing head blows were not enough, but Nebo, who was still fighting hard at the final bell, received warm applause for his great efforts.

5 March 1934. Barney Ross drew 10 Frankie Klick.
Venue: Civic Auditorium, San Francisco, California, USA. **Recognition:** California/Illinois. **Referee:** Toby Irwin.
Fight Summary: Notwithstanding the fact that the referee gave a draw, Ross (137½) looked to have defended his title with some ease. While no one would dispute that Klick (138) contested it all the way, Ross, who started to fight viciously in the sixth and had all of the seventh and eighth with two-fisted attacks driving Klick back on his heels, appeared to have been robbed.

14 March 1934. Barney Ross w pts 10 Kid Moro.
Venue: Municipal Auditorium, Oakland, California, USA. **Recognition:** California/Illinois. **Referee:** Oakland Frankie Burns.
Fight Summary: Little was known about the challenger other than the fact that he was durable, and with Ross (137) forcing the fight most of the way it became merely a workout for the champion. Moro (137) did open up in the fifth, a two-handed attack driving Ross back before hurting his man with a swinging left to the head, but the newly found aggression quickly subsided as the champion used the straight left to advantage. All in all it was an easy night's work for Ross, despite Moro clinching at every opportunity to escape hurtful body shots and, apart from in the tenth round when he staggered the Filipino with a vicious left to the jaw, he rarely moved out of first gear. It was no surprise when the referee immediately lifted Ross's arm at the final bell.

27 March 1934. Barney Ross w pts 10 Bobby Pacho.
Venue: Olympic Auditorium, Los Angeles, California, USA. **Recognition:** California/Illinois. **Referee:** George Blake.
Scorecard: 6-2-2.
Fight Summary: Looking to take the title, Pacho (139½), in great shape, ultimately forced Ross (138½) to revert to clever defensive work in order for him to maintain the slim lead he had built up in the early stages. This was the pattern of the fight despite Pacho's nose being broken as early as the first round. With Ross cut over the left eye in

the fourth, Pacho continued to bore in, flailing away with short chopping overarm rights right through to the final bell, before the referee decided that the title remained with the champion.

A match made for Ross to defend his title against Tony Herrera in Fort Worth, Texas on 20 April was officially cancelled four days before it was due to take place, citing an injured ear that made it impossible for the champion to appear. Having earlier asked to be released from his contract on the grounds that terms and conditions for his forthcoming defence of the welterweight title against Jimmy McLarnin on 28 May precluded interim fights, Ross was obviously looking for a way out. For Herrera, who had just beaten Sammy Mandell, the former lightweight champion, it had a bad effect on the rest of his career when winning just 11 of his remaining 27 fights.

10 December 1934. Barney Ross w pts 12 Bobby Pacho.
Venue: Public Hall, Cleveland, Ohio, USA. **Recognition:** Illinois/Ohio. **Referee:** Matt Brock.
Fight Summary: In front of 11,500 fans, Ross (138) had difficulty in catching Pacho (138¼) cleanly in the early rounds, but in the last three sessions he opened up to have the challenger reeling under heavy blows to head and body while on his way to another successful defence by a unanimous decision.

28 January 1935. Barney Ross w pts 10 Frankie Klick.
Venue: Municipal Stadium, Miami, Florida, USA. **Recognition:** Florida/Illinois. **Referee:** Leo Shea.
Fight Summary: Viewed by a 13,000 crowd, Ross (136) dropped the challenger for 'eight' in round two following a heavy right to the jaw. Ross then controlled all the rounds bar the sixth, when Klick (137) fought back strongly, to land the unanimous decision of the judges.

9 April 1935. Barney Ross w pts 12 Henry Woods.
Venue: Civic Auditorium, Seattle, Washington, USA. **Recognition:** Illinois/Washington. **Referee:** Tommy McCarthy.
Fight Summary: Having been hammered to the floor by a one-two to the jaw in the third round it appeared that Woods (137¼) had twisted his ankle, but on reaching the count of 'ten' the referee demanded the challenger to get to his feet instead of counting him out. Ross (136½) then tried for a kayo before Woods fought a rearguard action to somehow stay in the fight. Following that, Ross started each session slowly, only speeding up when caught, and finished with a burst of action to impress the judges who handed him the unanimous decision.

When Ross relinquished the Illinois version of the title, after regaining the world welterweight crown in June, the weight class went into hibernation until Maxie Berger resurrected it in Montreal, Canada some four years later.

5 July 1939. Maxie Berger w pts 10 Wesley Ramey.
Venue: The Forum, Montreal, Canada. **Recognition:** Montreal. **Referee:** Tommy Sullivan.
Fight Summary: Advertised as a world title fight and recognised as such by the Montreal Boxing Commission who recommended that the NBA revive the weight class, Berger (139¾), putting two defeats at the hands of Ramey (132¼) behind him, scored three knockdowns over his old foe to secure a unanimous points victory. Although his game plan was carefully thought through he was occasionally drawn on to punches by the wily Ramey, but scoring effectively with counter punches he ultimately had a little too much power for the American.

6 September 1939. Maxie Berger w co 3 (10) Felix Garcia.
Venue: The Forum, Montreal, Canada. **Recognition:** Montreal. **Referee:** Micky McGowan.
Fight Summary: Billed for the Montreal Boxing Commission's version of the title, Berger (140) successfully defended his claim against Garcia (140) after quickly getting down to business when flooring his rival towards the end of the first round with a cracking right cross to the jaw. Back on his feet the Puerto Rican was outclassed from then on as Berger took advantage of every opening, and in the third a crashing right uppercut sent Garcia down to be counted out on the 1.31 mark.

Berger failed to capitalise on his new title, moving his operating base to New York in search of welterweight honours.

Meantime, following a seven-round retirement win over California Jackie Wilson (135½) on 22 November 1940 at the Legion Stadium, Los Angeles, California, Quentin Baby Breese (138½) laid claim to the title. Although having little support, Breese was matched against Harry Weekly in July 1941 to decide the Louisianan version of the junior welterweight championship, for what it was worth.

28 July 1941. Harry Weekly w pts 15 Quentin Baby Breese.
Venue: The Auditorium, New Orleans, Louisiana, USA. **Recognition:** Louisiana. **Referee:** Red Dolan.
Scorecards: 142-140, 141-139, 135-135.
Fight Summary: The *New Orleans Daily Picayune*, in their pre-fight report, summed up that for his bout against Breese it would be the first time Weekly had been below the 140lbs mark. The paper went on to say that the winner would be presented with a gold belt. Starting quickly, Weekly (139¾) forced the issue over the first two thirds, his right under the heart being his most effective blow in the middle sessions, while Breese (138¾) came on strong in the last five rounds as the New Orleans lad weakened. In the final session Breese belted Weekly all over the ring, but somehow the latter held on to win a disputed decision.

There was no doubting that Weekly had great difficulty making 140lbs, and this was to be his only contest at the weight before he was inducted into the US Army in May 1942, his claim to the title being abandoned.

With the weight class clearly out of favour, and with war raging throughout the world, it would be another four years before there was further activity. The December edition of *The Ring* magazine stated that the little-known American Boxing Federation recognised Ohio's Jackie Taylor as champion. This could hardly be taken seriously as Taylor had won just five of ten starts while competing at lightweight.

29 April 1946. Tippy Larkin w pts 12 Willie Joyce.
Venue: The Garden, Boston, Massachusetts, USA. **Recognition:** NBA/NY. **Referee:** Johnny Martin.
Fight Summary: Sponsored by the Massachusetts Boxing Commission who provided the belt, and supported by the NBA and NYSAC, the weight class made another comeback with Larkin (139½) and Joyce (138¼) contesting the vacant title. Fought at a terrific pace, both men started well, but when Larkin was dropped three times for counts of 'eight' in the third round it looked like it was all over. Realising that he had been taking too many risks Larkin went back to his boxing, stabbing the all-action Joyce (138¼) to the head with stinging lefts and smashing in short rights to the jaw. Coming into the 11th it was still anybody's fight, but with Larkin impressing the judges more he was the one who picked up the unanimous decision.

According to press reports, Larkin was contracted to defend the title in California against Cleo Shans on 12 August. However, for whatever reason, when that fell through he was matched to meet Joyce in a return contest.

13 September 1946. Tippy Larkin w pts 12 Willie Joyce.
Venue: Madison Square Garden, Manhattan, NYC, New York, USA. **Recognition:** NBA/NY. **Referee:** Frank Fullam.
Scorecards: 9-3, 9-3, 10-2.
Fight Summary: Using the ring to good advantage the champion fought a clever battle against the hustling Joyce (139). And despite being caught by heavy rights and lefts at times he was well in front by the seventh round. However, by then it was clear that Larkin (139¼) was tiring when finding himself trapped in corners where he was forced to take some heavy wallops. Getting a second wind, Larkin came back with solid left jabs to keep the onrushing Joyce off balance, and slipping the swings more and more he eventually came home a comfortable winner.

It is difficult to assess when Larkin lost the support of the NBA and NYSAC, but by the end of 1946 it appears that he was only recognised in Massachusetts as champion. Due to meet Charley Fusari in an overweight match on 13 December he had pulled out at the last moment, only to be stopped inside nine rounds by the latter on 14 February 1947 at Madison Square Garden after the fight had been rescheduled. In his next contest, weighing 139lbs, he actually outpointed Billy Graham (139¾) over ten rounds at the same venue on 21 March 1947. Not contested at a championship distance it was not given credence as a title fight, although he still had the support of Massachusetts as champion.

If there had been any recognition left for him as a champion outside of Massachusetts to all intents and purposes Larkin (141) would certainly have forfeited it following a fourth-round kayo defeat by the NBA lightweight champion, Ike Williams (136¼), in a non-title bout at Madison Square Garden on 20 June 1947. The *Boxing News* report stated that Williams could now claim the 140lbs title if he so wished, but he obviously thought better of it. Despite Larkin not making 140lbs again after the Graham fight he was still being reported as the Massachusetts recognised champion right up until June 1948, but that is the last we hear of the weight division for some while.

There was a brief glimmer of it being resurrected in 1954 when the Australian Boxing Club initially billed a fight between George Barnes and Freddie Dawson as being for the junior welterweight championship. Dawson said he had claimed the title after beating Irvin Steen on points over 12 rounds at the Pelican Stadium, New Orleans Louisiana on 23 September 1950 when weighing in at 140lbs to his opponent's 145. Unable to make a case for the title being involved, with the match eventually going ahead at 142lbs, no more was heard of the weight class until the NBA, supported by the NYSAC, decided to reintroduce it in May 1959 when a match was made between Kenny Lane and Carlos Ortiz, the number one and two rated lightweights, who were both waiting for a crack at the 135lbs champion, Joe Brown.

The previous year, Lane, who had given Brown a close call for the lightweight championship in July, had beaten Ortiz on points over ten rounds at The Auditorium, Miami, Florida on 31 December in a contest that was considered by many to be an eliminator. With Brown in no hurry to defend against Lane or Ortiz, the official NBA line was that both men and others like them would benefit from having an additional weight class set between the lightweights and welters.

12 June 1959. Carlos Ortiz w rsc 2 (12) Kenny Lane.
Venue: Madison Square Garden, Manhattan, NYC, New York, USA. **Recognition:** NBA/NY. **Referee:** Harry Kessler.
Fight Summary: With both men getting away fast, Ortiz (139¼) matching the southpaw jabs of Lane (140), there were a number of lively exchanges in the opening session. However, early in the second round Ortiz dropped Lane for 'four' with a left-right combination and near the end of the session when their heads came together the latter was left with a badly gashed right eye. It was clear that Lane could not continue with such a deep wound that would ultimately require ten stitches, and during the interval the fight was called off by the referee on the ringside doctor's advice. Although Ortiz was also carrying a slight cut on his right eye, having been deemed fit to continue he was announced the winner.

By the end of the year when it was clear that for whatever reason the NYSAC had lost interest in the weight class, even Ortiz recognised that it was merely a stepping stone to the lightweight crown.

4 February 1960. Carlos Ortiz w co 10 (15) Battling Torres.
Venue: The Coliseum, Los Angeles, California, USA. **Recognition:** NBA. **Referee:** Mushy Callahan.
Fight Summary: Tantalising the 18-year-old challenger with the left jab Ortiz (137) proved what a good fighter he was, taking everything that came his way before opening up in the latter rounds with big punches of his own. Torres (138) put up a good fight, but showed his inexperience when trying to take Ortiz out with everything he threw. Cut over the left eye and battered by fierce rights to the head and hurtful body attacks, Torres was showing evidence in the ninth that he would not be around much longer, and in the tenth a barrage of lefts and rights saw him sink to the canvas to be counted out with just four seconds of the session remaining.

Ortiz's next challenger would be Duilio Loi, a long-term lightweight contender who had been bypassed for several years. With 110 contests behind him, and beaten just once, by Jorgen Johansen in a European lightweight title challenge, Loi had eventually been crowned as champion, defending the title eight times before becoming the European welterweight boss. A difficult man to tag, since starting out in 1948 Loi's record read like a veritable Who's Who, especially on the European front, beating men such as Bruno Bisterzo, Emilio Marconi, Agustin Argote (twice), Francis Bonnardel, Ernesto Formenti (twice), Bruno Visintin, Jacques Herbillon, Ivor Kid Germain, Mario Trigo, Glen Flanagan, Ray Famechon, Giancarlo Garbelli, Seraphin Ferrer, Orlando Zulueta, Manolo Garcia, Fred Galiana, Sauveur Chiocca, Hoacine Khalfi, Rudi Langer, Idrissa Dione, Felix Chiocca (twice), Wallace Bud Smith, Al Nevarez and Conny Rudhof.

15 June 1960. Carlos Ortiz w pts 15 Duilio Loi.
Venue: Cow Palace, San Francisco, California, USA. **Recognition:** NBA. **Referee:** Vern Bybee.
Scorecards: 145-143, 148-146, 143-145.
Fight Summary: Keeping the fight at long range with accurate left jabs, while Loi (140) preferred to bob and weave, the champion found his opponent difficult to tag with big shots due to his crouching style. While the upright Ortiz (137½) looked to land with straight punches, Loi would hook and uppercut to head and body, and at times the action was fast and furious as both men tried to take control. There were no knockdowns recorded, although Ortiz slipped over twice. With the contest slowing appreciably in the latter stages, after Loi took a hard right to the body in the penultimate session he had little left, leaving Ortiz to make sure of the decision in his favour.

1 September 1960. Duilio Loi w pts 15 Carlos Ortiz.
Venue: San Siro Stadium, Milan, Italy. **Recognition:** NBA. **Referee:** Andre Esparraquera.
Scorecards: 74-73, 74-73, 72-72.
Fight Summary: As per their first contest it was closely fought, but this time Loi (139½) had the edge over the champion who was shaken up by a left to the jaw in the fourth and given no room to work. The early rounds had seen both men content to spar for openings before Loi became more effective on the inside and began to box his man off. With the tide beginning to turn in the ninth, when Ortiz (138½) was forced on the defensive by Loi he was blitzed by a hail of left and right hooks that had him rocking. Although Ortiz was still boxing brilliantly at times, especially in the 11th and 13th rounds, Loi was beginning to get on top as he put everything into his attacks, his work over the last two sessions giving him a deserved victory.

10 May 1961. Duilio Loi w pts 15 Carlos Ortiz.
Venue: San Siro Stadium, Milan, Italy. **Recognition:** NBA. **Referee:** Frank Carter.
Scorecards: 70-67, 74-69, 74-66.
Fight Summary: With 60,000 fans shouting themselves hoarse both men got to work early, but it was not until the sixth round that anything decisive happened. Prior to that, Ortiz (136¾) had generally been on the attack while the champion held the centre of the ring, bobbing and weaving before unloading bursts of punches. In three fights between the pair there had been no knockdowns, but in the sixth Loi (138) had Ortiz over twice, firstly from a right to the jaw and then from a fusillade of blows from both hands. Thereafter, with the contest in Loi's hands, he gave a master class in footwork and countering as Ortiz, fighting furiously at times, tried to make up the deficit to no avail.

21 October 1961. Duilio Loi drew 15 Eddie Perkins.
Venue: Sports Palace, Milan, Italy. **Recognition:** NBA. **Referee:** Nello Barroveccio.
Scorecards: 70-69, 69-71, 71-71.
Fight Summary: There was little action to talk of during the opening rounds and in the seventh, with the crowd whistling and jeering, despite the referee warning both men to get busy it had little effect. With Perkins (139½) content to stand off and counter while the champion appeared unable to force matters, the contest degenerated into a shambling bore until the final stages when the pair tried to turn things around. Even when Loi (138½) finally went on the attack in the 15th the fans remained unhappy, and although he could not really explain his lethargic display the champion stated that things would be different if there was a return bout.

Following the NBA's directive for Loi to defend against Perkins on 5 July 1962, the fight was pushed on to September when the latter picked up an injury and Loi defended his European welter title against Fortunato Manca (w pts 15 at the Amsicora Stadium, Cagliari on 15 July) instead.

Meanwhile, the NBA was reconstituted as the World Boxing Association (WBA) in August 1962.

14 September 1962. Eddie Perkins w pts 15 Duilio Loi.
Venue: Vigorelli Stadium, Milan, Italy. **Recognition:** WBA. **Referee:** Pierre Verners.
Fight Summary: This time around there were no complaints as Perkins (140), settling down quickly with his left hand being the decisive weapon, fully deserved the unanimous decision in his favour. Every time the champion tried to force the issue he was boxed off by stabbing jabs and solid left hooks to both the head and body, and

although not particularly hurt he was forced to give ground in order to regroup. This was the pattern of the fight throughout. Despite Loi (140) having no answer to the speed and accuracy of Perkins' punches, a return clause would see the pair come together three months later.

15 December 1962. Duilio Loi w pts 15 Eddie Perkins.
Venue: Sports Palace, Milan, Italy. **Recognition:** WBA. **Referee:** Georges Gondre.
Fight Summary: Although he had some difficulty making the weight for this one, with Loi (137¼) showing that he had learned the lessons required to regain his title he was happy to take the fight to Perkins (138½). From the halfway stage through to the final bell it was give and take as both men looked to influence the referee, who was the sole official, and in the 12th Perkins had Loi hanging on from a barrage of solid head blows. Holding on gamely Loi came back strongly to rip in punches to Perkins' body right through to the end, it being this ability to keep going against the odds that saw him ultimately favoured with the referee's decision.

When Loi retired as undefeated champion in January 1963, Perkins was designated by the WBA to meet Battling Torres for the vacant title. Unfortunately, after the promoters had won the contracts for the contest and had scheduled it to take place on a Carnival of Champions show to be held in Los Angeles, California on 21 March, it was discovered that Perkins had a prior engagement contracted in Paris, France which was too close to the date. It was then agreed that Roberto Cruz should be drafted in, with Perkins being given a crack at the winner within 90 days.

21 March 1963. Roberto Cruz w co 1 (15) Battling Torres.
Venue: Dodgers' Stadium, Los Angeles, California, USA. **Recognition:** WBA. **Referee:** Lee Grossman.
Fight Summary: Contesting the title left vacant following the retirement of Duilio Loi, Cruz (138¼) did not waste much time when racing out of his corner to knock Torres (140) down with a solid right hand to the jaw. Although the Mexican got to his feet he was dropped twice more by vicious left hooks before being hammered to the floor again and counted out after just 2.07 of the opening round.

In 18 earlier recorded bouts Cruz had failed to show that he was a future world beater, knocking out just three opponents while losing six, including a kayo defeat at the hands of Shigemasa Kawakami and two losses on points to Solomon Boysaw.

15 June 1963. Eddie Perkins w pts 15 Roberto Cruz.
Venue: Rizal Coliseum, Manila, Philippines. **Recognition:** WBA. **Referee:** Teorico Reyes.
Scorecards: 73-63, 72-68, 73-67.
Fight Summary: Getting his long awaited chance to regain his old title, Perkins (138¼) soon got down to business when dropping the champion in the first session following blows to the head and body. Although Cruz (140) was up before a count could begin he was given a thorough mauling, and had Perkins put his mind to it he could surely have halted his clumsy rival who had no answer to the spearing punches coming his way. Unable to reach Perkins in the earlier rounds Cruz improved as the bout progressed, but lacking the tools to worry the American unduly he went down on all three cards.

4 January 1964. Eddie Perkins w rsc 13 (15) Yoshinori Takahashi.
Venue: Kuramae Arena, Tokyo, Japan. **Recognition:** WBA. **Referee:** Nicholas Pope.
Fight Summary: Showing good form from the start the champion began by scoring well with solid jabs and hooks to head and body as Takahashi (139¼) looked for a way into the fight. It was soon clear that Takahashi was no real match for Perkins (138¼), and apart from the fourth round which two judges thought he won he was kept at arm's length. For round after round Perkins was in control without really going for the kayo win, but in the 13th he staggered Takahashi with a right to the jaw before unloading barrages of blows to drop him. Somehow getting up at 'nine', Takahashi was taking an unmerciful beating until going down again and being rescued by the referee on the 1.35 mark.

Ranked as the number four lightweight by *The Ring* magazine, Bunny Grant would be Perkins' next challenger. In a career that started in 1958, Grant had put together 33 wins from 39 contests and numbered Lauro Salas, Percy Hayles, Gerald Gray, Tito Marshall, Angel Robinson Garcia, Dave Charnley and Doug Vaillant among his victims.

18 April 1964. Eddie Perkins w pts 15 Bunny Grant.
Venue: National Stadium, Kingston, Jamaica. **Recognition:** WBA. **Referee:** Willie Pep.
Scorecards: 147-140, 145-141, 148-139.
Fight Summary: Producing top quality the champion once again defended on foreign territory, and once again was too good for his opponent as he took control from the opening bell with smart one-twos that immediately put Grant (137½) under pressure. However, Grant showed his mettle when coming back to cut Perkins (139) over the left eye in the sixth. He then provided the fans with some good action as he counter-punched his way through the middle sessions before the latter got going again. In the tenth Perkins started to bang in left hooks that Grant found difficulty in avoiding, and over the remainder of the contest it was all Perkins as he shook his man up with combinations to run out a clear winner.

Unable to make a worthwhile title fight in his native America, in August Perkins' manager, Johnny Coulon, was reported as saying they would be looking abroad.

Meantime, having beaten Mauro Vazquez (w rsc 8 at the New Leon State Coliseum, Monterrey, Mexico on 6 September) and Mario Rossito (w pts 10 at the Santamaria Circus, Bogota, Colombia on 18 September) in non-title bouts, and looking to defend the championship against Carlos Hernandez in Venezuela in October, the fight had to be held on ice until the latter had served a suspension. To appease the NBA there was talk of the fight coming to Miami on 21 December, but after much wrangling it was eventually contracted to take place in January 1965.

Having been formed on 14 February 1963, at their convention in September 1964 the World Boxing Council (WBC) officially agreed to recognise the junior welterweight class from 1 January 1965. The WBC consisted of Britain and the Commonwealth, Europe, North America (not including New York and States affiliated to the WBA), Latin America and the Orient, and was formed to rival the WBA. Although the WBC, as a majority, accepted Perkins as the current champion, two of the membership, namely Britain (BBBoC) and the Commonwealth, did not recognise the junior welter class within their own confines. It would not be until 1968 that Britain contested championships at 140lbs, followed by the Commonwealth in 1975.

18 January 1965. Carlos Hernandez w pts 15 Eddie Perkins.
Venue: New Circus Bullring, Caracas, Venezuela. **Recognition:** WBA/WBC. **Referee:** Henry Armstrong.
Scorecards: 143-142, 146-143, 129-150.
Fight Summary: Continually defending his title on away soil finally proved too much for Perkins (140), who was deemed to have lost the contest after the two Venezuelan judges scored against him despite the referee having him winning by a wide margin on his card. At the halfway stage Perkins seemed well in front, and even though Hernandez (139½) came back with long lefts and rights, especially to the body, the former remained in control. There was no doubt that Hernandez's driving finish would have influenced the judges to some degree, but following the fight the former three-weight world champion referee claimed that it was the most brazen demonstration of partiality he had ever witnessed.

Very little was known about Mario Rossito, who was selected for Hernandez's first title defence, other than he had won 44 out of 55 contests and was relatively durable. Despite not being rated by *The Ring* magazine, Rossito had beaten J. D. Ellis, Vicente Rivas (twice), Bert Somodio and Eugenio Espinosa, but was not given much of a chance against the hard-hitting Hernandez.

15 May 1965. Carlos Hernandez w rtd 4 (15) Mario Rossito.
Venue: Alejandro Borges Stadium, Maracaibo, Venezuela. **Recognition:** WBA/WBC.
Fight Summary: Defending his newly won title, Hernandez (134¼) quickly showed his power with two-handed body attacks and cracking left uppercuts making inroads into the challenger's defences as early as the opening session. Despite being noted for his durability it was soon clear to see that Rossito (137½) was going to be unable

to cope with the champion's speed as he continued to take a battering, and at the end of the third he was badly marked up with his left eye closed and left cheek badly bruised. It came as no surprise when Rossito was retired prior to the fifth getting underway, having taken further severe punishment in the fourth and being on the verge of suffering a knockout.

10 July 1965. Carlos Hernandez w co 3 (15) Percy Hayles.
Venue: National Stadium, Kingston, Jamaica. **Recognition:** WBA/WBC. **Referee:** Willie Pep.
Fight Summary: Although Hayles (136½) made a bright start in the opening two rounds, it was clear that the big-punching champion was merely biding his time while feeling his way into a contest that was being watched by 17,000 excited fans. That all changed in the third session as Hernandez (137½) finally decided that Hayles was no danger to him and started to let his punches go. Driving Hayles around the ring under a stream of combinations to head and body, Hernandez ended the contest with a smashing left hook that saw the referee count the local out with seven seconds of the round remaining.

On 3 August, Jose Napoles outpointed Eddie Perkins over ten rounds at the Monumental Bullring, Juarez, Mexico, in what the WBC considered to be an eliminating bout.

Meantime, Hernandez, having failed to make a fight with Ismael Laguna for the lightweight title, found himself suspended for 'Drunk Driving' and then charged with 'Assault' in October. Unable to leave the country, when the charges were later dropped Hernandez got back into action early in 1966 after his suspension at the hands of the Venezuelan Boxing Commission had ended on 31 December.

Having turned down an offer to defend against Napoles, Hernandez then suffered a bad non-title defeat in Panama at the hands of Laguna (l rsc 8 at the Juan Diaz Stadium, Panama City on 19 February 1966), prior to signing for a defence against the Italian champion, Sandro Lopopolo. A former Olympic silver medallist, the southpaw Lopopolo had lost just twice in 44 pro contests, to Piero Brandi and Juan Albornoz, and had beaten J. D. Ellis, Doug Vaillant and Brandi. However, while there was no doubt that he was a clever, compact box-fighter with a future, Lopopolo, rated ninth in the division by *The Ring* magazine, appeared fortunate to get a title shot ahead of others, especially the European champion, Albornoz.

30 April 1966. Sandro Lopopolo w pts 15 Carlos Hernandez.
Venue: Sports Palace, Rome, Italy. **Recognition:** WBA/WBC. **Referee:** Manuel Risoto.
Scorecards: 71-68, 70-67, 69-69.
Fight Summary: Providing plenty of spirit and craftiness, and fighting in front of his own people, Lopopolo (139½) started to show in the second session with quick left-rights to the head after feeling the champion out in the first. He repeated this tactic throughout, but by the fifth Hernandez (139½) was warming to the task with some cracking left smashes to the head prior to cutting Lopopolo over the right eye in the seventh following a volley of lefts. Although Lopopolo was shading things Hernandez always looked dangerous with his power, and in the ninth a stream of left uppercuts had the Italian down on one knee. After chasing Hernandez in the 11th Lopopolo eased off for a round or so to conserve his energy before coming back with long lefts to keep the champion at bay. The final round saw both men fighting hard for supremacy, with Lopopolo getting a second wind and eventually outworking Hernandez who claimed afterwards that the referee had stopped him from fighting.

21 October 1966. Sandro Lopopolo w rtd 7 (15) Vicente Rivas.
Venue: Sports Palace, Rome, Italy. **Recognition:** WBA/WBC. **Referee:** Nello Barroveccio.
Fight Summary: Making his first defence, Lopopolo (139¾) hardly covered himself in glory against the 32-year-old Rivas (140), who offered very little in terms of aggression before retiring on his stool at the end of the seventh. Prior to that, the technically correct Lopopolo had finally caught up with Rivas in the sixth, with lefts and rights to the head, but had been unable to make his attacks pay off against the speedy Venezuelan. In explaining his retirement, Rivas, who had beaten Lopopolo on points in a ten-round non-title contest on 3 July, claimed that, having first hurt his right in the fourth, by the seventh the pain was too severe for him to continue.

Ordering Lopopolo to defend against Jose Napoles by 20 November or risk being stripped the WBC accepted 21 January 1967, but when Lopopolo then requested a postponement following a tonsillectomy operation on 12 December he was given a final date of 21 February 1967. It was then agreed that he could make a defence against Paul Fujii as long as both men posted a $15,000 bond with the WBC and accepted that whoever won would defend against Napoles next time out. Then, it was announced that Willi Quatuor, the undefeated European champion, would be meeting Napoles in Mexico City on 26 March 1967 to decide the WBC version of the title, but after that fell through when it was realised that the latter could not make the weight it was agreed that Quatuor would be first in line for the winner of Lopopolo v Fujii.

30 April 1967. Paul Fujii w rsc 2 (15) Sandro Lopopolo.
Venue: Kuramae Arena, Tokyo, Japan. **Recognition:** WBA/WBC. **Referee:** Jay Edson.
Fight Summary: Boxing away from home proved to be disastrous for the clever champion after he had convincingly won the opening round when concentrating on his fine left jab and excellent footwork. However, that all changed in the second session as Fujii (140), ducking below the left hands coming his way, suddenly crashed in a right hook to the jaw that dropped Lopopolo (139). After just beating the count Lopopolo was forced to take the mandatory 'eight' prior to coming under another barrage of blows from either hand. With Lopopolo defenceless up against the ropes, the referee came to his rescue at 2.33 of the session.

16 November 1967. Paul Fujii w co 4 (15) Willi Quatuor.
Venue: Kuramae Arena, Tokyo, Japan. **Recognition:** WBA/WBC. **Referee:** Jay Edson.
Fight Summary: Despite entering the ring as a big underdog the southpaw challenger held Fujii (140) on even terms in the opening two rounds, trading punches and giving the man from Japan plenty to think about. Having edged the third, especially after landing a cracking right to the jaw, when Fujii opened up in the fourth Quatuor (139¼) met him all the way, using his right jab effectively. Although flat footed at times, Quatuor was proving more than a match for Fujii until he was hurt by a long right to the jaw which sent him back on the ropes. Almost defenceless at that point, Quatuor took a smashing left hook to the body before dropping for the full count that was completed at 2.30 of the session.

The WBC vacated the title in November 1968 after Fujii had failed to make a defence for nearly a year, having suffered injuries in a car accident and then signing to meet Nicolino Locche. This followed the WBA's failure to approve a match between Fujii and Pedro Adigue, their number three contender.

To contest the vacant WBC title, Adigue was matched against Adolph Pruitt, *The Ring* magazine's number four ranked contender. Pruitt was on a run of seven wins, having beaten Luis Molina and Ernie Lopez, while Adigue numbered Arthur Persley, Rene Barrientos and Jaguar Kakizawa among his 27 wins from 40 contests.

12 December 1968. Nicolino Locche w rtd 10 (15) Paul Fujii.
Venue: Kuramae Arena, Tokyo, Japan. **Recognition:** WBA. **Referee:** Nicholas Pope.
Fight Summary: Springing something of a surprise, the experienced challenger quickly got his left jab going to put points in the bank while Fujii (139¾) seemed lethargic and disappointing after being out of the ring for so long. Maintaining his good start, Locche (138½) continued to pull away, mixing up long left hooks to the body and rights and lefts to the head as Fujii rushed him in a desperate attempt to bring him down. Being cut over the right eye in the fourth made Fujii's job even more difficult. Although he never stopped throwing punches they were often wild, having little effect other than the odd few which landed. After taking the best Fujii could offer Locche opened up in the ninth with hard right and left uppercuts to the jaw, and when the bell rang for the tenth to begin it was clear that the champion had retired, the contest coming to a close after five seconds of the session had elapsed.

Carlos Hernandez, who was *The Ring* magazine's fifth-rated lightweight contender and a former champion, would be Locche's first challenger. Since losing his title to Sandro Lopopolo, Hernandez had won 15 of 18 contests, beating the likes of L. C. Morgan, Lennox Beckles, Daniel Guanin, German Gastelbondo, Ray Adigun and Alfredo Urbina.

14 December 1968. Pedro Adigue w pts 15 Adolph Pruitt.
Venue: Araneta Coliseum, Manila, Philippines. **Recognition:** WBC. **Referee:** Nicholas Pope.
Scorecards: 72-69, 70-68, 71-66.
Fight Summary: Fighting for the title that was vacated after the WBC stripped Paul Fujii, with both Adigue (140) and Pruitt (140) having difficulty in making the weight, at one stage it appeared that the contest might not be going ahead. Outjabbed in the opening round but fighting on even terms in the next two sessions, Adigue came on strongly in the fourth with sharp left-right combinations to head and body before carrying on in the same vein until Pruitt evened things up between the seventh and ninth rounds when landing with excellent counters and solid, wide left hooks. The last six rounds saw Adigue throwing sharp, hurtful punches, while Pruitt picked it up in the 14th as he looked for the kayo. All this activity made for an exciting finish.

Taking on Pruitt in a non-title contest, scheduled for ten rounds at the International Centre Arena, Honolulu, Hawaii on 18 February 1969, Adigue, floored twice, received a bad beating before the fight was stopped in the fifth round to save him from suffering further punishment. He was also troubled by severe stomach pains. Rushed to hospital immediately after the fight, Adigue was operated on for appendicitis and only got back into action again at the end of October before being matched to defend his title against the European champion, Bruno Arcari. A clever southpaw with a punch, having reversed two early defeats Arcari had 36 wins on his record, beating the likes of Joe Brown, Angel Robinson Garcia, Johann Orsolics, Joe Tetteh, Willi Quatuor and Juan Albornoz.

3 May 1969. Nicolino Locche w pts 15 Carlos Hernandez.
Venue: Luna Park Stadium, Buenos Aires, Argentina. **Recognition:** WBA. **Referee:** Victor Avendano.
Scorecards: 298-290, 298-297, 298-290.
Fight Summary: Over the first five rounds the challenger looked to be in with a chance as he threw some pretty solid punches at Locche (139), but after the mini-storm subsided the latter took over, battering away with straight lefts and rights while scoring heavily on the inside. Although Hernandez (137) made another big charge, this time in the 12th when swinging wildly in a vain attempt to land a kayo, his efforts were negated by Locche who gave it both barrels during the remaining three sessions, firing in solid lefts and rights despite having the fight already in the bag.

11 October 1969. Nicolino Locche w pts 15 Joao Henrique.
Venue: Luna Park Stadium, Buenos Aires, Argentina. **Recognition:** WBA. **Referee:** Alfonso Araujo.
Scorecards: 296-294, 300-289, 299-296.
Fight Summary: Moving well and landing solid lefts to the face of the challenger, Locche (139¾) was clearly in front during the early rounds as he continued to spear in the punches. This tactic certainly paid dividends when Henrique (138¼) was cut over the right eye during the fourth. With Henrique trying to protect himself from suffering further damage, it was not until the ninth that he took up the offensive as Locche tired. For the next three or four sessions Henrique began to peg back Locche's lead, battering his rival with powerful lefts and rights, before the latter came alive and took over where he had left off to run out a good winner.

1 February 1970. Bruno Arcari w pts 15 Pedro Adigue.
Venue: Sports Palace, Rome, Italy. **Recognition:** WBC. **Referee:** Teddy Waltham.
Fight Summary: In a difficult contest to score, which saw both men banging away sometimes wildly from the opening bell, it was hardly surprising that there were many infringements, with Adigue (139½) being warned for careless use of the head nine times and twice for butting. The champion was jarred up by a number of heavy punches in the eighth as Arcari (138) let fly before coming back to rock the latter with a cracking right hand in the tenth. It was still difficult to separate the pair, but in the 12th Arcari attacked two-fistedly, mixing up southpaw hooks and uppercuts, to score well before he came again in the 15th when raining blow after blow on Adigue, who could hardly stand. The decision in Arcari's favour was rendered by the referee, who controlled the action superbly, and was met by loud applause. Both men finished puffed up around the eyes, but otherwise seemingly unharmed.

16 May 1970. Nicolino Locche w pts 15 Adolph Pruitt.
Venue: Luna Park Stadium, Buenos Aires, Argentina. **Recognition:** WBA. **Referee:** Joaquin Arvas.

Scorecards: 149-145, 149-144, 149-141.

Fight Summary: Although the challenger took up the offensive from the opening bell, Locche (139¼) quickly picked it up when coming back with solid lefts as his rival missed with far more than he threw. The pattern of the fight saw Locche ducking under or blocking blows from Pruitt (138) with ease while sending in hurtful punches virtually every round. Miraculously, the American showed little sign of being hurt or even tired despite the tremendous amount of blows he had taken to the head and body throughout, appearing quite fresh at the finish. The unanimous verdict in favour of Locche came as no surprise, but according to Pruitt it was he who landed the harder punches and without him forcing the fight there would have been little action.

Following this one, Locche failed to get back into the ring until February 1971 due to suffering a number of injuries in training, and would not be ready to defend the title again for a further couple of months after taking on board two warm-up contests.

10 July 1970. Bruno Arcari w disq 6 (15) Rene Roque.
Venue: Big Top Circus, Lignano Sabbiadoro, Italy. **Recognition:** WBC. **Referee:** G. Martinelli.
Fight Summary: Both men attacked from the start, trading hooks and sharp jabs, with the challenger at his most dangerous when fighting off the ropes while Arcari (138¾) sent in powerful blows from his southpaw stance. Roque (139), who was rocked by big rights in the fourth, was warned by the referee for butting a round later when trying to worsen Arcari's cut over the right eye received in the third, and by the fifth he was beginning to take a hammering, especially to the body. With Roque continuing to rough his man up the referee had seen enough, disqualifying the Frenchman at 1.29 of the sixth for illegal use of the head after Arcari was cut again, this time over the left eye. Arcari was reckoned to be well ahead at the finish.

30 October 1970. Bruno Arcari w co 3 (15) Raymundo Dias.
Venue: Sports Palace, Genoa, Italy. **Recognition:** WBC. **Referee:** Domenico Carabellese.
Fight Summary: This was a fight given plenty of publicity due to it being between a champion and one of his former sparring partners, and when the champion was cut over the right eye in the opening session after Dias (137½) had snaked in a right jab an imminent shock was on the cards. However, Arcari (139), protecting the damage, took time out in the second before going up a gear to punish Dias with two-handed attacks that concentrated on the body. There was more of the same in the third, Arcari's efforts quickly bearing fruit when he drove Dias into a corner and caught the Brazilian with a solid right-left combination to the head. Dropped heavily, Dias was counted out at 1.45 of the round after rolling over on to his stomach in a vain attempt to get up. Both men were southpaws.

6 March 1971. Bruno Arcari w pts 15 Joao Henrique.
Venue: Sports Palace, Rome, Italy. **Recognition:** WBC. **Referee:** Teddy Waltham.
Scorecard: 74-68.
Fight Summary: Producing the better work in the early exchanges the southpaw champion hurt Henrique (138¾) several times with solid lefts before opening up a cut over the Brazilian's right eye in the fifth, which saw the latter going in to defensive mode for a while. Arcari (139¼) himself suffered damage over the left eye in the ninth following a clash of heads, but he denied Henrique, the heavier puncher of the two, a chance of gaining the upper hand when fighting a rearguard action. In the 11th Henrique was in trouble when battered against the ropes for a long spell. However, after shrugging off the attack it was his turn to have Arcari on the run in the 13th as he chased him around the ring, firing in heavy lefts and rights to head and body. Still under pressure in the 14th, Arcari called up his reserves to battle through the pain and drive his way forward, fully deserving the referee's verdict following the final bell.

3 April 1971. Nicolino Locche w pts 15 Domingo Barrera.
Venue: Luna Park Stadium, Buenos Aires, Argentina. **Recognition:** WBA. **Referee:** Antonio Guzman.
Scorecards: 147-145, 148-146, 146-148.
Fight Summary: Despite suffering two torn tendons in his left arm during the second round and a bad cut over his right eye in the eighth, the champion battled on bravely to take a split decision over the tough Barrera (138). There was no doubting that Locche (139) was confused by Barrera's southpaw stance, but luckily for him when the

Spaniard began to tire from his exertions by the tenth he was able to land some solid shots. Surprisingly, Barrera came out firing in the 11th in an effort to finish off Locche, but the latter escaped any serious hurt by dint of excellent footwork. Following that, in the 13th and 14th rounds it was the champion who landed the most explosive punches before both men struggled through the final session.

26 June 1971. Bruno Arcari w rsc 9 (15) Enrique Jana.
Venue: Palermo Sports Palace, Sicily, Italy. **Recognition:** WBC. **Referee:** Georges Gondre.
Fight Summary: After surprising the southpaw champion with his powerful attacks immediately following the bell, Jana (137¾) dropped him in the second round and cut him over the right eye in the fifth before being found wanting himself. In a boxing sense Arcari (139½) was a cut above Jana, and as the latter stormed in time and again he was swiftly countered by solid hooks and uppercuts. Although still dangerous, by the fifth Jana was showing the effects of battle with swellings over both eyes, and while he bravely fought on for a while after 45 seconds of the ninth the referee pulled the brave Argentine out.

10 October 1971. Bruno Arcari w co 10 (15) Domingo Barrera.
Venue: Sports Palace, Genoa, Italy. **Recognition:** WBC. **Referee:** Teddy Waltham.
Fight Summary: Having gone close to winning the WBA title earlier in the year, Barrera (139) was given a crack at the WBC crown worn by Arcari (140) in what would be a battle of southpaws. In charge most of the way, especially with infighting exposing his crude opponent, Arcari really got on top in the fifth round as he caught the onrushing Barrera with heavy rights and lefts. By the ninth Barrera was on the verge of going down several times as he was forced to survive a battering, and following a further bombardment of heavy blows in the tenth he finally sunk to the floor to be counted out.

11 December 1971. Nicolino Locche w pts 15 Antonio Cervantes.
Venue: Luna Park Stadium, Buenos Aires, Argentina. **Recognition:** WBA. **Referee:** Jose Gomez.
Fight Summary: Defending his title for the first time since suffering a badly injured arm, Locche (139) boxed well on the back foot to beat the younger Cervantes (138), who was kidded out of it for large spells of the contest by the crafty champion. At times, Locche, with his hands by his side, would invite Cervantes on to the attack and counter his rival with head punches, while the latter would appear almost nonplussed. Round after round went this way, and although the challenger finished the fight almost as fresh as when he started he had nothing to show for it as Locche successfully notched up his fifth successful defence. All three judges gave Locche every round.

10 March 1972. Alfonso Frazer w pts 15 Nicolino Locche.
Venue: New City Gym, Panama City, Panama. **Recognition:** WBA. **Referee:** Jesus Celis.
Scorecards: 147-143, 148-141, 149-146.
Fight Summary: Taking the fight to the champion from the start, 'Peppermint' Frazer (137) continued his offensive right through to the final bell to run out a clear winner, despite never having been more than ten rounds previously. For Locche (139) it was one defence too many, and although he showed up well with counter attacks in the third and fifth sessions he was hampered by a gash over the right eye sustained in the eighth, an injury Frazer took full advantage of. Prior to beating Locche, the big-punching Frazer had won 25 of 30 contests, with only seven of them going the distance. However, he had also been halted four times.

On 17 June, Frazer (139¾) forced Al Ford (135¾) to retire in the fourth round at the New City Gym, but although both men came to the ring inside 140lbs the fight could not be considered as involving Frazer's world title as it was contracted at 141lbs and scheduled for ten rounds only.

10 June 1972. Bruno Arcari w co 12 (15) Joao Henrique.
Venue: Sports Palace, Genoa, Italy. **Recognition:** WBC. **Referee:** Harry Gibbs.
Fight Summary: Putting his title on the line against Henrique (139½) for the second time Arcari (139½) was under some pressure during the opening three rounds as the challenger looked for an early win, but came back well with solid body punches. As the fight wore on the southpaw champion continued to get on top despite having a few rocky moments in the fifth, and in the ninth he repeatedly belaboured Henrique on the ropes to further weaken him. Although Henrique gamely continued to fight back he was subjected to more of the same as Arcari stepped

up the pace. Having been given another heavy pounding in the 12th a left hook dropped Henrique for the full count, the finish being timed at 2.15.

28 October 1972. Antonio Cervantes w co 10 (15) Alfonso Frazer.
Venue: New City Gym, Panama City, Panama. **Recognition:** WBA. **Referee:** Waldemar Schmidt.
Fight Summary: In what was viewed a big upset, Cervantes (139), also known as Kid Pambele, took all that the champion could muster before coming back with heavy punches of his own to knock the 'Peppermint' out. The contest had got away to a slow start as both men felt each other out, but by the middle rounds Frazer (139½) was just about ahead on the cards, his aggressive work from head to body paying dividends. However, Cervantes was still very much in the contest as Frazer continued to miss with a fair percentage of heavy shots, and following a heavy exchange of blows in the tenth the latter sank to the floor where he was counted out at 1.15 of the session.

2 December 1972. Bruno Arcari w pts 15 Everaldo Costa Azevedo.
Venue: Bacoruffini Sports Palace, Turin, Italy. **Recognition:** WBC. **Referee:** Jean Deswert.
Fight Summary: After getting off to a slow start with little action during the opening three rounds, as Arcari (140) began to drive forward he was soon dominating Costa Azevedo (139) with heavy body attacks, especially when the latter was against the ropes. Although the taller Costa Azevedo did reasonably well, cutting the southpaw champion over the right eye in the 14th, he was always under pressure, stating afterwards that he was unable to get himself going. Both men were cautioned, Costa Azevedo for butting and Arcari for the use of elbows, before the latter ultimately gained a clear-cut unanimous points decision in what was not one of his better nights.

Having agreed to defend against Roger Zami, the European champion, for whatever reason the match never came off for Arcari. Then, after several months of dallying around, a title defence was eventually secured against Joergen Hansen and scheduled for November 1973.

16 February 1973. Antonio Cervantes w pts 15 Josue Marquez.
Venue: Roberto Clemente Coliseum, San Juan, Puerto Rico. **Recognition:** WBA. **Referee:** Luis Sulbaran.
Scorecards: 147-142, 149-145, 142-145.
Fight Summary: Making his first defence, Cervantes (140) used his height and reach advantages, coupled with punching power, to good effect when dealing with the elusive Marquez (137) who backed off for much of the time while only fighting in brief spurts. Stalking Marquez throughout Cervantes always looked the likely winner, but found it difficult to catch up with his man. And he was more surprised than hurt in the third round when a short left hook deposited him on the deck. Marquez continued to make life difficult for Cervantes before the latter eventually caught up with him in the final round, blitzing the Puerto Rican, now cut over the left eye, to the deck for the mandatory 'eight'. Strangely, one of the judges scored Marquez ahead at the finish regardless of the fact that Cervantes seemed a clear winner.

17 March 1973. Antonio Cervantes w rtd 9 (15) Nicolino Locche.
Venue: Cesar Giron Bullring, Maracay, Venezuela. **Recognition:** WBA. **Referee:** Luis Sulbaran.
Fight Summary: Trying to regain his old title, the veteran Locche (140) gave Cervantes (139) very few problems before a bad cut over the left eye, sustained in the third, saw his corner retire him after the ninth round had ended. Taller and faster than Locche the new kid on the block took the fight to the Argentine from the opening bell when pounding him from head to body, especially when getting to close quarters. Although consistently outpunched the game Locche never looked like going down, and when he was pulled out of the fight he had to be physically restrained from continuing.

19 May 1973. Antonio Cervantes w rsc 5 (15) Alfonso Frazer.
Venue: New City Gym, Panama City, Panama. **Recognition:** WBA. **Referee:** Luis Sulbaran.
Fight Summary: Frazer (137½), yet another former champion looking to regain his old title, made a good start when carrying the fight to Cervantes (139½), but by the second round he was really up against it as the current titleholder started to pick him apart. By the third, with Cervantes warming to the task Frazer was floored three times before getting on his bike in order to survive. Floored again in the fourth and then early in the fifth Frazer

had no defence against the power-packed punches coming his way, and after being decked twice more the referee came to his rescue at 1.38 of the session.

8 September 1973. Antonio Cervantes w rsc 5 (15) Carlos Gimenez.
Venue: Campin Coliseum, Bogota, Colombia. **Recognition:** WBA. **Referee:** Isaac Herrera.
Fight Summary: Getting into top gear quickly the champion never really gave Gimenez (140) much of a chance to settle, twice dropping the latter with hard rights to the jaw in the third round. Gamely getting to his feet both times Gimenez did well to stay in the fight, but it was Cervantes (139), showing an excellent array of jabs, hooks and uppercuts who dominated. The end for Gimenez came in the fifth when he was again put down by a heavy right to the head, and although he beat the count he was rescued by the referee on the 1.45 mark.

1 November 1973. Bruno Arcari w co 5 (15) Joergen Hansen.
Venue: KB Hall, Copenhagen, Denmark. **Recognition:** WBC. **Referee:** Raymond Baldeyrou.
Fight Summary: Despite opening up cautiously the southpaw champion stepped up the pace in the second round, and although Hansen (137¾) did well in the third he was unable to unlock his opponent's defence. Dropped by a short left to the jaw in the fifth, Hansen tried to rally before being badly hurt by another solid left and being forced to hold on as Arcari (138) went to town. After the referee managed to break the pair, almost immediately Arcari connected with a heavy right to send Hansen crashing down to be counted out. The 1987 *Ring Record Book* showed Hansen to weigh 141lbs, but having looked at the papers of the day the fight was clearly recognised as a defence for Arcari.

4 December 1973. Antonio Cervantes w pts 15 Lion Furuyama.
Venue: New City Gym, Panama City, Panama. **Recognition:** WBA. **Referee:** Jesus Celis.
Scorecards: 148-140, 147-141, 149-141.
Fight Summary: In a bruising battle Cervantes (139¾) piled up the points as he made good use of his better boxing ability and longer reach, while the challenger looked to move inside to get his punches off. Several times Cervantes was staggered, but it was not until the 14th round that Furuyama (140), despite boxing on with a completely closed right eye and damage to his left, really got to his man when having him in trouble sporadically right through to the final bell. Although Furuyama twice hit the deck, classed as slips they did not affect the scoring.

16 February 1974. Bruno Arcari w disq 8 (15) Antonio Ortiz.
Venue: Bacoruffini Sports Palace, Turin, Italy. **Recognition:** WBC. **Referee:** Rudolf Drust.
Fight Summary: Roughing the champion up from the start, Ortiz (136½), who twice fell out of the ring, forced the action with some wild punching but very little accuracy. Unfortunately, Arcari (138¾) got caught up in a brawl early on before he began to take control in the fourth when mixing up heavy body blows with solid shots to the head. It was also in this round that Arcari was cut over both eyes after Ortiz was guilty of dangerous headwork, a tactic which saw the Spaniard receive a public warning. Regardless of that, Ortiz still charged into Arcari when it would have probably been more advantageous to utilise his longer reach, and it was no surprise when he received another reprimand for his headwork in the clinches. By the eighth the southpaw champion was still landing the punches that counted, and with Ortiz continuing to ignore the earlier warnings about using his head as an additional weapon the referee threw him out on the 1.20 mark.

Arcari relinquished the WBC version of the title in August due to weight-making difficulties and injuries that saw him unable to go through with a defence against Lion Furuyama. Further to that announcement, Perico Fernandez, the heavy-handed European champion, and Furuyama were selected to contest the vacant title. Fernandez, who had come to the fore on taking the European title from Antonio Ortiz and defending it against Piero Ceru, had lost just twice in 40 contests, with Kid Tano, Manuel Calvo and Juan Albornoz among his victims.

3 March 1974. Antonio Cervantes w co 6 (15) Chang-Kil Lee.
Venue: Indian Bullring, Cartagena, Colombia. **Recognition:** WBA. **Referee:** Isidro Rodriguez.
Fight Summary: As the aggressor from the outset, and the heavier puncher of the pair, the champion went looking for an early finish, only to find Lee (139) content to use good footwork to stay out of harm's way. However, by the third, Cervantes (140), pressuring his rival and cutting the ring space down, was beginning to have some success.

Into the sixth, midway through the session with Lee taking a battering a straight right to the chin dropped him, and although he looked be getting up he failed to do so.

27 July 1974. Antonio Cervantes w co 2 (15) Victor Ortiz.
Venue: Indian Bullring, Cartagena, Colombia. **Recognition:** WBA. **Referee:** Ray Solis.
Fight Summary: Making his seventh defence, Cervantes (139) walked straight into Ortiz (140), firing in solid blows from both hands, and within a minute had dropped the latter for the mandatory 'eight' count. With Ortiz all at sea, at 1.35 of the second he was counted out after taking a tremendous left hook to the jaw.

21 September 1974. Perico Fernandez w pts 15 Lion Furuyama.
Venue: Sports Stadium, Rome, Italy. **Recognition:** WBC. **Referee:** Roland Dakin.
Scorecards: 148-147, 148-145, 145-148.
Fight Summary: Contesting the title vacated by Bruno Arcari, with both men making a slow start it was the hard-hitting Fernandez (140) who got away first, his crouching style making him a difficult target for Furuyama (140). In the early stages Furuyama was certainly wary of the Spaniard's hooking ability from either hand, but by the 13th he seemed to be ahead after picking up the pace as he began to concentrate on the body. The last two rounds saw Furuyama going for broke, throwing good uppercuts to head and body, and with Fernandez under a lot of pressure and not really able to respond effectively the split decision in his favour was met by loud boos throughout the arena.

26 October 1974. Antonio Cervantes w co 8 (15) Shinichi Kadota.
Venue: Nihon University Auditorium, Tokyo, Japan. **Recognition:** WBA. **Referee:** Luis Sulbaran.
Fight Summary: Dominating from the start, the hard-hitting Cervantes (140) quickly had the challenger in real trouble when dropping him for the mandatory 'eight' count in each of the opening five rounds. Despite being cut on the right eye early in the fourth, Kadota (138½) continued to try and force the fight. At times it looked as though he might get lucky, but having got through the sixth and seventh relatively unscathed he ran into a cracker of a right hand in the eighth, only just beating the count. Put down again by another right, Kadota made it to his feet before being smashed to the floor again by a similar punch and counted out on the 1.42 mark.

19 April 1975. Perico Fernandez w co 9 (15) Joao Henrique.
Venue: Sports Stadium, Barcelona, Spain. **Recognition:** WBC. **Referee:** Paul Talairach.
Fight Summary: Showing up well with his longer reach, the challenger, making his fourth attempt to win the title, boxed confidently for the first seven rounds as he kept Fernandez (139) at bay while scoring with jabs and body blows. It was not until the closing stages of the seventh that Fernandez came alive when battering Henrique (140) with both hands, and in the eighth he was a transformation when leaping from his corner throwing wild, swinging punches, many of which landed. It was more of the same in the ninth before a tremendous right to the jaw smashed the Brazilian to the deck where he was counted out after just one minute of the session had elapsed.

Having been the undefeated Thai-style champion, after 48 bouts Saensak Muangsurin decided to turn to boxing as we know it, and after two inside-the-distance wins over Rudy Barro and Lion Furuyama he got himself a number five rating and a world title shot. A hard-hitting southpaw, Muangsurin had already proved to be a revelation in his new sport.

17 May 1975. Antonio Cervantes w pts 15 Esteban De Jesus.
Venue: New City Gym, Panama City, Panama. **Recognition:** WBA. **Referee:** Isidro Rodriguez.
Scorecards: 148-135, 148-136, 147-138.
Fight Summary: Even though he had been beaten by Roberto Duran in a crack at the lightweight title just over a year earlier, De Jesus (139) was strongly fancied in some quarters to derail the champion. However, Cervantes (139) thought otherwise, forcing the Panamanian to take the mandatory 'eight' count when he dropped him with a right hander in the first round. Although De Jesus got back into the fight, rallying well over the next nine rounds, with his stamina flagging in the 11th he was put down again in the 12th. From there on it was all Cervantes, who raced away to a big points win as De Jesus continued to give ground.

15 July 1975. Saensak Muangsurin w rtd 8 (15) Perico Fernandez.
Venue: Hua Mark Stadium, Bangkok, Thailand. **Recognition:** WBC. **Referee:** Ernest Magana.
Fight Summary: For a man having just his third pro contest Muangsurin (140) looked a veteran as he attacked the champion from the second round onwards while nearly putting him down during that session with heavy-handed hooking. Instead of going on the defensive Fernandez (140) tried to outpunch his southpaw opponent before being forced to backpedal in the face of right-hand smashes. And in the fifth he was cut over the left eye. Subsequently, it was one-sided as rights and lefts crashed into Fernandez almost monotonously, and after suffering a badly broken nose he walked to the centre of the ring at the start of the eighth to announce his retirement.

15 November 1975. Antonio Cervantes w rtd 7 (15) Hector Thompson.
Venue: New City Gym, Panama City, Panama. **Recognition:** WBA. **Referee:** Isaac Herrera.
Fight Summary: Settling down with a long left jab the champion was soon in control, beginning to open up as the contest progressed to such an extent that Thompson (138¼) was badly hurt by combinations of lefts and rights in the fourth and nearly finished off. Although still gamely trying to get into the fight the Aussie was continually punished, being forced to take an abundance of heavy blows driven in by Cervantes (139¼). This culminated in him sustaining a bad cut over the right eye in the seventh. With Thompson in such bad condition his corner wisely retired him before the eighth could get underway.

25 January 1976. Saensak Muangsurin w pts 15 Lion Furuyama.
Venue: Nihon University Auditorium, Tokyo, Japan. **Recognition:** WBC. **Referee:** Enrique Jiminez.
Scorecards: 146-143, 148-139, 147-144.
Fight Summary: Fighting the man he beat in his second pro contest, the southpaw champion came under pressure in the opening three rounds as Furuyama (140) attacked the body with lefts and rights. With Muangsurin (139) hitting back hard from the fourth onwards, Furuyama was cut over the left eye in the sixth before sustaining similar damage over the right eye in the eighth, injuries which saw both eyes beginning to close over the last three sessions. In the latter part of the fight Muangsurin began to get right on top, landing lefts and rights almost at will as Furuyama had great difficulty in seeing properly, and while the decision in his favour was unanimous the Thai judge who gave it as 148-139 seemed way out of line.

6 March 1976. Wilfred Benitez w pts 15 Antonio Cervantes.
Venue: Hiram Bithorn Stadium, San Juan, Puerto Rico. **Recognition:** WBA. **Referee:** Isaac Herrera.
Scorecards: 148-144, 147-142, 145-147.
Fight Summary: Following a cautious opening start when both men had a good look at each other there was little in it before Benitez (138½) took over in the fifth, beating the listless champion to the punch while avoiding the wild blows coming his way. However, when Cervantes (140) began to improve by the ninth, scoring well with solid right hands to the head, he had more success during the next couple of sessions but was unable to drop Benitez. At this point in the fight it was probably even but, with Benitez picking it up from there on, as he got back to his boxing he began to pull away to fully deserve the split decision in his favour. A pro since the age of 15, by his victory, Benitez, at 17 years and six months, became the youngest ever fighter to win a world title.

31 May 1976. Wilfred Benitez w pts 15 Emiliano Villa.
Venue: Roberto Clemente Coliseum, San Juan, Puerto Rico. **Recognition:** WBA. **Referee:** Ismael Quinones-Falu.
Scorecards: 149-137, 148-137, 150-138.
Fight Summary: Operating an accurate left jab, Benitez (139) made a reasonable start to the contest as he stabbed in point scorers to the challenger's face despite having some difficulty with the Colombian's southpaw style. By the seventh, with Benitez beginning to score well with the right as well, he took over, apart from a period in the 12th round which saw Villa (139) giving as good as he got in several solid exchanges. Although Benitez peppered Villa, who was cut over the left eye in the 12th, with rights and lefts through to the final bell there were no knockdowns, and while the latter looked to be going down on a number of occasions he hung on to go the distance.

30 June 1976. Miguel Velazquez w disq 4 (15) Saensak Muangsurin.
Venue: Sports Palace, Madrid, Spain. **Recognition:** WBC. **Referee:** Abraham Echevarria.

Fight Summary: Starting strongly, Muangsurin (139) was quickly in control of the contest. However, with Velazquez (136) prepared to mix it with the hard-hitting southpaw champion a quick ending was being predicted. After Velazquez was dropped in the second and third rounds for mandatory 'eight' counts it seemed all over bar the shouting, but the finish when it came was not quite the one that was expected. With both men slugging away, Muangsurin smashed in a low left hook immediately following the bell to end the fourth, and with Velazquez lying prostrate on the canvas and out to the world the Thai was disqualified.

16 October 1976. Wilfred Benitez w rsc 3 (15) Tony Petronelli.
Venue: Hiram Bithorn Stadium, San Juan, Puerto Rico. **Recognition:** WBA. **Referee:** Ismael Quinones-Falu.
Fight Summary: Keeping the fight at distance and utilising his reach advantage the champion quickly took command. It was towards the end of the second that Benitez (139½) showed he was not going to hang about when he trapped Petronelli (139) in his own corner, crashing in solid head shots immediately prior to the bell. In the third it was more of the same when Benitez opened up with heavy-handed hooks to the head to drop Petronelli. Having surprisingly made it to his feet the Bostonian was again decked, this time by a left-right combination, and the referee called a halt with just 53 seconds on the clock.

After Benitez forfeited WBA recognition in December for failing to defend against Antonio Cervantes, due to not having enough time to prepare following a car accident, the latter would end up meeting Carlos Gimenez for the vacant title. Meanwhile, Benitez continued to be recognised as the champion in New York by the NYSAC.

29 October 1976. Saensak Muangsurin w rsc 2 (15) Miguel Velazquez.
Venue: Maristas School Sports Pavilion, Segovia, Spain. **Recognition:** WBC. **Referee:** Dick Young.
Fight Summary: Further to an opening round which saw Velazquez (139) feel his way into the fight, jabbing and moving, the southpaw challenger raced out for the second session full of intent. Throwing heavy-handed shots that drove Velazquez to the ropes, Muangsurin (139) then shortened his blows, switching from head to body to drop the champion four times in all before the referee stopped the unequal contest following the final knockdown. Ultimately, the power of Muangsurin was too much for Velazquez to handle.

15 January 1977. Saensak Muangsurin w rsc 15 (15) Monroe Brooks.
Venue: Municipal Stadium, Chiang Mai, Thailand. **Recognition:** WBC. **Referee:** Marcello Bertini.
Fight Summary: During the first eight rounds it seemed as though the slick challenger might be just too skilful for Muangsurin (139½) as he stepped around the ring tossing in fast combinations and flashy right hooks to the latter's head. However, by the ninth Muangsurin's pressure was beginning to pay off as Brooks (139½) started to feel the pace, and as the rounds progressed the American was forced to take more and more punches. With two rounds remaining, and the end in sight, after taking a tremendous southpaw left hook to the head in the 14th Brooks was given a standing count. Showing much resilience Brooks recovered to make the final session, but after being dropped twice he was wisely rescued at 1.55 when the referee realised he had nothing left.

2 April 1977. Saensak Muangsurin w co 6 (15) Guts Ishimatsu.
Venue: Kuramae Arena, Tokyo, Japan. **Recognition:** WBC. **Referee:** Larry Nadayai.
Fight Summary: Following a cautious start the challenger began to take the fight to Muangsurin (139), flashing in stinging lefts to the head before the latter came back strongly with southpaw lefts to the body in the next two sessions. By now Muangsurin was taking full advantage of his five-inch-reach advantage and in the sixth, after throwing some heavy blows that seriously weakened Ishimatsu (140), he dropped him with a cracking combination to the body. Up at 'nine', Ishimatsu was immediately dropped again from a battery of body blows and counted out on the 1.56 mark.

17 June 1977. Saensak Muangsurin w pts 15 Perico Fernandez.
Venue: Sports Palace, Madrid, Spain. **Recognition:** WBC. **Referee:** Jay Edson.
Scorecards: 147-144, 148-144, 147-145.
Fight Summary: Putting his title on the line in Spain against the man he won it from presented few difficulties for Muangsurin (140), who won all but the sixth and 15th rounds when Fernandez (135) opened up with hooks from both hands. In the main Fernandez was happy to stay on the ropes and hold when he had to rather than go all out

in an effort to get back his old belt, while the southpaw champion failed to take advantage of the situation. After the unanimous decision was announced the referee was knocked to the floor when he was hit by a missile, the ring almost being invaded by a group of fans who somehow felt that Fernandez should have won. Thankfully, the trouble was soon quelled.

25 June 1977. Antonio Cervantes w rsc 5 (15) Carlos Gimenez.
Venue: The Bullring, Maracaibo, Venezuela. **Recognition:** WBA. **Referee:** Marty Denkin.
Fight Summary: Fighting for the title that became vacant when Wilfred Benitez was stripped for failing to meet him, Cervantes (139¼) took on the hardy Gimenez (139¼), a man he had previously beaten. With a badly conditioned Cervantes looking but a shadow of his former self the fight was a huge disappointment as he struggled throughout to find any rhythm, while Gimenez, who was cut over the left eye in the third, hardly looked much better. Even so it came as a shock when the referee, without even consulting a doctor, decided to pull Gimenez out of the contest at the end of the fifth on the grounds that the damage to his eye made it impossible for him to box on. Seen by some as being a 'fix', following the fight a rematch was called for due to the scoring being even at the time of the stoppage. At that stage, Gimenez's eye damage appeared to be holding up, not worsening, and Cervantes seemed to be close to exhaustion.

3 August 1977. Wilfred Benitez w rsc 15 (15) Ray Chavez Guerrero.
Venue: Madison Square Garden, Manhattan, NYC, New York, USA. **Recognition:** NY. **Referee:** Arthur Mercante.
Fight Summary: Defending the NYSAC version of the title for the first time, and having had to take off seven pounds on the day of the fight, although Benitez (139½) started well enough with solid jabs and combinations he found Chavez Guerrero (139½) to be a cagey customer with a tight defence who would not be drawn in to a fight. Occasionally Chavez Guerrero would land a sneak punch or two, but after being picked off by counters he was soon back in defensive mode, bobbing and weaving with a high guard. In the final round Benitez at last got the bit between the teeth, and a terrific left hook saw Chavez Guerrero up against the ropes being battered by the hardest blows of the fight before falling over the bottom two strands. Having taken the mandatory 'eight' count Chavez Guerrero went back into the fray, but on dropping his hands to his sides the referee pulled him out of the contest with just 1.19 remaining.

As the number one contender for the world welterweight title, following a six-round stoppage win over Randy Shields at Madison Square Garden on 25 August 1978 Benitez announced that in future he would only fight at the higher poundage.

20 August 1977. Saensak Muangsurin w rsc 6 (15) Mike Everett.
Venue: Army Stadium, Roi-Et, Thailand. **Recognition:** WBC. **Referee:** Larry Nadayai.
Fight Summary: Although Muangsurin (140) began slowly Everett (136¼) failed to take any advantage, but once the southpaw champion stepped up the pace in the third the latter started to feel the full weight of his punches. For the next round or so it was much of the same and in the sixth Everett was being hammered without reply when he was rescued by the referee on the 2.50 mark. A clever boxer, Everett just did not have the punch to keep Muangsurin at bay.

22 October 1977. Saensak Muangsurin w pts 15 Saoul Mamby.
Venue: Open Air Stadium, Korat, Thailand. **Recognition:** WBC. **Referee:** Abraham Echeverria.
Fight Summary: In a contest that was initially announced as being unanimous in favour of Muangsurin (139½) it was changed the next day as being a split decision when it was discovered that one of the judges had actually voted for Mamby (138). Spending the majority of the fight trying to catch Mamby with heavy southpaw punches the champion discovered that the American was a difficult man to trap, and on several occasions he found himself countered after being made to miss. There was no doubt that Muangsurin landed the harder punches, especially with the left, but Mamby probably hit the target just as much if not more with lesser blows.

Ranked at number eight by *The Ring* magazine, the African champion, Jo Kimpuani, would be next up for Muangsurin, having won 38 (25 inside) of 39 contests. A durable, hard-hitting fighter, even though Kimpuani had beaten Cemal Kamaci he was relatively unknown.

5 November 1977. Antonio Cervantes w pts 15 Adriano Marrero.
Venue: Cesar Giron Bullring, Maracay, Venezuela. **Recognition:** WBA. **Referee:** Luis Sulbaran.
Scorecards: 148-140, 148-146, 147-142.
Fight Summary: Having outscored Marrero (139½) over ten rounds earlier in the year, Cervantes (139¾) was happy to give his former opponent a crack at the title this time round. Both men landed solid left and right combinations, with Marrero mainly concentrating on the body and the champion using the full target, being generally more accurate. There were no knockdowns, but the better quality blows came from Cervantes despite him damaging his right hand.

30 December 1977. Saensak Muangsurin w rsc 14 (15) Jo Kimpuani.
Venue: Tung Na-Chai Stadium, Chanthaburi, Thailand. **Recognition:** WBC. **Referee:** Marcelo Bertini.
Fight Summary: With his title on the line for the sixth time in a year, Muangsurin (138) began to get on top of Kimpuani (136½) from the third round when he forced his rival into a corner and battered him through to the bell with solid blows. Kimpuani had started well in the opening session, scoring with sharp jabs, but he was now under attack. In the fifth, having sustained a badly cut mouth, he was really up against it as Muangsurin went after him at every opportunity. To his credit, although under extreme pressure from the southpaw champion continuously, Kimpuani kept going despite the injury worsening until a series of big punches had him in desperate trouble in the 13th. The referee allowed Kimpuani to continue into the 14th even though he was way down on the cards, but with blood everywhere he called the doctor who immediately signalled that it was all over.

8 April 1978. Saensak Muangsurin w co 13 (15) Francisco Moreno.
Venue: Municipal Stadium, Hat Yai, Thailand. **Recognition:** WBC. **Referee:** Jay Edson.
Fight Summary: Despite having difficulty in making the weight, Moreno (139) did well at first with snappy hooks and combinations keeping Muangsurin (140) at bay in the early rounds. However, once the challenger began to tire Muangsurin opened up more and took complete control from the 11th, a round in which Moreno was badly cut on the mouth and left eye. From then on it was just a matter of time, and in the 13th a pair of lethal right hooks put Moreno down for the full count with just 20 seconds of the session remaining.

29 April 1978. Antonio Cervantes w co 6 (15) Tongta Kiatvayupakdi.
Venue: Provincial Stadium, Udon, Thailand. **Recognition:** WBA. **Referee:** Jesus Celis.
Fight Summary: Piling up points with his trusted left jab from the opening bell, Cervantes (140) was soon in control of his hard-hitting southpaw challenger. And by the second he was beginning to land heavily himself. Forced on the defensive, Kiatvayupakdi (140) was beginning to look slow and awkward as he struggled to avoid the accurate punches coming his way, and with blood pouring from his right eye following a solid right hook in the sixth he was ready to be taken. Sensing this was it, Cervantes followed up with two big rights and a left hook to send Kiatvayupakdi crashing down to be counted out after 2.40 of the round had elapsed.

26 August 1978. Antonio Cervantes w rsc 9 (15) Norman Sekgapane.
Venue: Independence Stadium, Botswana, South Africa. **Recognition:** WBA. **Referee:** Luis Sulbaran.
Fight Summary: Tit for tat during the opening three rounds, the champion landing with excellent left jabs while Sekgapane (139¼) busied himself on the inside, the tide changed in the fourth as Cervantes (139) cut loose to knock the South African over with a left hook. Continuing with the left hook, while supplementing it with the uppercut, Cervantes put Sekgapane down twice more in the sixth and again in the ninth after connecting with a volley of combinations. Although Sekgapane got to his feet he was soon down again, only this time the referee stopped it at 1.52 after the brave challenger got up on unsteady legs and tried to continue.

30 December 1978. Sang-Hyun Kim w co 13 (15) Saensak Muangsurin.
Venue: Munhwa Stadium, Seoul, South Korea. **Recognition:** WBC. **Referee:** Carlos Padilla.
Fight Summary: There was no doubt that Kim (140) meant business as he matched Muangsurin (139½) in the opener before forcing his fellow southpaw on the defensive with solid, scoring punches. After a period of being outboxed the champion tried to step up the pace in the middle rounds but found himself unable to land with the sweeping left hook as Kim defended tidily while looking to counter. By the 11th, Muangsurin, who had fallen

behind on points, was badly shaken up by a flurry of blows before being dropped in the 13th by a looping left hook which left him flat on his back to be counted out. The time of the finish was 2.05.

18 January 1979. Antonio Cervantes w pts 15 Miguel Montilla.
Venue: Madison Square Garden, Manhattan, NYC, New York, USA. **Recognition:** WBA. **Referee:** Tony Castellano.
Scorecards: 145-143, 147-142, 143-142.
Fight Summary: After Wilfred Benitez stepped up a division, the NYSAC recognised this fight as a championship contest. Almost back to his best, Cervantes (140) gave a master-class of long-range boxing when defending the WBA Belt against Montilla (138), being well in control most of the way. Having had to shed half a pound on the day of the fight it was thought that Cervantes might be weak at the weight, but there was no sign of that as he delivered accurate blows to Montilla's head in the opener. For his part, Montilla never stopped trying and was always looking to get inside the champion's defences where he could work the head and body. After the tenth Montilla realised that he was behind and went for broke. Despite nearly going over in the 12th from a cracking left uppercut, Montilla regrouped but, unable to close the deficit enough, he was well outboxed in the final round.

3 June 1979. Sang-Hyun Kim w pts 15 Fitzroy Guisseppi.
Venue: Changchung Gym, Seoul, South Korea. **Recognition:** WBC. **Referee:** Abraham Echevarria.
Scorecards: 146-142, 148-141, 146-140.
Fight Summary: Making a solid start, displaying superior hand-speed, the champion floored Guisseppi (139½) with a sharp southpaw left to the jaw in the second, but was unable to follow up his advantage as the veteran fighter showed good defensive ability. After a period of superiority for the champion there was little between them in the middle rounds, and although Kim (139½) appeared to have an edge he was dropped by a right smash in the 11th round. Lucky to be saved by the bell, the 12th saw Kim under attack as Guisseppi went all out with blows to head and body. Having survived the onslaught, in the final session it was Kim's turn to drop Guisseppi. However, the Trinidadian got up to make it to the gong.

25 August 1979. Antonio Cervantes w pts 15 Kwang-Min Kim.
Venue: Changchung Gym, Seoul, South Korea. **Recognition:** WBA. **Referee:** Stan Christodoulou.
Scorecards: 149-140, 149-138, 146-147.
Fight Summary: Unleashed after 15 unbeaten fights when matched against the champion, Kim (139½) was very aggressive from the start before he began running into a roadblock that came in the shape of a solid left hand to the head. Still Kim continued to bore-in tossing overarm blows, but with his extra reach Cervantes (139¼) cleverly outboxed the youngster to put points in the bank. After knocking Kim over with a cracking left hook to the jaw in the 11th Cervantes began to feel the pace, and in the 15th he was knocked down by a wild right before making it to his feet and the final bell where victory awaited him.

4 October 1979. Sang-Hyun Kim w co 11 (15) Masahiro Yogai.
Venue: Korakuen Hall, Tokyo, Japan. **Recognition:** WBC. **Referee:** Ray Solis.
Fight Summary: Cool from the start, with the southpaw champion producing an excellent defence in the face of the bombs being sent in by Yogai (140) before long he was cracking in some of his own. Boxing in a controlled fashion, Kim (139½) was in command in all but the sixth as Yogai chased him down. He then moved up a gear to dominate the action when countering his rival heavily. Although Yogai's left eye was showing signs of damage by the tenth, he was allowed to carry on after an inspection by the doctor only to run into some powerful blows followed by a left smash to the head which saw him counted out at 2.01 of the 11th.

23 February 1980. Saoul Mamby w co 14 (15) Sang-Hyun Kim.
Venue: Changchung Gym, Seoul, South Korea. **Recognition:** WBC. **Referee:** Harry Gibbs.
Fight Summary: Both men made a cautious start to the contest as they felt each other out for the opening two sessions, and even when the action took off it remained close. The champion was obviously dangerous with body punches and southpaw jabs, while Mamby (139) was proving difficult to nail down with his ducking and clever defence. In rounds seven and eight, after Mamby had points deducted when Kim's left eye started to close from the effects of butting he was told that he would be disqualified if he did it again. However, the damage was done. With Kim (140) suffering from a lack of vision, when Mamby came on strongly to take the 13th by a clear margin to

go ahead on the scoring, it was no surprise when Kim came out recklessly for the 14th as looked to make any leeway up. Although initially doing well in the session as he met Mamby punch for punch, Kim eventually walked into a straight right that deposited him on the floor to be counted out on the 1.44 mark in the act of rising.

29 March 1980. Antonio Cervantes w rsc 7 (15) Miguel Montilla.
Venue: Indian Bullring, Cartagena, Colombia. **Recognition:** WBA. **Referee:** Waldemar Schmidt.
Fight Summary: In a return match the champion again got the better of Montilla (139½), only this time it was by the short route. Making a studied start, Cervantes (139¼) was soon stabbing the left jab into Montilla's face as he made full use of his extra reach, and he dominated all the way to drop the latter in the fifth and seventh with cracking left hooks. Although getting up from the second knockdown, and with Montilla looking ready to be taken, at 1.28 of the seventh it was all over after the referee called it off.

7 July 1980. Saoul Mamby w rsc 13 (15) Esteban De Jesus.
Venue: Metro Centre, Bloomington, Minnesota, USA. **Recognition:** WBC. **Referee:** Rudy Ortega.
Fight Summary: For the opening two rounds De Jesus (140) made sure he was first to lead before clinching, but by the third the champion showed what he was made of as he began to dominate with the jab, a tactic he developed all night. Round after round went by with the once super De Jesus taking punches by the plenty and in the 12th Mamby (139½) finally dropped him with a cracking left-right-left. Up at 'four', although forced to take the mandatory 'eight', De Jesus made it to the bell but should have stayed on his stool. Racing out for the start of the 13th Mamby took his time before six straight lefts followed by a solid left-right dropped De Jesus on the seat of his pants, ushering the referee in for an immediate stoppage with 1.13 on the clock.

2 August 1980. Aaron Pryor w co 4 (15) Antonio Cervantes.
Venue: Riverfront Coliseum, Cincinnati, Ohio, USA. **Recognition:** WBA. **Referee:** Larry Rozadilla.
Fight Summary: Sensing that it was going to be his night the challenger tore into a hesitant Cervantes (139½) from the bell, but after doing some good work he was dropped by a short right-hand counter and saw the round out cautiously. In the second Pryor (138½) again came on strongly, and after giving Cervantes a bit of a pounding with lefts and rights a slashing left hook opened up a bad gash over the latter's right eye. By the end of the third Cervantes appeared exhausted, having tried to fend Pryor off, and at 1.47 of the fourth he was counted out after being dropped by a big overarm right which followed a heavy body attack.

2 October 1980. Saoul Mamby w pts 15 Maurice Watkins.
Venue: Caesar's Palace, Las Vegas, Nevada, USA. **Recognition:** WBC. **Referee:** Mills Lane.
Scorecards: 146-140, 147-139, 147-141.
Fight Summary: Looking far from impressive the champion eventually subdued the aggressive Watkins (140), who was always on the attack with the right hand before running out of steam as the contest progressed. Right from the start Mamby (138½) appeared content to go the distance, and even when Watkins picked up a cut eye in the fifth he failed to up the pace. Continually refusing to be drawn into a close-quarter battle, Mamby would pick Watkins off whenever he stormed in while occasionally banging in sweeping right uppercuts. However, he failed to take full advantage of the many openings that began to appear as the challenger tired and grew more desperate. The final bell came as a welcome relief to all of those who had expected something more lively.

22 November 1980. Aaron Pryor w rsc 6 (15) Gaetan Hart.
Venue: Riverfront Coliseum, Cincinnati, Ohio, USA. **Recognition:** WBA. **Referee:** Roberto Ramirez.
Fight Summary: Proving far too good for his challenger Pryor (138½) dropped him twice in the second round, the second time from a crashing overarm right to the head, before settling down with the left jab as the Canadian champion plodded forward. By the fifth it was apparent that the game Hart (138¼) had no real chance of winning as he had neither the firepower nor the movement to worry Pryor. Coming out for the sixth with a vengeance, Pryor soon sent Hart crashing from a right to the jaw, and although the latter got to his feet the referee rescued him on the 51-second mark when he was being punished remorselessly.

12 June 1981. Saoul Mamby w pts 15 Jo Kimpuani.
Venue: Joe Louis Arena, Detroit, Michigan, USA. **Recognition:** WBC. **Referee:** Eddie Yoo.

Scorecards: 149-134, 149-140, 149-138.

Fight Summary: Hampered by a nine-month layoff mainly due to contractual problems, although the champion took his time to get going by the eighth his left hook, especially to the body, was proving to be too much for Kimpuani (139¼). Prior to that Kimpuani had bothered Mamby (139¾) with left hooks of his own, supplemented by the occasional right hand, but after failing to make a permanent dent the latter's speed took him away from the danger zone to run out an easy victor. Mamby admitted afterwards that he was unable to put his combinations together as he would have liked.

27 June 1981. Aaron Pryor w rsc 2 (15) Lennox Blackmoore.
Venue: Hacienda Hotel, Las Vegas, Nevada, USA. **Recognition:** WBA. **Referee:** Stan Berg.
Fight Summary: Starting like a tornado, after the champion walked into the taller Blackmoore (139½) throwing punches from both hands the latter barely made it to the end of the opening session, having been dropped twice by left hooks and cut over the right eye. Resuming where he had left off Pryor (140) tore into Blackmoore at the start of the second, soon having him down from a right-left hook combination. Up at 'eight', Blackmoore was again under pressure as Pryor took him to the ropes, and following another hefty left hook the referee had seen enough, jumping in to rescue the badly beaten Guyanese after just 58 seconds of the session.

29 August 1981. Saoul Mamby w pts 15 Thomas Americo.
Venue: Senayan Stadium, Jakarta, Indonesia. **Recognition:** WBC. **Referee:** Ken Morita.
Scorecards: 146-141, 147-139, 146-146.
Fight Summary: Attacking from the opening bell Americo (139) made life extremely difficult for Mamby (139¼), especially after opening up a cut on his right eye. It was not until the fifth that the champion found his feet when getting the left jab working and cracking in uppercuts and body blows. The contest was fairly even through to the 11th when Mamby was staggered by lefts and rights to the head, but he fought back well and got right on top as Americo tired. It was during the last four rounds that Mamby cemented his dominance as he opened up with both hands to drive Americo back and, although one judge scored the fight even, the other two were much nearer the mark.

14 November 1981. Aaron Pryor w rsc 7 (15) Dujuan Johnson.
Venue: Public Auditorium, Cleveland, Ohio, USA. **Recognition:** WBA. **Referee:** Jackie Keough.
Fight Summary: No respecter of reputations after winning 17 in a row, Johnson (140) chased down the champion at the opening bell, dropping him with a solid right to the head. With his pride shaken Pryor (139¼) was soon back on his feet firing in punches from both hands, but was hurt again by a left hook before the round was over. It was a different matter thereafter as Pryor found his distance when beginning to put his punches together better while Johnson fired in one at a time and, although he was shaken up on the odd occasion, by the fifth he was taking over. Having hurt Johnson in the previous session, the sixth saw Pryor really going to work. In the seventh it was more of the same as he unleashed a barrage of blows to head and body, which only abated when the referee stopped the fight at 1.49 after the challenger failed to respond.

Miguel Montilla, who already had two attempts at the title, would be Pryor's next challenger. A hardened pro, Montilla had 37 wins from 46 contests, and despite having had just five fights in the last two years and losing a close one to Johnson he had beaten Alfonso Frazer and Domingo Ayala. He was ranked at number four by *The Ring* magazine.

20 December 1981. Saoul Mamby w pts 15 Obisia Nwankpa.
Venue: National Stadium, Lagos, Nigeria. **Recognition:** WBC. **Referee:** Harry Gibbs.
Scorecards: 144-143, 145-143, 145-146.
Fight Summary: Nwankpa (138¼) made a good start when taking the fight to the champion, and for the first six rounds he was in with a shout as he went after an opponent who seemed happy to stay out of trouble. However, all that changed in the seventh when Mamby (139¼), deciding that he had done enough defensive work, cut loose with lefts and rights to the head to floor the Commonwealth champion. Although Nwankpa rallied somewhat during the next few rounds it was Mamby, putting his punches together well, who finished the stronger to just about warrant the split decision in his favour.

21 March 1982. Aaron Pryor w rsc 12 (15) Miguel Montilla.
Venue: Playboy Hotel, Atlantic City, New Jersey, USA. **Recognition:** WBA. **Referee:** Waldemar Schmidt.
Fight Summary: Forced to travel more than ten rounds for the first time in his career, the champion eventually managed to subdue the tough Montilla (139) after 42 seconds of the 12th when the referee came to the latter's rescue. Pryor (139¾) had been unable to drop Montilla, who was cut over both eyes at the finish, despite racking him with solid punches from both hands and driving him back for long periods. At times it had been nothing more than a punch-up as Montilla stood right in front of Pryor, throwing looping left hooks and right-handers, but unable to take him out of the fight despite hurting him at times it was the Dominican who ultimately gave way.

26 June 1982. Leroy Haley w pts 15 Saoul Mamby.
Venue: Front Row Theatre, Cleveland, Ohio, USA. **Recognition:** WBC. **Referee:** Jackie Keough.
Scorecards: 145-142, 148-144, 143-144.
Fight Summary: Allowing Haley (139½) to get away to a good start in the early rounds while he was content to bide his time, it eventually became obvious that the champion had made the wrong decision when finding it difficult to get himself going. A notoriously slow starter, when Mamby (138) did finally begin to apply pressure it seemed to have little effect on the bobbing and weaving Haley, who threw left hooks and overarm rights from a crouching position while coping comfortably with everything coming his way. By the 11th the title seemed to be slipping away from Mamby, and although he began to throw more leather Haley just about deserved the verdict that came his way.

Haley's first defence would be against Juan Jose Gimenez, the durable Argentine who had lost to Obisia Nwankpa in a WBC eliminator in March 1981. Despite losing, Gimenez's performance had been good enough in a tough fight for him to be offered a title shot down the line. A pro since 1968, and a veteran of 86 wins in 98 contests, Gimenez had beaten Hugo Gutierrez, Barry Michael, Antonio Amaya and George Feeney.

4 July 1982. Aaron Pryor w rsc 6 (15) Akio Kameda.
Venue: Riverfront Coliseum, Cincinnati, Ohio, USA. **Recognition:** WBA. **Referee:** Ernesto Magana.
Fight Summary: Taking a standing 'eight' count in the opening session, after being put down by Kameda (139¼), was not in the champion's script but he quickly rallied to drop his opponent twice in the second and again in the third before setting the tall southpaw up for the finish in round six. Being cut over the right eye following a clash of heads in the fifth merely made Pryor (139½) more determined when coming out for the sixth, and although Kameda was able to stagger up from another couple of knockdowns, with there being no response the referee called it off after 1.13 of the round had elapsed.

20 October 1982. Leroy Haley w pts 15 Juan Jose Gimenez.
Venue: Public Hall, Cleveland, Ohio, USA. **Recognition:** WBC. **Referee:** Carlos Padilla.
Scorecards: 147-143, 147-140, 146-143.
Fight Summary: In what was a tough defence Haley (139¼) could never quite subdue the hardy Gimenez (139½), who was always prepared to battle it out even after being dropped by a low blow in the seventh. The classier boxing came from Haley no doubt, but it was Gimenez who forced the fight in the latter stages, and although he was rocked by combinations of left hooks and right hands he remained undeterred. In the 13th Gimenez was knocked sideways by a left hook, but he continued to walk through the punches until the final bell.

A short while later the WBC announced that, as from 1 January 1983, all world title bouts held under its auspices would be contested over 12 rounds.

12 November 1982. Aaron Pryor w rsc 14 (15) Alexis Arguello.
Venue: Orange Bowl, Miami, Florida, USA. **Recognition:** WBA. **Referee:** Stan Christodoulou.
Fight Summary: Attempting to become a world champion in four different weight divisions proved to be too much for Arguello (138½), who was rescued by the referee after 1.06 of the penultimate round despite not being put down. Prior to the finish there had been no knockdowns, it being closely fought with one judge showing Pryor (140) to be in front by 127-124 at the start of the 14th and another having Arguello ahead by 127-125. With Pryor somehow being able to withstand Arguello's best punches, which included vicious rights to head and body and any

number of other blows, and to come back blasting away proved him to be one of the best the division had seen. Having been severely shaken up by a tremendous right in the 13th many would not have expected Pryor to be still standing let alone going on the attack in the 14th, and with Arguello tottering under a hail of leather he was wisely pulled out.

13 February 1983. Leroy Haley w pts 12 Saoul Mamby.
Venue: Public Hall, Cleveland, Ohio, USA. **Recognition:** WBC. **Referee:** Carlos Padilla.
Scorecards: 115-114, 115-114, 115-113.
Fight Summary: Fighting over the shorter distance of 12 rounds, and a return bout, Mamby (140) tried to get off early with the jab but was met punch-for-punch by Haley (140) who countered well with both hands and kept on the move. Haley gradually went to the fore as Mamby, although landing the heavier punches of the fight, became more selective thus allowing the stocky champion to make the running to the final bell. There were no knockdowns, but both men were cut above their left eyes.

2 April 1983. Aaron Pryor w rsc 3 (15) Sang-Hyun Kim.
Venue: Sands Hotel & Casino, Atlantic City, New Jersey, USA. **Recognition:** WBA. **Referee:** Carlos Berrocal.
Fight Summary: Although struggling to make the weight, the champion immediately went after Kim (138¾), knocking him from one side of the ring to the other, and it was more of the same in the second round with the latter seemingly unable to fight back other than with wild swings. Having been cut over the right eye by a butt in the second, Pryor (140) was now determined to end matters as he tore into Kim at the start of the third, banging in solid rights and lefts, and with the South Korean not responding the referee was left with no alternative other than to call it off after just 37 seconds.

Towards the end of April, after the United States Boxing Association voted to form an international string to its bow, known as USBA/I, it was announced that they supported Pryor as the champion.

18 May 1983. Bruce Curry w pts 12 Leroy Haley.
Venue: Dunes Hotel, Las Vegas, Nevada, USA. **Recognition:** WBC. **Referee:** Davy Pearl.
Scorecards: 117-112, 115-114, 116-112.
Fight Summary: Looking to join his brother Donald as a world champion, the aggressive Curry (139) forced the fight from the start, being especially effective with the left hook after setting up the champion with the jab. The smaller of the two, Haley (140), scoring with solid punches to head and body, came back well in the middle rounds before giving way to Curry as he faded towards the end. The last two sessions were all Curry as he made up any lost ground to make sure of the verdict.

7 July 1983. Bruce Curry w rsc 7 (12) Hidekazu Akai.
Venue: Kinki University Arena, Osaka, Japan. **Recognition:** WBC. **Referee:** Octavio Meyran.
Fight Summary: The opening two rounds saw Akai (139¾) take the champion by surprise when attacking him for all his worth, despite him having been cut over the left eye by an accidental butt early on. However, Curry (138¼) had settled by the third, tossing in accurate left jabs and hooks at Akai, who responded in the fifth with a right-left which put the American on the seat of his trunks. Ruled a slip, Curry was up immediately, fighting back strongly prior to running into a firestorm in the sixth as Akai went after him with incessant lefts and rights. Recognising that Akai had punched himself out in the sixth, Curry quickly got down to business in the seventh, temporarily dropping the challenger with solid head shots. Back in the fray, Akai was immediately assailed by a barrage of blows, the final one being a cracking right which dropped him in a heap and led to the doctor advising the referee to call the fight off after 71 seconds.

9 September 1983. Aaron Pryor w co 10 (15) Alexis Arguello.
Venue: Caesar's Palace, Las Vegas, Nevada, USA. **Recognition:** WBA. **Referee:** Richard Steele.
Fight Summary: Dropped in the first by a crashing right over the top and by a left hook in the fourth, Arguello (139) somehow got through the mayhem to continue, but instead of boxing the champion he continually elected to punch it out with him. When Arguello boxed he did well, but Pryor (140) would not be denied. After taking everything that the former had to throw, which was considerable, he would merely grin and wave his rival in for

more. By the tenth there was no doubt that Arguello was weakening from his exertions, and when Pryor charged in and nailed him with a series of sharp punches he'd had enough, sinking to the floor to be counted out with 1.12 of the session remaining. It had been another tremendous fight between the pair, but Pryor had once again proved too tough and too hard-hitting for the legend that was Arguello.

Having earlier announced that they supported Pryor as champion, the USBA/I, renamed as the International Boxing Federation (IBF) in late October, stated that they would be supporting the aims of the current USBA champion, Johnny Bumphus. However, in January 1984, they changed their minds, again proclaiming Pryor, who had relinquished the WBA version of the title in December, as their champion after Bumphus and Lorenzo Garcia had been matched to contest the vacant WBA championship.

19 October 1983. Bruce Curry w pts 15 Leroy Haley.
Venue: Showboat Hotel, Las Vegas, Nevada, USA. **Recognition:** WBC. **Referee:** Davy Pearl.
Scorecards: 116-114, 115-113, 113-115.
Fight Summary: Although easing his way past Haley (138¼) for the second time, with this one being even closer the champion had to pull out all the stops before getting the nod on the scorecards. While Curry (139½) seemed to make the better start, Haley boxed well to make him miss repeatedly with some big shots before being hampered by a nasty cut over the left eye in the ninth. Haley had also done well in some of the hard-hitting exchanges between the pair, but it was Curry, throwing the greater number of punches in the last three sessions, who ultimately impressed the judges.

22 January 1984. Johnny Bumphus w pts 15 Lorenzo Garcia.
Venue: Sands Hotel & Casino, Atlantic City, New Jersey, USA. **Recognition:** WBA. **Referee:** Tony Perez.
Scorecards: 146-143, 144-142, 144-142.
Fight Summary: Contesting the title vacated by Aaron Pryor, neither man managed too much in the opening three sessions before Garcia (139¾) suddenly found a short right to drop the much taller Bumphus (139) for the mandatory count in the fourth. Back in action, Bumphus, who seemed more embarrassed than hurt, was jolted by several rights to the chin before getting himself going and upping his work-rate to take the next five rounds. The tempo of the fight was now increasing, and following a lively ninth the cagey Garcia came again to make things tighter over the next few rounds. But as he began to suffer from fatigue, it was the Tacoma southpaw who had enough left in the tank to make sure of victory.

29 January 1984. Billy Costello w rsc 10 (12) Bruce Curry.
Venue: Civic Centre, Beaumont, Texas, USA. **Recognition:** WBC. **Referee:** Richard Steele.
Fight Summary: Defending his title for the third time, Curry (139½) felt the weight of his challenger's punches as early as the first when a big left hook left him on unsteady legs. Bravely battling back, Curry began to take the fight to Costello (140) before being caught heavily again, in the fourth, and being cut over the left eye in the sixth. From the seventh onwards Costello began to assume control with his heavy-laden left hooks and right hands seemingly shaking Curry up every time he connected, and at the end of the ninth the champion looked all-in. With the tenth seeing no let-up in Costello's pursuit of Curry, when the latter had got to his feet after being dropped by a cracking left-right the referee eventually came to his rescue after 56 seconds of the round had elapsed. At the time of the stoppage, Curry was in dire straits as all manner of punches were finding the target.

1 June 1984. Gene Hatcher w rsc 11 (12) Johnny Bumphus.
Venue: Memorial Coliseum, Buffalo, New York, USA. **Recognition:** WBA. **Referee:** John LoBianco.
Fight Summary: Even though Hatcher (139½) made a good start when rocking the southpaw champion with a right to the jaw in the opening round and again in the fifth he failed to follow up his advantage before beginning to fall behind on the cards. Switching from southpaw to orthodox and back again, the six-foot tall Bumphus (139½) certainly confused Hatcher, who seemed to rely on landing with one punch, and by the end of the tenth he was well ahead. With that in mind Hatcher upped the pace in the 11th, but instead of remaining at distance he began to work on the inside, a tactic which bore fruit immediately when he dropped Bumphus with a heavy left hook. Barely making it to his feet, with Bumphus all over the place as Hatcher hounded him, the referee called it off on the 2.35 mark to save the champion from taking further punishment.

22 June 1984. Aaron Pryor w pts 15 Nick Furlano.
Venue: Varsity Stadium, Toronto, Canada. **Recognition:** IBF. **Referee:** Harold Davis.
Scorecards: 146-139, 146-138, 148-140.
Fight Summary: Having been out of the ring for nine months Pryor (139½) came back to defend the IBF title bestowed upon him, quickly having Furlano (140) in trouble when dropping him twice with left hooks in the opening round. To his credit Furlano came back well to make it competitive, showing good movement and the ability to keep away from further trouble. He certainly bothered Pryor at times when unloading his best punches. However, never really hurt, at the end of the day Pryor threw too many punches from all kinds of angles for Furlano to deal with.

15 July 1984. Billy Costello w pts 12 Ronnie Shields.
Venue: Midtown Centre, Kingston, New York, USA. **Recognition:** WBC. **Referee:** Davy Pearl.
Scorecards: 117-111, 117-110, 119-110.
Fight Summary: Fighting in stifling heat, both men eased through the opening round before the contest came alight in the second when Shields (140), dropped by a left hook, came back strongly to put down the champion with a left hook of his own. Dusting himself down, Costello (138¾) began to control the fight, but could never take over completely despite cutting Shields over the left eye in the third and decking him twice more in the sixth following heavy rights to the head. Although Shields made a real fight of it, especially in the last round when he had Costello backing off and covering up, the difference in power was the deciding factor.

3 November 1984. Billy Costello w pts 12 Saoul Mamby.
Venue: Midtown Centre, Kingston, New York, USA. **Recognition:** WBC. **Referee:** Tony Perez.
Scorecards: 118-110, 119-109, 119-109.
Fight Summary: Putting up his title against a former champion in Mamby (139¼) on his home turf the unbeaten Costello (140), showing a good left jab to go with heavy hands, nailed his man with plenty of big punches but was unable to apply the finisher. It was a tough fight for the 37-year-old Mamby, who came in as a substitute at six days' notice for the injured Leroy Haley, but he defied all of Costello's efforts to put him away while continuing to make life difficult right through to the final bell. Although both men suffered cuts above their left eyes the damage failed to alter the nature of the contest.

15 December 1984. Gene Hatcher w pts 15 Ubaldo Sacco.
Venue: Tarrant County Civic Centre, Fort Worth, Texas, USA. **Recognition:** WBA. **Referee:** Tony Perez.
Scorecards: 144-141, 144-140, 141-145.
Fight Summary: In a bitterly fought contest, Hatcher (139), cut over and under both eyes, had to fight for all he was worth to decision Sacco (140) in defence of his title. There were times when it looked as though Hatcher's crown was slipping away as Sacco scored with left jabs and combinations, but by the eighth he was beginning to make up lost ground when hammering his man around the ring and buckling his legs. It was in the 11th, however, that Hatcher finally made his run for home as he stormed after Sacco, cutting him over the left eye and flooring him with a right to the jaw, and although the latter fought back well it was the champion who landed the majority of blows through to the final bell.

16 February 1985. Billy Costello w pts 12 Leroy Haley.
Venue: Midtown Centre, Kingston, New York, USA. **Recognition:** WBC. **Referee:** Arthur Mercante.
Scorecards: 118-111, 116-111, 119-109.
Fight Summary: Although the harder hitter of the pair the champion could not put Haley (139) down, even suffering the ignominy of being dropped himself in the second with what seemed to be a push. With his crouching style and durability, Haley was a difficult man to pin down, but by the sixth Costello (138½) had assumed control and was beginning to dominate with the left jab and heavy left hooks to the body. Despite suffering a badly cut left eye in the seventh Haley would not be deterred, continuing to offer up a difficult target before punching away with both hands in the 12th to go down fighting.

2 March 1985. Aaron Pryor w pts 15 Gary Hinton.
Venue: Sands Hotel & Casino, Atlantic City, New Jersey, USA. **Recognition:** IBF. **Referee:** Rudy Battle.

Scorecards: 143-141, 146-139, 141-143.
Fight Summary: Suffering the effects of a long layoff the champion found it tough going against Hinton (140), having to come from behind to beat the Philadelphia southpaw. Right from the off Hinton was able to hit Pryor (140) with right jabs and two-handed hooks, and the latter's cause was not helped when he was cut on the right temple in the second following a clash of heads. Pryor's problems continued with his inability to find any rhythm in the early rounds, but in the ninth he began to look more like his old self when he hurt Hinton with a burst of two-handed hitting. Now back in the fight, Pryor hurt Hinton with left hooks and right hands in several rounds before catching the latter with a big right in the 14th, which dropped him and effectively sewed up the fight.

After Pryor forfeited IBF recognition in December due to inactivity, Hinton and Reyes Antonio Cruz were eventually matched to find a new champion.

21 July 1985. Ubaldo Sacco w rsc 9 (15) Gene Hatcher.
Venue: Municipal Casino, Campione, D'Italia, Italy. **Recognition:** WBA. **Referee:** Ernesto Magana.
Fight Summary: In a return contest that was requested after Sacco (139) had gone close previously, this time round he made no mistake, being well on the way to winning before the champion was pulled out by the referee at 1.28 of the ninth when a bad cut over the left eye worsened. Although the opening four rounds had been closely fought, Sacco took charge in the fifth when meeting the aggression of Hatcher (140) with solid left-hand counters and big head punches, and forced a knockdown when the latter went down on one knee to gain respite. It was in the sixth that Hatcher was first cut over the left eye and, while there were several exchanges which were bitterly contested, it was Sacco who was getting into control mode. And that was how it remained until the stoppage.

21 August 1985. Lonnie Smith w rsc 8 (12) Billy Costello.
Venue: Madison Square Garden, Manhattan, NYC, New York, USA. **Recognition:** WBC. **Referee:** Luis Rivera.
Fight Summary: Starting well, the champion soon had Smith (138½) over from a left hook, but the latter recovered his senses to get to the bell. In the second round it was his turn to do some damage, knocking Costello (138½) down twice with heavy left hooks of his own. Costello continued to stalk Smith in the third, but found his unorthodox hit-and-run style difficult to handle, and gradually becoming frustrated he began to charge in throwing wild punches. With Smith now sensing that he had got Costello's measure, when opening up in the fifth he dropped him with another left hook. On his feet again, Costello continued to take the fight to Smith, but in the eighth he reached the end of the road when a left jab-right uppercut combination downed him. Although Costello got up the referee rescued him with 29 seconds of the session remaining after he had been put down by uppercuts from both hands for the fifth time in the fight. A powerful puncher, Costello was made to look pedestrian by the accurate countering, faster hand-speed and movement shown by Smith, who was accurately dubbed "Lightnin'" in the build up to the fight.

15 March 1986. Patrizio Oliva w pts 15 Ubaldo Sacco.
Venue: Louis 11 Stadium, Monte Carlo, Monaco. **Recognition:** WBA. **Referee:** Frank Cappuccino.
Scorecards: 147-144, 145-141, 140-145.
Fight Summary: Dominating the early rounds with the left jab, supported by left hooks and solid rights, the unbeaten Oliva (139¼) also proved able to fight back when under pressure as he did in the sixth when the champion cornered him on occasion. Although he was the aggressor throughout, while looking to be the stronger, Sacco (139½) was unable to match the hand-speed of the Italian. As the fight wore on it appeared that Sacco was getting into the fight, especially when doing well in the tenth, but when Oliva had a point deducted in the 12th for holding he held his nerve, repelling most of the punches coming his way, and ran out a worthy winner.

26 April 1986. Gary Hinton w pts 15 Reyes Antonio Cruz.
Venue: Sports Palace, Lucca, Italy. **Recognition:** IBF. **Referee:** Randy Neumann.
Scorecards: 143-142, 145-140, 144-142.
Fight Summary: Contesting the vacant title it was Hinton (139½) who came through to take the verdict despite winning just one of the last four rounds. The previously unbeaten Cruz (139¼) boxed well, but was often confused by Hinton's southpaw stance as the latter scored well with barrages of right jabs and hooks. On reflection Cruz's

slow start probably cost him the fight, but there was never much in it with both men exchanging sharp blows up until the final bell.

5 June 1986. Rene Arredondo w co 5 (12) Lonnie Smith.

Venue: Olympic Auditorium, Los Angeles, California, USA. **Recognition:** WBC. **Referee:** Marty Denkin.
Fight Summary: Playing a waiting game, Arredondo (139¼) appeared content to allow the champion to stay on the outside, flicking out left jabs nervously and throwing wild rights and lefts from well out of range. All that changed in the third as Smith (139½) moved closer to take the round before being wobbled by a right hand in the fourth and then being hurt again by a good left uppercut. Arredondo again failed to make his move at the start of the fifth, but after gradually manoeuvring Smith into his own corner he eventually unloaded a smashing right to the jaw to send the latter crashing down to be counted out at 1.24 of the session.

24 July 1986. Tsuyoshi Hamada w co 1 (12) Rene Arredondo.

Venue: Kokugikan Arena, Tokyo, Japan. **Recognition:** WBC. **Referee:** Steve Crosson.
Fight Summary: As soon as the opening bell rang the southpaw challenger tore into Arredondo (139½) with overarm rights and lefts before being driven almost through the ropes by solid left hooks. Still banging away, Hamada (139¼) would not be deterred when continuing to try and close Arredondo down. In the last half minute of the session, the Mexican, caught up in a flurry of blows, fought back hard before wilting under a hail of leather and crashing down to be counted out after 3.09 of the first round; nine seconds into the interval.

6 September 1986. Patrizio Oliva w rsc 3 (15) Brian Brunette.

Venue: Sports Palace, Naples, Italy. **Recognition:** WBA. **Referee:** Guy Jutras.
Fight Summary: Having made the weight at the third attempt, Brunette (140) was taken to task by the champion almost from the opening bell. Having been speared several times by fast lefts he was then wobbled by left-right combinations before ending the round with his left eye closed. Oliva (139¼) soon got to Brunette in the second, continuing his attack in the third with heavy combinations which left the American all at sea with nowhere to go. The fight came to an end when the referee stopped it on the 2.38 mark after Brunette's cornermen jumped into the ring to make sure that their man did not continue.

30 October 1986. Joe Manley w co 10 (15) Gary Hinton.

Venue: Civic Centre, Hartford, Connecticut, USA. **Recognition:** IBF. **Referee:** Sal Maltempo.
Fight Summary: Both men got down to work from the opening bell, but it was Manley (138½) who struck first when he dropped the southpaw champion with a solid right in the second round. Although shaken up Hinton (139) was soon back into the fray, and for the next few sessions the fight see-sawed back and forth as first one man got the upper hand and then the other. Having been rocked in the seventh by a left hook, in the eighth it was Hinton's turn to hurt Manley with a similar punch before the pair continued to fire in solid blows throughout the ninth. Things changed dramatically in the tenth when it became clear that Hinton was all-in, and he was soon troubled by lefts and rights which saw him staggering across the ring prior to a heavy right putting him down for the full count on the 2.14 mark.

2 December 1986. Tsuyoshi Hamada w pts 12 Ronnie Shields.

Venue: Kokugikan Arena, Tokyo, Japan. **Recognition:** WBC. **Referee:** Arthur Mercante.
Scorecards: 111-108, 116-111, 113-115.
Fight Summary: While Shields (139¼) proved difficult to pin down and fought cautiously, with the southpaw champion being forced to make the running he relied too heavily on the left cross which missed its target more often than not. Deducted a point in the fourth for going low, Hamada (139¾) began to have difficulty in avoiding right-hand counters, something that led to him being cut over the right eye in round seven. Still coming forward, Hamada continued to work the body with fair success, but in the 11th Shields finally cut loose, also making the body a target, and although he had fair success right through to the final bell his efforts came too late.

10 January 1987. Patrizio Oliva w pts 15 Rodolfo Gonzalez.

Venue: Tenda Theatre, Agrigento, Italy. **Recognition:** WBA. **Referee:** Isidro Rodriguez.
Scorecards: 147-142, 146-139, 145-141.

47

Fight Summary: Using his superior speed and an accurate left jab Oliva (140) proved to be a cut above Gonzalez (138½), outboxing his rugged Mexican challenger in virtually all rounds bar the seventh when a big left hook had him down for the first time in his career. Although badly shaken Oliva picked himself up before eventually getting back into his routine, thereafter offering Gonzalez only limited opportunities. However, spurred on by his success, Gonzalez came on much stronger after the seventh, and despite not get getting close enough he made life more difficult for Oliva, who made it 47 victories from 47 contests since winning the gold medal at the 1980 Moscow Olympics.

4 March 1987. Terry Marsh w rsc 10 (15) Joe Manley.
Venue: Festival Hall Super Tent, Basildon, England. **Recognition:** IBF. **Referee:** Randy Neumann.
Fight Summary: Making a great start, showing plenty of commitment and passion, Marsh (140) outboxed the champion right from the first bell to be well in control by the end of the eighth as his opponent weakened. The only blots on the Englishman's performance at that moment in time had been two blatant butts for which he had been severely cautioned, but they had served a purpose. Marsh began the ninth as though he intended it to be the last, keeping Manley (138½) under unrelenting pressure before finally flooring him with a left hook for the mandatory 'eight'. There was not much left to come from Manley, and 20 seconds into the tenth it was all over as the referee dived in to rescue him when he was in the act of falling after Marsh had poured in punch after punch from the start of the session.

1 July 1987. Terry Marsh w rsc 6 (15) Akio Kameda.
Venue: Royal Albert Hall, Kensington, London, England. **Recognition:** IBF. **Referee:** Randy Neumann.
Fight Summary: With the tall Japanese southpaw making his second attempt to win the title, Marsh (140) was soon hard at work, landing hurtful straight punches, but would-be disaster struck in the second when he picked up a badly cut right eye. It was at that point Marsh showed what he was made of. Instead of taking it easy he tore into Kameda (140), shaking him up with left hooks and solid rights. It looked desperate for Marsh in the third as the gashed eye worsened, but ignoring Kameda's blows he hit back with straight lefts and rights mixed up with left hooks and uppercuts, and walked through his man into the fourth where he inflicted more punishment. Kameda, who was now cut by the right eye, struggled through the fifth into the sixth before being dropped by a right hand, prior to being given a standing count when unable to defend himself adequately. Saved by the bell to end the round, the fight was called off during the interval when the ringside doctor advised the referee that Kameda was done for.

Marsh retired as the undefeated IBF champion in September. This came about after his disclosure of being an epileptic, having already been booked to defend against Frankie Warren. Following this, Warren was matched against Buddy McGirt to find a new champion.

4 July 1987. Juan Martin Coggi w co 3 (15) Patrizio Oliva.
Venue: Sports Palace, Ribera, Italy. **Recognition:** WBA. **Referee:** Bernie Soto.
Fight Summary: Boxing well from long range the champion went through the opening two rounds relatively in control, although Coggi (138¾) occasionally showed up with solid left hooks from his southpaw stance. In the third Coggi moved up a gear, and after biding his time he unleashed a big left hook to the jaw which dropped Oliva (139¾) heavily. While Oliva made it to his feet in time he was all at sea. Looking for the finish, Coggi soon got through again with another heavy left hook, but this time the Italian was counted out at 2.41 of the session.

At their convention held in October, the WBA announced that in future all world title bouts held under their banner would be contested over 12 rounds.

22 July 1987. Rene Arredondo w rsc 6 (12) Tsuyoshi Hamada.
Venue: Kuramae Sumo Arena, Tokyo, Japan. **Recognition:** WBC. **Referee:** Joe Cortez.
Fight Summary: Looking to regain his old title Arredondo (139¾) was a lot sharper this time around, immediately taking the fight to the champion, bloodying his nose in the first and cutting him over the right eye in the second. Stung into action, Hamada (139¾) had a big third, slamming away from head to body, but in the next round Arredondo quickly reasserted himself with left jabs before opening up with left hooks. There was no let up, and

with Arredondo well ahead and Hamada, both eyes almost closed, being severely punished in the sixth the referee halted the contest after 43 seconds of the session.

12 November 1987. Roger Mayweather w rsc 6 (12) Rene Arredondo.
Venue: Sports Arena, Los Angeles, California, USA. **Recognition:** WBC. **Referee:** Lou Filippo.
Fight Summary: Due to the champion fighting cautiously during the opening four rounds, Mayweather (139), nicknamed the 'Black Mamba', was able to get into the fight on his own terms, using the jab well and occasionally crossing the right to effect. When Arredondo (139) finally opened up in the fifth, carrying that aggression into the sixth when throwing big punches from either hand, that was just what Mayweather had been waiting for. Letting fly with a right he dropped Arredondo, and although the latter got up he was put down twice more before the referee rescued him immediately following the third knockdown, after two minutes of the session.

14 February 1988. Buddy McGirt w rsc 12 (15) Frankie Warren.
Venue: Memorial Coliseum, Corpus Christi, Texas, USA. **Recognition:** IBF. **Referee:** Barry Yeats.
Fight Summary: Contesting the title vacated by Terry Marsh's retirement, McGirt (139¾) was dominant from start to finish, using the left jab as a punishing weapon and following it up with solid rights and left hooks when sweeping Warren (138½) before him. Warren fought a game battle, but after being badly hurt in the first prior to suffering damage to both eyes and dropped for the first time in his career in the eighth it was all uphill. After Warren's left eye was closed shut in the previous session, although he launched courageous two-handed attacks in the ninth and tenth his time was almost up. Allowed to come out for the 12th, Warren was soon under pressure as McGirt began to unload at will, and at 1.34 of the session it was all over after the referee decided that enough was enough.

24 March 1988. Roger Mayweather w co 3 (12) Mauricio Aceves.
Venue: Sports Arena, Los Angeles, California, USA. **Recognition:** WBC. **Referee:** Chuck Hassett.
Fight Summary: Taking charge from the opening bell, measuring his challenger with left jabs before hammering him with rights, Mayweather (139½) had quick success when scoring a knockdown in the first. Although Aceves (139¾) hit back in the second it was barely enough to bother Mayweather and it was all over at 1.32 of the third after the former, dropped by a heavy right to the temple, had been counted out.

7 May 1988. Juan Martin Coggi w co 2 (12) Sang-Ho Lee.
Venue: San Parignano Tented Arena, Roseto Degli Abruzzi, Italy. **Recognition:** WBA. **Referee:** Carlos Berrocal.
Fight Summary: Having been booed by the crowd for showing a distinct lack of action in the first round, the southpaw champion walked out for the second determined to make the first defence of his title a memorable one. With that in mind the fans were soon silenced. After stunning Lee (139¼) with a solid right hook, Coggi (138¾) unleashed a battery of blows to head and body which ultimately saw the South Korean sink to the floor to be counted out on the 1.35 mark.

In October, during the WBA convention held in Venezuela, 27 of the 71 delegates walked out in disgust and went on to form the World Boxing Organisation (WBO) a few weeks later. From that moment the new organisation failed to recognise Coggi, nominating Hector Camacho and Ray Mancini to contest the vacant title instead.

6 June 1988. Roger Mayweather w pts 12 Harold Brazier.
Venue: Hilton Hotel, Las Vegas, Nevada, USA. **Recognition:** WBC. **Referee:** Carlos Padilla.
Scorecards: 114-113, 116-111, 115-116.
Fight Summary: Despite dominating the opening three rounds with the left jab, the champion came under pressure from the fourth onwards as Brazier (140) began to get into the fight, especially with the right cross. Several times during the middle sessions Mayweather (140) looked to be on the verge of being knocked out as Brazier cut loose with lefts and rights, but he showed great resilience to keep going. The final stages saw both men having success with heavy head punches, and although Brazier hurt Mayweather in the tenth and 11th the latter proved himself to be a worthy champion when coming back with hurtful punches of his own in the 15th to just about warrant the decision.

31 July 1988. Buddy McGirt w co 1 (15) Howard Davis.
Venue: MSG Theatre, Manhattan, NYC, New York, USA. **Recognition:** IBF. **Referee:** Joe Santarpia.
Fight Summary: Making his first defence, McGirt (138) was pitted against Davis (139¾), a substitute for Meldrick Taylor, and the fans appeared to be in for a long night as the latter began the fight on his bike, throwing out the jab. Whether or not having to get a stone off in three weeks would make life much tougher for Davis would remain an unknown factor as McGirt, quickly closing him down, rammed in a big right to the head which sent him crashing to be counted out after 2.45 of the first. Afterwards, McGirt stated that he had been working on his right because he felt that Davis would feel that the left hook would be the danger punch.

Prior to the fight the IBF had announced that, as from 1 September, all world title bouts held under their banner would be contested over 12 rounds, thus bringing them into line with the WBA and WBC.

3 September 1988. Meldrick Taylor w rsc 12 Buddy McGirt.
Venue: Harrah's Marina Hotel, Atlantic City, New Jersey, USA. **Recognition:** IBF. **Referee:** Randy Neumann.
Fight Summary: Although shaken up by a left hook in the opener the challenger soon got his game together to give McGirt (138¼) a bit of a boxing lesson. As the fight wore on the latter began to take more and more punishment, his head being rocked sideways by left hooks and right hands. Even when McGirt got in hurtful punches Taylor (140) would come right back with some of his own and after two minutes of the final round, with the former looking completely fatigued and reeling around the ring from a two-handed attack, the referee came to his rescue. With McGirt ultimately outclassed, having suffered a bad cut over the left eye following a clash of heads in the final session, the stoppage was a good one.

22 September 1988. Roger Mayweather w rsc 12 Rodolfo Gonzalez.
Venue: Sports Arena, Los Angeles, California, USA. **Recognition:** WBC. **Referee:** Lou Filippo.
Fight Summary: Continuing his domination of Mexican fighters, the champion stopped a game but outclassed Gonzalez (140) at 2.13 of the final round after the latter had been dropped by a big right to the head and was taking punches without reply. From the start Mayweather (140) had dominated without setting the world alight, being content to box patiently before sending in some tremendous blows from both hands as the fight progressed. In the latter stages it became obvious that the under pressure Gonzalez, by now carrying a badly swollen left eye, was not going to win, the stoppage when it came being overdue.

7 November 1988. Roger Mayweather w pts 12 Vinny Pazienza.
Venue: Caesar's Palace, Las Vegas, Nevada, USA. **Recognition:** WBC. **Referee:** Mills Lane.
Scorecards: 118-108, 117-110, 117-110.
Fight Summary: Controlling the fight with his stabbing left hand the champion was generally the master of the tough Pazienza (140), apart from occasionally being caught by flurries of blows and left hooks. Once Mayweather (140) had got his right hand into play it got more difficult for Pazienza, who was dropped in the fourth and cut over the left eye in the sixth before being put down again, this time by a right uppercut in the 11th. The last two rounds were brutal for Pazienza, being forced to take plenty of punishment as Mayweather went looking for him. It was amazing that Pazienza, carrying a lump under his right eye, was still standing in the 12th, and although his legs buckled several times he continued to bravely soak up everything until the final bell.

21 January 1989. Juan Martin Coggi w pts 12 Harold Brazier.
Venue: Sports Palace, Vasto, Italy. **Recognition:** WBA. **Referee:** John Coyle.
Scorecards: 116-113, 118-114, 119-111.
Fight Summary: Fighting in spurts the champion was still too good for Brazier (139¾), who posed too much and rarely let the right hand go, especially when that punch was the one recognised as being the antidote for a southpaw. As the action, or lack of it, continued it developed into a bit of a brawl. The referee clearly had his hands full trying to keep order, but in the tenth Coggi (139¾) finally woke up to drop Brazier with a left-hand counter. Making it to his feet Brazier rallied somewhat, but with Coggi beginning to tire rapidly and unable to turn his superiority to advantage the contest petered out.

21 January 1989. Meldrick Taylor w rsc 7 John Meekins.
Venue: Trump Plaza Hotel, Atlantic City, New Jersey, USA. **Recognition:** IBF. **Referee:** Steve Smoger.
Fight Summary: Regardless that he was outscored from the start, winning only the third round, the hard-punching Meekins (138) remained competitive right up to being pulled out of the contest by the referee at the end of the seventh when suffering a badly swollen right eye. Meekins tried hard enough, but the champion's blinding hand-speed made it almost impossible for him to contend with. Firing off jabs and an assortment of other blows to head and body, whilst also showing up to be an excellent defensive fighter, Taylor (139¾) looked a cut above the rest of the division. Even when he received damage over the left eye in the third Taylor remained unfazed, while the claim that he could not punch his weight was a fallacy as Meekins would testify afterwards.

6 March 1989. Hector Camacho w pts 12 Ray Mancini.
Venue: Lawlor Events Centre, Reno, Nevada, USA. **Recognition:** WBO. **Referee:** Mills Lane.
Scorecards: 115-113, 115-113, 112-116.
Fight Summary: Camacho (140) became the WBO's first champion at the weight when outscoring Mancini (139), the former lightweight king, but he was made to work hard when constantly being chased down and harried at every turn. With this being Mancini's first fight in four years he gave it everything he had against the fast-moving southpaw, who jabbed and clinched his way through the contest. He also landed some good punches, but so did Mancini. By the seventh Camacho appeared to be handing out a boxing lesson, and although that did not last when Mancini came on strong again it was the latter picking up most of the damage. Following the tenth, which Mancini won, there was little in it. However, it was Camacho who had more left in the tank as he picked his man off to just about get home on two of the cards.

29 April 1989. Juan Martin Coggi w pts 12 Akinobu Hiranaka.
Venue: Sports Palace, Vasto, Italy. **Recognition:** WBA. **Referee:** John Coyle.
Scorecards: 117-109, 117-108, 116-109.
Fight Summary: In a thrilling contest the challenger almost caused a huge shock when he had Coggi (140) down twice in the third, firstly with a left hook and then with a straight right before the latter survived to get up and fight back. Following that, Coggi, who had started confidently enough before running into the storm, began to find his way again when using his greater experience to get back in charge. Coming into the final round and well in front Coggi wobbled Hiranaka (140), who was by now badly cut, but instead of backing off the latter came right back to hurt the Argentine southpaw with two heavy right hands to the head prior to going down on points.

13 May 1989. Julio Cesar Chavez w rtd 10 Roger Mayweather.
Venue: Great Western Forum, Los Angeles, California, USA. **Recognition:** WBC. **Referee:** Henry Elesperu.
Fight Summary: Stepping up after winning titles at two different weights, and having beaten the champion back in 1985, Chavez (140) was fancied to win this fight, but Mayweather (138¾) did better than expected. Although Chavez's two-handed punching, strength and pressure proved too much for Mayweather the latter managed to hit him with quite a few solid shots, but every time that happened he was repaid twice over. By the seventh Chavez was swarming all over Mayweather, who was then cut over the left eye in the eighth. Although he tried desperately to keep the Mexican at bay, with the strength draining from Mayweather after being punished at the end of the tenth he slumped on his stool following the bell and was retired by his corner. It had been a valiant stand by Mayweather, but after he was deducted two points for going low and holding earlier in the contest he was always up against it, doing well to get as far as he did against the relentless Chavez.

11 September 1989. Meldrick Taylor w pts 12 Courtney Hooper.
Venue: Caesar's Palace, Atlantic City, New Jersey, USA. **Recognition:** IBF. **Referee:** Frank Cappuccino.
Scorecards: 117-111, 118-110, 118-110.
Fight Summary: Having injured his left knee in March, when Taylor (140) was finally deemed to be fit to defend his title against Hooper (139½) following two operations he was certainly given a tough workout by a worthy challenger. Switching back and forth from orthodox to southpaw, Hooper targeted Taylor's body throughout, having fair success. Although the latter was obviously not happy with the treatment he was getting he still managed to outbox his rival, some of his punches being almost a blur. Towards the end Taylor began to come

through with eye-catching combinations, and in the final session he totally dominated the action with a storming finish that saw him land solid rights and flurries of blows from both hands through to the bell.

18 November 1989. Julio Cesar Chavez w rsc 10 Sammy Fuentes.
Venue: Caesar's Palace, Las Vegas, Nevada, USA. **Recognition:** WBC. **Referee:** Carlos Padilla.
Fight Summary: Although he had not been off his feet, by the end of the tenth Fuentes (139¾), his right eye closed shut, had been worn down to such an extent by the champion that after consulting the doctor the referee stopped the contest during the interval. It had not been one-sided all the way as Fuentes had landed a fair amount of punches on Chavez (139¾), but the latter had just walked through them while continuing the body attacks which would ultimately be the deciding factor. Yet again Chavez had steamrollered an opponent to defeat, and at that moment in time it was difficult to see where a successful challenge would come from.

16 December 1989. Julio Cesar Chavez w co 3 Alberto Cortes.
Venue: Sports Palace, Mexico City, Mexico. **Recognition:** WBC. **Referee:** Arthur Mercante.
Fight Summary: Straight into action from the opening bell the champion swarmed all over the southpaw Cortes (139¾), punching away with right hands through the middle while throwing hooks to the body and uppercuts from both hands. Unfortunately for Cortes he lacked the power to keep Chavez (140) at bay, and although he threw plenty of leather himself the latter just shrugged it off. In the second, with Chavez pressing forward remorselessly, Cortes almost capsized under the hail of blows coming his way. Thus, it was no surprise when left uppercuts and rights to the head eventually dropped him to be counted out after 1.56 of the third session had elapsed.

3 February 1990. Hector Camacho w pts 12 Vinny Pazienza.
Venue: Convention Hall, Atlantic City, New Jersey, USA. **Recognition:** WBO. **Referee:** Tony Perez.
Scorecards: 117-116, 115-112, 119-109.
Fight Summary: With Pazienza (138) knowing that if he was to have any success whatsoever he would have to close the champion down and work the body the stage was set. However, for round after round Pazienza was unable to find the range, and even when he closed more often than not he found Camacho (140) just too fast for him, to such an extent he was often left floundering. The tenth was probably Camacho's best round, the Puerto Rican ripping open a cut over Pazienza's left eye with a solid right uppercut, an injury he constantly hammered away at for the remainder of the round. Knowing he had to score a knockout to win, Pazienza tore into the tiring Camacho during the last two sessions but although it was a strong finish it was not enough.

17 March 1990. Julio Cesar Chavez w rsc 12 Meldrick Taylor.
Venue: Hilton Hotel, Las Vegas, Nevada, USA. **Recognition:** IBF/WBC. **Referee:** Richard Steele.
Fight Summary: Contesting two titles, Taylor (139¾) made a great start against the more fancied Chavez (139½), making him look slow while picking him off with lightning left jabs and bursts of hooks from both hands over the opening six rounds. It was only in the seventh that Chavez began to catch up with Taylor as the pace of the fight slowed, but after a brief bout of slugging the latter got back to his boxing when mixing it up with solid blows. At the start of the 11th Chavez had it all to do, but despite him pressing Taylor all the way, with him having little success things appeared bleak for him as the final session got underway. Well down on the scorecards, Chavez, who knew he had to stop Taylor inside the next three minutes, attacked the IBF champion non-stop before stunning him with a big right and dropping him with a similar blow. Badly shaken and carrying a damaged left eye Taylor made it to his feet at 'five', but on reaching the mandatory 'eight' when the referee decided that he was unfit to continue the contest was stopped with just two seconds left on the clock. With arguments raging as to whether the referee should have noticed that the end of the round was only moments away, and many calling for an immediate rematch, two fights later Taylor had won the WBA welter title.

24 March 1990. Juan Martin Coggi w pts 12 Jose Luis Ramirez.
Venue: Municipal Sports Complex, Ajaccio, Corsica, France. **Recognition:** WBA. **Referee:** John Coyle.
Scorecards: 118-111, 118-110, 118-111.
Fight Summary: In his fourth defence, Coggi (139¾) quickly took control by staying at distance and scoring well with solid jabs and hooks to keep Ramirez (138½) at bay, a tactic he employed for much of the contest. Although Ramirez, a fellow southpaw, provided stubborn resistance he lacked the speed and guile required to get inside the

champion's defences, and despite plugging away gamely he had very few successes before fading completely. Ultimately, it was a relatively easy night's work for Coggi who finished almost as fresh as he started.

11 August 1990. Hector Camacho w pts 12 Tony Baltazar.
Venue: Caesar's Palace, Lake Tahoe, Stateline, Nevada, USA. **Recognition:** WBO. **Referee:** Richard Steele.
Scorecards: 118-109, 117-110, 118-109.
Fight Summary: Hoping to give Camacho (140) a hard time, Baltazar (140) eventually went the way of the champion's previous 39 opponents as he found the fluid movement and hand-speed too much to handle virtually throughout the contest. The hard-punching Baltazar did have some successes, especially when digging in solid left hooks to the body but, unable to consolidate, he often found himself rushing in to be tied up by the cagey Camacho. For much of the time it was Camacho snapping back Baltazar's head with speedy southpaw jabs and blinding combinations, and although the fight was always competitive there was only ever going to be one winner.

17 August 1990. Loreto Garza w pts 12 Juan Martin Coggi.
Venue: The Acropolis, Nice, France. **Recognition:** WBA. **Referee:** Ernesto Magana.
Scorecards: 116-115, 116-114, 115-115.
Fight Summary: Making a reasonable start, Garza (139) soon began to force the fight when shaking up the southpaw champion with solid rights, and even when he was being pushed back his countering punches found their mark with accuracy. As the fight wore on, with Coggi (139½) becoming more anxious it was only in the eighth that he began to take control from the centre of the ring for the first time. Even so, Coggi was still taking too many punches without being busy enough himself. In his desperation to find a finisher in the ninth he threw himself off balance. That just about summed up Coggi's performance. Despite trying hard enough he could not find any answers, the only surprise being the closeness of his defeat on the cards.

1 December 1990. Loreto Garza w disq 11 Vinny Pazienza.
Venue: Arco Arena, Sacramento, California, USA. **Recognition:** WBA. **Referee:** Larry Rozadilla.
Fight Summary: Maintaining his hold on the title, Garza (139½) proved that he was a worthy champion when dominating the rough, tough Pazienza (140) throughout with a left jab that rarely missed its target. As early as the first round Pazienza was badly staggered and cut under the right eye, and by the end of the third he was also suffering a cut under the other eye, having come under fire from Garza's accurate jab. The big surprise was that Pazienza seemed unable to get inside the jab, being forced to fight on the outside for round after round. By the 11th it had become clear that Pazienza was going backwards, especially after he had been deducted two points earlier for illegal tactics, and when he almost lifted Garza out of the ring in frustration the referee disqualified him with one second of the session remaining.

8 December 1990. Julio Cesar Chavez w rsc 3 Kyung-Duk Ahn.
Venue: Convention Centre, Atlantic City, New Jersey, USA. **Recognition:** IBF/WBC. **Referee:** Tony Perez.
Fight Summary: Working well with the jab to head and body by the end of the first round Chavez (139) had switched his attack downstairs, and with the challenger already looking disconcerted as the punches ripped in it was clear as to which way the fight was heading. Keeping up the pressure Chavez did not disappoint, dropping Ahn (139) with a straight right at the start of the second. Although the South Korean was soon back in the fray he did not know how to cope with the controlled power and aggression of Chavez, being knocked over by a left hook before struggling up and surviving to the bell. Despite giving it his best shot in the third Ahn was quickly under pressure from body blows and after a rib-breaking left hook knocked all the stuffing out of him and sent him down, the referee stopped the fight at 2.14.

23 February 1991. Greg Haugen w pts 12 Hector Camacho.
Venue: Caesar's Palace, Las Vegas, Nevada, USA. **Recognition:** WBO. **Referee:** Carlos Padilla.
Scorecards: 114-113, 114-112, 112-114.
Fight Summary: Further to coming to the weigh-in four pounds over and having to work it off, the champion initially allowed Haugen (139) to make the running but failed to get close enough to make his punches count. However, by the third, with Camacho (140) looking good with darting southpaw jabs and straight lefts finding the target it was no surprise when a right hook to the jaw put Haugen down for the first time in his career. This was

Camacho's big chance, but when failing to take full advantage by the seventh he was beginning to tire. With the fight still close going into the tenth, while Camacho had his speed and adroitness Haugen was landing solid body shots in an effort to slow his man down. Coming out for the final round, when Haugen refused to shake hands with Camacho the latter then fired three punches over the referee's shoulder before being deducted a point. Although Haugen's aggression had given him the last round it was still something of a shock when he was handed the title, Camacho appearing to have done enough in the eyes of many good judges.

Haugen forfeited the WBO title in March when showing up positive for marijuana and failing a post-fight drugs test.

18 March 1991. Julio Cesar Chavez w rsc 4 John Duplessis.
Venue: Mirage Hotel & Casino, Las Vegas, Nevada, USA. **Recognition:** IBF/WBC. **Referee:** Carlos Padilla.
Fight Summary: Deciding that he was not going to trade punches with the champion, Duplessis (139) quickly got on his bike while throwing out ineffectual lefts, and after surviving the opening round continued in much the same vein. However, Chavez (139) was not a champion for nothing and he was soon closing the ring space down. With Duplessis now dropping the jab well short before scampering away, just before the end of the second a right-left to the jaw followed by a left hook to the body put him down for 'four' after Chavez had been surprised by a solid right to the head. It was more of the same in the third as Duplessis moved at pace, but after he was doubled up by a left hook to the body in the fourth the writing was firmly on the wall. Timing his attack perfectly Chavez pounced, and having driven Duplessis into a corner with a big right to the head a right to the body sent him halfway through the ropes, whereupon the referee called it off. The finish was timed at 2.42.

After Chavez relinquished the IBF version of the title in April 1991 rather than defend against Rafael Pineda on a Bob Arum promotion, the latter was matched against Roger Mayweather to find a new champion.

18 May 1991. Hector Camacho w pts 12 Greg Haugen.
Venue: Sparks Convention Centre, Reno, Nevada, USA. **Recognition:** WBO. **Referee:** Bobby Ferrara.
Scorecards: 115-112, 114-113, 112-115.
Fight Summary: Billed for the vacant title after Haugen had been stripped following his championship win over Camacho on 23 February, this time round the latter made sure of victory when getting off to a good start. Strangely, the man from Las Vegas never really came to terms with what he had to do until it was too late, and it was not until the eighth when Camacho (138½) began to tire that Haugen (139) got himself going. At that stage it was noticeable that body punches would be Haugen's best form of attack, especially when Camacho kept complaining about them. From thereon in, Camacho was clutching for dear life at times, but try as he might Haugen was unable to remove him. Having had a point deducted for slapping Haugen after the bell to end the 11th, after Camacho jumped out of the ring at the end of the fight, obviously thinking that Haugen had won, he had to be recalled on the announcement of the verdict.

When Camacho forfeited the WBO version of the title in March 1992 for failing to defend against Oba Carr, the latter was matched against Carlos Gonzalez to find a new champion. Carr was eventually replaced by his stablemate, Jimmy Paul, when he pulled out of the fight with three weeks to go.

14 June 1991. Edwin Rosario w rsc 3 Loreto Garza.
Venue: Arco Arena, Sacramento, California, USA. **Recognition:** WBA. **Referee:** Larry Rozadilla.
Fight Summary: Tearing out at the bell it took Rosario (139½) just ten seconds to register a stunning setback to the champion's chances when he dropped him with a crunching straight right. Although Garza (139) got up he was under pressure immediately before being put down again prior to the end of the first by a left-right combination. Decidedly hesitant, Garza somehow made it through the second, and even nailed Rosario with some stiff left jabs at the start of the third until being countered over the top by a big right which had him wobbling. Bombing away with both hands, Rosario soon had Garza down for the third time in the fight. Even though Garza made it to his feet, when he was sent crashing again just moments later the referee called it off 69 seconds into the session.

14 September 1991. Julio Cesar Chavez w pts 12 Lonnie Smith.
Venue: Mirage Hotel & Casino, Las Vegas, Nevada, USA. **Recognition:** WBC. **Referee:** Carlos Padilla.
Scorecards: 118-106, 119-107, 119-109.
Fight Summary: With Smith (140) sprinting non-stop around the ring for round after round, Chavez (140) had great difficulty in catching him, having to be satisfied with the odd occasion when he could get to grips with his challenger. Eventually, in the eighth, Smith began to get some punches off, but it did nothing to stop Chavez's charge. As Smith slowed inevitably he was caught by solid blows, mainly to the body, although in the tenth he showed that he could bang when smashing Chavez with a brutal left hook which would have downed just about anyone else. Thereafter, it was all Chavez as Smith weakened, the latter being severely punished by body punches before the final bell came to his aid.

7 December 1991. Rafael Pineda w rsc 9 Roger Mayweather.
Venue: Sparks Convention Centre, Reno, Nevada, USA. **Recognition:** IBF. **Referee:** Mills Lane.
Fight Summary: Contesting the title vacated by Julio Cesar Chavez, neither man did too much to deserve a championship shot prior to the sixth, Mayweather (140) being content to jab occasionally before moving backwards, while whenever Pineda (139) went forward he was often left lunging with wild punches hitting the air. The sixth finally saw both men landing with solid shots, Pineda with two left hooks and Mayweather with a right hand being the pick before the fans were forced to sit through a passive seventh. With boos ringing out, at least Pineda tried to get his left hooks away in the eighth, but following a lecture from the referee in the ninth for more action a huge, sweeping left hook left Mayweather flat out and obviously beaten. Not even bothering to count, the referee eventually stopped the fight on the two-minute mark after he made sure that Mayweather was okay.

10 April 1992. Akinobu Hiranaka w rsc 1 Edwin Rosario.
Venue: City Bullring, Mexico City, Mexico. **Recognition:** WBA. **Referee:** Enzo Montero.
Fight Summary: When both men came out firing off punches, and neither relenting, it became a real slugging match fought out in the centre of the ring. It could not last, and when the champion was sent wobbling into the ropes with Hiranaka (139½) in hot pursuit, smashing in rights and lefts, it seemed to be all over. However, with Rosario (140) even punching back at times Hiranaka suddenly appeared arm weary. Regardless, with Hiranaka continuing to throw big shots, when a salvo of left-rights sent Rosario lurching across the ring at 1.32 the referee brought the contest to a halt.

10 April 1992. Julio Cesar Chavez w rsc 5 Angel Hernandez.
Venue: City Bullring, Mexico City, Mexico. **Recognition:** WBC. **Referee:** Arthur Mercante.
Fight Summary: Switching from orthodox to southpaw in an effort to confuse Chavez (138¾), the unbeaten Hernandez (139½) made life difficult for the champion for a few rounds before he was eventually ground down. Chavez was out of sorts for much of the contest, having difficulty working Hernandez out, especially when the latter led with his head. However, he finally caught up with his man in the fifth when crashing blow after blow into the by now bloodied Hernandez, who was trapped in a corner. With Chavez in full flow, when a pulverising right to the body left the Puerto Rican in some difficulty the referee jumped in to stop the fight after 1.11 of the round had elapsed.

22 May 1992. Rafael Pineda w rsc 7 Clarence Coleman.
Venue: Four Roads Bullring, Mexico City, Mexico. **Recognition:** IBF. **Referee:** Jesus Arias.
Fight Summary: Controlling the fight throughout, the champion's biggest problems were not with Coleman (139) but with himself after he became wild and clumsy as he tried to find the punch to finish the fight with. To make matters worse, Pineda (139) suffered a damaged mouth in the fifth and was cut over the right eye by a butt in the sixth before eventually finding the blows to end the contest in the seventh. With the crowd restless, a left to the head sent Coleman down, and after he had been dropped again following a solid right to the temple the referee stopped it with 28 seconds on the clock.

30 June 1992. Carlos Gonzalez w rsc 2 Jimmy Paul.
Venue: Great Western Forum, Los Angeles, California, USA. **Recognition:** WBO. **Referee:** Lou Moret.

Fight Summary: Contesting the vacant title, both men began cautiously before the fireworks really started in the second round. Paul (140), who had substituted for Oba Carr, was soon under fire as Gonzalez (139½) began to release his big guns, and how he remained upright prior to being stopped at 2.12 of the session was a mystery. The 20-year-old Mexican was a revelation as he threw punches to head and body, with the uppercut from either hand and left jabs and right crosses all thundering in to such an extent that the referee should have halted the action much earlier than he did. Unbeaten in 32 contests, this was Gonzalez's 30th win inside the distance, with 17 of them coming in the first round.

18 July 1992. Pernell Whitaker w pts 12 Rafael Pineda.
Venue: Mirage Hotel & Casino, Las Vegas, Nevada, USA. **Recognition:** IBF. **Referee:** Joe Cortez.
Scorecards: 116-110, 117-108, 117-108.
Fight Summary: Spending much of the fight chasing the shadow that was Whitaker (140), the champion had few opportunities to land his heavy punches, being comprehensively outboxed by the fleet-footed southpaw. Bobbing and weaving in front of Pineda (139), Whitaker continually fired in the jab whilst avoiding most of the blows that came his way, and in the sixth he dropped the champion with a solid right hook to the ribs. Towards the end of the bout, with Whitaker taking it easy Pineda staged something of a rally, but by then only a knockout would have been enough.

After Whitaker relinquished the IBF version of the title on becoming WBC welterweight champion in March 1993, Charles Murray and Rodney Moore were matched in order to find a new champion.

1 August 1992. Julio Cesar Chavez w rsc 4 Frankie Mitchell.
Venue: Hilton Hotel, Las Vegas, Nevada, USA. **Recognition:** WBC. **Referee:** Mills Lane.
Fight Summary: Defending the title for the eighth time, Chavez (140) started quickly, while Mitchell (137½) tried to box from both orthodox and southpaw stances before having his gumshield knocked out prior to the end of the opening session. Mitchell, who also wasted a good many punches with a lack of accuracy, began to come apart in the third as Chavez started to unload. Dropped after a barrage of blows thudded home, Mitchell, now on borrowed time, got up but was soon down again after taking punches to head and body prior to fighting back gamely to hear the bell. Now cut over the right eye Mitchell made it to the fourth, but after taking a further beating he was again dropped, this time by a solid right lead, and although getting to his feet after a count of 'nine' the referee called it off with 56 seconds on the clock.

9 September 1992. Morris East w rsc 11 Akinobu Hiranaka.
Venue: Nihon Budokan Martial Arts Hall, Tokyo, Japan. **Recognition:** WBA. **Referee:** Carlos Berrocal.
Fight Summary: It was hardly surprising that East (140), with just 16 fights on his record, was under pressure early on as the champion looked to finish early. However, showing good upper body movement he was able to stay out of harm's way prior to the sixth before winning the next three rounds with solid left jabs paving the way. Although the ninth and tenth rounds were evenly contested, when Hiranaka (140) began to tire a solid left-hand counter to the face was all that was required to put him down in the 11th. With Hiranaka behind on all three cards and pretty well banged up, despite him getting up at the count of 'eight' the referee stopped the fight on the 1.47 mark.

12 September 1992. Julio Cesar Chavez w pts 12 Hector Camacho.
Venue: Thomas & Mack Centre, Las Vegas, Nevada, USA. **Recognition:** WBC. **Referee:** Richard Steele.
Scorecards: 119-110, 117-111, 120-107.
Fight Summary: In an eagerly anticipated contest Chavez (140) was relentless in his pursuit of Camacho (140), who was unable to keep the champion at bay and was pounded incessantly from head to body. Apart from the odd punch that hurt Chavez, the southpaw Camacho just did not have the armoury, ultimately being forced to take whatever came his way. By the ninth, with Camacho's left eye badly swollen and his right eye also cut it seemed as though he would not make it, but gritting his teeth he somehow got through to the final bell despite lurching around the ring during the final two sessions with both eyes almost closed shut. Derided by the fans for his outlandish showmanship, in defeat Camacho finally proved he was a real fighting man.

9 November 1992. Carlos Gonzalez w rsc 6 Lorenzo Smith.
Venue: Great Western Forum, Los Angeles, California, USA. **Recognition:** WBO. **Referee:** Raul Caiz.
Fight Summary: Coming into the fight with a seven-inch reach-advantage, the challenger immediately got his left jab working to outscore Gonzalez (138) in the opening three sessions. However, after feeling the latter's power in the third he was never as effective again. The jabs were still going in from Smith (139) in the next couple of rounds, but getting caught by heavy counters towards the end of the fifth he was cut in the corner of the right eye. Affected by the injury, Smith went to pieces as he frantically tore around the ring to keep his distance from Gonzalez, and at the end of the sixth the referee stopped the fight when it was clear that the challenger did not really want to continue.

14 December 1992. Carlos Gonzalez w rsc 1 Rafael Ortiz.
Venue: Fronton Arena, Mexico City, Mexico. **Recognition:** WBO. **Referee:** Ismael Fernandez.
Fight Summary: Making his second defence in the space of five weeks Gonzalez (138½) quickly set about Ortiz (138¾), driving him backwards with heavy combinations before dropping him headlong to the canvas. On his feet but badly shaken, Ortiz was hammered down again almost immediately by a crashing right to the jaw, and although he beat the count he was deemed unable to defend himself by the referee, who stopped the contest after just 93 seconds of fighting.

13 January 1993. Juan Martin Coggi w rsc 8 Morris East.
Venue: The Superdome, Mar Del Plata, Argentina. **Recognition:** WBA. **Referee:** Bernie Soto.
Fight Summary: Struggling to find a way through the former champion's defence, after East (139¾) was dropped by solid southpaw lefts to the body in the second from thereon in it was nearly all one way. Attacking the body throughout, Coggi (139¾) also made the head a target, and whenever East tried to get into range he was generally countered over the top. Having had a point deducted for butting in the sixth, East made a big effort in the seventh to have Coggi stumbling around the ring, but that would be his last success. Regrouping during the interval, once Coggi went to work in the eighth it was all over on the 2.50 mark when a heavy left to the jaw sent East downwards, the referee stopping the fight immediately without even bothering to count.

20 February 1993. Julio Cesar Chavez w rsc 5 Greg Haugen.
Venue: Azteca Stadium, Mexico City, Mexico. **Recognition:** WBC. **Referee:** Joe Cortez.
Fight Summary: Fighting in front of his own fans - and not forgetting that there were three other world title bouts on the same bill in Nelson v Ruelas, Norris v Blocker and Nunn v Morgan - Chavez (139½), who was the main reason for the world-record turnout of 136,000 people for a big fight, made a great start. After dropping Haugen (140) on to one knee in the opener, following a hard right to the head, the champion methodically worked the American over for the remainder of the session. Thereafter concentrating on the body, Chavez was happy to belt Haugen around the ring for the next three rounds before deciding to go for the finish in the fifth. Having sent his man into the ropes with solid head blows, Chavez proceeded to keep the punches going from head to body until Haugen was forced to drop to one knee again. Although the latter made it to his feet, he was driven into a corner by a relentless barrage before being belatedly rescued by the referee with 58 seconds of the round remaining.

22 March 1993. Carlos Gonzalez w rsc 1 Tony Baltazar.
Venue: Great Western Forum, Los Angeles, California, USA. **Recognition:** WBO. **Referee:** Raul Caiz.
Fight Summary: Roaring out two-fistedly at the bell, the challenger really let his punches go from head to body, especially with the left hook, and it took Gonzalez (139¾) a few moments to begin to compose himself before replying in kind. When Gonzalez started landing it had an immediate effect, Baltazar (139¾) being dropped by a sweeping left uppercut. Although Baltazar got to his feet quickly, when his legs betrayed him a five-punch combination to the head sent him crashing again. The contest was almost over. On getting up and being battered down again by accurate shots to the head the referee stopped the fight on the 'three knockdowns in a round' ruling, the finish being timed at 2.22.

10 April 1993. Juan Martin Coggi w rsc 7 Jose Rivera.
Venue: The Superdome, Mar Del Plata, Argentina. **Recognition:** WBA. **Referee:** Isidro Rodriguez.

Fight Summary: Although he started strongly the challenger soon had trouble dealing with the southpaw counters once Coggi (140) had settled down, and in the third round solid hooks and uppercuts opened a cut over the Puerto Rican's right eye. However, Rivera (139¼) was still dangerous, hurting Coggi with a big right to the head in the fifth before the latter came back in the sixth to work on his opponent's injured eye which began to worsen. With just two seconds of the seventh remaining it was all over when the referee decided that the damage to Rivera's eye was too bad for him to continue.

8 May 1993. Julio Cesar Chavez w rsc 6 Terrence Alli.
Venue: Thomas & Mack Centre, Las Vegas, Nevada, USA. **Recognition:** WBC. **Referee:** Carlos Padilla.
Fight Summary: Even though the challenger took the fight straight to Chavez (140), peppering him with left jabs and bursts of punches, the latter was soon hammering away with ferocity. For the next four rounds it was much of the same as Chavez dissected Alli (139) a bit at a time, and at the end of the fifth a barrage of head blows left the latter on unsteady legs and ready to go. Starting the sixth fast, Chavez dropped Alli on his back for 'eight' with a crunching left hook. And when Alli was back on his feet he was chased down with such viciousness that the referee was forced to stop the contest with just 45 seconds of the session on the clock. There was a certain amount of confusion over the stoppage as the third man had not been as emphatic as he should have been, but the fight was over.

15 May 1993. Charles Murray w pts 12 Rodney Moore.
Venue: Trump Castle Hotel, Atlantic City, New Jersey, USA. **Recognition:** IBF. **Referee:** Frank Cappuccino.
Scorecards: 115-113, 118-110, 116-112.
Fight Summary: Contesting the title relinquished by Pernell Whitaker, both men appeared happy to spend the first seven rounds working close, despite Murray (140) being expected to box from long range where he could jab and move. However, Murray's harder punches and good body movement gave him the edge in most rounds. From the seventh onwards, Murray began to pull away with accurate jabs and solid body shots getting to Moore (140), who was shaken up several times, and although the latter rallied over the last two sessions he was unable to close the gap.

7 June 1993. Zack Padilla w pts 12 Carlos Gonzalez.
Venue: Thomas & Mack Centre, Las Vegas, Nevada, USA. **Recognition:** WBO. **Referee:** Richard Steele.
Scorecards: 117-111, 115-114, 117-112.
Fight Summary: Moving around Gonzalez (140) and pumping out accurate left jabs and hard rights throughout, the challenger caused a huge upset when being awarded the decision, having thrown hundreds of blows, many of which landed. Even when his right eye started to swell in the second and he was hurt by left uppercuts and solid rights, Padilla (139) remained unfazed, coming back to nail Gonzalez (140) with a cracking right in the same session. The pattern of the fight remained constant, with Gonzalez working the body in the vain hope that Padilla would be worn down, while the latter threw eye-catching head shots and utilised his speed. Although Gonzalez made a big effort in the 12th it was beyond him, and with Padilla continuing to punch on the retreat the decision was a formality.

23 June 1993. Juan Martin Coggi w rsc 5 Hiroyuki Yoshino.
Venue: Korakuen Hall, Tokyo, Japan. **Recognition:** WBA. **Referee:** Rafael Ramos.
Fight Summary: For the first three rounds the contest was fairly even, with Yoshino (140) capitalising on his speed and vigour to score with hefty left hooks, while the southpaw champion used heavy straight lefts and uppercuts to head and body before opening up in the fourth as the challenger began to weaken. Coming out fast for the fifth, Coggi (140) soon had Yoshino floundering prior to flooring him with a cracking left to the head. Having gamely got up Yoshino was soon down again, courtesy of a right hook and heavy follow-up blows, and when he arose only to be knocked over by another left, at 2.15 of the session the referee called it off.

4 July 1993. Charles Murray w pts 12 Juan Laporte.
Venue: Showboat Hotel & Casino, Atlantic City, New Jersey, USA. **Recognition:** IBF. **Referee:** Tony Orlando.
Scorecards: 118-110, 120-107, 118-110.

Fight Summary: Making his first defence against Laporte (140), the sharp-shooting Murray (140) soon had the veteran Puerto Rican in his sights, with his excellent left jab at the forefront of every move. Although it was lopsided Laporte was always trying, especially with countering hooks, but having little success he had finally begun to work his way inside by the eighth. However, apart from having some joy in the tenth he ultimately had to settle for being second best.

13 August 1993. Juan Martin Coggi w pts 12 Jose Rafael Barboza.
Venue: Lanus Sports Centre, Buenos Aires, Argentina. **Recognition:** WBA. **Referee:** Waldemar Schmidt.
Scorecards: 119-114, 118-112, 117-111.
Fight Summary: Coming out fast from the opening bell, virtually allowing Barboza (139¼) no time to settle, the southpaw champion dropped his man with a solid left in the opening session as he looked to finish early. However, Barboza had other ideas and quitting was not one of them. Although Coggi (139¾) never looked like losing he had to be on his toes throughout as his rival rallied strongly and held his ground until the final bell.

24 September 1993. Juan Martin Coggi w co 10 Guillermo Cruz.
Venue: Villa Lujan Defenders Club Arena, Tucuman, Argentina. **Recognition:** WBA. **Referee:** Carlos Berrocal.
Fight Summary: Content to wait for Cruz (139¼) to come in during the early rounds the southpaw champion knew that he had the power to end the contest early, being prepared to let his rival burn himself out. There was no doubt that Cruz, deducted a point in the second for butting, was going for it, but by the fifth he was being forced to take solid lefts to head and body as Coggi (140) began to let fly. Still under pressure in the tenth, Cruz, stunned by a right hook to the head, was then put down by a short left to the solar plexus and counted out at 1.51 of the session.

19 November 1993. Charles Murray w rtd 5 Courtney Hooper.
Venue: Convention Centre, Atlantic City, New Jersey, USA. **Recognition:** IBF. **Referee:** Frank Cappuccino.
Fight Summary: Brought in as a late substitute for Rafael Pineda who was injured, Hooper (139) found the champion a difficult number to deal with, never really getting himself up for the task in front of him. While it took Murray (140) some time to warm up once he got the left jab going to head and body in the third, with Hooper's left eye beginning to swell there seemed to be no way back for the latter. Picking it up in the fourth with left hooks and uppercuts, Murray began to unleash punch after punch on the unfortunate Hooper in the fifth, and after taking a battering on the ropes the challenger was retired at the end of the round.

19 November 1993. Zack Padilla w rtd 8 Efrem Calamati.
Venue: Sports Palace, Arezzo, Italy. **Recognition:** WBO. **Referee:** William Connors.
Fight Summary: Following a reasonable start when scoring well with good lefts, the challenger found himself up against it from the fourth onwards as Padilla (139) began to unload. Having worn Calamati (139½) down after several heavy exchanges along the ropes, Padilla started to go for the body in the sixth and in the seventh the Italian was dropped by a right hand to the head. With Calamati now soaking up heavy punishment, after a nerve in his neck began to add to his problems he stayed in his corner as the bell went for the start of round eight.

16 December 1993. Zack Padilla w pts 12 Ray Oliveira.
Venue: Foxwoods Resort, Ledyard, Connecticut, USA. **Recognition:** WBO. **Referee:** Steve Smoger.
Scorecards: 118-110, 117-112, 116-113.
Fight Summary: Boxing beautifully for three rounds, spearing in jabs and sliding away before being caught, the constantly switching Oliveira (139) made a great start, but once the champion began to close the range and began to let the body shots go in the fourth things got tougher for him. By the fifth, Padilla (138½), who was finding the lanky Oliveira without fail, was beginning to pin him on the ropes while scoring with accurate blows to head and body. Although Oliveira got his second wind in time for the remaining two rounds his inability to hurt Padilla allowed the latter to cruise through to the final bell without any mishaps.

17 December 1993. Juan Martin Coggi w rsc 7 Eder Gonzalez.
Venue: Villa Lujan Defenders Club Arena, Tucuman, Argentina. **Recognition:** WBA. **Referee:** Isidro Rodriguez.

Fight Summary: Seen by some as the most controversial fight of the year, after both men had sized each other up in the opener Coggi (139¾) was the first to strike when he dropped the challenger with a right hook in the second. On getting to his feet Gonzalez (139¾) smashed home a tremendous right to the southpaw champion's jaw which sent him crashing to the floor, whereupon the referee appeared to issue a count that lasted about 15 seconds. Up at 'nine', Coggi was all over the place as Gonzalez laid into him. When the referee came between the two fighters on the 2.26 mark, saying later that he thought he heard the bell, the round ended 35 seconds early. Even then Coggi remained weak for the next two or three sessions prior to being dropped again. This time the referee called it a slip. By now Gonzalez was tiring from his exertions, and with Coggi fully recovered the Colombian was put down by a strong left in the seventh before clambering up and taking more blows. The fight was concluded by the referee when Gonzales's manager got into the ring to stop him from taking more punches. Five days later the WBA took away the referee's license and ordered an immediate rematch.

18 December 1993. Julio Cesar Chavez w rtd 5 Andy Holligan.
Venue: Cuauhtemoc Stadium, Puebla, Mexico. **Recognition:** WBC. **Referee:** Arthur Mercante.
Fight Summary: Wobbled by a solid left hook to the body in the opening minute the challenger must have realised it could only get tougher as Chavez (139¼) started to let the punches go, and when he returned to his corner at the end of the second bleeding above the right eye the reality was stark. However, the third and fourth rounds saw Holligan (140) do relatively well as Chavez took a breather, but towards the end of the fifth the latter got himself going again. With Chavez unleashing heavy hooks and uppercuts, although the Englishman fired back he was retired at the end of the round, a burst blood vessel in the nose making it too difficult for him to continue.

29 January 1994. Frankie Randall w pts 12 Julio Cesar Chavez.
Venue: MGM Grand, Las Vegas, Nevada, USA. **Recognition:** WBC. **Referee:** Richard Steele.
Scorecards: 114-113, 116-111, 113-114.
Fight Summary: Although Randall (140) was forced to take plenty, especially downstairs, his ability to sustain that along with his movement and tremendous combinations enabled him to stay in a fight that virtually nobody gave him a chance of winning. Not only that, but he gave Chavez (140) more to worry about than any of his previous challengers had managed, things getting even better for Randall in the seventh when the champion had a point deducted for going low. The next few rounds saw both men give and take before the fight was virtually decided in the 11th when Chavez had another point deducted for a further low blow and was then dropped by a right hand to the jaw. Back on his feet Chavez tried to close Randall down, but knowing that the 11th round had been decisive the latter spent the final session avoiding trouble.

13 February 1994. Jake Rodriguez w pts 12 Charles Murray.
Venue: Bally's Park Place Hotel, Atlantic City, New Jersey, USA. **Recognition:** IBF. **Referee:** Tony Orlando.
Scorecards: 115-113, 114-114, 116-112.
Fight Summary: Unable to get his act together, Murray (140) found himself bulled out of the fight by the aggressive southpaw challenger who was never discouraged whatever came his way. Rodriguez (140) was constantly going forward, and even when Murray was connecting with lead rights and crisp combinations he was not fazed. With both men looking to get on the inside, following the fight Murray was generous enough to admit that Rodriguez had outworked and outhustled him. Despite the head butts that Murray complained about there were no injuries. There were also no knockdowns.

18 March 1994. Juan Martin Coggi w rsc 3 Eder Gonzalez.
Venue: MGM Grand, Las Vegas, Nevada, USA. **Recognition:** WBA. **Referee:** Richard Steele.
Fight Summary: Further to their previous fight fireworks were expected. And in the opening round it went to plan with the southpaw champion being dropped by a looping right to the jaw as Gonzalez (140) went looking for an early win. Lasting out the round without absorbing too much further damage, Coggi (140) began to counter well in the second despite having to take the odd right-hand bomb coming his way, but he was still very wary. At the start of the third Coggi was again forced to take a heavy right counter to the head, which was followed by another huge right that gashed his left eye badly. Knowing he was in big trouble Coggi stormed into Gonzalez with five or six big shots landing, and when the latter gave way a brutal left decked him. Up but groggy, Gonzalez was hit with everything in Coggi's armoury, eventually being stopped on the 2.01 mark after he had been put down again.

18 April 1994. Zack Padilla w rtd 6 Harold Miller.
Venue: Ahoy Sports Palace, Rotterdam, Netherlands. **Recognition:** WBO. **Referee:** Norbert Krosch.
Fight Summary: In what was the Netherland's first world title fight, the champion had too much of everything for the limited Miller (136¾) who was painfully exposed before being retired on his stool at the end of the sixth. This was almost a workout for Padilla (137¾), and it was only a mixture of Miller's bravery and a humane champion not wishing to do permanent damage to his over-matched foe that enabled the fight to last as long as it did.

21 April 1994. Jake Rodriquez w pts 12 Ray Oliveira.
Venue: Foxwoods Resort, Ledyard, Connecticut, USA. **Recognition:** IBF. **Referee:** Steve Smoger.
Scorecards: 115-112, 116-111, 119-108.
Fight Summary: Making his first defence, the southpaw champion pounded away at the flashy Oliveira (140), hurting him with lefts to the body prior to dropping him with an overarm left in the fifth round. Subsequently, Oliveira was forced to fight on Rodriguez's terms, and although the latter continued to pound away at the body he was unable to force another knockdown before having to settle for the points. Afterwards, Rodriguez (140) stated that regardless of whom he fought and when, he would always aim to work the body for 12 rounds and if a stoppage came that would be a bonus.

7 May 1994. Julio Cesar Chavez w tdec 8 Frankie Randall.
Venue: MGM Grand, Las Vegas, Nevada, USA. **Recognition:** WBC. **Referee:** Mills Lane.
Scorecards: 76-75, 77-74, 75-76.
Fight Summary: Starting well, the champion caught Chavez (140) with fast volleys of head punches, rocking him badly on one occasion, while looking to finish early. Taking time to find his feet, Chavez began to work the body more effectively in the fourth round to get himself back into the fight. However, it was clear that Chavez was not at his best when he was dominated for much of the fifth, and although coming back well at times there was the general feeling that he might crack under the kind of pressure that Randall (140) was exerting. The eighth saw the pair trading blows, with Randall having the better of the exchanges before an accidental head butt opened a cut over Chavez's right eye. Immediately turning away, Chavez was seen by the doctor who advised the referee that the fight was over with just three seconds of the session remaining. Following that, the WBC's 'accidental head-butt ruling' came into play. With Randall being deducted a point, Chavez was handed the title on a split decision after looking a likely loser.

24 July 1994. Zack Padilla w rtd 10 Juan Laporte.
Venue: Olympic Auditorium, Los Angeles, California, USA. **Recognition:** WBO. **Referee:** Raul Caiz.
Fight Summary: Throwing punches from the first bell, with Padilla (140) beginning to apply non-stop pressure it soon became clear that Laporte (140) did not have the power required to keep the champion from swarming all over him. As hard as he tried Laporte was wilting by the tenth, having hit Padilla with his best shots, and he was retired on his stool at the end of the round completely exhausted.

When the WBO version of the title became vacant after Padilla was forced to retire in September, having suffered an aneurism in training, Hector Lopez and Fidel Avendano were initially matched to find a successor. However, after Lopez sprained an ankle in training for the fight Sammy Fuentes was drafted in as a late substitute.

27 August 1994. Jake Rodriguez w rsc 9 George Scott.
Venue: Fernwood Resort, Bushkill, New York, USA. **Recognition:** IBF. **Referee:** Tony Wolfe.
Fight Summary: In a battle of southpaws it was the champion who came out on top after the referee, on the advice of the ringside doctor, took Scott (139½) out of the contest at the end of the ninth round. By the fifth Rodriguez (140) was beginning to get on top of his unbeaten opponent, and in the eighth he dropped him with a short left to the jaw. On resuming Scott was then sent into the ropes after the bell had gone. Being forced to trade in the ninth, Scott, who was bleeding badly from the mouth, was almost out on his feet with exhaustion when the stoppage came.

17 September 1994. Frankie Randall w pts 12 Juan Martin Coggi.
Venue: MGM Grand, Las Vegas, Nevada, USA. **Recognition:** WBA. **Referee:** Mitch Halpern.

Scorecards: 115-109, 116-108, 116-108.

Fight Summary: After both men were floored in the opening two rounds, Coggi (140) in the first by a left hook and Randall (140) in the second by a southpaw left, the latter settled down to put points in the bag when working from head to body. Randall was certainly beginning to get to the champion, who was again dropped in the fifth and sixth, and it was only Coggi's defensive skills that kept him in the fight. With his left eye badly swollen by the ninth it looked to be curtains for the Argentine, but he kept going, even putting in a storming 11th to no avail as Randall cruised to victory.

17 September 1994. Julio Cesar Chavez w rsc 8 Meldrick Taylor.
Venue: MGM Grand, Las Vegas, Nevada, USA. **Recognition:** WBC. **Referee:** Mills Lane.
Fight Summary: Further to their controversial earlier fight both men were unsurprisingly cautious in the early rounds, but after the challenger had two points deducted for misdemeanours, in the third and sixth sessions, Chavez (140) seemed to slip into gear just as his rival began to lose composure. Then, having effectively worked the body, Chavez saw his efforts finally paying off in the eighth as Taylor (140) came apart at the seams. Grasping the opportunity with both hands, Chavez rammed home a couple of straight punches followed by right and left hooks and another left to put Taylor on the deck. Although Taylor was up at 'six', the referee rescued him on the 1.41 mark when realising that he was in no position to defend himself.

10 December 1994. Frankie Randall w rsc 7 Rodney Moore.
Venue: Baseball Stadium, Monterrey, Mexico. **Recognition:** WBA. **Referee:** Kenny Bayless.
Fight Summary: Having knocked Moore (139) down with a left hook inside 35 seconds the tone was set, and by the sixth Randall (140) was well on his way to victory, having cut and shaken up his challenger with sustained work to the body. When left-right combinations drove Moore to the ropes in the seventh, following a flurry of 20 punches that went unanswered the referee called it off on the 1.43 mark.

10 December 1994. Julio Cesar Chavez w rsc 10 Tony Lopez.
Venue: Baseball Stadium, Monterrey, Mexico. **Recognition:** WBC. **Referee:** Luis Guzman.
Fight Summary: Although the challenger gave it his best shot and was never floored he was unable to make a dent in Chavez's armour before being pulled out of the contest by the referee after 1.41 of the tenth round had elapsed. Lopez (139) had only won two rounds at best, and with his left eye almost shut tight and the right eye closing fast and bleeding badly the decision was not a difficult one. Despite Chavez (140) injuring his left shoulder he still had too many punches for the game Lopez. When Lopez complained afterwards that he should have been allowed to carry on it was only what you would have expected from a warrior.

28 January 1995. Kostya Tszyu w rsc 6 Jake Rodriguez.
Venue: MGM Grand, Las Vegas, Nevada, USA. **Recognition:** IBF. **Referee:** Richard Steele.
Fight Summary: Floored by a cracking right to the head inside 15 seconds, the champion did well to keep going for as long as he did as Tszyu (139½) picked his punches to deliver pain virtually every time he connected. Somehow the southpaw Rodriguez (139½) made it to the end of the fifth round, having been savaged at every opportunity, and only his bravery and instinct had kept him upright. The sixth, which would be the last, was full of incident. It started with a head clash that left Tszyu nursing a cut right eye and ended with Rodriguez being dropped four more times by solid rights before the referee called it off, the finish being timed at 1.50 of the session.

20 February 1995. Sammy Fuentes w rsc 2 Fidel Avendano.
Venue: Great Western Forum, Los Angeles, California, USA. **Recognition:** WBO. **Referee:** Lou Filippo.
Fight Summary: Contesting the title vacated by Zack Padilla, Fuentes (139½) started fast against Avendano (138) and by the end of the first round had the Mexican stumbling around the ring after larruping him with left hooks. There was no letting up in the second as Fuentes, a late substitute for Hector Lopez, fired in punch after punch at the almost defenceless Avendano before the referee called a halt with just 41 seconds of the session gone.

8 April 1995. Julio Cesar Chavez w pts 12 Giovanni Parisi.
Venue: Caesar's Palace, Las Vegas, Nevada, USA. **Recognition:** WBC. **Referee:** Joe Cortez.
Scorecards: 120-107, 118-109, 118-109.

Fight Summary: When Parisi (139) was floored in the second it looked as though it was going to be an early night, but the challenger got himself up and dusted himself down to lead Chavez (140) a merry dance for the full distance. However, while waging a defensive campaign throughout, Parisi won only one round on the cards, the third, spending most of the time moving, occasionally turning southpaw, and rallying in spurts to make life tedious for Chavez. For his part, Chavez, who was well in front due to his extra work-rate, gave up trying to catch Parisi towards the end, ultimately settling for the points win.

10 June 1995. Sammy Fuentes w pts 12 Hector Lopez.
Venue: Caesar's Palace, Las Vegas, Nevada, USA. **Recognition:** WBO. **Referee:** Mitch Halpern.
Scorecards: 112-113, 114-111, 113-112.
Fight Summary: After being cut as early as the opening round as well as dropping Lopez (139½) for 'eight' it turned into a tough night for the champion, especially when you take into account the two points he had deducted for infringements in the fourth and seventh. Fuentes (140) eventually gained the decision because he took the last six rounds on the cards, but it was a close call.

16 June 1995. Frankie Randall w pts 12 Jose Rafael Barboza.
Venue: Gerland Sports Palace, Lyon, France. **Recognition:** WBA. **Referee:** Julio Alvarado.
Scorecards: 116-114, 119-111, 114-116.
Fight Summary: Thought to be an easy defence for Randall (140), he was hard pressed to beat the 30-year-old Barboza (139½) who caused him all kinds of problems with his movement and rapid-fire punches from both hands to head and body. Even when Randall upped the pace Barboza was happy to go with it, and after the latter had a good tenth round it was only in the last two sessions that the champion finally got on top.

25 June 1995. Kostya Tszyu w pts 12 Roger Mayweather.
Venue: Entertainment Centre, Newcastle, Australia. **Recognition:** IBF. **Referee:** Billy Males.
Scorecards: 119-109, 118-110, 118-110.
Fight Summary: With a massive reach advantage the challenger was able to keep Tszyu (139½) at bay for long periods, but having done so much running in the earlier rounds he tired well before the end. Despite being cut over the left eye Tszyu won almost every round when sending in a variety of punches and, although he never quite solved the style of Mayweather (140), as the latter slowed he upped the pace before coasting to the final bell.

16 September 1995. Julio Cesar Chavez w pts 12 David Kamau.
Venue: Mirage Hotel & Casino, Las Vegas, Nevada, USA. **Recognition:** WBC. **Referee:** Mills Lane.
Scorecards: 117-110, 116-112, 116-114.
Fight Summary: Making good use of his extra reach the challenger often outscored the listless Chavez (140) in the first half of the bout, mainly due to a clash of heads that had seen the latter cut over the left eye in the opening session and boxing warily. The tide turned for Chavez in the eighth when dropping Kamau (140) with a straight left, and in the next three rounds he repeatedly connected with hard punches to head and body before the Kenyan came back in the 12th to land good lefts to the head as he tried to get back in the fight.

13 January 1996. Juan Martin Coggi w tdec 5 Frankie Randall.
Venue: Jai-Alai Fronton, Miami, Florida, USA. **Recognition:** WBA. **Referee:** Bill Connors.
Scorecards: 39-38, 38-37, 38-37.
Fight Summary: It was a strange fight while it lasted, the southpaw challenger swiping with wild lefts and rights as Randall (140) looked to hurt him with rights through the middle. When Randall went down in the third round from a wild Coggi (140) left hook it was actually scored as a knockdown even though the latter had tripped him. By the fourth Randall was beginning to hurt Coggi, and in the fifth after a head clash the Argentine went down on the 1.15 mark. Despite the referee telling Coggi that he had three minutes to get up the corner decided that their man was not fit to continue. Unfortunately for Randall, who looked certain to win, it went to the cards to be decided on a technical decision.

20 January 1996. Kostya Tszyu w rsc 11 Hugo Pineda.
Venue: The Stadium, Parramatta, Australia. **Recognition:** IBF. **Referee:** Billy Males.

Fight Summary: Put down by a short right hook in the first round by the unbeaten southpaw challenger, Tszyu (139¾) came back strongly to drop his man with a right to the jaw in the fourth, and although being outboxed in the fifth he repeated the dose in the seventh. With Tszyu taking over as Pineda (139½) tired, he smashed the Colombian to the floor twice in the 11th before the referee called it off with 22 seconds of the session remaining.

9 March 1996. Giovanni Parisi w rsc 8 Sammy Fuentes.
Venue: Palalido Sports Palace, Milan, Italy. **Recognition:** WBO. **Referee:** Raul Caiz.
Fight Summary: A gruelling fight for the first seven rounds as the champion chased Parisi (138) non-stop, looking to wear him down and force a stoppage, it all went horribly wrong for him in the eighth when he suddenly ran out of gas. At that stage there was not a great deal between them as Parisi had scored well off the back foot, but faced with the rapidly fading Fuentes (140) he was scoring at will when the referee stepped in on the 2.20 mark.

24 May 1996. Kostya Tszyu w co 4 Corey Johnson.
Venue: Entertainment Centre, Sydney, Australia. **Recognition:** IBF. **Referee:** Billy Males.
Fight Summary: Taking the fight to the southpaw challenger right from the opening bell, Tszyu (139¾) began driving in solid rights to the body, the pressure finally telling in the third round. Having been dropped for 'nine' in that session Johnson (140) lasted out the remainder of the round before a continued body assault, culminating with a left hook and two rights, saw him counted out with 39 seconds of the fourth still left on the clock.

6 June 1996. Oscar De La Hoya w rsc 4 Julio Cesar Chavez.
Venue: Caesar's Palace, Las Vegas, Nevada, USA. **Recognition:** WBC. **Referee:** Joe Cortez.
Fight Summary: From the moment the champion was badly cut over the left eye in the very first minute of the opening round he lost any chance he had of holding on to his title as De La Hoya (139) swarmed all over him. Half blinded, Chavez (139) continually walked into De La Hoya's lightning-fast punches from both hands, it being only a matter of time when the fight would be stopped. The brilliant De La Hoya just could not miss Chavez, and after 2.37 of the fourth had expired the referee, under instruction from the ringside doctor, called a halt, thus ushering in a future legend of the ring to replace one from the past.

20 June 1996. Giovanni Parisi drew 12 Carlos Gonzalez.
Venue: Assago Indoor Arena, Milan, Italy. **Recognition:** WBO. **Referee:** Larry Rozadilla.
Scorecards: 114-112, 112-114, 114-114.
Fight Summary: Caught cold early on, when the champion was dropped in the opener it looked very much on the cards that the hard-punching Gonzalez (138¾) was well on his way to a quick win. This view was compounded when Parisi (137¼) again found himself on the floor in the second. However, from thereon in Parisi showed what he was made of when coming back strongly to take the next three sessions by dint of his good boxing skills, switching first one way and then the other to confuse Gonzalez. Although the former champion came back in the sixth and seventh, Parisi edged the last five rounds on all three judges' cards to retain his title by the narrowest of margins.

16 August 1996. Frankie Randall w pts 12 Juan Martin Coggi.
Venue: German Society Gym, Villa Ballester, Buenos Aires, Argentina. **Recognition:** WBA. **Referee:** John Coyle.
Scorecards: 115-112, 117-111, 114-113.
Fight Summary: In this, the third meeting between the pair, Randall (140) regained the title he had lost to the awkward southpaw, Coggi (140), after surviving a clash of heads in the opening round. This time he left nothing to chance, dropping Coggi with a long right in the second and hurting him badly in the eighth and 11th sessions. Deducted a point in the fifth for low blows the game Coggi gave it his best shot, but Randall, who was the quicker, dominated much of the latter stages despite being fatigued.

14 September 1996. Kostya Tszyu w rsc 6 Jan Piet Bergman.
Venue: Entertainment Centre, Newcastle, Australia. **Recognition:** IBF. **Referee:** Billy Males.
Fight Summary: Having started with the jab-and-move routine, after getting cut on the left eye in the second round Bergman (139¾) lost his discipline and went looking for the champion. He even had some successes, going relatively well until Tszyu (139½) began to step it up in the fifth. Cut over the right eye early in the sixth Tszyu went

in to overdrive, dropping Bergman with a solid left hook to the jaw, and when the latter got himself up he was smashed down again by a right cross, whereupon the referee immediately called the fight off at 1.23 of the session.

12 October 1996. Giovanni Parisi w rsc 4 Sergio Rey Revilla.

Venue: Assago Indoor Arena, Milan, Italy. **Recognition:** WBO. **Referee:** Samuel Viruet.

Fight Summary: Defending the title again following his scare last time out, Parisi (139½) started slowly before getting into gear in the third round, his straight lefts finding the onrushing Rey Revilla (136¾) with some ease. Having hurt the Spaniard with a solid left hook at the end of the previous session Parisi moved up a gear in the fourth, having his man down from a left to the body for 'four' prior to putting him down again with a right hook to the jaw. Incredibly, after the referee waved Rey Revilla on despite getting up in a dazed state, it was only when he saw the Spaniard's cornermen waving the towel he stopped it, the finish being timed at 2.03.

11 January 1997. Khalid Rahilou w rsc 11 Frankie Randall.

Venue: The Arena, Nashville, Tennessee, USA. **Recognition:** WBA. **Referee:** Rafael Ramos.

Fight Summary: Further to Rahilou (139) starting the contest with the left jab and countering well before picking up the pace in the fifth, the champion was unable to find any form of rhythm. From that point on most of the rounds belonged to Rahilou as Randall (139½) became increasingly desperate, especially in the tenth when the latter was being picked apart. In the 11th the wheels came off for Randall, and after he had been slammed into a corner by four consecutive head punches, being hit without reply, the referee jumped in to call a halt after 58 seconds of the session had elapsed.

18 January 1997. Kostya Tszyu tdraw 1 Leonardo Mas.

Venue: Thomas & Mack Centre, Las Vegas, Nevada, USA. **Recognition:** IBF. **Referee:** Joe Cortez.

Fight Summary: Classified by the IBF as a no-decision result (for our purposes a technical draw), the fight came to abrupt halt after a big Tszyu (139) left hook sent Mas (139), who had already been decked twice, to the floor just on the bell ending the first round. It was then announced that due to an unintentional illegal blow the challenger was unable to continue.

18 January 1997. Oscar De La Hoya w pts 12 Miguel Angel Gonzalez.

Venue: Thomas & Mack Centre, Las Vegas, Nevada, USA. **Recognition:** WBC. **Referee:** Mills Lane.

Scorecards: 117-110, 117-111, 117-109.

Fight Summary: Although he could hardly miss with the left jab, setting Gonzalez (140) up on countless occasions, the champion could not find the punches to put the Mexican hard man away. Twice Gonzalez (140) had points deducted for transgressing the rules, but it would not have made any difference as De La Hoya (140) won almost every round effortlessly. Some of De La Hoya's work was blinding, the CompuBox stats showing that he landed with 212 of the 319 left jabs he threw.

After De La Hoya relinquished the WBC version of the title on winning the WBC welterweight crown in April, Gonzalez was matched against Julio Cesar Chavez to find a new champion. Unfortunately, with Chavez suffering an elbow injury that required an operation, and coupled with domestic problems, it took almost ten months to get the two men together.

19 April 1997. Giovanni Parisi w rsc 8 Harold Miller.

Venue: The Palalido, Milan, Italy. **Recognition:** WBO. **Referee:** Mario Maianti.

Fight Summary: With this being an easy defence for Parisi (138¼) it was difficult to see how Miller (138¼) was classified as a suitable opponent for a world championship opportunity. Winning every round with some ease, despite not being able to drop the American Parisi handed out a real beating as lefts and rights found their mark with regularity. The stoppage when it finally came was timed at 1.45 of the eighth round.

31 May 1997. Vince Phillips w rsc 10 Kostya Tszyu.

Venue: Trump Taj Mahal Casino Resort, Atlantic City, New Jersey, USA. **Recognition:** IBF. **Referee:** Benjy Esteves Jnr.

Fight Summary: In what was a huge shock, Phillips (140) proved that boxing was a game of styles and opportunities as he took his when forcing a stoppage at 1.22 of the tenth round over a champion whose star was on the rise. After Tszyu (140) had been dropped by a big right in the seventh the fight changed completely, and picking up where he left off Phillips was still sending in big punches during the eighth and ninth. With Tszyu having no defence against a right through the middle he was eventually rescued by the referee when on his way to the canvas, with both eyes cut and badly deflated. Phillips also had a nasty gash over the right eye.

5 July 1997. Khalid Rahilou w rsc 7 Marty Jakubowski.
Venue: King Mohammed V Sports Complex, Casablanca, Morocco. **Recognition:** WBA. **Referee:** Stan Christodoulou.
Fight Summary: Returning to the land of his parents, the champion defeated Jakubowski (139) by gradually wearing his man down while taking all completed six rounds on the cards before applying the finishing touches. Deciding to up the pace further in the seventh Rahilou (139¼) soon had Jakubowski on one knee, and following two more visits to the canvas by the latter in the same session the referee was forced to call a halt on the 'three knockdowns in a round' ruling, with just 20 seconds of the round remaining.

9 August 1997. Vince Phillips w rsc 3 Micky Ward.
Venue: The Roxy, Boston, Massachusetts, USA. **Recognition:** IBF. **Referee:** Dick Flaherty.
Fight Summary: Making his first defence, Phillips (139½) started well with left jabs and solid right crosses before opening up with body punches that forced Ward (139¾) to cover up. After switching between southpaw and orthodox in the third, and having done reasonably well, Ward was caught by a three-punch combination that opened up a two-inch gash on his left eye. With blood flowing the referee tried to let Ward carry on, but with a second of the session remaining he was forced to call a halt as the injury was deemed to be too bad for the latter to continue.

4 October 1997. Giovanni Parisi w rtd 7 Nigel Wenton.
Venue: Big Tent, Vibo Valentia, Italy. **Recognition:** WBO. **Referee:** Genaro Rodriguez.
Fight Summary: Defending his title in a specially constructed tent situated in front of San Leoluca Cathedral, Parisi (138) was always in control despite having some uncomfortable moments when Wenton (139½) got in several good shots in the second, fourth and sixth rounds. Switching from orthodox to southpaw, with Parisi finding gaps in the Englishman's defence, by the seventh he was well on top. After being dropped by a right uppercut at the end of that session, although a badly dazed Wenton was saved by the bell he was also carrying a nasty cut over the left eye. Following that, his corner wisely pulled him out during the interval.

6 December 1997. Giovanni Parisi w pts 12 Jose Manuel Berdonce.
Venue: Sports Palace, Catanzaro, Italy. **Recognition:** WBO. **Referee:** Roberto Ramirez.
Scorecards: 116-114, 118-111, 117-112.
Fight Summary: Having to carry an injured finger on his right hand for most of the contest was not what Parisi (137¼) really wanted, but he made light of it to outscore an awkward southpaw challenger in Berdonce (139½). With Berdonce trying to get in close several times heads came together. However, Parisi kept his distance with the use of a good jab and apart from the fourth round was never really inconvenienced.

13 December 1997. Vince Phillips w co 10 Freddie Pendleton.
Venue: The Amphitheatre, Pompano Beach, Florida, USA. **Recognition:** IBF. **Referee:** Tom Kimmons.
Fight Summary: Right from the start when Pendleton (140) was nailed by a cracking right to the jaw the writing was on the wall as Phillips (140) looked to make another successful defence. Cut over the left eye, by the fifth round the veteran Pendleton (140) was stumbling around, and in the sixth it was no surprise when he was dropped by a cracking right to the temple. Smashed down twice more, in the seventh and ninth rounds, Pendleton somehow managed to keep going into the tenth before being taken out of it when a left hook to the body dropped him for the full count.

21 February 1998. Khalid Rahilou w pts 12 Jean-Baptiste Mendy.
Venue: Bercy Sports Palace, Paris, France. **Recognition:** WBA. **Referee:** Carlos Berrocal.

Scorecards: 115-111, 115-112, 114-113.

Fight Summary: Following a cautious start by both men, Mendy (139) broke the tension when dropping the champion for 'four' with a right hook in the third but was unable to find a finishing blow. The contest then swayed back and forth as both men looked to get their punches off, there never being much between them. Even after the ninth when Rahilou (139¾) knocked Mendy over with a right and followed it up in the next session with an all-out attack the latter did not back down. Coming out for the 11th it could be seen that Rahilou had tired himself out, but he still found the punches to hurt Mendy. Although Mendy gave it everything in the 12th to win the round it was not enough.

7 March 1998. Julio Cesar Chavez drew 12 Miguel Angel Gonzalez.

Venue: The Bullring, Mexico City, Mexico. **Recognition:** WBC. **Referee:** Lupe Garcia.

Scorecards: 115-114, 114-116, 115-115.

Fight Summary: Contesting the title vacated by Oscar De La Hoya, Gonzalez (140) and Chavez (140) fought a draw according to the official verdict, but had the 115-115 scorecard been added up correctly it would have been marked 115-114 to Gonzalez, thus making him the new champion. As it was, Gonzalez seemed to have the better of the once great Chavez, especially early on, but with no knockdowns to help and the latter winning three of the last five sessions the championship would have to be decided another time.

In the wake of Chavez's decision to move up a weight, Gonzalez was matched against the mandatory challenger, Kostya Tszyu, to decide the vacant title. Unfortunately, Gonzalez was then forced to pull out with rib damage while Tszyu went on to win the WBC 'interim' championship, stopping Diosbelys Hurtado inside five rounds at the Fantasy Springs Casino, Indio, California on 28 November. The pair would eventually meet to decide the title on 21 August 1999.

14 March 1998. Vince Phillips w co 1 Alfonso Sanchez.

Venue: Trump Taj Mahal Casino Resort, Atlantic City, New Jersey, USA. **Recognition:** IBF. **Referee:** Joe Cortez.

Fight Summary: Given a crack at the title, Sanchez (139), a fast-moving stylist, was expected to make life difficult for the champion. Both men came out fast, immediately getting down to work, and after a couple of good exchanges Phillips (140) suddenly slipped the lead and smashed in a right-left that dropped Sanchez like a log to be counted out with 30 seconds of the opening round still remaining.

Later, with Phillips experiencing weight problems, Zab Judah stopped Wilfredo Negron in the fourth round of an IBF 'interim' title fight at the MGM Grand, Las Vegas, Nevada on 16 January 1999. Given that Phillips was already contracted to defend the title against Terron Millett on 20 February 1999, with it really being an official eliminator Judah would eventually get his opportunity.

29 May 1998. Carlos Gonzalez w rsc 9 Giovanni Parisi.

Venue: BPA Sports Palace, Pesaro, Italy. **Recognition:** WBO. **Referee:** Jose Rivera.

Fight Summary: Having been unlucky to come away with just a draw when challenging Parisi (138½) two years earlier, Gonzalez (139) meant to get his hands on the title this time around, taking the first three rounds on the cards. It was important that Gonzales cut down the ring to give the champion less space to work in, and although Parisi came back well in the fourth and fifth the Mexican picked it up again in the sixth. After Parisi was knocked down by a terrific right uppercut in the seventh, although he shared the next session he was all at sea in the ninth before advising the referee that he could not continue on the 2.14 mark.

10 October 1998. Sharmba Mitchell w pts 12 Khalid Rahilou.

Venue: Bercy Sports Palace, Paris, France. **Recognition:** WBA. **Referee:** Julio Alvarado.

Scorecards: 116-107, 116-110, 118-105. Although the champion fought a game rearguard action he was up against it right from the opening bell as Mitchell (139) showed both fast hands and power from a southpaw to stance to win the title. Knocked down twice in the second, and smashed to the floor from a body shot in the third round, it did not look as though Rahilou (140) would be in the fight for much longer. However, against all the odds he battled back well as Mitchell took a breather before being floored again in the seventh by a big right. He then somehow finished the full course despite taking a battering in the last three sessions.

6 February 1999. Sharmba Mitchell w pts 12 Pedro Saiz.
Venue: Convention Centre, Washington DC, USA. **Recognition:** WBA. **Referee:** Ken Chevalier.
Scorecards: 120-105, 119-107, 116-112.
Fight Summary: At just 16 days' notice Mitchell (140) put his title on the line against a fellow southpaw in Saiz (140), a Dominican residing in Brooklyn, New York, and had little trouble picking up the points decision when using a good left jab and firing in effective combination punches. The only knockdown was recorded in the fifth round when Saiz slipped over. Saiz also lost a point in the seventh when going low, but despite all that he proved himself to be a tough customer who could take a good punch.

20 February 1999. Terron Millett w rsc 5 Vince Phillips.
Venue: Madison Square Garden, Manhattan, NYC, New York, USA. **Recognition:** IBF. **Referee:** Jim Santa.
Fight Summary: Suffering serious weight problems that obviously weakened him, the champion, who was reported to have taken off 47 pounds in seven weeks, appeared to be in trouble right from the opening bell as Millett (140) set a very fast pace. Although bewildered by Millett's left jab, Phillips (140) actually dropped his man with a right-hand counter in the second round, only for it to be ruled a slip. In the third Phillips was floored by a right hand just as the bell sounded, and in the fourth he was put down twice again before being under pressure in the fifth prior to being rescued by the referee on the 1.58 mark after he had been sent reeling across the ring by two big lefts.

24 April 1999. Sharmba Mitchell w pts 12 Reggie Green.
Venue: MCI Centre, Washington DC, USA. **Recognition:** WBA. **Referee:** Ken Chevalier.
Scorecards: 116-111, 115-113, 114-114.
Fight Summary: Making a big start, the champion had Green (140) down and cut over the right eye in the opening session from a series of combination punches, but could not finish him off. Green actually came back to win the second, hurting Mitchell (140) into the bargain, before the fight went first one way and then the other as both men went looking for the win. By the sixth it had developed into a bruising war of attrition. Although Green took the next three rounds on the cards, with Mitchell edging the last three he just about held on to his title.

15 May 1999. Randall Bailey w co 1 Carlos Gonzalez.
Venue: Jai-Alai Fronton, Miami, Florida, USA. **Recognition:** WBO. **Referee:** Telis Assimenios.
Fight Summary: Given a crack at the world title the little-known Bailey (140) surprised everyone, including the champion, when scoring one of the quickest wins in championship history. Although he came into the fight unbeaten in 18 starts the lanky 24-year-old challenger was not expected to give Gonzalez (139¾) too many problems, despite most of his wins coming early. However, having made a good start and showing very fast hands Bailey smashed in a left hook that dropped Gonzalez heavily for a dramatic knockout after just 41 seconds of the fight.

24 July 1999. Terron Millett w rsc 12 Virgil McClendon.
Venue: Flamingo Hilton, Las Vegas, Nevada, USA. **Recognition:** IBF. **Referee:** Richard Steele.
Fight Summary: Even though he was slow out of the blocks Millett (139) withstood his southpaw challenger's early blitz, being well and truly in the groove by the sixth. The awkward McClendon (139½) had certainly given Millett a shaking up, especially in the second, but he was now beginning to ship more and more punishment. Hurt at the end of the 11th McClendon was under fire immediately in the 12th, and after taking a welter of blows to head and body without return the referee called it off with 1.50 on the clock.

Having suffered a long-term injury to his hands, when Millett forfeited the IBF version of the championship in December he was told that when fully fit he would become a preferential challenger to whoever held the title. Following that, Zab Judah and Jan Piet Bergman were matched for the vacant title.

21 August 1999. Kostya Tszyu w rsc 10 Miguel Angel Gonzalez.
Venue: Miccosukee Indian Gaming Reservation, Miami, Florida, USA. **Recognition:** WBC. **Referee:** Frank Santore Jnr.
Fight Summary: Following two years of postponements caused by injuries and promotional problems, the WBC finally had a 140lbs champion after the 'interim' titleholder, Tszyu (140), stopped Gonzalez (140) in the tenth. From

68

the second round onwards it could be seen that Tszyu had the measure of Gonzales, rocking him with heavy rights to the head, and after the latter had a point taken away in the fourth for illegal use of the shoulder it was all one-way traffic. Gonzalez, who had been cut over the right eye as early as the opening session, was really up against it in the fifth when taking heavy punishment from thereon in. It came as no surprise when the referee was forced to call a halt after 48 seconds of the tenth when the Mexican's corner was screaming for it to be stopped. For the purists, however, the fight should have seen Gonzalez disqualified at some stage for fouling throughout the fight with impunity, but for whatever reason he had just the one point deducted.

13 November 1999. Sharmba Mitchell w pts 12 Elio Ortiz.
Venue: Thomas & Mack Arena, Las Vegas, Nevada, USA. **Recognition:** WBA. **Referee:** Richard Steele.
Scorecards: 114-112, 118-108, 119-109.
Fight Summary: On dropping his challenger with a fast southpaw left after just 15 seconds Mitchell (139½) must have thought he was in for an early night, but he was forced to go all the way after suffering a badly cut right eye in the sixth following a clash of heads. Ortiz (139½) eventually had a point deducted for illegal use of the head, in the eighth. Following the injury, Mitchell, careful to protect himself from further damage, allowed Ortiz back into the fight, but the latter was a long way behind on two of the cards and would have needed a knockout to win.

11 December 1999. Randall Bailey w rsc 9 Hector Lopez.
Venue: Grand Hotel, Tunica, Mississippi, USA. **Recognition:** WBO. **Referee:** Fred Steinwinder.
Fight Summary: While made to look clumsy at times the champion ultimately had too much power for Lopez (140), who was unable to do too much damage despite battling back with left hooks. If he had not concentrated on landing single blows Bailey (140) could probably have finished earlier and, although he had Lopez down in the fifth from a right to the head, he failed to follow up any advantage. Eventually, Bailey finally nailed the rapidly tiring Lopez with a right to the jaw in the ninth, the latter being rescued by the referee after two minutes of the session when struggling to get to his feet.

12 February 2000. Kostya Tszyu w rsc 8 Ahmed Santos.
Venue: Mohegan Sun Casino, Uncasville, Connecticut, USA. **Recognition:** WBC. **Referee:** Frank Cappuccino.
Fight Summary: Although failing to win a round on the cards the challenger managed to hold out until the eighth. Prior to that, Santos (139) had shown an ability to assimilate any number of right hands and left uppercuts to his head, but it was also clear that Tszyu (140) was merely biding his time. Early in the eighth Santos was finally dropped by a right uppercut, and when he got up and was blasted back down the referee halted proceedings with just 36 seconds on the clock.

12 February 2000. Zab Judah w co 4 Jan Piet Bergman.
Venue: Mohegan Sun Casino, Uncasville, Connecticut, USA. **Recognition:** IBF. **Referee:** Steve Smoger.
Fight Summary: Contesting the title forfeited by Terron Millett, Judah (138½) quickly asserted himself when dropping Bergman (138¾) twice with solid lefts in the opening round, only to be floored himself in the second when getting caught by a desperate left hook. Getting over that embarrassment, the southpaw Judah soon picked it up again with one two-fisted attack after another and in the fourth Bergman was counted out with ten seconds of the session remaining, having been floored heavily in a neutral corner.

8 April 2000. Randall Bailey w rtd 6 Rocky Martinez.
Venue: Bercy Sports Palace, Paris, France. **Recognition:** WBO. **Referee:** Samuel Viruet.
Fight Summary: Most people would have expected at least a knockdown in this one, but Martinez (139½) defied all of the champion's best efforts even though he was dominated throughout. Making a fast start, Bailey (139½) was soon pumping out left jabs as a prelude for the right to follow, but Martinez made it difficult for him despite suffering from a cut left eye and damage to his nose. And he was still in there coming up for the sixth. Having absorbed a solid right to the head that rocked him, with the cuts beginning to worsen after Martinez got back to his corner at the end of the session he was retired.

24 June 2000. Zab Judah w pts 12 Junior Witter.
Venue: Hampden Park, Glasgow, Scotland. **Recognition:** IBF. **Referee:** Roy Francis.

69

Scorecards: 116-112, 118-110, 118-111.

Fight Summary: Taking the fight at a week's notice the challenger showed no sign of nerves in his first major championship battle, and at times made Judah (139¾) look quite ordinary as he made life difficult for the southpaw champion with his movement. Although Judah was constantly the aggressor he had great difficulty in getting solid shots on Witter (139¼), but while defending well the latter had to settle for being a very good loser whose time would come at a later date.

22 July 2000. Ener Julio w pts 12 Randall Bailey.
Venue: American Airlines Arena, Miami, Florida, USA. **Recognition:** WBO. **Referee:** Max Parker Jnr.
Scorecards: 113-111, 114-111, 111-115.
Fight Summary: It was a strange start for the champion as he missed Julio (139¾) consistently before being knocked down by a left hook in the opening session. However, Bailey (139) had got himself back in the fight by the sixth, dropping Julio heavily from a right to the head, only for the latter to show remarkable recuperative powers when continuing to land his left lead almost at will. By the ninth, Bailey, his right eye closed, was tiring but he still found a big right to drop Julio towards the end of the session. It turned out to be Bailey's last opportunity as the Colombian got up and carried on as if nothing had happened. Julio then came back with some venom to win the last three rounds clearly, even though he had a point deducted in the 11th for holding and hitting.

After Julio forfeited the WBO version of the title in June 2001 when it was discovered that he had cataracts on both eyes immediately prior to a championship defence against Felix Flores, DeMarcus Corley was drafted in at just four days' notice in order to find a new champion.

29 July 2000. Kostya Tszyu w rsc 6 Julio Cesar Chavez.
Venue: Veteran's Memorial Coliseum, Phoenix, Arizona, USA. **Recognition:** WBC. **Referee:** Bobby Ferrara.
Fight Summary: This was the fight that ended Chavez (140) as a fighter at the highest level as he vainly tried to recapture his old title from the brilliant Tszyu (139½). Apart from the third round when two judges voted for him, with Chavez beginning to take more punches than needed he was starting to look like he had run out of ideas coming into the sixth. Chavez was also punching low, but it was more to do with his timing than anything untoward. Smashed down by a big right to the head Chavez got up but was now being hit at will, and when he was dropped again, by a left-right, the referee stopped it with 1.30 of the session remaining.

5 August 2000. Zab Judah w rsc 4 Terron Millett.
Venue: Mohegan Sun Casino, Uncasville, Connecticut, USA. **Recognition:** IBF. **Referee:** Michael Ortega.
Fight Summary: Putting up his title against the man who forfeited it, the speedy Judah (138) got down to business immediately when sending in thudding southpaw left crosses that hurt Millett (139½) right down to his boots. Then, without warning, Judah was tagged and dropped by a solid left hook, but surprised more than badly hurt he got up to finish the opening round strongly. With Judah back in business it was Millett's turn to be smashed to the canvas, by a left cross in the second, and although the third saw both men exploding punches there were no knockdowns. The fourth, however, was destined to be the last. There was no doubt that Judah was looking to finish it, flooring his challenger twice more before the referee called it off with 13 seconds of the session remaining.

16 September 2000. Sharmba Mitchell w pts 12 Felix Flores.
Venue: MGM Grand, Las Vegas, Nevada, USA. **Recognition:** WBA. **Referee:** Tony Weeks.
Scorecards: 116-111, 116-111, 116-113.
Fight Summary: Knocked down in the fourth by right uppercuts to the body and jaw and saved by the bell, the champion soon got back on track when peppering Flores (139½) with good combinations to add to his points total. Although Flores was always dangerous, being credited with winning the seventh and eighth, he was never able to repeat his fourth-round performance as Mitchell (139) kept his hands up from thereon in to box his way to victory.

20 October 2000. Zab Judah w rsc 8 Hector Quiroz.
Venue: The Palace, Auburn Hills, Michigan, USA. **Recognition:** IBF. **Referee:** Dale Grable.

Fight Summary: Using his speed to good effect the southpaw champion made sure that he did not take too many unnecessary chances against the limited but dangerous Quiroz (140). After almost dropping Quiroz in the first and then being hurt himself in the second, Judah (139¼) settled down to box his way to victory before the fight was stopped at 1.56 of the eighth when the referee decided that damage to the Mexican's right eye was too great for him to carry on.

13 January 2001. Zab Judah w rsc 10 Reggie Green.
Venue: Mohegan Sun Casino, Uncasville, Connecticut, USA. **Recognition:** IBF. **Referee:** Arthur Mercante.
Fight Summary: While clearly in control the southpaw champion appeared to be doing only as much as he needed to do, and in the sixth round the 81-year-old referee, a veteran of many big fights of yesteryear, asked him to provide more action. Almost immediately Judah (138¼) began to up his work-rate, Green (139), with swellings around both eyes, being wobbled several times before he was sent crashing in the tenth by a left hook to the head. No sooner had Green got to his feet another left put him down again, whereupon the referee called a halt with 1.31 of the session left on the clock.

3 February 2001. Kostya Tszyu w rtd 7 Sharmba Mitchell.
Venue: Mandalay Bay Resort & Casino, Las Vegas, Nevada, USA. **Recognition:** WBA/WBC. **Referee:** Joe Cortez.
Fight Summary: In a battle to unify two of the four main titles, the unfortunate Mitchell (139), who carried an injured left knee into the ring, was forced to retire on his stool at the end of the seventh round when the pain and lack of mobility was just too much to bear. Although being docked a point in the fourth for pushing, Tszyu (140) was three rounds ahead on the cards but had failed to put his southpaw opponent away despite having him down for unrecorded knockdowns on several occasions.

23 June 2001. Kostya Tszyu w pts 12 Oktay Urkal.
Venue: Mohegan Sun Casino, Uncasville, Connecticut, USA. **Recognition:** WBA/WBC. **Referee:** Frank Cappuccino.
Scorecards: 116-112, 115-113, 116-113.
Fight Summary: Defending both the WBC and WBA Belts, Tszyu (139½) was expected to walk through Urkal (138½), but unfortunately for the champion the latter had not read the script. Starting how he meant to carry on, Urkal often embarrassed Tszyu with combination punches and quick counters while his awkward style made it difficult for the champion to fathom. Despite Tszyu being the harder puncher and the fresher in the closing stages, unable to pull away from the clever Urkal he had to be satisfied with a relatively close margin of points in his favour.

23 June 2001. Zab Judah w rsc 3 Allan Vester.
Venue: Mohegan Sun Casino, Uncasville, Connecticut, USA. **Recognition:** IBF. **Referee:** Charles Dwyer.
Fight Summary: Although he got through the opening round unscathed, actually sending in decent combinations, it would be merely a matter of time for the limited challenger as Judah (138½) came out briskly in the second. Decked by a hard left-right Vester (138) was soon down, and while getting up he was badly punished before being dropped again. Having been saved by the bell Vester once again came under the cosh and, after Judah found a perfect southpaw right hook that smashed into the Dane's temple and sent him to the canvas with no hope of beating the count, the referee halted the uneven contest with just two seconds of the third remaining.

30 June 2001. DeMarcus Corley w rsc 1 Felix Flores.
Venue: Mandalay Bay Resort & Casino, Las Vegas, Nevada, USA. **Recognition:** WBO. **Referee:** Jay Nady.
Fight Summary: Just five days before defending against Flores, after Ener Julio forfeited his title when it was discovered that he had cataracts in both eyes Corley was drafted in to contest the vacant championship, with the winner pledged to defend against Julio following surgery. Not one to miss a golden opportunity Corley (140) went straight on the attack with stiff jabs, and before Flores (140) could even get anything off he was smashed down by a tremendous right uppercut. Although the Puerto Rican was up quickly he was forced to take the mandatory 'eight' count before immediately running into a southpaw left cross that dropped him again. When Flores, who somehow staggered up at 'nine', was allowed to continue Corley was on to him like a flash, driving in a right-left-right that sent him reeling into the ropes to leave the referee with no alternative other than to stop the contest with 11 seconds of the first round remaining.

3 November 2001. Kostya Tszyu w rsc 2 Zab Judah.
Venue: MGM Grand, Las Vegas, Nevada, USA. **Recognition:** IBF/WBA/WBC. **Referee:** Jay Nady.
Fight Summary: Looking to unify three titles, and having been outboxed by the southpaw Judah (139½) in the opening round, Tszyu (140) picked it up in the second when staying as close as he could to the IBF champion. It was the correct tactic. After nailing Judah with a right to the head Tszyu crashed in another right to put the former down heavily. Although Judah got up quickly and spoke to the referee to say he was okay all of a sudden, with his legs betraying him, he staggered across the ring before collapsing in Tszyu's corner. Despite there being just one second remaining in the session the referee stopped the fight, leaving Tszyu the holder of three belts. Extremely upset, Judah lost his head and attacked the third man before being escorted away.

Having been awarded *The Ring* Championship Belt at the end of the year, with Tszyu now considered a 'super' champion by the WBA, Randall Bailey won the vacant 'second tier' title when stopping Demetrio Ceballos in the third round at the Sovereign Centre, Reading, Pennsylvania on 2 February 2002. Later, on 11 May 2002 at the Roberto Clemente Coliseum, San Juan, Puerto Rico, Bailey lost the so-called title to Diosbelys Hurtado when he was knocked out in the seventh round.

19 January 2002. DeMarcus Corley w pts 12 Ener Julio.
Venue: Jai-Alai Fronton, Miami, Florida, USA. **Recognition:** WBO. **Referee:** Jorge Alonso.
Scorecards: 119-105, 118-107, 117-107.
Fight Summary: Corley (140) started well when knocking his challenger down in the second and third rounds, but on both occasions he failed to finish the job when standing off to admire his work. Although Julio (140) had a five-inch advantage in height, unable to use it as he did not have the hand-speed to match, the southpaw champion continually beat him to the punch. In the sixth the Colombian came on stronger, but after Corley sank to his knees, having been punched down, Julio stupidly hit him before he had arisen and was docked two points. Thereafter, with Corley tiring, Julio came more into it, but due to his lack of mobility he failed to do too much damage before the fight ran its course.

18 May 2002. Kostya Tszyu w pts 12 Ben Tackie.
Venue: Mandalay Bay Resort & Casino, Las Vegas, Nevada, USA. **Recognition:** IBF/WBA/WBC/The Ring. **Referee:** Jay Nady.
Scorecards: 120-108, 120-108, 119-109.
Fight Summary: As the IBF's mandatory challenger Tackie (139½) won just one round as he bravely stayed on the front foot while being forced to take anything the champion cared to throw at him. Almost from the opening bell one could see that Tackie would have to get lucky if he wanted to win the title, being too one-dimensional, and while Tszyu (140) had to be careful that he did not get caught the Ghanaian was an easy target.

Diosbelys Hurtado lost the 'second tier' title to Vivian Harris when he was stopped in the second round of their contest at Reliant Park, Houston, Texas on 19 October.

4 January 2003. DeMarcus Corley w pts 12 Randall Bailey.
Venue: The Armoury, Washington DC, USA. **Recognition:** WBO. **Referee:** Joseph Cooper.
Scorecards: 117-111, 116-112, 117-111.
Fight Summary: In a match where fireworks were expected the action was at best lacklustre, the fast and clever southpaw champion making a point of not allowing Bailey (139) to target him with the right hand. Although Corley (140) occasionally fired in jarring left crosses that hurt Bailey it was all too infrequent, and even when the latter found himself in range to unload the right hand more often than not he failed to do so. With the crowd becoming restless from before the halfway stage the fighters made some effort in the eighth, but when that fizzled out the men were booed for the rest of the contest.

19 January 2003. Kostya Tszyu w rtd 6 Jesse James Leija.
Venue: Telstra Dome, Melbourne, Australia. **Recognition:** IBF/WBA/WBC/The Ring. **Referee:** Malcolm Bulner.
Fight Summary: There was little action in the opening three rounds as both fighters settled, but following a few flurries from Leija (139) the champion began to dictate matters with a controlled left jab paving the way. While

Tszyu (139¾) was beginning to go up a few gears in the sixth he appeared not to be looking to finish matters, although he was getting much closer to Leija who was beginning to flounder. The contest came to an abrupt halt during the interval between round six and seven when Leija's corner decided to retire their man, having realised that he had burst his right eardrum.

With Tszyu remaining inactive due to injury, after the WBC decided to give him an honorary 'Emeritus' status in order to free up the championship, it was decided by the body towards the end of the year that Arturo Gatti and Gianluca Branco would contest the vacant title.

Following that, Sharmba Mitchell outscored Lovemore Ndou over 12 rounds at Bally's Park Place Hotel, Atlantic City, New Jersey, USA on 7 February 2004 to win the vacant IBF 'interim' title, prior to successfully defending it against Michael Stewart (w pts 12 at the MEN Arena, Manchester, England on 3 April 2004). Those two wins would eventually get Mitchell a crack at Tszyu for the IBF title and *The Ring* Championship Belt.

Increasingly difficult to satisfy all three bodies, when Tszyu forfeited the WBA title in June 2004, Vivian Harris, who had successfully defended the 'second tier' crown when beating Souleymane M'baye (w pts 12 at Orleans Hotel & Casino, Las Vegas, Nevada, USA on 12 July 2003) and Oktay Urkal (w pts 12 at the Max Schmeling Hall, Berlin, Germany on 17 April 2004), was declared champion.

12 July 2003. Zab Judah w pts 12 DeMarcus Corley.
Venue: Orleans Hotel & Casino, Las Vegas, Nevada, USA. **Recognition:** WBO. **Referee:** Joe Cortez.
Scorecards: 115-112, 112-115, 115-112.
Fight Summary: Challenging for the title, and a battle between southpaws, by the third round the speedy Judah (140) was already proving to be too skilful, and towards the end of the session two left crosses had the champion down. However, with Judah failing to sustain the pressure it was close enough for the judges to disagree on many of the rounds. While Corley (139½) was never out of it he did not take advantage of the opportunities when presented to him, and although he had a good tenth round he failed to build on it. Despite the scores being much closer than anticipated, how one judge had Corley winning 115-112 was just amazing.

13 December 2003. Zab Judah w co 1 Jaime Rangel.
Venue: Boardwalk Hall, Atlantic City, New Jersey, USA. **Recognition:** WBO. **Referee:** Frank Cappuccino.
Fight Summary: In another battle of fellow southpaws the WBO champion, Judah (140), proved his right to the title when demolishing Rangel (140) at 1.12 of the opening round. With no sign of what was to come when the men came together at the start there were no real blows of note until Judah unleashed a cracking left cross that detonated on Rangel's jaw and sent him crashing down to be counted out. Having disappointed last time out this was a perfect response from the champion.

Judah vacated the title in June 2004 after beating Rafael Pineda for the WBO Inter-Continental welterweight crown at the Mandalay Bay Resort & Casino, Las Vegas, Nevada on 15 May. Following that, a match was made between Miguel Cotto and Kelson Pinto to find a new champion.

24 January 2004. Arturo Gatti w pts 12 Gianluca Branco.
Venue: Boardwalk Hall, Atlantic City, New Jersey, USA. **Recognition:** WBC. **Referee:** Rudy Battle.
Scorecards: 116-111, 115-112, 116-111.
Fight Summary: Contesting the title which became vacant due to Kostya Tszyu's enforced absence, although Gatti (140) won clearly enough, after breaking his right hand in the fifth round he was forced to rely on the left. Branco (140) was no slouch when it came to attack, having a rapier-like left jab and a fair right hand, but he was too upright, a failing that was more often than not exploited by Gatti. The only knockdown came late in the tenth when Gatti exploded a left hook on Branco's jaw. However, with Gatti failing to take advantage of the situation the Italian was let off the hook. Still dazed in the 11th Branco was caught by left jabs throughout the session, and even though another heavy left hook nearly dropped him in the 12th he was still there at the final bell.

24 July 2004. Arturo Gatti w co 2 Leonard Dorin.
Venue: Boardwalk Hall, Atlantic City, New Jersey, USA. **Recognition:** WBC. **Referee:** Randy Neumann.
Fight Summary: Right from the opening bell, with the challenger appearing to be too small for the weight division, Gatti (139¼) was looking to use the left as his main punch. After a quiet first round, as it became apparent that Dorin (139) would have to get closer to Gatti if he wanted to win he adopted this tactic in the second. Although he was able to push Gatti back a couple of times Dorin was obliged to take lefts and rights in return, but by now the champion was beginning to motor. The finish came after Gatti had thrown a left-right-left combination to the head before suddenly dropping in a terrific left hook to Dorin's side that sent him down for the full count with just five seconds of the session remaining on the clock.

11 September 2004. Miguel Cotto w rsc 6 Kelson Pinto.
Venue: The Coliseum, Hato Rey, Puerto Rico. **Recognition:** WBO. **Referee:** Roberto Ramirez.
Fight Summary: Fighting for the title that was left vacant when Zab Judah moved up a weight division, Cotto (140) showed himself to be a real star of the future when destroying Pinto (139). After just 15 seconds of the opener he had hurt the Brazilian with a solid left hook to the jaw before following it up with several more during the session. The fight could not continue like that, and having floored Pinto in the second and fifth rounds with big punches Cotto raced out for the sixth, lashing in blows to leave his opponent sprawling on the deck. Although the floundering Brazilian got up it was only when his corner demanded that it be stopped did the referee call it off, the finish coming 32 seconds into the round.

23 October 2004. Vivian Harris w rsc 11 Oktay Urkal.
Venue: The Tempodrom, Berlin, Germany. **Recognition:** WBA. **Referee:** Armando Garcia.
Fight Summary: Making his first defence, Harris (139¾) had already beaten Urkal (139) and knew exactly what he had to do this time round. There was never much between them, with Harris throwing the power punches and Urkal being the smarter boxer of the two, but as they entered the latter stages the challenger, cut on the right eye, was unable to raise his game. The 11th saw Harris up the pace to drop Urkal with a right to the jaw, and when the German got up and stumbled badly the referee stopped it with 56 seconds of the round gone.

6 November 2004. Kostya Tszyu w rsc 3 Sharmba Mitchell.
Venue: Glendale Arena, Phoenix, Arizona, USA. **Recognition:** IBF/The Ring. **Referee:** Raul Caiz.
Fight Summary: Defending his two remaining belts Tszyu (140) did not waste too much time when going to work on the southpaw 'interim' champion, but in cutting the ring down he received a bad vertical gash alongside his left eye initiated by a clash of heads towards the end of the opening round. With Tszyu desperate to get the fight over, after Mitchell (140) strangely stayed on the inside in the second instead of using his speed he was made to pay as big rights drove him back to the ropes before a left hook dropped him for 'five'. Almost as soon as the third had begun Mitchell had been smashed down by a right through the middle, and following two more knockdowns the referee stopped it with just two seconds of the round remaining.

11 December 2004. Miguel Cotto w rsc 6 Randall Bailey.
Venue: Mandalay Bay Resort & Casino, Las Vegas, Nevada, USA. **Recognition:** WBO. **Referee:** Norm Budden.
Fight Summary: Although Bailey (139½) went into the fight full of purpose, by the end of the third round it had virtually been knocked out of him, heavy punches to head and body having floored him twice, in the second and third. Now cut over the left eye and shaken up, the former champion backed off during the next two sessions prior to Cotto (140) eventually moving up a gear in the sixth to batter him all around the ring with solid blows from both hands. When Bailey was cut on his right eye it was an injury that forced the referee to call it off on the 1.39 mark.

29 January 2005. Arturo Gatti w co 5 Jesse James Leija.
Venue: Boardwalk Hall, Atlantic City, New Jersey, USA. **Recognition:** WBC. **Referee:** Earl Brown.
Fight Summary: Once again Gatti (140) met a challenger who appeared to be several divisions lighter, and once again the Canadian stuck to his newly developed boxing skills to make sure of victory. With Leija (140) looking to use a right over the top while Gatti used countering blows and jabs nothing much happened until the start of the fifth when the latter decided to open up. Having dropped Leija for 'nine' with a straight right early in the session

Gatti bided his time, exchanging blows with his rival before whacking in a heavy left to the temple that saw the American counted out on one knee with 1.12 of the fifth remaining.

26 February 2005. Miguel Cotto w rsc 5 DeMarcus Corley.
Venue: Ruben Rodriguez Coliseum, Bayamon, Puerto Rico. **Recognition:** WBO. **Referee:** Ismael Quinones-Falu.
Fight Summary: Having had trouble making the weight Cotto (140) started quickly as if to get his southpaw challenger out of the fight as soon as he could. And with Corley (137) on the back foot he was chased around the ring before being half-pushed over for a mandatory count. Both men were docked a point for low blows, Cotto in the second and Corley in the fourth, and in the third Corley actually had Cotto going with a right hook to the jaw when the latter had left himself wide open. Nothing, however, was going to stop Cotto in the fifth, and after stalking Corley to the ropes he twice put him down on one knee before the referee halted the contest on the 2.45 mark. Following the stoppage, Corley stated that he had gone down to take stock and was furious at the decision of the third man.

4 June 2005. Ricky Hatton w rtd 11 Kostya Tszyu.
Venue: MEN Arena, Manchester, England. **Recognition:** IBF/The Ring. **Referee:** Dave Parris.
Fight Summary: In one of the great British fight nights Hatton (140) forced the once top-class champion to retire on his stool at the end of the 11th, having beaten him to a standstill. It was a sad end for Tszyu (140), but the challenger had taken everything that was thrown at him before coming on like a train to control the last few rounds. In outboxing and outpunching his rival, Hatton showed many of the qualities that great fighters need, and as well as the IBF title he had won *The Ring* Championship Belt on the result.

11 June 2005. Miguel Cotto w rsc 9 Muhammad Abdullaev.
Venue: Madison Square Garden, Manhattan, NYC, New York, USA. **Recognition:** WBO. **Referee:** John Callas.
Fight Summary: Because Abdullaev (138¾) had eliminated Cotto (138¾) from the 2000 Olympics there were a good few people thinking that the man from Uzbekistan might just be capable of winning the title. There was no doubting that it was a good match between two good fighters, and although Cotto won virtually every round there was never that much between them until Abdullaev's right eye started to swell up in the eighth due to left hooks being concentrated on that area. Unable to see from that eye Abdullaev should have been retired during the interval, but after gesticulating that he did not wish to carry on and being inspected by the doctor the referee stopped the fight after 57 seconds of the ninth.

25 June 2005. Carlos Maussa w co 7 Vivian Harris.
Venue: Boardwalk Hall, Atlantic City, New Jersey, USA. **Recognition:** WBA. **Referee:** Albert Brown.
Fight Summary: Trying to knock out the ungainly Maussa (139) quickly in order to secure a match with the winner of Floyd Mayweather v Arturo Gatti, Harris (139) spent several rounds getting nowhere and had been cut over the right eye in the fourth. After being badly hurt by Maussa in the sixth, Harris started the seventh with some trepidation, and with the Colombian taking the initiative he was immediately put under pressure. Having softened Harris up with a series of wild-looking blows, when Maussa threw a long left hook that caught the champion flush on the jaw it dropped him to be counted out 43 seconds into the session.

25 June 2005. Floyd Mayweather Jnr w rtd 6 Arturo Gatti.
Venue: Boardwalk Hall, Atlantic City, New Jersey, USA. **Recognition:** WBC. **Referee:** Earl Morton.
Fight Summary: Exuding quality, class and confidence, Mayweather (139) backed up his boasts that he would win the title when forcing Gatti (140) to retire on his stool at the end of the sixth following a one-sided beating. Down in the first round from a left hook after being hit by punches coming in at blinding speed, if Gatti did not know it was going to be a hard night beforehand he knew it at that moment. For round after round it was torment for Gatti as Mayweather could not miss, and after being battered non-stop in the sixth the champion was wisely retired on his stool at the end of the session.

When Mayweather relinquished the WBC title in March 2006 on moving up a division to meet Zab Judah for the IBF title, Junior Witter, who had beaten Lovemore Ndou (w pts 12 at the Staples Centre, Los Angeles, California on 19 February 2005) in an eliminator and DeMarcus Corley were matched to find a new champion.

24 September 2005. Miguel Cotto w co 7 Ricardo Torres.
Venue: Boardwalk Hall, Atlantic City, New Jersey, USA. **Recognition:** WBO. **Referee:** David Fields.
Fight Summary: In a topsy-turvy affair that included five knockdowns, having dropped Torres (140) in the first the champion was battered all over the ring in the second round before being put down for the first time in his career. The third session was relatively quiet by their standards, but in the fourth Cotto (140) again put Torres on the floor, only for the latter to come back firing heavy shots. It could not last. In the sixth Torres was floored for the third time, and although he got back up to last the round out the seventh saw him finally ground down and counted out on the 1.52 mark, a left hook being the finisher.

26 November 2005. Ricky Hatton w co 9 Carlos Maussa.
Venue: Hallam FM Arena, Sheffield, England. **Recognition:** IBF/WBA/The Ring. **Referee:** Mickey Vann.
Fight Summary: Looking to unify three titles as well as putting his *Ring* Championship Belt up for grabs, Hatton (139½) took on the WBA champion, Maussa (139¾), and was given no end of trouble before scoring a knockout at 1.10 of the ninth round. Cut over the left eye in the first 20 seconds and over the right eye two rounds later would have been a disaster for most fighters, but not for Hatton who merely gritted his teeth while getting on with the job. The durable and ungainly Maussa continually caused problems, and although Hatton was well up on the cards he was having some difficulty setting the Colombian up. Every time Hatton hurt Maussa the latter would come back strongly, but once the man from Manchester realised towards the end of the eighth that he should not be making the running, the outcome proved positive as he picked out a terrific left hook that dropped Maussa for the full count in the ninth.

Having given up the IBF Belt in April 2006 when moving up a division to meet Luis Collazo for the WBA welter crown, Hatton then relinquished the WBA junior welter title in May 2006 when it became clear that he could only boss one division at a time. After the IBF decided on a vacant title fight between Juan Urango and Naoufel Ben Rabah, who had beaten Arturo Morua (w pts 12 at the MGM Grand, Las Vegas, Nevada on 17 September 2005), Souleymane M'baye and Raul Horacio Balbi were matched to find a new WBA champion.

4 March 2006. Miguel Cotto w rsc 8 Gianluca Branco.
Venue: Ruben Rodriguez Coliseum, Bayamon, Puerto Rico. **Recognition:** WBO. **Referee:** Luis Pabon.
Fight Summary: The champion started as he meant to carry on, blasting in lefts and rights at the 35-year-old Branco (140) as the latter went into defensive mode. Although Branco tried to hold his ground the more the contest moved on the more he failed to punch hard enough to deter Cotto (140), and although he had a good fifth round it was not sustained. Badly swollen on the right side of his face, Branco was really up against it before being pulled out of the contest by the referee after 49 seconds of the eighth had ensued.

10 June 2006. Miguel Cotto w pts 12 Paul Malignaggi.
Venue: Madison Square Garden, Manhattan, NYC, New York, USA. **Recognition:** WBO. **Referee:** Steve Smoger.
Scorecards: 116-111, 115-112, 116-111.
Fight Summary: It did not start too well for the flashy Malignaggi (138¼) after heads came together in the opening round and left him with cut over the left eye, and in the second a left hook from the champion dropped him. When getting up a solid shot that smashed into Malignaggi's right cheekbone caused a swelling that would worsen throughout the contest. Right up against it, Malignaggi even took the fifth and sixth as Cotto (138¼) hunted him down, banging in solid blows to head and body. Showing tremendous spirit to last the distance, non-puncher Malignaggi's bravery saw him walk away with his pride intact, having withstood a battering at the hands of Cotto despite carrying a suspected fracture of the right cheekbone.

Cotto handed in his belt towards the end of October after announcing that he would be meeting his fellow Puerto Rican, Carlos Quintana, to decide the vacant WBA welterweight title. Shortly after that the IBF stated that Ricardo Torres and Mike Arnaoutis would be contesting their vacant title.

30 June 2006. Juan Urango w pts 12 Naoufel Ben Rabah.
Venue: Seminole Hard Rock Live Arena, Hollywood, Florida, USA. **Recognition:** IBF. **Referee:** Tommy Kimmons.
Scorecards: 116-112, 115-113, 117-111.

Fight Summary: Contested for the vacant title after Ricky Hatton handed in his belt in order to fight for the WBA welterweight crown, Urango (139) outpointed Ben Rabah (138) in what was seen by many as a bad decision at the end of a poor spectacle. With Ben Rabah on the move and Urango, a southpaw stalking, there was little action but at least the former did whatever boxing there was. It was apparent that the judges gave Urango the win because it was he who had forced the fight despite him landing punches of little value.

2 September 2006. Souleymane M'baye w rsc 4 Raul Horacio Balbi.
Venue: Reebok Stadium, Bolton, England. **Recognition:** WBA. **Referee:** Paul Thomas.
Fight Summary: With the vacant title up for grabs after Ricky Hatton handed in his belt, M'baye (139½) took full advantage of the opportunity when battering Balbi (140) to defeat at 2.14 of the fourth. Feeling his way into the fight after being badly hurt by a left-right from Balbi in the opener, M'baye gradually got himself going in the second before dropping the Argentine with a solid right to the jaw. Showing an accurate long left M'baye was in full flow in the third, and in the fourth another heavy right to the head saw the hardy Balbi on the floor again. Having taken a count of 'eight' Balbi was back in the fray, but following a terrific right to his temple the referee stepped in to rescue him.

15 September 2006. Junior Witter w pts 12 DeMarcus Corley.
Venue: Alexandra Pavilion, Muswell Hill, London, England. **Recognition:** WBC. **Referee:** Massimo Barrovecchio.
Scorecards: 117-111, 118-112, 116-113.
Fight Summary: In what was a contest for the vacant title after Floyd Mayweather handed in his belt on moving up a division, it was the switch-hitting Witter (138¼) who got the better of his southpaw opponent to pick up a world title at his second attempt. Moving around at speed, Witter made life difficult for Corley (139½), his buzzing around tactics in differing stances confusing the American round after round. In the fifth it looked as though Witter was taking the bit by the teeth, hurting Corley with a right hook before sending the latter over for what the referee correctly ruled as a push. From the sixth onwards, however, it was Witter's power that threatened Corley. Although having Corley one punch away from defeat at times, Witter ultimately boxed his way to the unanimous decision in his favour.

18 November 2006. Ricardo Torres w pts 12 Mike Arnaoutis.
Venue: Thomas & Mack Centre, Las Vegas, Nevada, USA. **Recognition:** WBO. **Referee:** Tony Weeks.
Scorecards: 116-111, 114-113, 113-114.
Fight Summary: Fighting for the vacant title after Miguel Cotto decided to move up the weight scale, Torres (139) was let off the hook on several occasions before coming through to win narrowly on a split decision. Having won three of the opening four rounds it looked as though the hard-hitting Torres was on his way, but after hurting his right hand and then being floored heavily in the seventh by a southpaw right hook as Arnaoutis (138) countered things should have changed. Unfortunately for Arnaoutis he failed to build on that, and although pushing Torres back he was unable to pin him down long enough to do any damage while at the same time fearing countering blows. With his work-rate faltering, Arnaoutis let slip the chance of victory.

20 January 2007. Junior Witter w rsc 9 Arturo Morua.
Venue: Alexandra Palace, Muswell Hill, London, England. **Recognition:** WBC. **Referee:** Timothy Adams.
Fight Summary: Although the champion rolled off the rounds he failed to excite against Morua (139¾), a man who threw only jabs and the odd right before holding on and starting again. Landing solidly at times it appeared that Witter (139¾) could take Morua out as and when, but it was only in the seventh when the latter touched down for what the referee ruled to be a slip that he began to open up. After failing to find a way through in the eighth, when the switch-hitting Witter slammed in several solid rights and lefts to the head and body in the ninth, Morua was in trouble. With the referee observing that the ropes were holding Morua up, he issued a count before rescuing the Mexican moments later following three heavy head shots. The finish was timed at 2.12 of the session.

20 January 2007. Ricky Hatton w pts 12 Juan Urango.
Venue: Paris Hotel, Las Vegas, Nevada, USA. **Recognition:** IBF/The Ring. **Referee:** Tony Weeks.
Scorecards: 119-109, 119-109, 119-109.

Fight Summary: Coming back to the 140lbs division to defend his *Ring* Championship Belt, Hatton (139) took on the IBF champion, Urango (139), a man he looked to defeat in order to get his hands on his old title. Dropping one round at most, Hatton powered his way forward before being forced to take time out in the fifth after Urango went low. From thereon in Hatton boxed more sensibly, banging in solid lefts and rights before clinching as his southpaw opponent tried to move inside. The last few sessions saw plenty of mauling, but it was Hatton's fight.

By mid-February Hatton had relinquished the IBF title when being told that he had to sign for a defence against the mandatory challenger, Lovemore Ndou, who had won a final eliminator at the States Sports Centre, Sydney, Australia on 4 February when stopping Naoufel Ben Rabah at the end of the 11th. As Hatton had already signed to meet Jose Luis Castillo on 23 June his decision was an easy one, and following that Ndou was handed the IBF title on a plate.

10 March 2007. Souleymane M'baye drew 12 Andriy Kotelnyk.
Venue: Olympia, Liverpool, England. **Recognition:** WBA. **Referee:** Dave Parris.
Scorecards: 115-113, 112-117, 114-114.
Fight Summary: In what was a tough fight to score, M'baye (139¾) held on to his title when the judges saw it as a split draw, despite one of them having Kotelnyk (140) winning by nine rounds to three. Showing good hand-speed and marking Kotelnyk's face up with the jab, M'baye obviously did enough, but had the Ukrainian produced more work the result could have been different. Following the contest, Kotelnyk's management team lodged a protest with the WBA.

28 April 2007. Ricardo Torres w pts 12 Arturo Morua.
Venue: University of the North Coliseum, Barranquilla, Colombia. **Recognition:** WBO. **Referee:** Uriel Aguilera.
Scorecards: 120-109, 120-108, 118-110.
Fight Summary: Dominating Morua (139¼) from the start, although the hard-hitting champion tried to finish it on several occasions he was unable to find the punches required. Several times Torres (139½) had Morua going, but it came to nothing as the latter used the ring well to avoid many of the blows thrown at him. Despite tiring towards the end Morua deserved to make it to the final bell, having nullified much of Torres' work.

16 June 2007. Paul Malignaggi w pts 12 Lovemore Ndou.
Venue: Mohegan Sun Arena, Uncasville, Connecticut, USA. **Recognition:** IBF. **Referee:** Eddie Cotton.
Scorecards: 118-108, 120-106, 120-106.
Fight Summary: This was the first defence of the title for Ndou (138¼), who had been given full championship status after Ricky Hatton had handed in his belt. Right from the opening bell it could be seen that Malignaggi (138) had the tools to outbox the champion, his speed around the ring and fast hands serving notice that the belt was going to be his. He even threw the right hand despite it letting him down in the past, and in the ninth one such punch to the head dropped the increasingly desperate Ndou. Having had a point taken away in the sixth for hitting behind the head, Ndou was now right up against it, but although he gave it his best shot, winning just two rounds on one of the judges' cards, he was a wide loser at the final bell.

23 June 2007. Ricky Hatton w co 4 Jose Luis Castillo.
Venue: Thomas & Mack Centre, Las Vegas, Nevada, USA. **Recognition:** The Ring. **Referee:** Joe Cortez.
Fight Summary: Putting his *Ring* Championship Belt up for grabs against the tough Castillo (140) seemed to be a tough ask for Hatton (140), but he surprised many when knocking his Mexican opponent out at 2.16 of the fourth. Starting strongly, Hatton dropped Castillo (140) in the opener with a left hook, only for the referee to classify it as a slip. Although Castillo got himself back into the fight in the second and third with strong jabs it was not enough to win the rounds and in the fourth he came undone. With both men trading in that session Castillo was docked a point when going low, but moments later after a left hook to the shoulder lifted the Mexican's guard when Hatton fired in a similar blow to the body he was downed. Never looking likely to rise, Castillo was counted out at 2.16 of the session.

21 July 2007. Gavin Rees w pts 12 Souleymane M'baye.
Venue: International Arena, Cardiff, Wales. **Recognition:** WBA. **Referee:** Stan Christodoulou.

Scorecards: 117-112, 117-113, 118-110.

Fight Summary: Working away like a Trojan, Rees (139½) upset the applecart when outpointing the champion in a contest that saw the much shorter Welshman use his lack of height to get inside and work the body. Despite Rees tiring at the midway stage, he was still busy. He even took on board some hard shots from M'baye (139½) before coming back strongly, and although the latter tried to raise his game it was ultimately a lost cause as the ebullient Rees continued to come on even though his left eye was beginning to close from the tenth onwards. Following the verdict it was the Frenchman who was left wondering where it all went wrong, while being forced to recognise that Rees's tactics were spot on.

1 September 2007. Ricardo Torres w rsc 11 Kendall Holt.
Venue: Jumbo Saloon Country Club, Barranquilla, Colombia. **Recognition:** WBO. **Referee:** Genaro Rodriguez.
Fight Summary: Having dropped the opening three rounds, the champion picked it up in the third and fourth, hurting Holt (139¾) with a countering left hook in the latter session, before being dropped in the sixth with a left-right to the head. Although nothing much happened during the seventh through to the ninth, it was Holt who was winning the rounds as Torres (140) tried to get himself going. Finally, in the 11th Torres found the punch he had been looking for all night when smashing Holt to the floor with a left hook. On Holt getting to his feet, after Torres tore into him landing solidly, the referee rescued the American at 2.24 of the round. Following the contest, Holt's people were asking for a rematch on the grounds that their man was struck in the face by a can of beer in the sixth and had his ankle grabbed in the 11th.

7 September 2007. Junior Witter w co 7 Vivian Harris.
Venue: The Dome, Doncaster, England. **Recognition:** WBC. **Referee:** Daniel Van de Wiele.
Fight Summary: Boxing better than he had for some time, the champion took Harris (139½) apart before knocking him out with a terrific left hook to the jaw after one minute of the seventh round had elapsed. Witter (139½) started strongly, running up the rounds when putting Harris on the back foot and hurting him with lefts and rights to the head and body. Although Harris came back somewhat, having gone down early in the fourth from a left-right which the referee claimed was a slip, before the round was over Witter had downed him again with a left hook to the jaw. Regardless of the fact that Harris did rather better in the fifth and sixth once Witter had caught up with him in the seventh it was all over.

5 January 2008. Paul Malignaggi w pts 12 Herman Ngoudjo.
Venue: Bally's Park Place Hotel, Atlantic City, New Jersey, USA. **Recognition:** IBF. **Referee:** Allan Huggins.
Scorecards: 117-111, 115-113, 116-113.
Fight Summary: Even though hotly contested, the scorecards showed the champion's unanimous points win over Ngoudjo (140) to be wider than it probably was. While both men thought they had won, Malignaggi (139) boxed below form and admitted so after the fight. Badly hurt in the seventh, Malignaggi somehow stayed firm as Ngoudjo failed to take advantage of the opportunity. Coming back well from that, Malignaggi won four of the last five rounds on the cards, even banging home a solid right uppercut in the tenth on his way to the win.

22 March 2008. Andriy Kotelnyk w rsc 12 Gavin Rees.
Venue: International Arena, Cardiff, Wales. **Recognition:** WBA. **Referee:** Luis Pabon.
Fight Summary: Defending his title for the first time, although Rees (140) went well in three of the opening four sessions, once Kotelnyk (140) got a grip from the fifth onwards there was only going to be one winner. Blocking many of the punches that Rees threw, while not allowing him room to work inside, served Kotelnyk well, his accurate jabs and long solid rights regularly finding their mark. In the seventh Rees was showing signs of wear, his left eye beginning to swell, and he was badly hurt by two left hooks. Despite showing up well in the ninth by the 12th Rees was nearly out of puff, and after he had gone down without a count and was being battered by lefts and rights the referee called it off with just 26 seconds of the contest remaining.

10 May 2008. Timothy Bradley w pts 12 Junior Witter.
Venue: Trent FM Arena, Nottingham, England. **Recognition:** WBC. **Referee:** Massimo Barrovecchio.
Scorecards: 115-113, 114-113, 112-115.

Fight Summary: Starting well, repeatedly beating the switch-hitting Witter (139¾) to the punch, the challenger looked to be a class operator when taking the play away from the Englishman. Every now and again Witter seemed as though he was getting into the fight, but after a heavy right hand to the jaw had him over in the sixth it could be seen that Bradley (139½) possibly had his number. Strangely, at the end of the ninth, two of the three cards had Witter in the lead despite him not performing at his best, but when Bradley ran off two of the last three sessions it the latter who took the split decision. On losing, Witter, cut over the left eye, moved further away from a contest against Ricky Hatton.

24 May 2008. Paul Malignaggi w pts 12 Lovemore Ndou.
Venue: City of Manchester Stadium, Manchester, England. **Recognition:** IBF. **Referee:** Mickey Vann.
Scorecards: 116-112, 116-113, 114-115.
Fight Summary: Looking to get a match-up with Ricky Hatton, the IBF champion, Malignaggi (139¾), took on Ndou (139) in a return, and after making a bright start found himself being dragged into a tough battle that had one of the judges voting against him. It was Malignaggi's speed of hand and foot against the single shots dished out by Ndou. By the tenth, after Malignaggi's work-rate had fallen away he was forced to take some heavy blows as Ndou, his left eye now swollen, tried to pull the coals out of the fire right through to the final bell.

Malignaggi was stripped of the IBF title in September after signing to meet Hatton for *The Ring* Championship Belt rather than agreeing to make a defence against the number one challenger, Herman Ngoudjo, and the latter was matched against Juan Urango to find a new champion. Both men had won eliminating bouts to qualify for a title shot, Ngoudjo beating Souleymane M'baye (w pts 12 at the Uniprix Stadium, Montreal, Canada on 6 June) and Urango defeating Carlos Wilfredo Vilches (w co 4 at the Seminole Hard Rock Hotel & Casino on 23 April).

24 May 2008. Ricky Hatton w pts 12 Juan Lazcano.
Venue: City of Manchester Stadium, Manchester, England. **Recognition:** The Ring. **Referee:** Howard Foster.
Scorecards: 120-110, 118-110, 120-108.
Fight Summary: With his *Ring* Championship Belt on the line, Hatton (140) beat Lazcano (139¾) easily enough, but was unable to floor him while being forced to take several hard shots himself. It was not one of the champion's better performances, but he did what he had to. Proving his durability, Lazcano took whatever Hatton threw at him, and despite being badly hurt at times he lasted the course. In the tenth, having been hit by a left hook, Hatton was thrown down before getting back into the fray, banging away to the final bell.

5 July 2008. Kendall Holt w rsc 1 Ricardo Torres.
Venue: Planet Hollywood Resort & Casino, Las Vegas, Nevada, USA. **Recognition:** WBO. **Referee:** Jay Nady.
Fight Summary: Coming out fast at the bell it was not too long, 12 seconds in fact, before the champion sent Holt (139) crashing from a right to the jaw. Although getting up quickly Holt was soon under pressure as Torres (139) went for him, and following several wide punches that belted into him he was floored for the second time. Having hit Holt while he was in the act of rising with no reprimand, Torres chased his man down before being smashed into the ropes, courtesy of a short right to the head and an accidental head butt that stunned him further. Tearing off the ropes, a dazed Torres was caught by another right that dropped him on to a lower strand. The referee started the count before calling it off, the finish being timed at 1.01.

13 September 2008. Andriy Kotelnyk w pts 12 Norio Kimura.
Venue: Sports Palace, Lviv, Ukraine. **Recognition:** WBA. **Referee:** Stan Christodoulou.
Scorecards: 119-109, 118-110, 119-109.
Fight Summary: Moving into Kimura (140) from the opening bell the champion, looking to assert himself quickly, was soon banging in left hooks to head and body as he pushed on. Even though the tough Kimura was up against it for round after round as Kotelnyk (140) pressured him he showed great resolve in making it to the final bell, having been on the end of sharp, accurate punches throughout. This was Kotelnyk's first defence.

13 September 2008. Timothy Bradley w pts 12 Edner Cherry.
Venue: Beau Rivage Resort & Casino, Biloxi, Mississippi, USA. **Recognition:** WBC. **Referee:** Gary Ritter.
Scorecards: 118-109, 119-109, 117-110.

Fight Summary: Having stopped Stevie Johnston inside ten rounds to get a crack at the champion, Cherry (139¼) started aggressively with the overarm right being his weapon of choice. He also dug solidly to the body, as Bradley (139¾) would testify in the fourth. By the fifth, however, Bradley was in control as he banged out the jab and followed up with rights to the body to keep Cherry fully occupied. After knocking Cherry down in the eighth with a countering right Bradley settled down to box his man, and apart from taking a heavy shot to the head in the 11th he continued in that vein up to the final bell.

22 November 2008. Ricky Hatton w rsc 11 Paul Malignaggi.
Venue: MGM Grand, Las Vegas, Nevada, USA. **Recognition:** The Ring. **Referee:** Kenny Bayless.
Fight Summary: Once again putting his *Ring* Championship Belt on the line, Hatton (140) was always in control of Malignaggi (139), forcing him into corners and cutting down the ring until there was nowhere to go. Hatton also hit much harder than the clever American, who could never keep him at bay. In the latter stages Malignaggi was showing signs of wear and tear, his left eye cut and the right side of his face swelling up, and in the 11th with Hatton attacking the body the referee called the fight off after 28 seconds of the session on the advice of Malignaggi's corner.

13 December 2008. Kendall Holt w pts 12 Demetrius Hopkins.
Venue: Boardwalk Hall, Atlantic City, New Jersey, USA. **Recognition:** WBO. **Referee:** Allen Huggins.
Scorecards: 117-111, 116-112, 113-115.
Fight Summary: Though Holt (140) was due to defend against Ricardo Torres, the man he took the title from, when the latter pulled out a week before the fight Hopkins (140) was drafted in even though he had not boxed for 13 months. Not a spectacle by any means, it was more than boring, but at least Holt tried to force the fight despite being a natural counter puncher. There were no knockdowns and very few punches of quality on view, apart from in the seventh when Holt caught his man with a left hook to the jaw and a solid right to the body. There were some who felt that Hopkins had edged it, but at the final bell it did not seem to matter.

30 January 2009. Juan Urango w pts 12 Herman Ngoudjo.
Venue: Bell Centre, Montreal, Canada. **Recognition:** IBF. **Referee:** Marlon Wright.
Scorecards: 118-108, 116-110, 120-106.
Fight Summary: Contested for the vacant title after Paul Malignaggi was stripped, Urango (139), a southpaw, was clearly better than Ngoudjo (139¼) and the unanimous points decision in his favour was no more than he deserved. Having started strongly, Urango put Ngoudjo down twice with left hooks in the third, the latter being lucky to last the round. In fact, Ngoudjo never properly recovered, claiming later that his jaw had been broken in that session. From thereon in it was all Urango, banging in wide hooks from both hands to head and body, who took total control as Ngoudjo bravely made it to the final bell.

7 February 2009. Andriy Kotelnyk w pts 12 Marcos Maidana.
Venue: Stadium Hall, Rostock, Germany. **Recognition:** WBA. **Referee:** Hector Afu.
Scorecards: 115-114, 115-113, 113-115.
Fight Summary: Pressurising the champion from the opening bell, throwing in punches from all angles, Maidana (140) was always a danger, especially as some of his body shots went low. However, showing a good defence, Kotelnyk (139½) blocked much of what was coming his way while countering solidly to pick up the points. It was only in the latter rounds that Kotelnyk, his face badly swollen, was able to pick his punches before coming under assault again. In the tenth, having been under the cosh in the previous round, Kotelnyk was given time out as Maidana went low again before coming back strongly. The last two sessions saw both men battling away as they tried to influence the judges in a contest that was close enough to have gone either way.

On 27 June, Maidana won the vacant WBA 'interim' title when he stopped Victor Ortiz in the sixth round at the Staples Centre, Los Angeles, California, USA.

4 April 2009. Timothy Bradley w pts 12 Kendall Holt.
Venue: Bell Centre, Montreal, Canada. **Recognition:** WBC/WBO. **Referee:** Michael Griffin.
Scorecards: 114-112, 115-111, 115-111.

Fight Summary: In a contest to unify two titles, Bradley (138¾), the WBC champion, took on the WBO's Holt (140). The contest started with a surprise when Bradley was dumped on the canvas in the opening round by a countering left hook, but he was soon back on his feet and looking to regain control. From the second onwards it was clear that Bradley would have to take more care of his defences, and he began to push on with fast jabs and solid body shots while confusing Holt with his movement. Having got into a winning position, Bradley again found himself on the floor when a glancing blow to the head put him down in the 12th but, unhurt, he got up to take the decision.

At the Ruben Rodriguez Coliseum, Bayamon, Puerto Rico on 25 April, Lamont Peterson won the vacant WBO 'interim' title when stopping Willy Blain in the seventh round. Peterson would forfeit his 'interim' title when losing to Bradley for the main belt on 12 December.

Bradley was stripped of the WBC title on 28 April when unable to agree terms to fight their number one challenger, Devon Alexander. Alexander had been due to meet Junior Witter for the WBC 'interim' Championship Belt, a contest that was rebilled as being for the vacant title.

2 May 2009. Manny Pacquiao w rsc 2 Ricky Hatton.
Venue: MGM Grand, Las Vegas, Nevada, USA. **Recognition:** The Ring. **Referee:** Kenny Bayless.
Fight Summary: With his *Ring* Championship Belt on the line, Hatton (140) took on Pacquiao (138), a southpaw who had successfully come up though the weight divisions since starting out as a junior flyweight back in 1995. Much faster than Hatton, right from the start the Filipino moved in under the punches coming his way to deliver shots of his own, a right hook to the jaw having the Englishman over moments into the fight. Although he got up at 'eight' Hatton looked all at sea, and when Pacquiao tore in again, throwing punch after punch, it ended with another visit to the canvas, this time courtesy of a heavy left. Not a defeatist, Hatton came out for the second, having some success, before the fight came to an end at 2.59 of the session after he had been floored by a tremendous left to the jaw and was pulled out of the contest by the referee who stopped the count.

To all intents and purposes Pacquiao moved on after beating Miguel Cotto for the WBO welterweight title on 14 November, but continued to be recognised as champion by *The Ring* until 26 July 2010.

18 July 2009. Amir Khan w pts 12 Andriy Kotelnyk.
Venue: MEN Arena, Manchester, England. **Recognition:** WBA. **Referee:** Stan Christodoulou.
Scorecards: 120-108, 118-111, 118-111.
Fight Summary: Far too fast for the champion, Khan (140) came into the ring supremely confident and left it as the new title holder, having won virtually every round. Although Kotelnyk (139¾) had limited success in the third when getting off a few scoring blows it was Khan all the way, shooting in doubled-up jabs and great combinations that took all the play away from his opponent. For round after round it was much of the same, and it was only in the final session that Kotelnyk forced the fight as Khan backtracked to make sure he did not get caught nor did anything silly.

On 21 November, at the Liberty Sports Club, Sunchales, Argentina, Marcos Maidana defended his WBA 'interim' title when knocking out William Gonzalez in the third round.

1 August 2009. Devon Alexander w rtd 8 Junior Witter.
Venue: Agua Caliente Casino Resort, Rancho Mirage, California, USA. **Recognition:** WBC. **Referee:** Lou Moret.
Fight Summary: Contested for the vacant title after Timothy Bradley was stripped, it was Alexander (138½) who became the new champion when forcing Witter (139) to retire at the end of the eighth round. When the switch-hitting Witter, who was cut on the left eye in the second, suffered further problems in the fourth when his left arm was severely damaged his chances of winning all but disappeared. Having won the opening five rounds, the American southpaw was taken out of his stride in the sixth as Witter came back at him, but from there on it was all downhill for the latter prior to his retirement.

1 August 2009. Timothy Bradley tdraw 3 Nate Campbell.
Venue: Agua Caliente Casino Resort, Rancho Mirage, California, USA. **Recognition:** WBO. **Referee:** David Mendoza.

Fight Summary: Starting fast, the champion was soon banging out both hands and working the body as Campbell (138½) tried to find a way into the contest. Following a clash of heads in the second, in which there were no cuts suffered, the third saw Campbell complaining to the referee about a cut that had appeared over his left eye. With the complaint being ignored, Bradley (139) immediately went on the attack, smashing in blow after blow on the unfortunate Campbell until the bell. Following an inspection by the ringside doctor during the interval the fight was called off and announced as a stoppage win for Bradley. However, following an appeal the result was changed to that of a no-decision (technical draw) on the grounds that the cut had been caused by a head clash and not by a punch.

28 August 2009. Juan Urango w rsc 11 Randall Bailey.
Venue: Seminole Hard Rock Hotel, Hollywood, Florida, USA. **Recognition:** IBF. **Referee:** Tommy Kimmons.
Fight Summary: Both men being big punchers it had been fairly close during the opening five rounds, with the southpaw champion just ahead of Bailey (139½) due to a better work-rate. However, a dramatic turnaround in the sixth saw Urango (139) floored heavily by a right-hand counter for 'nine' before getting back into the action gingerly, sporting a cut on the right eye. Although having Urango at his mercy, Bailey failed to take advantage and soon found himself under the cosh. Dropped twice in the ninth, a countering left and then a right uppercut-left hook doing the trick, Bailey barely made it up from the first knockdown, and in the tenth a left-right put him over again. In the 11th it could be seen that both men had swellings around their eyes, but it was Bailey who was suffering the most. Having slipped over twice in that session, Bailey was rescued by the referee on the 1.51 mark after seeing the towel tossed into the ring by his corner.

4 December 2009. Amir Khan w rsc 1 Dmitriy Salita.
Venue: Metro Radio Arena, Newcastle, England. **Recognition:** WBA. **Referee:** Luis Pabon.
Fight Summary: Yet again making a fast start, the champion cracked in a left-right that had Salita (140) down after very few punches had been thrown. Although Salita was up at 'six' he was quickly put under pressure as Khan (139½) tore into him two-fistedly, and before long he had been pounded to the canvas again. This time Salita made it up at 'four'. Back in the fray, Salita was soon being driven around the ring as Khan went for the finish. Unable to match Khan's speed Salita tried to clinch, but when a short left to the head sent him into the ropes the referee came to his rescue at 1.16 of the first.

Marcos Maidana retained his WBA 'interim' title when knocking out Victor Manuel Cayo in the sixth round at the Hard Rock Hotel & Casino, Las Vegas, Nevada, USA on 27 March 2010.

12 December 2009. Timothy Bradley w pts 12 Lamont Peterson.
Venue: Agua Caliente Casino, Rancho Mirage, California, USA. **Recognition:** WBO. **Referee:** Pat Russell.
Scorecards: 120-107, 119-108, 118-110.
Fight Summary: Having taken terrific rights to the jaw from the champion in the opening two sessions, Peterson (139) was then dropped in the third by a short right to the back of the head. Back in the action, Peterson began to match Bradley (138) for body punches, but by the sixth the latter had gone to another level when bringing all of his armoury into play. Although falling well behind on the cards, Peterson never gave up and was still there at the end of the fight, outpointed but not vanquished.

6 March 2010. Devon Alexander w rsc 8 Juan Urango.
Venue: Mohegan Sun Arena, Uncasville, Connecticut, USA. **Recognition:** IBF/WBC. **Referee:** Benjy Esteves Jnr.
Fight Summary: Fighting to decide two championship belts, Alexander (139¼), the WBC champion, stopped the IBF representative and fellow southpaw, Urango (139¾), at 1.12 of the eighth round. There had been little between them up until then, Alexander boxing well with the jab and banging in right hands, while Urango tracked his man down and looked dangerous with heavy hooks from both hands. It seemed as though Alexander was stepping it up in the seventh, throwing more combinations than previously, and in the eighth a right uppercut to the jaw put Urango down. Although Urango was up at 'six' Alexander soon measured the Colombian up again, and after flooring him with a heavy straight right followed by the right uppercut the referee decided that he was not fit to continue despite beating the count.

15 May 2010. Amir Khan w rsc 11 Paul Malignaggi.
Venue: MSG Theatre, Manhattan, NYC, New York, USA. **Recognition:** WBA. **Referee:** Steve Smoger.
Fight Summary: Banging in punches as if there was no tomorrow, the champion raced away with the rounds despite Malignaggi (139) trying his best to stay in the fight. Dropped in the fifth from a left to the body that the referee saw as a slip, Malignaggi continued to fall behind as Khan (139½) moved at pace. At the end of the tenth, after a debate in Malignaggi's corner with the ringside doctor, the corner sent their man out for the 11th, only for him to come under fire from big lefts and rights before the referee came to his rescue on the 1.25 mark.

On 28 August, at the Luna Park Stadium, Buenos Aires, Argentina, Marcos Maidana retained the WBA 'interim' title when outpointing DeMarcus Corley on points over 12 rounds.

7 August 2010. Devon Alexander w pts 12 Andriy Kotelnyk.
Venue: Scot Trade Centre, St Louis, Missouri, USA. **Recognition:** IBF/WBC. **Referee:** Vic Drakulich.
Scorecards: 116-112, 116-112, 116-112.
Fight Summary: Putting his two championship belts on the line the southpaw champion threw more power shots than Kotelnyk (139½), but the latter contained him to some degree when defending well and scoring with accurate blows to head and body. The problems for Alexander (139¼) came about after allowing himself to be sucked into a fight when he should have stuck to his boxing. Although Alexander landed fewer punches than Kotelnyk, 202 to 225, despite throwing 1,113 to 763 according to CompuBox, all three judges gave him eight of the contested rounds because many of his shots were more powerful and had more effect. Afterwards, Alexander, who finished with a bad cut over the right eye, stated that he had fought the wrong fight and would improve next time out.

Alexander forfeited his IBF Belt on 22 October for not being prepared to make a defence against the number one contender, Kaizer Mabuza, who was then matched against Zab Judah for the vacant title. Mabuza had beaten Kendall Holt (w rtd 6 at Bally's Hotel & Casino, Atlantic City, New Jersey on 27 February) in an eliminator to get his chance, while Judah had recently outpointed Lucas Martin Matthysse.

11 December 2010. Amir Khan w pts 12 Marcos Maidana.
Venue: Mandalay Bay Resort & Casino, Las Vegas, Nevada, USA. **Recognition:** WBA. **Referee:** Joe Cortez.
Scorecards: 114-111, 114-111, 113-112.
Fight Summary: An extremely tough fight saw the champion hold off the relentless Maidana (139) to take the unanimous decision despite being forced to take 122 power punches. Khan (140) certainly started well, his fast hands bemusing Maidana, and towards the end of the first session two serious body shots had the latter down and almost out. Although Maidana came back strongly and was always dangerous he had dropped seven of the opening ten rounds by the start of the 11th, but looked to make up for that when smashing Khan all around the ring in what was a 10-8 round for the Argentine. Showing great mental toughness, Khan, who somehow remained upright to weather the storm while on wobbly legs, managed to get through the 11th and 12th without further damage. Maidana was deducted a point in the fifth for use of the elbow.

Maidana outpointed Erik Morales over 12 rounds at the MGM Grand, Las Vegas to win the vacant WBA 'interim' title on 9 April 2011.

29 January 2011. Timothy Bradley w tdec 10 Devon Alexander.
Venue: The Silverdome, Pontiac, Michigan, USA. **Recognition:** WBC/WBO. **Referee:** Frank Garza.
Scorecards: 97-93, 96-95, 98-93.
Fight Summary: It was the WBO champion, Bradley (139½), who made the better start as the WBC's Alexander (140) took a while to become accustomed to the pace and was forced to assimilate a tremendous left hook to the head. Towards the end of that session a clash of heads left Alexander with a swelling over the right eye, and into the sixth he had to absorb another heavy right hook to the head before fighting back. Having complained of yet another head butt in the ninth, and with his eye damage worsening, the St Louis southpaw came out for the tenth only for another clash of heads to leave him unable to see out of the right eye. Following the ringside doctor's advice, after the referee called for the cards at 1.29 of the session the technical decision went to Bradley, his headwork going unpunished.

Bradley forfeited the WBC Belt on 28 July due to inactivity after failing to make a match with Amir Khan and falling out with his promoter, an action that was followed by Erik Morales and Lucas Martin Matthysse being matched to find a successor. Unfortunately, the latter pulled out sick with a week to go and was replaced by Pablo Cesar Cano.

5 March 2011. Zab Judah w rsc 7 Kaizer Mabuza.
Venue: Prudential Centre, Newark, New Jersey, USA. **Recognition:** IBF. **Referee:** Samuel Viruet.
Fight Summary: Contested for the vacant title after Devon Alexander was stripped, the American southpaw, Judah (138), stepped up to the plate when stopping Mabuza (139) in the seventh. Boxing in a style reminiscent of Pernell Whitaker, Judah certainly looked the part before being forced to touch down in the fourth following a long right to the head. To the onlookers it looked more like a slip, and to back that up only one of the judges noted it as such. Although Mabuza did well in the fifth and sixth in the seventh Judah took over from him after forcing his opponent to take a standing count following a left-hand counter. Tearing into Mabuza, both hands firing, after 59 seconds of the session the referee jumped in to save the still upright South African from taking further punishment. Judah was once again a champion.

16 April 2011. Amir Khan w tdec 6 Paul McCloskey.
Venue: MEN Arena, Manchester, England. **Recognition:** WBA. **Referee:** Luis Pabon.
Scorecards: 60-54, 60-54, 60-54.
Fight Summary: Although he failed to put McCloskey (139) away, the champion was far too fast for the Northern Ireland southpaw, who was pedestrian by comparison. According to the judges Khan (139) won every round, his control of the contest increasing from the third onwards as McCloskey planted his feet and looked to make himself a difficult target. When heads accidentally came together in the sixth and left McCloskey nursing a badly cut left eye, the referee immediately called for the ringside doctor's advice on the 2.02 mark. As far as the medic was concerned it was over, and following the cards being called for Khan was awarded the technical decision.

23 July 2011. Amir Khan w co 5 Zab Judah.
Venue: Mandalay Bay Resort & Casino, Las Vegas, Nevada, USA. **Recognition:** IBF/WBA. **Referee:** Vic Drakulich.
Fight Summary: In a contest to unify two championship belts, Khan (140), the WBA champion, met the IBF's Judah (140), a southpaw who had been around since 1996. Right from the onset it was clear that Khan, his long arms pushing out lefts and rights, had far too much speed for the American, who was forced to take more punches than he would have wished for. Having continued his attack on Judah in the fifth, Khan found two rights, one to the head and the other to the body that sent his opponent down to be counted out at 2.47 of the session.

Following Khan being recognised by the WBA as their 'super' champion on 23 July, after Marcos Maidana was upgraded from 'interim' to 'second tier' champion he made his first defence on 23 September when stopping Petr Petrov in the fourth round at the German Gymnastic Club, Villa Ballester, Argentina.

On 22 October, the vacant WBA 'interim' title fight between Brunet Zamora and Alberto Mosquera at the Roberto Duran Arena, Panama City, Panama, failed to produce a champion following a 12-round draw.

Maidana vacated the 'second tier' title in July 2012 when moving up a division.

17 September 2011. Erik Morales w rtd 10 Pablo Cesar Cano.
Venue: MGM Grand, Las Vegas, Nevada, USA. **Recognition:** WBC. **Referee:** Kenny Bayless.
Fight Summary: Fighting to decide the vacant title after Timothy Bradley was stripped, Morales (140) added to his list of world titles when forcing Cano (140) to retire at the end of the tenth round. Although the bout had been closely fought, both men had showed signs of wear and tear by the seventh, Cano carrying cuts above and below the left eye while Morales had blood leaking from the right optic. Regardless that Cano had the better of the seventh, from thereon in Morales took over, his heavy right hand wreaking havoc with his rival's features. Continuing to hone in on Cano's left eye with heavy rights, when the cut turned into a gash in the tenth the damaged fighter was pulled out by his corner at the end of the round after the ringside doctor showed concern.

Morales lost his title on the scales when coming in at 142lbs for a defence against Danny Garcia (139½) at the Reliant Arena, Houston, Texas, USA on 24 March 2012. After the fight went ahead, Garcia took the title when outpointing the 35-year-old veteran over 12 rounds.

12 November 2011. Timothy Bradley w rsc 8 Joel Casamayor.
Venue: MGM Grand, Las Vegas, Nevada, USA. **Recognition:** WBO. **Referee:** Vic Drakulich.
Fight Summary: Despite retaining his title, Bradley (140) found it difficult to impress against a southpaw opponent who was happy to hang on from the opening round. Continuing in this vein, Casamayor (140) was docked a point in the fourth, and in the fifth Bradley had him over from a right to the head before having the Cuban on the floor again in the sixth from what appeared to be more of a push than a punch. Despite getting through the seventh unscathed, after going down following several heavy blows Casamayor was rescued at the count of 'eight' when the referee took note of the towel being waved from his corner. The finish was timed at 2.59 of the eighth.

Juan Manuel Marquez won the vacant WBO 'interim' title when outpointing Serhiy Fedchenko over 12 rounds at the New Arena, Mexico City, Mexico on 14 April 2012.

A few days after Bradley vacated the title on winning the WBO welterweight crown on 9 June 2012, Marquez, the 'interim' champion, was handed full championship status.

The vacant WBO 'interim' title was then won by Mike Alvarado, who outpointed Brandon Rios over 12 rounds at the Mandalay Bay Hotel & Casino, Las Vegas, Nevada on 30 March 2013.

Marquez relinquished the WBO title on 12 October 2013 when taking on Bradley for the welterweight crown. At the same time, Alvarado, who was due to defend his WBO 'interim' title against Ruslan Provodnikov a week later, was elevated to full championship status.

10 December 2011. Lamont Peterson w pts 12 Amir Khan.
Venue: Convention Centre, Washington DC, USA. **Recognition:** IBF/WBA. **Referee:** Joe Cooper.
Scorecards: 113-112, 113-112, 110-115.
Fight Summary: In what was a shock result, Peterson (140) picked up both of Khan's titles on being awarded the split decision. Khan (139) had started strongly enough, dropping Peterson with a left in the opener that the referee ignored before banging him over again with a right to the head for an 'eight' count. Although Peterson showed persistence when attacking the body and pressing Khan at all times, had it not been for two points deductions for pushing in the seventh and 12th the latter would have retained his titles. The seventh and eighth were big for Peterson, who hammered away non-stop, but Khan was throwing the cleaner punches throughout. Finishing the battle with his right eye swollen shut, Peterson had finally proved himself on the world stage.

On 10 December, at the Fair Stockade, Tepic, Nayarit, Mexico, Johan Perez won the vacant WBA 'interim' title after scoring three knockdowns prior to stopping Fernando Castaneda in the fourth round. Perez would lose his title on 21 July 2012, at the Oasis Hotel Complex, Cancun, Mexico, when beaten by Pablo Cesar Cano on a seventh-round technical decision.

Having failed a drugs test that forced a return with Khan to be cancelled shortly before the fight was due to take place, Peterson was eventually stripped of the WBA Belt on 10 July 2012. The WBA then made the decision to reinstate Khan as champion, while the IBF decided in early August that Peterson would remain as their champion following a report by an independent physician.

14 July 2012. Danny Garcia w rsc 4 Amir Khan.
Venue: Mandalay Bay Resort & Casino, Las Vegas, Nevada, USA. **Recognition:** WBA/WBC/The Ring. **Referee:** Kenny Bayless.
Fight Summary: This was Garcia's first defence of the WBC title he had won when defeating Erik Morales, who had failed to make the weight while Khan was defending the WBA title that had been handed to him after Lamont Peterson was stripped. *The Ring* Championship Belt, currently vacant, was also up for grabs in this one. Having

made a great start when outspeeding Garcia (139) in the opening two rounds and cutting him over the right eye Khan (139) came under pressure in the third when body punches began to hold him up. One such punch that strayed low saw Khan being given time out to recover, but towards the end of the session a cracking left hook had him down and almost out. Trying to fight back in the fourth, Khan was floored following a heavy right before his night came to an end after another big left hook had him down again. Although getting up at the count of 'eight', the referee pulled Khan out of the contest on the 2.28 mark after deciding that he was not in a fit state to carry on.

Lucas Martin Matthysse won the vacant WBC 'interim' title when stopping Ajose Olusegun inside ten rounds at the Hard Rock Hotel & Casino, Las Vegas on 8 September.

20 October 2012. Danny Garcia w rsc 4 Erik Morales.
Venue: Barclays Centre, Brooklyn, NYC, New York, USA. **Recognition:** WBA/WBC/The Ring. **Referee:** Benny Esteves Jnr.
Fight Summary: Putting his three championship belts on the line in what was a rematch Garcia (139¾) was far too strong for the shop-worn Morales (139¼), who despite banging in some good shots failed to make an impression on the champion. Having stumbled back to the wrong corner at the end of the third Morales seemed all at sea when coming out for the fourth, and having been smashed to the floor by a heavy left the referee stopped the contest without picking up the count at 1.23 of the session.

Khabib Allakhverdiev won the vacant WBA 'second tier' title when beating Joan Guzman by an eighth-round technical decision at the BB & T Centre, Sunrise, Florida, USA on 30 November.

On 26 January 2013, Lucas Martin Matthysse retained the WBC 'interim' title when knocking out Mike Dallas in the first round at the Hard Rock Hotel & Casino, Las Vegas, Nevada, USA.

22 February 2013. Lamont Peterson w rsc 8 Kendall Holt.
Venue: The Armoury, Washington DC, USA. **Recognition:** IBF. **Referee:** Tony Weeks.
Fight Summary: Not looking his normal self in the opening three sessions, the champion picked it up in the fourth when a right to the jaw dropped Holt (140) after the latter had scored with solid blows of his own earlier. With Holt hurt and on the back foot Peterson (139½) went for the win, belting in punches from both hands to head and body before putting his rival down again in the sixth, courtesy of a two-handed burst of blows. Although making a desperate attempt to get himself back in the contest, Holt again came under attack in the seventh when another right hand wobbled him, and in the eighth after taking stick on the ropes the referee rescued the New Jersey man at 1.42 of the session.

27 April 2013. Danny Garcia w pts 12 Zab Judah.
Venue: Barclays Centre, Brooklyn, NYC, New York, USA. **Recognition:** WBA/WBC/The Ring. **Referee:** Steve Smoger.
Scorecards: 116-111, 114-112, 115-112.
Fight Summary: Starting strongly, Garcia (139¾) took the fight to his southpaw challenger who seemed happy to make the three belt champion miss without doing much on the offensive side. Badly hurt in the fifth and sixth when hit by heavy right hands, Judah (140) was pushed back as Garcia looked for a finish, and in the eighth he was sent down from a left-right to the head. Having looked out of the fight, Judah came on to win the last three sessions as Garcia tired. The last round saw both men cut from a clash of heads as they tried to find a finishing blow, but although Judah had closed the gap it was not enough.

Khabib Allakhverdiev made a successful defence of the WBA 'second tier' title when stopping Souleymane M'baye inside 11 rounds at the Hall of Stars, Monte Carlo, Monaco on 13 July.

14 September 2013. Danny Garcia w pts 12 Lucas Martin Matthysse.
Venue: MGM Grand, Las Vegas, Nevada, USA. **Recognition:** WBA/WBC/The Ring. **Referee:** Tony Weeks.
Scorecards: 115-111, 114-112, 114-112.
Fight Summary: Even though he dropped the opening three rounds on the cards as the hard-hitting Matthysse (140) landed some heavy shots, Garcia (140), with his three championship belts on the line, was never far away.

There was never much between them, but from the seventh round onwards it was Garcia who began to take over, especially when Matthysse's right eye closed in that session. Becoming one-paced but still dangerous, Matthysse tried to find the punch he was looking for without success, and in the 11th he was belted to the deck after getting caught up in the ropes. The final round saw both men slugging, but at the bell it was Garcia who took the honours despite having a point deducted for a low blow in that session.

Following Pablo Cesar Cano's decision to move up to the welterweight division in October, Johan Perez regained his WBA 'interim' title when outpointing Paul Spadafora over 12 rounds at the Mountaineer Casino Racetrack & Resort, Chester, West Virginia, USA on 30 November.

19 October 2013. Ruslan Provodnikov w rtd 10 Mike Alvarado.
Venue: First Bank Centre, Broomfield, Denver, Colorado, USA. **Recognition:** WBO. **Referee:** Tony Weeks.
Fight Summary: Defending the title bequeathed him after both Timothy Bradley and Juan Manuel Marquez handed their belts in, the switch-hitting Alvarado (140) came under considerable pressure in the opener before hitting back hard in the second. By the seventh, however, Provodnikov (140), cut over the right eye, was ahead, having survived the body shots that threatened to take him out. It was in the eighth that Provodnikov took over completely when battering Alvarado to the deck following a barrage of blows, and although the latter got to his feet just in time he was to all intents and purposes done for. Down again from blows to head and body, Alvarado made it back to his corner only to face a further battering in the ninth and tenth before being retired by his corner at the end of the tenth.

25 January 2014. Lamont Peterson w pts 12 Dierry Jean.
Venue: The Armoury, Washington DC, USA. **Recognition:** IBF. **Referee:** Roberto Ramirez.
Scorecards: 118-112, 116-112, 115-113.
Fight Summary: Coming back from a non-title defeat at the hands of Lucas Martin Matthysse, the champion was never fully in control for long periods of this one as the unbeaten Jean (139) often gave as much as he took. It was when Peterson (139½) went to close quarters that he got more joy, many of the earlier rounds having swung back and forth. However, under instructions from his corner to keep things tight, the last three sessions went his way as Jean tired from his exertions.

15 March 2014. Danny Garcia w pts 12 Mauricio Herrera.
Venue: Ruben Rodriguez Coliseum, Bayamon, Puerto Rico. **Recognition:** WBA/WBC/The Ring. **Referee:** Roberto Ramirez.
Scorecards: 116-112, 116-112, 114-114.
Fight Summary: With his three championship belts on the line Garcia (139¾) was soon on the front foot when looking to take the play away from Herrera (139¼), but before too long the champion was struggling to deal with the tempo of the fight. Jabbing well to head and body, Herrera made life difficult for Garcia, especially when negating his famed left hook by good movement off the back foot. It was only in the ninth after Garcia's nose had been spread across his face that he kicked on when taking two of the last three rounds to make sure of the majority verdict.

The WBA 'second tier' title changed hands when Jessie Vargas outpointed the champion, Khabib Allakhverdiev, over 12 rounds at the MGM Grand, Las Vegas, Nevada, USA on 12 April.

Johan Perez made a successful defence of his WBA 'interim' title when forcing Fernando Monte De Oca to retire at the end of the tenth round at the Jose Maria Vargas Sports Complex, La Guaira, Venezuela on 10 May. Next time out, on 12 July, Perez lost the WBA 'interim' title when outpointed by Herrera over 12 rounds at the MGM Grand, Las Vegas, Nevada, USA.

Further successful defences of the WBA 'second tier' title for Vargas saw him beat Anton Novikov (w pts 12 at The Cosmopolitan, Las Vegas, Nevada on 2 August) and Antonio DeMarco (w pts 12 at the Cotai Arena, the Venetian Resort, Macao, China on 23 November).

In his first defence of the WBA 'interim' title, Herrera was outpointed over 12 rounds by Jose Benavidez at The Cosmopolitan, Las Vegas, Nevada, USA on 13 December. Benavidez's first defence of the WBA 'interim' title, which came against Jorge Paez Jnr, resulted in a 12th-round stoppage win for him at the US Airway Centre, Phoenix, Arizona, USA on 15 May 2015.

Vargas relinquished the WBA 'second tier' title when moving up to take on Timothy Bradley for the vacant WBO welterweight crown in June 2015.

Looking to take in another non-title bout, Garcia was forced to relinquish the WBC Championship Belt in May 2015 before handing in *The Ring* and WBA Belts in August 2015.

14 June 2014. Chris Algieri w pts 12 Ruslan Provodnikov.
Venue: Barclays Centre, Brooklyn, New York City, New York, USA. **Recognition:** WBO. **Referee:** Harvey Dock.
Scorecards: 114-112, 114-112, 109-117.
Fight Summary: Appearing in the top league for the first time in his career, the lanky challenger made a dreadful start when being dropped twice in the opener by Provodnikov (139¾), a left hook to the jaw and then a right to the side of the head doing the damage. Following the first knockdown it could be seen that Algieri's right eye had begun to swell, and by the end of the contest it was closed tight. Despite that, the elusive Algieri (140) got his boxing together to make life difficult for the Russian, flicking out jabs while moving around on the back foot at pace. It was only when Provodnikov could get him on the ropes that he had any success, and he was way down on the cards coming into the final four sessions. Although Provodnikov picked up points as Algieri tired he was too far behind on two of the cards to make up the leeway in what was one of boxing's biggest championship surprises.

On 2 November, Algieri was forced to abdicate his title, having signed to meet Manny Pacquiao for the latter's WBO welterweight crown later in the month.

9 August 2014. Lamont Peterson w rsc 10 Edgar Santana.
Venue: Barclays Centre, Brooklyn, NYC, New York, USA. **Recognition:** IBF. **Referee:** Pete Santiago.
Fight Summary: Never competitive, the 35-year-old Santana (139½) was reduced to plodding after the champion and swinging overarm rights from distance. Winning every round contested, Peterson (140) scored well on the inside with solid shots to head and body, but was unable to drop his man. Eventually, with Santana taking a pasting in the tenth the ringside doctor advised the referee to call a halt as he was simply taking too many punches for his own good. The finish was timed at 2.48 of the session.

Peterson was stripped of the IBF title immediately after being beaten on points over 12 rounds by Danny Garcia, the WBA, WBC and *Ring* champion. Held at the Barclays Centre on 11 April 2015, the decision was made regardless of the fact that it was contested at 143lbs, three pounds over the junior welterweight limit.

18 April 2015. Terence Crawford w rsc 6 Thomas Dulorme.
Venue: University of Texas Arena, Arlington, Texas, USA. **Recognition:** WBO. **Referee:** Rafael Ramos.
Fight Summary: Contested for the title that was stripped from Chris Algieri, it was Crawford (139¾), the former WBO lightweight champion, who won when Dulorme (139¼) was rescued by the referee at 1.51 of the sixth. Starting slowly while taking a good look at his rival, Crawford boxed his way into the fight while Dulorme made a solid start when banging in overarm rights and left hooks. By the third, however, Crawford began to pick it up when letting both hands go. Although he did less work in the fifth, Crawford went for Dulorme in the sixth, and after knocking the Puerto Rican down three times, a left hook to the head, a flurry of blows and then heavy shots up and down doing the job, it was all over.

18 July 2015. Cesar Rene Cuenca w pts 12 Ik Yang.
Venue: Cotai Arena, Venetian Resort, Macao, SAR China. **Recognition:** IBF. **Referee:** Danrex Tapdasan.
Scorecards: 117-108, 116-109, 115-110.
Fight Summary: Fighting for the title forfeited by Lamont Peterson, the 34-year-old Argentine southpaw made a good start when solid combinations sent Yang (139¾) reeling into the ropes upon which the referee gave the latter

an 'eight' count on claiming that the strands had stopped him from falling. After going well, his movement keeping Yang guessing for much of the time, Cuenca (139½) was caught by a right hand that dropped him momentarily. Coming back strongly with solid lefts, from thereon in it was Cuenca all the way when controlling the fight at his own pace as Yang came on to his punches. Being deducted a point in the 12th for throwing Cuenca to the floor summed up Yang's night.

3 October 2015. Adrien Broner w rsc 12 Khabib Allakhverdiev.
Venue: USA Bank Arena, Cincinnati, Ohio, USA. **Recognition:** WBA. **Referee:** Harvey Dock.
Fight Summary: In a fight for the title vacated by Danny Garcia, Broner (138½) picked up virtually all of the contested rounds without even getting out of first gear for much of the time. Having been out of the ring for 18 months Allakhverdiev (139) was never able to get to Broner, although one of the judges gave him the second and third rounds. The fight only warmed up when the Russian southpaw, cut under both eyes, realised he was miles behind on the cards and went after Broner, only to be picked off with solid shots as he came onto them. At the end of the 11th, the referee warned Allakhverdiev that he would stop the fight if he came under further attacks, and when he did the contest was halted with just 37 seconds of the 12th remaining.

It was reported on 2 March 2016 that Jose Benavidez had handed in the WBA 'interim' title having decided to fight in a higher weight division.

Broner forfeited the WBA title when failing to make the weight for a defence against Ashley Theophane at The Armoury, Washington DC, USA on 1 April 2016. The contest went ahead with Theophane being stopped inside nine rounds and unable to claim the title.

3 October 2015. Viktor Postol w co 10 Lucas Martin Matthysse.
Venue: US Bank Arena, Cincinnati, Ohio, USA. **Recognition:** WBC. **Referee:** Jack Reiss.
Fight Summary: Going for the title vacated by Danny Garcia, the lanky Postol (139½) controlled the tough Matthysse (139½) for much of the time before knocking him out in tenth round. When Matthysse did manage to get inside where he could do some damage, Postol had no compunction in grabbing the Argentine prior to moving on. It was not that Matthysse failed to win any rounds, there being little between them come the eighth, but from there onwards it was Postol all the way. The finish came at 2.58 of the tenth after Matthysse stayed down following a punch that had smashed into his left eye. Afterwards, Matthysse stated that he could have got up but feared damaging his eyesight.

24 October 2015. Terence Crawford w rsc 10 Dierry Jean.
Venue: CenturyLink Centre, Omaha, Nebraska, USA. **Recognition:** WBO. **Referee:** Tony Weeks.
Fight Summary: The switch-hitting champion got away well in this one, dropping Jean (140) with a short right-hand counter towards the end of the opener, and hurting him again in the second with another right out of a southpaw stance. Whether it be one stance or another, Crawford (140) was the master of the situation, his jab from either hand being both solid and accurate. By the eighth it was all going one way, and having given a superb exhibition of hitting and not being hit Crawford put Jean down in the ninth with a left-right-left before battering the Haitian through the ropes in the tenth with similar blows. At 2.30 of the session the referee called the fight off after not bothering to take up the count.

4 November 2015. Eduard Troyanovsky w rsc 6 Cesar Rene Cuenca.
Venue: Basket-Hall Arena, Kazan, Russia. **Recognition:** IBF. **Referee:** David Fields.
Fight Summary: With a record of 48 unbeaten, the southpaw champion came unstuck when facing Troyanovsky (139) on the latter's home turf. Having had difficulty with Troyanovsky's jab all night, the Argentine not only failed to equal the legendary Rocky Marciano's unbeaten record but found himself without a title after being stopped at 2.44 of the sixth. Although one of the judges saw the fight as an even one up until the sixth mainly due to work-rate, Cuenca (139¼) had been systematically taken apart, and after being hammered by a solid uppercut before being pushed over the referee pulled him out of the fight.

27 February 2016. Terence Crawford w rsc 5 Henry Lundy.
Venue: Madison Square Garden Theatre, Manhattan, NYC, New York, USA. **Recognition:** WBO. **Referee:** Steve Willis.
Fight Summary: Taking the champion a couple of rounds to readjust to the unorthodox Lundy (138¼), who threw blows from all angles, once he had, the writing was on the wall for the latter. Having switched to southpaw, by the third Crawford (139¼) was timing his blows better, and in the fifth he finally caught up with Lundy when dropping him with a solid straight left that was followed up by a left hook. Prior to that, two right jabs had opened Lundy up. Although he just about made it to his feet before the count reached 'ten' the referee halted the contest at 2.09 of the session after deciding that Lundy was in no fit state to continue.

8 April 2016. Eduard Troyanovsky w rsc 7 Cesar Rene Cuenca.
Venue: Krylya Sovetov Sports Arena, Moscow, Russia. **Recognition:** IBF. **Referee:** Malik Waleed.
Fight Summary: Giving Cuenca (139¾) another opportunity following their unsatisfactory first fight, the champion immediately got down to work with his long left jab picking the Argentine southpaw apart. Knocked down in the fourth from a hard right to the head, Cuenca resumed fighting before being dropped again in the sixth by a right uppercut as Troyanovsky (139¼) cut loose. Still not properly recovered, although Cuenca came out for the seventh he was soon in trouble following some serious body shots getting through, and when his corner advised the referee that they wanted their man pulled out after he had slipped over the third man obliged on the 2.14 mark.

28 May 2016. Ricky Burns w rsc 8 Michele Di Rocco.
Venue: SSE Hydro, Glasgow, Scotland. **Recognition:** WBA. **Referee:** Terry O'Connor.
Fight Summary: Battling for the title forfeited by Adrien Broner, it was Burns (139¼) who took the fight by the scruff of the neck to become a three-time world champion when stopping Di Rocco (139¼) at 1.57 of the eighth. While not losing a round Burns started the contest with a steady stream of left jabs prior to landing some solid blows that ultimately undid the Italian. Having been down in the third from a cluster of blows, Di Rocco probably knew that this was not going to be his night, and after struggling through to the eighth when a couple of heavy right hands left him on the floor it was all over.

23 July 2016. Terence Crawford w pts 12 Viktor Postol.
Venue: MGM Grand, Las Vegas, Nevada, USA. **Recognition:** WBC/WBO/The Ring. **Referee:** Tony Weeks.
Scorecards: 118-107, 118-107, 117-108.
Fight Summary: Although the WBC champion, Postol (139½), made a good start when winning two of the opening three rounds in his unification match against Crawford (140), the WBO title holder, by the fourth the latter had begun to stamp his mark on the contest. Having turned southpaw to confuse his man, in the fifth Crawford had Postol over twice, a right hook seeing the latter touch down before a heavy left hand secured the second knockdown. From thereon in it was all Crawford, and even in the 11th when Postol looked like winning the round he lost out when being deducted a point for hitting behind the head. This contest also involved the vacant *Ring* Championship Belt.

9 September 2016. Eduard Troyanovsky w rsc 2 Keita Obara.
Venue: Krylya Sovetov Sports Arena, Moscow, Russia. **Recognition:** IBF. **Referee:** Michael Ortega.
Fight Summary: Caught by a big right hand from Obara (139¼) towards the end of the opening session the champion was badly stunned before the bell came to his aid. Picking it up in the second, having sufficiently recovered, Troyanovsky (140) began landing heavy blows from his extended reach and before too long Obara was rocked by a cracking right to the head. Continuing the assault, Troyanovsky eventually smashed Obara through the ropes and on to one of the judge's table. Although Obara made it back in time to beat the count he was rescued by the referee on the 1.35 mark after being hurt by several big punches that threatened to do even more damage.

7 October 2016. Ricky Burns w pts 12 Kiryl Relikh.
Venue: SSE Hydro Arena, Glasgow, Scotland. **Recognition:** WBA. **Referee:** Howard Foster.
Scorecards: 116-112, 116-112, 118-110.
Fight Summary: Up against a hard-hitting challenger in Relikh (140), the durable Burns (139¼) had to be at the top of his game to both box and fight his way to a points win in an all-action contest. The unbeaten Relikh, bringing 19

short wins from 21 outings into the ring, did his utmost to blast Burns into submission but found the Scot a difficult target to catch. And when he did catch up with Burns the latter was more than happy to fire back. Although Burns deserved the victory, the scorecards did not do Relikh justice.

Junior Welterweight Boxers' Index:

(Country of birth where known/Domicile - birthplace and domicile are the same unless stated)

A

Davey Abad (Panama/USA)
Muhammad Abdullaev (Uzbekistan)
Mauricio Aceves (Mexico)
Pedro Adigue (Philippines)
Ray Adigun (Nigeria)
Kyung-Duk Ahn (South Korea)
Olusegun Ajose (Nigeria/England)
Hidekazu Akai (Japan)
Juan Albornoz (Spain)
Devon Alexander (USA)
Billy Alger (USA)
Chris Algieri (USA)
Khabib Allakhverdiev (Russia)
Terrence Alli (Guyana/USA)
Mike Alvarado (USA)
Antonio Amaya (Panama)
Thomas Americo (Indonesia)
Bruno Arcari (Italy)
Agustin Argote (Spain)
Alexis Arguello (Nicaragua)
Mike Arnaoutis (Greece/USA)
Rene Arredondo (Mexico)
Fidel Avendano (Mexico/USA)
Domingo Ayala (Puerto Rico)

B

Randall Bailey (USA)
Raul Horacio Balbi (Argentina)
Tony Baltazar (USA)
Jose Rafael Barboza (Venezuela)
George Barnes (Australia)
Domingo Barrera (Spain)
Rene Barrientos (Philippines)
Rudy Barro (Philippines/USA)
Marius Baudry (France)
Lennox Beckles (Guyana)
Naoufel Ben Rabah (Tunisia/Australia)
Jose Benavidez (USA)
Wilfred Benitez (USA/Puerto Rico)
Jose Manuel Berdonce (Spain)
Jack Kid Berg (England)
Maxie Berger (Canada)
Jan Piet Bergman (South Africa)
Bruno Bisterzo (Italy)
Lennox Blackmoore (Guyana)
Willy Blain (Reunion/France)
Francis Bonnardel (France)
Solomon Boysaw (USA)
Timothy Bradley (USA)

Gianluca Branco (Italy)
Piero Brandi (Italy)
Harold Brazier (USA)
Quentin Baby Breese (USA)
Adrien Broner (USA)
Monroe Brooks (USA)
Buster Brown (USA)
Joe Brown (USA)
Brian Brunette (USA)
Johnny Bumphus (USA)
Ricky Burns (Scotland)

C

Efrem Calamati (Italy)
Mushy Callahan (USA)
Manuel Calvo (Spain)
Hector Camacho (Puerto Rico/USA)
Nate Campbell (USA)
Pablo Cesar Cano (Mexico)
Tony Canzoneri (USA)
Oba Carr (USA)
Joel Casamayor (Cuba/USA)
Fernando Castaneda (Mexico)
Jose Luis Castillo (Mexico)
Victor Manuel Cayo (Dominican Republic)
Demetrio Ceballos (Panama/USA)
Piero Ceru (Italy)
Antonio Cervantes (Colombia)
Dave Charnley (England)
Ray Chavez Guerrero (Venezuela/Canada)
Julio Cesar Chavez (Mexico)
Edner Cherry (Bahamas/USA)
Felix Chiocca (Venezuela/France)
Sauveur Chiocca (Venezuela/France)
Kid Chocolate (Cuba)
Juan Martin Coggi (Argentina)
Clarence Coleman (USA)
Luis Collazo (USA)
DeMarcus Corley (USA)
Alberto Cortes (Argentina)
Everaldo Costa Azevedo (Brazil/Italy)
Billy Costello (USA)
Miguel Cotto (USA/Puerto Rico)
Terence Crawford (USA)
Guillermo Cruz (Mexico)
Reyes Antonio Cruz (Dominican Republic)
Roberto Cruz (Philippines)
Cesar Rene Cuenca (Argentina)
Bruce Curry (USA)

D

Mike Dallas (USA)
Howard Davis (USA)
Freddie Dawson (USA)
Esteban De Jesus (Puerto Rico)
Oscar De La Hoya (USA)
Al Delmont (USA)
Antonio DeMarco (Mexico)
Michele Di Rocco (Italy)
Raymundo Dias (Brazil)
Idrissa Dione (Gabon/France)
Andy DiVodi (USA)
Leonard Dorin (Romania/Canada)
Tim Droney (USA)
Thomas Dulorme (French Guiana/Puerto Rico)
John Duplessis (USA)
Roberto Duran (Panama)

E

Morris East (Philippines)
J. D. Ellis (USA)
Eugenio Espinosa (Ecuador)
Mike Everett (USA)

F

Ray Famechon (France)
Johnny Farr (USA)
Serhiy Fedchenko (Ukraine)
George Feeney (England)
Perico Fernandez (Spain)
Seraphin Ferrer (Algeria/France)
Glen Flanagan (USA)
Felix Flores (Puerto Rico)
Bruce Flowers (USA)
Al Ford (Canada)
Ernesto Formenti (Italy)
Alfonso Frazer (Panama)
Sammy Fuentes (Puerto Rico)
Paul Fujii (Hawaii/Japan)
Sammy Fuller (USA)
Nick Furlano (Canada)
Lion Furuyama (Japan)
Charley Fusari (Italy/USA)

G

Fred Galiana (Spain)
Giancarlo Garbelli (Italy)
Angel Robinson Garcia (Cuba/USA)
Danny Garcia (USA)
Felix Garcia (Puerto Rico/USA)
Lorenzo Garcia (Argentina)
Manolo Garcia (Spain)
Loreto Garza (USA)

German Gastelbondo (Colombia)
Arturo Gatti (Italy/USA)
Ivor Kid Germain (Barbados/England)
Joe Ghnouly (USA)
Carlos Gimenez (Argentina)
Juan Jose Gimenez (Argentina/Italy)
Fitzroy Guisseppi (Trinidad/Belize)
Joe Glick (USA)
Nate Goldman (USA)
Ruby Goldstein (USA)
Carlos Gonzalez (Mexico)
Eder Gonzalez (Colombia)
Miguel Angel Gonzalez (Mexico)
Rodolfo Gonzalez (Mexico)
William Gonzalez (Panama)
Billy Graham (USA)
Bunny Grant (Jamaica)
Gerald Gray (Jamaica)
Reggie Green (USA)
Philly Griffin (USA)
Daniel Guanin (Ecuador)
Hugo Gutierrez (Argentina)
Joan Guzman (Dominican Republic/USA)

H

Leroy Haley (USA)
Tsuyoshi Hamada (Japan)
Joergen Hansen (Denmark)
Vivian Harris (Guyana/USA)
Gaetan Hart (Canada)
Gene Hatcher (USA)
Ricky Hatton (England)
Greg Haugen (USA)
Percy Hayles (Jamaica)
Joao Henrique (Brazil)
Jacques Herbillon (France)
Angel Hernandez (Puerto Rico)
Carlos Hernandez (Venezuela)
Mauricio Herrera (USA)
Tony Herrera (USA)
Red Herring (USA)
Goldie Hess (USA)
Gary Hinton (USA)
Akinobu Hiranaka (Japan)
Andy Holligan (England)
Kendall Holt (USA)
Courtney Hooper (USA)
Demetrius Hopkins (USA)
Ace Hudkins (USA)
Diosbelys Hurtado (Cuba/Spain)

I

Guts Ishimatsu (Japan)

J

Johnny Jadick (Ukraine/USA)
Marty Jakubowski (USA)
Enrique Jana (Argentina/USA)
Dierry Jean (Haiti/Canada)
Jorgen Johansen (Denmark)
Corey Johnson (USA)
Dujuan Johnson (USA)
Stevie Johnston (USA)
Willie Joyce (USA)
Zab Judah (USA)
Ener Julio (Colombia)

K

Shinichi Kadota (Japan)
Jaguar Kakizawa (Japan)
Cemal Kamaci (Turkey/Austria)
David Kamau (Kenya/USA)
Akio Kameda (Japan)
Shigemasa Kawakami (Japan)
Hoacine Khalfi (Algeria/France)
Amir Khan (England)
Tongta Kiatvayupakdi (Thailand)
Kwang-Min Kim (South Korea)
Sang-Hyun Kim (South Korea)
Jo Kimpuani (DR Congo/France)
Norio Kimura (Japan)
Ray Kiser (USA)
Frankie Klick (USA)
Andriy Kotelnyk (Ukraine)

L

Tony Lambert (USA)
Kenny Lane (USA)
Rudi Langer (Germany)
Juan Laporte (Puerto Rico/USA)
Tippy Larkin (USA)
Juan Lazcano (Mexico/USA)
Chang-Kil Lee (South Korea)
Sang-Ho Lee (South Korea)
Jesse James Leija (USA)
Russie LeRoy (USA)
Cleto Locatelli (Italy)
Nicolino Locche (Argentina)
Bud Logan (USA)
Duilio Loi (Italy)
Ernie Lopez (USA)
Hector Lopez (Mexico/USA)
Tony Lopez (USA)
Sandro Lopopolo (Italy)
Henry Lundy (USA)

M

Souleymane M'baye (France)
Kaizer Mabuza (South Africa)
Fred Mahan (USA)
Marcos Maidana (Argentina)
Paul Malignaggi (USA)
Saoul Mamby (USA)
Fortunato Manca (Italy)
Ray Mancini (USA)
Sammy Mandell (Italy/USA)
Joe Manley (USA)
Emilio Marconi (Italy)
Josue Marquez (Puerto Rico)
Adriano Marrero (Dominican Republic/USA)
Terry Marsh (England)
Tito Marshall (Panama)
Rocky Martinez (Mexico/USA)
Leonardo Mas (Puerto Rico/USA)
Lucas Martin Matthysse (Argentina)
Carlos Maussa (Colombia)
Floyd Mayweather Jnr (USA)
Roger Mayweather (USA)
Virgil McClendon (USA)
Paul McCloskey (Northern Ireland)
Buddy McGirt (USA)
Jimmy McLarnin (Northern Ireland/USA)
Jimmy McNamara (USA)
John Meekins (USA)
Jean-Baptiste Mendy (Senegal/France)
Barry Michael (England/Australia)
Harold Miller (USA)
Terron Millett (USA)
Frankie Mitchell (USA)
Pinky Mitchell (USA)
Sharmba Mitchell (USA)
Luis Molina (USA)
Fernando Monte De Oca (Dominican Republic)
Miguel Montilla (Dominican Republic)
Rodney Moore (USA)
Erik Morales (Mexico/USA)
Francisco Moreno (Venezuela)
L. C. Morgan (USA)
Kid Moro (Philippines)
Arturo Morua (Mexico)
Alberto Mosquera (Panama)
Saensak Muangsurin (Thailand)
Charles Murray (USA)
Spug Myers (USA)

N

Jose Napoles (Cuba/Mexico)
Lovemore Ndou (South Africa/Australia)
Pete Nebo (Cuba/USA)

Wilfredo Negron (Puerto Rico)
Al Nevarez (Mexico)
Herman Ngoudjo (Cameroon/Canada)
Anton Novikov (Russia)
Obisia Nwankpa (Nigeria)

O
Keita Obara (Japan)
Patrizio Oliva (Italy)
Ray Oliveira (USA)
Ajose Olusegun (Nigeria/USA)
Johann Orsolics (Austria)
Antonio Ortiz (Spain)
Carlos Ortiz (Puerto Rico/USA)
Elio Ortiz (Venezuela)
Rafael Ortiz (Dominican Republic)
Victor Ortiz (Puerto Rico 1969-77)
Victor Ortiz (USA 2004-)

P
Bobby Pacho (USA)
Manny Pacquiao (Philippines)
Zack Padilla (USA)
Jorge Paez Jnr (Mexico)
Giovanni Parisi (Italy)
Jimmy Paul (USA)
Cecil Payne (USA)
Vinny Pazienza (USA)
Freddie Pendleton (USA)
Johan Perez (Venezuela)
Eddie Perkins (USA)
Herman Perlick (USA)
Arthur Persley (USA)
Lamont Peterson (USA)
Billy Petrolle (USA)
Tony Petronelli (USA)
Petr Petrov (Russia/Spain)
Vince Phillips (USA)
Hugo Pineda (Colombia/USA)
Rafael Pineda (Colombia/USA)
Kelson Pinto (Brazil)
Viktor Postol (Ukraine/USA)
Ruslan Provodnikov (Russia/USA)
Adolph Pruitt (USA)
Aaron Pryor (USA)

Q
Willi Quatuor (Germany)
Carlos Quintana (Puerto Rico)
Hector Quiroz (Mexico/USA)

R
Khalid Rahilou (Morocco/France)
Wesley Ramey (USA)
Jose Luis Ramirez (Mexico)
Frankie Randall (USA)
Jaime Rangel (Colombia/USA)
Gavin Rees (Wales)
Kiryl Relikh (Belarus)
Sergio Rey Revilla (Spain)
Brandon Rios (USA)
Vicente Rivas (Venezuela)
Jose Rivera (Puerto Rico)
Jake Rodriguez (Puerto Rico/USA)
Rene Roque (France)
Edwin Rosario (Puerto Rico)
Barney Ross (USA)
Mario Rossito (Colombia)
Conny Rudhof (Germany)

S
Ubaldo Sacco (Argentina)
Pedro Saiz (Dominican Republic/USA)
Lauro Salas (Mexico)
Dmitriy Salita (Ukraine/USA)
Alfonso Sanchez (Mexico)
Edgar Santana (Puerto Rico/USA)
Ahmed Santos (Mexico/USA)
George Scott (Liberia/Sweden)
Norman Sekgapane (South Africa)
Cleo Shans (USA)
Battling Shaw (USA)
Randy Shields (USA)
Ronnie Shields (USA)
Lonnie Smith (USA)
Lorenzo Smith (USA)
Wallace Bud Smith (USA)
Bert Somodio (Philippines)
Paul Spadafora (USA)
Irvin Steen (USA)
Michael Stewart (USA)

T
Ben Tackie (Ghana/USA)
Yoshinori Takahashi (Japan)
Kid Tano (Spain)
Jackie Taylor (USA)
Meldrick Taylor (USA)
Lew Tendler (USA)
Sid Terris (USA)
Joe Tetteh (Ghana/England)
Ashley Theophane (England/USA)
Hector Thompson (Australia)
Harvey Thorpe (USA)

Johnny Tillman (USA)
Battling Torres (Mexico)
Ricardo Torres (Colombia)
Mario Trigo (Mexico)
Eduard Troyanovsky (Russia)
Kostya Tszyu (Russia/Australia)

U
Juan Urango (Colombia/USA)
Alfredo Urbina (Mexico)
Oktay Urkal (Germany)

V
Doug Vaillant (Cuba/USA)
Al Van Ryan (USA)
Jessie Vargas (USA)
Mauro Vazquez (Mexico)
Miguel Velazquez (Spain)
Allan Vester (Denmark)
Carlos Wilfredo Vilches (Argentina)
Emiliano Villa (Colombia)
Bruno Visintin (Italy)

W
Billy Wallace (USA)
Micky Ward (USA)
Frankie Warren (USA)
Maurice Watkins (USA)
Teddy Watson (USA)
Harry Weekly (USA)
Nigel Wenton (England)
Pernell Whitaker (USA)
Ike Williams (USA)
California Jackie Wilson (USA)
Junior Witter (England)
Henry Woods (USA)

Y
Ik Yang (China)
Masahiro Yogai (Japan)
Hiroyuki Yoshino (Japan)

Z
Roger Zami (Guadeloupe/France)
Brunet Zamora (Cuba/Italy)
Orlando Zulueta (Cuba/USA)

Welterweight Division

Adapted from horse racing terminology, the 'welter' division first came into being in America in order to bridge the gap between light and middle. Thought to be fighting just above 140lbs, Paddy Duffy is generally recognised as the first bare-knuckle champion under London Prize Ring Rules after beating Bob Lyons by an 11th-round kayo in April 1884 (Boston, Massachusetts).

Having successfully defended the title against Bill Young, via a second-round kayo win in March 1886 (Baltimore, Maryland), he next claimed to be the division's first Marquess of Queensberry Rules (MoQ Rules) champion, but that claim was disputed by Johnny Reagan, albeit at a heavier weight

Weight Band/Amendments
140lbs to 146lbs (1887 to 14 April 1898)
140lbs to 148lbs (On 14 April 1898, Mysterious Billy Smith extended his welterweight claim to take in 148lbs)
140lbs to 150lbs (After Joe Walcott and Young Peter Jackson contested the welter title at 150lbs on 18 June 1903, the new British welterweight class also began operating up to that weight)
135lbs to 147lbs (On 11 February 1909, in London, the NSC formally stipulated that the lightweight class limit would be 135lbs and that the new welterweight division would be set at 147lbs)
140lbs to 147lbs (On 15 November 1922, the NBA launched the junior welterweight class for men between 135lbs and 140lbs)

Welterweight World Championship Fights and Title Claims:

2 June 1887. (146lbs) Johnny Reagan w co 44 (finish) John Files.
Venue: Greenwich Street Dancing Pavilion, Manhattan, NYC, New York, USA. **Referee:** Frank Stevenson.
Fight Summary: With both men wearing skin-tight gloves and contested under MoQ Rules within 100 yards of the Hudson River, this is the first reference to be found to the welterweight title. Some papers reported that the men fought at 144lbs, while the *New York Herald* stated that Reagan scaled 146lbs. The paper went on to say that the winner, who scored a kayo with a solid right-hand smash to the jaw, would confidently be able to call himself the champion welter. The men had fought for close on three hours and had both scored knockdowns, Files in the seventh and Reagan in the 34th, but once the older man weakened there was only going to be one winner.

21 July 1887. (144lbs) Arthur Bobbett w pts 12 Jim Kendrick.
Venue: Paradise Street School of Arms, Lambeth, London, England. **Referee:** H. Woodstock.
Fight Summary: Made at 144lbs, it was clear that Kendrick (143) was not the same fighter prior to his recent illness, but he still managed stiff resistance as Bobbett forced the fight from the opening bell, scoring to head and body with lefts and rights. There were no out-and-out knockdowns, just a few slips, and Bobbett impressed as a fighter who with some tuition could turn out to be a tough customer for any of the top men. There was no title billing as such, but Bobbett, who was reported to weigh 140, 143 and 148lbs depending what paper you read, claimed the English 144lbs title following this win over Kendrick.

8 August 1887. (146lbs) Johnny Reagan drew 39 (finish) Tom Henry.
Venue: Long Island, New York, USA. **Referee:** Frank Stevenson.
Fight Summary: Taking place 50 miles up the Hudson River in a dancing pavilion at a point on the Long Island shore almost opposite Larchmont, and with both men inside 146lbs, Reagan (142) put his American title claim up for grabs against Henry (145) in what was a hard-glove fight under MoQ Rules. Henry made the better start when forcing the fight, and apart from being knocked down in the opener he made all the running throughout the first 36 rounds, with Reagan being told to back off by his handlers in order to conserve his energy. There were no reports of any further knockdowns in the *New York Herald* report, the paper stating that the fighting was cautious from the 15th through to the 27th, with rounds 28 to 32 being characterised by even hitting while the 33rd and 34th sessions were desperate. In the 36th, according to the paper, Reagan came on strong, battering Henry

unmercifully before the howling mob forced both men over the ropes and down among the settees outside the ring. At that point the referee took the only course left open to him when bringing matters to a halt early after two hours and 35 minutes and calling it a draw.

Reagan moved on to fight Nonpareil Jack Dempsey for the American middles crown.

15 August 1887. (144lbs) Arthur Bobbett drew 13 (12) Sam Baxter.
Venue: Paradise Street School of Arms, Lambeth, London, England. **Referee:** J. T. Hulls.
Fight Summary: Reported to be the English 144lbs champion, despite a lack of billing and weights Bobbett's title claim would almost certainly have been at stake regardless of him not pursuing it. Bobbett, the heavier by about ten pounds, made the running but Baxter was always hitting back, and from the sixth round it was give and take all the way. Interestingly, an extra round was contested in order for the judges to find a winner.

On 26 November, George Wilson won a 144lbs championship competition when outpointing Anthony Diamond over three rounds at the Peter Street Grand Circus, Manchester. While Diamond looked to have well won it, Jim Kendrick, who was also claiming to be the English 144lbs champion, went to America in May 1888 to further his claim.

16 April 1888. (145/146lbs) Alf Suffolk w disq 11 (12) Ted Barrett.
Venue: Paradise Street School of Arms, Lambeth, London, England. **Referee:** George Dunning.
Fight Summary: Boxing at catchweights with no title billing it was said that following his victory, Suffolk (135), who was making his pro debut, claimed the English 145lbs title. Certainly, he was awarded a silver championship belt, presented by Harry Clarke, which might explain why he was boxing top-class men from thereon in. Showing good form for a man new to the pro game, Suffolk relied very much on his straight left with which to pick Barrett (145) apart, but as the two men got tired the latter resorted to wrestling and throwing. At the end of the tenth round, after more fouling, the referee came into the ring to warn both men that the first to commit a foul from that moment on would be thrown out. It was not long in coming. Halfway through the 11th when Barrett again back-heeled Suffolk he was promptly disqualified.

Another man to make good progress at 146lbs was Alec Burns, who outpointed Ted White over four rounds at Her Majesty's Theatre, Haymarket, London on 15 December to win a championship competition at the weight.

27 July 1888. (144lbs) Jim Kendrick drew 15 Jack McGee.
Venue: Fair Play Club, Boston, Massachusetts, USA. **Referee:** Jimmy Colville.
Fight Summary: Contested with small gloves at 144lbs, the Irish-born Kendrick, who was claiming to be the English champion at all weights between 138 and 144lbs, looked to have had the best of this against McGee, the only man to beat Paddy Duffy. Although both fighters agreed to continue the referee brought matters to a close at the end of the 15th, the stipulated distance.

Kendrick had also performed decidedly better than Duffy in a four-round no-decision bout on 11 July, before returning to Britain. Back home, however, despite continuing to challenge all and sundry he was never the same again before dying of consumption on 23 August 1898, aged 34.

30 October 1888. (144lbs) Paddy Duffy w disq 17 (finish) Billy McMillan.
Venue: Virginia, USA. **Referee:** Bob Callahan.
Fight Summary: Held in an old building on the shoreline near Fort Foote, 15 miles below Washington, the fight was given to Duffy in the 17th round after he had been fouled by McMillan. In bad shape at the time, it was felt that McMillan fouled himself out of it. Following the fight, Duffy stated that he had hurt his left hand early on, while McMillan's friends were claiming that their man had been poisoned after taking water between rounds. Although I found reference to Duffy claiming to be the American 140lbs champion earlier in the year, I could find nothing to support that claim. However, we do know that Duffy, weighing either 137 or 140lbs depending on what paper you read, was recognised as the American champion at all weights between 138 and 144lbs after his victory over McMillan (143lbs) in what was a hard-glove fight articled at 144lbs under MoQ Rules.

19 February 1889. (144/146lbs) Ted Pritchard w disq 4 (finish) Jim Hayes.
Venue: Paradise Street School of Arms, Lambeth, London, England. **Referee:** Bernard J. Angle.
Fight Summary: Billed for the English 145lbs title, Pritchard (144) soon got down to work, dropping Hayes twice with uppercuts in the opener and making life tough for his rival in the next two sessions. Because Hayes was badly outreached he was forced to get to close quarters, but was being countered with solid lefts on the way in, a tactic that saw him take a lot of punishment in the second and third rounds also. Knocked down twice in the fourth, after Hayes' seconds rushed to his aid thinking that he had been counted out on the first occasion, confusion reigned. It was only later that an announcement was made to the effect that Hayes had been disqualified due to the actions of his corner.

On winning, Pritchard challenged the world at 144 and 146lbs but was soon fighting among the middleweights.

Further activity in 1889 in the 144lbs class came when Ted White (who outpointed Andy Cannon over four rounds at the Royal Aquarium Theatre, Westminster, London on 23 February) and Sam Baxter (who outpointed White over four rounds at the Royal Agricultural Hall, Islington, London on 16 March) won English championship competitions.

A few days earlier, on 9 March, Johnny Robinson claimed to be the rightful holder of an English Championship Belt, having won it some six years earlier. However, the belt Robinson had won was at 146lbs and hardly had any bearing on his right to the 144lbs title.

29 March 1889. (142lbs) Paddy Duffy w disq 45 (finish) Tom Meadows.
Venue: California AC, San Francisco, California, USA. **Referee:** Hiram Cook.
Fight Summary: According to the *Sporting Life* this was a title fight, but the *San Francisco Chronicle* only made mention of it as being a contest at 142lbs between Duffy (139) and Meadows (l41½) with both men using small lace-up gloves. Incidentally, although Meadows, who was downed five times before being disqualified for a low blow, was billed out of Australia he had actually been born in England. For Duffy it would be his last fight as he tragically contracted tuberculosis before passing away at the early age of 26 on 19 July 1890.

19 August 1889. (144lbs) Harry Nickless w co 15 (finish) Alf Suffolk.
Venue: South London School of Arms, Kennington, London, England. **Referee:** C. Ford.
Fight Summary: The first nine rounds were evenly contested, both men going with the left, before the tenth saw the turning point as Nickless continually swung his Dexter mitt to Suffolk's head. Although Suffolk (138) struggled on gamely, after the bell sounded for the 15th Nickless crashed in several right hands before sending his rival to the floor to be counted out on the 2.15 mark. Contested at catchweights, Nickless, reportedly in only the third bout of his career, weighed 148lbs (almost certainly a misprint) and laid claim to the English 144lbs title following his victory.

31 October 1889. (144lbs) Harry Nickless w rtd 15 (finish) Jim Townsend.
Venue: Hop & Malt Exchange, The Borough, London, England. **Referee:** W. McNeff.
Fight Summary: Advertised as being for the English 144lbs title in four-ounce gloves, Nickless was recognised by most as the English champion at the weight. At the close of the 13th round there was very little to choose between either man, both having fought scientifically, but the 14th saw the tide change as Townsend landed to the head while Nickless went for the body, which led to fierce infighting. Towards the end of the session Townsend went to the boards after taking a vicious punch under the ribs, and although he was rescued by the bell he was unable to make it out for the 15th before being retired by his corner.

On 30 November, Anthony Diamond challenged the world at 144lbs, but would eventually make his mark at a higher weight, while Alf Suffolk outpointed Bill Cheese over four rounds to win a 144lbs English championship competition at the Saddlers Wells Theatre, Clerkenwell, London on 14 December.

20 January 1890. (144lbs) Harry Nickless w co 13 (finish) Alf Suffolk.
Venue: South London School of Arms, Kennington, London, England. **Referee:** T. J. McNeil.

Fight Summary: Made at 145lbs but reported to be for the English 144lbs title, despite the opening three rounds being more or less even, by the fourth Nickless (144) appeared to have the measure of Suffolk (143½) and although the latter came good in the seventh his left eye was fast closing. In the 11th, Suffolk, his left eye completely closed, was being punched around the ring at will. Then, having been floored time was called. With Nickless in the driving seat he set about Suffolk in the 12th, and following two knockdowns in that session the latter was knocked out by a blow to the neck in the 13th.

By now, with Nickless fairly well thought of as the English 144lbs champion he was challenged by Ted Pleydell (March), while Jim Kendrick (April), George Baxter (May), Jim Adds (June), Jim Connelly, Anthony Diamond and William Robinson (September) and Jim Townsend and Lachie Thomson (November) challenged all England.

In November, Diamond stated in the *Sporting Life* that he was the 144lbs English champion, while Nickless should only be recognised as the champion of London. A couple of weeks later Diamond was challenging Dick Burge at 146lbs.

30 May 1890. (145/146lbs) Lachie Thomson w rsc 2 (12) Alf Hanlon.
Venue: Peter Street Grand Circus, Manchester, England. **Referee:** Andrew Marsden.
Fight Summary: Articled at 145lbs, Thomson (144) started well, taking the opening round with ease, before going on to drop Hanlon (144) heavily in the second after landing with a solid blow to the jaw. Although Hanlon got to his feet he was badly dazed, and with Thomson looking to finish it the fight was stopped by the police, whereupon the referee awarded the decision to the latter. Despite there being no title billing attached, Thomson was claiming the English title at that weight thereafter.

Two men who came through to win championship competitions at 146lbs were William Robinson (who outpointed James Lowes over four rounds at Ginnett's Circus, Newcastle on 18 October) and Ted Dorkings (who outpointed Felix Scott over four rounds at the Central Hall, Holborn, London on 4 June 1892), while Jim Burchill (September) and Ted Bryant (January 1892) challenged all England.

18 February 1891. (142lbs) Tommy Ryan w rtd 76 (finish) Danny Needham.
Venue: Twin City AC, Minneapolis, Minnesota, USA. **Referee:** Joe Mannix.
Fight Summary: Ryan (139) admitted prior to the fight that if he was to be a world champion, Needham (138½) would have to be eliminated, just as Con Doyle (knocked out in 28 rounds) had been in a barn in Shelby on 6 September 1890. Although there was no title billing as such, the *Chicago Tribune* reported it as being the greatest (four ounce) glove fight seen in the USA up to that time, while the *New Orleans Daily Picayune* supported Ryan's claim to be recognised as the American 142lbs champion on the result. This was after Ryan had knocked Needham down time and again before the latter's seconds threw the sponge in at the end of the 76th round.

Born Joseph Youngs, Ryan also had a good claim to the American 140lbs title, but as a growing lad he did not box below that weight again.

11 March 1891. (142/144lbs) Harry Nickless w rtd 6 (20) Johnny Robinson.
Venue: Ormonde Club, Walworth, London, England. **Referee:** J. T. McNeil.
Fight Summary: Although billed for the English 144lbs title, with both men inside 142lbs Nickless (141) also had a valid claim to the 142lbs championship on his victory, which came when Robinson (141) was forced to retire after spraining his ankle. The contest had started with a rush as both men looked to get in early blows, and at the end of the fourth round it had become noticeable that Nickless was the more sprightly of the pair. In the fifth honours were even, solid blows from both hands finding their mark, but in the sixth it was Nickless who scored the first knockdown, a left-right to the jaw that sent Robinson down heavily. On getting up in a dazed state, after being battered along the ropes and going down again, Robinson was retired having hobbled back to his corner.

Another 142lbs English championship competition was decided when Joe Wilson knocked out Jack Ashman inside four rounds at Her Majesty's Theatre, Haymarket, London on 30 May.

Prior to this, two men - Ben Seth (who outpointed Dick Leary over four rounds at the Royal Agricultural Hall, Islington, London on 14 April 1888) and Ted Pritchard (who outpointed Dave Burke over four rounds at the Aquarium Theatre, Westminster, London on 8 December 1888) - had won 142lbs championship competitions. Bethnal Green's Burke, a veteran of the ring, should not be confused with his Lambeth namesake). Also, Ching Ghook (August 1888), Jim Kendrick (September 1888), Lachie Thomson (June 1889) and George Baxter (May 1890) either claimed the English 142lbs title or were challenging all England to decide it.

24 April 1891. (142lbs) Charley Kemmick w co 2 (finish) Jim Scully.
Venue: Twin City AC, Minneapolis, Minnesota, USA. **Referee:** Hank Sealey.
Fight Summary: Billed for the American 142lbs title, after a general feeling-out period in the opening round Kemmick (141½) got to work with the right hand in the second, and after a few moments of sparring he sent Scully (142) down to be counted out. Kemmick, who never really made his claim stick, died of consumption on 23 August 1895, aged 25.

9 August 1891. (144lbs) Tommy Ryan w co 3 (finish) Billy McMillan.
Venue: Richardson Milk Station, Texas, USA. **Referee:** Malachy Hogan.
Fight Summary: Made at 144lbs, and contested in two-ounce gloves, it was reported to be for the not very well defined welterweight title according to the *Chicago Tribune*, and took place 46 miles west of the Chicago St Paul and Kansas City railroad. Although McMillan was outclassed he did at least put Ryan down in the second before being dropped three times himself in the same round. The fight was settled in the third when McMillan was knocked out by a straight left drive to the jaw.

30 November 1891. (142lbs) Harry Nickless w co 9 (20) Bill Hatcher.
Venue: Bolingbroke Club, Clapham, London, England. **Referee:** Robert Watson.
Fight Summary: Advertised as being for the English 142lbs championship, with the men quickly getting to work Nickless (139¾), his right eye already cut, almost had Hatcher (140) down with a series of right hands to the jaw in the second round. Again, in the fifth, Hatcher, his eyes closing fast, was almost floored, but despite being hurt he continued to mock Nickless's efforts. At the end of the ninth it was a rapidly tiring Nickless who appeared to be in a worse plight than Hatcher and, although both men had slowed considerably, it was the former who found the strength to drop his rival for the full count. It was a big left to the body followed by a right to the jaw that did the damage. Immediately afterwards, Nickless claimed the English 140 and 142lbs titles to go with his 144lbs crown.

13 December 1891. (144lbs) Tommy Ryan w co 14 (finish) Frank Howson.
Venue: Chicago, Illinois, USA. **Referee:** George Siler.
Fight Summary: According to the *New York Herald* and *Sporting Life*, this fight, which took place in an old skating rink, was billed for the world welter title at 144lbs. With four-ounce gloves in use it climaxed after Ryan feinted with the left before unleashing a right to the jaw which led to the count out in the 14th.

11 February 1892. (142lbs) William Robinson w co 6 (20) Frank Callan.
Venue: Goodwin Club, Shoreditch, London, England. **Referee:** Bernard J. Angle.
Fight Summary: Contested in four-ounce gloves and attracting English 142lbs billing, Robinson (141) was soon busying himself before being warned for forcing Callan (142) to the floor in the second round. Although Robinson was floored in the fourth he got up quickly to put down Callan with a drive to the body, only for the latter to come back stronger than ever. It could not last, and in the sixth Callan was knocked out by a heavy right uppercut after ducking down in an effort to avoid the punches coming his way.

2 May 1892. (142lbs) Tom Williams w co 1 (20) Bill Hatcher.
Venue: NSC, Covent Garden, London, England. **Referee:** Tom Anderson.
Fight Summary: Free of title billing in a contest made at 143lbs, Williams (142) extended his Imperial British Empire title claim at 140lbs following his win over Hatcher (142). Although lasting less than a round there was plenty of action after the men had rushed in swinging punches from both hands. The moment Hatcher was badly dazed from several blows to the jaw it was all over for him as Williams kept punching, and after knocking his man down again and again the Londoner was eventually counted out.

27 June 1892. (146lbs) Dick Burge w co 2 (20) Lachie Thomson.
Venue: Social Club, Kennington, London, England. **Referee:** George Vize.
Fight Summary: Given English title billing at 146lbs, following a relatively quiet opening round Burge (137½) turned on the power in the second to first stagger Thomson (142) and then drop him with a right cross to the jaw. Although Thomson somehow made it to his feet two further heavy blows to the point saw him counted out after he had been sent to his knees with his right arm twisted around the top rope. According to the *Licensed Victuallers Gazette* and *Newcastle Daily Chronicle* Burge gave away six pounds to his rival, while the *Sportsman* showed Burge to be 138lbs and Thomson 145. The poundage I have used was as reported in the *Sporting Life*.

30 July 1892. (142lbs) Tommy Ryan drew 17 (finish) Jack Wilkes.
Venue: South Omaha AC, Germania Hall, Omaha, Nebraska, USA. **Referee:** Frank Parmalee.
Fight Summary: Reported by the *Omaha World-Herald* to be for the American 142lbs welter title, the referee declared a draw after the police intervened at the beginning of round 17 following pressure from Wilkes' supporters who were on the verge of losing their wagers. Contested in skin-tight gloves, Ryan (141) had knocked Wilkes (141) down in the eighth, and in the 15th and 16th sessions he had repeatedly sent in solid uppercuts to the latter's head and body. The *Ring Record Book* gave the result as being a kayo win for Ryan.

26 September 1892. (142/144lbs) William Robinson w rtd 8 (20) Alf Suffolk.
Venue: NSC, Covent Garden, London, England. **Referee:** Tom Anderson.
Fight Summary: Billed for the English 144lbs championship, with Robinson (142) assuming an aggressive role in the sixth round he brought Suffolk to the boards just as time was called. Prior to that, both men had landed solidly to head and body. Early in the seventh Robinson twice fought Suffolk down, and in the last minute of the session he did whatever he wished before leaving his rival on the boards as the round came to an end. Still badly dazed, Suffolk was retired after the bell to start the eighth, being in no fit condition to continue. The very next day Robinson was claiming the English 142 and 144lb titles on his victory.

Robinson, who was looking to defend against Dick Burge at 142lbs, was challenged by Austin Gibbons and Harry Neumier, both domiciled in America, while George Baxter (September 1893) challenged the world at the weight.

5 December 1892. (144lbs) William Robinson w rtd 3 (20) Tom Burrows.
Venue: NSC, Covent Garden, London, England.
Fight Summary: There was no title billing, but with both men inside 143lbs Robinson's 144lbs title claim would have been at risk. This was a fight that should never have happened, with Burrows, the world champion sculler, participating in his very first contest, and by the end of the second round he had already taken a beating, going to his corner decidedly in need of a rest. After rushing Robinson in the third, Burrows was only saved from being floored by the ropes before being smashed down for 'eight' by a right to the head. Put down again, on seeing that his man had no chance, Paddy Slavin, Burrows' cornerman, advised the referee that his man was retiring before rushing into the ring to tend to him.

At the same venue on 20 February 1893, Robinson forced Jim Townsend to retire in the tenth round of a contest in which he had been due to defend his English 144lbs title. Unfortunately, Townsend scaled 150lbs, thus making the title event null and void. This was followed by challenges at 144lbs from Bill Cheese and Lachie Thomson (23 and 28 February 1893 respectively) and Anthony Diamond (September 1893).

Meanwhile, 144lbs English championship competitions at the Central Hall, Holborn, London were won by Ginger Stewart (who walked over Charlie Rowles on 20 October 1894 and then stopped Harry Collins inside two rounds on 6 April 1895) and Jack Fitzgibbon (who outpointed Harry Harrison over four rounds on 17 November 1894).

Following his contest with Harry Nickless at 140lbs on 14 May 1894, Dick Burge threatened to walk away from boxing before challenging the world at 144lbs and claiming the English title at that weight, while Cheese (September 1895), Andrew Newton (February 1896) and Stewart (August 1896) challenged all England at 144lbs.

14 December 1892. (142lbs) Mysterious Billy Smith w co 14 (finish) Danny Needham.
Venue: Pacific AC, Wigwam Theatre, San Francisco, California, USA. **Referee:** Walter Watson.
Fight Summary: Although no title billing was given in the *San Francisco Chronicle*, by his victory Smith (142) staked his claim at the weight after starting round 14 like a whirlwind and dropping Needham (143) twice before knocking him out following a tremendous right-hand uppercut.

17 April 1893. (142lbs) Mysterious Billy Smith w co 2 (finish) Tom Williams.
Venue: Coney Island AC, Brooklyn, NYC, New York, USA. **Referee:** Johnny Eckhardt.
Fight Summary: As far as the *San Francisco Chronicle* and *New York Herald* were concerned this was an advertised 142lbs title bout for 20 rounds or more, with both men inside 140lbs. Although Williams came to the ring with a win over fellow-Australian, George Dawson, the American 142lbs welterweight championship would only be fully settled after Smith met Tommy Ryan. Reckoned to be a terrific contest with everything packed into a few moments, Williams was knocked down by a heavy right-hand uppercut and counted out at 2.35 of round two.

11 December 1893. (146lbs) William Robinson drew 20 Tom Williams.
Venue: NSC, Covent Garden, London, England. **Referee:** Bernard J. Angle.
Fight Summary: Made at 146lbs, with Williams' Imperial British Empire title claim at stake, the latter started the contest with a rush, having Robinson (144) down from a heavy right to the head in the second round. Williams (144) was like a hurricane, attacking his man non-stop. However, missing more and more, after a few sessions it was clear that he had damaged his left, which would not be in use for the rest of the fight. Still, he was a real handful for Robinson, who cleverly used his left from distance. Despite not being delivered with force the majority got home. Towards the end there was much clinching as the fighters tired, and while the great majority thought Robinson had done enough the referee could not split them.

On 11 February 1895, Robinson (145¾) was disqualified in the tenth round of his contest at the Central Hall, Holborn, London against the American, Charley Johnson (145), and with the result away went all of his title claims regardless of continued representations.

26 July 1894. (142lbs) Tommy Ryan w pts 20 Mysterious Billy Smith.
Venue: Twin City AC, Minneapolis, Minnesota, USA. **Referee:** Joe Choynski.
Fight Summary: Billed for the championship, with both men inside the articled 142lbs, Smith made the running as Ryan stayed on the back foot, going down twice in the eighth round to avoid punishment before coming on strongly to do serious damage to his opponent's eyes by the 12th. In the 15th, Smith, by now tiring, went down, and was dropped twice more in the 19th prior to Ryan being awarded the decision.

6 August 1894. (146lbs) Danny Needham w rsc 5 (10) Louis Groeninger.
Venue: Hercules AC, Cincinnati, Ohio, USA. **Referee:** Jim Hall.
Fight Summary: Although billed for the welterweight title of America no weights were reported, but as Needham was fighting at around 146lbs at this moment in time that was quite probably the limit set. According to the *Galveston Daily News*, with the fight being a hot one, much blood being spilled, it was eventually stopped by the police at the end of the fifth round. The referee then awarded the fight to Needham. By this time it was apparent that Needham's career was coming to an end, and following a further eight contests, of which he won just two, he had retired.

13 September 1894. (146lbs) Tommy Ryan w co 4 (finish) Billy Layton.
Venue: Near St Joseph, Missouri USA. **Referee:** Andy Kisimar.
Fight Summary: Held on a sand bar in the middle of the Missouri River (near St Joseph, Missouri) on neutral territory after the contest had been banned from taking place in the town, it was reported in the *New York Herald* as a welterweight defence for Ryan (146). The fight was ended when Ryan, who had set Layton (146) up, sent in several heavy blows before a right under the ear forced a count out in the fourth.

18 January 1895. (146lbs) Tommy Ryan w rsc 3 (15) Nonpareil Jack Dempsey.
Venue: Coney Island AC, Brooklyn, NYC, New York, USA. **Referee:** Tim Hurst.

Fight Summary: Given title billing at 146lbs, Dempsey (142) was in such poor condition, having been dropped and hit at will by Ryan (145), that the referee pulled him out of a contest that proved to be his last. Even before the referee acted the crowd were calling for it to be stopped, some even thinking that Dempsey was drunk. Less than a year later he was dead, the victim of tuberculosis.

21 January 1895. (142lbs) Dick Burge w co 4 (20) Tom Williams.
Venue: NSC, Covent Garden, London, England. **Referee:** Bernard J. Angle.
Fight Summary: Made at 142lbs, after a dull opening round Burge (138lbs) picked up the pace in the second before having Williams (139½) over in the third. Starting the fourth where he left off, Burge was quickly on the attack and after fair pressure he floored Williams with a right to the jaw, the latter being counted out after hitting his head on the floor with great force. Burge successfully defended his English version of the world title against Williams, and in doing so he also took over the latter's Imperial British Empire title.

When Burge was presented with a solid gold belt, prescribed to the ten-stone champion of the world, it was reported in the *Sporting Life* that he would be foolish to ever box below 140lbs again as he had outgrown the weight class.

On 28 March, Tommy Ryan was matched with Burge for an NSC purse at 142lbs, and on the same day the Englishman accepted a challenge from Joe Walcott. However, neither fight came off.

6 May 1895. 142lbs) Arthur Valentine w pts 10 Charley Johnson.
Venue: Central Hall, Holborn, London, England. **Referee:** Jack Jones.
Fight Summary: Despite being an international bout at 142lbs it was not over a championship distance, although Valentine's claim was still at risk. As a contest it was poor, with Valentine merely rushing in to get a punch or two off before racing around the ring to avoid what was coming his way. When Johnson got too close for comfort on occasion Valentine threw himself to the floor, and several times he held the American round the waist while hitting him with the right. Unfortunately for Johnson, the referee, who was a local, never once warned Valentine for use of foul tactics. On top of that he ultimately gave him the decision rather than calling the whole thing off.

27 May 1895. (142lbs) Tommy Ryan drew 18 (45) Mysterious Billy Smith.
Venue: Coney Island AC, Brooklyn, NYC, New York, USA. **Referee:** Tim Hurst.
Fight Summary: Articled for 142lbs, with both inside, the fight was halted on the two-minute mark of the 18th after interference from the police. It had been a brutal affair, with a badly dazed Smith, half unconscious, hanging onto the ropes when the stoppage came. Earlier, in the 11th round, Ryan was so stunned that the referee called a halt with two minutes of the session unused following advice from the policeman in charge. Often reported as being a no contest, the result should have been given as a draw owing to an agreement being in place between the men to that effect.

With Ryan unable to make 142lbs again, Smith had a clear right to the title at that weight.

16 March 1896. (142lbs) Joe Walcott w co 7 (20) Scott Bright Eyes Collins.
Venue: New Eureka Club, Queens, NYC, New York, USA. **Referee:** Jimmy Carroll.
Fight Summary: Reported to be for the 'American black 142lbs title', it was a hard fight up until the end of the fifth round before Walcott took over. Collins was down seven times in the sixth, and after being dropped five more times in the seventh, the final punch being a crashing right to the jaw, he was counted out with just five seconds of the session remaining.

25 November 1896. (146lbs) Tommy Ryan w disq 9 (finish) Mysterious Billy Smith.
Venue: Empire AC, Maspeth, Queens, NYC, New York, USA. **Referee:** Tim Hurst.
Fight Summary: Following his defeat at the hands of Charles Kid McCoy when weighing 148lbs it is doubtful whether Ryan had much credibility as the welter champ thereafter, especially when you take into account that he was unable to make 142lbs (the key welterweight limit in America's eyes) any longer. Although the *Mirror of Life* reported it as a catchweight contest, with the *New York World* giving it as a world title fight it was thought to

involve Ryan's 146lbs claim. There were no knockdowns and not a great deal in it, but Smith was eventually thrown out in the ninth by the referee after ignoring countless warnings for hitting low and not breaking when told to do so. While Smith had done most of the leading, Ryan, his left eye badly cut in the eighth round, showed a sound defence.

28 January 1897. (144lbs) Dick Burge drew 10 (20) Eddie Connolly.
Venue: Olympic Club, Birmingham, England. **Referee:** George Dunning.
Fight Summary: Although made at catchweights, with it being advertised for the world 144lbs title it involved the Englishman's Imperial British Empire championship claim. At the opening bell Connolly (137) got away fast, showing lightning-like speed, before Burge (143) could settle. Dropped to his knees in the second round and cut over the left eye in the third, Connolly continued to force the action. In the sixth it looked as though the fight was over when Connolly was floored heavily, but after making several vain attempts to rise he was eventually saved by the bell. Having been knocked down several times in the seventh, Connolly came back strongly in the eighth. However, during that session they both went down together striking their heads on the floor, and although both were dazed they continued apace. Again, in the ninth Connolly was dropped several times, but at the end of the tenth the referee stepped into the ring to say that, as the management had ordered him to stop the bout, he had no other choice than to declare a draw. Burge, who was far more comfortable at this poundage than he had been at the lightweight limit, was virtually recognised by all and sundry as being the best man at the weight in England, if not the world.

Regardless of Burge's reputation, Pat Daly disputed his right to the 144lbs title a few days later.

24 February 1897. (146lbs) Tommy Ryan w rtd 9 (20) Tom Tracey.
Venue: Empire AC, The Alhambra, Syracuse, New York, USA. **Referee:** Yank Sullivan.
Fight Summary: Recorded in the *Ring Record Book* as involving the championship, Luckett Davis, the noted record compiler, unearthed the following extract from the *Philadelphia Item*. According to the *Item* the match was a catchweight affair that was restricted to 145lbs, with Tracey (139) several pounds lighter than his opponent. Had the Australian won he would almost certainly have claimed the 'popular' 142lbs title. The fight itself saw Tracey being put down several times when receiving an awful drubbing at the hands of Ryan (144) before his corner jumped into the ring while throwing up the sponge in the ninth round.

8 March 1897. (142lbs) Bill Whatley w co 4 (10) Tom Williams.
Venue: NSC, Covent Garden, London, England. **Referee:** Bernard J. Angle.
Fight Summary: Limited to ten rounds at 142lbs, the opening two sessions were well contested before Whatley (140) found that Williams was uncomfortable under pressure to the body in the third. Having landed heavily in that region, Whatley put Williams (142) down with a solid crack on the jaw before lefts and rights to the body had the latter down twice more. Saved by the bell, Williams came back strongly in the fourth prior to a right under the heart seeing him counted out. For Whatley it was an impressive victory, but despite claiming the English title at the weight he was unable to secure it.

17 March 1897. (145lbs) George Green w rtd 11 (finish) Mysterious Billy Smith.
Venue: Racetrack Arena, Carson City, Nevada, USA. **Referee:** Malachy Hogan.
Fight Summary: With Tommy Ryan inexorably moving towards the full middleweight ranks according to the *Police Gazette*, and despite the absence of individual weights, Green claimed the welter title following his victory over Smith at 145lbs. Refraining from using his left arm which had been broken three months earlier, Smith had by far the worst of it, being an open target for Green's left jab. With Smith looking to get to close quarters continuously the referee had his hands full breaking the men up as there was much fouling. At the end of the 11th round Smith went back to his corner to retire himself, saying that his left arm had been broken again, in the fourth, and that it was hopeless for him to carry on any longer.

26 May 1897. (145lbs) George Green w rsc 15 (20) Charlie McKeever.
Venue: National AC, Woodward's Pavilion, San Francisco, California, USA. **Referee:** Hiram Cook.

Fight Summary: Now that Green was claiming the 145lbs title, the *San Francisco Chronicle* reported this to be a great welter contest. The end came in the 15th round after both men were weary from their exertions, and McKeever, having taken terrific punishment to the body fell down in a corner immediately prior to the contest being stopped by the referee. Green, who set a terrific pace, had cut McKeever over the left eye in the second and had forced the fight throughout, while the latter relied on countering. Despite the omission of weights and the fact that Green looked to be several pounds heavier than McKeever, who was a natural welter at the time, the billing suggests that Green's title claim was on the line in this one.

31 May 1897. (142/144lbs) Tom Causer w disq 7 (20) Dick Burge.
Venue: NSC, Covent Garden, London, England. **Referee:** Bernard J. Angle.
Fight Summary: Billed for the English 144lbs title, by the sixth round Burge (142), who appeared to be in control at that stage, was making the body his target. Cautioned for a low blow after Causer (140) had knocked his punch down, an angry Burge was caught off guard and took a few shots that he should have avoided. With Burge well on top in the seventh Causer twice pushed blows below the belt, blatantly jumping up on the second occasion to allow the blow to go low, an action that saw Burge disqualified immediately. Most fight reports stated that Causer was never in with a chance, while rumours abounded that it had been a fix in order to drum up a return bout.

Meantime, Pat Daly challenged Causer to settle the 142 and 144lb championships before being followed by Jim Styles in July.

21 June 1897. (145/146lbs) Tommy Ryan w co 2 (20) Tom Williams.
Venue: Empire AC, Syracuse, New York, USA. **Referee:** Yank Sullivan.
Fight Summary: Reported as being for the welterweight championship of the world by the *Syracuse Herald*, another paper, the *Syracuse Courier*, reported that the forfeited weight limit was 145lbs and that both men were tipping the scales on the day of the fight. At the sound of the bell Williams charged into Ryan, who was content to dodge until opening up at the end of the round. The second session saw Ryan sending in lefts and rights to Williams' head and body, with the latter going down three times in order to avoid further punishment. Ryan was now rampant, and after Williams had clambered up on the third occasion he was despatched by a left to the temple prior to being counted out.

Putting on the pounds, Ryan fought at a higher weight from thereon in.

26 August 1897. (145lbs) Joe Walcott w co 18 (20) George Green.
Venue: Woodward's Pavilion, San Francisco, California, USA. **Referee:** Jack Welch.
Fight Summary: Even though no weights were given, the *Police Gazette* reported this as 'practically' a championship affair, while the *San Francisco Chronicle* claimed that the contest was being treated with all the consideration due to a title fight, labelling it as a battle for welter honours. Green shipped a tremendous amount of punishment, being down three times in the sixth, three times in the tenth, and once in the 18th before being knocked out from a series of heavy jolts to the jaw. By his victory, Walcott took over Green's 145lbs title claim.

8 October 1897. (144lbs) Dick Burge w co 1 (20) Tom Causer.
Venue: Bolingbroke Club, Clapham, London, England. **Referee:** Robert Watson.
Fight Summary: Given English and world title billing at 144lbs, the return between the two lasted just 61 seconds as Burge quickly took full revenge for his earlier disqualification defeat at the hands of Causer. Hurt by the opening punch of the fight, Causer landed just once before Burge pushed him away prior to sending in a terrific right to the jaw that sent the Londoner down to be counted out.

Despite threatening to quit boxing during January 1898, in March and April of that year both the *Mirror of Life* and *Sporting Life* reported that Burge should be recognised as the 144lbs world champion.

29 October 1897. (140/145lbs) Kid Lavigne w rtd 12 (20) Joe Walcott.
Venue: Occidental Club, Mechanics' Pavilion, San Francisco, California, USA. **Referee:** Ed Graney.

Fight Summary: Regardless that this one was a billed lightweight championship fight at 135lbs, Walcott's Californian title claims at 140, 142 and 145lbs passed to Lavigne on the result. Setting a terrific pace Lavigne's body blows sapped Walcott's strength and in the ninth round he suffered muscular cramps. Wishing to organise a draw at the end of the 11th but having been refused Walcott came out for the 12th before retiring himself at the end of the session. Although Walcott was inside 135lbs on the night he had weakened himself considerably, hence the disappointing performance.

8 November 1897. (146lbs) Tom Woodley w pts 20 Jim Styles.
Venue: NSC, Covent Garden, London, England. **Referee:** Bernard J. Angle.
Fight Summary: Made at 146lbs, many saw this as involving the English title at the weight due to Styles having outpointed William Robinson over eight rounds at the same venue on 4 February to win the final of a 146lbs competition that included the Australian, Tom Williams. Evenly contested, there was little to choose between them as first one man then the other got off good punches, and just when it looked as though Styles had the advantage Woodley came on strong in the last three rounds to make sure of the verdict. Although Woodley was put down in the 19th he was up without a count to carry on as though nothing had happened.

Throughout 1898 and most of 1899 both Woodley and Styles, who were claiming the English 146lbs championship, were challenged by Owen Sweeney (February 1898) for an NSC purse.

14 April 1898. (148lbs) Mysterious Billy Smith drew 25 Joe Walcott.
Venue: Park City Theatre, Bridgeport, Connecticut, USA. **Referee:** Sam Austin.
Fight Summary: Although the *Boston Post* reported it to be a catchweight contest with neither man to exceed 148lbs, the result proved nothing other than both were now claiming the title at the weight. The first ten rounds belonged to Smith, who led throughout and showed up well on the inside, while Walcott merely contented himself waiting for the Mysterious one to blow up. From the 11th onwards Walcott evened it up with heavy body blows hurting Smith, and although the latter came again he was unable to change the course of the fight.

29 July 1898. (148lbs) Mysterious Billy Smith w pts 25 George Green.
Venue: Lenox AC, Manhattan, NYC, New York, USA. **Referee:** Charlie White.
Fight Summary: Regarded as a title fight by the *1985 Ring Record Book*, Smith (147) was stronger and better than Green (146) throughout, outfighting and outboxing his man in virtually every round. Working well to the body Smith pounded Green whenever he got to close quarters, and although the latter stood up manfully there was only one winner. There were no knockdowns. Despite successfully defending his 148lbs claim, Smith would not be generally recognised until he defeated Matty Matthews at 142lbs.

26 August 1898. (142lbs) Mysterious Billy Smith w pts 25 Matty Matthews.
Venue: Lenox AC, Manhattan, NYC, New York, USA. **Referee:** Charlie White.
Fight Summary: With the *New York Herald* reporting that both men were inside the agreed 142lbs, Smith, whose foul tactics were more than noticeable, made a good start and was the aggressor throughout. At the end of the 14th Matthews claimed that he had been hit low, but after the referee ignored him he used sprint tactics to keep his distance. Despite that, Smith had Matthews down in the 17th and 23rd rounds but was unable to find a finishing blow. On the result, Smith was generally recognised in America as the new leader of the weight class.

5 September 1898. (145lbs) Mysterious Billy Smith drew 25 Andy Walsh.
Venue: Greater New York AC, Brooklyn, NYC, New York, USA. **Referee:** Alec Brown.
Fight Summary: Recorded in the *Ring Record Book* as a title fight, it was contested at 145lbs and belonged to Smith's claim at that weight. Mainly fought at close quarters with both men concentrating on the body, it was no surprise that holding and hitting occurred on a regular basis. It was a tough one to handle, with even the referee getting struck at times, and while Smith was the cleverer, Walsh, whose face was badly swollen at the final bell, gave as good as he got.

3 October 1898. (142lbs) Mysterious Billy Smith w co 20 (20) Jim Judge.
Venue: American SC, Scranton, Pennsylvania, USA. **Referee:** Sam Austin.

Fight Summary: According to the *Scranton Times* this was a billed 142lbs title fight, with both men being inside the prescribed weight at the 3pm weigh-in. In showing a marked superiority throughout Smith punished Judge severely before eventually finding the finishing blow, a terrific right hook that sent the latter hurtling to the floor to be counted out in the 20th.

7 October 1898. (142lbs) Mysterious Billy Smith w pts 25 Charlie McKeever.
Venue: Lenox AC, Manhattan, NYC, New York, USA. **Referee:** Charlie White.
Fight Summary: While there was no mention of it being a title clash in the *New York Herald*, both men were announced as being inside the championship limit of 142lbs. With that being so, it obviously involved Smith's claim at the weight. Both men showed much cleverness in blocking punches, but the one blow that McKeever found difficult to avoid was the right delivered by Smith to the kidneys when infighting. The *Brooklyn Eagle* reported that Smith demonstrated his right to be called the champion when controlling the fight from start to finish. Although McKeever dropped Smith in the 22nd round, unable to sustain any pressure the latter was soon back to return the compliment in the 25th as he moved on to an easy win.

25 November 1898. (142lbs) Kid Lavigne w pts 20 Tom Tracey.
Venue: Woodward's Pavilion, San Francisco, California, USA. **Referee:** Jim McDonald.
Fight Summary: Reported by the *San Francisco Chronicle* as a 142lbs title fight, with Lavigne expected to scale 134lbs and Tracey between 138 and 140, this was a defence of the former's Californian welter claim at the weight. For the opening ten rounds it was fairly even as Tracey used all of his cleverness and fleet of foot to keep out of the main firing line, but from thereon in it was Lavigne's aggression that took him to the front as his rival tired. There were no knockdowns reported, but Tracey, who had been hurt by body shots, surprisingly came back in the final two sessions to keep Lavigne guessing.

6 December 1898. (145lbs) Mysterious Billy Smith w pts 20 Joe Walcott.
Venue: Lenox AC, Manhattan, NYC, New York, USA. **Referee:** Charlie White.
Fight Summary: Billed for the 145lbs championship, at this moment in time Smith was claiming the 142, 145 and 148lb titles. Both men showed wonderful ability to accept their punishment, with Walcott taking blows to the head that would have finished most men, but apart from the 11th round when he was dropped by a heavy right he looked impregnable. Badly handicapped in reach, Walcott was often unable to stop Smith from reaching him, and as the latter did most of the forcing it gave him a decided advantage. Prior to the contest it was thought that Smith had left his best days behind and that Walcott had a great chance, but the champion proved the doubters wrong when giving one of his finest displays.

12 December 1898. (144lbs) Bobby Dobbs w rtd 8 (20) Dick Burge.
Venue: People's Palace, Newcastle, England. **Referee:** George Dunning.
Fight Summary: Advertised as being for the world 144lbs title, with Burge having knocked Dobbs down at least three times in the opening three sessions it looked as though the fight would not be lasting much longer. Surprisingly, however, despite having clinched on innumerable occasions to save himself by the end of the fifth round Dobbs was beginning to get to Burge. The sixth and seventh were much better rounds for Dobbs as Burge weakened, and the eighth was full of fierce fighting, culminating in Charlie Mitchell, who was in the Englishman's corner, illegally entering the ring and calling for a foul. When Mitchell said he was not allowing Burge to continue the referee handed the decision to Dobbs amidst much cheering.

This fight effectively spelt the end of Burge in the weight class, regardless of him continuing to claim the English 144lbs title right up until August 1900. Having tried hard to make a match with Pat Daly, who repeatedly challenged him, Burge never seemed to be available when a match was on the cards.

24 January 1899. (148lbs) Mysterious Billy Smith w co 14 (25) Australian Billy Edwards.
Venue: Lenox AC, Manhattan, NYC, New York, USA. **Referee:** Charlie White.
Fight Summary: Made at 147lbs, this was a defence of his American claim at 148lbs for Smith, who despatched Edwards with a heavy right to the jaw in the 14th after flooring his rival several times and hurting him with body blows.

22 February 1899. (144lbs) Bobby Dobbs nc 1 (20) Pat McDonald.
Venue: Wellington Palace, Glasgow, Scotland. **Referee:** George Dunning.
Fight Summary: Recognised as a defence of Dobbs' 144lbs title despite being contested over two-minute rounds, the fight was halted when the police climbed into the ring and arrested both men for assault. The action came about when McDonald, having only his second contest, should have been disqualified after being knocked out of the ring and helped back in again. With the police not recognising the mood of the audience a full-scale riot ensued. It came as no surprise that the men were immediately rematched, the fight being switched to England.

1 March 1899. (144lbs) Bobby Dobbs w co 2 (20) Pat McDonald.
Venue: Standard Theatre, Gateshead, England. **Referee:** George Dunning.
Fight Summary: A return fight at 144lbs saw the badly-matched McDonald knocked out in the second round. Although McDonald began reasonably well it was soon clear that Dobbs had been carrying him throughout the first round when he opened up in the second. Knocked down heavily by a right to the head it was a surprise that McDonald made it to his feet, but following a tremendous left hook to the jaw he crashed down with no chance of ever beating the count.

At this point in time Dobbs' 144lbs title claim did not even make an impact in Britain, let alone America, and was quickly forgotten.

10 March 1899. (142lbs) Mysterious Billy Smith w disq 14 (20) Kid Lavigne.
Venue: Woodward's Pavilion, San Francisco, California, USA. **Referee:** Jim McDonald.
Fight Summary: Regarded as involving the 142lbs title, Lavigne (139) had a slight lead by the 14th round before being badly shaken up in that session. When Lavigne's brother jumped into the ring the referee stopped the fight, awarding the decision to Smith (142). Certain papers also recorded this as a stoppage win for Smith.

Meantime, in England, Pat Daly, who was still trying to get his hands on the vacant English 142lbs title, challenged Johnny Hughes and any man in the world on 20 November 1900. This was followed by challenges to all England from Jewey Cook (October 1901), Owen Sweeney and Harry Ward (November 1901) and Charlie Knock (December 1901), with nothing ever settled.

30 June 1899. (145lbs) Mysterious Billy Smith drew 20 Charlie McKeever.
Venue: Broadway AC, Manhattan, NYC, New York, USA. **Referee:** Johnny White.
Fight Summary: The *New York Herald* reported this one to involve Smith's 145lbs title claim, and for long spells McKeever did not look out of it as he cut his rival up badly around the eyes. While Smith's showing was disappointing he was at least the aggressor throughout, administering the most punishment, especially to the body, but McKeever proved almost equally as good downstairs while producing the better left-hand work to secure a share of the spoils.

6 November 1899. (146lbs) Pat Daly w pts 15 Tom Woodley.
Venue: NSC, Covent Garden, London, England. **Referee:** Bernard J. Angle.
Fight Summary: Although there was no title billing attached, Daly (145) claimed the English 146lbs title following his win over Woodley (146). Reported to be a bout full of give and take it was relatively even up until the ninth when Woodley was dropped to his knees by a left to the ribs, and on getting up was cautioned for going down again without being hit. Subsequently, although Daly slipped down in the 12th, followed by them both falling together in the same round, he had the edge, his skill and trickiness ultimately winning him the day over the game Woodley.

8 November 1899. (145lbs) Mysterious Billy Smith w pts 20 Charlie McKeever.
Venue: Broadway AC, Manhattan, NYC, New York, USA. **Referee:** Johnny White.
Fight Summary: In a return match, the *New York Herald* reported that while this contest was made at catchweights it still involved Smith's claim at 145lbs. Other press reports stated that McKeever (144) looked to be much heavier than his recorded weight. Making a solid start McKeever had the better of things early on, but Smith (145) came back strongly and was fighting flat out in the latter stages as he looked to knock his man out. In the 19th round

Smith had McKeever badly dazed from right uppercuts before swinging the latter heavily to the floor for a count, and in the final session he had the latter groggy again but was unable to finish it.

13 December 1899. (146lbs) Tom Woodley w pts 15 Jewey Cook.
Venue: Goodwin Club, Shoreditch, London, England. **Referee:** Tommy Orange.
Fight Summary: Even though this one was contested at catchweights, with Woodley challenging all England at 144/146lbs a few weeks later it mirrored the weight that he made for Cook. By all intents and purposes this one was said to be a poor fight, with far too much hugging and very little good work taking place. In the fourth round Woodley landed the best blow of the fight, sending Cook down with a countering right, and in the sixth the latter was stunned by solid blows to head and body before making it back to his corner on shaky legs. The remainder of the fight was less than interesting prior to the referee giving the casting vote to Woodley.

By August 1900, Woodley, along with Pat Daly, Billy Morgan, Jim Styles and Owen Sweeney, was looking to pick up the vacant English 144lbs title that had become available following Dick Burge's retirement.

Throughout 1901, Cook issued challenges to additional men such as Jack Palmer to sort out the English 144lbs championship to no avail.

There was renewed activity, however, in 1902 when Cook won an English championship competition at the weight on outpointing Dave Barry over seven rounds at Wonderland, Mile End, London on 11 January, and Daly and Charlie Knock (14 May) challenged all England.

15 January 1900. (145lbs) Rube Ferns w disq 21 (25) Mysterious Billy Smith.
Venue: Hawthorne AC, Buffalo, New York, USA. **Referee:** Ed McBride.
Fight Summary: Contested at 145lbs, Ferns, who had been floored 15 times, was declared the winner by disqualification in the 21st round, thus taking over Smith's claim at the weight. After continuously striking Ferns, badly cut around the eyes, with vicious body blows in the clinches, Smith was warned for going low but took no notice and paid the ultimate consequence. Although Ferns had given a wonderful exhibition of endurance, the majority of fans thought that Smith had been robbed.

26 January 1900. (148lbs) Mysterious Billy Smith w co 22 (25) Frank McConnell.
Venue: Broadway AC, Manhattan, NYC, New York, USA. **Referee:** Johnny White.
Fight Summary: According to the *New York Herald* this contest was made at 148lbs, thus involving Smith's claim at that weight. While McConnell generally showed himself to be clever he lacked the strength to keep Smith at arm's length indefinitely. Gradually weakening, McConnell took the count after being decked by a heavy left swing to the jaw in the 22nd round.

22 February 1900. (145lbs) Rube Ferns w pts 20 Mike Donovan.
Venue: Hawthorne AC, Buffalo, New York, USA. **Referee:** Ed McBride.
Fight Summary: Advertised as a world title fight at 145lbs according to the *Buffalo Courier*, Ferns' title claim at the weight was on the line in this one. And while Donovan gave a game and aggressive display he was generally playing second fiddle. The only knockdown of the contest saw Donovan down in the 19th round from a right swing to the side of the head.

12 March 1900. (145lbs) Mysterious Billy Smith drew 25 Jack Mahoney.
Venue: Hercules AC, Brooklyn, NYC, New York, USA. **Referee:** Joe Ward.
Fight Summary: With Smith still claiming the American 145lbs title despite his loss at the weight to Rube Ferns, the *New York Herald* reported this to be a 145lbs title defence by him. Proving a surprise package, Mahoney would surely have won if he could have punched harder and gone forward a bit more, but as it was he made life miserable for Smith with his clever blocking, feinting tactics and countering straight lefts. Although Smith made the running he could rarely find a way through, often being outscored at the rate of two to one. It was clear in the aftermath that Smith got a share of the decision purely because of his aggression.

17 April 1900. (142lbs) Matty Matthews w co 19 (20) Mysterious Billy Smith.
Venue: Broadway AC, Manhattan, NYC, New York, USA. **Referee:** Johnny White.
Fight Summary: Billed for the 142lbs 'popular' welter championship, Matthews took over the title as he outpointed and outgeneraled Smith from start to finish. The end came after Smith had wrestled Matthews to the floor, only to be knocked out in the 19th when the latter got up to land three heavy rights to his head that sent him crashing.

4 May 1900. (142lbs) Matty Matthews drew 10 Kid Parker.
Venue: Athletic Club, Denver, Colorado, USA. **Referee:** Billy Woods.
Fight Summary: Reported by the *Rocky Mountain News* to be a billed 142lbs welterweight title fight, Matthews had recently won the American 142lbs championship when beating Mysterious Billy Smith (w co 19 at the Broadway AC, Manhattan, NYC, New York on 17 April), and with both men inside the articled 140lbs his title claim at that weight was also up for grabs. Proving to be a useful opponent for Matthews, even though Parker was dropped in the sixth round by a right swing to the jaw and a body shot he was soon back on his feet, shooting out jabs and punches as if nothing had happened.

24 May 1900. (142lbs) Rube Ferns w co 1 (20) Jack Bennett.
Venue: Crescent AC, Mutual Street Rink, Toronto, Canada. **Referee:** Jack Sheehan.
Fight Summary: Calling himself the welter champion after beating Mysterious Billy Smith at 145lbs, Ferns defended his claim against Bennett at 142lbs in a fight billed for the title. There was very little fighting done for the first couple of minutes due to each man sizing the other up but, after both came together and were told to break by the referee, Bennett stepped back dropping his hands to his sides while Ferns jumped in and smashed in a solid right to the head, followed by a left hook to the jaw to drop his rival. With Bennett stretched out on the canvas and counted out after just two minutes and 20 seconds, Ferns later said that he did not step back on being asked to break as he was not obliged to do so according to the agreement.

5 June 1900. (142lbs) Eddie Connolly w pts 25 Matty Matthews.
Venue: Seaside AC, Brooklyn, NYC, New York, USA. **Referee:** Billy Madden.
Fight Summary: Although a billed 142lbs welterweight title fight, with both men inside 140lbs the Canadian was also looking to take over Matthews' claim at that weight as well. In four meetings between the pair Connolly had never won, but this time he got away well and was never headed. While Matthews appeared to have left his fight at home, Connolly found his face repeatedly with slashing left swings and scored three knockdowns, in the 11th, 18th and 25th rounds that made the referee's decision easy.

13 August 1900. (142lbs) Rube Ferns w rtd 15 (25) Eddie Connolly.
Venue: Olympic AC, Buffalo, New York, USA. **Referee:** Ed McBride.
Fight Summary: The *Buffalo Courier* stated that the American 142lbs title changed hands on the result, but with both men weighing in below 140lbs Ferns also took over Connolly's claim at that weight. The fight itself was evenly contested up to the 15th, but things changed in that round after Ferns landed three blows below the ribs that saw Connolly backed up and reeling against the ropes before his corner threw in the towel.

30 August 1900. (142lbs) Rube Ferns w pts 15 Matty Matthews.
Venue: Light Guard Armoury, Detroit, Michigan, USA. **Referee:** Malachy Hogan.
Fight Summary: Ferns successfully defended the American 142lbs title in this one after what had been a good, clean contest. While the press generally reported that a draw would have been fairer, the referee stated that he had awarded Ferns the decision on the basis of him having landed at the rate of three to one.

16 October 1900. (142lbs) Matty Matthews w pts 15 Rube Ferns.
Venue: Light Guard Armoury, Detroit, Michigan, USA. **Referee:** George Siler.
Fight Summary: Advertised as being for the 142lbs welterweight title, with the men inside 140lbs (as far as the *Toledo Bee* was concerned) on the afternoon of the fight, Matthews regained both titles on winning. According to the *Detroit Free Press*, however, both men weighed in at 141½lbs on the afternoon of the contest. Despite Ferns

coming into the fight handicapped by an injury to his left shoulder, Matthews, who did the lion's share of the leading, still had to work hard to secure victory as the former proved to be a difficult obstacle to overcome.

29 April 1901. (142lbs) Matty Matthews w pts 20 Tom Couhig.
Venue: New Monarch AC, Buckingham Theatre, Louisville, Kentucky, USA. **Referee:** George English.
Fight Summary: In a match made at 140lbs, this was also a defence of Matthews' 142lbs welterweight title and, although Couhig (139) had the better of it up to the eighth round, in the ninth after his nose was broken the tide turned. From then on Matthews (139½) moved ahead, almost having Couhig, badly cut on the left eye, out in the 13th before settling for a points win.

24 May 1901. (142lbs) Rube Ferns w co 10 (20) Matty Matthews.
Venue: Crescent AC, Mutual Street Rink, Toronto, Canada. **Referee:** Marvin Smith.
Fight Summary: Made at 142lbs, up until the end Matthews had much the better of Ferns, but in the tenth session everything changed after the latter rushed his rival through the ropes. On the resumption, Ferns quickly put Matthews down for a moment, and when the latter got to his feet he was immediately dropped again by a tremendous left prior to being counted out.

According to Patsy Sweeney (*The Ring* magazine, page 39, May 1925), he had a crack at Matthews' welter title on 2 September 1901 at the Nutmeg AC, Hartford, Connecticut. Whether Matthews was still claiming the title I am not sure, but in a fight made at 138/140lbs he came in six pounds over the weight and outpointed Sweeney over 20 rounds. If Sweeney, inside 140lbs, had won I guess he could have had a weak claim, but he was well beaten by Matthews, even going down in the 19th round to avoid punishment.

23 September 1901. (142lbs) Rube Ferns w co 9 (20) Frank Erne.
Venue: International AC, Fort Erie, Ontario, Canada. **Referee:** Ed McBride.
Fight Summary: The *Sporting Life* and the *Philadelphia Item* reported that the contest had been made at 142lbs with both men on the weight. Having been knocked down in the first round it was noticeable that Erne lacked the power of Ferns and, after getting up from a long left that had dropped him in the ninth, a heavy right sent him down for the full count.

28 November 1901. (145lbs) Rube Ferns w pts 15 Charles Dutch Thurston.
Venue: Light Guard Armoury, Detroit, Michigan, USA. **Referee:** Malachy Hogan.
Fight Summary: Even though no weights were given the *Chicago Tribune* stated that Ferns made a successful defence against Thurston, while the *Detroit Free Press* confirmed that this was a defence of Ferns' 145lbs title claim with both men making the weight. Whilst Thurston was the quicker and ducked and blocked beautifully at times, Ferns' blows were by far the more effective despite the crowd calling for a draw.

18 December 1901. (142lbs) Joe Walcott w rsc 5 (20) Rube Ferns.
Venue: International AC, Fort Erie, Ontario, Canada. **Referee:** Ed McBride.
Fight Summary: With both men inside the stipulated 142lbs the title changed hands after Ferns was rescued by the referee in the fifth, having been downed twice and battered by terrific body blows, as well as by heavy right and left swings to the head.

On 1 April 1903, Walcott drew over 20 rounds against Billy Woods at Hazard's Pavilion, Los Angeles, California. Listed as a title fight in the *Ring Record Book*, I have yet to ascertain the weights. Although advertised on the day of the fight as being for the welterweight championship of the world, a few days later Woods' manager was telling local reporters that his man would fight anyone who could make 158lbs at a 3pm weigh-in.

20 January 1902. (146lbs) Tom Woodley w co 14 (15) Jim Styles.
Venue: Ginnett's Circus, Newcastle, England. **Referee:** Ed Plummer.
Fight Summary: Billed for the English 146lbs title, with both men inside the weight, it was one of the best contests ever seen on Tyneside and placed Woodley at the top of the 146lbs championship tree. The two men started as they meant to carry on when unloading heavy punches, and in the second round Woodley had Styles on one knee

from a terrific left to the face. Both men continued fighting fiercely as the action swung back and forth with first one man landing heavily followed by the other, but after several first-class sessions it was felt that Styles was ahead on points at the end of the tenth. It looked as though Woodley was finished in the 12th, having been floored by a right to the jaw, but he recovered well in the 13th to have Styles down from a swinging right to the head before sending him down for the full count with a short left to the body in the 14th.

21 June 1902. (144lbs) Eddie Connolly w pts 15 Pat Daly.
Venue: NSC, Covent Garden, London, England. **Referee:** Tom Scott.
Fight Summary: Given world 144lbs title billing, neither man held back, and following some good fighting both hit the floor in the third round, Connolly for the second time. However, it was Connolly who showed up the better as the fight progressed, having Daly groggy on more than one occasion, and in the eighth the latter twice visited the floor. Although Daly was put on the deck twice in the tenth he was still strong while looking none the worse for wear. The last five sessions were of an excellent nature, Daly giving as good as he got at times, but at the final bell it was Connolly's cleverer work that entitled him to the verdict.

23 June 1902. (144lbs) George Penny w pts 10 Peter Brown.
Venue: New Adelphi Club, The Strand, London, England. **Referee:** Harry Cooper.
Fight Summary: Advertised for the English title (thought to be 140 to 144lbs) and Coronation Championship Belt, it was Penny who started the better of the pair with long left leads scoring consistently. After five rounds, with Penny ahead, Brown began to cut back the deficit when picking up the pace before eventually tiring from his efforts. Some rousing fighting took place in the last two rounds with Brown on the front foot, but it was Penny who received the unanimous decision, the judges recognising his excellent left-hand work. Cut from 15 to ten rounds in view of Penny being a substitute for Jim Maloney, the result carried no weight at all for the winner.

15 September 1902. (144lbs) Tom Woodley w pts 11 (10) Eddie Connolly.
Venue: Wonderland, Mile End, London, England. **Referee:** Tom Goodwin.
Fight Summary: Reported as a fight to decide the world 144lbs title, regardless of the fact that it was not contested under full championship conditions it did not stop Woodley from claiming the English title at the weight on winning. However, on reading the *Sporting Life* fight report it would seem that Connolly was robbed as he fought Woodley all over the ring at times, and while there were no knockdowns before the end of normal time he appeared to have landed most of the heavy punches. With the tenth undoubtedly being the best round of the fight, both men having gone hammer and tongs, the referee, considering it even, asked them box another session. In the decider, having had Woodley over from a hard body punch and fighting on even terms Connolly still lost.

22 December 1902. (145lbs) Matty Matthews w pts 10 Rube Ferns.
Venue: Kenyon's Hall, Pittsburgh, Pennsylvania, USA. **Referee:** Buck Cornelius.
Fight Summary: Made at 145lbs, the contest was fast and scientific, Matthews outclassing Ferns in all bar the clinches where the latter did his best work. Nine rounds clearly belonged to Matthews, but in the sixth after being badly troubled by a vicious attack from Ferns he had to defend for all his worth to get through. Following the contest between two former titleholders, Matthews claimed the 'white' version of the title at that weight.

22 December 1902. (148lbs) Bobby Dobbs drew 20 Joe White.
Venue: Grand Theatre, Cardiff, Wales. **Referee:** Edward Humphreys.
Fight Summary: Articled at 148lbs, the result proved nothing, especially as it was contested over two-minute rounds. The first six sessions were evenly fought before the seventh saw both men on the attack, the round ending with Dobbs (148) being floored twice after White (146) had got his right and left hands working in harmony. At this stage, with Dobbs weak he again visited the boards in the eighth. However, in the ninth, after Dobbs made a great recovery, it was White's turn to hit the floor following a tremendous left-hand swing. Dobbs was now in the ascendancy, winning many of the latter rounds, but White's early lead ultimately held him in good stead when a drawn verdict was given.

This was the first distance fight at the weight held in Britain for over ten years, and despite Tom Woodley (October 1898) and Jim Styles (September 1899) challenging all England for supremacy at the weight since 1898 nothing concrete had happened. However, with Woodley continuing to challenge all England at 148lbs throughout the following four years he appeared to have the best claim to the English title when throwing down the gauntlet to the winner of Dobbs v White.

26 January 1903. (146lbs) Eddie Connolly w pts 15 Tom Woodley.
Venue: NSC, Covent Garden, London, England. **Referee:** J. H. Douglas.
Fight Summary: Accorded world 146lbs title billing, and involving the Imperial British Empire championship at the weight, although Woodley (145) was always in the fight against the clever, hard-hitting Connolly (144) he was ultimately unable to swing things his way. After a third round in which Connolly seemed to have Woodley at his mercy, the next couple of sessions witnessed some fearfully hard exchanges before the latter was dropped in the sixth following a heavy blow to the jaw. On getting up Woodley then went down without being hit, for which he received a caution. Thereafter, however, Woodley held his own in many of the rallies, but it was the better boxing of the Canadian that won him the decision.

Matched for a return contest at 146lbs at the Warwickshire Horse Repository, Birmingham on 13 April, Woodley pulled out, leaving Connolly to face Pat Daly, who was almost a stone heavier. Despite the weight difference, Connolly was good value for the 20-round points decision even though he was twice floored.

Meanwhile, Woodley continued to claim the English 148lbs title, being joined by Peter Brown (who won a 148lbs championship competition at the International AC, Marylebone, London on 4 January 1904, outpointing Jack Kingsland over six rounds).

23 February 1903. (145lbs) Matty Matthews w pts 10 Tom Couhig.
Venue: Allegheny AC, Mason Hall, Pittsburgh, Pennsylvania, USA. **Referee:** Buck Connelly.
Fight Summary: Matthews, who was introduced as the 145lbs 'white welterweight champion', defended his title claim in this one according to the *Pittsburgh Gazette*. Matthews had the better of it throughout, catching Couhig's early rushes with heavy swings to the jaw before dropping him twice in the fifth. Although being put down again in the ninth, a heavy right to the jaw doing the job, Couhig held on to hear the final bell.

28 February 1903. (142lbs) Jack Nelson w pts 20 Tom Ireland.
Venue: Ginnett's Circus, Newcastle, England. **Referee:** J. R. Smoult.
Fight Summary: Contested at 142lbs, it became clear that Nelson (141) would be making the body his target for the night, while Ireland (142½) was always dangerous with right-hand counters. In the seventh Ireland was dropped by a heavy left to the ribs, but after gamely coming back he was fighting as hard as Nelson at the bell. Both men went well for the next few rounds, but when Ireland began to tire from his exertions in the 13th Nelson stepped up a gear when beginning to land more frequently on both the head and body. In the 17th Nelson had Ireland over again, but was unable to finish him off despite hitting him with everything he had. Although the Londoner surprisingly came back refreshed in the 18th, making it to the final bell, the decision was a formality. On winning, Nelson automatically took over from Ireland at the weight before concentrating on his 140lbs title claim as the 142lbs weight class went on hold.

25 April 1903. (146lbs) Charlie Knock w co 4 (10) Tom Woodley.
Venue: Wonderland, Mile End, London, England. **Referee:** Joe Hyman.
Fight Summary: Thought to have been made at 146lbs, right from the start it could be seen that Knock had a decided advantage in height and reach, and in the second round he dropped Woodley with a swinging right after setting him up with heavy lefts. Getting up in good condition, Woodley tore into Knock for the rest of the session. Despite that, the third round saw Woodley floored four times before a right under the heart in the fourth, that followed several heavy blows, dropped him for the full count. Although it was contested over ten two-minute rounds Knock claimed the English 144lbs title, a statement refuted by Woodley, who said that Knock had no right to call himself the English champion at 144lbs as he held the championship belt. Woodley went on to say that he would fight Knock, or anyone else, at 144lbs any time over 20 three-minute rounds for an NSC purse.

115

On 6 October, after Knock failed to show at the offices of the *Sporting Life* when due to sign for an English 144lbs title fight against Pat Daly he forfeited to the latter.

Later in the year, on 21 December, America's Jack Clancy also failed to turn up at the *Sporting Life* offices to sign for a bout with Daly that would decide the world 144lbs title.

27 April 1903. (145lbs) Rube Ferns w rsc 19 (20) Matty Matthews.
Venue: International AC, Fort Erie, Ontario, Canada. **Referee:** Ed McBride.
Fight Summary: Ferns once again laid claim to the 'white welterweight title' following his victory at 145lbs. It was Ferns all the way, with Matthews going down 16 times and taking plenty of punishment before the referee pulled him out in the 19th round after he had injured his leg in a tumble.

28 May 1903. (142lbs) Martin Duffy w co 13 (20) Rube Ferns.
Venue: Music Hall, Louisville, Kentucky, USA.
Fight Summary: Articled at 142lbs, the *Chicago Tribune* confirmed the billing to be for the 'white American welterweight title', currently in the possession of Ferns. Proving to be a cut above what was expected, Duffy showed himself to be the complete master of Ferns as he jabbed him silly and pounded his face into a bloody mess before knocking him out with a single right hand in the 13th. Mindful of Ferns' punching ability, Duffy had used his good footwork, longer reach and blocking ability to negate much of the champion's work as he gradually ground him down.

18 June 1903. (150lbs) Joe Walcott drew 20 Young Peter Jackson.
Venue: Pastime AC, Portland, Oregon, USA. **Referee:** Jim Neil.
Fight Summary: Reported as a 150lbs world title fight by the *Morning Oregonian*, for the opening eight rounds there was little in it with both men content to take punishment. However, after Jackson pulled himself together from the ninth onwards it appeared to be his fight. He certainly was the one looking to win, it being only Walcott's clever work on the inside that gave him hope. Trying desperately to land a knockout blow Jackson tore into Walcott during the last three sessions, and although the latter was punched all over the ring he survived. Maybe the fighters had a pre-fight agreement as to the decision if both were still standing at the end of the contest, but to all intents and purposes Jackson should have been returned the winner.

3 July 1903. (142lbs) Joe Walcott w co 3 (10) Mose LaFontise.
Venue: Broadway Theatre, Butte, Montana, USA. **Referee:** Duncan McDonald.
Fight Summary: Made at 142lbs, the *Anaconda Standard* reported that both men were inside the weight, and once underway it was clear to see who would win after Walcott dropped LaFontise several times early on. Able to get inside his rival's guard with apparent ease, Walcott rushed LaFontise at the start of the third round, swinging vicious punches to head and body, before a short right-arm blow to the solar plexus put the latter down and out.

25 August 1903. (145lbs) Martin Duffy w pts 10 Matty Matthews.
Venue: Athletic Club Auditorium, Port Huron, Michigan, USA. **Referee:** Ed McBride.
Fight Summary: According to the *Chicago Tribune* report this was billed for the 'white title' at 145lbs, while the *Detroit Free Press* called it a battle for the light welterweight championship. The *Port Huron Daily Herald* reported that Duffy made the pace in the majority of rounds, landing at the rate of four to one, and in the opening five sessions he dealt Matthews some heavy punishment. In the seventh, while looking for a knockout, although Duffy was nearly put out himself Matthews was unable to take advantage. It was unclear whether the referee deducted points from Duffy when he threw Matthews to the mat, once in the first and twice in the eighth, actions that left the audience screaming for a foul.

At the same venue on 31 August, Duffy risked his 'white title' at catchweights when he took on Gus Gardner, well inside 142lbs, while outweighing his rival by at least 15lbs.

16 November 1903. (146lbs) Charlie Allum w co 9 (12) Charlie Knock.
Venue: Wonderland, Mile End, London, England. **Referee:** Tom Craze.

Fight Summary: Given English 144lbs title status, give or take two pounds, despite being contested over two-minute rounds Allum (146) claimed the English 146lbs title following his win over Knock (144). Both men had given everything they had, and in the opening four rounds they virtually fought each other all over the ring before Allum dropped his game rival with a right to the head in the fifth. Although Knock got himself up he was receiving severe punishment at the bell. By this time the pace had begun to tell, both being groggy on occasion, but having had Knock at his mercy at the end of the eighth Allum finished the job in the ninth when several body shots followed by rights to the head and jaw put the Stratford man down for the full count.

13 January 1904. (142lbs) Honey Mellody w pts 12 Matty Matthews.
Venue: Central AC, Boston, Massachusetts, USA. **Referee:** Dan Donnelly.
Fight Summary: After beating the former champion in a match articled at 142lbs, Mellody claimed the 'white' version of the title at that weight. It had been a gruelling contest, with Mellody down in the second round and Matthews being dropped once in the fourth, three times in the seventh and twice in the 11th. Time and again Matthews was left staggering and reeling around the ring, and only his conditioning got him through to the final bell.

On 27 February, with both men weighing in at 138lbs, Mellody drew over six rounds with Dick Fitzpatrick at the Athletic Club, Chicago, Illinois in what was obviously a risk fight.

15 February 1904. (146lbs) Jack Clancy w pts 15 Pat Daly.
Venue: NSC, Covent Garden, London, England. **Referee:** J. H. Douglas.
Fight Summary: Billed for the world 146lbs title, with four-ounce gloves the order of the day, the contest was scrappy with too much holding to be considered top-notch. Although Clancy landed the harder, cleaner punches, especially in the fifth when he almost finished Daly off, with there being little momentum throughout the referee had to caution the men on a couple of occasions for foul play. Towards the end Daly came more and more into it, but Clancy, who had made too much headway in previous rounds to be overhauled, was unsurprisingly given the decision.

26 February 1904. (148lbs) Martin Duffy w pts 20 Rube Ferns.
Venue: Whittington Park Auditorium, Hot Springs, Arkansas, USA. **Referee:** Pat Early.
Fight Summary: Although Ferns fought gamely and several times had Duffy groggy he was always too tired to follow up any advantage. Suffering from cuts almost from the opening bell, Ferns' efforts were further hampered when his nose was badly split in the tenth, following the only knockdown of the contest, before his left eye closed in the 11th. Subsequently, it was Duffy all the way, and while the result was unquestionable the crowd yelled for a draw due to Ferns' outstanding gameness against all odds. Occasionally reported as a 145lbs 'white title' defence, further examination of the *Chicago Tribune* showed the fight to have been articled at 148lbs, a weight Duffy extended his claim to on winning after 20 rounds of the fiercest fighting ever seen at the venue.

22 April 1904. (142lbs) Honey Mellody w rsc 4 (6) Martin Duffy.
Venue: Battery 'D' Club, Chicago, Illinois, USA. **Referee:** Abe Pollock.
Fight Summary: Despite it being only a six rounder, the *Boston Post* reported that with Mellody inside 142lbs the 'white welter title' changed hands following the result. Articled at 142lbs, Duffy (147½), who looked ill trained and out of condition, was toppled for a count of 'nine' in the fourth before getting up to be rescued by the referee when deemed to be defenceless.

29 April 1904. (142lbs) Dixie Kid w disq 20 (20) Joe Walcott.
Venue: Woodward's Pavilion, San Francisco, California, USA. **Referee:** James Sullivan.
Fight Summary: Winning comfortably against the Kid (138), who was hanging on and in some distress, Walcott (144½) was disqualified for no discernible reason in the 20th round. As far as the crowd were concerned the punch in question was a legal one, being delivered above the kidneys, and the majority hooted long and loud.

Later, with the result being disregarded, Walcott continued as champion when it was discovered that the referee had placed a bet on the Kid. At the same time, due to the chicanery involved, despite claiming the 142lbs title the

Kid was accorded very little recognition whatsoever. His career then faltered when he was sent to prison for offences committed outside the ring before returning to boxing in September 1908.

2 May 1904. (144lbs) Jack Clancy w pts 10 Peter Brown.
Venue: Wonderland, Mile End, London, England. **Referee:** Victor Mansell.
Fight Summary: This was the final of a 144lbs world championship competition that had seen Charlie Knock and Charlie Allum eliminated earlier, and by the third round Clancy had landed all the telling punches up to that point, his left hand going in straight and hard to Brown's head and body. Although Brown came back well towards the end of the fifth, after he was put down by a right to the ribs he never really recovered, being sent down twice from similar blows in the seventh. Five more times Brown went to the floor from swinging right hands to the head or body, three times in the eighth and twice in the ninth, before gamely making it to the final bell.

14 May 1904. (144lbs) Jack Clancy w pts 20 Bobby Dobbs.
Venue: Ginnett's Circus, Newcastle, England. **Referee:** Billy Bell.
Fight Summary: In a match made at 144lbs, and billed for the world title, Clancy (146), announced as the champion, wasted little time as he rushed Dobbs (140), scoring well with jabs and body blows to take the lead during the opening eight rounds. Although Dobbs scored with smashing right-hand punches, on occasion he was unable to sustain any momentum. According to the *Sporting Life* Clancy held a decided advantage in 15 of the 20 rounds contested. Regardless of that statement, Dobbs claimed the title by forfeit due to Clancy failing to make the requisite weight.

4 June 1904. (146lbs) Jack Clancy w co 3 (20) Charlie Allum.
Venue: Ginnett's Circus, Newcastle, England. **Referee:** Billy Bell.
Fight Summary: Advertised as being for the world 146lbs title, it was scheduled for 20 rounds if you read the *Sporting Life* or 15 if you took the *Mirror of Life*. Right from the opening bell it was Clancy all the way, with Allum failing to keep his rival away and lacking the power to deter him. By the start of the third Clancy had inflicted heavy punishment on Allum, who was already palpably in distress, and after the latter was caught by a terrific blow to the body he slumped to the floor to be counted out on the 1.50 mark.

10 June 1904. (148/150lbs) Young Peter Jackson w co 4 (15) Joe Walcott.
Venue: Germania Maennerchor Hall, Baltimore, Maryland, USA. **Referee:** James O'Hara.
Fight Summary: Following his victory over the 142lbs champion in a catchweight contest at 150lbs, Jackson (148) claimed the world title at both 148 and 150lbs. Up until the fourth round Walcott just about had the better of matters before a left to the body dropped him to be counted out, still trying to claim a foul.

13 June 1904. (142lbs) Honey Mellody drew 20 Jack O'Keefe.
Venue: Silver Bow AC, Broadway Theatre, Butte, Montana, USA. **Referee:** Duncan McDonald.
Fight Summary: Billed for the 'white 142lbs welterweight title' in the possession of Mellody, it was reckoned to be one of the best fights ever seen in the area as neither man stopped punching for the full 20 rounds. If they ever clinched, which they often did, they were still looking to get their blows in, and while O'Keefe did his best work at distance Mellody would have been better off staying at close quarters where he was superior to the challenger. Both men took heavy punishment, but they somehow managed to keep going. A rematch was called for immediately.

18 June 1904. (142lbs) Bobby Dobbs w pts 20 Peter Brown.
Venue: Ginnett's Circus, Newcastle, England. **Referee:** Billy Bell.
Fight Summary: Regardless that this one was billed for the world 142lbs title, the report in the *Sporting Life* stated that Brown looked out of condition but failed to list the individual weights. Up to the sixth round neither man could claim any advantage according to the fight report, but in the seventh a left to the body followed by a right swing to the head brought Brown to his knees. By the ninth Brown was in the ascendancy, courtesy of his skill and power, and in the 12th he staggered Dobbs with a terrific right under the heart. Unfortunately for Brown his challenge was short lived. After being smashed to the floor by a right to the head in the 14th, Dobbs dominated from thereon in to take the decision.

There had been little activity in this weight class in recent years in Britain, mainly challenges and counter challenges with nothing being settled. By February 1905 both Jack Bayley and Brown were challenging all England without proving anything, prior to Aldgate's Young Joseph coming through the ranks in 1907.

23 July 1904. (144lbs) Bobby Dobbs w co 2 (15) Bill Chester.
Venue: Ginnett's Circus, Newcastle, England. **Referee:** Billy Bell.
Fight Summary: Originally billed for the world 140lbs title, unfortunately when Dobbs (144) failed to make the weight the fight went ahead at 144lbs, with Chester (139) taking on a man already claiming the title at that poundage. After Chester stormed out of his corner in the opening session so intense was his attack that Dobbs, who had already been decked, sought the canvas on his own account. However, in the second round when the onrushing Chester left his guard down he was countered heavily by a left-right from Dobbs (nicknamed 'Bobby Dazzler') and was counted out on the 1.20 mark.

5 September 1904. (142lbs) Joe Walcott drew 15 Sam Langford.
Venue: Queen City AC Coliseum, Manchester, Massachusetts, USA. **Referee:** Owen Kenney.
Fight Summary: Refusing to accept the loss to the Dixie Kid, Walcott signed Articles of' Agreement for a title defence at 142lbs against the much feared Langford, who was more than capable of making the weight at that stage of his career. Regardless of the official result Langford clearly outpointed Walcott, dropping his rival on one knee in the third, while hammering him with lefts and rights to keep him bleeding throughout. Langford, who had the advantage of the longer reach, also cleverly avoided many of the blows coming his way by good footwork. A draw had earlier been agreed if both men were still standing at the final bell.

10 September 1904. (144lbs) Jack Clancy drew 20 Bobby Dobbs.
Venue: Ginnett's Circus, Newcastle, England. **Referee:** Billy Bell.
Fight Summary: Given world 144lbs championship billing, during the opening six rounds Clancy (142) built up a good lead when driving in with straight lefts and never giving Dobbs (143) any respite. Dobbs came back some in the seventh, his right-hand work being very effective, and in the eighth Clancy's left eye was swelling fast. At this stage of the contest Clancy's blows were lacking steam. In the 13th, despite both of his eyes being in a bad way, he continued to score with light lefts even though the 44-year-old Dobbs was fighting hard, especially with the right. With both tired out by the 19th, although Dobbs made a determined effort to finish Clancy off he was unable to do so.

After Clancy returned to America Dobbs claimed the 144lbs title, but there is no evidence to be found that he ever defended it.

26 September 1904. (148lbs) Young Peter Jackson w co 3 (20) Charlie Knock.
Venue: Wonderland, Mile End, London, England. **Referee:** J. T. Hulls.
Fight Summary: Despite being billed as a world welterweight title fight at 148lbs, it was disqualified from full recognition with two, not three-minute rounds in place. Something common to contests at Wonderland in those days was the fact that quite often the newspapers could not agree on detail, as in this case. According to the *Sporting Life* it was scheduled for 20 rounds, while it was reported as 15 if you took the *Mirror of Life*. Knock was the first to show, trying to get inside, but it was Jackson who retaliated with interest, and in the second session he was visibly hurting the Englishman with severe body punches. The third was very much of the same order, and after about half a round had elapsed Knock was dropped by a tremendous right to the body that sent him down to be counted out.

On the home front, while Tom Woodley and Peter Brown were still claiming the English 148lbs title, despite his defeat Knock continued to challenge all England at the weight. He was later joined by Jack Bayley (February 1905) and Pat O'Keefe (August 1905).

30 September 1904. (142lbs) Joe Walcott drew 20 Joe Gans.
Venue: Woodward's Pavilion, San Francisco, California, USA. **Referee:** Jack Welch.

Fight Summary: Reported in some papers as being for the 142lbs title despite the Dixie Kid's continuing claim, the *San Francisco Chronicle* stated that the two champions would be doing battle on neutral ground at 141lbs. This was supported when Billy Pierce, an authority on pugilistic matters at the time, was quoted as saying that the title was not involved due to the men fighting at a weight below the recognised 142lbs. However, whatever was said it had to involve Walcott's title and was treated as such by the fighters. It was soon apparent that Gans (137) was the cleverer of the pair while Walcott (141) concentrated on the right swing to the body, and although there were no knockdowns it was exciting. Later in the contest Gans found a way to protect himself from the right by stepping inside it and countering with his own right to the jaw. At the final bell, with opinions divided as to who would win, a draw should be seen as a fair result.

In October, Walcott accidentally shot himself through the right hand (his friend and fellow boxer, Nelson Hall, was killed by the same bullet) and he was forced out of the ring for almost two years.

Meantime, Sam Langford, having drawn with Walcott at 142lbs on 5 September, claimed the title with some justification. In some quarters he was even called the legitimate champion. Also claiming the title was Honey Mellody, the 'white 142lbs champion'.

22 October 1904. (147lbs) Bobby Dobbs w pts 20 Jack Kingsland.
Venue: Ginnett's Circus, Newcastle, England. **Referee:** Billy Bell.
Fight Summary: Originally made at 147lbs, Kingsland (149), who came in two pounds heavier, was conspicuous early on with powerful left leads before opening up with both hands while Dobbs (142) took his time. Before too long Dobbs had seen all he needed to and began attacking Kingsland with powerful lefts and rights, cutting the latter's left eye and generally assuming control. Although Kingsland also scored frequently with both hands, with Dobbs judged to have been the most accurate he was therefore more deserving of the verdict. Following the contest, Dobbs claimed the English open title at 147lbs.

24 October 1904. (142lbs) Honey Mellody w pts 10 Jack O'Keefe.
Venue: Blue Island AC, Chicago, Illinois, USA. **Referee:** George Siler.
Fight Summary: With both men inside 142lbs, the *Chicago Tribune* reported it as being for the title after assuming Joe Walcott had retired. Mellody led from start to finish, having the better of every round, and punished O'Keefe severely. Down for 'nine' in the fourth, on several occasions it was only the bell that saved O'Keefe from being knocked out.

14 November 1904. (142lbs) Buddy Ryan w co 1 (10) Honey Mellody.
Venue: New Harlem Club, Chicago, Illinois, USA. **Referee:** Abe Pollock.
Fight Summary: Billed for the 142lbs title, the *Chicago Tribune* reported that while Mellody (142) was at weight Ryan came in six pounds heavier. Ryan's camp said that he came in one pound over the weight but eventually worked it off. Whatever the truth, the paper went on to say that Mellody was quite prepared to enter the ring knowing full well his title claim hinged on the result. The author of that statement, George Siler, also claimed that by his victory Ryan became the acknowledged American champion. Right from the opening bell Ryan went after Mellody, quickly having him down for 'nine' from a right hook to the jaw. On getting up the latter was immediately dropped again. Although Mellody again made it to his feet, by now totally bewildered, a straight right to the jaw put him down for the full count before he was carried back to his corner still unconscious.

Having been matched in a return at 142lbs, at the same venue on 12 December, the fight was called off at the 11th hour over the question of weights, Ryan being unable to get down in time.

21 November 1904. (146lbs) Bobby Dobbs w rsc 8 (20) Pat Daly.
Venue: Ginnett's Circus, Newcastle, England.
Fight Summary: Accorded world 146lbs championship billing, Dobbs (142½) and Daly (145), using an accurate left jab, made a fast start with both men letting their punches go and both having fair success. Although the contest degenerated somewhat, eventually Dobbs began to get on top. And in the eighth round, after he had smashed in a

heavy right hand to Daly's jaw leaving him hanging on the ropes in a bemused state, the referee stopped the contest.

Further to a catchweight bout against Charlie Knock at the Christian Street Gymnastic Club, Liverpool on 27 September 1906, Dobbs, despite winning on a ninth-round disqualification in a fight where it was thought both men were inside 146lbs, did not figure from there on even though he boxed on until September 1907 when failing eyesight forced him to retire.

21 November 1904. (150lbs) Young Peter Jackson w co 6 (20) Charlie Allum.
Venue: Wonderland, Mile End, London, England. **Referee:** J. T. Hulls.
Fight Summary: Advertised as an international contest at catchweights, with Jackson restricted to 150lbs and Allum called the English 150lbs champion, despite it being contested over two-minute rounds this one belonged to Jackson's claim at the weight. With little sparring involved both men made early moves before Jackson (149½) settled in defensive mode, boxing on the counter while allowing Allum to make the running. After Jackson became more active in the fourth towards the end of the session he crashed in a terrific left that opened a cut on Allum's right eye. The fifth marked the beginning of the end as a rapidly tiring Allum was twice dropped and extremely fortunate to hear the bell. Bravely coming out for the sixth it was not long before Jackson had Allum over again, but after surprising all and sundry in getting up the Englishman was sent down by another right to the jaw, this time to be counted out.

Earlier in the year, on 15 March, a fight between Jim Styles and Jack Kingsland, which had been set up to decide the vacant English 150lbs title, was called off after Styles severely injured his right knee. On the basis of Styles forfeiting, Kingsland claimed the title, being joined by Allum who was also advertising himself as the English champion, which had led to the fight with Jackson.

When Jackson drew with the Dixie Kid over 15 rounds on 26 December at the Germania Maennerchor Hall, Baltimore, Maryland, regardless of it being classified as a catchweight bout it was likely that his title claims at 148 and 150lbs would have been at risk. However, by early 1905 the American was fighting at 158lbs and although continuing to claim his lighter titles he never defended them again.

9 December 1904. (142lbs) Sam Langford drew 15 Jack Blackburn.
Venue: Highland AC, The Theatre, Marlboro, Massachusetts, USA. **Referee:** Jack Sheehan.
Fight Summary: In a match made at 142lbs, with Langford claiming the title at the weight, neither man tipped the beam. The fight was reported in the *Boston Post* as being a desperate encounter with both men looking for a finishing blow and both out on their feet at the final bell, and in line with the Articles of Agreement it was declared a draw. The fight report went on to say that the referee had no trouble with either man, but try as they might there were no knockdowns.

13 February 1905. (142lbs) Sam Langford drew 15 Dave Holly.
Venue: Apollo AC, Salem, Massachusetts, USA. **Referee:** Jack Sheehan.
Fight Summary: Made at 142lbs, with Langford supposedly defending his title claim at the weight, Holly was well inside at the weigh-in while the former, unable to make the contracted poundage, was forced to pay a forfeit. Following that, and for the fight to go ahead, Holly (137½) insisted that if both men were on their feet at the final bell a draw would be announced. Fast and hard all the way, Langford's extra weight favoured him over the last half of the contest, but by then he had already proved to be the more skilful. For most of the time Holly worked out of a crouch, sending in punches from both hands while trying to land his famous 'loop the loop' blow when at close quarters, but the real power belonged to Langford.

20 February 1905. (144lbs) Tom Woodley w disq 5 (15) Charlie Knock.
Venue: Wonderland, Mile End, London, England. **Referee:** G. H. Holloway.
Fight Summary: Although Woodley was still claiming the English 146lbs title, this one was billed as an English 144lbs title fight. With no individual weights given (it was stated that Knock could never have made 144lbs), and despite the majority of newspapers reporting it as being over three-minute rounds, the *Mirror of Life* gave it as

two-minute rounds, which was the normal practice at the venue. The contest started carefully with both men targeting the body, but before long virtually every close exchange ended in too much holding. In the fourth round the referee found fit to caution each fighter for holding and not breaking when asked. In addition to that Knock was twice warned for going low, and when he repeatedly went low in the fifth he was disqualified.

While Woodley appears to go into retirement, in August 1905 Peter Brown challenged all England at 144lbs, which he continued to do throughout 1906, being joined by Jack Meekins (January 1906). However, Brown fought at a higher weight thereafter.

27 February 1905. (150lbs) Charlie Allum w rsc 10 (15) Jack Kingsland.
Venue: NSC, Covent Garden, London, England. **Referee:** J. H. Douglas.
Fight Summary: Billed for the English 150lbs title, twice in the opening session Kingsland (149) went down in a somewhat questionable manner after Allum (149) had landed with solid body punches, but was made to fight on. Allum continued to visit the head and body with great force, and in the fifth he drove in a perfectly good right to the body that Kingsland again queried unsuccessfully with the referee. Twice Allum had Kingsland over in the sixth. And following a scrappy couple of sessions he repeated the act in the ninth, sending his rival back to his corner in a sorry state. On coming out for the tenth, with Kingsland having little left, after Allum had decked him twice more the referee awarded the contest to the latter.

Somewhat surprisingly, Kingsland was claiming the same title through the auspices of the *Sporting Life* on 13 March 1906, having recently knocked out the previously unbeaten Tom Lancaster. Almost immediately, Allum challenged his former victim to a contest that would decide the championship, but the match was never made. Regardless of that, both men carried on claiming the title.

17 June 1905. (145lbs) George Peterson w pts 20 Jack Clancy.
Venue: Mission Street Arena, Colma, San Francisco, California, USA. **Referee:** Billy Roche.
Fight Summary: As far as Clancy was concerned it was the English version of the 145lbs world title he was putting up against Peterson, who was supposedly making his professional debut after faring well as an amateur. Peterson made a quick start, pegging away with the jab and moving around the ring at speed, while Clancy showed excellent blocking skills. By the third round, however, Peterson had decided that Clancy was vulnerable to right-hand swings to the kidney region, and from thereon in he worked the right from head to body with great effect. It was no surprise that Peterson, who was deemed to have had virtually the best of every session, claimed the title at the weight on receiving the decision. The *San Francisco Chronicle* reported that Clancy was exasperatingly slow, his chief objective being to avoid punishment.

4 July 1905. (145lbs) Buddy Ryan w co 11 (20) George Herbert.
Venue: Clifford Arena, Butte, Montana, USA. **Referee:** Duncan McDonald.
Fight Summary: Reportedly billed for the 145lbs title, Herbert (143½) had the better of it up until the eighth despite being dropped twice in the opening round. Having come back to hurt Ryan (142) badly on several occasions, Herbert finally lost all interest in the contest when a terrific right to the jaw dropped him for the full count in the 11th.

19 July 1905. (145lbs) Buddy Ryan w rtd 20 (25) George Peterson.
Venue: Mission Street Arena, Colma, San Francisco, California, USA. **Referee:** Billy Roche.
Fight Summary: Given world title billing at 145lbs on account of Peterson's win over Jack Clancy, the *San Francisco Chronicle* reported that both men were down to weight. The paper, which also went on to describe Ryan as the holder of a much-neglected title, stated that Peterson was knocked down five times in the 19th round and again in the 20th before his seconds threw the towel in. While Peterson responded gamely throughout he was no match for Ryan. A short time afterwards, Peterson's career was halted due to him being stabbed by his manager and losing an eye.

25 August 1905. (142lbs) Jimmy Gardner w rtd 15 (20) Buddy Ryan.
Venue: Mission Street Arena, Colma, San Francisco, California, USA. **Referee:** Billy Roche.

Fight Summary: While not reporting this as a title fight the *San Francisco Chronicle* described Ryan as world champion, with both men agreeing to make 142lbs. The finish came when Ryan, having unsuccessfully tried to claim a foul after being dropped by a long left to the solar plexus, got up and was subjected to all manner of blows before being put down again prior to his retirement at the end of the 15th round. All bets were called off, but that did not stop Gardner claiming the 'white title' after his victory. It was reported that Gardner's blocking was remarkable, but it was his straight left which landed continuously, backed up by left and right swings, that undid Ryan.

29 September 1905. (142lbs) Sam Langford drew 10 Jack Blackburn.
Venue: Lyric Hall, Allentown, Pennsylvania, USA. **Referee:** James O'Hara.
Fight Summary: Although the *Allentown Morning Call* gave this one at 138lbs, with Langford having a slight advantage, it was really a version of the 142lbs title that the men were trying to win. Interestingly, Blackburn depended entirely on his infighting, striking few straight blows and repeatedly holding and punching after being told to break, while Langford used straight punches to good effect. It had been prearranged that in the event of both men still standing at the completion of ten rounds a draw would be imposed, and although Langford pounded Blackburn's left eye to a pulp he was unable bring about a finish.

Thereafter, both Langford and Blackburn appear to box at heavier weights, although it is clear that the latter could make 142lbs with ease. It is also clear that the top men did not want any part of him.

Despite challenging all bar Jack Johnson, Blackburn was still unable to make any headway. However, towards the end of 1907, with the 142lbs class again in dispute, he reclaimed the title. Supported by the *TS Andrews' Annual*, the claim appears to be based on his fights against Langford and Jimmy Gardner, and the fact that the former undefeated champion, Joe Gans, was naming him as the best man at the weight. Once again he found himself avoided when it came to important matches.

Unable to make his claim stick it was reported in December 1908 that Blackburn had killed a man and also shot his wife. Jailed for manslaughter and freed early in 1914, he came back to the ring that same year but was not the fighter he once was before retiring from the ring in 1923. Never leaving boxing completely he later became famous as Joe Louis' trainer, being in the heavyweight champion's corner for every one of his contests prior to falling ill with pneumonia early in March 1942. Louis was heartbroken when 'Chappie', as he called his trainer, passed away from a heart attack on 24 April 1942, aged 59.

24 November 1905. (142lbs) Mike Twin Sullivan w pts 20 Jimmy Gardner.
Venue: Woodward's Pavilion, San Francisco, California, USA. **Referee:** Jack Welch.
Fight Summary: Even though decided at catchweights both men were still inside 142lbs, and Gardner, who was reported by the *San Francisco Chronicle* as being the 'legitimate' holder of the 'white 142lbs title', forfeited his claim on the result. Sullivan was a revelation, using the left hand as a scoring punch and the right to block the best that Gardner could throw, including his lefts to the body, and when the latter stalled the Twin would be at him with the straight left. The only times that Gardner had his man going were in the 13th and 15th rounds when he unleashed his right swing to the jaw, and although the latter was badly hurt he managed to buy himself some time by stalling. While Gardner proved to be a disappointment, with Sullivan showing himself to be a far better man than his record suggested he well deserved the win.

19 January 1906. (142lbs) Joe Gans w co 15 (25) Mike Twin Sullivan.
Venue: Woodward's Pavilion, San Francisco, California, USA. **Referee:** Jack Welch.
Fight Summary: According to the *Philadelphia Item* and *San Francisco Chronicle* the fight was for a version of the title with Articles of Agreement calling for the men to come into the ring at 142lbs. It ended in the 15th after Gans landed heavily to head and body before smashing home a left to the jaw that dropped Sullivan for the full count. Gans was on top for most of the contest, standing right up to Sullivan and continually hurting him with rights to the body, while using the left to open up the latter's guard.

In early February it was reported that Honey Mellody was reclaiming the 'white title' on being unable to get Sullivan into the ring with him after the latter had defeated Jimmy Gardner.

On 17 March, Gans again met Sullivan, this time at Chutes Park, Los Angeles, California, knocking him out in the tenth of a scheduled 25-round contest. Although billed as a 142lbs title fight, Sullivan came in six pounds over the limit.

Defending his 142lbs title claim in a short distance fight, Gans (137) met Willie Lewis (nd-l pts 6 at the Twentieth Century AC, MSG Concert Hall, Manhattan, NYC, New York on 18 May). The majority of newspaper reports stated that Gans let Lewis (142lbs) do all the work and failed to put on a show.

Two other short-distance bouts for Gans that were thought to have been made at 142lbs, both held at the National AC, Philadelphia, Pennsylvania, came against Harry Lewis (nd-drew 6 on 15 June) and Jack Blackburn (nd-w pts 6 on 29 June).

Later in the year, on 23 October, it was reported that Gans had decided against continuing as a welter as he could comfortably make 133lbs. He was also happy to forfeit his title claim to Joe Thomas, whom he considered to be the best man around at that time.

19 February 1906. (145lbs) Honey Mellody w co 12 (15) Terry Martin.
Venue: Lincoln AC, Chelsea, Massachusetts, USA.
Fight Summary: Involving Mellody's 'white title' claim at 145lbs, Martin fought on gamely to the tenth before being dropped in that round and then knocked out in the 12th by a chance blow to the jaw. Having tumbled down several times, after Martin had taken so much punishment to the body that he was exhausted his exit in the 12th was hardly surprising.

Martin had put up such a good showing that he and Mellody were rematched a week or so later after the latter's fight against Mike Twin Sullivan, scheduled for 10 March, was called off.

26 February 1906. (148/150lbs) Pat Daly w co 5 (15) Mike Crawley.
Venue: Wonderland, Mile End, London, England. **Referee:** Edward Humphreys.
Fight Summary: Billed for the English 150lbs title, Daly took a good look at the hard-punching Crawley during the opening session before extending that to a round or two after being bundled down in the second. By the fourth he was beginning to get to Crawley, and in the fifth after working the latter's body Daly eventually found the blow to put his rival down for the full count.

Although the contest was disqualified from having real credibility as a championship affair due to it being contested over two-minute rounds, it did not stop Daly, who came in below 148lbs, putting in a claim for the English title at that weight also.

5 March 1906. (145lbs) Honey Mellody w co 11 (15) Terry Martin.
Venue: Lincoln AC, Chelsea, Massachusetts, USA.
Fight Summary: With Mellody's 145lbs 'white title' claim again at stake against Martin the latter surprised many when taking the first six rounds. Not only that but he almost had Mellody out on three occasions. It was contested at a whirlwind pace, but once Mellody got to grips with Martin the latter gradually weakened before being knocked out in the 11th following a vicious right to the jaw that had sent him crashing. Both men took tremendous punishment prior to the finish.

Further to two catchweight affairs against Charlie McKeever, Mellody next took on Jack Dougherty at the Badger AC, Panorama Building in Milwaukee, Wisconsin on 20 April, drawing over eight rounds. Thought to have been made at 145lbs, no weights were reported.

21 May 1906. (146lbs) Charlie Knock w rsc 17 (20) Curley Watson.
Venue: Wonderland, Mile End, London, England. **Referee:** J. T. Hulls.
Fight Summary: Advertised as being for the English 146lbs title following the retirement of Tom Woodley, despite being contested over two-minute rounds Knock claimed to be the English champion at the weight on winning. Controversy was never far away where the promoter, Harry Jacobs, was concerned, and after the referee awarded the fight to Knock following smelling salts being spilt into Watson's eyes by his second at the end of the 17th there were cries of 'fix'. Prior to the eighth round it had been Knock who landed the better shots, but thereafter Watson came more into it, with scoring punches of his own, and at the time of the finish he was probably ahead.

4 July 1906. (145lbs) Honey Mellody w co 3 (15) Willie Lewis.
Venue: Lincoln AC, Chelsea, Massachusetts, USA. **Referee:** Bill Daly.
Fight Summary: Made at 145lbs, and involving Mellody's 'white title' claim at the weight although, it was fast and furious while it lasted, it ended suspiciously. Lewis, who had been made to work off half a pound of excess, dropped Mellody in the second round before body punching took its toll and led to him being knocked out in the third after being decked by a left to the head.

10 July 1906. (142lbs) Joe Walcott w co 8 (15) Jack Dougherty.
Venue: Lincoln AC, Chelsea, Massachusetts, USA. **Referee:** Maffit Flaherty.
Fight Summary: Now that the Dixie Kid was in prison for offences committed outside the ring and Joe Gans thought to be back among the lightweights, after Walcott reclaimed the American title he was matched against Dougherty. The *Boston Post* reported the fight as being for the championship, with both men inside the prescribed 142lbs. Up until the end of the seventh round it appeared that Dougherty was ahead, and following the bell to start the eighth he launched himself into Walcott when driving for the body, a tactic that saw the latter swinging wildly. It would have been better for Dougherty had he backed away, but continuing in the same vein a left swing connected with his jaw and down he went face first. Although Dougherty tried desperately to rise, by the time he was on his knees he had been counted out.

4 August 1906. (150lbs) Pat Daly w co 9 (15) Charlie Knock.
Venue: Wonderland, Mile End, London, England. **Referee:** Dave Fineberg.
Fight Summary: Reported as being for the English 150lbs title over two-minute rounds, up until the fourth round Daly (150) was content to wait for Knock (148½) to come on to his punches. By the fifth, however, realising he was behind on points Daly began to open up, and in the seventh it was noticeable that Knock was fast weakening after taking several rights to the body. Although Knock came back coolly in the eighth, with Daly biding his time a left to the jaw and a right to the body dropped the Stratford man for the full count in the ninth. Years later, Daly always said that his contests against Mike Crawley and Knock were over three-minute rounds not the normal two-minutes mainly seen at Wonderland.

Following this, Daly was challenged by both Crawley and Charlie Allum to settle the title, while Jack Kingsland (October) was still claiming to be the champion.

In November 1907, Knock was said to have outpointed Allum over ten rounds at Wonderland. According to Harold Alderman, the fight had been advertised for two-minute rounds at 150lbs on 18 November. However, all I could find was a comment made in the 23 November edition of the *Sporting Life* stating that the contest had taken place on the 16th but had been missed out of the report covering the show. This was strange as Allum had been knocked out inside a round by James Tiger Smith at the NSC, Covent Garden, London two days previously and would have been in no fit condition at that time. Regardless of whether the fight took place or not, Knock was still claiming the English 150lbs title throughout the remaining months of 1906 and 1907 despite his defeat at the hands of Daly, while Allum continued to be listed as the English 150lbs champion in the *Sporting Life* on 4 April 1908, a title he claimed right up until the NSC set the new weight standards on 11 February 1909.

3 September 1906. (145lbs) Joe Thomas w rtd 11 (15) Honey Mellody.
Venue: Lincoln AC, Chelsea, Massachusetts, USA. **Referee:** Maffit Flaherty.

Fight Summary: While there was no billing as such Thomas technically took over Mellody's 'white title' claim at 145lbs on winning. Having almost won the fight in the fifth round Mellody was on the up, but after chasing Thomas to the ropes in the tenth he was knocked down and saved by the bell. Now it was Thomas's turn. Banging away with lefts and rights he dropped Mellody three times in the 11th, and with the latter hanging over the bottom rope his corner threw the towel in. Regardless of his defeat, Mellody went on to meet Joe Walcott on 16 October. Thomas was billing himself as the 145lbs champion, his position being strengthened further when Joe Gans stated that he should be recognised as the top man now that he (Gans) was remaining among the lightweights.

On 24 October, and contracted for 30 rounds, Thomas beat Dick Fitzpatrick (w co 16 at the Mission Street Arena, Colma, San Francisco, California) at 150lbs. One can only assume that the latter came in below 145lbs when the press reported that the title could have been his had he won.

30 September 1906. (142lbs) Joe Walcott drew 20 Billy Rhodes.
Venue: Island Park, Kansas City, Missouri, USA. **Referee:** Dave Porteous.
Fight Summary: As in his two previous contests, Articles of Agreement were signed for Walcott's title to be at stake and for both men to make 142lbs. Pitched on a sandbank island in the Missouri River where neither Kansas nor Missouri had jurisdiction, while Walcott was the aggressor from the opening bell Rhodes contented himself blocking. It was a strange tactic for a man who was supposed to be trying to win a world title, and it was stranger still when Rhodes continued to stay on the back foot until the final bell even after Walcott had damaged one of his hands in the 17th.

16 October 1906. (145lbs) Honey Mellody w pts 15 Joe Walcott.
Venue: Lincoln AC, Chelsea, Massachusetts, USA. **Referee:** Hector McInnis.
Fight Summary: Although billed as a title bout, the fact that Mellody and Walcott were contracted to meet at 145lbs did not please those who saw the championship weight as being 142lbs. It looked as though it was going to be an early night when Walcott dropped Mellody in the first round, but concentrating on the body the local fighter scored steadily with stiff lefts and rights to go to the front by the halfway stage. Although Walcott remained dangerous throughout he was unable to floor Mellody again before going down narrowly.

Afterwards, with the general consensus among the pressmen being that only a return at 142lbs would satisfy all concerned, they were immediately matched up again at the lesser weight.

29 November 1906. (142lbs) Honey Mellody w rsc 12 (15) Joe Walcott.
Venue: Lincoln AC, Chelsea, Massachusetts, USA. **Referee:** Jack Sheehan.
Fight Summary: In a return match, this time made at 142lbs, after both men came out fast it soon became a slugging match. With Mellody's footwork and blocking making things difficult for Walcott, the latter was unable to land a telling blow until the fifth round. Coming back strongly in the sixth Mellody dropped Walcott momentarily, but had to wait until the 11th before really getting on top, punching away at will. In the 12th it was clear to see that Walcott was a spent force, and after turning away and walking to his corner the fight was stopped in favour of Mellody. Walcott later said that he had disabled his left arm in the ninth which had made it impossible for him to carry on.

8 January 1907. (145lbs) Honey Mellody w pts 15 Terry Martin.
Venue: City Hall, Augusta, Maine, USA. **Referee:** Spin Mahaney.
Fight Summary: With championship billing given at 145lbs, the *Boston Post* stated that although the 'popular' title was not strictly involved the contest was still an important one. Unfortunately for the fans it was more of a hugging match than a fight, both men coming together in virtually every round, but when they did break free it was fast and furious. Mellody's idea was to get close and work rights and lefts up and down, while Martin proved himself to be a shifty boxer who could hold his own, as he did in the fifth and sixth when letting his punches go. There were no knockdowns reported.

11 February 1907. (144lbs) Curley Watson w pts 20 Andrew Jeptha.
Venue: Wonderland, Mile End, London, England. **Referee:** Edward Humphreys.

Fight Summary: Even though Jeptha (142½) was a South African this match was reported as being for the English 144lbs title. Contested over two-minute rounds, Watson (141) quickly got down to business when having little difficulty getting through his adversary's guard with the straight left. Round after round Watson scored well, and although Jeptha was groggy at times he stuck to his task, even putting the sailor down in the 11th with a drive to the ribs. It was now clear to Jeptha that to win a fight he was losing by a substantial margin of points his best chance lay in working the body, but as much as he tried he was unable to repeat the trick. The last five rounds were tough for the tiring Watson, who claimed the title at the weight after his victory.

11 February 1907. (145/147lbs) Honey Mellody w rtd 4 (15) Willie Lewis.
Venue: The Athletic Club, Valley Falls, Rhode Island, USA. **Referee:** Hector McInnes.
Fight Summary: Advertised as a title fight at 142lbs, it turned out that Articles of Agreement had been signed for the contest to go on at 147lbs. Although Lewis showed he had a punch and some class in the third round, it was all over in the fourth after he had been put down by a right and left to the jaw and his seconds had immediately thrown in the sponge.

Now that Mellody was claiming the title at 142, 145 and 147lbs, his next contest saw him losing the press decision when pitted against his old foe, Joe Thomas (nd-l pts 6 at the National AC, Philadelphia, Pennsylvania on 6 March). Despite it being contested over six rounds it was billed as a world title bout at 145lbs, with both men inside the weight. By this time Mellody was being pressured to defend his title against Thomas, but knowing that the latter could not get below 145lbs he was demanding that the weight be set at 142lbs. This was strange as Mellody had made 145lbs for the first Walcott fight, but sticking to his guns the match against Thomas was put on ice.

25 March 1907. (144lbs) Andrew Jeptha w co 4 (20) Curley Watson.
Venue: Wonderland, Mile End, London, England. **Referee:** Edward Humphreys.
Fight Summary: It was widely reported that Jeptha (141) claimed the English welter title following this win over Watson (142) at 144lbs, but his claim never really stood up due to the fact that it was contested over two-minute rounds and that he was a South African. While not gaining much recognition as the English champion, many saw Jeptha as holding the Imperial British Empire title at the weight. In the light of their previous contest, Jeptha knew that he could hurt Watson by working the body, and although the latter was scoring freely with the left the South African bided his time. The fourth round saw Jeptha's plan come to fruition when, following up a swinging left to the head with a terrific right uppercut to the jaw, he dropped Watson heavily to the boards where he was counted out.

23 April 1907. (145/150lbs) Mike Twin Sullivan w pts 20 Honey Mellody.
Venue: Pacific AC, Naud Junction Pavilion, Los Angeles, California, USA. **Referee:** Charles Eyton.
Fight Summary: Billed as a title fight at 145lbs, Sullivan well outpointed Mellody with the use of an excellent left at range and much cleverness when at close quarters. Although Mellody was strong and willing he was unable to ruffle Sullivan, who missed several opportunities to knock his man out. Afterwards, Mellody, who finished badly battered and with both eyes almost closed, claimed that the championship had not been on the line because the officials had allowed the challenger to weigh in close on 150lbs. This explanation was accepted by some but not by others, with much support for Sullivan in California. Regardless of this defeat, Mellody continued to be referred to by the *Boston Post* as the champion.

Sullivan was next matched against Joe Thomas, who was considered by many as the true champion, over ten rounds in Denver, Colorado on 30 May. Made at 145lbs, Sullivan pulled out of the contest with just two days to go claiming that the promoter had not allowed for a large enough attendance and that his take would be too small. By now, with it becoming more and more difficult for Thomas to make 145lbs he would concentrate on defending his title claim at 150lbs.

21 May 1907. (142lbs) Jimmy Gardner w pts 10 Harry Lewis.
Venue: The Coliseum, Denver, Colorado, USA. **Referee:** Red Gallagher.
Fight Summary: Gardner won virtually every round when forcing Lewis on to the back foot and defending himself well against the right hand. Unable to get his punches off, due to Gardner staying too close to him, Lewis was

forced to take continuous lefts and rights to the body that had a bad effect on him. Immediately afterwards, Gardner, who also showed good defensive skills, claimed the 142lbs title.

4 July 1907. (145lbs) Honey Mellody w rsc 7 (10) Jim Donovan.
Venue: Brown's AC, Far Rockaway, Queens, NYC, New York, USA. **Referee:** Johnny Pollock.
Fight Summary: Reported as a championship fight at 145lbs by the *New York Times*, with both men inside 143lbs (thought to be a misprint) according to the *New York World*, Mellody maintained his claim at the weight by defeating his English-born rival after the referee stopped hostilities in the seventh round. Earlier, Donovan had been saved by his ability to take punishment, being dropped a couple of times by hard rights to the jaw in the third, and he came back well before being floored in the seventh by a similar blow immediately prior to the stoppage.

4 July 1907. (150lbs) Joe Thomas drew 20 Stanley Ketchel.
Venue: Phoenix AC, Marysville, California, USA. **Referee:** Edward J. Smith.
Fight Summary: Made at 150lbs, with a 3pm weigh-in, Thomas almost lost his welterweight title claim to the charging Ketchel who threw punches for fun. Dropped in the 11th round and again in the 14th, a still groggy Thomas looked certain to lose, but on both occasions he managed to stall and wear out Ketchel while coming on strongly himself in the last two sessions. Afterwards, the referee stated that he gave the draw because of Thomas's extra class.

19 July 1907. (142lbs) Jimmy Gardner w pts 10 Clarence English.
Venue: Princess Rink, Fort Wayne, Indiana, USA. **Referee:** George Brown.
Fight Summary: This was a fight that was thought to have seen both men inside 142lbs. Although there were no weights reported in the local papers, English was quoted as saying that he was well aware of the fact that in Gardner he was meeting the toughest man in the world at 140lbs. With English assuming a crouching stance against the upright Gardner the stage was set, but there was nothing really to write home about as the latter virtually controlled most of the action with straight lefts to head and body. Although English had his moments, especially when setting up some good attacks in the sixth, he was generally outmanoeuvred and outscored by Gardner.

8 August 1907. (145lbs) Joe White w pts 15 Andrew Jeptha.
Venue: Welsh National AC, Merthyr Tydfil, Wales. **Referee:** Harry Wheeler.
Fight Summary: Given English 144lbs title billing, it had no right to be with White (despite living in Cardiff) having been born in Canada and Jeptha being a South African, and the contest being made up of two-minute rounds. However, it would certainly have had an Imperial British Empire claim of sorts. While there was generally too much holding the contest was an interesting one, White scoring well, especially with left leads to the head, while Jeptha gamely stuck to the task. It was noted by the *Mirror of Life* reporter that Jeptha had an excellent reach advantage if he cared to use it to his benefit, but throughout the 15 rounds he was unable to get to White in a heavy manner and was always running second best.

White had soon moved on, and following the directive from the NSC on 11 February 1909 that the new welterweight division would be for men between 135lbs and 147lbs, there were no more English championship fights at 145lbs.

2 September 1907. (150lbs) Stanley Ketchel w rtd 32 (45) Joe Thomas.
Venue: Mission Street Arena, Colma, San Francisco, California, USA. **Referee:** Billy Roche.
Fight Summary: Both men were inside 150lbs for this one. With it being non-stop from the start, it came as no surprise when Ketchel eventually dropped Thomas heavily in the 16th. After Thomas came back well to put Ketchel down in the 27th, at that stage either man could have won it before the latter ultimately prevailed. Twice in the 32nd round Thomas was on the floor, and when a terrific right to the solar plexus had him over again his seconds threw in the towel.

Although Ketchel automatically took over Thomas's 150lbs welter claim on winning, with him putting on weight the pair would meet again at middleweight.

21 October 1907. (142lbs) Young Joseph w pts 20 Jack Goldswain.
Venue: Wonderland, Mile End, London, England. **Referee:** Eugene Corri.
Fight Summary: Articled at 142lbs, with two-minute rounds in place, after Joseph (142) was cautioned for going low in the opener for several rounds the fight never really took off as both men hugged and worked away untidily. But after Goldswain (141½) was dropped in the fifth the next few sessions saw Joseph beginning to drive the Bermondsey man's head back with left hands, and in the tenth his rival was badly dazed following heavy blows to head and body. Although Goldswain made several desperate efforts to turn the fight around, he was unable to do so, being well beaten at the final bell. In the aftermath, Joseph claimed the English title at 142lbs on the result.

31 October 1907. (145/150lbs) Mike Twin Sullivan w pts 20 Frank Fields.
Venue: Casino AC, The Hippodrome, Goldfield, Nevada, USA. **Referee:** Jack McDonough.
Fight Summary: While not reported by the *Goldfield Daily Tribune* as a title bout, the fact that the former champion, Honey Mellody, who had earlier lost his crown to Sullivan in a match made at 145lbs, challenged the winner strongly suggests that articles had been signed at that weight. Originally announced as a finish fight before being set at 20 rounds, it was an uneven contest. According to press reports, Sullivan could have seen Fields off at any time during the last five rounds.

On 27 November, Sullivan forced Kid Farmer to retire in the 13th round at Naud Junction Pavilion, Los Angeles, California in a fight that was advertised as involving the title in the *Los Angeles Times*. However, in essence, it was made at catchweights with Farmer, reported to be inside 142lbs, looking to win the title. Sullivan was said to be in the region of 150lbs.

1 November 1907. (145lbs) Frank Mantell w co 15 (20) Honey Mellody.
Venue: Dayton AC, Ohio, USA.
Fight Summary: Held somewhere between Dayton and Cincinnati, and contested at 145lbs, it was billed as a title fight according to the *Boston Post*. The paper went on to state that the result was such a fluke that it was to laugh. However, fluke or not, Mellody, by his inability to defend at 142lbs, would not be considered as a champion thereafter. While there was no mention of the contest involving the title in the *Dayton Journal*, the *1987 Ring Record Book* supported the view that it was. The fight had seen Mellody controlling most of the action coming into the 15th round. Although he'd had a few rocky moments along the way it was something of a shock when he was attacked by right and left swings to the jaw before being counted out. At the end of the 14th Mantell had looked as though he had nothing left.

18 November 1907. (146lbs) Curley Watson w pts 15 Andrew Jeptha.
Venue: NSC, Covent Garden, London, England. **Referee:** J. H. Douglas.
Fight Summary: In a match made 146lbs, Watson (144), who was looking to regain his Imperial British Empire title claim, was the first to make some headway when using the left heavily before Jeptha (144½) started to cross his right over the top. With both men inclined to clinch the referee had his hands full, while Watson was forced to use the ring to avoid the body blows. In the sixth Watson added considerably to his score, and in the seventh he also had the best of the exchanges, but failed to take advantage of openings, as did Jeptha. Although the tenth saw Jeptha almost getting even when the two men came together, from thereon in Watson, using clever headwork to avoid punishment, went on to secure the required points.

Watson was soon fighting at 148lbs, and as far as I can ascertain there were no further English championship fights at 146lbs.

4 December 1907. (150lbs) Charlie Knock w co 11 (15) Peter Brown.
Venue: Wagram Theatre, Paris, France. **Referee:** Frantz Reichel.
Fight Summary: Contested at catchweights, both men were thought to be inside 150lbs, thus placing Knock's title claim at the weight on the line. Initially, Brown was supposed to have met Charlie Allum, but when the latter met

with an accident Knock stepped in. Brown made the better start, using his favoured right hand over the heart, and in the third round he sent Knock to the boards. It was becoming a stubborn affair. In the fifth, after hurting Knock badly, Brown himself was put down by a heavy left to the jaw. Although Brown was using the ring more, in the ninth Knock had him down for 'nine', and despite escaping further punishment in the tenth he was finished off in the 11th after taking a right to the point and being counted out.

Throughout 1908 Knock claimed the English 150lbs title despite being outpointed by Curley Watson over ten rounds and knocked out inside 12 rounds by Alf Hewitt, a well-known wrestler, at Wonderland, Mile End, London on 30 November 1908. Although made at 150lbs it was contested over two-minute rounds, lessening its importance, but it was still a bad defeat.

On 17 July 1909, a few months after the NSC had announced the new weight classes, Knock stated that he had the best claim to the new British 147lbs title, having beaten Brown several times as well as Andrew Jeptha, while winning and losing to Watson. However, the fact that he was then campaigning at 154lbs disqualified him from fighting at the welterweight limit.

7 January 1908. (142lbs) Jimmy Gardner w pts 12 Joe Walcott.
Venue: The Armoury AA, Boston, Massachusetts, USA. **Referee:** Jack Sheehan.
Fight Summary: Prior to the fight, which was made at 142lbs, the *Boston Post* stated that Gardner should be recognised as the leading man in the world at that weight. Proving far too clever for the old champion, Gardner had him beaten in the first six rounds when going to his head and body at will. In the second half of the contest the younger man was content to counter Walcott, who was desperate to land heavily, and romped to an easy win. Although Walcott, rumoured to have come in above the required weight, claimed a foul in the fourth he was overruled.

20 January 1908. (144lbs) Young Joseph w pts 20 Jack Goldswain.
Venue: Wonderland, Mile End, London, England. **Referee:** J. T. Hulls.
Fight Summary: Boxing at 144lbs, with two-minute rounds in place, an impetuous Goldswain was very nearly taken out in the opening session before being saved by the bell. By the sixth, Goldswain, who was on his knees during the round, was very much second best after Joseph had set a very fast pace, having scored well to the head and body while excelling on the inside. Continuing to hold the upper hand Joseph had almost closed Goldswain's right eye by the 12th, but from then on the latter began to fight back, scoring well with solid blows to the head. At this stage of the fight Goldswain was well behind, but according to the *Sporting Life* fight report he was rapidly making up the leeway by the 16th. Meanwhile, Joseph was too cute to become exposed to sucker punches, and for the remaining rounds he kept a tight guard which Goldswain was ultimately unable to break down. According to the paper it was age that stopped Goldswain, not Joseph, and his magnificent display in fighting an uphill battle almost got him the win he so desired. Afterwards there were rumours that both men were over the weight, but it did not stop Joseph from claiming the English 144lbs title following his victory.

With both men fighting at heavier weights from there on, there appears to be no more fights involving the English championship at 144lbs.

23 January 1908. (142/145lbs) Harry Lewis w co 3 (12) Frank Mantell.
Venue: Edgewood AC, Music Hall, New Haven, Connecticut, USA. **Referee:** Dave Fitzpatrick.
Fight Summary: Billed and advertised as a 12-round championship fight at 145lbs according to the *Boston Post*, the paper went on to say that Lewis, who had a lot of backers after his win, quickly laid claim to the 142lbs title as well. The paper also reported that despite all statements given to the press it was a good 10-1 bet that Lewis never came in as low as 142lbs against Mantell and his claim to that title should be disregarded. However, the *Philadelphia Item* reported that both men weighed in at 142lbs. On the statements made in the *Post*, Luckett Davis, who researched the subject, said: "It sounds like the sort of empty gossip that abounded in those days". You take your pick! The opening two rounds had been scientific, but in the third Lewis put down Mantell heavily, and when the latter surprisingly got up he was immediately smashed down by a left swing to the jaw and counted out.

26 March 1908. (145/147lbs) Harry Lewis w pts 15 Terry Martin.
Venue: Eureka AC, Baltimore, Maryland, USA. **Referee:** Jack McGuigan.
Fight Summary: According to the *Ring Record Book* this was a billed championship bout, while the *Philadelphia Item* merely stated that it assumed the character of a title fight. With no weights reported one should remain sceptical, but my guess would be that the fight was made at either 145 or 147lbs. The aggressor throughout, Lewis was too clever and hit too hard for Martin, who was dropped in the first and eighth rounds from heavy right-hand swings to the jaw. As game as they come, Martin was thought to have won five rounds, especially when both men were tiring, and was always trying.

20 April 1908. (145/147lbs) Harry Lewis w co 4 (12) Honey Mellody.
Venue: Armoury AA, Boston, Massachusetts, USA.
Fight Summary: Listed in the *Ring Record Book* as a title fight, the *Boston Post* stated that the contest did not involve the championship with both men making 147lbs. However, with many feeling that 147lbs should be the welter limit Lewis looked to capitalise on his claim at that weight when securing an early lead over Mellody. In the fourth round, having decided to wind it up, Lewis went in with a series of hard blows to head and body, eventually dropping Mellody to the canvas where he was counted out.

A few days later, on 27 April, at the City Hall, Augusta, Maine, Lewis met Larry Conley (nd-w co 3) in what was a six rounder, but with the loser articled to make 142lbs the *Daily Kennebec Journal* confirmed that Lewis's title claims had been at risk. Three other six-round contests for Lewis where his opponents could make the championship weight came against Unk Russell twice (nd-w pts 6 at the National AC, Philadelphia, Pennsylvania on 9 and 23 May) and Willie Lewis (nd-l pts 6 at the National AC, Manhattan, NYC, New York on 9 June).

23 April 1908. (142lbs) Mike Twin Sullivan w pts 25 Jimmy Gardner.
Venue: Vernon Arena, Los Angeles, California, USA. **Referee:** James J. Jeffries.
Fight Summary: Reported as a so-called championship fight by the *Los Angeles Times* both men made the required 142lbs, with Gardner down to 141½lbs the day before. Showing strength and coolness, Sullivan had Gardner at his mercy on several occasions but was unable to finish his foe off. Gardner's best period in the fight was between the 15th and 20th rounds, but after he slowed appreciably Sullivan had it all his own way.

Following the fight, although unable to make 142lbs any longer Sullivan continued to claim the title at 145lbs.

2 May 1908. (150lbs) Willie Lewis w co 5 (20) Walter Stanton.
Venue: The Circus, Paris, France. **Referee:** Tommy Burns.
Fight Summary: In a match given world welterweight (150lbs) title status, Lewis (148½) was soon on the attack, putting his fellow-American opponent down three times in the fourth round. The fifth session saw Lewis continuing to take the fight to Stanton, and after getting up from a further knockdown the latter was dropped again and counted out.

21 May 1908. (148/150lbs) Joe White w pts 20 Curley Watson.
Venue: Christian Street Gymnastic Club, Liverpool, England. **Referee:** J. T. Hulls.
Fight Summary: No championship billing as such, and made at catchweights, it is sometimes referred to as involving the English title. While not an English title bout it could have qualified for Imperial British Empire championship honours, especially as both men were inside 148lbs. Despite that, it is also unclear as to whether it was contested over two or three-minute rounds. For five rounds the exchanges were exceedingly tame, but after the referee cautioned them both in the sixth matters greatly improved, with White building up a commanding lead to take the verdict. Watson was a disappointment, being wild with his deliveries and unable to box his way into the contest. Coming into the fight Watson had received a fair amount of recognition as the English champion at 148lbs after outpointing Charlie Knock over ten rounds at Wonderland, Mile End, London in the final of a 148lbs championship competition on 18 April.

Immediately following his win over Watson, after White challenged the world at 150lbs he was quickly accepted by Jim Sullivan, but with the fight never coming off any claim he may have had stalled.

On 22 December, the *Sporting Life* reported that Sullivan should be recognised as the English 148lbs champion, having classified him as being the 150lbs champion a day earlier, and on 1 February 1909 the *Mirror of Life* reported that Jack Kingsland should be recognised as the English 148lbs champion. Neither claim had much substance though, and both were soon fighting among the middleweights.

Following the loss to White and two inside-the-distance defeats in catchweight contests at the hands of Willie Lewis and Honey Mellody, after being knocked out by Frank Inglis inside ten rounds at Wonderland on 5 March 1910 Watson never recovered, being pronounced dead the same day.

23 June 1908. (145lbs) Harry Lewis w pts 12 Larry Temple.
Venue: Armoury AA, Boston, Massachusetts, USA.
Fight Summary: Articled at 145lbs for the world welterweight title, further scrutiny of the *Boston Post* uncovered that while Lewis came in over the weight, Temple (145), who had worked hard to get into shape, could have taken the former's claim by forfeit had he wished. Putting up an aggressive fight, Temple was heavily countered to head and body from both hands as Lewis took a grip on the contest, and it was not until the last three rounds that he got on the attack.

Having met Unk Russell (nd-w pts 6 at the Auditorium, Bangor, Maine) on 14 July, Lewis was then matched against the same man in Boston, Massachusetts, winning on points over 12 rounds at the Armoury AA on 7 September. The Boston papers reported that Lewis had successfully held on to his title claim, but then went on to say that the contest had been made at catchweights, with Russell the bigger of the two. Getting used to each other by now, they went six rounds to a press draw at the Old City Hall, Pittsburgh, Pennsylvania on 1 October. With Russell quite capable of making 147lbs, it was not reported whether he did or not.

19 October 1908. (142lbs) Young Joseph w pts 15 Corporal Bill Baker.
Venue: NSC, Covent Garden, London, England. **Referee:** J. H. Douglas.
Fight Summary: Recognised as an English 142lbs title fight although not advertised as one, Joseph (140¾) was soon into his stride against the big-punching Baker (140) who concentrated on body shots to bring the champion down. By the ninth Baker's blows were beginning to have an effect on Joseph, and in the tenth the corporal was going even stronger before the latter came back at him in the 11th. With Joseph weakening, from thereon in he just about held up against the rib-bending punches of the much stronger Baker to justify the win.

7 November 1908. (142lbs) Jimmy Gardner w pts 15 Jimmy Clabby.
Venue: West Side AC, McDonoghville, New Orleans, Louisiana, USA. **Referee:** Otto Schoenfeldt.
Fight Summary: Billed for the vacant 142lbs title, it was a brilliant match as far as the *New Orleans Daily Picayune* were concerned, with Gardner (142), defending his title claim, leading from the start and showing more aggression than Clabby (138), who clinched, wrestled and clung on whenever on the inside. On the outside, however, Clabby was never far behind Gardner in clever work, but unable to pin his man down he took a fair few punches in trying to do so. Although the crowd were in favour of a draw it was Gardner who was given the verdict, but it had been such a good match that the pair immediately signed for a quick return at the same venue.

26 November 1908. (142lbs) Jimmy Gardner drew 20 Jimmy Clabby.
Venue: West Side AC, New Orleans, Louisiana, USA. **Referee:** Wallace Wood.
Fight Summary: According to the *New Orleans Daily Picayune* Gardner was defending the 142lbs championship in this one. As far as the press reports went it was generally seen as a fast and scientific battle between two equally matched fighters, with Gardner doing his best work when concentrating on the kidneys and Clabby when shooting in blows to the head. With both men taking terrific punishment, Clabby almost had Gardner out before the bell to end the 15th round came to his aid. Following that, after Gardner came back strongly, the draw was seen as a fair result.

In the aftermath of the contest, Gardner stated that he should be seen as the rightful 142lbs champion while recognising Jack Blackburn and Mike Twin Sullivan to be his main rivals. He also went on to say that Clabby would need watching in the future.

Meantime, Clabby could have claimed the title on the basis of his draw with Gardner but refrained from doing so until December 1909 when it was clear that the latter would not be making 142lbs again. It had also been difficult to tie Gardner down to a return match at that weight. Having Beaten Guy Buckles (w pts 10 at the Royal AC, New Orleans, Louisiana on 18 December 1909), Clabby (144) then drew over eight rounds with Jimmy Howard at the Phoenix AC, Memphis, Tennessee on 15 January 1910. While Howard claimed the title on the basis of this result it went nowhere as Clabby had won all the way and the latter had come to the ring in excess of 154lbs according to local reports.

After coming through catchweight contests against Sullivan on 4 February 1910 (for details see Sullivan v Terry Martin on 21 September 1909), Paddy Lavin (nd-w pts 10 at Wesp's Hall, Buffalo, New York on 8 February 1910) and Gardner on 11 March 1910 (for details see Gardner v Clarence English on 15 September 1909), Clabby was matched to defend his 145lbs title claim against Lavin.

14 December 1908. (145/148lbs) Willie Lewis drew 12 Harry Lewis.
Venue: Edgewood AC, Grand Opera House, New Haven, Connecticut, USA. **Referee:** Dave Fitzgerald.
Fight Summary: Advertised as being for the American 145lbs title, but made at catchweights, it also involved the 148lbs class. For seven rounds it looked as though Willie Lewis would beat his namesake, having taken the steam from him, but just as he was getting on top he broke his right hand. The remaining sessions were much slower, apart from the tenth when they mixed freely, and the decision seemed about right.

26 April 1909. (142lbs) Young Joseph w pts 20 Young Otto.
Venue: Wonderland, Mile End, London, England. **Referee:** J. T. Hulls.
Fight Summary: Made at 142lbs, despite it being contested over two-minute rounds and at a weight not recognised in Britain, Joseph claimed the world title on winning. Both men looked to be in good condition and both made good at the start, Joseph leading with sound left hands while Otto tried to work on the inside where his strength would be seen to better effect. Many of the rounds were close but by the halfway stage Joseph appeared to be in front, Otto's face being somewhat the worse for wear. From the 13th onwards Joseph definitely had the edge and by the 19th Otto's left eye was closing fast. Looking almost as fresh as when he began Joseph continued his good work in the final session, and although the American had provided a stern test it was the Englishman who was announced as the winner.

On 12 July, Joseph met Freddie Welsh, the future world lightweight champion, over 20 rounds at 142lbs at The Pavilion, Mountain Ash, Wales, losing on an 11th-round disqualification. Although the weight for the contest fell within the new 147lbs welterweight limit set by the NSC on 11 February, it was clear that Joseph could no longer make 142lbs and he moved up to contest the vacant Lonsdale Belt at 147lbs, while Welsh dropped down to campaign in the 135lbs lightweight division.

25 May 1909. (145lbs) Mike Twin Sullivan drew 20 Kyle Whitney.
Venue: Mission AC, Dreamland Pavilion, San Francisco, California, USA. **Referee:** Eddie Hanlon.
Fight Summary: With both men inside 145lbs, Sullivan successfully defended his claim at the weight when given a share of the verdict. It was reported that every session was like the previous one, with Whitney leading and Sullivan countering before falling into a clinch. After 16 rounds it appeared that Sullivan had the points over the cautious Whitney, but the latter came with a spurt in the 17th round to even things up somewhat, and a knockdown over his tired rival in the 19th got him the draw.

26 May 1909. (147/148lbs) Willie Lewis w co 3 (20) Andrew Jeptha.
Venue: Villiers Street Arena, London, England. **Referee:** J. T. Hulls.
Fight Summary: Reported by the *Mirror of Life* as being for the world 148lbs title, and elsewhere as involving the 147lbs crown, this contest caused much amusement in the USA as many felt that Lewis had no right to call himself the American champion at the weight. Although appearing to have a height-and-reach advantage, Jeptha failed to use it convincingly when allowing Lewis to get to close quarters early on. Having taken some heavy shots in both the first and second rounds, Jeptha was unable to keep the American at bay in the third, and upon rising after

being put down by a right to the side of the head he was dropped five more times, the last occasion seeing him counted out.

8 June 1909. (142lbs) Jimmy Gardner drew 12 Tommy Quill.
Venue: Armoury AA, Boston, Massachusetts, USA. **Referee:** Jack Sheehan.
Fight Summary: The *Boston Post* reported this as a defence of Gardner's 142lbs title claim, with both men inside the weight. While the challenger showed up well Gardner appeared to be off colour, and apart from the fifth round when Quill was knocked down twice he was well in the fight. In the tenth Quill went all out to have Gardner wobbling at the final bell, the decision appearing to favour the latter.

According to several papers of the day Quill had a reasonable claim to the title on the result, but failing to press home his advantage he lost to Young Loughrey next time out before moving up in weight.

15 September 1909. (142lbs) Jimmy Gardner nd-w pts 10 Clarence English.
Venue: Boyd's Theatre, Omaha, Nebraska, USA. **Referee:** Jack Sheehan.
Fight Summary: Although no weights were reported in the *Omaha World Herald*, the paper called Gardner the world champion and went on to say that English expected to win the 142lbs title in this one. The press reported that Gardner could have put English out anytime he wanted but held back and treated it as an exhibition, cuffing the latter as and where he pleased. In the absence of no blood and no knockdowns, Gardner later stated that as he had signed for a scientific contest with no real fighting allowed that is what he adhered to.

The following November Harry Lewis demanded that Gardner make 142lbs in order to decide the championship, but as neither could make that weight anymore it came to nothing.

While the *1910 TS Andrews' Annual* (covering 1909) continued to show Gardner as a title claimant, and the *Sporting Life* reported on 28 December that in the NSC scale of weights Americans now disputing the title at 147lbs included Lewis, Mike Twin Sullivan, Kyle Whitney as well as Gardner, from thereon in the later fought above the weight class. That was certainly true of his next four contests, against Young Loughrey (nd-w pts 6 at the National AC, Philadelphia, Pennsylvania on 2 October), Bill McKinnon (w rsc 4 at the Armoury AA, Boston, Massachusetts on 26 October), Sullivan (l pts 12 at the Grand Opera House, New Haven, Connecticut on 29 November) and Jimmy Clabby (nd-drew 10 at the Badger AC, Milwaukee, Wisconsin on 11 March 1910). Despite the last-named bout being advertised as one in which the title issue would be sorted out on the result, with Gardner coming to the ring weighing 155lbs it was a fallacy. Subsequently, Gardner was recognised as a middleweight.

21 September 1909. (145lbs) Mike Twin Sullivan w pts 12 Terry Martin.
Venue: Armoury AA, Boston, Massachusetts, USA. **Referee:** Dick Fleming.
Fight Summary: Sullivan proved that he was the master at 145lbs when outclassing Martin, peppering him with blows to face and body at will in every round after the first. Regardless that he was one of the best men around at the weight, Martin barely landed six punches all evening as the superior boxing ability of Sullivan told on him. That aside, with Sullivan unable to drop his opponent he had to be satisfied with a points win.

On 4 February 1910, Sullivan took on Jimmy Clabby at the National AC, The Hippodrome, Milwaukee, Wisconsin in what was referred to as being a championship contest, but was not as the Twin was fully ten pounds heavier than his rival. While Sullivan showed his superiority early on he was unable to hurt Clabby and, although the fight slowed considerably from the fifth through to the seventh, after the referee warned both men to start working it was the latter who came on strongly over the last three sessions. With the crowd behind Clabby, thinking that he was the best man, when it came to the attendant press a draw was deemed to be the popular decision.

11 January 1910. (145lbs) Harry Lewis w pts 10 Howard Baker.
Venue: Athletic Club, Denver, Colorado, USA. **Referee:** Red Gallagher.
Fight Summary: In a match made at 145lbs, the *Rocky Mountain News* reported that Lewis's title claim at the weight was on the line in this one. Although Baker put on a good show, consistently covering up in order to go the distance, the crowd were not enamoured with Lewis who failed to score a knockdown and never looked likely to.

19 February 1910. (147lbs) Harry Lewis drew 25 Willie Lewis.
Venue: The Circus, Paris, France. **Referee:** Snowy Lawrence.
Fight Summary: With the formation of the International Boxing Union (IBU) currently being proposed, and with Harry Lewis bringing his title claim from America, this was accepted as a title fight in France at 147lbs. After both men had been announced as making the weight at the 2pm weigh-in before the opening session was over Willie had been dropped twice from left-rights to the jaw. When Willie was dropped again in the second it looked to be all over, but he fought back courageously despite being outpointed all the way before being put down again, in the 11th. The 15th saw Willie in a different light, as for the first time in the contest he did all the leading while scoring heavily at times. Although Willie continued to lead for a few rounds Harry came back in the 20th to force matters once again, and in the 25th a right swing to the jaw put his rival down again. It was clear to most that Harry had won handsomely but, when Willie was given a share of the decision, it was seen as being more diplomatic than realistic.

21 March 1910. (147lbs) Young Joseph w disq 11 (20) Jack Goldswain.
Venue: NSC, Covent Garden, London, England. **Referee:** Tom Scott.
Fight Summary: The inaugural contest involving the Lonsdale Belt for the British 147lbs welterweight title saw Joseph (146½) matched against Goldswain (145). By the third round Joseph was hitting hard and straight, whilst Goldswain was having difficulty landing. However, there was far too much holding for it to be exciting. In the tenth Goldswain was beginning to take a battering, having already gone groggy on several occasions leading up to that round. After clutching again and again in the 11th and refusing to break the referee issued a final warning, and when that was ignored Goldswain was disqualified. On winning, Joseph claimed the world title at the new weight.

23 April 1910. (147lbs) Harry Lewis drew 25 Willie Lewis.
Venue: The Circus, Paris, France. **Referee:** Dr Phelin-Roux.
Fight Summary: A return championship match at 147lb, with Harry Lewis defending against his namesake, *Boxing* reported that it was no different from their previous fight. In the opening five rounds Harry had Willie down for three counts but failed to settle the latter, and throughout the contest he had several opportunities without dealing with them emphatically. In between times, Willie, taking advantage of Harry's missed opportunities, boxed rather well but certainly did not deserve to win.

26 April 1910. (145lbs) Jimmy Clabby nd-drew 10 Paddy Lavin.
Venue: Miller's Hall, Buffalo, New York, USA. **Referee:** Fred Ehrmann.
Fight Summary: Defending his 145lbs title claim against Lavin, a man who had given him trouble two and a half months earlier, Clabby failed to shine in what was more of a maul than a contest. Lavin was clearly up for it, pressing throughout, but was unable to find the punch to finish the clever Clabby. Whenever the pair came to close quarters there was very little fighting despite Lavin appearing to be the stronger man. At the conclusion of the bout, Clabby said that while Lavin was an extremely tough opponent he felt that he had been up against a heavier man despite the local paper reporting that both men would make even weight.

4 May 1910. (147lbs) Harry Lewis w co 3 (20) Peter Brown.
Venue: Wagram Theatre, Paris, France. **Referee:** F. G. Calhoun.
Fight Summary: Billed for the world 147lbs title, Brown, who was saved by the bell at the end of the opening round following a left-right to the jaw, met Lewis blow for blow in the second session as though nothing had happened. The third had been in progress about a minute when Brown, in the act of over-reaching, was dropped for 'nine' after being caught on the jaw by a right. It was later recognised that the true count was '14'. Almost immediately Brown went down again from a right to the ear. Despite appearing to be on his feet at 'ten' the referee sent him back to his corner amidst much protestation by all and sundry, saying that he had been counted out. Some reports state that Brown was over the limit, but at the end of the day it hardly mattered.

5 May 1910. (147lbs) Jimmy Clabby nd-w pts 10 Dixie Kid.
Venue: Empire AC, Maspeth, Queens, NYC, New York, USA.
Fight Summary: Initially due to fight Mike Twin Sullivan, who pulled out of a contest made at 147lbs due to financial reasons or otherwise, Clabby (139) met the Dixie Kid (147) instead. The *New York Times* reported that the

Kid, or Aaron Brown as he was christened, was the recognised champion (despite never defending his claim) and would probably still have lost to Clabby even if he had come in fully fit, not as an 11th-hour substitute. Although there was plenty of holding, Clabby's punches were far more frequent and accurate than those that the Kid threw, and in the sixth round the latter was being taunted by his young rival who hammered in punches with both hands as if for fun. There were no knockdowns, but at the end of the fight it was the Kid who was looking the worse for wear, with badly battered features and worn out. The unmarked Clabby, who was already claiming the title at 142lbs and 145lbs, also laid claim to the 147lbs championship following the contest.

Although Clabby and Sullivan were signed up to meet at 145lbs on 15 May at the Marathon AC, Brooklyn, NYC, New York, both men declined to fight on the night after police had raided the club and arrested the owners. Despite further efforts being made for them to contest the title it all came to nothing, apart from them going on to meet at the middleweight limit on 3 June 1911.

27 June 1910. (147lbs) Harry Lewis w rtd 7 (20) Young Joseph.

Venue: Wonderland, Mile End, London, England. **Referee:** Eugene Corri.

Fight Summary: Advertised as being for the vacant 147lbs world title between the American and British champions, Lewis was soon putting his punches together, dropping Joseph with a left hook to the jaw and having him hanging on desperately at the bell. It was more than clear at this stage of the contest that Lewis hit too hard for Joseph, who was dropped again in the third and sixth rounds before taking four more counts in the seventh prior to retiring on his stool at the end of the round.

After scoring a four-round kayo win over the 140¼lbs Johnny Summers at Olympia, Kensington, London on 25 January 1911, which was due to go on at 144lbs, Lewis (148¼) moved up among the middles.

1 September 1910. (145lbs) Mike Twin Sullivan nd-w pts 10 Paddy Lavin.

Venue: International AC, Buffalo, New York, USA. **Referee:** Fred Ehrmann.

Fight Summary: Still claiming the title at 145lbs, Sullivan met Lavin at the weight according to the *Buffalo Courier*. Set for a 3pm weigh-in, one can only assume that the men were safely inside. Ten fast rounds saw Sullivan showing much skill in warding off the tough Lavin after knocking his man down for 'eight' with a right hook in the opening session. Saved by the bell, Lavin was groggy for a while before coming back to keep Sullivan busy. Later in the fight Sullivan tried hard for the kayo, but was held up by a tough opponent who was still fighting strongly at the final bell.

5 September 1910. (142/145lbs) Jimmy Clabby w rtd 13 (20) Guy Buckles.

Venue: Kirby Opera House, Sheridan, Wyoming, USA. **Referee:** George English.

Fight Summary: According to the *Sheridan Post* this was for the 145lbs championship (3pm weigh-in), and by his victory Clabby further cemented his right to be recognised as the best man in America. Having reported that this would be the first time a championship belt had been offered at the weight, the paper went on to say that after being outclassed and taking terrific punishment without dropping, Buckles was pulled out of the fight when his corner threw the towel in early in the 13th.

Clabby then took his title claim to Australia where he participated in several over-the-weight fights, but by April 1911, with the weight class beyond him, he was seen as a fully-fledged middleweight.

9 September 1910. (142lbs) Dixie Kid nd-w pts 10 Willie Lewis.

Venue: National SC, Manhattan, NYC, New York, USA. **Referee:** Tom O'Rourke.

Fight Summary: Press reports showed this one to have been made at 142lbs, 3pm weigh-in, and that both men had no difficulty in making the required poundage. It was a fierce fight, with Lewis wobbling all over the ring at times as the Kid went to work with swings and hooks, and although many were blocked those that got through hurt. The last two sessions saw Lewis in big trouble, his excellent defence saving him, before the final bell came to his rescue.

Ten days later, on 19 September, the Kid took on Dick Nelson in a ten-round no-decision contest at the Olympia AC, Manhattan. After a hammer-and-tongs battle throughout the majority of the press felt that Nelson deserved the verdict, his straight lefts, right crosses and uppercuts at close quarters being most effective. He also scored the only knockdown of the fight. Following the contest, Nelson, who was inside 142lbs, claimed the title. However, to receive any form of recognition Nelson would have had to beat the Kid inside the distance. With no support forthcoming after he was defeated by Harry Lewis at the America AC, Schenectady, New York on 7 November any title hopes Nelson had disappeared. Lewis was Nelson's master at every stage, flooring the latter three times in the first and twice in the second before landing the kayo punch.

6 October 1910. (145lbs) Mike Twin Sullivan nd-w pts 10 Paddy Lavin.
Venue: International AC, Buffalo, New York, USA. **Referee:** Fred Ehrmann.
Fight Summary: In a rematch at 145lbs, 3pm weigh-in, the *Buffalo Courier* reported that Sullivan was fast out of the traps when looking to finish early. Although Lavin initially held his man up when boxing with caution, once into the middle rounds he went for Sullivan with gusto. However, the clever Sullivan was always one step ahead of Lavin, boxing him off when he had to. The final three rounds saw Sullivan going after Lavin in hurricane style, the latter taking some hard knocks in his stride before making it to the final bell.

Recognised by the *TS Andrews' Annual* as being one of three title claimants at the end of 1910, the author can find no more fights at the weight for Sullivan.

17 November 1910. (147lbs) Dixie Kid nd-l pts 10 Willie Lewis.
Venue: National SC, Manhattan, NYC, New York, USA. **Referee:** Tom O'Rourke.
Fight Summary: A return match believed to have been made at 147lbs saw Lewis put up a much better showing, even if both men appeared unwilling to fight at times. There were no knockdowns and there was frequent clinching, but when they did get going there was plenty of exciting action as first one and then the other sent in hard blows. With both Lewis and the Kid making it to the final bell their respective title claims remained intact.

29 April 1911. (147lbs) Willie Lewis w pts 20 Dixie Kid.
Venue: The Circus, Paris, France. **Referee:** Dr Phelin-Roux.
Fight Summary: After both men made the required 147lbs, the Kid went for Lewis right from the opening bell, lashing in blows from both hands, through the opening 15 rounds without ever knocking the latter down. During those sessions, Lewis seemed quite happy to cover up and wait for the Kid to burn himself out, and it was only in the 16th that he took a turn at the punching part of the game as *Boxing* put it. This was a defence of the title that Lewis was claiming after twice drawing with his namesake, Harry Lewis, and at the end of the contest when the decision went against the Kid it was heard in disbelief. While Lewis had boxed an excellent defensive fight the fact that he had not done the lion's share of the scoring should have counted against him. It later emerged that Lewis had scaled 154¼lbs.

Despite being disqualified in the third round of a contest made at 147lbs at Wonderland, Mile End, London, England on 3 July against fellow American Blink McCloskey (149), the Kid, who was still claiming to be the champion at the weight, was matched against Harry Duncan at the Rotunda Skating Rink, Dublin, Ireland on 10 July. When a riot ensued, with Duncan ahead on the scorecards, the referee stopped the contest in the fifth round and announced a no-decision verdict. Supposedly billed for the world welter title, the Kid claimed that Duncan was close on 154lbs, thus making the billing farcical if true.

9 November 1911. (142lbs) Dixie Kid w co 2 (20) Johnny Summers.
Venue: The Stadium, Liverpool, England. **Referee:** Eugene Corri.
Fight Summary: Billed for the world title at 142lbs, which the Kid still claimed, both men were announced as being inside the weight. And with Harry Lewis now perceived to be a middleweight the Kid was generally recognised in Britain as champion. Summers made a great start in the opening session, while the Kid was effectively having a good look at his opponent. Unfortunately for Summers the Kid came out firing in the second, and after he had coaxed his rival into an attempted counter a short, sharp right to the angle of the jaw put the Englishman for the full count.

28 November 1911. (145lbs) Willie Lewis nd-l pts 10 Mike Gibbons.
Venue: Fairmont AC, Bronx, NYC, New York, USA. **Referee:** Billy Joh.
Fight Summary: Confirming that both men were inside 145lbs at the 3pm weigh-in, the *New York Times* reported that despite looking like a novice at times Lewis held on to his 147lbs title claim thanks to the no-decision status of the contest. After being knocked down in the second round it looked all over for Lewis, but having got up he was battered from pillar to post as Gibbons looked to take him out. In the sixth Gibbons again went looking for Lewis, showering him with lefts and rights, but the latter somehow remained upright. Thereafter, Gibbons stood off, hitting Lewis whenever he pleased, and although trying for the knockout in the tenth he could not manage it.

29 November 1911. (142lbs) Ray Bronson nd-w pts 10 Tommy Howell.
Venue: Virginia Avenue Auditorium, Indianapolis, Indiana, USA.
Fight Summary: With both men inside 138lbs, in a match made at 142lbs, Bronson outboxed and outslugged the game Howell throughout, having him all but out in the tenth round. It was one of Bronson's best wins against a tough opponent, and following the fight he assumed the role of American champion at the weight, especially with all of the country's top men campaigning abroad.

1 January 1912. (142lbs) Ray Bronson nd-drew 10 Tommy Devlin.
Venue: Tri-Cities AC, Jeffersonville, Indiana, USA. **Referee:** Marvin Hart.
Fight Summary: Bronson soon got to close quarters in a match made at 142lbs, being the aggressor throughout, while Devlin held and frustrated him. Although Devlin did well in rounds three and five he was soon under attack again, and in the ninth as Bronson tried hard for a knockout he denied him by covering up well.

22 February 1912. (142lbs) Ray Bronson nd-w pts 10 Young Erne.
Venue: Virginia Avenue Auditorium, Indianapolis, Indiana, USA.
Fight Summary: Given 142lbs title billing, with both men making the weight at the 3pm weigh-in, apart from the fifth and eighth Bronson had matters very much his own way. The durable Erne, dropped just once, in the fourth, proved to be a tough customer as he shipped many blows that would have seen others off, and he was always looking to get his own punches in when he could. Although both men used their lefts to good advantage it was Bronson's infighting ability that took him well clear.

23 February 1912. (147lbs) Mike Gibbons nd-w co 2 (10) Willie Lewis.
Venue: Empire AC, Maspeth, Queens, NYC, New York, USA. **Referee:** Dan Lane.
Fight Summary: Made at 147lbs, with both men inside, this was the second meeting between the pair in recent months, Gibbons taking over Lewis's title claim after winning by a knockout. The first round saw Gibbons firing in lefts and rights to the head, while Lewis, swinging wildly, was dropped for 'nine' right at the end of the session. Coming out for the second still groggy Lewis was immediately attacked by Gibbons, and following a tornado of rights and lefts to the head a short left-right to the jaw sent him crashing to be counted out.

On 25 June, at the St Nicholas Arena, Manhattan, NYC, Gibbons received the ten-round press decision when up against Joe Stein. Despite Gibbons coming in at 149lbs, technically his 147lbs title claim was at risk when Stein made 143lbs. Stein proved to be a tough customer, being severely battered at times, and despite being dropped for 'nine' by a right uppercut in the second round he reached the final bell still on his feet.

Later on, Gibbons (154) won a ten-round press decision over Tommy Maloney (151) at Madison Square Garden, Manhattan, NYC on 23 September. That result meant nothing until it was reported in the 16 March 1916 edition of the *Manchester Sporting Chronicle* in England that Maloney had defended his title claim in this fight. However, on perusing Maloney's fight record and seeing that it was contested at middleweight, it is best forgotten.

1 April 1912. (142lbs) Ray Bronson w pts 15 Clarence English.
Venue: The Auditorium, St Joseph, Missouri, USA.
Fight Summary: Taking the fight to Bronson with effective left and right swings English started well, but by the fifth round he was spitting blood from a cut mouth and was beginning to weaken from body shots. It was only when Bronson was cut on the left eye in one of the latter sessions that he really began to look for a stoppage win, but

English held on. Following this win at 142lbs, Bronson put up a forfeit, without takers, to fight anyone in America for the title at 142lbs or 145lbs ringside.

24 April 1912. (147lbs) Dixie Kid w rsc 11 (20) Georges Bernard.
Venue: The Circus, Paris, France. **Referee:** Willie Lewis.
Fight Summary: Given world title billing at 147lbs title, with both men inside the weight, Bernard was dropped writhing in agony in the tenth round, whereupon the referee disqualified the Kid after the bell had already rung to get the 11th underway. Later, on being examined by three doctors, when Bernard was found to show no trace of having being fouled the decision was overturned and the Kid given the stoppage win. However, the referee had really disqualified the rapidly tiring Kid for butting, not low blows, but somehow that was not taken into account. It had been a strange fight, with the Kid dancing about without doing too much while Bernard appeared bewildered at his antics. The Kid had also been warned for using his elbows. In the aftermath, the referee stated that he had been amazed by Bernard's progress and felt that the Kid had deliberately fouled the Frenchman, hitting him below the belt and butting him, because he was tiring and looking likely to lose.

23 May 1912. (142/145lbs) Harry Brewer nd-w pts 8 Ray Bronson.
Venue: The Coliseum, St Louis, Missouri, USA.
Fight Summary: Reported in the *Chicago Tribune* as a billed title fight, the *St Louis Post-Dispatch* confirmed that Bronson was inside the stipulated 142lbs, while Brewer made 145lbs, the weight he claimed the title at following his fine performance, albeit over a shortened distance. In a contest that was meant to be a warm-up for a meeting with Packey McFarland, Bronson was shocked when knocked down in the first before being put through the ropes on two more occasions. Although Bronson came on strong near the end it was only his ring generalship that saved him from an early defeat.

On 24 September, at the same venue, Brewer met Art Magirl (nd-drew 8), a late replacement for Bronson, thus risking his 145lbs title claim after both men made the weight at the 2pm weigh-in.

29 May 1912. (142lbs) Ray Bronson nd-l pts 10 Packey McFarland.
Venue: Washington Ball Park, Indianapolis, Indiana, USA. **Referee:** Edward W. Smith.
Fight Summary: With both men inside 138lbs, this was effectively a defence of Bronson's 142lbs title claim, and with the fight going the distance the latter held on to his honours despite McFarland just about getting the press verdict. It was very close, with McFarland using a superb left lead and all-round skills to advantage while Bronson looked to get inside. There were no knockdowns incurred unless you count Bronson going to the floor and bouncing up like a rubber ball in the third round.

29 June 1912. (142lbs) Ray Bronson nd-w pts 10 Harry Brewer.
Venue: Washington Ball Park, Indianapolis, Indiana, USA.
Fight Summary: As per the *Indianapolis News*, both Bronson and Brewer were inside the articled 142lbs. And both held on to their title claims with the fight going the distance. After the opening round there was only one man in this fight and it was not Brewer, who was knocked down once in the fourth and twice in the sixth. Several times Bronson appeared to have Brewer at his mercy, and it was only the latter's heart and excellent condition that saved him.

2 September 1912. (142lbs) Ray Bronson nd-drew 10 Wildcat Ferns.
Venue: Virginia Avenue Auditorium, Indianapolis, Indiana, USA.
Fight Summary: It was reported in the *Indianapolis Star* that both men made the required 142lbs and that Bronson's title claim was once again at stake. It was nearly all over in the first round after Bronson was dropped for 'nine' by a tremendous right to the jaw. However, on getting up in a daze he showed his class with dazzling footwork keeping him out of harm's way until the bell. In the third Bronson was again downed by a right to the chin, but after that he stuck with his boxing, allowing Ferns to throw his right again and again while making him miss and sticking in the left jab. Ferns was always dangerous with the right, and although taking too much punishment when trying to set Bronson up he was given the majority press draw on account of the knockdowns rather than his boxing.

9 September 1912. (142lbs) Ray Bronson nd-l pts 12 Hilliard Lang.
Venue: The Auditorium, Winnipeg, Canada. **Referee:** Bun Foley.
Fight Summary: The *Winnipeg Telegram* reported that with both men inside 142lbs this was a battle between a world title claimant in Bronson and the best man in Canada to decide the championship. There were no knockdowns, only honest endeavour as both men tried to go clear. At the close Lang received the press decision on account of his greater work-rate and rushing tactics that allowed him to get inside Bronson's right swings. Afterwards, Bronson stated that he had injured his left arm prior to the contest but carried on as to not let anyone down.

Although Bronson's contest against Clarence English (nd-w pts 8 at the Athletic Club, St Louis, Missouri on 29 October) was only over eight rounds, the *St Louis Post-Dispatch* reported that Bronson's title claim was at risk due to the fact that both men made 142lbs.

4 October 1912. (147lbs) Marcel Thomas w pts 15 Dixie Kid.
Venue: Premierland, Paris, France. **Referee:** Emile Maitrot.
Fight Summary: In a title match made at 147lbs, with both men announced as having made the weight, right from the opening bell the match had a bad taste to it, especially as heavy bets in certain quarters were being made on Thomas to win or last into the later rounds. Prior to the contest, the Kid, who was recognised as the 147lbs champion in France, was expected to win without difficulty, but having pranced about for 11 rounds without doing any damage to Thomas the American suddenly woke up in the 12th only to find that he had nothing left in the tank. While the Kid had been taking time out Thomas had been scoring with the left, and in the final four sessions he opened up with both hands to win handily. At the highest level this was virtually the end of the road for the Kid, and despite him boxing on until early 1916 (not taking into account the single contest for him in 1920) he lost almost as many as he won.

10 October 1912. (145lbs) Harry Brewer w pts 15 Marty Rowan.
Venue: The Theatre, Salt Lake City, Utah, USA. **Referee:** Hardy Downing.
Fight Summary: After 15 rounds of fast boxing Brewer successfully carried his title claim at 145lbs when outscoring Rowan, a local fireman. Brewer threw far more blows than the tough Rowan, while what the latter did send out were harder. And at no time was Rowan ever in distress.

11 October 1912. (145lbs) Wildcat Ferns nd-w co 2 (8) Art Magirl.
Venue: Queen City AC, The Coliseum, St Louis, Missouri, USA.
Fight Summary: Even though carded for just eight rounds, with both men inside 145lbs, and following his ten-round press draw against Ray Bronson, Ferns claimed the American title on the result. Having been put down for two counts of 'nine' in the second round, Magirl was then knocked out by a terrific right uppercut.

13 November 1912. (145lbs) Wildcat Ferns nd-l pts 10 Tommy Howell.
Venue: Virginia Avenue Auditorium, Indianapolis, Indiana, USA.
Fight Summary: With both men inside 145lbs, the *Indianapolis News* reported that Ferns' title claim at the weight was at stake in this one. Despite Ferns possessing dynamite in his right hand, Howell, who was happy to take the fight to him from the opening bell, sent his rival down for 'nine' in the first session. Subsequently, they traded blows for most of the way, with Howell just keeping his nose in front due to him being more active.

1 January 1913. (145lbs) Wildcat Ferns w pts 10 Harry Brewer.
Venue: Labor Temple Auditorium, Kansas City, Missouri, USA. **Referee:** Walter Bates.
Fight Summary: According to the *Kansas City Star* both men made the prescribed 145lbs, and following the result Brewer's title claim at the weight rested with Ferns. The aggressor throughout, Ferns had the advantage in every round except the first when honours were even. Although there were no knockdowns, Brewer was in trouble in the second and last two sessions before making it to the final bell.

13 January 1913. (142/145lbs) Spike Kelly w pts 8 Ray Bronson.
Venue: Phoenix AC, Memphis, Tennessee, USA. **Referee:** Billy Haack.

Fight Summary: Despite being only an eight rounder, the *Memphis Daily Appeal* reported it to be a welter title debate at 142lbs. The contest saw Kelly stake a claim to the American 142/145lbs title after the referee awarded him the decision on the basis of him landing the cleaner blows and carrying the contest to Bronson for more than 70 percent of the battle. There were no knockdowns, but in the fifth Bronson had Kelly on the run from straight lefts and right hands to the body, while in the seventh Kelly had Bronson at full stretch, hitting him when and where he pleased. Meanwhile, Bronson continued to lay claim to the 142lbs title regardless of his defeat.

14 January 1913. (145lbs) Wildcat Ferns nd-w pts 15 Charley Pierson.
Venue: The Auditorium, St Joseph, Missouri, USA. **Referee:** Walter Bates.
Fight Summary: Both men made the required 145lbs mark according to the *St Joseph Gazette*, who went on to report that the fight did not warm up until the fourth round when Pierson was sent sprawling by a swinging right to the jaw. Fairly even up to the 11th, that was the best round to date as both men started fighting hard, and Pierson was momentarily knocked through the ropes before coming back strongly. Although a foul blow sent Ferns to his knees in the 12th he was quickly back in the fray playing on Pierson's features, and in the 14th a left uppercut dropped the latter to the floor. The final session saw Pierson under pressure again, before being saved by the bell with the count at 'seven' after being floored by a batch of solid uppercuts.

22 January 1913. (145lbs) Tommy Howell w pts 10 Ray Bronson.
Venue: The Labor Temple Auditorium, Kansas City, Missouri, USA. **Referee:** Dave Porteous.
Fight Summary: Made at 145lbs, on the basis of his win over one of the top men in the division Howell laid claim to the title at the weight. Bronson, who was dropped three times for 'nine' in round three and again in the ninth, had Howell down in the fourth as he regained his strength. Towards the end Bronson fairly cut the limited Howell up as he went in with left and right jabs and uppercuts, but it was not enough to force a stoppage or make sure of the verdict.

Happy to risk his new 145lbs title claim, Howell met Young Erne (nd-l pts 6 at the Olympia AC, Philadelphia, Pennsylvania on 3 February).

22 January 1913. (145lbs) Wildcat Ferns nd-drew 15 Al McCoy.
Venue: South Wayne Avenue Gym, Dayton, Ohio, USA.
Fight Summary: The *Dayton Journal* reported both men as being inside 145lbs, which automatically put Ferns' title claim at the weight at risk. McCoy, the future world middleweight title claimant at 158lbs, could also have taken over at 145lbs had he produced a winning punch, but despite both men showing much cleverness neither was ever in any danger of a knockout defeat. Early on McCoy's peculiar style bothered Ferns, but once the latter overcame that the fight evened itself up, and apart from the New Yorker's right eye being badly cut in the 11th round neither man was otherwise marked.

29 January 1913. (142lbs) Ray Bronson nd-w pts 10 Jimmy Perry.
Venue: Virginia Avenue Auditorium, Indianapolis, Indiana, USA. **Referee:** Dave Porteous.
Fight Summary: Bronson risked his claim in this one, with both men inside 142lbs at the 3pm weigh-in. Claiming afterwards that he'd had trouble making the weight, Perry was under pressure from the third round onwards as Bronson closed down the range and concentrated on the body. Several times it looked as though he would be floored, but in the tenth he actually fell down of his own accord before being saved by the bell.

A six-round no-decision affair between Bronson and Tommy Howell at the National AC, Philadelphia, Pennsylvania on 8 March 1913 was almost certainly contested at 145lbs. Howell received the verdict of the press.

7 February 1913. (145lbs) Spike Kelly drew 10 Tommy Howell.
Venue: The Labor Temple Auditorium, Kansas City, Missouri, USA.
Fight Summary: Without notification of actual weights, the *Chicago Tribune* reported this as a billed title fight at 145lbs, and while Kelly seemed to be well in the fight it was Howell who was the aggressor and landed more effectively. There were no knockdowns, but both men finished with damage to their eyes.

It is almost certain that Howell risked his title claim in five six-round no-decision contests in Philadelphia, Pennsylvania against Young Erne (nd-drew 6 at the Olympia AC on 17 February), Johnny Marto (nd-w pts 6 at the Olympia AC on 3 March), Ray Bronson (nd-w pts 6 at the National AC on 8 March), Kid Graves (nd-l pts 6 at the National AC on 22 March) and Erne again (nd-w pts 6 at the National AC on 5 April)

21 February 1913. (145lbs) Wildcat Ferns nd-drew 15 Billy Walters.
Venue: The Auditorium, St Joseph, Missouri, USA.
Fight Summary: Each man weighed between 144 and 145lbs as per the *St Joseph Gazette*, therefore putting Ferns' title claim on the line. In a fierce bout Walters took a severe beating in the first few rounds before evening things up later when going to the body. At the finish, Walters' left eye was closed and Ferns' body was battered and bruised.

10 March 1913. (145lbs) Wildcat Ferns w pts 10 Spike Kelly.
Venue: Labor Temple Auditorium, Kansas City, Missouri, USA.
Fight Summary: With both men making the required 145lbs, and their title claims at the weight automatically on the line, it was Ferns who made all the running to take six rounds with four even according to press reports. Kelly, who fought on gamely at all times, finished with a badly damaged mouth.

Fourteen days later, on 24 March, Kelly forced Jack Foreman to retire inside two rounds of an eight rounder at the Phoenix AC, Memphis, Tennessee. The *Memphis Daily Appeal* reported that Kelly put his title claim at risk in a fight made at 145lbs, regardless of his recent loss to Ferns.

18 March 1913. (145lbs) Wildcat Ferns drew 10 Jimmy Perry.
Venue: Orpheum Theatre, Atlanta, Georgia, USA. **Referee:** Mike Saul.
Fight Summary: This was billed as one of a series of eliminators to decide the 145lbs title. Putting his claim on the line, although Ferns had Perry down in the second round it was a relatively tame affair with few good blows landed. Ferns, the better boxer of the pair, piled up points with left jabs, but because he lacked venom in his fists Perry was able stay in the fight. There were no knockdowns and neither was badly hurt.

11 April 1913. (145lbs) Spike Kelly nd-w pts 10 Billy Walters.
Venue: Coliseum Skating Palace, Kenosha, Wisconsin, USA.
Fight Summary: In a match made at 145lbs, with both men inside, the *Chicago Tribune* reported that the winner would claim the title despite Kelly's recent defeat at the weight by Ferns. While Kelly was the better man at close quarters and at range it was not until the seventh round that he cut loose to go clear.

14 April 1913. (142lbs) Ray Bronson nd-drew 10 Billy Griffith.
Venue: Olympic Theatre, Cincinnati, Ohio, USA. **Referee:** Frank Kelly.
Fight Summary: The *Cincinnati Enquirer* claimed that with both men making the stipulated 142lbs Bronson's claim was at risk, and he started as though he meant to hold on to it when sending in right-hand swings to Griffith's face. For several rounds Griffith was a threat when sending in heavy wallops from either hand and in the sixth and eighth he virtually had Bronson at his mercy. Then it was Bronson's turn, battering Griffith around the ring while unsuccessfully looking to find a finisher.

16 April 1913. (145lbs) Wildcat Ferns drew 10 Tommy Howell.
Venue: Labor Temple Auditorium, Kansas City, Missouri, USA.
Fight Summary: Given as a catchweight contest by the *Kansas City Star* it then reported both fighters to be inside 145lbs. A hard-hitting affair saw Howell, who was dropped by a left swing to the jaw in the second round, come back strongly to send Ferns sprawling in the ninth from a similar blow. Both men were bleeding freely at the final bell.

Howell's claim at 145lbs subsequently faded away, as he continuously took part in six- rounders while putting on weight.

23 April 1913. (142lbs) Ray Bronson nd-w pts 10 Hilliard Lang.
Venue: Tomlinson Hall, Indianapolis, Indiana, USA.
Fight Summary: Made at 142lbs, with both inside, the *Indianapolis News* reported that Bronson proved himself to be the 'real' claimant in this one after decidedly getting the better of Lang in a return. There were no knockdowns, but Lang appeared all-in at the final bell while Bronson looked like he could fight another ten rounds. Once Bronson had worked out how to deal with Lang's early body attacks he stood at distance, jabbing, hammering and swinging at his rival almost at will according to press reports.

5 May 1913. (145lbs) Wildcat Ferns w pts 10 Jimmy Perry.
Venue: Labor Temple Auditorium, Kansas City, Missouri, USA. **Referee:** Billy Tissue.
Fight Summary: According to the *Kansas City Star* both men made the prescribed 145lbs, with Ferns holding on to his title claim at the weight after a very poor fight. It was only in three rounds that there was any live action, the rest of the contest being decidedly poor as both men missed with wild swings and lacked judgement. Ferns took the referee's decision on account of him landing more often and more effectively than Perry, who was badly hurt in the ninth by head punches and finished the session hanging on to the ropes for support.

12 May 1913. (145lbs) Ray Bronson nd-l pts 10 Young Denny.
Venue: Orleans AC, New Orleans, Louisiana, USA. **Referee:** Dick Burke.
Fight Summary: In a fight made at 145lbs, Bronson held on to his title claim despite being shaded by Denny, who almost had his man out in the second round before dropping him with a right cross to the jaw in the third. Although Bronson occasionally showed up well on the inside, Denny hurt him virtually in every round with heavy rights, and in the final session he staggered the title claimant three times before the bell came to his rescue.

Having successfully defended his claim to the American title, Bronson set sail for Australia in November.

28 May 1913. (145lbs) Wildcat Ferns drew 20 Al McCoy.
Venue: Lakeside Arena, Dayton, Ohio, USA. **Referee:** George Roehm.
Fight Summary: A contest at the welterweight limit of 145lbs, as was their first meeting, the *Dayton Journal* reported that it proved to be a boring, uninteresting affair with neither man bothering to do much fighting.

It is not known if McCoy claimed the welter title but, whether he did or not, it hardly mattered as he was soon up among the middleweights.

4 July 1913. (142lbs) Wildcat Ferns w pts 10 Young Denny.
Venue: Pelican Park, New Orleans, Louisiana, USA. **Referee:** Jimmy Bronson.
Fight Summary: The *New Orleans Daily Picayune* gave this as a billed championship match at 142lbs, with Ferns' title claim on the line. After a cat-and-mouse start the fight began with a vengeance in the fifth round as both men traded heavy blows, and following a couple of sessions of close-quarter work Denny seemed to have the better of things. Although Ferns continued to charge in throwing vicious punches, with Denny managing to avoid the great majority while countering heavily to the body, by the ninth the 'Wildcat' was carrying a badly gashed left eye. The tenth round saw Denny well on top, with the much weakened Ferns taking a beating and ready to drop before the final bell came to his rescue. When the referee indicated that Ferns was the winner at the expense of the local man all hell broke loose, the third man being lucky to escape injury as the crowd surged towards him.

22 July 1913. (142lbs) Mike Glover w rsc 4 (10) Marcel Thomas.
Venue: Atlas AA, Boston, Massachusetts, USA. **Referee:** Jack Sheehan.
Fight Summary: Although Thomas held the French version of the world 147lbs title, the *Boston Post* failed to report weights and billing. However, they did state: "This was as near a title fight you will get". Following the result, and taking into account his recent victory over England's Gus Platts (nd-w pts 10 at St Nicholas Arena, Manhattan, NYC, New York on 9 July), Glover laid claim to the 142lbs championship. It was a strange fight, with Thomas well outpointing Glover in the first two rounds but then being in distress as the latter responded with stiff body shots. After two minutes of the fourth Thomas suddenly dropped his hands and walked to his corner, whereupon the referee awarded the contest to Glover.

In his next contest, on 7 August, Glover took on Paddy Sullivan at the Atlantic AA, Rockaway Beach, Queens, NYC, New York, knocking him out in the seventh of a no-decision contest scheduled for ten rounds. It is not known what the weights were, but Sullivan was fighting just above the lightweight limit at that time.

9 September 1913. (145lbs) Spike Kelly nd-w pts 10 Tommy Sheehan.
Venue: Grand Opera House, Superior, Wisconsin, USA.
Fight Summary: As far as the *Milwaukee Sentinel* were concerned this one was made at 145lbs, and with his claim at risk Kelly made sure of the press verdict when using fast footwork to score points as well as avoid punches. Despite it being tame, Kelly shaded it after Sheehan was unable to come up with anything significant.

26 September 1913. (145lbs) Wildcat Ferns nd-w pts 10 Billy Walters.
Venue: Coliseum Skating Palace, Kenosha, Wisconsin, USA.
Fight Summary: It was reported in the *Chicago Tribune* that both men were inside 145lbs. Ferns started to fight the moment the bell went before dropping Walters with a left to the jaw after about half a minute. Thereafter, with Walters losing his drive, Ferns shaded six rounds with four even according to the fight report.

29 September 1913. (142lbs) Mike Glover nd-w pts 10 Young Denny.
Venue: Orleans AC, New Orleans, Louisiana, USA. **Referee:** Dick Burke.
Fight Summary: With both men inside 142lbs at 3pm, as per the *New Orleans Daily Picayune*, Glover's title claim was automatically at stake. Starting fast, Glover's left hand opened Denny up again and again, and on at least three or four occasions the latter almost went through the ropes after rushing in to the attack. In the middle stages the fight lost its impetus due to both men continually wrestling at close quarters, very few quality punches landing. After being told that he would be thrown out if he continued to transgress the rules, Denny finally woke up in the ninth, going after Glover with both hands and opening up the title claimant's left eye. The last round saw both men working hard with Glover relying on his skill to nullify Denny's aggression, and at the final bell there was no doubt in the minds of the attending pressmen as to the winner.

9 October 1913. (145lbs) Spike Kelly nd-l pts 10 Mike Gibbons.
Venue: Coliseum Skating Palace, Kenosha, Wisconsin, USA.
Fight Summary: Reported in the *Chicago Tribune* as being articled for the 145lbs version of the title, Kelly held on to his claim despite being outscored in most of the rounds. At first Gibbons stood off and boxed at range, but once Kelly began to bore in, forcing him to trade, he was soon rattling in short rights almost at will. Although Kelly was still active when sending in hard looking swings and uppercuts, too few of them landed to make a dent in Gibbons' defensive shield.

13 October 1913. (142lbs) Mike Glover nd-l pts 10 Kid Graves.
Venue: Irving AC, Brooklyn, NYC, New York, USA. **Referee:** Patsy Haley.
Fight Summary: Made at 142lbs, and a fight between title claimants, the opening three rounds saw Glover (142) doing the better work, drawing Graves' leads and countering him accurately. However, realising that a change in tactics were called for, after Graves (141½) began to swing in blows from both hands a right hook soon closed Glover's left eye. Although the last two sessions were contested more evenly, with both men doing some clever work, the press in attendance agreed that Graves' aggression had earned him the decision.

Graves had been claiming the title with limited recognition since March, stating that as he had bested Lee Barrett (nd-w pts 10 at the Irving AC, Brooklyn on 1 February) and Young Ahearn (nd-w pts 10 at the Beach AC, Brooklyn on 18 February) in no-decision contests he deserved to be ranked among the front runners, and challenged any of the top men to make 142lbs at 3pm or 145lbs ringside. Before meeting Glover he had met Tommy Howell (nd-w pts 6 at the National AC, Philadelphia, Pennsylvania on 22 March), Young Erne (nd-w pts 6 at the National AC on 19 April), Jack Britton (nd-l pts 6 at the National AC on 17 May) and Tommy Maloney (nd-drew 10 at the Irving Ac, Brooklyn on 26 July) in no-decision affairs.

Following his press win over Glover it was clear that Graves was strengthening his claim, but to most observers he was still no more than an Eastern Board candidate. Then, after challenging all America to a distance fight that would settle the championship, Graves found himself on the wrong end of no-decision meetings with Barrett (nd-l pts 10 at the Southside AA, Milwaukee, Wisconsin on 4 December), Mike Gibbons (nd-l pts 6 at the Olympia AC, Philadelphia on 16 February 1914) and Jack Britton (nd-l pts 10 at the Irving AC on 10 March 1914). Despite the press result, there were many good judges who felt that Graves had got the better of Britton. Contested at a fast pace it was always close, and while the clever Britton (137½) nullified much of Graves' aggression the harder punching came from the latter.

Looking to keep busy, Graves took in two no-decision six rounders and was felt by the press to have drawn over six-rounds with Soldier Bartfield (at the Olympia AA, Philadelphia on 30 March 1914) and been outpointed by Britton (at the National AC, Philadelphia, Pennsylvania on 25 April 1914). He then met Bartfield three more times in no-decision ten-rounders at the Broadway SC, Brooklyn, on 23 May, 9 and 20 June, winning the first and second contests, and drawing the third according to the press. While Graves made 140½lbs ringside for his opening contest against Bartfield, the latter came in at 145¾lbs. The next two affairs saw Graves make 142lbs to Bartfield's 148lbs and 147lbs. At the same venue, on 7 July 1914, Graves (143¾) was deemed by the press to have outscored Glover (147¼) after ten rounds of competitive boxing at catchweights.

Meanwhile, Bartfield, who was seen by those around him as having as good a claim to the title as others, was generally thought to be too heavy for the weight class, and with scant backing he concentrated on the middleweights. Also hindering Bartfield's cause was the fact that he boxed mainly in no-decision fights and did not beat any of the top men inside the distance.

23 October 1913. (145lbs) Spike Kelly nd-w pts 10 Billy Walters.
Venue: Grand Opera House, Superior, Wisconsin, USA. **Referee:** Tug McDonough.
Fight Summary: In a match made at 145lbs, the *Superior Telegram* reported that it was a terrific fight. Contested at a fast pace, with Walters (142½) forcing matters, Kelly (145) showed a clever defence and countered with clean shots that would have racked up the points if a decision had been involved. Neither man was in distress at any time.

17 November 1913. (145lbs) Wildcat Ferns drew 15 Johnny McCarthy.
Venue: Stockyards Stadium, Denver, Colorado, USA. **Referee:** Mike Geary.
Fight Summary: With the weight set at 145lbs, the *Rocky Mountain Herald* stated that both men were inside for what was a defence of Ferns' title claim. Every round saw Ferns forcing matters, with McCarthy, who was about ten pounds lighter, covering up well and fighting cleverly on the inside to nullify the incessant attacks before tiring towards the end.

24 November 1913. (145lbs) Spike Kelly nd-l pts 10 Lee Barrett.
Venue: Elite Rink, Milwaukee, Wisconsin, USA. **Referee:** Dan Hyde.
Fight Summary: Taking on Barrett in a match made at 145lbs, with Kelly's title claim up for grabs the first five rounds saw both men cautioned for continually holding. After that they opened up tooth and nail, with Kelly doing his best work at range while Barrett continually bored in to land solid body shots.

27 November 1913. (142lbs) Mike Glover nd-w pts 10 Jack Britton.
Venue: Irving AC, Brooklyn, NYC, New York, USA.
Fight Summary: Although Britton (134¾) was really considered to be a lightweight, Glover (137¼) put his 142lbs title claim on the line in this one, and following a close bout the press just about gave him the honours. Britton had started like a whirlwind before Glover came back strongly to even matters up in the closing stages, his best punch being a heavy right to the jaw that sent the lighter man reeling on the ropes during the seventh.

2 December 1913. (142lbs) Johnny Kid Alberts nd-w co 6 (10) Phil Cross.
Venue: Atlantic Gardens AC, Manhattan, NYC, New York, USA. **Referee:** Billy Moore.
Fight Summary: Contested at 142lbs, Alberts (141½) made a cracking start with body punches doubling Cross (140¾) up in the opening two rounds before heavy right swings to the jaw saw the later take two counts of 'seven' in the third. Somehow getting through the fourth, despite being all over the place according to the *New York*

Times' report, Cross came back well in the fifth, landing solidly with straight lefts to the body. Although Cross seemed to be right back in the fight when forcing matters in the sixth, after being again caught by a hard right swing to the head he crashed down, his head striking the ring floor heavily, and was counted out. In a contest that had been billed as one which would bring about a championship candidate, the *Lowell Sun* reported that Alberts had claimed the title.

It is not known whether contests against Al Roach (nd-w rsc 7 at the Fairmont AC, Bronx, NYC, New York on 6 December), Tommy Howell (nd-l pts 6 at the Olympia AC, Philadelphia, Pennsylvania on 8 December) and Joe Chick (drew 15 at the Marieville AC, Providence, Rhode Island on 19 December) belonged to Alberts' claim or not.

10 December 1913. (147lbs) Mike Gibbons nd-w co 2 (10) Wildcat Ferns.
Venue: Pelican Park, New Orleans, Louisiana, USA. **Referee:** Dick Burke.
Fight Summary: Billed for the 147lbs title, Ferns (146) was dropped four times in quick succession by Gibbons (147) in the second round, the final knockdown ending in a count out. However, with the popular limit still at 142lbs (3pm weigh-in) or 145 (ringside) in America, Gibbons received little recognition.

Meanwhile, Ferns carried on with his 145lbs claim. Although taking in fights against Young Denny (w pts 10 at the Pelican Stadium, New Orleans, Louisiana on 22 December), Harry Brewer (l pts 10 at the Academy of Music, Kansas City, Missouri on 1 January 1914) and Charley Pierson (w pts 15 in Joplin, Missouri on 29 January 1914) prior to being beaten by Spike Kelly, I am not sure whether they were made at 145lbs or not. If they were then Ferns technically lost his claim to Brewer, who had retired two fights later. In his penultimate contest, Brewer met Eddie Johnson (nd-drew 10 at the Colonial Theatre, Pueblo, Colorado on 17 September 1914), a fighter who had also been claiming the title on the back of a win over Spike Kelly. Regardless of the fact that Johnson's contest against Kelly cannot be traced at present, his claim went nowhere.

16 December 1913. (145lbs) Spike Kelly w pts 15 Billy Walters.
Venue: Eagles Hall, St Joseph, Missouri, USA.
Fight Summary: Made at 145lbs, Kelly held on to his title claim when dancing his way to a points win over Walters, often jabbing him at will and never being in any danger. While Walters was not disgraced, due to him giving it everything, he was unable to locate Kelly, and after he had butted the latter at the final bell there was a free-for-all that lasted about a minute.

On 22 December, Kelly knocked out Jimmy Burns in the final session of a ten-round no-decision affair at the Moose Lodge Hall, Kankakee, Illinois, following a left-right to the jaw with just ten seconds of the contest remaining. Initially thought to have involved Kelly's title claim when the *Kankakee Daily Republican* reported it to be a bout between men of the 142lbs class it turned out to be a catchweight contest above the weight.

29 December 1913. (142lbs) Johnny Kid Alberts nd-drew 10 Tommy Maloney.
Venue: National AC, New Amsterdam Opera House, Manhattan, NYC, New York, USA.
Fight Summary: Alberts (142) held on to his claim at the weight when getting a press draw against Maloney (142). The *New York Times* report stated that after eight sessions of mediocrity, the last two rounds were enlivened by fast mixing and clean hitting, in which Maloney made the running in the ninth. Although baffled by some clever boxing, Alberts eventually came back in the tenth to even matters up.

1 January 1914. (147lbs) Waldemar Holberg w pts 20 Ray Bronson.
Venue: West Melbourne Stadium, Melbourne, Australia. **Referee:** Ernie Fullalove.
Fight Summary: Bronson (146¾), who had been claiming the title, met Holberg (143½) in a fight given championship billing at 147lbs by the leading Melbourne promoter. While Holberg proved to be the better boxer of the two, his speed around the ring coupled with accurate left jabs giving the American plenty to think about, Bronson was the harder puncher. In the middle rounds Bronson came on strong, and his ability on the inside showed just how limited the Dane was in that field. But having come through a difficult time, Holberg began to get his boxing back on track from around the 13th to move into the ascendancy. Thereafter, with Bronson seemingly

unable to influence the fight the last three rounds saw him cutting down his work-rate as he went looking for a knockout without success. There were no knockdowns, but both men bled freely throughout.

19 January 1914. (142lbs) Mike Glover nd-l pts 10 Jack Britton.
Venue: National AC, New Amsterdam Opera House, Manhattan, NYC, New York, USA.
Fight Summary: A defence of Glover's 142lbs title claim ended with Britton (134½) being awarded the press verdict following an exceptional contest of skill and science that saw him get the better of every round bar the fifth and seventh. While Glover (137¼) was not far behind he was unable to make a breakthrough against a man at the top of his game.

Glover outpointed KO Sweeney over ten rounds at the North-End AC Auditorium, Waterbury, Connecticut on 29 October, in a fight that was described by the *Naugatuck Daily News* as being practically a battle for the welterweight title. However, with no weights available and Sweeney described in one fight report as being 16 pounds heavier than Glover we should discard any claims of it having title involvement until better information surfaces.

24 January 1914. (147lbs) Tom McCormick w disq 6 (20) Waldemar Holberg.
Venue: West Melbourne Stadium, Melbourne, Australia. **Referee:** Ernie Fullalove.
Fight Summary: Advertised as a championship bout at 147lbs by the local promoter, but not recognised as such in Sydney, by his victory McCormick took over Holberg's claim at the weight. According to the *Mirror of Life* the clever McCormick (145¼) totally outclassed Holberg (145¼) from the opening bell, and even at an early stage it could be seen that it would only be a matter of time before the latter would be at his mercy. Holberg, a bustling, determined fighter, could do nothing with McCormick, being outboxed with ease. In vain he tried to batter his way through the Irishman's defence, but after he struck a palpably low blow in the sixth he was immediately disqualified. Summing up the fight, the *Sydney Morning Herald* reported that Holberg gave the worst display of foul fighting that had ever been seen in Melbourne before being thrown out.

3 February 1914. (142lbs) Johnny Kid Alberts nd-w pts 10 Frankie Madden.
Venue: Atlantic Gardens, Manhattan, NYC, New York, USA.
Fight Summary: In a match made at 142lbs, Alberts' title claim at the weight was on the line against Madden, the latter being totally ineffective for nine rounds when boring in without delivering punches and laying on the Elizabeth (New Jersey) lad in such a manner that prevented him from doing his best work. There were no quibbles against the press decision in favour of Alberts as it was so obvious.

Following a catchweight contest against Young Jasper, Alberts took in a 15-round return match against Tommy Maloney at the Gardens, Marieville, Rhode Island on 15 April. The *Kennebec Journal* stated that Alberts was outclassed and did not win a round as Maloney toyed with him all night. One must assume that this was contested above 142lbs or was a no-decision contest as Alberts was still claiming the title at that weight when he met Frankie Notter (nd-w pts 10 at the Fairmont AC, Bronx, NYC, New York on 20 June) and Terry Mitchell (nd-drew 10 at the Twyford AC, Brooklyn, NYC, New York on 2 July) prior to meeting Kid Graves.

It was reported in the 16 March 1916 issue of the *Manchester Sporting Guardian* that Maloney had been claiming the welter title for the past three years and defending against all-comers, including Mike Gibbons. While Maloney may have boxed Gibbons, according to the *New York Times* he was given an awful drubbing. It is more than likely that Maloney's claim came from his two contests against Alberts, which was further weakened when he quickly moved to the upper end of the weight class.

14 February 1914. (147lbs) Tom McCormick w co 1 (20) Johnny Summers.
Venue: The Stadium, Sydney, Australia. **Referee:** Arthur Scott.
Fight Summary: Recorded in most record books as a 147lbs championship fight, it was, in effect, a semi-final leg of the Australian elimination series. However, regardless of that, McCormick (145¾) would be defending the title claim he won when beating Waldemar Holberg. On deciding that it was in his best interests to finish early, Summers (143¼) tore into McCormick from the clang of the bell, showering the latter with punches from both

hands at bewildering speed. It then became McCormick's turn to hurl himself at Summers, the pair meeting in a frenzied burst of punching. Although McCormick was taking pile-driving shots to the body he somehow found a short right-arm blow to the jaw to lay Summers low, and amidst a tremendous din the latter was counted out at 2.30 of the opening session, face down on the canvas.

11 March 1914. (145lbs) Spike Kelly nd-w pts 10 Lee Barrett.
Venue: Turner Hall, Madison, Wisconsin, USA. **Referee:** Harry Stout.
Fight Summary: According to the *Wisconsin State Journal,* with both fighters in trim neither was expected to bend the scale set at 145lbs. Defending his claim at the weight, Kelly had the power, stiff, jolting blows sending Barrett back on his heels at times, but unable to drop his opponent he only had him in distress during the last two rounds. Kelly could even have lost had it not been for Barrett's sportsmanship. Having gone low in the seventh the referee admonished Kelly and asked Barrett whether he wished to continue, but the latter gamely declined the opportunity when saying that he would prefer to battle on.

21 March 1914. (147lbs) Matt Wells w pts 20 Tom McCormick.
Venue: The Stadium, Sydney, Australia. **Referee:** Harold Baker.
Fight Summary: The final leg of the Australian 147lbs international elimination tournament saw both Wells (146) and McCormick (146) boxing below par, and although there was some heavy hitting involved as a spectacle it was not the best. Wells showed up better at distance, especially with the left jab, while McCormick relied on the short right uppercut that had demolished Johnny Summers. After taking the opening five rounds, Wells endured some uncomfortable moments at close quarters before finding that a solid right to McCormick's body was to his advantage. At the half-way mark, Wells was well ahead. Despite tiring towards the finish nearly all of his punches were of the scoring variety, whereas McCormick continued to cuff when less volume and more quality would have been a better bet. McCormick had just eight more bouts before re-joining the British Army and being killed in action on the Western Front in June 1916.

7 April 1914. (145lbs) Spike Kelly nd-w disq 1 (10) Wildcat Ferns.
Venue: The Grand Opera House, Superior, Wisconsin, USA.
Fight Summary: On the day of the fight the *Superior Telegram* reported that the match had been articled at 145lbs, a weight that both men could make without difficulty. The contest itself was a fiasco, Kelly, hit below the belt by a wild left before the opening round was a minute old, being forced to leave the ring on a stretcher. Ferns later denied that the low blow had been intentional. Although Ferns' career ends three fights later, his claim to the American title was effectively over following the contest.

26 May 1914. (147lbs) Mike Gibbons nd-w pts 10 Johnny Kid Alberts.
Venue: The Alhambra, Syracuse, New York, USA. **Referee:** Charles Huck.
Fight Summary: In a match made at 147lbs, thus involving Gibbons' claim at the weight, the latter was never in any danger of losing as he controlled matters throughout. Alberts (145), whose title claim at 142lbs was not on the line, landed no more than six clean punches all night according to press reports, while Gibbons (147) was content to show his marvellous boxing ability without hurting his rival until opening up in the last two rounds. Having no answer to the left jab, Alberts spent much of the time rushing at Gibbons, only to be forced to cover up.

Having great difficulty making 147lbs, Gibbons should be recognised as a middleweight from thereon in.

12 June 1914. (145lbs) Spike Kelly w co 15 (20) Eddie Madison.
Venue: Trocadero Hall, Murray, Utah, USA.
Fight Summary: Kelly took over proceedings from the start before having Madison down in the seventh with a hard swing to the body. Madison, who was obviously in some pain, appealed for a disqualification but was turned down by the doctors and told he could take a 15-minute rest. Although Madison, showing much courage, got himself back into the fight his night was over after Kelly sent in a terrific right to the solar plexus that put him down for the full count in the 15th round. The contest was made at 145lbs.

Prior to being inactive for 15 months Kelly boxed George Klett (drew 15 at the Gymnastic Club, Dayton, Ohio on 21 October), but at the moment I have yet to uncover whether the contest was made at 145lbs. What is known is that Kelly was still claiming the American 145lbs title at the end of the year, and was supported by the *TS Andrews' Annual* published early in 1915. However, Kelly's claim at 145lbs appears to be over from thereon in.

30 June 1914. (147lbs) Johnny Summers drew 20 Harry Stone.
Venue: Olympia, Kensington, London, England. **Referee:** Eugene Corri.
Fight Summary: With many of the top Britons fighting abroad, Summers was matched against Stone to contest the world 147lbs title. Although there were no knockdowns it was an exciting fight between top men, and while Summers worked well downstairs Stone showed a sound knowledge of the game when countering and defending well. With there never being much in it the announcement of a draw was widely accepted. Given world title billing mainly because it was an international contest between a man still seen by many as the British champion and a leading American the fight solved nothing. While Summers had been beaten in his two previous contests next time out he lost his version of the British welterweight title to Johnny Basham, being knocked out inside 14 rounds at the NSC, Covent Garden, London on 14 December.

Going straight back to America after meeting Summers, having been campaigning in Australia since April 1913, Stone was claiming to be the world welterweight champion (or 140lbs lightweight champion depending on what paper you read) after he said he had been presented with a diamond studded silver belt by Snowy Baker on beating Matt Wells (w pts 20 at the Sydney Stadium on 29 November 1913). Wells had weighed 136lbs to Stone's 132. A report in the *Sydney Referee* in December 1914 refuted Stone's claim to hold Australia's version of the world title at any weight, stating that he was well beaten on points over 20 rounds at The Stadium, Sydney by Herb McCoy (135½) at the Australian lightweight limit of 140lbs in his penultimate contest in the Antipodes and was unable to make a match with Hughie Mehegan, who was recognised as the best man in Australia at the time. The report went on to say that he was a champion liar and was fooling the boxing public.

Regardless of all that, Stone, who could comfortably make 135lbs if he wished, was challenging all men between 135lbs to 150lbs, preferably Mike Gibbons, and back in America wherever he went he billed himself as a leading claimant for the 142/145lbs title. Although Stone could make the lightweight limit of 135lbs with ease, because Freddie Welsh was recognised universally as the champion of that division, and with the welterweight class in disarray, he would concentrate on the latter weight class.

18 July 1914. (142lbs) Kid Graves nd-w co 2 (10) Johnny Kid Alberts.
Venue: Broadway SC, Brooklyn, NYC, New York, USA.
Fight Summary: There is limited information on this fight, other than the result and the fact that Graves did what a whole lot of top-notch boxers had tried in vain to accomplish when knocking Alberts out. The fight report in the *New York Telegram* stated that the end came so suddenly in the second the spectators were bewildered. It was also reported that the winner of the Graves v Albert fight was recognised by the American Boxing Association (ABA) as the welterweight champion, being the final of a competition to find such a man.

At this stage of its history, the ABA was a little known body that was eventually reformed on 21 September 1915. Having beaten Alberts, Graves stated that he should be recognised as the champion on the grounds that Mike Gibbons and Packey McFarland appeared to be fighting in a higher division and that other noted men had fallen by the wayside. Along with Spike Kelly and Mike Glover, he was supported by the *TS Andrews' Annual.*

On 29 September Graves (143½) again faced Alberts (146½) at the Broadway SC, winning the ten-round press decision. This time, however, it has to be treated as a catchweight contest with the latter fighting above 145lbs. Later in the year Graves challenged McFarland to a bout that would settle the championship, but nothing came of it.

8 September 1914. (142lbs) Harry Stone nd-l pts 10 Phil Bloom.
Venue: Broadway SC, Brooklyn, NYC, New York, USA.

Fight Summary: Back in America, having been away since the beginning of 1913, Stone's world title claim of 142lbs at 3pm or 145lbs ringside was automatically on the line against Bloom (135), and as far as the *New York Times* was concerned he took just two sessions, the fourth and fifth. Stone (137), who was nicknamed 'Hop Harry' due to his peculiar style, delayed fighting in every other round, only cutting loose in the last ten seconds of the others when being outboxed by a man who would not back away despite taking hard blows to the wind.

1 December 1914. (142lbs) Harry Stone w pts 12 Gilbert Gallant.
Venue: Atlas AA, Boston, Massachusetts, USA. **Referee:** Patsy Haley.
Fight Summary: In what was a close bout with Stone's 142lbs title claim on the line, there was very little good work. It was also clear that many in the crowd felt that Gallant deserved a share of the spoils on the basis that he was more attack-minded. Stone was happy to box on the back foot, showing a sound defence when needed, but was unable to hurt his opponent.

12 January 1915. (142lbs) Kid Graves nd-w pts 10 Johnny Kid Alberts.
Venue: Knickerbocker AC, Germania Hall, Albany, New York, USA.
Fight Summary: Both men made the required 142lbs according to the *Albany Evening Journal*. The fight report in the *Albany Times Union* stated that as entertainment it was disappointing. However, in terms of ability Graves totally outclassed Alberts, who apart from a burst of punching in the seventh failed to take any risks whatsoever. There were no knockdowns, and as far as the paper was concerned Graves won six rounds with the other four being seen as even. Graves showed himself to be a clever operator as well as a two-fisted one, tying up Alberts on the inside as and when needed while controlling the contest from start to finish.

27 January 1915. (142lbs) Harry Stone nd-w pts 10 Frankie Nelson.
Venue: Brown's Gym, Queens, NYC, New York, USA.
Fight Summary: Although the *New York Herald* reported this to be a lightweight contest, it was Stone's 142lbs title claim that was really at risk. Stone showed up well against the rushing, slugging and unscientific Nelson, who made all the running but was unable to do any damage. Despite Stone handing out a boxing lesson, hitting Nelson whenever and wherever he pleased, he showed such little power that the latter finished almost as strong as when he started.

30 January 1915. (142lbs) Kid Graves nd-l pts 10 Jack Britton.
Venue: Broadway SC, Brooklyn, NYC, New York, USA.
Fight Summary: Regardless that Graves (142) was more than three pounds heavier than Britton (139) both men were inside 142lbs at ringside, thus putting the former's title claim at that weight on the line. Britton forced the fight from the opening bell, his left jabs and right uppercuts being his most effective weapons, while Graves was at his best in the fifth, sixth and seventh rounds. At the end of the contest most scribes thought that Britton's cleaner work entitled him to the press decision. There were no knockdowns recorded.

22 February 1915. (142lbs) Harry Stone nd-l pts 10 Lockport Jimmy Duffy.
Venue: Broadway Auditorium, Buffalo, New York, USA. **Referee:** Dick Nugent.
Fight Summary: After both men made 136lbs, Stone's 142lbs title claim was technically at stake regardless of the fact that there was nothing in the *Buffalo News* to suggest that he was a championship claimant. Stone quickly realised that he was up against a tartar as Duffy was after him like a cyclone, brushing away his punches almost contemptuously from the second round onwards. Round after round Stone was backed up against the ropes with nowhere to go, and in the sixth a cracking right uppercut almost had him out. According to the newspaper report there was not a session where Stone had even a share. The paper went on to say that he somehow got through the fight by staying on the back foot and covering up as Duffy worked away non-stop.

26 February 1915. (142lbs) Harry Stone nd-w pts 10 Frankie Nelson.
Venue: Armoury B, Oshkosh, Wisconsin, USA. **Referee:** Harry Stout.
Fight Summary: Billed as a welterweight championship contest, Stone put up his 142lbs title claim in what was one of the fastest battles seen in the city for a long time. Both men were happy to fight at close quarters, and although

Nelson did much of the forcing in every round he was more often than not stopped in his tracks by straight lefts to head and body.

6 March 1915. (142lbs) Kid Graves nd-l pts 10 Walter Mohr.
Venue: Irving AC, Brooklyn, NYC, New York, USA.
Fight Summary: With both men inside the contracted weight, despite Mohr (136) taking the press decision Graves (142) came through unscathed to maintain his claim at the weight. The *Brooklyn Citizen* report of the fight stated that Mohr forced Graves all over the ring, roughing him up round after round, and although the latter complained continually he was overruled and told to get on with it by the referee.

By now claiming the title at 145lbs as well as 142lbs, it is possible that Graves' next outing, against Jimmy Capper (nd-w pts 10 at the Broadway SC, Brooklyn on 3 April), was made at that weight, but after Jack Kincaid, an expert on boxing in New York, had looked at all the papers of the day he was unable to find any notification of weights. Reports of the fight were sparse to say the least, stating that Capper failed to do enough to gain the press decision, his best work being a straight left to the body early on and his aggression towards the end.

12 April 1915. (145lbs) Willie Moore nd-w rsc 5 (6) Young Jack O'Brien.
Venue: Olympia AA, Philadelphia, Pennsylvania, USA.
Fight Summary: Even though it was just a mere six rounder Moore (142½) claimed the American 145lbs title after he had defeated O'Brien (145), having smashed his man down with a big left hook for 'nine' in the fifth before the fight was stopped. Christened Wilhelm von Franzke, Moore was a member of one of the most outstanding boxing families to come out of America, his brothers being Pal (Thomas), Frankie, Reddy and Albert, all top-line fighters.

There was no doubting Moore's power, but continually participating in six-round contests hardly enhanced his claim, and when Ted Kid Lewis (139¾) was deemed by the press to have outscored him over six rounds at the Olympia AA on 18 October it was further weakened. For that fight Moore weighed in at 144lbs.

24 April 1915. (145lbs) Kid Graves nd-w pts 10 Harry Stone.
Venue: Irving AC, Brooklyn, NYC, New York, USA.
Fight Summary: Articled for a ringside weigh-in at 145lbs, and with both fighters' aspirations to be the welterweight champion on the line, Graves (144) easily held on to his title claim at the weight according to the majority of press reports. Graves had at least six rounds in his favour over Stone (136), who failed to offer a threat and only showed in two sessions.

Putting his 142lbs title claim on the line, Stone was deemed by the press to have defeated Johnny Reese (nd-w pts 10 at the Vanderbilt AC, Brooklyn) on 28 May. In what was a lightweight contest, both men scaling 134lbs, Reese had stepped in at short notice for Walter Mohr.

Without weights being available, it is unclear at this moment as to whether Stone's contest against Kid Burns (nd-w pts 10 at Brown's Gym, Queens, NYC on 11 June) involved his title claim. At that moment in time the latter could make 140lbs with ease.

1 June 1915. (142lbs) Mike Glover w pts 12 Matt Wells.
Venue: Armoury AA, Boston, Massachusetts, USA. **Referee:** Patsy Haley.
Fight Summary: Although there was no mention of this one being a title fight in the *Boston Daily Globe*, the *Boston Post* claimed afterwards that as both men were inside 142lbs at 3pm, Glover should now hold the Australian version of the title. Regardless, there was no doubt that Glover's claim at the weight was considerably strengthened by his victory. Outreached by more than eight inches, Wells, who was forced to make all the running in order to get to close quarters, finished the contest with his right eye closed as well as suffering plenty of further facial damage. The opening few rounds were fairly even as both men looked for openings, but after the fourth, using a solid left jab mixed with uppercuts to head and body, Glover surged to the front and stayed there. However hard Wells tried he just could not gain the advantage, and despite a powerful rally in the 12th when throwing caution to the wind he had to settle for a points defeat.

9 June 1915. (145lbs) Kid Graves nd-l pts 10 Ted Kid Lewis.
Venue: St Nicholas Arena, Manhattan, NYC, New York, USA. **Referee:** Billy Roche.
Fight Summary: Graves (145) held on to his title claim at the weight when lasting the distance against a future champion in Lewis (140), but in the main he was outfought at close quarters and well beaten at range. While there were no knockdowns, Lewis was easily the better man on the night.

22 June 1915. (142lbs) Jack Britton w pts 12 Mike Glover.
Venue: Armoury AA, Boston, Massachusetts, USA. **Referee:** Patsy Haley.
Fight Summary: On the day of the contest the *Lowell Sun* reported that the bout would virtually settle the 142lbs welterweight title, the winner being the logical successor to previous champions. For five rounds, Glover, countering and moving well, matched Britton jab for jab, but thereafter as he began to tire the latter took full advantage. Winning five of the last seven rounds, having all his own way, Britton won easily even though Glover never stopped trying for a knockout. The newspaper report claimed that having to make 141lbs at 4pm on the day of the fight not only drained Glover but his championship hopes also disintegrated.

After winning it is unclear as to whether Britton took over Glover's welterweight claim, seemingly being more interested in getting his hands on the lightweight crown when signing for a match against NYC's Johnny Dundee at 133lbs ringside. Put back until 8 August due to Dundee being injured, it was later postponed indefinitely when Britton was unavailable, and a match with Ted Kid Lewis was agreed for the end of the month.

With regards to Britton's contest against Lewis, who outscored him over 12 rounds on 31 August at the Armoury AA, it would appear that historians down the years have tried to tidy up the descent of the weight division without examining the full facts, a perfectly good argument put forward by Luckett Davis. A quote from Lewis's memoirs said that Nat Fleischer got it wrong in the *Ring Record Book* when suggesting that this contest was for the welterweight title. At this stage of his career, Lewis, also looking for a crack at the lightweight title, had agreed articles for the bar to be set at 135lbs, a weight he made without any difficulty at 3pm, while Britton refused to weigh in. After much bargaining it took 20 minutes for the contest to get underway before Lewis finally gave in to Britton's wishes when removing his gumshield, which had been seen by the American as giving his opponent an unfair advantage.

Once in action, Lewis went on the attack before being dropped by a straight left when overbalanced. He was then hit on the neck when down. Subsequently, Lewis hardly gave his man a moment's rest, and the pair battled it out with the Englishman having a decided edge with his volume of blows often forcing Britton back.

Technically, Britton's claim would have passed to Lewis on the result, but neither man seemed interested in pursuing the welterweight title at that moment in time, both continuing to see themselves as lightweights.

On 27 September, Lewis again outscored Britton over 12 rounds at the same venue. This time it was Lewis who refused to get on the scales, while Britton weighed in at 136½lbs.

Following a six-rounder against Willie Moore (nd-w pts 6 at the Olympia AC, Philadelphia, Pennsylvania on 18 October), Lewis took on four 12-round contests in Boston (the first three being held at the Armoury AA and the fourth at the Atlas AA) against top-class Americans in Joe Mandot, Milburn Saylor, Lockport Jimmy Duffy and Mike Glover, the first two being at the lightweight limit and the last two at catchweights. Following the results against Mandot (w pts 12 on 26 October), Saylor (w pts 12 on 2 November), Duffy (w rsc 1 on 23 November) and Glover (l pts 12 on 30 November), and taking his wins over Britton into account, Lewis claimed the welterweight title in early December after being unable to get a crack at Freddie Welsh for the 135lbs championship.

His manager, Jimmy Johnston, who was also the new manager of Madison Square Garden, then matched Lewis against the former lightweight champion, Willie Ritchie, to contest the vacant title at that venue. Ritchie had added his name to the list of claimants on 3 November after challenging Packey McFarland, Lewis or Britton to decide who should be the champion.

Earlier, on 22 August, a group representing 14 boxing clubs in various States formed the American Boxing Association (ABA) at a meeting in Cleveland. Recognising a weight limit of 147lbs, which fell into line with the weight scale used in Europe, in November they stated that they would accept the winner of an elimination series involving the likes of Lewis, Britton, McFarland, Ritchie, Kid Graves, Harry Stone, Mike O'Dowd and Soldier Bartfield as champion. Despite the ABA calling for a 147lbs welterweight class, it would not be until 1920 that America as a whole fell into line with the rest of the boxing world at that weight.

29 June 1915. (145lbs) Kid Graves nd-l pts 10 Walter Mohr.
Venue: Broadway SC, Brooklyn, NYC, New York, USA. **Referee:** Dan Lane.
Fight Summary: In a very fast contest, Graves (143½) put his 145lbs title claim on the line against Mohr (139), being made to work hard before the latter took the press verdict at the final bell. While there were no knockdowns it was Mohr who did all the forcing, and although he was continually booed for using foul tactics he was always looking for a way to finish the contest early. Graves was by far the cleverer, showing to good advantage at distance with the left jab, but his punches lacked power. And on the inside he was always second best. The *New York Times* press report gave Graves just two rounds, Mohr four, with the rest even.

2 July 1915. (142lbs) Harry Stone nd-w pts 10 Johnny Kid Alberts.
Venue: Brown's Gym, Queens, NYC, New York, USA.
Fight Summary: Defending his 142lbs title claim, Stone easily outscored Alberts in what was an uninteresting contest with neither man exerting himself. It was only in the last two rounds that Stone came to life in an effort to impress the fans, landing effectively from both hands as he cut loose.

24 July 1915. (142lbs) Harry Stone nd-w pts 10 Eddie Fitzsimmons.
Venue: Fairmont AC, Bronx, NYC, New York, USA.
Fight Summary: The *New York Telegram* reported that Stone was never at risk of losing his 142lbs title claim in this one, even though Fitzsimmons was a shade in front after five rounds. Picking up the pace at that stage of the fight, after Stone inflicted a cut over Fitzsimmons' left eye in the seventh he had the latter on the back foot right through to the final bell.

2 August 1915. (142lbs) Harry Stone nd-w pts 10 Johnny Marto.
Venue: Olympic AC, Manhattan, NYC, New York, USA.
Fight Summary: Showing all of the skill that made him a leading welterweight title claimant, Stone (136) was far too good for Marto (138), who was reduced to rushing in with big swings that scarcely ever landed cleanly. Blocking, sidestepping and taking the blows on his arms and shoulders, the *New York Herald* reported that it was only when on the attack that Stone lacked effectiveness, producing very little power in his blows.

With weights unavailable, it is unclear whether Stone's contest against Jimmy Capper (nd-w pts 10 at the Broadway SC, Brooklyn, NYC on 21 August) involved his title claim.

24 August 1915. (142lbs) Harry Stone nd-w pts 10 Fighting Fitzpatrick.
Venue: Wallace AC, Queens, NYC, New York, USA.
Fight Summary: Stone's title claim at 142lbs was at stake in this one, and although Fitzpatrick (140) tore in, throwing punches from both hands for much of the fight, at no time did he look like flooring his man. Showing great skill and speed, most of the time Stone (136) smeared Fitzpatrick's features with the left while snapping in rights to the jaw before adroitly moving out of range. The *Queen's Chronicle* reported that Fitzpatrick was the recipient of a severe lacing in the eighth before coming back strongly to mix it with Stone right up to the final bell.

4 September 1915. (142lbs) Harry Stone nd-w pts 10 Fighting Fitzpatrick.
Venue: Clermont Rink, Brooklyn, NYC, New York, USA.
Fight Summary: Similar to their previous encounter a week or so earlier, Stone's cleverness again enabled him to score an easy press victory over the rugged Fitzpatrick. The *New York Tribune* reported that Stone was still very much alive, while his 142lbs title claim remained intact. There were no knockdowns.

Next time out, on 10 September, Stone was deemed by the press to have beaten Teddy Hayes (nd-w pts 10 at The Armoury, Marinette, Wisconsin) in what was a lightweight contest.

16 September 1915. (142/145lbs) Harry Stone nd-drew 10 Bert Stanley.
Venue: Armoury B, Oshkosh, Wisconsin, USA.
Fight Summary: Billed for the 145lbs title, with Stone (135) reported as the champion, both boys went the distance without a let up, punching away continuously. Stanley (145) was the harder hitter, but Stone more than made up for that with his cleverness and left jab that found its mark more often than not.

A return match at the lightweight limit saw Stone again prove too good for Teddy Hayes (nd-w pts 10 at Hagemeister Park Pavilion, Green Bay, Wisconsin on 7 October) according to the majority of the press in attendance.

3 December 1915. (142lbs) Harry Stone w pts 15 Young Denny.
Venue: Athletic Club, New Orleans, Louisiana, USA. **Referee:** Dick Burke.
Fight Summary: Made at 142lbs, although Stone's claim at the weight was at stake against Denny (142) the latter only showed in four rounds according to the *Times-Picayune*, and was unable to cope with the speed and all-round ability of his opponent. The difference between both fighters was a marked one. While Stone (136½) would rock Denny's head back with left jabs before following up with body attacks virtually in every session, the latter would be chasing shadows for much of the time. At the end of the contest there could only be one winner, Denny taking the sixth and sharing three others, with Stone clearly taking 11 rounds according to the attendant press.

On 17 January 1916, Stone beat Frankie Russell by an 18th-round disqualification at the Bienville Street Arena, New Orleans, Louisiana, USA. Made at 133lbs, Stone (137½) came in over the articled weight and was forced to pay forfeit to Russell (133), who was happy to take the fight despite giving a few pounds away. With Stone's 142lbs title claim at stake, the *Times-Picayune* fight report stated that Russell divided his time between trying to hit the title claimant fairly and hitting him unfairly, while being bewildered by the fusillade of left jabs coming his way. Time and again the referee warned Russell to stop going low, using his elbow and butting, but it had no effect. Having taken a boxing lesson for round after round, halfway through the 18th Russell was slung out of the ring after slamming his head into Stone's face.

10 December 1915. (145lbs) Willie Moore nd-l pts 10 Steve Latzo.
Venue: Vulcan Arena, Tamaqua, Pennsylvania, USA.
Fight Summary: Billed for the Pennsylvanian 145lbs title, which automatically took in Moore's American championship claim at the weight, Latzo should have taken over from the latter after having him down for an inexorably long count in the ninth round. Moore got up at 'nine' before surviving two further counts to make it to the final bell.

Moore was not given any credence as a claimant thereafter, and any aspirations he may have had at welterweight were ended when KO Willie Loughlin (nd-w co 1 at the Lincoln AC, Philadelphia on 17 November 1916) and then Ted Kid Lewis (nd-w co 1 at the Palace AC, Bronx, NYC, New York on 19 March 1917) exacted crushing first-round defeats on him in consecutive contests.

28 December 1915. (142lbs) Ted Kid Lewis nd-w pts 10 Willie Ritchie.
Venue: Madison Square Garden, Manhattan, NYC, New York, USA. **Referee:** William McPartland.
Fight Summary: Although a no-decision contest it was billed for the welterweight championship of' the world, 142lbs at 3pm, with the Englishman, who had recently claimed the title after failing to get a crack at Freddie Welsh for the lightweight crown, styled as champion despite the fact that Ritchie was by now also seeing himself as the title holder. With the State of New York's Rules and Regulations at the time calling for a welterweight limit of 145lbs at the ringside weigh-in, after both men gave it all they had it was fairly even up until the fourth. Thereafter, however, Lewis (139¾) made all the running, and although neither man was decked at the end of the contest the press saw the latter as a clear winner. Finishing with a cut over the right eye, Ritchie (143¾) had shown an excellent jab, but it was Lewis's greater volume that took the eye.

17 January 1916. (142lbs) Ted Kid Lewis nd-w pts 10 Kid Graves.
Venue: The Auditorium, Milwaukee, Wisconsin, USA.
Fight Summary: With both men inside 142lbs at 3pm their title claims were on the line, but although Lewis (140½) had Graves (142) beaten from the second round onwards he was unable to find a finishing punch. Despite Graves occasionally worrying Lewis, with him being consistently battered against the ropes it seemed a certainty that he would be eliminated from the title race before eventually making it to the final bell.

Even though Graves' title claim was greatly diminished after this contest he continued to style himself as the 145lbs champion.

20 January 1916. (145lbs) Ted Kid Lewis nd-l pts 10 Jack Britton.
Venue: Broadway Auditorium, Buffalo, New York, USA. **Referee:** Joe Suttner.
Fight Summary: In what was effectively a 145lbs title contest, Britton (144¾) shaded the early rounds before Lewis (142½) came on strong in the final third to almost even up the score.

15 February 1916. (145lbs) Ted Kid Lewis nd-l pts 10 Jack Britton.
Venue: Broadway SC, Brooklyn, NYC, New York, USA.
Fight Summary: Risking his 145lbs title claim against Britton (143½), although Lewis (141½) was extremely confident it was the latter who jabbed his way to the newspaper verdict when using his left at the expense of his right throughout. Looking stale, Lewis (141½) only came to life in the final session when he staged a grandstand finish, jabbing and belting Britton with both hands to the applause of the fans.

Having taken two press decisions off Lewis inside a month, the *Sandusky Star* reported that Britton was now claiming the title.

21 February 1916. (142lbs) Ted Kid Lewis nd-l pts 10 Lockport Jimmy Duffy.
Venue: Broadway Auditorium, Buffalo, New York, USA. **Referee:** Dick Nugent.
Fight Summary: Lewis (141) again held on to his title claim in New York despite losing the press decision against Duffy (142), who kept his man at bay with a stabbing left for much of the time. It was reckoned that Duffy won three rounds, Lewis one, with the rest even.

A few days later, on 24 February, Lewis (141½) travelled to St Louis, Missouri where he knocked out Harry Trendall (141) in the seventh round of a scheduled eight at the Future City AC show held in The Coliseum.

21 February 1916. (145lbs) Eddie Moha nd-w disq 11 (15) Kid Graves.
Venue: Shamrock AC, Dayton, Ohio, USA. **Referee:** Bud Lally.
Fight Summary: Although Graves had dropped press decisions to both Ted Kid Lewis and Jack Britton he was still claiming the title at 145lbs ringside, a weight that his fight against Moha was made at according to the *Dayton News*. Evenly matched, the contest came to a sudden end in the 11th when Graves hit low with a right-hand smash and was disqualified.

Moha now laid claim to the 145lbs title with little backing, while Graves, not satisfied in being disqualified, continued to see himself as the best man at the weight without any tangible support.

28 February 1916. (145lbs) Kid Graves nd-l pts 12 Al Doty.
Venue: East Market Street Rink, Akron, Ohio, USA.
Fight Summary: Still claiming the 145lbs title despite losing to Eddie Moha, Graves, floored in the third, eighth and 11th rounds, lost this one by a mile according to the *Massillon Evening Independent*. The paper stated that Graves seemed powerless to stop long, sweeping swings from both hands and that Doty won six rounds while the remaining six were even.

1 March 1916. (142lbs) Ted Kid Lewis w pts 20 Harry Stone.
Venue: Burns' Arena, New Orleans, Louisiana, USA. **Referee:** Dick Burke.

Fight Summary: Postponed from 28 February due to heavy rain, and with both men articled to make 142lbs at 3pm, Lewis (142) forced the fight in at least 13 of the rounds to win going away. Stone (139) was game enough, but was never in with a shout, the last four sessions seeing Lewis at his very best. There were no knockdowns.

22 March 1916. (145lbs) Jack Britton nd-w pts 15 Kid Graves.
Venue: Gymnastic Club, Dayton, Ohio, USA. **Referee:** Lou Bauman.
Fight Summary: Made at 145lbs, according to the *Sandusky Star Journal* Britton took nine of the rounds, jabbing away constantly with his left and occasionally crossing rights to the jaw. As far as the paper was concerned, Graves managed to win just two sessions. Both fighters' championship claims were on the line in this one.

While Britton would go on to fight Ted Kid Lewis for the title, any claim that Graves felt he had a right to disintegrated when he was knocked out by Lewis inside nine rounds at the Broadway SC, Brooklyn, NYC, New York on 6 February 1917, even though he weighed 147½lbs to the winner's 145.

24 April 1916. (145lbs) Jack Britton w pts 20 Ted Kid Lewis.
Venue: Louisiana Auditorium, New Orleans, Louisiana, USA. **Referee:** Dick Burke.
Fight Summary: In a match made at 145lbs, 3pm weigh-in, with both men on the limit, Britton picked up Lewis's title claim when keeping up a fusillade of left jabs round after round to take the decision. Although there were no knockdowns, Lewis was forced to defend almost throughout as Britton kept him on the back foot, and it was only in the 19th that the Englishman came to life as the latter tired, landing lefts and rights to head and body in a vain attempt to make up the leeway.

On 6 June, at the Armoury AA, Boston, Massachusetts, Jack Britton outpointed Mike O'Dowd over 12 rounds in a contest that the *Lowell Sun* claimed to be of championship status. However, I cannot uncover any details of the weight that the fight was made at, although O'Dowd could well have been inside 145lbs. According to some reports the crowd laughed when Britton's weight was announced as being 147lbs as he appeared a good deal heavier than O'Dowd, which suggests to me that the fight was probably made at 147lbs. Ever since taking a press decision off Soldier Bartfield (nd-w pts 10 at The Arena, Hudson, Wisconsin on 12 November 1915), O'Dowd had been staking a claim to the title, albeit a weak one. The fight itself saw Britton let O'Dowd force the fight from the opening bell, and while taking plenty at close quarters he continually stuck the left into the challenger's face. The last three rounds saw Britton finally open up, but with O'Dowd staying with him many thought he was unlucky not to get a share of the spoils.

Britton (147) next risked his title claim when taking on the 145lbs Battling Kopin at The Arena, Syracuse, New York on 23 June, the ten-round newspaper decision ultimately being in favour of the champion.

24 May 1916. (145lbs) Ted Kid Lewis nd-w rsc 13 (15) Eddie Moha.
Venue: Gymnastic Club, Dayton, Ohio, USA.
Fight Summary: Fighting for the first time since taking over Kid Graves' 145lbs title claim, Moha made a reasonable start when flooring Lewis in the second round. However, Lewis came back strongly with fast, clever work to outclass his rival in every facet of the game. After Lewis had put Moha down with a hard left to the jaw in the 13th the referee stopped the fight when it was clear that the latter could not continue.

Although Lewis derailed Moha's title plans in this one he did not claim the title as he considered Jack Britton to be the champion. The same principle applied when he beat Mike Glover on points over 12 rounds at the Armoury AA, Boston, Massachusetts on 13 June, despite the *Boston Evening Globe* stating on the day of the fight that the match had a championship flavour about it as the winner would be claiming the title. It was an easy win for Lewis as he outspeeded Glover throughout while having his rival down from a left hook in the final session to earn himself another crack at Britton. Having retired from the ring immediately after the fight, Glover passed away on 11 July 1917 following a short illness.

25 July 1916. (145lbs) Jack Britton drew 12 Johnny Griffiths.
Venue: Armoury AA, Boston, Massachusetts, USA. **Referee:** Phil Powers.

Fight Summary: Reported by the *Lowell Sun* as a contest where the championship could be won or lost by decision, it has to be assumed that both men were inside 145lbs. A fast and clever fight, neither man was ever in danger despite both scoring with hard blows on occasion, and the result was a fair one. With Britton jabbing and hooking well while Griffiths showed a smart defence, it was only towards the end that the pair went toe-to-toe.

Another fight for Britton (147) in which he risked his title came against the 134½lbs Joe Welling at the Queensberry AC, Buffalo, New York on 5 September. A ten-round no-decision affair, Britton was ultimately awarded the press verdict.

17 October 1916. (145lbs) Jack Britton w pts 12 Ted Kid Lewis.
Venue: Armoury AA, Boston, Massachusetts, USA. **Referee:** Larry Conley.
Fight Summary: The *Boston Post* classed this one as a title fight but failed to list any weights, while according to Lewis with both men inside the limit Britton's title was at stake. Britton nearly lost in the fifth when going low and using his forearm, but escaped with a warning, and while Lewis forced the contest from the start and set a furious pace the former's cleverness took him to the front. Winning the last few sessions handily, Britton just about got home.

Britton and Lewis met again at the Armoury AA on 14 November, drawing over 12 rounds. While there was no mention in the *Boston Post* that the title was up for grabs, the *Boston Herald* reported that Lewis made the required 142lbs even if Britton did not.

21 November 1916. (145lbs) Jack Britton w pts 12 Charley White.
Venue: Armoury AA, Boston, Massachusetts, USA.
Fight Summary: As far as the *Boston Post* was concerned the Articles of Agreement called for the two men to be inside 142lbs at 3pm on the day of the fight despite Britton winning the title from Lewis at 145lbs. Having ignored the weight stipulation, Britton (144½) handed White (136½) what was termed as an artistic whipping as he outboxed the hard-hitting Chicago man for round after round. There were no knockdowns, but how both men tried. Although White fought one of the gamest uphill battles seen in a Boston ring, Britton was his master even though he had four lower teeth chipped by a cracking left hook.

On 4 December, Britton (147) won a ten-round press decision over the 144lbs Steve Latzo at the Majestic Theatre, Wilkes-Barre, Pennsylvania. Had Latzo won inside the distance he would have had an excellent claim to the 145lbs title.

8 December 1916. (145lbs) Jack Britton nd-w pts 10 Sam Robideau.
Venue: The Athletic Club, Cleveland, Ohio, USA. **Referee:** Eddie Davis.
Fight Summary: Although Robideau was a replacement for Joe Sherman, Britton's title claim at 145lbs was still on the line. Adopting defensive tactics throughout ten slow rounds, the press came down hard on Britton (144) for not finishing the outclassed Robideau (143) off. In short, with Britton taking things easy it was only towards the end when Robideau hurt him with a left swing that he finally opened up.

At the beginning of 1917 Lew Williams was claiming the 'black title' despite continuously fighting middleweights in order to earn a living. After beating Kyle Whitney twice in 1914, Eddie Palmer had claimed the same title before he was twice outpointed over 20 rounds at the Orleans AC, New Orleans, Louisiana by Gorilla Jones (on 23 January and 15 February 1915). It was then reported early in 1916 that the Jamaica Kid was calling himself the 'black champion' after beating Jones, but as yet I can find no evidence of that fight happening. If that was not enough, the Kid was challenging all-comers at 158lbs. Other men who would claim the 'black title' in the next year or so to no great effect included Panama Joe Gans and Battling Thomas, and it would appear that very few black boys were getting a fair crack in the division at this time, something that would persist right up until the late 1920s.

1 January 1917. (145lbs) Jack Britton nd-w pts 10 Lockport Jimmy Duffy.
Venue: Broadway Auditorium, Buffalo, New York, USA.

Fight Summary: According to the *Buffalo Morning Express*, Duffy's attack on the 145lbs championship was ably warded off as Britton (144½) outgeneralled his rival all the way before dropping him in the seventh and ninth with solid blows. Earlier, there had been a bit of a wrangle when Duffy (144½) was allowed to use a mouth protector, but it failed to save him from a beating.

An almost certainly over-the-weight Britton risked his title at the Coliseum, Columbus, Ohio on 5 March when allowing Bryan Downey to make 144lbs, but he was still on his feet at the end of the 12th round prior to losing the press decision.

26 March 1917. (145lbs) Jack Britton nd-l pts 10 Ted Kid Lewis.
Venue: Queen City AC, Cincinnati, Ohio, USA. **Referee:** Lou Bauman.
Fight Summary: With the 145lbs title on the line the contest had been fairly even up until the eighth round, but Britton (145) had landed the cleaner blows and the left jab had gone especially well for him. Eventually opening up in the last three sessions, although Britton came on to repeatedly Lewis (144) would have none of it when hammering in right crosses to gain an advantage.

19 May 1917. (142lbs) Jack Britton nd-l pts 10 Ted Kid Lewis.
Venue: Massey Hall, Toronto, Canada. **Referee:** Walter C. Kelley.
Fight Summary: After both men agreed to be inside 142lbs (3pm weigh-in), thus putting Britton's title claim up for grabs, it was the Englishman who made all the running. Unfortunately for Lewis, although he managed to pierce Britton's guard on various occasions he was unable to find a finisher before having to content himself with the press verdict.

6 June 1917. (145lbs) Jack Britton nd-drew 10 Ted Kid Lewis.
Venue: Future AC, The Coliseum, St Louis, Missouri, USA.
Fight Summary: The *St Louis Globe Democrat* gave this as a match at 145lbs, which saw Britton again putting his title on the line against his main rival. Being a no-decision contest it was obvious that to lift the title Lewis would have to win inside the distance, but Britton made sure that by using every inch of the ring the Englishman would not get the opening he would have wished for. The paper reported that although there were no knockdowns it was Lewis who did the main work, leading before clinching hard and breaking free to start another attack, which seemed at odds with the majority of the press present who saw it as a draw.

On 14 June, at the St Nicholas Arena, Manhattan, NYC, New York, an over-the-weight Britton again risked his title against Lewis (144¼), losing the ten-rounder on points according to the press.

25 June 1917. (142lbs) Ted Kid Lewis w pts 20 Jack Britton.
Venue: Westwood Field, Dayton, Ohio, USA. **Referee:** Lou Bauman.
Fight Summary: With both men inside the agreed 142lbs at 3pm, and with all the leading claimants disposed of, this contest should be recognised as the one that finally cleared up the long-standing world title mess. The fight itself saw Lewis make the running before going into a clear lead, and although Britton scored a knockdown in the final round it was not enough to offset the former's good work. This time round, with Lewis being particularly effective with the left as he looked to deal with Britton's boring-in tactics, the steady volley of blows to the head saw him home. Summarising, Lewis, who took over from Britton on the referee's decision, was credited with winning seven rounds to five, with eight even.

4 July 1917. (145lbs) Ted Kid Lewis nd-l pts 15 Johnny Griffiths.
Venue: Grosvenor Park, Akron, Ohio, USA. **Referee:** Walter C. Kelley.
Fight Summary: In his memoirs Lewis gives no hint of this one involving the title, but elsewhere, including the *Akron Beacon Journal*, the fight has been shown as being part of the championship at 145lbs. The paper went on to say that had a decision been given Griffiths would have surely been crowned champion, having won six rounds to Lewis's four, with five considered even. There was little infighting, with Lewis strangely unable to get started despite landing several hard smashes to the head, while Griffiths was the aggressor from the opening bell, his snappy left hand always being in evidence.

Following Griffiths there were three over the weight affairs for Lewis before he came up against Albert Badoud, the European 147lbs champion, in a ten-round no-decision contest at the St Nicholas Arena, Manhattan, NYC, New York on 31 August. Billed for the title regardless of the fact that Badoud scaled 151lbs ringside, Lewis (144) knocked the Swiss out inside one round. It was no surprise that Lewis's manager claimed the European title for his man immediately afterwards.

3 September 1917. (145lbs) Ted Kid Lewis nd-drew 10 Soldier Bartfield.
Venue: Queensberry AC, Broadway Auditorium, Buffalo, New York, USA.
Fight Summary: Newspaper reports suggested that the first five rounds belonged to Lewis (145) by a fair margin, and in the fifth Bartfield (144½) was dropped by a cracking right to the jaw. Up again quickly, Bartfield took the fight to Lewis, slinging in punches from all angles right through to final bell.

So good was the action that the pair were matched again, eight days later, at the Airdome AC, Rochester, New York on 11 September. The *Rochester Democrat & Chronicle* reported that if Bartfield could find the punch the title could well change hands, which was not quite true as Bartfield came in at 146lbs ringside. This time round Lewis (145½) was far too good for his rival, winning the ten-round no-decision in the eyes of the press after finding Bartfield's face time and again with the left jab.

A 12-round no-decision contest for Lewis against Bryan Downey at the Memorial Hall, Columbus, Ohio on 17 December was reported to involve the world title by the *Newark Advocate*, but with the latter scaling 145½lbs he was above the recognised limit of the day.

Lewis risked his crown against Johnny Tillman (nd-w pts 6 at the Olympia AC, Philadelphia, Pennsylvania on 4 February 1918) when both men made the required 145lbs. The latter's showing was so good that he earned himself a title shot over the championship distance a short while later.

6 March 1918. (145lbs) Ted Kid Lewis nd-l pts 10 Jack Britton.
Venue: The Armoury Auditorium, Atlanta, Georgia, USA. **Referee:** Frankie Edwards.
Fight Summary: Crossing gloves with Britton for the 14th time, and involving the title at 145lbs, Lewis boxed cautiously from the start as the former champion looked for a kayo. While Lewis used his speed to avoid trouble, bearing in mind that the only way he could lose the championship would be if he lost inside the distance, the bout turned into a stalemate.

2 May 1918. (145lbs) Ted Kid Lewis nd-drew 10 Jack Britton.
Venue: The Public Hall, Scranton, Pennsylvania, USA.
Fight Summary: The earliest clue that this involved the championship came the night before when the *Scranton Times* reported that in the event of Britton scoring a kayo victory the fans would be able to say they had witnessed a title fight and that the latter would be the new champion. After both men made 145lbs ringside, it turned into a gruelling battle, with Lewis showing all his cleverness to keep Britton at bay. There were no knockdowns, but Britton never gave up trying.

17 May 1918. (142lbs) Ted Kid Lewis w pts 20 Johnny Tillman.
Venue: The Arena, Denver, Colorado, USA. **Referee:** Billy Roche.
Fight Summary: Billed for the title, both men made 142lbs at the 3pm weigh-in, and by the 14th round Lewis was well in front as he continued to pull away. Then, after the fireworks started as Tillman came on strong, the pair fought viciously right through to final bell. It had been a tough fight, but Lewis well deserved the unanimous decision in his favour.

4 July 1918. (145lbs) Ted Kid Lewis nd-w pts 20 Johnny Griffiths.
Venue: East Market Gardens, Akron, Ohio, USA.
Fight Summary: Lewis explained in his memoirs that, with both men inside 145lbs and the referee unable to render a decision, the only way Griffiths could land the title was by winning inside the distance. Taking it easy for

the first few rounds Lewis eventually stepped up the pace to subject Griffiths to a boxing lesson, as he held back the big punches before going on to pick up the press decision.

Three eight-round no-decision fights, against Walter Mohr (nd-w pts 8 at the Ballpark, Jersey City, New Jersey on 17 August), Benny Leonard (nd-w pts 8 at Weidenmayor's Park, Newark, New Jersey on 25 September) and Griffiths (nd-drew 8 at the Lyric Theatre, Memphis, Tennessee on 10 March 1919), saw both Lewis and his opponents scaling below 145lbs, thus putting his title claim at risk.

17 March 1919. (145lbs) Jack Britton nd-w co 9 (12) Ted Kid Lewis.
Venue: The Auditorium, Canton, Ohio, USA. **Referee:** Matt Hinkel.
Fight Summary: Despite it being a no-decision bout, with Lewis knocked down nine times before he was counted out in the ninth, Britton successfully claimed the title on the result. Prior to the fight, Lewis, suffering from anaemia, had been told by doctors to take a complete rest from boxing, but his management team stupidly disregarded the advice. Also, with the championship weight in America fluctuating between 142 and 145lbs regardless of whether a 3pm or ringside weigh-in, Lewis (inside 145lbs) should have realised that Britton (144½) would be accepted as champion if he won inside the distance.

24 March 1919. (142/145lbs) Jack Britton nd-w pts 10 Jack Perry.
Venue: Duquesne Gardens, Pittsburgh, Pennsylvania, USA. **Referee:** Eddie Kennedy.
Fight Summary: On the eve of the fight the *Pittsburgh Daily Gazette* claimed that Britton was already down to the articled 142lbs, while Perry was expected to comfortably make his normal fighting weight of 140lbs in what was effectively a title battle. Undaunted by Britton's reputation Perry walked in from the opening bell, punching away as if he was meeting a preliminary boy not a boxing great. According to the paper each won four rounds while sharing the remaining two, with Perry throwing the harder punches and Britton only using the right when there was a clear-cut opportunity. As in days gone by the champion used the left hand to perfection, either in opening his rival up or scoring solidly, and had Perry not been made of tough material he would have surely been finished off prior to the final bell. At the final bell the majority of the press saw it as a win for the champion.

Britton took on Johnny Griffiths (nd-w pts 10 at the Broadway Auditorium, Buffalo, New York on 6 May) in what was billed as a title match, the *Buffalo Boxing Record* giving Britton as being 145½lbs and Griffiths at 147. However, at this point in time the weight class limit in America was recognised as being 145lbs.

In another no-decision go, over 12 rounds at the Eureka AC, Baltimore, Maryland on 12 May, against Johnny Tillman, the *Baltimore Sun* reported that Britton could not lose his title unless kayoed. This remark inferred that Tillman was inside 145lbs, but the writer seemed uncertain of Britton's weight. Britton won the decision according to the majority of the press.

19 May 1919. (142lbs) Jack Britton nd-w pts 10 Joe Welling.
Venue: The Arena, Syracuse, New York, USA. **Referee:** Harry Stout.
Fight Summary: Both men were inside 142lbs at the 6pm weigh-in according to the *Chicago Tribune* report, which went on to say that the championship was on the line. Although Welling just about had the better of the opening four rounds when landing the cleaner punches, Britton, who was merely biding his time, continually stabbed out the left to keep his rival off balance from thereon in. In the sixth a solid right almost closed Welling's left eye, and despite the latter looking for a stoppage in the last three sessions Britton was far too cute and elusive to be caught napping.

Two fights later, Britton outpointed Walter Mohr at the French Theatre, Montreal, Canada on 13 June according to the majority of the press. Although no weights were reported it was clear that had the latter, who scaled around 140lbs at this time, won inside the distance the title may well have changed hands.

26 June 1919. (142/145lbs) Jack Britton nd-l pts 12 Jack Perry.
Venue: The Baseball Park, Cumberland, Maryland, USA. **Referee:** Eddie Kennedy.

Fight Summary: Promoted by the local athletic club, with this being a return match with the 142lbs title at stake, Perry's second crack at the championship in two months saw the challenger almost there according to the *Philadelphia Inquirer*. As in their previous contest, Britton stayed mainly on the defensive, countering with lefts and rights to the head, while Perry threw himself at the champion in the opening four rounds. In the fifth, after chasing Perry down, Britton rocked his man with a tremendous right to the jaw before dropping him for 'nine' with a body shot. Revitalised in the sixth, Perry came back strongly, giving as good as he got to take the final session by a big margin as he went looking for a kayo win.

Another two fights which had championship status attached despite being made at 148lbs, saw Britton take on Johnny Griffiths (nd-w pts 15 at the Auditorium, Canton, Ohio on 4 July) and Al Doty (nd-w rsc 2 at Fayette Field, Connellsville, Pennsylvania on 9 July), while the press verdict in an eight-round no-decision contest against Ted Kid Lewis (at the Armoury AA, Jersey City, New Jersey on 28 July), with both men inside 145lbs at the 3pm weigh-in, went Britton's way.

7 August 1919. (145lbs) Jack Britton nd-drew 12 Johnny Griffiths.
Venue: Stockyards Stadium, Denver, Colorado, USA. **Referee:** Jimmy Britt.
Fight Summary: This one was reported in the *Rocky Mountain News* as a defence for Britton at 145lbs, and after 12 rounds of clever boxing without a knockdown the majority of the press decided that both men deserved something out of the contest despite Griffiths being badly marked up.

5 November 1919. (145lbs) Jack Britton nd-w pts 10 Johnny Tillman.
Venue: Woodward & Hendrie Arena, Detroit, Michigan, USA.
Fight Summary: With both men agreeing to make 145lbs Britton's title was at risk in this one, but despite the latter boxing like a tired old businessman, as the *Detroit News* put it, Tillman was unable to take advantage. Round after round saw Britton poke his left into Tillman's face, while cocking the right as if to use it. There was very little action to note, and while the slow moving Tillman did the vast majority of the leading he did little damage as Britton either ducked beneath the jabs or made his man miss wildly. Having recently recovered from illness, while Britton was not up to speed he showed all and sundry what a great defensive fighter he still was.

Next time out, on 7 November, a contest against local fighter, Billy Doig (nd-drew 10 at the Auditorium, LaSalle, Illinois), was made at 150lbs in order to protect Britton's crown.

25 November 1919. (145/147lbs) Jack Britton nd-w pts 10 Harvey Thorpe.
Venue: Broadway Auditorium, Buffalo, New York, USA. **Referee:** Joe Suttner.
Fight Summary: The *Buffalo Boxing Record* handout gave this one as a title fight, which was also substantiated by the *Buffalo Evening News*. The fight report went on to say that Britton (144), giving a beautiful exhibition of his art, picked up a neat bundle of easy money when allowing Thorpe (140) to stay the full ten rounds with him. Never in any difficulty whatsoever, Britton handed out a boxing lesson to the younger man, jabbing him silly and only doing what was necessary.

Although 145lbs was recognised as being the welter limit in America at this time there were those who thought that the country should fall in line with Britain and Europe, who recognised 147lbs as being the limit. It was at that weight Britton met Billy Ryan at the Auditorium, Canton, Ohio on 1 December, winning their billed championship 12-round no-decision contest by an 11th-round kayo.

A further fight made at 147lbs saw Britton (147) take the ten-round press decision from Steve Latzo (144) at the Athletic Club, Johnstown, Pennsylvania on 9 December.

Continuing to protect his crown as best he could Britton's next two contests against, Johnny Gill and Johnny Kid Alberts, were made at 150lbs despite newspaper reports indicating that the title was on the line. With both being no-decision affairs, Britton was judged by the press to have beaten Gill (nd-w pts 10 at Roberts' Garage Complex, Steelton, Pennsylvania on 1 January 1920) and Alberts (nd-w pts 8 at the Schuetzen Park, Bayonne, New Jersey on 6 January 1920).

Although Britton's contest against Jimmy Conway (w pts 12 at the Auditorium, Savannah, Georgia on 30 January 1920) was stated to have been made at 145lbs it was almost certainly contested at 147lbs, as was his meeting with Dave Palitz (nd-w pts 10 at the Church Street Auditorium, Hartford, Connecticut on 8 March 1920). For that contest, Palitz weighed in at 143lbs while Britton made 146.

Up against Jack Perry (nd-w pts 12 at the Auditorium, Canton, Ohio on 17 March 1920), despite there being a distinct lack of weights available the latter stated that he expected to lift the title from Britton by means of a knockout.

Britton's next fight among the welters came against Dennis O'Keefe (nd-w pts 10 at the Coliseum, Kenosha, Wisconsin on 7 April 1920) when he made 146lbs as opposed to his rival's 146½, in a State which recognised 147lbs as being the championship limit. Even prior to the advent of the Walker Law in New York on 1 September 1920 some authorities recognised 147lbs as being the welterweight limit, but as far as Britton was concerned he could not lose his title if an opponent was above 145lbs at 3pm.

31 May 1920. (145/147lbs) Jack Britton nd-w pts 15 Johnny Griffiths.
Venue: League Park, Akron, Ohio, USA. **Referee:** Eddie Davis.
Fight Summary: Made at 145lbs, according to the *Akron Beacon Journal* the 34-year-old Britton held a decisive edge in every round, often hitting Griffiths at will with stinging left jabs and finishing festivities as fresh as when he started.

When Britton came up against Young Joe Borrell (nd-w pts 8 at the Palace, Philadelphia, Pennsylvania on 2 June) and Eddie Shevlin (nd-w pts 12, a back-to-back six rounder at Exposition Park, Portland, Maine on 1 July), both men were reported to have made 145lbs. Regardless of the fact that no weights were published, the papers reported that Britton comfortably held on to his title.

Facing Marcel Thomas (nd-w rsc 10 at the 1st Regiment Armoury, Newark, New Jersey on 26 July), Britton stipulated that the fight should be made at 150lbs despite many thinking that his title was at stake. Even in so called billed title fights, where it was stated that the opponent was inside 147lbs, Britton often had a habit of not weighing in.

On 23 August 1920, Britton drew over 12 rounds with Lou Bogash at the Bridgeport Arena, Connecticut. Despite the *Boston Daily Globe* not reporting it as a title fight, it was recognised as one by some of those who mattered in America, especially with both men inside 147lbs. Although Britton (146¾) claimed that this was a catchweight contest and he could only lose the title at 145lbs, had Bogash (147) won he too would have had plenty of support.

Another fight for Britton where the opponent made the championship weight, while it is unclear whether he himself did, came against the 145lbs Johnny Tillman (nd-w pts 10 at the Baseball Park, Cleveland, Ohio on 3 September).

6 September 1920. (145lbs) Jack Britton nd-w pts 10 Ray Bronson.
Venue: The Open Air Arena, Cedar Point, Ohio, USA. **Referee:** Ollie Pecord.
Fight Summary: The *Sandusky Register* reported that both men made the required 145lbs for this one, thus putting Britton's title on the line. Unfortunately for Bronson he was not the fighter of old, being made to look like a novice at times while Britton went through the motions, barely exerting himself and joking with the crowd. There was no doubt that Britton held back, but he enjoyed the workout.

Catchweight contests where Britton allowed his opponents to make 145lbs or less while he did not, came against Jack Perry (drew 12 at the Coliseum, Toledo, Ohio on 8 October), Morris Lux (nd-w pts 10 at the Convention Hall, Kansas City, Missouri on 18 November), Bud Logan (nd-l pts 10 at Beethoven Hall, San Antonio, Texas on 23 November) and Pinky Mitchell (nd-w pts 10 at the Auditorium, Milwaukee, Wisconsin on 6 December). Sandwiched between the last two contests for Britton was one against the local fighter, Jake Abel (w pts 10 at the Auditorium, Atlanta, Georgia on 29 November), that was contracted at 150lbs.

From here on in all title bouts would be contested at 147lbs. With Britain and the IBU recognising 147lbs as being the welterweight limit, after the Walker Law was passed on 24 May 1920 that weight was also accepted by the New York State Boxing Commission. However, it was not until 17 September 1920 that the first main event in New York was held under Walker Law. The National Boxing Association, which was formed on 11 January 1921, followed suit.

7 February 1921. Jack Britton w pts 15 Ted Kid Lewis.
Venue: Madison Square Garden, Manhattan, NYC, New York, USA. **Recognition:** World. **Referee:** Dick Nugent.
Fight Summary: In the first title fight at 147lbs held in New York since the Walker Law was passed, Lewis (145) made all the running in the first round, jabbing and hooking, before Briton (145) lost his temper in the second when rushing over to the challenger's corner where he hit Lewis's manager with a tremendous blow in the face. With all hell breaking loose a full-scale riot was only averted after the referee managed to get the round underway again. The trouble had started prior to the contest beginning when Britton insisted that Lewis remove his gumshield, and it was only when Lewis had acceded to that request that the action started. Having fought so often, this being the 20th time they had met, initially there was not a great deal between them as they matched jabs and worked away on the inside, but in the fifth after two heavy rights wobbled Lewis the tide turned. By the seventh Lewis was being hit far too often for comfort by accurate left jabs, and in the eighth his right eye became noticeably swollen. Lewis was also beginning to miss far too often as he looked for a finisher. He was also being given a bit of a boxing lesson. Despite Lewis coming on strong in the final session in a vain attempt to score a kayo, when the decision was announced all three judges voted for Britton who proudly collected a championship belt to mark his victory.

17 May 1921. Jack Britton nd-w pts 10 Johnny Tillman.
Venue: The Coliseum, Des Moines, Iowa, USA. **Recognition:** World. **Referee:** Harry Stout.
Fight Summary: Billed for the title at 145lbs, the champion won going away, jabbing with the left and sending in solid right hands when the opportunity beckoned. With Tillman continually boring in he was forced to take heavy punishment, especially early on, and was rarely able to land effectively himself. According to the *Des Moines News*, Britton won every round apart from one, which was drawn.

To protect his titles, apart from a four-round exhibition affair, Britton's next three contests were made at 150lbs, against Dave Shade (drew 10 at the Milwaukee Arena, Portland, Oregon on 3 June), Frank Barrieau (nd-drew 10 at the Milwaukee Arena on 8 June) and Mickey Walker (nd-drew 12 at the Armoury, Newark, New Jersey on 18 July).

Following the contest against Walker, Britton was out of action for seven months before coming back to defend against Shade.

17 February 1922. Jack Britton drew 15 Dave Shade.
Venue: Madison Square Garden, Manhattan, NYC, New York, USA. **Recognition:** World. **Referee:** Patsy Haley.
Fight Summary: A championship contest at 147lbs, saw Britton (146½) appear to win clearly despite being handed a draw by the judges. Moving around Shade (144½) like a master with his pupil, Britton made the youngster miss constantly. While the champion was occasionally hurt, the inexperienced 19-year-old Shade was unable to sustain the pressure before the skilful Britton quickly got back in to the groove, the left hand regularly finding the target. Although the majority of fans believed the older man to have won, there was much to admire in Shade, the youngest of three fighting brothers from California, and he was soon mixing with the division's leading fighters.

Despite being billed as title bouts, Britton's next three contests, against Cowboy Padgett, Morris Lux and Ray Long, were made at 150, 148 and 148lbs respectively, and were all no-decision affairs. Padgett was adjudged to have been outpointed over ten rounds at the Auditorium, Omaha, Nebraska on 5 May, while Lux was stopped inside five rounds at McNulty Park, Tulsa, Oklahoma on 16 May, and Long was seen to have drawn their 12 rounder at the Coliseum, Oklahoma City, Oklahoma on 26 May.

26 June 1922. Jack Britton w disq 13 (15) Benny Leonard.
Venue: The Velodrome, Bronx, NYC, New York, USA. **Recognition:** World. **Referee:** Patsy Haley.

163

Fight Summary: One of the unresolved mysteries remaining in boxing saw lightweight champion, Leonard (139¼), ruled out at 2.42 of the 13th for hitting the already floored Britton (146¼) for no apparent reason. Britton, who was out in front after ten rounds and beginning to tire was put down on one knee from a short left to the body when the challenger, reaching from behind the referee, landed a punch on the champion's head. Information which came to hand years later suggested that Leonard had no intention of winning the welterweight title, and getting disqualified without loss of face seemed to be his best way out.

Britton outpointed Jimmy Kelly over 12 rounds at the Marina Stadium, Havana, Cuba on 10 October. According to the *Havana Post* this was a billed championship match, but having been made at 150lbs, and with Kelly weighing 149½lbs to Britton's 149, the title was not on the line regardless of what the crowd thought.

1 November 1922. Mickey Walker w pts 15 Jack Britton.
Venue: Madison Square Garden, Manhattan, NYC, New York, USA. **Recognition:** World. **Referee:** Patsy Haley.
Fight Summary: The younger man by 16 years, Walker (144¼) started like a train when cracking in vicious short-arm hooks to the body before the champion began to get his boxing going in the second round. Jabbing Walker silly, Britton (146) looked like the fighter of old as he sped around the ring, combining defence with offence, but by the sixth he seemed spent when Walker came to the front, belting away with both hands during the next two sessions. The ninth saw Britton come back into the frame. However, it was just a fleeting memory of a former great and by the tenth he was holding on, taking punch after punch under the ribs, to the heart and to the head. Eventually, when his legs buckled under him, he dropped to one knee for a count of 'seven' having taken a terrific right hand to the jaw, before being saved by the bell. Slipping over twice in the 11th without taking a count, Britton was soon in trouble again in the following frame when a heavy swing to the body dropped him yet again. Most of the ringsiders were amazed to see Britton still there in the 13th as Walker went all out for an inside-the-distance win, but giving a magnificent display of guts and willpower he somehow made it to the final bell. Although Walker received the unanimous decision he showed a marked lack of skill, despite being rough, tough and willing, and the loudest cheers were for Britton who went out like all great champions should when they reach the end of the road.

When Walker won a ten-round press decision over Johnny Griffiths at the 109th Infantry Armoury, Scranton, Pennsylvania on 23 February 1923, despite the latter reported as being inside 147lbs the title was not at stake.

22 March 1923. Mickey Walker nd-w pts 12 Pete Latzo.
Venue: 113th Regiment Armoury, Newark, New Jersey, USA. **Recognition:** World. **Referee:** Harry Ertle.
Fight Summary: Putting his title on the line in a no-decision title bout, Walker (146¼) won all the way, his severe body assaults generally being too much for Latzo (144½) to handle. The onrushing Latzo, who was floored for a short count in the fourth following a left hook to the jaw before being staggered in the ninth from a similar blow, proved to be a tough and durable opponent, but lacked the guile to avoid taking heavy punishment.

Reported to be for the welterweight title in the *Wilkes Barre Times-Leader*, a ten-round no-decision contest against Johnny Riley, in which Walker secured a two-round kayo win at The Armoury, Wilkes Barre, Pennsylvania on 4 April, was made at 150lbs.

On 3 May, a six-round no-decision win for Walker at the Dexter Park Pavilion, Chicago, Illinois, against Morrie Schlaifer, was reported by the *Chicago Tribune* as being for the 147lbs title, with Walker's welter crown being the prize for Schlaifer if he could score an inside-the-distance win. In fact, the fight was also made at 150lbs with the title protected whatever the result. Schlaifer was kayoed in the final round.

A little over a month later, on 6 June, after repeated requests for Walker to defend his title against Dave Shade had failed the NYSAC stripped him and proclaimed Shade as champion.

27 July 1923. Jimmy Jones w pts 10 Dave Shade.
Venue: The Arena, Boston, Massachusetts, USA. **Recognition:** Massachusetts. **Referee:** Jack Sheehan.
Fight Summary: With never an idle moment in what was a furious contest, three times Shade (143) sent the muscular Jones (145½) to the canvas, but each time the rugged Jones got to his feet and fought back like a man

possessed against his cleverer opponent. The only clean knockdown came in the eighth when Shade dropped his rival with a solid left to the head, and after Jones got to his feet the fighting became so intense that both boys went through the ropes along with the referee. According to *The Ring* magazine report of the fight it was even going into the tenth, but with Jones taking the round the decision went in his favour.

Recognised in Massachusetts as a world 147lbs title fight, on 31 July after reports of the bout had satisfied the New York Commissioner that the decision in favour of Jones over Shade was fully justified, the former was acclaimed champion by the NYSAC. According to the *Boston Post*, Shade had already been signed up to defend his NYSAC version of the title against Georgie Ward at Johnson Field, Johnson City, New York on 24 August. Despite the lack of title billing, the fight went ahead with Shade winning on points over 15 rounds.

Outside the jurisdiction of Massachusetts and New York, Jones tangled with Johnny Tillman (nd-w pts 10 at the Broad AC, Newark, New Jersey on 30 August) and Bermondsey Billy Wells (nd-nc 6 at the Auditorium, St Paul, Minnesota on 10 September). Both fights were of the no-decision variety at 147lbs, and in the latter both men fell out of the ring at which stage the action was called off.

20 September 1923. Mickey Walker nd-w rsc 8 (10) Bobby Green.
Venue: The Coliseum, Davenport, Iowa, USA. **Recognition:** NBA. **Referee:** Jim Brennan.
Fight Summary: Reported in the *Davenport Democrat* as a billed 147lbs title fight, with both men inside the weight, Walker won every round by a margin that left no doubt of his superiority. Right from the opening bell the game Green was punished from head to body as the champion worked him over, and in the seventh the game youngster took a count of six after being dumped by a left to the jaw. In the next session, with Green under a sustained body attack and not fighting back, the referee came to his rescue.

Later, on 8 October, at Dreamland Park, Newark, New Jersey, Walker (148lbs) and Jimmy Jones (145¼lbs) were thrown out before the start of the tenth round of a scheduled 12-rounder for not trying. And, just to add insult to injury, it was New Jersey's Chief Inspector, Platt Adams, who ordered the referee to halt the contest. It did not stop there, however. On 10 October, after Walker was suspended for a year by the New Jersey Commission the NYSAC rescinded Jones' title claim the following day. Earlier, Jones had been warned by the NYSAC that he risked indefinite suspension if he went ahead with the fight against a man already serving one, a decision which would have undoubtedly been upheld by Massachusetts who had a close working relationship with the New York authority.

Following this, on 26 October, at Madison Square Garden, Manhattan, NYC, New York, Dave Shade outpointed Bermondsey Billy Wells over 15 rounds in an effort to reclaim the support of the NYSAC (some reports even gave it as a NY title fight), but a day later, following a special meeting at the Commission's offices, Walker was reinstated as champion, even though he would remain suspended in New York until April 1925. The upshot of the special meeting was that in future the Commission would no longer make champions by proclamation when existing champions failed to make defences within the stipulated period, but would merely place them under suspension until such time they co-operated.

2 June 1924. Mickey Walker w pts 10 Lew Tendler.
Venue: Baker Bowl, Philadelphia, Pennsylvania, USA. **Recognition:** World. **Referee:** Jim Brennan.
Fight Summary: Billed as Philadelphia's first title bout, a 25,000 crowd witnessed Walker (147) make a successful defence over Tendler (142½) by a unanimous decision, his vicious body attacks leaving the latter battered and bruised. Although there were no knockdowns, the only way Tendler, who at best shared one round, avoided being floored was to clutch for all he was worth, and it was only his superb condition that saved him.

1 October 1924. Mickey Walker w co 6 (10) Bobby Barrett.
Venue: Baker Bowl, Philadelphia, Pennsylvania, USA. **Recognition:** World. **Referee:** Dan Buckley.
Fight Summary: Down four times in the first round, when Barrett (147) was carried to his corner at the end of the session it looked all over, but he came back punch for punch until being eventually ground down by the champion. In the sixth Barrett was dropped for 'nine' by a right to the jaw followed by a left to the body, and on getting up he

was met by Walker (146¾), who feinted with the left before crashing in a heavy right to the jaw that sent him down to be counted out at 1.33 of the round.

Walker was now fighting more and more at the middleweight limit, but on 8 April 1925 his suspension was lifted in New York on the grounds that he would defend against Dave Shade prior to 16 August and would post a forfeit. This agreement with the NYSAC also paved the way for him to challenge Harry Greb for the middleweight title at the Polo Grounds, Manhattan, NYC, New York on 19 June, which was later moved to 2 July when Walker picked up a foot infection. There was no happy ending, Walker being outpointed over 15 rounds.

Meanwhile, at their conference in July, the IBU membership decided not to recognise Walker as a world champion as he had repeatedly ignored the challenges of Belgium's European titleholder, Piet Hobin.

Following his unsuccessful crack at the 160lbs title, and after much haggling over venues and finances, on 16 August 1925 Walker signed contracts to meet Shade at the Polo Grounds some five weeks later.

Leading up to his fight with Shade, Walker was awarded a 12-round press decision over Sailor Friedman at the Athletic Club Arena, East Chicago, Indiana on 24 August 1925. According to the *Chicago Tribune*, both men were inside 147lbs, but the *Chicago Daily News* gave it as Walker scaling 150lbs to Friedman's 151, which was more realistic.

21 September 1925. Mickey Walker w pts 15 Dave Shade.
Venue: Yankee Stadium, Bronx, NYC, New York, USA. **Recognition:** NY/NBA/GB. **Referee:** Patsy Haley.
Fight Summary: Prior to the 15th most of the audience were of the impression that Shade (147) only had to stand up to win the title. However, come the final bell *The Ring* magazine had both men winning six rounds with two even at the end of the 14th, and with Walker's big finish in the 15th when he hammered Shade at will, smashing him to head and body with heavy wallops, they saw it as a hard-earned but worthy win for the champion. Even the judges were divided, two voting for Walker (144½), including the referee, and one for Shade, but according to several papers the decision in Walker's favour had to be one of the worst seen in New York. Walker had started as aggressively as ever when delivering punishing blows to head and body, but Shade, bobbing up and down, was soon sending in accurate straight lefts and rights to the head. Although the champion was at his best in the fourth, sixth, seventh and 15th as he ripped in powerful blows from both hands, Shade almost always came back to nullify further advances with clever moves and hard hitting of his own. It should be noted that at least three times a dazed Walker made out for the wrong corner at the end of a round. Frustrating Walker continuously, even making him look foolish at times, Shade must have thought it was going to be his time prior to the verdict. Having twice failed narrowly to win the title, although recognised as the champion in New York for a short time, this would virtually be the last fight for Shade at 147lbs.

25 November 1925. Mickey Walker nd-w pts 12 Sailor Friedman.
Venue: 113th Regiment Armoury, Newark, New Jersey, USA. **Recognition:** NY/NBA/GB.
Fight Summary: Outmanoeuvred on the outside, the crafty Friedman (144) did much better at close quarters in nullifying the champion's aggression, and although well beaten he staged a belated rally which left Walker (146½) with a badly battered mouth at the final bell. While there were no arguments with the press decision, Walker, who appeared to lack the finishing ability needed to put paid to his hardy rival, was a big disappointment.

20 May 1926. Pete Latzo w pts 10 Mickey Walker.
Venue: The Armoury, Scranton, Pennsylvania, USA. **Recognition:** NY/NBA/GB. **Referee:** Frank Floyd.
Fight Summary: A savage contest, which saw plenty of heavy hitting on both sides, ended with Walker (144) losing his title to Latzo (146) following a majority verdict in the latter's favour. Interestingly, the referee had it as a draw. While Latzo started slowly, conserving his energy when crouching low to make himself a difficult target, he was still forced to withstand terrific body punishment before making his run for home. Eventually getting his counter offensive going, in the closing rounds Latzo swarmed all over the by now tiring Walker, slamming in stinging punches to head and body to have him frequently staggering around the ring prior to the final bell. Having been

out of action for six months prior to the contest, Walker put his defeat down to being over-trained after coming to a peak much too early, but regardless of that he lost to a better boxer who had his number on the night.

Reported in some places as involving the title, when Latzo (153½) knocked out Willie Harmon, who scaled 144¾, inside five rounds at Dreamland Park, Newark, New Jersey on 29 June, it was merely a no-decision non-title contest with the latter being inside the championship weight.

At their conference in July the IBU membership agreed to recognise Latzo as the world champion, having vacated the title the previous year.

9 July 1926. Pete Latzo w disq 4 (15) George Levine.
Venue: Polo Grounds, Manhattan, NYC, New York, USA. **Recognition:** World. **Referee:** Ed Purdy.
Fight Summary: Both men started well, Latzo (147) working to head and body and Levine (145½) relying more on the left jab, before the former started to get on top in the fourth round when looking for a knockout. Notwithstanding, the ending at 1.28 of the fourth was still sudden. As the champion worked Levine over, beginning to rock him on the ropes, the latter lashed out with a right to the body that sent Latzo to the floor claiming a foul. Although the referee picked up the count, reaching 'four' before he realised that Latzo was in a great deal of pain, he stopped the contest and awarded the decision to the champion on a disqualification.

Coming into 1927 the outstanding challenger was Joe Dundee, who reversed a shock loss when he outpointed Eddie Roberts at Madison Square Garden, Manhattan on 14 January. With Dundee in the frame it was then reported that Latzo would be defending against the winner of a contest between him and Ace Hudkins, but that never took place, while a mooted defence against Paul Doyle on 22 February also never happened.

Latzo took on Billy Piltz in a ten-round no-decision contest at The Coliseum in Oklahoma City, Oklahoma on 18 February 1927, in what was advertised in the *Daily Oklahoman* as a fight that the latter would have to win by a knockout, stoppage or disqualification if he wanted to take the title. At the final bell, it was Latzo who received the press decision. However, being one of two contests in three days while on tour it was highly unlikely that the championship was involved, especially as Latzo's ten-round no-decision meeting with Clyde Hull at Gardner Park Ice Arena, Dallas, Texas on 21 February 1927 was an overweight affair. Immediately following Hull's newspaper win over Latzo it was reported that the pair would contest the title in Scranton, but that was put on the backburner after it was announced that Humbert Fugazy would be putting on Latzo against Dundee in June 1927.

3 June 1927. Joe Dundee w pts 15 Pete Latzo.
Venue: Polo Grounds, Manhattan, NYC, New York, USA. **Recognition:** World. **Referee:** Eddie Forbes.
Fight Summary: After 15 torrid rounds a new champion was crowned when Dundee (143), who concentrated on the body in an effort to bring a weight-weakened Latzo (146½) down, set up a furious rally to storm home over the last seven rounds. Latzo made a good start, but tired as the fight progressed, and following a collision in the 11th which cut his left eye he was severely punished. According to most of the papers the decision was by a majority, the referee and one judge scoring it in favour of Dundee with the other judge seeing it as a draw.

In the October edition of *The Ring* magazine, Jack McVey, a brilliant fighter who was reported to be claiming the 'black title', went on to draw with Latzo and Dave Shade before moving up to middleweight.

13 July 1927. Joe Dundee nd-w pts 10 Billy Drako.
Venue: Redland's Baseball Park, Cincinnati, Ohio, USA. **Recognition:** World. **Referee:** Frank O'Brien.
Fight Summary: Not recorded in the *Ring Record Book* as a title fight, the *Cincinnati Enquirer* tells us it was advertised and went ahead as such with both men inside 147lbs. Contested in the open air, Drako (147), despite having his left eye virtually closed early on, proved himself to be a tough customer, who, although an easy target, took his punishment unflinchingly without ever being knocked off his feet by Dundee (147). With this being the champion's first contest since winning the title he showed up as a two-fisted fighter of the old school. Ice cool, he avoided his rival's swings with some ease while scoring accurately, if not sparingly, throughout. Dundee was well worth the press decision while the game Drako received plaudits for staying the course.

On 3 November, Dundee, due to defend against Ace Hudkins at Wrigley Field, Los Angeles, California, decided not to enter the ring after the promoter failed to deposit the $60,000 guarantee. Both men had weighed in, and Hudkins claimed the title without any real backing after climbing into the ring to show that he was ready and willing.

When Dundee stopped Hilario Martinez inside eight rounds at the Monumental Bullring, Barcelona, Spain on 7 July 1928, it was reported in some listings as involving the title. In truth, it was a ten-round over-the-weight contest. Martinez had earlier impressed in a trip to America when beating the likes of Jack Zivic, Sammy Vogel, Sid Terris, Jack Britton and Andy DiVodi before coming unstuck against Lew Tendler.

Further to a catchweight contest made at 148lbs against the 143lbs Young Jack Thompson at Comiskey Park, Chicago, Illinois on 30 August 1928, Dundee, who was stopped in the second round, forfeited NBA recognition when persistently refusing to defend against either Thompson or the leading contender, Jackie Fields, who were subsequently matched for the vacant NBA title.

By January 1929 Al Mello was the number one rated welterweight in *The Ring* magazine, having just defeated Vince Dundee, the brother of Joe, and his next two fights would be non-title affairs against the champion. Winning both on points over ten rounds should have put Mello in line for a shot at the championship, but by the end of June he had lost his high ranking after being beaten by Gorilla Jones.

Still recognised by the NYSAC as the champion, Dundee took in two warm-up bouts before looking to reunify the title in a match against the NBA's Fields, who had earlier eliminated Thompson.

25 March 1929. Jackie Fields w pts 10 Young Jack Thompson.
Venue: The Coliseum, Chicago, Illinois, USA. **Recognition:** NBA. **Referee:** Ed Purdy.
Fight Summary: Billed for the vacant NBA title, Fields (145¾) started well, almost dropping Thompson (145) on a couple of occasions in the opening two rounds when he had him groggy from a terrific battering to head and body. Thereafter, Thompson was up against it, but having won the seventh when launching a desperate rally he was going well until panic broke out in the audience in the eighth. The problem started when two paying customers drew weapons on each other, and although both Fields and Thompson continued fighting while this was going on the contest was halted when some of the fans found their way into the ring after the crowd had stampeded. However, once calm and order was resumed the fight started again some 15 minutes later. With a minute of round eight still left it was immediately noticeable that Thompson had been affected more than Fields by the enforced interlude. While Thompson began to find his feet towards the end of the tenth, after the final bell rang there was no surprise when the referee awarded Fields the decision. Having proved to be the better man on the night, Fields was thought to have won eight of the ten rounds contested with his unswerving offensive being too much for Thompson to handle.

25 July 1929. Jackie Fields w disq 2 (15) Joe Dundee.
Venue: The Fairgrounds, Detroit, Michigan, USA. **Recognition:** World. **Referee:** Elmer McClelland.
Fight Summary: In a battle to unify the title, with both men starting slowly the first round was generally a feeling-out session with Fields (145), the NBA champion, just about having the better of it. However, the second was different altogether as the pair set about each other from the gong, and following a volley of blows to the head Dundee (147) was decked for 'nine'. On his feet, again Dundee was sent crashing, this time for 'seven', from punches to head and body. Then, after getting up, for whatever reason he smashed in a hard right below the belt for which he was immediately disqualified when Fields went down in agony. The finish was timed at 1.55. Long after the fight was over rumours persisted that Dundee had fouled himself out of the fight intentionally, something he vehemently denied. It was said that with Dundee's purse wagered on him winning, he activated an 'all bets off' agreement in the event of a disqualification.

After being inactive for two months Fields came back to beat Vince Dundee, Gorilla Jones (twice) and Fred Mahan in non-title contests, but by the end of the year the calls for him to defend against Jimmy McLarnin were getting stronger, especially when Jack Dempsey ranked the latter as the leading challenger in *The Ring* magazine ratings.

Early in 1930 it was reported that promoters in San Francisco, Cleveland and Chicago were bidding to stage a title match between Fields and Tommy Freeman, who had just come off a win over Young Jack Thompson (w pts 10 at the Olympia Stadium, Detroit on 10 January 1930).

Meanwhile, in an overweight match, Fields was defeated by Young Corbett III (l pts 10 at the Recreation Ground, San Francisco, California on 22 February 1930). Despite elevating himself into the number one spot, Corbett fractured his left hand, an injury that would put him out of action for a couple of months.

Although he had failed to make an early defence, with Fields remaining active his next contest saw him beat Freeman (w rsc 5 at the Public Auditorium, Cleveland, Ohio on 8 April 1930) at 150lbs, thus temporarily putting the latter out of the title race. Pressure was now being brought from the leading boxing authorities for Fields to defend his crown, but ongoing talks for a fight against McLarnin continued to break down over the terms. Then came an announcement from Detroit that the Olympia promoters had Fields under contract to defend the title and would go to court if necessary to prevent a proposed fight between Fields and McLarnin taking place in New York on 11 September 1930. The threat of legal action obviously worked for the Detroit promoters, and faced with a choice Fields decided to hook up with Thompson at the Olympia rather than risk a meeting with McLarnin.

9 May 1930. Young Jack Thompson w pts 15 Jackie Fields.
Venue: Olympia, Detroit, Michigan, USA. **Recognition:** World. **Referee:** Elmer McClelland.
Scorecard: 10-3-2.
Fight Summary: Meeting for the third time, the champion having won both previous contests, Thompson (142¾) was seen as a far easier touch than Jimmy McLarnin, who had recently beaten the latter. Setting a blistering pace from the start Thompson carried the fight to Fields (145¾), but was almost knocked out in the second round after smashing lefts and rights had him on 'Queer Street' before the bell came to his rescue. Staying away from Fields' vicious attacks for the next few sessions, with Thompson beginning to pile up a comfortable lead from the sixth onwards by the end of the tenth it was anybody's fight. Although Thompson continued to go well as Fields tired the 15th saw the latter stage a blistering response, and it was only because his blows lacked snap that enabled Thompson to reach the final bell. After receiving the referee's decision Thompson spent the night in hospital suffering from a haemorrhage of the nose, while the virtually unmarked Fields blamed just three days of heavy training for his defeat.

5 September 1930. Tommy Freeman w pts 15 Young Jack Thompson.
Venue: League Park, Cleveland, Ohio, USA. **Recognition:** World. **Referee:** Patsy Haley.
Scorecard: 8-5-2.
Fight Summary: Proving to be as strong as a bull, the challenger not only surprised Thompson (143¼) but just about everyone out there after receiving the referee's decision following 15 gruelling rounds. Expected to be weak at the weight, Freeman (145¾) was more than happy to make it a fight of endurance, and apart from being knocked down for a count of 'six' in the second when chinned by a left hook he remained strong. With the contest even at the end of the tenth, it was Freeman who went for it in the 11th, belting in body punches for the remainder of the bout. The new champion attributed his strength to his time as a lumberjack.

Out of action until early 1931, having gone down with two bad cases of flu after vacationing, Freeman came back with five non-title wins over Pete August, Eddie Murdock, Duke Tramel, Al Kober and Alfredo Gaona before signing up to meet Thompson in a return bout for the title. These contests were incorrectly shown at a later date in some listings as involving the title.

Earlier it had been announced that Freeman would make a defence against either Jackie Fields, Jimmy McLarnin, Young Corbett III or Thompson. Eventually, it was the latter who got the opportunity, having been out of action even longer than Freeman before coming back in March 1931 with two warm-up fights to prepare him for the task ahead.

14 April 1931. Young Jack Thompson w rsc 11 (15) Tommy Freeman.
Venue: Public Hall, Cleveland, Ohio, USA. **Recognition:** World. **Referee:** Eddie Davis.

Fight Summary: In what was seen as a poor fight, being held in silence for the first eight rounds, the champion got a boxing lesson as Thompson (145¼) flipped in lefts without reply. After Freeman (146¾) was cut over the left eye in the third, Thompson gave a splendid display of mixing up his punches and feinting to take a clear lead into the ninth. It was then that Freeman came on strong with lefts and rights to the body, but when a hard right from Thompson further damaged his already half-closed right eye in the 11th session the referee called it off during the interval.

Having beaten the new champion and Gorilla Jones in successive fights to become *The Ring* magazine's top-rated welterweight in May, Bucky Lawless appeared to be the logical challenger at that moment in time. However, Thompson's next defence would be against Lou Brouillard, who had outpointed him over ten rounds at the Garden, Boston, Massachusetts in a non-title fight on 23 July, and Lawless' big chance had gone.

23 October 1931. Lou Brouillard w pts 15 Young Jack Thompson.
Venue: The Garden, Boston, Massachusetts, USA. **Recognition:** World. **Referee:** Johnny Brassil.
Fight Summary: Fighting on the defensive, Thompson (146), displaying none of his much vaunted punching power and boxing ability generally allowed Brouillard (146¾) to take the play away from him throughout. Three times he was dropped, twice for 'nine' in the tenth and 13th rounds, and was unable to cope with the rugged body attacks as the southpaw challenger made that his target when romping to the unanimous points victory. While Brouillard was on the way up, winning 12 of the 15 rounds, with it being apparent that Thompson had nothing much left he retired after five more fights.

By the end of December, Baby Joe Gans was Brouillard's number one challenger according to *The Ring* magazine ratings, having drawn with the champion over ten rounds in a recent non-title bout, but following two successive draws against ordinary opposition he dropped down the rankings.

28 January 1932. Jackie Fields w pts 10 Lou Brouillard.
Venue: The Stadium, Chicago, Illinois, USA. **Recognition:** World. **Referee:** Dave Miller.
Fight Summary: It had been fairly even for five rounds, before Fields (145½) opened up in the sixth, throwing vicious punches from both hands to have the southpaw champion wobbling and severely at risk. He kept up the pressure throughout the next two sessions before Brouillard (146) rallied in the ninth, only for Fields to make sure of regaining the championship by pecking away with the left in the tenth to fully deserve the unanimous decision.

After beating Fields (w pts 10 at The Garden, Boston, Massachusetts on 4 March) in a non-title fight, Johnny Indrisano was given number one status by *The Ring* magazine, but that was quickly forfeited when he lost to Brouillard on points over ten rounds at the same venue on 8 April.

At the end of July *The Ring* magazine had Billy Petrolle top-rated simultaneously in three weight divisions – light, junior welter and welter – having recently defeated Billy Townsend, the hard-hitting Eddie Ran, Battling Battalino (twice) and Tommy Grogan. From there on, however, he would concentrate on preparing for his coming lightweight title challenge against Tony Canzoneri.

Prior to the billed eliminator in NYC, New York on 4 August between Jimmy McLarnin and Brouillard, won by the latter on points over ten rounds, the matchmaker, Al Weill, went before the NYSAC to try and get the bout upped to 15 rounds and recognised as being for the world title. This came about after Weill had been told that Fields had serious eye trouble and would probably not be allowed to box again. The request was turned down on the grounds that until the Commission heard in an official capacity that Fields would not be boxing again he should still be seen as the champion.

A few weeks later the NBA ordered Fields to defend by 28 October, but eventually agreed to let him have a couple of warm-up bouts before making a defence. He was then matched against the number two rated Young Corbett III, who was a 13-year veteran with 102 wins, 17 draws and seven defeats to his name, and was undefeated in his last 28 contests. More of a boxer than a puncher, the hard-to-figure Corbett was a durable southpaw who could control the pace of a contest effectively.

22 February 1933. Young Corbett III w pts 10 Jackie Fields.
Venue: Seals Stadium, San Francisco, California, USA. **Recognition:** World. **Referee:** Jack Kennedy.
Scorecard: 6-3-1.
Fight Summary: Corbett (146) lived up to his name as the conqueror of champions when outboxing and outpunching Fields (146) in six of the ten sessions to take the referee's decision. Fighting in whirlwind fashion, the southpaw challenger took Fields completely by surprise as he fired in long lefts from the start while effectively countering anything coming his way. After losing the first five rounds Fields came to life in the sixth, belting Corbett to head and body at will before tiring after taking some heavy lefts in the seventh and eighth rounds, which stopped him in his tracks. The ninth and tenth sessions saw Fields battering Corbett around the ring in a desperate bid to hold on to his title, but with a minute to go he was badly hurt by lefts to the jaw and rights to the body before slumping on to his stool at the bell.

On beating the fast-rising Teddy Yarosz at the end of February, and in doing so breaking the latter's unbeaten streak at 59, Eddie Wolfe moved himself into title contention. Despite losing to Tony Herrera, Jack Portney, Frankie Hughes and Harry Dublinsky, the last two defeats being avenged, Wolfe had drawn with Yarosz and Paulie Walker. He had also beaten men of the calibre of Tracey Cox, Ray Kiser (twice) and Eddie Ran before being outpointed by Willard Brown in July 1934. Although Wolfe gained revenge over Brown and beat Tiger Joe Randall, Cox and George Salvadore, they were his only wins in his final ten fights.

After beating Wolfe, Brown was ranked as high as fourth by *The Ring* magazine, but having been stopped twice in succession in Australia by Jack Carroll (4 March 1935) and Portney (29 April 1935) he never again got close to a title shot.

29 May 1933. Jimmy McLarnin w rsc 1 (10) Young Corbett III.
Venue: Wrigley Field, Los Angeles, California, USA. **Recognition:** World. **Referee:** George Blake.
Fight Summary: Starting the contest with short southpaw jabs and jolting lefts the champion confused McLarnin (145¼) for the opening two minutes, but the latter remained calm while awaiting an opening to get his punches off. He would not have to wait long. As Corbett (146) came in McLarnin saw his chance and took it when smashing in a right hander to the jaw. Although the champion was up at 'nine' three rapid left hooks dropped him again. Getting up at 'eight', Corbett seemed to be out on his feet, and when he was sent sprawling halfway through the ropes by a short right the referee stopped the contest on the 2.37 mark.

Inactive for a year while waiting for a worthwhile challenger to appear, McLarnin finally signed up to meet Barney Ross, the lightweight and junior welter titleholder, in April 1934. With many wondering whether all three titles would be on the line the former was asked to come in above 140lbs.

28 May 1934. Barney Ross w pts 15 Jimmy McLarnin.
Venue: MSG Bowl, Queens, NYC, New York, USA. **Recognition:** World. **Referee:** Eddie Forbes.
Scorecards: 11-2-2, 13-1-1, 1-9-5.
Fight Summary: Making ring history, Ross (137¾), champion of the lightweights and junior welters, became the first man to hold three titles at one time when he took a split decision off McLarnin (142), who seemed to be just a shadow of his normal self after being on the sidelines for a year. Although McLarnin made a reasonable start to take the first two rounds, most reporters saw Ross winning the third through to the ninth when charging in with hefty wallops. He also surprised everyone when taking the heavy punches coming his way. The ninth was hectic, Ross being put down by a cracking left hook before getting up and tearing into McLarnin with both hands firing, prior to producing two left hooks of his own to drop the latter. In the tenth it was noticeable that Ross was tiring. Following instructions, for the next five sessions McLarnin made his big effort as the New Yorker began to wilt under the body punches and long-range lefts. However, eager to build on his earlier supremacy, Ross came out for the 15th like a man who knew he was only moments away from victory when charging into McLarnin savagely, throwing caution to the wind and crowding the champion to such an extent that he was unable to get any heavy shots off. It had been a thrilling affair, but McLarnin would make a better account of himself in the return.

17 September 1934. Jimmy McLarnin w pts 15 Barney Ross.
Venue: MSG Bowl, Queens, NYC New York, USA. **Recognition:** World. **Referee:** Arthur Donovan.
Scorecards: 10-5, 6-5-4, 6-8-1.
Fight Summary: In a bid to regain his old honours, McLarnin (146¼) came to the ring better prepared than in their first fight. This time round it was he who scored well with the left hand and smashing body blows while Ross (140¼) seemed slightly below par. The battle was a desperate one with left hooks, left jabs, body blows and solid rights to the head keeping the fans happy, and both men suffering plenty of damage. McLarnin, who had his left eye closed early on, was at his best in the first, sixth, seventh and eighth, where his boxing was superb and bewildered Ross. However, Ross was always dangerous, coming on strong in the closing sessions with two-fisted attacks to head and body to make it a close run thing. The split decision in McLarnin's favour was a disputed one, but if the low blow that saw a point deducted from the latter in the fifth had not been counted as was Ross's similar misdemeanour in the 14th all three judges would have voted for the Irishman.

Strangely, McLarnin again remained inactive, while Ross thrice defended his junior welter laurels before relinquishing his lightweight crown in April 1935 in order to take the rematch with the welter champion. It had always been known that the pair would meet up again in the summer of 1935 in a big-money, open-air fight, and with Ross not having defended his lightweight title since September 1934, being suspended in New York until he did so, it came as no surprise that he opted to go for the 147lbs belt instead. As in their first contest, with Ross still ruling the junior welters, McLarnin was asked to come in above 140lbs.

Earlier, in November 1934, Tony Falco had joined the top five as far as *The Ring* magazine was concerned, after beating Young Peter Jackson. Unfortunately for Falco he was unable to build on his win over Jackson, being beaten next time out by Harry Dublinsky, and despite defeating Young Joe Firpo, Johnny Jadick and Andre Jessurun he won just 14 of his remaining 38 bouts.

28 May 1935. Barney Ross w pts 15 Jimmy McLarnin.
Venue: Polo Grounds, Manhattan, NYC, New York, USA. **Recognition:** World. **Referee:** Jack Dempsey.
Scorecards: 7-5-3, 8-6-1, 9-4-2.
Fight Summary: Although the decision was unanimous in favour of Ross (141) it was disputed by many ringsiders, including Nat Fleischer, who thought that McLarnin (144¾) had retained his title. According to Fleischer, the champion started early with jabs, hooks and the occasional body punch, while Ross only got active when there was less than a minute of each round left in order to impress the judges. Each man was jarred up a number of times, but neither was on the verge of being knocked out. In the 11th, 12th and 14th rounds Ross attacked with vicious intent, but McLarnin evened matters up in the 15th when he had his rival holding on and looking exhausted.

Taking three months off before coming back to the ring, Ross, who saw 1935 out with three non-title wins, was accused in *The Ring* magazine of being hesitant about defending the title when there were so many good matches to be made. When Jimmy Johnston, on behalf of Madison Square Garden, offered Ross a fight against the lightweight champion, Tony Canzoneri, it was turned down out of hand, the latter being matched against McLarnin instead. Ross's management stated that they would not be doing business with the Garden while Johnston acted on their behalf.

Since the McLarnin v Ross rivalry had begun several men had been ranked number one by *The Ring* magazine, such as Bep van Klaveren, Harry Dublinsky and Kid Azteca. All of them had been totally ignored as far as championship requests were concerned and now Jack Carroll was in poll position. Following a challenge on behalf of Carroll, the Australian champion, for Ross to defend in Melbourne during November 1936 it was announced that the champion had agreed to take the fight on 8 December at the Sydney Sports Ground. After beating Phil Furr at the Griffith Stadium, Washington DC on 22 July 1936, his ninth non-title win since regaining the championship, Ross announced that he would not take any more fights and was preparing to leave for Australia at the beginning of October.

With the black welters of the day not getting much of a shout, the Cocoa Kid (144½) knocked out Young Peter Jackson (142½) in what was a billed 'black ten-round title fight' held at Heinemann Park, New Orleans, Louisiana on

26 July 1936. He later defended that claim with a ten-round points decision over Jackie Elverillo at the same venue on 22 September 1936.

Meanwhile, with the NYSAC setting up an eliminating series to find an opponent for Ross, Izzy Jannazzo beat Gustav Eder (w pts 15 at St Nicholas Arena, Manhattan on 21 September 1936) before going on to meet Ceferino Garcia in the final. Following a 15-round draw at Madison Square Garden, Manhattan on 30 October 1936 the NYSAC presented Jannazzo with an early Christmas present when they selected him to meet the champion for the title as they did not think Garcia would be ready in the time frame.

Whatever happened to the Ross v Carroll fight is unclear, but while the Australian would remain the number one challenger until September 1937 he did not figure again.

27 November 1936. Barney Ross w pts 15 Izzy Jannazzo.
Venue: Madison Square Garden, Manhattan, NYC, New York, USA. **Recognition:** World. **Referee:** Johnny McAvoy.
Scorecards: 8-4-3, 9-5-1, 9-6.
Fight Summary: Doing his best to make a fight of it against the wily Jannazzo (145¼), the champion put the latter down twice, for a count of 'two' in the second following a left hook and for 'four' in the fifth, but unable to find a finishing blow he was forced to go the distance. With Jannazzo travelling backwards, flicking out his left, although Ross (143) won the opening eight rounds he tired himself out in the process, being forced to conserve his energy. It was in the ninth that Jannazzo got busier, but he never had Ross in any difficulty whatsoever, while the latter, only opening up in flashes, cruised to the finishing line to collect the unanimous verdict.

Holman Williams claimed the 'black title' when beating the Cocoa Kid (w pts 12 at the Coliseum Arena, New Orleans, Louisiana on 12 March 1937), but then lost the return when outpointed over 15 rounds by the Kid at the same venue on 11 June 1937.

Around that time the Chicago Boxing Commission were making overtures to Ross for him to defend against Pedro Montanez, but the champion's people were saying that the New York agreement called for him to meet Ceferino Garcia first.

Inactive for two months before returning to beat Al Manfredo in a non-title contest, Ross was then out again for a further five months prior to coming back for three more overweight contests and signing to defend against Garcia.

23 September 1937. Barney Ross w pts 15 Ceferino Garcia.
Venue: Polo Grounds, Manhattan, NYC, New York, USA. **Recognition:** World. **Referee:** Billy Cavanagh.
Scorecards: 7-5-3, 9-4-2, 9-4-2.
Fight Summary: Defending his title in 'The Carnival of Champions' show, Ross (143) put on an excellent display to thwart the ambitious Garcia (145¾), who proved to be a tough opponent. Always looking to get away his famous 'bolo' punch, a devastating sweeping overarm right, Garcia hurt Ross on several occasions. However, the latter showed up well, keeping the challenger off balance with the left jab, and when in trouble his defensive ability enabled him to get out of tight spots more often than not. In the fourth Garcia was cut around the right eye, and a round or so later under the left as Ross worked away, but he was always dangerous. Several times during the contest it looked as though Ross would be dropped, but somehow he found a way out. With the 13th and 14th sessions being especially bad for him he was strictly on the defensive throughout, fighting open mouthed, and it was almost the same in the 15th until he found another gear to rip in lefts and rights prior to the final bell. The unanimous decision in his favour was testament to all of the good work he put in earlier, but Ross, who ended with a badly swollen face and a damaged left hand, knew he had been in a war.

On 15 November, the Cocoa Kid (143½) successfully defended his 'black title' claim when knocking out Sonny Jones (142½) in the sixth of a 15 rounder at the Valley Arena, Holyoke, Massachusetts.

Ross, who was currently inactive, forfeited IBU recognition in January 1938 when that authority decided to recognise the winner of the Felix Wouters v Gustav Eder European title bout as world champion.

Coming back in April 1938 for two warm-up fights, Ross had earlier signed to make a defence against Henry Armstrong, the current featherweight champion, on 31 May 1938, with the winner to meet Lou Ambers inside 60 days.

16 February 1938. Felix Wouters w pts 15 Gustav Eder.
Venue: Sports Palace, Brussels, Belgium. **Recognition:** IBU.
Fight Summary: In a fight to decide the vacant IBU version of the world title as well as being a defence of his European crown, Wouters (147), who had previously been knocked out by Eder (147), was the benefactor of a much disputed verdict. Although it was hardly surprising that he took few risks, having boxed carefully in front of his home crowd, he was belatedly floored in the 15th round by Eder, who, while looking for openings for his trusty right hand, had refrained from using it in the early stages. However, Wouters got up and despite being further wobbled made it to the final bell. Earlier, there had been some doubt as to whether the contest, which had already been postponed once due to Wouters being ill, would take place as Eder was suffering from an internal ailment.

During an international boxing convention held in Rome in April 1938, which was attended by many of the leading authorities within the sport, the IBU agreed to refuse to recognise all individually-made world champions, including their own, in an effort to stand by one universally acknowledged champion, who, in turn, would have to concede to regular defences decided by the new Federation.

31 May 1938. Henry Armstrong w pts 15 Barney Ross.
Venue: MSG Bowl, Queens, NYC, New York, USA. **Recognition:** World. **Referee:** Arthur Donovan.
Scorecards: 12-2-1, 11-2-2, 10-4-1.
Fight Summary: Already the holder of the featherweight title, Armstrong (133½) jumped one division to capture the welterweight crown also when being awarded the unanimous decision over the game Ross (142). The fight itself was one-sided with, Ross, despite winning the opening two rounds, finding himself up against a whirlwind of a fighter who just walked through his defences. Subsequently, it was gameness alone that kept him on his feet as Armstrong relentlessly marched forward throwing punches from both hands to head and body. Even when Ross came on with big punches of his own, Armstrong, sporting a fair amount of weight, appeared to be impervious to them. At the final bell the champion looked like he had been through a threshing machine, his right eye closed, his face distorted and mouth and nose badly puffed up. It was no surprise when Ross announced his retirement from the ring immediately after the fight.

17 August 1938. Henry Armstrong w pts 15 Lou Ambers.
Venue: Madison Square Garden, Manhattan, NYC, New York, USA. **Recognition:** World. **Referee:** Billy Cavanagh.
Scorecards: 8-6-1, 7-6-2, 7-8.
Fight Summary: Starting off at a whirlwind pace Armstrong (134) backed Ambers (134¼) against the ropes for most of the action, battering the body with great effect despite receiving three cautions for low blows, and had the champion down from a crunching right to the jaw in the fifth round and again in the sixth. That Ambers fought back gamely to give Armstrong more trouble than he had been forced to take on board previously was rewarded on one of the judges' scorecards, his efforts being highlighted in the 13th session when he stormed into the challenger, whipping in savage blows to force his rival back. However, with the men tiring that was the final spell of mass excitement, both being glad to hear the final bell when it came. On winning, Armstrong became a three-time champion while simultaneously holding the feather (which he relinquished in November), light and welterweight crowns. Although billed for the lightweight title, and with both men naturally inside 135lbs, the NBA stated that it recognised the fight as also involving the welter championship.

Despite falling on deaf ears, Nat Fleischer, writing in the *Ring* magazine, stated that because Armstrong was forced to come to the ring inside 135lbs how could the welterweight title have been at stake when he was prevented by the terms of the contract from defending his crown at the weight prescribed for that weight class.

A few days later, on 22 August, at Hickey Park, Pittsburgh, Pennsylvania, the Cocoa Kid (144) lost his 'black welterweight title' to Charley Burley (145½) on points over 15 rounds, but with Armstrong firmly in place as the number one fighter in the world at 147lbs the synthetic title meant very little. Regardless, the new claimant soon moved on.

At the beginning of September, Ceferino Garcia and Michele Palermo, known as Kid Frattini in American rings, were the two top-rated men in the division as far as *The Ring* magazine was concerned. With Garcia being lined up to become Armstrong's first challenger, Palermo, who had beaten Holman Williams, Bobby Pacho and Andre Jessurun in his last three contests, was next in line. Unfortunately for him he was stopped inside six rounds by Sonny Jones on 24 September, and one fight later he was back in his native Italy, eventually winning the EBU welter title at the age of 38.

25 November 1938. Henry Armstrong w pts 15 Ceferino Garcia.
Venue: Madison Square Garden, Manhattan, NYC, New York, USA. **Recognition:** World. **Referee:** Arthur Donovan.
Scorecards: 9-6, 9-6, 8-7.
Fight Summary: Giving away over 12 pounds to the dangerous Garcia (146½), the champion took the fight to his foe right from the opening bell regardless of the weight difference, pouring in punches with both hands at close quarters to nullify much of what came his way. At times Garcia gave as good as he got. In the 12th he came close to knocking Armstrong (134) out with slamming right hands to the head, but somehow the latter recovered his equilibrium, bobbed and weaved, and pushed on in the last two rounds to fully deserve the unanimous decision that eventually came his way. There was no doubt that Garcia was at his best when he was able to shake Armstrong off, but he missed a golden opportunity by not giving himself room to fire off his heavy rights. Despite being booed by a certain section of the crowd at the finish Armstrong had again proved himself to be the best man in the division, while Garcia announced that having to take off weight had hindered him. He went on to say that in future he would be fighting at 158lbs.

5 December 1938. Henry Armstrong w rsc 3 (15) Al Manfredo.
Venue: The Arena, Cleveland, Ohio, USA. **Recognition:** World. **Referee:** Tony LaBranch.
Fight Summary: Setting a terrific pace from the opening bell Armstrong (134¾) quickly wore down Manfredo (146), who tried to box from range but was overwhelmed. With the champion pumping in piston-like blows to head and body Manfredo was punched all over the ring in the second round before the referee brought the uneven contest to a halt at 1.45 of the third. At that stage of the fight Manfredo was not returning punches.

10 January 1939. Henry Armstrong w pts 10 Baby Arizmendi.
Venue: Olympic Auditorium, Los Angeles, California, USA. **Recognition:** World. **Referee:** George Blake.
Scorecard: 6-1.
Fight Summary: After ten rounds of head-to-head fighting the referee decided that Armstrong (134½), who weighed inside the lightweight limit, had outscored Arizmendi (136). Although the champion often threw questionable punches, Arizmendi, who finished up with battered features and both eyes cut, just stood in front of him taking whatever landed. It was non-stop action all the way, and while both men threw plenty of punches it was apparent that the champion threw more. This was the sixth meeting between the pair.

4 March 1939. Henry Armstrong w rsc 4 (15) Bobby Pacho.
Venue: Tropical Stadium, Havana, Cuba. **Recognition:** World. **Referee:** Jim Braddock.
Fight Summary: Tossing in hard rights and lefts from the opening bell, the champion quickly showed his intent as Pacho (147) missed repeatedly. Although Pacho had more success in the second, especially with the right uppercut, he was gradually being mown down. Opening up in the third, Armstrong (134) began to force Pacho around the ring, slamming in hard rights and lefts to the body, and the latter would almost certainly have gone down had he not been backed up against the ropes. Surprisingly, Pacho came out for the fourth, but having taken another beating and hanging helpless halfway through the ropes the referee rescued him from further punishment on the 1.10 mark.

16 March 1939. Henry Armstrong w co 1 (15) Lew Feldman.
Venue: Municipal Auditorium, St Louis, Missouri, USA. **Recognition:** World. **Referee:** Walter Heisner.

Fight Summary: Billed and reported as a fight that involved Armstrong's light and welterweight titles, the champion started well with sharp left jabs before getting down to business to floor Feldman (134) for a count of 'nine' after less than two minutes of action. There was no coming back from that, and with Feldman back on his feet Armstrong (135) piled in with powerful rights and lefts to leave the former on the deck to be counted out with just 2.12 on the clock.

31 March 1939. Henry Armstrong w rsc 12 (15) Davey Day.
Venue: Madison Square Garden, Manhattan, NYC, New York, USA. **Recognition:** World. **Referee:** Billy Cavanagh.
Fight Summary: Although waging a stubborn battle, while never threatening Armstrong (135), Day (136) showed a tremendous ability to assimilate everything thrown at him without ever going down. That was until the 12th round when a solid right to the body finally put the exhausted challenger on the floor after a hail of blows to the head had met with little or no resistance. Dispensing with the count when it was obvious that Day could not continue, the referee called a halt at 2.49 to help the beaten fighter back to his corner.

25 May 1939. Henry Armstrong w pts 15 Ernie Roderick.
Venue: The Arena, Harringay, London, England. **Recognition:** World. **Referee:** Wilfred Smith.
Fight Summary: Apart from the opening round which Roderick (145¾) won by dint of good left-hand work, the champion began to control the action thereafter when getting to close quarters where he surprisingly threw few bodyline shots, perhaps fearful of disqualification. With many thinking that Armstrong (135) would falter sooner or later, having set an exacting pace, they were ultimately proved wrong as the American kept going round after round, churning out lefts and rights to both head and body at speed. If anything, he even upped the pace at times. To the British champion's credit he was always trying to fight back, taking Armstrong's best punches without dropping, even when being hit full bloodedly on the jaw. In the final third of the fight Roderick's left eye, which was already cut, began to close, but he kept up his game resistance right through to the final bell when Armstrong deservedly took the referee's decision.

On 22 August, at the Yankee Stadium, Bronx, NYC, New York, Armstrong was outpointed over 15 rounds by Lou Ambers when making a defence of his 135lbs lightweight title. Following the fight there was much talk of the latter having also won the welterweight championship at the same time. In explaining the situation, Nat Fleischer, of *The Ring* magazine, stated: "Talk about Ambers having won two titles is nonsense. If the boys had been fighting for the welter crown and Ambers had scaled within the lightweight limit and had been returned the winner then there would be no doubt about both crowns belonging to him". This was supported by the NBA, who addressed their previous mistake by saying that they did not recognise Ambers as the welterweight champion. They went on to say that in future a champion can only defend his title against men rated in his division.

Meantime, having beaten Fritzie Zivic and Jimmy Leto, Charley Burley was number one in *The Ring* magazine ratings, but by December he had moved on, leaving the way clear for Zivic. Although Zivic would get his chance at a later date, he lost his top-rating to Milt Aron, who knocked him out in the eighth round at The Coliseum, Chicago, Illinois on 27 December. Aron seemed to be a real comer, but after beating Eddie Brink and Bep van Klaveren he lost to Emil Calcagni, and although getting immediate revenge he soon dropped down the ratings.

9 October 1939. Henry Armstrong w rsc 4 (10) Al Manfredo.
Venue: Riverview Park Arena, Des Moines, Iowa, USA. **Recognition:** World. **Referee:** Alex Fidler.
Fight Summary: Following two tame rounds as Manfredo (146¾) back-pedalled to keep out of the danger zone, Armstrong (141½) opened up in the third with an attack that left his challenger in a dazed state and ready to be taken. Resuming his assault in the fourth it was all one way as Armstrong swamped Manfredo in a hail of leather, and with the latter draped helplessly over the ropes the referee came to his rescue at 1.35 of the session.

13 October 1939. Henry Armstrong w co 2 (10) Howard Scott.
Venue: The Armoury, Minneapolis, Minnesota, USA. **Recognition:** World. **Referee:** John DeOtis.
Fight Summary: Just four nights after beating Al Manfredo the champion was again putting his title on the line, against 'Cowboy' Scott (147), and he made a fast start when pumping out rights and lefts to head and body to push the latter back. Dropped in the first by a left hook, Scott, who was expected to be a bit of a test for Armstrong

(141), was right up against it in the second. Unable to get going, at 1.38 of the session Scott was counted out after being downed by a heavy right to the head.

20 October 1939. Henry Armstrong w rsc 3 (15) Richie Fontaine.
Venue: Civic Stadium, Seattle, Washington, USA. **Recognition:** World. **Referee:** Tommy Clark.
Fight Summary: Not one to back away, Fontaine (141) took the fight to the champion in the first round but almost exhausted himself in the process. Coming out for the second he was immediately dropped by a left to the jaw as Armstrong (139¾) tore into the attack, and although he got up he was knocked down four more times in the session, none of the counts going above 'four'. Wobbly when he answered the bell for the third, Fontaine was dropped for 'six' following a cluster of blows, but on rising to his feet and being put down by a right to the jaw the referee stopped the fight after his seconds threw the towel in. The finish was timed at 2.03.

24 October 1939. Henry Armstrong w pts 10 Jimmy Garrison.
Venue: Olympic Auditorium, Los Angeles, California, USA. **Recognition:** World. **Referee:** George Blake.
Fight Summary: Content to let Garrison (139½) make the running in the opening session, the champion only got moving after taking a few solid blows in the fifth. Tearing out for the sixth, Armstrong (138¼) made all the running from thereon in, dropping Garrison for a count of 'two' in the eighth after banging in a crisp right to the head. However, as much as he tried Armstrong could not finish Garrison off, and although he punched his man from pillar to post in the last round he was forced to settle for the referee's decision in his favour.

30 October 1939. Henry Armstrong w rsc 4 (15) Bobby Pacho.
Venue: Municipal Auditorium, Denver, Colorado, USA. **Recognition:** World. **Referee:** Jack Bloom.
Fight Summary: Six nights after beating Jimmy Garrison, the champion was back in the ring defending his title again, this time against the battle-scarred Pacho (146). Despite being given the opportunity, Pacho did not look to be in the greatest of shape at the weigh-in. The first three rounds saw Armstrong (140) all over Pacho, who to his credit was still looking to make a fight of it, and although the latter tried to get to close quarters in the fourth he was quickly sent spinning into the ropes from a fusillade of punches. With Armstrong pounding away to head and body until Pacho's arms were dangling by his side the referee called it off after a minute and a half of the session had elapsed. This was Armstrong's fifth title defence in just 22 days.

11 December 1939. Henry Armstrong w rsc 7 (10) Jimmy Garrison.
Venue: The Arena, Cleveland, Ohio, USA. **Recognition:** World. **Referee:** Benny Leonard.
Fight Summary: This was Armstrong's 12th world championship fight in a year, which included a lightweight title defence, and is a record that will probably never be beaten. Although Garrison (141) put up a good fight there was no doubt that Armstrong (138¾) would beat him for the second time in two months, especially after he connected heavily in the third round with overarm lefts and rights. Garrison, who had his left eye cut in the fourth and his right eye damaged in the sixth, was gradually beaten up before being floored by a right swing to the jaw in the seventh. On getting up in a bad way and being met by a flurry of blows the referee stopped the contest after his corner threw in the towel, the fight coming to an end after 79 seconds of the session had elapsed.

4 January 1940. Henry Armstrong w co 5 (15) Joe Ghnouly.
Venue: Municipal Auditorium, St Louis, Missouri, USA. **Recognition:** World. **Referee:** Harry Cook.
Fight Summary: Given a crack at the 147lbs championship despite being a lowly-ranked lightweight, Ghnouly (135½) was quickly cut down to size as Armstrong (136¾) swarmed all over him from the opening bell. There was virtually no let up as the punches thudded in from all angles, Ghnouly being dropped three times in the opening round before fighting his way back in summary fashion. Downed again in the fourth and saved by the bell, he came out for the fifth, showing some resistance, prior to being counted out at 1.34 of the session.

Strange, when you consider the world already had a black champion in Armstrong that a fight between the Cocoa Kid and Holman Williams, won on points over 15 rounds by the former at the Coliseum, Baltimore, Maryland on 11 January, was advertised as being for the vacant 'black title'. While the title itself was not taken too seriously the result elevated the Kid to number two in *The Ring* Ratings, one above Williams, and would lend him much support in his quest to meet Armstrong.

24 January 1940. Henry Armstrong w rsc 9 (15) Pedro Montanez.
Venue: Madison Square Garden, Manhattan, NYC, New York, USA. **Recognition:** World. **Referee:** Billy Cavanagh.
Fight Summary: In a contest that was sizzling with action right from the opening bell, the champion slammed in lefts and rights to head and body from start to finish as Montanez (144½) stood his ground before being worn down. Although Montanez had some success at the beginning, by the third he was taking a licking but was still going toe-to-toe with Armstrong (139¾) despite being cut over the right eye. Even when dropped twice in the fourth, firstly for 'five' and then for 'seven', Montanez was still in there firing, while Armstrong was sending in trip-hammer punches from both hands remorselessly. In this fight the champion's left hook was seen at its best, with Montanez having no answer to it at any stage. Then, in the eighth, it was the left hook along with several others that put Montanez down just as the bell rang. Allowed out for the ninth Montanez could barely stand up, and with Armstrong lashing in blows from all angles he was rescued by the referee after 47 seconds of the session.

Next time out, Armstrong stepped up a division to have a crack at Ceferino Garcia's Californian version of the world middleweight title, drawing over ten rounds at the Gilmore Stadium, Los Angeles on 1 March.

26 April 1940. Henry Armstrong w rsc 7 (15) Paul Junior.
Venue: The Garden, Boston, Massachusetts, USA. **Recognition:** World. **Referee:** Johnny Martin.
Fight Summary: Twice knocked down in the first, Junior (141) came roaring back throwing terrific right hooks that rocked the champion time and again in the second, and continued his bombardment into the third to even up the round. Thereafter, it was Armstrong (139½) who made the running, despite Junior being dangerous when tearing in with uppercuts and hooks, and he continued to throw punches galore. In the sixth, when it was apparent that Junior was wilting, after being put down for 'nine' he bravely fought on into the seventh where he was dropped again before being rescued by the referee on the 1.05 mark. Had the referee not made the stoppage when he did, Junior would have almost certainly suffered the first knockout of his career.

24 May 1940. Henry Armstrong w rsc 5 (15) Ralph Zannelli.
Venue: The Garden, Boston, Massachusetts, USA. **Recognition:** World. **Referee:** Johnny Martin.
Fight Summary: Although Zannelli (145½) made an aggressive start, possibly shading the first round, he was soon under pressure as the champion's two-handed attacks forced him back. Dropped in the second and third, Zannelli made the mistake of trying to close Armstrong (140½) down, paying the price when being punched around from all kinds of angles, and it was only when he went to range that he found brief success. It could not continue though. In the fifth, having already been floored for the third time, Zannelli was almost out when back on his feet before being rescued by the referee on the 1.10 mark.

21 June 1940. Henry Armstrong w rsc 3 (15) Paul Junior.
Venue: Arena AA, Portland, Maine, USA. **Recognition:** World. **Referee:** Johnny Martin.
Fight Summary: The first world title bout to be held in Maine saw Junior (142½) being given another crack at Armstrong (144) despite having failed to win the title in their previous meeting just two months earlier. Regardless of the rights and wrongs of whether he deserved another opportunity or not, the stubborn Junior made a reasonable start when holding the champion even in the opening two rounds before coming apart at the seams in the third. Starting the session in whirlwind fashion Armstrong soon had Junior under severe pressure, and after being dropped four times the referee came to the latter's aid.

At the Polo Grounds, Manhattan, NYC, New York on 17 July, Armstrong (139) forced Lew Jenkins (135½), who held the NYSAC version of the lightweight title, to retire at the end of the sixth round. However, the meeting was contracted specifically as a non-title contest, both men to be inside 140lbs, thus not involving the welterweight championship.

23 September 1940. Henry Armstrong w co 4 (15) Phil Furr.
Venue: Griffith Stadium, Washington DC, USA. **Recognition:** World. **Referee:** Ray Powen.
Fight Summary: Showing plenty of courage, Furr (147) stood up to the incessant attacks of the champion before being counted out at 1.45 of the fourth, having been down twice earlier in that round. He had also been dropped twice in the third. Right from the start Armstrong (145) bulled his man around, slamming in blows to all sections of

the body while mixing his attacks up with short rights to the jaw, until it became just a matter of time that the contest would be concluded. Prior to being knocked out for the first time in a long career Furr constantly went toe-to-toe with Armstrong, regardless of the blows coming his way, and received much applause at the finish.

Tired of waiting for the Cocoa Kid to be granted a title shot by Armstrong, the Maryland Boxing Commission ruled that they would recognise the winner of a contest set for 14 October between the Kid and Izzy Jannazzo as a world title fight. After notching up wins over men such as Holman Williams, Jimmy Leto and Furr during the year the Kid fully warranted a crack at the championship, while Jannazzo had outpointed both Williams and Steve Mamakos in his last couple of fights.

4 October 1940. Fritzie Zivic w pts 15 Henry Armstrong.
Venue: Madison Square Garden, Manhattan, NYC, New York, USA. **Recognition:** World. **Referee:** Arthur Donovan.
Scorecards: 8-7, 8-7, 8-5-2.
Fight Summary: Recognising that the way to beat his opponent was to sidestep his onrushing attacks before landing with solid right uppercuts Zivic won the opening two rounds, but from there up to the end of the ninth with one exception the champion put himself in front by a fair margin. What Armstrong (142) probably did not realise at the time was that Zivic (145½) had been pacing himself, and from the tenth onwards it was his fight as he belted away at a champion, who was unable to see properly from either eye and was swinging like an open gate. By now Zivic was making up the deficit as he battered the swollen-eyed Armstrong at will. Several times Armstrong was asked if he wished to be retired, but he gamely carried on to reach the final bell despite being dropped on to his face just as the fight ended. The unanimous decision in Zivic's favour was no more than he deserved.

Yet again the lightweight champion, Lew Jenkins, took on a welter champion in a contest which, despite both men weighing inside 147lbs, was contracted as a non-title bout over ten rounds in Madison Square Garden on 20 December. Announced as a draw, Zivic scaled 142½lbs to Jenkins' 135¼.

14 October 1940. Izzy Jannazzo w pts 15 Cocoa Kid.
Venue: Carlin's Park, Baltimore, Maryland, USA. **Recognition:** Maryland. **Referee:** Jack Dempsey.
Fight Summary: Billed for the vacant world title as recognised in Maryland, the Cocoa Kid (147) made all the running from the opening bell, but was picked off by the fast-stepping Jannazzo (146½) who kept flicking out the left and showing a sturdy pair of legs when required. As much as the heavier-punching Kid tried, apart from the odd occasion, he could not get Jannazzo to stay in one place for too long despite constantly trying to get over right-hand smashes. When he did get home Jannazzo quickly recovered and was soon pumping his left into his rival's face. In the 13th and 14th rounds, the Kid went after Jannazzo with lefts and rights to head and body, but each time he got home the latter was able to save himself. After coming back strongly in the 15th, at the end of the fight it was the referee's casting vote that won it for Jannazzo.

Looking for a return match, in his very next fight the Kid (150) got himself knocked out inside three rounds by the 148lbs Jimmy Leto at the Century AC, Baltimore on 11 November, and it was the latter who eventually went forward to meet Jannazzo.

17 January 1941. Fritzie Zivic w rsc 12 (15) Henry Armstrong.
Venue: Madison Square Garden, Manhattan, NYC, New York, USA. **Recognition:** NBA/NY. **Referee:** Arthur Donovan.
Fight Summary: Trying to regain his old title, Armstrong (140½) was on the receiving end in all rounds from the third through to the 11th as Zivic (145¾) repeatedly stabbed his fists into the former's eyes, sent in right uppercuts to the jaw and targeted the body. Armstrong was soon cut over the left eye, then the right, before both eyes started to close due to Zivic constantly working the face without let-up. Round after round Armstrong took a battering, and at the start of the 11th he was given one final chance to turn things around by a referee who did not want to see him knocked out. For two minutes of that session Armstrong stirred the memories as he stormed all over Zivic, pounding blows into head and body, but after 52 seconds of the 12th the third man pulled him out of the fray when he was recklessly walking into an accurate bombardment and was unable to defend himself.

179

Zivic's next four contests were above the weight, and after three wins he came a cropper on points over ten rounds against Mike Kaplan at The Garden, Boston, Massachusetts on 18 April. Having got himself to the rank of number one contender in *The Ring* ratings Kaplan immediately challenged Zivic to put the title up against him, only to be told that the latter's next few outings were already contracted. Zivic would be meeting Tony Marteliano, Phil Furr (which ultimately failed to take place) and Al Bummy Davis in non-title fights before making a defence against Freddie Cochrane on 26 May.

However, things did not go to plan. After beating Marteliano in a real humdinger, when Zivic was forced to have an operation on his right forearm things got put back. When fit again, Zivic stopped Davis in the tenth round at the Polo Grounds, Manhattan, NYC on 2 July, and then outpointed Johnny Barbara over 12 rounds at The Garden, Philadelphia, Pennsylvania on 12 July prior to meeting Cochrane, who was not even rated in the top ten. The red-headed Cochrane had lost no fewer than 25 times in his nine years as a pro, but was on a run of nine consecutive victories coming into the fight since losing to Kaplan. For Kaplan, however, there were just seven more fights prior to him retiring in 1942 and enlisting in the Army.

14 April 1941. Izzy Jannazzo w pts 15 Jimmy Leto.
Venue: The Coliseum, Baltimore, Maryland, USA. **Recognition:** Maryland. **Referee:** Charlie Short.
Fight Summary: Both men started fast, Leto (145½) landing the harder and cleaner punches, and Jannazzo (145½) keeping up an effective left jab, supplemented with an occasional right cross, to the challenger's face. It soon became a nip-and-tuck affair, with first one man going to the front then the other. Although Leto (145½) shook Jannazzo up with the left hook several times he was unable to land a finishing blow but, despite that failing, when the split decision in the latter's favour was announced it was not well received, the referee feeling that Leto's aggression had warranted him victory.

Meanwhile, after Jannazzo failed to further his world title ambitions when unable to force a bout against Freddie Cochrane he was eventually reduced to mixing with middleweights, suffering losses against Coley Welch, Fritzie Zivic, Saverio Turiello, Johnny Jackson and Eddie Booker along the way. However, when Jannazzo (147) took on Sugar Ray Robinson (143½) at The Arena, Philadelphia, Pennsylvania on 10 October 1942, losing on points over ten rounds, he was reported as still holding the Maryland version of the world title despite the State showing scant interest at the time. What is clear, following that fight and his next one, also against Robinson (l rsc 8 at The Arena, Cleveland, Ohio on 1 December 1942), who weighed 145lbs, is that he was no longer recognised in Maryland afterwards.

29 July 1941. Freddie Cochrane w pts 15 Fritzie Zivic.
Venue: Ruppert Stadium, Newark, New Jersey, USA. **Recognition:** NBA/NY. **Referee:** Joe Mangold.
Scorecard: 7-4-4.
Fight Summary: Confounding all of his critics, Cochrane (142½) at times outclassed Zivic (145), especially at close quarters where he could make the latter miss and get in hard lefts to the jaw before tying his man up. Although he was penalised in the fourth for using his head he continued to take the fight to the champion. Cochrane even out-roughed Zivic, and only in the 15th when he was dropped by a right to the jaw while off balance did he look flustered. Following the referee's verdict in Cochrane's favour, Nat Fleischer, of *The Ring* magazine, stated that he had given seven rounds to the new champion and six to Zivic, with two even, thus making it much closer.

The following day, with the war raging in Europe, after Cochrane was passed fit in Class 1A in his bid to join the American Navy he was expected to be called up for active duty within a few months.

In yet another ten-round non-title handicap match made between Lew Jenkins, the lightweight champion, and a welterweight champion, with both men inside 147lbs, Cochrane (141½) outpointed Jenkins (135) at Madison Square Garden, Manhattan, NYC, New York on 6 October. Three fights later, in a non-title affair, Cochrane (146½) was outpointed over ten rounds by Zivic (147¼) at the same venue on 10 September 1942.

When Cochrane, who had already enlisted in the US Navy, was called away on active service the title was frozen. Men rated in *The Ring* magazine top five during World War Two who were unable to make much progress, losing their peak years, included Young Kid McCoy, Earl Turner, Freddie Archer, Bee Bee Wright, Jimmy McDaniels and Nick Moran.

Meanwhile, after rising through the ranks to become the leading lightweight challenger, the unbeaten Sugar Ray Robinson, having put on extra weight, became the number one welterweight contender after beating Zivic twice. By the end of 1942 Robinson had also beaten Maxie Berger, Norman Rubio, Izzy Jannazzo (twice), Marty Servo, Sammy Angott, the NBA lightweight champion, and Jake LaMotta to cement his position as the 147lbs champion in waiting.

With Cochrane likely to be out of circulation until the war was over, Robinson suffered his first defeat in 41 contests when outpointed by LaMotta at the Olympia Stadium, Detroit, Michigan on 5 February 1943. However, prior to Cochrane's return to the ring it was success all the way for Robinson, as he defeated California Jackie Wilson, LaMotta (twice), Ralph Zannelli, Henry Armstrong, Jannazzo, Tommy Bell and George Costner before being held to a draw by middleweight, Jose Basora.

Following a number of warm-up bouts in June 1945, at the end of that month Cochrane was knocked out inside ten rounds by the hard-hitting future middleweight champion, Rocky Graziano, at Madison Square Garden. With Cochrane ahead on the cards going into the tenth a rematch at the Garden was called for 24 August. Yet again Cochrane surprised the pundits when taking Graziano into the tenth round before being stopped. However, Cochrane, now being asked to defend his title, was matched against the sixth-rated Servo who had to guarantee him $50,000 to get the opportunity. Clearly, Cochrane wanted no part of Robinson, there being a great deal of anger when the match with Servo was made despite whoever won having to agree to defend against the number one challenger within 90 days. Nat Fleisher, writing in *The Ring*, summed up the general feeling when he stated: "The fact that Robinson has been guaranteed a shot at the title does not alter the situation any. It is the duty of the Commission at all times to see that outstanding talent is not side-tracked or given the run-around in the planning of championship fights in favour of inferior fighters."

1 February 1946. Marty Servo w co 4 (15) Freddie Cochrane.

Venue: Madison Square Garden, Manhattan, NYC, New York, USA. **Recognition:** World. **Referee:** Eddie Joseph.
Fight Summary: Staggered by a heavy left hook in the opening round, although the champion fought back strongly he was doubled over by savage blows to the body as Servo (143) went to work on him in the second. Increasing the pace in the third Servo was now stalking Cochrane (145), who continued to hit back gamely, but in the fourth a succession of heavy blows to the head had the latter reeling before a series of straight lefts drove him into the ropes in a bewildered state. With Cochrane now an easy mark for Servo, a left hook followed by a right cross dropped him, his head reclining on the bottom rope, to be counted out at 2.54 of the session.

Having won the title Servo was contractually committed to defend against Sugar Ray Robinson, the leading contender, within 90 days and a date was set for 24 May. Strangely, bearing that in mind, Servo accepted a non-title fight in NYC on 29 March against the future middleweight champion, Rocky Graziano, where he would spot his heavy-hitting opponent almost a stone in weight. It turned into a nightmare as the game Servo was stopped in the second round, suffering a badly injured nose which caused the Robinson fight to be postponed due to surgery.

After the NYSAC gave Servo until 6 September to defend his title the fight was rescheduled for that date. Because he was unable to take in a warm-up contest as per the contract binding him to the Robinson fight, Servo was forced to take in a couple of ten-round exhibition bouts behind closed doors, on 1 and 15 August, to get himself match fit. However, with the nose still giving him problems he asked for another postponement, which immediately saw him stripped by the NYSAC. That was followed by Mike Jacobs, the Madison Square Garden promoter, making an announcement that Beau Jack would meet Tommy Bell for the vacant title on 20 December. He later suggested Robinson against Johnny Greco, Tippy Larkin or Bell, but when negotiations got underway it appeared that only the latter fancied a match against Robinson, having already travelled ten close rounds with him. Meanwhile, after the NBA categorically stated that titles should be won and lost in the ring they continued to recognise Servo, giving him until 1 December to defend. Bringing matters to a head, Servo sportingly announced his retirement on 25 September, stating that his nose had refused to heal and there was no way he could make even the latter date. By then, the NYSAC had matched Robinson and Bell for their version of the title on 20 December, while the NBA fancied a Jack v Robinson sortie.

20 December 1946. Sugar Ray Robinson w pts 15 Tommy Bell.
Venue: Madison Square Garden, Manhattan, NYC, New York, USA. **Recognition:** NY. **Referee:** Eddie Joseph.
Scorecards: 10-5, 10-5, 8-6-1.
Fight Summary: Contesting the title vacated by Marty Servo, Robinson (146½) seemed only a shell of his normal self against Bell (146), but still had enough on him to win the unanimous decision. In Robinson's previous fight he had been knocked down and hurt by Artie Levine, and a left hook from Bell had him on the floor as early as the second round. This was not the Robinson of old, wincing every time Bell went for the body as well as being staggered often by the left hook to the jaw. Having gone the first ten rounds hugging each other at every opportunity, Robinson woke up in the 11th to floor Bell for 'seven' with a cracking right, but although the latter looked decidedly weak for the rest of the session he defied all attempts to put him away. Forced to go through another rough passage in the 12th, Bell got himself together to win the last two rounds against the sluggish Robinson, who might have won the unanimous decision but did not impress too many onlookers. Almost immediately following the fight, the NBA, recognising that Robinson was the best man around, gave him their unequivocal backing.

Rated number six by *The Ring* magazine, Jimmy Doyle would be Robinson's next challenger. Doyle had lost just six of 51 contests, beating men such as Aldo Spoldi, Nick Moran, Ralph Zannelli (twice), Chuck Hunter, Tommy Bell, Lew Jenkins and Danny Kapilow.

24 June 1947. Sugar Ray Robinson w rsc 8 (15) Jimmy Doyle.
Venue: The Arena, Cleveland, Ohio, USA. **Recognition:** World. **Referee:** Jack Davis.
Fight Summary: Jarred by a left hook in the opening round, Doyle (147) had the worst of matters for the next two sessions, during which he was badly punished by blows to head and body as the champion looked to work him over. Despite Robinson (146) being firmly in control, when Doyle began to force the fight in the fourth he was met by heavy counters, and in the fifth he was twice staggered. However, he came back strongly in the sixth to open a cut over Robinson's right eye before making the latter appear to be just another fighter in the seventh when blocking many of his shots with arms and elbows to take the round. Late in the eighth, after Robinson banged in two fast rights to Doyle's body when the latter launched a right he was met by a crunching short left to the jaw that sent him down heavily, his head crashing on the floor. With Doyle out cold the count reached 'nine' when the bell rang to end the session. On realising that his condition was serious the fight was immediately halted. In a bad way, the stricken fighter was taken to hospital where he died 17 hours later, having lapsed into a coma and failed to survive an operation to remove a blood clot. Out of boxing for nine months after suffering brain concussion when knocked out by Artie Levine, Doyle had returned to the ring in December 1946 and run up five wins in succession to justify his title challenge.

It was announced on 25 November that Robinson's next challenger would be Chuck Taylor, a man who had lost three of his last four contests, against Charley Fusari, Tony Pellone and Sammy Adragna, and was not even rated in the top ten. Although Taylor had wins over Tommy Bell, Freddie Archer (twice), Tony Marteliano and Pellone, in the wake of the Doyle tragedy one would have thought that the commissioners would have been more careful when it came to choosing the champion's future opponents. With 23 wins from 33 contests Taylor was a 6-1 underdog, and as far as the papers were concerned it was only Robinson's weight-making problems that stopped the odds from soaring higher.

19 December 1947. Sugar Ray Robinson w rsc 6 (15) Chuck Taylor.
Venue: Olympia, Detroit, Michigan, USA. **Recognition:** World. **Referee:** Johnny Weber.
Fight Summary: Giving a brilliant display of cleverness and hard hitting the champion overcame the aggressive Taylor (144¾), who made a good start in the opening two sessions before being hurt in the third by a solid right to the jaw and several searing body blows. Rescued by the bell in the fourth after being almost dropped by a right to the head, Taylor came out for the fifth but soon began to weaken as Robinson (146½) belted in heavy rights to the body and brought his hooks into play. Sensing that he had his man going Robinson upped the pace in the sixth, and

a variety of quality shots followed by a right to the head dropped Taylor heavily. Although Taylor made it up at 'nine' it was the beginning of the end, Robinson giving him no time to recover before an avalanche of blows put him down again, and at 2.07 of the round the fight was over when the referee brought matters to a halt.

By January 1948 the new number one as recognised by *The Ring* magazine was Gene Burton, who had just added Bernard Docusen to his list of victims after beating Tommy Campbell, Ike Williams, Johnny Bratton (twice) and drawn with Doug Ratford and Freddie Dawson in his previous 13 contests. It seemed feasible that he might be the next opponent for Robinson, but following a reverse at the hands of Docusen and a defeat by Charley Williams he had dropped out of the top ten by the middle of the year.

After his win over Burton, Docusen took in four more contests before becoming Robinson's next challenger when signing up at the beginning of May. Initially the fight had been proposed for 4 June 1948 before the 17th of the month was agreed, but bad weather saw a further delay of 11 days.

28 June 1948. Sugar Ray Robinson w pts 15 Bernard Docusen.
Venue: Comiskey Park, Chicago, Illinois, USA. **Recognition:** World. **Referee:** Walter Brightmore.
Scorecards: 85-65, 83-67, 81-69.
Fight Summary: Having trouble making the weight the champion found Docusen (145½) a more than worthy foe, and for the first ten rounds, which were contested at a fast gallop, there was little between the pair. Finally, at the start of the 11th Robinson (146½) turned loose a blistering assault which sent Docusen into the ropes and eventually saw him dropped for 'nine' by a vicious left hook to the jaw. Fighting back desperately upon rising, Docusen saved himself from being downed again when continuing to try and take the play away from the fast-tiring Robinson, who was cut under the right eye by left jabs in the 14th. Coming on strong again in the 15th as Docusen visibly ran out of gas, Robinson tried hard to finish his challenger off but was unable to do so, ultimately having to settle for the unanimous decision cast in his favour.

According to *The Ring* magazine, the top ten in the world were Doug Ratford, Docusen, Kid Gavilan, Robert Villemain, Beau Jack, Tippy Larkin, Frankie Fernandez, Gene Burton, Bert Linam and Johnny Greco. At that moment in time it looked as though Ratford would be next in line for Robinson, having twice beaten Gavilan, but when he got himself outpointed by Tommy Bell his chance had gone.

Fast running out of challengers in his own weight class, despite Gavilan giving him a tough time in a non-title fight on 23 September, Robinson (w pts 10 at the Yankee Stadium, Bronx, NYC, New York) was by now eying up the middleweights. Having agreed to make 150lbs for Gavilan, who claimed the $5,000 forfeit after Robinson was unable to get within the required poundage, many good judges were saying that he would never make 147lbs again.

Come November, the London promoter, Jack Solomons, cabled Robinson an offer to fight either Henry Hall, the new British champion, or Eddie Thomas. Solomons must have taken into account the fact that the Docusen fight had to be postponed three times to allow Robinson to make the weight. There was no response, which was probably just as well.

At the end of the year Robinson was quoted as saying that although he could still make 147lbs he would be prepared to give the title up if he could be guaranteed a contest with Marcel Cerdan for the middleweight championship. Also, the lightweight champion, Ike Williams, was casting envious eyes at the welter crown, but in what were virtual eliminators he was twice beaten on points over ten rounds on 28 January and 1 April 1949 at Madison Square Garden, Manhattan, NYC by Gavilan, who was now without doubt Robinson's leading challenger.

Following those two victories the trade papers were calling for the boxing commissions to force Robinson to either defend his title against Gavilan or to abdicate, and after much talk about him meeting Vince Foster or Docusen again the match was finally made at the beginning of June. Since arriving in America, Gavilan had also beaten Johnny Williams (twice), Charley Williams, Bell, Buster Tyler and Tony Pellone.

Prior to this, Robinson took on Young Gene Buffalo in a ten-round non-title fight at the West Side Armoury, Kingston, Pennsylvania on 10 February 1949. When the two men weighed in, Buffalo, who left his clothes on, was stated to be 148lbs, but when in the ring the announcer gave his weight as 145¾lbs. Fearing that he might lose his title, Robinson took no chances when getting down to work quickly and knocking Buffalo out in the opening session. Despite the Pennsylvanian Boxing Commission saying that Robinson could not lose his title in a non-title fight, even though Buffalo was inside the championship weight, the champion's management team would not make the same mistake again.

11 July 1949. Sugar Ray Robinson w pts 15 Kid Gavilan.
Venue: Municipal Stadium, Philadelphia, Pennsylvania, USA. **Recognition:** World. **Referee:** Charles Daggert.
Scorecards: 9-6, 9-6, 12-3.
Fight Summary: Well documented that Robinson (147) had trouble making the weight, in recognising this Gavilan (144½) set up a fair pace in the opening rounds when attacking strongly and cutting the champion over the right eye in the fourth. From the fifth onwards, however, Robinson began to dominate, milling on the retreat, pulling Gavilan up short with straight lefts and blocking the latter's best blows when at close range. Although Gavilan was always trying it was Robinson who hit with the greater accuracy and precision, and while the switch-hitting Cuban took advantage when the champion coasted at times he could never assume control. The last three rounds saw Robinson at his best as he opened up, staggering Gavilan with straight lefts and hooks to the jaw and a cracking right uppercut which almost took the latter off his feet. While Gavilan claimed that the fight was much closer than suggested by the cards, Robinson well deserved the unanimous decision.

Next time out Robinson proved he was a match for any middleweight in the world when he dismantled the leading contender, Steve Belloise. Subsequently, it was assumed that Robinson would soon abdicate the welter division as he continued to take on middleweights, despite having the occasional catchweight contest with men such as George Costner, the second-ranked welter, who was dispatched in a round. Then, on 5 June 1950, he won the Pennsylvanian version of the world middleweight title when beating France's Robert Villemain, a fight that came about after repeated challenges to Jake LaMotta, who had won the world middleweight championship from Marcel Cerdan in June, fell on deaf ears.

Earlier, in May 1950, the NBA had warned all champions that they were expected to defend every six months or else. This certainly applied to Robinson, who had consistently ignored the same ruling that the NYSAC operated. At the end of June 1950, Al Weill, the Madison Square Garden matchmaker, asked the NYSAC to approve an elimination tournament involving Billy Graham, Charley Fusari, Lester Felton, Bernard Docusen and Kid Gavilan to find a new champion, but within a matter of days it was announced that Robinson would be defending his welter title against Fusari.

Responding to those who said that he should defend the title at least twice a year, Robinson said that he had looked for worthy challengers even when the NYSAC and NBA had failed to designate an opponent, and had, on occasion, offered to meet certain fighters in defence of the championship only for them to be uninterested.

9 August 1950. Sugar Ray Robinson w pts 15 Charley Fusari.
Venue: Roosevelt Stadium, Jersey City, New Jersey, USA. **Recognition:** World. **Referee:** Paul Cavalier.
Scorecard: 14-1.
Fight Summary: Despite being weight-weakened, the champion had very little trouble on his way to taking the referee's verdict at the end of 15 one-sided rounds, and at times simply allowed Fusari (145¼) the opportunity to recover when hurt. When he did manage to land on Robinson (147) Fusari was forced to take plenty in return, being cut over the left eye as early as the second round. After the fourth, which was Fusari's best round, it was all downhill for him. And in the sixth and ninth especially, when staggered by lightning blows to the head, it looked as though he would be knocked out. However, Robinson chose to coast through the next few sessions before opening up again in the 14th and 15th when he beat off Fusari's attacks and inflicted punishment with either hand before settling down to box his way to the final bell.

Having successfully defended the Pennsylvanian version of the middleweight title against Jose Basora and Carl Bobo Olson, within weeks of Robinson beating Jake LaMotta to become the world middleweight champion in February 1951 the NBA selected Johnny Bratton, who had recently knocked out Lester Felton and Bobby Dykes, to fight Fusari for their version of the championship after observing that the five leading contenders in *The Ring* magazine ratings after Robinson were Kid Gavilan, Bratton, Billy Graham, Fusari and Eddie Thomas.

In making the running the NBA alienated several other bodies, namely the NYSAC, BBBoC and EBU, and even Robinson himself, who stated that he had no thoughts of handing in his welter title. That was surprising as immediately after the Fusari defence he was quoted as saying he would soon be giving up the crown due to weight problems. Although the New York Commission were angered by the NBA, who threw out Graham on the grounds that he had been beaten by Thomas in 1949, with the International Boxing Club in New York having Kid Gavilan under contract they eventually agreed that the winner of Bratton v Fusari would fight the Cuban in New York within 90 days.

14 March 1951. Johnny Bratton w pts 15 Charley Fusari.
Venue: The Stadium, Chicago, Illinois, USA. **Recognition:** NBA. **Referee:** Tommy Gilmore.
Scorecards: 77-73, 78-72, 74-76.
Fight Summary: Contesting the vacant NBA title, Bratton (146¼) was the first to show when cutting Fusari (146¼) over the left eye in the first round and opening up with vicious two-handed attacks to push the latter back. Thus, it came as no surprise when he dropped Fusari for 'four' after smashing in a heavy right to the jaw in the fourth. In the seventh Fusari's eye damage worsened, giving cause for concern from there onwards, and although he was gradually putting that to one side he was sent crashing by a savage left hook followed by a right cross in the tenth, barely making it up in time. After the tenth, when it became apparent that Bratton was now carrying an injury to his right arm, he boxed the remainder of the contest with the sole use of his left hand. Never one to miss an opportunity, Fusari got right back into the fight when winning three and drawing two of the final five sessions, but it was not enough. As far as two of the judges were concerned, Bratton's earlier good work entitled him to the verdict.

With Bratton due to meet Kid Gavilan to decide the title, the American plan was then to match the winner of that fight with Eddie Thomas, the British, British Empire and European champion, some three months later. This was followed by the BBBoC writing immediately to the NBA and NYSAC stating that they would not countenance Thomas being included in any eliminators, demanding that he be given a straight crack at the vacant title.

Meanwhile, Robinson insisted that he was still champion and would be defending his title in London against Thomas in July. Unfortunately for Thomas that became academic when he lost his European title to Charles Humez at the Coney Beach Arena, Porthcawl, Wales on 13 June 1951. While Robinson stayed among the middles, Thomas would go on to lose the British and British Empire titles when beaten by Wally Thom in October.

18 May 1951. Kid Gavilan w pts 15 Johnny Bratton.
Venue: Madison Square Garden, Manhattan, NYC, New York, USA. **Recognition:** NBA/NY. **Referee:** Ruby Goldstein.
Scorecards: 11-4, 11-4, 8-5-2.
Fight Summary: Looking to add to his NBA crown, Bratton (147) was unanimously outpointed by Gavilan (145¼), who was just too strong and vigorous for his rival. Gavilan won without experiencing any difficulty at any stage as he forced the fight throughout, while Bratton, who had no answer to the continuous punches coming his way, finished with a broken jaw and a fracture of the right wrist. Although badly wobbled in the first round Bratton came back for the next few sessions with some flashy defensive boxing, coupled with speedy left jabs and stinging rights, and while the going was fairly even at the halfway stage he began to fade thereafter. By now increasing the tempo, Gavilan chased the back-pedalling Bratton down to work him on to the ropes where he could pour in punches from both hands, the decision being a formality. Bratton had been the NBA champion for just 65 days.

Having just won the European title, Charles Humez demanded an immediate crack at the world title, being fully supported by the EBU to that end. Even though *The Ring* magazine had him rated second only to Gavilan, who they saw as the American champion only, those who ran boxing in New York decided that the latter's first defence would be against Billy Graham. Following that, the EBU reiterated that they would only recognise the winner as the American champion.

29 August 1951. Kid Gavilan w pts 15 Billy Graham.
Venue: Madison Square Garden, Manhattan, NYC, New York, USA. **Recognition:** NBA/NY. **Referee:** Mark Conn.
Scorecards: 9-6, 7-7-1, 7-7-1.
Fight Summary: Under the complicated New York system of scoring, after one of the judges and the referee scored it 7-7 they were asked to go to the points system. While judge Frank Forbes gave it to Graham by 11-10, when the referee saw Gavilan as a 10-7 winner that decided it. Although the champion was prominent early on with his bolo punch looking spectacular, Graham (145) eventually found a way of dealing with it by moving inside at every opportunity. Having lost the early rounds Graham came back to take the fifth, sixth and seventh when outboxing and outpunching the bewildered Gavilan (145½), using long lefts and sharp rights. Thereafter, the battle seesawed as first one man took the initiative then the other before the last five sessions, with the exception of the 13th, saw Graham seemingly doing enough to win. When the split decision in Gavilan's favour was announced there was much dissent, but on reflection it had been based on the champion's aggression against the counter-punching tactics of Graham.

On 24 September, Charles Humez defended the European title for the first time, knocking out Emile Delmine inside seven rounds at the Sports Palace, Paris, France, and although the EBU did not give the contest world title billing they continued to recognise Gavilan as the American champion only. When the NBA announced that Gavilan had to defend his title against Humez within three months, a prospective date of 17 December 1951 was later made known in the press. With Humez apparently concentrating on the middleweight division that date came and went, but at the end of 1951 it was reported that the pair would decide the vacant world title on 28 March 1952, which was followed by the NBA demanding that Gavilan v Humez had to be held prior to 15 March 1952.

Realistically, Humez, who obviously had difficulty making 147lbs at that stage, had already made his mind up before the year was out that he would be moving up to 158lbs, but it was not until 20 February 1952 that it was officially announced that he was giving up the European title due to increasing weight problems. At the same time the EBU intimated that Gavilan should now be recognised as the rightful champion.

4 February 1952. Kid Gavilan w pts 15 Bobby Dykes.
Venue: The Stadium, Miami, Florida, USA. **Recognition:** NBA/NY. **Referee:** Eddie Coachman.
Scorecards: 142-141, 145-139, 140-143.
Fight Summary: Yet again Gavilan (147) successfully defended his title by means of a split decision, this time against a rank outsider who was not expected to stay long. Starting shakily, the lanky Dykes (146¾) was decked for a count of 'eight' by left and right hooks in the second, while appearing at a loss as to how to deal with Gavilan's flurrying attacks, but as the fight wore on he started to come forward with the left jab. Having his best round in the tenth, Dykes jabbed and hooked well throughout as he looked to make up any leeway. He also fired in solid rights when the opportunity arose, but Gavilan was not done for. After Dykes had slipped to the canvas in the 11th Gavilan made his run for home, but on finding the challenger still full of fight in the final three sessions he would ultimately have to rely on the judges.

The Cuban's next defence would be against Gil Turner, who was unbeaten in 31 contests and had overcome former lightweight champions, Beau Jack and Ike Williams, and defeated Bernard Docusen, Mario Trigo, Del Flanagan, the brother of Glen, Don Williams and Chico Varona. *The Ring* magazine, who rated Turner at number two, commented that he was tireless and threw more punches in a contest than anyone else around.

7 July 1952. Kid Gavilan w rsc 11 (15) Gil Turner.
Venue: Municipal Stadium, Philadelphia, Pennsylvania, USA. **Recognition:** World. **Referee:** Pete Tomasco.
Fight Summary: Many good judges of boxing thought that Turner (144½) would be too good for the champion, but they were proved wrong when the youngster was stopped after 1.58 of the 11th round. As expected Turner set the pace from the start, attacking with lefts to the body, while Gavilan (146) countered with heavy left hooks to the body. Remaining the aggressor despite losing the third and fifth for low blows, Turner kept on battering away at

Gavilan before the latter started to get going from the sixth onwards, mainly with left hands to head and body. When they came out for the 11th, Gavilan, who was slightly in the lead, set up a big attack to the body before switching to the head, and although Turner fought back he suddenly wilted when a left hook smashed against his jaw. Subjected to a tremendous pounding, Turner wobbled before being beaten into a sitting position on the bottom strand, whereupon the referee called it off.

5 October 1952. Kid Gavilan w pts 15 Billy Graham.
Venue: Gran Ballpark Stadium, Havana, Cuba. **Recognition:** World. **Referee:** Mark Rojo.
Scorecards: 15-2, 16-3, 16-7.
Fight Summary: Looking to pressure the champion Graham (146½) went after him from the opening bell, but throughout the fight he found his opponent to be a different proposition from the one he encountered previously. Using his left sparingly and way off with the right when he needed it, Graham was battered by solid counters to head and body, touching down twice as Gavilan (146½) sent in heavy shots to the body. In the tenth, Graham, cut on the bridge of the nose, his left eye swollen and closing, made a great effort through to the next session, but from thereon in it was all Gavilan, the unanimous decision in his favour being a formality.

11 February 1953. Kid Gavilan w rtd 9 (15) Chuck Davey.
Venue: The Stadium, Chicago, Illinois, USA. **Recognition:** World. **Referee:** Frank Gilmer.
Fight Summary: Gavilan (146½) had little difficulty in dealing with his southpaw challenger, a Master of Arts from Michigan, and was on top throughout, dominating the exchanges and landing hurtful left hooks to the body to wear his man down. Unbeaten in 39 starts, Davey (147) was gradually ground down, a right to the jaw dropping him for 'nine' in the third before he was put down three more times in the ninth and retired on his stool by his handlers at the end of the round. On reflection, Davey's total lack of power enabled Gavilan to fight at his own pace. And despite being occasionally bamboozled by the challenger's stance he was always in control. When hard rights cut Davey under the right eye in the eighth it was clear that Gavilan was now intent on finishing the fight as quickly as possible, and attacking strongly in the ninth he knocked all the stuffing out of his game opponent to bring about the retirement.

Next up to challenge Gavilan would be the rugged, two-fisted Carmen Basilio, who had been a pro since 1948 and was unbeaten in his last eight contests, beating the likes of Ike Williams, Vic Cardell, Carmen Fiore and Billy Graham. He had also drawn with Graham in his last outing. With the fights against Graham carrying the New York State title, both were seen as the two best fighters in the division by the NYSAC. When the commission called for Gavilan to defend against either man it was Basilio who got the opportunity, while Graham had just six more contests, losing four of them.

18 September 1953. Kid Gavilan w pts 15 Carmen Basilio.
Venue: War Memorial Auditorium, Syracuse, New York, USA. **Recognition:** World. **Referee:** George Walsh.
Scorecards: 8-6-1, 7-6-2, 5-7-3.
Fight Summary: Showing distinct signs of having difficulty in making the weight the champion did not start that well against the rough and ready Basilio (147), being made to pay for it when a cracking left hook to the jaw deposited him on the canvas for 'nine' in the second round. Unfortunately for Basilio, after he failed to take advantage of the situation, Gavilan (146¾) gradually got himself back into the fight when showing cleverness and good use of the jab, which eventually cut and closed the challenger's left eye. At the end of the sixth Basilio was thought to have won four sessions, but from there onwards Gavilan rolled out at least six of the remaining nine when showing his infighting ability. To Basilio's credit, even when hurt, as he was in the tenth after being punished with lefts and rights to the body, he continued to fire back.

13 November 1953. Kid Gavilan w pts 15 Johnny Bratton.
Venue: The Stadium, Chicago, Illinois, USA. **Recognition:** World. **Referee:** Frank Gilmer.
Scorecards: 82-68, 85-65, 83-67.
Fight Summary: This was Gavilan (146) at his best as he won all rounds bar the first, fifth and tenth, and went into overdrive in the eighth, throwing so many punches to head and body that it was difficult to count. Amazingly, Bratton (145½) came back to take a share of the tenth, but took so much out of himself in that session he barely

showed again. With Bratton repeatedly stunned by any number of punches through to the final bell it was testament to his gameness that he was able to keep going.

Having struggled with the weight over the years, and having taken care of all leading challengers, prior to his next defence Gavilan was given time out to challenge for the middleweight title held by Carl Bobo Olson. After Olson won that one comfortably on points over 15 rounds at The Stadium, Chicago on 2 April 1954 Gavilan had an enforced lay-off when suffering from a hand injury before signing for a 1 September 1954 title defence against fourth-ranked Johnny Saxton.

After beating Bratton (w pts 10 in The Arena, Philadelphia, Pennsylvania on 24 February 1954) to get a crack at the title, a ten-round draw against the lightly regarded Johnny Lombardo at the High School Stadium, Mount Carmel, Pennsylvania on 4 August was hardly the best form of advertising for the Blinky Palermo-managed Saxton. So much so, that hardly anybody noticed the fight being postponed until October due to Gavilan picking up a virus infection.

20 October 1954. Johnny Saxton w pts 15 Kid Gavilan.
Venue: Convention Hall, Philadelphia, Pennsylvania, USA. **Recognition:** World. **Referee:** Pete Pataleo.
Scorecards: 9-6, 7-6-2, 8-6-1.
Fight Summary: Hampered by a novice-like referee, who continually warned him not to hold and pushed him off at times while taking no notice of low blows perpetrated by Saxton (146½), it was hardly surprising that the champion failed to perform at his best level. Although Gavilan (145½) appeared to be well in control, it was only in the last two sessions that he started putting punches together, landing several hard rights. However, it was too little and too late according to the judges. Nat Fleischer, writing in *The Ring* magazine, stated that Saxton won only three rounds and Gavilan was robbed and years later, when it came to light that the new champion's connections were people who boasted that they had controlled the welterweight division, the result has to be seen as highly suspicious. As it was, both men were hauled before the Pennsylvania State Athletic Commission the next day to explain their conduct, but the result stood regardless of the fact that virtually every boxing scribe present gave the fight to Gavilan.

Saxton's first defence would be against Tony DeMarco, a walk-in banger who was rated at number three in *The Ring* magazine. Despite losing five of 51 contests, DeMarco had drawn with the lightweight champion, Jimmy Carter, last time out and was undefeated in his last 16 contests.

1 April 1955. Tony DeMarco w rsc 14 (15) Johnny Saxton.
Venue: The Garden, Boston, Massachusetts, USA. **Recognition:** World. **Referee:** Mel Manning.
Fight Summary: Uncertain at the start, the challenger sustained a cut left eye in the second round, and when coming forward he found himself successfully countered by Saxton (145½) up until the seventh. At that point, however, when DeMarco (145) found the range for his left hooks he began to make up lost ground, forcing the fight and getting in punches to head and body. Still driving forward, in the 14th DeMarco finally got to Saxton. There had been no knockdowns at that stage, but after Saxton went for broke he came off worse when sent crashing to the canvas, having been forced to take at least a dozen solid blows to the head. Somehow getting up at 'nine', Saxton was being hit without reply when rescued by the referee on the 2.20 mark.

10 June 1955. Carmen Basilio w rsc 12 (15) Tony DeMarco.
Venue: War Memorial Auditorium, Syracuse, New York, USA. **Recognition:** World. **Referee:** Harry Kessler.
Fight Summary: Making his first defence, DeMarco (144¾) found himself outworked by Basilio (145½) throughout, and in the tenth round he was dropped for 'seven' after taking several heavy rights to the jaw. With cuts over both eyes, when DeMarco was immediately floored again, this time by a left hook, he took another 'seven' count before being saved by the bell. Although DeMarco came out firing in the 11th in a desperate attempt to hold on to his title, Basilio took no chances, blocking punches and hitting back with left hooks and jabs until the referee stopped the fight at 1.52 of the 12th. DeMarco had been champion for just 70 days.

30 November 1955. Carmen Basilio w rsc 12 (15) Tony DeMarco.
Venue: The Garden, Boston, Massachusetts, USA. **Recognition:** World. **Referee:** Mel Manning.
Fight Summary: Even though he injured his left hand in the second round and lost the first few rounds the champion started to pick it up in the fifth when beginning to beat DeMarco (145½) to the punch. Sensing the tide was turning, DeMarco, cut over the left eye, made an all-out effort in the seventh before fading as Basilio (145½) came on strong with both hands, and in the 11th he was badly hurt by body punches. As in their previous fight the 12th proved to be decisive. When a series of right hands to DeMarco's head saw him eventually slump to the deck for 'eight', although he was allowed to carry on he was immediately heading for the canvas again after being slammed by a left hook-right to the jaw. Following that, he was rescued by the referee with 66 seconds of the session still remaining.

14 March 1956. Johnny Saxton w pts 15 Carmen Basilio.
Venue: The Stadium, Chicago, Illinois, USA. **Recognition:** World. **Referee:** Frank Gilmer.
Scorecards: 144-142, 145-138, 147-140.
Fight Summary: Unable to fight in New York due to his manager, Blinky Palermo, being banned there, the challenger met Basilio (146¾) in Chicago and regained his old title in what was seen as an upset. Despite Basilio complaining about the decision he had been outboxed by Saxton (146), who stayed at distance and scored continuously with stiff left jabs, while proving too elusive to be caught after a tough second round. There was no doubt that Basilio intended to end the fight in the second as he threw everything at Saxton, who despite being shaken up came back towards the end of the session to cut the champion over the left eye. Subsequently, Saxton was never in serious trouble, but would have to defend against Basilio due to a private agreement existing between the two managers.

12 September 1956. Carmen Basilio w rsc 9 (15) Johnny Saxton.
Venue: War Memorial Auditorium, Syracuse, New York, USA. **Recognition:** World. **Referee:** Al Berl.
Fight Summary: Learning from their previous meeting, Basilio (146¼) won every round bar the second when cutting the space down and scoring consistently with left hooks and right crosses as the champion failed to use the ring as well as he had done when winning the title. In the eighth Saxton (145¾) was eventually forced to back-pedal after Basilio chased his man from pillar to post in the hope of finishing it. The ninth had only just started when a long right to the jaw sent Saxton reeling, and following his man up Basilio hit the champion with all manner of blows from head to body before the referee intervened on the 1.31 mark to save a knockout from occurring.

22 February 1957. Carmen Basilio w co 2 (15) Johnny Saxton.
Venue: The Arena, Cleveland, Ohio, USA. **Recognition:** World. **Referee:** Tony LaBranch.
Fight Summary: Although Basilio had decisively beaten Saxton last time out to regain his title, with another contract for a return in place the two men met again. This time, Basilio (147), showing no sign of the injury to his right hand that had forced a postponement, marched straight into Saxton (147), throwing hooks to the head and body in relentless fashion. Tearing out for the second, Basilio reproduced what he had done in the first, smashing away at his opponent until a big right found the mark. Down went Saxton, as if shot, and although he made a desperate effort to get up he was counted out with 18 seconds of the session still remaining.

After Basilio relinquished the title on becoming world middleweight champion when outpointing Sugar Ray Robinson at the Yankee Stadium, Bronx, NYC, New York on 23 September, a World Boxing Committee, which was set up to organise a series of eliminators, named Virgil Akins, George Barnes, Vince Martinez, Isaac Logart, Gaspar Ortega and Gil Turner to take part.

In the meantime, Massachusetts who felt strongly about Tony DeMarco being left out of the eliminators, matched him with Akins to contest their version of the championship. Since losing the title to Basilio, DeMarco had won seven of nine contests, reversed two defeats by Ortega, and had also beaten Wallace Bud Smith, Arthur Persley, Martinez, Kid Gavilan, Larry Boardman and Walter Byers. His opponent, Akins, had been a pro since 1948, winning 45 of 63 contests, but had fought the best, defeating the likes of Smith (twice), Tommy Campbell, Freddie Dawson, Luther Rawlings, Joe Brown, Henry Davis, Ronnie Delaney, Joe Miceli, Logart, Hector Constance, Al Andrews and Garnet Hart.

29 October 1957. Virgil Akins w co 14 (15) Tony DeMarco.
Venue: The Garden, Boston, Massachusetts, USA. **Recognition:** Massachusetts. **Referee:** Jimmy McCarron.
Fight Summary: Looking to find a new champion after Carmen Basilio had moved on, and backed by the Massachusetts Boxing Commission, DeMarco was matched against Akins, a 29-year-old church deacon from St Louis. At the end of the ninth round it had been hard but fairly even, with DeMarco (146) relying on the left hook and Akins (144½) sticking to his countering game-plan with neither giving ground. From there on, it really took off. It started with DeMarco being dropped twice in the tenth, the first time by a vicious right to the jaw, and on getting up he was clubbed down again. The 12th then saw Akins step into a DeMarco left hook to take a mandatory count before he put the local man on the floor again in the 13th following a right-left to the jaw. Having been saved by the bell, DeMarco was all at sea before coming out for the 14th. Racing out of his corner, Akins had DeMarco on the canvas twice from solid rights to the head, and after setting the latter up with a feinted left hook he smashed home a right cross that left him stretched out, head lying on the bottom strand, to be counted out on the 1.17 mark. Both men carried damage, Akins sporting a swollen right eye and DeMarco cut on both eyes.

Following Akins' win over DeMarco, the World Boxing Committee's quarter-final pairing of Cuba's Isaac Logart v Gaspar Ortega took place at The Arena, Cleveland, Ohio on 6 December, being won by the former on points over 12 rounds.

Not long afterwards, however, in early January 1958, the British Empire champion, George Barnes, decided that he was not interested in travelling to America to take his place in the eliminators and pulled out. This announcement was followed by calls to replace the Australian with the winner of the forthcoming European title fight between Peter Waterman and Emilio Marconi, but the Committee stood firm.

In the second quarter-final, Vince Martinez outpointed Gil Turner over 12 rounds at The Arena, Philadelphia, Pennsylvania on 15 January 1958.

21 January 1958. Virgil Akins w rsc 12 (15) Tony DeMarco.
Venue: The Garden, Boston, Massachusetts, USA. **Recognition:** Massachusetts. **Referee:** Eddie Bradley.
Fight Summary: The return bout between the pair, saw DeMarco (147) going well in the early stages before tiring and becoming a target for the hard-punching Akins (147). Down in the eighth round from a hard left to the jaw and floored twice in the 11th, DeMarco was staggered by a tremendous right to the jaw in the 12th prior to being rescued by the referee at 1.53 of the session.

Having rejoined the elimination tournament at the semi-final stage, Akins kayoed Isaac Logart inside six rounds at Madison Square Garden, Manhattan, NYC, New York on 21 March 1958, while Vince Martinez drew a bye into the final.

5 June 1958. Virgil Akins w rsc 4 (15) Vince Martinez.
Venue: The Arena, St Louis, Missouri, USA. **Recognition:** World. **Referee:** Harry Kessler.
Fight Summary: Contesting the universally recognised vacant title, Akins (146¾) had Martinez (146¾) on the floor four times in the opening round from heavy rights without reply, and although the latter somehow got through the second he was again smashed down for two more counts in the third before being saved by the bell. Coming out for the fourth in a weakened state, Martinez was punched around the ring prior to being dropped for 'nine' after taking some heavy blows to the body, and when on his feet again he was put down for the eighth time by a crunching left hook. The referee never bothered to count, calling it off with 52 seconds on the clock.

Akins' first defence would come against Don Jordan, *The Ring* magazine's top-rated welter. Having started 1958 losing to Dave Charnley, Jordan went on to beat Isaac Logart and Gaspar Ortega before repeating his win over the latter (w pts 12 at the Lafayette Hotel, Long Beach, California on 22 October) in what was seen as an eliminator.

5 December 1958. Don Jordan w pts 15 Virgil Akins.
Venue: Olympic Auditorium, Los Angeles, California, USA. **Recognition:** World. **Referee:** Lee Grossman.
Scorecards: 145-138, 145-132, 146-136.

Fight Summary: Defending for the first time, Akins (145½) was shocked by the 3-1 underdog who set up a left jab-left hook attack from the opening bell and gave him no room to manoeuvre his big punches as he was forced to defend. In the tenth the champion was hammered from pillar to post, and having survived he came again over the last few rounds as Jordan (145) tired. However, he was unable to find a finishing punch. Akins, who had two points deducted, in the eighth for going low and in the 14th for butting, finished with a gash over his right eye, while Jordan picked up a cut over his left eye.

24 April 1959. Don Jordan w pts 15 Virgil Akins.
Venue: Kiel Auditorium, St Louis, Missouri, USA. **Recognition:** World. **Referee:** Harry Kessler.
Scorecards: 70-68, 71-68, 71-65.
Fight Summary: Starting well, Akins (147) hammered away at the body in the first round before changing tack when going for the head in the second and having a fair bit of success, twice buckling the champion's legs. Although it looked promising in the third for Akins, from that moment on he began to fade as Jordan (146¾) came into it more and more, with his left jab working overtime. In the eighth, Akins was all but put down when staggered by a right cross. From there onwards it was virtually all one-way traffic as Jordan piled up points with the jab, and several times the crowd urged him to finish it. Afterwards, Jordan explained that he had been unable to stop Akins due to him having injured his right early on.

10 July 1959. Don Jordan w pts 15 Denny Moyer.
Venue: Meadows Racetrack, Portland, Oregon, USA. **Recognition:** World. **Referee:** Harry Volk.
Scorecards: 144-143, 147-144, 147-143.
Fight Summary: Bidding to become the youngest ever welterweight champion, Moyer (146½) showed his inexperience when going down on points against Jordan (147). While putting up a game performance he was often bewildered at times as left jabs, hooks and uppercuts all found their target with regularity. Moyer started fast, but after staggering Jordan in the second he was made to play second fiddle as the latter moved up through the gears. There were no knockdowns, and although Jordan tried hard for one in the eighth when he opened up to have Moyer holding on grimly he had to settle for the unanimous decision in his favour.

After Charley Scott defeated Garnet Hart (w rsc 9 at the Convention Hall, Philadelphia, Pennsylvania on 19 October) in a battle between the two leading contenders for Jordan's title, the winner's manager telegraphed a £25,000 offer to Jordan to make a title defence but received no reply. Scott's case for a crack at the title was then put before the NBA Executive Committee.

Meanwhile, all kinds of rumours were going round about gangsters trying to buy a piece of Jordan, who took off for a couple of fights in South America. Having beaten Fernando Barreto (w pts 10 at the Ibirapuero Stadium, Sao Paulo, Brazil on 5 December), he next moved to Buenos Aires, Argentina where he was knocked out at the Luna Park Stadium by Federico Thompson inside four rounds on 12 December. Jordan, who blamed his defeat on a virus infection that had affected him for the last four months, did not mention the threats on his manager's well-being.

Back in America, Scott was twice outpointed by Benny Kid Paret over ten rounds at Madison Square Garden, Manhattan, NYC, New York, on 18 December and 29 January 1960, while Carmen Basilio was booked to challenge Jordan for the title on 10 June 1960. However, the NBA refused to recognise a Basilio fight and threatened to strip Jordan if he did not meet a contender named by them prior to that date.

This was followed by Jordan getting himself into trouble on a drink-drive charge and the NBA giving him a final warning that he must sign to meet Luis Rodriguez or another of their top four contenders by the end of February 1960 or be stripped. The NBA then relented when recognising a fight at Madison Square Garden between Paret and Thompson on 25 March 1960 as a final eliminator, but demanded that Jordan defend against the winner by the beginning of June 1960. Following Paret and Thompson drawing over 12 rounds, the NBA gave their blessing to a Jordan defence against Paret with the winner having to meet Thompson within 90 days.

27 May 1960. Benny Kid Paret w pts 15 Don Jordan.
Venue: Convention Centre, Las Vegas, Nevada, USA. **Recognition:** World. **Referee:** Charles Randolph.

Scorecards: 72-66, 72-67, 71-68.

Fight Summary: Imitating a perpetual-motion attack, reminiscent to that used by Henry Armstrong, Paret (146½) went for the champion's body prior to switching his attacks upstairs with a long left jab and right uppercuts. Jordan (144½) tried hard, but lacking the power to perturb Paret he faded after the sixth, seemingly unable to change his fight plan to deal with Paret's aggression. Although Paret, whose left eye was damaged in the fifth, was warned frequently by the referee to keep his punches up it was not until the 14th that he had a point deducted, but the damage had already been done by then.

Having beaten Willie Toweel (w rsc 8 at Madison Square Garden, Manhattan, NYC, New York on 22 October), Emile Griffith guaranteed himself a title shot when eliminating *The Ring* magazine's top-rated Luis Rodriguez (w pts 10 at the same venue on 17 December).

10 December 1960. Benny Kid Paret w pts 15 Federico Thompson.
Venue: Madison Square Garden, Manhattan, NYC, New York, USA. **Recognition:** World. **Referee:** Arthur Mercante.
Scorecards: 9-6, 9-6, 7-6-2.
Fight Summary: Making his first defence, right from the opening bell Paret (147) forced the fight when setting up a relentless assault. Although Thompson (145½), nine years older, tried to keep up he lacked the stamina to be able to trade non-stop with the champion throughout. Thompson tried to use his longer reach, but that also failed to affect the way the contest went as Paret constantly got inside, and while there were no knockdowns both men were occasionally rocked in various exchanges. The turning point came in the third round when Thompson's mouth was badly gashed. Swallowing a large amount of blood from thereon in, often choking on it, made it more difficult for Thompson to up the pace. However, when the Panamanian did manage a grandstand finish in the 15th, pummelling away with a two-fisted attack for virtually three minutes, it was too late.

1 April 1961. Emile Griffith w co 13 (15) Benny Kid Paret.
Venue: Convention Hall, Miami Beach, Florida, USA. **Recognition:** World. **Referee:** Jimmy Peerless.
Fight Summary: Starting how he meant to carry on Paret (146½) targeted the challenger's body right from the opening bell. Apart from the third round, when his left eye was cut, and the fifth he was virtually in control right up to the end of the 12th. At that point Paret was well in the lead, having never let up, but a lapse of concentration in the 13th turned his world upside down. Both men came out fast for that session, but it was Griffith (145½) who first found the range when lashing in a long left to Paret's jaw, and when the latter staggered back a right-left sent him crashing downwards to be counted out on the 1.11 mark.

3 June 1961. Emile Griffith w rsc 12 (15) Gaspar Ortega.
Venue: Olympic Auditorium, Los Angeles, California, USA. **Recognition:** World. **Referee:** Tommy Hart.
Fight Summary: In what turned out to be a one-sided contest, Ortega (146) was stopped for the first time in an 83-bout career when the referee stepped in to save him from taking further punishment at the hands of the champion after 48 seconds of the 12th had elapsed. Ortega never really got into the fight following an excellent start by Griffith (145½), who used the left hook to wear him down before twice smashing him to the canvas in round seven for counts of 'eight'. Ortega tried to regroup, but having again been put under the cosh he was saved by the bell after being sent staggering into his own corner at the end of the 11th. Although Ortega came out for the 12th it was pointless as Griffith was soon pouring in punches from both hands, almost as if he was working on a punch-bag, and it was a welcome relief for just about everyone when the fight was called off.

30 September 1961. Benny Kid Paret w pts 15 Emile Griffith.
Venue: Madison Square Garden, Manhattan, NYC, New York, USA. **Recognition:** World. **Referee:** Al Berl.
Scorecards: 8-6-1, 9-6, 6-8-1.
Fight Summary: Defending the title against the man he had taken it from, Griffith (147) appeared to have won the fight handily on points despite a total lack of knockdowns, but when the decision was announced in the Cuban's favour there was uproar. Out of 22 reporters at ringside only four gave it to Paret (146). Although Nat Fleischer, of *The Ring* magazine, felt that it was relatively even he did make the point that he had Griffith ahead by two points on the basis of his superior work in rounds four and 11. It was noticeable that Paret excelled on the inside after the sixth, whereas Griffith, who punched harder throughout, worked mainly at range, and had the latter not injured his

left hand early on he would possibly have won inside the distance. The last four sessions saw Paret fighting with both eyes almost closed and damage to his mouth, while Griffith ended the contest unmarked.

Taking time out, Paret challenged Gene Fullmer for the NBA middleweight title at the Convention Centre, Las Vegas, Nevada on 9 December, being knocked out inside ten rounds after taking plenty of punishment along the way.

24 March 1962. Emile Griffith w rsc 12 (15) Benny Kid Paret.
Venue: Madison Square Garden, Manhattan, NYC, New York, USA. **Recognition:** World. **Referee:** Ruby Goldstein.
Fight Summary: Fighting each other for the third time, and following much animosity at the weigh-in after Paret (146½) made derogatory remarks about his challenger, this time round Griffith (144) was well in command for much of the contest. After taking the opening five rounds Griffith was almost knocked out in the sixth when Paret floored him for 'eight' with a left hook, but he was soon back in the groove. Coming into the 12th Griffith appeared to be well ahead. At that time there was no inkling of what was to come, despite the many fouls perpetrated by both men throughout the fight that had gone unpunished and the bad feeling between them. It started reasonably enough but that was before Griffith drove Paret to the ropes where his head went through the upper strands, and hammered punch after punch at his now defenceless target. With Griffith punching away unrestrained, it was estimated that 21 blows landed on Paret before the referee was able to call it off on the 2.09 mark, the final blow, a left to the jaw, seeing the latter slide to the canvas. At the finish, Paret, in a coma, was removed to the Roosevelt Hospital where he failed to regain consciousness after an operation before dying ten days later.

13 July 1962. Emile Griffith w pts 15 Ralph Dupas.
Venue: Convention Centre, Las Vegas, Nevada, USA. **Recognition:** World. **Referee:** Frankie Van.
Scorecards: 73-69, 74-65, 71-64.
Fight Summary: Returning to the ring for the first time since his title win over the unfortunate Benny Kid Paret, the champion was posed plenty of problems by the shifty Dupas (145¾), who danced and moved as if he was on a piece of elastic at times. The first ten rounds were relatively even but following that, Griffith (145¼), who was cut around both eyes at the finish, picked up the pace to go ahead. After working the body Griffith tried to finish Dupas off in the final session with a two-handed attack, but the latter weathered the storm, even thinking he had won at the final bell. There were no knockdowns.

Temporarily moving into the new junior middleweight division, Griffith outpointed Ted Wright over 15 rounds at the City Hall, Vienna, Austria on 17 October to win the Austrian version of the newly formed junior middleweight title.

8 December 1962. Emile Griffith w rsc 9 (15) Jorge Fernandez.
Venue: Convention Centre, Las Vegas, Nevada, USA. **Recognition:** World. **Referee:** Harry Krause.
Fight Summary: After what had been a tough and hard-fought contest for six rounds, with both men sending in solid punches, the champion got on top in the seventh session when dropping Fernandez (147) with a right swing to the jaw. Forced to take the mandatory 'eight' count, having bounced up immediately Fernandez battled on strongly until being floored by a hard right below the belt in the ninth. At that point there was chaos as Fernandez's handlers jumped into the ring, and when the Argentine was unable to continue, having been given five minutes to recover, following an inspection by the doctor the fight was halted. At that juncture, Griffith (145) was deemed to have retained his title. The announcement came after officials went to the Nevada State rule book, which stated that when a bout was ended by a questionable or accidental blow the man ahead on points at the time should be declared the winner.

Before taking on the top-rated Luis Rodriguez, Griffith fitted in another defence of his junior middleweight title, beating Chris Christensen on a ninth-round retirement at the KB Hall, Copenhagen, Denmark on 3 February 1963. Wishing to stay among the welters, Griffith relinquished the junior title immediately after the fight.

A pro since 1956, Rodriguez had an outstanding record, having lost just twice, against Griffith and Curtis Cokes, in 53 contests. Resilient, very fast and skilful, he numbered Gomeo Brennan, Benny Kid Paret (twice), Charley Scott,

Joe Miceli, Cecil Shorts, Virgil Akins (twice), Rudell Stitch, Larry Baker, Isaac Logart, Garnet Hart, Chico Vejar, Yama Bahama (twice), Johnny Gonsalves (twice), Guy Sumlin, Cokes, Federico Thompson, Gene Armstrong and Joey Giambra among his victims.

21 March 1963. Luis Rodriguez w pts 15 Emile Griffith.
Venue: Dodger Stadium, Los Angeles, California, USA. **Recognition:** World. **Referee:** Tommy Hart.
Scorecards: 9-5, 8-6, 8-5.
Fight Summary: Even though Griffith (145½) controlled the fight for the opening five rounds the challenger was gradually working his way into the fight, and from the sixth onwards he was jabbing hard and often with his left hand while beginning to show superior speed. Despite Rodriguez (146) boxing mainly on the back foot he was getting his punches in, and while Griffith looked to work the body in order to open his rival up he was only launching sporadic attacks. There was no doubt that Griffith hurt Rodriguez with solid blows in the tenth and 13th, but the Cuban was soon back on his game to catch the eye of the judges. While Griffith angrily claimed to have been jobbed yet again, he would get another crack at Rodriguez due to a 90-day return clause being in place in the event of him losing.

8 June 1963. Emile Griffith w pts 15 Luis Rodriguez.
Venue: Madison Square Garden, Manhattan, NYC, New York, USA. **Recognition:** World. **Referee:** Jimmy Devlin.
Scorecards: 8-7, 9-6, 5-10.
Fight Summary: In gaining the split decision Griffith (146½) became the first man to win the 147lbs title for the third time, but for long periods of the contest he appeared to have been outboxed by the champion. While he carried the harder punch, hurting Rodriguez (146½) from both hands in the first, eighth and 13th rounds, he did not sustain his attacks. And in the seventh he was forced back continuously. According to Angelo Dundee, Rodriguez dominated the fight, being at his best when forcing Griffith to lead before leaving him lunging and missing. Press reports generally gave the impression that Rodriguez had landed more blows, but many of them would not have counted as they lacked authority.

Having regained the title, Griffith went in search of the middleweight championship but came a cropper when blitzed in the opening round by Rubin Carter. With both men looking for two further warm-up bouts under their belts, a rubber match was sealed between Griffith and Rodriguez at the end of February 1964.

12 June 1964. Emile Griffith w pts 15 Luis Rodriguez.
Venue: Convention Centre, Las Vegas, Nevada, USA. **Recognition:** World. **Referee:** Harry Krause.
Scorecards: 69-67, 70-68, 70-71.
Fight Summary: Meeting for the fourth time, once again there was little to separate Griffith (146) and Rodriguez (146½), but this time the latter went toe-to-toe with the champion when trying to influence the judges. As in their previous contests there were no knockdowns, and the score would have been closer still had Rodriguez not had a point deducted for low blows in the third round. Again Griffith punched the harder, being more precise, but many of the sessions were ragged and bitterly contested as both looked to gain supremacy. Although cut over the left eye in the second and having struggled to make the weight, Rodriguez was always looking for a fight as fortunes swayed one way and then the other. Griffith was also fortunate not to have points taken away for fighting after the bell on the odd occasion.

Ranked number three by *The Ring* magazine, Brian Curvis, the British and British Empire welterweight champion, would be Griffith's next challenger. A solid-punching southpaw, Curvis had won 31 of 32 contests, having beaten George Barnes, Wally Swift (twice), Luis Folledo, Mick Leahy, Ralph Dupas and Dave Charnley, and had gained revenge over Guy Sumlin who was responsible for his only defeat.

22 September 1964. Emile Griffith w pts 15 Brian Curvis.
Venue: The Arena, Wembley, London, England. **Recognition:** World. **Referee:** Harry Gibbs.
Fight Summary: Despite being second best all the way the southpaw challenger proved his courage if nothing else as Griffith (145½) virtually overwhelmed him from the opening bell. Often presenting a stationary target, Curvis (145½) was set about on numerous occasions before he was dropped by a left-right to the head in the sixth round

and then saved by the bell. Body shots were also worrying Curvis, and after going for Griffith in the tenth he was put down from a couple of heavy blows to the solar plexus. Curvis came back magnificently in the 12th as he blasted Griffith before him, but another solid body punch had him down in the 13th. Getting up and doing his best to avoid a stoppage defeat, Curvis, swollen around both eyes, bravely fought his way through to the end of the contest, where he freely admitted that he had been beaten by a superior opponent who fully deserved the referee's decision.

Next up for Griffith was *The Ring* magazine's third-ranked Jose Stable, an aggressive Cuban who could box a bit, and a man with 26 wins from 29 contests. Although he had lost to Angel Robinson Garcia and Dave Charnley, men who had been defeated by him included Garcia, Kenny Lane, Eddie Pace, Curtis Cokes, Charley Scott, Stanley Hayward, Dick Turner and Gabe Terronez.

30 March 1965. Emile Griffith w pts 15 Jose Stable.
Venue: Madison Square Garden, Manhattan, NYC, New York, USA. **Recognition:** World. **Referee:** Arthur Mercante. **Scorecards:** 9-5-1, 8-6-1, 11-4.
Fight Summary: Taking command almost from the start, having been staggered by a short left hook to the body in the opening session, the champion punished Stable (146) throughout as he looked to shake the latter up with hard rights to the head. By the tenth Griffith (146½) had his full artillery on display as he went with jabs, hooks and uppercuts to Stable's head and body, and although he was walking through the latter he failed to find a finishing blow. All in all it was a listless performance by Griffith, who openly stated that he was looking at moving up a weight despite his loss to Rubin Carter.

Allowed time out to challenge for the vacant WBA version of the American middleweight title, Griffith was defeated by Don Fullmer (l pts 12 at the Fairgrounds Coliseum, Salt Lake City, Utah on 19 August). He also took in two further contests, beating Gabe Terronez and Harry Scott, before signing for a defence against Manuel Gonzalez, who had outpointed him over ten rounds at the Sam Houston Coliseum, Houston, Texas on 26 January 1965 to earn a title shot.

10 December 1965. Emile Griffith w pts 15 Manuel Gonzalez.
Venue: Madison Square Garden, Manhattan, NYC, New York, USA. **Recognition:** World. **Referee:** Arthur Mercante. **Scorecards:** 9-5-1, 12-3, 11-3-1.
Fight Summary: Although Gonzalez had outpointed Griffith in a non-title fight, there was no way that he was going to win this one as he continually clutched and grabbed the champion while doing little work. With Gonzalez (146) using hit-and-run tactics, the action was dull as Griffith (146) tried to catch up with him, and the left hook that landed in the ninth was the only solid blow the American-Mexican, who was cut over the left eye in the eighth, delivered all night. For his part, Griffith tried to make a fight of it but was ultimately unable to catch up with Gonzalez, having to settle for the points awarded for his aggression.

After Griffith had won the world middleweight title from Dick Tiger (w pts 15 at Madison Square Garden on 25 April 1966), the NYSAC asked him to immediately vacate his welterweight crown under a State ruling, only to be told by his lawyers that they had filed a motion in the State Supreme Court to have the ruling set aside.

A few weeks later, the Philadelphia promoter, Herman Taylor, announced that he was in the process of setting up an elimination tournament involving Luis Rodriguez, Percy Manning (who had recently beaten Rodriguez), Bennie Briscoe and Stanley Hayward, prior to it being reported that Griffith would be defending against Hayward on 30 September. Needless to say, the eliminating series proposed by Taylor failed to get support and never went ahead.

Then, in early June 1966, it was reported that the WBA had stripped Griffith of the title for not defending within the six-month period and were setting up fights between Curtis Cokes and Rodriguez and Gonzalez and Hayward to find a new champion. Although Hayward declined because he was contracted to fight Griffith, after Cokes stopped Rodriguez in the 15th round at the Municipal Auditorium, New Orleans, Louisiana on 6 July 1966 he went forward to meet Gonzalez for the WBA version of the championship, with the NYSAC agreeing to recognise the fight as an eliminator. Cokes and Gonzalez had already met four times with score 3-1 in favour of the former. Prior to meeting

Rodriguez, Cokes had won 40 of 50 contests, beating Rip Randall, Stefan Redl, Joe Miceli, Charley Tombstone Smith, Stan Harrington, Al Andrews, Fortunato Manca and Rodriguez. He had also been beaten by Jose Stable, Rodriguez and Hayward.

When the State Supreme Court rejected Griffith's claim to be allowed to hold two world titles at once in September 1966, it was followed by the news that the proposed Hayward fight was off. Meanwhile, with neither Charley Shipes nor Manning being involved in the WBA eliminators, the Chairman of the Californian Boxing Commission, Doug Hayden, stated that with California being the most important boxing centre in the USA the State had every right to stage its own world welter championship contest, especially as the weight class was without a fully recognised champion. He went on to say that the fight between Shipes, the Californian champion with 28 wins from 29 contests, and Manning, who had beaten the former world champion and number one contender, Rodriguez (w pts 10 at The Arena, Philadelphia, Pennsylvania on 11 April 1966), would be recognised by California as a world title fight. Hayden also said, after not receiving a reply from the NYSAC on the subject, that California would now become independent of all other organisations.

With the two leading men outside of America not invited to take part in the WBA elimination series to find a new world champion, the promoter billed a fight between Willie Ludick and Jean Josselin as an eliminator prior to the South African authorities granting it world title status on the result. Both men were deserving of a shot and both had beaten Brian Curvis, Ludick winning on points over ten rounds at the Rand Stadium, Johannesburg on 3 April 1965, while Josselin had forced the Welshman to retire at the end of the 13th round at the Sports Palace, Paris, France on 25 April 1966 to win the European title.

6 August 1966. Willie Ludick w pts 15 Jean Josselin.
Venue: Wembley Stadium, Johannesburg, South Africa. **Recognition:** South Africa. **Referee:** Wilf Garforth.
Fight Summary: From start to finish it was a bloody, bruising contest of sustained savagery, which saw both men giving and taking in equal amounts. In the seventh round, Ludick (146½), a southpaw, was dropped by a short right for 'eight', and after getting up on rubbery legs, his mouth badly cut and a nasty gash by the side of his right eye, it looked ominous. However, he fought on strongly to claw back the lead following several tremendous rallies, before dropping Josselin (146½) with a solid left hook in the final session to just about edge home on the scorecards.

24 August 1966. Curtis Cokes w pts 15 Manuel Gonzalez.
Venue: Municipal Auditorium, New Orleans, Louisiana, USA. **Recognition:** WBA. **Referee:** Pete Giarusso.
Scorecards: 8-2-5, 11-2-2, 14-1.
Fight Summary: Contesting the WBA version of the vacant title, with Cokes (145¾) and Gonzalez (147) meeting for the fifth time, at the final bell it was clear that the latter had been beaten for the fourth time. Although Gonzalez gave a good account of himself in the fourth and fifth rounds, he was far too negative, clutching at every opportunity, and did not do nearly enough to convince the judges. With the exception of an explosive 12th round when Cokes blasted Gonzalez to the canvas following a flurry of hard blows from both hands there was not much excitement, and even when the latter got up the man from Dallas could not finish him off.

Brian Curvis was to have been Cokes' next opponent, but when he was forced to withdraw with an injured foot it was quickly decided that he would be replaced by the unbeaten Ted Whitfield, Percy Manning, Francois Pavilla or Jean Josselin, the European champion. With Manning lined up to contest the Californian version of the title and Pavilla not even ranked, it was the top-rated Josselin who was ultimately selected. Whitfield was now rated in the top three, numbering Gaspar Ortega and Charley Scott among his 23 victims, but any chance of a crack at the winner disappeared when he lost five of his next six contests.

28 November 1966. Curtis Cokes w pts 15 Jean Josselin.
Venue: Memorial Auditorium, Dallas, Texas, USA. **Recognition:** WBA/EBU. **Referee:** Dick Cole.
Scorecards: 149-136, 148-138, 147-140.
Fight Summary: Even though the scorecards made it sound as though the fight was one-sided it was not, the ever willing Josselin (146¾) always being in with a chance, and in many rounds he was only shaded. Despite taking jabs, left hooks and uppercuts to the head, with Josselin always trying Cokes (145¾) had to be wary, but his height and

extra reach gave him a decided advantage. Josselin made his big effort in the 12th, but Cokes quickly responded with solid counters to make sure of victory. Following the fight, Cokes also became recognised as champion by the WBC.

7 December 1966. Charley Shipes w rsc 10 (15) Percy Manning.
Venue: High School Gym, Hayward, California, USA. **Recognition:** California. **Referee:** Vern Bybee.
Fight Summary: In a contest that would decide the Californian version of the world title, Shipes (146) started well with the left jab before moving to the body with solid right hands in the eighth and beginning to make his domination count. In the tenth round, Manning (146), staggered badly from a two-handed onslaught and forced to take a standing 'eight' count, was then dropped by a left to the body. At that point, with Shipes ahead on all cards, the referee moved in to stop the fight with just one second of the round remaining.

19 May 1967. Curtis Cokes w rsc 10 (15) Francois Pavilla.
Venue: Memorial Auditorium, Dallas, Texas, USA. **Recognition:** WBA/WBC. **Referee:** Pat Riley.
Fight Summary: Having previously drawn with Cokes (145) earlier in the year the challenger proved to be a sad disappointment according to *The Ring* magazine, winning just one round on the cards. Cokes was always in control, despite claiming he was hurt by Pavilla (146¾) in the sixth and seventh, his left jab totting up the points, but in the eighth he felt his opponent weakening in the clinches and ready to be taken. After getting through with some solid shots in the ninth Cokes caught Pavilla with a right in the tenth, and when the latter came off the ropes a cracking left dropped him. Up almost immediately, staring into the crowd glassy-eyed, Pavilla was eventually rescued by the referee with ten seconds of the session remaining after the Frenchman's manager had jumped into the ring.

An on-off title bout between Cokes and Gypsy Joe Harris due to take place on 24 July, was finally called off on the day of the fight when Harris, who was well over the weight, failed to arrive for the weigh-in. The problems had initially come about when Cokes demanded money up front, including monies still owed from the Pavilla contest.

2 October 1967. Curtis Cokes w rsc 8 (15) Charley Shipes.
Venue: The Arena, Oakland, California, USA. **Recognition:** WBA/WBC. **Referee:** Jack Downey.
Fight Summary: Recognised in California as the champion, Shipes (145) started promisingly, forcing the contest, before a right-left to the jaw dropped him in the fourth. Back in the fight, Shipes, now cut over the right eye, crowded Cokes (145) but took several right uppercuts for his pains, and in the sixth a left hook followed by a solid right sent him to the floor again. Shipes was still giving it everything he had in the seventh, although Cokes' extra reach was proving to be a real advantage, but in the eighth the lights finally went out for the Californian. After being floored twice, the second time by a terrific right to the jaw, Shipes was helped up by the referee and taken back to his corner when it was clear that he had no chance of getting back into the fight. The finish was timed at 1.37 of the session.

25 November 1967. Willie Ludick w pts 15 Carmelo Bossi.
Venue: Ellis Park Rugby Stadium, Johannesburg, South Africa. **Recognition:** South Africa. **Referee:** Bill Godfrey.
Fight Summary: Meeting in a return match, this time for the South African recognised version of the world title, the contest ran on similar lines to their previous meeting (over ten rounds) just seven weeks earlier. Ludick (146¼) started fast, taking the opening two sessions, before Bossi (146½), the European champion, came on to connect with hard rights that often shook the South African southpaw up. The only knockdown came in the 11th when Bossi was caught by a left and slipped over, but in the 13th it was Ludick who was in trouble when hit repeatedly by right hands to head and body. The last two sessions saw both men going toe-to-toe. At the final bell it was Ludick, who had produced the better work in the middle rounds, especially with the left hand, who got the verdict.

16 April 1968. Curtis Cokes w rsc 5 (15) Willie Ludick.
Venue: Memorial Auditorium, Dallas, Texas, USA. **Recognition:** World. **Referee:** Lew Eskin.
Fight Summary: Outboxed and outpunched right from the start, Ludick (146¼) did not have the tools to take the title from the accomplished champion, who was soon into his stride when sending in solid countering rights, one of which opened up a cut over the South African southpaw's right eye in the second round. It did not get much better for Ludick, despite him doing reasonably well in the fourth, when Cokes (145¾) crashed in a powerful right

uppercut in the fifth to drop him for 'six'. Although the referee gave Ludick a few moments just to see if he could come back with anything, when Cokes again sent him tumbling into the ropes he called a halt with just 34 seconds on the clock.

21 October 1968. Curtis Cokes w pts 15 Ramon La Cruz.
Venue: Municipal Auditorium, New Orleans, Louisiana, USA. **Recognition:** World. **Referee:** Herman Dutreix.
Scorecards: 11-3-1, 11-1-3, 11-4.
Fight Summary: Up against a challenger who had major disadvantages in height and reach, Cokes (146½) should have gone on the attack right from the beginning, but with both men looking to counter the fight as a spectacle became less than interesting. When La Cruz (147) did come forward he lacked the firepower to do any damage, having hurt his left arm in the first round, and was picked off by speedy jabs and hooks to head and body. It was clear that Cokes was the better man, but he refused to take any risks. After being cut over the right eye in the sixth, Cruz was really up against it, although Cokes still failed to take advantage of the opportunities when they presented themselves, saying at the end of the fight that the Argentine's peculiar style confused him.

18 April 1969. Jose Napoles w rsc 13 (15) Curtis Cokes.
Venue: Inglewood Forum, Los Angeles, California, USA. **Recognition:** World. **Referee:** George Latka.
Fight Summary: Rarely being able to find the range against the clever, hard-punching Napoles (143), the champion slumped to a 13th-round stoppage defeat, having barely won a round on the cards. By backing Cokes (145½) up throughout, Napoles forced the latter to fight his fight, and in the fifth round the Cuban started to open up with combinations of left hooks and right crosses. With Cokes unable to hurt Napoles, and having difficulty picking up the punches as his eyes swelled up, he took a bit of a battering in the ninth. Although the pace slowed from the tenth it was clear as to which way the fight was going. In the 13th, after Cokes was repeatedly backed against the ropes and hit flush with left hooks, the doctor was called in to inspect his injuries. Although letting Cokes fight on, at the end of the round the referee decided enough was enough.

29 June 1969. Jose Napoles w rtd 10 (15) Curtis Cokes.
Venue: City Bullring, Mexico City, Mexico. **Recognition:** World. **Referee:** Ramon Berumen.
Fight Summary: With a return clause in place Cokes (146½) got first crack at the new champion, but although doing better than in their previous contest he was unable to turn things around, being forced to retire on his stool at the end of the tenth round. Fighting outdoors in drizzling rain were not the best of conditions, but even when Cokes' right eye started swelling in the fourth round he still continued to rock Napoles (145) virtually in every session with hard rights until it was impossible for him to see. The only other problem for Cokes was the fact that Napoles was getting through to him, and in the tenth the latter poured in punch after punch when trying for a finish. To his eternal credit Cokes would not go down, making it to the bell before being retired by his corner.

17 October 1969. Jose Napoles w pts 15 Emile Griffith.
Venue: Inglewood Forum, Los Angeles, California, USA. **Recognition:** World. **Referee:** Dick Young.
Scorecards: 11-4, 11-3, 9-4.
Fight Summary: Pacing himself expertly, Napoles (144¾) poured in the punches early on against the former champion, always looking for the opportunity to rip in left hooks. And in the opening two sessions he delighted his supporters when hammering in left jabs and hard rights. In the third, with the men at close quarters, Napoles smashed in a vicious right uppercut to drop Griffith (144½), and when the latter got up he was pounded to the body for the remainder of the round. There were no more knockdowns, but with Napoles always dangerous in close Griffith often had to tie him up in order to avoid punishment, which, more often than not, detracted from the attacking side of his game plan. Although Griffith showed up at best in the fifth, when he came again in the 13th with some terrific left-right combinations Napoles held on in the knowledge that he already had the result sewn up.

Napoles' next challenger would be Ernie Lopez, who had won 38 of 45 contests, beating Jose Stable, Tito Marshall, Gabe Terronez, Hedgemon Lewis (twice) and Raul Soriano. Ranked as the number two contender by *The Ring* magazine, Lopez was an aggressive all-action fighter who rarely failed to excite.

15 February 1970. Jose Napoles w rsc 15 (15) Ernie Lopez.
Venue: Inglewood Forum, Los Angeles, California, USA. **Recognition:** World. **Referee:** Larry Rozadilla.
Fight Summary: Punching with machine-like precision, Napoles (145½) opened up to drop Lopez (146) in the first round. Although the latter did well in the opening four sessions, mainly with hard rights to the head, once the champion got on top there was no stopping him. His accurate left jab would find Lopez all night, and in the ninth and 15th he put 'Indian Red' over for two more knockdowns. Towards the end of the contest Lopez had shot his bolt, but although still trying to take Napoles out with one blow he was in a weakened state. Having disposed of his leading challenger, Napoles was given time by the commissions to sort out his next opponent.

In early July it was announced that he would be making a defence against Austria's European champion, Johann Orsolics, on 12 November following a couple of warm-up bouts. Then, at the end of August, it was reported that the only thing preventing the fight taking place would be if Orsolics was defeated by Eddie Perkins, which unfortunately happened at the Trade Hall, Vienna, Austria on 3 September when the European champion was knocked out in the fourth round.

It was then stated that Napoles would take on Perkins in Chicago on 20 October, but that too fell through when the promoters could not work out a TV deal. Finally, Napoles signed for what he considered an easy defence against Billy Backus, who was the nephew of former champion, Carmen Basilio. With an in-and-out record of 29 wins in 43 fights, Backus had actually retired earlier in his career before coming back to earn a number two rating after beating Percy Pugh (twice) and Manuel Gonzalez. An awkward southpaw and willing mixer, he had won the New York State title when beating Ricky Ortiz.

3 December 1970. Billy Backus w rsc 4 (15) Jose Napoles.
Venue: War Memorial Auditorium, Syracuse, New York, USA. **Recognition:** World. **Referee:** Jack Millicent.
Fight Summary: Following ten defeats and four draws from 45 contests, Backus (146½), a 27-year-old southpaw, stopped Napoles (144¼) after 55 seconds of the fourth round in what was seen as one of the division's great upsets. The opening session had seen Napoles pushing Backus round the ring with left jabs before both men were cut over their right eyes in the second. At that stage there was a transformation in Backus's fortunes when he began to connect with right jabs as the champion missed with his. The third round saw Backus open a cut over Napoles' left eye as well, and by the fourth the damage was so serious that the doctor advised the referee to call the contest off. It was alleged that the injuries suffered by Napoles, who had been a 9-1 favourite, were brought about by butts, which was stringently denied by Backus.

4 June 1971. Jose Napoles w rsc 8 (15) Billy Backus.
Venue: Inglewood Forum, Los Angeles, California, USA. **Recognition:** World. **Referee:** Dick Young.
Fight Summary: Having suffered a cut right eye in the opening round Napoles (146) soon put that behind him as he went in search of regaining his old title from Backus (145¾), giving the latter such a pounding in the second session that it seemed to be just a matter of time. Using a sharp left hand to set Backus up, after Napoles cut the southpaw champion on the left eye in the fifth before too long the right eye began to close. By the eighth Backus was ready to be taken, and having been floored twice, a short right to the chin and a left-right combination to the body doing the damage, he was stopped on the 1.43 mark.

14 December 1971. Jose Napoles w pts 15 Hedgemon Lewis.
Venue: Inglewood Forum, Los Angeles, California, USA. **Recognition:** World. **Referee:** Larry Rozadilla.
Scorecards: 8-6, 8-7, 9-4.
Fight Summary: After building up an early lead, Napoles (145¼) eventually became frustrated at his inability to knock his challenger out, becoming arm-weary from his efforts. Coming into the final third, Napoles slashed away with both sweeping and short left hooks to no avail as the speedy Lewis (140¾) either took his best shots or cleverly avoided them. In the 14th Lewis even staggered Napoles with a right flush on the jaw, but despite narrowing the points deficit it was not enough.

Due to his good connections, the unrated Ralph Charles would be Napoles' next challenger. Even though he had been a former European champion and was the current British and Commonwealth champion, Charles was seen to be out of his depth. However, to his credit he had good skills, was game and could punch a bit, and in 42 contests he had won 39 with Johann Orsolics and Jeff White among his victims.

28 March 1972. Jose Napoles w co 7 (15) Ralph Charles.
Venue: The Arena, Wembley, London, England. **Recognition:** World. **Referee:** James Brimmell.
Fight Summary: Sticking to a jab-and-move routine rather than going with his normal aggressive tactics probably brought the challenger some time, but in doing so he expended a fair amount of energy while Napoles (146¼) merely waited. In the fourth, although Charles (147) was dropped by a right to the body he was soon up, and despite losing his gumshield three times in the session he boxed reasonably well until Napoles cut loose in the seventh. After hurting Charles with a right to the jaw, Napoles poured in a whole range of sharp combinations before the British champion was sent crashing to be counted out with just eight seconds of the round remaining.

10 June 1972. Jose Napoles w rsc 2 (15) Adolph Pruitt.
Venue: Monumental Bullring, Monterrey, Mexico. **Recognition:** World. **Referee:** Octavio Meyran.
Fight Summary: Taking control from the opening bell, Napoles (146) quickly set about Pruitt (143½) with solid hooks to head and body, inflicting a bad cut over his challenger's left eye before the end of the first round. There would be no let-up for Pruitt as Napoles went to work with the left jab being concentrated on the injured eye, and at 2.10 of the second the referee deemed it to be too serious for the American to continue. Pruitt had not been off his feet, but the referee felt there was no way back for him.

On failing to get Napoles to give Billy Backus a return, further to the latter's win on points over 12 rounds against Danny McAloon at the War Memorial Auditorium, Syracuse, New York on 14 April, the New York Boxing Commission announced that they had matched Backus against Hedgemon Lewis for their version of the title.

Despite being the best man at the weight Napoles was now finding it more and more difficult to make 147lbs. Following a non-title fight in early August, both the WBA and WBC allowed Napoles time out as long as he defended his title against either Roger Menetrey, the European champion, Hedgemon Lewis, or Ernie Lopez before mid-1973.

16 June 1972. Hedgemon Lewis w pts 15 Billy Backus.
Venue: War Memorial Auditorium, Syracuse, New York, USA. **Recognition:** NY. **Referee:** Arthur Mercante.
Scorecards: 9-6, 8-6-1, 7-6-2.
Fight Summary: Fighting for the NYSAC version of the title, Lewis (145½) got away well using his longer reach to good advantage. And in the second round a solid left hook surprised Backus (146¼) who was forced to take the mandatory 'eight' count. Although Lewis continued to score well with left jabs and hooks, it was noticeable that the Canastota southpaw was getting stronger the longer the fight went on, especially when powering in body shots. Over the last third, with Backus pressing, there was no doubting that Lewis' early lead was gradually diminishing, but he kept his boxing together to hold on for a unanimous points win, albeit by only a round on two of the cards.

8 December 1972. Hedgemon Lewis w pts 15 Billy Backus
Venue: War Memorial Auditorium, Syracuse, New York, USA. **Recognition:** NY. **Referee:** Tony Phillips.
Scorecards: 10-4-1, 10-4-1, 12-2-1.
Fight Summary: A return fight between the pair saw Lewis (145) win more convincingly this time round, often scoring at will and repeatedly sending in solid blows from both hands to the head of Backus (145½). Although the southpaw challenger took the fight to Lewis early on he was forced to ship plenty of leather, being made to pay for his aggression when continuing to run into shots. By the seventh Backus was bleeding profusely from cuts around both eyes, and unable to work the body to any great affect he was falling further and further behind. Despite having a reasonable 11th, with Backus failing to build on it the result was a formality.

28 February 1973. Jose Napoles w co 7 (15) Ernie Lopez.
Venue: Inglewood Forum, Los Angeles, California, USA. **Recognition:** WBA/WBC. **Referee:** Dick Young.

Fight Summary: After opening a cut over the champion's left eye in the second round Lopez (146½) had something to target, but by the third he was being outboxed and hurt with sharp lefts and rights to head and body. Napoles (146½) had Lopez cut over the left eye and rocking in the fifth after upping his work-rate, and although the latter came on strong in the sixth the champion was well in control. With the eye injury obviously bothering him, Napoles went on the attack in the seventh. After sending in a left hook that was followed by a crunching right uppercut to the jaw Lopez crashed down on his back to be counted out at 1.36 of the session.

Ranked number two by *The Ring* magazine, the European champion, Roger Menetrey, was signed up as Napoles' next challenger. With 49 wins in 54 contests, and having reversed three of his four defeats, the Frenchman was tough, game and a good puncher who had beaten Jean Josselin, Robert Gallois (twice), Fighting Mack, Angel Robinson Garcia, Ralph Charles, Silvano Bertini, Joergen Hansen and Sandro Lopopolo.

23 June 1973. Jose Napoles w pts 15 Roger Menetrey.
Venue: Sports Palace, Grenoble, France. **Recognition:** WBA/WBC. **Referee:** Roland Dakin.
Scorecards: 149-139, 150-134, 150-137.
Fight Summary: Napoles (146) dominated almost every round in this one, solid blows to the body in the opening session alerting Menetrey (145) to what was around the corner. By the third Menetrey was in retreat after being raked with hooks and uppercuts, and while the champion tried his hardest to induce the Frenchman to come forward the bait was not taken. From the ninth onwards Napoles held the centre of the ring, potting Menetrey with left jabs and fast combinations whenever he could, but by now the contest was totally one-sided. As it was, the Frenchman, who finished with badly swollen features, showed great courage in staying the course.

The Mexican-based Cuban's next challenge would come from the hard-hitting Clyde Gray, rated at number one by *The Ring* magazine. Gray, who had 40 wins in 43 contests, had beaten Donato Paduano, Ray Chavez Guerrero, Marcel Cerdan Jnr, Manuel Gonzalez and Eddie Blay, and was the reigning Commonwealth champion.

22 September 1973. Jose Napoles w pts 15 Clyde Gray.
Venue: Maple Leaf Garden, Toronto, Canada. **Recognition:** WBA/WBC. **Referee:** Jay Edson.
Scorecards: 71-67, 71-67, 71-65.
Fight Summary: Although losing his unbeaten record, with Gray (147) running the champion relatively close there was not too much in it at the close after he really went for it in the 15th round when sending in some heavy, scoring blows. As was his way, Napoles (147) started well, connecting with hard shots to head and body, and had Gray down in the fifth with a cracking left hook to the jaw. Thereafter, although Gray did well when often beating his man to the punch it was not enough.

Allowed time out to challenge Carlos Monzon (l rtd 6 at the Puteaux Circus Tent, Paris, France on 9 February 1974) for the world middleweight title, a few weeks later the WBC warned Napoles that they would strip him unless his next defence was against the leading contender, Hedgemon Lewis, to unify the title. It had been rumoured that Napoles was trying to arrange a match against either Angel Espada or Bruno Arcari, to which the WBC described as playing with fire. In mid-April 1974 it was announced that Napoles would be defending against Lewis, the provisional date given was 8 June 1974 prior to it being changed due to Napoles requiring more time to take surplus weight off.

3 August 1974. Jose Napoles w rsc 9 (15) Hedgemon Lewis.
Venue: Sports Palace, Mexico City, Mexico. **Recognition:** World. **Referee:** Ramon Berumen.
Fight Summary: Struggling to find his normal rhythm, the strain of weight-making showed up early as the champion made a hesitant start. However, by the end of the second round he was beginning to match Lewis (141) punch for punch. In the fourth session it was noticeable that the altitude was causing problems for Lewis, Napoles (145) taking advantage of the situation when ripping in heavy lefts and rights to the head. After being in trouble in the seventh, Lewis rallied in the eighth to hurt Napoles with hooks and uppercuts before the Cuban came on strongly with a stream of hooks to the head in the ninth. Doing his best to survive Lewis tried to grab Napoles, but when he was pounded into a corner and was being hit almost at will the referee had seen enough, calling a halt at 2.34 of the session.

14 December 1974. Jose Napoles w co 3 (15) Horacio Saldano.
Venue: Sports Palace, Mexico City, Mexico. **Recognition:** World. **Referee:** Ramon Berumen.
Fight Summary: Despite having difficulties in making 147lbs, when Napoles (146½) came out fast he was soon penetrating the challenger's defences with left jabs and sparkling combinations. Even then Saldano (143) was catching Napoles with hurtful body blows, and it looked like being a quick and explosive fight. The third round saw Napoles smashing in a left uppercut that knocked Saldano's gumshield out, leaving him weak and open before a cracking left-right combination sent him down to be counted out on the 1.55 mark.

Another man making his mark in the division at this time was Fausto Rodriguez, the Dominican champion, who had just beaten Harold Weston and Alvin Anderson to be handed a top-three rating by *The Ring* magazine. Described as having a hypnotic upright stance, Rodriguez had won 16 of 17 recorded fights (29 of 30, with 24 inside the distance wins according to the press hand-outs) and reversed his only loss to Anderson. On the verge of a title shot, after being outpointed by Nick Ortiz ten fights later he was dead, killed in a car crash along with his family.

30 March 1975. Jose Napoles w tdec 12 (15) Armando Muniz.
Venue: Convention Centre, Acapulco, Mexico. **Recognition:** World. **Referee:** Ramon Berumen.
Scorecards: 149-142, 149-139, 148-142.
Fight Summary: The toughest defence yet for Napoles (147) saw him take on the hard-punching Muniz (145), with much of the action being at close range and neither man prepared to give an inch. Cut over the left eye in the second, Napoles was forced to meet Muniz head on as the latter continued to press forward to attack the body. Although Napoles rocked Muniz on occasion he was being denied the room in which to work. He was also weakening as well as being cut over the right eye by the seventh. Muniz, gashed on the left cheek in the fifth, was still giving it his all in the 11th, pounding in hard rights to Napoles' badly battered face. By now the champion's right eye was closed and giving cause for concern. After 50 seconds of the 12th had elapsed, with Napoles on the ropes taking what was on offer, the referee stopped the action to seek medical advice, being told to call the contest off as the champion's injuries were too bad for him to continue. It was reported that Napoles required 38 stitches afterwards. This appears to be the first world title bout where a technical decision was given after the referee was forced to go to the scorecards. It was later disclosed that Muniz had points deducted for butting in the third and fifth rounds which ultimately cost him, but according to other sources one judge had Muniz ahead 107-102 at the finish before the cards went missing. Despite angry protests from Muniz's camp, the WBC supported the decision on the grounds that the rulebook had been adhered to. From that point on many fights would be decided on a technical basis if circumstances warranted it. Injuries caused by headwork being the most common factor.

In May, after hearing the news that Napoles was handing back his WBA Championship Belt in order to concentrate on defending the WBC title, the WBA announced that a Clyde Gray v Angel Espada contest would be for their version of the vacant title. As far as the WBA were concerned they had stripped Napoles after he had failed to make a fight with either Gray or Espada.

Since losing to Napoles in September 1973, Gray had run up nine straight wins, beating Bunny Grant and Fate Davis, while Espada had won 33 of 44 fights, defeating Davis, Manuel Gonzalez, Dario Hidalgo, Jack Tillman, Alvin Anderson and Muniz along the way. Espada, who was a clever and hurtful counter puncher, was rated at number three by *The Ring* magazine as opposed to his rival's number one ranking.

28 June 1975. Angel Espada w pts 15 Clyde Gray.
Venue: Roberto Clemente Coliseum, San Juan, Puerto Rico. **Recognition:** WBA. **Referee:** Isaac Herrera.
Scorecards: 146-143, 147-139, 148-144.
Fight Summary: Contesting the vacant WBA title, Espada (145¾) concentrated on boxing on the back foot while occasionally opening up with fast right hands that caught Gray (144½) coming in. Despite being handicapped by a cut right eye from the fourth round onwards, Gray continually pressed forward, throwing combinations to head and body, while Espada moved and countered, his left jab being a handy tool that often brought the Canadian up short. It was only in the last five rounds that the Puerto Rican took over, and although he was down briefly in the 14th all three judges voted for him.

12 July 1975. Jose Napoles w pts 15 Armando Muniz.
Venue: Sports Palace, Mexico City, Mexico. **Recognition:** WBC. **Referee:** Octavio Meyran.
Scorecards: 149-142, 149-139, 148-142.
Fight Summary: After their previous contest ended so controversially the WBC made sure that Muniz (146½) got first crack at Napoles (146) once the latter's injuries had healed. Clearly, Napoles was much fitter and faster than before, rarely giving Muniz the chance to capitalise on his aggressive tactics when standing back and punishing him at long range. In the seventh round, after a two-handed blast put Muniz down, although he was saved by the bell he appeared dazed. From thereon in Muniz never gave Napoles many problems, spending most of his time up close to avoid further trouble. Muniz finished with a badly split right eyebrow and various facial cuts.

11 October 1975. Angel Espada w pts 15 Johnny Gant.
Venue: Ponce Arena, San Juan, Puerto Rico. **Recognition:** WBA. **Referee:** Waldemar Schmidt.
Scorecards: 145-142, 149-139, 147-140.
Fight Summary: Making his first defence Espada (143½) was supposed to have met Tony Petronelli, but when the latter got himself injured Gant (144) stepped in and did reasonably well before going down on points. Unfortunately, with two counter punchers on display it turned into something of a bore. Apart from that, Gant, who suffered a cut left eye in the fifth, had great difficulty in opening Espada up. In the third round Espada hurt Gant but was unable to finish him, and he opened up again in the tenth, 11th and 14th rounds with combinations without success before the contest ran its course.

Having been sidelined through illness and managerial problems, Espada came back to stop Alfonso Hayman in the eighth round at the Roberto Clemente Coliseum, San Juan on 27 April 1976 in a warm-up bout before making his second defence, against Pipino Cuevas.

6 December 1975. John H. Stracey w rsc 6 (15) Jose Napoles.
Venue: City Bullring, Mexico City, Mexico. **Recognition:** WBC. **Referee:** Octavio Meyran.
Fight Summary: Coming to the ring as an underdog, the challenger overturned the form book when taking the title from once great Napoles (147), who became an old man in boxing terms as the fight progressed. Napoles made a good start when dropping Stracey (145) in the first round with a solid left hook, and when he hurt the Englishman again in the second it looked like he was on his way. However, in the third, Stracey floored Napoles, who was forced to take the mandatory 'eight' count. At that stage of the fight, Stracey began to impose himself despite being shaken up by right hands. Stracey also shrugged off a cut over the left eye as he continued to keep the pressure on Napoles, never giving him a moment's rest, while keeping up a gruelling pace. At last it looked as though Stracey's tactics were paying off. In the sixth, after he had smashed Napoles on to the ropes and was hammering away at the veteran the referee stepped in with 30 seconds of the session still remaining.

20 March 1976. John H. Stracey w rsc 10 (15) Hedgemon Lewis.
Venue: The Arena, Wembley, London, England. **Recognition:** WBC. **Referee:** Harry Gibbs.
Fight Summary: Fighting with tremendous zeal, Stracey (146¼) survived a shaky opening round to gradually grind down his American opponent, who made life difficult for the champion right up until the eighth. Although Lewis (146¾) boxed well, making Stracey work hard, he slipped further and further behind as the latter never left him alone, and in the eighth through to the tenth the punches kept on coming. At certain stages it seemed as though Stracey would punch himself out, but eventually Lewis slumped against the ropes before falling down under a torrent of leather just as the referee was halting the contest on the 1.25 mark.

22 June 1976. Carlos Palomino w rsc 12 (15) John H. Stracey.
Venue: The Arena, Wembley, London, England. **Recognition:** WBC. **Referee:** Sid Nathan.
Fight Summary: Although he made a reasonable start, by the second round Stracey (146) was being caught by solid rights while finding himself out of distance as the challenger constantly moved out of range. As the contest progressed Palomino (145¼) was also outjabbing Stracey. Despite coming back strongly in some sessions, the *Boxing News* reporter had Stracey five rounds down going into the 12th, having taken a real battering in the previous three. It was in this session that having decided that body blows were his route to the title, Palomino

poured in vicious hooks to drop Stracey for two counts of 'nine' before the referee came to the champion's rescue with 1.25 still on the clock.

17 July 1976. Pipino Cuevas w rsc 2 (15) Angel Espada.
Venue: Califa Bullring, Mexicali, Mexico. **Recognition:** WBA. **Referee:** Isidro Rodriguez.
Fight Summary: Having chased the champion around the ring in the opening session, Cuevas (146) quickly got down to business in the second, dropping his man early on with a looping left hook. Getting up, carrying a nasty cut over the right eye and looking bewildered, Espada (145) was quickly put down twice more, whereupon the fight was automatically stopped on the one-minute mark under the 'three knockdowns in one round' ruling.

27 October 1976. Pipino Cuevas w rsc 6 (15) Shoji Tsujimoto.
Venue: Jissen Rinri Stadium, Kanazawa, Japan. **Recognition:** WBA. **Referee:** Carlos Berrocal.
Fight Summary: Making a good start the challenger utilised his southpaw style and added reach to make it difficult for Cuevas (145¾) during the opening five sessions, as he flicked in jabs and moved out of distance. It was only in the sixth that Cuevas picked it up when dropping Tsujimoto (146¾) with a left to the temple. He then put Tsujimoto down again twice more in the session to invoke the 'three knockdowns in a round' ruling for the second fight running.

22 January 1977. Carlos Palomino w rsc 15 (15) Armando Muniz.
Venue: Olympic Auditorium, Los Angeles, California, USA. **Recognition:** WBC. **Referee:** John Thomas.
Fight Summary: In his first defence after two postponements due to injuries, Palomino (146½) got off to a poor start when he was dropped by a left hook just before the end of the first before falling behind during the opening four rounds. Although he was being roughed at close quarters by Muniz (147), the champion got himself into gear in the fifth when keeping at range and punching with added authority. Having come back strongly in the 12th for a couple of sessions Muniz then began to weaken, and in the 15th he was dropped by a right cross-left hook combination. After taking the 'eight' count, Muniz was set upon by Palomino who bombarded him from both hands until the referee stopped it at 2.26 when he was in a helpless condition.

12 March 1977. Pipino Cuevas w rsc 2 (15) Miguel Angel Campanino.
Venue: Four Roads Bullring, Mexico City, Mexico. **Recognition:** WBA. **Referee:** Isaac Herrera.
Fight Summary: The bout began with the champion targeting the body with left hooks and right hands as Campanino (146½) defended his chin with a high guard and tried to distance himself from heavy shots. Having worked his opponent out, Cuevas (146½) started the second round strongly with body attacks, and as Campanino's arms came down he was hit with heavy rights to the head, the last being a smash to the temple that saw him take an 'eight' count. When ordered to continue Campanino dropped his hands, whereupon the referee halted the contest. The finish was timed at 2.05.

14 June 1977. Carlos Palomino w co 11 (15) Dave Boy Green.
Venue: The Arena, Wembley, London, England. **Recognition:** WBC. **Referee:** James Brimmell.
Fight Summary: Despite giving it his best shot the challenger finally succumbed in the 11th round to the better quality coming from Palomino (147). However, up until the tenth when his left eye suddenly started to close, Green (146¾) had pressed Palomino all the way with his long punches, and in the eighth after the latter was cut over the left eye he even sensed victory. Although he was also cut over the right eye in the ninth Palomino was beginning to reassert himself, firing in uppercuts from both hands and solid hooks and jabs. And at 2.05 of the 11th Green was counted out after being flattened by a crashing left hook which he later admitted he never saw coming. With Green giving one of the greatest displays of indomitable courage seen in a British ring, at times Palomino was almost done for before showing why he was the champion.

6 August 1977. Pipino Cuevas w co 2 (15) Clyde Gray.
Venue: Olympic Auditorium, Los Angeles, California, USA. **Recognition:** WBA. **Referee:** Chuck Hassett.
Fight Summary: Having rocked the challenger with a cracking left to the jaw in the opening round, Cuevas (145½) continued to seek an early win as he went forward with both fists in a bid to steamroller his rival. Using all of his experience Gray (147) somehow managed to get through the session, but he had been badly hurt. It came as no

surprise when he was counted out at 1.26 of the second after being flattened by a left to the jaw. Although the Commonwealth champion fought gamely, ultimately he could not cope with Cuevas's power.

13 September 1977. Carlos Palomino w pts 15 Everaldo Costa Azevedo.
Venue: Olympic Auditorium, Los Angeles, California, USA. **Recognition:** WBC. **Referee:** Dick Young.
Scorecards: 147-140, 145-140, 145-140.
Fight Summary: Showing no inclination to trade with the champion Azevedo (145½) boxed on the back foot, continually moving away from punches while clinching at every opportunity when he was closed down. In what was a poor fight to watch, Palomino (147) had been unable to catch up with Azevedo until the latter stages when the Brazilian finally ran out of gas due to his exertions. Brought down to his opponent's level, Palomino won the fight on conditioning and his work over the last few rounds, but he disappointed with his inability to corner Azevedo.

19 November 1977. Pipino Cuevas w rsc 11 (15) Angel Espada.
Venue: Roberto Clemente Coliseum, San Juan, Puerto Rico. **Recognition:** WBA. **Referee:** Jesus Celis.
Fight Summary: Looking to get his old title back, the challenger started well before being dropped by a cracker of a left hook in the second as Cuevas (147) tried to finish early. Although he got up at 'nine' Espada (146½) had to hang on until making a recovery in the middle rounds when shaking up Cuevas several times with heavy rights to the head. However, by the eighth, Espada's face was a mess, having been cut under the left eye, but he bravely kept going until reaching the end of the 11th. The fight then came to an end when the doctor advised the referee to stop the bout on the grounds that the latter's jaw was broken and it was impossible for him to carry on.

10 December 1977. Carlos Palomino w co 13 (15) Jose Palacios.
Venue: Olympic Auditorium, Los Angeles, California, USA. **Recognition:** WBC. **Referee:** John Thomas.
Fight Summary: Making his fourth defence in 1977, Palomino (147) was always in command against Palacios (146½), repeatedly landing with fast punches from both hands despite the challenger's reach advantage. In trouble in the third and ninth rounds, Palacios came back well in the tenth to hurt Palomino with a heavy right, but that would be his final shout. After tearing in to Palomino at the start of the 13th, when Palacios was caught heavily by a short left-right to the jaw he went down to be counted out after 49 seconds of the session. Palacios made a great effort to get his feet in time to beat the count, but after collapsing to the floor again he had to receive treatment before leaving the ring.

11 February 1978. Carlos Palomino w co 7 (15) Ryu Sorimachi.
Venue: Hilton Sports Pavilion, Las Vegas, Nevada, USA. **Recognition:** WBC. **Referee:** Ferd Hernandez.
Fight Summary: Getting away slowly, Palomino (147) did not really warm up until the fourth round when the challenger began to fire in punches, but the exchanges were wild and mainly ineffectual. It was in the sixth that Palomino began to get his punches off, sending in punishing blows to the body, Sorimachi (147) barely making it to his corner at the end of the session. Realising that he had his man where he wanted Palomino stormed into Sorimachi in the seventh, and having softened him up with a vicious body attack he sent the Japanese down to be counted out with a smashing left hook to the jaw. The finish was timed at 2.03.

4 March 1978. Pipino Cuevas w rsc 9 (15) Harold Weston.
Venue: Olympic Auditorium, Los Angeles, California, USA. **Recognition:** WBA. **Referee:** Marty Denkin.
Fight Summary: Following a testing opening two rounds, in which he was nearly floored in both, Weston (146½) came back well when occasionally outboxing Cuevas (146¼). However, with his punches carrying little weight the champion began to walk through them. Several rounds saw both men going head-to-head, but by the seventh Weston's left eye was damaged and he was beginning to ship punches. Although he had a good eighth round, Weston absorbed a terrific beating throughout the ninth before the doctor advised the referee to stop the contest at the end of the session due to the challenger's badly-cut mouth.

18 March 1978. Carlos Palomino w rsc 9 (15) Mimoun Mohatar.
Venue: Aladdin Hotel, Las Vegas, Nevada, USA. **Recognition:** WBC. **Referee:** Charles Roth.

Fight Summary: Defending his title for the second time in five weeks, Palomino (147) allowed Mohatar (145¼) to make the early running before dropping him with a left hook to the jaw in the fourth round. Decked for the first time in his career Mohatar was up at 'eight', but from thereon in he would be under constant pressure as Palomino worked on the body, and towards the end of the eighth it appeared that the Moroccan was almost through for the night. Coming out for the ninth against his better judgement, Mohatar was quickly dropped, following lefts and rights to the head, and after getting up the referee stopped the bout 57 seconds into the session.

20 May 1978. Pipino Cuevas w rsc 1 (15) Billy Backus.
Venue: Inglewood Forum, Los Angeles, California, USA. **Recognition:** WBA. **Referee:** Carlos Berrocal.
Fight Summary: On the attack from the opening bell Cuevas (146¾) quickly got to grips with his southpaw challenger, who was badly hurt following a hard right to the head. Although Backus (146¼) stayed on his feet he was soon under pressure again, and after being tagged by a left hook to the head he went down for 'eight' having suffered obvious damage to his right eye. Back in the fray, Backus managed to get through the round before the doctor advised the referee during the interval that the bout would have to be stopped. With Backus never landing a punch, Cuevas called it his easiest defence yet.

27 May 1978. Carlos Palomino w pts 15 Armando Muniz.
Venue: Olympic Auditorium, Los Angeles, California, USA. **Recognition:** WBC. **Referee:** Rudy Ortega.
Scorecards: 148-141, 148-139, 145-142.
Fight Summary: It was no surprise that Muniz (146) took the opening three rounds as Palomino (147) started slowly, but by the fifth the champion had begun to go up through the gears. Thereafter, Palomino was in control, landing from head to body without too much coming back, and although Muniz continued to bore in his attacks became more and more ineffectual. In the last couple of sessions it seemed as though Muniz was fighting from memory, but despite Palomino firing in punches from both hands the challenger held out to the final bell. If Palomino's punches lacked zip in the latter stages it was mainly down to the fact that he had fractured his left hand around the halfway mark.

9 September 1978. Pipino Cuevas w rsc 2 (15) Pete Ranzany.
Venue: Hughes Stadium, Sacramento, California, USA. **Recognition:** WBA. **Referee:** Isidro Rodriguez.
Fight Summary: Coming to the ring holding a good record, Ranzany (146), determined to force the fight against the hard-hitting champion, started by doing just that as both men let their punches go. However, having picked it up in the second where he left off in the first Ranzany found himself beaten to the punch before being dropped by a solid left hook. Although getting up, after Ranzany was quickly trapped against the ropes he was sent down again by a right to the head. It was clear that the fight was almost over and, with Cuevas (146¼) tearing in for the kill as the dazed challenger found his feet for the second time, the referee called a halt on the 1.57 mark.

14 January 1979. Wilfred Benitez w pts 15 Carlos Palomino.
Venue: Hiram Bithorn Stadium, San Juan, Puerto Rico. **Recognition:** WBC. **Referee:** Jay Edson.
Scorecards: 148-143, 146-143, 142-146.
Fight Summary: Being out of the ring for nine months affected Palomino (146½) badly, his timing off while his punching power rarely troubled the challenger. Benitez (146) was never in difficulty despite one judge alarmingly voting for the champion. With Benitez's speed a major plus in the fight, by the ninth he was dictating matters, hitting Palomino with left jabs and right crosses and generally pacing himself to the finishing post. Between the tenth and 13th rounds Palomino had his best time when pounding Benitez's body, but the last two sessions proved that the latter had been holding back.

29 January 1979. Pipino Cuevas w rsc 2 (15) Scott Clark.
Venue: Inglewood Forum, Los Angeles, California, USA. **Recognition:** WBA. **Referee:** Luis Sulbaran.
Fight Summary: Hardly warming up, the champion cruised through the opening session before going to work on the luckless Clark (145½) in the second and having his man over from a heavy left hook. After taking the mandatory 'eight' count Clark did his best to hold off Cuevas (146), but was quickly put down again when another left hook

slammed into his head. There was little doubt that Clark was badly dazed, and although he got to his feet and was trying to fight back the referee quickly jumped in to rescue him with 45 seconds of the round remaining.

25 March 1979. Wilfred Benitez w pts 15 (15) Harold Weston.

Venue: Hiram Bithorn Stadium, San Juan, Puerto Rico. **Recognition:** WBC. **Referee:** Richard Steele.
Scorecards: 149-138, 144-142, 146-145.
Fight Summary: Having struggled to make the weight the champion was not his normal self. To add to his woes he was cut over the left eye in the fourth round as Weston (147) tried to take a grip of the fight. Luckily for Benitez (147), the sweltering heat affected Weston more than it did him, the fight rarely ever coming to life. Weston claimed later that he had also had trouble making the weight. With both men sagging, after Benitez finally came back with some heavy combinations in the 12th from thereon in he just about kept ahead of Weston to earn the decision.

The brilliant Sugar Ray Leonard who had moved up to number one in *The Ring* magazine ratings would be Benitez's next challenger. Lightning fast of hand and foot, the 1976 Olympic gold medallist had cut a swathe through the welterweight ranks since turning pro with 25 straight victories, beating Floyd Mayweather, Randy Shields, Armando Muniz, Adolfo Viruet, Marcos Geraldo, Pete Ranzany and Andy Price. He was also the reigning North American champion.

30 July 1979. Pipino Cuevas w pts 15 Randy Shields.

Venue: International Amphitheatre, Chicago, Illinois, USA. **Recognition:** WBA. **Referee:** Luis Sulbaran.
Scorecards: 71-70, 73-67, 71-70.
Fight Summary: Expected to win easily, Cuevas (146½) had a tough time of it against a challenger who used his height and reach to a maximum while also following his battle plan to the letter. Apart from the second round when he hurt Shields (142½) with a terrific left hook, Cuevas looked lethargic by his standards, possibly due to the four postponements, and was forced to take stinging left jabs and countering rights as he tried to get to close quarters. Although Shields thought he had won the fight in the aftermath, Cuevas, who forced matters throughout when concentrating on the body without ever being able to close his man down, just about did enough to keep his belt according to press reports.

30 November 1979. Sugar Ray Leonard w rsc 15 (15) Wilfred Benitez.

Venue: Caesar's Palace, Las Vegas, Nevada, USA. **Recognition:** WBC. **Referee:** Carlos Padilla.
Fight Summary: A contest between undefeated fighters, and the richest ever outside of the heavyweight division at the time, although the champion showed excellent defensive skills against the harder-hitting Leonard (146) he was unable to keep the latter out indefinitely before slumping to a controversial last-round defeat. Down in the third from a solid left jab and cut on the forehead from a clash of heads, Benitez (144½) eventually began to get his left working to even up matters. However, by the ninth Leonard was letting the big punches go again. Despite Benitez being hurt in the ninth and 11th the fight was fairly even going into the 12th, but after Leonard picked it up to edge the 13th and 14th it appeared that he might just be in front. Thus it was set up for a grandstand finish, and with both men giving it all they had and nearing the end of the contest a left jab-left hook dropped Benitez. With Benitez forced to take the mandatory 'eight' count, when Leonard rushed in to land lefts and rights the referee jumped between the two men to rescue the champion with just six seconds of the fight remaining.

8 December 1979. Pipino Cuevas w rsc 10 (15) Angel Espada.

Venue: Sports Arena, Los Angeles, California, USA. **Recognition:** WBA. **Referee:** Terry Smith.
Fight Summary: This, the third fight between the pair, signalled the end of the challenger's career after he was comprehensively beaten by the hard-hitting Cuevas (146) yet again. Never in with a chance from the opening bell, Espada (144½) was badly hurt in the third and fifth rounds without being decked. By the ninth, cut over the left eye, he was struggling to stay in the fight. At that point Cuevas was just walking through his defences, and following a non-stop attack in the tenth Espada went down for the mandatory 'eight' after being caught by heavy left-rights to the head. On getting up in a dazed state and being smashed with lefts and rights without reply, Espada was finally rescued by the referee with 57 seconds of the round remaining.

31 March 1980. Sugar Ray Leonard w rsc 4 (15) Dave Boy Green.
Venue: Capital Centre, Landover, Maryland, USA. **Recognition:** WBC. **Referee:** Arthur Mercante.
Fight Summary: Showing terrific hand-speed, power and movement, the champion had a good look at Green (147) for three rounds before proving what a great fighter he was when dismantling the game Englishman in the fourth. Having been stung by two left jabs Leonard (147) finally began to open up with blinding combinations, and after a right uppercut rocked Green down to his boots a thundering left hook to the jaw sent him crashing down to be counted out on the 2.27 mark. It should have been seen as a clean knockout as Green was out cold, but when the referee stopped the count at 'six' to remove the gumshield, regardless of what was said afterwards, it has to be recorded as a stoppage.

6 April 1980. Pipino Cuevas w co 5 (15) Harold Volbrecht.
Venue: The Astrodome, Houston, Texas, USA. **Recognition:** WBA. **Referee:** Carlos Berrocal.
Fight Summary: Although the southpaw challenger fought aggressively during the first three rounds, twice rocking Cuevas (146½) with left hooks, by the fourth the latter was beginning to get to him with solid body shots. The tide of change came in the fifth. Following an exchange of jabs, after Volbrecht (146¾) missed badly with a sweeping right, Cuevas, ducking inside, crashed home a vicious left to the chin to put the South African down for the count, timed at 1.19.

20 June 1980. Roberto Duran w pts 15 Sugar Ray Leonard.
Venue: Olympic Stadium, Montreal, Canada. **Recognition:** WBC. **Referee:** Carlos Padilla.
Scorecards: 145-144, 148-147, 146-144.
Fight Summary: In a battle between two great fighters, it was Duran (145¼) who came out on top when taking the title from Leonard (145) with a close but unanimous decision. For 15 rounds there was no let-up as both men showed their quality. Duran started fast, staying in close and putting terrific pressure on Leonard, and it was only in the fifth that the latter began to find the jab to distance himself from the aggressive Panamanian. At the end of the contest, although Leonard had just about landed the most punches Duran's heavier hitting swung it for him.

2 August 1980. Thomas Hearns w rsc 2 (15) Pipino Cuevas
Venue: Joe Louis Arena, Detroit, Michigan, USA. **Recognition:** WBA. **Referee:** Stan Christodoulou.
Fight Summary: It started with both men throwing the left hook at the same time, the 6'1" Hearns (146½) getting there first with such force that the champion backed off. That punch set the pattern of the fight, with Cuevas (146) retreating under the volume of leather coming his way. Hearns was denying Cuevas room to work by staying right on top of him and letting a vast array of punches go with blurring speed. Cuevas just about got through the opening round, but in the second he was doomed as Hearns belted him to the ropes, landing punch after punch before a vicious right to the head sent the champion crashing to the floor. Although the referee had started the count, on seeing Cuevas' handlers trying to get to their man he stopped the fight immediately, the finish being timed at 2.39.

25 November 1980. Sugar Ray Leonard w rsc 8 (15) Roberto Duran.
Venue: The Superdome, New Orleans, Louisiana, USA. **Recognition:** WBC. **Referee:** Octavio Meyran.
Fight Summary: Helped by a large ring, Leonard (146) was a different man to the one who fought Duran (146) previously, being able to counter and move effectively against the champion regardless of him visiting the ropes more than he would have wanted. Despite both men letting their punches go it appeared relatively even until the sixth when Leonard picked it up, boxing well behind the jab, while Duran began to land less frequently. The seventh was dramatic, as Leonard, hands down and swaying from side to side, taunted a bemused Duran and made him look foolish when winding up the right hand before snapping left jabs into his face. With Leonard now in control, following an exchange of blows in the eighth Duran suddenly and inexplicably quit when walking back to his corner. Asked to fight on by the referee Duran said that he'd had enough, and at 2.44 of the session the third man was forced to bring the fight to an end. Later, Duran would say that he had cramps in his stomach and arms, but when the press did not believe him the fight quickly became labelled as the 'No Mas' (Spanish for "No more") affair due to the way in which the champion retired himself.

6 December 1980. Thomas Hearns w co 6 (15) Luis Primera.
Venue: Joe Louis Arena, Detroit, Michigan, USA. **Recognition:** WBA. **Referee:** Ismael Fernandez.
Fight Summary: Shaken up badly in the opening round after Primera (146¾) waded into him, the champion hit back solidly in the second to drop the Venezuelan on the seat of his pants for 'four'. After biding his time in the third and fourth, Hearns (146½) unleashed heavy lefts and rights to the head in the sixth to drop Primera again before cutting loose with more solid punches to put the latter down for the full count with one minute of the session remaining. The final punch landed was a smashing right to the body.

28 March 1981. Sugar Ray Leonard w rsc 10 (15) Larry Bonds.
Venue: Carrier Dome, Syracuse, New York, USA. **Recognition:** WBC. **Referee:** Arthur Mercante.
Fight Summary: The southpaw challenger did well to last so long, proving extremely game, and gave Leonard (145½) a few problems with his awkward style. Dropped by a right to the jaw in the fourth round following several heavy body shots, Bonds (144¾) was saved by the bell before coming back in the fifth to peck away with the jab and make a nuisance of himself. There was no doubt that Leonard was in control, but he had not pressured Bonds enough, something he rectified in the ninth when jumping on the latter with blows to head and body. Coming out for the tenth, with Bonds soon in trouble as Leonard stayed right on top of him he was eventually dropped from heavy blows to head and body. After taking the mandatory 'eight' count, Bonds was soon under attack and not hitting back when the referee called it off on the 2.22 mark.

Next time out, on 25 June, at The Astrodome, Houston, Texas, Leonard challenged Ayub Kalule for the WBA junior middleweight title, winning by a ninth-round stoppage. Leonard handed back the junior belt the following month to concentrate on his welterweight unification fight against Thomas Hearns.

25 April 1981. Thomas Hearns w rsc 12 (15) Randy Shields.
Venue: Veterans' Memorial Coliseum, Phoenix, Arizona, USA. **Recognition:** WBA. **Referee:** Bobby Ferrara.
Fight Summary: Three inches shorter than the champion, although the gritty Shields (146½) gave it his best shot he took a hammering in virtually every round as Hearns (146) let the punches go. Several times Shields was sent back on his heels as crashing rights to the jaw hit the target and left jabs homed in on him, but he continued gallantly even if the task was a hopeless one. By the ninth Shields was cut over both eyes, and after taking a heavy beating on the ropes near the end of the 12th the referee pulled him out following a discussion with the ringside doctor.

25 June 1981. Thomas Hearns w rsc 4 (15) Pablo Baez.
Venue: The Astrodome, Houston, Texas, USA. **Recognition:** WBA. **Referee:** Ken Morita.
Fight Summary: After putting up a spirited fight for three rounds despite being under constant pressure, the challenger finally began to crumble in the fourth as Hearns (147) opened up with his big guns. Swollen and cut around the left eye from the attention of stinging left jabs, Baez (144¾) soon began to be caught with heavy rights and lefts to head and body as Hearns went for the finish, and at 2.10 of the session the fight was halted with the Dominican slumped on the bottom rope. Both fighters were 6'1", tall for welters.

16 September 1981. Sugar Ray Leonard w rsc 14 (15) Thomas Hearns.
Venue: Caesar's Palace Omnimax, Las Vegas, Nevada, USA. **Recognition:** World. **Referee:** Davy Pearl.
Fight Summary: Battling to unify the title, Leonard (146) ultimately proved to be the superior man when stopping Hearns (145) at 1.45 of the 14th round after being behind on all three cards. Billed as 'The Super Fight', Leonard fought from the third with a swollen left eye that obscured his vision, but after being on the end of Hearns' long reach he eventually came into the contest in the sixth when almost putting the latter down. The seventh was a big one for Leonard as he let the punches go, and he continued to stalk his man for the next three sessions without doing too much. After being held at bay in the 12th, when Hearns jabbed and crossed him throughout, Leonard opened up again in the 13th, pouring punches in to enforce a count over the WBA champion before the bell rang to end the round. Although Hearns made one last defiant stand in the 14th he was clearly spent, the referee coming to his aid following a six-punch burst that left him defenceless.

15 February 1982. Sugar Ray Leonard w rsc 3 (15) Bruce Finch.
Venue: Centennial Coliseum, Reno, Nevada, USA. **Recognition:** World. **Referee:** Mills Lane.

Fight Summary: Although he started promisingly, after Finch (145¼) was dropped for 'nine' by the champion in the second, when blasted by a left hook-right to the head, the end appeared ominous, especially when he fell down immediately afterwards. Seemingly distressed, but up at 'eight', Finch somehow struggled through the round. Coming out for the third Finch tried to get himself going but, having taken punches a plenty, a crunching left uppercut from Leonard (146) dropped him. On lurching to his feet in an unstable condition the referee took a good look at Finch before deciding that he was not fit to continue, stopping the bout on the 1.50 mark.

Towards the end of the year, the WBC announced that, as from 1 January 1983, all world title bouts held under their banner would be contested over 12 rounds.

When Leonard relinquished the title on announcing his retirement in November, the WBA lined up Donald Curry (who had won a final eliminator on points over 12 rounds against Marlon Starling at the Convention Hall, Atlantic City, New Jersey on 23 October) to fight Jun-Suk Hwang for their version of the championship. Meanwhile, the WBC set up Colin Jones and Milton McCrory to contest their title, despite the European champion initially being lined up to meet Mauricio Bravo in a final eliminator.

13 February 1983. Donald Curry w pts 15 Jun-Suk Hwang.
Venue: Civic Centre, Fort Worth, Texas, USA. **Recognition:** WBA. **Referee:** Roberto Ramirez.
Scorecards: 146-139, 148-140, 146-139.
Fight Summary: Contesting the vacant title, Curry (146¼) had to get off the floor after being put down by a right swing to the jaw in the seventh and was forced to take several wild blows to the head before being awarded the decision. Using stiff left jabs and hooks to pile up the points, Curry was never at ease against the wild-swinging Hwang (147) who more often than not missed with big left hooks and overarm rights as he stormed into the American. Occasionally, Curry opened up with both hands, but after hurting his right in the 12th he stuck to his boxing.

Curry was given added support as champion in April by the recently constituted United States Boxing Association (USBA/I), who would be renamed as the International Boxing Federation (IBF) in late October.

19 March 1983. Milton McCrory drew 12 Colin Jones.
Venue: Convention Centre, Reno, Nevada, USA. **Recognition:** WBC. **Referee:** Octavio Meyran.
Scorecards: 116-113, 114-116, 115-115.
Fight Summary: Following Sugar Ray Leonard's retirement, McCrory (146½) and Jones (146) contested the vacant WBC version of the title, but nothing was decided after the judges came up with a draw following a tremendous scrap. While McCrory pumped in long left jabs throughout, Jones was looking for one big punch rather than work the body. Had he done so, the fight might well have finished early. Many of McCrory's blows lacked sting and many of them were blocked, and in the eighth a terrific shot to the body hurt the American. By the ninth, McCrory was on the run as Jones continued to bang away. However, at the final bell Jones knew that he had let the American off the hook.

13 August 1983. Milton McCrory w pts 12 Colin Jones.
Venue: Dunes Hotel, Las Vegas, Nevada, USA. **Recognition:** WBC. **Referee:** Isaac Herrera.
Scorecards: 115-114, 115-111, 113-114.
Fight Summary: Knocked down by a curving left uppercut towards the end of the first round of this vacant title contest was not what Jones (146½) expected, and it took him another couple of rounds to recover from it. The rest of the fight was spent with Jones chasing McCrory (147), it being only the latter's last round effort that gained him the title. Wobbling, retreating at speed and clutching for much of the time, when the cards were read out it appeared that McCrory's lightweight left and right counters had actually scored points. Interestingly, the day before the fight the WBC introduced a new ruling stating that in the event of the judges coming up with another draw they would be ordered to find a winner, a decision that possibly benefited McCrory more than Jones.

3 September 1983. Donald Curry w rsc 1 (15) Roger Stafford.
Venue: Municipal Stadium, Marsala, Italy. **Recognition:** WBA. **Referee:** Stan Christodoulou.

Fight Summary: Also supported by the USBA/I, soon to be known as the IBF, the contest lasted just 102 seconds, having been twice postponed due to a hand injury suffered by Curry. Despite stating that he would knock Curry out, the challenger was dropped by the opening blow, a stiff left jab. Although getting up and trying to box his way out of trouble he was soon caught again. Two left hooks followed by a right to the head had Stafford over for the second time, and after taking the mandatory 'eight' he blazed into Curry wildly before being shot down by a cracking right to the jaw that left the referee no option other than calling it off under the 'three knockdowns in a round' ruling.

Curry's next defence would be against his number one challenger, Marlon Starling. Starling, who had lost just once in 32 contests - a split decision defeat at the hands of Curry - had beaten Floyd Mayweather, Kevin Howard and Tommy Ayers to obtain his high ranking. A clever fighter with a punch, who was known as 'The Magic Man', Starling was the USBA and NABF champion.

14 January 1984. Milton McCrory w rsc 6 (12) Milton Guest.
Venue: Sterling Heights Premier Centre, Detroit, Michigan, USA. **Recognition:** WBC. **Referee:** Zack Clayton.
Fight Summary: Knocked down twice by left hooks to the head in the opening session did not augur well for Guest (147), the champion continuing to hammer him in the second before cutting him over the left eye while giving him a steady beating. Although outboxed and outclassed, Guest gamely stuck to his task, but was dropped again in the third, fifth and sixth sessions before McCrory, punishing him with both hands, stepped it up in the sixth. Now, with it being just a matter of time, McCrory eventually found the finishing blow, a right uppercut to the jaw. Despite Guest making it to his feet the referee stopped the contest six seconds after the bell had ended the round.

4 February 1984. Donald Curry w pts 15 Marlon Starling.
Venue: Bally's Park Place Hotel, Atlantic City, New Jersey, USA. **Recognition:** WBA. **Referee:** Joe Cortez.
Scorecards: 144-142, 145-140, 145-140.
Fight Summary: With Curry (147) forcing the fight all the way, landing the harder blows throughout, even though the challenger took heavy punishment he was always there throwing punches in response. It was always uphill for Starling (146), but fighting on gamely he even shook Curry up on occasion. While there were no knockdowns, Curry had Starling wobbling in the 15th as he looked to finish strongly, and despite one judge marking it much closer than it was the unanimous decision was a formality. Although not involved in the promotion, the recently formed IBF announced that they would be recognising the winner as champion.

15 April 1984. Milton McCrory w rsc 6 (12) Gilles Elbilia.
Venue: Cobo Hall, Detroit, Michigan, USA. **Recognition:** WBC. **Referee:** Carlos Padilla.
Fight Summary: After outboxing his challenger in the opening round, McCrory (146½) started to land heavily with left hooks and solid left jabs in the second, and even at this stage it did not look as though the fight would go the distance. Cut over the left eye in the second, Elbilia (146) appeared decidedly shaky. Although Elbilia made it into the sixth his time was almost up. Dropped by a left hook for the mandatory 'eight' count, he was being driven around the ring when the referee stopped it on the 1.08 mark.

21 April 1984. Donald Curry w rtd 7 (15) Elio Diaz.
Venue: Will Rogers' Coliseum, Fort Worth, Texas, USA. **Recognition:** WBA/IBF. **Referee:** Stan Christodoulou.
Fight Summary: Being dropped after just 20 seconds was not the best of starts for the challenger, but he continually moved and made himself as difficult a target as he could as Curry (147) went looking for him. Pressing forward and picking his punches with care, Curry appeared to hurt Diaz (145½) every time he landed, and he had him down again in the fifth and the seventh rounds before the Venezuelan was retired during the interval. With his right eye almost closed shut and having done his best it would have been foolhardy to have sent out Diaz for the eighth.

22 September 1984. Donald Curry w rsc 6 (15) Nino La Rocca.
Venue: Circus Tent, Monte Carlo, Monaco. **Recognition:** WBA/IBF. **Referee:** Stan Christodoulou.
Fight Summary: Stalking the challenger from the start, Curry (147) pressed forward, blocking punches with a high guard, and by the third round appeared to have matters under control. Having hurt La Rocca (146¾) in the fourth

with a hard right to the head, Curry repeated the dose in the fifth before opening up with his full armoury in the sixth. With Curry now in full swing, La Rocca was dropped by two solid lefts. After taking the mandatory count and in a groggy condition he was hunted down and quickly floored again by a cracking left hook, whereupon the referee called a halt at 1.27 of the session.

19 January 1985. Donald Curry w rsc 4 (15) Colin Jones.
Venue: National Exhibition Centre, Birmingham, England. **Recognition:** IBF/WBA. **Referee:** Ismael Fernandez.
Fight Summary: Catching Jones (146) with three fast jabs immediately the first round got underway set the tone as the champion quickly moved into punching range. With Curry (147) continuing to press in the second there were several heavy exchanges between the pair, but in the third it all went wrong for the Welshman when the bridge of his nose was split. Unfortunately, the cut was too bad to repair during the interval, and after just 36 seconds of the fourth on the ringside doctor's advice the referee halted the bout, thus ending Jones' dream of becoming a world champion.

9 March 1985. Milton McCrory w pts 12 Pedro Vilella.
Venue: Bercy Sports Palace, Paris, France. **Recognition:** WBC. **Referee:** Angelo Poletti.
Scorecards: 120-112, 118-112, 120-112.
Fight Summary: Hammering at his challenger almost from the opening bell, McCrory (147) soon had difficulty in reaching him with clean punches as the Puerto Rican southpaw carried a high guard and ducked low continuously. Although Vilella (142) was never in the hunt, his negative style stopped McCrory from expressing himself, and when he occasionally went forward it was more of a wild charge that ended in bouts of slapping rather than scoring punches. A rare exchange in the last round saw McCrory forcing Vilella to the ropes while punching away with both hands to finish the fight as it started, followed by the obvious decision in his favour.

14 July 1985. Milton McCrory w rsc 3 (12) Carlos Trujillo.
Venue: Louis 11 Stadium, Monte Carlo, Monaco. **Recognition:** WBC. **Referee:** Rudy Ortega.
Fight Summary: Outclassing his challenger from the start, McCrory (147) was quickly into action with sharp and accurate punches finding their mark, and near the end of the opening round he had his man down on one knee from a right to the head. Going southpaw in trying to confuse McCrory brought some time for Trujillo (146½), who mainly through swings and hooks, but the end was inevitable. Firing in punches through the middle in the third, McCrory saw his chance. After a right sent Trujillo back on his heels, being followed by lefts and rights, another right sent him to the floor. Although the count had started the referee called it off on the 1.59 mark to make sure that Trujillo received treatment.

6 December 1985. Donald Curry w co 2 (12) Milton McCrory.
Venue: Hilton Hotel, Las Vegas, Nevada, USA. **Recognition:** World. **Referee:** Mills Lane.
Fight Summary: Wobbled in the first round by a searing left hook, McCrory (146¾) found the WBA/IBF champion right in front of him throughout the contest, seemingly unable to keep him off with his best punches having no effect. In the second session, picking it up where he left off, Curry (146¾) soon had McCrory over from a solid left hook to the head. It was clear that McCrory had little left, and after he just about got himself up by the end of the mandatory 'eight' a smashing right to the jaw sent him down to be counted out on the 1.53 mark. Contested over the WBC distance of 12 rounds, it had been agreed that in order to unify the title that body and the IBF/WBA, who recognised 15 rounds as the world title distance, would take it in turns to promote world title fights for this weight class.

9 March 1986. Donald Curry w co 2 (15) Eduardo Rodriguez.
Venue: Will Rogers' Coliseum, Fort Worth, Texas, USA. **Recognition:** World. **Referee:** Hubert Earle.
Fight Summary: Having unified the title, with Curry (146¾) making a slow start he even went down in the first as Rodriguez (146½) threw lefts and rights to head and body. Despite it being ruled a slip it certainly woke Curry up. More focused in the second, Curry started to back Rodriguez up, nailing him cleanly, and although the latter was throwing punches he was looking increasingly under pressure before two left hooks dropped him for the full count on the 2.29 mark.

27 September 1986. Lloyd Honeyghan w rsc 6 (12) Donald Curry.
Venue: Caesar's Hotel, Atlantic City, New Jersey, USA. **Recognition:** World. **Referee:** Octavio Meyran.
Fight Summary: In what was one of the biggest shocks ever for the weight division, Honeyghan (146½) forced a stoppage after the sixth round had ended when the ringside doctors decided that Curry (146½), who had suffered a broken nose, a bad cut on the left eye and a gashed mouth, was too badly injured to carry on. That was the official reason given, but Curry, who looked weight-drained, had taken a beating virtually all night as Honeyghan kept right on top of him. The action in the second round was a sign of things to come when Honeyghan opened up to almost have Curry over early on, and then had him in further trouble immediately prior to the bell. Although Curry came back well in the next couple of sessions, he was again badly hurt in the fifth before being worked over throughout the sixth and being taken out of the fight. It was clear afterwards that Curry had suffered from taking off weight, but it should not detract from a magnificent performance given by the British-based, Jamaican-born fighter.

Honeyghan relinquished the WBA version of the title in December after being told that his first defence would have to be against their number one challenger, the white South African, Harold Volbrecht. When Honeyghan refused the edict on the grounds of the organisation's attitude towards apartheid, the WBA matched Volbrecht against Mark Breland for their version of the title.

6 February 1987. Mark Breland w co 7 (15) Harold Volbrecht.
Venue: Trump Plaza Hotel, Atlantic City, New Jersey, USA. **Recognition:** WBA. **Referee:** Tony Perez.
Fight Summary: Contesting the vacant title against Volbrecht (146½), America's Breland (146) became the new champion when winning by a knockout at 2.07 of the seventh round after two quick right hands to the jaw had done the damage. Having hurt his left hand in the opening session, the 6'2½" Breland was forced to rethink his game-plan against the South African southpaw, especially as he had great difficulty in catching up with him when he was on the back foot. Prior to the ending Volbrecht had been staggered several times, but the former Olympic champion was happy to wait for the opportunity he knew would eventually come.

22 February 1987. Lloyd Honeyghan w rsc 2 (15) Johnny Bumphus.
Venue: Grand Hall, Wembley, London, England. **Recognition:** IBF/WBC. **Referee:** Sam Williams.
Fight Summary: The fight began with the champion opening up straight away to blaze into Bumphus (145½), and eventually a left jab followed by a solid straight right dropped the latter, who was forced to take the mandatory 'eight' before being stunned again before the bell. With great expectations for Honeyghan (146½), the second round started controversially as he tore out of his corner to smash in a left hook that floored Bumphus, who was still in the process of getting off his stool. With Bumphus' cornermen still partially in the ring, when his manager climbed back in to claim a disqualification win it was half a minute before the referee asked the judges to deduct a point from Honeyghan and the fight recommenced. He need not have bothered as Bumphus was almost through for the night. After 55 seconds of the session the referee stopped the uneven contest when a Honeyghan blast saw the American sliding towards the floor under a barrage of blows. There was no doubt that blame for the incident in question lay entirely with the referee, as he had allowed Honeyghan to advance to mid-ring before the bell had been rung. Officially, only the IBF portion of the title was involved as the WBC no longer saw 15 rounds as the championship distance and had Honeyghan lost they would have stripped him rather than recognise the winner.

18 April 1987. Lloyd Honeyghan w pts 12 Maurice Blocker.
Venue: Royal Albert Hall, Kensington, London, England. **Recognition:** IBF/WBC. **Referee:** Bob Logist.
Scorecards: 117-114, 119-112, 119-114.
Fight Summary: Proving a different proposition to his last challenger, Blocker (146¾) gave Honeyghan (147) all the trouble he could handle, the latter ending up with his left eye almost closed. Not recognised by the IBF as a title fight, Honeyghan switched between orthodox and southpaw in a bid to confuse Blocker, but as the fight moved on it was the latter's better boxing, with excellent jabbing and right-hand counters that was asking the questions. Towards the finish Honeyghan appeared to have something in hand before he had a couple of shockers in the 11th and 12th, when utterly exhausted, and had to call upon all his reserves to get through. On the face of it, the scorecards in Honeyghan's favour appeared much wider than they should have been.

22 August 1987. Marlon Starling w co 11 (15) Mark Breland.
Venue: Columbia Township Auditorium, South Carolina, USA. **Recognition:** WBA. **Referee:** Tony Perez.
Fight Summary: Even though he moved ahead of his challenger the danger signs were always there for Breland (146), and he was either pushed or wrestled to the floor on seven occasions in the opening seven rounds. In the eighth, after Breland took a low blow he was given time out, but Starling (146) was looking much stronger at this stage of the fight. The ninth saw Breland weakening before he came back well in the tenth, but in the 11th he was all over the place as Starling laid into him. Staggered by a right to the head, Breland was driven across the ring before being dropped to the floor by a left hook to the head and being counted out after 1.38 of the session.

At their convention, held in October, the WBA announced that in future all world title bouts held under their auspices would be contested over 12 rounds.

30 August 1987. Lloyd Honeyghan w rsc 1 (15) Gene Hatcher.
Venue: New Andalveia Bullring, Marbella, Spain. **Recognition:** IBF/WBC. **Referee:** Jean Deswerts.
Fight Summary: All over after 45 seconds of the opening round, Honeyghan (147) set a record as the quickest winner of a world title bout up until now when stopping a challenger who had barely warmed up. Having knocked Hatcher (147) down with the first punch of the contest, a right hand that seemed to come from the floor, Honeyghan quickly went to work following the mandatory count. At least 20 punches smashed into Hatcher before the latter slid to the canvas as the referee was belatedly halting the bout. Due to it being contested over 15 rounds and not 12, although the WBC recognised Honeyghan as the champion they were not involved in the promotion.

28 October 1987. Jorge Vaca w tdec 8 (12) Lloyd Honeyghan.
Venue: Grand Hall, Wembley, London, England. **Recognition:** IBF/WBC. **Referee:** Henry Elesperu.
Scorecards: 67-65, 67-66, 65-67.
Fight Summary: Well below his best in a give-and-take battle, boxing wildly at times, the champion ended the second round with a swelling under the right eye as Vaca (147) matched him blow for blow. Indeed, it was Vaca who was often doing the better work and was taking the best punches that Honeyghan (146¾) had on offer. Honeyghan had a good round in the fifth, but in the sixth he went badly low. Although Vaca was given half a minute to rest the champion failed to have a point deducted. Honeyghan was in trouble at the end of the seventh as Vaca, now cut over the left eye, smashed in a tremendous left hook to the head. However, with the contest nicely poised in the eighth heads came together with a sickening crack, leaving Vaca with a deep, jagged cut over the right eye and unable to continue. Inexplicably, because the head clash was obviously an accidental one, the referee asked the judges to deduct a point from Honeyghan's total before adding up the scores, which gave the fight to the Mexican. Without the point deduction, Honeyghan would have held on to his title.

Not recognised as a title bout by the IBF due to the duration of the bout being over 12 rounds and not 15, as required by that body, Vaca was not given credence by them as champion. The new IBF champion would be decided once Simon Brown and Tyrone Trice settled their fight for the vacant title.

5 February 1988. Marlon Starling w pts 12 Fujio Ozaki.
Venue: Convention Centre, Atlantic City, New Jersey, USA. **Recognition:** WBA. **Referee:** Steve Smoger.
Scorecards: 118-110, 117-114, 117-112.
Fight Summary: Devoid of any real excitement, the champion's defence against Ozaki (146½) went the distance. Although he was in control most of the way and had the better skills he rarely looked to do anything other than win on points. While Ozaki often plodded, occasionally sending in hurtful punches, he was too one-paced and predictable to be a real threat, Starling (145) winning as he pleased.

29 March 1988. Lloyd Honeyghan w co 3 (12) Jorge Vaca.
Venue: The Arena, Wembley, London, England. **Recognition:** WBC. **Referee:** Joe Cortez.
Fight Summary: Fighting like a man possessed, Honeyghan (146½) tore into Vaca (145¾), barely letting up, before inflicting a cut over the champion's right eye in the opening two minutes. There was little science in his work, just slugging, and although Vaca complained that the cut had been caused by Honeyghan's illegal use of the head it made little difference as the latter kept punching away. The third round saw Honeyghan begin to think about his

214

boxing, but he was soon back looking to take the Mexican out. Towards the end of the session, Vaca was finally dropped by clubbing right hands and counted out with just two seconds remaining.

16 April 1988. Marlon Starling drew 12 Mark Breland.
Venue: Hilton Hotel, Las Vegas, Nevada, USA. **Recognition:** WBA. **Referee:** Mills Lane.
Scorecards: 116-113, 114-115, 114-114.
Fight Summary: In a rematch, and fighting a different kind of campaign, Breland (146) came on towards the finish to snatch a draw as the champion ran out of steam, but as a title fight it was unimpressive. There were no knockdowns, being messy throughout, with neither man being able to assert himself totally on the other. Although Starling (146½), who finished with both eyes swollen, threw the heavier blows there were not enough of them, while Breland stuck with the left jab and right-hand counters in a contest best forgotten.

23 April 1988. Simon Brown w rsc 14 (15) Tyrone Trice.
Venue: Sports Palace, Berck Sur Mer, France. **Recognition:** IBF. **Referee:** Steve Smoger.
Fight Summary: Contesting the vacant title, the signs were not good for Brown (146) after he was dropped by a heavy right to the head in the second round when the lanky Trice (146) got to him with a cluster of big punches. However, by the fourth he was back in the fight. With Brown beginning to land the heavier shots, following sustained pressure a tiring Trice was dropped three times in the 12th and saved by the bell. Somehow managing to survive the 13th when holding and back-pedalling, Trice came back bravely in the 14th to hurt Brown before running into a right to the jaw that sent him down flat on his face. Although Trice managed to beat the count he was now a sitting target for Brown's heavy punches, and after two powerful left hooks had him sagging at the knees the referee came to his rescue with 31 seconds of the session remaining.

16 July 1988. Simon Brown w rsc 3 (15) Jorge Vaca.
Venue: National Arena, Kingston, Jamaica. **Recognition:** IBF. **Referee:** Rudy Battle.
Fight Summary: Starting strongly, the champion soon had the ring-worn Vaca (147) in trouble, flooring him with a right to the jaw just before the bell rang to end the opening round. If the first round had been bad for Vaca the second was even worse, Brown (146¼) dropping him four times. Although Vaca made it into the third there would be no respite, and after being cut over the left eye by heavy left hooks another one sent him to the floor for the sixth time. That was it as far as the referee was concerned, the fight being halted on the 2.05 mark.

The IBF announced that, as from 1 September, all world title bouts held under their banner would be contested over 12 rounds. From here on in all world title bouts in this weight division would be contested over that distance.

29 July 1988. Lloyd Honeyghan w rsc 5 (12) Yung-Kil Chung.
Venue: Convention Hall, Atlantic City, New Jersey, USA. **Recognition:** WBC. **Referee:** Tony Orlando.
Fight Summary: The challenger started strongly, forcing Honeyghan (147) to stumble in the opening round before the latter began to get a better grip of things in the fourth when turning southpaw to land punches with ease. Coming into the fifth ahead on all three cards, after banging in a few right jabs to the face Honeyghan went badly low with a clumsy left that sent Chung (146¾) writhing to the canvas in pain 42 seconds into the session. With Chung having been given five minutes to recover but unable to continue at the end of that period, the referee then awarded the decision to Honeyghan by way of a technical knockout.

29 July 1988. Tomas Molinares w co 6 Marlon Starling.
Venue: Convention Hall, Atlantic City, New Jersey, USA. **Recognition:** WBA. **Referee:** Joe Cortez.
Fight Summary: Unbeaten in 23 fights, the challenger started well, picking his punches cleverly, while Starling (147) was more cautious and bided his time. Eventually, after Starling got his act together he was landing with combinations by the fifth, while Molinares (146¾), whose right eye was closing, appeared a little perturbed at that stage. The sixth round saw the fight end in most controversial circumstances. As the bell went to close the session, Starling dropped his hands just as Molinares stepped in with a tremendous right to his jaw to send him crashing, and at the same time twisting his right ankle. The referee then applied the logic that the punch was already on its way as the bell went, counting Starling out ten seconds into the interval. Despite the New Jersey State Boxing

Commission changing the result to that of a no contest following the fight, the WBA recognised Molinares as their new champion.

Further to the formation of the World Boxing Organisation (WBO) in November, which came about after 27 delegates walked out of the WBA convention disgusted with the way things were being handled, the new organisation nominated Genaro Leon to meet Danny Garcia in order to decide their version of the vacant title.

Meanwhile, when Molinares relinquished the WBA title in January 1989 on realising that he would be unable to make the weight for a defence against Mark Breland, the latter was matched against Seung-Soon Lee to find a successor.

14 October 1988. Simon Brown w pts 12 Mauro Martelli.
Venue: Malley Skating Rink, Lausanne, Switzerland. **Recognition:** IBF. **Referee:** Steve Smoger.
Scorecards: 115-113, 120-108, 120-108.
Fight Summary: Defending his title for the second time, Brown (147) was nearly always going better than Martelli (146¼), who made a poor start when being frequently pounded on the ropes in the early rounds and hurt by solid right uppercuts. Although the European champion overcame his initial problems when gradually beginning to get into the contest from the fifth onwards he was never able to cut back Brown's lead. While Brown won convincingly, destroying Martelli's unbeaten record in doing so, the European judge strangely had the latter only two points down at the finish.

5 February 1989. Mark Breland w rsc 1 Seung-Soon Lee.
Venue: Caesar's Palace, Las Vegas, Nevada, USA. **Recognition:** WBA. **Referee:** Richard Steele.
Fight Summary: Meeting for the title vacated by Tomas Molinares, Breland (147) and Lee (146) quickly got down to business, the latter making the early running with wild swinging lefts and rights which forced the former champion to hit back. Standing four-and-a-half inches taller than his opponent, Breland had been expecting to work with the jab, but because of the intensity of the early action he opened up with a left-right-left to drop Lee, and although the latter got up he was soon reeling from another bombardment of blows before being stopped after just 54 seconds.

5 February 1989. Marlon Starling w rsc 9 Lloyd Honeyghan.
Venue: Caesar's Palace, Las Vegas, Nevada, USA. **Recognition:** WBC. **Referee:** Mills Lane.
Fight Summary: After wobbling Starling (146) with a right to the head in the third round, the champion failed to follow up his advantage, being dominated in every round from thereon in. The real problem for Honeyghan (146½), it later transpired, came after being hit early on and suffering terrible pain from around the jaw every time Starling landed in that area. By the sixth Honeyghan had run out of ideas, and with his gumshield continuously coming out he went back to his corner with his right eye closing fast and a badly swollen jaw. Bravely fighting on, Honeyghan was dropped by quick combination punches at the beginning of the ninth, and on getting up and being hit at will without firing back the referee stopped the fight on the 1.19 mark to save him from taking further punishment. Following the fight it was announced that Honeyghan's post-fight mandatory urine sample had revealed a quantity of the pain killing lidocaine. Although Honeyghan later stated that the substance had been prescribed by an official doctor to help get rid of the pain he had been suffering in his right hand he was still fined.

18 February 1989. Simon Brown w rsc 3 Jorge Maysonet.
Venue: Csamok Sports Hall, Budapest, Hungary. **Recognition:** IBF. **Referee:** Rudy Battle.
Fight Summary: Moving in on Maysonet (147) right from the opening bell, the champion gave the Puerto Rican no room in which to work and once he had got his left hook going the finish was imminent. Although Maysonet threw plenty of leather, landing with some decent shots on Brown (147), he was soon overwhelmed. Knocked down twice in the second round and twice more in the third, the referee moved in on the 2.01 mark to save him from taking further punishment.

22 April 1989. Mark Breland w rsc 5 Rafael Pineda.
Venue: Trump Castle Hotel, Atlantic City, New Jersey, USA. **Recognition:** WBA. **Referee:** Ted Pick.

Fight Summary: Making his first defence, Breland (146¾) had a shaky first round before spraining his left knee in the second and being forced to trade when he would rather have been using the left jab. By the fourth, however, with Breland getting the jab working Pineda (145¼) was looking decidedly shaky. After complaining about being thumbed in the eye and turning his back on his opponent, Pineda was punished with blows to the head. In the fifth when Pineda again turned his back on Breland, his left eye badly swollen, the referee stopped the fight, the finish being timed at 1.14 of the session.

27 April 1989. Simon Brown w co 7 Al Long.
Venue: The Armoury, Washington DC, USA. **Recognition:** IBF. **Referee:** Tony Orlando.
Fight Summary: Despite being out of the ring for nearly a year, Long (146½) started fast, making Brown (147) appear sluggish and easy to hit before the champion began to find his way in the third round. By the fourth, although still slippery, Long was gradually being worn down, having been hurt by left hooks to head and body. Still applying pressure, it took Brown until the seventh before he eventually found the finishing punches to knock Long over, and at 2.21 the latter was counted out after blows to head and body followed by left and right uppercuts had sent him crashing.

6 May 1989. Genaro Leon w rsc 1 Danny Garcia.
Venue: The Stadium, Santa Ana, California, USA. **Recognition:** WBO. **Referee:** John Thomas.
Fight Summary: Contesting the inaugural title, Leon (147) and Garcia (147) quickly got down to work, both men giving and taking solid blows before the latter was floored by a big right hand. Back on his feet, Garcia looked shaky. When another big right sent him down again the referee dispensed with the count, stopping the fight with two seconds of the opening round remaining.

Further to Leon relinquishing the WBO version of the title in October in order to try for a crack at one of the other organisation's crowns, Manning Galloway and Al Hamza (Veabro Boykin) were selected to meet up in order to find a new champion. Galloway, an experienced fighter who had been a pro since 1978, had 41 wins from 53 contests, beating Al Long, Hamza, Rollin Williams and Said Skouma, while his opponent had 23 wins from 28 contests, but had beaten no one of note. Neither man was rated in *The Ring* magazine's top ten.

15 September 1989. Marlon Starling w pts 12 Yung-Kil Chung.
Venue: Civic Centre, Hartford, Connecticut, USA. **Recognition:** WBC. **Referee:** Arthur Mercante.
Scorecards: 119-109, 119-110, 117-112.
Fight Summary: Although dictating the fight virtually from start to finish, Starling (146), unable to put his challenger on the floor, had to be satisfied with an easy points win. Chung (147), who proved to be tough and resilient, never gave up trying and was always in front of Starling, but he lacked the know-how to get to his man effectively, many of his best punches being taken on the arms and shoulders. In the latter stages, having realised that he was not going to knock Chung out, Starling contented himself with putting more points in the bag while coasting home.

20 September 1989. Simon Brown w rsc 2 Bobby Joe Young.
Venue: War Memorial Auditorium, Rochester, New York, USA. **Recognition:** IBF. **Referee:** Joe Santarpia.
Fight Summary: Back in the ring for the first time in 14 months, the game Young (146½) gave it his best shot but was no match for Brown (146¼), who rode out the first-round storm and had a good look at his challenger before picking it up in the second. Coming out quickly, Brown soon got down to business, having Young's legs going when belting in hurtful left hooks before putting the latter down with a heavy right. Although Young got up and was allowed to continue, even when the referee was jumping between the two men to make a stoppage on the 2.39 mark after the challenger had been sent reeling from a left hook Brown fired in a big right that sent him crashing.

13 October 1989. Mark Breland w rsc 2 Mauro Martelli.
Venue: Skating Palace, Geneva, Switzerland. **Recognition:** WBA. **Referee:** John Coyle.
Fight Summary: Back in action after a knee operation, Breland (146½) soon got his left jab working and had reddened the challenger's face considerably by the end of the first round. Although Martelli (146½) had a reputation as a sound boxer he seemed to have no defence against Breland's whiplash punches, and following a

battery of blows to the head the Swiss-Italian, now cut under the left eye, was floored and stopped after 1.15 of the second session.

9 November 1989. Simon Brown w pts 12 Luis Santana.
Venue: Civic Centre, Springfield, Massachusetts, USA. **Recognition:** IBF. **Referee:** Matt Mullaney.
Scorecards: 119-110, 120-108, 120-105.
Fight Summary: That he beat his challenger was no surprise, but being unable to put him down obviously rankled with Brown (146) who eventually had to settle for the points. There was never any doubt about Brown winning, but even though he hit Santana (146) with his best punches, thudding left hooks and right hands to head and body, the tough Dominican never looked like going down, even making many of the rounds fairly competitive. By the sixth Santana was carrying a badly swollen left eye that bothered him for the rest of the contest, but although virtually one-eyed he managed to keep going much to the chagrin of Brown.

10 December 1989. Mark Breland w rsc 4 Fujio Ozaki.
Venue: Korakuen Hall, Tokyo, Japan. **Recognition:** WBA. **Referee:** Julio Alvarado.
Fight Summary: Proving much too clever for his challenger, and six inches to the good, Breland (146¼) used speedy left jabs and solid overarm rights to undo his man in the opening two sessions having hurt him with the first worthwhile punch of the contest. Although Ozaki (146¾) began his fight-back in the third, having easily avoided the wild punches coming his way towards the end of the round Breland had opened up a bad cut on the Japanese's right eye. After coming out for the fourth with his damaged eye patched up within moments Ozaki had been caught again by stinging lefts, and with the eye pouring blood the ringside doctor advised the referee to make the stoppage with just 35 seconds on the clock.

15 December 1989. Manning Galloway w pts 12 Al Hamza (Veabro Boykin).
Venue: The Coliseum, Yabucoa, Puerto Rico. **Recognition:** WBO.
Fight Summary: Fighting for the title vacated by Genaro Leon it did not take Galloway long to impress himself on Hamza, who was fooled by the southpaw style and was a sucker for the straight left. Moving well, Galloway often stepped inside with quick punches to take his man by surprise. Never at risk, Galloway won going away on the cards.

3 March 1990. Mark Breland w rsc 3 Lloyd Honeyghan.
Venue: The Arena, Wembley, London, England. **Recognition:** WBA. **Referee:** Julio Alvarado.
Fight Summary: After catching Breland (146½) heavily with the first punch of the fight, a looping right hander, the challenger was put under pressure from thereon in prior to being rescued by the referee after 2.15 of the third. With Breland jabbing and moving fluently, Honeyghan (147) appeared to be at a loss, and after being put down heavily by a long left he just about made it to the end of the first round. Cut on the left eye and confused, he came out for the second to face more of the same before ending the session on the floor for the third time, having been dropped earlier on. The nightmare continued for Honeyghan as Breland put him down three more times in the third, the last time coming when he was caught by almost 30 punches that were unopposed. With Honeyghan left dazed on the canvas, the referee made sure he would not be fighting anymore that night.

1 April 1990. Simon Brown w rsc 10 Tyrone Trice.
Venue: The Armoury, Washington DC, USA. **Recognition:** IBF. **Referee:** Steve Smoger.
Fight Summary: While the contest was not as brutal as their previous one there was still plenty of hard-hitting action to satisfy most of the fans, and the champion again proved to have the measure of Trice (147). Instead of boxing Trice made the mistake of trying to outpunch Brown (146½), always being second best despite opening up a cut over the champion's left eye in the sixth. By the eighth the writing was on the wall for Trice. After getting to his feet, having being dropped by a left hook to the head, he desperately hung on to get to the end of the session. Although Brown coasted through the ninth he wasted no time in the tenth, ripping into Trice with both hands, and following a burst of heavy punches that left the unprotected challenger in a bad way the referee called a halt 51 seconds into the round.

8 July 1990. Aaron Davis w co 9 Mark Breland.
Venue: Harrah's Hotel & Casino, Reno, Nevada, USA. **Recognition:** WBA. **Referee:** Mills Lane.
Fight Summary: Despite having a seven-inch-reach advantage on his challenger, Breland (146¼) still had difficulty in keeping him at bay, being rocked in virtually every round. By the third Davis (146) had a swollen right eye that would require regular inspections by the doctor, while Breland's left eye was also swelling up. As the fight progressed Davis seemed to be getting the upper hand, but as Breland began to come back into it the eighth saw both men in trouble. Somehow refreshed, Davis came out for the ninth swinging with the left before Breland got to him again, but towards the end of the session a desperate right from the challenger smashed into the latter's face, leaving him to be counted out on the 2.56 mark.

19 August 1990. Maurice Blocker w pts 12 Marlon Starling.
Venue: Bally's Park Place Hotel, Reno, Nevada, USA. **Recognition:** WBC. **Referee:** Mills Lane.
Scorecards: 115-113, 115-113, 114-114.
Fight Summary: Utilising a four-and-a-half-inch-reach advantage, the challenger came out firing left jabs, continuing to slot them in all night as Starling (146) seemed to have no defence against them. With Blocker (146) also outhitting Starling on the inside, it was not until the fifth that the latter actually connected with one of his right-hand specials. By the eighth Blocker's lefts were really paying off as Starling's left eye suddenly poured blood, and while the champion started to work well in an effort to cut back the deficit at the final bell he knew that he had not done enough.

25 August 1990. Manning Galloway w pts 12 Nika Khumalo.
Venue: Youth Centre, Lewiston, Maine, USA. **Recognition:** WBO. **Referee:** Roberto Ramirez.
Scorecards: 115-112, 115-112, 115-112.
Fight Summary: Although the crude challenger made the fight he did not land enough scoring blows to get himself in front, while the southpaw Galloway (147) often frustrated him with his defensive capabilities and made for a difficult target. Finally, in the eighth, Khumalo (145½) hurt Galloway with a left hook-right cross, the force of the blow putting him down for 'three'. Khumalo also landed well in the ninth and 12th, but was never able to put enough punches together to swing things around as Galloway eased his way to a relatively lackadaisical points win.

19 January 1991. Meldrick Taylor w pts 12 Aaron Davis.
Venue: Convention Centre, Atlantic City, New Jersey, USA. **Recognition:** WBA. **Referee:** Arthur Mercante.
Scorecards: 115-112, 116-111, 116-111.
Fight Summary: Outclassing the champion in every department and proving to be a multi-talented fighter, Taylor (145) started with cracking left hooks and solid rights to head and body before continually increasing the tempo. It was not that Davis (145½) was not working hard, but he was being outflanked and outpunched, and despite showing great determination he lacked the tools to stop Taylor's advance. Towards the end, however, with Taylor moving more and more out of range, although Davis was occasionally able to catch up with him, especially when doing good work in the 11th, he was unable to close the gap.

15 February 1991. Manning Galloway w rtd 8 Gert Bo Jacobsen.
Venue: Town Hall, Randers, Denmark. **Recognition:** WBO. **Referee:** Mariano Soto.
Fight Summary: Using his considerable height and reach to good advantage, the southpaw champion was in total control of Jacobsen (147) from the fifth, having come back from a standing 'eight' count in the third after he went down from more of a slip than a punch. In that same round, Jacobsen received a cut on the left eye that would eventually get so bad that he would be forced to retire at the end of the eighth. Although Galloway (145½) was also cut on the left eye in the fifth the damage would not worsen too drastically, and in the seventh he dropped Jacobsen on one knee with a left to the head. With the doctor continually inspecting the Dane's dangerously swollen eye in the eighth it was no surprise when his corner decided not to send him out for the ninth.

18 March 1991. Simon Brown w rsc 10 Maurice Blocker.
Venue: Mirage Hotel, Las Vegas, Nevada, USA. **Recognition:** IBF/WBC. **Referee:** Mills Lane.
Fight Summary: Boxing brilliantly with the long left lead, Blocker (146) came within two rounds of unifying a couple of titles before he ran out of steam in the ninth and was taken apart in the tenth. It was only in the tenth

that Brown (147) had any joy, having had to wait his turn, but when it came he took it with both hands, a right-left to the head putting Blocker down. On getting up and hoping to get through the session, Blocker looked to have a chance as Brown missed with just about everything he threw until tremendous left and right uppercuts saw the former staggering around the ring prior to being stopped on the 2.10 mark.

After Brown relinquished the IBF version of the title in May to concentrate on the WBC crown, Blocker was booked to meet Glenwood Brown in order to find a new champion.

17 May 1991. Manning Galloway w rtd 7 Racheed Lawal.
Venue: KB Hall, Copenhagen, Denmark. **Recognition:** WBO. **Referee:** Ismael Fernandez.
Fight Summary: Having won 19 of his 20 contests prior to challenging for the title, the Sierra Leone-born Lawal (143) was expected to give a good account of himself against the wily, shifty Galloway (146½) in front of the home fans. For the opening three rounds it was relatively even, but after that it became one-sided as the southpaw champion began to open up, catching Lawal with ease. It quickly became apparent that Lawal, with the build of a lightweight, did not have the strength to contain Galloway who was far superior. Although he was not floored, after the fans turned on him Lawal retired in his corner at the end of the seventh. At the time of Lawal's retirement the scorecards read 69-65, 69-65, 68-65, all in favour of Galloway.

1 June 1991. Meldrick Taylor w pts 12 Luis Garcia.
Venue: Radisson Resort, Palm Springs, California, USA. **Recognition:** WBA. **Referee:** Lou Moret.
Scorecards: 118-112, 115-113, 114-117.
Fight Summary: Taking on the unbeaten Garcia (146¾) in his first defence proved more difficult for Taylor (146¾) than those around him imagined, the Venezuelan putting up a great fight. The lanky Garcia, who turned out to have an excellent left jab, certainly knew how to use it to his advantage. He had also won 17 of his last 19 fights inside the distance. Although Taylor was always one step ahead he could never take it easy as the hardy Garcia was always likely to counter him. However, the champion had that extra bit of class that won it for him.

15 September 1991. Manning Galloway w pts 12 Jeff Malcolm.
Venue: Jupiter's Casino, Broadbeach, Australia. **Recognition:** WBO. **Referee:** Rudy Ortega.
Scorecards: 118-109, 116-112, 118-110.
Fight Summary: Snapping southpaw jabs through the challenger's guard during the opening four rounds, Galloway (146½) ultimately proved too classy an opponent for the Aussie before eventually easing off. Despite fighting in spurts, Galloway had the speed that allowed him to get in and out without taking too many risks, and although Malcolm (145¼) scored well at times he was always travelling second best.

4 October 1991. Maurice Blocker w pts 12 Glenwood Brown.
Venue: Resorts International, Atlantic City, New Jersey, USA. **Recognition:** IBF. **Referee:** Joe Cortez.
Scorecards: 117-111, 118-111, 114-115.
Fight Summary: Contesting the title given up by Simon Brown, the huge height-and-reach advantage that Blocker (147) had over Brown (147) was a major factor in him becoming a champion again. Towering over his rival, Blocker put out the jab all night while having little difficulty in avoiding punches coming his way apart from when Brown turned it into a brawl, tactics that suited him. In the ninth Brown began to sink in the body punches, having Blocker looking uncomfortable before he was able to get back on an even keel. The last two rounds were a bit of a letdown as both men were tired from their earlier exertions. Surprisingly, one of the judges, Rocky Castellani, a former top middleweight, made Brown the winner, but luckily for Blocker the other two judges had been at the right fight.

29 November 1991. Buddy McGirt w pts 12 Simon Brown.
Venue: Mirage Hotel, Las Vegas, Nevada, USA. **Recognition:** WBC. **Referee:** Mills Lane.
Scorecards: 119-108, 117-110, 117-110.
Fight Summary: Gliding in, getting his punches off and moving away from the champion before he could be caught, McGirt (145) boxed brilliantly, especially up until the sixth when he was forced to take left hands to the body. By this time Brown (147) was bleeding from a cut over the right eye, which was beginning to close. Brown was also turning southpaw to try his luck, but in the tenth he was dropped by a left hook to the jaw before making it to the

bell. The last couple of sessions saw Brown all at sea on occasion, with the referee appearing to be ready to halt the fight before it eventually ran its course.

14 December 1991. Manning Galloway w pts 12 Nika Khumalo.
Venue: Green Point Stadium, Cape Town, South Africa. **Recognition:** WBO. **Referee:** Al Munoz.
Scorecards: 115-113, 116-113, 112-115.
Fight Summary: Instead of keeping the southpaw champion under constant pressure, Khumalo (145¾) went looking to land single shots while missing several good opportunities. Even when he dropped Galloway (147) in the eighth after turning southpaw, Khumalo never pressed home his advantage, and he continually struggled to get past the champion's reach despite hurting his man again in the ninth. With there never being much between them, had Khumalo applied the expected push the title would surely have changed hands.

18 January 1992. Meldrick Taylor w pts 12 Glenwood Brown.
Venue: Civic Centre, Philadelphia, Pennsylvania, USA. **Recognition:** WBA. **Referee:** Rudy Battle.
Scorecards: 114-113, 116-113, 116-113.
Fight Summary: Forcing Taylor (146¼) to come to him, when appreciating that fighting in front of his own fans he wanted to please, was a shrewd move on behalf of Brown (146½). And it almost paid off after a cracking left hook to the jaw in the first round had the champion over. Eventually, Taylor began working his way in behind the left jab, but he was again decked in the fourth when a right to the ribs sent him down for a flash knockdown. Subsequently, Taylor, more alert to the counters, began to gradually take control of the fight despite having further nasty moments, his left hand working well as Brown's swollen right eye testified at the final bell.

25 June 1992. Buddy McGirt w pts 12 Patrizio Oliva.
Venue: Lincola Aquaflash, Naples, Italy. **Recognition:** WBC. **Referee:** Arthur Mercante.
Scorecards: 118-111, 116-112, 118-110.
Fight Summary: Making his first defence against an awkward, long-armed opponent, McGirt (144) eventually decided that his best form of attack was to work the body. The taller man of the two, Oliva (146¼) had certainly made life difficult for McGirt with his holding tactics, but apart from a bad moment in the eighth round when he was hurt by a right to the head the champion was rarely worried. By the halfway stage McGirt was hammering away at Oliva's body, and in the 11th he had the latter in some trouble before coasting through the 12th to a well-earned points win.

25 July 1992. Manning Galloway w pts 12 Pat Barrett.
Venue: G-Mex Centre, Manchester, England. **Recognition:** WBO. **Referee:** Stan Christodoulou.
Scorecards: 116-112, 119-111, 116-112.
Fight Summary: Despite struggling to make the weight, the cagey southpaw champion did not struggle in any way, simply knowing too much for Barrett (144¾) who was unable to fathom out the defensive map in front of him. Barrett did force Galloway (147) to stumble to the floor in the third after connecting with a long right to the pit of the stomach, but he was unable to follow any advantage up. In the seventh round, after a clash of heads left Galloway badly cut on the left eye he refused to stand still from thereon in, forcing Barrett to chase him to the final bell without having any success whatsoever.

28 August 1992. Maurice Blocker w pts 12 Luis Garcia.
Venue: Trump Plaza Hotel, Atlantic City, New Jersey, USA. **Recognition:** IBF. **Referee:** Frank Cappuccino.
Scorecards: 115-110, 116-110, 112-115.
Fight Summary: Fighting aggressively from the opening bell, the challenger forced Blocker (147) on to the back foot in the first four rounds, never giving him the space or time in which to work. By the fifth Blocker was having to fight back or be overwhelmed, and in this session he knocked Garcia (147) down three times with left hooks without being able to halt the latter's advance. As the IBF did not have the 'three knockdowns in a round' ruling in place, far from being discouraged Garcia tore into Blocker, continually pressurising him and pushing him back. Although Blocker got his jab working well towards the end he spent the last couple of rounds totally on the back foot when most bystanders expected him to be hunting for points, and many, including one of the judges, felt that he had not done enough to win.

31 October 1992. Crisanto Espana w rsc 8 Meldrick Taylor.
Venue: Exhibition Centre, Earls Court, London, England. **Recognition:** WBA. **Referee:** John Coyle.
Fight Summary: Coming off a four-round loss to Terry Norris in a battle for the WBC junior middleweight title, Taylor (146½) hardly looked like the man he once was when defending his welterweight crown against Espana (147). Although he started quite well with the jab, from the second round onwards he found himself unable to get inside Espana's longer reach without being caught and was soon taking left hooks and right hands. By the fourth, Taylor was not moving with any confidence, but he began to have a bit more success until taking time out after being dropped by a low blow in the sixth and then coming under fire for the remainder of the session. Now cut under the right eye and stiff-legged, Taylor was tagged heavily throughout the seventh before being dropped by a right hand-left uppercut combination in the eighth. He was then rescued by the referee on the 2.11 mark after getting up and running into a battery of punches that left him defenceless.

27 November 1992. Manning Galloway tdraw 1 Gert Bo Jacobsen.
Venue: Town Hall, Randers, Denmark. **Recognition:** WBO. **Referee:** Ismael Fernandez.
Fight Summary: The fight had not long been started when there was an accidental coming together of heads that opened a cut on Jacobsen's temple and led to the contest being halted after blood continued to spurt unabated from the wound. WBO rules stated that because the fight had failed to go beyond the third round it should be classified as a no-decision (technical draw for our purposes), and under those conditions the officials were looking for Galloway (146½) to defend against Jacobsen (145) as soon as the wound had healed and it was convenient for another show to go ahead.

12 January 1993. Buddy McGirt w pts 12 Genaro Leon.
Venue: Paramount Theatre, Manhattan, NYC, New York, USA. **Recognition:** WBC. **Referee:** Arthur Mercante Jnr.
Scorecards: 118-113, 117-114, 117-111.
Fight Summary: Regardless of the fact that he injured his left arm ten days before the fight was due to take place, the champion had a reasonably comfortable time against Leon (147) apart from in the final two rounds. Although Leon was the bigger puncher of the pair, McGirt (147) had far too many skills for him, and it was not long before he was becoming frustrated and being deducted a point in the third for hitting and holding. Up to the end of the tenth it had been relatively easy for McGirt as he weaved around Leon's fists without being unduly troubled, but after taking some heavy blows in the 11th he was given little respite in the 12th as the Mexican came out fast. Driven around the ring and hurt, McGirt was forced to fight back in order to save himself. And at the final bell the two men were still banging away at each other.

12 February 1993. Gert Bo Jacobsen w pts 12 Manning Galloway.
Venue: Town Hall, Randers, Denmark. **Recognition:** WBO. **Referee:** Ismael Fernandez.
Scorecards: 115-113, 115-113, 116-113.
Fight Summary: With this being third time lucky for Jacobsen (146¾) in his quest to beat the clever southpaw champion, he made a reasonable start, landing impressively to the body while keeping up the pressure. Meanwhile, Galloway (146¾) was showboating and it was not until the fifth when Jacobsen began to suffer from a swollen left eye that he came back into it more. Jacobsen was still going well into the final third, but Galloway was landing the harder punches even if he was continuing to work sporadically. Although Galloway came with a rush in the last couple of rounds, his hit-and-run style obviously did not impress the judges enough to give him the decision.

When Jacobsen relinquished the WBO version of the championship in October because of illness, the week before he was due to defend against Eamonn Loughran, a Loughran v Lorenzo Smith match was hastily made to decide the vacant title.

6 March 1993. Pernell Whitaker w pts 12 Buddy McGirt.
Venue: Madison Square Garden, Manhattan, NYC, New York, USA. **Recognition:** WBC. **Referee:** Larry Hazzard.
Scorecards: 117-111, 115-113, 115-114.
Fight Summary: Having gone reasonably well for the opening six rounds against Whitaker (146¼), after it could be seen that the champion was struggling with an old injury to his left arm, the punches that had kept him in

contention up until then, the left hook and jab, were going to be at a premium from there on. Even without the injury it would have been difficult for McGirt (147) to beat the highly-skilled southpaw, and at that moment it was bordering on the impossible. Although McGirt managed to stay in the fight it was reckoned by the end of the ninth he would need a knockout to retain his title, and while he won two of the remaining three sessions he never came close to stopping Whitaker.

5 May 1993. Crisanto Espana w pts 12 Rodolfo Aguilar.
Venue: Ulster Hall, Belfast, Northern Ireland. **Recognition:** WBA. **Referee:** John Coyle.
Scorecards: 117-111, 120-109, 119-110.
Fight Summary: Although retaining his title against the southpaw Aguilar (145¾) it was not a night to remember for Espana (147) as he was handicapped by sore knuckles on his left hand and showed no real sense of urgency. Adding to his woes he could not floor or even hurt Aguilar, who was not expected to last long, and had to be content with a fairly comprehensive points win. At the end of the contest Aguilar's right eye was virtually closed, having ballooned during the last round, but he had done his best despite his limitations.

19 June 1993. Felix Trinidad w rsc 2 Maurice Blocker.
Venue: Sports Arena, San Diego, California, USA. **Recognition:** IBF. **Referee:** Robert Byrd.
Fight Summary: Two inches the taller man, Blocker (146) used his superior height and reach to block the challenger's punches in the early stages of the opening round, but towards the end he was badly stunned by a right to the jaw and follow-up combinations. The second session saw Trinidad (145½) go on the attack right from the bell and having pounded Blocker non-stop a crushing right-left-right sent him down, whereupon the referee called the fight off immediately, the finish being timed at 1.19.

6 August 1993. Felix Trinidad w rsc 1 Luis Garcia.
Venue: Ruben Rodriguez Coliseum, Bayamon, Puerto Rico. **Recognition:** IBF. **Referee:** Waldemar Schmidt.
Fight Summary: Making his first defence less than two months after winning the title Trinidad (146½) did not hang around against Garcia (147), dropping his challenger after just 75 seconds with a left hook, aided by a solid right to the jaw. Although Garcia survived that one he was dumped three more times in the opening session and halted with 29 seconds left on the clock. A good puncher, Garcia was never given the chance to get going, let alone damage Trinidad.

10 September 1993. Pernell Whitaker drew 12 Julio Cesar Chavez.
Venue: Alamo Dome, San Antonio, Texas, USA. **Recognition:** WBC. **Referee:** Joe Cortez.
Scorecards: 115-113, 115-115, 115-115.
Fight Summary: In front of 60,000 paying customers Whitaker (145) retained his title after drawing with Chavez (142), but following the result it was difficult to find anyone who felt that the latter had come anywhere near getting a draw. And if one of the judges, Mickey Vann, had not taken a point away from Whitaker in the sixth for a low blow at his own discretion the champion would have won, rather than shared the verdict. Although Chavez did reasonably well in the earlier sessions Whitaker was always around, and from the seventh through to the ninth he was firmly in control, avoiding the challenger's rushes and planting southpaw rights and lefts to head and body from his crouching stance. While the last round saw Whitaker on the run after being thumbed, despite it being Chavez's best period he never came close to dropping his man.

9 October 1993. Crisanto Espana w rsc 10 Donovan Boucher.
Venue: Old Trafford Stadium, Manchester, England. **Recognition:** WBA. **Referee:** John Coyle.
Fight Summary: Taking the fight to Espana (147) from the opening bell, the challenger found to his cost that his rival's left jab was a potent weapon, and after being speared on numerous occasions and hurt with solid rights a crunching right hand to the head dropped him in the second round. Never in with a shout, Boucher (147) kept Espana busy for a while before being floored by a left hook in the seventh. Somehow, the courageous Boucher made it into the tenth, but a short while after being decked for the third time the referee had seen enough and rescued him on the 2.31 mark.

16 October 1993. Eamonn Loughran w pts 12 Lorenzo Smith.
Venue: King's Hall, Belfast, Northern Ireland. **Recognition:** WBO. **Referee:** Knud Jensen.
Scorecards: 118-110, 116-112, 117-112.
Fight Summary: After preparing to challenge Gert Bo Jacobsen, when the latter was taken ill and relinquished the title Loughran found himself meeting Smith, who had been hastily drafted in. With the fight now involving the vacant title, and Loughran (146) forcing the issue all the way, as early as the opening session a clash of heads saw Smith cut on the right eye. The story of the fight was almost the same round after round; Loughran continually advancing, hooking to the body before going for the head, with Smith (146½) jabbing away with the left and countering with right crosses. It was in the latter stages that Loughran's strength really told, and he made a sustained effort in the 12th when catching Smith again and again to make sure of the decision. Although Loughran was warned on more than one occasion to keep his punches up and was lucky not to have had points deducted he fully deserved the win.

23 October 1993. Felix Trinidad w rsc 10 Anthony Stephens.
Venue: Convention Centre, Fort Lauderdale, Florida, USA. **Recognition:** IBF. **Referee:** Bill Connors.
Fight Summary: This was a disappointing performance by a highly-touted champion, and he even had to get off the deck to beat Stephens (145) who had him over in the third with a big right despite it not being recorded by the referee. Trinidad (147) was then sent crashing into a corner after getting to his feet, it being noticeable that Stephens was happy to trade with him at that stage. Even when Stephens tired and began to take some punishment he was still prepared to swap punches with Trinidad whenever he could. Cut above the left eye in the eighth, Stephens was still in there making life difficult for Trinidad, but after taking some big punches in the tenth he was sent crashing by a left uppercut to the jaw before the referee called it off with just one second of the session remaining.

22 January 1994. Eamonn Loughran w pts 12 Alessandro Duran.
Venue: King's Hall, Belfast, Northern Ireland. **Recognition:** WBO. **Referee:** Ron Lipton.
Scorecards: 117-111, 117-112, 117-112.
Fight Summary: Although the champion won widely on points he was extremely unimpressive against the crafty, awkward Duran (144¼). Right from the start Duran gave Loughran all the trouble he could handle, often catching him napping with sneak rights to the head. Although stretched, Loughran (145¾) continued to pile forward, throwing left hooks, but Duran, badly cut over the right eye in the 12th, proved to be a durable character who only gave ground when it suited him. As in previous contests Loughran again got away with low blows, but may not have been so fortunate had the contest taken place in another country.

On 13 August, Manning Galloway stopped Anthony Jones inside six rounds at the Ruben Rodriguez Coliseum, Bayamon, Puerto Rico to win the vacant WBO 'interim' title, a victory that would see him become Loughran's next challenger.

29 January 1994. Felix Trinidad w pts 12 Hector Camacho.
Venue: MGM Grand, Las Vegas, Nevada, USA. **Recognition:** IBF. **Referee:** Joe Cortez.
Scorecards: 119-106, 117-109, 116-110.
Fight Summary: Ten years younger than his southpaw challenger, and with height-and-reach advantages, after Trinidad (147) hurt Camacho (147) with a left-right to the chin in the third he continued to hunt him down despite finding it difficult when facing an opponent whose sole intent was to survive in any manner possible. Both men had points deducted for holding, Trinidad in the fifth and Camacho in the tenth. Having hurt Camacho in the sixth, ninth and tenth sessions, but unable to finish him off, the champion stated the obvious when saying that he found his fellow Puerto Rican too elusive to nail down.

9 April 1994. Pernell Whitaker w pts 12 Santos Cardona.
Venue: The Scope, Norfolk, Virginia, USA. **Recognition:** WBC. **Referee:** Al Rothenberg.
Scorecards: 119-109, 119-111, 119-109.
Fight Summary: Easily winning the battle of the jabs, the southpaw champion put on a great display against the very good Cardona (146½), and despite having to take the occasional solid right hand he never once looked like

losing his title. Although his left eye began to swell in the sixth, Whitaker (147) kept on pumping in the right leads followed by sharp lefts. By the 11th Cardona was stumbling around the ring, seemingly lost. With the right lead continuing to find its mark, at the final bell Cardona was still there bravely doing his best, which unfortunately for him had not been good enough.

4 June 1994. Ike Quartey w rsc 11 Crisanto Espana.
Venue: Marcel Cerdan Sports Palace, Paris, France. **Recognition:** WBA. **Referee:** Julio Alvarado.
Fight Summary: Defending for the third time the long-armed Espana (147) made a good start when outscoring Quartey (147), but by the third round the latter was beginning to get to the champion. In the fourth Espana was cut on the left eye. It was also noticeable that the Ghanaian was pacing himself, whacking in punches to head and body whenever in range, and by the sixth he was even getting home with the jab. Despite being hurt in the seventh Quartey pressed on, finally getting his reward when a batch of heavy punches left Espana shaken up before being given the mandatory count in the 11th. Following that, Quartey tore into Espana, and when the latter eventually failed to fight back, being defenceless, the referee called a halt just as he slumped to the floor.

17 September 1994. Felix Trinidad w rsc 4 Luis Ramon Campas.
Venue: MGM Grand, Las Vegas, Nevada, USA. **Recognition:** IBF. **Referee:** Richard Steele.
Fight Summary: Smashed to the floor by a short left hook in the second round the champion was forced to fight back hard as Campas (146½) went after him. It was just the same in the third as both men let their punches go. Something had to give as Trinidad (146½) rocked Campas with heavy punches in the fourth, only for the latter to come on with hurtful body blows that would have finished off lesser men than the champion. However, Trinidad showed he was made of stern stuff as he hammered back and after busting Campas's nose a full dozen big shots thundered into the latter to leave him totally defenceless, but still standing, before the referee called it off on the 2.41 mark.

1 October 1994. Ike Quartey w rsc 5 Alberto Cortes.
Venue: Cosets Arena, Carpentras, France. **Recognition:** WBA. **Referee:** Stan Christodoulou.
Fight Summary: It did not augur well for the southpaw challenger when Quartey (144¾) had him bending over in some agony as early as the first round, and it did not get any better for the Argentine as he was gradually softened up by big punches and demoralised in the next few sessions. By the fifth Cortes (146) was in real trouble, almost going through the ropes on one occasion before dropping down on one knee. When the referee saw Cortes' corner throwing in the towel he halted the contest, the finish being timed at 2.03.

1 October 1994. Pernell Whitaker w pts 12 Buddy McGirt.
Venue: The Scope, Norfolk, Virginia, USA. **Recognition:** WBC. **Referee:** Larry O'Connell.
Scorecards: 117-110, 117-113, 118-112.
Fight Summary: Once again McGirt (146) showed that he had lost the use of his wonderful left hook through injury, and although he put the southpaw champion down with a lunging right in the second he was steadily outboxed over the duration. The moment Whitaker (147) got the right jab working, McGirt, whose left eye began to swell early in the fifth, spent the rest of the evening chasing shadows. McGirt's surgeon, who had said that the fighter would find it difficult with his left shoulder in such bad shape, was proved correct.

10 December 1994. Eamonn Loughran w tdec 5 Manning Galloway.
Venue: G-Mex Centre, Manchester, England. **Recognition:** WBO. **Referee:** Luis Fernandez.
Scorecards: 39-37, 39-37, 40-37.
Fight Summary: The southpaw challenger made the worst possible start against Loughran (146½) when falling short with the jab and being slammed by left hooks in the opening two rounds before both men were cut after an accidental clash of heads. While Loughran was cut on the forehead, Galloway, who had his right eye damaged, was worse off. And when another coming together of heads opened a cut above and below his left eye in the third the American was really up against it. With Galloway bleeding profusely in the fourth, although he came out for the fifth the referee called it off without a punch being thrown in that session and went to the cards.

10 December 1994. Felix Trinidad w rsc 8 Oba Carr.
Venue: Baseball Stadium, Monterrey, Mexico. **Recognition:** IBF. **Referee:** Robert Gonzalez.
Fight Summary: Despite being dropped in the second round by a straight right, the champion was quickly up, and after being outjabbed by Carr (145) in the third he came on in the next session to get his left going while hammering solid rights. By the sixth Trinidad (146½) was catching Carr repeatedly with long rights to the head and although he somehow survived a bad seventh the latter was sent down by two cracking rights to the head in the eighth. Having taken the mandatory count and back in the firing line, Carr was soon over from another right, and not long after was down again. Trinidad now had the bit between the teeth, and when Carr got up for the third time he was hammered by both hands until the referee called a halt with 19 seconds of the session remaining.

4 March 1995. Ike Quartey w rsc 4 Jung-Oh Park.
Venue: Convention Centre, Atlantic City, New Jersey, USA. **Recognition:** WBA. **Referee:** Earl Morton.
Fight Summary: Making a brave bid to land the title the challenger was up against it from the opening bell, taking terrific punishment in the first three minutes as Quartey (147) ripped punches in from both hands. Park (147) even succeeded in forcing Quartey back with clusters of blows in the second, but despite the latter returning accurate, hurtful counters he brushed them aside. However, by the fourth Quartey was landing with ease, and at 2.35 of the session the fight was stopped after Park, now cut on the right eye, had been forced back by heavy jabs and was not responding.

8 April 1995. Felix Trinidad w rsc 2 Roger Turner.
Venue: Caesar's Palace, Las Vegas, Nevada, USA. **Recognition:** IBF. **Referee:** Mitch Halpern.
Fight Summary: Starting the opening session nervously, the challenger flicked out the left jab from distance, half expecting Trinidad (147) to counter, before circling the ring and scurrying away. Coming out with more purpose in the second, with Trinidad detecting no danger from Turner (147), he went to work before dumping the latter for 'nine' with a heavy left hook. On the resumption Trinidad went in throwing punches, and after Turner had been rocked and smashed into a corner by a slamming right the referee made a fully justified stoppage at 2.28 of the session.

27 May 1995. Eamonn Loughran tdraw 3 Angel Beltre.
Venue: King's Hall, Belfast, Northern Ireland. **Recognition:** WBO. **Referee:** Roberto Ramirez.
Fight Summary: Having made a decent start, winning the opening two rounds, Loughran (147) began to hook solidly to the challenger's body in the third while ignoring the counters coming his way. Following a borderline left that crashed into his body, a furious Beltre (145¾) responded with a fast burst of punches before he turned away from Loughran with blood seeping from a long and deep cut on his right eye. After being led to his corner for an inspection by the ringside doctor, at 2.23 of the session the fight was over. The decision was first announced as a win for Loughran (w rsc 3), but on closer inspection the WBO decided that the injury to Beltre had been caused by an accidental clash of heads. Thus, after going to the rule book they changed the verdict to that of no contest (technical draw for our purposes) as the bout had been halted prior to the end of the third round. They then ordered that the pair meet again.

23 August 1995. Ike Quartey w rsc 4 Andrew Murray.
Venue: Sports Palace, Le Cannet, France. **Recognition:** WBA. **Referee:** Carlos Berrocal.
Fight Summary: Although the southpaw challenger started well when outworking Quartey with snappy punches from both hands, right on the bell to end the first round he was dropped by a right to the jaw and barely beat the count. Despite Murray showing a good recovery he was always running second best to Quartey, and when the latter opened up in the third the man from Guyana went back to his corner cut on the right eye. Forty-four seconds into the fourth the referee called it off after a solid right from Quartey sent Murray stumbling backwards, bleeding badly from the left eye.

26 August 1995. Eamonn Loughran w rsc 6 Tony Gannarelli.
Venue: Ulster Hall, Belfast, Northern Ireland. **Recognition:** WBO. **Referee:** Roy Francis.
Fight Summary: Strangely taking the contest whilst on his honeymoon, the little-known Gannarelli (146) probably wished that he was back home on going back to his corner at the end of the first round, both eyes looking sore and

blowing heavily after tasting the champion's punches. However, the American got better as the contest progressed, regardless of the fact that he was being edged out in every session. In the sixth Loughran (147) began to open up, throwing hard rights and left hooks, and a heavy right to the head saw Gannarelli down on one knee before the referee had seen enough and called it off on the 1.28 mark.

26 August 1995. Pernell Whitaker w pts 12 Gary Jacobs.
Venue: Convention Centre, Atlantic City, New Jersey, USA. **Recognition:** WBC. **Referee:** Ron Lipton.
Scorecards: 118-108, 118-109, 117-109.
Fight Summary: Closer than the scoreline indicated, the challenger gave Whitaker (147) a run for his money in a battle of southpaws, and at times had the upper hand, especially in the third, ninth and 11th. Proving to be stronger than Whitaker, the Scot often pushed the champion around, but was also made to pay when he walked forward discarding his guard. Once Whitaker started to use the ring more in the seventh he had more success, scoring well with the jab and solid left crosses, but back came Jacobs (147) in the ninth with a series of right hooks. In the tenth Whitaker's speed was the deciding factor, but in the 11th he was on the floor after missing his target prior to Jacobs going after him with the right. The final session saw Jacobs deducted a point for holding before being dropped twice from big left crosses and saved by the final bell.

7 October 1995. Eamonn Loughran w pts 12 Angel Beltre.
Venue: Ulster Hall, Belfast, Northern Ireland. **Recognition:** WBO.
Fight Summary: Following on from their previous contest the pair were rematched, but it was really a case of the challenger boxing on the back foot with Loughran (146¼) trying to catch him. When Loughran did manage to catch up with Beltre (145½) he seemed unable to pin him down, and in the fourth after being hit with a right uppercut he emerged from a clinch with a cut on his left eye. He also hurt his right hand in that session. Regardless of his problems, and despite boxing conservatively from thereon in, Loughran eased his way past Beltre who had not got the power to take the title.

18 November 1995. Felix Trinidad w co 4 Larry Barnes.
Venue: Convention Centre, Atlantic City, New Jersey, USA. **Recognition:** IBF. **Referee:** Benjy Esteves Jnr.
Fight Summary: Much shorter than the upright champion and looking a division or two smaller as well, Barnes (146) was soon under pressure, his face already swelling when the opening round ended. Although Barnes opened up wildly in the second Trinidad (147) picked him off almost nonchalantly. Trinidad then held back until the fourth when he opened up with both hands in a bid to finish it. Ramming punches in to head and body from both hands Trinidad set about Barnes in a clinical fashion but, although wobbling his game opponent, he could not find the finishing blow until a left hook to the body saw the latter on one knee and counted out on the 2.54 mark.

18 November 1995. Pernell Whitaker w co 6 Jake Rodriguez.
Venue: Convention Centre, Atlantic City, New Jersey, USA. **Recognition:** WBC. **Referee:** Frank Cappuccino.
Fight Summary: Once a sparring partner for the champion, Rodriguez (146¼) gave it his best in a battle of southpaws, but while he showed a pretty good jab he lacked the power for the title to change hands. Once Whitaker (147) got himself going he began to send in single hard shots to Rodriguez's jaw, and although the latter stood up to them by the fifth his right eye was swelling fast. By the sixth Rodriguez running second best in every department, with Whitaker's jabs landing flush, and after taking a pounding a wide left hook to the body sent him down. Getting up at 'seven', with Rodriguez all at sea, a series of telling body shots put him down again to be counted out by the referee with 15 seconds of the session remaining.

10 February 1996. Felix Trinidad w rtd 4 Rodney Moore.
Venue: MGM Grand, Las Vegas, Nevada, USA. **Recognition:** IBF. **Referee:** Mitch Halpern.
Fight Summary: Trying to make amends for losing two previous challenges, Moore (147) started fast when firing in wild rights. There was more of the same in the second before Trinidad (147) started to break Moore up with body punches in the third as the latter tried desperately to survive. Dropped from a series of blows in the fourth, Moore got up at 'nine' before he was hit very close to the border on a couple of occasions prior to being put down again for 'nine' by a cracking left uppercut to the temple. It came as no surprise when the corner retired Moore during the interval between the fourth and fifth rounds.

12 April 1996. Ike Quartey w rsc 3 Vince Phillips.
Venue: Atlantis Casino, St Maarten, Dutch Antilles. **Recognition:** WBA. **Referee:** Julio Alvarado.
Fight Summary: Throwing a staggering 244 punches in the opening two rounds the challenger was obviously looking to overwhelm Quartey (147), but the latter merely stuck out the jab and countered whenever he could with heavy rights. Towards the end of the second Quartey was beginning to close Phillips (147) down, and in the third after biding his time he struck with the right. Having landed heavily, Quartey went after Phillips, who was looking for a breather, dropping him with a flurry of blows. On staggering up and taking a few more unnecessary punches, the contest was halted on the 2.31 mark when the referee decided that Phillips was in no fit state to continue.

12 April 1996. Pernell Whitaker w pts 12 Wilfredo Rivera.
Venue: Atlantis Casino, St Maarten, Dutch Antilles. **Recognition:** WBC. **Referee:** Larry O'Connell.
Scorecards: 116-111, 115-113, 112-115.
Fight Summary: Although he dominated early on this was a poor performance by the champion, Rivera (147) giving him problems when switching from orthodox to southpaw and finishing the stronger. Following a clash of heads in the third round Whitaker (147) was left with a swelling over the left eye and Rivera with a cut on his forehead, and as the fight wore on the latter began to catch the champion with solid blows without ever giving him grief. However, it was not a great performance by Whitaker's high standards, the eye damage obviously concerning him, but he made sure of winning by just doing enough.

13 April 1996. Jose Luis Lopez w rsc 1 Eamonn Loughran.
Venue: Everton Park Sports Centre, Liverpool, England. **Recognition:** WBO. **Referee:** Roy Francis.
Fight Summary: Despite making a more positive start than his challenger, connecting with left hooks and solid jabs, Loughran (146¾) was soon in trouble when being caught and dropped by a big left uppercut. After getting up shakily Loughran tried to regroup, but was quickly smashed down by a cracking right to the head. Although Loughran made it to his feet at 'five' Lopez (146½) dropped him for the third time, thus invoking the 'three knockdowns in a round' ruling that ended the fight after just 51 seconds.

18 May 1996. Felix Trinidad w co 5 Freddie Pendleton.
Venue: Mirage Hotel & Casino, Las Vegas, Nevada, USA. **Recognition:** IBF. **Referee:** Richard Steele.
Fight Summary: Both men came out shooting hard jabs before the champion upped the pace when beginning to open up with the right hand to catch Pendleton (147) more and more. Pendleton, though, was still boxing well. However, despite Pendleton coming on strongly in the fourth, Trinidad (147) really began to let the punches go in the fifth, and at 1.30 of the session the former was counted out after being dropped heavily by a solid left hook to the body.

7 September 1996. Felix Trinidad w rsc 6 Ray Lovato.
Venue: MGM Grand, Las Vegas, Nevada, USA. **Recognition:** IBF. **Referee:** Mitch Halpern.
Fight Summary: Moving from side to side the champion held back for a few rounds before beginning to get to Lovato (146½), but by the fifth he was nailing the latter with solid lefts and rights. Although Lovato fought back in the sixth, Trinidad (147) started firing in heavy blows to the head and body, and after backing his man up with jarring hooks and uppercuts the referee called the contest off on the 1.57 mark when the dazed challenger was not fighting back.

20 September 1996. Pernell Whitaker w pts 12 Wilfredo Rivera.
Venue: Hyatt Regency Knight Centre, Miami, Florida, USA. **Recognition:** WBC. **Referee:** Frank Santore Jnr.
Scorecards: 113-112, 115-111, 115-113.
Fight Summary: Showing signs that he was beginning to slow up a bit the southpaw champion elected to slug it out with Rivera (147) at times, nearly paying the price, especially in the fifth when he was dropped. Quickly back on his feet Whitaker (147) went after Rivera in the sixth, and after the latter had been docked a point for going low he was floored by a cracking left counter moments later. Rivera had soaked up a lot of punishment in that session, but was soon back on course. By the tenth, after Whitaker had slowed, the Puerto Rican came on strong to win three

of the last four rounds. Despite it not being enough it showed that Whitaker was not the fighter he once was and, at 32 years of age, would struggle once his legs gave up on him.

4 October 1996. Ike Quartey w pts 12 Oba Carr.
Venue: MSG Theatre, Manhattan, NYC, New York, USA. **Recognition:** WBA. **Referee:** Arthur Mercante.
Scorecards: 116-109, 117-109, 112-112.
Fight Summary: Strangely lethargic, the champion only came to life after being deducted a point for rabbit punching in the fourth. Stung into action, he began to reach Carr (147) with hard jabs and chopping right hands. Although Carr had done reasonably well up to the sixth, in the eighth it was the weary American who was deducted a point for low blows. Carr was now being hammered as Quartey (147) started to set him up with solid jabs, while also ripping in hooks and uppercuts to the head and body, but he came back well to win the tenth and 11th. In that penultimate round Carr put Quartey down after the latter slipped, and despite what certain reports claimed it was considered to be a knockdown by the judges. However, the final session saw Carr almost out from exhaustion and glad to hear the final bell.

6 October 1996. Jose Luis Lopez w rtd 5 Luis Ramon Campas.
Venue: Sports Arena, Los Angeles, California, USA. **Recognition:** WBO. **Referee:** Raul Caiz.
Fight Summary: In a battle of Mexicans it was the champion who came out on top after Campas (147) was forced to retire at the end of the fifth round, having taken a battering and carrying a badly damaged right eye. Right from the start Lopez (147) took the fight to the brawling Campas with solid jabs, and in the second a left-right-left to the jaw sent the latter crashing. Back on his feet Campas tore after Lopez, but was soon driven back. It was just a matter of time by now. When Campas kept running into left jabs and left hooks in the fourth and fifth sessions, barely able to see from his right eye, it was obvious to his corner that he was through for the night.

When Lopez forfeited the WBO version of the title in January 1997 after testing positive for marijuana, Michael Loewe and Santiago Samaniego were matched to find a new champion.

11 January 1997. Felix Trinidad w rsc 3 Kevin Lueshing.
Venue: The Arena, Nashville, Tennessee, USA. **Recognition:** IBF. **Referee:** Denny Nelson.
Fight Summary: Having just shaded the first round the challenger caused a near sensation in the second when stepping in with two heavy left hooks that floored Trinidad (147) for a count of 'two'. Unfortunately for Lueshing (146¼), unable to follow up his advantage in the third session, he was dropped by a big left hook and forced to take the mandatory 'eight' count. With Trinidad following up another heavy left sent Lueshing sprawling for a further 'eight' count before a right cross dropped him again, a situation that saw the referee call the fight off with one second of the session left without even bothering to pick up the count.

24 January 1997. Pernell Whitaker w rsc 11 Diosbelys Hurtado.
Venue: Convention Centre, Atlantic City, New Jersey, USA. **Recognition:** WBC. **Referee:** Arthur Mercante Jnr.
Fight Summary: Once again the southpaw champion disappointed but, behind on points on all three cards and very close to losing his title to Hurtado (146), he finally found the punches that mattered to force a stoppage at 1.52 of the 11th round. Down from a short right to the head within the opening 12 seconds, Whitaker (147) boxed his way back before he was dropped again by a fast left-right to the head in the sixth. While the taller Hurtado appeared to have the beating of Whitaker at this stage of the contest, with the latter still working the body hard in an attempt to weaken his rival, eventually his pressure paid off. Coming in to the 11th it was obvious that Whitaker needed a stoppage, and after firing in a hard left to the head followed by a whole blast of punches Hurtado finally wilted and was left hanging over the middle strand when the referee intervened. Prior to the finish, both men had been docked points for illegal blows, Hurtado in the fifth and seventh and Whitaker in the ninth.

22 February 1997. Michael Loewe w pts 12 Santiago Samaniego.
Venue: Wandsbek Sports Hall, Hamburg, Germany. **Recognition:** WBO. **Referee:** Genaro Rodriguez.
Scorecards: 114-113, 117-110, 116-112.
Fight Summary: Fighting for the title taken away from Jose Luis Lopez, Loewe (145½), the 1987 amateur world junior champion, came up against a tough, awkward customer in Samaniego (145), eventually winning on points

after being badly cut up from repeated head clashes. Lacking the power to stop Samaniego in his tracks did not help Loewe's cause as the Panamanian constantly charged forward. The latter also had points deducted for low blows. Despite having height-and-reach advantages, and using the left jab well, Loewe was caught over the top more than he would have wished, but after losing two of the opening three rounds he gradually began to accrue the points required. There were no knockdowns.

12 April 1997. Oscar De La Hoya w pts 12 Pernell Whitaker.
Venue: Thomas & Mack Centre, Las Vegas, Nevada, USA. **Recognition:** WBC. **Referee:** Mills Lane.
Scorecards: 115-111, 116-110, 116-110.
Fight Summary: At the end of the contest, Whitaker (146½), his right eye almost closed, could hardly believe he had lost his title to De La Hoya (146½), having dropped the latter in the ninth round and kept him at bay with an accurate right jab and a sound defence. Many people, other than the judges, agreed with him. Repeatedly going southpaw to confuse Whitaker, the 'Golden Boy' was the one who landed the heavier blows. And he always seemed to catch the eye with bursts of punches towards the end of rounds, but was unable to knock his man over however hard he tried. While Whitaker continually showed his experience, often forcing De La Hoya to punch down at him, he did not do enough scoring. This was ultimately the difference between the pair.

18 April 1997. Ike Quartey w rsc 5 Ralph Jones.
Venue: Hilton Hotel, Las Vegas, Nevada, USA. **Recognition:** WBA. **Referee:** Joe Cortez.
Fight Summary: Never really in with a chance, the challenger started badly after walking in to Quartey (146½). He was soon in trouble, a left-right to the jaw knocking him over for 'four' before another volley of blows sent him down again prior to him being saved by the bell to end the first round. Jones (147) was soon under pressure in the second, but showed real grit to get through the storm that headed his way, even surprising Quartey in the third with a fight back. However, it was back to survival in the fourth for Jones before he became an open target in the fifth. On his way down again, it was no surprise when the referee rescued him after 68 seconds.

14 June 1997. Oscar De La Hoya w co 2 David Kamau.
Venue: The Alamodrome, San Antonio, Texas, USA. **Recognition:** WBC. **Referee:** Laurence Cole.
Fight Summary: Despite having a huge reach advantage the challenger was unable to make it work for him, as De La Hoya (147) carefully weighed him up in the opening round before going to work in the second. Sending in solid, fast jabs that hit the target, De La Hoya was soon busy, a cracking left hook having Kamau (146¾) over for the mandatory 'eight'. Back on his feet Kamau was still gamely trying to present De La Hoya with a few problems, but following a round of heavy blows a smashing right-left to the head sent him to the floor to be counted out on the 2.54 mark.

13 September 1997. Oscar De La Hoya w pts 12 Hector Camacho.
Venue: Thomas & Mack Centre, Las Vegas, Nevada, USA. **Recognition:** WBC. **Referee:** Richard Steele.
Scorecards: 119-108, 120-106, 120-105.
Fight Summary: Close to being dropped on several occasions before a three-punch attack sent him down in the ninth for only the third knockdown in his career, the challenger did little to show that he was up to beating De La Hoya (147). Concentrating on the body, De La Hoya tried hard to finish Camacho (147) off, but was unable to do so as the latter held like a limpet, moved at speed whenever challenged, and when he was deducted a point for holding and hitting in the 12th it just about summed up his title challenge. However, if it was just survival he wanted then Camacho achieved his aim, but in terms of winning a world title he wasted the opportunity.

20 September 1997. Michael Loewe w pts 12 Michael Carruth.
Venue: Tivoli Sports Hall, Aachen, Germany. **Recognition:** WBO. **Referee:** Rudy Battle.
Scorecards: 115-114, 117-111, 114-114.
Fight Summary: By failing to impose himself on Loewe (145¼) early enough the southpaw challenger possibly lost his best chance of winning the title, despite making a reasonable start. Cut on the right eye in the fourth obviously hampered Loewe from there onwards, but Carruth (145) failed to take advantage of the situation when allowing the champion to keep him at bay with a long left lead while tying him up in the clinches. Carruth was also guilty of throwing one punch at a time, and although he occasionally countered well he did not work hard enough until

coming with a rush to win the last two rounds. Although it was always close, Loewe, with his better work, just about deserved the win.

After Loewe relinquished the WBO version of the title when unfit for a defence against Leonard Townsend in February 1998, a Townsend v Akhmed Kotiev bout went ahead to decide the vacancy. Loewe later announced his retirement.

17 October 1997. Ike Quartey drew 12 Jose Luis Lopez.
Venue: Foxwoods Resort Casino, Ledyard, Connecticut, USA. **Recognition:** WBA. **Referee:** Steve Smoger.
Scorecards: 116-112, 113-113, 114-114.
Fight Summary: Opening up with a ramrod left lead, the champion concentrated on that punch all night as Lopez (146½) seemed unable to handle it despite being taller than his rival, and according to the punch stats he was hit at the rate of six punches to one. Twice Lopez dropped Quartey (146), in the second round with a stiff right counter and in the 11th with a left-right. Quartey was up quickly on both occasions, while Lopez, in trying to finish, was wild and wasted much energy when missing the target. Initially the decision was announced as a win for Quartey but, after the WBA supervisor checked the cards and there were found to be discrepancies, the result was changed to that of a majority draw.

When Quartey forfeited the WBA version of the title in August 1998 for failing to go through with a defence against Andrey Pestryaev, the latter was matched against James Page to decide the vacancy. Initially, the WBA had mandated that it was Lopez who would be meeting Pestryaev, but following much discussion it was agreed that the Mexican would get first crack at the winner.

6 December 1997. Oscar De La Hoya w rsc 8 Wilfredo Rivera.
Venue: Convention Centre, Atlantic City, New Jersey, USA. **Recognition:** WBC. **Referee:** Joe Cortez.
Fight Summary: Taking his time, De La Hoya (147) picked it up towards the end of the first round, but after he had opened up with fast left jabs the challenger hit back with some blows of his own before disaster struck for him in the second when his right eye was sliced open by a short left uppercut. Surprisingly allowed to carry on, Rivera (147) somehow continued. However, when he was smashed to the floor by a solid right to the jaw in the fourth it looked all over. Beating the count, Rivera stayed in the contest mainly because De La Hoya let him. Although Rivera fought on bravely the end came when De La Hoya unleashed more combinations in the eighth, and with blood pouring from the Puerto Rican's eye the referee called a halt with two seconds of the session remaining.

14 February 1998. Akhmed Kotiev w pts 12 Leonard Townsend.
Venue: Wandsbek Sports Hall, Stuttgart, Germany. **Recognition:** WBO. **Referee:** Joe Cortez.
Scorecards: 116-109, 119-106, 117-110.
Fight Summary: Battling for the title vacated by Michael Loewe, Kotiev (146¼) proved too good for Townsend (146¾). As early as the first round Kotiev had the American on the deck before being lucky to escape with nothing more than a warning when hitting him while he was on one knee taking the count. An excellent counter puncher, Kotiev lost just two rounds, the fifth and the 11th, and apart from those two sessions was always one step ahead of Townsend, who was down again in the 12th. Kotiev also had a point deducted for low blows in that session, although it hardly made a difference to the scoreline.

3 April 1998. Felix Trinidad w rsc 4 Mahenge Zulu.
Venue: Ruben Rodriguez Coliseum, Bayamon, Puerto Rico. **Recognition:** IBF. **Referee:** Luis Pabon.
Fight Summary: In what seemed to be a palpable mismatch, the challenger, who was reported to be 32 although he looked much older, did nothing of note in the opening two rounds other than throw wild punches at Trinidad (147) that missed by a mile. Meanwhile, Trinidad was merely biding his time. In the third he began to open up on Zulu (147), sending in some fairly hefty wallops that served notice of what was to come. After a spot of posing in the fourth, Trinidad finally went for the finish, and having hurt Zulu and sent him stumbling with punches to head and body a crashing left hook to the jaw decked him. Although the referee took up the count, at about 'three' when Zulu suggested that he was not going to make it, the fight was called off at 2.20 of the session.

23 May 1998. Akhmed Kotiev w pts 12 Paulo Alejandro Sanchez.
Venue: Sports Hall, Offenburg, Germany. **Recognition:** WBO. **Referee:** Andre Van Grootenbruel.
Scorecards: 118-109, 119-109, 119-108.
Fight Summary: Close to being a shut-out victory for the champion, Sanchez (146¾) won only the sixth round which was mainly due to the German-based Russian hurting his right hand in that session. A very clever boxer, Kotiev (147) threw far more punches than Sanchez, making him miss badly at times while sending in point-scoring counters. Hardly exciting, but efficient, Kotiev always held the upper hand against an opponent who was out of his depth.

13 June 1998. Oscar De La Hoya w rsc 3 Patrick Charpentier.
Venue: The Sunbowl, El Paso, Texas, USA. **Recognition:** WBC. **Referee:** Laurence Cole.
Fight Summary: Showing his ruthless streak, the champion edged up on Charpentier (146) in the opening two rounds, having a good look at what the shorter man had to offer before unleashing his big punches in the third. Although Charpentier started the session with a rush, a fast right-left hook exploded on his head to put him down for 'five'. On getting back into the fray two rib benders followed by a crunching left uppercut to the chin had the Frenchman over again, this time for 'six'. Moments later, after De La Hoya (147) had sent Charpentier down for the third time with a right over the top the referee immediately called a halt, the finish being timed at 1.56.

18 September 1998. Oscar De La Hoya w rtd 8 Julio Cesar Chavez.
Venue: Thomas & Mack Centre, Las Vegas, Nevada, USA. **Recognition:** WBC. **Referee:** Richard Steele.
Fight Summary: Making a cautious start against Chavez (144½) the champion was soon one step ahead, whether countering, throwing combinations with blurring speed or getting left hooks off. By the fifth, De La Hoya (146½) had probably shaded every round, but Chavez was still there connecting with left hooks and rights over the top despite being gradually ground down. Even though De La Hoya went up a gear in the sixth and seventh Chavez was staying put, and it was not until the champion began to sit on his punches more in the eighth that the fight ended. Having taken some terrific blows to the head and sent staggering back to his corner at the end of the session, it was announced during the interval that Chavez had retired.

10 October 1998. James Page w co 2 Andrey Pestryaev.
Venue: Bercy Sports Palace, Paris, France. **Recognition:** WBA. **Referee:** Stan Christodoulou.
Fight Summary: Four days prior to this match going ahead for the vacant title, a New Jersey judge had ruled that the number two contender, Jose Luis Lopez, should be involved in any championship contest. However, luckily for all concerned a French judge overruled that decision on the eve of the fight. Economical in style, Pestryaev (146¾) started by staying out of range before making an attack, but was soon in trouble as Page (145½), concentrating on heavy, single shots, had him over with three solid blows to the head just before the bell ended the first round. With there being no hiding place for Pestryaev, after he was countered with a tremendous left hook to the jaw he crashed over to be counted out after 45 seconds of the second.

28 November 1998. Akhmed Kotiev w pts 12 Santos Cardona.
Venue: Hanseatic Hall, Lubeck, Germany. **Recognition:** WBO. **Referee:** Bill Connors.
Scorecards: 115-112, 115-112, 116-112.
Fight Summary: Defending his title for the second time, Kotiev 146½) was up against a man who enjoyed a four-inch-reach advantage and knew how to use it. To combat this, Kotiev boxed on the back foot for much of the contest, scoring with counters and using his footwork to keep him away from trouble as Cardona (146½) made the running. Although Kotiev was shaken up in the second round by a heavy left hook he came back well with left uppercuts and left-right combinations, and despite the Puerto Rican making a strong run from the eighth through to the final bell he failed to make up the deficit. Cardona's cause was not helped when he had a point deducted for landing repeated low blows in the 11th.

5 December 1998. James Page w pts 12 Jose Luis Lopez.
Venue: Convention Centre, Atlantic City, New Jersey, USA. **Recognition:** WBA. **Referee:** Tony Perez.
Scorecards: 116-111, 115-112, 115-111.

Fight Summary: Starting strongly, Page (147) punched away at Lopez (146½) who seemed content to take whatever was coming his way. Then, having nearly knocked his opponent down with a left jab in the second, but under immediate pressure himself, Lopez dropped Page in the third and rained in punch after punch before the bell came to the champion's rescue. Although Lopez struck with solid blows over the next few rounds, having Page stumbling around at times before dropping him again in the ninth, after he began to fade the latter came on strongly to take the last three sessions to make sure of retaining the title.

13 February 1999. Oscar De La Hoya w pts 12 Ike Quartey.
Venue: Thomas & Mack Centre, Las Vegas, Nevada, USA. **Recognition:** WBC. **Referee:** Mitch Halpern.
Scorecards: 116-112, 116-113, 114-115.
Fight Summary: This was not the fight that most people expected, the challenger more than giving De La Hoya (147) a run for his money, and many even agreed with one of the judges who had the man from Ghana winning by one point. Prior to the sixth neither man had dominated, it being extremely intense, but in that session first Quartey (146½) was dropped and then De La Hoya before the latter had to endure many heavy right hands. His left eye was also beginning to swell. Two of the next three sessions saw De La Hoya taking more heavy blows prior to him coming through to win the last three rounds on all of the cards. Knowing that the 12th had to be a big round for him De La Hoya charged from his corner, throwing punches, before dropping Quartey with a cracking left hook. Back on his feet, although the Ghanaian was unsteady he somehow weathered everything that was coming his way. It was also clear that near the end of the session De La Hoya, having punched himself out, would not be getting the 10-7 score he so badly wanted.

20 February 1999. Felix Trinidad w pts 12 Pernell Whitaker.
Venue: Madison Square Garden, Manhattan, NYC, New York, USA. **Recognition:** IBF. **Referee:** Benjy Esteves Jnr.
Scorecards: 118-109, 117-110, 118-109.
Fight Summary: Although the challenger fought bravely against the odds, after being floored in the second by a countering right from Trinidad (147) and damaging his jaw in the sixth, ultimately it was just too big a bridge to cross. Fighting with much skill and courage, Whitaker (147) gave as good as he got in the opening four sessions, but then faded after taking some hefty shots in the fifth and sixth sessions. Whitaker did come back with a jolting counter in the seventh, but was almost overwhelmed on occasion as Trinidad, throwing solid rights, put in a spurt that took him through to the final bell.

13 March 1999. James Page w pts 12 Sam Garr.
Venue: Madison Square Garden, Manhattan, NYC, New York, USA. **Recognition:** WBA. **Referee:** Steve Smoger.
Scorecards: 117-111, 119-108, 116-113.
Fight Summary: Forced to overcome several difficult moments the champion was given a tough test by Garr (146¼), being forced to get back to basics as his early blitz failed to bring results. While Garr probably won only three rounds he was extremely well schooled with sound defensive qualities, and it was not until the sixth round that Page (147) connected solidly with rights to the head after bringing his left jab into play. From the eighth through to the 11th Page continued to score with heavy punches, but in the final session Garr came back with fast flurries before showboating down the stretch as if to prove that he belonged at this level.

24 April 1999. Akhmed Kotiev w rsc 3 Peter Malinga.
Venue: Krone Circus Tent, Munich, Germany. **Recognition:** WBO. **Referee:** Genaro Rodriguez.
Fight Summary: Coming out fast the champion made it his contest right from the off, punching solidly from head to body as Malinga (145½) did his best to cover up. Previously thought to lack power Kotiev (147) proved that he could punch once he set his feet, and in the third round a big right to the head put Malinga down for 'eight'. Back in the fray, Malinga was dropped twice more during the session before the referee called a halt on the 1.15 mark in order to save the beleaguered South African from taking further punishment.

22 May 1999. Oscar De La Hoya w rsc 11 Oba Carr.
Venue: Mandalay Bay Resort & Casino, Las Vegas, Nevada, USA. **Recognition:** WBC. **Referee:** Richard Steele.
Fight Summary: Up against a clever fighter in Carr (147), the champion showed a marked improvement after tightening his defence and letting the punches go right from the opening bell. Putting Carr down with a left hook to

the head halfway through the first round before hurting him again with a big uppercut on the inside, even though De La Hoya (147) showed his intent he seemed happy to cruise along with the jab picking up the points. In the seventh a clash of heads saw De La Hoya cut under the left eye, for which Carr had a point deducted. Then, a little later in the session a left hook that went low saw the challenger lose another point. Although he won the ninth, by the tenth Carr knew that he could only capture the title if he could score a knockout, but it was De La Hoya who struck next. Having driven in some hurtful body shots in the 11th, De La Hoya then found a great left counter to the jaw to drop Carr and after the latter got to his feet and was unable to co-ordinate the referee stopped the contest, the finish being timed at 0.55.

29 May 1999. Felix Trinidad w co 4 Hugo Pineda.
Venue: Roberto Clemente Coliseum, San Juan, Puerto Rico. **Recognition:** IBF. **Referee:** Roberto Ramirez.
Fight Summary: At 6'1", Pineda (147) towered over Trinidad (147), but that was just about all he had on the champion as he boxed on the back foot, throwing punches from distance before moving away with alacrity. Having hurt Pineda just about every time he connected Trinidad moved up a gear in the fourth, and after landing heavily with punches to head and body a crunching left uppercut to the body sent the challenger down to be counted out with seven seconds of the session remaining.

24 July 1999. James Page w rsc 11 Freddie Pendleton.
Venue: Flamingo Hilton Hotel & Casino, Las Vegas, Nevada, USA. **Recognition:** WBA. **Referee:** Joe Cortez.
Fight Summary: Despite looking for a knockout win from the opening bell, Page (147) had to settle for almost having to go the distance prior to retaining his title against the game Pendleton (146½). On realising he would have to work his way into openings and quit slugging, Page eventually settled down with the jab to outbox a challenger, who at best won just two rounds, the third and the ninth. At the start of the tenth Page got to Pendleton, backing him up with hooks, jabs and uppercuts, and in the 11th he again belaboured the latter who was carrying damage around both eyes. Having dropped Pendleton and seeing him spring up immediately, after Page repeated the dose the old-timer was forced to take a 'seven' count before a cracking left hook dumped him for 'eight'. This time there was no way back for Pendleton, the referee stopping the contest on the 2.25 mark.

Page forfeited the WBA version of the title in September 2000 for failing to fulfil a mandatory defence against Andrew Lewis due to contractual problems, prior to meeting the latter to decide the vacancy.

18 September 1999. Felix Trinidad w pts 12 Oscar De La Hoya.
Venue: Bay Resort & Casino, Las Vegas, Nevada, USA. **Recognition:** IBF/WBC. **Referee:** Mitch Halpern.
Scorecards: 115-113, 115-114, 114-114.
Fight Summary: In most eyes De La Hoya (147) retained his WBC title and won the IBF crown, but the judges saw it differently when giving their votes for aggression rather than quality boxing. It was really a case of Trinidad (147) throwing more punches, many of them not landing cleanly, and De La Hoya doubling up with the jab, more often than not finding the target. By the end of the fifth Trinidad's left eye was damaged, and in the sixth De La Hoya moved in with excellent combinations which he repeatedly threw from there onwards before tiring towards the end. The last three rounds saw De La Hoya moving away from Trinidad, which could have given the impression that he was being chased down, whereas in reality he was allowing the one-dimensional Puerto Rican to merely follow him around until the final bell.

After Trinidad relinquished the IBF/WBC versions of the title in March 2000 on moving up to junior middle, De La Hoya was reinstated as the WBC champion. Meantime, the IBF set up a fight between Vernon Forrest and Raul Frank to find their new champion.

27 November 1999. Akhmed Kotiev w pts 12 Daniel Santos.
Venue: Hanseatic Hall, Lubeck, Germany. **Recognition:** WBO. **Referee:** Earl Jewell.
Scorecards: 115-113, 115-113, 111-117.
Fight Summary: Showing good movement, the southpaw challenger made the fight from the opening bell. In the first half of the contest Kotiev (145¾) appeared to have no answer as to how to get inside the jab, and in the fourth round he walked on to a solid left that nearly put him over. Picking it up, Santos (147) fired in more lefts that found

their mark, but by now Kotiev was coming more into it when firing in rights to head and body. By the end of the 11th Kotiev appeared to have closed the deficit after steadily getting on top. However, that was before Santos came back in the final session with solid left hands to put himself back in with a shout. Following the fight, because many WBO officials thought he might have been lucky to hold on to his title, Kotiev was told by that body his next defence would have to be against Santos.

6 May 2000. Daniel Santos w co 5 Akhmed Kotiev.
Venue: Swiss Hotel, Neuss, Germany. **Recognition:** WBO. **Referee:** Bill Connors.
Fight Summary: Having already beaten his southpaw challenger six months earlier, although Kotiev (147) might have been expecting to repeat the dose things did not quite work out for him this time round. Making a good start, Santos (147) knew that to beat Kotiev he had to press him while using the jab to find his way in and crossing the left. As before Kotiev had difficulty with reaching Santos, and already down on two of the cards he was floored twice in the fifth from solid left hands, the second occasion seeing him counted out on the 2.07 mark.

17 June 2000. Shane Mosley w pts 12 Oscar De La Hoya.
Venue: Staples Centre, Los Angeles, California, USA. **Recognition:** WBC. **Referee:** Lou Moret.
Scorecards: 116-112, 115-113, 113-115.
Fight Summary: Outspeeding the champion after stepping up two weight divisions, Mosley (147) came from behind over the last half to snatch victory by what turned out to be a close margin. Both men went for the body and both threw blurring punches to the head, but just when it looked likely that De La Hoya (146½) would get on top Mosley upped his work-rate. The longer it went on the more frantic it became, and by the tenth De La Hoya was feeling the pace whilst Mosley was getting in and out with sharp scoring punches. The final session saw both men tired, but it was Mosley, punching more cleanly and deliberately than De La Hoya, who was making more of a show at that stage. The punch stats had Mosley landing in total 284 to 257 blows for De La Hoya, having the best of the jabs with 110 to 92 and power punches with 174 to 165.

29 July 2000. Daniel Santos w rsc 4 Giovanni Parisi.
Venue: Oreste Granillo Stadium, Reggio Calabria, Italy. **Recognition:** WBO. **Referee:** Raul Caiz.
Fight Summary: Despite having a good opening round Parisi (145¾) was found wanting thereafter as he struggled against the southpaw champion, four inches the taller, quickly falling behind on the cards. Coming into the fourth and clearly up against it, Parisi took a beating from Santos (146½), and after being knocked over twice and lying defenceless on the ropes the referee called it off on the 2.32 mark to save him from taking further punishment.

26 August 2000. Vernon Forrest tdraw 3 Raul Frank.
Venue: Bay Resort & Casino, Las Vegas, Nevada, USA. **Recognition:** IBF. **Referee:** Kenny Bayless.
Fight Summary: Contesting the title left vacant by Felix Trinidad, while expected to use his jab the taller Forrest (146½) was soon mixing it up with Frank (147) at close quarters. In the second it could be seen that Frank was already cut on the left eye, and as Forrest continued to land the left hook to head and body the signs for the underdog were ominous. Showing fast hands, Forrest still held sway in the third, but when he bent low to smash in another left hook there was a terrible clash of heads that left Frank badly cut and unable to continue. Due to the fight not making it to the end of the fourth round, the IBF rules stated that it would be classified as a no-decision (technical draw for our purposes) and that both men would have to meet again.

4 November 2000. Shane Mosley w rsc 6 Antonio Diaz.
Venue: MSG Theatre, Manhattan, NYC, New York, USA. **Recognition:** WBC. **Referee:** Arthur Mercante.
Fight Summary: Stepping up from junior welter seemed to be too much of an ask for Diaz (146½), especially when facing someone of the champion's calibre, and after being smashed to the canvas by a fast burst of combination punches in the second round it became blatantly obvious that he was out of his depth. For the next few sessions it was almost as if Mosley (146½) was allowing Diaz a stay of execution, but in the sixth he struck with a terrific right to the head to drop the latter. Up almost immediately, the tough Diaz took several more hard rights before another smash sent him crashing. With Diaz floundering but wishing to continue, the referee, a magnificent 80-years of age, made a perfect stoppage on the 1.36 mark.

16 December 2000. Daniel Santos w co 2 Neil Sinclair.
Venue: The Arena, Sheffield, England. **Recognition:** WBO. **Referee:** John Coyle.
Fight Summary: Working everything around his southpaw left hand, mixing up uppercuts and crosses, the champion soon got down to business to send Sinclair (146) down with a left cross. Up at 'two', but forced to take the mandatory 'eight' count, Sinclair allowed time for his head to clear before spotting an opening to send in a heavy right to the head that dropped Santos (147) for 'seven'. Saved by the bell, Santos came out warily as Sinclair looked for a finish, and with both men landing heavily it was the latter who came off worse when a short left to the head sent him down to be counted out with 35 seconds of the session remaining.

17 February 2001. Andrew Lewis w rsc 7 James Page.
Venue: MGM Grand, Las Vegas, Nevada, USA. **Recognition:** WBA. **Referee:** Kenny Bayless.
Fight Summary: Formerly a champion prior to being stripped, Page (146) was given another chance to win back his old title when meeting Lewis (147), but ultimately found the latter too much for him. Called 'Six Heads' because his frenetic movement and southpaw stance made him difficult to hit, Lewis came out blasting in the opening session, as did Page, and in the second a cracking right uppercut to the jaw had the latter over heavily. Back on his feet, Page took a real hammering for the remainder of the second and third. Then, in the fifth he was actually pushed to the canvas as Lewis continually changed stance and came in from varying angles. It was fairly obvious that Page would not last much longer, taking far too many punches for his own good. And at 1.15 of the seventh, after Lewis had smashed him to the canvas, the referee wisely stopped the fight.

10 March 2001. Shane Mosley w rtd 5 Shannan Taylor.
Venue: Caesar's Palace, Las Vegas, Nevada, USA. **Recognition:** WBC. **Referee:** Vic Drakulich.
Fight Summary: Giving a breath-taking display of boxing the champion had too much of everything for Taylor (147), who had courage a plenty but lacked the skill, power and speed required to deal with an opponent with such qualities. Towards the end of the first round, and having already been blinded by the speed of Mosley (147), the Australian was dumped by a flashing right hand to the head before being saved by the bell. Punching to the body to slow Taylor down, Mosley was merely biding his time. Although Taylor tried to rally, in the fourth he was deducted a point for roughhouse tactics before punches rained in on him again during the fifth, ending the session having to take a terrific blow to the body that almost doubled him up. It was no surprise when Taylor's corner retired their man during the interval leading up to the sixth, stating that the protection of the fighter was paramount.

28 April 2001. Andrew Lewis w pts 12 Larry Marks.
Venue: Hammerstein Ballroom, Manhattan, NYC, New York, USA. **Recognition:** WBA. **Referee:** Steve Smoger.
Scorecards: 119-109, 120-108, 119-109.
Fight Summary: Prior to the contest it was felt that Marks (144¼) should not have been sharing the same ring as the champion but, after a left hook to Lewis' temple that had him floundering around two minutes into the fight, there was certainly a reassessment going on. Unfortunately, following that the next 11 rounds failed to live up to the initial excitement, and although Lewis (146½) virtually won all of them, occasionally having Marks in trouble, he was never able to finish the latter off. A proven tough guy, Marks stayed in the fight by clutching and being able to absorb whatever Lewis threw at him.

12 May 2001. Vernon Forrest w pts 12 Raul Frank.
Venue: Madison Square Garden, Manhattan, NYC, New York, USA. **Recognition:** IBF. **Referee:** Ken Zimmer.
Scorecards: 120-108, 118-110, 118-110.
Fight Summary: Again coming together to contest the vacant title, Forrest (145¼) beat Frank (147) to become the new champion when winning all rounds bar the fifth, in what was a messy affair. Tall for his weight and fast, Forrest failed to make full use of these advantages, being content to box on the back foot while happy to let Frank come to him. Even when in control Forrest failed to land effectively with right hands, preferring not to take any unnecessary risks against a wild swinging opponent who despite being dangerous at close quarters was limited at that level. Bearing in mind that their previous contest had seen one head clash too many, Forrest obviously had good reason not to get involved this time around.

When Forrest was stripped of the championship in December after deciding to challenge Shane Mosley for the WBC crown the IBF set up a fight for the vacant title between Michele Piccirillo and Cory Spinks.

21 July 2001. Daniel Santos tdraw 1 Antonio Margarito.
Venue: Ruben Rodriguez Coliseum, Bayamon, Puerto Rico. **Recognition:** WBO. **Referee:** Jose Rivera.
Fight Summary: After just 131 seconds, and following two terrible head clashes that left the challenger badly cut, the fight was called off and announced as a no-decision under the Association of Boxing Commission Rules. For our purposes it should be seen as a technical draw. The first coming together of heads occurred when Margarito (146), working his way in to back the southpaw champion on the ropes, was cut over the right eye. Although the referee allowed it to go on, when Margarito dipped under a Santos (147) left cross moments later before inadvertently bringing his head up the second clash of heads occurred. At that point, with blood pouring from a deep wound, the fight was stopped by the referee following a discussion with the doctor.

Before a rematch could be made, Santos relinquished the WBO version of the title in November in order to step up and challenge for the vacant WBO junior middleweight title. That was eventually followed by an announcement that Margarito would fight Antonio Diaz to decide the vacant title.

21 July 2001. Shane Mosley w rsc 3 Adrian Stone.
Venue: Caesar's Palace, Las Vegas, Nevada, USA. **Recognition:** WBC. **Referee:** Jay Nady.
Fight Summary: Starting fast, the challenger went forward with the jab trying to take Mosley (147) out of his stride during the opening two rounds. Although those sessions were given to Mosley his work was not of the standard expected, missing with far too many punches as Stone (147), pressing forward, went for the body. However, the third round saw Mosley beginning to move better, but despite hurting Stone to the body he bided his time, waiting for the opportunity to strike rather than punching away at his opponent who was moving from side to side and showing a high guard. Eventually measuring Stone with lefts Mosley banged in three rights to the top of the head, and when the target opened up he cracked in a fast left hook-right to the jaw that sent the Englishman crashing. Not bothering to pick up the count, the referee called the fight off on the 2.01 mark so that Stone, out cold, could be attended to as quickly as possible.

28 July 2001. Andrew Lewis tdraw 2 Ricardo Mayorga.
Venue: Staples Centre, Los Angeles, California, USA. **Recognition:** WBA. **Referee:** Marty Denkin.
Fight Summary: Storming out from the opening bell, Mayorga (146¾) began to throw rights at the champion who withstood the attacks and countered with southpaw lefts. However, moments into the second round with both fighters coming together there was a clash of heads, Lewis (147) receiving bad cuts over both eyes as well as a swelling on the left optic. Too bad for him to continue, the referee called it off with seven seconds on the clock when ruling it to be a no-decision (technical draw for our purposes) under the Association of Boxing Commission Rules. It was later announced that the pair would have to meet again.

26 January 2002. Vernon Forrest w pts 12 Shane Mosley.
Venue: MSG Theatre, Manhattan, NYC, New York, USA. **Recognition:** WBC/The Ring. **Referee:** Steve Smoger.
Scorecards: 118-108, 117-108, 115-110.
Fight Summary: In what was a huge upset, Forrest (147) dropped the WBC champion twice and hurt him badly on more than one occasion prior to winning the fight by a unanimous decision. When Forrest, who had been the last man to beat Mosley (146) in the amateurs, used his height-and-reach advantages he neutralised much of the champion's work by not allowing him to fire away at close quarters. With equally fast hands, Forrest's added power also stopped Mosley in his tracks at times, and when the latter did get through, more often than not he was held in a vice-like grip. In the second session heads came together, leaving Mosley cut on his scalp and dazed before being dropped by heavy rights, which obviously affected his game plan from thereon in. Never at any time was Mosley able to work Forrest out, being in trouble again in the tenth after taking heavy belts to the body and smashed with solid right hands. In only three rounds did Mosley land more than a dozen punches, testament to the new champion's control over him. Forrest also won the vacant *Ring* Championship Belt on the result.

16 March 2002. Antonio Margarito w rsc 10 Antonio Diaz.
Venue: Bally's Park Place Hotel, Las Vegas, Nevada, USA. **Recognition:** WBO. **Referee:** Jay Nady.
Fight Summary: Contesting the vacant title, with Margarito (146½) pumping out both hands from the start although Diaz (147) came back to win the second by dint of a better technique the Mexican charged ahead, throwing punches frenetically at times. Margarito continued to dictate the pace, even outboxing the well-schooled Diaz in the seventh while also hurting him with long left uppercuts. In the tenth, with Margarito still busy behind the jab he finally got to Diaz with a doubled-up uppercut that dropped him to the floor. After gamely climbing to his feet and being battered by head punches, the referee called a halt at 2.17 of the session to save Diaz from taking further punishment.

30 March 2002. Ricardo Mayorga w rsc 5 Andrew Lewis.
Venue: Sovereign Centre, Reading, Pennsylvania, USA. **Recognition:** WBA. **Referee:** Rudy Battle.
Fight Summary: Following on from their no-decision encounter in July 2001, Mayorga (145½) walked into the southpaw champion from the opening bell, throwing crude punches, and by the third round it had developed into a wild, hard-slugging affair as both men got drawn in. Although Lewis (147) appeared to be settling down in the fourth, landing solidly at times, he was failing to use the jab enough before being made to pay in the fifth as Mayorga jumped on him with rights and lefts. Badly hurt by wild combinations, after a terrific right to the jaw rocked Lewis he was sent crashing by more heavy rights. Struggling to his feet at 'six', Lewis was rescued by the referee at 1.08 of the session when unable to focus and being in no fit state to continue.

13 April 2002. Michele Piccirillo w pts 12 Cory Spinks.
Venue: The Casino, Campione D'Italia, Italy. **Recognition:** IBF. **Referee:** Rafael Argiolis.
Scorecards: 116-111, 115-112, 115-112.
Fight Summary: Meeting for the title forfeited by Vernon Forrest, Spinks (146½) began behind the southpaw jab to win the opening two rounds, but by the third Piccirillo (147) had picked up the pace, being always dangerous with a solid right cross as he took the next four sessions. Having been cut on the right eye in the fifth and lost a point in the sixth for illegal use of the head Spinks was now behind, and although he came back strongly when outworking the Italian over the final round or so he was unable to make up the deficit.

20 July 2002. Vernon Forrest w pts 12 Shane Mosley.
Venue: Conseco Fieldhouse, Indianapolis, Indiana, USA. **Recognition:** WBC/The Ring. **Referee:** Laurence Cole.
Scorecards: 115-113, 116-112, 117-111.
Fight Summary: Having proved to be the master of Mosley (147) in their first fight the WBC champion and holder of *The Ring* Championship Belt continued to be the latter's bogeyman when repeating the dose in what was a contest without thrills, possibly due to both men knowing each other too well. As before, Forrest (147) used his extra reach to keep Mosley at bay. Due to the continual clutching by both men the fight never flowed, and because there were no knockdowns the interest ebbed away despite hard punches being thrown on occasion. Mosley's best round was the ninth when he landed several good shots, but unable to follow up as Forrest moved away by the 12th it was clear that the belts were not going to change hands.

12 October 2002. Antonio Margarito w pts 12 Danny Perez.
Venue: Arrowhead Pond, Anaheim, California, USA. **Recognition:** WBO. **Referee:** Jon Schorle.
Scorecards: 120-108, 118-110, 120-108.
Fight Summary: Although Perez (145½) gave it his best shot when proving to be a plucky challenger, Margarito (146½) never once relaxed his hold on the title while walking to a shut-out victory. Both men concentrated on the left jab, but while Margarito scored again and again, following up with left hooks to head and body, Perez found his route normally blocked off and was too one-paced. By the sixth, with Perez almost out of ideas, Margarito was unrelenting when working up and down with hooks and hard rights to the head. Several times Perez looked as though he was going to go, especially in the 11th when he was caught heavily, but he remained on his feet to hear the final bell.

25 January 2003. Ricardo Mayorga w rsc 3 Vernon Forrest.
Venue: Pechanga Resort & Casino, Temecula, California, USA. **Recognition:** WBA/WBC/The Ring. **Referee:** Marty Denkin.
Fight Summary: Fighting to unify three belts, the WBA's Mayorga (146) proved to be too strong for Forrest (146½), the WBC champion and holder of *The Ring* Championship Belt, the latter being dragged into a war of attrition by his powerful rival. On the attack from the opening bell the wild-swinging Mayorga, smashing in big left hooks and heavy rights, put Forrest down with a head punch. Although it did not look a genuine knockdown it was classified as one. Following this, Forrest took the fight to Mayorga in the second round, matching him when whacking in left hooks to the body and right uppercuts to the head. There was more of the same in the third, but after having no effect on Mayorga and being hurt by a solid right to the temple, the WBC champion was sent to the floor by lefts and rights as the Nicaraguan unloaded. Despite getting back on his feet Forrest appeared unstable, and at 2.06 of the session the referee called the fight off to make sure that the latter took no further punishment that night.

On 13 September, a contest for the vacant WBA 'second tier' title saw Jose Antonio Rivera beat Michel Trabant (w pts 12 at the Estrel Convention Centre, Berlin, Germany).

8 February 2003. Antonio Margarito w rsc 2 Andrew Lewis.
Venue: Bay Resort & Casino, Las Vegas, Nevada, USA. **Recognition:** WBO. **Referee:** Joe Cortez.
Fight Summary: Despite making a reasonable start, punching much harder and faster than the champion, when trying to repeat his earlier successes in the second round Lewis (147) came unstuck. Tearing into Margarito (146½) and letting go several big shots it looked like a shock was on the cards, but after Lewis was eventually driven back against the ropes by a fusillade of heavy blows the referee rescued him on the 2.31 mark when he was not fighting back.

22 March 2003. Cory Spinks w pts 12 Michele Piccirillo.
Venue: The Casino, Campione D'Italia, Italy. **Recognition:** IBF. **Referee:** Mario Maianti.
Scorecards: 117-112, 117-111, 115-113.
Fight Summary: Dominating from the opening bell with the southpaw jab, the tricky challenger proved too awkward and too slick for Piccirillo (146½) this time round when setting a very fast pace. Although Piccirillo occasionally connected with solid right crosses he was being outworked by Spinks (146¼), and although the Italian came on strong in the last few sessions it was a matter of too little, too late. On winning the title, Spinks emulated his father (Leon) and uncle (Michael), who were also world champions.

13 December 2003. Cory Spinks w pts 12 Ricardo Mayorga.
Venue: Boardwalk Hall, Atlantic City, New Jersey, USA. **Recognition:** IBF/WBA/WBC/The Ring. **Referee:** Earl Morton.
Scorecards: 117-110, 114-112, 114-114.
Fight Summary: In a fight involving four championship belts the IBF's Spinks (146) eventually won the majority verdict. However, in so doing he had to rely on Mayorga (146) being deducted two points for hitting after the bell in the fifth and holding behind the head in the 11th. Spinks, who was too slippery and by the far the better stylist of the pair, had to contend with wild rushes from Mayorga throughout, but sticking to his boxing he was often able to bang in countering blows before moving on. According to Mayorga, Spinks should have been counted on at least three times. He certainly had a legitimate case in the last round when Spinks was dropped by a right to the body. Unfortunately for the Nicaraguan, because his style was not always conducive to the rules the officials saw it as being more of a push than a punch.

31 January 2004. Antonio Margarito w rsc 2 Hercules Kyvelos.
Venue: Dodge Theatre, Phoenix, Arizona, USA. **Recognition:** WBO. **Referee:** Raul Caiz.
Fight Summary: Even though the challenger was unbeaten in 22 contests he had never fought anyone as good as Margarito (146¾), and while he had a decent jab he was unable to stop all the leather going in his direction, virtually being punched around the ring in the opening session. To his credit, Kyvelos (147) gave it his best shot in the second, but he was soon under pressure before being sent crashing by a left uppercut and a heavy right to the

head. After getting up and being put under attack without any let-up, the referee, having seen the Canadian's corner intimating that they wanted Kyvelos out of the fight, stopped it 54 seconds into the session.

At the Reliant Centre, Houston, Texas on 17 July, Kermit Cintron stopped Teddy Reid in the eighth round of a contest to decide the vacant WBO 'interim' title and to secure a crack at Margarito.

10 April 2004. Cory Spinks w pts 12 Zab Judah.
Venue: Bay Resort & Casino, Las Vegas, Nevada, USA. **Recognition:** IBF/WBA/WBC/The Ring. **Referee:** Joe Cortez.
Scorecards: 116-111, 114-112, 114-112.
Fight Summary: This clash of southpaws saw Spinks (147) outscore his challenger in a contest that was more like a fencing match between very clever tacticians. Behind on the cards, Judah (146) tried to step it up in the 11th, only to be put down by a countering left to the jaw, and although getting up smartly and boxing well for the rest of the session it seemed that he had lost his chance. Having to win by a knockout Judah opened up in the 12th, going close on a couple of occasions before ramming in a solid left that dropped Spinks heavily. On his feet at 'five', but on unsteady legs, Spinks was forced to take a solid right hook that had him holding on immediately prior to the bell to end the fight.

4 September 2004. Cory Spinks w pts 12 Miguel Angel Gonzalez.
Venue: Bay Events Centre, Las Vegas, Nevada, USA. **Recognition:** IBF/WBA/WBC/The Ring. **Referee:** Joe Cortez.
Scorecards: 118-109, 118-109, 118-109.
Fight Summary: Putting up his four championship belts for the second time, Spinks (147) was just too big and too fast for Gonzalez (146½) to handle. In the main, as Gonzalez pushed forward with the right the champion would counter him with southpaw left-right combinations. The former world lightweight champion obviously thought his best chance lay in going for the body, having had fair success in this direction before being docked a point in the eighth for a serious low blow. Although the Mexican went well in the ninth, following that it was nearly all Spinks, the latter giving an excellent display when landing jab after jab prior to moving away and countering with quality shots from both hands.

5 February 2005. Zab Judah w rsc 9 Cory Spinks.
Venue: Savvis Centre, St Louis, Missouri, USA. **Recognition:** IBF/WBA/WBC/The Ring. **Referee:** Armando Garcia.
Fight Summary: Gaining revenge for the defeat Spinks (147) inflicted on him five months earlier, and at the same time taking over the latter's four championship belts, Judah (146) proved emphatically that he was the better man on the night. Making a good start in this battle of southpaws after deciding that speed was in his favour, Judah was soon beating Spinks to the jab. Judah was travelling so fast, Spinks just could not find him. Although it looked as though Judah was possibly fading in the fifth and sixth he came back strongly in the seventh when he appeared to have dropped Spinks with a left cross-right hook, but the referee failed to recognise it as a knockdown, stating that the bell had already sounded. By the ninth, however, Judah had taken over completely and, after landing punch after punch to put Spinks down, when the latter got to his feet he was chased, lurching along the ropes, before being rescued by the referee with 11 seconds of the session remaining.

Jose Antonio Rivera lost the WBA 'second tier' title to Luis Collazo when he was outpointed over 12 rounds at the DCU Centre, Worcester, Massachusetts on 2 April.

18 February 2005. Antonio Margarito w rsc 10 Sebastian Lujan.
Venue: Boardwalk Hotel, Atlantic City, New Jersey, USA. **Recognition:** WBO. **Referee:** David Fields.
Fight Summary: Up until the third round it was anybody's fight, but once the slow-starting champion got himself going when pumping out the left jab and getting his uppercut on the move Lujan (146) was up against it. By the fifth Margarito (147) was working well to the body, and in the sixth according to the CompuBox stats he threw a staggering 144 punches, landing with 54 of them. Things were not going well for Lujan. After being rocked badly in the tenth when the referee noticed that part of his left ear was flapping the fight was called off, with three seconds of the session remaining.

23 April 2005. Antonio Margarito w rsc 5 Kermit Cintron.
Venue: Caesar's Palace, Las Vegas, Nevada, USA. **Recognition:** WBO. **Referee:** Kenny Bayless.
Fight Summary: Having knocked out 22 of 24 opponents, the 'interim' titleholder, Cintron (146½), who was seen as the division's biggest puncher, went looking for Margarito (147) at every opportunity. Unfortunately for Cintron the champion took his best shots before hurting him in the third and opening up a cut over his right eye. Dropped by a right to the head in the fourth, although Cintron got up he was soon put down again before Margarito went for the jugular in the fifth. On the deck for the third time from another hard right to the head, Cintron was then blasted from both hands prior to being floored for the fourth time by a terrific right to the body, whereupon the referee called off the contest on the 2.12 mark.

14 May 2005. Zab Judah w rsc 3 Cosme Rivera.
Venue: MGM Grand, Las Vegas, Nevada, USA. **Recognition:** IBF/WBA/WBC/The Ring. **Referee:** Joe Cortez.
Fight Summary: Defending four championship belts for the first time, and not wishing to lose one of them by default, Judah (146½) quickly had Rivera (147) in some difficulty when smashing him down in the opener with a southpaw left to the jaw. Back on his feet but dazed, Rivera was soon on the deck again following a flurry of blows. Although he lasted out the round and got through the second he would not be so lucky thereafter. Appearing to take it easy in the early stages of the third Judah eventually moved in on Rivera, and following a left uppercut to the jaw another flurry of punches had the latter down. That was it as far as the referee was concerned, the contest being called off at 2.11 of the session.

Luis Collazo made a successful defence of the WBA 'second tier' title when Miguel Angel Gonzalez retired at the end of the eighth round at the United Centre, Chicago, Illinois on 13 August.

7 January 2006. Carlos Baldomir w pts 12 Zab Judah.
Venue: MSG Theatre, Manhattan, NYC, New York, USA. **Recognition:** IBF/WBA/WBC/The Ring. **Referee:** Arthur Mercante Jnr.
Scorecards: 115-113, 115-112, 114-113.
Fight Summary: After reeling off five of the opening six rounds, when the southpaw champion was caught heavily by a Baldomir (146¼) overarm right in the seventh he was all at sea as the latter desperately tried to finish him off in what was a 10-8 round on all three cards. Despite Baldomir being cut over both eyes, the left in the ninth and the right in the 11th, he continued to crank up the pressure as Judah (146¾) tired. Coming into the final session there was still a chance that Judah could pull it off, but that was before he was outworked by a rampant Baldomir.

When Baldomir refused to pay sanctioning fees to both the WBA and IBF, the WBA title passed to their 'second tier' champion, Luis Collazo, while the IBF continued to recognise Judah despite his defeat at the hands of the Argentine.

18 February 2006. Antonio Margarito w rsc 1 Manuel Gomez.
Venue: Aladdin Hotel & Casino, Las Vegas, Nevada, USA. **Recognition:** WBO. **Referee:** Richard Steele.
Fight Summary: In a battle between fellow Mexicans, the champion demolished Gomez (147) inside 74 seconds. The contest had begun with both men swinging heavy blows at each other, but after Margarito (146½) caught Gomez with a heavy left hook to the jaw that was followed by a right to the same area the latter crashed to the floor. When the referee dispensed with the count at 'six' it was all over.

8 April 2006. Floyd Mayweather Jnr w pts 12 Zab Judah.
Venue: Thomas & Mack Centre, Las Vegas, Nevada, USA. **Recognition:** IBF. **Referee:** Richard Steele.
Scorecards: 116-112, 117-111, 119-109.
Fight Summary: Due to Mayweather (146) starting slowly, the reinstated champion picked up the opening two rounds before the three-weight world title holder came back, throwing combinations to head and body that forced him to the ropes and negated his movement. Apart from the final session which Judah (145½) won as he looked to turn things around it was all Mayweather, who had no difficulty with his opponent's southpaw stance. The only problem Mayweather had was when his uncle and trainer, Roger Mayweather, a former junior welterweight champion, jumped into the ring during the tenth to complain that his fighter had been hit below the belt and on

the back of the neck. The result was a five-minute breathing period before resumption with neither Judah being warned for foul blows or Mayweather being disqualified for the actions of his corner.

On 15 August it was announced that Mayweather had relinquished the IBF title in order to challenge Baldomir for the WBA crown, rather than defend against the little known Mark Suarez, who had beaten James Webb (w rsc 1 at Madison Square Garden, Manhattan, NYC, New York on 7 January) in an eliminating bout. Following this action, Suarez was booked to meet Kermit Cintron to contest the vacant title. Cintron had also won an eliminator against David Estrada (w rsc 10 the Convention Centre, Palm Beach, Florida) on 7 January.

13 May 2006. Ricky Hatton w pts 12 Luis Collazo.
Venue: TD Bank North Garden, Boston, Massachusetts, USA. **Recognition:** WBA. **Referee:** John Zablocki.
Scorecards: 115-112, 115-112, 114-113.
Fight Summary: Collazo (147), who was making his first defence of the title that was handed to him after Zab Judah had been stripped, was dropped by a short left in the opening seconds as Hatton (147) got away quickly. There was never that much between them, two rounds at most, and Hatton admitted afterwards that the southpaw champion's punches hurt him throughout. In the final session Collazo hammered in a barrage of blows that saw Hatton go down for what the referee felt was a slip, and although the latter, tired from his exertions, stayed upright from thereon in he took further heavy blows prior to the bell. In what had been a tough, close fight, the unanimous decision could have gone either way.

Hatton relinquished the title on 31 August rather than defend against the mandatory challenger, Oktay Urkal. Following that decision it was decided that Miguel Cotto would meet Carlos Quintana for the vacant title, with the winner making his first defence against Urkal.

22 July 2006. Carlos Baldomir w rsc 9 Arturo Gatti.
Venue: Boardwalk Hall, Atlantic City, New Jersey, USA. **Recognition:** WBC/The Ring. **Referee:** Wayne Hedgpeth.
Fight Summary: Outboxed from the beginning, his hard career catching up with him as the rounds passed by, Gatti (147) gave it everything he had left against a two-belt champion who continually caught him with the jab and was a hardy customer to boot. In the eighth it was clear that Gatti, cut under the right eye, was struggling as Baldomir (147) raised the tempo, and he twice went to the floor from what were classified as slips but seemed more than that. Coming out for the ninth intending to finish there and then, with Baldomir smashing in several heavy blows a left hook saw Gatti crash to the floor. Although Gatti just about made it up he was rescued by the referee at 2.50 of the session after he had gone down again.

28 October 2006. Kermit Cintron w rsc 5 Mark Suarez.
Venue: The County Convention Centre, Palm Beach, Florida, USA. **Recognition:** IBF. **Referee:** Frank Santore Jnr.
Fight Summary: Contested for the vacant title after Floyd Mayweather handed in his belt, Cintron (146) was the man who took advantage of the situation when stopping Suarez (146¼) at 2.53 of the fifth. Although Cintron was knocked down from a blatant rabbit punch in the opener, for which Suarez got off with a warning, it was not until the third round that he began to take over. Going with the jab in the fourth, Cintron walked through some heavy blows to get his left hook on target and in the fifth, after knocking Suarez over for the 'eight' count with a solid left, the latter was being battered without response when the referee stepped in to rescue him.

4 November 2006. Floyd Mayweather Jnr w pts 12 Carlos Baldomir.
Venue: Bay Hotel, Las Vegas, Nevada, USA. **Recognition:** WBC/The Ring. **Referee:** Jay Nady.
Scorecards: 120-108, 120-108, 118-110.
Fight Summary: Despite being outjabbed and losing the opening two rounds, the two-belt champion was working the body well while looking to slow Mayweather (146) down in the latter stages. However, by the sixth Baldomir (147) was being outboxed and unable to find a way through Mayweather's defences. It was later learned that Mayweather was using his right hand sparingly from here onwards as had injured it, but it made no difference to the way the fight was going. An easy win for Mayweather, the CompuBox stats showed that the latter scored with 199 from 458 thrown, while Baldomir had landed just 79 times from his 670 output.

Shane Mosley outpointed Luis Collazo over 12 rounds at the Bay Hotel on 10 February 2007, winning the WBC 'interim' title in the process.

2 December 2006. Antonio Margarito w pts 12 Joshua Clottey.
Venue: Boardwalk Hall, Atlantic City, New Jersey, USA. **Recognition:** WBO. **Referee:** Benjy Esteves Jnr.
Scorecards: 116-112, 116-112, 118-109.
Fight Summary: Clottey (147) started well when winning three of the opening four rounds before damaging his left hand, an injury that let the champion back into the contest. With Margarito (147) sensing that Clottey had a problem he slammed into the latter round after round without being able to floor the teak-tough Ghanaian. In the ninth, Margarito dished out so much punishment that one of the judges marked it as a 10-8 round. Although Clottey hung in and came back well in the final session the decision was never in doubt.

2 December 2006. Miguel Cotto w rtd 5 Carlos Quintana.
Venue: Boardwalk Hall, Atlantic City, New Jersey, USA. **Recognition:** WBA. **Referee:** Steve Smoger.
Fight Summary: With the vacant title up for grabs after Ricky Hatton had handed in his belt, Quintana (147), a southpaw, made a fairly solid start when keeping it long as Cotto (146) tried to close the distance. The fourth saw Cotto getting close enough to land his heavier shots, having had to take time out in the third after being hit low. Tearing out for the fifth with the bit between the teeth, with Quintana's right eye closing Cotto had him over with a left to the body. Although Quintana just about made it to his feet he was quickly put down again with a similar blow that took everything from him, and despite making it to the bell he was retired by his corner at the end of the session.

3 March 2007. Miguel Cotto w rsc 11 Oktay Urkal.
Venue: Roberto Clemente Coliseum, San Juan, Puerto Rico. **Recognition:** WBA. **Referee:** Luis Pabon.
Fight Summary: Making his first defence, Cotto (147) began strongly, scoring with solid blows to the body as he looked to slow the tough Urkal (146) down, and although the latter was still in the contest the champion was picking up the rounds. Cut over the left eye from a head butt in the sixth Cotto turned southpaw to avoid further damage, but when Urkal continued with dangerous headwork he had points deducted in the seventh and 11th. Following the last transgression, when Urkal's corner signalled that they wanted the fight stopped as their man was too far behind the referee obliged, the stoppage coming at 1.01 of the session.

9 June 2007. Miguel Cotto w rsc 11 Zab Judah.
Venue: Madison Square Garden, Manhattan, NYC, New York, USA. **Recognition:** WBA. **Referee:** Arthur Mercante Jnr.
Fight Summary: Looking to get his hands on his old title, the southpaw challenger made a decent start, a countering left uppercut hurting Cotto (146½) in the opener before he was dropped by a low blow and given five minutes of time out to recover. Surprisingly, Judah did not take up the allocated time fully. Following a tough second, Cotto was deducted a point in the third when hitting Judah (145) low again. By the sixth, with both men cut on their right eyes and Cotto's heavy jabs beginning to take over, Judah came back with some big punches of his own in the seventh but was unable to discourage the champion. Getting right on top in the eighth despite taking the occasional heavy shot, Cotto dropped Judah in the ninth following a two-fisted attack. With Judah's right eye closing fast, Cotto carried on with the battering into the 11th before dropping his man, a left-right-left combination doing the business. On his feet again, but still dazed, Judah was rescued by the referee on the 49 second mark when he was shipping punches having fallen into the ropes.

14 July 2007. Kermit Cintron w rsc 2 Walter Dario Matthysse.
Venue: Boardwalk Hall, Atlantic City, New Jersey, USA. **Recognition:** IBF. **Referee:** Earl Morton.
Fight Summary: Up against a tough banger in Matthysse (147), the champion mixed it up from the bell, his straighter blows being the difference. With Cintron (146) going well, towards the end of the opening round a crashing right to the jaw had the Argentine over for the 'eight' count. No sooner had Matthysse come out for the second was he dropped by another heavy right as Cintron unloaded, and on getting to his feet and being smashed down again by a left hook to the head the referee dispensed with the count to allow the medics into the ring. The finish came just 29 seconds into the session.

14 July 2007. Paul Williams w pts 12 Antonio Margarito.
Venue: Home Depot Centre, Carson, California, USA. **Recognition:** WBO. **Referee:** Lou Moret.
Scorecards: 115-113, 115-113, 116-112.
Fight Summary: A tall southpaw, Williams (145½) got his jab working quickly as he looked to outbox the hard-hitting champion, but it was his solid left-hand punching that was one of the main reasons that the title ended up with him. Margarito (145¾) was always dangerous and worked the body well, but many of his crude swinging blows were evaded. Regardless of that it still appeared to be close for many of those watching despite the CompuBox stats showing that Williams landed with 228 punches to Margarito's 181.

10 November 2007. Miguel Cotto w pts 12 Shane Mosley.
Venue: Madison Square Garden, Manhattan, NYC, New York, USA. **Recognition:** WBA. **Referee:** Benjy Esteves Jnr.
Scorecards: 115-113, 116-113, 115-113.
Fight Summary: The champion started well enough against the 36-year-old Mosley (146¼), keeping his left going while looking to notch up the points and bang over the occasional right hand. Although Mosley was never out of the contest and landed heavy overarm rights on Cotto (146¼) at times he was too slow to follow up any opportunities. All three judges had Mosley winning five rounds, while Cotto, who could have upped the pace had he needed to, always appeared to be in control.

On 8 December, at the Sports Palace, Le Cannet, France, Yuriy Nuzhnenko outpointed Frederic Klose over 12 rounds to win the WBA 'interim' title.

23 November 2007. Kermit Cintron w rsc 10 Jesse Feliciano.
Venue: Staples Centre, Los Angeles, California, USA. **Recognition:** IBF. **Referee:** Jon Schorle.
Fight Summary: With a three-inch reach advantage over Feliciano (147) it was no surprise that the champion used long lefts and rights to keep the latter at bay. In the second, however, Feliciano was at close quarters where he was able to nullify much of Cintron's efforts, even hurting the latter with solid shots. Come the fifth, although Cintron (146¾) was catching Feliciano with heavy shots the latter was prepared to walk through them to land more of his own. While Cintron was winning the rounds on the scorecards Feliciano was always there looking to halt his progress, but in the tenth all of his good work came undone after he was caught by several big punches that left him dazed and open. Despite trying to hold on, Feliciano was rescued by the referee on the 1.53 mark after two more heavy rights crashed into him.

8 December 2007. Floyd Mayweather Jnr w rsc 10 Ricky Hatton.
Venue: MGM Grand, Las Vegas, Nevada, USA. **Recognition:** WBC/The Ring. **Referee:** Joe Cortez.
Fight Summary: Rattling up the rounds against the tough Hatton (145) the two-belt champion showed his class when overcoming a rival who was still in the fight come the fifth round, even if he was behind on the cards. It was after Hatton was deducted a point for hitting Mayweather (147) on the back of the head in the sixth that the latter began to warm up, picking his punches with deliberation and drawing his man on to him. Having been cut over the right eye in the third Hatton ploughed on, but in the tenth he ran headlong into a tremendous left hook that smashed him to the floor, via a ring post. Although Hatton made it to his feet and was allowed to box on, when he was caught heavily by a left-right-left the referee stopped the contest just as he was collapsing to the floor. The finish was timed at 1.35 of the tenth.

Further to Mayweather's announcement on 6 June 2008 that he was retiring, a forthcoming match between Andre Berto and Miguel Angel Rodriguez was recognised by the WBC as being for the vacant title. In the light of the above, *The Ring* magazine's version of the world title became vacant on 29 June.

9 February 2008. Carlos Quintana w pts 12 Paul Williams.
Venue: Pechanga Resort & Casino, Temecula, California, USA. **Recognition:** WBO. **Referee:** Jack Reiss.
Scorecards: 115-113, 116-112, 116-112.
Fight Summary: In this all-southpaw battle it was the challenger who started the better, jumping in with solid rights and lefts that Williams (146¾) seemed powerless to stop, and making it difficult for the latter to pick him up. Having set a terrific pace, by the seventh with Quintana (146¾) beginning to tire it was Williams who looked to pick

it up from thereon in, but he failed to take advantage. In fact, the contest was ultimately decided in the last four rounds, Williams winning just one of them on the cards as Quintana came back strongly. According to one ringside critic, it was Quintana who landed the heaviest punches throughout and thus deserved the win.

12 April 2008. Antonio Margarito w co 6 Kermit Cintron.
Venue: Boardwalk Hall, Atlantic City, New Jersey, USA. **Recognition:** IBF. **Referee:** Earl Brown.
Fight Summary: Having already had a beating at the hands of Margarito (146½) three years earlier, the champion took another one in this rematch before he was counted out at 1.57 of the sixth. Standing right in front of Cintron (146½), banging in solid body shots throughout while virtually ignoring the heavy leather coming his way, Margarito took all the rounds on the cards other than the first. Finally, in the sixth Margarito found the punches he had been looking for, a cracking right to the head that was followed by a left hook to the body bringing the contest to an end.

Margarito relinquished the title in May in order to make a match with Miguel Cotto for the latter's WBA crown. Following that, Joshua Clottey, who had beaten Shamone Alvarez (w pts 12 at the Hard Rock Hotel & Casino, Las Vegas, Nevada on 20 December 2007) in an eliminator, and Zab Judah were signed up to battle for the vacant crown.

12 April 2008. Miguel Cotto w rsc 5 Alfonso Gomez.
Venue: Boardwalk Hall, Atlantic City, New Jersey, USA. **Recognition:** WBA. **Referee:** Randy Neumann.
Fight Summary: Dominating from the opening bell, the champion got his left jab going early as well as banging in solid body shots to slow Gomez (147) down and open him up. Hurt at the end of the opener, Gomez was dropped in the second after several lefts and rights were finished off by a right to the body, and he was down again in the third courtesy of a left hook to the body. Constantly switching between southpaw and orthodox Cotto (146½) confused Gomez who was floored for the third time by a straight left in the fifth, and at the end of the session the referee stopped the contest on the advice of the ringside doctor.

Defending the WBA 'interim' title, Yuriy Nuzhnenko retained his crown following a ten-round technical draw against Irving Garcia on 19 April at the Sports Palace, Kiev, Ukraine.

7 June 2008. Paul Williams w rsc 1 Carlos Quintana.
Venue: Mohegan Sun Casino, Uncasville, Connecticut, USA. **Recognition:** WBO. **Referee:** Eddie Claudio.
Fight Summary: A return match and an all southpaw affair, Williams (145¾) took swift revenge on the champion when regaining his title after just 135 seconds of the opening session. There would be no mistakes this time round as Williams found a big left to stagger Quintana (146), who stumbled around before three more powerful lefts smashed him to the deck. Although Quintana was up at 'eight' he was quickly set upon, and when two more heavy lefts had him over again, dragging Williams down as he went to the floor, the referee stopped the contest.

Williams relinquished the WBO title in November to contest the WBO 'interim' junior middleweight championship, which was followed by an announcement that Miguel Cotto would be meeting Michael Jennings in order to find a new champion.

21 June 2008. Andre Berto w rsc 7 Miguel Angel Rodriguez.
Venue: FedEx Forum, Memphis, Tennessee, USA. **Recognition:** WBC. **Referee:** Laurence Cole.
Fight Summary: Contested for the vacant title after Floyd Mayweather handed in his belt, Berto (146) proved to be a cut above Rodriguez (145) before stopping the latter at 2.13 of the seventh. With his speed around the ring and fast hands, Berto looked to be an accomplished performer when setting up attack after attack. By the sixth, even though Berto was totally dominant, Rodriguez was always trying to fight back, but in the seventh his days were numbered. Dropped by a right uppercut that followed a right hook, although Rodriguez made it up and was allowed to fight on, the moment he was downed again by a solid one-two the referee stepped in.

26 July 2008. Antonio Margarito w rsc 11 Miguel Cotto.
Venue: MGM Grand, Las Vegas, Nevada, USA. **Recognition:** WBA. **Referee:** Kenny Bayless.

Fight Summary: Having given up the IBF title to take Cotto (147) on, Margarito (147) justified his decision when stopping the champion at 2.05 of the 11th. The faster and more precise Cotto had gone well at first, taking four of the opening five rounds, but after Margarito stepped it up in the sixth he took over when gradually grinding his man down. By the latter stages of the tenth Cotto was being overwhelmed, and into the 11th he was dropped by a heavy left and two straight rights. Although he was quickly back into the fray, Cotto was soon decked again when he was blasted to the floor by two rights to the jaw, having been sent to the bottom strand earlier in the round without a count. At that point, with the towel on its way into the ring, the referee called a halt to proceedings.

2 August 2008. Joshua Clottey w tdec 9 Zab Judah.
Venue: Palms Hotel & Casino, Las Vegas, Nevada, USA. **Recognition:** IBF. **Referee:** Robert Byrd.
Scorecards: 87-84, 86-85, 86-85.
Fight Summary: In a contest to decide the vacancy that arose when Antonio Margarito handed in his belt, Clottey (147) won the title on a technical decision at 1.12 of the ninth after Judah (143) sustained a badly cut right eye. Prior to that there was little between them, both landing solidly at times, Judah with southpaw shots up and down and Clottey banging in straight rights. With Clottey getting on top in the ninth, when Judah's right eye was gashed by a left uppercut the referee called for the cards on the ringside doctor's advice. Despite Judah claiming it was a butt that caused the damage he was correctly overruled by the third man. Following the contest it was learned that Clottey would be out of action for several months, having injured his left bicep in the fourth or fifth round.

Clottey forfeited his title on 16 April 2009 after signing for a fight against the WBO champion, Miguel Cotto. Further to that, Isaac Hlatshwayo and Delvin Rodriguez were contracted to settle the vacancy after boxing a debatable 12-round draw at the Emperor's Palace, Kempton Park, Gauteng, South Africa on 17 November in an eliminating contest. Rodriguez had gone on to beat Shamone Alvarez (w pts 12 at the Mohegan Sun Casino, Uncasville, Connecticut on 6 March 2009).

27 September 2008. Andre Berto w pts 12 Steve Forbes.
Venue: Staples Centre, Los Angeles, California, USA. **Recognition:** WBC. **Referee:** James Jen-Kin.
Scorecards: 116-111, 118-109, 118-109.
Fight Summary: Making his first defence against a former junior lightweight champion in Forbes (147), a 31-year-old veteran, Berto (145½) initially had his hands full before sorting himself out to win going away. Exhibiting great hand-speed and movement, allied to good power, Berto began to mix up his punches more and more as the contest moved on, while Forbes, cut on the left eye in the third following a head clash, showed his skill when making the champion work for victory. The common consensus afterwards was that Berto should be looking to meet the top men in the division before too long.

17 January 2009. Andre Berto w pts 12 Luis Collazo.
Venue: Beau Rivage Resort & Casino, Biloxi, Mississippi, USA. **Recognition:** WBC. **Referee:** Keith Hughes.
Scorecards: 116-111, 114-113, 114-113.
Fight Summary: Giving as good as he got the southpaw challenger tested Berto (146) in this one, and although the latter won unanimously it was too close for comfort. Having started well with a right-left in the opener that almost had Berto over, Collazo (145½) was continually held early on, the champion eventually being deducted a point for the offence in the fourth. Berto began to come on in the fifth, knocking Collazo's gumshield out with a solid right, before running off the next three sessions when slowing the latter down with body shots. Although Collazo came back well in the ninth and tenth, by taking the final two rounds when pressing hard, Berto made the decision his.

24 January 2009. Shane Mosley w rsc 9 Antonio Margarito.
Venue: Staples Centre, Los Angeles, California, USA. **Recognition:** WBA. **Referee:** Raul Caiz.
Fight Summary: At the age of 38, Mosley (147) showed that he was still a player when stopping the champion in the ninth round, having given a tip-top performance in the art of boxing from the opening bell. Taking control from the off, with jabs and solid rights going in up and down, just when it looked as though Mosley was tiring from his exertions in the fourth Margarito (145¾) was staggered by some heavy right-handers. In the sixth Margarito was badly hurt by another batch of rights, and in the eighth he was eventually dropped after taking several punches from both hands full on. Getting up to be saved by the bell, Margarito had nowhere to hide in the ninth, being

caught by blow after blow until the referee, seeing the towel coming in, came to his rescue 43 seconds into the round. It was no surprise that Margarito collapsed to the deck once Mosley had been pulled off him.

When Mosley was promoted to 'super' champion status by the WBA, Yuriy Nuzhnenko, the 'interim' titleholder, was outpointed over 12 rounds by Vyacheslav Senchenko at the Sports Palace, Donetsk, Ukraine on 10 April. In a battle between Ukrainians, Senchenko would be seen as the new 'second tier' champion.

Later in the year, on 3 October, at the Druzhba Sports Palace, Donetsk, Ukraine, Senchenko outpointed Motoki Sasaki over 12 rounds to retain the 'second tier' title.

After Mosley was beaten by Floyd Mayweather Jnr (l pts 12 at the MGM Grand, Las Vegas, Nevada on 1 May 2010) in a fight at the welterweight limit, when he was stripped of his 'super' champion title on 22 May Senchenko was promoted to full championship status. The Mosley v Mayweather contest had gone ahead as a non-title fight after the latter refused to pay the sanctioning fee.

Souleymane M'baye outpointed Antonin Decarie over 12 rounds at the Marcel Cerdan Sports Palace, Levallois-Perret, France on 28 May 2010 to win the vacant WBA 'interim' title.

21 February 2009. Miguel Cotto w rsc 5 Michael Jennings.
Venue: Madison Square Garden, Manhattan, NYC, New York, USA. **Recognition:** WBO. **Referee:** Benjy Esteves Jnr.
Fight Summary: Fighting to decide the vacant title after Paul Williams decided to move up a division, Cotto (146) had far too much experience at this level for Jennings (146½) and it showed. With Jennings on the back foot from the opening bell Cotto took his time when cutting off the ring, but after pouncing in the fourth he had the Englishman over twice from left hooks to the body. The knockdowns followed a battery of blows from both hands that had already stunned Jennings, who finished the session with a cut left eye. Dropped again, this time in the fifth, from a straight right to the head, although Jennings got to his feet the referee decided that he was not fit to continue and pulled him out on the 2.36 mark.

30 May 2009. Andre Berto w pts 12 Juan Urango.
Venue: Seminole Hard Rock Arena, Hollywood, Florida, USA. **Recognition:** WBC. **Referee:** Tommy Kimmons.
Scorecards: 118-110, 118-110, 117-111.
Fight Summary: Moving around the ring at speed for round after round, banging in countering blows before moving on, Berto (145¼) made his southpaw challenger look foolish at times. As the IBF junior welterweight champion, Urango (146½) gave it his best shot but was wide open to the left jab-left hooks that came his way, winning two rounds at most. Having disappointed in recent fights, Berto showed what he was made of in this one.

13 June 2009. Miguel Cotto w pts 12 Joshua Clottey.
Venue: Madison Square Garden, Manhattan, NYC, New York, USA. **Recognition:** WBO. **Referee:** Arthur Mercante Jnr.
Scorecards: 116-111, 115-112, 113-114.
Fight Summary: Cotto (146) putting his title on the line against the former undefeated IBF champion, Clottey (147), who had been stripped for taking this fight, made an excellent start when dropping the Ghanaian with a straight left in the opener. However, from thereon in there was never much between them, as Clottey marched forward to take the play away from Cotto, blocking many blows while dishing out his own. Cut over the left eye in the third after heads came together, Cotto was forced to make changes. In the fifth Clottey crashed to the floor after being pushed, injuring his left knee, but in winning the sixth through to the eighth he was in poll position. For whatever reason, Clottey failed to take advantage of the situation, and it was the more aggressive Cotto who came home to take the split decision.

1 August 2009. Isaac Hlatshwayo w pts 12 Delvin Rodriguez.
Venue: Mohegun Sun Arena, Uncasville, Connecticut, USA. **Recognition:** IBF. **Referee:** Steve Smoger.
Scorecards: 116-112, 116-113, 113-115.

Fight Summary: Contested for the vacant title after Joshua Clottey was stripped, it was Hlatshwayo (146¼) who won the split decision after the pair had fought a draw in an eliminating contest a few months earlier. Although Rodriguez (147) shaded the opening three rounds, once the South African got his left jab going he began to control the bout within reason. There was still plenty of scrappy fighting going on, especially on the inside, but in the last three sessions it was Hlatshwayo who landed the cleaner blows.

14 November 2009. Manny Pacquiao w rsc 12 Miguel Cotto.
Venue: MGM Grand, Las Vegas, Nevada, USA. **Recognition:** WBO. **Referee:** Kenny Bayless.
Fight Summary: With his title on the line against the hammering southpaw, Pacquiao (144), although starting well Cotto (145) was soon under the cosh, being dropped in the third by a right to the body and a left to the head, and then again in the fourth by a crunching left uppercut to the head. Despite taking a battering, Cotto was always trying to fight back, but it was getting harder and harder for him as the rounds progressed. Even though Pacquiao was caught by solid lefts at times he merely shrugged them off before setting up further assaults. Gamely fighting on while ignoring a badly cut left eye and facial swellings, when Cotto was stunned in the 12th by heavy combinations the referee stopped the fight 55 seconds into the session.

11 December 2009. Jan Zaveck w rsc 3 Isaac Hlatshwayo.
Venue: Wembley Indoor Arena, Johannesburg, South Africa. **Recognition:** IBF. **Referee:** Jen Chevalier.
Fight Summary: Making his initial defence, Hlatshwayo (146) was soon under pressure after the hard-hitting Zaveck (146½) hurt him with three heavy blows that sent him to the ropes early in the opener. Going on the back foot, Hlatshwayo survived the round, but was soon under attack in the second as Zaveck smashed in punches from both hands to the head, many of them being overarm swings. Battered down by a right hook to the jaw the South African looked a sorry sight, and in the third he was sent to the floor for an 'eight' count. After the fight resumed, when Hlatshwayo was sent crashing for the third time following heavy shots from both hands the referee rescued him at 2.55 of the session.

13 March 2010. Manny Pacquiao w pts 12 Joshua Clottey.
Venue: Cowboys Stadium, Arlington, Texas, USA. **Recognition:** WBO. **Referee:** Rafael Ramos.
Scorecards: 120-108, 119-109, 119-109.
Fight Summary: Happy to give Clottey (147) a crack at his new title, Pacquiao (145¾) proceeded to hammer in solid southpaw blows, more than 1,200 of them to be precise, as the Ghanaian made for a difficult defensive target. The only round that Clottey might have won was the third, a batch of rights to the head earning Pacquiao's attention, but he was quickly back on the front foot when looking to open his challenger up with body shots, the right hook being his favoured weapon. For round after round the pattern was the same, Pacquiao's speed against Clottey's defence, and although the champion ended the fight cut below the right eye and carrying bruised features it was probably due to Clottey being much the heavier man on the night than punishment that was dished out, although the latter did get off some heavy blows in the tenth.

9 April 2010. Jan Zaveck w rsc 12 Rodolfo Ezequiel Martinez.
Venue: Tivoli Sports Hall, Ljubljana, Slovenia. **Recognition:** IBF. **Referee:** Ingo Barrabas.
Fight Summary: Starting on the front foot the champion had too much power for Martinez (147), who was treated to heavy combinations for round after round in what was a fast-paced bout. Showing great fortitude, despite having little success against the hard-hitting Zaveck (147), the brave Martinez struggled on through the rounds until the referee had seen enough, stopping the contest with just 45 seconds remaining. Although Martinez wished to continue it was the right decision as he had been unable to stem the flow of punches coming his way.

10 April 2010. Andre Berto w rsc 8 Carlos Quintana.
Venue: Bank-Atlantic Centre, Sunrise, Florida, USA. **Recognition:** WBC. **Referee:** Tommy Kimmons.
Fight Summary: In a tough no-holds-barred contest, the champion showed his resolve when coming through strongly to stop Quintana (146½) at 2.16 of the eighth round. Berto (146½) started well enough, but had to fight back after being hurt by a cracking southpaw overarm left that stunned him in the second. Fight back hard he did, two-fisted attacks forcing Quintana to give ground before the latter was deducted a point for hitting behind the head in the third. The battle raged on through the fourth as Quintana, now cut on the left eye, gave it all he had

but was gradually being ground down. Having continually come back hard when under pressure, Quintana was eventually rescued by the referee in the eighth when he was shipping blows and had just taken a heavy right to the head.

30 August 2010. Vyacheslav Senchenko w pts Charlie Jose Navarro.

Venue: Donbass Arena, Donetsk, Ukraine. **Recognition:** WBA. **Referee:** Steve Smoger.
Scorecards: 115-113, 115-113, 116-113.
Fight Summary: Defending the title that was handed to him after Shane Mosley was stripped, Senchenko (146½) started carefully, working the jab, before opening up in the third and hurting Navarro (146) with a heavy uppercut followed by a right cross. Although Senchenko was able to box Navarro off for several rounds, in the sixth he came under pressure as the latter finally got to close quarters. With Senchenko tiring and Navarro getting to him, the last few sessions were closely contested but it was the champion's better quality that ultimately won the day.

On 14 July 2011, Ismael El Massoudi won the WBA 'interim' title when stopping the champion, Souleymane M'baye, in the 12th round at the Open Air Arena, Jemaa el-Fnaa Plaza, Marrakech, Morocco.

4 September 2010. Jan Zaveck w pts 12 Rafal Jackiewicz.

Venue: Sportpark Arena, Ljubljana, Slovenia. **Recognition:** IBF. **Referee:** Jean-Pierre Van Imschoot.
Scorecards: 117-111, 117-111, 114-114.
Fight Summary: As the only man to beat him in his career thus far, the champion gained revenge over Jackiewicz (146¾) when taking the majority decision in what was a hard-fought contest that see-sawed throughout. Dictating the action for the opening two rounds, banging away with both hands, Zaveck (146) soon found himself in a fight as Jackiewicz came back hard with punches of his own. All three judges had Zaveck winning the last two sessions as he pushed on, but regardless of the scorecards there never seemed to be much in it.

27 November 2010. Andre Berto w rsc 1 Freddy Hernandez.

Venue: MGM Grand, Las Vegas, Nevada, USA. **Recognition:** WBC. **Referee:** Russell Mora.
Fight Summary: Taking his time while feeling Hernandez (147) out, there was very little action before Berto (145) suddenly whipped in a left-right to the jaw that sent the challenger crashing. Although Hernandez made it up at 'five' the referee stopped the contest on the 2.07 mark when believing that the latter was unprepared to continue. Following the decision, despite sending out the wrong message, Hernandez was adamant that he could have carried on.

18 February 2011. Jan Zaveck w rsc 5 Paul Delgado.

Venue: Sportspark Arena, Ljubljana, Slovenia. **Recognition:** IBF. **Referee:** Benny Decroos.
Fight Summary: Getting away to a strong start, the champion hurt Delgado (145¾) early on with a right to the head before marching out in the second to drop the latter twice from further heavy rights to the head following barrages of blows that had softened him up. Fighting on bravely despite being cut over both eyes, Delgado stayed around until the fifth before the referee rescued him at 3.00 of the session after he had been hammered to the canvas by another big right. Zaveck (146¾), showing a high guard when required, had been in control throughout, his solid two-handed punching ultimately being too much for the brave but outgunned Delgado.

16 April 2011. Victor Ortiz w pts 12 Andre Berto.

Venue: MGM Grand Theatre, Mashantucket, Connecticut, USA. **Recognition:** WBC. **Referee:** Michael Ortega.
Scorecards: 114-112, 114-111, 115-110.
Fight Summary: Tearing out of his corner from the bell the southpaw challenger took the play away from Berto (145½) before dropping him with a left to the head that the referee ruled as a slip. Not giving Berto much rest in the opener, Ortiz (146) dropped his man again, this time with a right uppercut to the chin following a left-right that had paved the way. Just when you thought that Ortiz was en-route to a quick win he himself was floored by a straight right in the second. Despite Ortiz getting on top, the sixth saw him downed again by a crashing right. But when Berto came in to finish him off following the count he too was decked by a big left hook. Competitive all the way from thereon in, although Ortiz was deducted a point for hitting behind the head in the tenth it made no difference to the result.

7 May 2011. Manny Pacquiao w pts 12 Shane Mosley.
Venue: MGM Grand, Las Vegas, Nevada, USA. **Recognition:** WBO. **Referee:** Kenny Bayless.
Scorecards: 120-107, 120-108, 119-108.
Fight Summary: Despite not being at his best the southpaw champion still had too much for the 39-year-old Mosley (147), who was dropped heavily in the third by a short left to the side of the head that almost terminated the contest there and then. Somehow Mosley made it up, and although taking a battering at the hands of Pacquiao (145) he was still there at the bell. With Pacquiao suffering from leg cramps and Mosley still shell-shocked the fight turned into a boring affair that had the fans booing before it livened up in the last two rounds as the Filipino tried to stop it going to the cards.

26 August 2011. Vyacheslav Senchenko w rsc 6 Marco Antonio Avendano.
Venue: Donbass Arena, Donetsk, Ukraine. **Recognition:** WBA. **Referee:** Steve Smoger.
Fight Summary: Regardless that the 38-year-old Avendano (146¾) started the better, moving in and out with the jab, the champion began to take over in the third when banging in some heavy shots to the head. Both men had been cut over their left eyes following a clash of heads in the opener, but neither seemed affected. With the fight going the way of Senchenko (146¾) he picked it up in the sixth when hurting Avendano with a solid straight right, and having avoided the latter's attempts to hold on he landed two rights and a left to the body to send him down. Not even bothering to pick up the count, the referee called the fight off on the 2.40 mark.

3 September 2011. Andre Berto w rtd 5 Jan Zaveck.
Venue: Beau Rivage Resort & Casino, Biloxi, Mississippi, USA. **Recognition:** IBF. **Referee:** Fred Steinwinder.
Fight Summary: Having lost his WBC welterweight title last time out, Berto (146¾) came back to take the IBF version away from Zaveck (146½) after the latter was retired at the end of the fifth. Working well behind the jab, Berto made life difficult for Zaveck in the opening three rounds, the latter unable to get going due to the challenger's tactics. When Zaveck finally got to grips with Berto in the fourth it seemed as though the tide might have turned. Picking it up again in the fifth, Zaveck bundled into Berto, whose left eye was now swollen, and was dishing it out when both of his eyes were cut. Back in his corner at the end of the session, with his right eye now closed, it was all over.

After Berto relinquished the IBF title on 8 November in order to pursue a rematch with Victor Ortiz, Randall Bailey and Mike Jones were in pole position to find a new champion. Both men had come through eliminating contests, Bailey beating Jackson Osei Bonsu (w rsc 1 at the Lotto Arena, Merksem, Antwerp, Belgium on 19 March 2010) and then being involved in a two-round no-decision affair at the same venue against Said Ouali on 10 December 2010, while Jones had defeated Sebastian Andres Lujan (w pts 12 at Madison Square Garden, Manhattan, NYC, New York on 3 December). Although the fight went out to purse bids in January 2012, it would not go on until the following June for a number of reasons.

17 September 2011. Floyd Mayweather Jnr w co 4 Victor Ortiz.
Venue: MGM Grand, Las Vegas, Nevada, USA. **Recognition:** WBC. **Referee:** Joe Cortez.
Fight Summary: Right from the opening bell this was Mayweather's fight as Ortiz (147) continually walked into countering blows and was outspeeded throughout. There were moments of joy for the southpaw champion, but they were few and far between as Mayweather (146½) placed himself exactly where he wanted to be. Having rushed Mayweather in the fourth and failed to land effectively, Ortiz was deducted a point for a deliberate head butt. There would be no way back for him after that as moments later an angry but focussed Mayweather slammed in a heavy left hook to the head, and with Ortiz still looking towards the referee he was decked by a right cross. Unable to get to his feet, Ortiz was counted out at 2.59 of the session after ignoring the maxim of protecting yourself at all times.

At the HP Pavilion, San Jose, California on 28 July 2012, Robert Guerrero outpointed Selcuk Aydin over 12 rounds to win the vacant WBC 'interim' title. Guerrero retained his 'interim' title when outpointing Andre Berto at the Citizens Business Bank Arena, Ontario, California, USA on 24 November 2012.

12 November 2011. Manny Pacquiao w pts 12 Juan Manuel Marquez.
Venue: MGM Grand, Las Vegas, Nevada, USA. **Recognition:** WBO. **Referee:** Tony Weeks.
Scorecards: 115-113, 116-112, 114-114.
Fight Summary: In what was their third meeting, and made at 144lbs in order to suit both men, it was the southpaw champion who received the majority decision after winning four of the last five rounds on two of the cards as Marquez (142) tired. Extremely close, as their previous contests had been, it was also difficult to score as neither man landed eye-catching shots. With his hands held high and going with single jabs and right-hand counters, Marquez posed problems for Pacquiao (143) all night, the latter often following the Mexican around rather than making him fight his fight. Although cut on the right eye in the tenth and not at his best it did not stop Pacquiao's advance as Marquez ran out of gas.

29 April 2012. Paul Malignaggi w rsc 9 Vyacheslav Senchenko.
Venue: Donbass Arena, Donetsk, Ukraine. **Recognition:** WBA. **Referee:** Steve Smoger.
Fight Summary: Fighting on enemy territory it was a major shock when Malignaggi (146) wrested the title away from Senchenko (146¾), especially as the champion was up against a known non-puncher. Going with the left jab and moving well, Malignaggi led Senchenko a merry dance for several rounds, and by the sixth the left side of the latter's face was swollen and bruised. On top of that Senchenko was cut both on top and under the left eye. From thereon in, Malignaggi continued to counter Senchenko as he came on to the left hand, and at 1.10 of the ninth the referee halted the contest when it was clear that the Ukranian could hardly see out of his left eye and consequently was taking too many punches.

On 21 July, Diego Gabriel Chaves won the WBA 'interim' title when knocking out Ismael El Massoudi inside two rounds at the German Gymnastic Society Arena, Buenos Aires, Argentina. Chaves made a successful defence of the WBA 'interim' title when stopping Jose Miranda inside two rounds at Luna Park, Buenos Aires, Argentina on 22 September.

Due to defend the WBA title against Pablo Cesar Cano on 20 October at the Barclays Centre, Brooklyn, NYC, New York, USA, Malignaggi went ahead with the contest despite his rival coming in over the weight. Unable to lose the added weight in the allotted time given him, Cano also lost the 12-round points decision.

9 June 2012. Randall Bailey w rsc 11 Mike Jones.
Venue: MGM Grand, Las Vegas, Nevada, USA. **Recognition:** IBF. **Referee:** Tony Weeks.
Fight Summary: Contested for the vacant title after Andre Berto had handed in his belt, Jones (146½) controlled the former IBF junior welterweight champion, Bailey (146), virtually from the off. It was Jones' speed of hand and foot that Bailey could not deal with, being forced to take the jab time and again as his opponent put rounds in the bag. Coming into the tenth all Jones had to do was make sure that he did not get caught by the hard-hitting Bailey, but that is exactly what he failed to do when getting dropped by a straight right to the head. Having been put under a lot of pressure in the 11th, eventually Jones succumbed when he was floored by a right uppercut that landed squarely on his chin, and although trying to make it to his feet the referee called the action off at 2.52 of the session.

9 June 2012. Timothy Bradley w pts 12 Manny Pacquiao.
Venue: MGM Grand, Las Vegas, Nevada, USA. **Recognition:** WBO. **Referee:** Robert Byrd.
Scorecards: 115-113, 115-113, 113-115.
Fight Summary: In a contest in which the CompuBox stats had the southpaw champion out-landing Bradley (146) in ten of the 12 rounds, many were shocked when the latter was awarded the split decision. Even though Pacquiao (147) had appeared to ease off during the final three sessions it was difficult to work out how and where the fight was lost. As *Boxing News*, the British weekly magazine, stated: "Received wisdom is that American judges habitually favour aggression, but Pacquiao was clearly the aggressor on this night, albeit in bursts rather than the non-stop mode of old. He definitely landed blows that had greater impact, heavy lefts forcing Bradley back far more often than the latter had him backing up." The general feeling afterwards was that there should be an immediate return.

20 October 2012. Devon Alexander w pts 12 Randall Bailey.
Venue: Barclays Centre, Brooklyn, NYC, New York, USA. **Recognition:** IBF. **Referee:** Arthur Mercante Jnr.
Scorecards: 116-110, 115-111, 117-109.
Fight Summary: Making sure that he stayed well clear of the champion's much vaunted power punches, Alexander (146¾), a southpaw and a former IBF/WBC junior welterweight title holder, racked up the rounds in negative fashion when jabbing before moving on. Unable to get close enough, Bailey (147) merely stalked his man, landing little of note throughout. There was also a lot of holding, both fighters having a point deducted for such an offence in the sixth. Despite not being interested in trading, the speedier Alexander did just enough to convince the judges without taking risks.

Alexander forced Lee Purdy to retire at the end of the seventh round at the Boardwalk Hall, Atlantic City, New Jersey on 18 May 2013. Purdy had taken the place of Kell Brook, who was earlier ruled out by a foot injury. Intended to involve the IBF title, although Purdy (147¾) failed to make the weight the contest still went ahead with Alexander fulfilling his mandatory defence obligation.

16 March 2013. Timothy Bradley w pts 12 Ruslan Provodnikov.
Venue: Home Depot Centre, Carson, California, USA. **Recognition:** WBO. **Referee:** Pat Russell.
Scorecards: 115-112, 114-113, 114-113.
Fight Summary: Although the champion made a fast start, both hands pumping out, he was dropped by a right to the head that the referee saw as a slip and came under terrific pressure from Provodnikov (146½) before the opener came to an end. Hurt again in the second, Bradley (146½) fought back hard prior to getting blasted by a big left in the sixth that almost had him over. From thereon in Bradley boxed to instructions, sending out the jab while constantly moving as the Russian tried to turn it into a war. By the ninth, Provodnikov, who was cut over the left eye, was taking plenty of point-scoring punches, but back he came with solid blows to stagger Bradley in the 11th before dropping him in the 12th with a heavy right. Saved by the bell, Bradley received a narrow unanimous verdict for his pains.

4 May 2013. Floyd Mayweather Jnr w pts 12 Robert Guerrero.
Venue: MGM Grand, Las Vegas, Nevada, USA. **Recognition:** WBC/The Ring. **Referee:** Robert Byrd.
Scorecards: 117-111, 117-111, 117-111.
Fight Summary: With the vacant *Ring* Championship Belt on the line as well as his WBC title being at stake, Mayweather (146) controlled the fight with some ease against the WBC 'interim' champion, Guerrero (147), who was outclassed most of the way. Although Guerrero, a southpaw, won the seventh and 12th rounds according to the judges it was more to do with Mayweather taking time out than the challenger, who was cut over the left eye in the eighth. Picking his punches carefully throughout as Guerrero came on to them, Mayweather proved that there was still plenty of life left in his 36-year-old legs.

22 June 2013. Adrien Broner w pts 12 Paul Malignaggi.
Venue: Barclays Centre, Brooklyn, NYC, New York, USA. **Recognition:** WBA. **Referee:** Benjy Esteves Jnr.
Scorecards: 115-113, 117-111, 113-115.
Fight Summary: Getting away quickly, the champion took three of the opening four rounds before Broner (146¾) was up and running, his punch-rate and speed keeping the latter at bay. As the contest wore on, the harder blows were being landed by Broner, especially on the inside, but he was never able to dominate the fast-moving Malignaggi (146½). Towards the end, while it was obvious that Malignaggi was throwing punches just to keep Broner at bay, the man from Cincinnati was unable to break through. At the final bell it was Broner who received the split decision, although it had been much tougher for him than expected.

Diego Gabriel Chaves lost his WBA 'interim' title when he was knocked out inside ten rounds by Keith Thurman at the AT & T Centre, San Antonio, Texas on 27 July.

12 October 2013. Timothy Bradley w pts 12 Juan Manuel Marquez.
Venue: Thomas & Mack Centre, Las Vegas, Nevada, USA. **Recognition:** WBO. **Referee:** Robert Byrd.
Scorecards: 115-113, 116-112, 113-115.

Fight Summary: Up against a 40-year-old challenger in Marquez (144½), and wary of his power, Bradley (146) boxed accordingly. At times both men let their punches go, but in the main it was safety first for Bradley, who kept his boxing together rather than taking the bait offered by Marquez. Despite there being no knockdowns, it was still interesting to see the contest play out, and there was never that much between them as the split decision in favour of Bradley would testify. In a difficult fight to score, there were only five rounds that all three judges could agree on, four of them going to Bradley and one to Marquez.

7 December 2013. Shawn Porter w pts 12 Devon Alexander.
Venue: Barclays Centre, Brooklyn, NYC, New York, USA. **Recognition:** IBF. **Referee:** Harvey Dock.
Scorecards: 115-113, 116-112, 116-112.
Fight Summary: Losing his title at the first time of asking, Alexander (146½), who was hurt by a big right in the opening session and almost decked in the third found Porter (146¾) just too lively for him. Porter also found Alexander's southpaw stance a perfect target for his right hands, and it was only in the middle rounds that the champion had some joy with the jab. With heads cracking together in the seventh, it was Alexander who came off worse when he was cut over the left eye. Whether it held Alexander back or not was debatable, but it certainly revitalised Porter who went on to take three of the last four rounds and the title.

14 December 2013. Marcos Maidana w pts 12 Adrien Broner.
Venue: The Alamodome, San Antonio, Texas, USA. **Recognition:** WBA. **Referee:** Laurence Cole.
Scorecards: 117-109, 115-110, 115-109.
Fight Summary: Beginning the contest strongly, banging in blows from both hands, Maidana (146¼) gave the champion no respite as he looked to unsettle him. In the second a cracking left hook to the chin dropped Broner (144½), who had received a warning earlier after an overarm left had sent him crashing into the ropes. Although being forced to take several hard shots upon getting to his feet Broner picked it up in the third when coming back with punches of his own, but by the seventh Maidana had taken over the reins again. Put down by another left hook in the eighth, on rising Broner was on the floor again, courtesy of a head butt for which Maidana had a point deducted. Still looking to put Broner away, Maidana slammed his way through the next three sessions before the American hit back hard in the 12th. Despite giving it everything Broner had left it too late, losing not only his title but also his unbeaten record.

On the same bill, Keith Thurman successfully defended his WBA 'interim' title when stopping Jesus Soto Karass in the ninth round. Thurman made another successful defence of the WBA 'interim' title when forcing Julio Diaz to retire at the end of the third round of their contest at the StubHub Centre, Carson, California on 26 April 2014.

12 April 2014. Manny Pacquiao w pts 12 Timothy Bradley.
Venue: MGM Grand, Las Vegas, Nevada, USA. **Recognition:** WBO. **Referee:** Kenny Bayless.
Scorecards: 116-112, 116-112, 118-110.
Fight Summary: Gaining revenge for his earlier defeat at the hands of the champion, Pacquiao (145) made sure this time round that he would impress the judges when taking the fight to his opponent, banging a southpaw hook in right from the off. Not perturbed, Bradley (145½) quickly hit back when both giving and taking, and hurt Pacquiao in the fourth with a wide right to the head. Back came a renewed Pacquiao, who battered away with solid combinations before almost dropping Bradley in the seventh. From thereon in it was nearly all Pacquiao. The only dampener for Pacquiao came in the 12th round when he received a bad cut over his right eye that would require 32 stitches after heads came together.

19 April 2014. Shawn Porter w rsc 4 Paul Malignaggi.
Venue: The Armoury, Washington DC, USA. **Recognition:** IBF. **Referee:** Sam Williams.
Fight Summary: Defending his title for the first time, Porter (146¾) was soon driving into Malignaggi (146¼) with both hands blazing, a cut opening up on the latter's left cheek in the first round as heads and punches went in. Hurt in the second by left and right hooks, Malignaggi tried to fight back but found Porter too big and strong for him. Forced to take a count in the fourth after being put down by a right to the head Malignaggi was in trouble, and when a big right smashed him down again the referee halted the contest at 1.14 of the session without bothering to take up the count.

3 May 2014. Floyd Mayweather Jnr w pts 12 Marcos Maidana.
Venue: MGM Grand, Las Vegas, Nevada, USA. **Recognition:** WBA/WBC/The Ring. **Referee:** Tony Weeks.
Scorecards: 116-112, 117-111, 114-114.
Fight Summary: With Mayweather's WBC title and *Ring* Championship Belt on the line in a contest that also saw Maidana's WBA crown thrown into the mix for good measure, the latter made the running when never giving his opponent a minute's rest. Defending himself at all times as Maidana (146½) continually tore in, by the halfway point Mayweather (146) was beginning to put some distance between himself and the Argentine, banging out the jab and looking to go to the body before moving on. With the ninth and tenth going to Mayweather on all three cards, Maidana continued to force the pace in the last two sessions but was unable to turn things around. Mayweather, who finished with a cut over his right eye and a swelling on the left cheek, was ultimately far too clever for the tough Maidana who fought above expectation.

16 August 2014. Kell Brook w pts 12 Shawn Porter.
Venue: StubHub Centre, Carson, California, USA. **Recognition:** IBF. **Referee:** Pat Russell.
Scorecards: 116-112, 117-111, 114-114.
Fight Summary: Boxing at a level above what the Americans expected from him, Brook (146½) gradually took the steam out of the champion before coming on strong to take the majority points decision. Outworked in the early rounds and cut over the left eye in the second, Brook began to make up ground from the fourth before winning every round bar two on two of the judges' cards from the seventh onwards. Cut over the right eye in the sixth, Porter (146¾) was almost blasted out in the seventh by a cracking right uppercut, and after Brook took over from the American on the inside he made the fight his.

13 September 2014. Floyd Mayweather Jnr w pts 12 Marcos Maidana.
Venue: MGM Grand, Las Vegas, Nevada, USA. **Recognition:** WBA/WBC/The Ring. **Referee:** Kenny Bayless.
Scorecards: 116-111, 116-111, 115-112.
Fight Summary: This was also surprisingly seen by the WBC as involving Mayweather's 154lbs title. Yet again a relatively tough fight, the champion being forced to work at all times, Maidana (146) was always there or thereabouts. Although Mayweather (146½) was by far the better boxer, Maidana was continually trying to rough him up even though he was forced to take some heavy shots in return. In the ninth Mayweather complained that Maidana had bitten into his left glove, hurting his fingers and numbing his hand from thereon in. When Mayweather was blatantly pushed over in the tenth a point was deducted from Maidana's total, which only made the latter even wilder. Following a wild right that hurt Mayweather, and with blows being tossed in from all angles, the champion calmly boxed his way through to the final bell without putting himself in the firing line.

Keith Thurman retained his WBA 'interim' title when outpointing Leonard Bundu over 12 rounds at the MGM Grand on 13 December, prior to being promoted to 'second tier' champion on 16 January 2015. He successfully retained his new title when outpointing Robert Guerrero over 12 rounds at the MGM Grand on 7 March 2015.

Selected to meet Josesito Lopez for the vacant WBA 'interim' title, Andre Berto stopped his man inside six rounds at the Citizens Business Bank Arena, Ontario, California, USA on 13 March 2015.

23 November 2014. Manny Pacquiao w pts 12 Chris Algieri.
Venue: Cotai Arena, Venetian Resort, Macau, China. **Recognition:** WBO. **Referee:** Genaro Rodriguez.
Scorecards: 120-102, 119-103, 119-103.
Fight Summary: Taking every round against a game challenger who was dropped six times in all, Pacquiao (143¾) continued to show that he was a cut above all of his challengers. Using a countering southpaw jab as Algieri (143½) tried to fight his way out of the corners, Pacquiao dropped the American with a barrage of blows in the second before catching up with him again in the sixth when knocking him down twice, a solid left and a clubbing right doing the damage. Somehow Algieri made it into the ninth after taking further heavy shots, only to be decked twice more in that session when a straight left had him over before a cluster of blows had him down on one knee. Dropped again in the tenth from another big left, Algieri got up and dusted himself down to make it to the final bell.

28 March 2015. Kell Brook w rtd 4 Ionut Dan Ion.
Venue: Motorpoint Arena, Sheffield, England. **Recognition:** IBF. **Referee:** Earl Brown.
Fight Summary: Brook (145½) was far too good for his southpaw challenger in this one despite coming back from a stab wound to his left leg just six months earlier. Going straight on the attack, Brook began pushing Dan Ion (146¼) back in the opener before dropping him with a big right that followed a left hook. Having got to his feet, Dan Ion was again put down by another right, and although he made it to the end of the round and then through the third he was in trouble in the fourth. Sent to the boards following a barrage of blows, even though Dan Ion was allowed to box on it would not be for long. Having been smashed to the floor by a left-hander right at the end of the session Dan Ion's corner retired him during the interval.

2 May 2015. Floyd Mayweather Jnr w pts 12 Manny Pacquiao.
Venue: MGM Grand, Las Vegas, Nevada, USA. **Recognition:** WBA/WBC/WBO/The Ring. **Referee:** Kenny Bayless.
Scorecards: 116-112, 118-110, 116-112.
Fight Summary: Despite some claiming that this would be 'The Fight of the Century, it was nothing of the kind as the ultra-clever Mayweather (146), the three-belt title holder, thwarted the WBO's Pacquiao (145), taking over the latter's crown in the process. Every now and again Pacquiao would bang in a barrage of blows from his southpaw stance, most of which would not hit the target due to Mayweather's brilliant defensive skills, especially when on the ropes. Although there was not much in it at the halfway stage, Mayweather upped his work-rate from thereon in, his left jab and single shots picking Pacquiao out, and he rubber stamped it when clearly taking the last two sessions. According to the CompuBox stats, Mayweather landed 148 to Pacquiao's 81, the Filipino's low punch rate being explained by the fact that he sustained a torn muscle in his right shoulder three weeks earlier.

Timothy Bradley outpointed Jessie Vargas over 12 rounds at the StubHub Centre, Carson, California, USA on 27 June to win the vacant WBO 'interim' title.

Further to an ultimatum to comply with WBO rules, Mayweather was stripped of the WBO title on 6 July. At the same time, Bradley was confirmed as the new WBO champion.

Keith Thurman made a successful defence of the WBA 'second tier' title when forcing Luis Collazo to retire at the end of the seventh round of their contest at the USF Sundome, Tampa, Florida, USA on 11 July.

30 May 2015. Kell Brook w rsc 6 Frankie Gavin.
Venue: O2 Arena, Greenwich, London, England. **Recognition:** IBF. **Referee:** Steve Gray.
Fight Summary: Up against a fellow Brit in Gavin (146¾), a former world amateur champion, Brook (146¼), his IBF title on the line, proved too good for his southpaw opponent after taking control from the opening bell. There was no doubt that the champion's switch-hitting confused Gavin, who was gradually taken apart. Having put Gavin under pressure in the sixth following some solid shots to head and body, when a right hook-right uppercut slammed into the Birmingham fighter the referee, who had seen enough, called a halt to proceedings at 2.51 of the session. Following the contest, Brook called out Amir Khan to settle their differences in a big money fight.

12 September 2015. Floyd Mayweather Jnr w pts 12 Andre Berto.
Venue: MGM Grand, Las Vegas, Nevada, USA. **Recognition:** WBA/WBC/The Ring. **Referee:** Kenny Bayless.
Scorecards: 120-108, 117-111, 118-110.
Fight Summary: In what Mayweather (146) stated would be his last contest, he took on Berto (145), the WBA 'interim' champion, in defence of his three championship belts. To be fair, Berto was never in with a chance against a master of defensive boxing, an expert in laying traps before drawing opponents into them. Even when Berto got close in the seventh he was punished by solid uppercuts to deter such a notion. Berto's battle plan had been to attack the body, but whenever he got close to Mayweather the opportunity quickly disappeared. One of the judges gave Berto three rounds and another gave him two, probably in sessions where Mayweather stopped working while the challenger was at least trying to make the fight. Having made the toughest of sports look easy it was rumoured that Mayweather would retire on 49 straight wins.

Following Mayweather's announcement that he had retired from boxing, *The Ring* Championship Belt was eventually vacated on 19 September. The WBC eventually accepted that Mayweather was not coming back and vacated their title on 4 November.

The WBA 'interim' title was next won by David Avanesyan when he stopped Charlie Jose Navarro inside nine rounds at the Room of Stars, Monte Carlo, Monaco on 7 November.

Immediately after their convention, in January 2016 the WBA dropped Mayweather from their list of champions, a move that saw Keith Thurman being recognised as the top man.

Avanesyan made his first defence of the WBA 'interim' title a successful one when outpointing Shane Mosley over 12 rounds at the Gila River Arena, Glendale, Arizona on 28 May 2016.

7 November 2015. Timothy Bradley w rsc 9 Brandon Rios.
Venue: Thomas & Mack Centre, Las Vegas, Nevada, USA. **Recognition:** WBO. **Referee:** Tony Weeks.
Fight Summary: Hoping to make a successful defence of the title that he was handed after the WBO stripped Floyd Mayweather for not complying with their rules and regulations, Bradley (146) ultimately proved too good for Rios (147) when winning in the ninth round. Starting fast with the jab and follow-up combinations before moving on, Bradley took the contest by the scruff of the neck, punishing the laborious Rios in virtually every round. Eventually, in the ninth, Bradley began the run for home when hurting Rios with a left to the body, and after sinking in another heavy left the latter took 'a knee' to recuperate. Although Rios made it to his feet, when another barrage of blows put him down again the referee came to his rescue at 2.49 of the session.

Bradley was forced to hand back his WBO title when signing for a third fight against Manny Pacquiao instead of making a mandatory defence against Sadam Ali on 11 February 2016. However, the WBO announced that because of the importance of the fight the winner would be given special recognition.

23 January 2016. Danny Garcia w pts 12 Robert Guerrero.
Venue: Staples Centre, Los Angeles, California, USA. **Recognition:** WBC. **Referee:** Jack Reiss.
Scorecards: 116-112, 116-112, 116-112.
Fight Summary: Contested for Floyd Mayweather Jnr's old title that was vacated on his retirement, Garcia (146¾) clearly outscored Guerrero (146¾). Having worked his southpaw opponent out early on, by the sixth Garcia began to get to Guerrero with countering hooks and uppercuts. From the sixth to the tenth it was virtually all Garcia before Guerrero started the fightback in the tenth and 12th when firing in solid blows. Although Guerrero thought that he had won, the CompuBox stats had him landing just 108 blows to Garcia's 163.

5 March 2016. Jessie Vargas w rsc 9 Sadam Ali.
Venue: The Armory, Washington DC, USA. **Recognition:** WBO. **Referee:** Kenny Chevalier.
Fight Summary: Fighting for the title that was vacated when Timothy Bradley fought Manny Pacquiao instead of meeting the unbeaten Ali (147), it was Vargas (146¼) who became champion when forcing a stoppage at 2.09 of the ninth. Working well with two-fisted attacks and having hurt Vargas towards the end of the fourth, Ali looked as though he had settled in nicely. However, once Vargas had got himself going, using his extended reach to fire in blows from the outside while outworking Ali, his overarm right started to do some damage, the latter was dropped in the eighth from one such punch. Although making it to the ninth, once Ali took another heavy shot to the head before being floored again and then staggered from another big right, the third man had seen enough.

26 March 2016. Kell Brook w rsc 2 Kevin Bizier.
Venue: The Arena, Sheffield, England. **Recognition:** IBF. **Referee:** Marcus McDonnell.
Fight Summary: Having been inactive since a damaged rib forced him out of a defence against Diego Gabriel Chaves, the champion was soon in complete control of Bizier (146¼) before stepping it up. Although Bizier began by making the running in the second he was countered solidly by Brook (146½), two rights to the head eventually having him over. When the game Bizier got to his feet there was no hiding place and after being hit with a cluster

of shots he was dropped again. This time it was curtains, the referee calling the count off at 'five' and halting the contest with 45 seconds of the session remaining.

25 June 2016. Keith Thurman w pts 12 Shawn Porter.
Venue: Barclays Centre, Brooklyn, NYC, New York, USA. **Recognition:** WBA. **Referee:** Steve Willis.
Scorecards: 115-113, 115-113, 115-113.
Fight Summary: Making his first defence since being appointed champion, Thurman (146) outpointed Porter (147) by a very narrow margin in what was a hard-fought affair that was contested at an extremely fast pace. Both men were cut on their left eyes towards the end, Porter below and Thurman above, but it made no difference to the result. There was no doubting Porter's pressure took the eye as he continually came forward, but it was Thurman's defence and countering that won the day in a fight that will be remembered for a long time by those who witnessed it. In a battle between friends, neither was able to dominate and both were hurt at times. There were no knockdowns.

Welterweight Boxers' Index:

(Country of birth where known/Domicile - birthplace and domicile are the same unless stated)

A

Jake Abel (Russia/USA)
Jim Adds (England)
Sammy Adragna (USA)
Rodolfo Aguilar (Panama)
Young Ahearn (England/USA)
Virgil Akins (USA)
Johnny Kid Alberts (Hungary/USA)
Devon Alexander (USA)
Chris Algieri (USA)
Sadam Ali (USA)
Charlie Allum (England)
Shamone Alvarez (USA)
Lou Ambers (USA)
Alvin Anderson (USA)
Al Andrews (USA)
Sammy Angott (USA)
Bruno Arcari (Italy)
Freddie Archer (USA)
Baby Arizmendi (Mexico/USA)
Gene Armstrong (USA)
Henry Armstrong (USA)
Milt Aron (USA)
Jack Ashman (England)
Pete August (USA)
David Avanesyan (Russia)
Marco Antonio Avendano (Venezuela)
Selcuk Aydin (Turkey/Germany)
Tommy Ayers (USA)
Kid Azteca (Mexico)

B

Billy Backus (USA)
Albert Badoud (Switzerland/France)
Pablo Baez (USA)
Yama Bahama (Bahamas/USA)
Randall Bailey (USA)
Corporal Bill Baker (England)
Howard Baker (USA)
Larry Baker (USA)
Carlos Baldomir (Argentina)
Johnny Barbara (USA)
George Barnes (Australia)
Larry Barnes (USA)
Fernando Barreto (Brazil)
Bobby Barrett (England/USA)
Lee Barrett (USA)
Pat Barrett (England)
Ted Barrett (England)
Frank Barrieau (Canada/USA)
Dave Barry (Ireland/England)
Soldier Bartfield (Hungary/USA)

Johnny Basham (Wales)
Carmen Basilio (USA)
Jose Basora (Puerto Rico/USA)
Battling Battalino (USA)
George Baxter (England)
Sam Baxter (England)
Jack Bayley (England)
Tommy Bell (USA)
Steve Belloise (USA)
Angel Beltre (Dominican Republic)
Wilfred Benitez (USA/Puerto Rico)
Jack Bennett (England/USA)
Maxie Berger (Canada)
Georges Bernard (France)
Silvano Bertini (Italy)
Andre Berto (USA)
Kevin Bizier (Canada)
Jack Blackburn (USA)
Eddie Blay (Ghana)
Maurice Blocker (USA)
Phil Bloom (England/USA)
Larry Boardman (USA)
Arthur Bobbett (England)
Lou Bogash (Italy/USA)
Larry Bonds (USA)
Eddie Booker (USA)
Young Joe Borrell (USA)
Carmelo Bossi (Italy)
Donovan Boucher (Jamaica/Canada)
Timothy Bradley (USA)
Johnny Bratton (USA)
Mauricio Bravo (Venezuela/USA)
Mark Breland (USA)
Gomeo Brennan (Bahamas/USA)
Harry Brewer (USA)
Eddie Brink (USA)
Bennie Briscoe (USA)
Jack Britton (USA)
Adrien Broner (USA)
Ray Bronson (USA)
Kell Brook (England)
Lou Brouillard (Canada/USA)
Glenwood Brown (USA)
Joe Brown (USA)
Peter Brown (Ireland/England)
Simon Brown (Jamaica/USA)
Willard Brown (USA)
Ted Bryant (England)
Guy Buckles (USA)
Young Gene Buffalo (USA)
Johnny Bumphus (USA)
Leonard Bundu (Sierra Leone/Italy)

Jim Burchill (England)
Dick Burge (England)
Dave Burke (Welterweight)
Charley Burley (USA)
Alec Burns (England)
Jimmy Burns (USA)
Kid Burns (USA)
Tom Burrows (Australia)
Gene Burton (USA)
Walter Byers (USA)

C

Emil Calcagni (USA)
Frank Callan (England)
Hector Camacho (Puerto Rico/USA)
Miguel Angel Campanino (Argentina)
Luis Ramon Campas (Mexico/USA)
Tommy Campbell (USA)
Andy Cannon (England)
Tony Canzoneri (USA)
Jimmy Capper (USA)
Vic Cardell (USA)
Santos Cardona (Puerto Rico)
Oba Carr (USA)
Jack Carroll (Australia)
Michael Carruth (Ireland)
Jimmy Carter (USA)
Rubin Carter (USA)
Rocky Castellani (USA)
Tom Causer (England)
Marcel Cerdan Jnr (Morocco/France)
Marcel Cerdan (Algeria/France)
Ralph Charles (England)
Dave Charnley (England)
Patrick Charpentier (France)
Diego Gabriel Chaves (Argentina)
Ray Chavez Guerrero (Venezuela/Canada)
Julio Cesar Chavez (Mexico)
Bill Cheese (England)
Bill Chester (England)
Joe Chick (USA)
Chris Christensen (Denmark)
Yung-Kil Chung (South Korea)
Kermit Cintron (Puerto Rico/USA)
Jimmy Clabby (USA)
Jack Clancy (USA)
Scott Clark (USA)
Joshua Clottey (Ghana/USA)
Freddie Cochrane (USA)
Curtis Cokes (USA)
Luis Collazo (USA)
Harry Collins (England)
Scott Bright Eyes Collins (USA)
Larry Conley (USA)
Jim Connelly (England)
Eddie Connolly (Canada)

Hector Constance (Trinidad/Austria)
Jimmy Conway (USA)
Jewey Cook (England)
Young Corbett 111 (Italy/USA)
Alberto Cortes (Argentina)
Everaldo Costa Azevedo (Brazil/Italy)
George Costner (USA)
Miguel Cotto (Puerto Rico)
Tom Couhig (USA)
Tracey Cox (USA)
Mike Crawley (England)
Phil Cross (USA)
Pipino Cuevas (Mexico)
Donald Curry (USA)
Brian Curvis (Wales)

D

Pat Daly (Ireland/England)
Ionut Dan Ion (Romania/Canada)
Chuck Davey (USA)
Aaron Davis (USA)
Al Bummy Davis (USA)
Fate Davis (USA)
Henry Davis (Hawaii)
Freddie Dawson (USA)
George Dawson (Australia)
Davey Day (USA)
Oscar De La Hoya (USA)
Antonin Decarie (Canada)
Ronnie Delaney (USA)
Paul Delgado (Cape Verde/USA)
Emile Delmine (Belgium)
Tony DeMarco (USA)
Nonpareil Jack Dempsey (Ireland/USA)
Young Denny (USA)
Tommy Devlin (USA)
Anthony Diamond (England)
Antonio Diaz (Mexico/USA)
Elio Diaz (Venezuela/USA)
Julio Diaz (Mexico/USA)
Andy DiVodi (USA)
Bobby Dobbs (USA)
Bernard Docusen (USA)
Billy Doig (USA)
Jim Donovan (England/USA)
Mike Donovan (Ireland/USA)
Ted Dorkings (England)
Al Doty (USA)
Jack Dougherty (England/USA)
Bryan Downey (USA)
Jimmy Doyle (USA)
Paul Doyle (Italy/USA)
Billy Drako (Germany/USA)
Harry Dublinsky (USA)
Lockport Jimmy Duffy (USA)
Martin Duffy (USA)

Paddy Duffy (USA)
Harry Duncan (England)
Joe Dundee (Italy/USA)
Johnny Dundee (Italy/USA)
Vince Dundee (Italy/USA)
Ralph Dupas (USA)
Alessandro Duran (Italy)
Roberto Duran (Panama)
Bobby Dykes (USA)

E

Gustav Eder (Germany)
Australian Billy Edwards (Australia/England)
Ismael El Massoudi (Morocco/France)
Gilles Elbilia (France)
Jackie Elverillo (USA)
Clarence English (USA)
Frank Erne (Switzerland/USA)
Young Erne (Welterweight)
Angel Espada (Puerto Rico)
Crisanto Espana (Venezuela/Northern Ireland)
David Estrada (USA)

F

Tony Falco (USA)
Kid Farmer (USA)
Lew Feldman (USA)
Jesse Feliciano (USA)
Lester Felton (USA)
Frankie Fernandez (Hawaii)
Jorge Fernandez (Argentina)
Rube Ferns (USA)
Wildcat Ferns (USA)
Frank Fields (USA)
Jackie Fields (USA)
John Files (USA)
Bruce Finch (USA)
Carmen Fiore (USA)
Young Joe Firpo (Italy/USA)
Jack Fitzgibbon (England)
Dick Fitzpatrick (USA)
Fighting Fitzpatrick (USA)
Eddie Fitzsimmons (USA)
Del Flanagan (USA)
Luis Folledo (Spain)
Richie Fontaine (USA)
Steve Forbes (USA)
Jack Foreman (USA)
Vernon Forrest (USA)
Vince Foster (USA)
Raul Frank (Guyana/USA)
Tommy Freeman (USA)
Sailor Friedman (USA)
Don Fullmer (USA)
Gene Fullmer (USA)

Phil Furr (USA)
Charley Fusari (Italy/USA)

G

Gilbert Gallant (USA)
Robert Gallois (France)
Manning Galloway (USA)
Tony Gannarelli (USA)
Baby Joe Gans (USA)
Joe Gans (USA)
Panama Joe Gans (Barbados/Panama)
Johnny Gant (USA)
Alfredo Gaona (Mexico)
Angel Robinson Garcia (Cuba/USA)
Ceferino Garcia (Philippines/USA)
Danny Garcia (USA 2007-16)
Danny Garcia (Puerto Rico 1983-2002)
Irving Garcia (Puerto Rico)
Luis Garcia (Venezuela)
Jimmy Gardner (Ireland/USA)
Sam Garr (USA)
Jimmy Garrison (USA)
Arturo Gatti (Italy/USA)
Kid Gavilan (Cuba)
Frankie Gavin (England)
Marcos Geraldo (Mexico)
Joe Ghnouly (USA)
Ching Ghook (England)
Joey Giambra (USA)
Austin Gibbons (England/USA)
Mike Gibbons (USA)
Johnny Gill (USA)
Mike Glover (USA)
Jack Goldswain (England)
Alfonso Gomez (Mexico)
Manuel Gomez (USA/Mexico)
Johnny Gonsalves (USA)
Manuel Gonzalez (USA)
Miguel Angel Gonzalez (Mexico)
Billy Graham (USA)
Bunny Grant (Jamaica)
Kid Graves (USA)
Clyde Gray (Canada)
Rocky Graziano (USA)
Johnny Greco (Canada)
Bobby Green (USA)
Dave Boy Green (England)
George Green (USA)
Billy Griffith (USA)
Emile Griffith (Virgin Islands/USA)
Johnny Griffiths (USA)
Louis Groeninger (USA)
Tommy Grogan (USA)
Robert Guerrero (USA)
Milton Guest (USA)

H

Henry Hall (England)
Nelson Hall (USA)
Al Hamza-Veabro Boykin (USA)
Alf Hanlon (England)
Joergen Hansen (Denmark)
Willie Harmon (USA)
Stan Harrington (Hawaii)
Gypsy Joe Harris (USA)
Harry Harrison (England)
Garnet Hart (USA)
Bill Hatcher (England)
Gene Hatcher (USA)
Ricky Hatton (England)
Jim Hayes (England)
Teddy Hayes (USA)
Alfonso Hayman (USA)
Stanley Hayward (USA)
Thomas Hearns (USA)
Tom Henry (England/USA)
George Herbert (USA)
Freddy Hernandez (Mexico)
Tony Herrera (USA)
Alf Hewitt (England)
Dario Hidalgo (Dominican Republic)
Isaac Hlatshwayo (South Africa)
Piet Hobin (Belgium)
Waldemar Holberg (Denmark)
Dave Holly (USA)
Lloyd Honeyghan (Jamaica/England)
Kevin Howard (USA)
Tommy Howell (Italy/USA)
Frank Howson (England)
Ace Hudkins (USA)
Frankie Hughes (USA)
Johnny Hughes (England)
Clyde Hull (USA)
Charles Humez (France)
Chuck Hunter (USA)
Diosbelys Hurtado (Cuba/Spain)
Jun-Suk Hwang (South Korea)

I

Johnny Indrisano (USA)
Frank Inglis (England)
Tom Ireland (England)

J

Beau Jack (USA)
Rafal Jackiewicz (Poland)
Johnny Jackson (USA)
Young Peter Jackson (USA 1895-1914)
Young Peter Jackson (USA 1929-39)
Gary Jacobs (Scotland)
Gert Bo Jacobsen (Denmark)
Johnny Jadick (Ukraine/USA)

Izzy Jannazzo (USA)
Young Jasper (USA)
Lew Jenkins (USA)
Michael Jennings (England)
Andrew Jeptha (South Africa/England)
Andre Jessurun (USA)
Charley Johnson (USA)
Eddie Johnson (USA)
Anthony Jones (USA)
Colin Jones (Wales)
Gorilla Jones (USA)
Jimmy Jones (USA)
Mike Jones (USA)
Ralph Jones (USA)
Sonny Jones (Canada)
Don Jordan (USA)
Young Joseph (England)
Jean Josselin (France)
Zab Judah (USA)
Jim Judge (USA)
Paul Junior (Canada/USA)

K

Ayub Kalule (Uganda/Denmark)
David Kamau (Kenya/USA)
Danny Kapilow (USA)
Mike Kaplan (USA)
Jesus Soto Karass (Mexico/USA)
Jimmy Kelly (USA)
Spike Kelly (USA)
Charley Kemmick (USA)
Jim Kendrick (Ireland/England)
Stanley Ketchel (USA)
Amir Khan (England)
Nika Khumalo (South Africa)
Cocoa Kid (Puerto Rico/USA)
Dixie Kid (USA)
Jamaica Kid (Belize/USA)
Jack Kingsland (England)
Ray Kiser (USA)
George Klett (USA)
Frederic Klose (France)
Charlie Knock (England)
Al Kober (USA)
Battling Kopin (USA)
Akhmed Kotiev (Russia)
Hercules Kyvelos (Canada)

L

Ramon La Cruz (Argentina)
Nino La Rocca (Mauritania/Italy)
Mose LaFontise (USA)
Jake LaMotta (USA)
Tom Lancaster (England)
Kenny Lane (USA)
Hilliard Lang (Canada)

Sam Langford (Canada/USA)
Tippy Larkin (USA)
Pete Latzo (USA)
Steve Latzo (Austria/USA)
Kid Lavigne (USA)
Jimmy Lavin (Ireland/USA)
Racheed Lawal (Sierra Leone/Denmark)
Bucky Lawless (USA)
Billy Layton (USA)
Mick Leahy (Ireland/England)
Dick Leary (England)
Seung-Soon Lee (South Korea)
Genaro Leon (Mexico)
Benny Leonard (USA)
Sugar Ray Leonard (USA)
Jimmy Leto (USA)
Artie Levine (USA)
George Levine (Russia/USA)
Andrew Lewis (Guyana/USA)
Harry Lewis (USA)
Hedgemon Lewis (USA)
Ted Kid Lewis (England)
Willie Lewis (USA)
Bert Linam (USA)
Michael Loewe (Romania/Germany)
Bud Logan (USA)
Isaac Logart (Cuba/USA)
Johnny Lombardo (USA)
Al Long (USA)
Ray Long (USA)
Ernie Lopez (USA)
Jose Luis Lopez (Mexico)
Josesito Lopez (USA)
Sandro Lopopolo (Italy)
KO Willie Loughlin (USA)
Eamonn Loughran (Northern Ireland)
Young Loughrey (USA)
Ray Lovato (USA)
James Lowes (England)
Willie Ludick (South Africa)
Kevin Lueshing (England)
Sebastian Lujan (Argentina)
Morris Lux (Russia/USA)

M
Souleymane M'baye (France)
Fighting Mack (Curacao/Netherlands)
Frankie Madden (USA)
Eddie Madison (USA)
Art Magirl (USA)
Fred Mahan (USA)
Jack Mahoney (England/USA)
Marcos Maidana (Argentina)
Jeff Malcolm (Australia)
Paul Malignaggi (USA)
Peter Malinga (South Africa)

Jim Maloney (England)
Tommy Maloney (USA)
Steve Mamakos (USA)
Fortunato Manca (Italy)
Joe Mandot (USA)
Al Manfredo (USA)
Percy Manning (USA)
Frank Mantell (Germany/USA)
Emilio Marconi (Italy)
Antonio Margarito (USA/Mexico)
Larry Marks (USA)
Juan Manuel Marquez (Mexico)
Tito Marshall (Panama)
Tony Marteliano (USA)
Mauro Martelli (Switzerland)
Terry Martin (Norway/USA)
Hilario Martinez (Spain)
Rodolfo Ezequiel Martinez (Argentina)
Vince Martinez (USA)
Johnny Marto (USA)
Matty Matthews (USA)
Walter Dario Matthysse (Argentina)
Ricardo Mayorga (Nicaragua)
Jorge Maysonet (Puerto Rico)
Floyd Mayweather Jnr (USA)
Danny McAloon (USA)
Johnny McCarthy (USA)
Blink McCloskey (USA)
Frank McConnell (USA)
Tom McCormick (Ireland/England)
Al McCoy (USA)
Charles Kid McCoy (USA)
Herb McCoy (Australia)
Young Kid McCoy (USA)
Milton McCrory (USA)
Jimmy McDaniels (USA)
Pat McDonald (Scotland)
Packey McFarland (USA)
Jack McGee (USA)
Buddy McGirt (USA)
Charlie McKeever (USA)
Bill McKinnon (Canada)
Jimmy McLarnin (Northern Ireland/USA)
Billy McMillan (Scotland/USA)
Jack McVey (USA)
Tom Meadows (England/Australia)
Jack Meekins (England)
Hughie Mehegan (Australia)
Al Mello (USA)
Honey Mellody (USA)
Roger Menetrey (France)
Joe Miceli (USA)
Jose Miranda (Panama)
Charlie Mitchell (England)
Pinky Mitchell (USA)

Terry Mitchell (USA)
Eddie Moha (USA)
Mimoun Mohatar (Morocco/Spain)
Walter Mohr (USA)
Tomas Molinares (Colombia)
Pedro Montanez (Puerto Rico)
Carlos Monzon (Argentina)
Charlie Moody (USA)
Rodney Moore (USA)
Willie Moore (USA)
Nick Moran (Mexico)
Billy Morgan (Wales)
Shane Mosley (USA)
Denny Moyer (USA)
Armando Muniz (Mexico/USA)
Eddie Murdock (USA)
Andrew Murray (Guyana/USA)

N

Jose Napoles (Cuba/Mexico)
Bill Natty (England)
Charlie Jose Navarro (Venezuela)
Danny Needham (USA)
Dick Nelson (Denmark/USA)
Frankie Nelson (USA)
Jack Nelson (England)
Harry Neumier (England)
Andrew Newton (England)
Harry Nickless (England)
Terry Norris (USA)
Frankie Notter (USA)
Yuriy Nuzhnenko (Ukraine)

O

Young Jack O'Brien (USA)
Mike O'Dowd (USA)
Dennis O'Keefe (USA)
Jack O'Keefe (USA)
Pat O'Keefe (England)
Patrizio Oliva (Italy)
Carl Bobo Olson (Hawaii)
Johann Orsolics (Austria)
Gaspar Ortega (Mexico)
Nick Ortiz (USA)
Ricky Ortiz (USA)
Victor Ortiz (USA)
Jackson Osei Bonsu (Ghana/Belgium)
Young Otto (USA)
Said Ouali (Morocco/USA)
Fujio Ozaki (Japan)

P

Eddie Pace (USA)
Bobby Pacho (USA)
Manny Pacquiao (Philippines)
Cowboy Padgett (USA)

Donato Paduano (Italy/Canada)
James Page (USA)
Jose Palacios (Mexico)
Michele Palermo (Italy)
Dave Palitz (USA)
Eddie Palmer (USA)
Jack Palmer (England)
Carlos Palomino (Mexico/USA)
Benny Kid Paret (Cuba/USA)
Giovanni Parisi (Italy)
Jung-Oh Park (South Korea)
Kid Parker (USA)
Francois Pavilla (Martinique/France)
Tony Pellone (USA)
Freddie Pendleton (USA)
George Penny (England)
Danny Perez (USA)
Eddie Perkins (USA)
Jack Perry (Italy/USA)
Jimmy Perry (USA)
Arthur Persley (USA)
Andrey Pestryaev (Uzbekistan/Russia)
George Peterson (Sweden/USA)
Billy Petrolle (USA)
Tony Petronelli (USA)
Vince Phillips (USA)
Michele Piccirillo (Italy)
Charley Pierson (USA)
Billy Piltz (USA)
Hugo Pineda (Colombia/USA)
Rafael Pineda (Colombia/USA)
Gus Platts (England)
Ted Pleydell (England)
Shawn Porter (USA)
Jack Portney (Russia/USA)
Andy Price (USA)
Luis Primera (Venezuela)
Ted Pritchard (Wales/England)
Ruslan Provodnikov (Russia/USA)
Adolph Pruitt (USA)
Percy Pugh (USA)
Lee Purdy (England)

Q

Ike Quartey (Ghana/USA)
Tommy Quill (USA)
Carlos Quintana (Puerto Rico)

R

Eddie Ran (Latvia/USA)
Rip Randall (USA)
Tiger Joe Randall (USA)
Pete Ranzany (USA)
Doug Ratford (USA)
Luther Rawlings (USA)
Johnny Reagan (USA)

Stefan Redl (Hungary/USA)
Johnny Reese (USA)
Teddy Reid (Jamaica/USA)
Billy Rhodes (USA)
Johnny Riley (USA)
Brandon Rios (USA)
Willie Ritchie USA)
Cosme Rivera (Mexico)
Jose Antonio Rivera (USA)
Wilfredo Rivera (Puerto Rico/USA)
Al Roach (USA)
Eddie Roberts (USA)
Sam Robideau (USA)
Johnny Robinson (England)
Sugar Ray Robinson (USA)
William Robinson (England)
Ernie Roderick (England)
Delvin Rodriguez (Dominican Republic/USA)
Eduardo Rodriguez (Panama)
Fausto Rodriguez (Dominican Republic/Puerto Rico)
Jake Rodriguez (Puerto Rico/USA)
Luis Rodriguez (Cuba/USA)
Miguel Angel Rodriguez (Mexico)
Barney Ross (USA)
Marty Rowan (USA)
Charlie Rowles (England)
Norman Rubio (Puerto Rico/USA)
Frankie Russell (USA)
Unk Russell (USA)
Billy Ryan (USA)
Buddy Ryan (USA)
Tommy Ryan (USA)

S

Horacio Saldano (Argentina)
George Salvadore (USA)
Santiago Samaniego (Panama/USA)
Paulo Alejandro Sanchez (Argentina)
Luis Santana (Dominican Republic)
Daniel Santos (Puerto Rico)
Motoki Sasaki (Japan)
Johnny Saxton (USA)
Milburn Saylor (USA)
Morrie Schlaifer (USA)
Charley Scott (USA)
Felix Scott (Bahamas/England)
Harry Scott (England)
Howard Scott (USA)
Jim Scully (England/USA)
Vyacheslav Senchenko (Ukraine)
Marty Servo (USA)
Ben Seth (England/Australia)
Dave Shade (USA)
Tommy Sheehan (USA)
Joe Sherman (USA)
Eddie Shevlin (USA)

Randy Shields (USA)
Charley Shipes (USA)
Cecil Shorts (USA)
Neil Sinclair (Northern Ireland)
Said Skouma (Morocco/France)
Charley Tombstone Smith (USA)
James Tiger Smith (Wales)
Lorenzo Smith (USA)
Mysterious Billy Smith (Canada/USA)
Wallace Bud Smith (USA)
Raul Soriano (Mexico)
Ryu Sorimachi (Japan)
Cory Spinks (USA)
Aldo Spoldi (Italy/USA)
Jose Stable (Cuba/USA)
Roger Stafford (USA)
Bert Stanley (USA)
Walter Stanton (USA)
Marlon Starling (USA)
Joe Stein (USA)
Anthony Stephens (USA)
Ginger Stewart (England)
Rudell Stitch (USA)
Adrian Stone (England/USA)
Harry Stone (USA)
John H. Stracey (England)
Jim Styles (England)
Mark Suarez (USA)
Alf Suffolk (England)
Jim Sullivan (England)
Mike Twin Sullivan (USA)
Paddy Sullivan (USA)
Guy Sumlin (USA)
Johnny Summers (England)
KO Sweeney (USA)
Owen Sweeney (England)
Patsy Sweeney (Ireland/USA)
Wally Swift (England)

T

Chuck Taylor (USA)
Meldrick Taylor (USA)
Shannan Taylor (Australia)
Larry Temple (USA)
Lew Tendler (USA)
Sid Terris (USA)
Gabe Terronez (USA)
Wally Thom (England)
Battling Thomas (USA)
Eddie Thomas (Wales)
Joe Thomas (USA)
Marcel Thomas (France)
Federico Thompson (Panama)
Young Jack Thompson (USA)
Lachie Thomson (Scotland)
Harvey Thorpe (USA)

Keith Thurman (USA)
Charles Dutch Thurston (USA)
Dick Tiger (Nigeria/USA)
Jack Tillman (USA)
Johnny Tillman (USA)
Willie Toweel (South Africa)
Billy Townsend (England/Canada)
Jim Townsend (England)
Leonard Townsend (USA)
Michel Trabant (Germany)
Tom Tracey (Australia/USA)
Duke Tramel (USA)
Harry Trendall (USA)
Tyrone Trice (USA)
Mario Trigo (Mexico)
Felix Trinidad (Puerto Rico)
Carlos Trujillo (Panama)
Shoji Tsujimoto (Japan)
Saverio Turiello (Italy)
Dick Turner (USA)
Earl Turner (USA)
Gil Turner (USA)
Roger Turner (USA)
Buster Tyler (USA)

U

Juan Urango (Colombia/USA)
Oktay Urkal (Germany)

V

Jorge Vaca (Mexico)
Arthur Valentine (England)
Bep van Klaveren (Netherlands)
Jessie Vargas (USA)
Chico Varona (Cuba/USA)
Chico Vejar (USA)
Pedro Vilella (USA)
Robert Villemain (France)
Adolfo Viruet (USA)
Sammy Vogel (USA)
Harold Volbrecht (South Africa)

W

Joe Walcott (Guyana/USA)
Mickey Walker (USA)
Paulie Walker (USA)
Andy Walsh (USA)
Billy Walters (USA)

Georgie Ward (USA)
Harry Ward (England)
Peter Waterman (England)
Curley Watson (England)
James Webb (USA)
Coley Welch (USA)
Joe Welling (USA)
Bermondsey Billy Wells (England)
Matt Wells (England)
Freddie Welsh (Wales)
Harold Weston (USA)
Bill Whatley (England)
Pernell Whitaker (USA)
Jeff White (Australia)
Joe White (Canada/Wales)
Ted White (England)
Ted Whitfield (USA)
Kyle Whitney (USA)
Jack Wilkes (USA)
Charley Williams (USA)
Don Williams (USA)
Holman Williams (USA)
Ike Williams (USA)
Johnny Williams (USA)
Lew Williams (USA)
Paul Williams (USA)
Rollin Williams (USA)
Tom Williams (Australia)
California Jackie Wilson (USA)
George Wilson (England)
Joe Wilson (England)
Eddie Wolfe (USA)
Tom Woodley (England)
Billy Woods (USA)
Felix Wouters (Belgium)
Bee Bee Wright (USA)
Ted Wright (USA)

Y

Teddy Yarosz (USA)
Bobby Joe Young (USA)

Z

Ralph Zannelli (USA)
Jan Zaveck (Slovenia/Germany)
Fritzie Zivic (USA)
Jack Zivic (USA)
Mahenge Zulu (DR Congo/Italy)

Junior Middleweight Division

Recognised by the amateurs since 1951 because the weight gap between welter and middle was too great, the 147 to 154lbs weight class was introduced to the pro ranks in 1962 thanks to the World Boxing Association (WBA). Men boxing in this division are also known as super welterweights or light middleweights.

However, before the WBA could get a vacant title contest between Denny Moyer and Joey Giambra underway the Austrian Boxing Commission supported a bout between America's Ted Wright and Emile Griffith, the world welterweight champion who was having difficulty making 147lbs, as being for their version of the championship. Although the Austrians had hoped to get the support of the European Boxing Union (EBU) and the New York State Athletic Commission (NYSAC), unable to do so they ultimately went it alone.

Weight Band
147lbs to 154lbs

Junior Middleweight World Championship Fights:

17 October 1962. Emile Griffith w pts 15 Ted Wright.
Venue: City Hall, Vienna, Austria. **Recognition:** Austria. **Referee:** H. De Bakker.
Fight Summary: Scoring repeatedly with left hooks to head and body, Griffith (149¼) was always in front of Wright (153¼) in a contest that was seen in Austria as involving the vacant title. Although Wright showed a good boxing brain and some smart moves he was never able to hurt Griffith, who kept his left going throughout to score points, and at times one felt that he could have raised the tempo anytime he wished. There were no knockdowns, the verdict being unanimous.

20 October 1962. Denny Moyer w pts 15 Joey Giambra.
Venue: Memorial Coliseum, Portland, Oregon, USA. **Recognition:** WBA. **Referee:** Sonny Liston.
Scorecards: 149-144, 148-146, 146-144.
Fight Summary: Getting off to an early lead, Moyer (153¾) sent out the left jab for several rounds until Giambra (154) came into the fight in the fifth and pushed on until the ninth saw the tide turn in the youngster's favour. As Giambra tired so Moyer came on strong, and although the 31-year-old veteran rallied in the 11th from thereon in it was the latter who took control through to the final bell.

With it being the WBA's inaugural championship fight at the weight it raised little excitement in America, or anywhere else for that matter, and it remained to be seen whether the new weight class would come into fashion.

As the reigning Hawaii welter champion, Stan Harrington, who had won 42 of his 53 contests, would be Moyer's next challenger. A pro since 1953, Harrington had beaten Henry Davis, Carlos Chavez, L. C. Morgan (twice), Rocky Kalingo (three times), Chico Vejar, Joe Miceli, Tony Dupas, Charley Tombstone Smith, Paddy DeMarco, Larry Baker and Charley Scott. He was known as a tough, wily campaigner with a hard dig.

3 February 1963. Emile Griffith w rsc 9 (15) Chris Christensen.
Venue: KB Hall, Copenhagen, Denmark. **Recognition:** Austria/Denmark. **Referee:** Robert Seidel.
Fight Summary: Putting his Austrian recognised 154lbs title on the line against Christensen (152½), the world welter champion quickly got down to business, having the Dane over from a right hand for the 'eight' count in the third and doing very much as he pleased from thereon in. Hooking strongly with both hands, Griffith (152) pursued his unfortunate foe who stayed in the contest mainly by holding on at every opportunity. From the sixth it was just a matter of time. In the ninth Griffith smashed Christensen down twice for counts of 'nine', and although the latter tried to fight on the referee stopped the fight after his corner threw the towel in.

Immediately following the fight, Griffith gave up the Danish/Austrian version of the title to concentrate on his welterweight crown.

19 February 1963. Denny Moyer w pts 15 Stan Harrington.
Venue: Honolulu Civic Auditorium, Oahu, Hawaii. **Recognition:** WBA. **Referee:** Louis Freitas.
Scorecards: 72-69, 71-69, 74-68.
Fight Summary: Defending his new title for the first time, Moyer (153½) had to wait a while before getting into his stride as Harrington (150¼) made the early running, especially in the second and fifth rounds when he caught the champion with solid right hands to the chin. From there onwards, though, he had less success, tiring badly from the tenth as Moyer came on strong to win the unanimous decision.

29 April 1963. Ralph Dupas w pts 15 Denny Moyer.
Venue: Municipal Auditorium, New Orleans, Louisiana, USA. **Recognition:** WBA. **Referee:** Pete Giarusso.
Scorecards: 9-4-2, 8-5-2, 6-7-2.
Fight Summary: The slow-starting champion was puzzled early on by the bobbing-and-weaving tactics employed by Dupas (151), and by the time he had worked his man out it was too late for him to turn the fight around. It was the body attacks that won the fight for Dupas, who was far more aggressive than normal, as he moved from side to side before jumping in with both hands to tie Moyer (154) up. With neither man in difficulty, despite Moyer finishing strongly with solid rights to the head to win two of the last three sessions, he effectively left it far too late.

17 June 1963. Ralph Dupas w pts 15 Denny Moyer.
Venue: Civic Centre, Baltimore, Maryland, USA. **Recognition:** WBA. **Referee:** Benny Goldstein.
Scorecards: 70-66, 69-68, 69-68.
Fight Summary: Starting fast as in their last contest, the champion began to outspeed and outdance Moyer (154) right from the opening bell, throwing long lefts and straight rights, often out of a crouch. Dupas (150), circling both ways, again proved a difficult target to nail, and it was not until he tired that Moyer made a determined run for home during the last five or six rounds. Had Moyer made his move two rounds earlier it might have been a different story.

7 September 1963. Sandro Mazzinghi w rsc 9 (15) Ralph Dupas.
Venue: Vigorelli Velodrome, Milan, Italy. **Recognition:** WBA. **Referee:** Rolf Neuhold.
Fight Summary: Regardless of displaying every trick in his locker the champion was unable to keep the hard-punching Mazzinghi (153¼) at arm's length, and as early as the first round he was floored for 'eight' by a left hook to the body. From that moment on, Dupas (152¼) knew he had problems. Relying on his hit-and-run style he was able to survive for several sessions before being chased down and hurt in the sixth and seventh. Although rallying somewhat in the eighth, opening up a cut over Mazzinghi's left eye, after Dupas was floored by a right to the head in the ninth, despite rising at 'seven' the referee continued to count to 'ten'. With Dupas on his feet at the finish, timed a 1.45, this has to be seen as a stoppage rather than a kayo.

2 December 1963. Sandro Mazzinghi w rsc 13 (15) Ralph Dupas.
Venue: The Stadium, Sydney, Australia. **Recognition:** WBA. **Referee:** Vic Patrick.
Fight Summary: Fighting bravely, although outgunned, the challenger made life difficult for Mazzinghi (153) for a few rounds, scoring heavily in the sixth when cutting the latter over the left eye. However, by the ninth he was tiring badly. Having shown excellent ring-craft against his hard-punching opponent to get so far, Dupas (150¼) hung on bravely into the 13th. But after being smashed to the canvas three times in that session he was rescued by the referee on the 1.20 mark with Mazzinghi still full of fight.

Forced out of action due to a car accident in which his wife was killed, Mazzinghi, given an extension to his 'title defence every six-month' clause got back into training in March 1964.

On 3 October, at the Sports Palace, Genoa, Italy, Mazzinghi knocked out America's Tony Montano inside 12 rounds of a fight that had been advertised for the WBA championship. Unfortunately, when Montano weighed in two and a half pounds over the weight although the contest went ahead the title was not involved.

11 December 1964. Sandro Mazzinghi w pts 15 Fortunato Manca.
Venue: Sports Palace, Rome, Italy. **Recognition:** WBA. **Referee:** Giorgio Tinelli.
Fight Summary: Evenly balanced during the first eight rounds, despite the champion displaying greater speed and agility he was unable to get on top of Manca (152¾) who was always fighting back. Unfortunately, from thereon in the contest developed into a punch-up as Manca began to use his right hand more, and in the last round he almost got to Mazzinghi (153½) with vicious right hooks. Following the referee's decision in favour of Mazzinghi, who should have stuck to his boxing instead of getting too involved, Manca felt that he might have done considerably better had he not injured his right hand in the days leading up to the fight.

Having turned pro after winning a gold medal at the 1960 Olympic Games, Nino Benvenuti had run up 61 straight wins and was the obvious opponent for Mazzinghi in what would be a match between countrymen. A classy box-fighter, Benvenuti, who had beaten Isaac Logart, Jimmy Beecham (twice), Victor Zalazar, Gaspar Ortega, Ted Wright, Denny Moyer, Juan Carlos Duran, Art Hernandez and Mick Leahy among others, was generally seen as the champion in waiting.

18 June 1965. Nino Benvenuti w co 6 (15) Sandro Mazzinghi.
Venue: San Siro Stadium, Milan, Italy. **Recognition:** WBA. **Referee:** Salvatore Brambilla.
Fight Summary: This one started at a fair pace, with Mazzinghi (153½) going for the body while Benvenuti (153) held him at bay with his superb left hand in all rounds other than the third when he was hurt by blows to head and body. By the sixth it was felt that Mazzinghi had built up a small lead due to his pressing tactics, but at 2.40 of the session he was counted out after running into a terrific right uppercut to the jaw. Prior to the contest it was felt by the Mazzinghi camp that the best way to retain the title was to nullify Benvenuti's left hand, but in doing so the champion ultimately paid the price when failing to spot the right coming.

At their convention in September, the World Boxing Council (WBC), who had been formed in February 1963, agreed to recognise the 154lbs weight class forthwith, although member bodies such as the Commonwealth (1972), the British Boxing Board of Control (BBBoC) (1973) and parts of the USA (1974) would not fall into line for several years. The WBC also recognised Benvenuti as the world champion.

17 December 1965. Nino Benvenuti w pts 15 Sandro Mazzinghi.
Venue: Sports Palace, Rome, Italy. **Recognition:** WBA/WBC. **Referee:** Giacinto Aniello.
Fight Summary: Making a good start, the champion dropped Mazzinghi (153¾) in the second round with a sharp left, but unable to repeat the trick he ultimately had to be satisfied with a disputed points decision. The *Ring Record Book* gives the decision as being a unanimous one, whereas other reports indicate the sole arbiter as being the referee. Early on it appeared that Mazzinghi could not get past the Benvenuti (153¾) left hand, and by the sixth the latter had established a comfortable lead. In the seventh through to the ninth, however, Mazzinghi finally managed to find a way to break down his rival's defence, working the head and body well with both hands before he was held up during the tenth and 11th. Although Mazzinghi had the best of the 12th and 13th sessions, Benvenuti was back in charge prior to the final bell. Despite the former champion being upset with the result most independents went with the winner.

25 June 1966. Ki-Soo Kim w pts 15 Nino Benvenuti.
Venue: Changchung Gym, Seoul, South Korea. **Recognition:** WBA/WBC. **Referee:** Nicholas Pope.
Scorecards: 74-68, 72-69, 68-72.
Fight Summary: Scoring with accurate southpaw left hooks to the body the challenger had the better of it early on when setting a pace that was difficult for Benvenuti (153) to work at his best, his solid right-hand punches often failing to hit the target. As the fight wore on, Kim (152¼) continued to work at a fast tempo as he bored in, and in the tenth Benvenuti was cut on his nose, being bothered by it from thereon in. The fight was held up for six minutes in the 13th when one of the ropes worked loose, but it brought no real respite to Benvenuti. Although the Italian tried to pull the fight out of the fire in the last two sessions, a badly-tiring Kim clutched and held on to the final bell.

At the beginning of December, the Italian Boxing Federation asked the WBC not to recognise the forthcoming Kim v Stan Harrington title contest on the grounds that Benvenuti should have been given an immediate return. Although the WBC was happy to support Benvenuti, with it becoming clear that he was now looking to win the world middleweight title the would-be action fizzled out.

Since his unsuccessful attempt to relieve Denny Moyer of the title, Harrington had been busy, beating men such as Manuel Gonzalez, Rip Randall, Isaac Logart, Moyer, Eddie Pace, Gaspar Ortega (twice), Charley Scott, Sugar Ray Robinson (twice), Gabe Terronez, Ferd Hernandez, Rubin Carter and Jimmy Lester. Despite losing six times during that period he fully deserved another crack, especially with Benvenuti not being too concerned.

17 December 1966. Ki-Soo Kim w pts 15 Stan Harrington.
Venue: Changchung Gym, Seoul, South Korea. **Recognition:** WBA/WBC. **Referee:** Yung-Soo Chung.
Scorecards: 74-67, 73-69, 73-66.
Fight Summary: In front of his home crowd, Kim (153½) made a fair start to lead from the fourth round through to the eighth prior to tiring in the tenth. It was then that Harrington (154), who had showed great stamina and a strong right hand, had his best spell of the fight before he was cut over the left eye on being butted in the 13th. With Harrington still dangerous, Kim used a combination of hit-and-clinch tactics to get through the remaining two rounds, the unanimous decision in his favour being warmly greeted by the locals.

Afterwards, Kim was challenged by Sandro Mazzinghi, the European champion, the date being provisionally set for 9 June 1967 in Italy. Unfortunately, the fight did not come off due to the WBA insisting that Kim must first meet Freddie Little before all others, and an uneasy truce between the WBA and WBC saw Mazzinghi set aside to meet the winner.

3 October 1967. Ki-Soo Kim w pts 15 Freddie Little.
Venue: The Stadium, Seoul, South Korea. **Recognition:** WBA/WBC. **Referee:** Yung-Soo Chung.
Scorecards: 72-68, 71-69, 64-75.
Fight Summary: Cut on his forehead in the opening round was not the best of starts for the challenger, but banging away at Kim (153½) with solid, hurtful punches he often forced him to give ground. However, the southpaw Kim was soon back, bulldozing his way forward. Little (152), who had predicted a win inside four rounds, was finding Kim a tough nut to crack. Regardless of that, after hurting Kim in the tenth a long, jolting right to the head had him over in the 11th for the mandatory 'eight'. Although Kim was groggy at the resumption he managed to remain upright before coming out strong for the 12th. Thereafter, there was a lot of clinching as both men tired. In the 15th Little again opened up with big punches to stun Kim, but it was not enough to influence two of the judges.

25 May 1968. Sandro Mazzinghi w pts 15 Ki-Soo Kim.
Venue: San Siro Stadium, Milan, Italy. **Recognition:** WBA/WBC. **Referee:** Harold Valan.
Scorecards: 71-67, 71-67, 68-73.
Fight Summary: With the champion starting in his normal roughhouse fashion, before the first round was over Mazzinghi (151½) was cut on the left eye by an unintentional butt which bled throughout. Having slipped over in the first Kim (153¾) was then dropped in the third following a barrage of blows to the head, but quickly recovered. Kim was soon back to using his head as an effective weapon, intentional or otherwise. Wading into Mazzinghi in the 11th, when Kim butted the Italian on the jaw he was again reprimanded. Having been on top from the seventh through to the 12th, Kim then ran out of steam, and Mazzinghi, fighting for all he was worth, came on strongly to take the decision.

25 October 1968. Sandro Mazzinghi nc 9 (15) Freddie Little.
Venue: Sports Palace, Rome, Italy. **Recognition:** WBA/WBC. **Referee:** Herbert Tomser.
Fight Summary: Dealing out punishment for eight rounds, Little (151¼) worked the champion over with body shots, cutting him up around the eyes, nose and mouth, and dropping him in the fifth. As much as Mazzinghi (151¼) tried he could not stem the tide as a steady stream of jabs, hooks and straight punches came his way. It was no surprise when a tired and badly cut-up Mazzinghi did not come out for the ninth round, but when the referee

declared a no contest on the grounds that he had acted under EBU rules there was uproar. Although EBU rules stated that a contest could be stopped before the halfway stage, the referee said that he considered the end of the eighth sufficient. This statement was debunked by the majority of officials in attendance on the grounds that EBU rules did not apply in this instance and that Mazzinghi had been beaten fairly and squarely.

A week or so later the WBC declared the title vacant and ruled that Mazzinghi and Little should meet again within 120 days. However, when Mazzinghi refused to meet Little on even-purse terms in mid-January the WBC set up a fight between Little and Stanley Hayward to find a new champion. Meantime, the WBA, who had vacated the title at the end of the year when it was clear that Mazzinghi was going to move up to middleweight on a permanent basis, also gave their backing to a fight between Little and Hayward for the title.

17 March 1969. Freddie Little w pts 15 Stanley Hayward.
Venue: Convention Centre, Las Vegas, Nevada, USA. **Recognition:** WBA/WBC. **Referee:** Harry Krause.
Scorecards: 73-63, 73-64, 74-62.
Fight Summary: Contesting the vacant title, Little (153½) carried the fight to Hayward (154) throughout, never giving him a moment's respite, while whacking in sharp left counters and solid combinations to head and body. Having been cut on the left eye in the third round and suffering from nasal damage in the 11th Hayward did his best to fight back, but was generally outpunched and well outscored. He had been badly staggered in the third, seventh and 11th, and his only real success had come when he caught Little with a cracking right to the jaw in the sixth.

9 September 1969. Freddie Little w co 2 (15) Hisao Minami.
Venue: Prefectural Gym, Osaka, Japan. **Recognition:** WBA/WBC. **Referee:** Nicholas Pope.
Fight Summary: Making a very fast start, Little (152¼) obviously intended to take his challenger out of the fight as quickly as possible as he chased him from the opening bell, jabbing out solid lefts. Still retreating into the second round, Minami (150), who had hardly landed a punch of note, was caught cold and dropped like a log to be counted out on the 1.26 mark.

20 March 1970. Freddie Little w pts 15 Gerhard Piaskowy.
Venue: Sports Palace, Berlin, Germany. **Recognition:** WBA/WBC. **Referee:** L. Sanchez Villard.
Fight Summary: Giving his challenger a boxing lesson, Little (152¾) sent out flicking lefts and solid rights without anyone realising that he had fractured his left hand as early as the second, least of all Piaskowy (153¼). The European champion had gameness but little else and failed to win a round according to one expert's view, which was a bit strange when the sole arbiter, the referee, had Little winning by just one round at the finish. It seemed that Little was carrying Piaskowy, having him groggy on occasion and badly swollen on the left eye until the extent of his injury was known.

9 July 1970. Carmelo Bossi w pts 15 Freddie Little.
Venue: The Stadium, Monza, Italy. **Recognition:** WBA/WBC. **Referee:** Roland Dakin.
Scorecard: 73-69.
Fight Summary: Although the champion kept Bossi (153) well under control in the early rounds it was the latter who eventually made most of the running to build up a lead from the ninth onwards. Warned several times to keep his head up, Little (152) failed to raise his game when he needed to, relying on countering and clinching prior to being battered in the final session with solid right hooks to the jaw. Little, who was upset at the decision, claimed that the reason he had struggled through the latter stages was due to his left hand being injured yet again.

Further to an over-the-weight defeat against the South African middleweight champion, Pierre Fourie (l pts 10 at the Ellis Park Tennis Court, Johannesburg, South Africa on 14 November), Bossi was given a bit of breathing space to allow a cut left eye to heal before announcing that he would be making his first defence against the European champion, Jose Hernandez, on 5 March 1971. The date was subsequently moved on, first to 29 March and then to 29 April, due to Bossi's fall out with the promoter over live television affecting ticket sales.

29 April 1971. Carmelo Bossi drew 15 Jose Hernandez.
Venue: Sports Palace, Madrid, Spain. **Recognition:** WBA/WBC. **Referee:** Bernard Mascot.
Scorecards: 70-71, 70-70, 75-75.
Fight Summary: In a closely fought contest, the deaf-mute Hernandez (154), showing excellent movement as well as a fighting heart, went so close to becoming the new champion when taking Bossi (154) right down to the wire. Both men had opened slowly, testing each other out, and the taller Hernandez soon realised he would profit by using his longer reach when staying on the outside, while Bossi did his best work at close quarters. Bossi, who complained of hurting his right arm in the fifth, was the classier fighter and threw more punches, but with many of them missing the target the result was a fair one.

31 October 1971. Koichi Wajima w pts 15 Carmelo Bossi.
Venue: Nihon University Auditorium, Tokyo, Japan. **Recognition:** WBA/WBC. **Referee:** Harold Valan.
Scorecards: 72-70, 68-67, 70-73.
Fight Summary: Carrying the fight to Bossi (153¼) from the start, Wajima (152¾) bobbed and weaved his way in to the attack in such a manner that belied the fact that he had only been boxing for three years. There was no doubt that Wajima's unorthodox tactics completely took the wind out of the champion's sails, perplexing him and bewildering him to the point that he was forced to hold at every opportunity. With Wajima getting stronger as the contest moved into the latter stages, Bossi was forced into all-out retreat, and at the final bell his face was reddened and swollen from the punches that he had endured.

7 May 1972. Koichi Wajima w rsc 1 (15) Domenico Tiberia.
Venue: Fukuoka Sports Centre, Tokyo, Japan. **Recognition:** WBA/WBC. **Referee:** Yusaka Yoshida.
Fight Summary: Following a feeling-out period, with Wajima (153) soon pounding away at Tiberia (154) it was quickly seen that the latter had no immediate answer as to how to deal with the vicious blows coming his way. Having been backed to the ropes by the champion Tiberia was dropped by a right-left hook to the head, and on getting up at 'nine' he was under immense pressure before going down again. Although the referee had already counted to 'three', once the towel was thrown in by Tiberia's corner he immediately called the fight off on the 1.49 mark to allow the Italian to receive treatment.

3 October 1972. Koichi Wajima w co 3 (15) Matt Donovan.
Venue: Nihon University Auditorium, Tokyo, Japan. **Recognition:** WBA/WBC. **Referee:** Takeo Ugo.
Fight Summary: Wading in to Donovan (151¾) almost from the opening gong, throwing lefts and rights to the body, the champion took the first round by a wide margin. It was much of the same in the second round as Wajima (150½) continued to go for Donovan with hard punches to head and body, and apart from landing with a few straight lefts the latter was again very much on the run. With there being no respite in the third as Wajima kept his work-rate going, after 53 seconds of the session Donovan was counted out, having been dropped by a cracking left hook to the jaw following a flurry of heavy blows.

9 January 1973. Koichi Wajima drew 15 Miguel De Oliveira.
Venue: Municipal Gym, Tokyo, Japan. **Recognition:** WBA/WBC. **Referee:** Hiroyuki Tezaki.
Scorecards: 73-71, 71-71, 71-71.
Fight Summary: While most of the cleaner punching came from De Oliveira (153½), the champion never stopped working despite being ineffectual in the early stages. However, Wajima (152), sending in blows from both hands, started to land more effectively from the tenth onwards as De Oliveira tired, and by sheer aggression he forced his way back into the contest. At the final bell neither man complained at the result.

19 April 1973. Koichi Wajima w pts 15 Ryu Sorimachi.
Venue: Prefectural Gym, Osaka, Japan. **Recognition:** WBA/WBC. **Referee:** Nobumitsu Inukai.
Scorecards: 72-71, 72-71, 71-71.
Fight Summary: Crowding Sorimachi (151¼) from the start the aggressive champion, deciding as always that attack was the best form of defence, hammered away at his fellow countryman who was only too happy to fire back. With both men being known punchers the exchanges had the fans on the edge of their seats in anticipation, but it

was the strength of Wajima (154) that eventually won the day by a slight margin. Although Sorimachi ripped through Wajima's defences at times, especially with right crosses, it was the latter who finished the fresher.

14 August 1973. Koichi Wajima w rtd 12 (15) Silvano Bertini.
Venue: Makomanai Ice Arena, Sapporo, Japan. **Recognition:** WBA/WBC. **Referee:** Takeo Ugo.
Fight Summary: Making his fifth defence, Wajima (153¾) once again proved too strong for a challenger when forcing Bertini (153) to retire at the end of the 12th round. Although Bertini had taken a fair amount of punishment the end came as a surprise as he had gone well in the earlier sessions, scoring with solid body shots, and had never looked to be in trouble. After six rounds it had seemed as though the title was going to change hands, but from there onwards it was Wajima who picked it up, crowding his opponent and ripping in solid uppercuts. Bertini later explained that he had retired because his right hand was badly swollen and that blisters on his feet were making life even more difficult.

5 February 1974. Koichi Wajima w pts 15 Miguel De Oliveira.
Venue: Metropolitan Gym, Tokyo, Japan. **Recognition:** WBA/WBC. **Referee:** Seiji Ebine.
Scorecards: 73-70, 74-71, 73-73.
Fight Summary: In what was a return match after De Oliveira (153¾) had drawn with the champion previously, Wajima (153) crowded the Brazilian from the opening bell and smashed in punches relentlessly. Not to be deterred, De Oliveira still made life difficult for Wajima, who was wild at times, when coming back strongly to mix it up. Unfortunately for the taller De Oliveira, having been cut on the right eye early on the sheer aggression of the champion eventually forced him to defend for all he was worth, but he still proved a dangerous foe when ramming accurate blows home. With some of the rounds being extremely hard fought it was only in the last three or four sessions that Wajima made sure of the verdict.

3 June 1974. Oscar Albarado w co 15 (15) Koichi Wajima.
Venue: Nihon University Auditorium, Tokyo, Japan. **Recognition:** WBA/WBC. **Referee:** Yusaku Yoshida.
Fight Summary: Lacking his normal drive, speed and power, the champion came unstuck against the hard-hitting Albarado (151¾) when caught early on by stinging left leads before being eventually knocked out at 1.54 of the final session. Starting well, the first three rounds were dominated by Albarado, with his best punch being a left uppercut to the body. However, by the seventh through to the 11th Wajima (153¾) was right back in the frame, especially when the American was deducted a point for going low. Although the next two rounds were hard fought, Wajima came on strongly in the 14th when nailing Albarado against the ropes, but faded badly in the 15th when he was dropped by a long right to the head for the compulsory 'eight'. Back on his feet, Wajima was soon down again when hurt by a series of combination punches, and on getting up he was quickly floored again, this time for the full count.

8 October 1974. Oscar Albarado w rsc 7 (15) Ryu Sorimachi.
Venue: Nihon University Auditorium, Tokyo, Japan. **Recognition:** WBA/WBC. **Referee:** Dick Young.
Fight Summary: Defending his newly won title for the first time, Albarado (154) soon made his presence felt when meeting up with Sorimachi (152¾). And after a hard-hitting opener Sorimachi was dropped in the second by a solid left for the statutory 'eight'. By the fourth it looked all over for Sorimachi, who had been chased from pillar to post, but he remained upright before being smashed down by a heavy one-two in the fifth. Now bloody and battered, when Sorimachi tried to get on his bike he was soon hunted down, being decked by Albarado again in the seventh prior to the referee coming to his rescue at 2.17 of the session.

21 January 1975. Koichi Wajima w pts 15 Oscar Albarado.
Venue: Nihon University Auditorium, Tokyo, Japan. **Recognition:** WBA/WBC. **Referee:** Dick Young.
Scorecards: 69-67, 70-69, 74-68.
Fight Summary: A return contest saw Wajima (153), initially changing his style to completely confuse the champion, using evasive tactics to bob and weave away from trouble instead of mixing as previously. Making Albarado (154) miss badly on numerous occasions Wajima was well in front by the sixth before deciding to go toe-to-toe. Thereafter, both men fought on strongly and, although Albarado did better, Wajima maintained his lead to run out a good winner. There were no knockdowns this time round, Wajima stating the following day that his

decision to hold back his punches until the last moment had come from watching Muhammad Ali beat George Foreman.

By this time the 154lbs weight class was generally recognised throughout the boxing world, *The Ring* magazine having recently included it in their World Ratings. This was followed with an inclusion in the USA Ratings. When Wajima decided against meeting Miguel De Oliveira, who had already been involved in two very close fights against him, the WBC declared the title vacant towards the end of February, matching the latter against Jose Manuel Duran, the European champion, for their version of the championship.

7 May 1975. Miguel De Oliveira w pts 15 Jose Manuel Duran.

Venue: Louis 11 Stadium, Monte Carlo, Monaco. **Recognition:** WBC. **Referee:** Herbert Tomser.
Scorecards: 149-146, 149-143, 147-142.
Fight Summary: Contesting the inaugural WBC championship contest at the weight, De Oliveira (154) very nearly ended the contest in the first round when he dropped Duran (154) for 'nine' with a cracking right to the jaw. However, he failed to follow up his advantage prior to being badly cut over the left eye in the second. Boxing cleverly, Duran got himself back in the fight as De Oliveira's injury steadily worsened, but in the eighth he was counted on again after running into some heavy shots before picking himself up. With it now apparent that Duran did not have the power to see De Oliveira off, the latter backed the Spaniard up continually to run home a good winner on the cards.

7 June 1975. Jae-Doo Yuh w rsc 7 (15) Koichi Wajima.

Venue: Municipal Gym, Kitakyushi, Japan. **Recognition:** WBA. **Referee:** Yusaku Yoshida.
Fight Summary: Both men started fast, but it was the champion who was the most successful early on as he chased the taller Yuh (154) down when trying to get to close quarters where he could work him over. However, the tricky Yuh had other ideas, Wajima (154) being left bleeding from the left ear in round three. At the end of the fifth there was a sensation when Wajima was floored moments after the bell rang to end the session. Following that, it was felt Wajima was not fully recovered by the start of the sixth. When Yuh came on strong in that session, although Wajima survived the round he was being hit and wobbled by fast combinations. It was clear that Wajima was now on his last legs, and in the seventh after being battered and dropped three times the referee was forced to call a halt on the two-minute mark under the 'three knockdowns in a round' ruling.

11 November 1975. Jae-Doo Yuh w rsc 6 (15) Masahiro Misako.

Venue: Sumpu Arena, Shizuoka, Japan. **Recognition:** WBA. **Referee:** Takeo Ugo.
Fight Summary: Using hit-and-run tactics, Misako (153½) bewildered the champion with speedy punches in the opening two sessions before getting back on his bike and using every inch of the ring. By the third, however, with Yuh (154) beginning to find the range there were some good exchanges. Expecting to get to grips with Misako in the fourth, Yuh was badly wobbled by a big right to the head, and although it took him a while to find his bearings by the fifth he was finally firing on all cylinders, especially when smashing in solid body shots. After those punches weakened Misako, who for the first time was not moving so well, Yuh took advantage of the situation to batter the challenger to the canvas three times in the sixth to enforce the 'three knockdowns in a round' ruling on the 2.16 mark.

13 November 1975. Elisha Obed w rtd 11 (15) Miguel De Oliveira.

Venue: New Hippodrome, Paris, France. **Recognition:** WBC. **Referee:** Kurt Halbach.
Fight Summary: With both fighters looking to impress the opening two rounds were evenly contested, but the second session was marred for Obed (154) when he had a point deducted for hitting the champion below the belt. Spurred on by the loss of a point, Obed had De Oliveira (154) at his mercy when the bell rang to end the third round. However, to everyone's surprise De Oliveira came out firing in the fourth, the pair blasting away at each other right through to the eighth. In that session it was De Oliveira's turn to almost finish Obed off, but when the opportunity was lost it was the champion who was smashed down twice and retired by his corner after the bell rang to start the 11th.

17 February 1976. Koichi Wajima w rsc 15 (15) Jae-Doo Yuh.
Venue: Nihon University Auditorium, Tokyo, Japan. **Recognition:** WBA. **Referee:** Jae-Duk Kim.
Fight Summary: Surprisingly one-sided, Wajima (153) was always in the face of the champion, throwing punches from a crouching position and forcing him to back off almost throughout. From the second through to the fourth, Wajima threw combinations of lefts and rights at Yuh (153), and on stepping up the pace he continued to march forward for round after round, smashing in hard blows and often scoring at will. Way down on the cards, Yuh gamely stuck to the task, despite taking a pounding, before a thundering left sent him crashing in the 15th. Although Yuh managed to get to his feet the referee continued with the count while he was leaning over the ropes, the fight coming to an end at 1.47 of the session.

28 February 1976. Elisha Obed w co 2 (15) Tony Gardner.
Venue: Queen Elizabeth Centre, Nassau, Bahamas. **Recognition:** WBC. **Referee:** Jay Edson.
Fight Summary: Never giving the challenger a chance to get set, Obed (154) controlled the fight with a searing left jab that seemed to find the target as if by radar. By comparison, Gardner (154) almost seemed slow as Obed dictated, and apart from landing a couple of good body shots and a thumping right to the jaw early in the second that was it as far as he was concerned. Having had the wake-up call, when Obed opened up in the second a right uppercut followed by a left-right to the chin had Gardner over and counted out with five seconds of the session remaining.

25 April 1976. Elisha Obed w pts 15 Sea Robinson.
Venue: National Stadium, Abidjan, Ivory Coast. **Recognition:** WBC. **Referee:** Jay Edson.
Scorecards: 148-146, 149-143, 146-147.
Fight Summary: Winning the majority of the first eight rounds, scoring well to the challenger's head and body with left uppercuts and hooks, Obed (150) was nearly put out in the ninth after being sent reeling by a left hook that was backed up by solid blows from both hands. Just about getting through the session and the next one, Obed came back to win the 11th and 12th and, although Robinson (149½) made the last three rounds interesting, the champion was worth the win.

18 May 1976. Jose Manuel Duran w co 14 (15) Koichi Wajima.
Venue: Nihon University Auditorium, Tokyo, Japan. **Recognition:** WBA. **Referee:** Yusaku Yoshida.
Fight Summary: Having already had a crack at the WBC version of the title the challenger did better this time around when meeting up with Wajima (154). Although Wajima started the first round strongly, Duran (154) soon picked up the pace before opening up with combinations and solid rights to the head in the second prior to dropping the Japanese fighter for the mandatory 'eight' with a right to the jaw. From the third through to the 12th, Duran, not known as a puncher, continued to catch the advancing Wajima with shots to the head, while the latter concentrated on the body. In the 13th Duran made his move, sending Wajima down with blows to the head from both hands, and even though the champion made it to the end of the round he was through. Tearing out of his corner in the 14th, Duran threw punch after punch at Wajima, who was sent down to be counted out on the 50-second marker after taking a crashing right to the jaw.

18 June 1976. Eckhard Dagge w rsc 10 (15) Elisha Obed.
Venue: National Hall, Berlin, Germany. **Recognition:** WBC. **Referee:** Jay Edson.
Fight Summary: Fighting as though he meant business the champion came out with the left jab going into the face of Dagge (154) on a regular basis, and while he was less accurate with his right hand it seemed as though it was just a matter of time. In the fourth, Obed (154) finally dropped Dagge with a right to the jaw just as the bell rang. Despite being clearly hurt the German came back to shade the next two sessions, especially when catching the champion off balance with a solid right. Although Obed was still picking up the points with the left hand the next three rounds saw a shift in fortunes as Dagge sent in some damaging body blows, but nobody was more surprised than he when after 1.47 of the tenth the fight came to an abrupt end when the referee halted the action as the champion turned away and made for his corner. Following the fight, Obed stated that he'd had real trouble in focusing on Dagge in the tenth and was fighting on instinct alone, a statement that was backed up by a German doctor who said that the Bahamian's blood circulation could have been interrupted by heavy blows to the arms. According to the referee, Obed ran out of gas.

18 September 1976. Eckhard Dagge w pts 15 Emile Griffith.
Venue: National Hall, Berlin, Germany. **Recognition:** WBC. **Referee:** Angelo Poletti.
Scorecards: 149-143, 148-145, 145-145.
Fight Summary: Defending for the first time, Dagge (154) came up against the 38-year-old Griffith (151½) who at times made him look positively ordinary when turning the clock back. Having scored so well in the early rounds it looked as though Griffith might be on to a winner, but gradually the tall, rangy Dagge came back with solid rights and left hooks. Twice Dagge went low, in the second and 12th, but he could not put Griffith away, even unintentionally, and soon went back to the jab. The ninth was probably the turning point for Dagge when he finally hurt Griffith with a big right hand. From thereon in, Dagge began to pick his punches better, with the last two sessions being impressive for the champion as the American began to fade through tiredness.

8 October 1976. Miguel Castellini w pts 15 Jose Manuel Duran.
Venue: Sports Palace, Madrid, Spain. **Recognition:** WBA. **Referee:** Stan Christodoulou.
Scorecards: 146-142, 147-144, 146-147.
Fight Summary: Boxing on the back foot, once Duran was knocked down in the third round following a right to the head, and realising the added power of Castellini (153¼), the champion stayed in the countering position for the rest of the contest. Duran (153) became even more negative after a clash of heads in the fifth left him cut on the forehead and Castellini suffering a two-inch gash over the left eye. Instead of picking it up at that point, Duran continued to land light, tapping blows to the head whilst on the run, while Castellini, always looking to make the fight, put in a fast finish over the last few sessions to make sure of the decision.

5 March 1977. Eddie Gazo w pts 15 Miguel Castellini.
Venue: National Baseball Stadium, Managua, Nicaragua. **Recognition:** WBA. **Referee:** Jay Edson.
Scorecards: 148-144, 148-143, 149-144.
Fight Summary: The aggressor throughout, Gazo (153) landed the hardest punches of the fight and totally confused the champion with his unorthodox style, keeping him off balance for much of the time. After Castellini (151) was cut over the left eye in the seventh he allowed Gazo to dominate continuously, while often throwing nothing back. For such an experienced fighter as Castellini it was a strange way to make his first defence, and following the contest he admitted that he could not get started and did not seem to have any real interest.

15 March 1977. Eckhard Dagge drew 15 Maurice Hope.
Venue: National Hall, Berlin, Germany. **Recognition:** WBC. **Referee:** Dino Ambrosini.
Scorecards: 145-144, 142-145, 145-145.
Fight Summary: For round after round Hope (152) landed with his southpaw jab, and it was not until the champion began to work out an effective way of dealing with it in the second half of the contest that he began to cut back the deficit. Although Dagge (153), badly marked around both eyes, hurt Hope on several occasions with heavy rights to the head he was unable to follow up and the latter was soon back in his jabbing routine. Towards the end the German threw far more punches in a desperate bid to knock Hope out but, after failing to achieve that, most expert bystanders felt that he did not even deserve the draw when it was announced.

7 June 1977. Eddie Gazo w rsc 11 (15) Koichi Wajima.
Venue: Martial Arts Hall, Tokyo, Japan. **Recognition:** WBA. **Referee:** Jay Edson.
Fight Summary: Right from the start the challenger did not appear to be his normal self, despite confusing Gazo (152½) with his stance and sudden punching from a crouching position, and as the contest proceeded his power gradually diminished. Both men suffered cuts early on, Wajima (154) on the forehead in the second and Gazo over the left eye in the third. From the fourth through to the tenth, with Gazo piling up points as Wajima tired, the deficit became even greater. This was especially noticeable when Wajima was being belted against the ropes in the eighth and ninth sessions. Right on the bell to end the tenth Wajima was dropped by a right to the jaw, and although he came out for the 11th he was soon in further trouble. After being floored for the second time, by a cracking left hook, when Wajima was back on his feet the referee halted the contest after the latter's corner threw the towel in on the 45-second mark to save their fighter from taking further punishment.

275

6 August 1977. Rocky Mattioli w co 5 (15) Eckhard Dagge.
Venue: National Hall, Berlin, Germany. **Recognition:** WBC. **Referee:** Richard Steele.
Fight Summary: Getting straight on with the job the much smaller Mattioli (154), throwing plenty of punches from both hands, stormed into the champion from the opening bell and began to dictate matters. As it was known that Dagge (152) was a slow starter there were no real worries initially, but when there was no response a few rounds later, other than a few wild right hands being thrown in the direction of Mattioli, there was some consternation. Ripping in blows from head to body Mattioli would not be denied, and in the fifth a terrific left hook to the jaw sent Dagge to the deck to be counted out in a sitting position at 2.20 of the session.

13 September 1977. Eddie Gazo w pts 15 Kenji Shibata.
Venue: Martial Arts Hall, Tokyo, Japan. **Recognition:** WBA. **Referee:** Carlos Berrocal.
Scorecards: 71-69, 72-71, 73-71.
Fight Summary: The southpaw challenger made a fair start when shooting jabs into the five-inch shorter Gazo (153¾), but although it took a round or so to sort himself out by the fourth the latter was beginning to work the body and having some success. At this point Shibata (153½) was lost when it came to infighting, preferring to keep Gazo at distance where he could connect with his longer punches. The fight had evened itself out in the latter stages, and although Shibata had a very good 13th he then faded from sight as Gazo moved up a gear to win a close decision.

18 December 1977. Eddie Gazo w pts 15 Jae-Keum Lim.
Venue: Sunin Gym, Inchon, South Korea. **Recognition:** WBA. **Referee:** Marty Denkin.
Scorecards: 147-146, 147-144, 148-150.
Fight Summary: Putting his title on the line for the third time, Gazo (153¾), using his favoured hit-and-run tactics, just about got home against Lim (152½) on a split decision. There were no knockdowns in what was a dreary affair, and although Lim got through with some good punches he was more often than not tied up when getting set. That Lim got a crack at the title at all was surprising as he had been knocked out in the seventh round of his previous contest by Jae-Doo Yuh.

11 March 1978. Rocky Mattioli w co 7 (15) Elisha Obed.
Venue: Kooyong Stadium, Melbourne, Australia. **Recognition:** WBC. **Referee:** Dick Young.
Fight Summary: After a fairly uneventful opening round, when Mattioli (151½) began to release some heavy punches in the second it could be seen that the challenger had become extremely wary. With Mattioli continually forcing his way inside and pounding Obed (153) with shots from both hands, despite being held at every opportunity he concentrated on the body knowing that the man from the Bahamas was weakening. Eventually, Mattioli caught up with Obed, staggering him with a right to the jaw, and after landing a few more heavy blows the latter went down face first to be counted out at 1.07 of the seventh.

14 May 1978. Rocky Mattioli w rsc 5 (15) Jose Manuel Duran.
Venue: Adriatic Stadium, Pescara, Italy. **Recognition:** WBC. **Referee:** Jean Deswert.
Fight Summary: Challenging Mattioli (152¾) for the WBC title, the former WBA champion, Duran (153), was soon in trouble, seemingly hurt every time he was tagged. Having been shaken up in the first round, when Duran was dropped by a left hook to the chin in the second he was quickly under pressure again on getting up. Staggered virtually every time Mattioli caught up with him Duran was decked again in the fourth, and although he made it through to the fifth he was eventually battered down on one knee by a right to the head. When Duran, thoroughly demoralised, shook his head in recognition of defeat the referee needed no further signs, the fight being called off at 2.24 of the session.

On 2 November, the *Tuscaloosa News* reported that Edgar Ross, the fifth-ranked junior middle according to *The Ring* magazine, had been given the go-ahead by the WBC to make a match against Mattioli. Unfortunately for Ross his management team were unable to come to terms with Mattioli's people and nothing was agreed. A crunching body puncher with the nickname of 'Mad Dog', Ross had just three more fights before retiring after being knocked out inside ten rounds by Tony Chiaverini. With 58 wins, two defeats and two draws from 62 contests, his record was outstanding.

9 August 1978. Masashi Kudo w pts 15 Eddie Gazo.
Venue: City Gym, Akita, Japan. **Recognition:** WBA. **Referee:** Marty Denkin.
Scorecards: 146-143, 147-145, 145-146.
Fight Summary: Being cut over the left eye as early as the second did not do the champion many favours, but luckily for him many of the left jabs and one-twos tossed in by Kudo (153¼) throughout the opening four rounds missed the target. Boxing out of a crouch as normal, Gazo (152¼) seemed strangely lethargic before getting home in the fifth with some wide rights. Although working well inside with short hooks and uppercuts over the next round or so Gazo eventually allowed himself to be pegged back again. By the 11th Gazo was fading, being deducted a point in the 12th for holding and, although Kudo began to increase his lead in the eyes of two of the judges, the last three sessions saw more negative action as both men continually hit and grabbed.

13 December 1978. Masashi Kudo w pts 15 Ho Joo.
Venue: Prefectural Gym, Osaka, Japan. **Recognition:** WBA. **Referee:** Paul Field.
Scorecards: 148-144, 149-144, 145-148.
Fight Summary: Although expected to go forward from the opening bell, Kudo (153½) began cautiously and was happy to pick up points from distance while having a good look at his challenger. From the fourth onwards, Joo (154), a hard-hitting counter-puncher, perked up when sending in left hooks to Kudo's face, and at the same time was looking to smash in heavy uppercuts. By the eighth it looked as though Kudo had finally worked Joo out, darting in to land fast one-twos until getting on the back foot again, with the latter lacking the mobility to catch him. While the ninth through to the 11th were slow rounds, Kudo piled up more points in the 12th with great combinations to Joo's head before things became extremely messy with lots of clinching as the champion ran the fight down.

4 March 1979. Maurice Hope w rtd 8 (15) Rocky Mattioli.
Venue: Ariston Theatre, San Remo, Italy. **Recognition:** WBC. **Referee:** Ray Solis.
Fight Summary: Starting like a bomb, the challenger had Mattioli (152) on the floor from a southpaw left to the jaw within the first ten seconds. Although the latter responded well, having broken his right wrist when falling he was right up against it from there onwards. Following a frantic next couple of sessions, when both men landed heavily, Hope (154) came on strongly to batter away at Mattioli in the fifth and sixth before the Australian-based Italian had an excellent seventh when forcing his man to the ropes with heavy lefts. However, it later transpired that the seventh and eighth sessions had been Mattioli's swan song, and with the wrist in a bad way he was retired by his corner before the ninth could get underway.

When it was announced that Hope would be making his first defence against Mike Baker there was much surprise as he had never set the world alight, being an honest-to-goodness fighter. While Baker had won 34 of 47 contests, the only two wins of any note were against Leo Saenz and Casey Gacic. Regardless of that, the WBC had rated him at number eight.

13 March 1979. Masashi Kudo w pts 15 Manuel Gonzalez.
Venue: Korakuen Hall, Tokyo, Japan. **Recognition:** WBA. **Referee:** Luis Sulbaran.
Scorecards: 148-147, 146-144, 146-146.
Fight Summary: Bouncing left jabs off the champion repeatedly to take most of the opening seven rounds, Gonzalez (153) showed the Japanese crowd just what a skilled operator he was despite his lack of a concussive punch. Gonzalez was also adept at defending when on the ropes while sending in countering blows from both hands at the same time. Unable to connect with Gonzalez solidly other than on the odd occasion, Kudo (154) often resorted to sending out batches of punches in the hope of catching his man, and even when he went flat out in the last two sessions his title seemed to have slipped away from him. When the scores were announced there were gasps of amazement, and in order to save face the WBA fixed up a return almost immediately.

20 June 1979. Masashi Kudo w rsc 12 (15) Manuel Gonzalez.
Venue: City Gym, Yokkaichi, Japan. **Recognition:** WBA. **Referee:** Stan Christodoulou.
Fight Summary: Although he had controversially retained his title against the same opponent three months earlier the champion started better in the return match when sending in sharp one-twos to the head and not hanging

around to trade. Gonzalez (152) came back well in the fifth through to the ninth when countering with solid rights to the head as Kudo (153¾) missed with stinging left leads, and in the tenth he sent the latter staggering into the ropes with solid lefts and rights. Hammering away non-stop at Kudo it seemed as though Gonzalez was on the verge of winning the title, but having absorbed everything thrown at him the champion suddenly cut loose, a cracking left to the Argentine's jaw just before the bell changing the course of the fight. Badly stunned, Gonzalez did not know where he was from that point on. After taking a beating in the 11th, when Gonzalez was staggering around the ring in the 12th the referee halted the contest after his corner threw in the towel nine seconds into the session to save him from taking further punishment.

As the outstanding challenger for over a year, Ayub Kalule would finally get his chance of a shot at Kudo. This followed a WBA demand on 25 July that the latter defend his title against the Ugandan within 90 days. Kudu had been reported to have signed up to meet Emiliano Villa which, if true, was stopped in its tracks. The Commonwealth middleweight champion was unbeaten in 30 (17 inside the distance) contests and had defeated Elisha Obed, Rudy Robles, Alvin Anderson, Miguel Castellini, Jose Hernandez, Milton Owens, Sugar Ray Seales, Kevin Finnegan, Ho Joo, Monty Betham and David Love, all top men. A southpaw who was feared for his ability with right hooks and uppercuts, Kalule was a big pre-fight favourite.

25 September 1979. Maurice Hope w rsc 7 (15) Mike Baker.
Venue: The Arena, Wembley, London, England. **Recognition:** WBC. **Referee:** Raymond Baldeyrou.
Fight Summary: Making his first defence, Hope (153½) was far too good for Baker (152½), who had come from America with the reputation of possessing a big left hook, being content for the first few rounds to just work his man over without going the whole hog. Hope did not really start to let the punches go until the fifth, and it was clear that Baker could not cope with the combined accuracy and power. Although Hope eased off in the sixth he came back with a vengeance in the seventh, driving Baker into a corner and blasting heavy shots in from both hands before a southpaw right hook sent the latter down. Getting up late in the count, Baker, to his credit, came right back at Hope. Eventually, with punches from both hands raining in on him, the referee pulled Baker out with 30 seconds of the session remaining.

Early in 1980 Hope suffered a detached retina while sparring, but having undergone an operation to correct the damage it was announced in June that his second defence would be against Rocky Mattioli, the man he won the title from.

24 October 1979. Ayub Kalule w pts 15 Masashi Kudo.
Venue: Prefectural Gym, Akita, Japan. **Recognition:** WBA. **Referee:** Bobby Ferrara.
Scorecards: 149-139, 146-139, 149-145.
Fight Summary: With the upright champion adopting a defensive approach, Kalule (153¾) took charge from the opening bell. Cutting the ring down from the second through to the fourth Kalule began firing in some solid shots, the prime one being the southpaw straight left to the body. In the fifth, realising that he was in trouble, Kudo (154) started to let straight rights go, one of which had Kalule stumbling. Although Kudo began to punch it out later in the fight, invariably he was coming off worse when being caught by heavy counters. Despite his left eye beginning to close Kudo did reasonably well in the 12th and 13th, but when Kalule dropped him on the bell to end the 13th it seemed to be all over. Surprisingly, Kalule did not press his advantage in the 14th or the 15th, being happy to cruise to victory.

6 December 1979. Ayub Kalule w pts 15 Steve Gregory.
Venue: Brondby Hall, Copenhagen, Denmark. **Recognition:** WBA. **Referee:** Tony Perez.
Scorecards: 149-135, 150-135, 150-147.
Fight Summary: Having floored Gregory (152) in the opening round with a looping southpaw right, whenever the champion got the opportunity he would force his rival to the ropes in order to work him over with body shots. When Kalule (153) upped his work-rate in the third, pumping in blows to Gregory's body before firing in uppercuts, the latter had no defence for the punches coming his way other than covering up or retreating if he could. Gregory, who was as game as they come, had some success in the 11th and 12th with good left hands, but before

too long he was again taking punishment. The fight entered the final session with Kalule still trying to win inside the distance, Gregory being under attack from a barrage of uppercuts to the head before making it to the bell.

17 April 1980. Ayub Kalule w rtd 11 (15) Emiliano Villa.
Venue: Brondby Hall, Copenhagen, Denmark. **Recognition:** WBA. **Referee:** Joe Santarpia.
Fight Summary: In a battle of southpaws, Kalule (153½) took it relatively easy at the start as Villa (150¾) made the early running, concentrating on the body while looking to put the champion under pressure. By the fourth, however, Kalule was beginning to take over when making good use of his jab. From there on, although Villa was still in the contest, his work was becoming wild and less effective. As the fight moved on, Kalule was more and more in control, his jabs and hooks slowly but surely grinding Villa down, and at the end of the 11th session the latter's corner advised the referee that he had suffered enough. At the time of closure Villa had cuts over both eyes and a badly swollen mouth.

12 June 1980. Ayub Kalule w pts 15 Marijan Benes.
Venue: The Stadium, Randers, Denmark. **Recognition:** WBA. **Referee:** Max Stranfeld.
Scorecards: 149-145, 149-142, 149-147.
Fight Summary: Starting well, the southpaw jab finding Benes (153) time and again in the opening five rounds, the champion built up a good lead before the stocky Yugoslav came on strongly in the sixth. Piling in, throwing hooks from both hands, Benes started to make life difficult for Kalule (153½), and if he had been wearing normal gloves other than the ten-ounce variety agreed for the contest there might have been a different result. As it was, Kalule boxed his way back into a good lead and survived a strong finish from Benes in the last two sessions to finish a worthy winner.

12 July 1980. Maurice Hope w rsc 11 (12) Rocky Mattioli.
Venue: Grand Hall, Wembley, London, England. **Recognition:** WBC. **Referee:** Arthur Mercante.
Fight Summary: Coming back from an operation to repair a detached retina, the champion quickly put all his problems behind him as he opened up with southpaw left crosses and solid rights to halt the rampaging Mattioli (151¾) in his tracks. Not deterred, Mattioli, his right cheekbone swollen and cut early on, continued to steam into Hope (153), only to be met by right-hand counters before having a fair amount of success in the middle rounds when landing some heavy shots. When Mattioli began to tire from his exertions, Hope was back on top by the ninth and starting to let his punches go again. Having cruised through the tenth Hope really picked it up in the 11th, and after battering Mattioli with hooks and body blows the referee stepped in to rescue the latter on the 2.52 mark.

6 September 1980. Ayub Kalule w pts 15 Bushy Bester.
Venue: Athletics Stadium, Aarhus, Denmark. **Recognition:** WBA. **Referee:** Davy Pearl.
Scorecards: 147-138, 147-138, 147-139.
Fight Summary: Although Bester (152½) was not expected to pose much of a threat to Kalule (153¼) he provided a real challenge, almost having the latter over in the sixth round when he had him on the ropes bewildered and hurt. While Kalule had the class and moved up a gear from thereon in, Bester never gave up and was always in there working away against his fellow southpaw, leaving him badly bruised and cut over the left eye. Not being a puncher did not help Kalule's cause. Despite repeatedly landing hooks and uppercuts to Bester's head, unable to stop the South African in his tracks he ultimately had to settle for a points victory. Making the fight from start to finish, Bester, who was cut over the right eye towards the end, left the ring to great applause, having forced Kalule to fight on his terms.

Ranked at number two by the WBA at this time, Roger Leonard, the older brother of Sugar Ray, was eying a shot at the title after beating Sean Mannion, Mario Maldonado, Rudy Robles, Johnny Gant and Clyde Gray. Known as 'The Dodger' for his ability to make punches miss, Leonard was well on track before being beaten by Maldonado and retiring one fight later.

26 November 1980. Maurice Hope w pts 15 Carlos Herrera.
Venue: Grand Hall, Wembley, London, England. **Recognition:** WBC. **Referee:** Arthur Mercante.

Scorecards: 142-139, 145-142, 147-146.

Fight Summary: In a bitterly-fought contest, Hope (153½) retained his title against the hard-hitting Herrera (151¾) after being on the brink of defeat in the fifth, 11th and 15th rounds when his fellow southpaw had used his longer reach to crack in vicious and damaging rights and lefts. There was no doubt that Hope was badly hurt, but each time he weathered the storm to come back with solid jabs and crosses. By the 13th both men were cut over their right eyes in what had become a war of attrition and, although Hope took that session, the last two rounds went to Herrera who, despite coming close to seeing the champion off, was unable to find the finishing blow.

24 May 1981. Wilfred Benitez w co 12 (15) Maurice Hope.
Venue: Caesar's Palace, Las Vegas, Nevada, USA. **Recognition:** WBC. **Referee:** Richard Greene.
Fight Summary: Taking the fight to the challenger with stiff southpaw jabs, although Hope (153½) made a reasonable start before too long he was being undone by powerful body shots that began to weaken him. By the sixth Benitez (153¼) was well on top, almost having Hope over from a battery of lightning-quick punches delivered from both hands in that session. Somehow Hope kept plugging away, but fighting a losing battle he was sent down for 'four' by a right to the head at the end of the tenth. Having cruised through the 11th Benitez moved up a gear in the 12th, and after setting Hope up with body blows a long right to the jaw sent the latter crashing to be counted out on the 1.56 mark.

25 June 1981. Sugar Ray Leonard w rsc 9 (15) Ayub Kalule.
Venue: The Astrodome, Houston, Texas, USA. **Recognition:** WBA. **Referee:** Carlos Berrocal.
Fight Summary: Moving up a weight division to challenge Kalule (153) for the junior middleweight title, Leonard (153) had to overcome a few initial problems. However, once he had settled and made the body his target the writing was on the wall for the Ugandan southpaw. Although Kalule came back with hooks and uppercuts from both hands at times Leonard proved to be more versatile, and in the ninth a series of blows had the champion rocking before a right-left-right combination dropped him. Back on his feet but looking decidedly shaky, the referee decided that Kalule was not fit to continue and the fight was over. Announced as a stoppage at 2.59 of the ninth round, in reality it was effectively six seconds into the interval as the timekeeper had forgotten to ring the bell.

After Leonard relinquished the WBA version of the title at the end of August to concentrate on unifying the welterweight division, Tadashi Mihara and Rocky Fratto were matched to find a new champion.

7 November 1981. Tadashi Mihara w pts 15 Rocky Fratto.
Venue: War Memorial Auditorium, Rochester, New York, USA. **Recognition:** WBA. **Referee:** Arthur Mercante.
Scorecards: 144-143, 145-140, 142-142.
Fight Summary: Contesting the title vacated by Sugar Ray Leonard both men started fast, with Fratto (153¼) the aggressor and Mihara (154) boxing well on the back foot, making for an interesting mix. Having surprisingly been dropped by a right in the fourth, Fratto began to work well on the inside during the middle rounds before Mihara picked it up in the tenth to come on strong from thereon in. There was never much between them, but the fight swung Mihara's way when Fratto's work-rate slackened off during the final third, as he looked to land heavy shots rather than point-scoring blows. It was this tactic that ultimately cost him.

14 November 1981. Wilfred Benitez w pts 15 Carlos Santos.
Venue: Showboat Hotel, Las Vegas, Nevada, USA. **Recognition:** WBC. **Referee:** Ferd Hernandez.
Scorecards: 145-140, 145-139, 147-138.
Fight Summary: A poor fight, it was not until the sixth round that there was any real action, and that ended with the referee ruling that Santos (153¼) had been floored when most of the crowd saw it as a slip. After further pontificating by both men it was only in the 11th and 13th that Benitez (153½) went to work on his southpaw challenger, staggering him and at least trying to close the ring down as his fellow countryman got on the move. Although Benitez continued to work in the last two sessions, Santos, realising he was outgunned, was more than happy to survive until the final bell.

30 January 1982. Wilfred Benitez w pts 15 Roberto Duran.
Venue: Caesar's Palace, Las Vegas, Nevada, USA. **Recognition:** WBC. **Referee:** Richard Greene.
Scorecards: 145-141, 143-142, 144-141.
Fight Summary: An interesting fight rather than an explosive one, the champion appeared to beat Duran (152½) by a bigger margin than what was spelt out on the scorecards. Most sessions saw the much bigger, stronger Benitez (152¼) commanding the centre of the ring and countering Duran, who lacked the hand-speed of previous years. Although Duran gave it one last fling in the 15th he was unable to punish Benitez, who coolly picked him off as he charged in. Even when they went toe-to-toe through to the final bell the former 135 and 147lbs champion was unable to make a dent. There were no knockdowns, but both men were cut over the left eye, Duran in the seventh and Benitez in the 12th.

2 February 1982. Davey Moore w rsc 6 (15) Tadashi Mihara.
Venue: Metropolitan Gym, Tokyo, Japan. **Recognition:** WBA. **Referee:** Carlos Berrocal.
Fight Summary: For a man having his ninth pro fight Moore (152¾) started with great confidence, soon finding the champion with left jabs and heavy hooks from both hands. Although Mihara (153¾) came back strongly in the third with solid rights to the chin, followed by the pair fighting it out in the fourth, Moore came on in the fifth to drop his man with a right to the head before pressuring him for the rest of the round. In the sixth Moore really turned it on, and after knocking Mihara down three times the referee stopped the contest after 53 seconds of the session on the 'three knockdowns in a round' ruling. Mihara had held the title for just 87 days.

26 April 1982. Davey Moore w co 5 (15) Charlie Weir.
Venue: Ellis Park Rugby Ground, Johannesburg, South Africa. **Recognition:** WBA. **Referee:** Luis Sulbaran.
Fight Summary: Although shading the opening round the challenger was found wanting early in the second when Moore (152) opened up quickly to drop him twice with rights to the head. Thereafter, it was all one way as Moore went about his business, dropping Weir (151¾) once in the third and twice in the fourth before finishing the South African off in the next session. Charging out for the fifth, when Moore, who had only made the weight after three attempts, found Weir with a left to the body followed by a right to the jaw the latter was counted out after 35 seconds.

Prior to the fight, Tony Ayala had won an injunction in New Jersey on the grounds that he was the leading available challenger and that the WBA had no right to allow Moore v Weir to go ahead as a championship contest. However, the WBA immediately applied for a stay in a Pennsylvanian court and when this was granted the fight went ahead as initially planned.

That had not been the only wrangle, as the WBA had already given assurances to Ayub Kalule that he would be facing the winner within 60 days, having overlooked the ruling that if a champion loses his title to anyone but the official leading contender then the new champion's first defence must be against the leading available contender.

17 July 1982. Davey Moore w rsc 10 (15) Ayub Kalule.
Venue: Bally's Park Place Hotel, Atlantic City, New Jersey, USA. **Recognition:** WBA. **Referee:** Luis Sulbaran.
Fight Summary: Cut over the left eye in the third round and behind on the cards, when Moore (154) started to pick things up against his southpaw challenger from the fourth, although hard fought, he then had matters in hand from there onwards. While there were no knockdowns it was clear that Moore's punches were having the most effect, and in the ninth he was banging in rights and lefts that seemed to be draining all resistance from Kalule (154). At this stage Kalule looked a beaten man. After Kalule was wobbled by a big right in the tenth, Moore continued to pour in punches until the former champion, who was not fighting back, was rescued by the referee with just two seconds of the session remaining.

3 December 1982. Thomas Hearns w pts 15 Wilfred Benitez.
Venue: The Superdome, New Orleans, Louisiana, USA. **Recognition:** WBC. **Referee:** Octavio Meyran.
Scorecards: 144-137, 144-139, 142-142.
Fight Summary: Using a brilliant left lead and helped by an eight-inch-reach advantage, Hearns (153¾) picked his punches with cool precision to outbox the champion in all but the middle rounds. How one judge had them level

on points at the end beggared belief. Despite having a point deducted in the fourth for pulling Benitez's head down and being counted on in the ninth after slipping over, Hearns appeared to win handsomely. Benitez (152), who was dropped in the fifth by a right to the jaw, had great difficulty in catching Hearns, and even when he managed to get to close quarters he was more often than not outpunched. Not an exciting contest by any means, but in Hearns the New York-born Benitez had undoubtedly met his match.

Having injured his right hand during the contest Hearns had it placed in a cast before coming back to beat Murray Sutherland in a non-title bout on 10 July 1983. Unfortunately, when it was again damaged and placed in a cast it was seven months before he was fit enough to defend the title against Luigi Minchillo.

Towards the end of 1982, the WBC announced that, as from 1 January 1983, all world title bouts held under their banner would be contested over 12 rounds.

29 January 1983. Davey Moore w co 4 (15) Gary Guiden.
Venue: Bally's Park Place Hotel, Atlantic City, New Jersey, USA. **Recognition:** WBA. **Referee:** Vincent Rainone.
Fight Summary: Far too strong for his challenger, Moore (153¼) started briskly, punching away with both hands, and was looking for a quick finish before being pegged back at the end of the second. However, Moore was soon back on track in the third as he started to move with the jab, while Guiden (152) looked to get on the inside. With Moore upping the tempo, towards the end of the session a terrific right to the jaw jolted Guiden badly. The fourth saw the hardest fighting to date, both men landing well before two right uppercuts and a left hook sent Guiden down to be counted out in the act of rising on the 2.18 mark.

16 June 1983. Roberto Duran w rsc 8 (15) Davey Moore.
Venue: Madison Square Garden, Manhattan, NYC, New York, USA. **Recognition:** WBA. **Referee:** Ernesto Magana.
Fight Summary: Thought to be too young and too strong for his veteran challenger, Moore (154) found himself outpunched and outclassed by a man who had got himself into tip-top condition as well as recovering total faith in his ability. With Duran (152½) digging in brutal blows to the body early on it drained Moore, who was never in the fight before being floored in the seventh by a big right. Although the champion somehow made it to the bell the eighth brought him no respite, a rampant Duran smashing him around the ring before the referee came to his rescue on the 2.02 mark.

Supported as champion by the United States Boxing Association, who had set up an international body (USBA/I) back in April (later renamed as the International Boxing Federation (IBF) in late October), once Moore had lost to Duran and the IBF found that they could not do business with the latter they nominated Mark Medal and Earl Hargrove to meet for their version of the title.

After Duran relinquished the WBA version of the title in June 1984 to challenge Marvin Hagler for the world middleweight crown, Mike McCallum and Sean Mannion were matched to find a new champion.

11 February 1984. Thomas Hearns w pts 12 Luigi Minchillo.
Venue: Joe Louis Arena, Detroit, Michigan, USA. **Recognition:** WBC. **Referee:** Waldemar Schmidt.
Scorecards: 120-109, 120-110, 118-109.
Fight Summary: Despite the challenger being game to the core he lacked the power to really trouble Hearns (153¾), something that gave the latter an ideal platform on which to exhibit his skill as well as keeping his suspect right hand under wraps. Minchillo (153), who finished with a badly swollen left eye, was always trying. However, even when Hearns appeared to be tiring he could not close him down, and although fighting hard in the tenth and 11th he was a spent force in the final session.

11 March 1984. Mark Medal w rsc 5 (15) Earl Hargrove.
Venue: Sands Hotel, Atlantic City, New Jersey, USA. **Recognition:** IBF. **Referee:** Paul Venti.
Fight Summary: Medal (152¾) became the first champion at the weight for the IBF when stopping Hargrove (153½) in the fifth round of what had been a fierce contest, with both men giving it everything they had. It was Hargrove who made the best start when hammering in blows to the head to take the opening three sessions, but

the taller Medal weathered the storm to come on strongly in the fourth. Banging in punches to head and body, Hargrove, now cut on the right eye, was in dire straits in the fifth, and after being badly hurt by a right to the jaw he was not fighting back when rescued by the referee 49 seconds into the session.

15 June 1984. Thomas Hearns w rsc 2 (12) Roberto Duran.
Venue: Caesar's Palace, Las Vegas, Nevada, USA. **Recognition:** WBC. **Referee:** Carlos Padilla.
Fight Summary: Having finally recognised that his right hand would stand up under duress, the much taller champion marched into Duran (154), using his left lead as a pathfinder. Keeping up the pressure, before the end of the opening round Hearns had smashed Duran down with a right to the jaw. Having made it to his feet, Duran, cut over the left eye, was soon put down again by a short left prior to being saved by the bell. Although he looked to have recovered during the interval it could be quickly seen that Duran was still dazed, and Hearns (153¼) took full advantage of the situation when blasting in punches to the head from both hands. With Hearns in full flow it was no surprise that, after a big right to the chin had dropped the Panamanian like a log, the referee did not even bother to count, calling it off on the 1.07 mark.

15 September 1984. Thomas Hearns w rsc 3 (12) Fred Hutchings.
Venue: Civic Centre, Saginaw, Michigan, USA. **Recognition:** WBC. **Referee:** Arthur Mercante.
Fight Summary: Standing 6'2", an inch taller than the champion, Hutchings (153¾) gave it his best shot but was simply outgunned by a man at the top of the tree. Coming out with the left jab, looking to find a way inside, Hutchings was nailed by countering left hooks and solid rights as Hearns (154) got into gear, being dropped twice before the first round was over. Although Hutchings made a fair fist of it in the second, despite being hurt, it was already clear that he was not going to be around much longer, and when Hearns started to throw punches from both hands without respite the referee stepped in with four seconds of the third session remaining. In no fit state to continue, Hutchings was damaged inside the mouth and had swellings and cuts around both eyes.

Hearns' next fight would be against Marvin Hagler for the latter's world middleweight title at Caesar's Palace, Las Vegas on 15 April 1985, but following a third-round stoppage defeat he was out of the ring for close on a year to allow his injured right hand enough time to heal.

Back in action, Hearns beat James Shuler for the NABF title on 10 March 1986 before declaring that he was ready to defend against Mark Medal, a man who had fought just once since March 1984. Sadly, Shuler was killed a week after fighting Hearns when he crashed his motorcycle.

19 October 1984. Mike McCallum w pts 15 Sean Mannion.
Venue: Madison Square Garden, Manhattan, NYC, New York, USA. **Recognition:** WBA. **Referee:** Tony Perez.
Scorecards: 150-134, 149-136, 149-123.
Fight Summary: Although Mannion (154) went the distance and stayed on his feet in a fight that involved the vacant title he was punished every time he went forward. Mannion, a southpaw, had no answer to McCallum's left jab, which practically landed at will throughout, and finished the fight with his right eye nearly closed and badly bruised features. The indomitable Mannion even staggered McCallum (153¾) in the ninth, but unfortunately for him it was a one-off.

2 November 1984. Carlos Santos w pts 15 Mark Medal.
Venue: MSG Theatre, Manhattan, NYC, New York, USA. **Recognition:** IBF. **Referee:** Joe Cortez.
Scorecards: 146-138, 147-139, 142-140.
Fight Summary: Making his first defence, after Medal (153½) was decked by a left to the jaw in the opening round he continued to be confused by the southpaw stance of Santos (152½), who generally shifted from side to side and banged in blows from both hands before retreating. The big-punching Medal had great difficulty locating the shifty Santos as round followed round, but in the 14th he finally dumped the tiring challenger with a left hook to the jaw. Back on his feet, with Medal also weary from his exertions, Santos just about held his boxing together to make it to the final bell and a well-earned victory. Both fighters were cut over the right eye, Santos' damage coming after a clash of heads.

Santos' first challenger would be Louis Acaries, unranked by *The Ring* magazine, but a man who had just defeated the former WBA champion, Davey Moore, albeit by disqualification. In 44 contests, Acaries, a former European middleweight champion, had won 39 and also beaten Everaldo Costa Azevedo, Jose Hernandez, Marijan Benes, Oscar Albarado and Frank Wissenbach.

1 December 1984. Mike McCallum w rtd 13 (15) Luigi Minchillo.
Venue: Sports Palace, Milan, Italy. **Recognition:** WBA. **Referee:** Frank Cappuccino.
Fight Summary: Badly behind on the cards, the challenger was retired by his corner at the end of the 13th having taken a battering at the hands of McCallum (153). The Italian was almost being hit at will at times. Although Minchillo (153) performed at his best and was never down he was totally outclassed by a champion who just had too much of everything for him, and by the halfway stage he was being hit by jabs, hooks, right hands and uppercuts to head and body without much being returned. Earlier in the fight, Minchillo used his strength to bulldoze McCallum, but once those tactics failed to pay dividends and he began to tire the end was always in sight.

1 June 1985. Carlos Santos w pts 15 Louis Acaries.
Venue: Princes Park Stadium, Paris, France. **Recognition:** IBF. **Referee:** Larry Hazzard.
Scorecards: 147-139, 147-138, 143-142.
Fight Summary: Dominating for long periods, the slippery southpaw champion piled up points during the first seven rounds as Acaries (153½), cut over the left eye early on, spent much of the time plodding after him. Subsequently, however, Acaries got himself going as Santos (154) tired from his exertions, but while the former occasionally landed well and hurt his man with heavy rights and left hooks he was unable to make them pay. The last two sessions saw the rejuvenated Santos totally in charge as he backed up the by now demoralised Acaries with blows from both hands to make the decision a foregone conclusion.

When Santos forfeited IBF recognition in February 1986 for failing to defend against Davey Moore, the latter was matched against Buster Drayton for the vacant title. However, when Moore was injured Santos stepped in as a replacement.

28 July 1985. Mike McCallum w rsc 8 (15) David Braxton.
Venue: Tamiani Fairgrounds Auditorium, Miami, Florida, USA. **Recognition:** WBA. **Referee:** Roberto Ramirez.
Fight Summary: Putting his title on the line against a former sparring partner, McCallum (154) started well when banging in body shots and solid rights to the head of Braxton (154), almost stopping the latter in the fourth as volleys of punches hit the target. It got worse for Braxton in the fifth when his left eyelid was badly damaged, and although hitting back with some venom he could not dent McCallum's defences. After Braxton had fought desperately to no avail in the next two sessions, with the eye damage worsening in the eighth and his legs beginning to go, the referee waved the fight over on the 2.26 mark.

4 June 1986. Buster Drayton w pts 15 Carlos Santos.
Venue: Byrne Meadowlands Arena, East Rutherford, New Jersey, USA. **Recognition:** IBF. **Referee:** Tony Orlando.
Scorecards: 145-141, 145-140, 143-143.
Fight Summary: Contesting the title he had earlier forfeited and was now vacant, Santos (153) failed to match Drayton (152¾), who forced matters and hit just that bit too hard for his rival. Originally matched to meet Davey Moore, Drayton was not going to let his opportunity slip against the slippery southpaw, often switching himself to even things up. Although Santos gave a courageous display, having been rocked several times, he was unable to keep Drayton at bay for long, and even when getting through he would invariably have to take heavy shots in return. After being cut over the left eye in the 11th round, with Santos being forced to defend more he most likely lost the fight between the 12th and 14th when Drayton dominated. Despite having a good last session, unable to change the course of the contest Santos had to settle for being a good loser.

23 June 1986. Thomas Hearns w rsc 8 (12) Mark Medal.
Venue: Caesar's Palace, Las Vegas, Nevada, USA. **Recognition:** WBC. **Referee:** Davy Pearl.
Fight Summary: Defending his title after nearly two years since his previous defence, his last two contests being at middleweight, Hearns (154) started well enough when flooring Medal (154) with a heavy right to the jaw in the

first round. Getting back on his feet and forced to take the mandatory 'eight', Medal had difficulty lasting out the session. Allowed to continue, Medal made his way into the eighth where he shipped plenty of punishment without going down as Hearns hit him at will at times. The fact that Hearns damaged his right hand in the second probably explains why Medal remained upright for so long, but at 2.20 of the eighth the referee stopped the contest when it became apparent that the latter had no chance of winning.

Hearns relinquished the WBC version of the title in September due to difficulty making the weight. Following this, Duane Thomas and John Mugabi were matched to find a new champion.

23 August 1986. Mike McCallum w rsc 2 (15) Julian Jackson.
Venue: Convention Centre, Miami Beach, Florida, USA. **Recognition:** WBA. **Referee:** Eddie Eckert.
Fight Summary: This was a hard-hitting affair right from the opening bell as the challenger, having stopped 27 of his 29 previous opponents, soon hurt McCallum (152½) with a cracking left hook. Using all of his experience, McCallum somehow weathered the storm before dropping Jackson (152) for the mandatory 'eight' with a right-left in the second. Now it was McCallum's turn to be the aggressor, and giving Jackson no chance to recover he unloaded incessant two-handed attacks from head to body that had the latter going before the referee jumped in to rescue him at 2.03 of the session.

24 August 1986. Buster Drayton w rsc 10 (15) Davey Moore.
Venue: Pinede Open Air Arena, Juan Les Pins, France. **Recognition:** IBF. **Referee:** Bobby Ferrara.
Fight Summary: Despite having had only two rounds of boxing in the last 20 months, it was Moore (154) who made the early running before the champion came to life in the third. That did not last long, however, and Drayton (154) was soon easing off as Moore put in all the better work right through to the seventh. In the eighth Drayton finally got his act together when beginning to hurt Moore with heavy rights, something he repeated in the ninth prior to wobbling the latter badly in the tenth. At that point Moore came apart at the seams. Although Moore tried to hit back it was Drayton who was landing the more meaningful punches, and with the challenger on the ropes and not fighting back the referee called the fight off at 1.15 of the session.

25 October 1986. Mike McCallum w co 9 (15) Said Skouma.
Venue: The Zenith, Paris, France. **Recognition:** WBA. **Referee:** Roberto Ramirez.
Fight Summary: Even though the challenger made a reasonable start when taking the fight to McCallum (154) in the first three rounds, it soon became apparent in the fourth that his days would be numbered. Stepping it up, McCallum began to smash in fast, accurate punches that hurt Skouma (153¾) and opened up a deep cut over his right eye. Thereafter, it was all McCallum, who handed out a boxing lesson despite losing a point in the eighth when going low. Cruising into the ninth, McCallum had Skouma at his mercy before crashing in a right to the jaw to send the latter downwards to be counted out on the 2.25 mark.

5 December 1986. Duane Thomas w rsc 3 (12) John Mugabi.
Venue: Caesar's Palace, Las Vegas, Nevada, USA. **Recognition:** WBC. **Referee:** Carlos Padilla.
Fight Summary: Fighting for the title vacated by Thomas Hearns, it was Thomas (152¼), a stablemate of the latter, who came though the odds against the vicious, hard-punching Mugabi (153½) to become the new champion. Although rocked by heavy rights in the second and third rounds, Thomas fought a cool and patient fight, while waiting to land his left hook when Mugabi threw wide punches. Several times Thomas was hurt by the power of Mugabi's blows, but in the third the tide changed when the latter was sent into the ropes after being caught by several left hooks. With Thomas now rampant, Mugabi, claiming he had been thumbed in the left eye, suddenly turned away from him and leaned over the ropes, whereupon the referee stopped the fight after 56 seconds of the session. While Mugabi's damaged left eye was clear for all to see afterwards, the referee was adamant that it was a punch that had caused the damage.

Matched to challenge Thomas in April 1987, Lupe Aquino stopped Davey Moore inside five rounds on that date after the champion had pulled out injured a week earlier. With 30 wins (22 inside the distance) from 33 contests, despite one of his two defeats coming at the hands of Marlon Starling, Aquino had earlier beaten Steve Hearon and had made rapid strides to earn a title shot.

27 March 1987. Buster Drayton w rtd 10 (15) Said Skouma.
Venue: Festival Palace, Cannes, France. **Recognition:** IBF. **Referee:** Joe O'Neil.
Fight Summary: Getting another chance to win the title, it nearly paid off for Skouma (153¼) in the fourth round when he rocked the champion badly with rights and lefts. Up to that point Drayton (153½) had been in charge, and he came back well to weather the storm before Skouma got his left jab and right crosses going in the sixth. Skouma was still pressing in the eighth, even though he had been cut over the right eye by dangerous headwork for which Drayton was deducted a point. Clearly up for it, even in the ninth Skouma was scoring well with short punches on the inside. However, behind on all the cards, the tenth saw Drayton come out firing, several left hooks to the head hurting Skouma before a cracking right sent him down. Although Skouma beat the count, Drayton was on him like a flash, and after the beleaguered Moroccan's corner threw the towel in to stop the contest from continuing, it was only after the bell to end the round went that the retirement was accepted.

19 April 1987. Mike McCallum w rsc 10 (15) Milton McCrory.
Venue: Pointe Resort, Phoenix, Arizona, USA. **Recognition:** WBA. **Referee:** Joe Cortez.
Fight Summary: While McCrory (154) got away well against the slow starting champion, by the seventh round he was being pegged back by body shots that were undoubtedly sapping his strength, and when he was cut over the left eye in the eighth his challenge was almost over. Seemingly unable to hurt McCallum (153¾) the game McCrory gave it everything he had in the ninth, despite being under great pressure and taking plenty of stick. With McCrory, now badly swollen over the right eye as well as the left, McCallum cut loose with both hands in the tenth to eventually force the latter to his knees. Although McCrory was up at 'four' the referee took a good look at him on completion of the mandatory count and called it off, the finish being timed at 2.20.

27 June 1987. Matthew Hilton w pts 15 Buster Drayton.
Venue: The Forum, Montreal, Canada. **Recognition:** IBF. **Referee:** Denny Nelson.
Scorecards: 147-138, 146-139, 144-140.
Fight Summary: The challenger made the best of starts when dropping Drayton (154) with a big right to the head in the opening session, but was unable to produce a finish as the veteran came back from the brink. Although Drayton was hit throughout by body shots and solid blows to the head he was never on the floor again, and while it was always competitive he failed to hurt Hilton (154) until the latter stages when the Canadian was tiring. It was certainly gruelling. In the 14th, thinking it was the last round Drayton went for Hilton before being driven around the ring himself as the latter hit back and continued in the same vein throughout the 15th. In the aftermath it was discovered that Drayton had suffered a broken nose, two broken ribs and a broken hand, while Hilton's hands were badly swollen.

12 July 1987. Lupe Aquino w pts 12 Duane Thomas.
Venue: Merignac Sports Complex, Bordeaux, France. **Recognition:** WBC. **Referee:** Larry O'Connell.
Scorecards: 116-111, 117-110, 114-113.
Fight Summary: A big underdog, Aquino (154) surprised the champion when taking the fight to him right from the opening bell. Aquino then shook Thomas further when putting him down in the second round with a big left hook. Although Thomas (154) made it to his feet and fought back bravely, landing some big punches of his own, he was unable to quell the spirited Aquino, and even when it looked as though he might be getting on top the latter came back strongly in the eighth. After the ninth was evenly contested, Thomas faded badly in the remaining three sessions, being knocked down by a solid right in the last and finishing with cuts over both eyes to go with badly swollen features.

18 July 1987. Mike McCallum w co 5 (15) Donald Curry.
Venue: Caesar's Palace, Las Vegas, Nevada, USA. **Recognition:** WBA. **Referee:** Richard Steele.
Fight Summary: Curry (154) looked as good as ever when mixing up his punches, almost having the champion over in the second round when landing a crashing right to the head. Even when McCallum (153¾) had regained his equilibrium Curry looked to be in control, and in both the third and fourth he scored with crisp punches to head and body, a swelling over his left eye not seeming to bother him. The fifth saw more of the same as Curry continued to make the pace, but out of the blue he was dropped by a tremendous left hook to the jaw that saw him counted out at 1.14 of the session. McCallum, who had obviously been biding his time and was behind on the

cards, explained afterwards that having shown Curry the right uppercut he went to the body with a left hook before shifting to the head.

After McCallum relinquished the WBA version of the title in September to campaign in the middleweight division, Julian Jackson and In-Chul Baek were matched to find a successor.

Following the WBA convention, held in October, the body announced that in future all world title bouts held under their auspices would be contested over 12 rounds.

2 October 1987. Gianfranco Rosi w pts 12 Lupe Aquino.
Venue: Sports Palace, Perugia, Italy. **Recognition:** WBC. **Referee:** Joe Cortez.
Scorecards: 115-114, 115-114, 118-113.
Fight Summary: Using the ring well and showing great judgement, the challenger made Aquino (154) look clumsy at times as he jabbed, countered and often had the better of matters on the inside with right uppercuts through the middle. There was no doubting that Aquino was the bigger puncher of the pair, but having difficulty in finding the target on a regular basis he only threw one punch at a time while Rosi (153½) was always prepared to work. Overcoming a bad cut on his right eye, suffered in the fourth round, Rosi went on the attack in the 11th and 12th, punching it out with Aquino and forcing him up against the ropes to earn an ovation at the final bell.

16 October 1987. Matthew Hilton w rsc 2 (15) Jack Callahan.
Venue: Convention Hall, Atlantic City, New Jersey, USA. **Recognition:** IBF. **Referee:** Rudy Battle.
Fight Summary: Although the slow moving challenger was unbeaten in 24 contests none of the men on his record were remotely of world class. Thus, it was hardly surprising that Hilton (154) brought about a finish after just two completed rounds. The first punch of the fight, a left jab, jolted Callahan (154) backwards, and whilst he somehow got through the opening session he was soon cut over the right eye in the second prior to being dropped by a left hook. Up on his feet Callahan was quickly under the cosh before a right to the head dropped him again. The bell rang at the count of 'six' but the referee continued to count. Even though the badly dazed Callahan made it up at 'nine' and staggered back to his corner, the fight was called off by the third man following a consultation with the doctor.

This would be the last 15-round world title fight for the weight class after the IBF announced the following year that, from 1 September 1988, all world title bouts held under their banner would be contested over 12 rounds, bringing them into line with the WBA and WBC.

21 November 1987. Julian Jackson w rsc 3 In-Chul Baek.
Venue: Hilton Hotel, Las Vegas, Nevada, USA. **Recognition:** WBA. **Referee:** Mills Lane.
Fight Summary: With Mike McCallum moving up a weight division, Jackson (153) met Baek (154) to decide the vacant title and, although the contest started slowly, before the opening round was over the latter had been dropped by a long left. Saved by the bell, Baek plodded forward in the second but Jackson, again switching to southpaw on occasion, was soon firing with both hands from head to body. Coming out for the third it was not long before Jackson wobbled Baek with heavy combinations, prior to dropping him with a left hook. Although the South Korean got to his feet, seeing that he was all at sea the referee rescued him at 1.17 of the session.

3 January 1988. Gianfranco Rosi w rsc 7 Duane Thomas.
Venue: Sports Palace, Genoa, Italy. **Recognition:** WBC. **Referee:** Larry O'Connell.
Fight Summary: Making his first defence and against all expectation Rosi (153¼) was soon tearing into Thomas (154) with wide left hooks and overarm rights that completely took the latter by surprise. By the fourth both men were cut, Rosi between the eyes and Thomas over the right eye, but continued to trade. Having been taken out of his stride, Thomas was beginning to fade by the sixth, and in the seventh after being rocked by heavy rights he was slammed into the ropes by a barrage of blows as Rosi opened up with both hands. With it being clear that Thomas was through for the night, the referee called the fight off just as the American was slumping to the canvas. The finish was timed at 57 seconds.

8 July 1988. Donald Curry w rtd 9 Gianfranco Rosi.
Venue: The Portosole, San Remo, Italy. **Recognition:** WBC. **Referee:** Octavio Meyran.
Fight Summary: The champion started well enough when shaking Curry (153¾) with a right hand in the opening round but after that it was all downhill as the latter began to put his punches together. Knocked down by a short left hook in the second, Rosi was floored again in the fourth, three times in the seventh and once in the eighth. It was now clear that Rosi could not take Curry's punches and after his legs were buckled by another big right in the ninth it had become a hopeless position. Thus it was no surprise when he retired, claiming an injured hand, at the end of the session. Curry, despite being cut over both eyes at the finish, obviously hit too hard for Rosi, and while not the classy box-fighter of a year or so earlier he was far too good for the Italian.

30 July 1988. Julian Jackson w rsc 3 Buster Drayton.
Venue: Harrah's Marina Hotel, Atlantic City, New Jersey, USA. **Recognition:** WBA. **Referee:** Tony Perez.
Fight Summary: An exciting, free-hitting affair from the start, it was the champion who made an early mark when sending Drayton (153) to the boards in the second round, having set the latter up with heavy left hooks. Up at 'two', although forced to take the mandatory count, Drayton surged into Jackson (153) and gave as good as he got before being taken out by a crunching left hook that separated him from his senses. Although announced as being a knockout at 2.57 of the third because the referee never picked up the count, and stopped the fight immediately to allow Drayton medical attention, it should be seen as a stoppage.

Following the WBA convention in October, when 27 of the 71 delegates walked out in disgust, the World Boxing Organisation (WBO) was formed. To find a champion, John David Jackson and Lupe Aquino, the NABF titleholder, were nominated to contest the vacant title.

4 November 1988. Robert Hines w pts 12 Matthew Hilton.
Venue: Hilton Hotel, Las Vegas, Nevada, USA. **Recognition:** IBF. **Referee:** Carlos Padilla.
Scorecards: 116-110, 113-111, 112-111.
Fight Summary: Floored twice, in the second and third rounds, and badly hurt on several occasions by booming right hands from the wild-swinging Hilton (154), at that stage it seemed that the southpaw challenge of Hines (152) would be a short one. However, with both eyes swollen Hines somehow managed to stay in the fight against all the odds before beginning to take over from the sixth as Hilton tired badly. Deducted a point for low blows in the eighth, Hilton was now up against it as Hines drilled in solid shots to head and body, and although the champion came back with a vicious final attack in the 11th once that subsided the fight was virtually over.

8 December 1988. John David Jackson w rtd 7 Lupe Aquino.
Venue: Cobo Arena, Detroit, Michigan, USA. **Recognition:** WBO.
Fight Summary: Jackson (153) became the WBO's first champion at the weight when forcing Aquino (154), who was arrested immediately after the fight on vehicular manslaughter charges, to retire on his stool at the end of the seventh. Afterwards, Aquino said his thoughts had been elsewhere, which probably summed up why he was never in the contest against his sharp-punching southpaw opponent who seemed to be able to hit him at will at times. Put down by a left hand in the first round, Aquino, cut on the bridge of the nose in the fourth, was badly outboxed from there onwards as Jackson banged away with both hands. Thus, it came as no surprise when Aquino's corner pulled him out of the fight.

5 February 1989. Darrin Van Horn w pts 12 Robert Hines.
Venue: Trump Castle Hotel, Atlantic City, New Jersey, USA. **Recognition:** IBF. **Referee:** Randy Neumann.
Scorecards: 118-110, 118-111, 116-112.
Fight Summary: Looking slow and lethargic, Hines (153) lost his title at the first time of asking when being outboxed by the 20-year-old Van Horn (153¼), who mixed up slugging with boxing effectively on the outside to take the opening five rounds. The unbeaten Van Horn continued in that vein during most of the remaining sessions as the southpaw champion desperately tried to get going. Even when the youngster was caught napping he always came back firing fiercely. Although Hines was not dropped he was caught time and again by right hands, and at the finish he was left bleeding heavily from the nose and lumpy around both eyes.

11 February 1989. Rene Jacquot w pts 12 Donald Curry.
Venue: Sports Palace, Grenoble, France. **Recognition:** WBC. **Referee:** Jean Deswert.
Scorecards: 117-113, 118-115, 118-116.
Fight Summary: Often outhustled and outpunched, the champion was a shell of the man who won the welterweight title a few years back, having great difficulty stemming the tide as the vigorous Jacquot (153) took over in the sixth and proceeded to build up points. Although he made a reasonable start, taking four of the opening five rounds, Curry (154) had difficulty landing effectively once the Frenchman got into his stride. Curry also had problems lifting himself when he needed to. By the eighth it was clear that the flat-footed Curry was tiring badly, and Jacquot took full advantage of the situation when driving his rival around the ring, landing lefts and rights to the head. Occasionally, Curry smashed in solid blows but the mechanical Jacquot, despite being shaken up at times, merely backed off until coming again.

25 February 1989. Julian Jackson w co 8 Francisco De Jesus.
Venue: Hilton Hotel, Las Vegas, Nevada, USA. **Recognition:** WBA. **Referee:** Mills Lane.
Fight Summary: Even though the champion controlled the action virtually all the way he was not at his best, which would probably explain why De Jesus (153½) lasted for so long. After taking the first round, courtesy of his powerful left jab, De Jesus found himself in trouble in the second when a short right sent him sprawling, but he was soon back on his feet. Then, after surviving another scare in the third he began to give Jackson (153½) all kinds of problems with his elusiveness. By the fifth Jackson was starting to look ponderous as he plodded after De Jesus, but he hurt the latter in the sixth before really getting on top in the seventh. With both eyes now swollen, although De Jesus came out for the eighth and continued to make things awkward for Jackson, a clubbing right to the head eventually sent him crashing down to be counted out on the 2.19 mark.

22 April 1989. John David Jackson w rsc 8 Steve Little.
Venue: Auburn Hills Palace, Detroit, Michigan, USA. **Recognition:** WBO. **Referee:** Dale Grable.
Fight Summary: Dominating from the start against a challenger who had been beaten in his last two outings, although Jackson (152) won easily enough he was unable to knock his man over and had to rely on a cut eye stoppage after 37 seconds of the eighth to maintain his title status. Why the WBO should give Little (152¾) an opportunity to win one of their titles was the question being asked at ringside, especially as he was so negative, clutching and defending throughout. Outboxed all the way by the southpaw champion, it was almost a relief when the referee deemed that the damage to Little's right eye was too severe for him to carry on.

8 July 1989. John Mugabi w rsc 1 Rene Jacquot.
Venue: Cergy-Pontoise Mirapolis Amusement Park, Paris, France. **Recognition:** WBC. **Referee:** Arthur Mercante.
Fight Summary: Pitted against the hard-hitting Mugabi (153½) was not the ideal contest for Jacquot (152½) to make his first defence, and right from the opening bell it looked as though he would be overpowered. The contest started with Mugabi stalking Jacquot before a looping right hand to the head sent the latter crashing, his left leg bent under him. Although Jacquot got up quickly it could be seen that he was hobbling. Despite the WBC commissioner shouting for it to be stopped the referee called 'time out' to allow the champion's corner to work on what turned out to be knee-ligament damage. It was certainly a contentious decision. After approximately two minutes, still unable to stand properly, Jacquot was sent out again only to be floored immediately and stopped. The finish was given as 2.53.

15 July 1989. Gianfranco Rosi w pts 12 Darrin Van Horn.
Venue: Trump Castle Hotel, Atlantic City, New Jersey, USA. **Recognition:** IBF. **Referee:** Tony Perez.
Scorecards: 117-109, 118-108, 116-109.
Fight Summary: In what was a huge upset, the former WBC champion, Rosi (153), took the title from Van Horn (154) by a wide margin, controlling the fight throughout after knocking the latter down in the opening round with a left-right combination. Van Horn doggedly held on to get to the end of the session but was given a boxing lesson despite hurting Rosi occasionally with big punches of his own. However, Van Horn continued to be hit as Rosi cleverly mixed up his punches, especially when pulling out of clinches to land lefts and rights and making it difficult for the youngster when at range. Finishing the fight the stronger of the pair, Rosi came on in the 11th and 12th to

totally dominate the action as Van Horn tired, landing good, solid shots from both hands before scoring another knockdown following a big left hook prior to the final bell.

30 July 1989. Julian Jackson w rsc 2 Terry Norris.
Venue: Convention Centre, Atlantic City, New Jersey, USA. **Recognition:** WBA. **Referee:** Joe Cortez.
Fight Summary: Starting smartly, the challenger showed plenty of lateral movement and even shook Jackson (153¼) up on occasion to win the session on all three cards. It later transpired that Jackson wanted to see what his rival could do. After sizing Norris (152) up he took the latter to the ropes in the second before smashing in a cracking right to the head that dropped him heavily. Surprisingly up at 'nine', although shaky and unsteady on his legs, the referee had a good look at Norris before deciding that he was not fit to continue on the 1.37 mark.

Jackson relinquished the WBA version of the title in September 1990 to challenge for the vacant WBC middleweight crown, an action that was followed by Gilbert Dele and Carlos Elliott coming together to decide who would be the new champion.

27 October 1989. Gianfranco Rosi w pts 12 Troy Waters.
Venue: Sports Palace, St Vincent, Italy. **Recognition:** IBF. **Referee:** Tony Orlando.
Scorecards: 118-110, 119-113, 117-111.
Fight Summary: Controlling the opening nine rounds as the challenger failed to get into the fight, it was only in the tenth that Rosi (153¼) came close to a setback after being caught by a big left to the head. Calling on all of his experience to get through, Rosi, cut over the right eye, boxed his way out of a tight spot but had to take further heavy shots on the way as the game Waters (153½) came on strong. Following the contest, Rosi stated that although he had tried to knock Waters out he had found him too tough a nut to crack and settled for the points.

17 February 1990. John David Jackson nc 11 Martin Camara.
Venue: Deauville Hotel, Chapilion, France. **Recognition:** WBO. **Referee:** Ted Pick.
Fight Summary: In what was pure farce, Camara (152), who had been floored three times and outboxed, came back strongly to put Jackson (153¾) on the floor towards the end of the 11th round. When Jackson got up he was in a dazed state and did not understand what the French official was telling him but following a long delay he somehow got through the remaining seven seconds left of the round. However, after the crowd, who had felt that the challenger had been robbed of the championship, invaded the ring the fight was eventually terminated and classified as a no-contest by the WBO.

31 March 1990. Terry Norris w co 1 John Mugabi.
Venue: The Sundome, Tampa, Florida, USA. **Recognition:** WBC. **Referee:** Eddie Eckert.
Fight Summary: Having won the title in less than a round, Mugabi (154) lost it in the same manner when destroyed by Norris (153¾) who came well prepared in how to deal with the slow moving champion. Caught by early punches that whistled through his guard, Mugabi should have been warned, but he persisted in carrying his right low and paid the price when Norris had him down with two chopping rights. Having taken the mandatory count, a dazed Mugabi was all over the place, and at 2.47 of the opening round he was counted out after being dropped by another heavy right to the head.

14 April 1990. Gianfranco Rosi w rsc 7 Kevin Daigle.
Venue: Loew's Hotel, Monte Carlo, Monaco. **Recognition:** IBF. **Referee:** Rudy Battle.
Fight Summary: Far too good for his limited challenger, Rosi (153¾) did as he pleased for much of the contest, often landing ten punches at a time without response. Cut over the right eye in the first round and staggered in the third by a right, although Daigle (153½) tried hard enough he could not get to grips with Rosi, resorting to wrestling and holding on. With Rosi's lack of power saving Daigle from being knocked out, even when the latter was down in the sixth it was from more of a push than a punch. The referee finally called it off at 2.29 of the seventh when Daigle was being battered up against the ropes without returning fire.

13 July 1990. Terry Norris w pts 12 Rene Jacquot.
Venue: Skating Rink, Annecy, France. **Recognition:** WBC. **Referee:** Joe Cortez.

Scorecards: 117-109, 120-107, 119-108.

Fight Summary: After losing his title to John Mugabi in peculiar circumstances, Jacquot (153¾) was given a crack at Norris (152½), who had taken over from the Ugandan a few months previously. Although Jacquot was knocked down in the first and second rounds, with great heart he struggled back into the contest without ever looking likely to win, using stalling and clutching tactics as a substitute for good defence. It was easy for Norris, but his lack of experience enabled the hardy Jacquot to stay the distance, even though he was dropped again in the 11th by a left-right-left combination to the head.

21 July 1990. Gianfranco Rosi w pts 12 Darrin Van Horn.
Venue: Ghiacchio Sports Palace, Marino, Italy. **Recognition:** IBF. **Referee:** Randy Neumann.
Scorecards: 116-113, 115-110, 115-110.
Fight Summary: Using every trick in the trade to disrupt the challenger's rhythm, Rosi (153½) mauled and brawled his way to a unanimous points victory without ever having to raise his game. With heads coming dangerously close on occasion Rosi was cut on the right eye as early as the opening round, and in the fifth it was Van Horn's turn to be injured in the same place. Rosi also had a point taken away for going low in the fifth. Although Van Horn (154) got lucky in the seventh when the referee ruled that Rosi had been knocked down when it looked like a clear push, he was unable to build on it, continuing to be outwitted as he walked forward in straight lines. A difficult contest to score, according to Rosi he was not only fighting Van Horn, who he claimed butted him throughout, but the referee as well.

23 October 1990. John David Jackson w pts 12 Chris Pyatt.
Venue: Granby Halls, Leicester, England. **Recognition:** WBO. **Referee:** Ismael Quinones-Falu.
Scorecards: 117-111, 118-109, 116-112.
Fight Summary: Boxing brilliantly, Jackson (154) made Pyatt (152¼) look a very ordinary challenger indeed as he allowed the latter's punches to miss while countering effectively with southpaw rights and lefts. The hard-punching Pyatt was always in with a chance, but Jackson was just too clever for him. In the 11th he even dropped the Englishman with a right-left. Whatever he tried, Pyatt had little success, and although he stormed out for the last session with only a knockout win on his mind he just could not get to grips with Jackson, who sauntered home for a thoroughly deserved points win.

30 November 1990. Gianfranco Rosi w pts 12 Rene Jacquot.
Venue: Sports Palace, Marsala, Italy. **Recognition:** IBF. **Referee:** Joey Curtis.
Scorecards: 118-110, 117-112, 115-113.
Fight Summary: In one of the poorest championship bouts on record, Rosi (152¾) held on to his title in a fight that had too much holding and mauling and too little boxing. There was also bad feeling between the two men. The contest started with Jacquot trying to force the action and looking for opportunities to land his right hand, only to be held up by Rosi who wanted to remain at close quarters where his strength gave him the upper hand. Unfortunately for all concerned the two styles failed to mix and, while Rosi deserved the win on account of his better work and Jacquot's inability to land cleanly, as a spectacle it was a disaster.

9 February 1991. Terry Norris w pts 12 Sugar Ray Leonard.
Venue: Madison Square Garden, Manhattan, NYC, New York, USA. **Recognition:** WBC. **Referee:** Arthur Mercante Jnr.
Scorecards: 116-110, 120-104, 119-103.
Fight Summary: Coming back to the ring for the first time since defending his WBC super middleweight title on 7 December 1989, the 35-year-old Leonard (154) was given a chance to win the 154lbs title when taking on the champion, Norris (152½). Once the finest fighter on the planet, Leonard was a shadow of his former self, being dropped twice, in the second and seventh, and hammered without let-up throughout. Well beaten, it was only Leonard's pride and courage that got him through, and he was often picked off by long punches from either hand as Norris boxed on the outside. The last two sessions were especially difficult for Leonard, his left eye swelling fast, as Norris staggered him repeatedly and belted him along the ropes, but although the decision was a lopsided one he made it to the final bell to receive an ovation from the crowd. Leonard returned for one last fling in 1997, but was demolished by Hector Camacho inside five rounds.

23 February 1991. Gilbert Dele w rsc 7 Carlos Elliott.
Venue: Football Stadium, Point A Pitre, Guadeloupe. **Recognition:** WBA. **Referee:** Isidro Rodriguez.
Fight Summary: Contested for the vacant title after Julian Jackson had abdicated, Dele (153¼) dominated proceedings from the start with the jab before opening up with right hands in the third round to drop Elliott (152½) twice. Although the Japanese-based Elliott came back well in the fifth with solid left hooks he was unable to make up any leeway, and before too long his right eye began to close. Subsequently, the American was more often than not reduced to clinching. Having battered away at Elliott throughout the sixth, Dele's punches had a dramatic effect in the seventh when heavy rights sent the latter to his knees, whereupon the referee stopped the contest on the 1.48 mark. It was later disclosed that Elliott's jaw had been fractured in two places.

16 March 1991. Gianfranco Rosi w pts 12 Ron Amundsen.
Venue: Sports Palace, St Vincent, Italy. **Recognition:** IBF. **Referee:** Randy Neumann.
Scorecards: 118-111, 118-111, 116-113.
Fight Summary: Making a solid start, the champion showed off his ring-craft as he boxed his way into a clear lead after eight rounds, although he was always aware that the Amundsen (154) left hook was a punch he needed to avoid as best he could. Then, in the ninth, Amundsen's left hook almost dropped Rosi (154), who stopped himself from going down by hanging on to the challenger for dear life. Sensing an opportunity, Amundsen relentlessly moved forward, but the crafty Rosi kept on his toes to weather the storm. Despite being further hurt a couple of times, at the final bell Rosi was back in control of the situation.

5 May 1991. Gilbert Dele w pts 12 Jun-Suk Hwang.
Venue: Carpentier Hall, Paris, France. **Recognition:** WBA. **Referee:** Eddie Eckert.
Scorecards: 118-114, 119-109, 119-109.
Fight Summary: Starting sensibly against his tough challenger, Dele (154) showed an excellent left jab, backed up by solid uppercuts, to control the fight virtually throughout despite having a few anxious moments. By the fourth Hwang (154) was already showing signs of wear and tear, and in the seventh when under severe pressure it looked as though he would not be around much longer. However, after Hwang came back strongly in the eighth to confound Dele and his supporters, although the latter sensibly kept it at long range from thereon in to win comfortably he knew he had been in a fight.

1 June 1991. Terry Norris w co 8 Donald Curry.
Venue: Radisson Resort, Palm Springs, California, USA. **Recognition:** WBC. **Referee:** Chuck Hassett.
Fight Summary: Having won every round coming into the sixth, the champion had outspeeded and outpunched Curry (154), taking the best the latter had to offer almost nonchalantly. He was also ready to step up a gear. Shrugging off Curry's best punch of the fight, a cracking left hook, when Norris (151) went to work in the seventh the former champion was saved by the bell after being dropped by a long right hand. Although fighting back gamely in the eighth it was clear that Curry's days were numbered, and following a barrage of two-fisted blows and three crashing right hands to the head he went down to be counted out with seven seconds of the session remaining.

13 July 1991. Gianfranco Rosi w pts 12 Glenn Wolfe.
Venue: Main City Square Open Air Arena, Avezzano, Italy. **Recognition:** IBF. **Referee:** Sam Williams.
Scorecards: 118-109, 118-110, 119-109.
Fight Summary: Wolfe (153¼) started well enough when putting Rosi (153½) down with a left hook in the third round, but apart from a similar punch in the fifth that had the champion sagging at the knees he failed to produce any further fireworks. Picked off by jabs, right hands and left hooks, Wolfe, who finished with both eyes badly swollen, was a demoralised figure in the latter stages as Rosi almost did as he pleased. While Wolfe never gave up trying to land a punch that would end the fight, Rosi was far too cute to be caught again, being content to box his way through to the final bell without taking added risks.

20 July 1991. John David Jackson w pts 12 Tyrone Trice.
Venue: The Racecourse, Atlantic City, New Jersey, USA. **Recognition:** WBO. **Referee:** Joe Cortez.
Scorecards: 116-111, 116-111, 117-110.

Fight Summary: A disappointing fight saw Jackson (153) constantly boxing on the outside at speed while Trice (154) plodded after him in the hope that he would eventually tire. As the rounds went by it looked hopeless for Trice as Jackson continued to pepper him with light southpaw jabs before moving out of range. However, never giving up hope Trice eventually got to Jackson when dropping him with a right to the head in the 11th, but after beating the count with several seconds to spare the latter quickly went back to his tried and trusted tactics to make it to the final bell.

16 August 1991. Terry Norris w rsc 1 Brett Lally.
Venue: Sports Arena, San Diego, California, USA. **Recognition:** WBC. **Referee:** Rudy Ortega.
Fight Summary: Despite making a tentative start, the champion soon picked it up when under pressure, and having being knocked off balance by a lead right he fired in a left hook that dropped Lally (154). Stunned, but back on his feet, when Lally tried to brawl his way out of it he was sent to the boards. With Norris (153) in full cry and Lally allowed to carry on it was just a matter of time, a barrage of blows followed by a thudding right to the jaw dropping the latter for the third time before the referee called it off. The finish, timed at 2.40, was the third quickest in the division's history.

3 October 1991. Vinny Pazienza w rsc 12 Gilbert Dele.
Venue: Civic Centre, Providence, Rhode Island, USA. **Recognition:** WBA. **Referee:** Luis Rivera.
Fight Summary: Considered by many to be over the hill, the battle-scarred Pazienza (154) proved his critics wrong when taking the title from the fancied Dele (154), who was found to be wanting despite having an 11-inch-reach advantage. Darting in and out with fast jabs and thumping body shots Pazienza bewildered Dele at times, and while the champion always tried to fight back he was being outmanoeuvred at every turn. Although the doctor had a close look at Dele before the tenth got underway he was allowed to continue, but in the 12th, having turned away from Pazienza and claimed that he had been thumbed in the eye, the referee stopped the fight. With just 50 seconds of the contest remaining it was clear that Dele had lost heart and had given up fighting.

After Pazienza relinquished the WBA version of the title in October 1992 when an injury stopped him from defending inside the stipulated deadline, Julio Cesar Vasquez and Hitoshi Kamiyama were matched to find a successor.

21 November 1991. Gianfranco Rosi w pts 12 Gilbert Baptist.
Venue: Sports Palace, Perugia, Italy. **Recognition:** IBF. **Referee:** Denny Nelson.
Scorecards: 118-111, 120-108, 120-108.
Fight Summary: In what was a fairly mundane affair, the champion used an accurate left jab and right cross to catch the hard-punching Baptist (152¾) time and again as he rumbled in. Although the game Baptist never stopped trying, Rosi (153½) was just too fast and too good for the American, having him covered all the way. Regardless that he was given credit by one of the judges for never taking a backward step, Baptist received a boxing lesson.

13 December 1991. Terry Norris w pts 12 Jorge Castro.
Venue: Bercy Sports Palace, Paris, France. **Recognition:** WBC. **Referee:** Joe Cortez.
Scorecards: 117-111, 118-109, 120-108.
Fight Summary: Superior in every department, the champion boxed brilliantly, whether in defence or attack, and although he failed to knock Castro (154) down it was due more to the Argentine being tremendously tough rather than a lack of power. Picking his punches and jabbing strongly at all times, Norris (151¼) was a revelation. Even when put on the defensive by the charging Castro he either moved out of range or was able to cover up without taking too much. While always dangerous Castro lacked the ability to open the champion up.

22 February 1992. Terry Norris w rsc 9 Carl Daniels.
Venue: Sports Arena, San Diego, California, USA. **Recognition:** WBC. **Referee:** Lou Filippo.
Fight Summary: Not one to miss an opportunity, the challenger took the opening two rounds when scoring well with southpaw jabs and crosses to leave Norris (152) confused. However, Norris came back well in the third and was soon forcing Daniels (152) to the ropes where he consistently scored with heavy two-handed blows to the head. It was clear by the eighth that the inexperienced Daniels, his left eye badly swollen, was being worn down.

And when a barrage of punches sent him to the canvas in the ninth the referee pulled him out of the contest on the 2.37 mark without even bothering to take up the count.

9 April 1992. Gianfranco Rosi w rsc 6 Angel Hernandez Gonzalez.
Venue: Sports Palace, Celano, Italy. **Recognition:** IBF. **Referee:** Dale Grable.
Fight Summary: Making his 11th title defence and with Rosi (153¼) in command, by the fourth round his combinations to head and body had already started to wear Hernandez Gonzalez (152½) down. To his credit, Hernandez Gonzalez was always looking to get inside, but with Rosi's left lead finding its mark time and again he had little luck. At this stage it was clear to see that the Spaniard was gradually having the fight knocked out of him. After being dropped in the sixth by a left hook, Hernandez Gonzalez got to his feet and immediately walked to his corner, an action that prompted the referee to call the fight off after 26 seconds of the session

9 May 1992. Terry Norris w rsc 4 Meldrick Taylor.
Venue: Mirage Hotel, Las Vegas, Nevada, USA. **Recognition:** WBC. **Referee:** Mills Lane.
Fight Summary: Impressing even more than previously, the champion made quick work of the once gifted Taylor (149), who was clinically taken apart. Although Taylor came out fast to knock Norris (149) off balance by the third he was under pressure as two-handed punches thudded in to his head and body. Coming out for the fourth Norris ripped into Taylor, a battery of solid punches seeing the latter slide to the floor. Up at 'seven', Taylor tried to fight back but was soon put down again. Having taken the mandatory count for the second time, Taylor was allowed to continue before the contest was called off on the 2.55 mark when he was being battered without response.

9 June 1992. John David Jackson w rtd 9 Pat Lawlor.
Venue: Civic Auditorium, San Francisco, California, USA. **Recognition:** WBO. **Referee:** Raul Caiz.
Fight Summary: Assuming control at the sound of the bell, the elusive Jackson (154) made a difficult target for his challenger before landing terrific hooks to the body. Despite having victories over men such as Wilfred Benitez and Roberto Duran, the game Lawlor (151) proved to be limited at this level, especially in trying to solve the southpaw puzzle that was Jackson. By the ninth it was clear that Lawlor, badly cut over the left eye, would not have still been upright had Jackson possessed anything approaching punching power. Still receiving a beating, though, it came as no surprise when Lawlor was retired at the end of that session by his corner.

11 July 1992. Gianfranco Rosi w pts 12 Gilbert Dele.
Venue: Louis 11 Stadium, Monte Carlo, Monaco. **Recognition:** IBF. **Referee:** Rudy Battle.
Scorecards: 116-111, 116-114, 113-114.
Fight Summary: Getting away strongly, despite being cut over left eye in the second round by an accidental butt the challenger had Rosi (152¼) over in the third from a right to the head. Certainly, for the first half of the contest Dele (153¼) impressed when standing off with left jabs and right crosses, but he expended a great deal of energy when trying to find a way through Rosi's defence, something that went against him in the latter stages. Although continually trying to force the fight, with Dele gradually getting pegged back the last three sessions saw Rosi scoring well with combinations to impress at least two of the judges.

19 December 1992. John David Jackson w rsc 10 Michele Mastrodonato.
Venue: Sports Palace, San Severo, Italy. **Recognition:** WBO. **Referee:** Stan Christodoulou.
Fight Summary: Although the challenger went on the attack right from the start he never really inconvenienced Jackson (153¼), who easily controlled the fight with the southpaw jab and precise combinations. With just 16 fights under his belt, Mastrodonato (153¼) did not have the experience to deal with a man of Jackson's class, the contest becoming very one-sided despite him showing grim determination. After allowing his charge to start the tenth, once he could see that it was a hopeless case, Mastrodonato's manager threw the towel in on the 1.14 mark prompting the referee to call the fight off. The Italian was cut under both eyes and had taken a steady battering.

After Jackson relinquished the WBO version of the title in July 1993 due to difficulty making the weight, Verno Phillips and Lupe Aquino were matched to find a successor.

21 December 1992. Julio Cesar Vasquez w rsc 1 Hitoshi Kamiyama.
Venue: Hector Etchart Stadium, Buenos Aires, Argentina. **Recognition:** WBA. **Referee:** Isidro Rodriguez.
Fight Summary: Fighting to decide the title vacated by Vinny Pazienza, the aggressive Vasquez (152¾) soon had Kamiyama (152¼) in trouble, and after landing solidly with southpaw uppercuts and hooks he dropped his man with a heavy right to the jaw. On getting up, when it could be seen that Kamiyama was cut over the left eye Vasquez wasted no more time when battering him down again almost immediately. The contest was automatically ended on the 'three knockdowns in a round' ruling on the 2.59 mark, after a cracking left to the head had floored Kamiyama for the third time.

20 January 1993. Gianfranco Rosi w pts 12 Gilbert Dele.
Venue: Sports Palace, Avoriaz, France. **Recognition:** IBF. **Referee:** Robert Byrd.
Scorecards: 116-111, 114-113, 112-114.
Fight Summary: A return match that was brought about by dissatisfaction over the previous verdict, this time round there appeared to be no dissent as the champion outscored Dele (153½). Although there was never much between them, Rosi (151¾) controlled the fight by staying close to Dele and working the body, a tactic that saw the latter unable to land his big punches. In the tenth round Rosi staggered Dele badly when catching him with a heavy right, and although the latter was able to hang in for the remainder of the contest he was unable to turn things around.

20 February 1993. Terry Norris w rsc 2 Maurice Blocker.
Venue: Azteca Stadium, Mexico City, Mexico. **Recognition:** WBC. **Referee:** Richard Steele.
Fight Summary: Never making proper use of his three-inch-reach advantage Blocker (151½) was unable to trouble the champion, who soon found that his left hook would be his best weapon on the night when dropping his rival with that punch in the opening session. Having taken the mandatory count, Blocker was all at sea and reeling around the ring before being dumped again by Norris (150), this time by a crashing right to the head. Somehow, Blocker made it to the bell, but with there being little time for him to recover he was rescued by the referee after 49 seconds of the second when he was swaying badly following a non-stop attack from Norris.

22 February 1993. Julio Cesar Vasquez w co 1 Aquilino Asprilla.
Venue: The Superdome, Mar Del Plata, Argentina. **Recognition:** WBA. **Referee:** Waldemar Schmidt.
Fight Summary: Making his first defence, Vasquez (154) wasted little time when facing up to Asprilla (153¼). Fired up, after a few perfunctory exchanges the champion opened up with a barrage of blows from both hands before a left to the jaw sent the Panamanian down to be counted out after just 45 seconds. Although Asprilla had been stopped previously he was expected to give Vasquez a bit of a test, but appeared bewildered by the latter's southpaw stance.

24 April 1993. Julio Cesar Vasquez w pts 12 Javier Castillejo.
Venue: Ermita Retirement Park, Leganes, Madrid, Spain. **Recognition:** WBA. **Referee:** John Coyle.
Scorecards: 114-113, 115-114, 120-115.
Fight Summary: In what turned out to be a gruelling affair, with both men exchanging heavy punches at times, Vasquez (153) held off the challenge of Castillejo (152) to retain his title. Although Castillejo started well and had the southpaw champion under some pressure early on he was unable find a finishing blow before being put down in the sixth round. Thereafter, Vasquez just about held the upper hand, but it was too close for comfort as the fight swung first one way and then the other.

19 June 1993. Terry Norris w rtd 3 Troy Waters.
Venue: Sports Arena, San Diego, California, USA. **Recognition:** WBC. **Referee:** Marty Denkin.
Fight Summary: Treating the London-born Waters (152) with disdain, Norris (154) ripped into his challenger from the opening bell looking for a quick finish. Punching with blinding speed, Norris eventually found a blow to drop Waters, a cracking overarm right to the temple, but was lucky to escape a severe censure when hitting his man while down. With the end seemingly near, Waters not only made it to his feet but lasted out the round with clever defensive boxing. Then, in the second, with the champion firing in solid punches, Waters put him down with a right to the temple. Badly embarrassed, when Norris got up the pair went at each other to see the session out. After

295

being dropped by a right to the head in the third, Waters, gashed on the cheek and over both eyes, somehow lasted the round out before being retired by his corner during the interval.

10 July 1993. Julio Cesar Vasquez w pts 12 Alejandro Ugueto.
Venue: Villa Lujan Defenders Football Ground, Tucuman, Argentina. **Recognition:** WBA. **Referee:** Julio Alvarado.
Scorecards: 118-111, 119-111, 119-111.
Fight Summary: Unbeaten on 13 prior to challenging for the title, Ugueto (154) gave it his best shot but was unable to move the southpaw champion, who laboriously tried to find a finishing blow without success. Although winning comfortably, the crude, wild-swinging Vasquez (153½) found himself up against an opponent who not only knew how to resist but was able to fight back at times despite shipping solid lefts to the head and body. While possessing limited boxing skills, once again Vasquez had traded on his aggression, toughness and great strength to win a contest that many initially thought he might lose.

21 August 1993. Julio Cesar Vasquez w pts 12 Aaron Davis.
Venue: Etoiles Sporting Club, Monte Carlo, Monaco. **Recognition:** WBA. **Referee:** Stan Christodoulou.
Scorecards: 115-114, 116-115, 115-115.
Fight Summary: Boxing behind a high guard the challenger did well in the opening rounds, but was unable to make a dent in Vasquez (153) despite catching him with solid left uppercuts on the inside. As the fight wore on the crude, swinging Vasquez came more into it, but lacking the quality to take advantage of openings he had to rely on his strength to eventually wear Davis (154) down. Fairly even with three rounds to go, it was only in the last two sessions that the southpaw champion made sure of victory as Davis finally cracked under the pressure.

10 September 1993. Terry Norris w rsc 1 Joe Gatti.
Venue: The Alamodome, San Antonio, Texas, USA. **Recognition:** WBC. **Referee:** David Avalos.
Fight Summary: Not up to championship standard, Gatti (153¾) only lasted 88 seconds while hardly landing a blow in anger as the champion dismantled him with ease. Within moments of the opening bell, when Norris (153½) slipped a lead and countered heavily it could be seen that it was going to be an early night for him, confirmation of that coming when Gatti was dropped by a left hook. Having taken the mandatory count Gatti tried to fight back, but was overwhelmed by all manner of heavy shots before crashing down from a vicious right hand to the temple. That was it as far as the referee was concerned, waving it off without starting to count.

30 October 1993. Verno Phillips w rsc 7 Lupe Aquino.
Venue: America West Arena, Phoenix, Arizona, USA. **Recognition:** WBO. **Referee:** Al Munoz.
Fight Summary: Contested for the title vacated by John David Jackson, Aquino (154) got away to a good start when dropping Phillips (151½) in the opening session before gradually being outworked and suffering a broken nose in the fifth. Matters went from bad to worse in the sixth as Phillips handed out a real shellacking, and after 57 seconds of the seventh had elapsed the fight was stopped when a dejected Aquino turned his back on his opponent just as his handlers were entering the ring. At the time of the stoppage, the scores in favour of Phillips read 58-55, 57-56, 57-57.

18 December 1993. Simon Brown w co 4 Terry Norris.
Venue: Cuauhtemoc Stadium, Puebla, Mexico. **Recognition:** WBC. **Referee:** Lupe Garcia.
Fight Summary: After overcoming heart ailments and a detached retina, and with his best days apparently behind him, Brown (153½) came back to win the title from the seemingly unbeatable Norris (151¼) in what was recognised by *The Ring* magazine as the 'Upset of the Year'. Having survived the opening assaults of Norris and further heavy bombardments, Brown struck with a big right, which was followed up with a left hook to put the champion down. Probably saved by the bell, Norris was still dazed when getting back to his corner. However, he ripped into Brown again in the second round, looking to take the latter out, before being hurt at the end of the session when wobbled by a solid left hook. Although Norris was still laying into Brown in the third he was having less success, being caught more and more, and a left-right-left hook had him finishing the round in bad shape. The fourth saw Brown picking it up as Norris's punches began to have less effect on him, and following a heavy exchange the latter was sent crashing by a right to the head to be counted out on the 1.06 mark.

22 January 1994. Julio Cesar Vasquez w pts 12 Juan Ramon Medina.
Venue: Sports Palace, Alma Ata, Kazakhstan. **Recognition:** WBA. **Referee:** Armand Krief.
Scorecards: 119-102, 117-107, 120-105.
Fight Summary: It had only been going for a minute or so when the champion had Medina (152½) over from a solid southpaw straight left, and although the latter was dropped a further seven times – again in the first, in the second, twice in the third, in the eighth, and twice in the 11th - his durability enabled him to last the distance. Unable to hurt Vasquez (153¼), the Dominican-based Medina had little going for him other than sticking out the jab and skittering backwards as fast as he could. If the contest had been stopped early there would have been little dissent.

29 January 1994. Simon Brown w pts 12 Troy Waters.
Venue: MGM Grand, Las Vegas, Nevada, USA. **Recognition:** WBC. **Referee:** Mitch Halpern.
Scorecards: 118-111, 116-112, 114-114.
Fight Summary: Following on from his upset victory over Terry Norris, it was something of a surprise when Brown (153) only outpointed the tough Waters (153) on a majority decision despite having many advantages. With so little action the early rounds were difficult to score, and it was only from the ninth onwards when Waters was tiring that Brown began to up the pace. Working well on the inside and turning southpaw in order to rest his left hand that had been damaged earlier, Brown kept the punches going regardless of his right eye being opened up in the 12th from an accidental head butt.

4 March 1994. Gianfranco Rosi tdraw 6 Vincent Pettway.
Venue: MGM Grand, Las Vegas, Nevada, USA. **Recognition:** IBF. **Referee:** Mills Lane.
Fight Summary: This was classified as a technical draw by the IBF after an accidental clash of heads left Rossi (154) with a gaping cut over the left eye 19 seconds into the sixth round and brought the contest to a halt. Had the sixth round been completed the result would have been determined by the scorecards at that point, which had Rossi ahead on all three cards by 49-45, 49-45 and 48-46. It was a typical Rosi type of contest, pushing out the jab and holding on whenever Pettway (150) looked dangerous, and in the opening session the latter was counted upon after being pushed to the floor following a left hook. The action then became extremely scrappy. Even though Pettway hurt Rossi in the third with solid right hands he was doing too little and did not look a likely winner when the contest was terminated.

4 March 1994. Julio Cesar Vasquez w rsc 2 Armand Picar.
Venue: MGM Grand, Las Vegas, Nevada, USA. **Recognition:** WBA. **Referee:** Mitch Halpern.
Fight Summary: Having slammed Picar (153½) into the ropes with solid lefts in the opening session, the champion quickly stepped up the pace in the second. Lining Picar up with the southpaw jab, Vasquez (154) was soon sending in big lefts, one of which had the Filipino over for 'two' early on. Following that success, Vasquez had Picar down again, this time for 'six', from a short left to the head, and when the latter was floored for the third time following a series of blows the referee called it off on the 2.05 mark under the 'three knockdowns in a round' ruling.

8 April 1994. Julio Cesar Vasquez w pts 12 Ricardo Raul Nunez.
Venue: Villa Lujan Defenders Football Ground, Tucuman, Argentina. **Recognition:** WBA. **Referee:** Fernando Peyrous.
Scorecards: 118-114, 118-113, 118-112.
Fight Summary: Starting slowly, the champion soon began to pick up the pace, dropping Nunez (152¼) in the third with a southpaw left to the body. However, Nunez came back well when scoring with both hands in the fifth and sixth rounds. Gradually, Vasquez (152¾) began to take over from the awkward Nunez, and after knocking his fellow Argentine down for the second time, in the ninth, he made sure of victory with a storming last two sessions.

7 May 1994. Terry Norris w pts 12 Simon Brown.
Venue: MGM Grand, Las Vegas, Nevada, USA. **Recognition:** WBC. **Referee:** Mitch Halpern.
Scorecards: 116-112, 117-111, 119-109.
Fight Summary: Putting the earlier loss of his title behind him, Norris (152) came back a totally different fighter to completely outbox Brown (154) and regain the WBC Championship Belt by a unanimous decision. This time round

Norris looked to outspeed Brown rather than trying to knock him out, and although he failed to work hard enough in some rounds he was almost always going too well for the champion. Using a good left hand, coupled with fast combinations, Norris gave Brown few chances to land solidly, being one step ahead when it counted.

21 May 1994. Julio Cesar Vasquez w rsc 10 Akhmet Dottuev.
Venue: King's Hall, Belfast, Northern Ireland. **Recognition:** WBA. **Referee:** John Coyle.
Fight Summary: Even though the champion made a reasonable start, Dottuev (153), also a southpaw, was soon beginning to put impressive combinations together. Matching Vasquez (153¾) punch for punch, Dottuev dropped his man in the third round with a right hook to the jaw. He then stepped up the pace before being cut on the left eye in the fifth and floored by punches to head and body in the sixth. It looked grim for Dottuev, but after taking the mandatory count he came right back to knock Vasquez over with a straight left. It was in the seventh, as Dottuev tired from his exertions, that Vasquez began to take over, the Russian being sold-out by the end of the ninth. Coming out for the tenth, appearing to be at the mercy of Vasquez, the game Dottuev was floored three times in all prior to being stopped on the 47 mark under the 'three knockdowns in a round' ruling.

25 July 1994. Verno Phillips w rsc 7 Jaime Llanes.
Venue: Great Western Forum, Los Angeles, California, USA. **Recognition:** WBO. **Referee:** Lou Moret.
Fight Summary: Although starting in countering mode, once he realised that Llanes (154) was there for the taking the champion began to open up, sending the Mexican crashing from a big left hook in the fourth. Back on his feet, Llanes was now being outclassed. When three heavy left hooks in a row from Phillips (154) battered him down again, in the fifth, although Llanes managed to make it to the end of the session he was gradually being taken apart. All Llanes had left was his bravery, and after being dropped twice in the seventh the referee called the fight off on the 2.46 mark as he was trying to rise from the second knockdown.

21 August 1994. Julio Cesar Vasquez w pts 12 Ronald Wright.
Venue: Jai-Alai Stadium, St Jean De Luz, France. **Recognition:** WBA. **Referee:** Enzo Montero.
Scorecards: 115-110, 113-110, 114-110.
Fight Summary: Regardless of claiming an injured right hand prior to the fight the champion was instructed to meet Wright (154) on the contracted date or forfeit his title. Turning up just four days prior to meeting another fellow southpaw seemed strange, but Vasquez (153½), who came to the ring in magnificent shape, floored Wright in the second and seventh rounds before dropping him twice more in the 12th to fully deserve the win. For his part, Wright was always looking to take the fight to Vasquez even after being knocked down.

17 September 1994. Vincent Pettway w co 4 Gianfranco Rosi.
Venue: MGM Grand, Las Vegas, Nevada, USA. **Recognition:** IBF. **Referee:** Jay Nady.
Fight Summary: Appearing in America for only the second time, Rosi (154) put his title on the line against his mandatory challenger, Pettway (152), after their previous contest had been halted prematurely due to an accidental butt. Starting in negative fashion, on the back foot and rarely attempting a counter, Rosi did not look like a champion, especially when he was badly shaken up by a solid right to the head in the second round. With Rosi continuing to use spoiling tactics, an accidental head clash saw Pettway deducted a point in the second before he dropped the Italian for 'seven' with a right to the side of the head. At least Rosi tried to make a fight of it in the third, but in the fourth after being docked a point for hitting on the break he was counted out at 3.59 following a three-punch combination.

9 November 1994. Verno Phillips w pts 12 Santos Cardona.
Venue: Lakefront Arena, New Orleans, Louisiana, USA. **Recognition:** WBO. **Referee:** Robert Gonzalez.
Scorecards: 114-113, 116-112, 116-110.
Fight Summary: Shocked in the second round when sent crashing by a left hook to the solar plexus, the champion was on his feet in a dazed condition before being saved by the bell just as Cardona (152½) was ready to get to work on him. Making a good recovery, Phillips (153¾) came out fast for the third, but with Cardona still matching him it was not until the eighth that the champion began to forge ahead. At the end of the tenth Phillips was in front, aided by a point deduction suffered by Cardona when going low, and although the last two sessions were tough he just about deserved the decision.

11 November 1994. Julio Cesar Vasquez w pts 12 Tony Marshall.
Venue: The Casino, Tucuman, Argentina. **Recognition:** WBA. **Referee:** Renato Caddeo.
Scorecards: 118-110, 119-112, 117-111.
Fight Summary: Aiming to impose himself on Marshall (148¼) from the opening bell, the rugged, brawling southpaw champion immediately walked into his rival in an effort to bulldoze him. It was soon clear that Vasquez (153¾) was the stronger of the pair, but Marshall remained unfazed throughout, having some successes, though they were few and far between. Unable to pick up his work-rate, despite much cajoling from his corner, the composed Marshall was never busy or aggressive enough to warrant anything from the contest.

12 November 1994. Luis Santana w disq 5 Terry Norris.
Venue: City Bullring, Mexico City, Mexico. **Recognition:** WBC. **Referee:** Mitch Halpern.
Fight Summary: This was a fight that should not have taken place due to the fact that Santana (152½) had lost seven of his last ten and had been out of the ring for a year, but amazingly he was handed the title after Norris (151) was disqualified for rabbit punching in the fifth round. Right from the opening bell Norris made the mistake of trying to knock Santana out, especially in the third when both men stumbled down and the champion was given the mandatory count. Then, in the fourth, Norris was deducted a point following a clash of heads with the clumsy challenger. Realising that he had to do better Norris began to get his punches off more cleanly in the fifth, but disaster struck when he unleashed a chopping left to the back of Santana's head that sent him crashing down. At the moment of impact, Santana had been totally defenceless, having stumbled through the ropes. Although the ringside doctor claimed that the Dominican was faking it, after 12 minutes of inaction it eventually became apparent that he was not when failing to recover quickly enough. The time of the disqualification was later given as being 2.02 of the fifth.

3 February 1995. Verno Phillips w pts 12 Santos Cardona.
Venue: Bushkill, Pennsylvania, USA. **Recognition:** WBO. **Referee:** Rudy Battle.
Scorecards: 116-112, 115-113, 113-115.
Fight Summary: A mandatory rematch between the pair saw the champion come on strong towards the end to beat the game, non-stop punching Cardona (153) in a fight that had been difficult to score. Cardona was always in front of Phillips (152½), firing in punches from both hands, but so many failed to hit the target as the champion either pulled away or got on the back foot. It was only in the last few rounds that Phillips began to assert himself, seemingly unable to miss Cardona with thudding right uppercuts in that period. Realising that it was close Phillips went toe-to-toe with Cardona in the 12th, and although both men landed well it was the champion's blows that carried the day.

4 March 1995. Pernell Whitaker w pts 12 Julio Cesar Vasquez.
Venue: Convention Centre, Atlantic City, New Jersey, USA. **Recognition:** WBA. **Referee:** Tony Orlando.
Scorecards: 118-110, 116-110, 118-107.
Fight Summary: Despite becoming the fourth man in history to win titles at four different weights Whitaker (153¾) did not seem to be the fighter of old, having slowed down appreciably. Still he was good enough to beat a fellow southpaw in Vasquez (153¾), who had two points deducted for rabbit punching and was made to measure for his jab. Although Vasquez had a six-inch-reach advantage he failed to make it work for him, apart from when he dropped Whitaker in the fourth with a short left uppercut, and he was often reduced to chasing shadows. By the eighth the jabs were really bamboozling Vasquez, but while occasionally hurting his man the champion was unable to follow through.

When Whitaker relinquished the WBA version of the title soon afterwards to concentrate on his WBC welter crown, Julio Cesar Green and Carl Daniels were matched up to find a new champion.

8 April 1995. Luis Santana w disq 3 Terry Norris.
Venue: Caesar's Palace, Las Vegas, Nevada, USA. **Recognition:** WBC. **Referee:** Kenny Bayless.
Fight Summary: Once again it was pure madness that cost Norris (153) as he threw away the opportunity of regaining his old title from Santana (153), with the latter becoming the first man to win back-to-back championship fights by disqualification while being carried out of the ring on a stretcher. The fight had started with Norris boxing

smartly and hurting Santana with solid punches before dropping the champion in the second round. Although Santana fought back he was cut over the left eye and being battered. In the third it was more of the same as Santana was floored again, this time by a solid right to the head. With Santana back on his feet and being pummelled, Norris went for the kill, but before any further damage could be done the bell sounded to end the session. It was then that Norris completely lost it when, five or six seconds into the interval, he went for Santana and left the Dominican prostrate on the deck from a big right hand to the jaw.

29 April 1995. Vincent Pettway w co 6 Simon Brown.
Venue: Air Force Arena, Landover, Maryland USA. **Recognition:** IBF. **Referee:** Ray Klingmeyer.
Fight Summary: Making his first defence, Pettway (152¼) was soon on the back foot as Brown (154) chased him down and dropped him heavily with a left-right-left prior to the end of the first round. Having got to his feet, but still badly dazed, Pettway somehow lasted out the session before putting himself back in the fight when smashing Brown to the floor with a dynamite right hand in the third. Now it was Brown's turn to be under the cosh. However, before long he was firing on all cylinders, punching Pettway out of the ring and on to the ring apron in the fifth. By the sixth nobody knew which way the fight was heading as first one man teed off and then the other, but that was before Pettway sent Brown crashing down from a left hook to be counted out on the 2.07 mark.

17 May 1995. Gianfranco Rosi w pts 12 Verno Phillips.
Venue: Sports Palace, Perugia, Italy. **Recognition:** WBO. **Referee:** Paul Thomas.
Scorecards: 115-113, 116-112, 116-114.
Fight Summary: Trying to win his third world title at the age of the 37, and having been out of the ring since the previous September, Rosi (152¾) was in control of the fight for much of the way despite being cut over the left eye in the second round. Once Rosi began to force the bemused Phillips (154) around the ring, the die was cast, the latter taking terrific punishment. Although he tried hard to turn things around, Phillips, looking strangely off colour, was unable to get his boxing together.

Rosi forfeited the title in June, having tested positive for amphetamines after the fight. Following that, Phillips was reinstated as champion and the result changed to that of no contest.

16 June 1995. Carl Daniels w pts 12 Julio Cesar Green.
Venue: Sports Palace, Lyon, France. **Recognition:** WBA. **Referee:** Stan Christodoulou.
Scorecards: 118-109, 119-107, 115-111.
Fight Summary: Contesting the title vacated by Pernell Whitaker, Daniels (153½) proved a worthy successor to the former champion when outboxing the tough and willing Green (153¾), who had two points deducted for roughhousing. After being cut over the left eye in the second round, Daniels found that the southpaw jab, followed by the left cross, were his best weapons as he boxed masterfully to gain control. Smashed to the canvas in the ninth, Green looked a sorry sight, his left eye swollen badly, but although Daniels went for him with a vengeance in the last session the Dominican held up to last the course.

12 August 1995. Paul Vaden w rsc 12 Vincent Pettway.
Venue: MGM Grand, Las Vegas, Nevada, USA. **Recognition:** IBF. **Referee:** Richard Steele.
Fight Summary: Having boxed his way to the front, despite a clash of styles, the champion was beginning to be pegged back by the eighth round as Vaden (154) came more and more into the fight. By now Pettway (153) had strangely gone off the boil, and while Vaden's jabs were making inroads he needed to lift his work-rate if he was to win the title. Although picking it up in the tenth, it was not until the 12th that Vaden really got himself going, firing in heavy punches from both hands to force a stoppage with just 27 seconds remaining. Afterwards, it was disclosed that Pettway would have remained champion had he made it to the final bell, but the referee rightly felt that he had no choice other than saving him from taking further punishment when he was not fighting back.

19 August 1995. Terry Norris w rsc 2 Luis Santana.
Venue: MGM Grand, Las Vegas, Nevada, USA. **Recognition:** WBC. **Referee:** Joe Cortez.
Fight Summary: Bringing the men together for the third time was probably more than Norris (152) deserved, but this time round he took advantage of the situation. Fighting with controlled aggression Norris let Santana (154)

come on to him in the opening session, almost finishing the fight there and then when a left-right sent the champion staggering into a corner only for the referee to hold the action up for no discernible reason. In the second Santana was under pressure right from the off, and after being dropped three times he was rescued by the referee on the 2.09 mark.

16 September 1995. Terry Norris w rsc 9 David Gonzalez.
Venue: Mirage Hotel & Casino, Las Vegas, Nevada, USA. **Recognition:** WBC. **Referee:** Richard Steele.
Fight Summary: Back in the ring again just 26 days after regaining the title Norris (151) was surprisingly sluggish when defending against Gonzalez (152), and after having the latter over with a booming right in the first round he failed to follow up. Again, in the fourth, Norris had Gonzalez down twice, only to let his man off the hook before really opening up in the ninth. On several occasions the tough Gonzalez had looked a beaten man, but this time there was no reprieve as Norris bombarded him with heavy blows from both hands before the referee came to his rescue with just one second of the session remaining. Gonzalez had given of his best, but with blood pouring from his nose, which was feared to be broken, and badly swollen eyes the ending did not come a moment too soon. The general feeling was that regardless of the result, Norris, who allowed himself to be pushed over five or six times, was a fighter in decline.

22 November 1995. Paul Jones w pts 12 Verno Phillips.
Venue: Hillsborough Leisure Centre, Sheffield, England. **Recognition:** WBO. **Referee:** Ismael Fernandez.
Scorecards: 114-113, 116-111, 113-113.
Fight Summary: It was not a great start for Jones (153½) when floored by a sharp right-hand counter in the opening round, but boxing his way back into the contest he never looked back against a surprisingly lethargic champion. With Jones as slippery as an eel, Phillips (154) found him too difficult a target, the majority of what little scoring there was in the first half of the contest coming from the Englishman. Although Phillips remained the aggressor he was unable to strike home more than a single punch at a time against the elusive Jones, who despite being docked a point for butting in the ninth was good value for his majority points win. Following the contest, Jones claimed that he had suffered a burst left eardrum in the fifth.

Booked to defend the WBO version of the title against Bronco McKart on 1 March 1996, Jones forfeited his belt when withdrawing immediately prior to the contest claiming an injury to his right hand. So that a title fight could go ahead on that date, Santos Cardona was drafted in to meet McKart for the vacant crown.

16 December 1995. Julio Cesar Vasquez w rsc 11 Carl Daniels.
Venue: CoreStates Spectrum, Philadelphia, Pennsylvania, USA. **Recognition:** WBA. **Referee:** Charlie Sgrillo.
Fight Summary: In a battle of southpaws it was the challenger who came through against all the odds when he found a big left hook that dropped Daniels (153) to force a stoppage after 34 seconds of the 11th. However, it had been Daniels, getting behind the jab, who made the better start when putting Vasquez (154) down with a straight left in the third. As hard as Vasquez tried he seemed to make no impression on Daniels, and it was the latter who continued to control the fight, winning all but two rounds on the cards prior to the finish.

16 December 1995. Terry Norris w pts 12 Paul Vaden.
Venue: CoreStates Spectrum, Philadelphia, Pennsylvania, USA. **Recognition:** IBF/WBC. **Referee:** Rudy Battle.
Scorecards: 119-109, 120-108, 118-110.
Fight Summary: With both men putting their respective titles up for grabs it was Norris (151½) who won through, while Vaden (154), whose performance was considered woeful, had his entire purse withheld pending a hearing. At least Norris tried to make a fight of it, continually hunting Vaden down and getting off punches to head and body, but he was unable to sustain the pressure against a man content to stay on the ropes with his gloves held high. That was generally the story of the fight, and although Vaden made something of an effort in the tenth when going after Norris the action quickly petered out.

27 January 1996. Terry Norris w co 2 Jorge Luis Vado.
Venue: Veterans' Memorial Coliseum, Phoenix, Arizona, USA. **Recognition:** IBF/WBC. **Referee:** Roger Yanez.

Fight Summary: Technically defending both belts, despite the contest not being recognised by the WBC, Norris (152½) was soon teeing off against the limited Vado (153½), who winged in long, wide punches normally associated with a club fighter. With Norris having taken a good look at his challenger in the first round it seemed clear that he would be going for a kayo. Thus, it was no surprise when a burst of punches followed by a terrific right to the jaw saw Vado counted out after 42 seconds of the second.

24 February 1996. Terry Norris w rsc 8 Vincent Pettway.
Venue: The Coliseum, Richmond, Virginia, USA. **Recognition:** IBF/WBC. **Referee:** Larry Doggett.
Fight Summary: Putting both of his belts on the line, Norris (150¾) came out firing, but with Pettway (151) moving back at speed he made a difficult target. However, towards the end of the first round when a cracking right to the jaw sent Pettway skidding downwards, although he got to his feet the bell came to his aid. Coming back in the second with surprise punches Pettway twice stunned Norris, but in the third after the challenger went down from a punch to the head it looked as though it would be an early night. Strangely, Norris allowed Pettway back into the contest, taking it in turns to fire off blows for several rounds before the latter began to tire. Still Norris was getting caught by punches he should have avoided. Then, in the eighth after a perfect left hook to the body sent Pettway crashing the referee called a halt with 19 seconds of the session remaining.

1 March 1996. Bronco McKart w rsc 9 Santos Cardona.
Venue: Fantasy Springs Casino & Resort, Indio, California, USA. **Recognition:** WBO. **Referee:** Lou Moret.
Fight Summary: Disputing the title vacated by Paul Jones, McKart (153¼) eventually found the punches to force a stoppage after 41 seconds of round nine when Cardona (154) was being pelted by heavy shots from both hands and was not fighting back. The referee's action was also influenced by the fact that Cardona's second was already climbing into the ring in an effort to bring closure to what was rapidly becoming a bad beating. Prior to that though, the tough Cardona had caused a few problems when marching into his southpaw opponent and banging in right hooks before McKart quickly assumed control. Afterwards, McKart felt that it had been harder than expected, while Cardona, who came in at short notice, said that while he found it difficult fighting a southpaw he had no excuses.

17 May 1996. Ronald Wright w pts 12 Bronco McKart.
Venue: Glen Stock Arena, Monroe, Michigan, USA. **Recognition:** WBO. **Referee:** Dale Grable.
Scorecards: 115-113, 115-113, 113-116.
Fight Summary: Regardless of the closeness of the scorecards and the fact that one judge even had McKart (154) winning, this was the challenger's fight all the way in the eyes of experienced onlookers. Right from the opening bell, with Wright (152) firing in fast right jabs to the face of his fellow southpaw it was clear early on that McKart had never faced anyone so quick. It was McKart's right hook against Wright's jab, and although the champion pitched in some useful blows of his own more often than not the latter was doubling up to hit the target without fail. Wright, who was so accurate that he did not even bother to go for the body, remained out of distance during the last three rounds to make sure of the win.

21 August 1996. Laurent Boudouani w rsc 5 Julio Cesar Vasquez.
Venue: Sports Palace, Le Cannet, France. **Recognition:** WBA. **Referee:** Franco Priami.
Fight Summary: Making the better start, the champion charged into Boudouani (153), throwing overarm lefts from his southpaw stance, as he tried to force the latter on to the back foot. Having done his homework, Boudouani knew that the best time to get his punches off was when Vasquez (153½) attacked, the Frenchman starting to make good use of that knowledge when crashing in solid uppercuts in the second round. Sticking to countering the onrushing Vasquez, Boudouani had more successes in the third and fourth but they were nothing compared to the damage he inflicted in the fifth. Beating Vasquez to the punch and dropping him for 'eight' Boudouani knew his chance had arrived, and when the Argentine was allowed to fight on, a left hook-short right to the jaw smashed him down again. This time, the referee immediately called it off, the finish being timed at 2.07.

7 September 1996. Terry Norris w rsc 5 Alex Rios.
Venue: MGM Grand, Las Vegas, Nevada, USA. **Recognition:** IBF/WBC. **Referee:** Mills Lane.

Fight Summary: Having taken a good look at his southpaw challenger Norris (153) began to warm to the task, and several times in the third round it looked like he was going to have his man over. Norris moved up a gear in the fourth, getting on his toes while looking to draw Rios (153½) on to him. Following that, he put Rios down for 'five' after finding him with a heavy left hook-left uppercut combination. With Rios now walking through the punches to get his own off, although he stunned Norris briefly in the fifth he was eventually pinned in a corner and rescued by the referee on the 2.08 mark when not fighting back.

9 November 1996. Ronald Wright w pts 12 Ensley Bingham.
Venue: Nynex Arena, Manchester, England. **Recognition:** WBO. **Referee:** Genaro Rodriguez.
Scorecards: 119-109, 119-110, 120-109.
Fight Summary: Giving a boxing masterclass in his first defence, Wright (152¾) exposed his challenger's limitations when outscoring him in virtually every round. He also proved to be the fastest man in the weight class, never being in one place longer than he had to be. Disappointingly, Bingham (154) failed to make himself a single opening to get his heavy punches off, something that was not helped by the fact that he injured his left hand in the third. Meantime, Wright was nearly always sending out accurate southpaw jabs to keep Bingham at distance. Towards the end, Wright occasionally rattled in hurtful combinations as if to show Bingham that he could step up a gear if needed.

11 January 1997. Terry Norris w rsc 10 Nick Rupa.
Venue: The Arena, Nashville, Tennessee, USA. **Recognition:** IBF/WBC. **Referee:** Marty Denkin.
Fight Summary: Although not really up to championship class, Rupa (152¼) proved to be a real tough guy as he stood in front of the champion virtually from the opening bell and took his best punches unflinchingly for almost ten rounds. Finding his man repeatedly, especially with overarm rights, Norris forced a mandatory count in the fourth when Rupa was adjudged to have touched down. With Rupa being outclassed, by the middle sessions there was little coming back. At that stage of the contest Norris's much harder shots were beginning to take their toll on Rupa, who was told by the referee before the start of the eighth that he would be given one more round to change things. Strangely, after taking a battering for the next couple of sessions Rupa was still there, and it was only in the tenth after a heavy one-two combination had dropped him that the third man thought fit to rescue him, the finish being timed at 2.34.

After Norris forfeited the IBF version of the title in March when negotiating a fight against Felix Trinidad and refusing to meet Raul Marquez, the mandatory challenger, the latter was matched against Anthony Stephens to find a new champion.

29 March 1997. Laurent Boudouani w pts 12 Carl Daniels.
Venue: Hilton Hotel, Las Vegas, Nevada, USA. **Recognition:** WBA. **Referee:** Richard Steele.
Scorecards: 118-108, 115-111, 117-109.
Fight Summary: Despite injuring his left arm in training, Boudouani (154) decided to go through with his defence against Daniels (154), relying heavily on right uppercuts and superior hand-speed to walk away with a unanimous decision. Having made his mind up to stay close to his man, the American southpaw was surprisingly unable to land more than one punch at a time, being made to pay as Boudouani backed him up with solid blows that shook him rigid. After being hurt in the seventh a left-right to the head had Daniels down in the eighth, and although Boudouani took a bit of a breather in the ninth he battered away with combinations to the end. The final session saw Daniels being deducted a point for spitting out his gumshield following an earlier warning, which merely emphasized the fact that he had little left.

12 April 1997. Raul Marquez w rsc 9 Anthony Stephens.
Venue: Tropicana Hotel & Casino, Las Vegas, Nevada, USA. **Recognition:** IBF. **Referee:** Richard Steele.
Fight Summary: Fighting for the title that formerly belonged to Terry Norris, Marquez (153) won when the referee rescued Stephens (154) at 1.47 of the ninth round after the latter had gone to the floor following a clash of heads and was being battered by heavy blows without return on getting up. At the finish, Marquez required 30 stitches to repair cuts on the forehead and right eye, while Stephens was also badly cut on the right eye. The contest started with Stephens countering his southpaw opponent well, but by the fourth Marquez was beginning to get on

top. And in the eighth he was looking to finish it. At that stage Stephens had little left, something that influenced the referee to call the fight off when he did.

3 May 1997. Ronald Wright w rsc 6 Steve Foster.
Venue: Nynex Arena, Manchester, England. **Recognition:** WBO. **Referee:** Genaro Rodriguez.
Fight Summary: Working away with the southpaw jab and smashing in vicious body shots, the champion gradually chopped Foster (153¾) down to size. He was also far too fast to be caught out himself. Never at any stage was Foster given an opportunity to take over, and in the fifth Wright (154) began to open up with both hands as he went for the finish. Somehow Foster made it to the bell, but having come under pressure in the sixth after taking a solid uppercut to the head two long lefts to the body dropped him. Back in the fray following a count of 'nine', when another left to the body sent Foster to the floor immediately afterwards the referee had seen enough, stopping the fight on the 2.52 mark.

5 July 1997. Raul Marquez w rsc 4 Romallis Ellis.
Venue: Isle of Capri Casino, Lake Charles, Louisiana, USA. **Recognition:** IBF. **Referee:** Elmo Adolph.
Fight Summary: Making his first defence against a fellow southpaw, and an Olympian from the class of 1988, Marquez (153) took his time to settle while Ellis (153) moved in with fast, scoring punches. Thirty seven seconds into the second, however, Ellis was put down for a count of 'three' after taking a straight left flush on the jaw, and although he got through the remainder of the session he was looking badly shaken. By the fourth, with Marquez in full flow, after Ellis had been dropped again (incorrectly ruled a slip by the referee) and was being battered in a corner the referee made his move, calling time at 1.14 of the session.

13 September 1997. Raul Marquez w pts 12 Keith Mullings.
Venue: Thomas & Mack Arena, Las Vegas, Nevada, USA. **Recognition:** IBF. **Referee:** Mitch Halpern.
Scorecards: 115-113, 116-112, 113-115.
Fight Summary: Coming in as a late replacement for Luis Ramon Campas, and having lost three of his previous five, Mullings (154) made a great showing when running the southpaw champion close. He also confounded those who thought he had no chance. With Marquez (154) consistently scoring well from to head and body and Mullings relying on solid one-twos that eventually caused swellings over the champion's eyes, the fight went first one way and then the other. Interestingly, all three cards had both men dead level at the end of the eighth. After a clash of heads in the ninth Marquez's right eye was cut, but he was still looking for Mullings. Clearly up for it, both men fired off punches right through to the final bell in a fight that was difficult to call.

6 December 1997. Keith Mullings w rsc 9 Terry Norris.
Venue: Boardwalk Convention Centre, Atlantic City, New Jersey, USA. **Recognition:** WBC. **Referee:** Tony Perez.
Fight Summary: Getting another opportunity to win a title following his excellent showing against Raul Marquez three months earlier, Mullings (153½) took full advantage when blasting the champion to defeat in the ninth round. There was no real hint of what was to come during the opening four rounds, Norris (154) seeming to have things well in hand even if he was not at his best. Although Mullings came on to win the fifth, Norris handed out a boxing lesson in the sixth. Things changed in the seventh when Mullings got home with several solid blows, and in the eighth as the pair traded Norris was suddenly dropped by a straight right to the jaw. Badly hurt, Norris was in dire trouble when the bell came to his aid. Even though he came out for the ninth, with Mullings throwing punches like there was no tomorrow there was only going to be one ending. Almost out on his feet, the brave Norris was finally put out of his misery when rescued by the referee after 51 seconds.

6 December 1997. Luis Ramon Campas w rsc 8 Raul Marquez.
Venue: Boardwalk Convention Centre, Atlantic City, New Jersey, USA. **Recognition:** IBF. **Referee:** James Condon.
Fight Summary: The fight began slowly with both men having a good look at each other, Campas (154) taking his time and the champion sending out southpaw jabs. That all changed at the end of the third when Marquez (153½) picked up a swollen right eye and a bad gash over his left eye following an exchange of blows. Somehow Marquez kept going, but with Campas getting to him and the blood flowing he was badly rocked by combinations in the seventh. Bravely fighting on, the unbeaten Marquez was finally rescued by the referee at 2.29 of the eighth while being battered by a torrent of punches on the ropes with nowhere to go. Prior to the fight it had been feared that

the facial damage, which saw Marquez have 70 stitches inserted after his previous contest, had not had enough time to heal.

19 December 1997. Ronald Wright w rtd 6 Adrian Dodson.
Venue: London Arena, Millwall, London, England. **Recognition:** WBO. **Referee:** Lou Moret.
Fight Summary: In what was his third appearance in succession in a British ring, the champion gave yet another superlative display when dismantling a fellow southpaw in Dodson (153) to retain his title. Dodson was seen as a dangerous opponent, but Wright (153¾) handled him with ease while displaying his trademark fast jab and solid left crosses to head and body, backed up by sound defensive work and movement. Cut over the left eye in the fifth, having taken a breather Wright quickly got down to business in the sixth, beginning to work Dodson over, but despite the latter going back to his corner with his left eye closed it still came as a surprise when he quit at the end of the session.

13 February 1998. Laurent Boudouani drew 12 Guillermo Jones.
Venue: University Auditorium, Albuquerque, New Mexico, USA. **Recognition:** WBA. **Referee:** Al Martinez.
Scorecards: 114-114, 114-114, 114-115.
Fight Summary: Way below his best, Boudouani (153¼) appeared to be lucky when holding on to his title by a majority draw against the 6'4" Jones (153). While Jones predictably went forward with a mechanical jab, although Boudouani landed the harder punches he failed to follow up any advantage. Obviously perplexed at Jones' huge reach advantage the Frenchman continually went into a shell when he should have been looking at ways to get inside. At the finish it was only due to Boudouani's 10-9 score on all three judges' cards in the 12th that the result did not go against him.

14 March 1998. Keith Mullings w rtd 5 Davide Ciarlante.
Venue: Trump Taj Mahal Casino & Resort, Atlantic City, New Jersey, USA. **Recognition:** WBC. **Referee:** Larry O'Connell.
Fight Summary: Boxing in determined fashion the challenger gave Mullings (154) a run for his money before a broken nose and gashes under each eye saw him pulled out of the contest by his corner at the end of the fifth round. If the corner had not made that decision the referee certainly would have. Although Ciarlante (153¾) threw the greater volume to put himself level on the cards at the time of the finish, it was Mullings' blows that carried the greater weight and proved to be more effective.

23 March 1998. Luis Ramon Campas w rtd 3 Anthony Stephens.
Venue: Foxwoods Resort Casino & Hotel, Ledyard, Connecticut, USA. **Recognition:** IBF. **Referee:** Ron Lipton.
Fight Summary: Outboxed in the opening round, Campas (152¾) absorbed what was coming his way when taking time to settle while whacking in the occasional body shot as the challenger worked behind the jab and threw solid right hands. Stepping it up in the third, Stephens (153¼) staggered Campas with a solid right cross before the latter came back with a concentrated attack on the body, digging in punches non-stop. Such was the ferocity of Campas' attack that Stephens, despite remaining upright, was battered from pillar to post prior to being retired during the interval after sustaining a dislocated shoulder.

30 May 1998. Laurent Boudouani w pts 12 Guillermo Jones.
Venue: Hilton Hotel, Las Vegas, Nevada, USA. **Recognition:** WBA. **Referee:** Richard Steele.
Scorecards: 116-112, 115-113, 111-117.
Fight Summary: Having had a close call against Jones (154) last time out the champion knew what he was up against this time around and prepared accordingly. With that in mind he gave away four of the first five rounds as he kept on the move in order to avoid the long jab. Boudouani (153½) began to come into the fight more from the sixth as he found a way to block Jones' jab, shaking the Panamanian up with heavy blows to the head in the eighth. From thereon in Boudouani was outpunching the tiring Jones, who was doing more stalking than fighting, and in the 11th and 12th the latter was badly hurt by overarm rights to the head and solid combinations. How one of the judges could score so widely in favour of Jones was a mystery.

5 June 1998. Luis Ramon Campas w rsc 11 Pedro Ortega.
Venue: Municipal Auditorium, Tijuana, Mexico. **Recognition:** IBF. **Referee:** Gwen Adair.
Fight Summary: Once again making a slow start, having pulled himself together by the second round Campas (153¼) was already beginning to make inroads into the challenger, using his left lead to set up heavy right crosses. In the third session both men took heavy shots. However, while Ortega (151) was proving to be extremely durable he was beginning to ship a lot of punishment. Badly cut around the left eye Ortega took a terrible pounding in the eighth, looking to be on his way out, before calling up all of his reserves to make it into the 11th. At this stage Campas had almost become too tired of hitting the brave Ortega, but picking it up again he surged in with such ferocity that after just 52 seconds the female referee felt fully justified in rescuing a man who just would not quit.

22 August 1998. Harry Simon w pts 12 Ronald Wright.
Venue: Carousel Resort Casino, Hammanskraal, South Africa. **Recognition:** WBO. **Referee:** Samuel Viruet.
Scorecards: 117-113, 115-113, 114-114.
Fight Summary: On becoming the first Namibian to win a world title, Simon (153¾) not only achieved a childhood dream but also created one of the biggest upsets ever associated with the weight class. Boxing to strict orders, the well-conditioned Simon took the fight to Wright (153¾) from the opening bell, never giving the speedy southpaw the time and room in which to work when staying right on top of him. Although Wright fought a good fight, Simon was inspired, throwing so many punches that it was difficult to score, and despite many rounds being close the ninth saw the champion forced to soak up terrific punishment. While there were no knockdowns, with the vast majority believing that Simon had won it came as a bit of a shock when it was announced that Wright had held on to his title by a majority draw. However, after it quickly transpired that one of the cards had been added up incorrectly Simon was given the win he so craved.

18 September 1998. Luis Ramon Campas w rtd 3 Larry Barnes.
Venue: Thomas & Mack Arena, Las Vegas, Nevada, USA. **Recognition:** IBF. **Referee:** Mitch Halpern.
Fight Summary: Tossing aside his normal slow start the champion went to work on the squat Barnes (153½) right from the opening bell, throwing steady combinations to head and body, and the latter's face was swollen and cut by the end of the first round. Although Barnes tried to put punches together in the second, Campas (153½) was just too strong for him. With the pressure mounting, after solid body shots got to Barnes in the third and his left eye closed he was retired by his corner during the interval.

30 November 1998. Laurent Boudouani w rsc 9 Terry Norris.
Venue: Port of Versailles Sports Palace, Paris, France. **Recognition:** WBA. **Referee:** Waldemar Schmidt.
Fight Summary: Forced to take off three pounds excess at the weigh-in, Norris (154) was not only weakened but he was a shadow of the top fighter he once was, winning at best just two rounds before being stopped at 2.59 of the ninth. By the fourth Boudouani (153½) was already on top, having staggered Norris with several punches, most notably the left hook. Although the challenger came back reasonably well in the fifth he was taking a hiding from there onwards, and by the ninth Boudouani was landing almost at will with the right hand. It was only when Norris retreated to the ropes and was coming apart at the seams did his father throw in the towel, an action that was followed by an immediate response from the referee.

12 December 1998. Fernando Vargas w rtd 7 Luis Ramon Campas.
Venue: Trump Taj Mahal Casino Resort, Atlantic City, New Jersey, USA. **Recognition:** IBF. **Referee:** Eddie Cotton.
Fight Summary: Charging out at the start of the fight the champion soon found himself being nailed by long left jabs to the face, and even when he responded more aggressively Vargas (151) found the time to spin off the ropes to fire in solid rights. With it becoming apparent that Vargas could not miss Campas (151) with the jab, after being tagged solidly by left-rights in the third the latter was badly cut over the right eye. Still Vargas took no untoward risks as he stuck with the jab but by the sixth, bit by bit, he was gradually breaking Campas down, having survived a last-ditch onslaught in the previous session. Campas, with both eyes now busted up, was having difficulty seeing Vargas in the seventh and the latter, sensing it was time to go, smashed in punches right to the bell to leave the champion in such a dazed state that he was retired by his corner immediately.

29 January 1999. Javier Castillejo w pts 12 Keith Mullings.
Venue: Cubierta Bullring, Leganes, Spain. **Recognition:** WBC. **Referee:** Bob Logist.
Scorecards: 116-112, 115-114, 114-114.
Fight Summary: Much faster than the pedestrian champion, Castillejo (153¾) was making inroads as early as the first round when showing excellent hand-speed and good movement to leave his man chasing shadows. After a few more sessions Castillejo knew he had the beating of Mullings (153½), continuing to dart in with straight lefts and occasional left-rights to take a good lead by the end of the seventh. At that stage Mullings had won two rounds at best, but with Castillejo beginning to showboat he came on much stronger, hooking to the head and body before slowing towards the finish. Realising it could be closer than it seemed Castillejo won the final session in the eyes of all three judges but had he not done so the title would have remained in the hands of Mullings.

6 March 1999. David Reid w pts 12 Laurent Boudouani.
Venue: Boardwalk Convention Centre, Atlantic City, New Jersey, USA. **Recognition:** WBA. **Referee:** Randy Neumann. **Scorecards:** 117-112, 117-111, 118-112.
Fight Summary: Given a crack at the title, the 1996 Olympic champion, Reid (154), soon made his presence felt when lashing in a cracking left hook in the second round. Even though Boudouani (152) came right back he continued to be caught by long, fast jabs. As the fight progressed the champion was being outworked, relying too much on countering Reid with the right hand, and in the ninth he was almost taken out by another left hook. Surprisingly, in the tenth Boudouani rallied to win that session along with the 11th, but just when he needed to make a big effort it was Reid who produced all the better punches in the final session to win handsomely.

13 March 1999. Fernando Vargas w rsc 4 Howard Clarke.
Venue: Madison Square Garden, Manhattan, NYC, New York, USA. **Recognition:** IBF. **Referee:** Wayne Kelly.
Fight Summary: Making his first defence against the little-known Clarke (154), the new champion had said that he wanted to fight a top opponent but ended up meeting a man who squeezed into the ratings after defeating Jason Papillion. Although Clarke started confidently enough, before too long Vargas (154) was firing in solid combinations to head and body. By the end of the third round Vargas was going far too well for Clarke. Dropped on one knee from a left to the body in the fourth, Clarke was in real trouble on getting up, and after being floored three more times he was rescued by the referee at 2.29 of the session.

1 May 1999. Harry Simon w rsc 3 Kevin Lueshing.
Venue: National Sports Centre, Crystal Palace, London, England. **Recognition:** WBO. **Referee:** Lou Moret.
Fight Summary: Although the champion won the opening two rounds on the cards it was Lueshing (153) who landed the hardest punch of the fight at that stage, a left-hook counter that stiffened his opponent's legs. Lueshing was still dangerous in the third, but having taken a few risks he was dropped by a right over the top for the mandatory count before coming back hard with the jab. Having tried to settle, after Simon (153) had floored Lueshing twice more in the session, heavy right hands doing the business, the referee called it off on the 2.08 mark.

15 May 1999. Javier Castillejo w rsc 4 Humberto Aranda.
Venue: Cubierta Bullring, Leganes, Spain. **Recognition:** WBC. **Referee:** Lupe Garcia.
Fight Summary: Defending the title for the first time, Castillejo (153¾) was always in control of this one, dominating Aranda (153¾) behind the jab and banging in harder shots when the openings were there. By the third Aranda was on the back foot, having been hurt by a left hook to the jaw and rights to head and body, and towards the end of the round a bad cut opened up on the Costa Rican's left eye. Clearly on borrowed time, Aranda went for Castillejo in the fourth, but was being battered around the ring before three right uppercuts sent him crashing to the floor. Although Aranda bravely made it to his feet, after the referee called for the doctor to inspect the injured eye the fight was stopped with just eight seconds of the session remaining.

16 July 1999. David Reid w pts 12 Kevin Kelly.
Venue: Boardwalk Convention Centre, Atlantic City, New Jersey, USA. **Recognition:** WBA. **Referee:** Tony Orlando.
Scorecards: 116-111, 115-112, 116-111.

Fight Summary: Looking to finish early Reid (153) was soon on the attack, opening up with solid left-rights, but he found his challenger a difficult foe to tie down as he flitted around the ring away from the danger zone. What was even more worrying for Reid was that despite four operations to repair a drooping left eyelid he was still finding it difficult to focus, and in the fifth Kelly (153) took advantage of this dilemma when putting the champion down with a wide left hook. Although he was quickly on his feet, with his left eye closing fast Reid began to fight with some urgency, but he still had difficulty in pinning Kelly down despite landing some solid shots. The last three sessions became a nightmare for Reid as he was jarred him up a couple of times before steadying himself to make it safely to the final bell.

17 July 1999. Fernando Vargas w rsc 11 Raul Marquez.
Venue: Caesar's Palace, Lake Tahoe, Nevada, USA. **Recognition:** IBF. **Referee:** Joe Cortez.
Fight Summary: It did not take long to see who was the better fighter, and as early as the first round after the champion had scored with straight lead rights Marquez (153) was cut over the left eye which then began to swell. With Vargas (154) continuing his offensive it was not until the fifth that Marquez came through with right-left combinations from his southpaw stance. Unfortunately for Marquez, who was now cut over the right eye, he was deducted a point in the sixth after dropping Vargas with a low blow. Having gone well in the ninth, when Vargas opened up in the 11th with solid combinations to force Marquez around the ring the latter was not fighting back when the referee made a sensible stoppage on the two-minute mark.

28 August 1999. David Reid w pts 12 Keith Mullings.
Venue: Hard Rock Hotel, Las Vegas, Nevada, USA. **Recognition:** WBA. **Referee:** Jay Nady.
Scorecards: 117-111, 117-111, 117-111.
Fight Summary: Seemingly back to his best, the champion got the jab going from the opening bell to rack up the first three sessions, but by the middle rounds Mullings (154) had turned up the heat when blasting away with two hands. Mullings was also resorting to foul tactics, mainly with the use of the head. However, with the infringements not being dealt with by the referee in the eighth session Reid's left eye was cut. At that point Reid (154) went back to the jab to sail through the next three sessions before having to endure a foul-filled 12th when he was thrown to the deck in anger and forced to take a knee. For whatever reason Mullings escaped disqualification, but it did him no good.

10 September 1999. Javier Castillejo w rsc 7 Paolo Roberto.
Venue: Europa Pavilion, Leganes, Spain. **Recognition:** WBC. **Referee:** Daniel Van de Wiele.
Fight Summary: Although Roberto (154) started well with the southpaw right jab, the champion was content to take his time before picking it up in the fourth round when landing hard blows to the body. The tactic paid off as Roberto was visibly pained, and in the fifth and sixth Castillejo (153¾) was totally dominant as he fired in blows almost at will to leave the challenger a spent force. Following a three-punch combination that left Roberto dazed the referee called it off at 1.47 of the seventh to save the latter from taking unnecessary punishment.

4 December 1999. Fernando Vargas w pts 12 Ronald Wright.
Venue: Chinook Winds Casino, Lincoln City, Oregon, USA. **Recognition:** IBF. **Referee:** Joe Cortez.
Scorecards: 116-112, 115-113, 114-114.
Fight Summary: Even though the unbeaten champion started confidently, the clever Wright (154) was soon making life difficult for him, forging ahead by the end of the seventh having used the southpaw jab as a great point scorer. Wright had also matched Vargas (154) punch for punch generally at that stage, but by the tenth the latter had just about got his nose in front after stepping up his work to the body. The last three rounds were extremely close, and following the majority verdict in Vargas's favour there were many who felt that Wright's cleaner punching deserved better.

17 December 1999. Javier Castillejo w rsc 7 Michael Rask.
Venue: Cubierta Bullring, Leganes, Spain. **Recognition:** WBC. **Referee:** Alfred Asaro.
Fight Summary: Never out of control for one moment the champion was soon busying himself, hurting Rask (153¼) with a big left uppercut at the end of the first round before going for the body in the next couple of sessions. By the fourth, with Rask cut on the left eye, Castillejo (154) was opening up with solid shots to head and

body, and at the end of the sixth the Dane was saved by the bell after being hurt by heavy lefts and rights to the head. With Castillejo spearing Rask with accurate jabs in the seventh, and the latter now cut over the right eye as well as the left, the referee halted the contest at 1.41 on the advice of the ringside doctor.

19 February 2000. Harry Simon w rtd 10 Enrique Areco.
Venue: Goresbrook Leisure Centre, Dagenham, England. **Recognition:** WBO. **Referee:** Raul Caiz.
Fight Summary: Working well with the southpaw jab and showing plenty of movement, the 37-year-old challenger made life difficult for Simon (153½) despite failing to win a round on the cards. Although Simon was doing his best to take Areco (154) out he was having great difficulty in trapping a man who could work inside or on the back foot equally well, and it was only when the latter began to feel the pace that things changed. By the eighth Simon was beginning to connect heavily, a left hook producing a nasty swelling under Areco's eye in the ninth as he stepped up a gear. With Simon now looking to finish it after a left uppercut dropped Areco for 'nine' towards the end the tenth, leaving the Argentine with a bad swelling on his good eye, he was retired during the interval.

3 March 2000. Felix Trinidad w pts 12 David Reid.
Venue: Caesar's Palace, Las Vegas, Nevada, USA. **Recognition:** WBA. **Referee:** Mitch Halpern.
Scorecards: 114-107, 114-106, 114-107.
Fight Summary: Having been dropped by a lead right in the third, Trinidad (153) came back to floor the champion, once in the seventh and three times in the 11th, as he pushed on to a well-earned points win after being deducted two points for low blows, in the sixth and 11th. Reid (153) also lost a point in the ninth for going low. Although Reid showed up well, especially when blocking and moving adroitly to avoid punches, it was the harder hitting Trinidad who gradually took over to take every round from the fifth onwards when moving up a gear. How Reid managed to survive the 11th was amazing, and with his right eye closing fast he bravely endured another battering in the 12th to make sure he reached the final bell.

Within days, Trinidad relinquished his IBF/WBC welterweight titles to concentrate on the 154lbs weight class, feeling that he had increased his punch power by moving up.

15 April 2000. Fernando Vargas w pts 12 Ike Quartey.
Venue: Mandalay Bay Resort & Casino, Las Vegas, Nevada, USA. **Recognition:** IBF. **Referee:** Joe Cortez.
Scorecards: 116-111, 114-113, 116-111.
Fight Summary: Defending his title against the dangerous Quartey (152) was always going to be a tough one for Vargas (153½), but despite his left eye being badly swollen and losing a point in the fourth round when going low he came through with flying colours to take a unanimous points decision. It was the left lead that won it for Vargas, as it not only scored him points but also stopped Quartey from getting off power punches. The last three sessions saw Vargas pick it up with combinations and left hooks to head and body to make sure of victory.

21 July 2000. Javier Castillejo w pts 12 Tony Marshall.
Cubierta Bullring, Leganes, Spain. **Recognition:** WBC. **Referee:** Daniel Van de Wiele.
Scorecards: 116-114, 117-112, 118-110.
Fight Summary: Stronger than his American-based challenger, Castillejo (153¾) quickly got down to work with the jab, being in the main unconcerned by anything coming his way. There was no doubting that Marshall (154) had a good, tight defence and was especially adept at moving his head to let punches miss, but he lacked the aggression to gain a foothold in the contest to any extent, apart from throwing the odd right uppercut. How one judge made it just two points between them was strange, as Castillejo, throwing sharp combinations and solid right hands to head and body, had won clearly in the eyes of the vast majority.

22 July 2000. Felix Trinidad w rsc 3 Mamadou Thiam.
Venue: American Airlines Arena, Miami, Florida, USA. **Recognition:** WBA. **Referee:** Jorge Alonso.
Fight Summary: Making his first defence, Trinidad (154) hardly gave Thiam (152½) time to settle before he jumped on him and began blasting away with power-laden blows from both hands. How Thiam stayed on his feet as he was blasted around the ring was amazing, but when he finally made it to the bell his right eye was already closed shut with the prospect of more to come. Although Thiam remained upright in the second round, even firing back at

Trinidad on occasion, with just 12 seconds remaining in the third the referee called it off. With Thiam staggering about and turning towards his corner, having been knocked sideways by a long left uppercut, the third man's decision was an easy one.

26 August 2000. Fernando Vargas w rsc 4 Ross Thompson.
Venue: Mandalay Bay Resort & Casino, Las Vegas, Nevada, USA. **Recognition:** IBF. **Referee:** Joe Cortez.
Fight Summary: Refusing to touch gloves with Thompson (153½), who had attacked him at the pre-fight press conference, with the champion being too pent up to settle immediately it was not until the third round that he eventually got going with a vengeance. After being messed about early in the session by Thompson and then having a point deducted for hitting behind the head, Vargas (153) got the message. Storming into the attack, Vargas hurt Thompson with a big left and moments later floored him. Back on his feet and attacked by a barrage of blows, Thompson was saved by the bell, having been floored again, and was still badly dazed when a hard left-right decked him early in the fourth. Clearly looking to bring the fight to a conclusion, when Vargas rifled in punch after punch to leave Thompson half sitting on the bottom rope, the referee jumped in quickly to call it off, the finish being timed at 1.07.

23 September 2000. Harry Simon w pts 12 Rodney Jones.
Venue: The Casino, Rama, Ontario, Canada. **Recognition:** WBO. **Referee:** Mark Nelson.
Scorecards: 117-111, 117-111, 114-114.
Fight Summary: Despite winning clearly on points, Simon (154) disappointed against a journeyman southpaw challenger whom he was expected to deal with in quick fashion, and more often than not was unable to cut the ring down. With Jones (153½) sticking out the jab, occasionally Simon walked straight into one as well as being caught by a number of other punches, but he generally outworked the American to deserve the win. Although two of the judges had Simon winning nine rounds, the third had them dead level, which made you wonder what fight he had been watching.

21 October 2000. Javier Castillejo w rsc 4 Javier Martinez Rodriguez.
Venue: Salon 21 Nightclub, Mexico City, Mexico. **Recognition:** WBC. **Referee:** Lupe Garcia.
Fight Summary: Contested the day before the WBC Convention, as soon as the fight got underway it was apparent that Castillejo (154) was looking to retain his title in the quickest possible fashion. In a battle between Spaniards on foreign soil, Martinez (152¾) was forced to suffer three knockdowns and a badly cut right eye before being rescued by the referee after 1.43 of the fourth round had elapsed. In the aftermath, Castillejo (154) was lined up to defend his title in a big-money match against Oscar De La Hoya.

2 December 2000. Felix Trinidad w rsc 12 Fernando Vargas.
Venue: Mandalay Bay Resort & Casino, Las Vegas, Nevada, USA. **Recognition:** IBF/WBA. **Referee:** Jay Nady.
Fight Summary: Meeting to decide two title belts, Vargas (154) had a disastrous opening round when he was twice hammered to the floor by cracking left hooks to the jaw, before fighting back to have Trinidad (154) over from a left hook in the fourth. Trinidad came roaring back to get himself in front again, dropping Vargas with two terrific right hands in the 12th, prior to decking him again almost immediately he had got to his feet. He then forced the stoppage at 1.33 when smashing Vargas down with a long right to the head. Both men had points deducted for low blows, Trinidad in the fourth and seventh and Vargas in the tenth, and many felt that the latter was badly disadvantaged when having to be given time out to recover on the first occasion. It had been a great fight regardless of recriminations and took Trinidad to his 19th world championship victory at the young age of 27.

Trinidad relinquished the IBF/WBA versions of the title in May 2001 in order to take part in the middleweight unification tournament. In order to find new champions, the WBA made a match between Vargas and Jose Flores, while the IBF settled on Ronald Wright and Robert Frazier.

10 February 2001. Harry Simon w rsc 5 Wayne Alexander.
Venue: Kingsway Leisure Centre, Widnes, England. **Recognition:** WBO. **Referee:** Paul Thomas.
Fight Summary: Coming in at 24 hours' notice for America's Robert Allen who pulled out following a dispute over his weight, Alexander (154) made a good start before the champion began to get himself going in the second

round. Having taken a cracking right from Alexander that shook him right down to his boots, Simon (152¼) started to open the Englishman up with uppercuts and by the fourth he was ripping in solid body shots. In the fifth, after being floored by hits to the body and a left hook to the jaw, Alexander took the mandatory count before facing Simon again, but when not firing back the referee stopped the contest at 2.43 of the session.

On winning the WBO middleweight championship on 21 July, it was expected that Simon would give up the junior middleweight title immediately, but when his win over Hacine Cherifi was later declared to have been for the 'interim' title it was not until November that the championship was officially vacated. Once that decision was made, Daniel Santos and Luis Ramon Campas were signed up to contest the vacant title.

23 June 2001. Oscar De La Hoya w pts 12 Javier Castillejo.
Venue: MGM Grand, Las Vegas, Nevada, USA. **Recognition:** WBC. **Referee:** Vic Drakulich.
Scorecards: 119-108, 119-108, 119-108.
Fight Summary: Moving up to win the title, having already presided over four separate weight divisions, De La Hoya (154) had just too much of everything for the upright, pedestrian champion, who was outspeeded throughout. After making a poor start, when Castillejo (154) began to motor in the third although he was unable to get his normal punches off he occasionally hurt De La Hoya, especially with left-rights to the head. It was only in the tenth that all three judges gave Castillejo the round, when he tore into De La Hoya with solid blows from both hands. However, De La Hoya was well on top again thereafter, eventually dropping the Spaniard for the mandatory count immediately prior to the final bell.

At the Americas Stadium, Parla, Spain on 12 July 2002, Castillejo won the vacant WBC 'interim' title when outpointing Roman Karmazin over 12 rounds.

22 September 2001. Fernando Vargas w rsc 7 Jose Flores.
Venue: Mandalay Bay Resort & Casino, Las Vegas, Nevada, USA. **Recognition:** WBA. **Referee:** Joe Cortez.
Fight Summary: Just two fights earlier Vargas (153½) had lost the WBA title to Felix Trinidad, but when the latter handed his belt back in to move up amongst the 160lbs men 'The Aztec Warrior' was matched to meet Flores (153½), his former sparring partner, in order to find a new champion. After making a tentative start and being knocked off balance in the second round, Vargas came back immediately with a cracking left uppercut to the head to drop Flores on one knee. Although Vargas was finding it difficult to get himself up for the fight, being hit more than he would have liked, he eventually found the punches to finish it after lambasting Flores throughout the sixth. Coming out for the seventh, it was clear that Flores, his right eye badly swollen, would not be around much longer, and after Vargas smashed in blows to head and body he sunk to the floor to be rescued by the referee with one second of the session remaining. Despite the WBA calling it a kayo win for Vargas, the referee actually called the fight off before the count was completed.

On 10 August 2002, at the Gaston Defere Skate Park, Marseilles, France, Santiago Samaniego stopped Mamadou Thiam in the 12th round to land the vacant WBA 'interim' title.

12 October 2001. Ronald Wright w pts 12 Robert Frazier.
Venue: Fantasy Springs Casino, Indio, California, USA. **Recognition:** IBF. **Referee:** Jon Schorle.
Scorecards: 120-107, 119-108, 119-108.
Fight Summary: Contesting the title vacated by Felix Trinidad, Wright (153¾), who dropped his man in round one, proved far too good for Frazier (153) when winning the unanimous decision by a wide margin. Starting aggressively, although not as smooth as normal due to him being out of the ring for ten months, while Wright tried to get the southpaw jab going he had some difficulty in catching up with Frazier who spent most of his time retreating without even bothering to counter. By the fifth, however, Wright was slotting his right home as Frazier tired, but it was not much of a spectacle. A big loser, despite taking a pounding in the final session Frazier somehow survived to the bell.

2 February 2002. Ronald Wright w rsc 5 Jason Papillion.
Venue: American Airlines Arena, Miami, Florida, USA. **Recognition:** IBF. **Referee:** Bill Connors.

Fight Summary: Although Papillion (149½) threw nearly as many punches as Wright (153¼) he was far less effective, landing just 55 to the champion's 157. With Wright's southpaw jab being the deciding factor he was soon in control, pushing Papillion back around the ring before opening up with lefts and rights in the fifth. The outclassed Papillion was under constant pressure from the moment the round started, as Wright blasted in punches from head to body, and while not going down the referee stopped the contest on the 2.44 mark to save him from taking unnecessary punishment.

16 March 2002. Daniel Santos w rsc 11 Luis Ramon Campas.
Venue: Bally's Park Place Hotel, Las Vegas, Nevada, USA. **Recognition:** WBO. **Referee:** Joe Cortez.
Fight Summary: In a battle to decide the vacant title, Santos (154), who moved up from welter to meet Campas, made a solid start with the southpaw jab against a man who looked like his best days were behind him. There was no doubt that Campas could still bang a bit, but always on the move Santos gave him too few opportunities. At the end of the seventh Santos had won virtually everything, but in the eighth Campas came on strong for the first time after landing a terrific left hook to the body. It was not to be though, and by the end of the tenth Santos had Campas cut up and disillusioned. After taking an elbow and recovering in the 11th, Santos was soon back cherry picking, and when a big left cross tore into Campas's already injured right eyebrow, forcing the blood to gush, the referee called a halt at 1.36 of the session.

17 August 2002. Daniel Santos w pts 12 Mehrdud Takaloo.
Venue: Cardiff Castle, Cardiff, Wales. **Recognition:** WBO. **Referee:** Genaro Rodriguez.
Scorecards: 116-112, 117-110, 116-111.
Fight Summary: Cut over the right eye as early as the opening round, although Takaloo (154) bravely stuck to the task he never looked likely to upset the smooth-moving southpaw champion. It was a solid performance from Santos (154), his accurate punching and excellent movement keeping him in control, and although the English-based Iranian did his best he was up against a man who was always one move ahead.

7 September 2002. Ronald Wright w disq 8 Bronco McKart.
Venue: Rose Garden, Portland, Oregon, USA. **Recognition:** IBF. **Referee:** Mike Fischer.
Fight Summary: Having already outpointed the challenger twice, with Wright (153¾) confidently expected to do the hat-trick he made a good start against his fellow southpaw when taking the opening round. Although McKart (153½) came back well in the second, Wright was soon beginning to vary his shots, especially when driving in body blows. Unfortunately, McKart did not have the same accuracy as Wright when going to the body, receiving two point deductions in the sixth, one in the seventh and another in the eighth, before being disqualified at 2.33 of that session. On being outboxed comprehensively, at that stage it was just one warning too many.

14 September 2002. Oscar De La Hoya w rsc 11 Fernando Vargas.
Venue: Mandalay Bay Resort & Casino, Las Vegas, Nevada, USA. **Recognition:** WBA/WBC/The Ring. **Referee:** Joe Cortez.
Fight Summary: With both men putting up their titles, as well as *The Ring* Championship Belt being up for grabs, even though it was not one of De La Hoya's better nights he did more than enough to win. Both men had their successes, but at the end of the tenth De La Hoya (154) was ahead by a couple of rounds, having had Vargas (154) wobbling when sending in solid blows to head and body in the last session. Starting the 11th very much as he had ended the tenth, De La Hoya kept the punches going before finding a cracker of a left hook to the jaw to drop Vargas, and despite the latter getting up he was under so much pressure that the referee stopped it on the 1.48 mark.

Now that De La Hoya was recognised by the WBA as their 'super' champion, Alejandro Garcia won the vacant WBA 'second tier' title when stopping Santiago Samaniego, the WBA 'interim' champion, in the third round at the Thomas & Mack Centre, Las Vegas on 1 March 2003.

1 March 2003. Ronald Wright w pts 12 Juan Carlos Candelo.
Venue: Thomas & Mack Centre, Las Vegas, Nevada, USA. **Recognition:** IBF. **Referee:** Robert Byrd.
Scorecards: 118-110, 117-111, 117-111.

Fight Summary: Setting off at a fair pace Wright (153½) was expected to have a relatively easy time with Candelo (153), but was made to fight all the way as the challenger stayed in there throwing punches. Countering with rights and lefts as Wright pumped out the southpaw jab, Candelo had a fair amount of success, especially in the fourth and sixth when forcing the champion to fight every inch of the way. While Wright, who finished the contest with a badly swollen right eye, was always in front he could never relax as Candelo matched him, and had the latter packed a punch there might have been a different ending. Having hurt Candelo in the 11th with a right-left to the head, unable to find a finishing punch Wright concentrated on outboxing his man by a wide margin in the final session just in case any of the judges felt there was little in it.

3 May 2003. Oscar De La Hoya w rsc 7 Luis Ramon Campas.

Venue: Mandalay Bay Resort & Casino, Las Vegas, Nevada, USA. **Recognition:** WBA/WBC/The Ring. **Referee:** Vic Drakulich.
Fight Summary: Defending his three championship belts against Campas (153½), despite not being able to put the latter down the 'Golden Boy' virtually used his challenger as target practice as he flitted through the rounds with jabs and combinations to head and body. The problem for the brave Campas was that he only ever threw one punch at a time, while his lack of defence saw him hit flush again and again as De La Hoya (154) teed up. In the sixth, finding it hard to breathe, Campas was deducted a point for spitting out his gumshield. Finally, in the seventh, with Campas almost being hit at will his chief second stood up on the ring apron to implore the referee to stop the unequal contest, which he did with just ten seconds of the session remaining.

At the Cubierta Bullring, Leganes, Spain on 9 May, Javier Castillejo successfully defended the WBC 'interim' title when stopping Diego Castillo in the first round.

28 June 2003. Daniel Santos w pts 12 Fulgencio Zuniga.

Venue: Hiram Bithorn Stadium, Bayamon, Puerto Rico. **Recognition:** WBO. **Referee:** Luis Pabon.
Scorecards: 118-110, 118-110, 118-110.
Fight Summary: Despite coming out like a train, blasting in punches from both hands, the southpaw champion was unable to drop the ponderous Zuniga (153), who ate the jab all the way to the final bell. Although Zuniga tried hard enough he lacked the class to be able to tie Santos (154) down, being so predictably one-paced that the latter often took time out. Only in the eighth and ninth did Zuniga show, when mounting frenetic attacks to steal the rounds on the cards, and from there to the end of the fight Santos began to land solidly in an effort to finish inside the distance.

13 September 2003. Shane Mosley w pts 12 Oscar De La Hoya.

Venue: MGM Grand, Las Vegas, Nevada, USA. **Recognition:** WBA/WBC/The Ring. **Referee:** Joe Cortez.
Scorecards: 115-113, 115-113, 115-113.
Fight Summary: Regardless that all three judges went with the challenger it was difficult to see how Mosley (154) outscored De La Hoya (154) when one examines the punch stats; De La Hoya connecting with 106 jabs to Mosley's 33 and with 115 solid blows to 94. According to the round-by-round punch stats, De La Hoya won the fight 11 to one, landing at the rate of three to one in the third, fourth and seventh. There were no knockdowns, and there was never that much between them on the face of it, but according to all three cards Mosley won the last four rounds. It was during these sessions that he landed with his best punches, a tremendous right to the body in the ninth almost dropping De La Hoya. Having being cut over the right eye in the fourth following a clash of heads, De La Hoya may well have been more protective than usual, but even when on the retreat he scored well with countering jabs and deserved better.

On 20 September, at the Mohegun Sun Casino, Uncasville, Connecticut, Alejandro Garcia retained the WBA 'second tier' crown when retiring Rhoshii Wells in the tenth round, but was parted from the so-called title when crushed by Travis Simms (l co 5 at the Boardwalk Hall, Atlantic City, New Jersey on 13 December).

8 November 2003. Ronald Wright w pts 12 Angel Hernandez.

Venue: Mandalay Bay Resort & Casino, Las Vegas, Nevada, USA. **Recognition:** IBF. **Referee:** Tony Weeks.
Scorecards: 119-109, 118-110, 118-111.

Fight Summary: Taking a few rounds to find his rhythm, although the champion eventually got the southpaw jab working he still spent too much time at close quarters with the battle-hardened Hernandez (154), who relished the opportunity given him. Going forward and swinging in the fifth, as Wright (154) tried to switch, Hernandez had his best session to date but unable to maintain any momentum he was soon back on the receiving end. Cut on the right eye in the seventh, Hernandez's chances were further weakened when he was nailed by several solid left hands as Wright looked for a finish. The final five sessions saw Wright well in control without having to be anywhere near his best.

13 March 2004. Ronald Wright w pts 12 Shane Mosley.
Venue: Mandalay Bay Resort & Casino, Las Vegas, Nevada, USA. **Recognition:** IBF/WBA/WBC/The Ring. **Referee:** Tony Weeks.
Scorecards: 117-111, 117-111, 116-112.
Fight Summary: In addition to three titles being on the line as well as *The Ring* Championship Belt, Wright (154) joined the elite when unanimously outscoring Mosley (154), having gone well with his solid southpaw jab throughout allied to a sound defence. From the second round onwards it was clear that Mosley somehow had to find a way through Wright's tight guard but even with a two-inch-reach advantage he had little success. Wright was also proving the stronger on the inside. Having piled up the points with the jab, backed up with solid left crosses, by the end of the tenth Wright was way in front, and although Mosley won the last two sessions on pure aggression he was unable to turn things around.

Following Wright being stripped of the IBF title in April when unable to meet his number one challenger due to contractual commitments, Verno Phillips and Kassim Ouma were contracted to contest the vacancy. Unfortunately for Ouma he damaged his back in training and was replaced by Carlos Bojorquez, who came in at four days' notice.

Travis Simms, the WBA 'second tier' champion, made a successful defence against Bronco McKart (w pts 12 at Madison Square Garden, Manhattan, NYC, New York on 2 October).

17 April 2004. Daniel Santos w pts 12 Michael Lerma.
Venue: Florida State Fairgrounds Entertainment Hall, Tampa, Florida, USA. **Recognition:** WBO. **Referee:** Max Parker Jnr.
Scorecards: 120-107, 120-107, 118-110.
Fight Summary: Although outboxing his fellow southpaw challenger in virtually every round and cutting him over the left eye in the third Santos (153½) was unable to find a finishing blow despite being just one punch away in the eighth. The lanky Lerma (153¾), nicknamed the 'Body Snatcher', with eight losses on his record did not really warrant a title shot. Throughout the fight Lerma had great difficulty in pinning Santos down. The one time he did manage it was in the fifth when getting off some solid shots but Santos rode them well and was soon back in control with the jab.

5 June 2004. Verno Phillips w rtd 6 Carlos Bojorquez.
Venue: Leggett & Platt Athletic Centre, Joplin, Missouri, USA. **Recognition:** IBF. **Referee:** Mark Nelson.
Fight Summary: Fighting for the title that became available when Ronald Wright was stripped, Phillips (153½) was supposed to have met Kassim Ouma, but when he pulled out with a back problem Bojorquez (154) substituted at just four days' notice. Very much a club fighter, with Bojorquez not in Phillips' class, he was soon being banged around but as game as a pebble he was always trying to get his punches off. In the fifth, after Bojorquez was almost overwhelmed, at the end of the session the referee told him that if he did not start defending himself better he would have to pull him out. It got worse in the sixth when Bojorquez was sent down for 'four' following a smashing right to the head, and having been saved by the bell he was retired by his corner during the interval.

11 September 2004. Daniel Santos w tdec 9 Antonio Margarito.
Venue: Jose Miguel Agrelot Coliseum, Hato Rey, Puerto Rico. **Recognition:** WBO. **Referee:** Luis Pabon.
Scorecards: 85-86, 86-85, 87-84.
Fight Summary: Not wishing to fight up close to avoid the possibility of heads coming together as in their previous contest, it was no surprise that the champion went on the move with southpaw jabs and solid left crosses, while

Margarito (153) looked to land big rights. However, before too long, with Santos (154) beginning to stand his ground to get his punches off it was he who delivered the more solid blows in the opening three rounds. Margarito, however, came back well in the fourth before rocking Santos in the fifth. In the sixth, just when it looked like Margarito might be getting a foothold in the contest, he led with his head and pulled away with a badly gashed right eye. Knowing that the fight could be stopped at any moment, Margarito slammed into Santos during the next two sessions, but ran into a cracking right hook in the ninth that nearly dropped him. When the cut was deemed to be too serious for Margarito to continue during the interval, Santos was announced as the winner after the referee went to the cards.

2 October 2004. Kassim Ouma w pts 12 Verno Phillips.
Venue: Caesar's Palace, Las Vegas, Nevada, USA. **Recognition:** IBF. **Referee:** Joe Cortez.
Scorecards: 114-113, 114-113, 117-110.
Fight Summary: Despite having been outscored over ten rounds by Ouma in 2001, Phillips was more than happy to put his title on the line against the same man in a bid to avenge that defeat. Unfortunately, it turned out to be a poor fight, with the 34-year-old Phillips (152½) growing older by the minute and Ouma (152) merely pushing out southpaw jabs with no real weight behind them. At the end of the tenth Phillips was marginally ahead on the cards, but it was Ouma who found something extra in the 11th, battering away at the champion until he fell before blasting in heavy shots during the final session to impress the judges.

20 November 2004. Ronald Wright w pts 12 Shane Mosley.
Venue: Mandalay Bay Resort & Casino, Las Vegas, Nevada, USA. **Recognition:** WBA/WBC/The Ring. **Referee:** Joe Cortez.
Scorecards: 115-113, 114-114, 115-113.
Fight Summary: Defending his belts against the man he took them off, Wright (154) outpointed Mosley (154) yet again, although the margin was not so great this time around. At the start of the ninth Mosley was just ahead according to the cards, but he took so much out of himself in the eighth, as Wright put up a clever defence, that he was not the same afterwards. It was clear that Wright had paced himself well when pumping out the southpaw jab in the ninth to great effect as Mosley failed to get the majority of his punches off. In the tenth there was only one man in it and it was not Mosley, and while he came back in the 11th to nick the session after dragging Wright into a brawl it was the latter who dominated the final round to retain his titles.

After Wright forfeited the WBA title in April 2005, having signed to meet Felix Trinidad in an official WBC middleweight eliminator on 14 May 2005, Travis Simms, the 'second tier' champion, was handed the belt.

The vacant WBA 'interim' title was then contested by Rhoshii Wells and Alejandro Garcia at the United Centre, Chicago, Illinois on 21 May 2005, being won by the latter on a ninth-round stoppage.

When Simms was stripped by the WBA in late June 2005, due to a contractual problem, Garcia was awarded the title.

Earlier, in April 2005, after deciding to move up a weight, when Wright relinquished the WBC title the 'interim' titleholder, Javier Castillejo, was accorded full championship status despite being inactive for a long period.

Meanwhile, Wright continued to hold *The Ring* Championship Belt until handing it back in October 2005.

Castillejo was then stripped at the end of May 2005, having signed up for a fight against Fernando Vargas instead of making required defence against Ricardo Mayorga. Following that, Mayorga was matched against Michele Piccirillo to find a new WBC champion.

29 January 2005. Kassim Ouma w pts 12 Kofi Jantuah.
Venue: Boardwalk Convention Centre, Atlantic City, New Jersey, USA. **Recognition:** IBF. **Referee:** Randy Neumann.
Scorecards: 117-111, 116-112, 118-110.

Fight Summary: Handing out a steady beating to his challenger, throwing punches from all angles, while it could be argued that Ouma (152) was not punching his weight it was certainly effective. From the first bell to last Ouma never stopped working, and although Jantuah (153) started well, taking the opening two rounds, the fifth was probably the only other session that he showed up in when taking the bull by the horns with some terrific right hands. By the eighth Jantuah was showing his age as he kept walking into prodding blows delivered from a southpaw stance. And even though he hurt Ouma he continued to be outscored until the final bell. The punch stats showed that Ouma threw an incredible 1,000 plus punches, landing with half of them.

14 July 2005. Roman Karmazin w pts 12 Kassim Ouma.
Venue: Orleans Hotel & Casino, Las Vegas, Nevada, USA. **Recognition:** IBF. **Referee:** Robert Byrd.
Scorecards: 118-108, 116-110, 117-109.
Fight Summary: Making a slow start, Ouma (154) was under pressure from the opening bell as Karmazin (153½) used his three-and-half-inch-reach advantage and awkward style to take control early before flooring the southpaw champion twice in the third round. Knocked down firstly by a left to the side, Ouma was caught off balance, but the right to the jaw that sent him crashing for the second knockdown took a lot of the stuffing out of him. Subsequently, it was hard going for Ouma, and although he battled back well during the middle of the fight he was never able to close Karmazin down. Working hard, the Russian-born Karmazin came on strongly over last three sessions with jabs and solid rights to walk off with the decision.

13 August 2005. Alejandro Garcia w pts 12 Luca Messi.
Venue: United Centre, Chicago, Illinois, USA. **Recognition:** WBA. **Referee:** Pete Podgorski.
Scorecards: 117-110, 119-108, 117-110.
Fight Summary: In what was his first defence, Garcia (154) suffered from a slow start when dropping the first two rounds to the hard-working Messi (151) before eventually finding the room to jab and work the body. With the challenger always in the thick of it, in the seventh he hurt Garcia with a solid right only for the latter to come right back with heavy rights of his own to drop him for 'eight'. Although Garcia was less effective from thereon in, claiming to have broken his left hand in the second, he did more than enough to win the decision.

13 August 2005. Ricardo Mayorga w pts 12 Michele Piccirillo.
Venue: United Centre, Chicago, Illinois, USA. **Recognition:** WBC. **Referee:** Gerald Scott.
Scorecards: 117-108, 117-110, 120-105.
Fight Summary: Contesting the vacant title, Mayorga (154) got himself up for this one despite claiming that he was through with boxing after being beaten by Felix Trinidad some ten months earlier. Making a solid start, the crude, wild punching Mayorga dropped Piccirillo (154) twice in the second round and once in the fourth with heavy rights to the head, and although the latter came back well in the fifth he was never able to do much other than fight in defensive mode. Unable to take the fight to Mayorga, although Piccirillo was put down again just before the final bell no count was registered.

3 December 2005. Serhiy Dzinziruk w pts 12 Daniel Santos.
Venue: Borderland Hall, Magdeburg, Germany. **Recognition:** WBO. **Referee:** Genaro Rodriguez.
Scorecards: 115-112, 115-112, 115-112.
Fight Summary: A fast-paced battle of southpaws saw a new champion crowned when the German-based Dzinziruk (154) took the title from Santos (154), beating the latter at his own game. Strong and determined, from the fourth round on the former undefeated European titleholder used the jab well to stop Santos from getting into his stride, having lost the opening three or four sessions. Coming on strong, in the eighth Dzinziruk countered superbly with a cracking right to the jaw to drop Santos, and although the Puerto Rican had no difficulty in beating the count the punch would ultimately prove decisive in what was a hard-fought contest. Now fighting with great confidence, Dzinziruk battled on, surviving a tremendous left hook to the head in the 11th as Santos put in a great finish. Despite losing the 12th, Dzinziruk was deemed to have done enough.

6 May 2006. Jose Antonio Rivera w pts 12 Alejandro Garcia.
Venue: DCU Centre, Worcester, Massachusetts, USA. **Recognition:** WBA. **Referee:** Richard Flaherty.
Scorecards: 116-106, 116-106, 115-107.

Fight Summary: The challenger made an excellent start when dropping Garcia (152½) twice in the opening round, a solid jab and an overarm right to the head doing the trick. Coming back strongly, Garcia put that behind him to get some good punches off in the second and third before flooring Rivera (152½) for the first time in his career with a straight right to the face. With both men punching away in the fifth, by the seventh Rivera was pushing on as Garcia tired, and in the ninth he decked the latter with a long right that landed on the jaw. Although knocked down again in the tenth, this time by a left hook, Garcia came back strongly in the 11th before another big overarm right put him over in the final session prior to the bell.

6 May 2006. Oscar De La Hoya w rsc 6 Ricardo Mayorga.
Venue: MGM Grand, Las Vegas, Nevada, USA. **Recognition:** WBC. **Referee:** Jay Nady.
Fight Summary: Coming back from a bad defeat at the hands of Bernard Hopkins, De La Hoya (153½), a champion at six-weights, gave a superb display in battering the dangerous Mayorga (153½) from his title. With both men swinging in blows in the opener it was De La Hoya who struck first when a cracking left hook to the jaw dropped Mayorga heavily. Although Mayorga got to his feet quickly he was soon under pressure from solid combinations as well as being outboxed for round after round. Having been floored in the sixth from another left hook, after Mayorga struggled up and was then battered down by a series of lefts and rights that landed on the jaw the referee stopped the fight. The finish came at 1.25 of the session.

27 May 2006. Serhiy Dzinziruk w pts 12 Sebastian Andres Lujan.
Venue: Zenith Culture Hall, Munich, Germany. **Recognition:** WBO. **Referee:** Joe Cortez.
Scorecards: 118-110, 117-110, 116-111.
Fight Summary: Stepping out for his first defence, the southpaw champion did not get himself going for three rounds as Lujan (153¾) dictated early on, but following a coming together of heads that left him with a cut over the left eye he began to take over. From the fifth through to the final bell Dzinziruk (154) dropped one session at most, his lead being enhanced when Lujan lost a point in the ninth for hitting behind the head. Although the Argentine was always dangerous, once Dzinziruk had got his right-left combinations up to speed there was only one man in it.

8 July 2006. Cory Spinks w pts 12 Roman Karmazin.
Venue: Savvis Centre, St Louis, Missouri, USA. **Recognition:** IBF. **Referee:** Mark Nelson.
Scorecards: 115-113, 115-113, 114-114.
Fight Summary: At the start it looked as though the champion would be too strong for Spinks (153), but the latter's greater speed and southpaw stance left the Russian flummoxed at times when winning four of the opening five rounds. By the middle stages, however, Karmazin (153) was beginning to come on when working the body and roughing Spinks up in the clinches. Cut under the right eye in the seventh, Karmazin was starting to hurt Spinks with big right hands, and finishing strongly he appeared to have done enough to retain his title as the latter took time out in the 12th. It was not to be though, as Spinks won by a very close decision on the cards.

21 October 2006. Serhiy Dzinziruk w pts 12 Alisultan Nadirbegov.
Venue: Fire in the Mountains Arena, Halle, Germany. **Recognition:** WBO. **Referee:** Terry O'Connor.
Scorecards: 120-108, 119-108, 119-109.
Fight Summary: Setting the pace from the opening bell, the southpaw champion was soon peppering Nadirbegov (151½) with solid jabs and combinations that had the latter desperately looking for a punch to turn things around. Occasionally catching Dzinziruk (153) with countering blows was not enough, and as the contest moved into the final stages it was clear that Nadirbegov lacked the know-how and speed to fight his way back into contention. Trying to finish matters Dzinziruk went on the attack in the last couple of sessions, but found Nadirbegov determined to last the course.

6 January 2007. Travis Simms w rsc 9 Jose Antonio Rivera.
Venue: Seminole Hard Rock Live Arena, Hollywood, Florida, USA. **Recognition:** WBA. **Referee:** Frank Santore Jnr.
Fight Summary: Coming back after well over two years out of the ring, Simms (153¾) started fast when hurting the current title holder in the first before dropping him with a southpaw straight left in the second. Showing faster hands and heavier punching power than Rivera (153), the 'champion in recess' came back with a bang as he took

round after round with heavy counters continually finding their target. Having been floored in the ninth by a straight left to the jaw, Rivera made it to his feet before the referee rescued him at 2.00 of the session when he was being battered from both hands unmercifully as Simms went for the finish.

3 February 2007. Cory Spinks w pts 12 Rodney Jones.
Venue: Silver Spurs Arena, Kissimmee, Florida, USA. **Recognition:** IBF. **Referee:** Tommy Kimmons.
Scorecards: 120-108, 1180110, 120-108.
Fight Summary: In a meeting between southpaws it was the champion who came out on top when outboxing the 38-year-old Jones (153) for round after round, his speed too much for the latter to handle. With Spinks (153¾) on the outside, Jones lacked the mobility to get in range and was consistently being beaten to the punch in what turned into a boring affair. Following the fight, Spinks stated that he wanted the best men in the division from there on.

5 May 2007. Floyd Mayweather Jnr w pts 12 Oscar De La Hoya.
Venue: MGM Grand, Las Vegas, Nevada, USA. **Recognition:** WBC. **Referee:** Kenny Bayless.
Scorecards: 116-112, 115-113, 113-115.
Fight Summary: Becoming a champion at five weights when outscoring De La Hoya (154), his skill being undeniable, Mayweather (150) failed to run off the rounds as he had predicted and won on the back foot rather than making the fight. Having taken three of the opening four rounds, De La Hoya failed to build on that with a smaller output of jabs than were required to push Mayweather back. There was never that much between them, but when De La Hoya tired in the latter rounds it allowed Mayweather more freedom to pick his shots. Had one of the judges agreed with the other two and given a 10-9 round for the 12th De La Hoya would have retained his title on a split draw, it was that close.

Mayweather vacated the title in June, preferring to hold on to the WBC welterweight crown, and following his decision he was given 'emeritus' status. Originally an eliminator, a match between Carlos Baldomir and Vernon Forrest, rated number two and three respectively by the WBC, was eventually given full title status after De La Hoya, the top-rated man, was undecided on his future.

19 May 2007. Serhiy Dzinziruk w rsc 11 Carlos Nascimento.
Venue: Color Line Arena, Hamburg, Germany. **Recognition:** WBO. **Referee:** Brian Garry.
Fight Summary: Boxing well within himself the southpaw champion racked up the rounds against the limited Nascimento (151½), who had little on offer than being able to soak up punishment and keep going. It was only in the 11th that Dzinziruk (153¾) opened up with solid rights and lefts to floor Nascimento who, by this time, had little left and was worn out. Although making it to his feet the referee called the action off on the 1.42 mark when realising that Nascimento was through for the night.

7 July 2007. Joachim Alcine w pts 12 Travis Simms.
Venue: Harbor Yard Arena, Bridgeport, Connecticut, USA. **Recognition:** WBA. **Referee:** Michael Ortega.
Scorecards: 115-110, 116-109, 114-111.
Fight Summary: Making his first defence in a contest between unbeaten fighters, and one filled with many transgressions, Simms (152½) allowed himself to be outworked by Alcine (152¼) in the latter stages. Having won four of the opening six rounds on two of the judges' cards, Simms should have pulled away at this point, but failed to take advantage of openings when they presented themselves. Both men were deducted points, Alcine in the sixth for a late punch and Simms in the ninth when hitting on the break. In that same round when Simms slipped on the wet canvas after missing with a punch the referee incorrectly scored it a knockdown. Following the fight, Simms, a southpaw, stated that after he had felt his left hand go in the fourth his momentum subsequently waned.

28 July 2007. Vernon Forrest w pts 12 Carlos Baldomir.
Venue: Emerald Queen Casino, Tacoma, Washington, USA. **Recognition:** WBC. **Referee:** Jose Rivera.
Scorecards: 118-109, 116-111, 118-109.
Fight Summary: Contested for the vacant title after Floyd Mayweather handed in his belt, it was Forrest (154) who walked off with the prize after widely outscoring the tough Baldomir (154) on two of the cards. Although Baldomir

was always on the front foot he found it difficult to reach the taller Forrest, who was landing solid, accurate jabs all night. Carrying a swollen right eye from the third did not deter Forrest as he speeded up before being caught heavily by Baldomir in the ninth and then losing a point for going low in the same session. Picking it up in the tenth when throwing punches from both hands, Forrest continued in that vein through to the final bell to fully deserve the plaudits that came his way.

1 December 2007. Vernon Forrest w rsc 11 Michele Piccirillo.
Venue: Foxwoods Casino, Mashantucket, Connecticut, USA. **Recognition:** WBC. **Referee:** Arthur Mercante Jnr.
Fight Summary: Defending his title for the first time, the 36-year-old Forrest (153) was nearly always going too well for Piccirillo (152). Although coming back in the third, Piccirillo, hardly making a dent on Forrest, was unable to get into the fight, and in the sixth he was push-punched to the deck for what should have been seen as a slip. It hardly got any better for Piccirillo when he was dropped by a solid right in the ninth, having done reasonably well in the previous session. Eventually, matters came to head in the 11th when another cracking right to the head had Piccirillo down again. Following that, when it was seen that he had injured a leg in the fall, the referee called the fight off on 2.21 mark.

7 December 2007. Joachim Alcine w rsc 12 Alfonso Mosquera.
Venue: Bell Centre, Montreal, Quebec, Canada. **Recognition:** WBA. **Referee:** Michael Griffin.
Fight Summary: In what was a difficult first defence for Alcine (152¼), he found himself trading with Mosquera (153) right from the off as the latter fired in quick combinations that initially confused him. However, by the fourth Alcine was in control for a few rounds, handing out solid combinations of his own as he pushed Mosquera back. Doing his best work on the inside, Mosquera really made it pay in the ninth when trapping Alcine on the ropes and banging away, but that seemed to be his last throw of the dice as the latter came back with a vengeance when stepping on the gas. Decidedly unsteady at the start of the 12th, Mosquera slipped over moments before being dropped by a right-left hook. Floored for the second time following a big right hook, upon getting up and taking a battering Mosquera was rescued by the referee at 2.17 of the session.

27 March 2008. Verno Phillips w pts 12 Cory Spinks.
Venue: Scot Trade Centre, St Louis, Missouri, USA. **Recognition:** IBF. **Referee:** Gerald Scott.
Scorecards: 115-113, 116-112, 113-115.
Fight Summary: According to the great majority of scribes and experts outside the ring this appeared to be an easy win for the southpaw champion, one such man saying that he had the 38-year-old Phillips (153) winning two rounds at most. Regardless of that the split decision went to Phillips. Much faster and much younger, Spinks (153) could have made sure had he put more work in, but he stopped dominating in the sixth when allowing Phillips the room to get heavy punches off, something that was highlighted in the seventh. Although Spinks was given the last three rounds, Phillips was seemingly favoured because his blows landed were of the heavier variety.

Phillips relinquished the IBF title on 19 November having already signed to meet Paul Williams for the vacant WBO 'interim' crown on 29 November. Following that, Spinks was eventually matched against Deandre Latimore with the vacant title at stake. Lattimore had earned his right to a title shot after beating the IBF's top-ranked Sechew Powell (w rsc 7 at the Hard Rock Café in Times Square, Manhattan, NYC, New York on 11 June).

26 April 2008. Serhiy Dzinziruk w pts 12 Lukas Konecny.
Venue: Freiberger Arena, Dresden, Germany. **Recognition:** WBO. **Referee:** Jose Rivera.
Scorecards: 118-110, 115-113, 114-114.
Fight Summary: A tough fight to score, and one that had twice been delayed, there was much dissent after the southpaw champion had been handed the majority decision at the end of 12 well-contested rounds. With Konecny (153) coming forward at all times, although Dzinziruk (153) countered strongly and moved well it appeared that the man from the Czech Republic had done enough on aggression alone. Following the contest calls went out for a return.

7 June 2008. Sergio Mora w pts 12 Vernon Forrest.
Venue: Mohegan Sun Casino, Uncasville, Connecticut, USA. **Recognition:** WBC. **Referee:** Dick Flaherty.

Scorecards: 116-112, 115-113, 114-114.

Fight Summary: It was clear from the start that things were not quite right with 37-year-old champion, who appeared to decline by the minute as Mora (154) set about him from the fourth onwards. Having controlled the opening three rounds, Forrest (153¾) had looked a good bet, but now he was being caught from head to body by solid combinations. Although Forrest came back somewhat in the fifth, after taking some heavy shots, and with his right eye swelling fast, his strength began to ebb away as Mora took the bull by the horns right through to the final bell.

11 July 2008. Daniel Santos w rsc 6 Joachim Alcine.
Venue: Uniprix Stadium, Montreal, Canada. **Recognition:** WBA. **Referee:** Marlon Wright.
Fight Summary: Up against a southpaw in Santos (153), the champion made a cautious start before both men went to work in the third. Having got home with a cracking right to Santos's jaw, Alcine (153) ended the session being pinned on the ropes while taking solid shots to head and body. Following the fourth, which went to Santos, Alcine went after the Puerto Rican in the fifth with long rights finding their mark but in the sixth he suddenly came undone. After Santos banged out a short right hook, just as Alcine was preparing to throw a left hook he was beaten to the punch by a thunderous straight left to the jaw that sent him crashing to the deck. Although the referee began the count, when he saw that Alcine had partially got up before falling down again he stopped the contest on the 2.10 mark.

At the Prefectural Gym, Osaka, Japan on 30 August 2009, Nobuhiro Ishida won the vacant WBA 'interim' title when outpointing Marco Antonio Avendano over 12 rounds.

13 September 2008. Vernon Forrest w pts 12 Sergio Mora.
Venue: MGM Grand, Las Vegas, Nevada, USA. **Recognition:** WBC. **Referee:** Vic Drakulich.
Scorecards: 118-109, 117-110, 119-108.
Fight Summary: In a complete reversal of fortunes, Forrest (154) regained his title from Mora (154), the man he lost it to, when receiving the unanimous decision at the end of a contest he had largely dominated. This time round it was Forrest's left jab that was decisive, and in the fourth he began working the body to good effect. Sent on to the ropes in the seventh from a left hook, the referee counted over Mora after ruling that it was effectively a knockdown. Although Mora landed heavily with a big right in the ninth, Forrest immediately responded when ramming in blows right through to the final bell.

On 4 October, at the Pechanga Resort & Casino, Temecula, California, Sergio Martinez forced Alex Bunema to retire at the end of the eighth round of a contest to decide the vacant WBC 'interim' title. Martinez then made a successful defence when drawing over 12 rounds against Kermit Cintron at the Bank Atlantic Centre, Sunrise, Florida on 14 February 2009.

After being out of the ring since his win over Mora due to a persistent rib injury, Forrest was stripped of the title on 21 May 2009, the WBC announcing that the 'interim' champion, Martinez, had been upgraded to full championship status.

Towards the end of June 2010, having won the WBC middleweight title a week earlier, Martinez handed back the junior belt after deciding to continue at 160lbs. Following that, Manny Pacquiao and Antonio Margarito were matched to contest the vacant title.

1 November 2008. Serhiy Dzinziruk w pts 12 Joel Julio.
Venue: Koenig Pilsener Arena, Oberhausen, Germany. **Recognition:** WBO. **Referee:** Genaro Rodriguez.
Scorecards: 116-112, 117-111, 116-112.
Fight Summary: There was little between the two men at the halfway stage, the southpaw champion and Julio (154) swapping blows as the action swayed back and forth. It was in the seventh, however, that the tide changed for Dzinziruk (153¼) as he began using his hand and foot speed to take the play away from Julio, who gradually began to fade when getting caught with more punches than before. With two judges giving Dzinziruk the last four sessions the margin of victory was complete.

Paul Williams stopped Verno Phillips on the ringside doctor's advice at the end of the eighth round of their fight for the vacant WBO 'interim' title at the Citizens Business Bank Arena, Ontario, California, USA on 29 November. After Williams relinquished the 'interim' title, he was succeeded by Alfredo Angulo who knocked out Harry Joe Yorgey inside three rounds at the XL Centre, Hartford, Connecticut, USA on 7 November 2009, and then went on to make a successful defence when stopping Julio in the 11th at the Citizens Business Bank Arena on 24 April 2010. Angulo forfeited the WBO 'interim' title on 17 July 2010 after beating Joachim Alcine in a final eliminator for the WBC crown and failing to agree a match against Dzinziruk.

24 April 2009. Cory Spinks w pts 12 Deandre Latimore.
Venue: Scot Trade Centre, St Louis, Missouri, USA. **Recognition:** IBF. **Referee:** Earl Morton.
Scorecards: 114-113, 115-112, 112-115.
Fight Summary: Contested for the vacant crown after Verno Phillips had returned his belt, Spinks (152¾) regained his old title when taking a split decision over Latimore (153½) in an all-southpaw battle. Making the early running, Latimore got off several solid shots while Spinks stood with him instead of moving on. After being cut over the left eye in the fourth, Spinks began working the jab to good effect before going back to punch-for-punch as Latimore started to fade around the ninth and was also cut over the left eye. From thereon in it was first one and then the other who landed the better punches, until Spinks sorted himself out to put the last couple of sessions in the bank.

14 November 2009. Yuri Foreman w pts 12 Daniel Santos.
Venue: MGM Grand, Las Vegas, Nevada, USA. **Recognition:** WBA. **Referee:** Jay Nady.
Scorecards: 117-109, 117-109, 116-110.
Fight Summary: Losing his title at the first time of asking after suffering weight-making problems, the southpaw champion was knocked down twice, once in the second by a right to the back of the head (when unsuccessfully claiming a foul) before a right to the body in the final round also did the trick. It was reported by some of the press that it was a left hook that did the job. Although both men were cut, Foreman on the left eye in the third and Santos on the right optic in the 11th, it made no difference to the way the contest went, Foreman (154) becoming the first Israeli to win a title when the unanimous decision went in his favour. Nothing to write home about, it was an extremely messy affair that saw Santos (154) doing the chasing and Foreman moving around, popping out scoring blows to make sure of the rounds.

Nobuhiro Ishida retained the WBA 'interim' crown when outpointing Oney Valdez over 12 rounds at the Prefectural Gym, Osaka, Japan on 29 December.

14 May 2010. Serhiy Dzinziruk w rsc 10 Daniel Dawson.
Venue: Chumash Casino, Santa Ynez, California, USA. **Recognition:** WBO. **Referee:** Jose Cobain.
Fight Summary: With Dawson (154) the aggressor from the start being held up by the champion's southpaw right jab, even when he managed to break through he was met by hooks and crosses from both hands. Dzinziruk (153) also proved that he had a good chin when required. By the sixth Dawson had run out of ideas, but he continued to push on despite taking a beating as the rounds passed. At 2.12 of the tenth the referee finally halted the action when a badly tiring Dawson was taking a whole string of solid lefts without response and was crumbling fast.

Zaurbek Baysangurov knocked out Mike Miranda in the opening round of a contest to decide the vacant WBO 'interim' title at the Sports Palace, Odessa, Ukraine on 30 July 2011.

On 5 October 2011, Dzinziruk was stripped of the WBO title after pulling out of a defence against Lukas Konecny, which had been scheduled for 30 September, following a long period of inactivity at the weight. Further to this, Baysangurov was promoted to full championship status. Meanwhile, Konecny won the vacant WBO 'interim' title when knocking out Salim Larbi in the seventh round of their contest at the Vodova Arena, Brno, Czech Republic on 5 April 2012.

5 June 2010. Miguel Cotto w rsc 9 Yuri Foreman.
Venue: Yankee Stadium, Bronx, NYC, New York, USA. **Recognition:** WBA. **Referee:** Arthur Mercante Jnr.

Fight Summary: Fairly even for the opening four rounds as both men looked to settle, from the fifth onwards it was clear that the champion's best shots were not making a dent on Cotto (153½) who continued to roll forward. Cut on the right eye in the fifth, Foreman (154) was being pushed around in the sixth and losing track. As a contest it was virtually over in the seventh when Foreman's right leg gave way when attempting a defensive movement, and although he was given time out it became difficult for him to fight on. Fight on he did though, despite falling over on occasion and taking a beating for his pains. He was also cut over the left eye. Having tried to stop the contest in the eighth when throwing the towel in, Foreman's corner was ignored by the referee after the latter said he wanted to fight on. Although Foreman came out for the ninth, when he was dropped by a left hook to the body the referee immediately called the fight off 42 seconds into the session.

Rigoberto Alvarez won the WBA 'interim' crown when outpointing Nobuhiro Ishida, the defending champion, over 12 rounds at the Sports Inn, University Campus, Tepic, Nayarit, Mexico on 9 October. Into 2011, on 5 February, Austin Trout outpointed Alvarez over 12 rounds to win the vacant WBA 'second tier' title at the Medrano 67 Coliseum Arena, Guadalajara, Mexico; the loser forfeiting the 'interim' belt.

7 August 2010. Cornelius Bundrage w rsc 5 Cory Spinks.
Venue: Scot Trade Centre, St Louis, Missouri, USA. **Recognition:** IBF. **Referee:** Mark Nelson.
Fight Summary: In something of a surprise, Spinks (153½) was beaten by Bundrage (153½) in a bout that had been twice postponed. It was also a match-up between fighters who had been inactive for well over a year. Starting strongly, Bundrage charged into Spinks from the opening bell, and had the challenger been more accurate with his blows the fight would undoubtedly ended very quickly. Not a shadow of his former self, his southpaw stance making him an easy target, when Spinks was dropped on to the ring apron in the fifth and made it up at 'eight' the referee stopped the contest at 1.28 of the session after he had stumbled.

13 November 2010. Manny Pacquiao w pts 12 Antonio Margarito.
Venue: Cowboys Stadium, Arlington, Texas, USA. **Recognition:** WBC. **Referee:** Laurence Cole.
Scorecards: 119-109, 120-108, 118-110.
Fight Summary: This one was contested for the vacant title after Vernon Forrest had been stripped and his successor, Sergio Martinez, who had been handed the belt, decided to move up a division without making a defence. Having won a WBC 112lbs title back in 1997, Pacquiao (144¾) added the 154lbs crown to his collection when winning virtually every round against the tough Margarito (150), his speed around the ring and southpaw stance being too much for the latter. There were no knockdowns, but Margarito, who was cut up and swollen on both eyes at the final bell, looked like he had been in a car crash. The CompuBox stats showed that Pacquiao landed 474 punches to 229 in what was an outstanding output against a seven-inch taller opponent.

With no ambitions to defend the WBC Belt, when Pacquiao was stripped on 8 February 2011 a ready-made fight between Saul Alvarez and the European welterweight champion, Matthew Hatton, was given title status despite the latter not being rated.

5 March 2011. Saul Alvarez w pts 12 Matthew Hatton.
Venue: Honda Centre, Anaheim, California, USA. **Recognition:** WBC. **Referee:** Lou Moret.
Scorecards: 120-108, 120-108, 120-108.
Fight Summary: Contested for the vacant title after Manny Pacquiao handed the belt back without making a defence, Alvarez (151½) had too much of everything for Hatton (149¾). Although the Mexican did not lose a round on the cards despite being docked a point in the seventh when going low, it should not detract from Hatton's performance. Even though Alvarez continually stalked Hatton, throwing solid, accurate bows from both hands, the latter was always ready to engage and was never off his feet. Cut on the left eye in the fourth, Hatton showed his toughness both mentally and physically when remaining in the fight against the odds, his career enhanced.

12 March 2011. Miguel Cotto w rsc 12 Ricardo Mayorga.
Venue: MGM Grand, Las Vegas, Nevada, USA. **Recognition:** WBA. **Referee:** Robert Byrd.
Fight Summary: Getting away well with the jab while Mayorga (154) looked to throw blows from both hands, the champion controlled the fight when outboxing the latter and working for three minutes each round. Mayorga

came with a rush in the seventh and ninth when scoring solidly, but Cotto (154) came back hard in the next two sessions to take the play away from the Nicaraguan. The fight came to an end in the 12th after Mayorga was dropped heavily by a left hook to the jaw as he rushed in blindly and, although getting up, he was being battered along the ropes when signalling that he was through for the night. At that point, 53 seconds into the session, the referee came to his aid.

On 11 June, at the Miguel Barragan Auditorium, San Luis Potosi, Mexico, Austin Trout retained his WBA 'second tier' title when outpointing David Lopez over 12 rounds.

Anthony Mundine outpointed Rigoberto Alvarez over 12 rounds to win the WBA 'interim' title at the Entertainment Centre, Newcastle, Australia on 19 October.

Trout went on to defend the 'second tier' title when stopping Frank LoPorto in the sixth round at the Cohen Stadium, El Paso, Texas, USA on 11 November.

Mundine forfeited his title in early May 2012 when refusing to take on the WBA 'second tier' champion, Trout.

18 June 2011. Saul Alvarez w rsc 12 Ryan Rhodes.
Venue: Vicente Fernandez Garcia Arena, Tlajomulco De Zuniga, Mexico. **Recognition:** WBC. **Referee:** Hector Afu.
Fight Summary: The champion started as he meant to carry on against the switch-hitting Rhodes (152½), a southpaw by trade, when looking to bang solid right hands through the middle to bring the latter down. With Rhodes trapped on the ropes in the fourth one such punch following a two-handed battering put him down. Although finding his feet and trying to fight back Rhodes was rarely able to keep Alvarez (153¼) at bay, and in the seventh he was showing signs of battle with damage under both eyes before being pushed over. From thereon in it was one-way traffic. Sensing that he had his man going at the start of the 12th, Alvarez poured in the punches with not much coming back until the referee stepped in after the towel had been thrown in by Rhodes' corner, 48 seconds into the session.

25 June 2011. Cornelius Bundrage w pts 12 Sechew Powell.
Venue: Family Arena, St Charles, Missouri, USA. **Recognition:** IBF. **Referee:** Ernie Sharif.
Scorecards: 119-109, 117-111, 115-113.
Fight Summary: Looking to avenge a stoppage defeat at the hands of Powell (152½) back in 2005, Bundrage (152¼) took the fight to his southpaw challenger from the opening bell and before too long both men were slogging it out with rare abandon. Not only that, but there was such animosity between them that there were hardly any jabs thrown. There were no knockdowns, but plenty of holding made it a fight to forget. Carrying a swelling under his right eye, Bundrage, who always appeared to be in command of this untidy affair, finished the contest moving in-and-out with the jab before closing it with some heavy shots immediately prior to the final bell.

17 September 2011. Saul Alvarez w rsc 6 Alfonso Gomez.
Venue: Staples Centre, Los Angeles, California, USA. **Recognition:** WBC. **Referee:** Wayne Hedgpeth.
Fight Summary: Regardless of all the bad talking beforehand, Alvarez (153¾) quickly got down to work when dropping his challenger in the opening round with a solid left jab. Although Gomez (152¾) came back strongly in the second, Alvarez picked it up in the third when banging in lefts and rights before going on to control the contest. Having hurt Gomez in the sixth with a right uppercut, when Alvarez followed up with some heavy blows from both hands the referee stopped the contest on the 2.15 mark with many feeling that the former should have been given more time.

26 November 2011. Saul Alvarez w rsc 5 Kermit Cintron.
Venue: Monumental Bullring, Mexico City, Mexico. **Recognition:** WBC. **Referee:** Hector Afu.
Fight Summary: Both men made reasonable starts, but by the third it could be seen that the heavy-handed champion was beginning to hurt Cintron (154). Towards the end of the fourth Alvarez (154) finally struck when a big right over the top dropped Cintron heavily, and although the latter got up at 'nine' and tried to fight back the

end of the round saw him in trouble on the ropes. The fight ended when the referee stepped in at 2.53 of the fifth to rescue Cintron after he had been wobbled in a session that saw many heavy shots being landed by both fighters.

3 December 2011. Miguel Cotto w rsc 9 Antonio Margarito.
Venue: Madison Square Garden, Manhattan, NYC, New York, USA. **Recognition:** WBA. **Referee:** Steve Smoger.
Fight Summary: Gaining revenge for a 2008 stoppage defeat at the hands of Margarito (152½) in controversial circumstances, the champion was on top most of the way in this one as he marched to a ninth-round stoppage win. With his suspect right eye starting to swell in the third, when Margarito urged Cotto (152¼) to do his worst that is just what the latter did, left hooks and jabs damaging the Mexican's features the more the fight went on. Continuing to miss with much of what he threw, by the ninth the still advancing Margarito was being picked off and blasted by Cotto, and at the end of the session following a long discussion with the ringside doctor the fight was halted by the referee. Although Margarito's corner pleaded for just one more round it was not to be.

5 May 2012. Floyd Mayweather Jnr w pts 12 Miguel Cotto.
Venue: MGM Grand, Las Vegas, Nevada, USA. **Recognition:** WBA. **Referee:** Tony Weeks.
Scorecards: 117-111, 117-111, 118-111.
Fight Summary: With the champion on the attack from the opening bell, looking to crank up the pressure, the plan was obviously to give the four-weight champion, Mayweather (151), as little room to work in as possible. Showing an exceptional defence, Mayweather avoided much of what was coming his way before hitting back with solid blows as Cotto (154) came forward. Although Mayweather won most of the rounds on the cards he could not relax for one moment, especially in the sixth and eighth when Cotto outscored him. The punch of the contest was a tremendous left uppercut in the final session that Cotto survived, and he was still there at the final bell fighting his heart out.

On 2 June, Austin Trout successfully defended his WBA 'second tier' title when outpointing Delvin Rodriguez over 12 rounds at the Home Depot Centre, Carson, California. Trout made a further successful defence of the 'second tier' title on 1 December when outpointing Cotto over 12 rounds at Madison Square Garden, Manhattan, NYC, New York.

The vacant WBA 'interim' title was decided when Erislandy Lara stopped Alfredo Angelo in the tenth round of their contest at the Home Depot Centre, Carson, California on 8 June 2013.

5 May 2012. Saul Alvarez w pts 12 Shane Mosley.
Venue: MGM Grand, Las Vegas, Nevada, USA. **Recognition:** WBC. **Referee:** Jay Nady.
Scorecards: 119-109, 118-110, 119-109.
Fight Summary: Up against the 40-year-old Mosley (154), the young champion showed off his impressive ability against a man who was a top amateur boxer way before he was born. Although Alvarez (154) won with plenty to spare it was still competitive until the older man tired. Cut by the left eye from an accidental clash of heads in the third Alvarez was never perturbed, and as the fight wore on he was handing out plenty of stick as Mosley tried to stay in the contest. Particularly impressive was Alvarez's work to the body, while his all-round game showed much improvement. According to CompuBox, he landed 348 blows to Mosley's 183 despite the latter throwing more.

12 May 2012. Zaurbek Baysangurov w pts 12 Michel Soro.
Venue: Terminal Ice Palace, Brovari, Ukraine. **Recognition:** WBO. **Referee:** Mickey Vann.
Scorecards: 116-111, 117-111, 115-112.
Fight Summary: Making his first defence of the title that was handed to him after Serhiy Dzinziruk was stripped, Baysangurov (153¾) got away quickly before being surprised, hurt and dropped by a big left that seemed to come from nowhere. Despite coming back strongly to take the play away from Soro (154), the Russian was forced to fight off a resurgent opponent in the middle sessions when coming under pressure from solid combinations. Picking it up again in the eighth, when Baysangurov banged in heavy body blows that took away Soro's legs the fight was his as the less experienced challenger tired.

30 June 2012. Cornelius Bundrage w rsc 7 Cory Spinks.
Venue: Fantasy Springs Casino, Indio, California, USA. **Recognition:** IBF. **Referee:** Ray Corona.
Fight Summary: In what was a return fight the 39-year-old champion proved that his previous win over Spinks (153¾) was no fluke when he repeated the exercise, only this time it was inside the distance. Starting strongly, Bundrage (153½) dropped his southpaw challenger with a big right to the head in the first and generally roughed his foe up as the contest continued. Although Spinks came back to pick up rounds with the jab he was never in control, and when he came under fire from Bundrage in the seventh, after going down twice from solid rights to the head, the referee called matters off at 2.32 of the session when he fell down.

15 September 2012. Saul Alvarez w rsc 5 Josesito Lopez.
Venue: MGM Grand, Las Vegas, Nevada, USA. **Recognition:** WBC. **Referee:** Joe Cortez.
Fight Summary: Too big and too powerful for the challenger, after a feeling-out round Alvarez (154) came back from a heavy shot in the second before dropping his rival with a tremendous left hook to the body towards the end of the session. When Alvarez repeated the exercise with the same blow in the third, Lopez (153) was right up against it. Still on the front foot Alvarez dropped Lopez in the fourth with a cracking right to the jaw and, although the latter got up and fought on spiritedly, when he was driven into a corner in the fifth and was being pounded incessantly the referee rescued him with five seconds of the session remaining.

6 October 2012. Zaurbek Baysangurov w pts 12 Lukas Konecny.
Venue: Sports Palace, Kiev, Ukraine. **Recognition:** WBO. **Referee:** Genaro Rodriguez.
Scorecards: 119-109, 117-111, 118-110.
Fight Summary: Despite starting well and having an especially strong second round, Konecny (153¾) was soon pegged back as the champion began to control matters with the jab and solid uppercuts. Even though Konecny appeared to be landing the cleaner, harder shots throughout it was Baysangurov (152½) who was picking up the points on the judges' scorecards. There were those who though Konecny deserved more from the contest than just two rounds, but ultimately it was not to be.

Due to defend the WBO title against Demetrius Andrade, Baysangurov was forced to pull out when injuring his back in training. On 18 June 2013 the WBO announced that Baysangurov had relinquished the title and that Andrade would be meeting Vanes Martirosyan to decide the vacancy. They went on to say that once fully fit Baysangurov would be given the opportunity to win his old title back.

23 February 2013. Ishe Smith w pts 12 Cornelius Bundrage.
Venue: Masonic Temple, Detroit, Michigan, USA. **Recognition:** IBF. **Referee:** Sam Williams.
Scorecards: 116-111, 116-111, 114-114.
Fight Summary: Coming back from a career that had been on the slide, Smith (152½) shocked the champion when winning the majority decision in a fight that was hardly one for the purist. Bundrage (152¾) never really got going, and in the second after knocking Smith down with a blow to the back of the head he was deducted a point for then hitting him while on the floor. The fight really turned in the fourth when Smith smashed in a heavy round-hand counter that hurt Bundrage, who then dropped six of the next seven rounds when going on the back foot. Decidedly messy towards the end, with both men throwing wild blows, Smith picked it up when pushing Bundrage to the ropes and making sure of the win.

20 April 2013. Saul Alvarez w pts 12 Austin Trout.
Venue: The Alamodome, San Antonio, Texas, USA. **Recognition:** WBC/The Ring. **Referee:** Laurence Cole.
Scorecards: 115-112, 118-109, 118-111.
Fight Summary: Apart from Trout's WBA 'second tier' title and Alvarez's WBC crown being on the line, *The Ring* Championship Belt was also up for grabs in this one. With height and reach advantages in his favour Trout (153¾) got away well, his southpaw jab keeping Alvarez (153½) at bay to some degree, but before too long the latter was closing the distance to get his heavier shots off. As far as the cards were concerned Alvarez was always in front, although he had not landed enough on Trout to discourage him. That all changed in the seventh, however, when a straight right to the jaw sent Trout down, and although the latter got up and fought back from thereon in it was all Alvarez.

14 September 2013. Carlos Molina w pts 12 Ishe Smith.
Venue: MGM Grand, Las Vegas, Nevada, USA. **Recognition:** IBF. **Referee:** Jay Nady.
Scorecards: 116-112, 117-111, 112-116.
Fight Summary: According to CompuBox there were more than 700 punches thrown by both men, the vast majority of them being ineffectual. In what was a contest that will hardly be remembered, the champion was unable to raise his game against Molina (153), who did enough to convince two of the judges that he was the better man. Although Molina scored with measured blows and Smith threw flurries in virtually every round in an effort to impress the judges it was a tough one to score. Following the contest there were many disgruntled fans who thought Smith should have been given the decision as he appeared to land the higher percentage, but at the end of the day there were few shots of note delivered by either man.

14 September 2013. Floyd Mayweather Jnr w pts 12 Saul Alvarez.
Venue: MGM Grand, Las Vegas, Nevada, USA. **Recognition:** WBA/WBC/The Ring. **Referee**: Kenny Bayless.
Scorecards: 116-112, 117-111, 114-114.
Fight Summary: With Mayweather's WBA title and Alvarez's two championship belts on the line it was all to fight for. Although Alvarez (152) did well, the experienced Mayweather (150½) was just too good for him, his jabs and superb movement being too difficult to match. As Mayweather ran up the rounds it was only when he backed off in the latter sessions that Alvarez got into the fight, but even then the latter was forced to take some heavy uppercuts and right hands in return for his pressing. Announced as a majority points win for Mayweather, when it was clearly a hands-down victory, the judge who made it a draw had to ride out the volume of criticism that came his way in the aftermath.

On 7 December, Erislandy Lara, the WBA 'interim' champion, won the vacant WBA 'second tier' title when outpointing Austin Trout over 12 rounds at the Barclays Centre, Brooklyn, NYC, New York.

9 November 2013. Demetrius Andrade w pts 12 Vanes Martirosyan.
Venue: American Bank Centre, Corpus Christi, Texas, USA. **Recognition:** WBO. **Referee:** Jon Schorle.
Scorecards: 114-113, 117-110, 112-115.
Fight Summary: Contested for the title that Zaurbek Baysangurov forfeited, it was Andrade (153¼), a southpaw, who won the title despite being knocked over by a cracking left hook in the opener. Taking a round to recover Andrade came back well as Martirosyan (153¾) stood off while looking to land a finishing blow, but both men were guilty of standing back and not pressing enough throughout. Although the scores were somewhat disparate, the belt was Andrade's when he took the last four sessions on all three cards.

14 June 2014. Demetrius Andrade w rsc 7 Brian Rose.
Venue: Barclays Centre, Brooklyn, NYC, New York, USA. **Recognition:** WBO. **Referee:** Michael Griffin.
Fight Summary: Starting on the front foot the champion had Rose (153½) over from a southpaw straight left in the opening round and again in the third when a long right to the temple had the Englishman in dire trouble. Although Rose fought on bravely he was being outclassed by Andrade (153¾), who could have stepped it up had he wished. However, having pushed on in the sixth, Andrade went for Rose in the seventh with a vengeance, and after battering the latter to the ropes and banging in many hurtful punches the referee stopped the contest at 1.19 of the session. This followed Rose's corner intimating that they wanted their man out of it.

Andrade was stripped of the WBO title at the end of July 2015, having been inactive for close on 14 months.

13 September 2014. Floyd Mayweather Jnr w pts 12 Marcos Maidana.
Venue: MGM Grand, Las Vegas, Nevada, USA. **Recognition:** WBA/WBC/The Ring. **Referee:** Kenny Bayless.
Scorecards: 116-111, 116-111, 115-112.
Fight Summary: Having already successfully defended his WBA/WBC and *Ring* welterweight Championship Belts against Maidana, this return match that was billed for the same titles was also surprisingly seen by the WBC as involving Mayweather's 154lbs crown. Because of that I have also shown the WBA and *The Ring* under 'Recognition' as it could well have affected the rest of Mayweather's title claims had he lost. Yet again a relatively tough fight, the champion being forced to work at all times, Maidana (146) was always there or thereabouts.

Although Mayweather (146½) was by far the better boxer, Maidana was always trying to rough him up even though he was forced to take some heavy shots in return. In the ninth Mayweather complained that Maidana had bitten into his left glove, hurting his fingers and numbing his hand from thereon in. When Mayweather was blatantly pushed over in the tenth a point was deducted from Maidana's total, which only made the latter even wilder. Following a wild right that hurt Mayweather, and with blows being tossed in from all angles, the champion calmly boxed his way through to the final bell without putting himself in the firing line.

Erislandy Lara made his first defence of the WBA 'second tier' title when outpointing Ishe Smith over 12 rounds on 12 December at The Alamodome, San Antonio, Texas, USA. He then made further successful defences against Delvin Rodriguez (w pts 12 at the UIC Pavilion, Chicago, Illinois, USA on 12 June 2015) and Jan Zaveck (w rsc 3 at the Park Racing & Casino, Hialeah, Florida, USA on 25 November 2015).

At the Festival Hall, Frankfurt, Germany, on 9 May 2015, Jack Culcay outpointed Maurice Weber over 12 rounds to win the vacant WBA 'interim' title.

Mayweather forfeited *The Ring* Championship Belt on 11 August 2015, having not fought at 154lbs since beating Alvarez almost two years earlier, while the WBC eventually accepted his retirement on 4 November 2015 and vacated the title. In January 2016 the WBA finally removed Mayweather as champion, leaving Lara as their top man.

Culcay successfully defended the WBA 'interim' title when outpointing Dennis Hogan over 12 rounds at the Island Park Hall, Wilhelmsburg, Hamburg, Germany on 5 December 2015 and then defeated Jean Carlos Prada (w rtd 9 at the MBS Arena, Potsdam, Brandenburg, Germany on 9 April 2016). Following his win over Prada, Culcay was upgraded to second-tier status.

11 October 2014. Cornelius Bundrage w pts 12 Carlos Molina.
Venue: Oasis Hotel Complex, Cancun, Quintana Roo, Mexico. **Recognition:** IBF. **Referee:** Kenny Chevalier.
Scorecards: 117-106, 117-109, 117-110.
Fight Summary: In a return and a reversal of fortunes, Bundrage (154) regained his old title from the man who took it from him when being awarded the unanimous decision, despite losing a point in the eighth for punching behind the head. Clearly, Bundrage had done his homework this time round, and after getting away fast he dropped Molina (152¾) with a straight right to the head after hurting the latter with a big overarm right. Although Molina came back well he could never fully keep Bundrage at bay, being hurt on several occasions before being floored in the tenth following some heavy rights to the head. From thereon in Molina had little left, while Bundrage, who was worn out from his exertions, kept out of trouble until the final bell.

12 September 2015. Jermall Charlo w co 3 Cornelius Bundrage.
Venue: Foxwoods Resort, Mashantucket, Connecticut, USA. **Recognition:** IBF. **Referee:** John Callas.
Fight Summary: The championship changed hands in this one when Bundrage (153) was dropped in the opening round by a right to the head as Charlo (153) looked to impose himself on his opponent quickly. Although Bundrage got to his feet he was soon in trouble again, another big right flooring him in the second, and while he came back swinging he was no match for the younger, quicker Charlo. It was all over in the third after Bundrage had been knocked over twice by heavy rights, the referee rescuing him at 2.33 of the session.

10 October 2015. Liam Smith w rsc 7 John Thompson.
Venue: The Arena, Manchester, England. **Recognition:** WBO. **Referee:** Marcus McDonnell.
Fight Summary: Fighting for the title that was vacated after Demetrius Andrade was stripped, Smith (153½) ultimately took full advantage of the opportunity even though Thompson (152¼) won the opening two rounds by dint of his long left jab. Once Smith had found his distance with some powerful body shots he was more than happy to let Thompson burn energy on the back foot prior to opening up in the sixth with bursts of heavy shots. Having gone back to his corner shakily, Thompson came out for the seventh only to be tracked down as Smith looked to finish it. After being wrestled to the canvas, when Thompson got up he was soon in difficulty as Smith

went gunning for him. Following two or three heavy rights to the head the American went down before being rescued by the referee on the 1.44 mark halfway through the count.

28 November 2015. Jermall Charlo w rsc 4 Wilky Campfort.
Venue: Bomb Factory, Dallas, Texas, USA. **Recognition:** IBF. **Referee:** Mark Colo-Oy.
Fight Summary: Putting his title on the line for the first time, Charlo (154) went through a feeling-out process before dropping Campfort (153¼) with a solid left jab in the second. Even though Campfort gamely continued to come forward he was on borrowed time, and when a left hook followed by a right uppercut smashed him down in the third the end was nigh despite him making it to the bell. The finish came in the fourth when the referee stopped the contest at 1.16 after Campfort went down complaining that his right eye was giving him trouble, having been caught by a left uppercut.

19 December 2015. Liam Smith w rsc 7 Jimmy Kilrain Kelly.
Venue: The Arena, Manchester, England. **Recognition:** WBO. **Referee:** Marcus McDonnell.
Fight Summary: Defending his title for the first time, it was clear from the start that Smith (154) was too good for the game Kelly (153) who was caught and hurt in virtually every round. Under pressure all the way, Kelly had two points deducted in the sixth when charging into Smith head-first before being rescued in the next session. Having gone on the rampage in the seventh, Smith dropped Kelly with a solid left and, although the referee ruled it a slip, on seeing that the latter's corner wanted the fight to end he called a halt on the 2.35 mark.

21 May 2016. Erislandy Lara w pts 12 Vanes Martirosyan.
Venue: The Cosmopolitan, Las Vegas, Nevada, USA. **Recognition:** WBA. **Referee:** Vic Drakulich.
Scorecards: 116-111, 116-111, 115-112.
Fight Summary: Making the first defence of the full WBA title he inherited on Floyd Mayweather's retirement, Lara (153½) gained revenge over Martirosyan (153¾), having drawn with his opponent nearly four years earlier. Although Martirosyan targeted the body and looked to make a fight of it, Lara scored with southpaw jabs on the outside as he made for an elusive target while doing just enough to deserve the unanimous decision. The points totals would have been closer still had the hard-working Martirosyan not been docked a point in the 11th for going low.

21 May 2016. Jermall Charlo w pts 12 Austin Trout.
Venue: The Cosmopolitan, Las Vegas, Nevada, USA. **Recognition:** IBF. **Referee:** Russell Mora.
Scorecards: 116-112, 116-112, 115-113.
Fight Summary: Up against a former WBA champion in Trout (154) the current IBF title holder once again showed his mettle in what turned out to be a hard-fought, close contest. While Trout boxed mainly on the outside using his southpaw jab to good effect, Charlo (153¼) went looking for the one punch that would end matters there and then. Although outboxed at times, Charlo always hit back hard, and in the penultimate round a left uppercut to the jaw almost had Trout over. There was never that much between them, but ultimately it was Charlo's heavier blows that won the day.

21 May 2016. Jermell Charlo w co 6 John Jackson.
Venue: The Cosmopolitan, Las Vegas, Nevada, USA. **Recognition:** WBC. **Referee:** Tony Weeks.
Fight Summary: Contesting the vacant title following Floyd Mayweather's retirement, it was Jermall's twin brother, Jermell, who also became a world champion when stopping Jackson (153½), the son of former champion, Julian Jackson, after 51 seconds of the eighth round. Jackson made the better start, winning the opening four rounds with his classy boxing and, although dropping the fifth as Charlo hit back, he was well clear coming into the eighth. The fight was then turned on its head after Jackson, stunned by solid lefts and rights to the head, turned away from Charlo before the referee stepped in after the Virgin Islander was sent crashing into the strands.

4 June 2016. Liam Smith w co 2 Predrag Radosevic.
Venue: Echo Arena, Liverpool, England. **Recognition:** WBO. **Referee:** Steve Gray.
Fight Summary: Getting away fast the champion racked Radosevic (153) with several solid body shots in the opener before setting about the latter in the second. Recognising that Radosevic was there for the taking, Smith

(154) was quickly at his man with blows from both hands, and following a further left hand to the body the Montenegrin was counted out at 1.34 of the session while trying to get the wind back in his sails.

17 September 2016. Saul Alvarez w co 9 Liam Smith.
Venue: AT&T Stadium, Arlington, Texas, USA. **Recognition:** WBO. **Referee:** Luis Pabon.
Fight Summary: This fight proved to be one step too far for the champion who was up against one of the best pound-for-pound fighters around in Alvarez (154). Although Smith (154) made a good start, his accurate blows finding their target, all the while it was Alvarez who was in front, his fast hands inflicting pain. By the sixth an old wound over Smith's right eye had reopened, and in the seventh he was dropped by a right hand that landed behind the left ear. Back in action, Smith saw the round out, only to be dropped again in the eighth by a solid left to the body. Making a valiant effort to get up Smith somehow made it into the ninth before another smashing left to the ribs sent him crashing for the third time, the referee counting him out on the 2.28 mark.

Junior Middleweight Boxers' Index:

(Country of birth where known/Domicile - birthplace and domicile are the same unless stated)

A

Louis Acaries (Algeria/France)
Oscar Albarado (USA)
Joachim Alcine (Haiti/Canada)
Wayne Alexander (England)
Robert Allen (USA)
Rigoberto Alvarez (Mexico)
Saul Alvarez (Mexico)
Ron Amundsen (USA)
Alvin Anderson (USA)
Demetrius Andrade (USA)
Alfredo Angelo (Mexico/USA)
Alfredo Angulo (Mexico/USA)
Lupe Aquino (Mexico/USA)
Humberto Aranda (Costa Rica)
Enrique Areco (Argentina)
Aquilino Asprilla (Panama)
Marco Antonio Avendano (Venezuela)
Tony Ayala (USA)

B

In-Chul Baek (South Korea)
Larry Baker (USA)
Mike Baker (USA)
Carlos Baldomir (Argentina)
Gilbert Baptist (USA)
Larry Barnes (USA)
Zaurbek Baysangurov (Russia/Ukraine)
Jimmy Beecham (USA)
Marijan Benes (Serbia/Bosnia)
Wilfred Benitez (USA/Puerto Rico)
Nino Benvenuti (Slovenia/Italy)
Silvano Bertini (Italy)
Bushy Bester (South Africa)
Monty Betham (Samoa/New Zealand)
Ensley Bingham (England)
Maurice Blocker (USA)
Carlos Bojorquez (Mexico/USA)
Carmelo Bossi (Italy)
Laurent Boudouani (France)
David Braxton (USA)
Simon Brown (Jamaica)
Cornelius Bundrage (USA)
Alex Bunema (DR Congo/USA)

C

Jack Callahan (USA)
Hector Camacho (Puerto Rico/USA)
Martin Camara (France)

Luis Ramon Campas (Mexico/USA)
Wilky Campfort (Haiti/USA)
Juan Carlos Candelo (Colombia/USA)
Santos Cardona (Puerto Rico)
Rubin Carter (USA)
Miguel Castellini (Argentina)
Javier Castillejo (Spain)
Diego Castillo (Colombia)
Jorge Castro (Argentina)
Jermall Charlo (USA)
Jermell Charlo (USA)
Carlos Chavez (USA)
Hacine Cherifi (France)
Tony Chiaverini (USA)
Chris Christensen (Denmark)
Davide Ciarlante (Italy)
Kermit Cintron (Puerto Rico/USA)
Howard Clarke (England)
Everaldo Costa Azevedo (Brazil/Italy)
Miguel Cotto (USA/Puerto Rico)
Jack Culcay (Ecuador/Germany)
Donald Curry (USA)

D

Eckhard Dagge (Germany)
Kevin Daigle (USA)
Carl Daniels (USA)
Aaron Davis (USA)
Henry Davis (Hawaii)
Daniel Dawson (Australia)
Francisco De Jesus (Brazil)
Oscar De La Hoya (USA)
Miguel De Oliveira (Brazil)
Gilbert Dele (Guadeloupe/France)
Paddy DeMarco (USA)
Adrian Dodson (Guyana/USA)
Matt Donovan (Trinidad/USA)
Akhmet Dottuev (Russia)
Buster Drayton (USA)
Ralph Dupas (USA)
Tony Dupas (USA)
Jose Manuel Duran (Spain)
Juan Carlos Duran (Argentina/Italy)
Roberto Duran (Panama)
Serhiy Dzinziruk (Russia/Germany)

E

Carlos Elliott (USA/Japan)
Romallis Ellis (USA)

F
Kevin Finnegan (England)
Jose Flores (Mexico/USA)
Yuri Foreman (Belarus/USA)
Vernon Forrest (USA)
Steve Foster (England)
Pierre Fourie (South Africa)
Rocky Fratto (USA)
Robert Frazier (USA)

G
Casey Gacic (Germany/USA)
Johnny Gant (USA)
Alejandro Garcia (Mexico)
Tony Gardner (USA)
Joe Gatti (Canada/Mexico)
Eddie Gazo (Nicaragua)
Joey Giambra (USA)
Alfonso Gomez (Mexico)
David Gonzalez (USA)
Manuel Gonzalez (Argentina 1973-79)
Manuel Gonzalez (USA 1957-74)
Clyde Gray (Canada)
Julio Cesar Green (Dominican Republic/USA)
Steve Gregory (USA)
Emile Griffith (Virgin Islands/USA)
Gary Guiden (USA)

H
Marvin Hagler (USA)
Earl Hargrove (USA)
Stan Harrington (Hawaii)
Matthew Hatton (England)
Stanley Hayward (USA)
Thomas Hearns (USA)
Steve Hearon (USA)
Angel Hernandez Gonzalez (Spain)
Art Hernandez (USA)
Ferd Hernandez (USA)
Jose Hernandez (Spain)
Carlos Herrera (Argentina)
Matthew Hilton (Canada)
Robert Hines (USA)
Dennis Hogan (Ireland/Australia)
Maurice Hope (Antigua/England)
Fred Hutchings (USA)
Jun-Suk Hwang (South Korea)

I
Nobuhiro Ishida (Japan)

J
John Jackson (Virgin Islands)
John David Jackson (USA)
Julian Jackson (Virgin Islands/USA)
Rene Jacquot (France)
Kofi Jantuah (Ghana/USA)
Guillermo Jones (Panama)
Paul Jones (England)
Rodney Jones (USA)
Ho Joo (South Korea)
Joel Julio (Colombia/USA)

K
Rocky Kalingo (Philippines)
Ayub Kalule (Uganda/Denmark)
Hitoshi Kamiyama (Japan)
Roman Karmazin (Russia/USA)
Jimmy Kilrain Kelly (England)
Kevin Kelly (Australia)
Ki-Soo Kim (North Korea/South Korea)
Lukas Konecny (Czech Republic)
Masashi Kudo (Japan)

L
Brett Lally (USA)
Erislandy Lara (Cuba/USA)
Salim Larbi (France/USA)
Deandre Latimore (USA)
Pat Lawlor (USA)
Mick Leahy (Ireland/England)
Roger Leonard (USA)
Sugar Ray Leonard (USA)
Michael Lerma (USA)
Jimmy Lester (USA)
Jae-Keum Lim (South Korea)
Freddie Little (USA)
Steve Little (USA)
Jaime Llanes (Mexico)
Isaac Logart (Cuba/USA)
David Lopez (Mexico)
Josesito Lopez (USA)
Frank LoPorto (Australia)
David Love (USA)
Kevin Lueshing (England)
Sebastian Andres Lujan (Argentina)

M
Marcos Maidana (Argentina)
Mario Maldonado (USA)
Fortunato Manca (Italy)
Sean Mannion (Ireland/USA)
Antonio Margarito (USA/Mexico)
Raul Marquez (Mexico/USA)

Tony Marshall (Guyana/USA)
Javier Martinez Rodriguez (Spain)
Sergio Martinez (Argentina/USA)
Vanes Martirosyan (Armenia/USA)
Michele Mastrodonato (Italy)
Rocky Mattioli (Italy/Australia)
Ricardo Mayorga (Nicaragua)
Floyd Mayweather Jnr (USA)
Sandro Mazzinghi (Italy)
Mike McCallum (Jamaica/USA)
Milton McCrory (USA)
Bronco McKart (USA)
Mark Medal (USA)
Juan Ramon Medina (Dominican Republic/Spain)
Luca Messi (Italy)
Joe Miceli (USA)
Tadashi Mihara (Japan)
Hisao Minami (Japan)
Luigi Minchillo (Italy)
Mike Miranda (Brazil)
Masahiro Misako (Japan)
Carlos Molina (Mexico/USA)
Tony Montano (USA)
Davey Moore (USA)
Sergio Mora (USA)
L. C. Morgan (USA)
Shane Mosley (USA)
Alfonso Mosquera (Panama)
Denny Moyer (USA)
John Mugabi (Uganda/USA)
Keith Mullings (Jamaica/USA)
Anthony Mundine (Australia)

N
Alisultan Nadirbegov (Russia)
Carlos Nascimento (Brazil)
Terry Norris (USA)
Ricardo Raul Nunez (Argentina)

O
Elisha Obed (Bahamas)
Gaspar Ortega (Mexico)
Pedro Ortega (Mexico)
Kassim Ouma (Uganda/USA)
Milton Owens (USA)

P
Eddie Pace (USA)
Manny Pacquiao (Philippines)
Jason Papillion (USA)
Vinny Pazienza (USA)
Vincent Pettway (USA)
Verno Phillips (Belize/USA)

Gerhard Piaskowy (Germany)
Armand Picar (Philippines)
Michele Piccirillo (Italy)
Sechew Powell (USA)
Jean Carlos Prada (Venezuela/USA)
Chris Pyatt (England)

Q
Ike Quartey (Ghana/USA)

R
Predrag Radosevic (Montenegro)
Rip Randall (USA)
Michael Rask (Denmark)
David Reid (USA)
Ryan Rhodes (England)
Alex Rios (USA)
Jose Antonio Rivera (USA)
Paolo Roberto (Sweden)
Sea Robinson (Ivory Coast)
Sugar Ray Robinson (USA)
Rudy Robles (USA)
Delvin Rodriguez (Dominican Republic/USA)
Brian Rose (England)
Gianfranco Rosi (Italy)
Edgar Ross (USA)
Nick Rupa (Trinidad/Canada)

S
Leo Saenz (USA)
Santiago Samaniego (Panama/USA)
Luis Santana (Dominican Republic)
Carlos Santos (Puerto Rico)
Daniel Santos (Puerto Rico)
Charley Scott (USA)
Sugar Ray Seales (Virgin Islands/USA)
Kenji Shibata (Japan)
James Shuler (USA)
Travis Simms (USA)
Harry Simon (Namibia)
Said Skouma (Morocco/France)
Charley Tombstone Smith (USA)
Ishe Smith (USA)
Liam Smith (England)
Ryu Sorimachi (Japan)
Michel Soro (Ivory Coast/France)
Cory Spinks (USA)
Marlon Starling (USA)
Anthony Stephens (USA)
Murray Sutherland (Scotland/USA)

T

Mehrdud Takaloo (Iran/England)
Meldrick Taylor (USA)
Gabe Terronez (USA)
Mamadou Thiam (Senegal/France)
Duane Thomas (USA)
John Thompson (USA)
Ross Thompson (USA)
Domenico Tiberia (Italy)
Tyrone Trice (USA)
Felix Trinidad (Puerto Rico)
Austin Trout (USA)

U

Alejandro Ugueto (Venezuela)

V

Paul Vaden (USA)
Jorge Luis Vado (Nicaragua)
Oney Valdez (Colombia)
Darrin Van Horn (USA)
Julio Cesar Vasquez (Argentina)
Chico Vejar (USA)

Emiliano Villa (Colombia)

W

Koichi Wajima (Japan)
Troy Waters (England/Australia)
Maurice Weber (Germany)
Charlie Weir (South Africa)
Rhoshii Wells (USA)
Pernell Whitaker (USA)
Paul Williams (USA)
Frank Wissenbach (Germany)
Glenn Wolfe (USA)
Ronald Wright (USA)
Ted Wright (USA)

Y

Harry Joe Yorgey (USA)
Jae-Doo Yuh (South Korea)

Z

Victor Zalazar (Argentina)
Jan Zaveck (Slovenia/Germany)
Fulgencio Zuniga (Colombia)

Middleweight Division

The weight class can be traced back at least to 1853 when Leicestershire's Nat Langham defeated the future heavyweight champion, Tom Sayers (his only loss), under London Prize Ring Rules, prior to successfully defending the bare-knuckle crown against George Gutteridge the following year. Langham, who weighed around 155lbs, popularised the middleweight division, which effectively came into being to fill the void between lightweights and the heaviest of men.

At the start of the 1870s sparring sessions with gloves were beginning to catch on, mainly in public houses, with Bat Mullins soon being recognised as a leading exponent. This quickly developed into competitive boxing under Marquess of Queensberry Rules (MoQ Rules), with Mullins winning an English middleweight championship competition over three rounds at 154lbs when outpointing Ted Whyman (at the Jolly Butchers Public House, Camden Town, London on 11 November 1871). Mullins then went on to beat Ben Bendoff (at the Camden Arms Public House, Leicester Square, London on 14 November 1871) and Plantagenet Green (at the same venue on 12 December 1871) in what were called catchweight competitions that were open to the world. This was followed by Charley Davis winning a 161lbs championship competition when outpointing Mullins over three rounds at the Victoria Tavern, Kilburn, London on 1 February 1872. Just a week later, at 160lbs, Davis lost to Jack Hicks (who outpointed him over three rounds at the Beavers Arms Public House, Bakers Row, Whitechapel, London on 8 February 1872). Another championship competition winner, this time at 154lbs, was Bill Brooks (who outpointed Jem Stewart over five rounds at the Prince of Wales Running Grounds, Bow, London on 16 April 1872). He was followed by Davis (who won a 144lbs competition when outpointing Denny Harrington over three rounds at Jemmy Shaw's Brown Bear Public House, Soho, London on 13 May 1872).

Prior to the advent of the welterweight division in 1887, I have set the middleweight band at the start of the gloved era for those boxing between 140lbs and 166lbs. While there were many who saw men who weighed between 160 and 166lbs as heavyweights, in Britain fighters of those weights often boxed in what came to be known as 'catchweight' contests and competitions before the advent of the light-heavyweight class. These contests are included in this section.

Weight Band/Amendments
140lbs to 166lbs (1873 – 1 June 1887)
146lbs to 166lbs (This came about with the advent of the welterweight division in America and Johnny Reagan claiming the American title at 146lbs on 1 June 1887)
148lbs to 166lbs (146 to 148lbs was recognised as belonging to the welterweight division when Mysterious Billy Smith extended his claim on 24 January 1889)
148lbs to 160lbs (On 18 August 1899, Joe Choynski was matched against Australian Jim Ryan to decide the new light heavyweight title, covering men weighing between 160lbs and 170lbs)
150lbs to 160lbs (After Joe Walcott and Young Peter Jackson contested the welter title at 150lbs on 18 June 1903, the new British welterweight class also began operating up to that weight)
147lbs to 160lbs (On 11 February 1909, the NSC formally introduced their eight named weight classes, with the welterweight limit set at 147lbs and the middleweight class remaining at 160lbs)
154lbs to 160lbs (Reformed and renamed in August 1962, one of the first tasks of the WBA, formerly NBA, was to legislate for a junior middleweight class for fighters between 147 and 154lbs)

Middleweight World Championship Fights and Title Claims:

7 January 1873. (160lbs) Charley Davis w co 14 (finish) Scotty McConnell.
Venue: Albert Austin's Blomfield Street Rooms, London, England.
Fight Summary: Billed for the 160lbs Bow Cup and English championship, Davis (160) had the taller McConnell (157) down in the opening round before the latter got even in the third. The Mile End man was soon back in harness, and in the fifth he put McConnell down with a left to the side of the head. With both men tiring by the

ninth, in that session as well as the 11th Davis had his man over, but McConnell was not yet done for. However, after two even rounds Davis jumped on McConnell right at the beginning of the 14th, dropping him with a heavy right to the head before delivering the finisher when the latter attempted to get up. It was reported that Davis was badly out of condition, his best fighting weight being a good stone lighter.

Regarding championship competition winners at the weight, after Jack Madden outpointed George Hope over three rounds at the Hall of Science, St Luke's, London on 12 January 1875, Young Griffiths outscored Florrie Barnett over three rounds at the Running Grounds, Hackney Wick, London on 26 July.

Strangely, there was not another championship competition winner at the weight until Jim Kendrick outpointed Alf Mitchell over three rounds at the Waites Brewer Street Rooms, Soho, London on 26 October 1887. This was followed by Charlie Bartlett, who forced Josh Alexander to retire in the first round at the Royal Aquarium Theatre, Westminster, London on 23 February 1889.

21 April 1873. (154lbs) Charley Davis w rtd 25 (finish) Ted Napper.
Venue: Grafton Street Hall, Soho, London, England.
Fight Summary: Made at 154lbs, and thought to involve the English 148lbs title as well, Davis (147) was ultimately just too strong for his older opponent. Having dropped Davis for a short count in the 23rd, Napper (140) led off for much of the time, but in some sessions there was very little activity as the men paced themselves. No doubt Davis was biding his time, and in the 24th he had Napper down before the latter was forced to quit in the 25th. Davis was presented with the 154lbs Bow Cup on 28 April in recognition of being the English champion at the weight.

Davis continued to be recognised as the best English middleweight until outgrowing the weight class.

1 February 1877. (148lbs) Hugh Burns drew 35 (finish) Jem Goode.
Venue: McDonald's Music Hall, Hoxton, London, England. **Referee:** J. D. E. Vesey.
Fight Summary: Contested at 148lbs for a silver cup under MoQ Rules, the fight was even for the opening seven rounds before Goode took the next six due to his effective body punching. Despite one of Burns' seconds jumping into the ring in the 14th the contest continued with Goode in control until breaking his right hand in the 26th. From there onwards, with both men being exhausted, it became a severe struggle without either gaining an advantage, and at the end of the 35th they agreed to terminate the fight. According to *Bells Life* it had been the greatest glove fight seen up to that time, having lasted two hours without either man being able to totally dominate, a draw being a fair result.

Earlier, on 30 August 1875, at the Running Grounds, Hackney Wick, London, Bill Kennedy outpointed Tim Harrington to win a 148lbs championship competition.

26 October 1877. (158lbs) Jem Goode drew 29 (finish) Mickey Rees.
Venue: Saddlers Wells Theatre, Clerkenwell, London, England. **Referee:** Robert Watson.
Fight Summary: Given English 158lbs gloved championship billing according to *Bells Life* and the *Sportsman*, it was stopped by the police 25 seconds into the 29th round and declared a draw the next day. Goode (158), who had broken his right arm in the second round, was obviously relieved at the verdict which came about after Rees (158) accepted an extra £5. Before breaking his arm the man from Billingsgate had twice put Rees down with right hands, but after that he was forced to box with the left only. Although continuing to hurt Rees he was unable to repeat the trick. It was reported that Rees's backers felt that 13 years in the ring had finally caught up with him.

There was little activity at 158lbs until 1885 when England's Bill Springhall challenged the world on 18 March, having arrived in America. However, despite beating the 43-year-old George Rooke by a third-round kayo on 11 May, by early July he was back in Britain complaining that all the top men in the States, including Nonpareil Jack Dempsey, had refused to fight him.

A further lull in action at the weight was halted when Alf Ball challenged the world on 29 November 1889, stating that if there were no acceptances he would claim the 154lbs English title.

This was followed by Jim Richardson drawing with Jack Martin in a four-round championship competition at Hengler's Circus, Hull on 6 February 1890.

12 March 1878. (154lbs) Denny Harrington w co 6 (finish) George Rooke.
Venue: Royal Surrey Gardens, Camberwell, London, England. **Referee:** Charles Conquest.
Fight Summary: Reported to be for the world 154lbs title under MoQ Rules, and in 'ordinary' gloves, *Bells Life* gave Harrington at 153⅓lbs to Rooke's 150½, while others reported Harrington to be 152lbs and Rooke 151½. Although both men were born in Ireland, the latter had been living in America for some 16 years before returning to Britain 18 months previously. The fight started with what was described as hard slogging, and after Rooke was dropped flat and had got up both men went down together before the bell ended the opening session. The second through to the fifth round saw savage infighting, with each suffering from exhaustion. In the sixth after Rooke had bitten Harrington's left wrist the latter asked for a disqualification but was denied. Ordered to fight on after spectators had been ejected from the ring, the two of them went hell for leather before Rooke fell down against the ropes to be counted out.

6 April 1878. (148lbs) William McClellan w disq 16 (finish) Mike Donovan.
Venue: 13th Street Masonic Hall, Manhattan, NYC, New York, USA. **Referee:** Harry Buermeyer.
Fight Summary: Articled to be contested under MoQ Rules for the American 148lbs title, in the event it appeared to get confused with London Prize Ring Rules when lasting 30 minutes (55 minutes according to the *New York Herald*), with several rounds ending earlier than the required three minutes. The paper also tells us that 'ordinary' gloves were used. Coming into the 16th round it was clear that McClellan (148) was already badly beaten, but after he had been smashed to the floor by Donovan (140) the latter was disqualified for hitting on the break. At that point, McClellan, carrying a swollen left eye and a badly damaged nose, would have found it difficult to continue for much longer.

18 May 1878. (148lbs) Mike Donovan w disq 7 (finish) William McClellan.
Venue: 36th Street Fencing Academy, Manhattan, NYC, New York, USA. **Referee:** Billy Borst.
Fight Summary: The *New York Herald* reported the fight as being contested at 148lbs under special rules, but as in their first go there was much confusion, with the action lasting just 15 minutes (18 minutes according to the Herald) after McClellan's seconds pulled him out and got their man disqualified. The report went on to say that, contested in hard gloves, with Donovan (145) punishing McClellan (146) throughout, the latter could have been badly hurt had it carried on.

26 May 1879. (160lbs+) Denny Harrington w disq 2 (finish) Florrie Barnett.
Venue: Bermondsey Street Railway Arches, The Borough, London, England. **Referee:** J. J. Enn.
Fight Summary: Challenging Harrington (163) for the English middleweight title, Barnett (161) was disqualified at 2.10 of the second round when his seconds entered the ring to tend to his pre-fight dislocated right shoulder after he had been floored. From the onset Harrington had forced the fighting, generally getting the better of the exchanges despite having his right eye split open in the first round. Setting about his man with both hands in the second session, Harrington eventually landed a swinging left followed by a heavy right to Barnett's jaw that sent him crashing. Had his seconds not jumped into the ring, Barnett would surely have been counted out.

18 August 1879. (148lbs) Mike Donovan drew 94 (finish) William McClellan.
Venue: Platt's Hall, San Francisco, California, USA. **Referee:** William Barnes.
Fight Summary: In a fight that was articled at 148lbs, and using 'ordinary' gloves, it was declared a draw after 94 rounds (228 minutes) after being more London Prize Ring Rules than those relating to the Marquess of Queensberry. At that point the referee decided neither man had any real advantage and it was pointless to continue, a decision that caused a great deal of dissent among the backers. Fouls had been claimed several times on behalf of McClellan (147), due to Donovan (147) hitting him whilst he was on the floor, but the referee refused to listen. While both men had their moments neither had been able to find a finisher.

Further to a two-round spar with George Rooke at Terrace Gardens, Brooklyn, NYC, New York on 25 April 1881, Donovan pursued a career of boxing exhibitions with heavyweights such as John L. Sullivan, thus leaving the way clear for Rooke to claim the American title.

Rooke may well have claimed to be champion but when he met McClellan (153) at Hunter's Point, Long Island, New York on 1 December 1881, he was almost certainly in the heavyweight class. Contested in a hall belonging to the Kelly and Bliss Company, it was articled under London Prize Ring Rules using hard gloves. No weights were given or stipulated, although Rooke was thought to scale around 170lbs. Lasting seven minutes, it was called off after McClellan was knocked unconscious and had failed to come up for the fourth round. Prior to this, Rooke had recently been knocked out by Sullivan in a bare-fist fight.

Meanwhile, in Britain, there were several championship competition winners at 148lbs, such as Charlie Mitchell (who outpointed Bill Harnetty over four rounds at the King's Road Baths, Chelsea, London on 3 April 1883) and Alec Roberts (who outpointed George Cashley over three rounds at Waites Brewer Street Rooms, Soho, London on 13 April 1885). And, on 29 March 1886, after repeatedly challenging all England at 148lbs to no avail, the *Sporting Life* was reporting that Toff Wall should now be recognised as the English champion at the weight.

27 November 1879. (154lbs) Denny Harrington w disq 18 Alf Greenfield.
Venue: The Baths, Lambeth, London. **Referee:** Charlie Conquest.
Fight Summary: Supposed to have been made at 154lbs, Harrington (168) risked his title claim when taking on Greenfield (150) and coming in 18lbs heavier than his rival. Even then Harrington should have been beaten, only winning after having been hit several times while on the ropes in the 18th and successfully claiming he was fouled.

On 25 February 1880, articles were signed for a world title match between Harrington and Leicester's Tug Wilson at 154lbs, but it never took place due to police vigilance.

A few days earlier, on 18 February 1880, Jem Brock had outpointed Young Dyer over three rounds at the Somerset Arms Public House, Whitechapel, London to win an English championship competition at 154lbs.

20 January 1880. (142lbs) Jim Goodwin drew 41 (finish) Joe Thorley.
Venue: Loveday Street Argyll Rooms, Birmingham, England.
Fight Summary: Contracted for 142lbs, to a finish in gloves under MoQ Rules, the fight had barely started when Thorley (142) was dropped. However, on getting up to fight his way back there was never much between them. Round after round ensued with both men carrying severe facial damage and Goodwin (140½) suffering a sprained right hand. Still they battled on until 35 rounds were completed, but from there to the 40th hardly a blow was landed. Told to summon up everything they had left it was clear that both men were extremely weakened, and after they slumped down at the end of the 41st the referee decided upon a draw.

There was no further activity at 142lbs until 1884 when Bill Chesterfield Goode and Johnny Robinson challenged each other several times without ever getting round to deciding anything.

17 December 1880. (152/154lbs) William Sherriff w rtd 11 (finish) Denny Harrington.
Venue: Lapworth, near Solihull, England. **Referee:** Charles Bedford.
Fight Summary: Held in a meadow near the Boot Inn and recognised as a world title fight at either 152 or 154lbs, the contest went ahead under MoQ Rules, using 'ordinary' gloves. The battle commenced on high ground in a 24-foot ring, and up until the eighth round Sherriff (152) had begun to get the better of it although the game Harrington (149) appeared to be still dangerous. However, from there onwards it was all downhill for Harrington. At the conclusion of the 11th, after Harrington had been floored three times, the police, who had been watching throughout, stopped proceedings. Later that evening the referee insisted that the fight should be renewed the next day at Marston Green, but when Harrington's backers, realising that their man had little chance, refused to let him carry on the stakes were awarded to Sherriff.

337

For whatever reason, Sherriff remained inactive for nearly three years before coming back as a heavyweight and retiring in 1884.

Following this, Leicester's Tug Wilson claimed the English 154lbs title on 7 September 1881.

Men to win championship competitions at that weight were George Say (who knocked out George Cashley inside a round at the Spread Eagle Public House, Shoreditch, London on 19 December 1881), Bill Springhall (who knocked out Jack Massey inside two rounds at the St Andrew's Hall, Westminster, London on 7 November 1882), Tom Longer (who outpointed Arthur Cooper over three rounds at The Bell Public House, St Luke's London on 3 February 1883) and Jack Burke (who outpointed Massey over four rounds at the St Andrew's Hall on 14 February 1883).

On 21 February 1883, Springhall, who was now claiming the English 154lbs title, challenged all England and put down a deposit to bind a match with Burke. To further his aims at the weight, Springhall then took off for America. By July 1886, Toff Wall was reported in the *Sporting Life* as claiming the English 154lbs title, which was a surprise as he had previously fought at 148lbs.

19 November 1883. (146lbs) Bill Chesterfield Goode drew 9 (finish) Dick Roberts.
Venue: Hackney, London, England. **Referee:** Tommy Trew.
Fight Summary: Using a 12-foot ring in private rooms it was stopped when there were cries of police and the gaslights were turned out. Articled under MoQ Rules with gloves, the *Sporting Life* reported that a more determined contest for endurance had never taken place, with each round being fiercely fought. Goode (146) was beginning to get on top at the time of the stoppage, having dropped Roberts (140) twice in the seventh and once again in the eighth, but when the lights went out after 1.22 of the ninth the referee called it off, declaring that the contest would be continued at a later date.

Earlier, men who had won championship competitions at the weight were Young Johnny Walker (who outpointed George Say over three rounds at The Griffin Public House, Shoreditch, London on 20 October 1881) and Arthur Cooper (who outpointed George Roberts over three rounds at the Goldsmith Arms Public House, Clerkenwell, London on 23 January 1882). Walker, whose real surname was Badman, was the son of a well-known bare-fist fighter.

27 November 1883. (146lbs) Bill Chesterfield Goode w rtd 21 (finish) Dick Roberts.
Venue: The Rodney Arms Public House, Walworth, London, England.
Fight Summary: Continuing their battle of eight days earlier, Goode claimed the English 146lbs title on his victory. Once again both men fought all the way, concentrating on the body as well as mixing their punches up, and in the fifth Roberts was knocked down by a right hand to the jaw. Although Roberts was the more skilful, by the 12th round he was tiring badly. Under pressure, at the end of the 13th Roberts had to be carried to his corner after Goode got through with some heavy rights. With the money all on Goode, Roberts was dropped in the 14th before gamely fighting on in a beaten condition until 2.50 of the 21st session, when his seconds threw up the sponge and jumped into the ring to save him from being battered at will.

Two championship competitions at 146lbs in London during 1884 saw Johnny Robinson stop Arthur Cooper inside two rounds at the Horse Shoe Public House, Clerkenwell, London on 16 April and Alec Roberts outpoint Cooper over three rounds at the St Andrew's Hall, Westminster, London on 16 June.

Goode challenged the world at 146lbs on 7 March 1885, something he repeated in the *Sporting Life* a little over two months later, on 21 May.

2 February 1886. (150lbs) Nonpareil Jack Dempsey w rtd 27 (finish) Jack Fogarty.
Venue: Clarendon Hall, Manhattan, NYC, New York, USA. **Referee:** Al Smith.
Fight Summary: With just one reporter present, from the *New York World*, and set for a finish under London Prize Ring Rules at 150lbs in kid gloves, MoQ Rules seem to have applied. Well on top for much of the time, Dempsey (146) gave Fogarty (140½) a real pounding, which saw his face and body badly lacerated and his nose broken in

two places before he was pulled out. Fogarty, who had been knocked down in the 11th and battered continuously while growing weaker and weaker, was retired by his corner at the end of the 27th after being smashed down again in that session. Although he had regained his feet and was trying to fight back, Fogarty was pulled out by his seconds when it was apparent that he was through for the night. The finish was timed at 107 minutes.

Prior to this, the only fight of any significance at the weight had taken place in England on 21 May 1878, when Pat Condon had won a 150lbs championship competition when outpointing Andy Elms over three rounds at The Peacock Tavern, Bethnal Green, London.

14 March 1886. (156lbs) Nonpareil Jack Dempsey w co 13 (finish) George LaBlanche.
Venue: Larchmont Sound, Long Island, New York, USA. **Referee:** James O'Neil.
Fight Summary: Reported to be a catchweight bout by some papers, but a middleweight defence for Dempsey by the *New York Herald*, it was fought under MoQ Rules in kid driving gloves (two-ounce). With just nine people in attendance, and the men going at it hammer and tongs from the moment the fight started, the pattern was immediately set as LaBlanche (155) went to work with short arm blows at close quarters, while Dempsey (149) concentrated on solid left leads. By the end of the fourth LaBlanche's left eye was beginning to close due to the champion's excellent left-hand work and by the eighth he was spitting out teeth. It was a terrific battle with much give and take. In the tenth, in response to the referee's order to break, when LaBlanche dropped his hands he was belted to the floor vainly claiming a foul. Thereafter, it was blow for blow until LaBlanche sank to the boards from sheer exhaustion at 1.05 of the 13th to be counted out.

Almost a month later, on 10 April, Richard K. Fox presented Dempsey with the *Police Gazette* Championship Belt, for which he had to contend with all challengers for four years and remain unbeaten in order to keep it.

On 22 November, Dempsey (158) took on the 164lbs Jack Burke at the Mechanics' Pavilion, San Francisco, California in what was billed as a ten-round catchweight exhibition contest. Interestingly, as neither man would accept the club's choice of referee there were two men appointed, Frank Crockett to look after Burke's interests and Jack Hallinan doing likewise for Dempsey. It was an interesting contest, Burke being the aggressor and harder puncher of the two while Dempsey was by far the cleverer, and at the end of ten rounds it was declared a draw. Following the match-up, Professor Harry Maynard offered the men a purse of $1,000 and a percentage of all receipts over $250 if they agreed to meet in a fight to the finish. For whatever reason, nothing came of the offer.

6 May 1886. (148lbs) Jim Kendrick drew 20 (finish) Bill Chesterfield Goode.
Venue: Paradise Street School of Arms, Lambeth, London, England.
Fight Summary: Hinted at being for the English 148lbs title, Kendrick (145) had the best of it before the police stopped the fight at the end of the 20th round. It was clear that Goode (147) had played into Kendrick's hands by forcing the fight from the opening bell, inasmuch he began to tire early, losing every session from the 11th onwards. The general feeling was that if the police had not intervened Goode would have lost. According to the *Sporting Life* report it was contested in ordinary gloves under MoQ Rules with the utmost determination, and due to their excellent condition neither man showed much damage afterwards. Following the contest Kendrick and Goode met on 12 May and agreed a draw, but were arrested and charged at Lambeth on 19 May. After two adjournments, the case was heard at the Surrey sessions on 9 June, and after a jury had found them not guilty, the judge, Sir William Hardman, summed up by saying that soft-glove boxing of limited rounds was legal.

Further action at the weight saw Alec Roberts outpoint Jack Donoghue to win a championship competition at the St Andrew's Hall, Westminster, London on 9 January 1887.

14 January 1887. (148/150lbs) Jim Kendrick drew 12 Jack Hickey.
Venue: Paradise Street School of Arms, Lambeth, London, England.
Fight Summary: Made at catchweights, although Kendrick (143) slipped down in the first round he was soon in the thick of the action before Hickey (149) came on strong with body punching paving the way forward for him. In the eighth, after Kendrick was put down by a right to the jaw, upon rising in a dazed state he was at Hickey's mercy but managed to survive. At this stage Hickey appeared to be in front and even though Kendrick slightly improved in the

tenth it was still a surprise when both judges voted for a draw when the fight had been concluded. It was said that Kendrick, who put up his 148lbs English title claim in this one, had been suffering from a bout of influenza prior to the fight. Following the fight Hickey was challenging the world at 148lbs, and in the 6 June edition of the *Sportsman* he was called the English 150lbs champion.

Another man to win a championship competition, this time at 150lbs, was William Brown who outpointed Bill Cheese over three rounds at the Imperial Theatre, Westminster, London on 22 February. Brown had been the Amateur Boxing Association (ABA) middleweight champion in 1884.

Coming into 1887 two fighters in America, Johnny Banks and Ed Binney, were both claiming the 'black middleweight title' at around 150lbs. Banks (144) was the first to get going when taking on James Desverney (146) in a finish fight with kid gloves that took place somewhere in NYC, New York on 26 January. While Desverney won the so-called title on a ninth-round disqualification, reported to be a sparring match by at least one paper, he does not appear to go anywhere with it. Meanwhile, Binney beat Jim Keyes (w rtd 6 at the Early AC, Boston, Massachusetts on 31 January) to gain general recognition among the black community.

14 February 1887. (154lbs) Bill Natty w pts 12 Pat Condon.

Venue: Paradise Street School of Arms, Lambeth, London, England. **Referee:** J. T. Hulls.

Fight Summary: Agreed on 154lbs, despite being reported as 146lbs in some papers, and contested for an English silver championship belt, Natty (146) got away the better of the two, scoring effectively to take the opening four rounds before Condon (145) came on to win the fifth. Thereafter, the action was relatively even, but with Natty the stronger and having produced the better work at the start it was he who won the decision.

In America, Harris Martin, known as 'The Black Pearl', laid claim to the 'black middleweight title', thought to be around 154lbs, after knocking out Frank Taylor in 38 rounds of a finish fight held on the banks of the Mississippi River, Minneapolis, Minnesota on 2 May.

31 March 1887. (144lbs) Anthony Diamond w pts 10 Sam Baxter.

Venue: St Andrew's Hall, Westminster, London, England. **Referee:** Bernard J. Angle.

Fight Summary: Although contested at catchweights, Diamond (144), the former ABA lightweight and heavyweight champion who was making his official pro debut, defeated Baxter (130) and within a week he was already claiming the English 144lbs title. It was later reported to have been for the world 144lbs title as well as involving the English version. According to the papers of the day, Diamond won six rounds, Baxter two, with two even, Diamond using his extra weight to good advantage to take the verdict from the two judges at ringside. However, it was Baxter who was the closest to winning when he dropped Diamond with a right swing to the head in the sixth before his adversary was saved by the bell after being stunned by another big right at the end of the seventh.

Earlier, there had only been championship competitions held at the weight, which are listed herewith. They were all contested over three rounds.

On 23 December 1882, Charlie Mitchell outpointed Dick Roberts at St George's Hall, Westminster, London in the final of Billy Madden's heavyweight competition. Mitchell (143) was deemed to have outscored Roberts (142) when receiving the referee's casting vote. Strangely, Mitchell and Roberts were the two lightest men in a competition that included 21 entries.

In 1883, Bill Natty (outpointed Jack Donoghue on 23 January at the St Andrew's Hall), George Wilson (outpointed Ching Ghook at the Alexandra Rink, Nottingham on 29 May) and Jim Picton (outpointed Ghook at the Blue Anchor Public House, Shoreditch, London on 26 November).

Come 1884, Toff Wall (outpointed Tom Picton at the Blue Anchor Public House on 15 February) and Arthur Cooper (outpointed Jack McFarlane at the St Andrew's Hall on 29 February and then Jim Picton at the Blue Anchor Public House on 7 December).

Further activity in championship competitions at 144lbs that were held at the Blue Anchor Public House came when Wall, who had been advertised in the *Sporting Life* on 26 February 1885 as being the English champion at the weight, outpointed Ted Burchill on 21 January 1886. That was followed by Baxter (outpointing Ted Burchill on 16 December 1886 and then outpointing Jim Burchill on 19 January 1887).

29 August 1887. (156lbs) Bill Chesterfield Goode w rtd 15 (finish) Tom Lees.

Venue: Paradise Street School of Arms, Lambeth, London, England. **Referee:** J. T. Hulls.

Fight Summary: Regardless that this one was given English 156lbs championship billing, as Lees (155) was not eligible it was the Imperial British Empire title that he and Goode (152) should have been contesting. With Goode forcing the fight from the start, especially with body blows, by the ninth round his superior strength began to tell. In the 15th, after a right to the jaw almost knocked Lees out, in following up his advantage Goode dropped his man again. From then on Lees became the receiver general before being retired at 2.10 of the session when one of his seconds threw up the sponge. Both the *Sportsman* and the *Sporting Life*, who had reporters on the scene, stated that the fight was terminated during the 15th round, while the *Daily Telegraph* man had it lasting 17 rounds. The 5 September edition of the *Sporting Life* reported that the contest lasted 58 minutes, ten seconds, not one hour, 12 minutes as had been given elsewhere.

15 October 1887. (148lbs) Tom Lees drew 5 (finish) Bill Chesterfield Goode.

Venue: Waites Brewer Street Rooms, Soho, London, England. **Referee:** J. T. Hulls.

Fight Summary: A return match at catchweights, Lees (164) surprised Goode (148) when taking up the attack from the opening bell, the Englishman being left rather nonplussed for a few minutes before he began working the body. Nonetheless, with Lees doing far better than in their first contest it took Goode a while to catch up but by the fifth he was right back in it. At the start of that session, with Lees forcing Goode around the ring there was some heavy fighting before both tired from their exertions. When someone shouted 'time' both fighters went to their respective corners, which prompted the timekeeper to stand up and announce that it was not he who had called 'time' and that both men should carry on. Goode immediately responded by rushing the still seated Lees, who had obviously not heard the timekeeper amongst the ensuing din, and hit him so hard that his head came into contact with the ring post. With Lees' corner claiming a foul and Goode saying that he had only obeyed the orders of the timekeeper the referee told the men to box on, but when this decision caused an uproar the third man left the building, stating that he would see the fighters and their representatives at noon the next day. At the meeting, after George Dunning, the timekeeper, stated that only two minutes and 25 seconds of the round had elapsed the referee decided that a draw would be a fair result as he had no jurisdiction to force the men to meet again.

The following March (1888) the *Midland Sporting News* reported that Goode should be recognised as the English 148lbs champion. Regardless of that statement, it would be the Imperial British Empire title that the Australian-born Lees would be claiming.

17 October 1887. (148/150lbs) Alec Roberts drew 11 (12) Alec Burns.

Venue: Paradise Street School of Arms, Lambeth, London, England. **Referee:** E. Sampson.

Fight Summary: Even though made at catchweights this one was thought to involve the English 150lbs title, and it got underway in a fast and furious fashion with Burns forcing the pace. Extremely even up until around the seventh the fighters then started to hold on in order to conserve their energy, but there was so much noise that it was impossible to hear the referee above the din. At that stage the referee decided to depart regardless of all the efforts that were made to get him to stay, and at the conclusion of the fight the award of the judges was never made known. The *Sporting Life* reported that the fight ended in the 11th round while other papers gave it as the 12th or 13th, so take your pick. Roberts, the claimant of the English 148lbs title, was considered to have defended his claim in this one even though Burns (149½) was slightly over.

Roberts outpointed Arthur Cooper over three rounds at the St Andrew's Hall, Westminster, London on 25 January 1888 to win a 148lbs championship competition.

13 December 1887. (154lbs) Nonpareil Jack Dempsey w rtd 45 (finish) Johnny Reagan.

Venue: Manhasset, Long Island Sound, New York, USA. **Referee:** Frank Stevenson.

341

Fight Summary: Fought in two rings under London Prize Ring Rules – the first session lasting 18 minutes, the second 55 minutes due to the rising tide flooding the ring the first time round - the *New York Herald* claimed it to be the first 'proper' middleweight title fight in America for 20 years. Articled for both men to be inside 154lbs ringside, and using heavy driving gloves, when the fight restarted Dempsey closed the majority of rounds that followed by throwing Reagan and falling on him with as much force as he could muster. After taking much punishment from these tactics as well as having his head held and pummelled, Reagan often dropped on one knee to avoid what was coming. It could not go on like it was, and when Reagan had taken a further battering in the 45th round his seconds threw up the sponge, Dempsey being awarded an American 154lbs championship belt.

After the fight, real efforts were made to match him in England with Toff Wall, but when Dempsey refused to travel because of family commitments Wall said he could not go to America either as he was frightened of the water.

Still on the subject of English fighters scaling 154lbs, Alec Burns (who outpointed Jim Burchill over four rounds at the Royal Aquarium Theatre, Westminster, London on 8 December 1888), Burchill (who outpointed Arthur Bobbett over five rounds at the Royal Agricultural Hall, Islington, London on 16 March 1889) and Ted White (who outpointed Bat Mullins over four rounds at the same venue on 27 April 1889) all won championship competitions.

In the 10 July 1889 edition of the *Sporting Life* it was reported that Bill Chesterfield Goode should be recognised as the English 154lbs champion, while in January 1890 Alf Ball stated that he was claiming the title as no one had accepted his challenge at the weight.

15 December 1887. (152lbs) Ted Burchill w co 12 (finish) Arthur Bobbett.
Venue: London, England. **Referee:** Bernard J. Angle.
Fight Summary: Although no title billing was attached, years later Burchill (152) claimed he had won the English 152lbs title when beating Bobbett somewhere in the West End of London. The contest started with Bobbett using the left hand well as a scoring punch, but by the seventh round things were evening up as Burchill, concentrating on landing heavy blows from both hands, appeared to be the stronger. Down in the ninth, Bobbett was clearly weakening. Eventually, in the 12th, he was driven around the ring by heavy lefts and rights to the jaw before falling. After getting to his feet Bobbett was soon put down again, and although scrambling up and being treated leniently by Burchill, moments later it became apparent that he had already been counted out.

A championship competition at the weight in 1888 was won by Jim Kendrick, who outpointed Bill Corcoran over four rounds at the Royal Agricultural Hall, Islington, London on 14 April.

18 February 1888. (150lbs) Alec Roberts w pts 12 Alec Burns.
Venue: Paradise Street School of Arms, Lambeth, London, England. **Referee:** George Dunning.
Fight Summary: In a rematch, Roberts (146) eliminated Burns (149) from the title race when collecting the decision after a rattling good contest. Both men were down in the eighth, but in forcing the fight from early on Burns had weakened himself by the halfway stage, Roberts taking full advantage. Roberts showed a great left jab and much cleverness, while Burns proved himself to be a great competitor who carried a heavy punch in both hands.

Over in America, on 20 February, Ed Binney beat Johnny Banks (w rtd 14 at the Pelican Club, Boston, Massachusetts) in defence of his 150lbs 'black title' claim. Billed for 12 rounds, the referee, Joe Lannon, was unable to separate the two men at that point and asked them if they could box on until a winner could be found. This came about when Banks quit having taken a shellacking in the 14th session. Another 'black title' fight for Binney that took place in Boston on 22 June resulted in a stoppage win over Wiley Evans at the Crib Club. As yet, however, I have been unable to locate a fight report.

Meanwhile, back in England, Ted White (who outpointed Bill Husbands over four rounds at the Pelican Club, Soho, London on 14 January 1889) won a championship competition at the weight.

Towards the end of February 1889, Ted Pritchard challenged the world, preferably Nonpareil Jack Dempsey, to decide the title at 150lbs. A few days later Bill Chesterfield Goode accepted the challenge, on the proviso that the winner should meet Dempsey.

18 August 1888. (156lbs) George LaBlanche w rtd 3 Jack Varley.
Venue: New York, USA. **Referee:** Pete Donohue.
Fight Summary: The fight took place on a barge moored on the Hudson River near Yonkers. Varley (157), who arrived in America claiming to be the English middleweight champion, was soon found wanting, and by the end of the opening round he had been cut over the right eye and was receiving a bad beating at the hands of LaBlanche (156). It continued in the same vein in the second session. After Varley, now cut on the left eye, was saved by the bell and had been dropped heavily by a smashing blow under the heart he turned away in the third admitting defeat. Having also suffered damage to his mouth and nose, it was not a good start to the day for Varley, especially when the barge was boarded by the river police moments later. The fight, which had begun at 5.30am, lasted just eight minutes and was contested in skin-tight gloves. LaBlanche was now claiming the title at his stated weight.

Meanwhile, on 21 January 1890, Ted Pritchard was matched to fight Alf Mitchell in March to decide the English 156lbs title. However, when the fight was called off after Pritchard was taken ill Mitchell claimed the championship using bare-knuckles or gloves, and by the end of the year was signing himself off as the world middleweight champion.

25 September 1888. (148lbs) Alec Roberts drew 53 (finish) Arthur Bobbett.
Venue: Paradise Street School of Arms, Lambeth, London, England. **Referee:** Bernard J. Angle.
Fight Summary: Later given as a 148lbs English title defence by Roberts (147½), the bout was declared to be a draw with 15 seconds of the 53rd round still remaining. At that point, both men were out on their feet with nothing between them. There had only been two knockdowns, neither being of note, with Roberts generally the aggressor, using both hands well to head and body, while Bobbett showed himself defensively adept, especially when making his man miss. In the 50th it was clear that Roberts was suffering from cramp, and with Bobbett standing his ground despite his right hand being of little use the fight almost fizzled out, which ultimately led to the referee's decision.

This was the final bout of Roberts' career and he passed away on 5 October 1899, aged 39, of acute pneumonia.

On 14 October, Jack Hickey challenged all England at weights between 148 and 154lbs, but his career was over by the following year after he was charged with manslaughter.

23 November 1888. (152lbs) Bill Chesterfield Goode w pts 12 Arthur Bobbett.
Venue: Peter Street Grand Circus, Manchester, England. **Referee:** George Dunning.
Fight Summary: Billed for the English 152lbs middleweight title, it was even-steven before Bobbett (152) scored the opening knockdown in the fifth round when dropping Goode (150) with a left hander. In the next session it was Goode's turn to floor his man, a terrific uppercut putting Bobbett on his knees, and in the eighth the latter was floored three times in all. Despite this, Bobbett was still in the fight, but after flooring his opponent twice more in the 12th the decision in Goode's favour was a formality.

Following little real activity at the weight, on 3 February 1891 Arthur Akers challenged the world at 152lbs having recently won a championship competition at 158lbs.

A few months later, on 30 May 1891, Ted White won a championship competition when outpointing Bill Husbands over four rounds at Her Majesty's Theatre, Haymarket, London.

31 December 1888. (160lbs+) Alf Mitchell w pts 12 Ted O'Neill.
Venue: Lyceum Theatre, Liverpool, England.
Fight Summary: Reported in the *Sporting Life* as a contest to decide the catchweight championship of Lancashire it was really the English title that was involved. It was close and hard-fought, with Mitchell (161) hitting very straight,

concentrating on the body, while O'Neill (168), who was not in the best of condition, gave it everything. It was only in the last few rounds when O'Neill weakened that the Cardiff-born Mitchell took over, the paper stating that finer a contest was never witnessed.

Earlier in the year there had already been three catchweight championship competitions, Mitchell outpointing Alf Ball over four rounds at the Pelican Club, Soho, London on 4 June, Toff Wall outpointing Mitchell over four rounds at the Royal Aquarium Theatre, Westminster, London on 8 December and Ted Burchill also outpointing Mitchell at Her Majesty's Theatre, Haymarket, London on 15 December. The last contest had originally been set for three rounds, but because there was little to choose between them at the end of the third the referee ordered an extra round to be boxed.

In 1889 Mitchell came back to win a championship competition when he outpointed Charlie Bartlett over four rounds at the Royal Agricultural Hall, Islington High Street, London on 16 March. That was followed by Jim Haines (who forced Jack Welland to retire in the first round at the Pelican Club, Denman Street, Soho, London on 1 April), and Bill Chesterfield Goode (who forced O'Neill to retire in the first round at the Royal Agricultural Hall on 27 April). Haines then outpointed Alf Bowman over four rounds at Her Majesty's Theatre on 30 May).

28 May 1889. (160lbs+) George LaBlanche w co 13 Mike Lucie.
Venue: California AC, San Francisco, California, USA. **Referee:** Hiram Cook.
Fight Summary: After a brief warm-up, LaBlanche (155½) began to get on top of Lucie (said to weigh in the region of 162lbs), handing out severe punishment to the ribs before knocking him over with a left uppercut in the tenth. Lucie was soon floored again before being saved by the bell. Although the 11th was slow, after LaBlanche had Lucie down for the third time, in the 12th, once again the bell came to the latter's aid. With Lucie barely able to stand up in the 13th he was pushed to the floor and counted out. Four-ounce gloves were used.

Given much credit for a fine performance, LaBlanche, claiming to be the 156lbs champion, would receive another crack at Nonpareil Jack Dempsey on 27 August at the same venue.

Jim Haines (162) claimed to be the 'black English champion' when he outpointed Jack Welland over three rounds to win a catchweight competition at the Pelican Club, Soho, London on 8 June. At the end of the month, Haines challenged all England at the weight.

6 June 1889. (148lbs) Ted Pritchard w co 2 (finish) Alec Burns.
Venue: Paradise Street School of Arms, Lambeth, London, England. **Referee:** Bernard J. Angle.
Fight Summary: Contested for the English 148lbs middleweight title, the fight started at a fair pace and immediately prior to the end of the opening round Burns (147) was dropped in his own corner. It was obvious that Burns had not shaken off the effects of his knockdown, being quickly in trouble in the second as Pritchard (146) set about him with both hands. After being smashed down again, when Burns got up he was beaten down for the third time and counted out on the 1.30 mark. Burns' corner unsuccessfully tried to claim a foul on the grounds that each time their man went down he was being punched when on his haunches.

27 August 1889. (160lbs+) George LaBlanche w co 32 Nonpareil Jack Dempsey.
Venue: California AC, San Francisco, California, USA. **Referee:** Hiram Cook.
Fight Summary: Taking place in four-ounce gloves, and felt by some in later years to have involved Dempsey's title claim, it was announced by the Master of Ceremonies before the fight with LaBlanche (161) got underway that it would not involve the championship or the belt, just a purse. This was due to the French-Canadian being unable to make the required weight of 154lbs. Until the finish it was nearly all Dempsey (151), who jabbed and moved out of danger well while continually working the body. When Dempsey scored a knockdown in the 18th, he looked a sure fire winner at that stage. Although the Irish-American continued to box well the fight came to an abrupt end in the 32nd (also variously reported as the 30th and 31st) round when LaBlanche, under pressure in a corner and facing the crowd, suddenly pivoted with great force to land solidly on Dempsey's nose. The punch had a devastating effect, and with Dempsey unable to get up before being counted out the referee handed the decision to LaBlanche. Amidst cries of 'foul', the blow which came to be known as the 'pivot punch' was controversial to say

the least, being reported by some papers as a terrific right swing and by others, including the *New York World*, as being delivered by the right forearm. Years later, writing in the May 1925 edition of *The Ring*, A. D. Phillips, who claimed to have been present, stated that LaBlanche had whirled off the ropes with his right hand swinging backwards, while Nat Fleischer, writing in the March 1927 edition of *The Ring*, claimed that LaBlanche had pivoted on his left heel and swung his left arm, held stiffly at full length. Whatever the truth of the matter, Dempsey had lost his unbeaten record. Following the fight it was claimed that LaBlanche had worked on the finishing blow with his trainer, Jim Carroll, who had used the same tactic in his contest with Sam Blakelock. This was debunked by many, who claimed that the blow was a fluke.

Despite any claim put forward by LaBlanche the Californian Athletic Club refused to support him stating that regardless of the result, as they considered 154lbs to be the middleweight limit, the Canadian did not belong to that weight class. However, that failed to stop him continuing to bill himself as the man who beat Dempsey to win the title.

In England, a catchweight championship competition was won by Jack Welland, who outpointed Jim Richardson over four rounds at Saddlers Wells Theatre, Clerkenwell, London on 14 December 1889. Then, in 1891, Welland won two championship competitions, outpointing Jim Haines over six rounds at Her Majesty's Theatre, Westminster, London on 4 April and Alf Bowman over seven rounds at the Goodwin Gym, Shoreditch, London on 5 December.

On 1 November 1894, Arthur Bobbett challenged all England at 162lbs.

28 October 1889. (148lbs) Ted White w disq 8 (12) Tom Meadows.
Venue: South London Gym, Kennington, London, England. **Referee:** Robert Watson.
Fight Summary: Although there was no title billing attached, White (148) claimed the English 148lbs crown after beating Meadows who, although born in London, was doing his fighting in Australia. Meadows, a good stone lighter than his opponent, was never really in with a chance despite showing clever defensive qualities, and by the end of the sixth round, having been badly hurt, he looked to be on his way out. Somehow getting through the seventh, with Meadows resorting to holding on at every opportunity at the end of the eighth, after repeated warnings, the referee disqualified him.

A championship competition at the weight saw Jim Burchill outpoint Bill Husbands over four rounds at the Royal Aquarium Theatre, Westminster, London on 7 December.

7 February 1890. (158lbs) Toff Wall w pts 12 Bill Chesterfield Goode.
Venue: Pelican Club, Soho, London, England. **Referee:** Bernard J. Angle.
Fight Summary: Billed for the English 158lbs championship, and involving Goode's Imperial British Empire title claim, Wall (157) was on top almost all the way, often staggering his rival with well-placed punches. In the ninth, even though a tiring Wall slipped over and was cut over the left eye he still had the better of Goode (156), who was much the worse for wear and almost all-in.

Described by many as the most scientific boxer in England this was in fact the final bout of Wall's career, other than him participating in the odd exhibition and continuing to sign himself as champion for quite a while afterwards.

Arthur Akers outpointed Alf Suffolk over three rounds at Rowland's Carr Lane Circus, Hull on 10 January 1891 to win a 158lbs championship competition.

18 February 1890. (154/156bs) Nonpareil Jack Dempsey w rtd 28 (finish) Billy McCarthy.
Venue: California AC, San Francisco, California, USA. **Referee:** Hiram Cook.
Fight Summary: Made at 154/156lbs, the fight was delayed when it was discovered that the air had been let out of the regulation five-ounce gloves. It eventually went ahead with more stuffing inserted and weighing in the region of three to four ounces. There was plenty of good fighting during the first 20 rounds, with the men getting off

heavy punches from both hands, but beyond that period it was evident that McCarthy (151½) was weakening, especially from body blows. Following a few rounds of little activity, when Dempsey (147½) picked it up in the 26th McCarthy was belted all over the ring. Knocked down four times in the 27th and twice in the 28th, even though McCarthy was a beaten man he continued to get up, and it was only when Dempsey implored the referee to stop the carnage that the Englishman's corner finally pulled their man out.

With Dempsey in the driving seat at 154lbs it was reported in the *Sporting Life* on 27 August that he had been challenged for the world title at 158lbs by the Irish Lad, Jack Burke. Dempsey responded by saying he would not fight above 154lbs.

Later in the year, on 14 October, in England, Alf Mitchell stated in the *Sporting Life* that as Bill Chesterfield Goode had failed to turn up the previous day to make a match to decide the English 154lbs championship he would box any man who would match his deposit. The offer was immediately snapped up by Ted Pritchard.

28 February 1890. (156lbs) Alf Ball w co 12 (12) Jack Welland.
Venue: Goodwin Club, Shoreditch, London, England. **Referee:** Bernard J. Angle.
Fight Summary: Reportedly made at catchweights, the opening seven rounds had little going for them other than there being too much holding for which both men received warnings from the referee. Pulling himself together, Ball (156) finally woke up in the eighth when scoring repeatedly with the left, and from that moment there was only one man likely to win and it was not the plodding Welland (154), who although game lacked the basic rudiments of boxing. After knocking Welland out in the final session the *Sporting Life* reported that when Ball boxed coolly he did well, but when trying to knock Welland out he was wild and precipitate. Both men finished the contest with damage to their left eyes. Regardless of any criticism, the winner claimed the English 156lbs title on the strength of this result.

3 November 1890. (150lbs) Anthony Diamond w co 10 (finish) Arthur Bobbett.
Venue: Bill Reader's School of Arms, Fulham, London, England.
Fight Summary: In a fight given English 150lbs title billing, with height-and-reach advantage Bobbett (148) started to utilise those strengths when punching straighter. By the third round, though, he was being matched by Diamond (147¾), whose cleverness was beginning to come to the fore. In the fourth, despite Diamond being dropped by a left to the head he managed to come back strongly. With Bobbett's left eye closing fast by the sixth, while he was still going well Diamond was beginning to wear him down. Although both men came up fresh for the ninth it was Diamond who was now controlling the fight, and having tested Bobbett with an assortment of blows up and down in the tenth, he floored the latter for the full count with a right uppercut to the jaw.

Towards the end of the month Diamond was being reported as the world 150lbs champion, which was repeated in the *Sporting Life* during December.

7 November 1890. (150lbs) Lachie Thomson w co 3 (finish) Harry Downie.
Venue: London, England.
Fight Summary: Held in private, and billed for the English 150lbs title, both men were born in Scotland, with Downie fighting out of Australia at the time. The contest started with Downie forcing the pace, never leaving Thomson alone, and by the end of the opening session the latter was carrying two badly swollen eyes that were testament to his rival's good work. However, it was Thomson, with solid lefts, who showed up the better in the second to have Downie on the floor four times prior to going for the finish in the third. It was now clear that Thomson had the power to control the fight, and after dropping Downie a further four times in the third the last occasion produced a count out.

In the wake of this, two championship competitions at 150lbs were decided when William Robinson outpointed Felix Scott over six rounds at Her Majesty's Theatre, Westminster, London on 6 December and Bill Husbands outpointed Alf Suffolk over six rounds at the same venue on 4 April 1891.

On 4 May 1892, Fred Greenbank challenged all England at 150lbs, being followed by Ted Rich on 24 October.

The next time the weight class came to life was when Dido Plumb challenged all England, according to the *Sporting Life*, on 10 September 1894.

25 November 1890. (148lbs) Ted Bryant w co 1 (15) John O'Brien.
Venue: St Andrew's Hall, Westminster, London, England.
Fight Summary: Although made at catchweights, Bryant (148) claimed the English 148lbs title following his shock win over a man reckoned to be at least 14 pounds heavier. The contest had begun with the taller O'Brien chasing his man round the ring with lefts and rights, but after dashing in to attack Bryant downstairs the former was counted out after just 37 seconds following a cracking right to the jaw.

Alf Suffolk knocked out William Robinson in the first round at the National Sporting Club (NSC), Covent Garden, London on 22 June 1891 to win a 148lbs championship competition.

15 December 1890. (154lbs) Ted Pritchard w rsc 4 (finish) Alf Mitchell.
Venue: St Andrew's Hall, Westminster, London, England. **Referee:** Bernard J. Angle.
Fight Summary: Billed for the English and world 154lbs championships, Mitchell (153½) surprised Pritchard (153) when flooring him with a left to the head at the end of the opening round. However, Pritchard was soon back in the contest. Following wild bursts of fighting in the second, Pritchard found his mark in the third to knock Mitchell down three times, and in the fourth he had his man on the floor twice more before the ring was invaded. Following that, with Mitchell almost out on his feet the referee announced that he had awarded the fight to Pritchard on the grounds that an organised interruption had taken place in order to stop the Cardiff man from being knocked out.

14 January 1891. (154lbs) Bob Fitzsimmons w co 13 (finish) Nonpareil Jack Dempsey.
Venue: Olympic Club, New Orleans, Louisiana, USA. **Referee:** Alex Brewster.
Fight Summary: Fighting in an American ring for only the fourth time, Fitzsimmons (150½), a terrific two-handed fighter with immense hitting power, ultimately destroyed Dempsey (147½) to take the title. As early as the seventh round Dempsey looked a beaten man after he was dropped by a body blow, and although he gamely fought back the writing was on the wall. Dropped three times in the tenth, twice more in the 11th and again in the 12th, Dempsey was now completely at the mercy of Fitzsimmons. With Dempsey all at sea in the 13th, two heavy lefts and rights saw the champion floored again before being sent to the boards to be counted out. The final blow was more of a push than a punch, but Dempsey was completely used up, having had his nose broken and taken a battering to head and body.

Later in the year, on 30 November, Ed Binney knocked out Harris Martin inside 25 rounds of a 'black title' match held at the California AC, San Francisco, California. By his victory Binney was generally recognised in America as the 154lbs 'black champion' after eliminating one of his main rivals. Despite Binney's win over Martin, when Charles Turner knocked the latter out inside 19 rounds at the Occidental Club, San Francisco on 29 February 1892 he too claimed the 'black title' before going nowhere with it. On 13 November 1892, Joe Butler beat Binney (w co 2 in Philadelphia, Pennsylvania) to take over the latter's 'black title' claim, following it up with a successful defence against Frank Craig (w co 2 in Philadelphia on 18 March 1893).

20 February 1891. (154lbs) Young Mitchell w co 12 (finish) George LaBlanche.
Venue: California AC, San Francisco, California, USA. **Referee:** Hiram Cook.
Fight Summary: With LaBlanche (153) claiming the title and the *Chicago Tribune* reporting it to be a championship fight, following his defeat at the hands of Mitchell (151) the Canadian lost any vestige of credibility he might have had despite continuing with his claim, while the victor established no recognition whatsoever. The fight itself saw both men down at the same time in the first round, and both down separately in the seventh before LaBlanche was dropped in the ninth, tenth and 12th. The final knockdown, following a light left, brought about a knockout win for Mitchell, which most of the boxing press described as a likely fake and a disgrace to the sport.

7 March 1891. (160lbs) John O'Brien w co 9 (15) Ted White.
Venue: Pelican Club, Soho, London, England. **Referee:** George Vize.

Fight Summary: This one was articled at 160lbs. The contest had seen White (151), weakening by the fourth following a very fast start, using the left to keep O'Brien (159) at bay, but by the end of the eighth he was seen to be all-in after slipping down at the end of the session. Although O'Brien was way behind on points, after mounting a sustained attack in the ninth he had White over for 'nine' with a right to the jaw. Now thoroughly used-up White was there for the taking, and it was no surprise when O'Brien immediately sent him to the floor again, this time for the full count.

Calling himself the English 160lbs champion on the result, later in the year O'Brien was also claiming to hold the 158lbs title, even though he had been knocked out in the first round of a catchweight contest by Ted Bryant at the St Andrew's Hall, Westminster, London on 25 November 1890.

On 5 January 1892, Ted Fenton challenged all England at 160lbs.

12 March 1891. (154lbs) Ted Pritchard w co 3 (finish) Jack Burke.
Venue: Albany Club, Holloway, London, England. **Referee:** George Vize.
Fight Summary: Reported to be for the English 154lbs title, both men were reported as being inside the weight. By the second round Pritchard was well in control of the contest, closing Burke down, and towards the end of the session he sent the Irishman to the floor from a blow to the neck. Told to set about Burke right from the bell to begin the third, Pritchard was soon picking his punches, having his rival over three times before another right to the neck produced the knockout that he had been looking for.

Following this, Arthur Bobbett won a 154lbs championship competition when outpointing Bill Husbands at the Pelican Club, Soho, London on 14 March.

28 May 1891. (156lbs) John O'Brien w co 7 (finish) Alf Ball.
Venue: Pelican Club, London, England. **Referee:** George Vize.
Fight Summary: Made at catchweights, the turning point in the fight came in the fifth round after Ball (167¾) had ended the session in a dazed condition. At this point O'Brien (156) had begun to get on top, dropping Ball heavily in the sixth. Although Ball got up he was then battered from pillar to post as O'Brien looked for the finisher, and with the seventh underway it was clearly seen that the latter was merely biding his time. Eventually, a right hand to the jaw put Ball down. Despite Ball making it to his feet, following several heavy blows from the same hand O'Brien dropped his rival for the full count. The Welshman not only extended his 160lbs English title claim on beating Ball, who retired after the bout, but also took over the loser's 156lbs claim.

23 September 1891. Young Mitchell w co 13 (finish) Reddy Gallagher.
Venue: Occidental Club, San Francisco, California, USA. Referee Peter Jackson.
Fight Summary: Taking the centre of the ring for the first eight rounds, Gallagher (153) kept Mitchell (154) away with the use of solid left hands to head and body. From thereon in, however, Mitchell began to find the range, cutting Gallagher on the left eye and sending in some heavy shots of his own. The 13th round saw Gallagher beginning to fall apart at the seams, and he was eventually sent crashing to the floor to be counted out after taking terrific blows to the neck and chin.

It appears that Mitchell's title claim ends here, with just two more bouts being recorded for him.

30 November 1891. (148lbs) Lachie Thomson w co 6 (30) Arthur Akers.
Venue: Pelican Club, Soho, London, England. **Referee:** George Vize.
Fight Summary: Billed for the English 148lbs title, both men making the weight, the early exchanges were most lively with Akers especially going well. By the fifth, however, it was Thomson who was showing up better, but Akers was still dangerous with swinging right hands. The sixth saw Thomson picking up the pace as Akers began to fade, and after the latter had been dropped heavily three times he was counted out on the last occasion he visited the boards.

A few days later at the Goodwin Club, Shoreditch, London, on 5 December, William Robinson outpointed Walter Gunn over seven rounds to win a championship competition at 148lbs.

On 20 September 1893, it was reported by the *Sporting Life* that Alf Bowman should be seen as being the English 148lbs champion, which came to nothing.

With little action at 148lbs, the next man to come through was Alf Suffolk, who knocked out George Haskell inside 60 seconds to win a championship competition at the Central Hall, Holborn, London on 15 December 1894.

The weight class then fell silent until men such as Bill Husbands (30 November 1897), Harry Neumier (21 January 1898) and Tom Woodley (25 October 1898) challenged all England without any of them making it stick.

21 December 1891. (158lbs) John O'Brien w co 8 (20) Alf Mitchell.
Venue: NSC, Covent Garden, London, England. **Referee:** Bernard J. Angle.
Fight Summary: Involving the English 158lbs title and a championship belt, at the end of the second round it already looked to be going well for O'Brien (157) as he had not only knocked Mitchell (158) down with a solid right to the head in that session but was also in control. Driven around the ring thereafter, Mitchell was repeatedly floored in the fifth, six times in all, but still managed to last out until the call of time. Somewhat strangely O'Brien took his foot off the pedal in the next two rounds, but in the eighth, obviously ready to bring the contest to a conclusion, he laid into Mitchell with a vengeance. After dropping Mitchell with a cracking right to the jaw, when the latter finally made it to his feet he was set about before falling flat on his back where he was counted out.

Following this there was much talk of O'Brien meeting Ted Pritchard to decide the English title at the weight, but as the Welshman would only box at the NSC and their purse offer was lower than elsewhere the proposed match fell through. Not to be messed about, Pritchard quite rightly took over O'Brien's claim at this juncture. There was also talk of Pritchard meeting Bob Fitzsimmons in America, but that also fell through.

George Chrisp won a 158lbs championship competition when knocking out Jack Hart inside two rounds at the Central Hall, Holborn, London on 4 June 1892. He was followed in 1893 by Ted White (who outpointed Alf Bowman over four rounds at the NSC on 6 March) and Arthur Akers (who outpointed Chrisp over four rounds at The Coliseum, Leeds on 7 October). By December, Akers was claiming the 158lbs English title, while Pritchard challenged the world at 158lbs.

However, Chrisp came back strongly to win a championship competition when knocking out Ted Rich in the first round at the St Andrew's Hall, Westminster, London on 21 April 1894.

20 August 1892. (160lbs) Jim Hall w co 4 (finish) Ted Pritchard.
Venue: Sussex, England.
Fight Summary: This one took place at a racing stable on The Downs near Brighton. With Bob Fitzsimmons recognised as world champion at 154lbs, Hall and Pritchard were matched for the British version of the title at 160lbs, and following the contest, Hall, who had a kayo victory over Fitzsimmons to his credit, claimed the 158lbs world title. Also involving the Imperial British Empire title, both men weighed 157lbs. Almost immediately it could be seen that Hall had the reach on Pritchard, but in the second round the Australian was sent to the grass by a powerful right to the jaw. However, coming back strongly, Hall began to demoralise Pritchard with heavy blows of his own, and in the fourth two severe blows, one to the jaw and one to the side of the head, saw the latter crash to the turf to be counted out.

Now fighting in America, Fitzsimmons knocked out Hall in the fourth round of a finish fight at the Crescent Club, New Orleans, Louisiana on 8 March 1893. Although billed as a title match in some quarters, it should not be recognised as involving the championship due to it being contested at catchweights well above the recognised weight. When Fitzsimmons weighed in at a massive 167lbs to his opponent's 163½ it was now quite clear that he would be unable to make 154lbs again without losing strength.

Taking advantage of the champion's privilege of the day in being able to carry the weight to suit his own convenience, Fitzsimmons named 158lbs as the premier poundage within the weight class following his defeat of Hall.

22 April 1893. (154lbs) Ted White w pts 20 George Chrisp.
Venue: NSC, Covent Garden, London, England. **Referee:** Bernard J. Angle.
Fight Summary: In a match made at 154lbs, despite a lack of title billing many would have seen this one to have involved the English title, especially when White (152) claimed it on winning before challenging the world. By the fifth round White had built up quite a lead, his left hand bemusing Chrisp (152) at times, and although the latter gamely kept ploughing in he was being outboxed. The last third of the contest saw Chrisp rushing his man. While Chrisp had some success with his work to the body it failed to slow White, who cruised to an easy points win.

Across the water in America, Frank Craig took over Joe Butler's 154lbs 'black title' claim when outpointing his rival over four rounds in Philadelphia, Pennsylvania on 20 February 1894. Like Butler, Craig was soon solely campaigning among the heavyweights where the bigger purses were, and there appears to be little action for a year or two despite there being some good men around at the time.

According to the *Sporting Life* on 10 September 1894, Dido Plumb was challenging all England at 154lbs. At the same time he was being named as the world champion at the weight in the *Mirror of Life*.

15 January 1894. (152lbs) Ted White w pts 20 Anthony Diamond.
Venue: NSC, Covent Garden, London, England. **Referee:** Bernard J. Angle.
Fight Summary: Despite its lack of billing, this was recognised by the vast majority as being for the English 152lbs title. Very much a clash of styles, after realising that White (151) carried more power than he did Diamond (150) began to use dodging and holding tactics to stay in the contest as his rival weakened. In the 11th Diamond was twice dropped before being put down again in the 14th. However, with White unable to finish Diamond off the bout developed into a cat and mouse struggle. The last six rounds saw White sending out straight left-rights and making all of the running, while Diamond, who by this stage was not going to win, used the ring well and made punches miss by clever use of the head to go the distance.

On 10 September 1895 Dido Plumb challenged all England and the world, continuing doing so for several years.

Another excellent win at 152lbs for White came when he outpointed America's Charles Kid McCoy over ten rounds at the same venue on 25 November 1895. Not contested over a championship distance, there would be no world title claim forthcoming from White.

27 April 1894. (160lbs) Dan Creedon w co 9 (20) Dick Moore.
Venue: Twin City AC, Minneapolis, Minnesota, USA. **Referee:** Sandy Griswold.
Fight Summary: Billed for the 160lbs middleweight championships of Australia and America, Moore stepped in after Bob Fitzsimmons had refused to meet Creedon for such a small monetary reward. Contested at a brisk pace, by the seventh round it could be seen that Creedon (160) was getting on top, especially with Moore's left eye closed. In the eighth, Moore (157) was put down by a short right to the face and saved by the bell before being dropped again by a similar blow in the ninth. Getting to his feet quickly Moore rushed at Creedon, only to be caught by a left uppercut to the jaw that sent him to the floor for the full count.

26 September 1894. (158lbs) Bob Fitzsimmons w co 2 (finish) Dan Creedon.
Venue: Olympic Club, New Orleans, Louisiana, USA. **Referee:** Jim Duffy.
Fight Summary: Contested for the 158lbs title, Fitzsimmons (155½) quickly took the initiative in the opening round when forcing Creedon (157) back, and early in the second dropped the latter with heavy rights to the jaw. On his feet, but in a poor condition, Creedon was punched about from head to body before a smashing left to the chin sent him down to be counted out at 1.40 of the session.

By early 1896 it was clear that Fitzsimmons, unable to make 158lbs anymore, had set his sights on the heavyweight title. Regardless of Fitzsimmons continuing to call himself the middleweight champion, Tommy Ryan, who had already beaten the former titleholder, Nonpareil Jack Dempsey, claimed the crown.

8 October 1894. (158lbs) Frank Craig w co 2 (finish) John O'Brien.
Venue: NSC, Covent Garden, London, England. **Referee:** Bernard J. Angle.
Fight Summary: Reported as the British version of the world 158lbs title, Craig, making his debut in England, certainly did not waste much time. Earlier, Craig had claimed the world title after all the American white middleweights refused to fight him in anything other than four round contests. Forced down at the end of the opening round, by that time O'Brien (158) probably knew what was coming. Springing at O'Brien like a tiger, Craig opened up in the second in determined fashion, and after being dropped by lefts and rights to the jaw four times the gallant Welshman was sent down again and counted out at 1.32 of the session.

Dido Plumb won a 158lbs championship contest when knocking out Alec Young in the second round at the Central Hall, Holborn, London on 17 November.

26 November 1894. (160lbs) Ted Pritchard w co 2 (10) Dick Burge.
Venue: Eden Palace, Holborn, London, England. **Referee:** Joe Steers.
Fight Summary: Although there was no title billing for this one, there was a clause specifying that Pritchard would not exceed 160lbs. Regardless of that there appears to have been no official weigh-in. The first round opened with Burge dancing around Pritchard, shooting in counters while keeping out of harm's way, and the Newcastle man started the second in the same vein. Having missed a lot and been hurt by several hard wallops, Pritchard eventually got to Burge, putting him down with a heavy right to the jaw after the latter had left him an opening. Then, with Burge trying to regain his feet, he was smashed to the floor by another cracking right to the jaw and counted out on the 1.45 mark. There was much debate following the fight due to Pritchard standing over Burge and not going to a neutral corner. Despite there being many calling for a foul to be given they were ultimately overlooked. Whatever the rights and wrongs, Pritchard was now calling himself the English 160lbs champion.

Meanwhile, men who won championship competitions at the weight included Dido Plumb (who stopped Jack Bryan inside two rounds at the Central Hall, Holborn on 15 December) and Ted Rich (who knocked out Fred Greenbank in the first round at the same venue on 2 February 1895).

17 December 1894. (158lbs) Frank Craig w co 1 (10) Ted Pritchard.
Venue: Central Hall, Holborn, London, England. **Referee:** Bernard J. Angle.
Fight Summary: Advertised as being for the British version of the world 158lbs title even though it was scheduled for only ten rounds, the fight lasted just 96 seconds. Both men had started carefully, not wanting to leave an opening, but after a fair bit of clinching in which Pritchard tried to work the body Craig found the mark to send him heavily on to the ropes. Somewhat dazed upon rising, Pritchard tried to cover up but before he could do so he was hammered to the floor by a straight right and counted out.

Despite the result, after a rematch was agreed at 158lbs the pair were pencilled in to meet on 13 April 1895 at the same venue, only for John O'Brien to be drafted in at the last moment when Pritchard was taken ill. Hastily rearranged for 20 two-minute rounds at catchweights, O'Brien entered the ring blind drunk before retiring on his stool at the end of the first round and effectively walking away from the sport thereafter.

8 April 1895. (158lbs) Anthony Diamond w pts 12 Jack Varley.
Venue: Curzon Hall, Birmingham, England.
Fight Summary: Recognised as a catchweight bout with the weights not to exceed 158lbs, although his opponent appeared to be the stronger of the two Diamond (154) boxed extremely cleverly, showing an excellent defence and countering Varley (158) whenever given the opportunity. The last three sessions saw Diamond assert his superiority, cutting out most of the work, and even when he was brought down by Varley his responding blows more that laid the balance in his favour. The contest was later reported to have involved the English 158lbs title.

351

14 October 1895. (158lbs) Dan Creedon w pts 20 Frank Craig.
Venue: NSC, Covent Garden, London, England. **Referee:** Bernard J. Angle.
Fight Summary: Recognised as being for the British version of the world 158lbs title, after a slow start it warmed up with Craig (157) rushing Creedon (156), which was not his normal style. Nonetheless, he floored Creedon with a right to the jaw in the sixth and almost had the latter over again in the seventh with similar punches before weakening himself and slipping down after missing his rival. Despite looking to be a beaten man in the eighth, and being brought to his knees in the ninth, Creedon came on strongly after the 12th when taking most of the subsequent rounds to run out a good winner. Craig, who was not helped by the fact that he was cautioned on several occasions, reclaimed the title on Creedon leaving for America.

2 March 1896. (154/156lbs) Charles Kid McCoy w co 15 (20) Tommy Ryan.
Venue: Empire AC, Maspeth, Queens, NYC, New York, USA. **Referee:** Tim Hurst.
Fight Summary: This fight was made famous by the fact that McCoy, Ryan's old sparring partner, tricked the welterweight champion into taking him on at 154lbs by claiming he was out of condition. To add insult to injury, the *Brooklyn Eagle* tells us that McCoy was a pound over the articled weight at 155lbs to Ryan's 148. Following this, the famous expression: 'The Real McCoy' was probably coined, but with Bob Fitzsimmons still considered champion in some quarters the winner would not be generally recognised despite the fact that the contest was billed as being for the championship. The fight reports stated that Ryan, giving away height and weight, proved himself as great in defeat as in victory when getting up again and again to battle on. Although McCoy did little of the leading early on, after the seventh round he concentrated on the body, flooring Ryan in the eighth, ninth and 12th before opening up in the 15th. After some body work early in the session Ryan was dropped by a heavy left to the jaw, and on just about getting to his feet on time he was sent down for the full count, completed at 1.54, by a right-left to the jaw.

18 May 1896. (154lbs) Charles Kid McCoy w disq 6 (15) Mysterious Billy Smith.
Venue: Suffolk AC, West Newton Street Armoury, Boston, Massachusetts, USA. **Referee:** Bill Daly.
Fight Summary: Reported in the *Boston Post* as being for the championship of their weight class, with both Smith (150) and McCoy (153) starting slowly there was little action during the first three rounds. Regardless of that, however, it was clear that Smith was using foul tactics from the beginning, and in the sixth, having been warned several times, he hit McCoy on being told to break and was disqualified. Following the bout McCoy stated he would immediately be issuing a challenge to Bob Fitzsimmons, whom he still recognised as champion.

1 June 1896. (158lbs) Ted White w rsc 16 (20) Dido Plumb.
Venue: NSC, Covent Garden, London, England.
Fight Summary: Given English 158lbs championship billing, White, with the advantage in height and reach, soon had the left hand working well, and whatever Plumb tried he could not avoid it. Adding to his lead, White sent Plumb to the floor in the seventh round but could not repeat the trick until the 14th when he belted the latter through the ropes. Although Plumb threw caution to the wind in the 15th, after he had been dropped twice in the 16th the referee called a halt to the uneven struggle.

After what turned out to be the final bout of White's career, Plumb was challenging all England at 158lbs by November.

23 October 1896. (160lbs) Dan Creedon w pts 20 Harry Baker.
Venue: Empire AC, Maspeth, Queens, NYC, New York, USA. **Referee:** Tim Hurst.
Fight Summary: Having his first fight in America since arriving from Britain, Creedon, who held the British version of the title, was claiming to be world champion at 160lbs. Although there was no mention of the title in the *New York Herald*, the fight report stated that both men were inside the articled 160lbs despite Creedon looking a good ten pounds heavier. Apart from the opening session when Creedon was sent to his knees from a hard right swing to the head, he was in total control throughout, sending out left jabs and right crosses almost at will. In what was a tame affair, Baker lacked the class required to beat his opponent.

11 December 1896. (160lbs) Dan Creedon w rsc 9 (20) Dick O'Brien.
Venue: Broadway AC, Manhattan, NYC, New York, USA. **Referee:** Dick Roche.
Fight Summary: Although articled for 20 rounds at catchweights, Creedon's 160lb title claim was at stake in this one after O'Brien, who had been in training for a fight with Joe Walcott, was well inside the 158lbs class limit. Despite showing wonderful gameness, O'Brien was being pounded all around the ring in the ninth round when the referee stopped it. Even though he tired and was out of condition, Creedon was the better fighter by far.

26 December 1896. (158lbs) Charles Kid McCoy w co 9 (20) Bill Doherty.
Venue: The Amphitheatre, Johannesburg, South Africa. **Referee:** Clem D. Webb.
Fight Summary: Billed as a world title fight at 158lbs, McCoy (156), on top from the opening bell, soon had the outclassed Doherty (158) under pressure, dropping him in the third, fourth and fifth rounds. Showing tremendous courage, Doherty somehow stayed in the fight, but with McCoy biding his time he was twice floored by heavy rights to the jaw in the ninth, the second occasion seeing him counted out. It was a bad knockout and one that took Doherty almost thirty minutes to properly come round from. While the winner would be recognised in South Africa as champion, Bob Fitzsimmons was still generally perceived to be the titleholder elsewhere.

On 26 May 1897, McCoy stopped Dick O'Brien in the tenth round of a scheduled 25-rounder at the Palace AC, Manhattan, NYC, New York, USA. Although reportedly made at 158lbs this fight should not be seen as a defence of McCoy's claim to the 158lbs title as it was really a catchweight contest, with O'Brien coming in at 163lbs to McCoy's 156. Even then it was stated that McCoy looked much heavier.

12 January 1897. (160lbs) Dan Creedon w rsc 4 (20) Jim Williams.
Venue: Myers AC, Park Street Rink, Albany, New York, USA. **Referee:** Johnny Eckhardt.
Fight Summary: The *Buffalo Courier* reported the fight as being for the world 160lbs title between the champion, Creedon, who claimed to weigh 159lbs, and Williams (158). Following two heavy knockdowns in the fourth round from left-hand swings to the head, and having sustained a bad beating from there on, Williams was rescued by the referee just as the police were about to move in.

By March, however, Creedon admitted he could not get down to 160lbs anymore and in future would be boxing at 165lbs.

23 June 1897. (160lbs) George Chrisp w disq 12 (20) Edward Starlight Rollins.
Venue: Ginnett's Circus, Newcastle, England. **Referee:** Edward Humphreys.
Fight Summary: Made at 160lbs, although there was no championship billing attached it was generally recognised that the winner would have some right to the Imperial British Empire title at the weight. By the fifth both men had got into their stride, Chrisp (158) working well to the body while Rollins (157½) made a target of the head. However, it was not until the tenth that the Australian won a round even though it had been competitive from the opening bell. With Chrisp concentrating on the body there had been a fair bit of holding on by Rollins throughout, but in the 11th and 12th after being spoken to by the referee on a number of occasions for holding and hitting the latter was disqualified when the warnings were clearly having no effect on him.

20 August 1897. (150lbs) Paddy Purtell w rsc 6 (20) Lachie Thomson.
Venue: Olympic Club, Birmingham, England. **Referee:** John S. Barnes.
Fight Summary: Given world 150lbs title billing, Purtell, announced as being 149½lbs and fighting in Britain for the first time, really weighed in at 150½lbs. However, Thomson (149) waived the forfeit to allow the contest to go ahead. Purtell got away well, winning the opening three rounds and flooring Thomson with a solid right as the gong sounded the end of the third. Completely on top during the fifth, Purtell had Thomson at his mercy in the sixth, and 30 seconds into the session the referee saved the latter from taking further punishment when stopping the contest in the American's favour.

On 13 September, Arthur Akers knocked out Bill Singleton at the above venue in the first of a 20-round contest that was reported in some places as being for the English 150lbs title. In truth, it was a catchweight affair with both men coming in well above the weight. It was also a mismatch that lasted just 117 seconds.

When Akers (170) met Purtell (160) at catchweights at the Olympic Club on 30 November, it was all over in the opening round after the American had been floored three times prior to his second entering the ring and earning him a disqualification.

8 September 1897. (158lbs) Charles Kid McCoy drew 5 (20) Tommy Ryan.
Venue: The Alhambra, Syracuse, New York, USA. **Referee:** George Siler.
Fight Summary: The *Syracuse Evening News* reported that Ryan, although at his best at 145lbs, surprisingly agreed to enter the ring at 154lbs with McCoy scaling inside the articled 158lbs. Political and police interference saw the fight halted during the fifth round with neither man badly hurt, despite Ryan suffering damage to his left eye. Press reports stated that it was rumoured prior to the fight that the police would enforce a stoppage in the fifth or sixth rounds, but that could not be substantiated. When asked why he stopped the fight, Police Inspector O'Brien said that he had seen Ryan beginning to land heavy blows to McCoy's kidney region and felt that those punches were unacceptable. Reported as no contest in some record books, Siler gave it as a draw. It was generally thought that Ryan, now claiming the title at 150lbs, was ahead at the time of the stoppage and would have gone on to win. Although the leading promoters of the day were anxious for the men to be rematched they could not make the fight due to McCoy sticking out for 158lbs and Ryan wanting 154lbs.

Another fight made at 158lbs, and scheduled for six rounds, saw McCoy knock out Australian Billy Smith inside two rounds at the 2nd Regiment Armoury, Chicago, Illinois on 15 November.

23 October 1897. (158lbs) Dick O'Brien w rsc 2 (20) Frank Craig.
Venue: Olympic Club, Birmingham, England. **Referee:** John S. Barnes.
Fight Summary: Billed for the world 158lbs title claim held by Craig (157¾), although both men made a reasonable start by the end of the first round it was noticeable that O'Brien (158) was scoring well and looking most dangerous with the left. Picking up where he left off, O'Brien hammered in a right that almost closed Craig's left eye in the second, and before too long he had found the latter's chin with a similar blow that sent him down heavily. Having made a tremendous effort to pull himself up it was clear that upon getting to his feet Craig was finished. When he was put down again almost immediately the referee called off the count, stating that it would be foolish to allow the contest to proceed further.

O'Brien's claim went nowhere, especially as he had been stopped by Charles Kid McCoy some six months earlier. And in his very next contest, weighing 160lbs, he was disqualified inside four rounds against Dick Burge (146) at the above venue on 21 December.

In America, on 9 December, George Byers was claiming to be the 'black champion' after beating Harry Peppers (w co 19 at the Jacques Auditorium, Waterbury, Connecticut) in a bout scheduled for 20 rounds. However, Byers seems to be fighting heavyweights from hereon in despite Baltimore promoters trying to match him against Jim Janey for the 'black title'.

17 December 1897. (158lbs) Charles Kid McCoy w rtd 16 (25) Dan Creedon.
Venue: Puritan AC, Queens, NYC, New York, USA. **Referee:** Sam Austin.
Fight Summary: With Bob Fitzsimmons recognised as being unable to make 158lbs any longer, the promoters billed this as a battle to decide the middleweight championship at that weight. Made at catchweights, despite the fact that the *New York Herald* had earlier called it hardly legitimate, they later reclassified it as being one of the most important fights since the days of Nonpareil Jack Dempsey. Although pre-fight newspaper reports had stated that McCoy was expected to make 160lbs to Creedon's 165, the official announcement at ringside was that McCoy had scaled 155½lbs to Creedon's 157. Having advantages in height and reach, McCoy used them well against the stocky Creedon, jabbing lefts to the head and reaching for the body, and was always in control. In round nine, after heavy left swings opened up a cut over Creedon's left eye it came as no surprise when the latter was sent to the floor in the 11th following a right to the head. With Creedon's eye bleeding freely McCoy saw his opportunity in the 15th, dropping the New Zealander in his own corner. Only just making it to his feet in time Creedon was now at McCoy's mercy, but although he managed to make it to the end of the session he was unable to respond to the start of the 16th before being retired by his corner.

20 December 1897. (150lbs) Tommy Ryan w co 3 (20) Bill Heffernan.
Venue: Olympic AC, Buffalo, New York, USA. **Referee:** Jack Sheehan.
Fight Summary: This one was reported by the *Buffalo Courier* to be a defence of Ryan's 150lbs world title claim. For two rounds the lanky Heffernan kept Ryan at bay before being dropped for 'nine' in the third. Then, after being sent down again moments later he was counted out.

17 January 1898. (150lbs) Jerry Driscoll w pts 20 Tom Woodley.
Venue: NSC, Covent Garden, London, England. **Referee:** Bernard J. Angle.
Fight Summary: Despite a lack of billing this contest was regarded by those in the know as involving the English 150lbs title. Prior to the 17th round the men were difficult to split in what had been an even match-up, but from thereon in it was Driscoll (149½) who did the better work. On several occasions Woodley (146) was seen to be groggy. Never wasting a punch, the sailor fired away with both hands and pinned Woodley back to such a degree that there could only be one winner at the final bell.

Driscoll, an unassuming man, never pushed his claim.

25 February 1898. (154lbs) Anthony Diamond w pts 12 Dido Plumb.
Venue: Olympic Club, Birmingham, England. **Referee:** John S. Barnes.
Fight Summary: Although the final of an 154lbs championship competition, with Diamond, having his final bout, and Plumb being acknowledged by most as the best two men in the country the result was seen as settling the championship. Plumb was the first to make a move, using both hands to head and body before Diamond could find any sort of rhythm, and in the third round the latter's right eye was cut. By the fifth Diamond had got his left hand working well while scoring a mass of points, he was also avoiding Plumb's rushes better than before. From there on to the final bell it was Diamond's left hand holding up Plumb, who tried on numerous occasions to find his adversary's jaw without too much success. At the conclusion, both judges decided that Diamond's better boxing warranted the verdict.

On 6 September, when Diamond confirmed that he was retiring Plumb reclaimed the title.

25 February 1898. (158lbs) Tommy Ryan w co 18 (20) George Green.
Venue: National AC, San Francisco, California, USA. **Referee:** Jim McDonald.
Fight Summary: The *San Francisco Chronicle* report on the day of the fight stated that this was a catchweight contest between the welterweight champion and a man some seven pounds heavier. However, with both men inside 158lbs, Ryan's claim to the title at that weight stems from this one. The first 13 rounds saw the advantage alternating between both men, but thereafter it was noticeable that Green was tiring fast and Ryan's short right-arm blows to the body and straight lefts were beginning to drain the Californian. Ryan was now giving a great exhibition of boxing, and in the 18th a left-right combination to the jaw put Green down for the count. Although Green had already been counted out, Ryan stepped in with a right swing once he was up to put him down again, upon which matters were quickly concluded when the referee's decision became clear.

As far as the *Sporting Life* were concerned, Green (152) claimed the 158lbs middleweight title when outpointing Dan Creedon at Woodward's Pavilion, San Francisco on 30 December. However, I can find nothing to support that statement, especially when Green lost twice to Al Neill in his next three contests.

11 April 1898. (158/160lbs) George Chrisp w co 8 (20) Jim Richardson.
Venue: Standard Theatre, Gateshead, England. **Referee:** Ed Plummer.
Fight Summary: Advertised in some quarters as being for both the English 158 and 160lbs titles it was give and take all the way, Richardson (158) having the better of the contest between the third and sixth rounds before Chrisp came again. Although Chrisp had been groggy on several occasions he kept at it despite receiving severe punishment at times, and in the seventh he matched Richardson blow for blow. In the eighth it was Richardson's turn to go weak following several cracks on the jaw, a left half-arm punch eventually sending him to the floor. On getting up in a dazed state, with Richardson at the mercy of Chrisp he was immediately knocked down again, this

355

time for the full count. The *Mirror of Life* reported that it was the best contest ever seen in Gateshead, there not being a single foul blow or clinch all night.

23 May 1898. (154lbs) Dido Plumb w co 4 (20) Australian Billy Edwards.
Venue: NSC, Covent Garden, London, England.
Fight Summary: Recognised as an Imperial British Empire title fight at 154lbs, Edwards (149) made all the early running when concentrating on the body, having Plumb (152) down in the first round from a right to the point of the jaw. On getting up, Plumb boxed on the back foot for a while before coming back hard in the third, but after about a minute gone in the fourth he was dropped again. However, unperturbed, Plumb got to his feet and dodged around the ring for some respite before smashing in a countering right to Edwards' jaw as the Australian carelessly rushed forward. Now it was Edwards' turn to visit the canvas, and a complete reversal of form saw him go down three more times in that session prior to being counted out on the 2.10 mark.

23 May 1898. (160lbs+) Arthur Akers w co 2 (20) Bill Chesterfield Goode.
Venue: NSC, Covent Garden, London, England. **Referee:** Bernard J. Angle.
Fight Summary: Akers (162½) made the better start, appearing to be faster than Goode (166), and following some solid work inside he dropped the latter who went back to his corner at the end of the first round blowing hard having taken a short count. With Goode again under pressure in the second session, after being floored by a hard right to the cheek he gamely got up only to be met by the two-fisted Akers, now champing at the bit. This time round Goode never stood a chance and a hard right to the jaw saw him counted out with 40 seconds of the round remaining. On the result, the winner had a fair claim to both the English 164 and 166lb titles.

13 June 1898. (154lbs) Tommy Ryan w rsc 14 (20) Tommy West.
Venue: Lenox AC, Manhattan, NYC, New York, USA. **Referee:** Charlie White.
Fight Summary: The Articles of Agreement specifically called for a catchweight contest with neither man to exceed 154lbs, and with both inside it should be recognised as a defence of Ryan's title claim. West (152) gave a remarkable exhibition of courage when standing up to Ryan (146) and taking a terrible beating for almost 14 rounds. On realising that West was right at home on the inside Ryan stuck to boxing at range, gradually cutting his man up, going from head to body as he looked for any weakness. In the earlier rounds West was always a danger, but by the 12th he was fighting on instinct alone, having been smashed to the floor by a heavy right to the head. Eventually, with a minute to go in the 14th the referee called the fight off when West was being hit at will.

5 September 1898. (160lbs+) Dick Burge w co 1 (20) Arthur Akers.
Venue: New Adelphi Theatre, The Strand, London, England. **Referee:** George Dunning.
Fight Summary: Made as a catchweight contest, Akers, who was reckoned to be inside 164lbs and felt that he had a reasonable claim to the English title at that weight, was soon under attack from Burge. Although Akers fought back, after being dropped twice more a right to the jaw sent him down to be counted out after 1.45 of the first round. Deemed to be a 'fix' by some, Burge remained at his natural weight despite challenging all the 160lbs men in England, while Akers, who also played rugby for Leicester, later contracted pneumonia and died on 8 October 1899.

24 October 1898. (158lbs) Tommy Ryan w pts 20 Jack Bonner.
Venue: Greater New York AC, Brooklyn, NYC, New York, USA. **Referee:** Alex Brown.
Fight Summary: According to the *New York Herald* report of the fight, Ryan (149) v Bonner (158) involved the 158lbs title. The *Ring Record Book* lists this contest as being for the vacant world title, but in reality it was only the American version which was at stake, and even that was not conclusive with Bob Fitzsimmons continuing to class himself the champion and Charles Kid McCoy having a stronger claim than Ryan. There was no doubting that Bonner's wonderful condition got him through a fight he would eventually lose and that Ryan had to be careful throughout. In the second round, Bonner, who was confident of victory, dropped Ryan with a right to the head for 'nine', but although dazed the latter came roaring back to match his man blow for blow. Thereafter, Ryan had the upper hand, and after dropping Bonner for 'three' in the fifth with a right to the jaw he upped the pace and worked the head and body consistently to weaken his man. Cut badly on the left eye in the tenth, with Bonner right up against it, the last three sessions saw Ryan chopping him up bit by bit without taking too many risks.

On the same date, at the Athletic Club, Louisville, Kentucky, Jimmy Watts stopped Jim Janey inside seven rounds to claim the 'black title'. Watts lost his title claim when he was knocked out inside eight rounds by Joe Walcott at the same venue on 30 May 1899. With Walcott only interested in fighting for a more generally recognised title there were no defences as such for him.

23 November 1898. (158lbs) Tommy Ryan w rtd 8 (20) Johnny Gorman.

Venue: Turn Hall, Syracuse, New York, USA. **Referee:** Yank Sullivan.

Fight Summary: All the New York papers reported this one as a catchweight contest, but with Gorman inside 158lbs it should be considered a defence of Ryan's title claim at the weight. Ryan once again proved how good he was, controlling the contest against a dangerous man while waiting for the right time to strike. With jabs opening Gorman up for rights to head and body, in the eighth Ryan cut loose to drop the man from Brooklyn heavily following a terrific right-hand smash to the jaw with just three seconds of the round remaining. After Gorman's seconds got him back to the corner, on discovering that their man had a broken rib the sponge was thrown up and the decision given to Ryan.

25 November 1898. (160lbs) Frank Craig w co 12 (20) George Chrisp.

Venue: Ginnett's Circus, Newcastle, England. **Referee:** J. T. Hulls.

Fight Summary: Reported as involving the world 160lbs title, and in what was described as one of the best contests seen in the City for a long while, Chrisp (158) put up a good fight. After taking the lead and cutting Chrisp's mouth badly in the sixth it seemed odds on a Craig (158½) victory, but the local man had the American reeling around the ring in the seventh before the latter came back strongly with accurate lefts over the next few rounds. With Craig firmly in control, having finally caught up with Chrisp at the start of the 12th, a right swing to the jaw brought the fight to a conclusion.

23 December 1898. (158lbs) Tommy Ryan w rsc 14 (25) Dick O'Brien.

Venue: Charter Oak AC, The Coliseum, Hartford, Connecticut, USA. **Referee:** Dick Roche.

Fight Summary: With Ryan weighing 148lbs to O'Brien's 158, this should be classed as a defence of the former's title claim at the weight. Proving to be as durable as they come it took Ryan close on 14 rounds before he was able to drop O'Brien, having given him a shellacking for most of the fight. Badly cut around the eyes from the fourth onwards, O'Brien was eventually stopped in the 14th after Ryan had smashed him to the canvas three times, the final knockdown bringing the police into the ring and forcing the referee to call it off.

1 March 1899. (150lbs) Tommy Ryan w co 8 (20) Charley Johnson.

Venue: Whittington Park Arena, Hot Springs, Arkansas, USA. **Referee:** Jake Holtman.

Fight Summary: Following his contest with Johnson at 150lbs, Ryan was now claiming the title at all weights between 150lbs and 158lbs. It was soon apparent that Johnson was no match for Ryan, who let him force the fight for two or three rounds before opening up in the fourth with stiff blows to the ribs. In the eighth Johnson was dropped three times from body blows, the last time seeing him counted out.

1 May 1899. (154lbs) Dido Plumb w co 9 (15) Bill Heffernan.

Venue: NSC, Covent Garden, London, England. **Referee:** J. H. Douglas.

Fight Summary: Billed for English, Imperial British Empire and world (in some reports) 154lbs titles, Plumb (152) eventually asserted his superiority over the tough Heffernan (151) by the eighth round despite having been sent to his knees in the third and being hurt on several occasions. Ultimately, it was Plumb's ability to effectively counter the onrushing Heffernan that turned the fight his way. Coming out for the ninth, with Heffernan forcing, Plumb finally got to his man with left-rights to put him down, and when the Colonial managed to get to his feet he was quickly sent to the floor again to be counted out.

Around this time, Tom Woodley, who was more at home when weighing around the 144lbs mark, challenged all England at 150lbs. However, it would be another two or three years before he settled into that weight.

31 August 1899. (152lbs) Tommy Ryan w pts 20 Jack Moffat.

Venue: The Auditorium, Dubuque, Iowa, USA. **Referee:** George Siler.

Fight Summary: Despite being given as a welterweight title defence for Ryan, according to the *Chicago Tribune*, it was effectively Ryan's middleweight claim that was at stake here. After 20 rounds of fast fighting the decision went to Ryan (152), who was given more punishment than he would normally take and hurt his right hand in the 17th. There were no knockdowns, but with Moffat (152) giving Ryan all the trouble he could handle the champion had to change tactics several times to avert a defeat.

5 September 1899. (158lbs) Charles Kid McCoy w co 3 (20) Geoff Thorne.
Venue: Broadway AC, Manhattan, NYC, New York, USA. **Referee:** Johnny White.
Fight Summary: Articled at 158lbs, with both men inside at the 3pm weigh-in, McCoy's claim at the weight was automatically at stake. Having made a reasonable start, in the second round Thorne was sent to the ropes before dropping on one knee to avoid further punishment. Thorne was then put down by lefts to head and body. In the third, with both men looking for an opening, two terrific lefts to the head sent Thorne crashing to be counted out flat on his face.

18 September 1899. (158lbs) Tommy Ryan w rsc 10 (25) Frank Craig.
Venue: Coney Island AC, Brooklyn, NYC, New York, USA. **Referee:** George Siler.
Fight Summary: The *New York Herald* stated that both men, candidates for middleweight honours, were to meet at 158lbs. Despite rumours that Craig would come in over the weight the fight went ahead, the 'Coffee Cooler' starting well before having Ryan down in the second round from a right swing to the ear. By the fifth, Ryan, who was dictating the pace, was beginning to land heavy rights under Craig's heart that saw him eventually weaken. In the ninth Craig was dropped three times and appeared to be quitting before coming out for the tenth. Ryan lost no time in going after Craig, slamming away with both hands until putting him down with a right to the head. Although Craig got up at the count of 'nine' he was all over the place, and with 30 seconds of the session still remaining the referee rescued him.

In the aftermath, Ryan, who was also claiming the title up to 154lbs, challenged Charles Kid McCoy at that weight knowing full well that his rival would have difficulty in making it. McCoy, not surprisingly declined the offer, stating that 158lbs was now the real middleweight limit and that he still recognised Bob Fitzsimmons as champion, not Ryan.

On 29 May 1900, at Tattersall's Arena, Chicago, Illinois, Ryan took on McCoy in a six-round contest where both men were inside 158lbs, thus risking their title claims at the weight. Having raised McCoy's hand at the final bell, the referee, Malachy Hogan, was overruled when it came to light that the contract had stated that if both men were on their feet at the end of the contest a draw would be given.

Following this one, Ryan (150) won the six-round points decision over Young Mahoney (146) at the Dearborn AC, Chicago on 29 June 1900, before another short-distance fight saw him outpoint Kid Carter (158) over six rounds at Tattersall's Arena, Chicago on 27 November 1900.

19 March 1900. (154lbs) Dido Plumb w co 8 (15) Australian Jim Ryan.
Venue: NSC, Covent Garden, London, England. **Referee:** J. H. Douglas.
Fight Summary: Advertised for the Imperial British Empire and world 154lbs title, to be contested in six-ounce gloves, it was Plumb (153) who showed up better than Ryan (153¾) throughout, his left-hand leads continually opening the latter up. Several times Ryan was told to stop holding and hitting as he looked to gain an advantage, and by the seventh he had fallen behind due to the better work of the Englishman. The eighth round proved to be the last, as Ryan, in taking the fight to Plumb, was put down twice by heavy rights to the jaw before being counted out on the second occasion.

18 May 1900. (158lbs) Charles Kid McCoy w rtd 6 (25) Dan Creedon.
Venue: Broadway AC, Manhattan, NYC, New York, USA. **Referee:** Sam Austin.
Fight Summary: With McCoy's title claim at 158lbs on the line in this one he had no trouble in disposing of Creedon who looked very much the smaller man of the two. Creedon was knocked down in the third and sixth

rounds, the last time seeing his corner throw in the towel after 34 seconds of the session had elapsed. With Creedon never posing a threat, it appeared that McCoy could have finished his rival off at any time.

1 June 1900. (158lbs) Charles Kid McCoy w rtd 13 (25) Jack Bonner.

Venue: Broadway AC, Manhattan, NYC, New York, USA. **Referee:** Charlie White.

Fight Summary: Made at 158lbs, with Bonner looking to carry off McCoy's title claim at the weight in this one he gave it his best shot. Bonner was game to the core and fought viciously at times, even putting McCoy on the floor in the eighth round with a left swing to the head. In the ninth through to the 11th, although Bonner was under duress he refused to buckle, but in the 12th McCoy was all over him, sending him to his knees prior to the bell. Springing into action in the 13th McCoy sent in rights and lefts, and after Bonner had capsized from the effects of the battering his seconds threw up the sponge.

McCoy appears to have left the middleweight division in the possession of Tommy Ryan when taking on James J. Corbett for the heavyweight crown in his very next contest.

Following a three-round knockout win over England's Geoff Thorne at the Athletic Club, Chicago, Illinois on 10 November at 152lbs, Ryan was next in action on 27 November. The *Chicago Tribune* reported that while Ryan's six-round points win over Kid Carter at Tattersall's, Chicago on that date could hardly be classified as a championship match, both men had made 158lbs at the 6pm weigh-in.

15 October 1900. (152lbs) Charlie McKeever w pts 15 Dido Plumb.

Venue: NSC, Covent Garden, London, England. **Referee:** J. H. Douglas.

Fight Summary: Billed for the world title at 152lbs, McKeever (150) always seemed to be a step ahead of Plumb (152) who tended to go for the single punch and seemed unable to hit the target with maximum effect. This was possibly due to the fact that McKeever was very quick, both on his feet and with his hands. However, while Plumb remained strong he was always a threat, but even at his best he was only sharing rounds. Despite being dropped by a left hook at the end of the 11th and going over in the 13th Plumb still persevered, putting McKeever down in the 14th and badly hurting him. While there was no doubt that McKeever was shaken up he was soon on the go again, cruising through the final session to take the decision.

However, with Tommy Ryan considered the champion in America McKeever's victory carried no weight on the other side of the Atlantic. Regardless of that, according to Young Peter Jackson he took over McKeever's claim at the weight when beating the latter by a sixth-round disqualification at the Washington SC, Philadelphia, Pennsylvania, USA on 21 April 1902, even though it was just a six-rounder.

Despite Plumb losing out to McKeever, he continued to claim the English version of the 152lbs title until moving on. He was challenged several times by Pat Daly, but for whatever reason they never got together.

The next men to challenge all England were Harry Neumier (November 1901), Joe Platford (August 1903), Charlie Allum (April 1905 and onwards), Arthur Daley (August 1907), Charlie Knock (1908) and Peter Brown (1908), but with there being no further activity the weight class faded away following the NSC setting the middleweight limit at 160lbs on 11 February 1909.

28 January 1901. (158lbs) Dick Burge nc 2 (15) Jerry Driscoll.

Venue: Standard Theatre, Gateshead, England. **Referee:** Ed Plummer.

Fight Summary: Given billing as an English 158lbs title in some quarters, while Burge (151) made the early running after a relatively even first round, when there was too much holding, the second started in the same vein. However, after both men had been forced down on a couple of occasions, when Driscoll (157) rushed Burge they proceeded to fight hard on the ground as time was called. Having warned both fighters throughout, the referee then decided to call the contest off when it was clear that neither man was listening to his commands.

For Burge it was his last fight, and having spent three months on remand for fraud he was sentenced to ten years imprisonment in February 1902.

4 March 1901. (158lbs) Tommy Ryan w rtd 17 (20) Tommy West.
Venue: Southern AC Auditorium, Louisville, Kentucky, USA. **Referee:** Tim Hurst.
Fight Summary: Reported as a title match at 158lbs, although some papers gave it as being at catchweights, the *Chicago Tribune* reported afterwards that Ryan had strengthened his claim to the world title on the result. With both men said to be inside 157lbs, Ryan was sent to the floor twice in the second and looked all-in at the bell. However, despite losing the next two rounds he came back strongly in the fifth. In the sixth Ryan's right cheek was opened, and in the seventh West had his nose broken, his right eye closed, his forehead cut in two places and cheek split. For the next ten sessions Ryan played continually on West's injuries, it being amazing that the latter was able to continue for as long as he did before his seconds eventually retired him at the end of the 17th.

24 June 1901. (154/156lbs) Jack Palmer w co 5 (20) Lachie Thomson.
Venue: Ginnett's Circus, Newcastle, England. **Referee:** George Dunning.
Fight Summary: In a match made at catchweights, Palmer (154) started as if he meant to finish early, leading off without any response prior to having Thomson on the floor as the bell ended the third. Although Thomson came back from that strongly he was unable to sustain his attacks for long, and in the fifth, tiring rapidly, he was fought all over the ring before a terrific uppercut sent him crashing to the boards to be counted out.

After Palmer claimed the English 154lbs title he moved up in weight to take on the American, Charlie McKeever, at the same venue on 9 December. Stopped by the police in the second round, McKeever had been restricted to 156lbs (actually coming in at 158lbs), while Palmer was allowed to make any weight.

Subsequently, a number of men, including Palmer (August 1902) and Tom Woodley (November 1902), challenged all England at 156lbs, but it was not until 1906 that Pat O'Keefe put his stamp on the weight class.

4 July 1901. (159lbs) George Gardner w rsc 3 (20) Jack Moffat.
Venue: Old Baseball Ground, San Francisco, California, USA. **Referee:** Jack Welch.
Fight Summary: Advertised for the middleweight title according to the *San Francisco Chronicle*, Gardner (158) and Moffat (156) failed to conform to the Articles of Agreement when they weighed-in only four hours before the action got underway. The fight saw Moffat down in the first round from a right to the jaw before he dislocated his left shoulder and then rescued by the referee when on one knee in the third. This was the third time Moffat had dislocated his left shoulder, and following two more contests he was forced to retire.

Regardless of any claim at 158lbs coming in from Gardner, with Tommy Ryan now generally recognised as champion there would have been little support for him outside California, especially after he lost a 20-round points decision to Joe Walcott (who was well inside the middleweight limit) on 27 September at the Mechanic's Pavilion, San Francisco.

Following that, at the same venue on 31 January 1902, Gardner lost to another future light heavyweight champion, Jack Root, on a seventh-round disqualification in an advertised 158lbs title fight, despite the articles calling for catchweights. With neither man making the weight, Gardner continued his career in the new light heavyweight division.

19 August 1901. (154lbs) Philadelphia Jack O'Brien w co 6 (15) Dido Plumb.
Venue: Ginnett's Circus, Newcastle, England. **Referee:** Ed Plummer.
Fight Summary: Billed for the British version of the world 154lbs title, O'Brien (153) was far too good for Plumb (152) in both skill and power. After punching it out in the opening two rounds with Plumb, and dropping him near the end of the third, it was clear that O'Brien would ultimately win the day. In the fourth session Plumb took some heavy punishment as O'Brien began to open up with both hands, and although the Englishman came back strongly in the fifth he could not find a way through his rival's guard. The sixth saw Plumb continually tearing into O'Brien but, after several attempts to bring his man down had failed, he was sent to the boards to be counted out following a battery of heavy blows to the jaw.

10 October 1901. (158lbs) George Green w disq 6 (10+) Tommy Ryan.
Venue: Jackson County Democratic Club, Kansas City, Missouri, USA. **Referee:** Dave Porteous.
Fight Summary: Contracted at 158lbs, with both men inside, Ryan was winning easily until accidentally striking Green (147) with his knee after knocking him down in the sixth and being ruled out. Scheduled for ten rounds, or until a decision could be reached, with Ryan's title claim at the weight obviously at stake one can only assume that Green took it over. Ryan had been the aggressor throughout and had slightly the better of proceedings, often cornering Green and pounding away without respite. Although Green frequently countered Ryan's persistent onslaughts, being worn down gradually, he would have been hard pressed to have gained a victory by any other route.

27 January 1902. (154lbs) Philadelphia Jack O'Brien w disq 3 (15) Charlie McKeever.
Venue: Yorkshire County Athletic Club, Leeds, England.
Fight Summary: Seen as being for the British version of the 154lbs title, O'Brien (157½), who was forced to pay forfeit, won a contest that was fast, furious and clever when McKeever (154), who had been warned several times for holding, back-heeled him and was disqualified towards the end of the third round. Following this, O'Brien returned to America to seek a fight with Tommy Ryan.

Despite Dido Plumb continuing to claim the English 154lbs title for the next couple of years, when he remained inactive the weight class leadership was eventually taken up by Charlie Knock, who won a championship competition at Wonderland, Mile End, London on 1 February 1904 after outpointing Charlie Allum over 12 two-minute rounds. Knock (153½) received a silver cup on beating Allum (153), but it was the loser who began challenging all England at 154lbs.

Another man to catch the eye was Jim Courtney, who beat the future British champion, Pat O'Keefe, three times at the Welsh NSC, Queens Hall, Cardiff, Wales in 1904 - on points over 15 rounds on 16 March, a tenth-round knockout on 2 May and an 11th-round knockout on 23 May - prior to outpointing Jim Styles over ten rounds at the same venue on 3 October to win an international championship competition.

While not much more is heard from Courtney at the weight, men such as Joe Platford (February 1905), Mike Crawley (December 1905), O'Keefe (January 1906), Pat Daly (April 1906), Arthur Daley (August 1907), Sid Doyle (January 1908) and Jack Kingsland (July 1908) continued to challenge all England at 154lbs.

30 January 1902. (158lbs) Tommy Ryan w co 7 (10) George Green.
Venue: 3rd Regiment Armoury Hall, Kansas City, Missouri, USA.
Fight Summary: If Green, participating in what would be his last contest, ever took his 158lbs title claim seriously, and nobody else appeared to do so, this result put the record straight. Angry that he had been disqualified in their last encounter, when Ryan came out firing he soon had Green down from a left to the jaw after knocking him over the ropes with a hard right to the body. Having dropped Green in the second and fourth rounds Ryan was now biding his time, and in the seventh he sent the San Franciscan crashing to the boards to be counted out on the 2.20 mark following a heavy right to the jaw.

12 April 1902. (156lbs) Jack Palmer w co 11 (20) Joe White.
Venue: Ginnett's Circus, Newcastle, England. **Referee:** J. R. Smoult.
Fight Summary: Made at catchweights, Palmer (156), who was restricted to 158lbs, looked to be in the pink of condition at the start while White (154½) appeared drawn. The fight started with White going with the left hand, but it was quickly apparent that Palmer was the stronger man and at the end of the third round he landed a terrific right to the head just as the bell went. From there onwards, White did much holding, showing a lot of cleverness as he slipped punches. However, in the 11th Palmer finally got a reward for his aggression when dropping his rival to the boards with a terrific blow to the pit of the stomach. Although White called for the foul, the referee continued to count him out, an action that was followed by Palmer claiming the English title at the weight.

Later that year, Charlie Wilson claimed to be the English champion at 156lbs in the 4 November edition of the *Sporting Life*, while Tom Woodley challenged all England at the weight in the same issue.

26 May 1902. (158lbs) Tommy Ryan w rsc 4 (10) Jimmy Handler.
Venue: Turner Hall, Kansas City, Missouri, USA. **Referee:** W. H. Gibson.
Fight Summary: The *Kansas City Star* reported that with both men inside 158lbs Handler would have had a strong claim to the title if he won. However, with Ryan sending in rights and lefts to his jaw and body in rapid succession, as early as the second round any game-plan that Handler may have had went out of the window. It was all over in the fourth after Handler, who had been sent down four times, was rescued by the referee when a right to the jaw had dropped him for the fifth time.

23 June 1902. (154lbs) Joe Walcott w pts 15 Tommy West.
Venue: NSC, Covent Garden, London, England. **Referee:** Tom Scott.
Fight Summary: Advertised as a world title fight, it was, in fact, contested at catchweights with no weights announced, although both men were known to be inside 154lbs. While Walcott deserved the win he did not impress the audience to any great degree, being far too eager to hold on when fighting was what they wanted to see. Regardless of that, Walcott proved to be a good exponent of body punching, with the accomplished West remaining extremely wary throughout. In the seventh round West's left eye began to swell, but it did not stop him from taking the fight to Walcott at various stages despite having little success. The *Sporting Life* reported that even when West was hammering in blows to Walcott's head it was like hitting a post, seemingly having no effect on the latter whatsoever. There were no knockdowns.

Walcott next challenged the winner of Tommy Ryan v Johnny Gorman to decide the middleweight championship.

23 June 1902. (160lbs) Jack Palmer w co 7 (20) Dave Peters.
Venue: Prince of Wales Circus, Merthyr Tydfil, Wales. **Referee:** Tom Davies.
Fight Summary: Billed for the English 160lbs title, and articled for two-minute rounds to be in place, most aficionados ruled it out as a championship contest, the *Cardiff Evening Express* reporting the result as an eight-round kayo in an eliminator for the English championship. It was only in the first and second rounds that Peters appeared to have a chance reported the *Sporting Life*, and from there onwards Palmer began to pile up the points with a strong left lead. That the fight lasted as long as it did was entirely due to appeals for fouls and unsportsmanlike behaviour on behalf of Peters' supporters claimed the paper. On two occasions, Peters, who was almost finished and had been knocked out of the ring, gained three or four minutes respite due these tactics. However, in the seventh it was all over for Peters after a solid right-left sent him down to be counted out.

While Palmer moves up in weight following this one there is little activity at 160lbs until the NSC standardised weights on 11 February 1909, other than challenges and claimants in Britain such as Pat O'Keefe (September 1906), Charlie Wilson (November 1906), Jack Costello (June 1908) and Charlie Allum (July 1908).

24 June 1902. (150lbs) Tom Woodley w pts 10 Jim Styles.
Venue: New Adelphi Club, The Strand, London, England. **Referee:** Harry Cooper.
Fight Summary: Given 150lbs English middleweight championship billing, with a belt to match, and cut from 15 rounds to ten, Woodley set a fast pace right from the opening bell. Although Styles responded with splendid executions of his own at times he had difficulty maintaining the pace set by Woodley, and tiring fast he was dropped in the ninth and tenth prior to the verdict going against him.

Despite challenging all England at 150lbs, Woodley, who had weighed in at around 144lbs, remained in the lower weight class. With there being no more major fights at 150lbs in Britain, the weight class passed into history.

24 June 1902. (158lbs) Tommy Ryan w rsc 3 (15) Johnny Gorman.
Venue: NSC, Covent Garden, London, England. **Referee:** Charlie White.
Fight Summary: Recognised as a world title bout despite the Articles of Agreement calling for catchweights, it was Ryan (151) who started the better, showing great cleverness when countering Gorman (158) solidly during the opening session. The second round was full of good work from both men before Ryan stepped up the pace in the third. After landing a terrific left hook to the head, followed by several severe body blows and a right cross to the jaw Gorman was sent to the floor prior to being rescued by the referee.

15 September 1902. (158lbs) Tommy Ryan w co 6 (20) Kid Carter.
Venue: International AC, Fort Erie, Ontario, Canada. **Referee:** George Siler.
Fight Summary: Advertised as being for the championship at 158lbs, Ryan successfully defended his American title claim at the weight when knocking out Carter in the last minute of the sixth round. There was no doubting that Carter was a dangerous opponent, Ryan having to be careful as he looked for openings. In the third a glancing left to the head sent Carter down, and after gradually taking the steam out of him Ryan went to work in the sixth prior to putting his man down for 'nine' from a heavy right to the jaw. Following a further knockdown Carter just about made it to his feet before the final blow of the fight, another heavy right to the jaw, put his lights out.

23 October 1902. (158lbs) Jack Palmer w co 2 (10) Tom Smith.
Venue: National AC, Marylebone, London, England. **Referee:** Professor Murray.
Fight Summary: Billed for the English 158lbs title, despite it being scheduled for only ten rounds, both men were said to have made the weight. Standing several inches over the powerfully built Smith, the man from Benwell, near Newcastle upon Tyne, went straight on to the attack, doing a tremendous amount of damage to his rival in the opening session. Although Smith came back well at times he was unable to halt Palmer's charge, and in the second round he was knocked out by solid blows to the head after being softened up by body punches.

24 November 1902. (158lbs) Jack Palmer w pts 15 Eddie Connolly.
Venue: NSC, Covent Garden, London, England. **Referee:** J. H. Douglas.
Fight Summary: Following two battles between the pair in Newcastle, which Palmer won, they were matched in London in a catchweight contest with Palmer being restricted to 158lbs. The *Mirror of Life* reported the contest to be for the English version of the 158lbs title. It would also be recognised by many as one that involved the Imperial British Empire crown at the weight. Fast and furious throughout, Connolly, fighting with grim determination and strength, was ultimately unable to make up the early rounds surrendered to Palmer. However, right up to the final bell it was unclear as to who would be proclaimed the winner. According to the *Sporting Life*, Connolly made such a good showing that he had nothing to be ashamed about despite losing to Palmer for the third time. Both men gave and received heavy blows, often wincing, but the only knockdown recorded came in the 13th round when Palmer momentarily floored Connolly, having just been shaken up himself.

20 April 1903. (158lbs) Philadelphia Jack O'Brien drew 10 Joe Walcott.
Venue: Health & Physical Culture Club, Boston, Massachusetts, USA. **Referee:** Rube Waddell.
Fight Summary: Reported to be the biggest American middleweight fight seen in that city, with both men thought to be inside 158lbs, O'Brien outboxed Walcott despite breaking a knuckle on his left hand in the second round. The referee had announced before the bout that if both men were still standing at the end of ten rounds he would give a drawn verdict. Afterwards, Walcott stated that he had an agreement with O'Brien not to try for a knockout. With that in mind it was hardly surprising that O'Brien boxed on the back foot for much of the time, jabbing with the left, while Walcott pounded hard to the body when he could get close enough. Following the fight, the *Boston Post* stated that O'Brien should be recognised as the world champion.

25 May 1903. (158lbs) Jack Palmer drew 15 Jack Twin Sullivan.
Venue: NSC, Covent Garden, London, England.
Fight Summary: Contested for the English version of the world title at 158lbs, the opening exchanges favoured Palmer (156) who did the cleaner work, but before too long Sullivan (153) was right back in the fight after deciding that body punching would be his favoured attack. The seventh was a desperate round for Palmer as Sullivan began to catch him heavily to the head, but the Englishman fought back strongly to hurt his rival with a solid blow to the jaw in the tenth. That punch took a lot out of Sullivan, but back he came, concentrating on the body, while Palmer did his best work with the left hand.

14 December 1903. (158lbs) Jack Palmer w rtd 2 (15) Sergeant Tom Harris.
Venue: Standard Theatre, Gateshead, England. **Referee:** Bert Dorman.
Fight Summary: Although the soldier from the 2nd Essex Regiment made a favourable showing in the opening round, weaving in and scoring with both hands, Palmer soon had his measure. In the second, Palmer continually jabbed Harris off balance before a swinging right landed squarely on the latter's jaw to send him down heavily in

his own corner. Although the bell came to Harris's rescue he was in such a bad way that his seconds sensibly retired him during the interval. When the match was made it was reported to be for the English 158lbs title, but the *Sporting Life* failed to mention that. The paper also stated that the fight ended in the third round.

By February 1904 the same paper was claiming that Charlie Wilson should be seen as the English 158lbs champion, while Palmer was also reported as being the English 158lbs champion just a week later.

22 December 1903. (158lbs) Philadelphia Jack O'Brien w pts 15 Jack Twin Sullivan.
Venue: Criterion Club, Boston, Massachusetts, USA. **Referee:** Eugene Buckley.
Fight Summary: The *Boston Post* reported that this fight should be seen as involving the world title. After a few even rounds, O'Brien (158) took over, landing at the rate of three-to-one and, apart from the eighth through to the 13th when Sullivan (153) had some success, he was on top all the way. At the end of the 14th Sullivan was in a bad way after O'Brien had concentrated on the body, but he somehow made it to the final bell.

Finally, on 27 January 1904, O'Brien was matched against his arch-rival, Tommy Ryan, at the National AC, Philadelphia, Pennsylvania. Although only a six-round no-decision fight, as it had been made at 158lbs the *Chicago Tribune* reported that Ryan's right to the title was clearly at stake. After losing the press decision, Ryan was challenged to a fight at the weight by Bob Fitzsimmons, who claimed to never have resigned the middleweight title and that Ryan had been ducking him for years.

Several years later, O'Brien was quoted as saying that Ryan had tricked him by threatening to pull out of their Philadelphia six-rounder at the last moment unless he (O'Brien) deposited $1,000 to be forfeited in case Ryan was knocked out. According to O'Brien, rather than have the match called off he complied with Ryan's wishes. Ignoring all challenges, more than a year passed by before it was rumoured that Ryan would defend the championship in a distance fight against O'Brien. But that fell through when Ryan insisted on 154lbs, a weight that O'Brien had difficulty in making. Early in 1906, it was reported that Ryan had posted a forfeit to meet O'Brien at 158lbs. However, with O'Brien looking to win the heavyweight crown and not interested in having further dealings with Ryan, it came to nothing and at the age of 36 and inactive for over a year Ryan handed his crown to his protégé, Hugo Kelly.

29 December 1903. (158lbs) Philadelphia Jack O'Brien drew 10 Hugo Kelly.
Venue: Vineyard's Hall, Kansas City, Missouri, USA. **Referee:** Dave Porteous.
Fight Summary: According to the *Kansas City Star* both men were safely inside the articled 158lbs, thus putting their title claims at the weight on the line. Making an extremely fast start, O'Brien landed a dozen blows before Kelly could get going. Prior to the end of the third round, when dropped to his knees by a hard right uppercut, O'Brien had continued to send in lefts to Kelly's face. However, after the knockdown he was more wary. From the eighth through to the final bell, Kelly was the stronger of the two, and although he hit the target less than O'Brien his punches carried more steam. The referee's decision of a draw seemed to be taken in good stead by the crowd regardless of O'Brien appearing to be the winner.

14 April 1904. (158lbs) Philadelphia Jack O'Brien w co 3 (15) Jack Twin Sullivan.
Venue: West End Club, St Louis, Missouri, USA. **Referee:** Harry Sharpe.
Fight Summary: With O'Brien's 158lbs title claim on the line in this one, for two rounds Sullivan successfully blocked the punches coming his way but in the third, after similar blows got through his defences and landed on his jaw, he went down to be counted out. Immediately prior to the contest, the *St Louis Post-Dispatch* stated that the winner should meet Tommy Ryan in an effort to sort out the championship as far as America was concerned.

7 May 1904. (158lbs) Jack Palmer w pts 20 Jack Lalor.
Venue: Wanderers' Hall, Johannesburg, South Africa. **Referee:** D. C. Maturin.
Fight Summary: Contesting South Africa's version of the International 158lbs title against England's Palmer, the South African-based Irishman, Lalor (150), was floored in the opening round by a right to the jaw, going down on four more occasions before the final bell came to his rescue. Palmer (156) was always hitting too hard for Lalor, who complained of being constantly struck in the region of the kidneys. Regardless of that, with his two-fisted

attacks and height-and-reach advantages Palmer was always going too well for his game rival. It was only towards the end when Palmer began to tire that Lalor produced his best work.

Palmer fought in the heavyweight division from thereon in.

24 March 1905. (158lbs) Philadelphia Jack O'Brien w disq 2 (20) Young Peter Jackson.
Venue: 4th Regiment Armoury, Baltimore, Maryland, USA. **Referee:** James O'Hara.
Fight Summary: In a match articled at 158lbs, and the men contracted to break cleanly, after O'Brien was put down by a right to the jaw by Jackson (152) in the second round he appeared to have been knocked out. Unfortunately for Jackson he was disqualified on the grounds that he delivered the blow when the referee had been standing between the two men while trying to prise them apart and that 'break' had been called. In the aftermath, officials stated that not only was Jackson told to break, but he had actually thrown the punch when O'Brien was obscured by the referee.

7 April 1905. (158lbs) Philadelphia Jack O'Brien w pts 10 Young Peter Jackson.
Venue: 4th Regiment Armoury, Baltimore, Maryland, USA. **Referee:** Charlie White.
Fight Summary: The *Baltimore Sun* reported that with both men inside 158lbs, O'Brien's American title claim at the weight was automatically at stake. The fight started slowly, but after the opening round it warmed up with nearly every session going in O'Brien's favour. The nearest thing to a knockout came in the ninth when Jackson was extremely groggy but O'Brien was unable to find a finishing punch. Although Jackson generally had the better of things at close quarters he was outboxed and outmanoeuvred, at times being bewildered by O'Brien's movement and evasive tactics.

25 April 1905. (158lbs) Hugo Kelly w pts 10 Philadelphia Jack O'Brien.
Venue: Tomlinson Hall, Indianapolis, Indiana, USA. **Referee:** Jack Ryan.
Fight Summary: Made at 158lbs, with O'Brien reckoned to be heavier, Kelly effectively took over the former's title claim at the weight. O'Brien later claimed that both he and Kelly had agreed in advance not to try for a kayo and that the referee should declare a draw if they were both still standing at the end of ten rounds. Having felt he had clearly outpointed Kelly, O'Brien went on to say that surprise turned to anger when the referee awarded the decision to the latter. Fight reports stated that O'Brien, who was cautioned several times for using rough tactics, had Kelly much distressed in the sixth. Although O'Brien did well from thereon in he was almost out at the end. The referee was reported to have given the decision to Kelly because of his staying power, whereas he had occasionally warned O'Brien to buck his ideas up.

Meanwhile, in Britain on 27 April, Pat O'Keefe challenged all England at 158lbs. He was then followed by Charlie Wilson in September.

7 June 1905. (158lbs) Hugo Kelly drew 10 Tommy Burns.
Venue: Light Guard Armoury, Detroit, Michigan, USA. **Referee:** Eddie Ryan.
Fight Summary: Advertised as a match made at 158lbs, the *Detroit News* stated that, although limited to ten rounds and Burns being a couple of ounces over limit, the fight had more to do with the championship than any other recently held in the region. During the opening three rounds Burns jabbed Kelly at will and tied him into knots by using clever footwork, all that being before the strenuous dieting to make the weight caught up with him. In the fourth Kelly finally got down to business, two-fistedly belting Burns to the body. Kelly stayed with that tactic right through the seventh until the latter looked a spent force. However, in the eighth the pendulum swung as Burns came out fighting in a rejuvenated fashion, nearly taking Kelly out when raining in blows to head and body, before the tenth saw two tired fighters settling for the draw. The *Detroit Times* went on to say that whenever there looked likely to be a knockdown the police in attendance stood up to make sure that scientific principles were being exclusively employed and that neither man was looking to secure a result by a kayo.

17 October 1905. (158lbs) Jack Twin Sullivan w pts 20 Tommy Burns.
Venue: Pacific AC, Los Angeles, California, USA. **Referee:** Charles Eyton.

Fight Summary: Taking into account his 20-round points win over Hugo Kelly at the Athletic Club, Kansas City, Missouri on 7 April 1904, Sullivan (153lbs) claimed the 158lbs title on the strength of this win over Burns (163). With Sullivan being Burns' master throughout, by the end of the eighth round the latter's nose was bleeding, one eye had closed and he was seriously inconvenienced by the considerable punishment he had received in the way of body blows. For whatever reason, Burns saw the head as his target, but with Sullivan's ability to duck and sidestep expertly he had little success in that area. There were no knockdowns.

11 December 1905. (158lbs) Hugo Kelly drew 10 Young Mahoney.
Venue: Tomlinson Hall, Indianapolis, Indiana, USA. **Referee:** James Ryan.
Fight Summary: Kelly's 158lbs title claim was at stake in this one, with both men inside the weight, and the referee gave a draw after deciding that Mahoney had made up any lost ground when rallying strongly in the last two sessions. With Mahoney always willing to take a punch to land one of his own, even when rocked he came back strongly to bother Kelly who had gone to the front early on with his better boxing.

9 March 1906. (158lbs) Hugo Kelly drew 20 Jack Twin Sullivan.
Venue: Pacific AC, Los Angeles, California, USA. **Referee:** Charles Eyton.
Fight Summary: Articled at 158lbs, with both men inside the weight according to the *Los Angeles Times*, the two leading claimants came together with a view to settling their championship dispute. It seemed that Kelly had a clear lead at the final bell and should have been awarded the decision, having outboxed Sullivan in most of the rounds and knocked him to the floor in the 14th for 'eight' with a right to the jaw. Kelly carried the fight to Sullivan in all but the last three sessions, landing effectively to head and body while showing an excellent defence. From the 18th through to the final bell Sullivan fought like a madman when trying to score a knockout, but even then he was thwarted at every turn.

19 March 1906. (158lbs) Pat O'Keefe w pts 15 Mike Crawley.
Venue: NSC, Covent Garden, London, England. **Referee:** J. H. Douglas.
Fight Summary: Billed for the English 158lbs title, the taller O'Keefe (157½) was soon exploiting Crawley's distaste for body punches, and in the fourth the latter was cautioned for going down without being hit. Although the plodding Crawley (157½) did better as the fight wore on he was unable to break O'Keefe down. Even though the action petered out in the final third as both tired the Canning Town man had done more than enough to be awarded the decision.

23 April 1906. (156lbs) Pat O'Keefe w co 6 (15) Charlie Allum.
Venue: NSC, Covent Garden, London, England. **Referee:** Tom Scott.
Fight Summary: Meeting for the English 156lbs title, the early part of the contest was a scrambling affair that was epitomised when Allum (153½) was warned in the fourth for holding O'Keefe (156) around the neck with the left while punching away with the right. Before the round was over, however, O'Keefe was battering Allum with both hands to the body as the latter held on like a limpet. Cautioned repeatedly in the fifth for holding on while trying to avoid the body blows Allum was all at sea in the sixth and after another series of punches to the wind he dropped to the floor to be counted out.

Eventually, Tom Lancaster (who had outpointed South Africa's Andrew Jeptha over 20 rounds at Ginnett's Circus, Newcastle on 24 February 1908) challenged all England at 156lbs when recognising that O'Keefe had moved on. Although accepted by Jack Kingsland to decide the English 156lbs title nothing came of it.

With there being no further activity the weight class faded away following the NSC setting the middleweight limit at 160lbs on 11 February 1909.

28 May 1906. (158lbs) Tom Thomas w pts 15 Pat O'Keefe.
Venue: NSC, Covent Garden, London, England. **Referee:** J. H. Douglas.
Fight Summary: Given English 158lbs championship billing, although O'Keefe (155½) had the pull over Thomas (156) in reach, landing several solid lefts as the fight progressed, it was the latter's left-hand work that was the more effective. The *Sporting Life* reported that at every opportunity Thomas dashed in with a left to the face,

which caused the Londoner to measure his length upon the floor on one occasion. From the outset the exchanges were of a fast and vigorous nature for men of their weight, and round after round went the same way before Thomas received the decision. It could not be seen as a great fight as there had been far too much holding, but it was always exciting.

Following this, Thomas remained out of the ring for close on two years after being laid up with rheumatic fever. However, he was still generally recognised as being the champion despite the rise through the ranks of Tom Lancaster and James Tiger Smith, who both claimed the English title with little support. Despite having no experience to talk of, Smith would get a shot at the fearsome Sam Langford on 22 April 1907.

Lancaster's 158lbs English title claim started when he beat Jack Kingsland (w co 18 at Ginnett's Circus, Newcastle on 23 June). He then went on to defend his claim against Alf Rogers (w co 4 at the Running Grounds, Durham on 18 August), Bombardier Davis (w co 7 at Ginnett's Circus on 4 December), Kingsland (w co 14 at Ginnett's Circus on 11 February 1907), Mike Crawley (w pts 20 at Ginnett's Circus on 25 March 1907), Seaman Fred Broadbent (w pts 15 at the NSC on 3 June 1907) and Crawley (w pts 20 at Ginnett's Circus on 23 December 1907) before Thomas resurfaced.

Having recovered sufficiently to came back to the ring, Thomas took in a catchweight contest over ten rounds against Crawley (w co 5 at the West End School of Arms, Marylebone, London on 30 April 1908) before preparing himself for a defence against Smith on 1 June 1908.

25 June 1906. (158lbs) Hugo Kelly w co 3 (10) Young Mahoney.
Venue: Tomlinson Hall, Indianapolis, Indiana, USA.
Fight Summary: In a successful defence of his 158lbs title claim, Kelly eliminated Mahoney from the championship running after knocking him out towards the end of the third round. Previously, the men had fought two draws. The first session saw Mahoney forcing the fight, but in the second round Kelly came right back into it when deciding to counter rather than swing, immediately having his rival down for 'eight' from a right to the jaw. Following up with a body shot Mahoney was dropped again, and in the third he was floored twice, the second time seeing him counted out after falling back down.

24 August 1906. (158lbs) Hugo Kelly w co 6 (20) Tony Caponi.
Venue: Crawford's Opera House, Leavenworth, Kansas, USA.
Fight Summary: It was reported in the *Leavenworth Times* that both men were inside the required 158lbs, thus putting Kelly's claim at the weight up for grabs. While Caponi showed himself to be an aggressive fighter, newspaper reports stated that the result was never in doubt after Kelly showed great ability to make his man miss on countless occasions in the early rounds. In the sixth, however, Kelly decided it was time to pick up on his aggressive side, dropping Caponi three times in quick succession, the last time being for the full count.

11 September 1906. (158lbs) Hugo Kelly w disq 5 (15) Sailor Burke.
Venue: Lincoln AC, Boston, Massachusetts, USA. **Referee:** Maffit Flaherty.
Fight Summary: The *Boston Post* confirmed that with Kelly's 158lbs title claim being on the line he had all the best of what was a slugging match before knocking Burke down in the fifth with a heavy blow to the head. At that stage the referee stopped the bout and awarded the decision to Kelly, explaining that his action was based on the fact that Burke had gone to his knees three times earlier without being hit.

22 April 1907. (158lbs) Sam Langford w co 4 (20) James Tiger Smith.
Venue: NSC, Covent Garden, London, England. **Referee:** J. H. Douglas.
Fight Summary: Billed for the English version of the 158lbs middleweight title, having rushed out wildly at the opening bell before the end of the round Smith (151) was badly cut over the right eye. Meanwhile, Langford (154), who had been taking a good look at Smith, began to open up himself, especially at close quarters, and in the fourth he was really letting the punches go. With Smith still endeavouring to mix it with his dangerous rival, after taking a terrific right to the head he was dropped heavily by a left hook to the jaw and counted out.

In the aftermath, Langford challenged anyone in the world at the weight. On 27 August, at the Winnisimmet AC, Chelsea, Massachusetts, USA, Langford outpointed Larry Temple over ten rounds in a contest that was thought to carry his 158lbs title claim, despite him being above the weight.

Following his defeat at the hands of Langford, Smith defended his English title claim against Charlie Allum (w co 1 at the National Sporting Club, Merthyr on 14 November) and Jack Costello (w co 11 at the Norfolk Road Drill Hall, Sheffield on 27 January 1908). It was these two wins that would gain him a crack at Thomas on the latter's return to the ring.

10 May 1907. (158lbs) Hugo Kelly drew 20 Jack Twin Sullivan.
Venue: Naud Junction Pavilion, Los Angeles, California, USA. **Referee:** Tommy Burns.
Fight Summary: Reported by the *Los Angeles Times* to have involved the championship, with both men being inside 158lbs at the weigh-in, Kelly dropped Sullivan with a left to the jaw in the fourth prior to the latter fighting back strongly. In the eighth round Sullivan was again dropped to his knees, before almost having Kelly out in the 12th. Despite the two knockdowns Sullivan was considered to be ahead coming into the 16th, but Kelly made a strong run for home to deserve a share of the spoils.

12 November 1907. (158lbs) Sam Langford w pts 20 Young Peter Jackson.
Venue: Pacific AC, Los Angeles, California, USA. **Referee:** Charles Eyton.
Fight Summary: Made at 158lbs, with both men inside the weight, Langford outfought Jackson when sending in terrific blows to the body, and although the latter looked for a foul on the odd occasion it was only his gameness that kept him going. Langford cemented his claim to the title in this one, while Jackson retired just one fight later.

On 11 March 1908, at the Roanoke AC, Boston, Massachusetts, a marginally overweight Langford outpointed Larry Temple over eight rounds in what the *Boston Post* called a fight for the 'black title'.

Continuing to challenge all and sundry, in January 1909 the *Mirror of Life* declared Langford to be the world champion because Tom Thomas, Stanley Ketchel and Billy Papke were all drawing the 'Colour Bar'. Langford immediately challenged Ketchel, undertaking to stop him inside ten rounds or forfeit his purse, depositing $200 with that intent. In July 1909, Ketchel refused to defend against Langford, asking for ten rounds at catchweights instead, and from there onwards the latter concentrated on the bigger men while still hoping for a meaningful crack at the title.

An over-the-weight Langford defended his title claim twice against the welterweight title claimant, Dixie Kid, stopping him in the fifth at the Armoury AA, Boston, Massachusetts on 28 September 1909

12 December 1907. (155lbs) Stanley Ketchel w pts 20 Joe Thomas.
Venue: Recreation Baseball Park, San Francisco, California, USA. **Referee:** Sam Berger.
Fight Summary: Fighting at 155lbs, Ketchel started fast, looking for the body, while Thomas boxed coolly, keeping his defences in place and sending in short-arm rights and left jabs. At times it seemed as though Thomas had too much skill for Ketchel, but with the latter always dangerous at the halfway stage he was coming on. In the 15th round, Thomas, although tiring, caught Ketchel with a terrific right hook to the jaw, it only being the locking of arms that saved the Michigan man from a knockdown. Thereafter, however, it was all Ketchel. When a barrage of blows to head and body floored Thomas in the 16th it was only his superb conditioning that allowed him to make it through to the final bell.

30 December 1907. (158lbs) Hugo Kelly drew 10 Billy Papke.
Venue: Schlitz Park, Milwaukee, Wisconsin, USA. **Referee:** Malachy Hogan.
Fight Summary: Made at 158lbs, with both men inside, Kelly just about held on to his title claim at the weight, having been groggy and saved by the bell on several occasions in a very fast-paced contest. Despite a lack of knockdowns there was no let-up as the men looked for a winning punch, and both were bleeding heavily at the final bell. The general consensus was that Papke's vicious attacks warranted more than a draw. Earlier, the *Chicago Tribune* stated that the winner would have a realistic claim to the championship.

22 February 1908. (154lbs) Stanley Ketchel w co 1 (25) Mike Twin Sullivan.
Venue: Mission Street Arena, Colma, San Francisco, California, USA. **Referee:** Billy Roche.
Fight Summary: With both men inside 154lbs, Ketchel substantiated his claim at the weight after putting Sullivan down twice before knocking him out at 1.18 of the opening round with a terrific left to the head.

16 March 1908. (158lbs) Billy Papke w pts 10 Hugo Kelly.
Venue: The Hippodrome, Milwaukee, Wisconsin, USA. **Referee:** Al Bright.
Fight Summary: In a contest very similar to their previous go it was fought at a fast pace, Papke being allowed to use his strength in the clinches and getting away with butting, while Kelly had both eyes badly damaged in the process. Dropped momentarily in the opening session, Kelly got up quickly, going punch for punch with Papke before gashing him over the right eye in the second round. With Papke using foul tactics the crowd sided with Kelly, and although the decision went against him it was wafer thin. The *Philadelphia Item* report said "The winner was entitled to the best claim to the middleweight title", while the *Chicago Tribune* stated "With both men inside 158lbs, Papke eliminated Kelly from the championship race."

9 May 1908. (156lbs) Stanley Ketchel w co 20 (35) Jack Twin Sullivan.
Venue: Mission Street Arena, Colma, San Francisco, California, USA. **Referee:** Billy Roche.
Fight Summary: Reckoned by the *Ring Record Book* to be for the vacant title there was no mention of that in the *San Francisco Chronicle*, apart from the fact that both Sullivan and Ketchel were already claiming it. With both men required to make 156lbs, Sullivan managed to keep Ketchel at bay by using a repertoire of tricks, including dropping down without being hit on a few occasions while claiming a foul. In the 13th round it looked all over when Sullivan was decked by a vicious body blow, but back in action he was still causing problems before Ketchel finally caught up with him in the 20th. Knocked down heavily, although Sullivan somehow struggled up at 'nine' he was powerless to get up from a right under the heart which saw him dropped again and counted out.

1 June 1908. (158lbs) Tom Thomas w co 4 (20) James Tiger Smith.
Venue: NSC, Covent Garden, London, England. **Referee:** Eugene Corri.
Fight Summary: Billed for the English 158lbs title, at the start of the contest Thomas (157) seemed to be nonplussed by his opponent's tactics before being toppled over by a hard right in the second round. By the third, however, Thomas had worked Smith (154) out, sending the latter down with a right that landed squarely on the jaw. Coming out for the fourth it was apparent straight away that Smith had not fully recovered, and having been dropped four times from an assortment of blows he was counted out on the 1.08 mark.

Meantime, Tom Lancaster continued his weakened claim, beating Bombardier Davis (w co 8 at The Running Grounds, Durham on 20 June), while Thomas's next contest came against Jack Costello (w co 6 at the Ivor SC, Swansea on 17 October). Earlier thought to be a title fight, it was made at catchweights with no weights given.

Following wins over Bartley Connolly and Tom Dyer, and another lengthy absence, Thomas met Jack Kingsland (w rtd 11 at the Millfield AC, Pontypridd, Wales on 5 October 1909). According to *Boxing* it was a title defence, but in truth it was a hastily arranged catchweight contest of 20 two-minute rounds with no weights reported.

Keeping busy, Lancaster beat Fred Wilmott (w co 3 Ginnett's Circus, Newcastle on 19 October 1909) in what was considered to be another defence of his claim.

A matter of days after Lancaster defeated Harry Croxon (w co 6 at the Sporting Club, Elswick, Newcastle on 28 November 1909) in another 'defence', the *Sporting Life* reported that Thomas should now meet him to settle the English title. However, nothing ever came of it, and by mid-1910 following defeats at the hands of Eddie McGoorty and Jim Sullivan Lancaster retired. With victories over men such as Andrew Jeptha (twice), Frank Craig (thrice), Bartley Connolly, McGoorty and Ted Nelson, he should have been ensured of a crack at the Lonsdale Belt.

Having standardised the weight classes on 11 February 1909, the NSC eventually selected Thomas to meet Charlie Wilson at the Club on 20 December 1909 to decide the vacant British 160lbs title and first middleweight Lord

Lonsdale Belt. Although winning by a second-round kayo, Thomas was once again laid low by rheumatism. Further to this, a prospective title defence against Jim Sullivan was set aside.

Fit again, Thomas recorded four quick wins over decent opposition prior to the Sullivan fight being fixed for 14 November at the NSC. Made at 160lbs, Sullivan took over the British title after a 20-round points win. For Thomas there would be just four more fights before he sadly passed away on 13 August 1911 following another rheumatic attack.

Sullivan, who received quite a battering at the hands of Thomas, took six months out before Hugh McIntosh, a leading promoter, matched him against Billy Papke to contest the world title in London.

4 June 1908. (158lbs) Stanley Ketchel w pts 10 Billy Papke.
Venue: The Hippodrome, Milwaukee, Wisconsin, USA. **Referee:** Jack McGuigan.
Fight Summary: Recognised by the *Chicago Tribune* as the first championship battle for close on six years, with both men inside 158lbs, this should now be accepted as being for the vacant title. In what was a tremendous slugging match, it was judged that Ketchel landed two blows for one of Papke's, the fight said to be the most furious seen in the region. There were two clean knockdowns scored, Ketchel getting home in the first round with a right to the jaw that put Papke on his knees and the latter doing likewise with a left hook to the chin in the fourth. Ketchel's favourite blow was one he called 'the shift' as it had the appearance of landing in a certain area before changing direction. Papke dreaded it after the first round knockdown, covering up like a turtle every time Ketchel was getting set. Another danger blow was the short left uppercut delivered at close quarters by Ketchel, who was relentless in his pursuit of Papke.

31 July 1908. (158lbs) Stanley Ketchel w co 3 (20) Hugo Kelly.
Venue: The Coliseum, San Francisco, California, USA. **Referee:** Jack Welch.
Fight Summary: With both men inside 158lbs, the *San Francisco Chronicle* said "Just one punch snuffed out Kelly's title aspirations for good." Despite having done well in the opening two sessions, Kelly was counted out in the third following a terrific left hook to the jaw which dropped him in a heap.

In his next fight, on 18 August, Ketchel knocked out Joe Thomas inside two rounds at the Mission Street Arena, Colma, San Francisco. Initially thought to be a world title bout, with Ketchel weighing 168lbs to Thomas's 172 it should not be accepted as one.

7 September 1908. (158lbs) Billy Papke w rsc 12 (25) Stanley Ketchel.
Venue: Vernon Arena, Los Angeles, California, USA. **Referee:** James J. Jeffries.
Fight Summary: Billed for the title at 158lbs, Papke shocked Ketchel when, ignoring the accepted 'sporting' handshake at the start of the contest, he smashed in a terrific left hook followed by a right cross which closed one of the latter's eyes. Lifted off his feet three times in the first round, from there onwards Ketchel took a bloody beating for round after round, being dropped again in the sixth and 11th rounds before he was decked twice more in the 12th and rescued by the referee just as the police were about to get involved. Ketchel, with both eyes closed, was so badly beaten that he had to be carried to the dressing room.

26 November 1908. (158lbs) Stanley Ketchel w co 11 (20) Billy Papke.
Venue: Mission Street Arena, Colma, San Francisco, California, USA. **Referee:** Jack Welch.
Fight Summary: Made at 158lbs, and billed for the title, Ketchel regained the championship when he battered Papke with savage body blows in virtually every round before putting him down twice in the 11th, the second occasion enforcing the full count following a storm of lefts and rights to head and body. It had been a tough, hard-hitting contest that saw both men fall out of the ring in the fifth, but Ketchel held sway throughout with his heavier punches landing regularly.

Ketchel's next four fights were made at 160lbs, against Philadelphia Jack O'Brien (nd-w pts 10 at the National AC, Manhattan, NYC, New York on 26 March 1909), Hugh McGann (nd-w pts 6 at Duquesne Gardens, Pittsburgh,

Pennsylvania on 18 May 1909), Tony Caponi (nd-w co 4 at the American SC, Schenectady, New York on 2 June) and O'Brien again (nd-w rsc 3 at the National AC, Philadelphia, Pennsylvania on 9 June 1909).

5 July 1909. (158lbs) Stanley Ketchel w pts 20 Billy Papke.
Venue: Mission Street Arena, Colma, San Francisco, California, USA. **Referee:** Billy Roche.
Fight Summary: Given championship billing at 158lbs, it was a poor fight from Ketchel's point of view. Although Ketchel blamed his performance on breaking his right hand early on, the truth of the matter was that Papke had found a way of negating his power by staying close. The tactic also enabled Papke to get his own blows off to advantage. Gilbert Odd, the well-known historian, described it as "Give and take, no clever stuff, no real boxing; just a toe-to-toe bruising battle, each waiting for the other to show a weakness", while the referee stated "Never did I imagine that two human beings could stand such punishment." In his book, *The Michigan Assassin*, Nat Fleischer wrote "The men fought like bulldogs from gong to gong. Each delivered punch after punch that would almost have felled an ox, yet neither could get across the wallop soporific." In what was the fourth fight between the pair, Papke winning one of them, the general consensus was that it could have gone either way. It was also felt that had it been a finish fight Papke would have won.

Having had his crack at Jack Johnson for the heavyweight crown, in January 1910 it was announced that Ketchel was relinquishing the title due to increased weight. On hearing the news it was no surprise that Papke, who was campaigning abroad, claimed the crown.

19 March 1910. (158lbs) Billy Papke w co 3 (20) Willie Lewis.
Venue: The Circus, Paris, France.
Fight Summary: As Papke was now claiming the title, the leading French promoter matched him against fellow American, Willie Lewis, giving the fight championship billing at 158lbs. It was Papke (156½) virtually all the way, with Lewis (155) under attack from the opening bell. Down for 'seven' in the first round and saved by the bell, Lewis fought back savagely in the second before being blasted to the ropes by sledgehammer blows to the jaw in the third and dropped for the full count.

Back in America, on hearing news of the result Ketchel decided to stay in the middleweight division, allowing Frank Klaus to weigh 157lbs for their six-round no-decision clash at Duquesne Gardens, Pittsburgh, Pennsylvania on 23 March. The contest, seen as a draw by the press, was followed by the promoter, Tex Rickard, promising to deliver a title bout between Sam Langford and Ketchel. An over-the-weight Langford had recently defended his title claim against the Dixie Kid, knocking his man out in the third round at the Phoenix AC, Memphis, Tennessee on 10 January.

Despite all the promises the nearest Langford got to Ketchel was a six-round press decision loss at the National AC, Philadelphia, Pennsylvania on 27 April. Langford, by all accounts, allowed the champion off the hook in order to procure a championship match which ultimately failed to materialise.

27 May 1910. (158lbs) Stanley Ketchel nd-w rsc 2 (10) Willie Lewis.
Venue: National AC, Manhattan, NYC, New York, USA. **Referee:** Tom O'Rourke.
Fight Summary: In what was effectively a title defence for Ketchel (158), the fight was concluded after Lewis (148) had been dropped heavily by a crashing right to the jaw. Having reached the count of 'five' the referee called for Lewis's seconds to start administering aid to their stricken fighter.

On 15 October, the boxing world was shocked to hear that Ketchel had been murdered. The *TS Andrews' Annual* tells us that the men who served up notice of intent at that time included Billy Papke, Hugo Kelly, Jack Twin Sullivan and Sam Langford.

Langford filed a claim with all the major boxing papers for the world 158lbs title, which was restated in February 1911, but with neither Papke nor the others interested in taking the bait he concentrated on the heavier men from then on.

26 October 1910. (158lbs) Billy Papke w co 6 (20) Ed Williams.
Venue: The Stadium, Sydney, Australia. **Referee:** Harold Baker.
Fight Summary: According to the *Sydney Daily Telegraph*, this was to be the first world middleweight title bout held in Australia. However, following the fight, and after Papke had scaled 160lbs to Williams' 158, the same newspaper stated that Papke's title claim had not been at stake on the grounds that 158lbs was the recognised limit. According to press reports, Papke toyed with Williams for five rounds before raining in blows from both hands in the sixth, one of which caused the latter to be counted out.

Another fight at the Sydney Stadium, on 11 February, saw Papke outpointed over 20 rounds by fellow-American Cyclone Johnny Thompson. Prior to the fight, the *Sydney Daily Telegraph* referred to Papke as the champion, but with no mention of this having involved the championship the paper went on to say that Papke held all the advantages in height, weight and reach in a match made at 164lbs. Reports from another source have Papke scaling 165lbs to Thompson's 158, with the fight made at catchweights. That aside, the reason for Thompson claiming the championship appears to stem from the fact that he was inside 158lbs and weighed 153½lbs after the fight.

Meanwhile, Papke, continuing to style himself as champion, avenged an earlier defeat by Dave Smith when knocking the New Zealander out in seven rounds at The Stadium on 11 March 1911, in a match made at 165lbs.

20 December 1910. (158lbs) Hugo Kelly w pts 12 Frank Klaus.
Venue: Armoury AA, Boston, Massachusetts, USA.
Fight Summary: The *Boston Daily Advertiser* reported that by defeating Klaus at 158lbs Kelly fully justified his claim, especially when fighting the last seven rounds with a damaged hand. It was no surprise that Klaus forced the fight, but what was surprising was the way Kelly handled him, shooting in lefts to the face and holding his ground while making his man miss again and again. He also landed left hooks and right crosses regularly on Klaus when in range. With Klaus coming on strong in the fifth it looked as though Kelly would not survive, but weathering the storm he had an excellent last round when making sure of the verdict.

22 February 1911. (158lbs) Harry Lewis w pts 25 Blink McCloskey.
Venue: The Hippodrome, Paris, France.
Fight Summary: Having stopped McCloskey rather unsatisfactorily in three rounds at the Wagram Theatre, Paris on 1 February, Lewis undertook to do a better job this time round. Despite the fight carrying no title billing, along with a lack of weights, both men were thought to be inside 158lbs in what was seen as an important fight. By the 15th round, Lewis, who had done most of the leading, was reckoned to be just about ahead. Up to that point, McCloskey had shown himself to be a sound defensive fighter, with great blocking skills, but in the 13th he fractured the elbow of his right arm and was forced to go even more defensive. Meantime, Lewis, having realised that his opponent had a cast-iron jaw, started to work the body, a tactic that ultimately took him to victory. Both men showed that they could give and take and, although Lewis had been a bit slack according to *Boxing,* he immediately laid claim to the middleweight title. Interestingly, McCloskey came to be known as 'Blink' due to the fact that having gone blind in one eye and been fitted with a glass version which he used to place in a glass of water at ringside before boxing.

21 March 1911. (158lbs) Hugo Kelly w pts 12 Bill McKinnon.
Venue: Armoury AA, Boston, Massachusetts, USA.
Fight Summary: Articled to make 158lbs ringside, the *Boston Post* confirmed that this was a defence of Kelly's title claim at the weight. Although McKinnon tried his hardest it was one-sided as Kelly controlled the action for at least ten of the 12 rounds, despite being badly hurt by a couple of chance blows. With Kelly countering McKinnon's leads for several sessions the latter was almost in use as a punch-bag, but taking his punishment gamely he made the title claimant work hard for his win.

28 April 1911. (158lbs) Hugo Kelly nd-w pts 10 Cyclone Johnny Thompson.
Venue: The Auditorium, Racine, Wisconsin, USA.

Fight Summary: With both men claiming the title, this contest was made at 158lbs. While Kelly (156) made the weight at 3pm, Thompson, who scaled 159½, proved that he was either having problems or was just uninterested. Refusing to accept the forfeit, Kelly used short right uppercuts to counter Thompson, who continually looked to get inside, and although much of it was give and take the latter was generally outboxed. After Thompson, whose left eye was closed by straight lefts, lost a tooth in the eighth he resorted to covering up for the remainder of the contest. There were no knockdowns.

On 27 July, Thompson met Willie Lewis (nd-w pts 10 at the National AC, NYC, New York), and while it is unclear at what weight the contest was made at, Lewis, who could easily make 158lbs at that time, would undoubtedly have claimed the title had he won inside the distance. The *Utica Herald-Dispatch* claimed that that Thompson was at least 20lbs the heavier man.

3 May 1911. (158lbs) Leo Houck w pts 20 Harry Lewis.
Venue: The Hippodrome, Paris, France. **Referee:** Emile Maitrot.
Fight Summary: After claiming the title Lewis found himself challenged by Houck, who had been unsuccessful in seeking a match with the British champion, Jim Sullivan, and had twice bettered his fellow American back home. Unable to avoid the challenge, Lewis met Houck at 158lbs in a bout given championship billing. While Lewis scaled a low 147lbs (the welterweight limit), Houck, allowed to weigh-in privately, was announced as being within the agreed target. Although fairly even up until the eighth, from there on Houck showed his superiority, an uppercut nearly finishing Lewis off in the ninth. A clever boxer, Lewis came back, sidestepping and clinching to avoid further punishment, and although he had Houck going with solid blows to the stomach in the 19th he was too weak to follow up his advantage. Supported by the *Philadelphia Public Ledger*, Houck promptly laid claim to the title.

Before taking on Frank Mantell, Houck met Joe Thomas (nd-w pts 6 at the Athletic Club, Lancaster, Pennsylvania, USA on 16 June 1911) and George Chip (nd-w pts 6 at the National AC, Philadelphia, Pennsylvania on 16 September 1911) in contests where the men were more than capable of making 158lbs.

8 June 1911. (158lbs) Billy Papke w rsc 10 (20) Jim Sullivan.
Venue: The Palladium, London, England. **Referee:** Eugene Corri.
Fight Summary: Made at 158lbs, and billed for the title, both men were announced as being inside the agreed weight limit. Fast and furious from the opening bell, once Sullivan had settled down he got his left hand working, as well as the right cross, to fend off the slashing attacks of the American. However, fighting at range, Sullivan could never subdue Papke, who was at his best on the inside, and the referee continually had to break them as they clashed at close quarters. Towards the end of the ninth, Papke finally got through Sullivan's defences when a savage uppercut sent the latter down for 'five'. After Sullivan staggered back to his corner and was unable to answer the bell for the tenth round, the referee stopped the bout in the American's favour.

Back in America, on 22 August, at the Twentieth Century SC, Manhattan, NYC, New York, Papke (160) lost a ten-round press decision to Sailor Burke (165) in a fight the *New York Times* reported as one which involved Papke's title claim, which it obviously did not.

Another fight for Papke, a 12-round points defeat at the hands of Bob Moha at the Armoury AA, Boston, Massachusetts on 31 October, that was thought to have involved his 158lbs claim was later proved to be false. Regardless, it did not stop Moha from claiming the championship. With both men well in excess of 158lbs, and reckoned to be one of the worst fakes ever seen in Boston Moha's claim failed to stand up.

17 August 1911. (158lbs) Cyclone Johnny Thompson nd-l pts 10 Frank Klaus.
Venue: National AC, Manhattan, NYC, New York, USA.
Fight Summary: The *New York Times* reported that Thompson was still claiming the title and that both men were inside 158lbs for this one. Klaus hammered Thompson for ten rounds, having the better of every session, but could not knock over the latter who covered up, crouched low, clinched when under fire, and took heavy blows to the jaw without flinching.

Following this, Thompson took in another tour of Australia, involving four fights that were contested above the middleweight limit.

Reported in some quarters as a fight involving the title, Thompson drew over 20 rounds with Frank Mantell at Buffalo Park, Sacramento, California on 3 July 1912. Billed as a catchweight contest, the *Sacramento Union* reported that Mantell came to the ring somewhere in the region of 160lbs while Thompson was a good 12 pounds heavier. The paper went on to say that it did not involve the title.

Despite Thompson continuing to claim the title it was clear that his ten-round meeting with George KO Brown at the Marquette SC, Peoria, Illinois on 10 September 1912 did not come into the 158lbs category either. This one came to an end in the sixth round when the police asked the referee to stop the fight after several foul blows had been landed by Brown. Right from the opening bell it could be seen that Brown was the stronger of the two, but with both men continually sending in low punches it could not last.

On 16 September 1912, at Hippodrome Park, Cincinnati, Ohio, an over-the-weight Thompson was adjudged by the press to have drawn over ten rounds against Eddie McGoorty in a match made at 160lbs. Interestingly, the fight took in an extra round before anyone realised that a mistake had been made. The *New York Times* reported that Thompson's title aspirations appeared over, a statement that was backed up when the latter fought just four more times at weights well in excess of 158lbs.

21 September 1911. (160lbs) Leo Houck nd-w pts 10 Frank Mantell.

Venue: National AC, Manhattan, NYC, New York, USA. **Referee:** Patsy Haley.

Fight Summary: Articled at 160lbs, with both men inside, the *New York Times* reported that Houck was defending his claim to the title in this one. But with 158lbs being thought of as the limit in America at the time it was the European version that was on the line. A hard contest from start to finish, with each taking turns to lead, Houck had the better of it in eight of the ten rounds, and although he had Mantell in bad shape from terrific right uppercuts to the jaw in the ninth he was unable to finish his man off.

Contests in which Houck's title claim could have been at risk if his opponents made 158lbs, came against Harry Ramsey (nd-w pts 6 at the Athletic Club, Lancaster, Pennsylvania on 28 September), Frank Klaus (nd-l pts 6 at the American AC, Philadelphia, Pennsylvania on 18 October), Battling Levinsky (w pts 12 at the Armoury Arena, Boston, Massachusetts on 24 October), Ramsey (nd-drew 6 at the Nonpareil AC, Philadelphia on 3 November) and Buck Crouse twice (nd-l pts 6 at Duquesne Gardens, Pittsburgh, Pennsylvania on 15 November and nd-drew 6 at the National AC, Philadelphia on 9 December). The fight against Levinsky, then known as Barney Williams, only came about when Jack Dillon failed to appear and the latter stepped in at the last moment.

13 December 1911. (158lbs) Georges Carpentier w pts 20 Harry Lewis.

Venue: The Circus, Paris, France.

Fight Summary: Bearing in mind that Lewis had recently lost to Leo Houck and George Gunther, and this would be the 17-year-old Carpentier's first appearance at middleweight, the fight was still given world title billing at 158lbs by the promoters. Literally boxing rings around Lewis, with the Frenchman making a great start, it was only his experience and durability that enabled the American to last the course. Having outscored his rival from head to body Carpentier began to tire towards the end, but the final two sessions saw him show great awareness to avoid a last-minute catastrophe as Lewis threw everything at him bar the kitchen sink. Carpentier claimed the title despite coming in half an ounce over the weight.

With boxing having recently become very popular in France there were two main bodies running the sport at this time, The French Federation Society of Boxing (FFSB) and the French Federation of Boxing Clubs (FFBC). The second named was fronted by Victor Breyer and Theo Vienne, who promoted boxing at the above venue, while Paul Rousseau led the other body. It would be these two groups who, along with the Swiss, would be instrumental in setting up the International Boxing Union (IBU) in June 1913.

1 January 1912. (158lbs) Jack Dillon nd-w rtd 7 (10) Leo Houck.
Venue: Virginia Auditorium, Indianapolis, Indiana, USA.
Fight Summary: Dillon took over Houck's claim at the weight on winning after both men had made the requisite 158lbs. Sent through the ropes on a couple of occasions, Houck was up against it from the opening bell as Dillon concentrated on his midsection, throwing solid blows from both hands with great accuracy. From the second round onwards it was clear that Dillon was too strong for Houck, but the latter stayed on gamely when taking on board all the punishment that came his way. The sixth saw the beginning of the end as Dillon piled into his man, hitting him almost at will, and after Houck somehow made it back to his corner he was unable to respond to the bell starting the seventh. Houck's manager stated afterwards that Dillon was the best man in the world at 158lbs.

A fight for Dillon where it was unclear whether he was inside 158lbs or not, but where his opponent was thought to have made that weight, came against Howard Wiggam (nd-w co 2 at the Tomlinson Hall, Indianapolis on 26 January).

1 February 1912. (158lbs) Jack Dillon nd-w pts 12 Billy Berger.
Venue: The Auditorium, Youngstown, Ohio, USA.
Fight Summary: Although the fight was relatively even in six of the rounds contested, when Dillon did pick it up, landing vicious rights and lefts to Berger's body, the challenger showed great fortitude to hang in. In both the eighth and 12th Dillon looked for the punches that would finish Berger off, but somehow the latter survived by good use of the ring and clever movement. The *Pittsburgh Post* even saw it as a draw, so well did Berger perform.

8 February 1912. (158lbs) Jack Dillon nd-w pts 10 Paddy Lavin.
Venue: Convention Hall, Buffalo, New York, USA. **Referee:** Maurice Collins.
Fight Summary: After both men made 156lbs, Dillon held on to his 158lbs title claim with some ease, as Lavin was unable to mount much of an offensive, being too busy trying to ward off the blows coming his way. Wading into Lavin from the opening bell, ripping in terrific lefts and rights to the body, Dillon dropped the home fighter in the seventh with a right under the heart and twice drove him through the ropes. However, he was unable to find a decisive blow. The crowd were right behind Lavin, willing him to get through the contest, and when he did they cheered him to the rafters.

Two days later, on 10 February, Dillon took on George Chip (nd-w pts 6 at the Old City Hall, Pittsburgh, Pennsylvania) in a contest that the latter was expected to be inside 158lbs even if the 'Hoosier Bearcat' was not.

Not resting on his laurels, on 22 February, at the Chamber of Commerce, Columbus, Ohio an over-the-weight Dillon was given a ten-round press draw in his contest with Grant Clark, thought to be inside 158lbs.

21 February 1912. (158lbs) Hugo Kelly nd-w pts 10 George KO Brown.
Venue: Coliseum Skating Palace, Kenosha, Wisconsin, USA.
Fight Summary: Made at 158lbs, Kelly (158) successfully defended his title claim at the weight when keeping the dangerous Brown (155) at bay for ten rounds. While Brown was wild with his swinging blows, Kelly failed to take advantage when relying too much on his cleverness. He also failed to take advantage of many opportunities to step in with punches of his own. When Brown missed the pair would invariably clinch and hammer away one-handedly, every round being the same, but at distance the Greek Brown was outboxed.

22 February 1912. (158lbs) Frank Klaus w pts 20 Sailor Ed Petroskey.
Venue: Auditorium Pavilion, San Francisco, California, USA. **Referee:** Jack Welch.
Fight Summary: Occasionally listed as a title fight it was merely part of a 158lbs elimination series, but Klaus was claiming the title after his victory in what was a tough one. Ripping into Petroskey from the opening bell, Klaus hit the Sailor with all he had but to no avail, and although it was nearly all one way he could not drop his man, being booed for roughing it up. It was an easy win for Klaus, who claimed that he had hurt both hands early on and that had restricted his plan of action.

375

22 February 1912. (158lbs) Frank Mantell w pts 20 Billy Papke.
Venue: Buffalo Park, Sacramento, California, USA. **Referee:** Sol Levison.
Fight Summary: According to the *San Francisco Chronicle*, this fight was part of a 158lbs elimination tournament. Press reports stated that Papke, who won two rounds at most, failed to take advantage of the situation and less than a dozen of his wild swings hit the target, he was that poor. Even though Mantell failed to set the town alight he had the better of the fighting, being able to tie Papke up on the inside throughout. In fact, he did not have to be at his best to win. Afterwards, the *Philadelphia Item* reported "That whatever claim Papke had to the title is now the undisputed property of Mantell." However, although Papke continued to claim the title even though it was rumoured that he had failed to make 158lbs on the day of the fight, his cause was now considerably lacking support in America.

29 February 1912. (160lbs) Georges Carpentier w co 2 (20) Jim Sullivan.
Venue: Monte Carlo, Monaco. **Referee:** Fernand Cuny.
Fight Summary: Held in a makeshift arena erected in a public square on the Condamine fronted by the Mediterranean, it was billed for the European 160lbs title, with Carpentier weighing 155lbs to Sullivan's 157. Although specifically involving the European championship, this contest also has to be seen as belonging to Carpentier's world title claim at the weight. Outclassed from the start, Sullivan had difficulty in reaching Carpentier, let alone hurting him, and early in the second round a tremendous right hook to the point of the jaw sent him down to be counted out.

7 March 1912. (158lbs) Jack Dillon w pts 10 Walter Coffey.
Venue: Piedmont Pavilion, Oakland, California, USA. **Referee:** Toby Irwin.
Fight Summary: After both men made 158lbs according to the *Oakland Tribune*, Dillon again defended his title claim at the weight against sub-standard opposition in Coffey. An easy winner, Dillon disappointed when he had Coffey hanging on round after round, and despite throwing plenty of leather he was unable to finish him off. It was poor entertainment for the crowd who thought that Coffey should have been despatched early, but although Dillon showed plenty of science he seemingly lacked the power to floor his rival, let alone kayo him.

20 March 1912. (158lbs) Hugo Kelly nd-l pts 10 Eddie McGoorty.
Venue: Coliseum Skating Palace, Kenosha, Wisconsin, USA. **Referee:** Eddie Santry.
Fight Summary: With Kelly's 158lbs title claim at stake, although McGoorty (157) was easily the better man he could not finish his rival despite scoring a first-round knockdown. Kelly (156½), who stayed down for 'nine', was never really threatened again by McGoorty, who used the left hand consistently to score points. It was clear, however, that Kelly was obviously weakened by the weight-making. In fact, Kelly did not land six clean, hard punches throughout the fight, looking but a shadow of the man who outpointed Frank Klaus a year or so earlier.

23 March 1912. (158lbs) Frank Klaus w pts 20 Jack Dillon.
Venue: Daly City Arena, San Francisco, California, USA. **Referee:** Jack Welch.
Fight Summary: Billed as a middleweight elimination fight at 158lbs, on the result Klaus took over Dillon's claim at the weight. A wrestling match for much of the time, although Dillon was the better boxer of the pair he could not hurt Klaus, who just kept boring in. There were no knockdowns. However, both men butted each other on occasion and, while Dillon looked to have secured the points, press reports intimated that the referee was swayed by Klaus's last-ditch finish when giving the decision.

In a return match at 158lbs between the pair, a ten-round press win for Klaus at Madison Square Garden, Manhattan, NYC, New York on 3 May, the ringside scales showed both men to be ten pounds adrift. Klaus was adamant that he had been 157½ earlier in the day, while Dillon claimed to have been 158½lbs at the same time.

30 March 1912. (158lbs) Frank Mantell w pts 20 Jack Herrick.
Venue: Pacific AC, Vernon Arena, Los Angeles, California, USA. **Referee:** Charles Eyton.
Fight Summary: While the *Los Angeles Times* reported the contest as being another round in the elimination series at 158bs, Mantell, whose title claim at the weight was on the line for this one, lost much credibility in putting up a poor display. Although victorious again he was not widely accepted as being championship material. Even though

Herrick was marginally ahead after seven rounds from there onwards it was all downhill as Mantell battered him from the waist up, but despite hitting him with all he had he could not finish him off. Mantell's best chance of an early night came in the 16th when a solid right smashed against Herrick's jaw and forced him to hold on for dear life. Not the best of fighters to watch, Mantell specialised in wearing opponents down by his clutching tactics.

On 9 April, at the Athletic Club, Marysville, California, Mantell, well over 158lbs, risked his title claim against Russell Kane before securing an eight-round kayo win.

Another contest for Mantell that was reported in some quarters as involving the title came when he drew over 20 rounds with Cyclone Johnny Thompson at Buffalo Park, Sacramento, California on 3 July. Billed as a catchweight contest, the *Sacramento Union* reported that Mantell came to the ring somewhere in the region of 160lbs with Thompson a good 12 pounds heavier.

A contest against Vic Hansen at the Salt Palace, Salt Lake City, Utah on 15 July, which ended in a 20-round draw, was thought by some to have involved the title. Hansen may well have made 158lbs, but Mantell stated that he would probably come in around 161lbs.

3 April 1912. (160lbs) Georges Carpentier w pts 20 George Gunther.
Venue: The Circus, Paris, France.
Fight Summary: Having recently won the European title, Carpentier was next matched to defend his 160lbs belt against the recognised French champion, Marcel Moreau. When Moreau was injured in training, after hunting around for a replacement, the promoters brought in George Gunther at ten days' notice. Gunther had been claiming the world title since November 1911, having made repeated challenges to Billy Papke that had been turned down. However, with the promoters sticking to their original billing - as an Australian Gunther was hardly eligible to contest the European crown - this should be seen as a legitimate defence of both men's claim at the weight. Regardless of billing, Carpentier (158¼) continued to be recognised throughout France as a world champion of sorts after easily outscoring Gunther (158). Despite Gunther being ahead at the halfway point, Carpentier, who had been pacing himself, stepped up a gear from there on. At times the Australian was totally bewildered by the speed of the punches coming at him, left jabs, combinations, hooks and uppercuts all finding their mark, and on several occasions he was rocked on to his heels. Although Gunther tore into Carpentier in the last two sessions he had very little success as the skilful Frenchman kept out of harm's way, being cheered to the rafters at the final bell.

22 May 1912. (160lbs) Georges Carpentier w pts 20 Willie Lewis.
Venue: The Circus, Paris, France. **Referee:** Fernand Cuny.
Fight Summary: Given world title billing at 160lbs, both men were announced as being inside 158lbs. Working well with a stabbing left lead Lewis kept Carpentier busy over the first few rounds, and in the eighth after coming out of a clinch he slammed in a terrific right to the Frenchman's head that almost won the fight for him there and then. Sent down on his knees, Carpentier was rescued by the bell at the count of 'four' before spending several sessions boxing in defensive mode. With Lewis beginning to tire, Carpentier made his run for home in the 13th, beginning to outspeed the American while flashing in accurate punches from both hands to go well clear by the final bell.

Now that Lewis was out of the way, Carpentier and his manager, Francois Descamps, decided that it was time to take on the very best, suggesting to Theo Vienne and Victor Breyer, who promoted at the above venue, that a contest against Billy Papke was the one they wished for. It was not until Papke was on his way to France that Descamps accepted a better offer from a group calling themselves the French NSC for a match against Frank Klaus in Dieppe.

Not to be outdone, Vienne and Breyer brought in Marcel Moreau to fight Papke, thus creating a situation in which two world title contests held at the same weight took place in France within five days of each other.

28 May 1912. (158lbs) Jack Dillon nd-w co 3 (10) Hugo Kelly.
Venue: Empire Theatre, Indianapolis, Indiana, USA. **Referee:** Tom Dillon.

377

Fight Summary: Often reported incorrectly as being a fight that saw Dillon claim the light heavyweight title on the result, with both men inside 158lbs it was Kelly's middleweight claim that was at stake in this one. Right from the opening bell Dillon looked to work on Kelly's midsection, and once he got inside the latter's defences there was no shifting him. Coming out for the third, Dillon was quickly in action, a right-left to the jaw putting Kelly over for 'nine'. With Dillon now in full cry, Kelly was soon bowled over by a left hook for the full count.

17 June 1912. (158lbs) Jack Dillon nd-w pts 12 George KO Brown.

Venue: The Auditorium, Winnipeg, Canada. **Referee:** Battling Nelson.

Fight Summary: Although Dillon risked his title claim at 158lbs he was never in danger of losing despite the Greek always coming back from heavy shots. As the fight progressed, Dillon got better and better, sending in many telling blows to both head and body, and often standing toe-to-toe with his dangerous opponent without ever flinching. Afterwards, the general feeling was that only Eddie McGoorty amongst the current crop would give Dillon a real fight.

24 June 1912. (160lbs) Frank Klaus w disq 19 (20) Georges Carpentier.

Venue: Motor Racing Track Grand Hall, Dieppe, France. **Referee:** Jean Moues.

Fight Summary: Billed for the 160lbs title, Klaus was announced as being well inside the weight while Carpentier was said to have scaled 159lbs. Later, it was discovered that the scales were weighing some four pounds light, a discovery that appeared to suit the Frenchman who was already experiencing problems in making 160lbs. Unable to make an impression upon the tough Klaus, his best punches merely bouncing off the latter's head, Carpentier was pushed and battered around the ring for the opening four rounds before being blasted to the floor by a vicious right to the body in the fifth. Up at 'two', the young Frenchman threw himself at Klaus, wrestling his way through to the bell, but thereafter he was right up against it. And by the 17th he was out on his feet. Somehow making a speculative last-ditch effort, when Carpentier was taking a battering in the 19th his manager jumped into the ring to save him from taking further punishment. However, in doing so he got his charge disqualified.

29 June 1912. (160lbs) Billy Papke w rtd 16 (20) Marcel Moreau.

Venue: The Circus, Paris, France. **Referee:** Frantz Reichel.

Fight Summary: Given title billing at 160lbs, having made the weight at the second attempt Papke (160) was shocked when Moreau (157¾) dropped him in the opening session with a terrific right to the jaw. It would have been better for Moreau to have stuck to his boxing, but after looking to swap blows in the second he was put down, and when continuing in the same vein he was floored again in the eighth. Having looked tired in the ninth, after Moreau came back strongly to take the tenth he battered away at Papke for the next four rounds, looking very much a likely winner. Hurt at the end of the 14th after being caught low, Moreau then began to come apart at the seams in the 15th, being twice dropped heavily. Despite getting back to his corner and being worked on during the interval, when the bell rang for the 16th to commence Moreau was retired on his stool.

Back in America, having just met Leo Houck (nd-l pts 6 at the Olympia AC, Philadelphia, Pennsylvania on 27 September) at 160lbs, Papke was booked to meet Frank Mantell at the New Star Casino, Manhattan, NYC, New York on 1 October. Reported by the promoters as being a no-decision title bout over ten rounds, according to Mantell both he and Papke had been passed fit by the doctor and were waiting to go to the ring when the latter said he was going out to buy some smelling salts and never returned. Papke's excuses of hurting himself on the day of the fight and that the gate was too small to pay good money did not wear with the New York Boxing Commission, who suspended him immediately.

Already on his way to fight Georges Carpentier in France, the Commission wrote to the French Federation of Boxing Clubs asking them to support the suspension of Papke before stating that they would be recognising Mantell as the champion on 10 October. In response to being asked to uphold the suspension of Papke, the Federation replied that although they were in harmony with the New York Boxing Commission they were unable to take action against the latter as contracts for the Carpentier fight had already been signed.

4 July 1912. (158lbs) Jack Dillon nd-w rsc 8 (10) Joe Thomas.

Venue: Wabash AC, Terre Haute, Indiana, USA.

Fight Summary: Trying to recapture former glories, when Thomas came up against a hard-hitting title claimant in Dillon he was forced to soak up heavy punishment. Having been sent through the ropes in the seventh the writing was on the wall for Thomas, and after getting to his feet following a count of 'nine' in the eighth and looking a likely kayo victim he was rescued by a humane referee. The contest had been made at 158lbs, 12 noon weigh-in.

Two fights where Dillon was heavier than the 158lbs mark, but where his opponents were inside, came against Joe Gorman (w co 6 at the Southern AC, Memphis, Tennessee on 22 July) and George Chip (nd-w pts 10 at the Empire Theatre, Indianapolis on 25 July). Dillon's fight against Gorman was scheduled for eight rounds.

12 August 1912. (158lbs) Jack Dillon nd-w co 4 (10) Billy Donovan.
Venue: The Coliseum, Richmond, Indiana, USA.
Fight Summary: Made at 158lbs, according to the *Richmond Palladium* Dillon outclassed his opponent, knocking him down three times in the third round and sending him into dreamland after a flurry of blows during the fourth. There was never any doubt as to who would win, Dillon being on top from the opening bell and hitting far too hard for the game Donovan.

Having taken a short break, Dillon came back against Harry Ramsey (nd-w pts 6 at the Nonpareil AC, Philadelphia, Pennsylvania on 11 October), with the latter inside 158lbs. Next came Emmett Kid Wagner (nd-w pts 10 at the Point Grounds, Johnstown, Pennsylvania on 17 October) at 160lbs. Dillon was forced to pay forfeit when unable to make the weight. Two days later, on 19 October, Dillon took on an old opponent in George Chip (nd-w pts 6 at the Old City Hall, Pittsburgh, Pennsylvania) in a match made at 158lbs.

9 September 1912. (160lbs) Frank Klaus w disq 4 (15) Marcel Moreau.
Venue: Open-Air Arena, Aix les Bains, France.
Fight Summary: Not billed as a title fight, but with both men inside 160lbs Klaus's title claim at the weight was automatically at stake. According to *Boxing*, as in his contest against Billy Papke, once again Moreau got his tactics wrong when trying to outfight the fighter, being almost knocked out in the second and fourth rounds before intentionally going low and getting himself disqualified.

23 September 1912. (158lbs) Eddie McGoorty nd-w co 1 (10) Jack Harrison.
Venue: Madison Square Garden, Manhattan, NYC, New York, USA. **Referee:** Billy Joh.
Fight Summary: Although not a billed title bout, with 160lbs not being the recognised championship weight in New York at the time, McGoorty (158), who had long been recognised as a legitimate contender, staked his claim to the title following this victory over Harrison (158), the British champion and Lonsdale Belt holder. Right from the opening bell McGoorty went after Harrison, throwing rights and lefts to the head, and before too long the latter was down for 'nine' following a right uppercut to the jaw. Getting up groggy, Harrison was chased around the ring by McGoorty before being dropped for 'nine' again, this time by a left hook. And when another similar punch exploded on his jaw he was counted out with just five seconds of the first round remaining.

7 October 1912. (158lbs) Eddie McGoorty nd-w rsc 5 (10) Jack Denning.
Venue: Madison Square Garden, Manhattan, NYC, New York, USA. **Referee:** Billy Joh.
Fight Summary: In a match made at 158lbs, this should be seen as a defence of McGoorty's claim at the weight. Having weathered McGoorty's heavy punching in the opening two rounds, Denning (157¾), who had come back to outbox the title claimant in the third and fourth sessions, was going along nicely in the fifth when he suddenly bent over claiming a foul. McGoorty (157¾) later explained that he had sunk a long left into the pit of Denning's body that had taken all the steam out of him. Having been told that he did not wish to carry on, the referee stopped the fight and awarded the decision to McGoorty.

Two days later, on 9 October, McGoorty met Leo Houck (nd-l pts 6 at the Olympia AC, Philadelphia, Pennsylvania) at 158lbs over a short distance, staying put despite losing the press decision.

23 October 1912. (158lbs) Jack Dillon w pts 15 Gus Christie.
Venue: Lakeside AC, Dayton, Ohio, USA.

Fight Summary: Made at 158lbs, this was the first of five contests in which Christie made the middleweight limit for Dillon, who thus risked his title claim. Reported as a terrific mill which Dillon deserved to win, the *Racine Journal-News* went on to say that Christie put up a brave battle when fighting back after each vicious attack. Dillon, concentrating mainly on the body, tried so hard for a finish during the 11th and 12th rounds that he lost much steam. In the 12th Dillon twice had Christie almost out, and again in the 15th, but the game Milwaukee man made it to the final bell to well-deserve the cheers he received for his valiant efforts.

When Dillon outpointed Jimmy Howard over eight rounds at the Southern AC, Memphis, Tennessee on 8 November, the *Memphis Daily Appeal* reported it to be the start of a series of fights at 158lbs that would sort out the championship. In his next couple of outings, Dillon met George Chip (nd-w pts 10 at the Panhandle AC, Columbus, Ohio on 11 November) and Grant Clark (nd-w rsc 2 at the Empire Theatre, Indianapolis, Indiana on 22 November) in catchweight affairs where there was thought to be some element of risk involving his title claim.

23 October 1912. (160lbs) Billy Papke w rtd 18 (20) Georges Carpentier.

Venue: The Circus, Paris, France. **Referee:** Frantz Reichel.

Fight Summary: Billed for the title at 160lbs, although Papke (161) was over the weight the fight went ahead with the American paying £200 forfeit. Realising his best chance for victory was an early win, Carpentier (160) went for Papke before realising he would be unable to knock the teak-tough American out. Allowed to get away with holding and hitting tactics on the inside, Papke began to wear down the Frenchman, whose right eye was closed by the end of the eighth. Even though Carpentier came back quite strongly in the 15th and 16th rounds he soon shot his bolt, a terrific left hook to the jaw in the 17th dropping him heavily. Saved by the bell to end the 17th, and with his eye bleeding badly, Carpentier was retired following the gong to start the 18th.

Afterwards, Carpentier was handed the title due to Papke coming in over the weight, but refused to accept it on the grounds that he would no longer be fighting at 160lbs. He also felt he did not deserve the title as he had lost fairly and squarely. Following that, Papke continued to be seen as the champion by the French Federation of Boxing Clubs.

4 December 1912. (158lbs) Eddie McGoorty nd-w pts 10 Mike Gibbons.

Venue: Madison Square Garden, Manhattan, NYC, New York, USA. **Referee:** Billy Joh.

Fight Summary: Given middleweight title billing, Gibbons (148¼) was never in the hunt after the fifth as McGoorty (155), realising that he could not be hurt, constantly followed his rival around the ring and gave him little breathing space. As it turned out, McGoorty was too heavy for Gibbons and too powerful a hitter to be outflanked by the latter's classy boxing, generally roughing his man up in the clinches to win at least six of the rounds on offer.

On 27 February 1913, McGoorty picked up a ten-round press draw with Gus Christie at the Armoury, Fond Du Lac, Wisconsin. The *Milwaukee Sentinel* reported that Christie was inside the 158lbs required to enforce McGoorty to defend his title claim. However, there was nothing at stake as it was a catchweight contest with Christie weighing 160lbs to McGoorty's 168.

Another fight for McGoorty where he was above 158lbs while his opponent came in below was against Young Mahoney (nd-w pts 10 at the Grand Opera House, Superior, Wisconsin on 5 March 1913). The *Superior Telegram* reported that McGoorty was forced to step lively in order to hold up the challenger, who was at the weight.

4 December 1912. (160lbs) Billy Papke w rtd 7 (20) Georges Bernard.

Venue: The Circus, Paris, France. **Referee:** Frantz Reichel.

Fight Summary: Advertised as involving Papke's 160lbs title claim, the American seemed to be under wraps up until the fifth before cutting loose in that session. Badly hurt, Bernard (157) went back to his corner a beaten man, and in the sixth Papke (l59) was at him like a shot. Sent through the ropes by right to the jaw, although Bernard tried to fight back he was dropped twice, the second time seeing him saved by the bell with the count having reached 'nine'. Despite his seconds working on him feverishly he was unable to answer the call for the seventh. Later reports claimed that it had been an extremely unsatisfactory affair with more than a hint that Bernard had been drugged, as he was sound asleep in his corner and unable to be revived in time.

11 December 1912. (158lbs) Jack Dillon nd-w pts 10 Gus Christie.
Venue: Tomlinson Hall, Indianapolis, Indiana, USA. **Referee:** Tom Dillon.
Fight Summary: According to the *Indianapolis Star*, with Dillon's title claim on the line both men made the required 158lbs at the 3pm weigh-in. In a fast and furious slugging match that had been relatively even, the fourth and fifth rounds saw Christie getting the better of it before Dillon came back strongly with solid right uppercuts. With Dillon well on top he dropped Christie with lefts and rights to the jaw in the tenth, but although the latter got up and was under pressure the final bell came to his rescue.

19 December 1912. (158lbs) Jack Dillon nd-w pts 10 Harry Ramsey.
Venue: Reichrath's Park, Cincinnati, Ohio, USA. **Referee:** Walter C. Kelley.
Fight Summary: Made at 158lbs, the *Cincinnati Enquirer* reported that Dillon yet again restated his claim at the weight in this one after meeting Ramsey. The contest started with Dillon on the attack against the fast-stepping Ramsey, who favoured fighting at distance, and in the opening few rounds it looked as though it would be curtains for the latter as volleys of body blows came his way. After being cautioned several times for not breaking, Dillon lost his rhythm as honours remained even from the fifth through to the tenth with no major incidents occurring.

1 January 1913. (158lbs) Jack Dillon nd-w pts 10 Gus Christie.
Venue: Virginia Avenue Auditorium, Indianapolis, Indiana, USA. **Referee:** Tom Dillon.
Fight Summary: With both men inside 158lbs, this was another defence of Dillon's title claim at the weight. The *Indianapolis Star* report of the contest had Dillon winning by four rounds to two and four even, with the majority of the press agreeing that he was the winner. This was their third meeting, and Christie's tactics of holding on did not go down well with either Dillon or the crowd. While Christie's jab made Dillon look foolish early on, once the latter decided to rush his man and go from head to body the course of the fight changed. However, Dillon was unable to press home his advantage. There were no knockdowns.

9 January 1913. (160lbs) Jack Dillon w rsc 15 (15) Frank Mantell.
Venue: Rhode Island AC, Thornton, Rhode Island, USA. **Referee:** Johnny Joyce.
Fight Summary: Having earlier been recorded as a points victory for Dillon it now transpires that the fight was actually stopped by the referee, on instruction from a certain Sheriff McCusker, with 35 seconds to go in order to save Mantell from sustaining further punishment. Prior to that, Dillon had boxed a cautious fight for the opening seven rounds before moving up a gear to rattle in right hands continuously without ever having Mantell over. There was no doubt that Mantell, who was hurt at the time of the stoppage, was stalling but still strong he was angry at not being allowed to complete the course. Although the middleweight limit outside the USA was set at 160lbs, much of America saw 158lbs as being the mark apart from a few odd States that included Rhode Island. Thus, 160lbs was stipulated in this one, and following the result which effectively saw Mantell eliminated from the title race Dillon extended his claim from 158lbs.

Three short-distance fights for Dillon that might have carried a risk came in the space of six days against men who were all recognised middleweights. Taking on Al Rogers (nd-w pts 6 at the Old City Hall, Pittsburgh, Pennsylvania on 18 January), Leo Houck (nd-w pts 6 at the Olympia AC, Philadelphia, Pennsylvania on 22 January) and Frank Logan (nd-w pts 6 at the Nonpareil AC, Philadelphia on 24 January), at this stage of his career Dillon was happy to meet all-comers.

10 February 1913. (160lbs) Jack Dillon drew 15 Bill McKinnon.
Venue: Rhode Island AC, Providence, Rhode Island, USA. **Referee:** Johnny Joyce.
Fight Summary: Dillon held on to his title claim at 160lbs with a draw, but had it been a press decision it would surely have gone to Dillon as the majority of papers saw the fight in his favour. Although Dillon did not find a finishing blow he dealt out severe punishment in the clinches, sinking lefts and rights into McKinnon's body. All McKinnon had in his armoury was the left jab, but knowing how to avoid punches he made life difficult for Dillon at times without ever looking likely to win.

19 February 1913. (158lbs) Jack Dillon nd-w co 2 (10) Jack Denning.
Venue: Virginia Avenue Auditorium, Indianapolis, Indiana, USA.

Fight Summary: Another successful defence of Dillon's title claim, this time at 158lbs, saw the latter charge into Denning in the second round with a view to finishing early. Having dropped Denning twice with right swings during the session and worn him down with body shots, Dillon found a short left that stretched his rival out for the count with no further ado.

When meeting Al Rogers (nd-w pts 6 at the Mishler Theatre, Altoona, Pennsylvania on 10 March) for the second time in two months it was unclear whether this fight was a risk for Dillon against a man who could make 158lbs with ease, or whether it was contracted above the weight.

5 March 1913. (160lbs) Frank Klaus w disq 15 (20) Billy Papke.
Venue: The Circus, Paris, France. **Referee:** Frantz Reichel.
Fight Summary: Recognised by most of the authorities within reason, except the New York Boxing Commission who still supported Frank Mantell, this was billed as a title fight at 160lbs. Klaus (159), starting as he meant to continue by attacking Papke's body and invariably connecting with some heavy deliveries, was never headed. By the end of the 12th round Papke (159) had taken considerable punishment, and having been in distress on several occasions he began to fight wildly. Extremely riled he lost his head, starting to go low in the 13th. After being warned several times, when Papke took no notice, he was disqualified in the 15th.

Back home, Klaus met Eddie McGoorty (nd-w pts 6 at the Exposition Park, Pittsburgh, Pennsylvania on 24 May) at 158lbs and Jimmy Gardner (w rsc 3 at the Atlas AA, Boston, Massachusetts on 1 July). The last named was an over-the-weight contest in which Gardner expected to land the 158lbs title. Another fight where Klaus (162½) risked his title claim came on 29 September at the Southside AA, Milwaukee, Wisconsin, again against McGoorty (157¾) this time picking up a ten-round press draw.

12 March 1913. (158lbs) Jack Dillon nd-w pts 10 Willie KO Brennan.
Venue: Virginia Avenue Auditorium, Indianapolis, Indiana, USA.
Fight Summary: Soon to be known as 'The Giant Killer', Dillon made yet another successful defence of his 158lbs claim in this one when punching Brennan from pillar to post, especially during the last three rounds. Initially, Brennan showed tremendous gameness when taking the fight to Dillon, but the battering he received was intense. The *Indianapolis Star* reported that despite Dillon's aggressiveness he could not finish Brennan off.

With Dillon's 158/160lbs title claim at stake in his fight against Buck Crouse (nd-w pts 6 at Kenwood Lawn, Pittsburgh, Pennsylvania on 10 April) he made no mistakes once he had worked his man out.

24 March 1913. (160lbs) Eddie McGoorty nd-drew 10 Bob Moha.
Venue: South Side AC, Elite Rink, Milwaukee, Wisconsin, USA.
Fight Summary: Made at 160lbs, the *Milwaukee Sentinel* reported this to be the middleweight championship of Milwaukee, if not the world. It was certainly a tough fight, Moha giving McGoorty stacks of trouble, and even though the latter got home considerably with the left hook it barely made a dent on his opponent. Moha kept after McGoorty from the opening bell, continually swinging both hands and never wavering in his attempt to stake a claim to the middleweight title. Strangely, McGoorty once again failed to give his right a workout, preferring to go with the left.

10 April 1913. (158lbs) Eddie McGoorty nd-w pts 10 Gus Christie.
Venue: The Armoury, Fond Du Lac, Wisconsin, USA. **Referee:** Harry Stout.
Fight Summary: On the day of the fight the *Fond du Lac Daily Commonwealth* claimed that both men were down to weight in what would be Christie's second attempt inside six weeks to carry off McGoorty's title claim. Previously, McGoorty had come in at 168lbs, but this time he was in good condition. Christie made a very fast start, but every time he closed he was met by a trip-hammer uppercut that rocked him back. Apart from the fourth McGoorty won every round, and it was a surprise that Christie was still standing at the end, his face busted up but his courage intact. Even when Christie gave it everything in the fourth, as he swung hard for a knockout, McGoorty proved far too slippery in defence to be caught, and the latter was soon back smashing lefts and rights into his opponent's face.

McGoorty next took on Freddie Hicks (nd-w pts 8 at the Athletic Club, Windsor, Ontario, Canada on 16 April) at 158lbs in a contest that carried a certain amount of risk.

14 April 1913. (158lbs) Jack Dillon nd-w pts 12 George Chip.
Venue: Moose Hall Auditorium, Youngstown, Ohio, USA. **Referee:** Walter C. Kelley.
Fight Summary: This was another defence for Dillon at 158lbs, and once again he was too good for his opponent, Chip, his left being in evidence throughout as well as his cleverness in avoiding blows. As the fight moved on Dillon drew further ahead, the last two sessions being hugely exciting as the men looked to finish inside the distance. Both were staggered in the 12th as they wound up their punches, but it was Chip who came off worse. And if there had been a round or so left he would have had difficulty in getting through still standing.

14 April 1913. (160lbs) Pat O'Keefe w pts 20 Frank Mantell.
Venue: The Ring, Southwark, London, England. **Referee:** Dick Burge.
Fight Summary: Billed as a title fight at 160lbs, with both men announced as being within the limit, it was reported that O'Keefe was fighting for Mantell's New York version of the world title. Unfortunately, for O'Keefe, however, by the time the fight took place Mantell had already forfeited any support he may have had. Having hurt O'Keefe in the opening session with wide rights to the head Mantell hardly did anything much of note from thereon in and, although he made the body his target, more often than not the Englishman's left kept him out. With O'Keefe slowing over the last three rounds Mantell took advantage when working the body for all his worth, but it was not enough.

O'Keefe's victory ultimately proved meaningless, his next two contests, defeats at the hands of Bombardier Billy Wells and Georges Carpentier, coming in the heavyweight division.

28 April 1913. (160lbs) Jack Dillon nd-w pts 10 Bob Moha.
Venue: Elite Rink, Milwaukee, Wisconsin, USA.
Fight Summary: Almost at his best, Dillon successfully defended his 160lbs title claim when taking the newspaper decision from Moha after winning eight rounds with two even. According to reports, Dillon fought a cool and clever battle, whether it was up close or at long range, and when Moha tried to hit back in the last three sessions he blocked most of his blows before using a jolting left lead to make room for the right cross.

2 May 1913. (158lbs) Eddie McGoorty drew 10 Jimmy Clabby.
Venue: Athletic Club, Denver, Colorado, USA. **Referee:** Abe Pollock.
Fight Summary: Reported to be a 158lbs title fight, with both men inside, Clabby was announced as being 154lbs. Described as one of the fastest and most scientific contests ever seen in the territory, Clabby's cleverness was offset to a degree by the extra strength possessed by McGoorty. There were no knockdowns, and there was never any likelihood of one occurring as both men were so evenly matched. Although Clabby landed the greater volume of blows and appeared to be a better judge of distance, McGoorty was the heavier hitter, his punches carrying more authority when they landed. Afterwards, a prominent Wisconsin sportsman stated that the referee was incompetent and that McGoorty received the worst beating of his career, being made to look like a novice at times.

29 May 1913. (160lbs) Jack Dillon nd-w pts 10 Frank Klaus.
Venue: Washington Park, Indianapolis, Indiana, USA. **Referee:** Tom Dillon.
Fight Summary: Both fighters' claims at 160lbs were on the line in this one. Although the opening five sessions were slow and uninteresting, Dillon outfought and outboxed Klaus from round six through to the tenth, outpunching the latter at the rate of eight-to-one according to press reports. While Klaus spent much of his time clinching and blocking punches, Dillon, landing crisply, was a wide winner as far as the press were concerned.

13 June 1913. (158lbs) Jimmy Clabby w pts 12 Eddie McGoorty.
Venue: Holland Rink, Butte, Montana, USA. **Referee:** John H. McIntosh.
Fight Summary: According to the *TS Andrews' Annuals* Clabby (151) had been claiming the middleweight title since 1912, but it was only after defeating McGoorty (158) in this billed 158lbs title bout that his claim was taken

seriously. Despite being floored twice in the opening round, his left eye closed shut and groggy in the second, Clabby was bravely back in the fight by the fourth, boxing and moving well. With the punches flying in, when McGoorty's left eye was badly cut in the ninth there seemed no way back for him. At that stage of the fight, Clabby, excelling on the inside, was in full swing. According to the referee, Clabby won six rounds to McGoorty's one, with five evenly scored.

3 July 1913. (160lbs) Jack Dillon nd-w rsc 10 (10) Bill McKinnon.
Venue: Washington Park, Indianapolis, Indiana, USA. **Referee:** Tom Dillon.
Fight Summary: Dillon's 160lbs title claim was at stake here as both men came in under the prescribed weight. Regardless of the fact that McKinnon was fleet of foot and travelled around the ring at speed, Dillon eventually caught up with him. Having been cut over the left eye in the second round McKinnon was always at risk, and in the sixth he went to his knees three times as Dillon hammered in punches to the body. Down again twice in the seventh, and twice more in the ninth, when the final session arrived it was almost too much for McKinnon to get off his stool. And after being dropped five more times he was rescued by the referee. Other reports gave this as a last-minute kayo win.

Fighting at the Auditorium, Winnipeg, Canada on 8 August, Dillon, weighing above 160lbs, allowed the Canadian, George Ashe, to weigh inside 158lbs, thus risking his title claim. The fight went the distance, Dillon being awarded a 12-round draw by the attending press.

While it is not clear whether Dillon's 12-round no-decision contest against Tony Caponi (w co 8 at the Auditorium, Winnipeg on 17 September) was contracted for 160lbs, his short-distance bout against Leo Houck (nd-l pts 6 at Rocky Springs Park, Lancaster, Pennsylvania on 9 October) almost certainly was.

At The Casino, Akron, Ohio, on 14 October, Dillon forced Walter Monaghan to retire in the fourth of a 12-round no-decision affair refereed by Walter Kelley. In reference to the fighters' weights, the *Akron Beacon* newspaper reported that it was a catchweight contest in which Dillon would weigh around 160lbs and his opponent a little under. With no title billing given, it was this kind of reporting that has made it so difficult to fathom whether title claims were at risk or not.

Three weeks later, on 3 November, Dillon was deemed by the press to have outscored Gus Christie in a ten round no-decision contest at the South Delaware Street Auditorium, Milwaukee, Wisconsin. Although the press stated that the fight had been made at 160lbs, according to the *Indianapolis Star* Dillon outweighed his rival by 12 pounds but had Christie, well inside 158lbs, won he would have undoubtedly claimed the title.

2 August 1913. (158lbs) Jimmy Clabby drew 12 Freddie Hicks.
Venue: Holland Rink, Butte, Montana, USA. **Referee:** John H. McIntosh.
Fight Summary: The *Anaconda Standard* inferred that this involved Clabby's title claim when it stated that Clabby made 154lbs, while Hicks was inside the stipulated 158lbs. In the sixth round the referee asked for more action as nothing much had happened up to that point, but regardless of that the boys continued to come together. There were those who thought that Clabby carried Hicks, who was known to be his friend, and the referee had thought about calling the fight off, but after discussing the situation with the Commissioner a draw was decided upon.

As far as the 'black title' was concerned it was reported in *The Freeman* newspaper around this time that Jack Hannibal was the champion of the world, despite there being nothing in his record to sustain that statement. Hannibal was an interesting fighter as he was also a pro baseball and American football star at the same time as he boxed. A few months later, a certain Kid Hoy wrote to the same paper stating that he was the rightful 'black world champion'. At the same time he issued a challenge to all-comers. I have yet to find anything to back those statements up, although it is clear that both men were top fighters of the day.

1 September 1913. (158lbs) Jimmy Clabby w pts 20 Sailor Grande.
Venue: Buffalo Park, Sacramento, California, USA. **Referee:** Charley Schwallenburg.

Fight Summary: Made at 158lbs, Clabby (152) showed plenty of class as he concentrated on his left jab and right cross early on, but when he realised that Grande (157) could withstand any amount of punishment he changed tactics when allowing the latter to make the running. Using his extra weight, Grande, who was miles behind, clutched and hung on to survive in the latter rounds.

3 October 1913. (158lbs) Jimmy Clabby w pts 20 Sailor Ed Petroskey.
Venue: Coffroth's Arena, Daly City, California, USA. **Referee:** Benny Seelig.
Fight Summary: Clabby (151) dominated the contest, winning all but four rounds according to the papers, and handing out a real boxing lesson to the tough Petroskey (158). Several times Petroskey looked like going down, but he was never off his feet, somehow managing to weather the storm of punches coming his way. Realising he had to find a knockout blow if he wanted to win, Petroskey tore into Clabby in the last two rounds before being straightened up by solid left jabs, left hooks and right uppercuts from head to body as the title claimant boxed his way to victory.

11 October 1913. (160lbs) George Chip nd-w co 6 (6) Frank Klaus.
Venue: Old City Hall, Pittsburgh, Pennsylvania, USA. **Referee:** Tom Bodkins.
Fight Summary: This was not billed as a title bout as it was only a six-round no-decision affair, but Klaus's claim to the championship was deemed to have changed hands after he was counted out. In a situation such as this the only way a champion could lose his crown, unless he stipulated a poundage above the limit of the weight class, was if he failed to last the distance. It was on this basis that Chip (161½) received recognition as champion. Klaus (163) had the better of the fight during the first three rounds before Chip came on strong to batter him all over the ring prior to smashing him down for 'nine' in the sixth with a short right uppercut. Getting back on his feet, Klaus had hardly got going when Chip sent him down for the full count with a right to the head. Despite both men weighing over the middleweight limit, Chip immediately announced his right to the title and was accepted by a good many scribes.

Another six-rounder for Chip in Pennsylvania that was advertised as involving the title came against Leo Houck (nd-l pts 6 at the National AC, Philadelphia on 15 November), but there was no mention of weights.

Regardless of the defeat at the hands of Chip, the recently formed French-based International Boxing Union continued to recognise Klaus as the world champion.

13 October 1913. (158lbs) Joe Borrell nd-w rsc 5 (6) Harry Lewis.
Venue: Olympia AC, Philadelphia, Pennsylvania, USA. **Referee:** Frank O'Brien.
Fight Summary: Lewis was badly beaten by Borrell in a contest made at 158lbs, taking serious punishment in the second, third and fourth rounds. Belted to the floor twice in the fourth, and being hit at will, the referee stopped the fight early in the fifth to save an exhausted Lewis from being knocked out. After Lewis collapsed and was taken to hospital suffering from concussion of the brain he never boxed again. In the aftermath, Borrell claimed the title despite the bout being scheduled for only six rounds, but on receiving little or no support at all in America he eventually took his claim abroad.

15 November 1913. (160lbs) Jeff Smith w pts 20 Georges Bernard.
Venue: Wonderland, Luna Park, Paris, France. **Referee:** Franz Reichel.
Fight Summary: Billed for the title at 160lbs, with both men announced as being inside the weight, Smith (159½) controlled most of the fight with his left hand before opening up somewhat in the last three sessions as Bernard tired. Prior to that the contest had been mundane with Smith doing enough to keep ahead and Barnard occasionally throwing heavy blows without ever following them up. *Boxing* reported that in the last three rounds the real Smith was seen when sending in stinging left jabs to Bernard's face and doing good work with right uppercuts. Bernard, who was far too conservative to take the fight to Smith when given the opportunities, finished with a badly swollen left eye. Most observers felt that the referee should have awarded a draw as neither man did enough. After the fight, with Frank Klaus back in America the promoters awarded Smith a championship belt and proclaimed him to be the new champion.

25 November 1913. (160lbs) George Chip nd-w pts 10 Tim O'Neil.
Venue: Athletic Club, Racine, Wisconsin, USA. **Referee:** Louis Hagey.
Fight Summary: Claiming the title at 160lbs, in a match made at that weight Chip outboxed and outfought the game O'Neil (159), putting him down twice in the second round before the latter came back strongly in the tenth, having weathered the storm by covering up and keeping out of danger.

27 November 1913. (158lbs) Jimmy Clabby w rsc 14 (20) Frank Logan.
Venue: Daly City Arena, San Francisco, California, USA. **Referee:** Jim Griffin.
Fight Summary: With the *San Francisco Chronicle* reporting this one to be at 158lbs, Clabby's title claim was at risk. One-sided from start to finish, Logan was knocked down in the 13th and punished badly before being stopped after about a minute of the next round. Having been forced to make the weight obviously weakened Logan, the finish being in sight in the tenth session after he was dazed from terrific uppercuts to the jaw. Logan also received a broken nose for his pains.

27 November 1913. (160lbs) Jack Dillon w pts 12 Sailor Ed Petroskey.
Venue: Holland Arena, Butte, Montana, USA. **Referee:** Jack McDonough.
Fight Summary: Set at 160lbs, the recognised middles limit in Montana at the time, the *Anaconda Standard* reported that both men were actually inside 158lbs. Showing dazzling speed and power, Dillon gave Petroskey a terrible going over but was unable to knock his man out despite having him down in the eighth following a terrific volley of rights and lefts. There was never any doubt that Dillon would win, as he was hardly extended. However, although he tried to drop Petroskey, ultimately lacking the ammunition required, he had to settle for the points win.

23 December 1913. (160lbs) George Chip nd-w rsc 5 (6) Frank Klaus.
Venue: Duquesne Gardens, Pittsburgh, Pennsylvania, USA. **Referee:** Tom Dillon.
Fight Summary: In a return six-round no-decision fight, Chip (160) bettered his previous win over Klaus (162½) when stopping him in the fifth round. Up to the fifth round it had been a hard fight, but Chip had remained cool and shown his strength at close quarters. The fifth session saw Chip raining in blows to head and body to drop Klaus, and after the latter got up at the count of 'seven' he was immediately under pressure yet again. With Chip smashing in trip-hammer blows to the jaw when Klaus's hands dropped to his side, rendering him defenceless, the referee called a halt. Chip received widespread recognition at 160lbs in America even though the class limit was generally seen as being 158lbs.

1 January 1914. (158lbs) Jack Dillon nd-w pts 10 Gus Christie.
Venue: South Delaware Street Arena, Indianapolis, Indiana, USA.
Fight Summary: The *Indianapolis Star* reported that both men were down to the required 158lbs, thus putting Dillon's title claim at the weight at risk. While Dillon proved to everyone present that he could be comfortable at 158lbs, he was seldom forced to exert himself, being easily contented, as was Christie, to clinch rather than work for openings. After damaging Christie's right eye in the fourth round and blasting in power punches to the head it was expected that Dillon would move up a gear, but it just did not materialise. Christie was obviously intent on staying the course when they entered the latter stages, and although Dillon opened up again in the last two sessions he was unable to bring his opponent down.

1 January 1914. (160lbs) Eddie McGoorty w co 1 (20) Dave Smith.
Venue: Baker's Stadium, Sydney, Australia. **Referee:** Arthur Scott.
Fight Summary: Now that many of the leading fighters at the weight were campaigning abroad, the Australian authorities in Sydney declared McGoorty versus Smith to be for the vacant Australian version of the 160lbs title. Having knocked Smith (158) down twice in rapid succession, McGoorty (158) finished the New Zealander off with a right to the jaw after just 90 seconds of the opening round.

12 January 1914. (158lbs) George Chip nd-w pts 10 Gus Christie.
Venue: Southside AA, Elite Rink, Milwaukee, Wisconsin, USA.

Fight Summary: Both men were reckoned to be inside 158lbs at the 3pm weigh-in, with Chip's title claim being the prize for Christie if he could find a finishing blow. There hardly seemed to be any likelihood of that happening as Chip blasted him all around the ring, but the latter for all his domination was unable to find a knockout drop, mauling Christie about for round after round. The last two sessions saw Christie giving it a go, especially with the straight left, but Chip was soon breaking through his guard without doing any damage before settling for the press verdict.

Next up for Chip were six-round no-decision contests against Tim O'Neil (nd-w rsc 2 at the Powers Theatre, Grand Rapids, Michigan on 19 January) and Joe Borrell (nd-w pts 6 at the Olympia AC, Philadelphia, Pennsylvania on 26 January). While O'Neil was reported to weigh 159lbs, the *Philadelphia Public Ledger* stated that both Chip and Borrell were inside 158lbs.

20 January 1914. (158lbs) Jack Dillon w pts 12 Vic Hansen.
Venue: Colorado AC, Denver, Colorado, USA. **Referee:** Tommy McDonnell.
Fight Summary: Billed for the middleweight championship of the world, the *Denver Post* reported that both men made the required 158lbs. Outboxing Hansen right from the opening bell, and after dropping him twice for 'nine', Dillon broke his right hand in the second round. Following that, Dillon used his left hand exclusively from there on. Even then Hansen was occasionally in trouble, and in the latter sessions he held on to avoid taking too much punishment to the body.

A few days after this one Dillon took on Harry Baker (nd-w co 1 at the Tomlinson Hall, Indianapolis, Indiana on 30 January). It is not clear whether Dillon bothered to make weight for Baker, a natural middleweight, or not.

Another fight at 158lbs for Dillon came against Freddie Hicks (nd-w pts 8 at the Athletic Club, Windsor, Ontario, Canada on 4 February), before he allowed George KO Brown (w pts 8 at the Phoenix AC, Memphis, Tennessee on 23 March) to weigh 159lbs to his 170. Sandwiched somewhere between these two was an eight-round contest against Tommy Danforth (nd-w rsc 8 at the Phoenix AC, Memphis, Tennessee on 9 February). The fight report stated that Dillon was much the heavier, but knowing that Danforth was a big welter at this time I guess there was some risk attached.

Dillon next laid claim to the American light heavyweight title after beating Battling Levinsky, another future champion at 175lbs, on 14 April. Although there would be a few more defences of his middleweight claim, Dillon would soon be concentrating his efforts at the higher poundage.

7 February 1914. (160lbs) Eddie McGoorty w pts 20 Pat Bradley.
Venue: Baker's Stadium, Sydney, Australia. **Referee:** Arthur Scott.
Fight Summary: Reported as being the Australian version of the middleweight title, with McGoorty (158) defending, the challenger was not given much chance against a man who stood taller and outreached him by a considerable amount. Regardless of that, Bradley (158) proved to be a difficult man to dislodge, more than bothering McGoorty with his swings and smothering tactics. Several times during the contest McGoorty was caught by solid blows to the head that forced him to step cautiously, but he was well ahead by the three-quarter mark. While there was always the chance that Bradley might get lucky, especially in the 17th when he had a tiring McGoorty almost off his feet, he was given no further opportunities as the American boxed his way out of trouble to take the referee's decision.

12 February 1914. (158lbs) Jimmy Clabby w pts 20 Sailor Ed Petroskey.
Venue: Vernon Arena, Los Angeles, California, USA. **Referee:** Charles Eyton.
Fight Summary: Made at 158lbs, 10am weigh-in, the fight had first been booked for January but had been cancelled after an appendicitis scare for Petroskey. Right from the start, Clabby proved to be fast and clever, landing punches all over Petroskey at the rate of ten-to-one during the opening five rounds. Although Petroskey came back with some good blows of his own, especially to the body as Clabby tired, the last five sessions saw the latter all over his man, beating him to the punch and cutting him on the right eye in the 19th. However, he was unable to knock him over.

26 February 1914. (160lbs) Joe Borrell w pts 15 Georges Bernard.
Venue: The Stadium, Liverpool, England. **Referee:** George Dunning.
Fight Summary: Given world championship billing at 160lbs, with both men inside the weight, it received very little recognition as one even in Britain. Regardless of that it was well contested, the fourth round being sensational as Bernard was decked four times from body blows and once by a tremendous left-right to the jaw that would have finished off most men. Not only did Bernard fight on but he more than gave the American a run for his money, especially in the last three sessions when he scored freely with solid shots to head and body. While there were many who thought Bernard might have won, the referee scored it 69 to 57 in favour of Borrell.

14 March 1914. (160lbs) Jeff Smith w pts 20 Eddie McGoorty.
Venue: Baker's Stadium, Sydney, Australia. **Referee:** Arthur Scott.
Fight Summary: While there was never much in it with the crowd on the side of Smith (157¾), every time he landed on McGoorty (159) roars of approval went up. In the third round Smith's right eye began to close, but after taking a fair bit of punishment in the fourth this was rectified prior to the start of the fifth by his corner's clever work with the lancet. From that point on Smith got himself back in the fight, using a points scoring straight left, and in several sessions McGoorty was unable to lift himself. In the 17th McGoorty was badly hurt by a series of solid uppercuts, being still groggy in the 18th before coming back strongly in the final two sessions. Although the initial decision was given in McGoorty's favour it proved to be so unpopular that it was quickly rescinded by the officials in charge.

Next time out, McGoorty (158) took on Dave Smith (160) at Baker's Stadium on 11 April in a 20-round contest that has sometimes been shown as a world title fight. Although McGoorty knocked Smith out inside ten rounds, having lost the Australian version of the world title a month earlier at the same venue, it should not be recognised as such.

3 April 1914. (158lbs) Jimmy Clabby drew 20 Billy Murray.
Venue: Mission Street Arena, Colma, San Francisco, California, USA. **Referee:** Jim Griffin.
Fight Summary: Clabby's 158lbs title claim was on the line in this one. Although Murray was a bit of an unknown quantity, having recently beaten Leo Houck he would command some respect. Even to start with, Clabby got on top from the third round when beginning to outbox Murray, especially with the left hand, and he was also effective with short right crosses. However, after several good rounds Clabby started to take it easy and was made to pay. In the 15th Murray came on strongly, a hard left to the jaw nearly taking Clabby out of the fight, and at the bell the latter was on the ropes in a groggy condition. Murray was now pressing, but Clabby came back well prior to being caught with a crashing right cross in the 20th and having to hold on grimly until the final bell. Following the drawn verdict, Murray announced that he would be adding his name to the list of those already claiming the 158lbs title.

7 April 1914. (158lbs) Al McCoy nd-w co 1 (10) George Chip.
Venue: Broadway SC, Brooklyn, NYC, New York, USA. **Referee:** Johnny Haukaup.
Fight Summary: As in the contests between Chip and Frank Klaus this was not a billed title bout, but Chip's version of the championship was deemed to have changed hands after he ran on to a left hook counter from the Brooklyn southpaw and was knocked out on the 1.04 mark. Despite Chip (162½), who was a substitute for his brother Joe, coming in over the middleweight poundage in a ten-round no-decision affair with no weight stipulation in force McCoy (157½) received recognition as the first southpaw champion in boxing history.

13 April 1914. (160lbs) Jeff Smith w rsc 16 (20) Pat Bradley.
Venue: Baker's Stadium, Sydney, Australia. **Referee:** Harold Baker.
Fight Summary: In defence of his Australian world title claim, Smith (157½) recovered from a shock first-round knockdown to first outbox Bradley (157¼), with the left rarely out of the latter's face, and then to outpunch him. Having jabbed and uppercut Bradley to distraction in the seventh Smith really went to town, a burst of heavy punches, especially left hooks, having his man over for two long counts. Although Bradley came back with some heavy blows of his own, by the 11th round he was almost finished. How Bradley stayed upright for several more sessions was a mystery, but after terrific body shots had weakened him in the 16th he was dropped heavily by a

right cross. Almost immediately the police official in charge ordered the referee to stop the count and award the contest to Smith.

20 April 1914. (160lbs) Joe Borrell nc 4 (20) Bandsman Blake.

Venue: The Ring, Southwark, London, England. **Referee:** J. T. Hulls.

Fight Summary: Billed as a title bout at 160lbs, with both men announced as having made the weight, it was described in the *Mirror of Life* as being 12 minutes of wrestling before coming to life in the fourth. At the bell to end that session, when Blake dropped his hands to go to his corner he was promptly dropped by a cracking left hook to the jaw. With Blake in no position to box on in the fifth, and the crowd screaming for a foul, the referee called the bout off, claiming it to be a no contest. He later admitted that he had not heard the bell.

5 May 1914. (160lbs) Joe Borrell w rsc 8 (20) Marcel Moreau.

Venue: The Circus, Paris, France. **Referee:** Fernand Cuny.

Fight Summary: Although there was no title billing attached, with both men safely inside the required 160lbs Borrell's claim at the weight was certainly at risk. Moreau made a good start, sending in blows from both hands while Borrell was notable more for his use of elbow work. Unfortunately for Moreau, the third round saw him hit badly low, and had he gone down he would surely have won by disqualification, so obvious was the delivery from Borrell. *Boxing* stated that from that moment only one man remained in the fight. With his left eye badly damaged in the fifth each proceeding round saw Moreau falling further behind when being badly weakened by body shots. The end came in the eighth when Moreau, although still standing, was absolutely defenceless before being led back to his corner by the referee.

After arriving back in the USA and concentrating mainly on six-round affairs, Borrell's championship claim faded away.

8 May 1914. (158lbs) Al McCoy nd-w co 1 (10) George Pearsall.

Venue: New City AC, Roodner's Hall, South Norwalk, Connecticut, USA. **Referee:** William Rothwell (Young Corbett).

Fight Summary: Reported in the *Norwalk Hour* as being a 158lbs title fight, with both men making the agreed weight, Pearsall was knocked down in the first few seconds only to be dropped again by a cracking left to the jaw, this time for the full count. It was recognised as being one of the quickest finishes of all time.

21 May 1914. (158lbs) Al McCoy nd-l pts 10 Billy Murray.

Venue: Stadium AC, St Nicholas Rink, Manhattan, NYC, New York, USA. **Referee:** Billy Joh.

Fight Summary: With the title claim at stake for both men, Murray (157) had little difficulty with McCoy (154½), battering him around the head with two hands at times in the first eight rounds until the latter came back in the ninth. Up until then Murray had proved superior to the New Yorker, especially on the inside. The last two sessions witnessed a slugfest, McCoy coming close to stopping Murray immediately before the final bell rang. Both men finished with badly swollen right eyes.

6 June 1914. (160lbs) Jeff Smith w pts 20 Jimmy Clabby.

Venue: Baker's Stadium, Sydney, Australia. **Referee:** Harold Baker.

Fight Summary: In defending the Australian version of the championship Smith (156¼) met a very good man in Clabby (153¼), who not only possessed the longer reach of the pair but had punching power to match. Although there were no knockdowns, both landed lusty blows and both showed great cleverness. Those sitting further back from ringside probably thought it boring, but it was nothing of the kind as the men set about negating each other's strengths. Knowing that he had no chance of winning if he allowed his fellow-American to stand off him, Smith realised that he had to keep the fight at close quarters. And that is ultimately what he did, Clabby not being able to do much damage after the 15th round.

11 June 1914. (158lbs) Al McCoy nd-l pts 10 Billy Murray.

Venue: Stadium AC, St Nicholas Rink, Manhattan, NYC, New York, USA. **Referee:** Billy Joh.

Fight Summary: After both men put their title claims on the line for the second time in three weeks, McCoy (157) generally went missing, holding repeatedly, running away and refusing to exchange blows in order to avoid being stopped. With Murray (158) consistently forcing matters, despite his right eye being closed early on, if an official decision had been given he would have won hands down. Although McCoy made a better showing in the last two sessions, busting up Murray's nose, he was unable to find the punch to earn a stoppage win. At this stage of his career, McCoy was beginning to be seen as the 'cheese' champion.

3 July 1914. (160lbs) Jack Dillon w pts 10 Sailor Ed Petroskey.
Venue: Association Park, Kansas City, Missouri, USA.
Fight Summary: The *Kansas City Star* gave this one at 160lbs, carrying a heavy forfeit if not adhered to, thus putting Dillon's title claim at risk. Winning virtually every round to take an easy points verdict, Dillon found Petroskey a tough man to finish off despite having him down with a left uppercut in the seventh. Up until then Petroskey had been successful in blocking many of Dillon's best efforts, but from there onwards he took punch after punch while showing a remarkable ability in shipping punishment.

On 21 July, Dillon (168) took a ten-round press decision over the 157lbs George KO Brown at the Ballpark, Terre Haute, Indiana. The *Indianapolis News* reported it to be a billed middleweight title fight despite Dillon being eight pounds over the weight class.

Another fight for an over-the-weight Dillon where the opponent was inside 158lbs came against Howard Morrow (nd-w pts 6 at the Fuller Theatre, Kalamazoo, Michigan on 12 August).

4 July 1914. (158lbs) George Chip w co 15 (20) Billy Murray.
Venue: Daly City Arena, San Francisco, California, USA. **Referee:** Jim Griffin.
Fight Summary: Now claiming the 158lbs title, the weight the fight was made at, Murray, looking to establish himself ran into a tartar in the shape of Chip. Although he won five of the first nine rounds when forcing the fight, Murray could not hurt Chip despite cutting him over the left eye in the sixth, and after having a big eighth when he threw everything he had at his opponent he weakened. Rallying hard in the tenth, Chip began catching Murray with heavy uppercuts and straight rights, dropping the latter in the 11th for 'nine' after smashing home rights and lefts to the head. The next three rounds saw Murray under pressure and bleeding badly prior to Chip opening up in the 15th with solid lefts, before a right cross to the jaw sent the man from Petaluma crashing to be counted out.

At the Dreamland Rink, San Francisco on 31 July, Chip outpointed Sailor Ed Petroskey over 20 rounds in a match made at 160lbs. Had Chip lost, his new claim would have been shot down in flames.

7 September 1914. (158/160lbs) Jack Dillon nd-w pts 10 Sailor Einert.
Venue: Baseball Park, Terre Haute, Indiana, USA.
Fight Summary: Made at 158lbs, with Dillon (160) claiming the title at 158 and 160lbs, Einert was inside the required poundage. What was initially seen as being an interesting match turned into a farce as the novice-like Einert ran away, clowning for much of the time, with Dillon in hot pursuit. With the crowd restless, Dillon started gesturing to Einert to make a fight of it, but when that failed the title claimant, unable to find a finishing blow, went through the motions until the final bell.

An over-the-weight Dillon then risked his title claim against George KO Brown (nd-drew 10 at Knox County Fairground, Vincennes, Indiana on 15 September).

A few weeks later Dillon again took on Brown (nd-nc 3 at The Coliseum, St Louis, Missouri on 14 October) and was held by the local police for a couple of days when it appeared the fight may have been a fake.

Dillon next risked his claim against Young Ahearn (nd-drew 6 at the Olympia AC, Philadelphia, Pennsylvania on 1 January 1915).

30 September 1914. (158lbs) George Chip w co 4 (20) Billy Murray.
Venue: Mission Street Arena, Colma, San Francisco, California, USA. **Referee:** Jim Griffin.

Fight Summary: With both men inside 158lbs, Chip successfully defended his claim at the weight when knocking Murray out in the fourth round. Although Murray looked comfortable when fighting at range for the opening couple of rounds he was unable to resist a tear-up in the third, but found he could not make much of an impression on the teak-tough Chip. After about a minute of the fourth had elapsed, Chip battered down Murray's defences with heavy lefts and rights, and following a clinch he missed with a right before crashing in a left to the point that sent Murray down for the count.

13 October 1914. (158lbs) Al McCoy nd-w rtd 5 (10) Willie Lewis.
Venue: Broadway SC, Brooklyn, NYC, New York, USA.
Fight Summary: Risking his title claim in a match made at 158lbs, McCoy (157¾) hit far too hard for Lewis (157¼), lambasting him for round after round and knocking him down four times before the sponge was thrown in during the fifth.

19 October 1914. (158lbs) Al McCoy nd-l pts 10 Willie KO Brennan.
Venue: Broadway Auditorium, Buffalo, New York, USA. **Referee:** Maurice Collins.
Fight Summary: McCoy (158) had a hard time of it against Brennan (157), being outslugged in seven of the ten rounds according to press reports. Keeping an eye on the southpaw left that had flattened George Chip, Brennan found the perfect antidote when McCoy was getting set to drop in the left by jumping in with lefts of his own. With McCoy always dangerous, Brennan was shaken up in the fourth and eighth before hanging for the last two rounds to make sure of the press decision.

Next time out, McCoy (158¾) risked his title claim against Soldier Bartfield (nd-l pts 10 at the Broadway SC, Brooklyn, NYC, New York on 10 November), who was announced as being 146lbs.

6 November 1914. (158lbs) Jimmy Clabby w pts 20 George Chip.
Venue: Daly City Arena, San Francisco, California, USA. **Referee:** Benny Selig.
Fight Summary: Described in the *San Francisco Chronicle* as another step towards the settlement of the 158lbs title with both men inside the weight, Clabby said afterwards that he saw himself not only as the American champion but world leader also. Taken in context, Chip had lost his claim to Al McCoy in April but was back into contention after twice beating Billy Murray, while Clabby had recently been turned back by Jeff Smith for the Australian 160lbs version of the title. Unable to fathom out his elusive and tantalising foe, Chip was left chasing shadows before being floored by a left to the jaw in the ninth round as he was stumbling backwards. Following the fight it was reckoned that Clabby took 17 of the rounds with three even. Chip had been on the run after a bad 16th when he was hurt by hard rights to the head and follow-up body punches. Just as bad for Chip in the final session, it was a disappointing end to the last professional fight permitted in California under the new regulations enforced by the winners of the State election.

28 November 1914. (160lbs) Mick King w pts 20 Jeff Smith.
Venue: Baker's Stadium, Sydney, Australia. **Referee:** Harold Baker.
Fight Summary: After Smith (157), defending the Australian version of the title, dropped King (157¼) with a terrific left hook in the opening session the fight appeared to be one that would not last very long. If that was what Smith thought then he was wrong as King, with clever defensive boxing and the use of sharp lefts and rights, came right back to get himself in front. At the halfway mark, Smith, realising that he was fighting the wrong tactical battle, reverted to the jab, and apart from the 12th and 13th had the remainder of the contest very much his own way, especially in the last four rounds when he came close to knocking King over. While the decision in favour of King was greeted with much applause those who knew the game well enough called for an immediate rematch, realising the verdict was flawed.

22 December 1914. (158lbs) Al McCoy nd-l pts 10 Soldier Bartfield.
Venue: Broadway SC, Brooklyn, NYC, New York, USA.
Fight Summary: Although McCoy (156½) got his left haymaker working overtime, unable to put Bartfield (146¾) away the latter, who had a clear advantage in at least seven rounds, was still strong and fighting hard at the finish.

391

When McCoy met Joe Borrell (nd-w pts 6 at the Olympia AC, Philadelphia, Pennsylvania on 25 January 1915), while he scaled 156¾lbs his opponent came in just above the middleweight limit at 158¼. This seemed strange bearing in mind that Borrell was looking to lay claim to the 158lbs title.

Despite not involving the title, a ten-round no-decision contest of much interest pitted McCoy (158½) against Al Thiel (160¼) at the Broadway SC on 16 February 1915. McCoy, who was given the press decision, used to be managed by Jack Dougherty, but after he successfully picked up George Chip's title claim Dan Morgan became his manager and Dougherty was shown the door. Extremely angry at being treated in such a way, Dougherty had the name of one of his young middleweights legally changed from Al Thiel to 'Al McCoy' and he became known as the 'New' Al McCoy, thus creating a problem with billing, especially as he also came from Brooklyn, NYC, New York.

Another fight for McCoy that could have involved his title claim came against Silent Martin (nd-l pts 10 at the Broadway SC on 23 March 1915). According to some reports, Martin scaled 153lbs to McCoy's 163, while other papers gave the weights in reverse order.

On 6 April 1915, in a return match, McCoy (157) lost the ten-round newspaper decision to George Chip (159) at the Broadway SC, Brooklyn. Press reports stated that although Chip did all the leading from the second round onwards, twice dropping McCoy in the ninth, he was unable to finish his man off. Regardless of the fact that it was contested above 158lbs, had McCoy been beaten inside the distance his title claim would have been further weakened.

26 December 1914. (160lbs) Jeff Smith w pts 20 Mick King.
Venue: Baker's Stadium, Sydney, Australia. **Referee:** Harold Baker.
Fight Summary: By his victory over King (154¾) the Australian version of the title returned to Smith (158), the referee's decision being fully warranted. Once again the contest was of extreme cleverness reported the *Sydney Telegraph*, but this time round Smith made sure of winning when dropping King in the third round with a solid left hook and keeping his rival busy thereafter. By dint of clever left-hand work, King was never really outclassed, and in the 16th and 17th sessions he came back strongly before being badly hurt in the following round and going on the defensive through to the final bell.

21 January 1915. (158lbs) Jimmy Clabby nd-l pts 10 Mike Gibbons.
Venue: The Auditorium, Milwaukee, Wisconsin, USA. **Referee:** Harry Stout.
Fight Summary: This contest was billed for the 158lbs championship. While the *Milwaukee Sentinel* referred to Clabby (153¾) as the champion prior to the contest, it was Gibbons (153½) who was also claiming the title afterwards, having outboxed his rival all the way. In one of the greatest exhibitions of pure boxing seen in the region up to that point in time, Gibbons fully lived up to his nickname of the 'Phantom' when it came to cleverness. On top of that he showed he was stronger than his clever opponent and hit harder as well. Despite being cut over the right eye following a clash of heads in the ninth round, Gibbons was unmarked, while only great defence by Clabby saved him from a knockdown. Fast and furious from the opening bell, the fight proved that clever boxing could be just as exciting as a slugfest.

Two short-distance fights for Clabby, where both he and his opponents were reckoned to be inside 158lbs, came against Young Ahearn (nd-drew 6 at the National AC, Philadelphia, Pennsylvania on 17 March) and George Chip (nd-w pts 6 at the Coliseum, Grand Rapids, Michigan on 22 March).

23 January 1915. (160lbs) Jeff Smith w rtd 5 (20) Les Darcy.
Venue: Baker's Stadium, Sydney, Australia. **Referee:** Harold Baker.
Fight Summary: Defending the Australian version of the title, Smith (160) took on Darcy (155), a 19-year-old youngster who was seen as a good bet to become a world champion in the near future. For the opening four rounds, with not much action, halfway through the fifth, when Darcy complained to the referee that he had been struck low he was made to continue. At the end of the session Darcy dropped his shorts to show the crowd his dented protector before being retired by his seconds.

13 February 1915. (160lbs) Young Ahearn w co 2 (20) Willie Lewis.
Venue: Maine Park, Havana, Cuba. **Referee:** Sam Lewis.
Fight Summary: Billed as Cuba's first world title fight, when Ahearn (155) opened Lewis (159) up with lefts and rights to head and body in the second round, following a quiet start, it brought about a kayo win with an overarm right to the jaw.

On 17 March, at the National AC, Philadelphia, Pennsylvania, USA, Ahearn met Jimmy Clabby (nd-drew 6) in a contest made at 158lbs.

20 February 1915. (160lbs) Jeff Smith w pts 20 Mick King.
Venue: West Melbourne Stadium, Melbourne, Australia. **Referee:** Vic Newhouse.
Fight Summary: Smith (158½) boxed at his own pace throughout a contest that had little excitement. In the sixth and 11th rounds the referee asked both men for a little more action, but there was virtually no response. Every time King (156½) got through Smith merely gave him more back in return. From the 15th onwards Smith was happy to evade anything that King threw in anger, and at the final bell the *Melbourne Fight* declared that in their opinion the latter had won just one round.

2 March 1915. (158lbs) Mike Gibbons nd-w pts 10 Eddie McGoorty.
Venue: The Arena, Hudson, Wisconsin, USA. **Referee:** Harry Stout.
Fight Summary: Given title billing at 158lbs, after two even rounds Gibbons (151½) started to get to McGoorty (155½) in the third when opening up with five unanswered blows to the head immediately prior to the bell. There was no doubt that Gibbons' speed troubled McGoorty, who missed repeatedly when trying to land, and the latter also found himself losing the battle on the inside as well as at range. Up against a fine opponent, Gibbons showed that he would be just too fast and scientific for almost all of the top men around.

20 March 1915. (160lbs) Young Ahearn nd-w pts 10 Italian Joe Gans.
Venue: Irving AC, Brooklyn, NYC, New York, USA.
Fight Summary: Putting his 160lbs title claim on the line, with both men inside the weight, Ahearn continued his advance to the top of the middleweight tree when decisively outscoring Gans, his cleverness being just too much for the latter. Having got on top from the beginning, Ahearn started to send in clusters of punches from both hands without reply, something he did again and again. With Gans unable to fathom Ahearn out he never came close to putting a dent in the title claimant's plans.

When Ahearn met Gus Christie (nd-w pts 6 at the National AC, Philadelphia, Pennsylvania, USA on 17 April) both men were thought to be inside 160lbs.

6 April 1915. (160lbs) Jack Dillon nd-w pts 10 Billy Murray.
Venue: The Arena, Hudson, Wisconsin, USA.
Fight Summary: Made at 160lbs, Murray was well inside the weight while Dillon was announced as being 159lbs. More fighting was done in the opening round than in all those following it as the two men seemed quite content to clinch, with Murray being awarded just one round and Dillon four by the press. It was only in the last three rounds that Dillon picked it up, but the damage had already been done with the crowd shouting for more action and both fighters stalling.

28 April 1915. (158lbs) Jimmy Clabby nd-l pts 10 George Chip.
Venue: The Armoury, Marinette, Wisconsin, USA. **Referee:** George Duffy.
Fight Summary: The *Marinette Eagle Star* reported that Clabby was defending his 158lbs title claim in this one. Clabby started well with his clever boxing at the forefront, but after a few even rounds the last four went to Chip who proved to be a master at close quarters. Although Clabby's excellent footwork and general movement made Chip look like a prelim boy at times he could not sustain his energy levels for the full ten rounds, having to protect his chin in the last few sessions as the latter went all out for a knockout.

On the 'black title' front, Eddie Palmer beat Willie Langford (w co 14 in New Orleans, Louisiana on 1 May) in a billed championship bout before going on to defend against Christy Williams (w pts 20 in Memphis, Tennessee on 1 July), Young Kid McCoy (w co 4 in New Orleans on 31 December and w co 6 in Dallas, Texas on 21 January 1916) and Gorilla Jones (w co 8 in McElroy, Louisiana on 1 April 1916). Palmer eventually lost his title claim when twice outpointed over 15 rounds by the Jamaica Kid at The Auditorium, New Orleans on 12 May and 19 May 1916, respectively. Although the Kid continued to call himself the 'black champion' for some time he was soon up among the light heavies.

4 May 1915. (158lbs) Al McCoy nd-l pts 10 Jimmy Clabby.

Venue: Broadway SC, Brooklyn, NYC, New York, USA.

Fight Summary: Defending their 158lbs title claims, both men were inside the championship limit. Although somewhat confused by McCoy's awkward style, Clabby (154¾) was far too skilful for the New Yorker when winning virtually every round, his educated left hand landing almost at will. With McCoy (157¾) looking mainly to survive, while the contest showed up Clabby's lack of power it also highlighted the fact that as soon as the former took on a reasonable opponent in a decision contest he would almost certainly lose his title claim.

12 May 1915. (158lbs) Jimmy Clabby nd-nc 8 (10) George Chip.

Venue: St Nicholas Arena, Manhattan, NYC, New York, USA. **Referee:** Billy Roche.

Fight Summary: For a contest that would be best forgotten, Chip made 158lbs at 2pm while Clabby came in around 154lbs. That was before both men were thrown out in the eighth for not trying and suspended from fighting in New York for 30 days. Although Clabby had rolled up a clear points lead in the opening few rounds he then began to allow Chip to hold at every opportunity, and for whatever reason refused to take advantage of any openings that were presented to him. After being told to make a fight of it in the seventh, when both fighters started throwing 'air' punches in the eighth the referee had seen enough.

Before taking off for Australia again, Clabby received a press draw in a ten-round no-decision contest against Frank Farmer at the Armoury B, Oshkosh, Wisconsin on 12 July. It was a contest that was earlier thought to have been made at 158lbs, but was in fact 160lbs.

22 May 1915. (160lbs) Les Darcy w disq 2 (20) Jeff Smith.

Venue: Baker's Stadium, Sydney, Australia. **Referee:** Harold Baker.

Fight Summary: By the end of the opening round it had become clear that Smith (159) was going to drop the Australian version of the world 160lbs title to Darcy (159), who appeared to have too much power for him to handle. Having started fast, landing four punches to one and hitting the American pretty much as he liked, Darcy was looking to put Smith away in the second. However, before he could do too much further damage Smith head-butted him and followed it up with punch to the groin. Smith, who had obviously decided that he wanted out, got his wish when immediately disqualified.

31 May 1915. (158lbs) Al McCoy nd-drew 10 Silent Martin.

Venue: Ebbets Field, Brooklyn, NYC, New York, USA.

Fight Summary: Initially due to meet Johnny Howard, when he pulled out McCoy (157½) put his championship claim at risk against Martin (155), a man known for his aggressive, uncompromising way of fighting. According to the *New York Times* he certainly had McCoy hot and bothered at times despite only being given a draw by the pressmen in attendance. Like McCoy, Martin was capable of soaking up punishment, as well as showing a clever defence. Several times he had McCoy wincing from solid blows and scrambling for cover, but to take over the latter's title claim he would have needed to find the punch to put his man away with, something that well over a 100 fighters had failed to do up to that point.

31 May 1915. (158lbs) Mike Gibbons nd-l pts 10 Soldier Bartfield.

Venue: Ebbets Field, Brooklyn, NYC, New York, USA.

Fight Summary: Gibbons (155) defended his 158lbs title claim against Bartfield (148) in this one, and although exhibiting his usual cleverness he was never able to fathom the latter's defensive tactics before the contest developed into a game of chess. With Gibbons not appearing to exert himself, something Bartfield took advantage of, it was only in the last few sessions when the man from St Paul cut loose when staggering the soldier with heavy blows.

There was much talk about an elimination series being held in New York following this contest, but although Bartfield claimed the title, billing himself as the man who beat Gibbons, he was more of a welterweight than a 158lbs man. Continuing to fight in no-decision contests, when Bartfield (148) was stopped inside eight rounds by the 152lbs Italian Joe Gans at the Clermont Rink, Brooklyn, NYC on 25 December he lost any support he may have had.

12 June 1915. (160lbs) Les Darcy w rtd 10 (20) Mick King.
Venue: Baker's Stadium, Sydney, Australia. **Referee:** Harold Baker.
Fight Summary: Making his first defence of the Australian version of the world 160lbs title Darcy (159) was far too strong for King (159), being all over his rival like a rash right from the opening bell. Despite showing much cleverness, King was subjected to a fierce hammering, both to the head and body from either hand. It could not go on like this, and with King on the verge of being knocked out in the tenth round his corner threw the towel in. The finish, timed at 20 seconds, came just as the police were ready to pounce.

5 July 1915. (158/160lbs) Jack Dillon drew 10 George Chip.
Venue: Association Park, Kansas City, Missouri, USA. **Referee:** Walter Bates.
Fight Summary: Made at 158lbs, the *Kansas City Star* reported that with the men inside the limit Dillon risked his title claim at the weight. Having to make the weight by 3pm weakened both, the first six rounds seeing little action. This was the tenth meeting between the pair, and first one man looked to get his punches off and then the other, with little between them. After having a good ninth round Chip was looking to build on that in the tenth, but Dillon's rushing tactics forced him on to the back foot where he had to use all of his experience to extract himself from several difficult situations.

A few days later, on 12 July, at Brown's Gym, Queens, NYC, New York, an over-the-weight Dillon scored a ten-round press win over Johnny Howard, who weighed in at 160lbs.

Dillon, who was now finding it increasingly hard to make 158/160lbs anymore, campaigned as a light heavy from hereon in.

31 July 1915. (160lbs) Les Darcy w rsc 15 (20) Eddie McGoorty.
Venue: Baker's Stadium, Sydney, Australia. **Referee:** Harold Baker.
Fight Summary: In what was his second defence of the Australian version of the 160lbs title, Darcy (159¼) showed remarkable skill for one so young in blocking the American's best efforts early on before being caught by a tremendous left hook to the jaw in the sixth. While McGoorty (159½) took the next few sessions on sheer aggression he could not put Darcy down, and by the 12th the latter was well in control of his tiring opponent. Driving forward Darcy would not be denied, sending McGoorty to the floor three times by vicious right hands to the head in the 15th prior to the ringside police inspector advising the referee to call it off as the challenger was struggling to get to his feet.

4 September 1915. (160lbs) Les Darcy w pts 20 Billy Murray.
Venue: Baker's Stadium, Sydney, Australia. **Referee:** Harold Baker.
Fight Summary: Living up to his reputation as a tough opponent, Murray (160) was just not good enough to stop Darcy (159) from retaining the Australian version of the 160lbs title. According to the *Sydney Telegraph*, Darcy probably won 16 of the 20 rounds, but having battered Murray for long periods he was unable to finish him off. To his credit, Murray showed an amazing capacity to soak up punishment, even coming back strongly in the last few sessions to pose the odd problem.

9 September 1915. (158lbs) Al McCoy nd-l pts 10 Young Ahearn.
Venue: Ebbets Field, Brooklyn, NYC, New York, USA.

Fight Summary: With Ahearn (154) having a valid claim to the middleweight title, his match with McCoy (157½), regardless of it being of the no-decision variety, was given championship billing. The contest effectively proved just how limited McCoy was as Ahearn boxed rings around him in virtually every round. There were no knockdowns, McCoy being far too rugged to be floored at any stage.

In a meeting between McCoy and Soldier Bartfield (nd-drew 10 at the Clermont Rink, Brooklyn on 23 October), it is not known what the champion weighed. However, Bartfield could make 158lbs with ease.

Another contest at the same venue, this time against the Zulu Kid (nd-drew 10 on 13 November 1915) saw McCoy scaling 161lbs to his opponent's 157lbs.

11 September 1915. (154lbs) Mike Gibbons nd-drew 10 Packey McFarland.
Venue: Brighton Beach Motordome, Brooklyn, NYC, New York, USA. **Referee:** Billy Joh.
Fight Summary: Reported in the *New York Times* as a 154lbs title fight, McFarland, who had been out of the ring for almost two years, scaled 152lbs to Gibbons' 153. Witnessed by over 30,000 fans, after Gibbons got off to a flier it was only in the middle rounds that McFarland came into the fight as the 'St Paul Phantom' tired. Gibbons' left eye had been cut in the seventh, but despite having the better of things from thereon in McFarland had to settle for a press draw.

9 October 1915. (160lbs) Les Darcy w rtd 6 (20) Fred Dyer.
Venue: Baker's Stadium, Sydney, Australia. **Referee:** Harold Baker.
Fight Summary: Defending the Australian version of the 160lbs title, Darcy (159¼) had a big pull in the weights over Dyer (150) for this one, which soon became painfully obvious when the latter was unable to do much other than run for cover or clinch. With Dyer always playing second fiddle, in the sixth round when on the verge of being knocked out his seconds threw the towel in. At that stage of the fight the police were already asking the referee to call a halt to proceedings.

23 October 1915. (160lbs) Les Darcy w pts 20 Jimmy Clabby.
Venue: Baker's Stadium, Sydney, Australia. **Referee:** Arthur Scott.
Fight Summary: Still eight days short of his 20th birthday, Darcy (159¼) came through relatively unscathed while making another successful defence of the Australian version of the 160lbs title. This time the opponent was Clabby, one of the world's leading middles, and while he was defensively sound he was unable to trouble Darcy with his punches. Clabby's skill was best summed up in the eighth round when, after being almost knocked out by a thunderous left hook and sent staggering around, he was just too clever for Darcy to catch. Although Clabby made a big effort from the 15th onwards it was to no avail as almost all of his best punches merely bounced off Darcy, who insisted on getting even most of the time.

At the West Melbourne Stadium, Melbourne on 1 November, Darcy (162) knocked out Billy Murray (160) inside six rounds. Whether Murray would have had a claim on the 160lbs title had he won is not known, although it is almost certain that the fight was contracted above that weight.

25 November 1915. (158lbs) Al McCoy nd-l pts 15 Silent Martin.
Venue: The Auditorium, Waterbury, Connecticut, USA.
Fight Summary: Articled at 158lbs ringside, the report from the *Norwich Bulletin* stated that Martin easily took nine of the 15 rounds, with six being even. In the tenth McCoy almost lost his title claim when he was battered by vicious uppercuts and forced to hold on to the ropes to save himself from falling.

On 1 January 1916, at the Broadway SC, Brooklyn, McCoy, weighing 162lbs, lost a ten-round press decision to Ahearn (156lbs), who would have claimed the title had he secured an inside-the-distance win.

Two further contests at the same venue that had an element of risk for an over-the-weight McCoy came against George Chip (nd-l pts 10 on 20 January 1916) and Leo Bens (nd-drew 10 on 21 March 1916). For Chip (157¾), McCoy made 159¼lbs and for Bens (156) he scaled 163½.

Meeting Al Thiel (nd-drew 10 at the Military AC, Brooklyn on 17 April 1916), although many thought that McCoy's title claim would be on the line it was almost certainly contested above 158lbs.

Following an overweight contest against Ahearn, the 'real' McCoy next took on Canada's Young Al Ross (drew 20 at the Athletic Club Arena, New Haven, Connecticut on 22 May 1916). According to the *New Haven Evening Register* Ross made 158lbs at the ringside weigh-in, but because a decision was in place to decide the contest the author feels that it was almost certainly made at 160lbs in order to protect McCoy's title claim. Despite that, had Ross won inside the distance he would have had a claim.

Next time out McCoy suffered a 15-round no-decision points defeat at the hands of Hugh Ross at The Casino Hall, Bridgeport, Connecticut on 26 June 1916. On the day of the fight the *Bridgeport Evening Post* claimed that Ross, who was in good shape and inside 158lbs, could well win the championship. It is quite clear that this one was made at 160lbs, and that the paper was trying to build up the fight by claiming a title was involved. As in several of McCoy's contests, had his opponent weighed in at 158lbs or less and won inside the distance he would undoubtedly have had a title claim. A report from the *Brooklyn Eagle*, which was probably wired in by the champion's manager, states that McCoy knocked down Ross twice on his way to an easy win.

Although the *Brooklyn Daily Eagle* reported that when McCoy fought Dave Kurtz (nd-w pts 10 at the Harlem SC, Rockaway Beach, Queens, New York, USA on 3 July 1916) his title would be on the line in a contest articled for 158lbs ringside, I have yet to find out whether it was or not.

When McCoy met Jackie Clark (nd-l pts 10 at the Town Hall, Scranton, Pennsylvania on 28 September 1916), the *Scranton Times* reported it as a title battle but failed to mention any weights. While I am pretty certain that Clark made 158lbs, one cannot be sure that McCoy did.

Then, on 28 November 1916, at the High School Auditorium, Allentown, Pennsylvania, McCoy, much heavier than his opponent and refusing to weigh in, risked his title claim when allowing Jack McCarron to scale 157lbs. Ultimately, there was no danger as McCoy obtained a ten-round press draw.

25 November 1915. (160lbs) Young Ahearn nd-w pts 10 Emmett Kid Wagner.
Venue: Clermont Rink, Brooklyn, NYC, New York, USA.
Fight Summary: Ahearn (156½) risked his title claim when allowing Wagner to weigh in at 160lbs, but he never appeared to be in any danger, jabbing, uppercutting and countering his rival throughout. While Wagner was in the fight during the early sessions, showing a good defence and a propensity to swing in the left to head and body, as the rounds went by Ahearn found the target more often than not, being an easy winner of the press verdict.

27 December 1915. (160lbs) Les Darcy w rtd 8 (20) Eddie McGoorty.
Venue: Baker's Stadium, Sydney, Australia. **Referee:** Arthur Scott.
Fight Summary: Defending the Australian version of the world 160lbs title, with Darcy (159¼) giving the challenger no respite from the opening bell it soon became clear that barring accidents he was on his way to another win over his rival. Forced to take risks, in the fifth round McGoorty (159¾) was dropped by a terrific uppercut to the face before getting up at 'nine' and holding on for all his worth until the bell came his rescue. Although he came back strongly in the next two sessions McGoorty was unable to deter Darcy, who seemed to be impervious to any amount of heavy punches coming his way, and in the eighth a right uppercut to the body had the American over again. Despite McGoorty beating the count, after staggering around the ring to no purpose his corner wisely threw the towel in.

18 January 1916. (158lbs) Mike Gibbons nd-w co 1 (10) Young Ahearn.
Venue: The Auditorium, St Paul, Minnesota, USA. **Referee:** Jack McGuigan.
Fight Summary: Billed to decide the championships of England and America over ten rounds, following his victory Gibbons (155½) had more support in the States than Al McCoy, of that there was no doubt. The contest was almost over before it started. Following a whirlwind exchange of blows from range both men swung and missed before clinching. That was followed by more clinching. Then, after about 90 seconds of the opening round had

elapsed Gibbons worked Ahearn (154¾) over to a corner before sending him down to be counted out on connecting with a smashing right to the jaw.

17 March 1916. (158lbs) Mike Gibbons nd-w pts 10 Jeff Smith.
Venue: The Auditorium, St Paul, Minnesota, USA.
Fight Summary: Putting his 158lbs title claim on the line, Gibbons (156½) quickly took control, making Smith (156¾) look like a novice when jabbing and hooking him at will at times. While Smith was always dangerous with right swings, Gibbons never gave him the opportunity to get set, his speed being simply electric as he zipped in lefts and rights through the former Australian world champion's defences.

18 March 1916. (158lbs) Mike Gibbons nd-drew 10 Ted Kid Lewis.
Venue: Madison Square Garden, Manhattan, NYC, New York, USA. **Referee:** Bill Brown.
Fight Summary: Although not seriously seen as a risk to Gibbons' (152½) 158lbs title claim, Ted Kid Lewis (143) gave the former plenty to think about as he jumped in and out with both hands. Giving away almost ten pounds, Lewis did not hang around long enough to be tagged, and while carrying the heavier artillery Gibbons found it difficult to manage more than one shot at a time. Lewis says in his memoirs that everyone in that arena knew who really won.

On 10 February 1917, Gibbons was felt by the press to have beaten Harry Greb (nd-w pts 6 at the National AC, Philadelphia, Pennsylvania) in a match made at 158lbs.

13 May 1916. (160lbs) Les Darcy w rsc 4 (20) Alex Costica.
Venue: Baker's Stadium, Sydney, Australia. **Referee:** Arthur Scott.
Fight Summary: Making his seventh successful defence of the Australian version of the 160lbs title, Darcy (158) was far too good for Costica (154¼), who really should not have been allowed to share the same ring with him. Hanging on like a limpet allowed Costica to get through the first round, but after being dropped in the second and again in the third, when saved by the bell, he came out for the fourth staring defeat in the face. It was not long in coming, and having been floored twice more Costica was pulled out by the referee on the instructions of the police.

9 September 1916. (160lbs) Les Darcy w pts 20 Jimmy Clabby.
Venue: Baker's Stadium, Sydney, Australia. **Referee:** Arthur Scott.
Fight Summary: In what would be Darcy's penultimate defence of the Australian version of the world 160lbs title, Clabby (153¼) provided poor opposition having already decided to survive come what may. The fight was one long display of clinching, in which Clabby negated much of the champion's work, but the biggest disappointment to the crowd was that Darcy (159¼), although doing all the leading, did not have a 'Plan B'. At the end of the contest, Clabby was so weak that he flopped to the floor while Darcy was just glad to put it behind him.

30 September 1916. (160lbs) Les Darcy w co 9 (20) George Chip.
Venue: Baker's Stadium, Sydney, Australia. **Referee:** Arthur Scott.
Fight Summary: Fighting in what would prove to be the last contest of his career, Darcy (159½) was far too good for Chip (159½). Chip, who found that he was unable to deal with the Australian's straight left and was an open target to follow up rights, was showing signs of wilting as early as the second round. Shaken up badly through to the sixth, Chip was finally dropped by a right to the jaw, and although he somehow managed to make it through to the ninth he was knocked out by a right-hand counter midway through the session.

Having made yet another successful defence of the Australian version of the 160lbs title, Darcy was put on standby for the Great War being fought in Europe. However, sometime later, in November, he was reported missing and thought to be on his way to America. After turning up in the USA on an oil boat, via Chile, Tex Rickard, the promoter, tried to match him with Georges Carpentier, but was turned down by the latter who was heavily committed to the war at that time.

Eventually, in 1917, Darcy was matched against Jack Dillon in New York for early March, but when it became clear that he had left Australia in disguise to avoid the call-up the State Governor barred the fight from taking place. Darcy then signed to meet Mike Gibbons at 160lbs in Wisconsin for 10 April, but that too was blocked. Then, after agreeing to meet Chip in Ohio on 25 April, pressure from patriotic groups in the State saw that match also cancelled. Following that, he was matched to defend his title against Jeff Smith over 20 rounds in Louisiana on 23 April. Once again Darcy met with disappointment when the promoter, bowing to pressure from the State Governor, called the fight off on 14 April, substituting him with Young Ahearn. Having applied for American citizenship and enlisted with the Aviation Reserve Corps in Memphis, Tennessee on 24 April, it seemed that Darcy's luck was about to change when he was matched to fight Len Rowlands in that State on 7 May. Tragically, it was not to be. Taken ill on 4 May Darcy was forced to postpone the fight, spending the next three weeks fighting for his life before passing away on 24 May. Although many people were offering up all kinds of suggestions as to the reasons for his untimely death at the age of 21, it was reported in the press that decayed teeth and badly infected tonsils had ultimately led to him contracting septicaemia from which there was no way back.

After the Australian version of the 160lbs championship fell vacant on Darcy's death, Jeff Smith, who had knocked out Ahearn in the fifth round at the Louisiana Auditorium, New Orleans, Louisiana on 23 April, immediately reclaimed the title. But with Ahearn having been knocked out inside a round by Harry Greb just three weeks earlier, on 2 April, at the Power Auditorium, Pittsburgh, Pennsylvania, his claim was not taken seriously, especially as he continued to fight at a higher weight.

30 April 1917. (158lbs) Al McCoy nd-l pts 10 Harry Greb.
Venue: Exposition Hall, Pittsburgh, Pennsylvania, USA. **Referee:** Johnny McAvoy.
Fight Summary: Both men weighed below the 158lbs middleweight limit according to the *Pittsburgh Post*. Getting away fast, with the exception of the opening round, Greb did all the forcing in what was the first ten-rounder to be held in Pittsburgh under the new law. Fighting in determined fashion and pounding in blows from both hands Greb hit McCoy enough times to have sunk a battleship, but the latter remained on his feet against all the odds. Other than a swinging left, McCoy offered nothing of any value, only surviving by either grabbing Greb or backing off at every opportunity.

On 4 July, McCoy met Jackie Clark (nd-l pts 10 at the Goodwill Firemen's' Armoury, Lonaconing, Maryland). While the *Baltimore American* reported the contest as one that would decide the American middleweight championship there was nothing mentioned about weights. This one should be treated with suspicion as a title fight until better details emerge.

4 July 1917. (158lbs) Mike Gibbons nd-w pts 12 George Chip.
Venue: Wright Field, Youngstown, Ohio, USA. **Referee:** Mike McHale.
Fight Summary: According to the *Chicago Tribune* Gibbons successfully defended his 158lbs title claim in this one, his wonderful skill enabling him to hit Chip repeatedly while ducking and side-stepping the latter's lunges with ease. Most rounds were the same, Chip chasing shadows, but in the seventh the latter got closer than he had previously managed, only for Gibbons to cover up until the cyclone expended itself. Despite jabbing Chip silly at times, with Gibbons lacking the power to finish early he had to go the whole 12 rounds.

12 October 1917. (158lbs) Mike Gibbons nd-w rsc 3 (10) Frank Mantell.
Venue: The Auditorium, St Paul, Minnesota, USA. **Referee:** Hugh McMahon.
Fight Summary: Proving far too good for Mantell, his speed and hitting power bewildering, Gibbons won all the way before the referee stepped in and brought matters to a conclusion in the third round. Defending his 158lbs title claim, Gibbons never gave Mantell a look in as he danced in with stiff rights or scoring lefts, and although no knockdowns were reported it was a popular decision.

For over a year Gibbons was inactive, having decided to concentrate on his post of boxing instructor at Camp Dodge, Iowa.

14 November 1917. (158lbs) Mike O'Dowd nd-w rtd 6 (10) Al McCoy.
Venue: Clermont Rink, Brooklyn, NYC, New York, USA. **Referee:** Johnny McAvoy.
Fight Summary: As in the contests of George Chip v Frank Klaus and McCoy v Chip, even though this was not a billed championship fight the title was deemed to have changed hands with no additional weight stipulation in force and McCoy failing to last the distance. Adding to the interest, this was the last major fight that took place in New York under Frawley Law. While McCoy came in above 158lbs, weighing either 162 or 167lbs dependant on which paper report one took, O'Dowd (157) was recognised by many as being the champion on the result. Forcing the fight all the way, O'Dowd hurt McCoy with body blows and short right and left smashes to the head throughout the opening three rounds before dropping the title claimant four times in the fourth. O'Dowd also visited the canvas twice in the same session, but at all times the men got up quickly. Having given McCoy a going over in the fifth, O'Dowd went for his man in the sixth, decking him four times before smashing him down again with a hard left to the body followed by a right to the jaw. At 1.25 of the round, with referee's count at 'seven', McCoy's corner threw the towel in despite their man being in the act of rising. Many people saw this fight as being a fix as McCoy had proven durability while O'Dowd had never previously been seen as a big puncher, especially with some of the knockdowns appearing to be stage-managed.

This was followed by three six-round no-decision fights at the National AC, Philadelphia, Pennsylvania, against Jack McCarron (nd-w pts 6 on 24 November), Billy Kramer (nd-w pts 6 on 15 December) and Joe Welsh (nd-w pts 6 on 19 December), where O'Dowd was felt to have risked his newly-won title claim.

25 February 1918. (158lbs) Mike O'Dowd nd-drew 10 Harry Greb.
Venue: The Auditorium, St Paul, Minnesota, USA.
Fight Summary: A billed 158lbs championship fight of the no-decision variety saw Greb (156¾) doing most of the leading, but unable to break down the champion's guard he was forced to swing wildly at times. O'Dowd (157) continued to fight a strong defensive battle, while playing on Greb's ribs early on before opening up in the ninth round when looking to land a knockout blow.

With America joining the First World War O'Dowd enlisted as a private at Camp Dodge, spending nine months in the 55th Engineers serving in France prior to arriving home in May 1919.

Having beaten Al McCoy (nd-w co 3 at the Auditorium, St Paul on 17 July 1919) in a comeback fight at catchweights, O'Dowd then knocked out Young Fisher in the fifth of a no-decision ten rounder at The Arena, Syracuse, New York on 21 July 1919. While O'Dowd refused to weigh in, giving his weight as 157½lbs, Fisher made 156lbs, which automatically meant that the former's 158lbs title was at stake if not contracted otherwise.

11 August 1919. (158lbs) Mike O'Dowd nd-w pts 10 Jackie Clark.
Venue: The Arena, Syracuse, New York, USA. **Referee:** Jack Lewis.
Fight Summary: At the 6pm weigh-in both men were inside the required 158lbs, thus placing O'Dowd's title claim on the line. Boxing superbly well, especially when moving in and out with the jab in the third and fourth rounds, Clark gave O'Dowd much to think about for the first half of the contest. However, once the latter got close up it was a different story. That was where O'Dowd excelled, and having taken a shellacking in the eighth Clark thought it more prudent from thereon in to use his skill to evade punches rather than risk exposing his chin when trying to win inside the distance.

O'Dowd (155) immediately followed this up when taking an eight-round no-decision match at the 1st Regiment Armoury, Newark, New Jersey on 22 August against the welterweight champion, Jack Britton (146). At the final bell, O'Dowd was on the wrong end of the press verdict.

1 September 1919. (158lbs) Mike O'Dowd nd-w pts 10 Ted Kid Lewis.
Venue: The Arena, Syracuse, New York, USA. **Referee:** Jack Lewis.
Fight Summary: Showing great fortitude, the willing Lewis (145) found that giving 11 pounds away to O'Dowd (154) was just too much even though he did reasonably well. According to press reports it was probably fair to say

that Lewis won one round, the fourth, and that O'Dowd controlled the fight with his heavier, straighter hitting, while at close quarters his power proved conclusive despite a total lack of knockdowns.

19 September 1919. (158lbs) Mike O'Dowd nd-w pts 10 Soldier Bartfield.

Venue: The Auditorium, St Paul, Minnesota, USA.

Fight Summary: Made at 158lbs, the *St Paul Pioneer* reported that at no time during the contest were O'Dowd's titular laurels ever at risk from a man outweighed by ten pounds. During the course of the fight it was O'Dowd who landed the harder, cleaner and more frequent punches, and when at close quarters it was usually Bartfield who broke ground first. However, it was certainly not one-sided, Bartfield managing to rush O'Dowd to the ropes several times to slam away, scoring with blows from both hands before going back to his boxing. Although Bartfield clearly won the second and eighth sessions, using his famous back-hand punch, which was legal at the time, O'Dowd won most of the others.

Ten days later, on 29 September, at the Armoury AA, Jersey City, New Jersey, an over-the-weight O'Dowd (164) collected an eight-round press decision over Augie Ratner (154lbs), having risked his title claim. He presumably did the same when facing the 146lbs Steve Latzo (nd-w pts 6 at the National AC, Philadelphia, Pennsylvania on 18 October).

Before meeting Mike Gibbons for the world title, O'Dowd scored a two-round knockout win over Billy Kramer at the Lyceum Theatre, Paterson, New Jersey on 6 November in a no-decision fight where it is unclear whether the latter made 158lbs or not. O'Dowd (158½) next stopped Jimmy O'Hagan (159½) inside two rounds at the Roller Palace Rink, Detroit, Michigan on 10 November, after knocking his rival down three times. Initially thought to have involved the 158lbs title, it is now believed to have been articled at 160lbs.

21 November 1919. (158lbs) Mike O'Dowd nd-w pts 10 Mike Gibbons.

Venue: The Auditorium, St Paul, Minnesota, USA. **Referee:** Curley Ulrich.

Fight Summary: According to the *New York Times* the two men, both from St Paul, entered the ring inside 158lbs in what looked like being a classic. It was the master boxer, Gibbons, versus his former pupil, O'Dowd. And to win O'Dowd's title the older man by eight years would have to score an inside-the-distance victory. After boxing well during the opening couple of rounds, Gibbons was cut over left eye in the third, an injury that changed the course of the fight, and after breaking his right hand in the seventh there was no chance of victory. While neither man failed to get close to scoring a knockdown, it was Gibbons' skill that saw him capable of boxing on the inside and at range to keep himself in the fight against O'Dowd's aggression.

14 January 1920. (158lbs) Mike O'Dowd nd-w pts 10 Frank Carbone.

Venue: Roller Palace Rink, Detroit, Michigan, USA.

Fight Summary: The *Detroit Free Press* reported this to be a 158lbs title fight, and with O'Dowd failing to stop Carbone in their previous five fights it was unlikely that this one would end early. Having rushed the champion in the opening session, forcing him to give ground repeatedly when landing several solid blows to head and body, Carbone must have thought that this was his time. However, O'Dowd took up the offensive in the second right through to the final bell, but was unable to dislodge Carbone despite hitting him flush on the jaw at least a dozen times during the bout. Although O'Dowd was an easy winner in the eyes of the press, he found the awkward style of Carbone difficult to contend with at times, especially when having to deal with an extended left lead and back-handed blows to the head.

20 January 1920. (160lbs) Mike O'Dowd w rsc 3 (12) Stockyards Tommy Murphy.

Venue: Mechanics Building, Boston, Massachusetts, USA. **Referee:** Hector McInnes.

Fight Summary: Advertised in the *Boston Post* and *Boston Daily Advertiser* as being a battle for the world middleweight championship at 160lbs (ringside), it is clear that the State of Massachusetts recognised that poundage as being the upper limit of the weight class at that point in time. O'Dowd started as he meant to carry on, slamming in heavy rights to head and body, while Murphy hardly threatened him. The second round was much the same, with Murphy taking heavy punishment and looking likely to go at any time. After being accidentally butted, O'Dowd went for Murphy with a vengeance, and in the third the latter was smashed to the floor three times before the referee called it off at 1.05 of the session, just as the towel fluttered into the ring.

O'Dowd next took on Young Fisher (nd-w co 3 at The Arena, Syracuse, New York on 26 January) and Jack McCarron (nd-w rsc 2 at the Olympia AC, Philadelphia, Pennsylvania on 1 March) in catchweight contests where the opposition was thought to weigh in less than the championship weight.

When O'Dowd met Murphy for the second time a few weeks later at the Auditorium, Atlanta, Georgia, on 5 March, the *Cedar Rapids Evening Gazette* reported that Murphy lost another opportunity to become the middleweight champion when being stopped in nine rounds. Again weights were never mentioned.

Another opponent for O'Dowd, thought to be inside 158lbs, was Tommy Madden who was knocked out inside three rounds at the Stockyards Stadium, Denver, Colorado on 12 March. This contest was a billed 12-round championship battle according to the *San Antonio Evening News*, despite no weights being reported.

17 March 1920. (158lbs) Mike O'Dowd nd-w pts 10 Augie Ratner.
Venue: The Auditorium, St Paul, Minnesota, USA.
Fight Summary: Advertised as a title fight, the *St Paul Pioneer* stated that with O'Dowd (157½) inside the stipulated 158lbs, Ratner (155½) threw many punches in the hope one might just give him the championship. Starting strongly, O'Dowd shaded the opening rounds when taking the fight to Ratner, and although the latter fought back in the seventh through to the ninth, when banging in heavy rights, the champion stayed ahead by dint of clever boxing.

30 March 1920. (160lbs) Mike O'Dowd w co 5 (12) Joe Egan.
Venue: Mechanics Building, Boston, Massachusetts, USA. **Referee:** Hector McInnes.
Fight Summary: According to the *Boston Post* and *Boston Globe* this was a billed championship fight at 160lbs. Despite Egan getting himself into tip-top shape for the champion it was soon clear that he had no chance of landing the title, being belted around the ring with little response. When he did fight back he occasionally hurt O'Dowd, a straight right opening up a cut on the latter's left eye. By the fourth round, however, Egan was blowing badly, having taken some heavy blows to the midsection, and in the fifth a right to the jaw bowled him over for the full count. Although Egan had given of his best he was not in the champion's class.

On 3 April, O'Dowd took the six-round newspaper decision over Frankie Maguire at the National AC, Philadelphia, Pennsylvania, USA, in a fight made at 160lbs.

15 April 1920. (158lbs) Mike O'Dowd w rsc 6 (12) Walter Laurette.
Venue: State Street Casino, Bridgeport, Connecticut, USA. **Referee:** Dave Fitzgerald.
Fight Summary: This one was reported by the *Bridgeport Evening Post* to be a title fight. O'Dowd (155) was far too good for Laurette (153), dropping him twice in the opening round before easing off and letting the Canadian survive the next three sessions. Coming into the fifth with the intention of taking Laurette out, O'Dowd had great difficulty landing punches on a man covering up at all costs. In the sixth it was more of the same as O'Dowd hit Laurette everywhere but on the jaw, and with the latter merely a punch-bag the referee called it off just as the bell terminated the round.

6 May 1920. (160lbs) Johnny Wilson w pts 12 Mike O'Dowd.
Venue: Mechanics Building, Boston, Massachusetts, USA. **Referee:** Hector McInnes.
Fight Summary: Announced from the ring as a 160lbs title fight, although the champion was the aggressor throughout Wilson (158) repeatedly tagged him with southpaw rights. After knocking O'Dowd (159½) down in the second round for 'four' with a straight right, Wilson surprised most of those in attendance by his ability to continually break through his opponent's guard. Generally recognised as the champion on his victory, Wilson, the recipient of the referee's decision, was reckoned to have won eight rounds to O'Dowd's two, with two even.

1 July 1920. (158lbs) Johnny Wilson nd-w pts 12 Soldier Bartfield.
Venue: Sportsman's Club, 1st Regiment Armoury, Newark, New Jersey, USA. **Referee:** Jim Brennan.
Fight Summary: Making his first title defence at 158lbs, the *Boston Post* reported that Wilson (157¼), who had a huge pull in the weights against Bartfield (149½), certainly made it work to his advantage when bulling the latter about. Using a southpaw left to the body as his best form of attack Wilson was too strong for Bartfield, the latter taking three rounds at most, and although the challenger came forward in the final session he was unable to find a winning punch. Both men took punishment to the body, but when Bartfield, who normally excelled on the inside, tried to tie his man up he was generally shaken off and belted heavily.

20 July 1920. (158lbs) Johnny Wilson nd-l pts 10 Young Fisher.
Venue: The Arena, Syracuse, New York, USA. **Referee:** Walter C. Kelley.
Fight Summary: The *Syracuse Post-Standard* gave this one as a billed 158lbs title fight. Although the southpaw champion won the opening session all other rounds, except the sixth, were either shared or went the way of Fisher, who put on the best show of his career. Fisher's best round was the third in which he shook Wilson up with several right-hand smashes, and throughout the contest he was always looking to drop a man who was just intent to remain standing until the final bell. It was also noticeable that having brought his own referee with him enabled Wilson, who finished with damage over both eyes and a badly lacerated mouth, to violate the rules at every opportunity.

2 August 1920. (158lbs) Johnny Wilson nd-w co 5 (10) Steve Choynski.
Venue: Bison Stadium, Buffalo, New York, USA. **Referee:** Dick Nugent.
Fight Summary: Billed as a title fight, the *Buffalo Morning Express* reported that the southpaw champion handed out a bad beating to Choynski after disappointing in his previous contest. The fight had only just started when a ring post collapsed and both men, who were against the ropes, fell off the platform, an incident that saw time out being called while repairs were put in place. Unperturbed, Wilson had Choynski down twice for counts of 'nine' in the second, both knockdowns coming after he had rammed in a left to the head followed by a right to the body. Having survived, Choynski spent the next couple of rounds covering up, but in the fifth Wilson came on to knock his man out with a terrific left uppercut to the body, a blow that had been practised several times earlier. Although Choynski's corner claimed a foul it was not accepted as no indication of a low blow could be found.

Prior to meeting Battling Thomas (nd-w pts 10 at The Arena, Syracuse, New York on 6 July), with Panama Joe Gans already claiming to be the 'black champion' for his contest against George Robinson (w pts 12 at Madison Square Garden, Manhattan, NYC, New York on 8 October) Tex Rickard put up a diamond studded belt to be held by the winner. Furthermore, Rickard stated that whoever won could keep the belt as long as he made two more successful defences at the same venue in one of his promotions. Gans obliged by beating both George Christian (w co 3 on 26 November) and Sailor Darden (w pts 10 on 29 December). Other contests for Gans against black opposition came against Lew Williams (w co 4 at the Commonwealth SC, Manhattan, NYC on 19 October), Morris Tasco (nd-w co 3 in Detroit, Michigan on 22 October) and Young Jackson (w co 3 Garden Street Arena, Auburn, New York on 13 December).

At the Mount Royal Arena, Montreal, Canada on 9 December, an over-the-weight Wilson met Robinson (158), and although taking the ten-round press verdict he was within an ace of losing his title according to certain newspaper reports when suffering two knockdowns and being sent crashing at the start of the fight. Another catchweight contest for Wilson (162) where the opposition was inside 158lbs came against Joe Chip (nd-w pts 10 at the Motor Square Garden, Pittsburgh, Pennsylvania on 17 January 1921), who scaled 158lbs.

Articled to meet Navy Rostan at 158lbs at the old Auditorium, Kenosha, Wisconsin on 10 February 1921, Wilson (160¼) was forced to pay forfeit to the so-called challenger before knocking him out in the second round of a no-decision contest. Rostan, who weighed in at 154½lbs, would no doubt have claimed the title had he won.

From here on in all title bouts would be contested at 160lbs. With Britain and the International Boxing Union (IBU) recognising 160lbs as being the middleweight limit, after the Walker Law was passed that weight was also accepted by the New York State Boxing Commission (NYSAC). The National Boxing Association (NBA), which was formed on 11 January 1921, followed suit.

17 March 1921. Johnny Wilson w pts 15 Mike O'Dowd.
Venue: Madison Square Garden, Manhattan, NYC, New York, USA. **Recognition:** World. **Referee:** Johnny McAvoy.
Fight Summary: Although the decision was split, in at least ten of the 15 rounds Wilson (158) battered O'Dowd (159¼) around the ring, ripping home blows to head and body with uppercuts and stiff southpaw right hooks. While O'Dowd, gashed over the right eye in the 11th and above the left in the 13th, plugged away his attacks became more futile the longer it went on, especially with the flow of blood almost blinding him. There were no knockdowns, but several times the challenger complained of low blows to little avail as Wilson went about his work. The general consensus at ringside was that Wilson should have been disqualified. This was the first middleweight title fight held under Walker Law.

Next time out Wilson was deemed by the press to have outscored Joe Chip over ten rounds at the Roller Palace Rink, Detroit, Michigan on 25 May. Risking his title when allowing Chip to make 158lbs, in what had earlier been reported as a championship match, the ten pounds heavier Wilson gave his rival a severe thrashing. The tough Chip had no answers to the steady beating, being hit hard and often, but he survived to the final bell where he looked a sorry sight.

Two fights later, on 27 July, at Dunn Field, Cleveland, Ohio, Wilson ran into trouble against Bryan Downey. After the no-decision contest came to an end when the referee disqualified Downey (154), the Cleveland Boxing Commission refused to accept the decision, declaring Downey the winner by a kayo. This action was eventually supported by the Ohio Boxing Commission on 23 August, who awarded Downey champion status. The referee, Jimmy Gardner, who had been brought in to protect Wilson (165), claimed he had disqualified Downey for attempting to hit the champion while he was down, but Wilson had already been decked three times and appeared well beaten at the finish. It was stated in the *Ring Record Book* that the first two knockdowns saw Wilson down for counts of 13 and 11, according to the timekeeper.

On the 'black title' front, a billed championship contest saw Panama Joe Gans beat Tiger Flowers (w co 6 at The Auditorium, Atlanta, Georgia on 8 August), while other fights where he put his title claim at risk came against Kid Alberts (nd-w rsc 10 in Detroit, Michigan on 6 June), Carl Hertz (nd-w co 6 at The Armoury, Jersey City, New Jersey on 15 August) and Alex Gibbons (w pts 12 at the Commonwealth SC, Manhattan, NYC, New York on 27 August).

5 September 1921. Johnny Wilson nd-drew 12 Bryan Downey.
Venue: Boyle's Thirty Acres, Jersey City, New Jersey, USA. **Recognition:** NBA/NY. **Referee:** Jim Savage.
Fight Summary: A return fight, this time with the title at stake, Wilson (159) had his purse suspended for 'spoiling' and not wishing to make a fight of it, while Downey (154½) was exonerated. While there had been nothing to choose between the pair, whether Wilson had failed to extend himself was debatable. But with few clean blows landed and the champion fighting defensively, despite occasionally jabbing with an extended southpaw right, the New Jersey Boxing Commission thought otherwise. Although Wilson was twice staggered, in the first and fifth rounds, Downey, who was cut over the right eye in the fifth, lacked direction and was all hit and miss when failing to finish the champion off.

In defence of his unofficial 'black title' claim, towards the end of the year, Panama Joe Gans beat Sailor Darden (w pts 15 at the Convention Hall, Rochester, New York on 13 September and w pts 15 at The Arena, Syracuse on 5 October), Nero Chink (w pts 12 at the Commonwealth SC, Manhattan, NYC, New York on 22 October), Allentown Joe Gans (nd-w pts 12 at McGuigan's Arena, Harrison, New Jersey on 6 December), Tiger Flowers (w co 5 at The Auditorium, Atlanta, Georgia on 15 December) and Young Sam Langford (nd-w co 9 in Detroit, Michigan on 28 December).

Mike Gibbons outpointed Happy Littleton over 15 rounds at the Louisiana Auditorium, New Orleans, Louisiana on 31 October in a fight that was billed as a 160lbs title fight after Wilson had refused to box either man. However, according to the *New Orleans Daily Picayune*, with the winner scaling 160½lbs to Littleton's 160, it was the loser who went forward to fight Downey in a contest that would be recognised by both the Cleveland Boxing Commission and the Louisianan Boxing Commission as being a world title bout.

Although Downey (157¾) stopped Littleton (160½) inside five rounds at the Louisiana Auditorium on 12 December, the loser fluffed his opportunity when coming in over 160lbs, something strangely reminiscent of what happened in his previous contest.

Meanwhile, on 4 January 1922, Wilson was barred by the NYSAC from fighting in New York for not agreeing to defend his title against Harry Greb, an action that was followed by the NBA, which represented 16 States, banning him 12 days later. Massachusetts also banned Wilson from fighting in their State until July 1922.

With the championship now in total disarray, Downey (159¾) drew over 15 rounds against the 159¼lbs Young Fisher at The Arena, Syracuse, New York on 10 February 1922, with both men inside 160lbs, but while there was some risk attached to his title claim it was outside the jurisdiction of both the Cleveland and Ohio Boxing Commissions.

22 February 1922. Bryan Downey w pts 12 Frank Carbone.
Venue: The Auditorium, Canton, Ohio, USA. **Recognition:** Ohio. **Referee:** Eddie Davis.
Fight Summary: Billed for the Ohio version of the 160lbs title, with both men reportedly inside at the 3pm weigh-in, Downey held on to his claim at the weight when he easily mastered Carbone, winning nine rounds and drawing two on the scorecards. Time after time Downey connected with Carbone's jaw and stomach, but the only apparent damage seemed to be the cut over the latter's left eye. From the opening bell, Downey generally poked away with the left to head and body before cutting loose with right hands, while Carbone, who amazed all and sundry with his toughness, appeared to have no defence.

At the Tomlinson Hall, Indianapolis, Indiana on 13 March, Downey risked his 160lbs title claim when he again took on Carbone, this time outside the jurisdiction of the Ohio Boxing Commission. Carbone collected the ten-round decision according to the press.

21 April 1922. Johnny Wilson nd-nc 4 (10) KO Jaffe.
Venue: American AC, Hazleton, Pennsylvania, USA. **Recognition:** Pennsylvania. **Referee:** Joe O'Donnell.
Fight Summary: Given title billing, and contested in one of the few States where Wilson could still ply his trade, the *Hazleton Standard Sentinel* reported the men as being inside 158lbs. The paper went on to say that Wilson had an easy time of it apart from being dumped in the second round from a right hand on the chin. Getting to his feet quickly, despite being dazed, the southpaw champion tore into Jaffe so viciously that the latter was compelled to hold on for dear life. From then on, with Wilson doing all the leading, Jaffe had no chance. As the fourth began Jaffe fell to his knees from a shove, and just as Wilson moved in for kill the referee called it off, claiming it to be a no contest, as the angry crowd hissed and booed.

Taking place at The Fairgrounds, Rutland, Vermont, on 4 July, an over-the-weight Wilson knocked out one Al DeMaris in the fourth round of what the *Chicago Tribune* reported as being Vermont's first ever world title fight. However, it was just an eight-round catchweight no-decision contest for Wilson against a man with no record to speak of, with just 500 people in attendance. Also reported as Al Demerest, apart from this contest there is no record of either, and it is more than likely that this man was either Sailor Demarest or Joe DeMaris who were around at the same time.

Wilson was stripped of his title by the NYSAC after finally deciding not to go ahead with a contracted match against Harry Greb in New York. His reasoning for this was that he had been forced to sign for the fight in order to recover his purse monies due from the second Bryan Downey fight, an argument that did not wear with the authority.

15 May 1922. Bryan Downey w pts 12 Mike O'Dowd.
Venue: Fairmount Arena, Columbus, Ohio, USA. **Recognition:** Ohio. **Referee:** Sammy Trott.

Fight Summary: Contested for the title, with both men inside 160lbs, Downey (156½) eliminated one of the leading contenders on the result, a solid left hook almost spelling curtains for O'Dowd (156) in the fifth round. There was no doubting that the veteran was considerably shaken up but he managed to get to his feet and deny Downey, the aggressor throughout, a kayo for the remainder of the bout, his wily skills just about keeping him out of harm's way. According to the *Chicago Tribune* it was a 15-round bout that was decided by the judges unanimously, while the *Ring Record Book* and various other papers recorded it as a 12-rounder that was decided by the referee.

On 13 June, after Downey, weighing 154½lbs, lost a ten-round press decision to Jock Malone (153) at the Mullen-Sager Arena, Aurora, Illinois, a rematch was set up to decide the Ohio version of the title.

14 August 1922. Dave Rosenberg w pts 15 Phil Krug.
Venue: The Velodrome, Bronx, NYC, New York, USA. **Recognition:** NY. **Referee:** Kid McPartland.
Fight Summary: Krug (155), a replacement for Harry Greb who had pulled out after being matched against Rosenberg (160), showed amazing courage to last the distance in a battle for the New York version of the title that had been vacated following the Commission's decision to strip Johnny Wilson. Rosenberg won every round, although Krug, cut over the right eye in the sixth, somehow remained upright despite reeling around the ring and being on the verge of a kayo throughout. Right from the opening bell it was apparent that Krug had no defence against Rosenberg's non-stop, all-action style, but for bravery alone he had no peers on the night. The unanimous decision in Rosenberg's favour was a formality.

18 September 1922. Jock Malone w pts 12 Bryan Downey.
Venue: Fairmont Arena, Columbus, Ohio, USA. **Recognition:** Ohio. **Referee:** Sammy Trott.
Fight Summary: Following the fight, which was made at 160lbs, the *Ohio State Journal* claimed that Malone was the real middleweight champion as far as Ohio and several other States were concerned. The contest itself saw Downey, moving like a lightweight, take the opening four rounds, but from then on it was all Malone as the body punches took effect. When Downey tried to get back into it he was boxed off soundly. It was only in the last two rounds when liniment from the champion's body found its way into Malone's eyes that any turnaround seemed possible. However, Malone gamely kept going to land a well-earned decision from the referee, being awarded a diamond-studded belt on the promise that he would defend his title claim in Ohio within 90 days.

Afterwards, Downey's manager was suspended for 60 days when found guilty of placing liniment on Downey during the fight. It is difficult to know just when the Ohio Boxing Commission decided not to recognise Malone as champion, but after the Downey fight and a three-round no contest against Johnny Karr at the Mechanics Building, Boston, Massachusetts on 13 October, he met with a sixth-round disqualification defeat at the hands of Bob Sage in a no-decision contest at 160lbs at the Roller Rink, Detroit, Michigan on 16 October.

There is no doubt that a lot of people still continued to see Malone as a champion, and he went on to beat a whole posse of good men at 160lbs or less in 1922, such as Navy Rostan (w co 4 at the George Oswego Arena, East Chicago, Indiana on 27 October), Johnny Shea (w co 5 at the Broadway Auditorium, Buffalo, New York on 6 November) and Augie Ratner (nd-w pts 10 at Danceland, Detroit, Michigan on 10 November), before taking a 12-round press decision at 158lbs off Bryan Downey at the Jefferson SC, Louisville, Kentucky on 5 December.

In 1923 Malone went on to fight Johnny Klesch (w rsc 6 at the George Oswego Arena on 26 February) at 158lbs, prior to knocking out Mike O'Dowd in the first round at The Auditorium, St Paul, Minnesota on 16 March. Despite the *Chicago Tribune* reporting him to be the holder of the Ohio version of the title, the fight was not billed for the championship, and even when Malone, who had lost two ten-round press decisions (on 16 April and 4 May at The Auditorium, St Paul) to Bermondsey Billy Wells, came back to The Coliseum, Columbus, Ohio on 24 July to meet Anthony Downey, Bryan's younger brother, the fight was not given title billing. Nevertheless, the *Columbus Ohio State Journal* reported that Malone was putting up the belt in a fight where both men weighed well inside 158lbs. After Malone won on points over 12 rounds he then went on to outscore Frank Carbone over ten rounds at the Riverside Arena, Covington, Kentucky on 6 August before beating Tilly Herman by a third-round disqualification at Noble's Arena, Aurora, Illinois on 17 August. All of these matches were made at 158lbs or less, but following Harry Greb's win over Johnny Wilson on 31 August Malone was seen as a challenger rather than a claimant.

30 November 1922. Mike O'Dowd w disq 8 (15) Dave Rosenberg.
Venue: Clermont SC, Brooklyn, NYC, New York, USA. **Recognition:** NY. **Referee:** Patsy Haley.
Fight Summary: Prior to the fight, Rosenberg (156), the NYSAC world champion, had asked for a postponement due to suffering a badly swollen right hand in training, but was told to get on with it by the Commission. He even started well, cutting the onrushing O'Dowd (159) on the left eye in the first round before being knocked down in the third from a heavy right to the head. From there onwards, in a bout not up to championship standard, with Rosenberg's punching erratic to say the least he was warned several times by the referee to keep them up. It was thus no surprise when he put O'Dowd, who was beginning to weaken, down in a heap with a low right hand in the eighth session, and with the latter writhing on the floor in considerable pain the referee disqualified Rosenberg on the 2.20 mark.

On winning, O'Dowd took over the New York version of the title, but then forfeited all recognition after being knocked out by Jock Malone (152½) in the first round of a no-decision contest at The Auditorium, St Paul, Minnesota on 16 March 1923. At this juncture, O'Dowd, who had scaled 158½lbs for the fight, announced his retirement from boxing. That was followed in early May 1923 by the NYSAC reinstating Johnny Wilson as champion after he had agreed to defend the title against Harry Greb at the Polo Grounds in New York City during August. At the same time, the NBA stated that they would also recognise the winner as the champion.

While all of this was going on, Panama Joe Gans was still considered by many as the 'black champion', and having risked his claim against Joe Libby (nd-w pts 8 in Atlantic City, New Jersey on 6 November) he next defended it against Whitey Black (nd-w pts 10 at the Olympia AC, Detroit, Michigan on 14 May 1923), Tiger Flowers (nd-l pts 12 at The Coliseum, Toledo, Ohio on 25 May 1923) and Willie Walker (w co 9 at the Commonwealth SC, Manhattan, NYC, New York on 30 June 1923).

31 August 1923. Harry Greb w pts 15 Johnny Wilson.
Venue: Polo Grounds, Manhattan, NYC, New York, USA. **Recognition:** World. **Referee:** Jack O'Sullivan.
Fight Summary: Most reports state that Greb (158) won 13 of the 15 rounds on offer, with the southpaw champion appearing bewildered at times as his opponent came in from all angles and kept punching. There was also plenty of the rough stuff, Greb being guilty of butting and thumbing in the clinches while Wilson (158) was not averse to sending in the occasional low blow. What was clear, however, was that Greb was the superior fighter of the two, and at the final bell Wilson was badly marked, his left eye closed, his mouth slashed open and there were lumps under his right eye. 'The Human Windmill', as Greb was known, was never at risk, but although making Wilson suffer he could not put him down despite hitting him with every punch in the book. The verdict was unanimous.

Regarding the unofficial 'black title', Panama Joe Gans put up his claim against Whitey Black (w co 8 at Jake Carey's Club, Rochester, New York on 22 October) in what would be his last successful defence. A good look at his record shows that he had been avoided by the majority of top men while at his peak, but at least one of his victims, Tiger Flowers, would go on to become the first fully recognised black champion for the weight class.

Despite Greb weighing in at 161lbs for his fight against Bryan Downey (158½) at the Motor Square Garden, Pittsburgh, Pennsylvania on 3 December, it went ahead as a billed championship contest with the champion winning on points over ten rounds. This would not be the last time that Greb abused his commitments at 160lbs.

18 January 1924. Harry Greb w pts 15 Johnny Wilson.
Venue: Madison Square Garden, Manhattan, NYC, New York, USA. **Recognition:** World. **Referee:** Ed Purdy.
Fight Summary: Up until the seventh round the challenger looked a sure winner, having sickened Greb (159) with terrific southpaw lefts to the body while setting him up for an eventual knockout. Inexplicably, Wilson (159) started to go on the back foot in the seventh, a tactic that encouraged Greb to swarm all over him. Rattled and carrying a badly damaged left eye, Wilson resorted to fouling while possibly looking for a way out. To his credit, Greb, ignoring the low blows, went on to take the unanimous points decision. While other sources show Patsy Haley as being the referee, I have stayed with Purdy for the time being.

Matched to fight Fay Keiser at the Armoury, Baltimore, Maryland on 24 March in a contracted title bout, an oversight saw Greb, believing it to be a catchweight contest, weigh-in at 173lbs. Obviously, the Maryland Boxing Commission took a firm stance, but with Keiser (158½lbs) willing to accept the weight difference and with the promoter anxious for the fight to go ahead they demanded that Greb put his title at stake. Thus, under threat of suspension, Greb, his weight announced as being 159½lbs, stepped up to secure victory when winning via a 12th-round stoppage.

26 June 1924. Harry Greb w pts 15 Ted Moore.
Venue: Yankee Stadium, Bronx, NYC, New York, USA. **Recognition:** World. **Referee:** Ed Purdy.
Fight Summary: Taking place in front of more than 50,000 fans, Greb (159½) immediately moved on to the offensive, producing a seemingly inexhaustible supply of energy as he kept on top of Moore (160), who was forced to defend himself against a champion intent on driving him to the canvas. However, as the fight progressed the Englishman began to prove the master of Greb on the inside when fighting back doggedly, absorbing all the punishment going his way while hitting hard when and where he could in an exciting fight that went the distance. Although the decision was unanimous in Greb's favour, there was always the chance that Moore could have landed the one that counted, and that in itself kept the fans glued to their seats despite a lack of knockdowns.

On the same bill, Larry Estridge wrested the unofficial 'black title' from Panama Joe Gans when taking the ten-round points decision, and a few weeks later, on 11 August, he replicated his victory over the same man at the Queensboro Stadium, Queens, NYC, New York. I cannot find any defences as such for Estridge, but following his match-ups with Gans he went on to beat Young Fisher (twice), Dave Rosenberg and Charley Nashert before his career imploded when winning only once in his final 14 contests.

In a bout where it was unclear whether stipulated weights were contracted or not, an over-the-weight Greb (172lbs) appeared to risk his title prior to stopping Billy Hirsch, who scaled 155lbs, in the eighth round of a no-decision contest at Wabash Park, Mingo Junction, Ohio on 15 September.

Another contest for Greb that did not get into the record books as a title fight came against Bob Sage at the Roller Rink, Detroit, Michigan on 9 January 1925. Although the *Ring Record Book* gives this one as a ten-round no-decision fight, the *New York Times* reported that the verdict, in the champion's favour, was given by a referee of Greb's own preference. This concession allowed Sage to weigh less than 160lbs, which gave the promoter the right to attach championship billing.

Early on in 1925 it was reported that Greb's leading challenger was now Tiger Flowers, who had recently beaten Johnny Wilson. Twice Flowers took on Jack Delaney at Madison Square Garden, Manhattan, NYC when trying to find Greb's next opponent, and twice the latter won by a knockout, in the second round on 16 January 1925 and in the fourth session on 26 February 1925. But Delaney was quickly becoming a fully-fledged light heavy, as was another leading contender in Jimmy Slattery, and a 160lbs title challenge was out of the question.

Continuing to look for a worthy challenger, Greb eventually settled on Mickey Walker, the welter king-pin, with the fight being made for July.

2 July 1925. Harry Greb w pts 15 Mickey Walker.
Venue: Polo Grounds, Manhattan, NYC, New York, USA. **Recognition:** World. **Referee:** Ed Purdy.
Fight Summary: Despite having difficulties making the weight, the champion still had enough left to take a unanimous decision over the youthful Walker (152), the holder of the world welterweight title. Even though he was put down on one knee in the second round Walker was soon tearing into Greb (159), giving the champion such a drubbing in the fifth that it looked as though the title would be changing hands. A round later, however, the tide had turned as Greb began to outbox Walker, and although staggered several times he continued to hold the upper hand right through to the final bell. Walker finished with badly lacerated features and the referee with a limp, having been kneed in the groin, accidentally or otherwise, when warning Greb to cut out the holding.

Following this recognised title defence for Greb there were two further fights for him that were initially thought by some to have had some bearing on the championship. According to certain reports, Greb allowed Ed Smith, who was counted out in the fourth round of their no-decision contest at the Memorial Hall, Kansas City, Kansas on 4 August, to come into the ring weighing 160lbs. There was no way that Smith, who was fighting in the heavyweight division at the time, could have made that weight and it must be seen as a misprint.

As in the case of the Smith affair, his fight against Tony Marullo at The Coliseum Arena, New Orleans, Louisiana on 13 November 1925 was also a strange one. Billed for the world title, both the *Ring Record Book* and the *New Orleans Daily Picayune* reported Greb as weighing 169lbs to Marullo's 168. With the middleweight limit set at 160lbs there was a strong suspicion that there had been a misprint, but with Marullo fighting at around the 170lbs mark at the time and Greb often weighing in that region I feel it best that this one is ignored as involving the championship.

26 February 1926. Tiger Flowers w pts 15 Harry Greb.
Venue: Madison Square Garden, Manhattan, NYC, New York, USA. **Recognition:** World. **Referee:** Gunboat Smith.
Fight Summary: With Greb again finding it difficult to make the weight, this time it would prove to be his undoing against a challenger who made the running from the opening bell when sending in jolting southpaw lefts to the jaw. As the fight wore on Greb (159½) tried desperately to find a punch that would finish Flowers (158½), but his timing was out and he endlessly missed the target while the latter pecked away with scoring right jabs. Although Greb came back strongly from the 12th onwards, having Flowers reeling at times, unable to make up the lost rounds he forfeited his title by a split decision despite the referee giving him his vote.

19 August 1926. Tiger Flowers w pts 15 Harry Greb.
Venue: Madison Square Garden, Manhattan, NYC, New York, USA. **Recognition:** World. **Referee:** Jim Crowley.
Fight Summary: Sharper than when they met before, Greb (159) started fast when hammering the southpaw champion with two-fisted attacks to head and body. Going well, he kept up the pressure for the opening five rounds. Cut over left eye in the third, Flowers (159¼) regrouped to come back strongly in the middle rounds, and in the 13th he sliced open a cut over Greb's right eye. Many thought that was the end for Greb, but he surprised all of those critics when chasing Flowers non-stop for the remaining six minutes as he looked for a finishing punch. Although the unanimous decision went against him, Greb went out in a blaze of glory. However, there would be no more fights for Greb, who died following a car accident and subsequent operation on 22 October.

3 December 1926. Mickey Walker w pts 10 Tiger Flowers.
Venue: The Coliseum, Chicago, Illinois, USA. **Recognition:** World. **Referee:** Benny Yanger.
Fight Summary: Launching a furious two-fisted attack from the opening bell, knowing that the best way for him to win the title was by a knockout, Walker (154) soon put Flowers (159) down with a right to the jaw. Back on his feet quickly, the second round saw Flowers take control when a southpaw right opened a cut over Walker's left eye. Thereafter, with both men taking it in turns to go on the offensive it seemed to be about even coming into the ninth. Knowing that his bid to win the title depended on the last couple of rounds, Walker waded into Flowers in the ninth to drop him with a left hook-right cross. Although the champion recovered quickly, going toe-to-toe until the end of the tenth, the referee had no hesitation in raising Walker's hand at the bell. Some 18 fights later, and four days after beating Leo Gates, Flowers tragically lost his life on 16 November 1927 following an operation to remove a growth over his right eye.

Walker's first defence would be against Scotland's Tommy Milligan, the British, British Empire and European title claimant, who had been the leading challenger for the welterweight title at the end of 1925 as far as Tex Rickard was concerned. However, Milligan had moved up in weight, as had Walker, and had victories over men such as Alex Ireland, Hamilton Johnny Brown, Ted Kid Lewis, Bruno Frattini, Morrie Schlaifer, Jack Zivic, a highly-ranked member of the famous fighting family, and Ted Moore. Despite the EBU not recognising him as their champion, it was more to do with Britain not conforming to their rules and regulations at that time.

30 June 1927. Mickey Walker w co 10 (20) Tommy Milligan.
Venue: Olympia, Kensington, London, England. **Recognition:** World. **Referee:** Eugene Corri.

Fight Summary: For almost all of the opening five rounds it was anybody's fight as both men exchanged hard blows and fought at close quarters, but towards the end of the fifth the champion caught Milligan (159¼) with a terrific right hand under the heart that ultimately turned the tide of battle. Walker came out fast for the sixth, repeatedly sending in similar blows, and it was no surprise when Milligan (159½) was dropped twice for long counts in the seventh. Still Milligan continued, being floored twice in the eighth and twice in the ninth. And in the tenth following a barrage of lefts and rights the game Milligan was again sent down. Bravely struggling to his feet, Milligan was finally put out of his misery when a right-hand smash dropped him for the last time to be counted out.

After fighting above the weight for the remainder of the year, Walker was told by the NYSAC on 26 October that he must sign contracts within 30 days to defend his title against George Courtney, who had placed $2,500 with the Commission as surety, or risk being suspended in New York.

At the same time the NBA were being asked to look into an agreement that Walker had signed prior to his title-winning fight against Tiger Flowers, which called for a return within 90 days if he won. In the event, the NBA enquiry came to nought when Flowers did not recover from an eye operation and died on 16 November, while Walker failed to agree a championship match with Courtney and was suspended in New York on 30 November.

Meanwhile, the NBA notified Walker on 24 January 1928 that he must sign articles for a title defence within 30 days or risk being stripped. On 18 February, it was reported that Walker had signed with a Chicago promoter to defend his title in June against an unnamed opponent, but having been asked to post a forfeit of $5,000 when it did not arrive he was suspended for an indefinite period. Eventually, after fulfilling his contractual obligations in mid-May 1928 when signing for a defence in Chicago against Ace Hudkins, Walker was free to pick up his middleweight career.

Earlier, on 6 July 1927, Jack McVey was recognised by many as the unofficial 'black champion' after knocking out Walcott Langford in the tenth and final round of their contest at Taylor's Bowl, Cleveland, Ohio. At the end of the year only Dave Shade and Courtney were rated ahead of McVey by Tex Rickard, the latter being the leading black fighter at the weight. Since beating Langford he had drawn with Pete Latzo and Shade in contests where the press saw him as a clear winner.

5 June 1928. Mickey Walker nd-w pts 10 Jock Malone.
Venue: Lexington Park, St Paul, Minnesota, USA. **Recognition:** World.
Fight Summary: Billed for the title in an open-air event, with Malone (157) only able to become champion if Walker (159½) was stopped, kayoed or disqualified, the champion made a good start when stunning the former with two lefts and a right cross to the jaw in the second round. From then on, Malone fought an adroit defensive battle, jabbing, blocking and sidestepping, as Walker tried to wear him down with body punches. Towards the end of the fight, Malone realised he would have to open up if he wanted to land the title, but after Walker's bodywork had taken the steam out of him the action fizzled out, the latter easily winning the press decision.

21 June 1928. Mickey Walker w pts 10 Ace Hudkins.
Venue: Comiskey Park, Chicago, Illinois, USA. **Recognition:** World. **Referee:** Ed Purdy.
Fight Summary: To most discerning fans it appeared that the challenger had taken the title after ten rounds of fierce fighting, during which Walker (158) had been forced to soak up incessant body attacks. Apart from the fourth when Walker had Hudkins (155) wobbling from a bombardment of heavy blows to the head, it was the 'Nebraska Wildcat' who took the eye. According to the referee, Hudkins won by five rounds to three, with two even. However, the other two judges saw it for Walker. Both men were cut up, which was hardly surprising, and the wild, swinging Hudkins impressed when walking right through Walker, who was unable to keep his fearless rival at bay despite landing some of his best shots.

On 28 December, at Madison Square Garden, Manhattan, NYC, New York, Hudkins outpointed Rene De Vos over ten rounds in a bout that both the NYSAC and NBA saw as finding Walker's next championship opponent.

However, it appeared that Walker had other plans. In his previous two contests, De Vos had beaten Phil Kaplan and Dave Shade in contests considered by the NYSAC as being eliminators.

Wishing to challenge Tommy Loughran for the world light heavyweight title on 28 March 1929, and having gone beyond the six-month title defence period, on 24 February 1929 the NBA demanded that Walker post $25,000 in good faith that he would defend his title against Hudkins again by 4 July 1929. It was later reported that the figure both demanded and received by the Illinois Boxing Commission, before Walker was allowed to meet Loughran, had been reduced to $10,000.

Following his unsuccessful challenge for light heavyweight honours, Walker remained inactive until meeting Leo Lomski (w pts 10 at the Sesquin-Centennial Stadium, Philadelphia, Pennsylvania on 19 August 1929) in a match more to do with the 175lbs weight class. Then, on 17 September 1929, the NBA announced that as they had lost patience with Walker for not keeping his appointment with Hudkins they were stripping him of the title, listing the latter, De Vos and Harry Ebbets as the leading contenders. Although the NBA's decision remained firm, it was reported a week later that Walker had finally signed to meet Hudkins.

29 October 1929. Mickey Walker w pts 10 Ace Hudkins.
Venue: Wrigley Field, Los Angeles, California, USA. **Recognition:** California/NY. **Referee:** Jack Kennedy.
Fight Summary: Another ten rounder, it was not a patch on their previous contest, with Hudkins (156), cut around the eyes and carrying damage to the mouth, unable to produce the debilitating bodywork that many thought would gain him a win over Walker (159½). One report stated that 'The Wildcat' fought like a tired old bulldog, while Walker, who took the referee's decision, failed to live up to his billing, boxing a wily fight as he blocked a high percentage of Hudkins' body shots on his arms which must have been sore at the finish.

There would be no more fights for Walker at the middleweight limit, and regardless of what was being reported it is certain that he saw his future at a higher weight. Suspended in New York since November 1927, it was even reported on 20 January 1930 that Walker was trying to make up with the NYSAC and looking at the possibilities of a defence against the top-ranked Rene De Vos on 14 March, but as in previous attempts to patch up differences that also came to nothing.

Meantime, De Vos was beaten in a huge upset by Doc Conrad, who then went on to defeat Harry Ebbets. These two victories saw Conrad recognised as the number two contender by *The Ring* magazine, but just when it looked as though he would be part of any title plans he was knocked out of the ratings, quite literally, by Vincent Forgione. Needless to say, Forgione failed to take advantage of his shock victory when failing to win any of his next 15 contests.

Although the NBA continued not to recognise Walker as the champion it was not until 14 February 1931 when they announced that due to his failure to defend within the every six-month ruling they would be setting up an elimination tournament to find a successor. Walker had gone 15 months without defending his title and was fighting in the heavyweight division. Prior to the NBA tournament getting off the ground, Walker officially vacated what was left of his title on 19 June 1931.

Obviously looking for the best way to find a new champion, the NBA eventually set up a tournament with contests of ten-round duration, which would kick off at Borchert Field, Milwaukee, Wisconsin on 25 August 1931. After much debate they named Gorilla Jones, Tiger Thomas, Clyde Chastain, George Nichols, Frankie O'Brien, Rudy Marshall, Tait Littman, Ham Jenkins, Angel Clivilles, Frank Battaglia, Jack McVey, Tiger Roy Williams, Oliver Wright, Gary Leach, Young Johnny Burns and Henry Firpo as taking part. Following the announcement, the NBA were slated by *The Ring* magazine for not making sure that Dave Shade, Vince Dundee, Young Terry, Ben Jeby, Harry Smith, their top-rated fighter at that moment in time, and the Europeans, Marcel Thil, Len Harvey and Jack Hood, were involved.

Smith had won the unofficial 'black title' when beating McVey (w pts 15 at the Olympia BC, Manhattan, NYC, New York on 16 November 1929), before making a successful defence against Joe Tinsley (w co 7 at Woodcliff Park,

Poughkeepsie, New York on 13 August 1930). Despite being thrown out of the ring in a no contest affair against Gorilla Jones (nc 9 at Queensboro Stadium, Queens, NYC on 4 September 1930), Smith redeemed himself when beating Jones (w pts 10 at the Olympia BC, Manhattan, NYC on 23 October 1930) in another defence of the 'black title'. That appears to be the last time Smith defended the unofficial title.

When the first round of the NBA tournament got underway on 25 August 1931, Chastain (w pts Marshall), Jones (w pts Thomas), Littman (w pts Jenkins) and Clivilles (w co 1 Battaglia) joined the others, who received byes, in the next round. The last contest was held at The Auditorium, Milwaukee on 3 September 1931 and all the remaining contests would be held at that venue. Interestingly, Jones v Thomas has often been reported to have involved the world title, something that came about because Jones (who had claimed the unofficial 'black title' when outpointing McVey over ten rounds at Braves Field, Boston, Massachusetts on 25 June 1929) was meeting another black man in Thomas at 160lbs.

Making progress, the second round saw O'Brien (w pts McVey on 3 September 1931), Firpo (w pts Williams on 3 September), Clivilles (w co 5 Littman on 17 September), Jones (w co 6 Chastain on 17 September), Nichols (w pts Wright on 25 September) and Leach (w pts Burns on 25 September 1931) winning through. Prior to the quarter-finals beginning, the Italian, Oddone Piazza, who had been back home when the tournament started, was allowed in and would meet another newcomer in Cuba's Raul Rojas.

The quarter-finals were concluded after O'Brien (w co 9 Clivilles on 12 October 1931), Firpo (w co 2 Leach on 12 October), Jones (w pts Nichols on 3 November) and Piazza (w pts Rojas on 3 November), while the semis, held on 19 November 1931, saw Firpo and Piazza draw and Jones outpoint O'Brien. With three men still left at the final stage, it was decided on a draw which would see the first two men out of the hat meeting in a box-off, while the third man out of the hat would go straight into the final. Subsequently, Jones, who outpointed Firpo on 11 December 1931, would meet Piazza in the final leg on 25 January 1932.

25 January 1932. Gorilla Jones w rsc 6 (10) Oddone Piazza.
Venue: The Auditorium, Milwaukee, Wisconsin, USA. **Recognition:** NBA. **Referee:** Julius Fidler.
Fight Summary: Contesting the vacant NBA version of the title, Jones (152½) won every round except the first as he wore Piazza (153¾) down with a mixture of strong attacks to the body and heavy jolts to the jaw. Come the sixth, Piazza, staggering away from a hail of punches, fell in a neutral corner for a count of 'four', and on getting up the referee came to his rescue when it was clear that he was at Jones' mercy and on the verge of a serious beating.

26 April 1932. Gorilla Jones w pts 12 Young Terry.
Venue: The Armoury, Trenton, New Jersey, USA. **Recognition:** NBA. **Referee:** Hank Lewis.
Scorecard: 6-5-1.
Fight Summary: Getting away to an excellent start, Terry (158) was the early aggressor in a fast and furious affair before weakening badly after the eighth and seeing his lead dwindle as Jones (151) came on like a train. Well down on the cards at this point, Jones, who ultimately picked up the referee's decision, began to pile up the points with hard rights to head and body that doubled the challenger up and had him hanging on in front of a large crowd who had come to cheer him.

Jones' next defence of the NBA title would come in Paris, France against *The Ring*'s number one rated contender, Marcel Thil. The durable Frenchman, who had 85 wins from 118 contests, was a 29-year-old veteran of the ring, having started out in 1920. Since losing the European title to Mario Bosisio in November 1930 he had racked up 15 wins, which included victories over Vince Dundee and Jack Hood, and was an aggressive body puncher.

11 June 1932. Marcel Thil w disq 11 (15) Gorilla Jones.
Venue: Princes Park Stadium, Paris, France. **Recognition:** IBU/NBA. **Referee:** Juan Casanovas.
Fight Summary: Although clutching at every opportunity and boxing on the retreat, Jones (149) was unable to keep the ebullient Thil (158) at bay, being pressed at every turn. The challenger was also scoring freely with the jab, both at close quarters and at long range, and having been warned several times for hitting on the break Jones got

himself thrown out by the referee in the 11th after hammering the Frenchman with four left hooks to an unprotected jaw.

Despite Jones complaining bitterly about the way he was treated in France, especially not being allowed to work the body after being told that the first foul blow would bring a warning and the next a disqualification, the NBA, contrary to all kinds of stories, continued to support Thil as the world champion.

4 July 1932. Marcel Thil w pts 15 Len Harvey.
Venue: White City Stadium, Shepherds Bush, London, England. **Recognition:** IBU/NBA. **Referee:** Francois Devernaz.
Fight Summary: Having been outpointed over 15 rounds by Harvey more than four years earlier, Thil was seen by the British camp as just another hurdle on the way to the world title, but the man of granite had not read the script, fighting non-stop to earn the referee's decision. Harvey (158¾), cut over the right eye in the seventh, appeared to have everything in his favour - speed of mind, fast hands and power in the right mitt - but after the third round, having made a confident start, he gave up on his advantages when allowing Thil (159¼) to take control on the inside. Those who knew Harvey well could not understand why he failed to overcome the tough champion, whose main asset was to fight on until he dropped, but beaten he was and decisively at that.

Dissatisfied that the title had left America, and more than a year after Mickey Walker had handed back his belt, in September the NYSAC named Ben Jeby, Paul Pirrone, Chick Devlin and Frank Battaglia as the men who would fight it out to decide their version of the championship. Following the announcement, *The Ring* magazine spoke up on behalf of Dave Shade, who had been ignored yet again. They also went on to voice their concerns over the NYSAC's actions when there was already a world champion in Thil.

Regardless, the two semi-final legs went ahead at Madison Square Garden, Manhattan, NYC, New York on 13 October, Jeby knocking out Pirrone inside six rounds and Battaglia and Devlin drawing over ten rounds. Battaglia, who was reckoned by most good judges to have won handily, withdrew from the competition over terms for a return match with Devlin. Meantime, a contest was set up at the St Nicholas Arena, Manhattan between Jeby and Devlin, which was reported by many papers as carrying NYSAC championship recognition. The fight went ahead on 21 November, Jeby outpointing Devlin over 15 rounds, but following that it was announced that Battaglia would be meeting Devlin for the right to meet Jeby to decide the vacant NYSAC version of the title. It now appears certain that the Jeby v Devlin contest went ahead without full NYSAC recognition being granted, despite the advertisements, and after Battaglia outpointed Devlin over ten rounds on 9 December at Madison Square Garden he was booked to meet Jeby to decide the title.

Meanwhile, in a catchweight contest, Thil lost a 12-round points decision to Kid Tunero at the Sports Palace, Paris, France on 16 January 1933. It is interesting to note that in order to safeguard Thil at all costs, when Tunero scaled inside 160lbs he was sent away to have a meal and to come back in excess of that weight.

Two weeks later, on 30 January 1933, at the Public Hall, Cleveland, Ohio, the NBA matched Gorilla Jones with Sammy Slaughter for the American title, the former winning by a seventh-round kayo. Although *The Ring* magazine and certain record books reported this fight as being for the NBA version of the world title, the Association was adamant in stating that Jones was only the American champion and that they still recognised Thil as being the world champion.

However, having not defended the NBA version of the title for almost a year, Thil was ordered to make a match by 15 August 1933 or risk losing the championship. When this was not forthcoming he was stripped, an action that was confirmed when the NBA announced on 18 September 1933 that they would be recognising Lou Brouillard as champion, thus falling in line with the NYSAC.

13 January 1933. Ben Jeby w rsc 12 (15) Frank Battaglia.
Venue: Madison Square Garden, Manhattan, NYC, New York, USA. **Recognition:** NY. **Referee:** Jack Britton.
Fight Summary: Because he had previously knocked out Jeby in a round Battaglia was obviously confident of lifting the New York version of the vacant title. Taking all that Battaglia (159¼) could muster, Jeby (158¾) kept

coming back for more. Having dropped Battaglia for 'nine' in the second round with a terrific, if somewhat controversial body shot and then closing his rival's right eye a round later, by the sixth Jeby was clearly in front. A crude and plodding fighter, Jeby was not everyone's cup of tea, but he was too good for Battaglia, and after dropping him for 'nine' in the 11th with a right uppercut to the chin followed by a left hook to the body the referee halted the fight a round later on the 1.46 mark when the latter was ready to fall again.

17 March 1933. Ben Jeby drew 15 Vince Dundee.
Venue: Madison Square Garden, Manhattan, NYC, New York, USA. **Recognition:** NY. **Referee:** Eddie Forbes.
Scorecards: 9-3-3, 5-9-1, 7-7-1.
Fight Summary: According to most newspaper reports the decision of a draw was a disgrace. Nat Fleischer, writing in *The Ring* magazine, reflected that when a fighter wins by such a large amount of points as did Dundee there should be no reason for such a divergence of opinion among the officials. Incidentally, Fleischer had Dundee winning by eight rounds to five with two even. The referee, who gave it as seven rounds apiece with one even, said afterwards that as he had cautioned Dundee many times for holding that was the reason for his scoring. The fight itself saw Jeby (159½) as the aggressor, throwing many low punches for which he was not cautioned, while Dundee (159¾) sent out left jabs that seemed to be forever in the champion's face. Although the fight started slowly, Dundee held the upper hand most of the time, apart from the seventh and eighth sessions when Jeby got through with solid lefts and rights to the head. At the final bell Jeby looked a sorry sight, his left eye almost closed and carrying swellings to his nose and mouth.

Any hopes that Gorilla Jones had of furthering his title claims were abandoned following his six-round no contest at the Public Hall, Cleveland against Jeby on 19 April 1933, when it seemed to many bystanders that both men were looking to set up a rematch with the championship at stake. This was a scheduled 12 rounder where both men were stalling and with the crowd showing its displeasure the referee called it off at the end of the sixth.

This was followed a few weeks later at The Arena, Boston, Massachusetts, when Lou Brouillard outpointed Sammy Slaughter over ten rounds on 16 May. Perhaps, not surprisingly, with the middleweight division in some disarray, prior to the fight Brouillard's people had asked the Massachusetts Boxing Commission to recognise it as being for their version of the world title but were turned down.

10 July 1933. Ben Jeby w pts 15 Young Terry.
Venue: Dreamland Park, Newark, New Jersey, USA. **Recognition:** NY. **Referee:** Whitey Healey.
Scorecard: 9-4-2.
Fight Summary: Advertised as being for the NYSAC version of the title, and given dispensation to go ahead on NBA territory under full championship conditions, the champion showed a good boxing brain when staging a smart fight from beginning to end to nullify the aggressive tactics of the two-fisted Terry (157). Meeting Terry's attacks with left jabs and right uppercuts, Jeby (158¼) piled up the points during the first eight rounds, winning all but two of them, and conserving his energy he kept things on an even keel for the next five sessions before having to withstand a terrific assault over the last two. Realising he needed a kayo to win, and disregarding his cut and bleeding face, Terry tore into Jeby to attack the body with both hands. Despite Jeby being tired and worried for the first time, he met Terry's charge like a veteran, well deserving the referee's decision even if it did prove unpopular with the crowd.

9 August 1933. Lou Brouillard w co 7 (15) Ben Jeby.
Venue: Polo Grounds, Manhattan, NYC, New York, USA. **Recognition:** NY. **Referee:** Pete Hartley.
Fight Summary: For six rounds the southpaw challenger chopped away at Jeby, stabbing out openings with his right before unleashing left-hand smashes to the body. At the end of the sixth Jeby (159) was gasping after taking a series of such blows to the body, and when he came out for the seventh Brouillard (158½) jumped on him. There was no respite, Jeby being battered around the ring before being caught full on the chin by a sweeping left and sent crashing over. With the count underway, and Brouillard warned to keep his distance, Jeby managed to get to knees before slumping back to the floor and being counted out on the 2.21 mark.

Just under two weeks later, on 21 August, at Forbes Field, Pittsburgh, Pennsylvania, Teddy Yarosz outpointed Vince Dundee over ten rounds to get himself into the championship shake-up when winning the Pennsylvania State title, mistakenly referred to by the *Ring Record Book* as the Pennsylvanian version of the world title. According to the *Philadelphia Inquirer*, this fight involved the State title only due to an agreement between Massachusetts, New York and Pennsylvania, a group that recognised Brouillard as champion at the time.

2 October 1933. Marcel Thil w pts 15 Kid Tunero.
Venue: Sports Palace, Paris, France. **Recognition:** IBU. **Referee:** Roger Nicod.
Fight Summary: Defending his championship against a man who had beaten him in a non-title affair earlier in the year, this time round Thil (159½) proved he was the better man, especially in the first six rounds as Tunero (157) came on to his punches. It was only in the seventh that Tunero changed tactics, using excellent footwork and clever left-hand work to get back into the fight. The final few rounds saw the men go toe-to-toe, with Thil's greater strength earning him the unanimous decision.

With the IBU recognising Thil and the NYSAC supporting Lou Brouillard as champion at this time, another man to be awarded a world title was Vearl Whitehead (163), who had defeated the 160lbs Gorilla Jones (w disq 10 at the Dreamland Auditorium, San Francisco, California on 28 July). According to the 27 October issue of the *Milwaukee Journal*, the Californian Boxing Committee decided to recognise Whitehead as world champion on the basis of his win over Jones, but on the very same day Whitehead was outpointed over ten rounds at the Legion Stadium, Los Angeles, California by another Californian, Chick Devlin, who came in above 160lbs. Whether that changed anything or not soon became irrelevant when, within two months of that date, all but one of the committee had been removed from office.

30 October 1933. Vince Dundee w pts 15 Lou Brouillard.
Venue: The Garden, Boston, Massachusetts, USA. **Recognition:** NBA/NY. **Referee:** Johnny Martin.
Fight Summary: Regardless that he fought aggressively, Brouillard (159) was still unable to fathom out the clever Dundee (160), often floundering when exposed by the fast-moving, side-stepping challenger. Unfortunately for Brouillard he had left much of his fight in the gym, and on top of that was forced to take off almost three pounds in weight. There was no doubt all of that hindered him somewhat, but even then he should have handled himself better. In the main it was Dundee, moving left and right with stabbing lefts to the head that kept the champion off balance and out of distance. In winning the unanimous decision, Dundee followed his brother Joe, the former welter titleholder, as a world champion.

8 December 1933. Vince Dundee w pts 15 Andy Callahan.
Venue: The Garden, Boston, Massachusetts, USA. **Recognition:** NBA/NY. **Referee:** Jack Decker.
Fight Summary: Putting his title on the line for the first time and honouring his agreement with the promoters, Dundee (158½) came close to losing against Callahan (152½), it being his extra weight and added reach that ultimately gained him the split decision. Starting at a gallop, when the southpaw challenger realised his best chance lay in scoring a quick win he tore into Dundee with hard rights and lefts to head and body while continually pushing the latter against the ropes. Despite having much success, Callahan was blown out by the ninth, and having bided his time Dundee came on like a train over the last five rounds to just about get home. Callahan had never gone 15 rounds before and it showed. The press reported that Callahan won the first four rounds, split the next four and lost five out of the last seven.

Another Pennsylvanian title fight for Teddy Yarosz, mistakenly reported in the *Ring Record Book* as involving the State's version of the world title, saw him outpoint Jimmy Smith over 15 rounds at the Motor Square Stadium, Pittsburgh, Pennsylvania on 12 February 1934.

Meanwhile, there was a strong effort made in the USA to only recognise championship bouts if they were contested over 15 rounds.

26 February 1934. Marcel Thil w pts 15 Ignacio Ara.
Venue: Sports Palace, Paris, France. **Recognition:** IBU. **Referee:** Roger Nicod.

Fight Summary: Although Ara (156¾), a heavy hitter, gave the champion a good fight and tried endlessly to find a way through his rival's guard he was undone by sound bodywork, ultimately going down on all three judges' scorecards. Thil (159), a veteran of 15 years in the ring, showed no signs that he was about to lose his title when handing out a boxing lesson in all the rudiments of the game to the tough Spaniard.

3 May 1934. Marcel Thil w pts 15 Gustave Roth.
Venue: Sports Palace, Paris, France. **Recognition:** IBU. **Referee:** Eduard Mazzia.
Fight Summary: Despite Thil (157½) appearing to win handsomely, outslugging Roth (157½) round after round, one of the judges actually saw it as a draw. There had been high hopes for Roth, but he made the mistake of mixing it with the champion instead of getting on his bike. Regardless of that, with the challenger never looking likely to win Thil retained his title by a majority decision while picking up Roth's European crown at the same time.

3 May 1934. Vince Dundee w pts 15 Al Diamond.
Venue: State Armoury, Paterson, New Jersey, USA. **Recognition:** NBA/NY. **Referee:** Phil Erhardt.
Scorecard: 11-1-3.
Fight Summary: Even though Dundee (157) ultimately proved too experienced for the youthful challenger, the early rounds saw Diamond (156½) seemingly pile up a lead with good, clean punches to the head. Halfway through the fight, Diamond, appearing to be well in front, was belabouring Dundee with right-hand swings to the jaw despite lacking the power to finish matters. Dundee, who was obviously pacing himself, kept banging away with right hands, and from the eighth round through to the 14th his superior ring-craft gave him the advantage. In the 14th, Dundee, who was tiring, was cut under the left eye. Although Diamond speeded up, having left his charge too late, the referee's decision went to the champion.

11 September 1934. Teddy Yarosz w pts 15 Vince Dundee.
Venue: Forbes Field, Pittsburgh, Pennsylvania, USA. **Recognition:** NBA/NY. **Referee:** Al Grayber.
Scorecards: 7-4-4, 9-3-3, 7-8.
Fight Summary: Carrying the fight to the champion from the opening bell, Yarosz (157¼), attacking the body, sent Dundee (158½) into the ropes with hard lefts on at least six occasions. Yarosz had beaten Dundee twice before and knew how to deal with him. While Dundee was prepared to stay at distance and pick Yarosz off, it did not quite work out like that as he was given little space. Even when Dundee came on strong in the final third Yarosz made him work, but it was noticeable that had the former possessed a bigger punch he could well have retained his title rather than losing it by a split decision.

A few days after his win over Dundee, Yarosz turned down an offer to defend his title against Oscar Rankins in Los Angeles, California. Rankins had just beaten Gorilla Jones who, the *Charleston Gazette* reported, had been recognised in some States as the champion, and was rated at number three by *The Ring* magazine.

Taking in an overweight contest against Babe Risko at the Town Hall, Scranton, Pennsylvania on 1 January 1935, Yarosz, having damaged his right knee at some stage of the contest, was dropped six times before being rescued by the referee in the seventh round.

Due to make his return to the ring in March, Yarosz again had problems with the knee and was forced to have an operation before he could get back into action. Although he had passed the defence every six-month ruling, the authorities allowed him two comeback fights before he signed up to meet Risko again. Since beating Yarosz, Risko had lost to Vince Dundee, Jimmy Belmont and Paul Pirrone - who was elevated to the number one spot on the result - and was not expected to repeat his shock victory over the champion.

15 October 1934. Marcel Thil drew 15 Carmelo Candel.
Venue: Sports Palace, Paris, France. **Recognition:** IBU. **Referee:** M. Chavannas.
Fight Summary: Defending against his stablemate, Thil (157) had a tough time of it against an opponent who knew his every move, and for round after round the pair were locked together with the champion trying to find a way through. However, in the 13th Thil finally got on top of Candel (158), as his strength prevailed. At the final bell, Thil just about deserved a share of the spoils accorded to him by the judges, but it had been close.

4 May 1935. Marcel Thil w rsc 14 (15) Vilda Jaks.
Venue: Sports Palace, Paris, France. **Recognition:** IBU. **Referee:** Jean Chavanne.
Fight Summary: Dropped in the second, the challenger got on his bike to put as much distance between himself and Thil (159) as he could. He was actually outboxing the champion round after round until dumped again in the ninth for a count of 'nine'. From then on, Jaks (158½) took a murderous beating to the body. Put down again in the 13th, Jaks was floored three more times in the penultimate session after being nailed by big overarm rights. Finally, his corner had seen enough, the referee stopping the contest after they had tossed in the towel to save their man from taking a further beating.

1 June 1935. Marcel Thil w pts 15 Ignacio Ara.
Venue: The Bullring, Madrid, Spain. **Recognition:** IBU. **Referee:** Juan Casanovas.
Fight Summary: With his IBU version of the title on the line for the seventh time, while giving Ara (159¼) another crack, Thil (158½), carrying a badly cut mouth, was on a hiding to nothing as the tough challenger took up the offensive to make things extremely difficult. Nevertheless, Thil, whose stamina was never suspect, gradually got to work on the body and in the last three sessions, although both men were exhausted, it was Ara who could barely stand. The unanimous decision in Thil's favour was a formality.

28 June 1935. Marcel Thil w pts 15 Carmelo Candel.
Venue: Roland Garros Stadium, Paris, France. **Recognition:** IBU.
Fight Summary: Often reported as a ten-round non-title contest, research by Paul Kennett proved that it involved Thil's version of the world title over 15 rounds. The fight itself saw Thil (159) winning 13 of 15 rounds on the judges' cards, with Candel (159¾), shipping an ocean of punishment and outclassed, somehow getting through to hear the final bell, mainly by holding tactics. Despite forcing throughout and administering heavy blows to head and body, Thil was only able to put Candel down once, a solid left hook to the jaw sending the latter to the boards for a count of 'eight' in the ninth session.

13 July 1935. Marcel Thil w pts 15 Kid Tunero.
Venue: Prado Arena, Marseille, France. **Recognition:** IBU. **Referee:** Roger Nicod.
Fight Summary: In what was the third fight between the pair, Thil (156¼lbs) went 2-1 ahead when outscoring Tunero (154). The L'Intransigeant newspaper report gave little details of the fight other than it was a comfortable victory for the champion and that Tunero had not shown enough aggression. Recently discovered to be a title fight by Deepak Nahar, a boxing historian, there was no mention of knockdowns or any real damage to either man.

19 September 1935. Babe Risko w pts 15 Teddy Yarosz.
Venue: Forbes Field, Pittsburgh, Pennsylvania, USA. **Recognition:** NBA/NY. **Referee:** Red Robinson.
Fight Summary: Unfortunately for Yarosz (158½) the trouble he had previously suffered with his right knee resurfaced as early as the first round of his defence against Risko (158¼), and from there onwards he was up against it. Sent to the floor in the fourth from a right to the body Yarosz got up without taking a count, but after being forced to drag his right leg along it was no surprise when he was dropped again in the sixth. Rather than quit, Yarosz fought on with the crowd right behind him. With things getting tougher by the minute for Yarosz, when Risko dropped in a heavy right followed by an overarm left he took a 'nine' count. Following that, with his leg bandaged up and supported, as the fight progressed he came a little more into it. However, without proper balance he could not take advantage of any openings and slumped to a unanimous points defeat. The press scorecard showed Yarosz winning just one round, the first, and drawing the eighth.

20 January 1936. Marcel Thil w disq 4 (15) Lou Brouillard.
Venue: Sports Palace, Paris, France. **Recognition:** IBU. **Referee:** Juan Casanovas.
Fight Summary: Having outpointed the Canadian southpaw in an overweight contest two months previously, Thil (158¾), who was more than happy to put his title on the line against the hard-hitting Brouillard (154½), appeared to be piling up the points until he was butted several times in the third round. Brouillard was quite rightly admonished by the referee, but when he laid Thil out with a body punch, adjudged to have been low, in the next session he was immediately disqualified. Although many of the bystanders felt that the blow was legal, due to the earlier warning the challenger was not given the benefit of the doubt.

10 February 1936. Babe Risko w pts 10 Tony Fisher.
Venue: Laurel Gardens, Newark, New Jersey, USA. **Recognition:** NBA/NY. **Referee:** Whitey Healey.
Scorecard: 8-1-1.
Fight Summary: Failing to add to his reputation in front of a disappointed crowd, the champion fought crudely at times, looking stiff and wild with little control. Although Risko (159¾), cut over the left eye in the third from a clash of heads, did enough to warrant the referee's decision when concentrating on the body, Fisher (159¾), not living up to expectation, took a beating throughout.

Risko's next defence would be against Freddie Steele, a hard-hitter who could also box when needed. Steele well warranted his title chance, having beaten Risko (w pts 10 at the Civic Ice Arena, Seattle, Washington on 24 March) and Fisher (w pts 10 at the same venue on 28 April) in his last two contests.

11 July 1936. Freddie Steele w pts 15 Babe Risko.
Venue: Civic Stadium, Seattle, Washington, USA. **Recognition:** NBA/NY. **Referee:** Tommy McCarthy.
Scorecards: 93-72, 92-73, 91½-71½.
Fight Summary: Starting as he meant to carry on Steele (158¾) floored Risko (158) for 'seven' in the opening round, and continued aggressively before flooring the champion again in the ninth. Although Risko took plenty of punishment, gamely sticking to his task, he was gradually getting back into the fight over the last four sessions.

1 January 1937. Freddie Steele w pts 10 Gorilla Jones.
Venue: The Auditorium, Milwaukee, Wisconsin, USA. **Recognition:** NBA/NY. **Referee:** Jim Keefe.
Scorecard: 59-41.
Fight Summary: Making his first defence Steele (157) won all but one round following what was a slow start, and in the seventh made his extra speed pay off when he dropped Jones (153) for 'three' with a cracking right hand. It was the first time that the former champion had been floored. Working away with both hands, Steele proved far too slick for his rival as he walked off with the unanimous decision.

15 February 1937. Marcel Thil w disq 6 (15) Lou Brouillard.
Venue: Sports Palace, Paris, France. **Recognition:** IBU. **Referee:** Marcel Falony.
Fight Summary: Outclassed from the start, Brouillard (157¼), fighting back wildly at times, was cautioned for butting in the third and fifth rounds, and in the sixth when he was under severe pressure from Thil (159) he was warned again. With Brouillard clearly rattled, when Thil was struck by what seemed a low blow the southpaw challenger was immediately disqualified.

Thil announced his retirement from the ring a few days later, having seen the film of the fight which proved conclusively that the punch that did the damage was above the waistline and did not merit a disqualification. However, due to his manager talking him round, with Thil's decision never made official he continued to be recognised as the champion by the IBU. In May the IBU named Kid Tunero as his outstanding challenger, giving Thil until 21 October to sign for the fight.

Apparently disinterested, Thil took on the American, Fred Apostoli, at the Polo Grounds, Manhattan, NYC, New York on 23 September, being stopped in the tenth round of a 15-rounder. Prior to the fight, in order to protect Freddie Steele, whom the NYSAC recognised as champion, the two men were asked to sign an agreement that the fight would not involve the world title despite the fact that it was contested under championship conditions.

Even though the French Boxing Federation continued to recognise Thil as the world champion until he retired on 17 February 1938, in the light of his defeat in America the IBU stripped him on 21 October. Looking to set up a competition to find a new champion, the IBU received enquiries from Tunero, Edouard Tenet, Jupp Besselmann, Angel Clivilles and Adrien Anneet. Ultimately, the IBU ignored the idea of a competition when agreeing to a fight between Besselmann, who was already contracted to meet Gustave Roth for the European light heavyweight title on 21 January 1938, and Tenet that would decide both the European and world titles.

Following his victory over Thil, the NYSAC were anxious for Apostoli and Steele to get together when calling for a meeting. The pair did get it on, albeit above the weight class, at Madison Square Garden, Manhattan, NYC on 7 January 1938, Apostoli winning by a ninth-round kayo. However, Steele continued to avoid his number one challenger, signing to meet Carmen Barth instead.

Meanwhile, Apostoli (160¼lbs) next took on Young Corbett III (159½lbs) in a catchweight contest at the Seals Stadium, San Francisco, California on 22 February 1938, losing on points over ten rounds. Following this result, Corbett III (157lbs), who was proclaimed world champion by the Californian State Boxing Commission on 25 April 1938, outpointed the 149lbs Jackie Burke over 10 rounds at The Arena, Salt Lake City, Utah on 25 May 1938. However, outside of California it mattered little as to whether either man was inside 160lbs or not. Not remaining idle, Apostoli next outpointed Glen Lee in a 15-rounder at Madison Square Garden on 1 April 1938, while awaiting a crack at Steele.

19 February 1937. Freddie Steele w pts 15 Babe Risko.
Venue: Madison Square Garden, Manhattan, NYC, New York, USA. **Recognition:** NBA/NY. **Referee:** Arthur Donovan.
Scorecards: 11-4, 11-4, 11-4.
Fight Summary: After already experiencing the power of the champion over 25 rounds, Risko (158) decided that boxing on the back foot would be the best way to deal with Steele (157). With Steele unable to get himself going early on, missing badly at times, Risko was ahead after five rounds. He had taken advantage of the situation when smashing in right-hand swings to head and body as his rival over-reached and left himself open. It was not until the sixth that Steele was able to find himself, Risko dangerously close to being knocked out, but the latter undid all his good work when getting penalised for a low blow. From the seventh through to the 14th it was all Steele as he pushed Risko back, often having him on shaky legs, but in the 15th when making one last effort the latter started to crack in hard rights and lefts to the champion's head in a vain attempt to land a kayo. Ultimately, it was far too little and too late to make any difference to the cards, the unanimous decision in favour of Steele being fully expected.

11 May 1937. Freddie Steele w co 3 (15) Frank Battaglia.
Venue: Civic Auditorium, Seattle, Washington, USA. **Recognition:** NBA/NY. **Referee:** Tommy Clark.
Fight Summary: With Steele (156) originally booked to defend his title against Ken Overlin, after the latter arrived in Seattle and was taken ill with an attack of jaundice Battaglia (159¾) was drafted in. Taking the fight to Steele, and despite being dropped for 'nine' just 31 seconds into the opening session by a left to the jaw, Battaglia really shook his man up in the second round, having him on the verge of a knockout before being dropped himself by a vicious left hook and fast right to the head. At the count of 'eight' the bell came to Battaglia's aid, but it did not stop him tearing out for the third, looking to finish Steele with one of his big rights. That was before a bombardment of blows, followed by a crushing left hook, left him flat on his face to be counted out with 34 seconds on the clock.

11 September 1937. Freddie Steele w co 4 (15) Ken Overlin.
Venue: Civic Auditorium, Seattle, Washington, USA. **Recognition:** NBA/NY. **Referee:** Tommy Clark.
Fight Summary: Having been postponed twice previously, alarm bells were going off when Overlin (160) came to the scales one and a half pounds over the weight. It then took him two attempts before he was ready to meet the champion. Not surprisingly, Overlin fought a careful battle against a noted puncher in Steele (157¼), and after taking the opening two rounds he staggered the champion with a cracking right to the body and followed it up with a solid right to the jaw just as the bell rang to end the third. It did not take Steele long to recognise the danger signs, and at the start of the fourth he took full advantage of his first real opening to hurt Overlin with a left. On following this up with another big left that dazed Overlin, two bullet-like rights saw the challenger counted out on one knee 20 seconds into the session.

On 23 November, with both Gorilla Jones and the Alabama Kid trying to get a crack at Steele, they met at the Memorial Hall, Springfield, Ohio in a billed 'black title' fight. The Kid, who had been claiming the title since the beginning of the year, won on points over ten rounds before repeating the performance on 9 June 1938 at another

Memorial Hall, this time in Dover, Ohio. Following that, the Kid packed his bags bound for Australasia where he remained for close on ten years.

19 February 1938. Freddie Steele w rsc 7 (15) Carmen Barth.
Venue: The Auditorium, Cleveland, Ohio, USA. **Recognition:** NBA/NY. **Referee:** Jim Braddock.
Fight Summary: Getting away fast, Barth (159¼) won the opening four rounds when forcing Steele (159) to cover up on several occasions from heavy left-handed attacks, and it was not until the sixth that the champion got into his stride. That session saw Barth down three times, with stiff punches from both hands doing the damage. Although fighting back gamely in the seventh, it was not long before the former Olympic champion was in trouble again, being eventually dropped for 'eight'. On rising and taking a battering, Barth was floored by a thudding right to the head, whereupon the referee came to his rescue after his corner reacted quickly by throwing the towel in on the 2.19 mark.

After Steele was stripped of his New York title in May for continuing to refuse Fred Apostoli a crack at it the latter was eventually matched against Young Corbett III to decide a new champion.

Although he had beaten Solly Krieger in a catchweight contest, Steele's next defence of the NBA version of the title would be against the hard-hitting Al Hostak. Rated at number three by *The Ring* magazine, Hostak had drawn eight and lost one of 54 since turning pro in 1932. And his last 14 fights, which had all ended inside the distance, included victories over Tony Fisher, Young Terry, Babe Risko, Allen Matthews and Swede Berglund.

7 April 1938. Edouard Tenet w rtd 12 (15) Jupp Besselmann.
Venue: Sports Palace, Berlin, Germany. **Recognition:** IBU.
Fight Summary: In a battle for the vacant IBU version of the world title, Tenet (157½) proved to be too strong, fast and clever for Besselmann (156½), and following hard-fought exchanges of hooks and swings in the early rounds he gradually got on top. Still keeping up a fast pace, the Frenchman, despite being hurt to the body, roared into the 12th session to batter Besselmann, who retired on his stool during the interval after claiming to have been hit low.

During an international Boxing Convention held in Rome in April, which was attended by many leading authorities within the sport, the IBU agreed to refuse to recognise all individually-made world champions, including their own, in an effort to stand by one universally acknowledged champion, who, in turn, would have to concede to regular defences decided by the new Federation.

19 July 1938. Young Corbett III w pts 10 Glen Lee.
Venue: Teachers' College Stadium, Fresno, California, USA. **Recognition:** California. **Referee:** Freddie Bottero.
Fight Summary: Contesting the vacant Californian version of the title, Corbett (160) used all of his ring-craft to completely bewilder Lee (156) for most of the ten rounds when taking the referee's decision by a comfortable margin. Lee was never really in it, apart from when landing three heavy overarm rights to Corbett's jaw in the third, and he was outboxed and outpunched during every session by the 33-year-old southpaw.

26 July 1938. Al Hostak w co 1 (15) Freddie Steele.
Venue: Civic Stadium, Seattle, Washington, USA. **Recognition:** NBA. **Referee:** Jack Dempsey.
Fight Summary: Right from the opening bell Hostak (158¼) looked to get his big punches off, and the fight had hardly begun when he spotted an opening to crash in a left to the jaw that dropped Steele (159) in a heap. Instead of looking to buy himself time, when Steele jumped up straight away he was knocked down twice more before being counted out after just 103 seconds, having been smashed down again by a terrific right to the jaw.

1 November 1938. Solly Krieger w pts 15 Al Hostak.
Venue: Civic Auditorium, Seattle, Washington, USA. **Recognition:** NBA. **Referee:** Rod Murphy.
Scorecards: 83-82, 88-77, 89½-75½.

Fight Summary: Making his first defence, Hostak (159¾) was defeated in a stunning upset when unable to fathom out the peculiar jumpy style of Krieger (160). In what became a hard-hitting slugfest, Hostak complained that he had broken his right hand on Krieger's head in the fourth round and badly damaged his left later on. Having made a good start, it was the fourth session that saw Hostak suddenly wilt and take a pounding from there on. Dropped in the 14th, by this time Hostak could barely see with both eyes almost closed, but he gamely made it to the final bell when the unanimous decision went against him. Hostak had been a massive betting favourite, with 17 consecutive inside-the-distance wins to his name, but in Krieger he met a durable battler of more than ten years in the ring who had never been floored.

18 November 1938. Fred Apostoli w rsc 8 (15) Young Corbett III.
Venue: Madison Square Garden, Manhattan, NYC, New York, USA. **Recognition:** NY. **Referee:** Eddie Joseph.
Fight Summary: Quickly solving the challenger's southpaw style, by the third round Apostoli (159) was hammering his man to the body and generally working him over. With this one never going to go the distance it came as no surprise when the referee stepped in to save Corbett from taking further punishment at 1.21 of the eighth round. Prior to the referee stepping in, Corbett (159½) had been decked twice in the seventh and again in the eighth when he collapsed in a neutral corner following a savage assault.

It was announced at the end of the first week of August 1939 that Apostoli would be defending his title against Ceferino Garcia. While Apostoli had taken part in seven non-title contests, losing to Billy Conn twice, Garcia had had only moved up to middleweight at the start of the year after failing to relieve Henry Armstrong of the welterweight crown. Garcia certainly warranted his opportunity, having beaten Lloyd Marshall (twice), Walter Woods and Bobby Pacho (twice) to become the leading contender.

Nate Bolden, who had recently outpointed the future champion, Tony Zale, went on to beat Oscar Rankins (w pts 12 at the White City Arena, Chicago, Illinois on 14 April 1939) in a contest billed for the 'black title'. It is not clear whether Bolden made any defences, but after being outpointed over ten rounds by Charley Burley at the Duquesne Gardens, Pittsburgh, Pennsylvania on 12 February 1940 any claim he might have had would have been meaningless.

27 June 1939. Al Hostak w rsc 4 (15) Solly Krieger.
Venue: Civic Stadium, Seattle, Washington, USA. **Recognition:** NBA. **Referee:** Jim Braddock.
Fight Summary: The champion did not seem to be the same man who took the title from Hostak the previous November, possibly because he had to steam off 18 pounds before he could make the weight. Straight from the opening bell Hostak (158¼) went looking for Krieger (160), staggering him with a crunching right to the jaw early on before going for the body in the second round in an effort to slow him down. The third session saw the beginning of the end as Hostak blasted in big punches to drop Krieger twice, the second time seeing him saved by the bell. In the fourth it was all over as Hostak hammered Krieger to the boards for 'nine' and then smashed him down again to bring the referee into play with a 46-second stoppage.

2 October 1939. Ceferino Garcia w rsc 7 (15) Fred Apostoli.
Venue: Madison Square Garden, Manhattan, NYC, New York, USA. **Recognition:** NY. **Referee:** Billy Cavanagh.
Fight Summary: Having moved up to the 160lbs weight division the challenger showed the audience that he had not lost his power when getting straight down to work to win three of the opening four rounds from Apostoli (160). Not to be denied, Apostoli came back strongly in the fifth to have Garcia (153¾) floundering around the ring from heavy blows from both hands, and he would have won the sixth had he not had a point deducted for hitting on the break. Roles were reversed when the hard-hitting Garcia leapt into action in the seventh to drop the Californian with a cracking right-handed bolo punch to the jaw. Getting up far too quickly, Apostoli was an easy target for the same blow, this time staying down for 'nine', but when he was smashed straight down again the referee called it off on the 2.07 mark with the count at 'three'. Incidentally, the bolo punch was named after the knife action for cutting down vegetation in the Philippines and could be termed as a wide, swinging uppercut.

11 December 1939. Al Hostak w co 1 (15) Erich Seelig.
Venue: The Arena, Cleveland, Ohio, USA. **Recognition:** NBA. **Referee:** Tony LaBranch.

Fight Summary: Making his first defence, Hostak (159) took in a bout of sparring before unleashing a left hook to the jaw which sent Seelig (160) sprawling for a count of 'nine'. Somehow getting to his feet Seelig was immediately met with a right-hand uppercut that dropped him heavily, and although making every effort to get up he was counted out after just 81 seconds of boxing.

Hostak's next defence would be against the rugged Tony Zale, who outpointed him in a catchweight affair over ten rounds in January 1940, a victory that was mainly due to the NBA champion injuring his left hand in the fifth after battering his man throughout up until then. Coming into the title fight Zale was ranked at number two, having recently beaten Ben Brown. A pro since 1934, he had recorded 47 wins in 64 contests and was on 11 straight.

23 December 1939. Ceferino Garcia w co 13 (15) Glen Lee.
Venue: Rizal Stadium, Manila, Philippines. **Recognition:** NY. **Referee:** Jack Dempsey.
Fight Summary: According to press reports, Lee (156) won only the first and sixth rounds while being subjected to heavy attacks, by a champion fighting on home soil, in virtually every session. He was also introduced to the bolo punch. Having cut Lee's mouth badly in the first, Garcia (152½) went on to knock him down in the fourth, the eighth and three times in the 11th. Lee was put down a further three times in the 13th, being counted out only a few seconds before the end of the session. A veritable iron man, Lee had been forced to clinch on numerous occasions in order to stem the tide of punches coming his way. It had been thought initially that the fight had been stopped, but the referee confirmed that as he had completed the count it should be recognised as a knockout win for Garcia.

1 March 1940. Ceferino Garcia drew 10 Henry Armstrong.
Venue: Gilmore Stadium, Los Angeles, California, USA. **Recognition:** California. **Referee:** George Blake.
Fight Summary: Although billed as a title fight and given Californian backing, there was no New York championship at stake as it was not supported by the NYSAC, despite them recognising Garcia as champion. There were two good reasons why that was the case: at that time, New York title bouts were of 15-rounds duration, whereas this was contested over ten stanzas, and under the rules of boxing a champion was entitled to defend at the class limit, but for this go against the welterweight king, Garcia (153½) was contracted to weigh-in at 152lbs. Having already won the world championship at 126lbs, 135lbs and 147lbs, Armstrong (142) was looking to win a title at middleweight, an unprecedented achievement if successful. In what was their second meeting, the contest went ahead despite Garcia coming in one and a half pounds over the contracted weight. With the fight under way the first round saw Garcia receive a cut on his left eye, an injury that would bother him throughout the contest. There was never much between them, every round being virtually the same, Garcia cutting loose with his heavier armoury for the opening minute or so and Armstrong picking it up from there on. After the referee had been unable to find a winner, it was really back to square one for both men. Writing in *The Ring* magazine, Nat Fleischer stated that the consensus among reporters covering the contest was that the official erred in calling it a draw. It was generally thought that Armstrong should have been given the decision.

23 May 1940. Ken Overlin w pts 15 Ceferino Garcia.
Venue: Madison Square Garden, Manhattan, NYC, New York, USA. **Recognition:** NY. **Referee:** Arthur Donovan.
Scorecards: 9-5-1, 10-5, 7-6-2.
Fight Summary: A veteran of nine years in the ring Overlin (159) was not expected to bother the champion, but in giving a clever exhibition of boxing and fighting he nullified Garcia's aggression much to the surprise of the fans. Setting his own pace, Overlin prevented Garcia (154½) from getting his famed bolo punch to work for much of the time, and it was only towards the end when tiring that blows began to get through. Even then Overlin remained cool, stabbing in sharp lefts and dancing out of range before tying Garcia up. There were no knockdowns, although Garcia was momentarily on the floor in the opening session from a left hook to the body that was ruled a slip by the referee.

19 July 1940. Tony Zale w rsc 13 (15) Al Hostak.
Venue: Civic Stadium, Seattle, Washington, USA. **Recognition:** NBA. **Referee:** Benny Leonard.
Fight Summary: Beaten by Zale (158) in an overweight match the previous January, Hostak (159¾) knew what he was up against but went out like a champion. Forcing matters all the way, Zale opened up a cut over Hostak's left

eye in the eighth before closing the other eye as he handed out a severe beating. Dropped in the 12th round, and down for a count of 'nine' in the 13th, Hostak, his left hand badly injured, was in a helpless state when the referee stopped the contest on the 1.20 mark.

With Zale having some difficulty in finding an opponent for his first defence, Sam Pian, his manager, eventually settled on Steve Mamakos, a man the champion had beaten on points in a January non-title bout. Despite losing, Mamakos had proved to be a teak-tough opponent who was sure to come forward when they met again, and although not a top-ten rated fighter he had recently beaten Sammy Luftspring (twice) and Milt Aron.

1 November 1940. Ken Overlin w pts 15 Steve Belloise.
Venue: Madison Square Garden, Manhattan, NYC, New York, USA. **Recognition:** NY. **Referee:** George Walsh.
Scorecards: 11-4, 9-6, 7-7-1.
Fight Summary: Floored twice in a dramatic sixth, the veteran champion then proceeded to outbox the hard-punching Belloise (153) for the next five sessions. Although Belloise rallied in the 12th, smashing in heavy body shots that threatened to blow Overlin away, the latter somehow made it to the final bell to win a majority decision. Many fans thought that Belloise had won clearly due to him taking many of the sessions by overwhelming margins, but under NYSAC Rules which determined the winner on a round-by-round basis it was clear that Overlin just about deserved the nod. However, such a fuss was stirred up that the pair were immediately rematched.

13 December 1940. Ken Overlin w pts 15 Steve Belloise.
Venue: Madison Square Garden, Manhattan, NYC, New York, USA. **Recognition:** NY. **Referee:** Arthur Donovan.
Scorecards: 9-4-2, 10-4-1, 4-9-2.
Fight Summary: Far from being as exciting as their previous encounter the contest was an ordinary one with Belloise (154) unable to find a punch to finish the champion off, other than hurting Overlin 158) with body blows. When Overlin came into the fight carrying a bad cold it was felt that Belloise would have too much for him, but the crafty champion confounded the critics by making his man miss time and time again. Although the two judges saw Overlin as the winner, the referee gave the fight to Belloise by nine rounds to four with two even.

Overlin's next challenger would be Billy Soose, who beat Ernie Vigh (w pts 12 at Madison Square Garden on 7 March 1941) in an official NYSAC eliminator.

21 February 1941. Tony Zale w co 14 (15) Steve Mamakos.
Venue: The Stadium, Chicago, Illinois, USA. **Recognition:** NBA. **Referee:** Tommy Gilmore.
Fight Summary: The hard-hitting champion took the opening four rounds before coming under attack in the fifth when Mamakos (157½) badly hurt him with a right to the jaw. The next two sessions saw Mamakos hit Zale (159) with everything he had, but having remained upright the latter came right back in the eighth. With the men sounding each other out with solid rights to the head by the tenth both had eye problems. Picking up the fight in the 12th Zale was never headed thereafter, and in the 13th he twice dropped the gallant Mamakos, left hooks and straight rights doing the damage. Saved by the bell, a glassy-eyed Mamakos was all at sea in the 14th prior to being dropped by a straight right in his own corner and counted out on the 26-second mark.

9 May 1941. Billy Soose w pts 15 Ken Overlin.
Venue: Madison Square Garden, Manhattan, NYC, New York, USA. **Recognition:** NY. **Referee:** Arthur Donovan.
Scorecards: 8-7, 8-7, 9-5-1.
Fight Summary: Right from the opening bell Soose (157¾) went after the cagey champion, but for eight rounds he was made to look like a novice when being hit by countering left jabs and held up. Once he had Overlin (159½) worked out, Soose did manage to connect with right hands but there was little sting in them. Although Soose hurt Overlin several times in the latter sessions, having him ready for the finisher, when he failed to follow up the chance was gone. According to Nat Fleischer, of *The Ring* magazine, Soose should have won due to him scoring more cleanly, while the judges gave it to Soose on account of his aggression.

After winning the title, Soose never defended it, mainly due to increasing weight problems, and following an eight-round technical draw against Ceferino Garcia at Gilmore Field, Los Angeles, California on 15 September, in which he weighed 169½lbs, he relinquished the title on 31 October. Soose would have just two more contests prior to retiring.

The NYSAC were now firmly behind Georgie Abrams, a three-time winner over Soose and the last man to defeat him, saying that they would support the winner of a Tony Zale v Abrams contest as the world champion.

28 May 1941. Tony Zale w co 2 (15) Al Hostak.
Venue: The Stadium, Chicago, Illinois, USA. **Recognition:** NBA. **Referee:** Johnny Behr.
Fight Summary: Making his second defence, Zale (158¾) was badly hurt in the opening round when caught by a terrific right to the jaw and sent stumbling across the ring. Although Hostak (158¼) threw everything he had he was unable to find the finisher, and Zale, showing remarkable recuperative powers, was able to last out the round. It was a different story in the second when Zale countered a Hostak left jab with a right to the kidney, dropping the latter for 'nine' before putting him down four more times prior to enforcing the count out at 2.32 of the session

28 November 1941. Tony Zale w pts 15 Georgie Abrams.
Venue: Madison Square Garden, Manhattan, NYC, New York, USA. **Recognition:** World. **Referee:** Billy Cavanagh.
Fight Summary: Seen as a fight to unify the title, the supposedly light-hitting Abrams (159) had the NBA champion down for 'nine' from a left hook to the jaw in the first round but was unable to keep him there. Once again, Zale (158¼) showed his powers of recovery when coming right back to battle Abrams all around the ring with savage body attacks, while the latter sent in solid lefts to the jaw. Although Zale was badly hurt again in the eighth he quickly recovered prior to the pair going toe-to-toe. The remaining sessions saw Abrams under fire from heavy rights under the heart, but he bravely made it to the final bell where the unanimous decision went against him. It might have been different for Abrams had he not suffered a severe injury to his right eye in the third, a bad haemorrhage of the cornea making it virtually impossible for him to pick punches up on that side.

When Zale was called up to serve in the US Navy, following an over-the-weight 12-round points defeat at the hands of the former light heavyweight champ, Billy Conn, on 13 February 1942, the title was frozen.

Later that year, two of his leading challengers, Charley Burley and Holman Williams, were matched for the unofficial 'black title' at the Victory Arena, New Orleans, Louisiana. On 14 August 1942, Burley scored a ninth-round stoppage win, while in a return on 16 October Williams outpointed his rival over 15 rounds at the Municipal Auditorium, New Orleans. The 'black title' then passed to the Cocoa Kid when he outscored Williams over 12 rounds at the Victory Arena on 15 January 1943, and that seems to be the last time it is mentioned.

Another leading black fighter, Joe Carter, topped *The Ring* magazine ratings in January 1945 before being beaten by Burley. Carter was one of several whose careers were severely hampered by the war. Other men who were included in the top five during the war years and were unable to make progress included Ossie Stewart, Ben Brown, Tony Martin and Vince Hawkins.

Apart from several Californian State title fights, which saw a succession of champions during the wartime period from Eddie Booker, Jack Chase, a future light heavyweight champion in Archie Moore, Chase (again), to Burley, no moves were made to hold a 'duration' tournament.

With Zale due to return to boxing at the beginning of 1946, the top five men in *The Ring* magazine ratings were Jake LaMotta, Williams, Burley, Rocky Graziano and Marcel Cerdan. Sometime in April 1946, and well on his way to knocking out six opponents in a warm-up period, Zale was matched to defend the title against the exciting fourth-ranked Graziano, the fight being made in the knowledge that it would be a sell-out. The wild, swinging Graziano, who had turned pro in March 1942, had won 43 (32 inside the distance) of 54 fights, drawing five and losing six. Having lost two in a row to Harold Green towards the end of 1944, Graziano began his rise to fame when knocking out Green to avenge those two defeats, as well as beating Billy Arnold, Solomon Stewart, Freddie Cochrane (twice), Al Bummy Davis, Sonny Horne and Marty Servo. Both Cochrane and Servo were reigning world welterweight champions at the time of their meetings with Graziano. Close on 40,000 fans were expected to brave the elements in order to witness a fight that promised to be a tear-up right from the opening bell.

27 September 1946. Tony Zale w co 6 (15) Rocky Graziano.
Venue: Yankee Stadium, Bronx, NYC, New York, USA. **Recognition:** World. **Referee:** Ruby Goldstein.
Fight Summary: In one of the most savage contests seen in the gloved era, the champion knocked the wild swinging Graziano (154) out at 1.43 of the sixth round. Zale (160) had been on the brink of defeat several times. Graziano, who had been knocked down for 'four' by two heavy blows to the jaw in the opening round, came right back at Zale to smash him to the floor at the end of the second session. Having been out of the ring for well over four years, when Zale came out for the third he was forced to sustain a tremendous bombardment before fighting back in the fourth despite sustaining a broken thumb. The fifth had Graziano all over Zale, and how the champion made it back to his corner still standing was remarkable as he had been belted non-stop from pillar to post. Coming out for the sixth, with all the money on Graziano to complete the job, Zale took the challenger out after landing with a heavy right under the heart and a cracking left to the temple. Graziano tried desperately to get up before the 'ten' had been called, but with his body numbed that was that.

Signed up for a return in New York on 21 March 1947 almost before the final punch was delivered, both Marcel Cerdan, the European champion, and Jake LaMotta, the outstanding contenders, would have to wait until this one got sorted.

Zale v Graziano (2) was called off after the latter was suspended in New York on 7 February 1947 for not reporting that he had been offered bribes on three separate occasions, once when up against Al Bummy Davis and twice more prior to taking on Reuben Shank. Graziano, who defeated Davis on 25 May 1945 and pulled out of the Shank fight claiming a back injury just three days before it was due to take place on 27 December 1946, told the NYSAC that he did not report the offers as he thought they were a joke. However, when the NBA decided not to accept the sentence, allowing Graziano free to box in any other State outside of New York, New Jersey, Connecticut, Michigan, Massachusetts and Pennsylvania, a fresh hunt for a new venue was on. Intended to be held at Wrigley Field, Chicago, Illinois on 16 July, it was eventually moved indoors keeping the same date.

16 July 1947. Rocky Graziano w rsc 6 (15) Tony Zale.
Venue: The Stadium, Chicago, Illinois, USA. **Recognition:** NBA. **Referee:** Johnny Behr.
Fight Summary: Up until the sixth round the champion had appeared to be in control, having cut Graziano (155¼) over the left eye in the second, dropping him in the third with a right to the jaw and punishing him severely. Coming out for the sixth Zale (159) went for the kill, but it was the snarling, wild-eyed Graziano, his right eye now almost closed, who found the blows to finish the contest. Rights after rights landed on Zale, who stumbled around the ring in a defenceless state, and when he finally dropped to the floor the referee called it off on the 2.10 mark when the count had reached 'two', mindful of the recent Sugar Ray Robinson v Jimmy Doyle world welterweight title tragedy when Doyle died shortly after the fight had ended.

Even though suspended by the NYSAC, the NBA, apparently oblivious to any other reasons why Graziano should be banned, were therefore shocked shortly after he had won the championship under their jurisdiction to find out that he had gone absent without leave during the war before being given a dishonourable discharge. In line with their own rules, the NBA were then forced to release a statement saying that they rejected any participant in boxing who had not fulfilled his trust to his country. However, following a favourable poll among associated NBA States, with the NYSAC still sitting on the sidelines, the third Graziano v Zale fight was eventually accepted by New Jersey.

Meantime, other men lining up for a crack at the title who were in the top five, included the likes of Cecil Hudson, Jake LaMotta, Bert Lytell and Marcel Cerdan, the European champion. Hudson beat LaMotta but then went on a losing run, while the latter lost to Billy Fox in a fight that would become infamous down the years. It was Lytell, having seen off Watson Jones, Major Jones and Jackie Darthard, who was given the number one slot in *The Ring* magazine ratings after Cerdan lost his European title to Cyrille Delannoit on points over 15 rounds at the Heysel Stadium, Brussels, Belgium on 23 May 1948. Ultimately, that came to nothing when Lytell was beaten by Charley Doc Williams.

10 June 1948. Tony Zale w co 3 (15) Rocky Graziano.
Venue: Ruppert Stadium, Newark, New Jersey, USA. **Recognition:** NBA. **Referee:** Paul Cavalier.
Fight Summary: Making a great start, Zale (158¾) had the champion over in the middle of the opening round after a cracking left hook had done the damage before having to withstand a battery of blows coming his way in the second. Although badly hurt at times Zale regrouped to come back strongly in the third. From the moment a powerful straight left had Graziano (158½) reeling there was no way back and, after being belted from head to body non-stop, a right to the jaw had him down for 'seven'. On rising, Graziano was quickly set upon, a solid right to the jaw eventually sending him down to be counted out at 1.08 of the session. Following his victory, Zale was quickly recognised by the NYSAC as the champion.

Having regained the title, Zale was contracted to meet the winner of the European title fight between Marcel Cerdan and Cyrille Delannoit within six months. Cerdan, who beat Delannoit (w pts 15 at the Sports Palace, Brussels, Belgium on 10 July), had been knocking on the middleweight door for several years and was a welcome challenger. Prior to meeting Zale, Cerdan had run up 111 contests with just three defeats, having beaten many good men including Omar Kouidri (six times), Eddie Ran, Cleto Locatelli (twice), Gustave Humery (twice), Al Baker (twice), Saverio Turiello (twice), Felix Wouters, Larry Cisneros (twice), Joe DiMartino, Edouard Tenet (twice), Assane Diouf, Robert Charron, Holman Williams, Georgie Abrams, Harold Green, Anton Raadik, Giovanni Manca and Laverne Roach, just to name a few.

21 September 1948. Marcel Cerdan w rtd 12 (15) Tony Zale.
Venue: Roosevelt Stadium, Jersey City, New Jersey, USA. **Recognition:** World. **Referee:** Paul Cavalier.
Fight Summary: Although the champion was in the fight for several rounds, especially the fourth, it was clear that after the seventh it was a lost cause as Cerdan's body punches began to take their toll. Showing plenty of skill, allied to effective blows from head to body, Cerdan (158) was gradually wearing Zale (159) out, and in the 11th he had the latter all over the place before dropping him with a left-right to the jaw. Saved by the bell, Zale was helped back to his corner and retired. Under New Jersey rules a fighter could only be retired during the round, so it was the 12th rather than the 11th that the fight was officially over.

After buying himself out of his managerial contract, back in Europe Cerdan had warm-up bouts against Dick Turpin, the British champion, and Lucien Krawczyk before flying out to America where he was obligated to meet Zale in a return. Meanwhile, the New York promoters were trying to buy Zale, who was on the verge of retirement, out of his contract to allow Cerdan to defend against Jake LaMotta or Steve Belloise. Eventually an agreement was reached for Cerdan to meet LaMotta in Detroit, Michigan in June 1949.

A veteran of 72 wins in 88 fights, years later LaMotta admitted that he had taken a dive against Billy Fox in order to obtain himself a crack at the middleweight title. Despite losing four times to Sugar Ray Robinson, LaMotta had been the first man to beat the great man. Other rated men he had beaten included Henry Chmielewski, Jimmy Edgar (twice), California Jackie Wilson, Jimmy Reeves, Fritzie Zivic (three times), Coley Welch, George Costner, Bert Lytell, Jose Basora (twice), George Kochan (three times), Walter Woods, Holman Williams, Anton Raadik, Tommy Bell (three times), Tony Janiro, Johnny Colan, Tommy Yarosz, Robert Villemain, O'Neill Bell (twice) and Joey DeJohn.

16 June 1949. Jake LaMotta w rtd 10 (15) Marcel Cerdan.
Venue: Briggs Stadium, Detroit, Michigan, USA. **Recognition:** World. **Referee:** Johnny Weber.
Fight Summary: Outfought in every department, body punches sickening him, from the fourth onwards the champion was unable to throw punches with any effect due to torn ligaments in his left shoulder. Cerdan (159½) had won just one session, the second, and was at the mercy of LaMotta (158½), despite the latter having injured his left hand in the fifth, before slumping on to his stool at the end of the ninth. He had been blasted from head to body in that round, Nat Fleischer, of *The Ring* magazine, counting 104 blows that were not returned. Once it was clear that the referee was not going to stop the fight the Frenchman was retired after the bell rang to start the tenth. Blaming his injury on being pushed to the floor in the first round, when Cerdan stated that he would be back the return was made for 28 September.

Then tragedy struck. After the fight had been moved on to 2 December due to LaMotta suffering a shoulder injury in training, Cerdan was killed in a plane crash over the Azores on 27 October while on his way to America.

It was then agreed that LaMotta would meet Robert Villemain in a non-title contest at Madison Square Garden, Manhattan, NYC on 9 December as long as he signed up to defend his title by March 1950. Villemain won the ten-round points decision, but by the end of December the NYSAC were forced to warn LaMotta that if he did not sign for a title defence by 1 February 1950 he would be stripped. Although LaMotta signed up to defend his title in March 1950, New York's International Boxing Club had an agreement that the champion could make an open-air defence in the summer.

By now, Sugar Ray Robinson was recognised as the outstanding challenger, having recently beaten Steve Belloise (w co 7 at the Yankee Stadium, Bronx, NYC, New York on 24 August) in an eliminating bout, but it would be Rocky Graziano who was selected by LaMotta for a 28 June 1950 title fight. In May 1950, following LaMotta's inability to sign for a defence against Robinson, the Pennsylvanian Boxing Commission decided to match the welterweight champion against Villemain for their version of the title.

Meanwhile, Graziano suffered a fractured left thumb at the beginning of June 1950 and had to withdraw from the LaMotta fight, his place being taken by Tiberio Mitri, the European champion, with the date being moved on two weeks. Mitri was already in America, having outpointed Dick Wagner at Madison Square Garden on 19 May 1950, and was ready and willing. A clever boxer who lacked real power, Mitri had lost just once in 52 contests, turning back men such as Jean Stock (twice), Giovanni Manca, Laurent Dauthuille, Dick Turpin and Cyrille Delannoit.

5 June 1950. Sugar Ray Robinson w pts 15 Robert Villemain.
Venue: Municipal Stadium, Philadelphia, Pennsylvania, USA. **Recognition:** Pennsylvania. **Referee:** Charles Daggert.
Scorecards: 12-3, 12-3, 10-5.
Fight Summary: Despite not being in distress at any time and finishing the contest unmarked, the stocky, bobbing-and-weaving Villemain (159½) was as good as outclassed by Robinson (155) in their battle for the vacant Pennsylvanian version of the title. Forcing the action from the start, Villemain, who was dropped in the 12th for 'two', was continually caught by jabs and hooks as Robinson eased his way through the contest. That it went the distance was down to the Frenchman's ruggedness.

12 July 1950. Jake LaMotta w pts 15 Tiberio Mitri.
Venue: Madison Square Garden, Manhattan, NYC, New York, USA. **Recognition:** NBA/NY. **Referee:** Mark Conn.
Scorecards: 8-7, 12-3, 9-6.
Fight Summary: Absorbing punishment without flinching, Mitri (159), who had no defence to the straight left, bravely stayed with the champion despite not carrying a stopping punch. The Italian, who blamed his lack of power on a broken right hand suffered in the first round, surprised many when winning two of the last five sessions, but it was always LaMotta's fight. Right from the opening bell it was clear that LaMotta (159) was not going to use his normal rough style, and at the same time it quickly became apparent that his change of tactics had completely flummoxed Mitri.

25 August 1950. Sugar Ray Robinson w co 1 (15) Jose Basora.
Venue: The Stadium, Scranton, Pennsylvania, USA. **Recognition:** Pennsylvania. **Referee:** Johnny Kelly.
Fight Summary: Making the first defence of the Pennsylvanian version of the world title, Robinson (154¾) made quick work of Basora (159¾) after setting up an immediate attack from the opening bell. Dropped twice, the second time for 'nine, with Basora being an open target a couple of left hooks followed by a solid right to the head saw him counted out with just 52 seconds on the clock.

Carl Bobo Olson would be Robinson's next opponent. Rated at number ten by *The Ring* magazine, Olson had won 41 of 44 contests, losing only to George Duke and Boy Brooks, which were reversed, and Dave Sands, the sensational Australian. A pressure fighter with stamina to spare and good punching ability he had beaten Bobby Jones, Anton Raadik, Tommy Yarosz, Milo Savage, Earl Turner and Henry Brimm before getting the chance to meet Robinson.

13 September 1950. Jake LaMotta w co 15 (15) Laurent Dauthuille.
Venue: Olympia, Detroit, Michigan, USA. **Recognition:** NBA/NY. **Referee:** Lou Handler.
Fight Summary: The NBA only gave their agreement to this fight on the grounds that if he won LaMotta had to meet Sugar Ray Robinson by the end of February 1951. In one of the most amazing finishes of all time, Dauthuille (160), who was way out in front on all three scorecards, was knocked out by the champion with just 13 seconds left on the clock. The Frenchman had already beaten LaMotta on points over ten rounds early in 1949, and apart from the 12th, 13th and 15th he was the champion's master. With LaMotta failing to crowd Dauthuille, especially after cutting both of the Frenchman's eyes, it was only when he kidded his rival into taking up the gauntlet in the last few sessions that he had any success. Just when it was certain that Dauthuille was going to win, LaMotta, who blamed his earlier lack of aggression on an injury to his right hand, suddenly found a terrific left hook to the body. Then, after setting up a heavy-handed attack, another left hook put the Frenchman down and out.

26 October 1950. Sugar Ray Robinson w co 12 (15) Carl Bobo Olson.
Venue: Convention Hall, Philadelphia, Pennsylvania, USA. **Recognition:** Pennsylvania. **Referee:** Charles Daggert.
Fight Summary: Setting himself up for a contest with Jake LaMotta for the universally recognised title, Robinson (158) successfully defended the Pennsylvanian version of the championship when knocking out Olson (159) on the 1.19 mark in round 12. Although Olson was not in Robinson's class he plugged away despite lacking the speed with which to put the latter under pressure, and prior to the 11th round he had probably shared just two sessions. In the 11th, Robinson, who had been happy to pile up points from long range, had a round taken away for inadvertently going low, but in the 12th he stepped up the pace with stunning consequences for Olson. Having smashed in a terrific left to Olson's jaw, as the latter was sagging Robinson drove in a tremendous right to the body that brought the contest to a conclusion.

With Robinson already on his way to Europe for a series of five contests between 27 November and 25 December, it was announced in November that a unification fight with Jake LaMotta had been made for February. Back in the States after beating Jean Stock, Luc Van Dam, Jean Walzack, Robert Villemain and Hans Stretz, Robinson was made the clear favourite to defeat LaMotta, having won four of their five previous contests.

14 February 1951. Sugar Ray Robinson w rsc 13 (15) Jake LaMotta.
Venue: The Stadium, Chicago, Illinois, USA. **Recognition:** World. **Referee:** Frank Sikora.
Fight Summary: In what was their sixth meeting, Robinson (155½) scored a decisive win over LaMotta (160) to unify the title after the latter, displaying all of his bulldog spirit, had gone well during the opening ten rounds. All of that time Robinson had been in control without being able to take risks, but when LaMotta suddenly weakened in the 12th the 'Sugarman' seized his opportunity. Lashing in punches to both head and body, Robinson landed 56 heavy blows to nine in return, none of which were of any consequence according to *The Ring* magazine, and in the 13th it was more of the same. With LaMotta spread-eagled against the ropes and helpless, his face a terrible mess, he was finally taken out of his misery by the referee on the 2.04 mark.

It was announced by the British promoter, Jack Solomons, in early June that Robinson, currently in the midst of a European tour, would be defending his title against Randy Turpin before making for home. Although he beat Kid Marcel, Jean Wanes, Jan De Bruin, Jean Walzack, Gerhard Hecht and Cyrille Delannoit, the tour was not without hitch, as he was initially disqualified for decking Hecht with kidney punches before the decision was reversed to that of no contest.

Not given much chance of beating Robinson by the British press, Turpin was considered to be too raw and untested at that level. That aside, the brother of Dick Turpin, the former British and British Empire middleweight champion, had run up 40 wins in 43 fights, reversed two defeats at the hands of Albert Finch and Jean Stock, and had become the British and European champion. Extremely heavy-handed and strong, only nine of his victims had managed to stay the course. Along the way he had defeated Vince Hawkins, Doug Miller, Delannoit, Pete Mead, Tommy Yarosz, Billy Brown, Jackie Keough, Luc Van Dam and De Bruin, the last two in European title fights.

10 July 1951. Randy Turpin w pts 15 Sugar Ray Robinson.
Venue: Exhibition Centre, Earls Court, London, England. **Recognition:** World. **Referee:** Eugene Henderson.

Fight Summary: Having had eight contests since winning the title, six of them in Europe, Robinson (154½) was the victim of one of boxing's biggest shocks when coming up against Turpin (158¾). Carrying the fight to Robinson from the opening bell Turpin never let up, consistently using the straight left with power and accuracy to find the target while outpunching his man in the clinches. It was quickly apparent that Turpin was the stronger of the pair, being able to push Robinson about in the clinches, which embarrassed the champion. What was also noticeable was the fact that when the two started letting the punches go it was almost always Robinson who broke off first. From the halfway stage as Robinson began to tire it became clear to the onlookers that Turpin, barring an accident, was on his way to one of the most famous victories seen in a British ring. When the referee lifted his arm at the final bell the crowd nearly brought the roof down when singing "For He's a Jolly Good Fellow".

12 September 1951. Sugar Ray Robinson w rsc 10 (15) Randy Turpin.
Venue: Polo Grounds, Manhattan, NYC, New York, USA. **Recognition:** World. **Referee:** Ruby Goldstein.
Fight Summary: The champion made a reasonable start, even overcoming a bad second round when Robinson (157½) almost sent him crashing from a short right to the jaw. Although only drawing one of the opening four sessions, Turpin (159) came right back in the fifth. Coming into the tenth the two fighters were even on points, with Turpin looking to be the stronger. The tide turned in that round after Robinson went berserk on being badly cut over the left eye. Bowled over by a crashing right counter the Englishman got up at 'nine', but instead of taking a breather by going down again he allowed Robinson to fire in punch after punch to head and body as he swayed back and forth against the ropes. With nothing coming back from Turpin the referee jumped between them with just eight seconds of the round remaining. Turpin's title reign had lasted just 64 days, a record for the division.

Towards the end of the year the Australian-born British Empire champion, Dave Sands, was rated the number two challenger to Robinson (one place behind Turpin), having won 19 straight with victories over Robert Villemain, Pete Mead and Carl Bobo Olson (twice). It seemed that all he had to do was to beat a young inexperienced Yolande Pompey at catchweights and a match with Turpin for the right to fight Robinson would be the next step. Unfortunately for Sands, when Pompey picked up a seventh-round stoppage win at The Arena, Harringay, London on 13 November, it was the unrated Olson who went on to meet Robinson. Sands never did get a world title shot, being killed in a tragic road accident just four contests later.

13 March 1952. Sugar Ray Robinson w pts 15 Carl Bobo Olson.
Venue: Civic Auditorium, San Francisco, California, USA. **Recognition:** World. **Referee:** Jack Downey.
Scorecards: 86½-79½, 84½-80 ½, 85½-79½.
Fight Summary: Inactive for six months, when the champion started to tire after the sixth round Olson (159½) came more and more into the fight as he took everything thrown at him. After starting strongly, boxing quite brilliantly at times, Robinson (157½) began to come under pressure from steady body attacks, and it was not until the 11th that he rallied as Olson showed signs of the fast pace he had set. Although Olson made a good showing in the 14th, the final session was all Robinson as he banged in vicious barrages to head and body.

16 April 1952. Sugar Ray Robinson w co 3 (15) Rocky Graziano.
Venue: The Stadium, Chicago, Illinois, USA. **Recognition:** World. **Referee:** Tommy Gilmore.
Fight Summary: A tough, hard-hitting affair while it lasted, the champion ultimately came through as Graziano (159¾) ran out of ideas in the third round. Swinging wildly, Graziano even had Robinson (157¼) over in the third despite the referee not calling it, but following this it was all one-way traffic. Stepping up the pace, Robinson went straight after Graziano, whipping in blows to head and body, and when the latter was opened up by a left to the body he was sent down for the count, timed at 1.53, following a solid right to the jaw.

After failing gallantly to take the light heavyweight crown from Joey Maxim at the Yankee Stadium, Bronx, NYC, New York on 25 June, Robinson relinquished his title on announcing his retirement in December. Following that, it was agreed by the NBA and the NYSAC that the winner of a series of eliminating bouts to decide the American championship should fight the victor of a European title bout between Randy Turpin and Charles Humez for the vacant crown. Initially, Carl Bobo Olson, Ernie Durando and Rocky Castellani were decided upon, but the choices created howls of protests regards to the latter two. The immediate response saw several top American fighters demanding admittance to the tournament. Also, the Olson camp argued that as the leading American he should not have to fight an eliminator. Ultimately, Olson backed down. Since losing to Robinson, Olson was unbeaten in nine contests, whipping the likes of Walter Cartier, Jimmy Beau, Robert Villemain, Gene Hairston, Lee Sala, Norman Hayes (twice) and Garth Panter.

With time now of the essence, the NBA and NYSAC went back to the drawing board and selected Paddy Young to meet Durando, the winner to tangle with Olson. With that settled, on 27 March 1953 Young outscored Durando over 12 rounds at Madison Square Garden, Manhattan, NYC, New York. He then went on to meet Olson to decide the American title at the same venue on 19 June 1953, losing on points over 15 rounds.

However, while all that was going on the British Boxing Board of Control (BBBoC), not supported by the EBU, stated that it would recognise the winner of the Turpin v Humez fight as world champion prior to taking on the new American titleholder.

9 June 1953. Randy Turpin w pts 15 Charles Humez.
Venue: White City Stadium, Shepherds Bush, London, England. **Recognition:** GB. **Referee:** Andrew Smythe.
Fight Summary: Fighting in safety-first mode it was not a vintage performance by Turpin (160), but he had far too much for the tough, courageous Humez (159½) in a contest that saw him win the British version of the world title. Several times throughout the contest, Turpin hurt Humez badly, and even in the 11th when he had the Frenchman over from a left hook he allowed his man to recover. Despite all of that, Turpin, who claimed afterwards that he had jarred his right in the opening session, won virtually every round on his way to the referee's decision.

21 October 1953. Carl Bobo Olson w pts 15 Randy Turpin.
Venue: Madison Square Garden, Manhattan, NYC, New York, USA. **Recognition:** World. **Referee:** Al Berl.
Scorecards: 9-4-2, 11-4, 8-7.
Fight Summary: In a contest to unify the title, Olson (159½) beat Turpin (157) after the Englishman had made a good start and looked to be on his way to victory. Unfortunately for Turpin he seemed to go to pieces after the third round when allowing the fast-punching Olson to crowd him out and take the initiative from thereon in. Once Olson realised that Turpin was content to cover up he just plastered him with blows from all angles, and in the ninth and tenth had his rival down and almost out. Turpin, to his credit, weathered the storm, even coming back strongly in the 12th, but it was all too little and too late to make a difference.

2 April 1954. Carl Bobo Olson w pts 15 Kid Gavilan.
Venue: The Stadium, Chicago, Illinois, USA. **Recognition:** World. **Referee:** Bernard Weissman.
Scorecards: 147-141, 147-139, 144-144.
Fight Summary: Making his first defence against the welterweight champion, while Olson (159½) was hardly ever in trouble against Gavilan (155) there was never much between them. Gavilan had kept clear of Olson in the opening three rounds, but thereafter found the going tougher as the latter opened up with blows from head to body. Regardless, Gavilan, cut over the right eye in the ninth, while showing clever ring-craft was unable to find the punch that would hurt his rival. Afterwards, Gavilan stated that his right hand had been injured in the run-up to the fight.

20 August 1954. Carl Bobo Olson w pts 15 Rocky Castellani.
Venue: Cow Palace, San Francisco, California, USA. **Recognition:** World. **Referee:** Ray Flores.
Scorecards: 87½-77½, 84-80, 89-76.
Fight Summary: When the champion initially failed the weight at the official weigh-in, Castellani's manager tried to claim the title for him but was overruled by the chairman of the Californian Boxing Commission. Olson (160) was then allowed two hours to get the extra eight ounces off. It did not seem to worry Olson, who stalked and punished Castellani (160) from the opening bell. Despite this, Castellani fought hard and proved to be an excellent counter-puncher, often catching Olson on the way in. In the 11th he put Olson down for 'three'. However, on getting up the latter went after his man, and in the 12th following a furious body attack Castellani was dropped for 'nine' by a hard right to the jaw. Having fractured a bone in his left hand, although Castellani tried to get back he was never in the fight from thereon in.

15 December 1954. Carl Bobo Olson w rsc 11 (15) Pierre Langlois.
Venue: Cow Palace, San Francisco, California, USA. **Recognition:** World. **Referee:** Ray Flores.
Fight Summary: Getting away fast, the champion kept flicking his left into the Frenchman's face before moving out of range of solid right uppercuts. By the fourth round the pace had heated up as both men looked to get their pet punches off, with Olson (159½) working well on the inside and Langlois (157¾) boxing well on the counter while looking to score heavily with uppercuts. After being cut over the left eye in the sixth Langlois' work became ragged as Olson stepped it up, but he continued to make the fight competitive. However, with Langlois' eye damage worsening the referee brought the fight to a halt after 58 seconds of the 11th had elapsed, having consulted the ringside doctor.

Given until 11 June 1955 to defend his title, Olson was allowed more time by the authorities after defeating the former light heavyweight champ, Joey Maxim, in order to challenge Archie Moore for the light heavyweight crown on 22 June 1955.

Earlier, on 20 October 1954, Sugar Ray Robinson announced he was returning to the ring, and despite losing to Ralph Tiger Jones in his second comeback fight he beat Rocky Castellani (w pts 10 at the Cow Palace on 22 July 1955) in what was loosely termed an eliminator to set up a fight with Olson, who had been knocked out in the third round against Moore. When the Olson v Robinson fight was made, supported by the NYSAC, Charles Humez, the European champion, was the number one challenger, but the NBA who should have supported his claim were strangely silent.

Following a ten-round points win over Gene Fullmer in November 1955, Eduardo Lausse, a hard-hitting Argentine, looked as though he was on his way to a title shot after moving up *The Ring* magazine ratings into third spot. Having already beaten Aldo Minelli, Jimmy Beau (twice), Chico Varona, Joe Rindone, Georgie Small, Ralph Tiger Jones and Kid Gavilan he had plenty of pedigree. Somewhat surprisingly, a draw against Milo Savage followed by three defeats in his next five contests, against Bobby Boyd and Andres Antonio Selpa (twice), saw him fall away before retiring just nine fights later.

9 December 1955. Sugar Ray Robinson w co 2 (15) Carl Bobo Olson.
Venue: The Stadium, Chicago, Illinois, USA. **Recognition:** World. **Referee:** Frank Sikora.
Fight Summary: Back in business after two and a half years out of the ring and seven comeback fights, Robinson (159¾) quickly made his mark after a quiet opening round. Following a few brief flurries by the champion, when Robinson stepped in with a left to the body, before Olson (159¼) could pull himself together, he was sent crashing from a right uppercut. Although Olson began to move he was counted out with just nine seconds of the second round remaining.

18 May 1956. Sugar Ray Robinson w co 4 (15) Carl Bobo Olson.
Venue: Wrigley Field, Los Angeles, California, USA. **Recognition:** World. **Referee:** Mushy Callahan.
Fight Summary: Proving his win over Olson (160) last time out was no fluke the champion once again took the latter out, albeit it took a couple of rounds longer. The first three sessions saw little action, although it was clearly noticeable that Robinson was setting the pace with accurate punches from both hands while Olson was trying to work inside. In the fourth Olson took the initiative for the first time, but following a clinch he was put down heavily to be counted out on the 2.51 mark after a left-right to the jaw had almost lifted him into the air.

It took three months of hard negotiation before Robinson could be induced to meet Gene Fullmer, who had recently eliminated Rocky Castellani (w pts 10 at The Arena, Cleveland, Ohio on 4 January), Ralph Tiger Jones (w pts 10 at the Public Hall, Cleveland, Ohio on 20 January) and Charles Humez (w pts 10 at Madison Square Garden, Manhattan, NYC, New York on 25 May) to head *The Ring* magazine ratings. Fullmer also had wins over Garth Panter, Jackie LaBua, Peter Mueller, Paul Pender, Gil Turner (twice), Del Flanagan, Al Andrews and Moses Ward to his credit. In 40 contests he had won 37, losing to Turner, Bobby Boyd and Eduardo Lausse.

Robinson had earlier said he would never fight for the International Boxing Club again due to their miserly purses, but a return clause with 47½% of the gate and 60% of TV revenue persuaded him to change his mind. Scheduled for 12 December in Madison Square Garden a week or so before the fight was due, when Robinson pulled out suffering a heavy cold the date was moved to 2 January 1957.

2 January 1957. Gene Fullmer w pts 15 Sugar Ray Robinson.
Venue: Madison Square Garden, Manhattan, NYC, New York, USA. **Recognition:** World. **Referee:** Ruby Goldstein.
Scorecards: 8-5-2, 10-5, 9-6.
Fight Summary: Having failed to knock Fullmer (157¼) out early the champion started to box on the back foot, sending in jabs and clips to the head whenever he could. It was apparent that Fullmer wanted to come off the leash once his manager had given him the go-ahead, and in the seventh he dropped Robinson (160) for 'six' after connecting with a right and left to the body. Twice the bottom rope had to be repaired, which did not help the fighters' concentration. Although Robinson improved in the ninth he was almost spent, the last five sessions seeing Fullmer extend his lead when climbing all over him at times. However, unable to put Robinson down again he had to settle for the points win.

1 May 1957. Sugar Ray Robinson w co 5 (15) Gene Fullmer.
Venue: The Stadium, Chicago, Illinois, USA. **Recognition:** World. **Referee:** Frank Sikora.
Fight Summary: Putting their last fight behind him, Robinson (159½) regained the title for the fourth time in his career when knocking the champion out at 1.27 of the fifth round. At that point Fullmer (159¾) was just in front with Robinson seemingly tiring, but had been badly caught by a jarring combination of punches in the fourth. That should have served as a warning. However, instead of being more cautious Fullmer came out on the attack, but after running into two solid rights to the body and a cracking left hook to the jaw he was sent down heavily to the canvas where he was counted out on the 1.27 mark.

23 September 1957. Carmen Basilio w pts 15 Sugar Ray Robinson.
Venue: Yankee Stadium, Bronx, NYC, New York, USA. **Recognition:** World. **Referee:** Al Berl.
Scorecards: 9-5-1, 8-6-1, 6-9.
Fight Summary: Despite coming into the fight as the reigning welterweight champion, Basilio (153½) was not given a great chance by the press, who although recognising that Robinson (160) had gone back a fair bit did not expect him to lose his title. It turned out to be one of the best fights of the year, as Basilio worked the champion all over while taking everything that came his way. Basilio, cut over the left eye early on, refused to give ground as Robinson, with his longer reach, smacked in jab after jab, and as the fight drew to a close it was still uncertain as to who would win. In the 12th, the weary Robinson rained in punch after punch on Basilio to send him hurtling back across the ring, but the latter came back strongly, the last three sessions seeing them going blow-for-blow until the final bell.

25 March 1958. Sugar Ray Robinson w pts 15 Carmen Basilio.
Venue: The Stadium, Chicago, Illinois, USA. **Recognition:** World. **Referee:** Frank Sikora.
Scorecards: 71-64, 72-65, 66-69.
Fight Summary: The first five rounds were very much in favour of the champion, who again attacked the body before Robinson (159¾) began to get up a head of steam in the sixth. Picking his punches carefully he opened up a bad cut over his rival's left eye, but while scoring well he was badly hurt at times when Basilio (153) got through. Although rocked in the tenth, Robinson came out strongly to force the fight all the way to the finishing post. Regardless of that, when unable to knock the gallant Basilio over he had to settle for the points that enabled him to regain the title for the fifth time.

In 1959, having remained inactive for over a year, and been given a deadline by the NBA to sign for a defence against Basilio by 25 April, Robinson ignored the edict and was stripped at the beginning of May. At that juncture, the NBA declared the championship vacant, matching Basilio with Gene Fullmer for their version of the title, while the NYSAC stated that as far as they were concerned Robinson had until 15 May to sign. George Gainford, Robinson's manager, had recently announced that the champion would meet Basilio on 21 September, but admitted nothing had been signed. At the end of May, Basilio still had not signed to meet either Robinson or Fullmer, leaving the authorities guessing. While Robinson was saying Basilio did not want to fight him again, the latter retorted that he had spent 14 months negotiating with the champion to no avail. When Basilio was said to be looking for a match with Fullmer to decide the NBA title, the NYSAC said they stood by Robinson as they had proof that he had signed for a defence against Basilio. With Massachusetts, having recently left the NBA, supporting the NYSAC, there had been talk that Robinson would meet Paul Pender, who barely made the top ten, and this came to fruition in early August when it was announced the two men would meet on 15 December in Boston. However, with Robinson needing a warm-up fight, not having boxed for more than 18 months, the date was eventually pushed into January 1960.

28 August 1959. Gene Fullmer w rsc 14 (15) Carmen Basilio.
Venue: Cow Palace, San Francisco, California, USA. **Recognition:** NBA. **Referee:** Jack Downey.
Fight Summary: Contesting the vacant NBA title, Fullmer (159½) ultimately proved to be stronger than Basilio (156), who was eventually pulled out of the contest by the referee in the 14th after his corner had asked the third man to stop the fight 36 seconds into the session. Fighting in an unusual fashion, for the first eight rounds Fullmer would retreat to the ropes before catching Basilio coming in. From the ninth, however, Fullmer made the running, switching his attacks from head to body, and by the 13th he had his man well under control. It was all Fullmer in the 14th. After a crashing right had sent Basilio into the ropes, with the latter desperately trying to remain upright under a torrent of punches, time was called.

With the NBA committing the winner to meet Spider Webb within 90 days or face being stripped contracts were signed fairly quickly. Fullmer had already posted a victory over Webb before he won the title, but the latter was now the leading challenger, having won 33 of 37 contests. Webb's victims included Jimmy Martinez (twice), Bobby Boyd (twice), Holly Mims, Rory Calhoun (twice), Charley Cotton, Pat McAteer, Neal Rivers (twice), Wilf Greaves, Randy Sandy, Charley Joseph, Willie Vaughn, Jimmy Beecham, Dick Tiger, Franz Szuzina, Joey Giardello and Terry Downes, all good men. Fast moving with classy skills and a sharp puncher to boot, Webb relished the opportunity to get back into the ring with Fullmer, especially with the title at stake.

4 December 1959. Gene Fullmer w pts 15 Spider Webb.
Venue: George Nelson Fieldhouse, Logan, Utah, USA. **Recognition:** NBA. **Referee:** Ken Shulsen.
Scorecards: 148-136, 150-132, 147-141.
Fight Summary: Pushing Webb (157¾) back in the first part of the fight worked well for the champion, who had his man in trouble in the third before slipping over in the fourth when hit by a solid right cross. In the middle rounds Webb began to slip Fullmer's leads, making him look ungainly at times, but the latter came back strongly, especially in the ninth when scoring with heavy punches to the head. Several even rounds were followed by Webb forcing Fullmer (159¾) to backtrack in the 13th, but after an even 14th Fullmer staged a grandstand finish to make sure of the decision. Webb, who inflicted damage to both of Fullmer's eyes, felt that the fight was much closer than the scores suggested and demanded a rematch.

22 January 1960. Paul Pender w pts 15 Sugar Ray Robinson.
Venue: The Garden, Boston, Massachusetts, USA. **Recognition:** EBU/NY. **Referee:** Joe Zapustas.
Scorecards: 147-138, 148-142, 142-146.
Fight Summary: In what was a huge upset, Pender (159¾) relieved Robinson (159¼) of his title when he allowed the latter to do all the work for the first seven rounds. With Robinson beginning to tire Pender made his move in the eighth, and despite being cut over left eye in the ninth he began to open up with rights and lefts to the chin that slowed the champion down even more. Dominating the rest of the contest, often landing three-punch combinations to the head, Pender took his fight record to 36 wins in 43 contests on receiving the decision.

20 April 1960. Gene Fullmer drew 15 Joey Giardello.
Venue: State College Fieldhouse, Bozeman, Montana, USA. **Recognition:** NBA. **Referee:** Harry Kessler.
Scorecards: 145-142, 142-144, 145-145.
Fight Summary: There was plenty of action in this one despite a lack of knockdowns. It was certainly rough, Fullmer (160) being warned for butting in the third and Giardello (158¼) in the fourth. The fight soon developed into an all-out war as the men went head-to-head for long periods, and while Fullmer looked to attack the body Giardello went for the head. At the final bell both men carried the signs of battle, Fullmer having five stitches to repair left eye damage and Giardello suffering from abrasions and cuts around both eyes.

433

10 June 1960. Paul Pender w pts 15 Sugar Ray Robinson.
Venue: The Garden, Boston, Massachusetts, USA. **Recognition:** EBU/NY. **Referee:** Jim McCarron.
Scorecards: 149-138, 147-142, 144-146.
Fight Summary: Just as before, the fight followed the same pattern, with Robinson (158½) trying to knock Pender (160) out early and the latter biding his time as the former champion faded. Robinson gave it everything at the start, tearing into Pender and cutting his left eye in the second while he looked for the punch that could settle matters. One thing for sure, Pender proved his durability in sustaining these attacks, and from the sixth onwards he jabbed incessantly with the left as he dodged Robinson's attacks, which became more sporadic as time went on. Towards the end, Robinson looked all of his 39 years, his punches having no sting in them while his legs looked likely to give way on him. Even though he desperately tried to turn things around in the 15th it was clear that he had nothing left on the clock.

29 June 1960. Gene Fullmer w rsc 12 (15) Carmen Basilio.
Venue: Derks Field, Salt Lake City, Utah, USA. **Recognition:** NBA. **Referee:** Pete Giacoma.
Fight Summary: Fighting much the same as he did the last time, the champion used his reach to keep Basilio (156½) at bay before countering to head or body. In the sixth both men sustained cuts, and in the eighth Basilio was nearly dropped by two heavy blows to the head before a left hook saw him turn a complete somersault. The referee failed to rule it a knockdown. Although Basilio had a good tenth, Fullmer (159¼) was now on the move, throwing punches from both hands. And in the 12th after catching his badly tiring challenger continually to the head the referee called it off with just six seconds of the session remaining.

3 December 1960. Gene Fullmer drew 15 Sugar Ray Robinson.
Venue: Sports Arena, Los Angeles, California, USA. **Recognition:** NBA. **Referee:** Tommy Hart.
Scorecards: 8-8, 9-5, 4-11.
Fight Summary: Having knocked the champion out in their previous encounter, Robinson (158¾) was up for this one, fooling almost all of the critics when still fresh at the final bell. Although the opening two rounds went to Fullmer (159), after the 39-year-old Robinson came right back with jolting rights and lefts to head and body in the third he seemed to be well in control until the ninth when the champion threw everything at him. Not to be deterred, Robinson went on the attack in the 11th to have Fullmer wobbling, before continuing in the same vein for the next three sessions. And while the latter won the last two rounds, the referee had Robinson winning the fight 11-4 under California's simplified scoring system only for the two judges to see the fight differently.

14 January 1961. Paul Pender w rsc 7 (15) Terry Downes.
Venue: The Arena, Boston, Massachusetts, USA. **Recognition:** EBU/NY. **Referee:** Bill Connelly.
Fight Summary: Despite being decked in the opening round Downes (160) steamed into Pender (160), continually forcing him back regardless of being caught with accurate jabs. Unfortunately for Downes, albeit still going well, his nose was badly cut in the fourth, an injury that would ultimately be his undoing. Coming out for the fifth with damage to both eyes adding to his problems, with the Englishman making the champion's body his target for the next two sessions, he was having some success before the referee called it off after 57 seconds of the seventh. At that stage it was obvious that the fight would not go the distance with the cut on Downes' nose being about one and a half inches long, but had he not suffered such an injury he was well on his way to breaking Pender's defences down.

4 March 1961. Gene Fullmer w pts 15 Sugar Ray Robinson.
Venue: Convention Centre, Las Vegas, Nevada, USA. **Recognition:** NBA. **Referee:** Frank Carter.
Scorecards: 70-66, 70-67, 70-64.
Fight Summary: This would be the last time that Robinson (159¾) contested the title. Having impressed in the first two rounds with classic left jabs, Robinson was then under constant attack as the champion came on like a train in the third, the fighters even trading blows after the bell. That was the end of Robinson as a threat, and while he was never floored he was forced to muster up all of his reserves as Fullmer (159¾) initiated attack after attack. When Robinson was cut over the left eye in the 11th, although it made life even more difficult for him he gamely battled on to the final bell.

22 April 1961. Paul Pender w pts 15 Carmen Basilio.
Venue: The Garden, Boston, Massachusetts, USA. **Recognition:** EBU/NY. **Referee:** Ed Bradley.
Scorecards: 149-135, 147-132, 147-138.
Fight Summary: Forced to visit the scales four times in order to make the weight, the champion was then badly cut on the left eye in the second round, an injury that required five stitches. He was also badly hurt by Basilio (156½) in that same session. Although Basilio kept up the pressure in the third Pender (160) was back in business, and by the fifth he had taken over, hooking, jabbing and throwing hurtful counters. In the 13th Basilio was downed by a right to the chin before being floored again by lefts and rights to the head in the final session. However, he still continued to attack, despite running into a barrage of left jabs. Floored for the first time in his career, Basilio never fought again.

11 July 1961. Terry Downes w rtd 9 (15) Paul Pender.
Venue: The Arena, Wembley, London, England. **Recognition:** EBU/NY. **Referee:** Ike Powell.
Fight Summary: In what was a return match the champion started well when opening up the old injury on Downes' nose with a left jab in the second round, but the Englishman shrugged it off and began throwing left jabs of his own. Maintaining a relentless pursuit of Pender (159), Downes (158¾) varied his work to such a degree that the former often became flummoxed. By the fourth Downes was pushing Pender before him, and while he was forced to take some heavy counters he kept up the charge. As the fight wore on a back-pedalling Pender appeared to be waiting to catch Downes as the latter charged in, although too often he failed to take any chance that came his way. The eighth round saw the beginning of the end. Cut over both eyes, Pender went mad, but with Downes now walking through his man despite his left eye being almost closed at the end of the ninth session the champion was retired on his stool.

With the return clause in place for 23 September, negotiations to conclude the rubber were arduous due to Pender continuing to get the champion's share of the gate and purse. Then, having agreed a deal in mid-August a few days later Downes broke a thumb when falling down stairs at home which resulted in an operation. Following that, with the fight put back until early in the New Year when Downes requested a warm-up bout in January 1962 he was suspended by the Massachusetts boxing authority. In the meantime, with the new date being some time in March or April, Pender turned down a match against Gene Fullmer, the NBA champion, which would have enabled the winner to unify the title against Downes.

5 August 1961. Gene Fullmer w pts 15 Florentino Fernandez.
Venue: The Stadium, Ogden, Utah, USA. **Recognition:** NBA. **Referee:** Ken Shulsen.
Scorecards: 148-140, 145-142, 143-145.
Fight Summary: Fullmer (159¾) just about held on to his title when meeting the hard-punching Fernandez (157¼) blow for blow. Having made an excellent start Fullmer gained a fair lead, but when Fernandez started to catch him with left hooks, especially to the body, in the latter sessions he was forced to fight for his life. The 14th was Fernandez's best round, the champion being forced to sustain a real battering before hanging on in the 15th. Afterwards, it was learnt that Fullmer had broken a bone in his right elbow in the penultimate round when fending off terrific left hooks.

9 December 1961. Gene Fullmer w co 10 (15) Benny Kid Paret.
Venue: Convention Centre, Las Vegas, Nevada, USA. **Recognition:** NBA. **Referee:** Harry Krause.
Fight Summary: Setting up a non-stop attack from the opening bell, Fullmer (159¾) took on the welterweight champion in defence of his title with a view to wearing his lighter rival down. Although Paret (156¾) tried to stay with Fullmer the task was just too much as he was backed into the ropes for long periods by barrages of blows from both hands. Up until the tenth there had been no knockdowns, but in the early part of that session Paret was dropped by a left hook to the head, immediately being downed again when back on his feet. Unwisely getting up at 'two', Paret was quickly put down for the full count, completed on the 2.30 mark. Many people blamed the shellacking that Paret received in this one for his demise in his very next fight, against Emile Griffith. Fullmer finished the contests with cuts over both eyes.

Early in 1962 it was reported that Fullmer would be defending his title against Denny Moyer in May. However, within days of that announcement, after promoter Sam Silverman said that he had lined up Paul Pender to fight Fullmer during the second week in June, no more was heard of Pender v Moyer. Unfortunately, when Pender was involved in a road accident in mid-May, which left him with a severe scalp injury, the Fullmer fight was postponed until 28 August. Around the same time, the NBA instructed Fullmer that he had to defend his title against Dick Tiger by 5 August or risk being stripped. With no mention of Fullmer's proposed fight with Pender, the NBA stated that Fullmer and Tiger had signed to meet on 27 August, while Pender was talking of a defence against the European champion, Laszlo Papp. This was followed by Jose Torres saying that he was due to fight Pender in Boston, Massachusetts on 19 October. Then, in mid-August, it was reported that the Fullmer v Tiger meeting was being moved on to October in order to allow both men, who had remained inactive while all this was going on, to prepare properly.

7 April 1962. Paul Pender w pts 15 Terry Downes.
Venue: The Garden, Boston, Massachusetts, USA. **Recognition:** EBU/NY. **Referee:** Jim McCarron.
Scorecards: 144-143, 145-143, 146-141.
Fight Summary: Despite being in front after five rounds, with the champion lacking the punch to finish Pender (159) off, even though he continued to force matters the latter came back into the fight with good left jabs and hooks. Unfortunately for Downes (159), as the American was allowed to clutch and stall for long periods of the contest he was pushed and pulled down on a couple of occasions. By the seventh, Downes was cut on the left eye and had sustained damage to his nose, but it was Pender's left jab that worried him more. It was a hard fight, with Pender vastly improved from their previous contest, and at the final bell it was his skill that won over Downes' aggression.

After negotiations for a unifying contest with Gene Fullmer broke down, Pender eventually elected to defend his share of the championship against Jose Torres on 2 November. Moved on when Torres picked up a cold the fight was called off within days when Cus D'Amato, Torres manager, failed to come up with the guarantee.

Although the NYSAC and EBU withdrew their support of Pender on 9 November, for failing to defend within the stipulated period, the Massachusetts Boxing Commission continued to support him as world champion.

On 6 March 1963, the Court of Appeal ordered the NYSAC to continue to recognise Pender, as in their eyes he was not the guilty party. Within days of that decision the NYSAC again vacated the title, stating that Pender had failed to sign articles of agreement with Joey Giambra, a rated boxer who had filed a challenge with the Commission. An article in the July edition of *The Ring* magazine printed a quote by John Cronin, Pender's legal adviser, stating that the purported challenge made by Giambra on 24 August 1962 was premature, invalid and ineffectual, and was so regarded and treated by the Commission. Even after the Appellate Court had decided in favour of Pender, the NYSAC failed to meet Pender for the purpose of resolving the matter. When it was announced on 11 April that Pender would be defending the title against Joey Giardello on 7 June, it quickly fell through due to the promoter being unable to obtain television support for the contest. Following that, with the prospect of more of the same Pender announced his retirement on 7 May.

23 October 1962. Dick Tiger w pts 15 Gene Fullmer.
Venue: Candlestick Park, San Francisco, California, USA. **Recognition:** NBA. **Referee:** Frank Carter.
Scorecards: 10-1, 9-5, 7-5.
Fight Summary: Fullmer's reign as the NBA champion came to an end as Tiger (159) took everything he had to throw and came back with more, having attacked from the opening bell. In the third round Fullmer (160) was driven into the ropes by blows to head and body before being subjected to a non-stop barrage of heavy shots in the fourth that took a great deal out of him. Giving it his best shot in the eighth, when Fullmer failed to halt the British Empire champion it was all downhill thereafter. At the end of the ninth, with Fullmer cut over the left eye, he was allowed to carry on after being examined by the doctor only to pick up a badly cut right eye in the tenth. From there onwards Tiger just kept the pressure going to run out an easy winner.

23 February 1963. Dick Tiger drew 15 Gene Fullmer.
Venue: Convention Centre, Las Vegas, Nevada, USA. **Recognition:** NBA. **Referee:** Vern Bybee.
Scorecards: 71-67, 68-70, 69-69.
Fight Summary: A poor fight saw Fullmer (160) back-pedal throughout while the champion merely plodded after him for much of the time without showing any of the form he had displayed in their first contest. There were no official knockdowns, although Fullmer slipped to the canvas on four occasions. The fight never took off until Tiger (160) came to life in the last four rounds after being cut over the left eye in the 11th following a head clash. Also cut over the left eye, his face bruised and swollen, Fullmer somehow survived with a mixture of holding and moving as Tiger tired.

10 August 1963. Dick Tiger w rtd 7 (15) Gene Fullmer.
Venue: Liberty Stadium, Ibadan, Nigeria. **Recognition:** World. **Referee:** Jack Hart.
Fight Summary: Relentlessly chasing Fullmer (160) for round after round, belting in punches to head and body whenever he had the opportunity, the champion forced the American to retire on his stool at the end of the seventh. This was the first world title fight ever held in West Africa. Fullmer never expected Tiger (159¾) to maintain such a fast pace, and battered from pillar to post, with his right eye almost closed, he eventually announced his retirement on 23 July 1964 without taking in anymore fights.

7 December 1963. Joey Giardello w pts 15 Dick Tiger.
Venue: Convention Hall, Atlantic City, New Jersey, USA. **Recognition:** World. **Referee:** Paul Cavalier.
Scorecard: 8-5-2.
Fight Summary: Using hit-and-run tactics, Giardello (158), a huge underdog, led the champion on a merry old dance for much of the fight, using his speed and boxing ability to get him home. Only in the sixth and tenth rounds did Tiger (159) hurt Giardello badly, and although it looked as though the latter might be on the way out on both occasions he somehow weathered the storm. At the finish Giardello said "I paced the fight my way, slow at the start, faster in the middle, then kept out of trouble at the end. To go in and fight it out with Tiger would have been suicidal. The only thing that surprised me was the referee not giving me 11 rounds instead of eight."

In July 1964, the NYSAC threatened to strip Giardello unless he signed to meet a leading contender within 20 days. Mindful of the consequences, he agreed to defend his title against the number two contender, Rubin Carter, in Nevada on 23 October, before it was eventually transferred to another State when the promoter failed to make good the guarantees.

14 December 1964. Joey Giardello w pts 15 Rubin Carter.
Venue: Convention Hall, Philadelphia, Pennsylvania, USA. **Recognition:** World. **Referee:** Bob Polis.
Scorecards: 72-66, 71-66, 70-67.
Fight Summary: Making his first defence, Giardello (160) boxed on the back foot throughout against the hard-hitting Carter (158½), being at risk from the sixth through to the 12th as the latter went looking for the kayo. Giardello was cut on the left eye in the fourth, but continued to pick Carter off as he pressed forward. In the 13th Giardello hurt Carter with left hooks, but then came back strongly in the 14th before the champion produced a grandstand finish in the final session. The decision was seen by many as unfair, with *The Ring* magazine tabling Carter as the winner by 68-64.

Having promised Dick Tiger a return in the aftermath of their 7 December 1963 contest, in mid-April 1965 Giardello rejected offers to defend his title against the welterweight champion, Emile Griffith, and stated that he would be happy to take on Tiger in late June. However, Tiger was already contracted to meet Carter (at Madison Square Garden, Manhattan, NYC, New York on 20 May), a fight he eventually won on points over ten rounds, while Giardello was still receiving treatment on the arm injured in the non-title win over Gil Diaz on 23 April. With the WBC looking on, at the end of June it was announced that Giardello would be defending against Joey Archer or George Benton on 20 September as he felt Tiger's 30% demand of the gate money too high. Then, at the end of July, the Madison Square Garden promoters announced that Giardello was close to signing for a defence against Tiger in October, which was confirmed shortly afterwards.

437

Meantime, the WBA set up a final eliminator between Griffith and Don Fullmer, won by the latter on points over 12 rounds at the Fairgrounds Coliseum, Salt Lake City, Utah on 20 August 1965, which was also billed for the American title. But the winner failed to get the support his victory warranted, especially after losing to Nino Benvenuti and Jose Gonzalez.

21 October 1965. Dick Tiger w pts 15 Joey Giardello.
Venue: Madison Square Garden, Manhattan, NYC, New York, USA. **Recognition:** World. **Referee:** John LoBianco.
Scorecards: 9-5-1, 10-5, 8-6-1.
Fight Summary: Starting strongly, after Tiger (158½) opened up a cut on the champion's left eye in the second round he was always in control, often catching his man with several punches without reply. In the seventh, Giardello (160), who was now cut on the right eye, was in danger of being stopped. Tiger made a terrific effort in the tenth to end matters, but when the 34-year-old Giardello fought back strongly he decided to coast through to the final bell.

25 April 1966. Emile Griffith w pts 15 Dick Tiger.
Venue: Madison Square Garden, Manhattan, NYC, New York, USA. **Recognition:** World. **Referee:** Arthur Mercante.
Scorecards: 9-5-1, 7-6-2, 7-7-1.
Fight Summary: In what was a slow contest, with both men showing too much respect for each other, Griffith (150½), the welterweight champion, used his superior speed to negate much of the champion's work. Neither man was cut or badly hurt, although Tiger (160) was dropped to his knees in the ninth. Back on his feet immediately, the referee still gave Tiger the mandatory 'eight' count. Up until the seventh Tiger was in front, but from thereon in Griffith picked up the pace, beating his man to the punch and speeding away from any danger. Realising he was behind, Tiger went for broke in the 11th, 12th and 13th rounds, but unable to do any real damage apart from delivering a few hurtful blows Griffith came back to cruise to the finish.

13 July 1966. Emile Griffith w pts 15 Joey Archer.
Venue: Madison Square Garden, Manhattan, NYC, New York, USA. **Recognition:** World. **Referee:** John LoBianco.
Scorecards: 8-7, 9-5-1, 7-7-1.
Fight Summary: Getting away quickly, the champion was soon in action with the left hook showing up well and in the fifth round he buckled Archer's knees with such a punch. Cut over the left eye following a clash of heads in the eighth, Archer (159½) became more aggressive, doing well in three of the last six rounds, stabbing in left jabs to head and body while slamming in blows at every opportunity. Despite Griffith (152) boxing at his best it was certainly close enough for Archer to be granted an immediate return.

23 January 1967. Emile Griffith w pts 15 Joey Archer.
Venue: Madison Square Garden, Manhattan, NYC, New York, USA. **Recognition:** World. **Referee:** Arthur Mercante.
Scorecards: 8-6-1, 8-7, 8-7.
Fight Summary: Right from the start the champion carried the fight to Archer (160), but although staggering the latter several times he was unable to drop him. In the second round Archer was cut over the right eye, thereafter boxing mainly on the retreat with Griffith (152) waiting to trade punches whenever they got close enough. Archer was at his best in the seventh through to the ninth when he was able to pile up the points with the left jab, but ultimately he was unable to keep it going as Griffith pressured him.

17 April 1967. Nino Benvenuti w pts 15 Emile Griffith.
Venue: Madison Square Garden, Manhattan, NYC, New York, USA. **Recognition:** World. **Referee:** Mark Conn.
Scorecards: 10-5, 9-6, 10-5.
Fight Summary: Benvenuti (159) took the opening two rounds, scoring a knockdown in the second, before the champion came back strongly to knock him down with a right to the jaw in the fourth. Rounds five and six went to Benvenuti, who was landing well with left jabs and straight rights, before Griffith (153½) opened up a cut on the Italian's nose. The contest was fairly even up until the 11th, but from there onwards the Italian did the better work, and although Griffith continued to look for a finishing punch he failed to find it.

29 September 1967. Emile Griffith w pts 15 Nino Benvenuti.
Venue: Shea Stadium, Queens, NYC, New York, USA. **Recognition:** World. **Referee:** Tommy Walsh.
Scorecards: 9-5-1, 9-5-1, 7-7-1.
Fight Summary: Griffith (154) was quickly off the mark with effective combinations before the champion settled down to be in front at the halfway stage. Apart from having an excellent 13th, Benvenuti (159¾) seemed to be running second best in the final seven rounds, being beaten to the punch and out of range with many of his attacks. In the 14th he was dropped by a solid left, and although on his feet very quickly he was forced to endure an 'eight' count. Coming back strongly, Benvenuti tried to convince the judges when fighting furiously, but it was all in vain as Griffith tied his man up before crashing in several heavy blows prior to the final bell.

4 March 1968. Nino Benvenuti w pts 15 Emile Griffith.
Venue: Madison Square Garden, Manhattan, NYC, New York, USA. **Recognition:** World. **Referee:** John LoBianco.
Scorecards: 8-6-1, 8-6-1, 7-7-1.
Fight Summary: In what was a close fight with the champion starting well, Benvenuti (160) did not make the same mistake as he did last time when allowing his rival to dominate large parts of the fight. Although he was very nearly dropped in the sixth and took some heavy punches in the seventh, Benvenuti came right back into it in the ninth when he floored Griffith (154½) with a left-right combination. The Italian shook Griffith up again in the 12th, and at the final bell despite both men being tired it was the latter who was on the receiving end.

After injuring a thumb in a non-title contest against Jimmy Ramos on 5 July, Benvenuti was suspended in Canada until he fulfilled his obligations to meet Art Hernandez, something he did on 17 September. The injury, however, had disturbed his routine, but given until the end of the year by the authorities to agree a defence against Don Fullmer negotiations began in September.

14 December 1968. Nino Benvenuti w pts 15 Don Fullmer.
Venue: Ariston Theatre, San Remo, Italy. **Recognition:** World. **Referee:** Piero Brambilla.
Scorecards: 73-68, 71-65, 72-69.
Fight Summary: Right from the start it was clear that Fullmer (159) was finding it difficult to get inside the champion's left jab, and eventually when he began to charge in it resulted in him being cut over the left eye in the sixth. The first six rounds went very much the way of Benvenuti (160), but in the seventh he was dropped by an overarm right to the head and forced to take the mandatory 'eight' count before coming back with steady left jabs and rights to the body. With Fullmer continuing to charge in without success he was cut over the right eye in the 12th. By now both men were tiring, and with Fullmer struggling to land Benvenuti kept his left going to win all the remaining rounds.

Remaining inactive before meeting Dick Tiger, who won on points over ten rounds at Madison Square Garden, Manhattan, NYC, New York in a non-title contest on 26 May 1969, Benvenuti complained of breaking his right hand in the first round and requiring more time out before a title defence. He then angered the WBA (who were insisting that he must meet the number one contender, Luis Rodriguez, before any others) in August when negotiating a defence against Fraser Scott for early October. The outcome was that Benvenuti must meet Rodriguez before the end of 1969 regardless of any arrangements made with Scott, and if the latter won the title he would have to meet the Cuban within the same time frame.

4 October 1969. Nino Benvenuti w disq 7 (15) Fraser Scott.
Venue: San Paolo Stadium, Naples, Italy. **Recognition:** World. **Referee:** Tonci Gilardi.
Fight Summary: It was never much of a fight as the wild Scott (158) was rarely able to pierce the champion's guard, merely charging in and being caught by sharp left jabs for his efforts. Although Scott was unbeaten in 17 contests, the only man of any note he had beaten was Denny Moyer, and even that was an early cut-eye stoppage. Warned and cautioned several times for butting, Scott was finally disqualified at 1.04 of the seventh after both men had fallen to the canvas after missing with jabs.

22 November 1969. Nino Benvenuti w co 11 (15) Luis Rodriguez.
Venue: Sports Palace, Rome, Italy. **Recognition:** World. **Referee:** Mario Carabellese.

Fight Summary: Using his height and reach to good effect, the champion took the opening two rounds before being cut over the left eye by a slashing right from Rodriguez (156) in the third and being forced to box more defensively to protect the wound. With Benvenuti (159½) continuing to cover up, Rodriguez began to get more shots off, and in the sixth he opened up a cut on the Italian's nose. By the seventh Benvenuti had become more aggressive, catching his rival with blows to head and body, but the next three sessions were evenly contested, both men scoring with hard punches. It was still anybody's fight. Benvenuti was still scoring, but it was Rodriguez, throwing hooks and jabs, that caught the eye. Then, in the 11th, as Rodriguez moved in with a right hook he was caught by a terrific left to the jaw and sent down to be counted out on the 1.08 mark.

Following an eighth-round stoppage win over Benvenuti in a non-title contest in Australia on 13 March 1970, Tom Bethea earned himself a crack at the championship as the Italian looked to rectify things after pulling out with a damaged rib. At that point Bethea had participated in just 16 pro fights, winning ten of them, but apart from Benvenuti his only other victim with any form had been Eddie Owens. However, he was confident that his power, especially to the body, would give him a good chance of a repeat win inside ten rounds.

23 May 1970. Nino Benvenuti w co 8 (15) Tom Bethea.
Venue: The Arena, Umag, Yugoslavia. **Recognition:** World. **Referee:** Georges Gondre.
Fight Summary: Having beaten the champion in a non-title fight 90 days earlier Bethea (160) fully earned his chance, however, it was a different Benvenuti (160) who turned up this time. Scoring well with left jabs and hooks, Benvenuti made this fight his from the start, and in the fourth he opened up a cut over Bethea's right eye. Bethea, who felt that attacking the body was his best option, did get through occasionally but failed to hurt his rival. With both men being warned for hitting in the clinches the tempo had certainly dropped when Benvenuti backed Bethea into the ropes in the eighth before unleashing a left-right to the head that floored the challenger for the full count, timed at 2.43 of the session.

7 November 1970. Carlos Monzon w co 12 (15) Nino Benvenuti.
Venue: Sports Palace, Rome, Italy. **Recognition:** World. **Referee:** Rudolf Drust.
Fight Summary: Producing only flashes of his ability at the highest level, the champion was put under pressure by Monzon (159¾) for much of the fight and after the second round he was unable to halt the relentless march of the Argentine. Despite the fans being in uproar at the end of the sixth after Monzon struck Benvenuti (159¾) following the bell, the challenger just got on with the job. Almost finished off in the seventh when badly hurt by blows to head and body, by now Benvenuti was tiring and although he had a good tenth round, stopping Monzon in his tracks several times, he was on the receiving end throughout the 11th. There was no doubting that Benvenuti was now in serious difficulty and he was counted out in the 12th on the two-minute marker after being put down by a thunderbolt of a right hand to the jaw.

8 May 1971. Carlos Monzon w rsc 3 (15) Nino Benvenuti.
Venue: Louis II Stadium, Monte Carlo, Monaco. **Recognition:** World. **Referee:** Victor Avendano.
Fight Summary: This was just a shadow of the old Benvenuti, having been beaten by the little-known Jose Chirino on points over ten rounds after losing his title to Monzon. Benvenuti (160) did reasonably well in the opening round, but in the second he was badly stunned by a swinging left to the head before a left from Monzon (159½) sent him through the ropes near the end of the session. Saved by the bell, Benvenuti was under the hammer right at the start of round three as Monzon punished him unmercifully, and when he was dropped flat on his face his manager threw in the towel. Although Benvenuti, who would never fight again, kicked the towel out of the ring it was too late as the referee had already stopped the contest.

25 September 1971. Carlos Monzon w rsc 14 (15) Emile Griffith.
Venue: Luna Park Stadium, Buenos Aires, Argentina. **Recognition:** World. **Referee:** Ramon Berumen.
Fight Summary: Giving the hard-hitting champion one of the toughest fights of his career, Griffith (154), with a height-and-reach disadvantage, showed tremendous courage. It was only in the seventh that Monzon (159) caught up with Griffith, and although he twice had the veteran in trouble he let him off the hook. After the tenth when Griffith began to tire Monzon stepped it up, landing thumping rights to the head and body, but at that stage there was no real sign of the contest finishing. However, in the 14th, when Monzon finally let the punches go, Griffith,

his right eye partially closed and his left eye showing signs of wear, was backed against the ropes and hit non-stop for what seemed an age before the referee called a halt with 11 seconds of the round remaining.

4 March 1972. Carlos Monzon w rsc 5 (15) Denny Moyer.
Venue: Sports Palace, Rome, Italy. **Recognition:** World. **Referee:** Lorenzo Fortunato.
Fight Summary: Holding his own for the opening four rounds, banging in left hooks and solid rights while boxing behind a high guard, Moyer (158¾) made things difficult for the champion. Although Monzon (159) got in some heavy blows Moyer always came straight back, shaking the Argentine up with a smashing right to the jaw in the third. In the fifth, however, Moyer was forced to take a compulsory eight count as Monzon (159) cut loose. When Moyer got up, immediately being put under pressure again, the referee called it off at 1.05 of the session. Afterwards, Moyer stated that even though Monzon had wrestled him to the ground he was fighting back at the stoppage.

The European champion and top-rated contender according to *The Ring* magazine, Jean-Claude Bouttier, was next in line to take on Monzon. With a record of 56 wins from 60 contests, he was a solid puncher, especially to the body, and had beaten Karl-Heinz Klein, Jacques Marty, Stanley Hayward, Jo Gonzales, Pascal Di Benedetto, Tom Bethea, Lonnie Harris, Juan Carlos Duran, Doyle Baird and Fabio Bettini.

17 June 1972. Carlos Monzon w rtd 13 (15) Jean-Claude Bouttier.
Venue: Colombes Stadium, Paris, France. **Recognition:** World. **Referee:** Rudolf Drust.
Fight Summary: Bouttier (159), the European champion, found that even his best punches were not stopping the champion's onward march, and in the sixth round he was blasted to the floor by a vicious right to the jaw. Forced to take the mandatory 'eight' count, Bouttier claimed he had slipped. The Frenchman was soon swapping punches with Monzon (159¼) again but continued to struggle to get inside the latter's longer reach, being hit by long looping rights and lefts. Down in the eighth without a count, Bouttier was now more cautious in his approach. Then, in the tenth, he had great difficulty focussing, later claiming a thumb in the eye had caused the problem. Although shaking Monzon up with a right in the 11th, the beleaguered Bouttier, now also cut on the right eye, remained on his stool at the start of the 13th.

19 August 1972. Carlos Monzon w rsc 5 (15) Tom Bogs.
Venue: Idraets Park Stadium, Copenhagen, Denmark. **Recognition:** World. **Referee:** Harry Gibbs.
Fight Summary: Making his fifth defence, Monzon (159) proved far too powerful for Bogs (159½), who was under pressure from the third round onwards after landing several heavy blows on the champion that had no effect. Although his legs began to go in the third Bogs fought on bravely, but at the end of the fourth, having been nailed by a Monzon (159) right to the head the end was in sight. Dropped four times in the fifth, Bogs was overwhelmed by Monzon's powerful rights, and although he got up from the fourth knockdown the referee had seen enough and brought the fight to a close on the 2.30 mark.

Bennie Briscoe, who had drawn over ten rounds with Monzon back in May 1967, would be the next challenger. Ranked at number seven by *The Ring* magazine, Briscoe had won 43 of 55 contests, beating Charley Scott, Percy Manning (twice), George Benton, Jimmy Lester, Jose Gonzalez (twice), Vicente Rondon, Tito Marshall, Joe Shaw, Tom Bethea, Carlos Marks and Luis Vinales. Having reversed six of his ten defeats, he was a dangerous opponent, being a durable and solid puncher with both hands, especially to the body.

11 November 1972. Carlos Monzon w pts 15 Bennie Briscoe.
Venue: Luna Park Stadium, Buenos Aires, Argentina. **Recognition:** World. **Referee:** Victor Avendano.
Scorecards: 150-139, 149-139, 149-143.
Fight Summary: Felt to be Monzon's hardest defence to date, the shaven-headed Briscoe (157) continually bulled his way in to work with short hooks to the body and head despite taking heavy punishment. After Monzon (158) was forced to hold on in the ninth, Briscoe immediately went looking for him in the tenth. Having weathered the storm, Monzon then had Briscoe, his right eye cut, in real trouble for the first time in the fight in the 13th, only for the latter to come back strongly right through to the final bell.

With a projected fight against Monzon under negotiation, Emile Griffith was placed under suspension for three months by the French Boxing Federation following his ten-round draw against Nessim Max Cohen at the Sports Palace, Paris, France on 12 March 1973. The announcement came after an alleged stimulant was found in a urine test prior to the fight. Obviously, this action held up Monzon v Griffith, but negotiations got back on track after the NYSAC could find nothing wrong with Griffith and the French authority merely treated it as a suspended sentence. These actions made it easier to promote the fight in Monte Carlo after negotiations for it to be held in San Remo, Italy fell through.

2 June 1973. Carlos Monzon w pts 15 Emile Griffith.

Venue: Louis II Stadium, Monte Carlo, Monaco. **Recognition:** World. **Referee:** Piero Brambilla.
Scorecards: 147-145, 147-143, 147-144.
Fight Summary: Looking like a fighter who'd had better days, the champion had great difficulty in holding off the 35-year-old Griffith (157) as the veteran frequently beat him to the punch and had him worried. For the opening ten rounds it looked as though there might be a new champion, especially with Griffith absorbing the punches coming his way to outfight Monzon (159). It was only in the tenth that Monzon began to look his real self, and by the 12th the fight was shifting away from Griffith. In the 14th, Griffith, who was cut on the right eye, came under immense pressure as Monzon loaded up, but with both men tiring the latter was comfortably contained in the final session.

29 September 1973. Carlos Monzon w pts 15 Jean-Claude Bouttier.

Venue: Roland Garros Stadium, Paris, France. **Recognition:** World. **Referee:** Harry Gibbs.
Scorecards: 145-139, 147-138, 148-145.
Fight Summary: In a return bout, Bouttier (159) was right in the frame at the end of the 12th, having given as good as he got against a champion who was unable to impress himself on his rival and who was caught by far too many punches. This time around it was Bouttier who made the running, and despite being hurt on occasion Monzon (159¾) failed to follow up. It was only in the final three sessions that Monzon made sure of the win, knocking Bouttier down in each round with clubbing right hands doing the damage while generally staying on the attack. With both men cut over the left eye, at the finish Bouttier's manager complained that Monzon had been allowed to get away with too many fouls. He went on to say that had the bout been held in America his man would have become champion due to them counting the number of rounds won as opposed to the Continental system of points totalled.

9 February 1974. Carlos Monzon w rtd 7 (15) Jose Napoles.

Venue: Puteaux Circus Big Top, Paris, France. **Recognition:** World. **Referee:** Raymond Baldeyrou.
Fight Summary: This was a bridge too far for the welterweight champion, Napoles (153), who was just too small for the strong and powerful Monzon (159). Whatever Napoles tried he failed to hurt the champion, and although there were no knockdowns it was only the fighting spirit of the Cuban that kept him in the contest. From the fourth round onwards Monzon got down to business, snapping in the jab followed by vicious uppercuts. In the sixth Napoles took such a battering that it was no surprise that he retired as the bell rang for the seventh round. Following the fight, Napoles' cornerman, Angelo Dundee, said that after his man had been thumbed in the eye it was impossible for him to continue.

When Monzon forfeited WBC recognition in April for failing to arrange a defence against Rodrigo Valdez within the stipulated period, the latter was matched with Bennie Briscoe in order to find a successor. A classy box-fighter, Valdez had beaten Briscoe on points over 12 rounds for the North American title in Noumea, New Caledonia on 1 September 1973, but the verdict had been disputed. With 59 wins from 67 contests, Valdez was rated at number one by *The Ring* magazine, while Briscoe sat one place behind him. Having turned pro in 1963 the experienced Valdez was on 20 straight victories, which included wins over Bobby Cassidy and Carlos Marks, and had waited a long time for this opportunity.

That decision of the WBC was blasted by the WBA, who stated that Monzon had met every obligation as far as they were concerned. With their blessing he negotiated a defence against Tony Mundine, to be held in Argentina on 14 September, before it was moved on to early October due to organisational problems.

25 May 1974. Rodrigo Valdez w co 7 (15) Bennie Briscoe.
Venue: Louis II Stadium, Monte Carlo, Monaco. **Recognition:** WBC. **Referee:** Harry Gibbs.
Fight Summary: Fighting for the vacant WBC title, Valdez (156¾) outboxed Briscoe (156½) in virtually every round apart from a spell in the second round when he was cut over the left eye and pinned against the ropes. By the fifth Valdez was getting to Briscoe more frequently, jabbing hard and throwing heavy combinations, but the latter somehow remained on his feet to fight on. Briscoe was still able to hurt Valdez, but the Colombian's punches were more accurate. The seventh saw Briscoe looking to take his man out, hammering in big right hands only for Valdez to hit back with a vengeance. Setting himself up for the finish, Valdez slammed in a series of solid shots to the head before a final right to the jaw dropped Briscoe on his back, and although the American was on his feet at 'eight', defenceless and unsteady on his legs, he was counted out.

5 October 1974. Carlos Monzon w co 7 (15) Tony Mundine.
Venue: Luna Park Stadium, Buenos Aires, Argentina. **Recognition:** WBA. **Referee:** Isaac Herrera.
Fight Summary: Prior to the contest there was much talk of the champion having weight problems, but despite that it turned out to be one of Monzon's easiest defences. Letting Mundine (159¼) make the running for several rounds and countering occasionally there was nothing in it until the sixth. Once Monzon (160) had decided to open up the end was in sight, long punches from both hands leaving Mundine dazed and disorientated at the bell. Monzon really opened up in the seventh, heavy lefts and rights driving Mundine into the ropes before a cracking combination sent him down to be counted out on the 1.20 mark.

Talk of Monzon taking on John Conteh for the WBC light heavyweight crown was a bit premature as the WBA expected him to defend against their number one ranked Tony Licata in May 1975 before that could happen. Having recently defended the American title, the unbeaten Licata went and lost to Ramon Mendez before turning the tables a few weeks later to stay on course for Monzon. Meantime, in April 1975, Monzon was banned from fighting in Europe for failing to take an anti-dope test after his fight with Jose Napoles. Following promotional problems, Monzon v Licata was eventually booked for 30 June 1975.

30 November 1974. Rodrigo Valdez w co 11 (15) Gratien Tonna.
Venue: Exhibition Centre, Paris, France. **Recognition:** WBC. **Referee:** Jean Deswert.
Fight Summary: Making his first defence, Valdez (160) came up against a tough customer in Tonna (159), who contested the fight all the way while making life very difficult for the champion. Having taken a beating for the opening three rounds, Tonna really went to work, consistently hurting Valdez thereafter, especially with big right hands. By the ninth it appeared that Tonna was ahead but, when Valdez came roaring back with big punches of his own to take the initiative again, by the end of the session he was punching the Frenchman around the ring. It was more of the same in the tenth, and in the 11th Valdez again laid into Tonna, whose cut left eye had worsened. The contest came to an end when the referee called for the men to break and Valdez, obviously not hearing the command in the din, jumped in with a left-right to put Tonna down on one knee for the full count, which was followed by uproar. The referee stated afterwards "There was no doubt that Valdez hit Tonna after the order to break, but I am certain he did not hear the command." He went on to say "Tonna did not want to get up after taking his corner's advice. It was a bad mistake as there was no question of my disqualifying Valdez."

31 May 1975. Rodrigo Valdez w rsc 8 (15) Ramon Mendez.
Venue: The Coliseum, Cali, Colombia. **Recognition:** WBC. **Referee:** Humberto Caceres.
Fight Summary: After sizing Mendez (159) up in the first round, the champion quickly got down to work, twice dropping the Argentine in the second from left hooks. Although Mendez went through the next two sessions relatively unscathed he was out of his depth and Valdez (160) picked up where he left off in the second when opening up in the fifth to drop his man again. Having been floored in the seventh and twice in the eighth, Mendez, his left eye almost closed, was rescued by the referee following the second knockdown.

30 June 1975. Carlos Monzon w rsc 10 (15) Tony Licata.
Venue: Madison Square Garden, Manhattan, NYC, New York, USA. **Recognition:** WBA. **Referee:** Tony Perez.
Fight Summary: Putting up stubborn resistance, Licata (160) forced Monzon (159¾) to raise his game, surviving much longer than the champion had forecast he would. The power was all with Monzon though. After taking time

to warm up he began to walk through Licata, the latter being put down in the eighth for the mandatory count having been floored by a right to the jaw. Most fighters would have been finished at this point, but back came Licata, throwing punch upon punch in the ninth only to be outhit by Monzon. With nowhere to go, in the tenth a crashing right to the jaw put Licata down for a second time. Back in action it was now just a matter of time, and when Licata finally fell on one knee having taken volleys of lefts and rights the referee called a halt with 17 seconds of the session remaining.

16 August 1975. Rodrigo Valdez w pts 15 Rudy Robles.
Venue: Indian Bullring, Cartagena, Colombia. **Recognition:** WBC. **Referee:** Victor Amor.
Fight Summary: In what was a difficult fight for the champion, the 22-year-old Robles (159½) made life tough for him by constantly changing styles and dancing away before being caught heavily. Recognising there was a danger that he might punch himself out, in the last four sessions Valdez (159½) virtually ceased to attack. By that time, however, he had a wide margin of points in the bag. Although Robles did well from thereon in he was never able to do much damage, the verdict in favour of the champion being unanimous.

13 December 1975. Carlos Monzon w co 5 (15) Gratien Tonna.
Venue: Nouvel Hippodrome, Paris, France. **Recognition:** WBA. **Referee:** Waldemar Schmidt.
Fight Summary: With the hardy Tonna (159) expected to give the champion a tough fight, although going well in the opening three rounds he came unstuck when things got difficult in the fourth. Going to work with a vengeance, the slow-starting Monzon (160) steamed in with heavy lefts and rights to head and body with Tonna, who was warned for butting, being visibly shaken. The fifth saw Monzon really picking up the pace, and when a heavy right hit Tonna in the region of the left ear he remained down on one knee until the count had been rendered. Immediately following the count, Tonna walked to his corner claiming that he had been hit on the back of the head, a complaint that received no backing.

Rated at number three by *The Ring* magazine, and on the verge of getting a shot at Monzon, George Cooper blew his opportunity when losing on points over 12 rounds to Sugar Ray Seales for the vacant North American title at The Coliseum, Seattle, Washington on 9 March 1976. Prior to this one, Cooper had won 31 of 35 contests, showing both skill and aggression, when beating Nate Collins (twice), Lonnie Harris, Jimmy Lester, David Love (twice) and Rudy Robles.

28 March 1976. Rodrigo Valdez w rsc 4 (15) Nessim Max Cohen.
Venue: The Pavilion, Paris, France. **Recognition:** WBC. **Referee:** Marcello Bertini.
Fight Summary: Looking to set up a unification fight against Carlos Monzon, the WBC champion ruthlessly destroyed the French-Moroccan Cohen (158¼). Although Cohen, countering well under pressure, made a good start Valdez (159½) was soon catching him with heavy rights to the head before flooring him twice in the third. The first time was more of a slip even though the referee counted to 'eight', but on the second occasion after a full-blooded right sent Cohen crashing down for the mandatory count he was lucky that the bell to end the session followed very quickly. The fourth saw Cohen on the receiving end of some blinding punches. Having tried to fight his way back with no success he lifted his right arm in surrender and turned away with 15 seconds left on the clock, leaving the referee to call the fight off.

26 June 1976. Carlos Monzon w pts 15 Rodrigo Valdez.
Venue: Louis II Stadium, Monte Carlo, Monaco. **Recognition:** World. **Referee:** Raymond Baldeyrou.
Scorecards: 146-144, 147-145, 148-144.
Fight Summary: Despite the fight being close, most good judges saw the WBA champion as the winner due to him standing up to Valdez's best shots before coming back with even bigger punches of his own. The fight certainly lived up to expectation, being one of the division's most exciting since the late 1950s. Valdez (160) was well in the running right up to the 14th when Monzon (159½) floored him for the compulsory 'eight' count with a heavy right to the jaw. If Valdez had not made such a slow start, regardless of him gradually eating away at Monzon's lead over the ensuing rounds, things might have been different, but following the knockdown his fate was sealed even though he fired back hard in the final session.

Having unified the title, it was reported that Monzon was looking for a March defence after getting back in training at the start of the New Year. With all the hard work beginning to get to him, Monzon admitted that he would now be concentrating just on title defences, nothing else. At the beginning of 1977, reports came out of South Africa that Monzon would be defending his title against Elijah Makathini in March or June, which was immediately followed by news of Monzon breaking the big toe on his right foot. Shortly afterwards it was announced that a return against Valdez, supported by both the WBA and WBC, would take place in July.

30 July 1977. Carlos Monzon w pts 15 Rodrigo Valdez.
Venue: Louis II Stadium, Monte Carlo, Monaco. **Recognition:** World. **Referee:** Roland Dakin.
Scorecards: 144-141, 147-144, 145-143.
Fight Summary: The return between the pair was almost as exciting and as close as their previous go, the champion always being wary of Valdez's power. Having been dropped by a whistling right to the jaw in the second round for what he claimed was the first time he had been decked since 1963, Monzon (159) gradually gained control as the contest wore on. Indeed, in the tenth it looked as though Valdez (158) might be stopped with blood pouring from his left eye and swellings around both eyes. It was Monzon's countering that ultimately gained him the initiative, and although Valdez fought like a man possessed in the last three sessions he failed to make up the leeway.

Monzon retired as undefeated champion in August when the WBC forced him to vacate their portion of the title after he failed to agree terms for a championship contest against Valdez. With the WBA supporting Bennie Briscoe and the WBC backing Valdez, neither body saw the need for an eliminator.

5 November 1977. Rodrigo Valdez w pts 15 Bennie Briscoe.
Venue: The Casino, Campione D'Italia, Switzerland. **Recognition:** World. **Referee:** Wally Thom.
Scorecards: 148-145, 149-142, 146-148.
Fight Summary: Contesting the vacant title in the wake of Carlos Monzon's retirement, Valdez (160) boxed brilliantly to outscore the battle-hardened Briscoe (160), who continually came forward only to be met by jabs, hooks and uppercuts that would knock him back. Despite being cut and bruised under the right eye and gashed on the nose Briscoe never hit the floor, always making Valdez work for the points. In the 12th, Briscoe, scoring well with heavy left hooks, came back to knock out Valdez's mouthpiece, and while there was never a great deal between them at that stage of the fight the latter came on strongly in the remaining three sessions to make sure of the verdict.

26 November 1977. Marvin Hagler w co 12 (15) Mike Colbert.
Venue: The Garden, Boston, Massachusetts, USA. **Recognition:** Massachusetts. **Referee:** Tommy Rawson.
Fight Summary: Although supported by Massachusetts, Oregon, New Jersey, Virginia and a few New England States, the billing was more in protest that Hagler had not been considered for an elimination series following the retirement of Carlos Monzon. His opponent was on 22 straight wins, and with victories over Rocky Mosley Jnr and Tony Licata he was certainly no pushover. Unfortunately it was a poor fight, with Hagler (160) having to chase after Colbert (157½), who was constantly going backwards while scoring as he went. Having begun to lose his way, at the end of the 11th round Hagler was reckoned by many to be trailing by three or four rounds despite the officials having him ahead by one point. However, that all counted for nothing when Hagler finally caught up with Colbert in the 12th. Floored from the cumulative effect of Hagler's blows, on getting up and trying to fight back Colbert was quickly put down for the full count, timed at one minute, following a smashing southpaw right to the jaw that dropped him flat on his face.

Regardless of the win, it turned out to be a one-off for Hagler following the promise of a title shot in the very near future. By the time Hagler got his opportunity against Vito Antuofermo, he had won 46 of 49 fights and had defeated Sugar Ray Seales, Matt Donovan, Willie Monroe (twice), Kevin Finnegan (twice), Bennie Briscoe and Norberto Cabrera along the way.

22 April 1978. Hugo Corro w pts 15 Rodrigo Valdez.
Venue: Ariston Theatre, San Remo, Italy. **Recognition:** World. **Referee:** Angelo Poletti.

Scorecards: 148-145, 147-144, 147-144.
Fight Summary: Reckoned to be one of the division's biggest ever upsets, Corro (159¾) boxed defensively for the opening nine rounds before coming on strongly to take all the remaining sessions, countering well and beating the champion to the punch repeatedly. There were no knockdowns and although Valdez (159¼) scored with heavy blows sporadically and stalked his man continuously he was unable to do any real damage. In the latter stages, looking ringworn, Valdez was badly shaken up in the 13th and from thereon in he failed to show.

5 August 1978. Hugo Corro w pts 15 Ronnie Harris.
Venue: Luna Park Stadium, Buenos Aires, Argentina. **Recognition:** World. **Referee:** Waldemar Schmidt.
Scorecards: 145-143, 146-144, 146-145.
Fight Summary: Up against a tough and clever southpaw in Harris (159½), the champion held on to his title when making a storming finish, landing well with lefts and rights to head and body to win the last three rounds. Up until then it had been relatively even, with Harris, despite lacking the power, making it extremely difficult for Corro (159). There were no knockdowns as such, apart from both men slipping over on occasion due to the wet canvas, and both were careless with their heads at times without causing damage. At ringside, the former champion, Carlos Monzon, felt that Corro deserved the win due his aggression, while slating the former Olympic champion, Harris, for being too negative.

11 November 1978. Hugo Corro w pts 15 Rodrigo Valdez.
Venue: Luna Park Stadium, Buenos Aires, Argentina. **Recognition:** World. **Referee:** Stan Christodoulou.
Scorecards: 149-140, 150-143, 150-140.
Fight Summary: Using hit-and-run tactics, the champion piled up the points against Valdez (158¾), who never looked like regaining his title with his rival being far too quick and elusive for him. Apart from landing a few heavy shots spasmodically, Valdez was always running second best as Corro (159¼) rarely missed with accurate jabs and hooks to the head and body without taking any risks. Not the fighter he once was, Valdez retired shortly afterwards before coming back to have two meaningless fights in 1980.

For Corro, Vito Antuofermo would be next. Having beaten Bennie Briscoe and Willie Warren earlier in the year, Antuofermo deserved a shot at the title, but had to wait as the match was postponed several times after Corro's badly damaged ankle, which happened in training, failed to respond to treatment. Afterwards, Corro stated that if he had been fighting either Marvin Hagler or Alan Minter he would have called the fight off until the ankle was completely okay.

30 June 1979. Vito Antuofermo w pts 15 Hugo Corro.
Venue: Royal Palace, Monte Carlo, Monaco. **Recognition:** World. **Referee:** Ernesto Magana.
Scorecards: 143-142, 146-145, 145-146.
Fight Summary: In what was a difficult fight to handle, and one that seemed likely to get out of control on occasion, Antuofermo (159¼) was ultimately just too aggressive and strong for the champion to handle as he bulled his way forward. Earlier on, though, Corro (158¾) had used the jab well to open up a cut over his rival's right eye in the third. Unable to hurt Antuofermo, he eventually began to tire before fading after the tenth following a solid right to the jaw. Subsequently, Corro, continuously complaining about Antuofermo's use of the head, was merely in defence mode, being almost dropped in the 15th. Even though Antuofermo had a round taken away for dangerous use of the head, it was felt at ringside that the referee would have been perfectly justified had he done likewise on at least two other occasions.

One of the conditions placed on Corro v Antuofermo was that the winner had to defend within 90 days against Marvin Hagler, who stopped Norberto Cabrera inside eight rounds on the same bill. Although the Antuofermo v Hagler fight was made for 22 September, an injured back suffered by the champion moved the fight on a couple of months or so.

30 November 1979. Vito Antuofermo drew 15 Marvin Hagler.
Venue: Caesar's Palace, Las Vegas, Nevada, USA. **Recognition:** World. **Referee:** Mills Lane.
Scorecards: 144-142, 141-145, 143-143.

Fight Summary: With a six-inch-reach advantage, Hagler (158½), who was the sharper puncher of the two, was cutting the champion up badly at range although unable to make it count in the long term. In what was an exciting affair, Antuofermo (158½) began to come through strongly from the eighth, bulling his way past Hagler's southpaw defences and slugging away to take the latter completely out of his stride. Antuofermo continued where he left off in the ninth, and despite Hagler wobbling him in the 11th he was punching it out with his challenger in the 12th. The last three rounds swung backwards and forwards, but in a grandstand finish, Antuofermo, carrying a multitude of cuts to his face, fought Hagler to a standstill in the final session. Hagler, who suffered a cut over the right eye in the 14th, felt that he was extremely unlucky not to have won.

Even though there was a lot of activity to promote a return immediately following the fight, the WBC stated that Antuofermo's next defence had to be against Alan Minter. Minter had lost six of 43 fights, all through cuts, but had battled through to win British and European titles before relinquishing them to concentrate on a world title challenge. Three British title wins over Kevin Finnegan proved his class while other men cast aside included Frank Reiche, Tony Licata, Sugar Ray Seales, Emile Griffith, Gratien Tonna, Rudy Robles and Monty Betham. A hard-punching southpaw with good skills to match, he had also overcome the shock of Angelo Jacopucci passing away following a contest for the vacant European title.

16 March 1980. Alan Minter w pts 15 Vito Antuofermo.
Venue: Caesar's Palace, Las Vegas, Nevada, USA. **Recognition:** World. **Referee:** Carlos Padilla.
Scorecards: 144-141, 149-137, 143-145.
Fight Summary: For the opening five rounds, for whatever reason the champion allowed the southpaw Minter (159¾) to make the running, especially with solid right jabs hitting the mark time and time again. Minter was also able to hammer in uppercuts and combinations during that spell. In the sixth Antuofermo (158¾) woke up to the fact that he was behind on the cards when tearing into Minter. Despite a lack of accuracy from Antuofermo, which Minter took advantage of with accurate counters, the latter was forced to change tactics. When a bad cut was opened over Minter's right eye in the ninth, by the 12th the damage was causing some concern due to Antuofermo charging in with his head at every opportunity. Following the 13th, which saw both men going toe-to-toe, in the 14th Minter was dropped by a straight right which he felt was a slip. With Antuofermo desperately trying to pull the iron out of the fire the final session turned into a brawl, but at the end of it Britain had a new undisputed world champion. In the aftermath, the WBC President, Jose Sulaiman, declared that the English judge, Roland Dakin, who had scored the fight 149-137, would be suspended indefinitely.

28 June 1980. Alan Minter w rtd 8 (15) Vito Antuofermo.
Venue: The Arena, Wembley, London, England. **Recognition:** World. **Referee:** Octavio Meyran.
Fight Summary: On top all the way, cutting Antuofermo (159¼) over the right eye as early as the opening session, it was soon clear that the latter was fighting a losing battle against a rampant Minter (160). Avoiding Antuofermo's reckless charges to counter with solid left crosses and right hooks, as the fight moved on the champion piled up the points with these tactics. Round after round Minter battered away at Antuofermo's features, it coming as no surprise when the latter was pulled out by his corner at the end of the eighth, his face a mass of cuts and abrasions.

Marvin Hagler would be next for Minter, having beaten Loucif Hamani, Bobby Watts and Marcos Geraldo since his title draw with Antuofermo.

27 September 1980. Marvin Hagler w rsc 3 (15) Alan Minter.
Venue: The Arena, Wembley, London, England. **Recognition:** World. **Referee:** Carlos Berrocal.
Fight Summary: With his title on the line, Minter (159¾) was cut on the left cheek from sharp rights in the opening 30 seconds, and by the end of the first round he had also been cut over the left eye as Hagler (160) clinically went about his work. With Minter not helping himself when taking the fight to Hagler, at the start of the third the first punch thrown by the American opened up another cut over his right eye. Although Minter, who needed 15 stitches to his face afterwards, tried to regroup the referee stopped the contest on the 1.45 mark, leaving Hagler the winner. Unfortunately, it became a night of shame for British boxing after fans rioted in a racial manner and Hagler had to be rushed away to safety as bottles and cans were thrown into the ring. Both men were southpaws.

17 January 1981. Marvin Hagler w rsc 8 (15) Fulgencio Obelmejias.
Venue: The Garden, Boston, Massachusetts, USA. **Recognition:** World. **Referee:** Octavio Meyran.
Fight Summary: Hagler (159½) quickly got down to business, his southpaw jab opening up the unbeaten Obelmejias (159½). Having damaged his right hand in the second, after Obelmejias' best punches failed to deter the champion there was no way back. By the fourth he was coming apart at the seams as Hagler nailed him at close range with both hands. A left to the jaw dropped Obelmejias in the fifth for the mandatory 'eight' count, and although there was constant pressure from Hagler it was not until the eighth round when the Venezuelan was sent staggering across the ring that the referee called the one-sided affair off 20 seconds into the session.

13 June 1981. Marvin Hagler w rtd 4 (15) Vito Antuofermo.
Venue: The Garden, Boston, Massachusetts, USA. **Recognition:** World. **Referee:** Davy Pearl.
Fight Summary: It was almost a lost cause for Antuofermo (158) after he suffered a bad cut in the opening round from a clash of heads. He was eventually pulled out by his corner at the end of the fourth following his right eye being opened up badly by heads coming together again. Several times the fighters locked horns as Antuofermo rushed in. While it appeared that Hagler (160) merely left his head in, he later said that he was getting set to throw left hooks. Whatever, it was clear that Antuofermo was not going to last, especially when solid southpaw punches put him down heavily in the third. Following the fight Antuofermo asked for a return on the grounds that he had been intentionally butted, but his request fell upon deaf ears.

3 October 1981. Marvin Hagler w rsc 11 (15) Mustafa Hamsho.
Venue: Horizon Arena, Rosemont, Illinois, USA. **Recognition:** World. **Referee:** Octavio Meyran.
Fight Summary: Right from the start Hamsho (160) waded into the champion throwing in wide arcing punches, only to be met by solid right counters that sent him back on his heels. Then, in the third round, Hamsho was cut over the right eye before a clash of heads saw Hagler (157) also damaged on the right eye. By the fifth Hagler was beginning to batter Hamsho, now cut over the left eye, slamming in jabs and uppercuts while beating him to the punch again and again. Surprisingly, Hamsho's cuts were under control by the seventh. However, Hamsho was being outpunched despite picking up the attack and in the 11th, when he was sent crashing to the floor following a savage burst of punching, the fight was stopped on the 2.09 mark. Both men were southpaws.

7 March 1982. Marvin Hagler w rsc 1 (15) Caveman Lee.
Venue: Bally's Park Place Hotel, Atlantic City, New Jersey, USA. **Recognition:** World. **Referee:** Larry Hazzard.
Fight Summary: Making a very fast start the champion was soon looking to put the quietus on Lee (159½), knocking his rival's head back with solid punches before a right hook sent him down. Up at the mandatory 'eight' count on shaky legs Lee was at the mercy of Hagler (158), who tore across the ring to finish the job. Having rained in punches, mainly to the head, two cracking right hooks left Lee helpless on the ropes, and just when Hagler was looking to finish the job the referee did it for him when calling a halt after just 67 seconds of action.

Hagler was now interested in hooking up with Thomas Hearns, the former WBA welterweight champion, and a title meeting was projected for 24 May before being called off in mid-June after the fighters were unable to agree the venue. Almost immediately, Hagler signed for a defence against Fulgencio Obelmejias in Italy at the end of July, which was undone within days when the champion suffered a broken rib in training. Bearing in mind that the injury would take two or three months to heal both parties agreed to an early October date.

30 October 1982. Marvin Hagler w co 5 (15) Fulgencio Obelmejias.
Venue: Ariston Theatre, San Remo, Italy. **Recognition:** World. **Referee:** Ernesto Magana.
Fight Summary: A return match between southpaws saw the champion yet again have too much for the gallant Obelmejias (159¼), who for the opening two rounds looked as though he would give Hagler (158½) problems. However, in the third Hagler began to take a grip of matters. Having punched Obelmejias all over the ring in the fourth it was only the bell that saved the Venezuelan. Tired and running out of ideas, with Obelmejias a sitting target for Hagler in the fifth a rapid succession of blows from both hands, followed by a right hook, sent him down to be counted out with 25 seconds of the session remaining.

Towards the end of the year, the WBC announced that as from 1 January 1983 they would be recognising 12-round contests as the accepted distance for world title fights. However, as Hagler had already signed a three-fight agreement, stipulating 15-round defences, with his promoter, Bob Arum, the WBC would ultimately have to accept that situation.

Hagler's next defence would come against Tony Sibson, who had outpointed Dwight Davison over 12 rounds at the National Exhibition Centre, Birmingham, England on 21 February 1982 to win a final eliminator as recognised by the WBC. A two-handed, solid puncher, Sibson had won 47 of 51 contests, beating men such as Roy Gumbs, Willie Classen, Chisanda Mutti, Norberto Cabrera and Alan Minter. He was also the former British, Commonwealth and European champion.

11 February 1983. Marvin Hagler w rsc 6 (15) Tony Sibson.

Venue: The Centrum, Worcester, Massachusetts, USA. **Recognition:** World. **Referee:** Carlos Padilla.

Fight Summary: With Britain's Sibson (160) next in line for the champion there were a few good judges who felt he had the equipment to handle the southpaw champion, or at least take him into the latter part of the contest. Unfortunately for Sibson by the end of the second round he was being outboxed while carrying a steadily worsening swelling on his left cheek. The next two sessions saw Sibson improving, by at least getting some heavy left hooks off, but he was still being pressured by Hagler (158¼) who was beginning to look for the finish. Moving up a gear in the fifth, Hagler opened up the lump under Sibson's left eye, and in the sixth following a battery of blows he put the latter down for the mandatory 'eight' count. Although Sibson, now with cuts on both eyes, was up at 'four' he was a sitting duck for Hagler's incisive punches. And after being knocked down again, despite getting up the referee stopped the contest. The finish was timed at 2.40.

After outpointing Frank Fletcher over 12 rounds on 13 February, Wilford Scypion not only won the United States Boxing Association (USBA) title but elevated himself into the number one slot to become Hagler's next challenger. A smart box-fighter, Scypion, who had beaten the ill-fated Willie Classen and Curtis Parker along the way, had won 26 of 29 contests.

27 May 1983. Marvin Hagler w co 4 (15) Wilford Scypion.

Venue: Civic Centre, Providence, Rhode Island, USA. **Recognition:** World. **Referee:** Frank Cappuccino.

Fight Summary: Once the contest got underway Scypion (160) quickly found himself outboxed, and although the challenger had been expected to move in on Hagler (160) to make life difficult for him he was unable to mount any real attacks. In the third Scypion continued to be outclassed, being hit by all manner of punches before picking up a cut on the left eye. Switching from southpaw to orthodox in the fourth, with Hagler pouring in the punches eventually a left-right-left combination sent Scypion down to be counted out with 13 seconds of the session remaining.

While the fight was not sanctioned by either the WBA or the WBC who considered that Scypion was not a worthy challenger for Hagler, it was supported by the United States Boxing Association/International. The said organisation was renamed as the International Boxing Federation (IBF) at their first ever convention in late October. The IBF would continue to support Hagler throughout his tenure.

10 November 1983. Marvin Hagler w pts 15 Roberto Duran.

Venue: Caesar's Palace, Las Vegas, Nevada, USA. **Recognition:** World. **Referee:** Stan Christodoulou.

Scorecards: 144-142, 146-145, 144-143.

Fight Summary: Having moved up through the weights the WBA junior middleweight champion, Duran (156½), stepped up one more division for a crack at Hagler (157½). At the end of the 13th, with the judges having Duran slightly ahead on the cards it was only due to Hagler's driving finish over the last three sessions that he ultimately took the decision. Bleeding from a cut around a badly swollen left eye, Hagler was given his toughest contest despite Duran damaging his right hand in the fifth. It was Duran's speed and movement that gave Hagler his biggest problems, and consequently he found the lighter man a difficult target to hit until both were tiring in the latter stages. There were no knockdowns. Afterwards, while Hagler stated that if there had been one more round he would have knocked Duran out, the latter responded by saying that he considered Sugar Ray Leonard to be a better fighter than the champion.

30 March 1984. Marvin Hagler w rsc 10 (15) Juan Domingo Roldan.
Venue: Riviera Hotel, Las Vegas, Nevada, USA. **Recognition:** World. **Referee:** Tony Perez.
Fight Summary: Making the ninth defence of his title, Hagler (159¼) was probably expecting a far easier ride than the one he got, especially when slipping over in the first round and being given a standing count for his pains. Thereafter, there were plenty of fierce exchanges, but Hagler gradually got on top when Roldan's right eye began to swell and close rapidly in the third. Roldan (159¼) was still dangerous with his swinging punches, but by the seventh Hagler was picking his punches better while keeping out of trouble. From there onwards it would be just a matter of time, and after 39 seconds of the tenth had elapsed a disorientated Roldan was pulled out of the fight by the referee, having just got up at 'eight' from a solid right to the head. Although retaining the WBC's support, Hagler again reiterated that he favoured 15-round fights. He went on to say that while he remained the champion he would defend over that distance.

19 October 1984. Marvin Hagler w rsc 3 (15) Mustafa Hamsho.
Venue: Madison Square Garden, Manhattan, NYC, New York, USA. **Recognition:** World. **Referee:** Arthur Mercante.
Fight Summary: Given another opportunity to meet the champion, Hamsho (159½) immediately went on the attack to take his fellow southpaw out of his stride. However, by the end of the opening round he was already cut over the left eye and up against it. This time, angry that Hamsho was using foul tactics and not being warned, Hagler (159½) caught his onrushing opponent with right hook counters in the second that stunned the 31-year-old Syrian and set him up for the finish. Finally, Hamsho was warned for butting in the third, but by now Hagler's fists were doing the talking. Smashed to the floor by solid right hooks, Hamsho beat the count only to be dropped to the canvas again by another cracking right hook, whereupon the referee immediately called it off on the 2.31 mark.

While the WBC had supported Hagler as the champion, even though he had refused to defend his title over 12 rounds, immediately following the fight they decided to vacate the title. When a deal was eventually brokered in December after Hagler agreed to abide by their ruling he was reinstated as champion forthwith.

15 April 1985. Marvin Hagler w rsc 3 (12) Thomas Hearns.
Venue: Caesar's Palace, Las Vegas, Nevada, USA. **Recognition:** World. **Referee:** Richard Steele.
Fight Summary: In a fight that would see Hagler (159¼) assuming the mantle of greatness, he defended his title against Hearns (159¾), the WBC junior middleweight champion. With both men tearing into each other with an intensity rarely seen, and both landing heavy blows, it was clear to all and sundry that this one was not going to go the distance. Towards the end of the opening session, with Hearns in trouble on the ropes but fighting back Hagler was badly cut between the eyes. In the second, when Hagler was cut under the right eye in his anxiousness to put Hearns away there were fears that he may have punched himself out with the latter remaining on his feet. Bleeding heavily, Hagler tore into Hearns in the third, and following a southpaw right hook that had the latter losing control of his legs three more heavy blows had him over. Even though Hearns amazingly got up at 'six' there was no way the referee was going to let him continue, the fight being over with 1.08 of the session remaining.

Due to defend the world title against John Mugabi in Nevada on 14 November, the match was called off two weeks before due to Hagler suffering a broken nose in sparring. There were also fears that the champion had suffered a ruptured disc in his lower back, which had already caused him to miss two weeks of training. After the doctors had advised him that his back condition should heal within three weeks and that he should not spar for at least six weeks, the promoter announced that the fight would take place in February or March 1986.

10 March 1986. Marvin Hagler w co 11 (12) John Mugabi.
Venue: Caesar's Palace, Las Vegas, Nevada, USA. **Recognition:** World. **Referee:** Mills Lane.
Fight Summary: Up against a man who had either stopped or knocked out all of his 25 opponents to date, this turned into another epic fight for Hagler (159½) in defence of his WBC, WBA and IBF titles. Both men started well, sending in plenty of hard punches, and in the fourth Mugabi (157) landed the heaviest punches of the fight at that

stage when shaking Hagler up with two tremendous right hooks. Although Hagler looked to be getting on top in the fifth, the sixth saw an all-out war with ferocious blows going in and both men looking stunned at times. After going flat out, Hagler was then penalised a point in the seventh for a low blow before his right eye began to rapidly close in the ninth. With there now being no more time for Hagler to stick to his boxing he tore into Mugabi in the tenth, only really hurting him at the end of the session, prior to picking it up again in the 11th. As Mugabi weakened badly Hagler took his chance, and following a battery of punches a long southpaw right to the head dropped the challenger for the full count, timed at 1.29.

Hagler forfeited WBA recognition in February 1987 for failing to meet Herol Graham within the stipulated period and subsequently signing for a defence against Sugar Ray Leonard. Following that, Sumbu Kalambay and Iran Barkley were matched to find a successor.

6 April 1987. Sugar Ray Leonard w pts 12 Marvin Hagler.
Venue: Caesar's Palace, Las Vegas, Nevada, USA. **Recognition:** IBF/WBC. **Referee:** Richard Steele.
Scorecards: 118-110, 115-113, 113-115.
Fight Summary: This one turned out to be the last fight in a great career for Hagler (160), and he seemed to be unfortunate to lose to Leonard (160) after what had been a very close affair, regardless of what one of the judges thought. As expected, Leonard started fast to take the opening four rounds before Hagler, hurting his rival with big southpaw hooks in the fifth, began to get more and more into the fight from there onwards. In the seventh, following a good sixth, Leonard appeared to be weakening, and in the eighth although his left eye was beginning to swell he continued to rally before meeting Hagler punch for punch in the ninth and being hurt by left hooks. However, from there on Leonard began to fade, fighting in bursts and dancing away out of trouble. Feeling that Hagler was hard done by, *Boxing News*, Britain's trade paper, gave him seven rounds to Leonard's four.

After opposing the match in the first place, it being a WBC promotion, the IBF stated that they were vacating their portion of the title because they could not lend their support to Leonard.

Then, on 26 May, Herol Graham forfeited his chance of a crack at the WBA title when losing his European crown to Sumbu Kalambay on points over 12 rounds at The Arena, Wembley, London, England.

A short while later, in June, all versions of the title were left vacant when Leonard announced that he was giving up the WBC title in order to take a long break from boxing.

With the division in turmoil, Iran Barkley, who had earlier been matched against Michael Olajide for the IBF title, was finally booked to meet Kalambay for the WBA crown on the proviso that the winner gave Mike McCallum first crack. Following matches made between Thomas Hearns v Juan Domingo Roldan (WBC) and Olajide v Frank Tate (IBF), the championship would be split three ways. While Hearns and Roldan had been involved in world title bouts previously, it was a new experience for the others.

An aggressive all-action fighter, Barkley had won 22 of 25 contests, beating Wilford Scypion and James Kinchen, whereas Kalambay was a crafty, clever boxer who had won 42 of 46, beating Buster Drayton and Graham.

Of the Tate versus Olajide pairing, the latter appeared to be the harder puncher with 16 inside-the-distance wins from 23 fights. Known as 'The Silk', Olajide had beaten Elio Diaz, Curtis Parker, James Green and Don Lee, and had a good left jab which was used to unleash solid hooks to head and body. Tate, with 12 quick wins from 20 contests, who had an excellent left jab and follow-up punches, had also defeated Parker, along with Marvin Mack and Troy Darrell.

10 October 1987. Frank Tate w pts 15 Michael Olajide.
Venue: Caesar's Palace, Las Vegas, Nevada, USA. **Recognition:** IBF. **Referee:** Richard Steele.
Scorecards: 146-135, 148-134, 147-136.
Fight Summary: Contesting the vacant title, the opening three rounds saw Olajide (157½) taking the fight to Tate (160) before the latter came back with better quality punches from head to body. Olajide, the son of Ola Michael, a

top-class lightweight who fought in British rings in the 1950s and '60s, began to give ground from the fifth onwards as Tate stepped it up. By the seventh the fight was in Tate's hands, and after staggering Olajide in the ninth with a left hook the latter was dropped by a big right in the tenth. Having got up and stayed out of trouble, Olajide went down again in the 12th. Although Olajide made it to his feet and came back fighting, knowing he had the contest in the bag Tate was happy to box his way through to the final bell.

23 October 1987. Sumbu Kalambay w pts 15 Iran Barkley.
Venue: Sports Palace, Livorno, Italy. **Recognition:** WBA. **Referee:** Ismael Rodriguez.
Scorecards: 147-140, 147-140, 147-142.
Fight Summary: Boxing an intelligent fight, Kalambay (160) picked up the vacant WBA title when outscoring Barkley (159) in a one-sided contest. It was Kalambay's excellent use of the left jab, solid counters and general cleverness that kept Barkley at bay, and although the American was unable to really influence the fight he never stopped trying. There were no knockdowns, but Barkley was rocked on occasion, finishing the fight with his left eye swollen.

At their conference, held during October, the WBA stated that all world title fights held under their banner would be contested over 12 rounds in future, thus bringing them into line with the WBC.

29 October 1987. Thomas Hearns w co 4 (12) Juan Domingo Roldan.
Venue: Hilton Hotel, Las Vegas, Nevada, USA. **Recognition:** WBC. **Referee:** Mills Lane.
Fight Summary: On winning the vacant WBC title, Hearns (159½) became the first man to win world championships in four different weight divisions. It was an exciting fight, Roldan (159½) being knocked down twice in the first round and again in the second before storming back to win the third and having Hearns going in the fourth. At that stage Hearns was fighting Roldan's fight, but after being forced to hold on for dear life, his legs quivering, he recovered to find a big right to the jaw that sent the latter down face first to be counted out on the 2.01 mark. An interesting statistic showed that Roldan threw 242 punches of which just 67 landed.

7 February 1988. Frank Tate w co 10 (15) Tony Sibson.
Venue: Bingley Hall, Stafford, England. **Recognition:** IBF. **Referee:** Frank Cappuccino.
Fight Summary: Although he was in the fight for eight rounds despite having to take some heavy punches along the way, Sibson (160) found the champion a far different proposition in the ninth when the American finally began to open up, having appeared almost lethargic at times. At this stage, *Boxing News* had Tate (160) two points up but that counted for nothing as Sibson appeared to stand off before a long right hand dropped him for the full count with just seven seconds remaining of round ten. Sibson, who had been a pro for 12 years, announced his retirement immediately after the fight.

5 March 1988. Sumbu Kalambay w pts 12 Mike McCallum.
Venue: Sports Palace, Pesaro, Italy. **Recognition:** WBA. **Referee:** John Coyle.
Scorecards: 116-115, 115-114, 118-114.
Fight Summary: In what was a huge upset, Kalambay (159) retained his title against the odds-on favourite McCallum (158¾), who had been expected to win inside the distance. Although McCallum constantly stalked Kalambay there were no knockdowns, the latter giving a great display of defensive boxing while making his rival miss and picking up points with left jabs and counters. Even when McCallum landed Kalambay was able to manoeuvre himself out of harm's way, and it was he who landed the more significant punches, a big right clearly rocking the Jamaican in the tenth. The last two sessions saw McCallum trying desperately to find the punch to turn things his way, but Kalambay was happy to coast to the final bell without taking any further risks.

6 June 1988. Iran Barkley w rsc 3 (12) Thomas Hearns.
Venue: Hilton Hotel, Las Vegas, Nevada, USA. **Recognition:** WBC. **Referee:** Richard Steele.
Fight Summary: Even though the champion made a dominant start, opening up with big punches, with Barkley (160) still right in front of him he was taking too many risks by not maintaining a proper defensive strategy. Still, there was no sign as to what was to come in the third. As Hearns (160) continued where he left off in the second, before too long Barkley, cut over both eyes, was under big pressure following a battery of lefts and rights to the

body. Then it happened. Having exchanged punches with Barkley in the centre of the ring in the third, Hearns, pulling away to survey his work, was caught by a big right over the top of his low defence that smashed into the side of his face and sent him crashing to the floor. Somehow getting up, Hearns was bundled through the ropes on to the ring apron, whereupon the referee stopped the fight with 21 seconds of the session remaining.

12 June 1988. Sumbu Kalambay w pts 12 Robbie Sims.
Venue: Sports Palace, Raveona, Italy. **Recognition:** WBA. **Referee:** John Coyle.
Scorecards: 118-110, 117-113, 119-113.
Fight Summary: The half-brother of Marvin Hagler, Sims (159¼) took the fight to the champion right from the start, staggering him with a southpaw right in the second round. That was Sims' best chance. With Kalambay (158¾) settling down from the third onwards the American was being caught by left jabs, hooks and solid rights. Although Sims kept up the attacks he was being picked off, and in the eighth he was badly hurt by a heavy right uppercut. He was under pressure again in the tenth and 11th when shipping hard lefts and rights, but continued to press right to the final bell in the vain hope of finding a winning punch.

28 July 1988. Michael Nunn w rsc 9 (15) Frank Tate.
Venue: Caesar's Palace, Las Vegas, Nevada, USA. **Recognition:** IBF. **Referee:** Mills Lane.
Fight Summary: Dictating the fight from the outset, the southpaw Nunn (160) showed all the qualities of an old-timer as he won virtually every round before finishing the champion off. Although Tate (160) occasionally got through Nunn's defences he was generally given a lesson as the latter picked up the pace, with cracking combinations, as the fight wore on. Nunn also showed excellent defensive skills. At the end of the eighth Tate was dropped by a left uppercut to the body, and while the bell came to his aid he was soon under pressure in the ninth when Nunn stormed into him. With Nunn not going to let his man off the hook this time, having hammered Tate on to the ropes and battered away at him the referee took a good look before calling it off after 40 seconds.

This would be the last 15-round fight for the weight class after the IBF announced that as at 1 September all world title bouts held under their auspices would be contested over 12 rounds.

4 November 1988. Michael Nunn w co 8 Juan Domingo Roldan.
Venue: Hilton Hotel, Las Vegas, Nevada, USA. **Recognition:** IBF. **Referee:** Richard Steele.
Fight Summary: Making his first defence the unbeaten Nunn (160) was in control virtually throughout, having started well when dropping Roldan (160) in the opening session. As the fight progressed the southpaw champion showed his ability to either box at long range or at close quarters, where he gave the dangerous Roldan a taste of his own medicine. The Argentine fought back somewhat in the seventh with strong rights to Nunn's head before again tagging the champion at the beginning of the eighth. Instead of backing off, Nunn was stirred into action, coming back hard to blast Roldan with a whole range of punches, and as the latter wilted he was despatched for the full count at 2.28 of the session after being caught by a left uppercut to the jaw. Unfortunately for Nunn he picked up an inch-long cut over his left eye in the final seconds of the contest.

8 November 1988. Sumbu Kalambay w rsc 7 Doug DeWitt.
Venue: Louis II Stadium, Monte Carlo, Monaco. **Recognition:** WBA. **Referee:** Carlos Berrocal.
Fight Summary: Kalambay (158½), the champion, was always in control of the fight, having outboxed DeWitt (159) right from the opening bell with left jabs and combinations. DeWitt had his moments, especially with left hooks, but unable to change the way the fight was going by the seventh he was cut under the left eye and had taken some heavy shots to head and body. Although DeWitt tried to pick up the pace in that session Kalambay was still unruffled, and when he found an opening for the left hook the American was sent crashing to the canvas. Even though DeWitt made it to his feet, when it was clear that he had nothing left the referee called a halt on the 1.31 mark.

After the World Boxing Organisation (WBO) was formed in November, following a major split in the ranks of the WBA, when the new organisation failed to recognise Kalambay as their champion they nominated DeWitt to meet Robbie Sims to decide their version of the title.

453

Meanwhile, Kalambay forfeited WBA recognition at the end of February 1989 when failing to sign for defence against Herol Graham, the British champion, and deciding to meet Michael Nunn for the IBF title instead. Following that, the WBA selected Graham and Mike McCallum to contest the vacancy. Since losing to Kalambay back in March, McCallum had won three out of three, while Graham looked forward to his first shot at a world title, having lost just once in 42 fights. That defeat also came against Kalambay. A former undefeated British, Commonwealth and European junior middleweight champion, Graham had victories over Kenny Bristol, Lindell Holmes, Irving Hines and Ayub Kalule, and at his best was a switch-hitter of the highest order with a brilliant defence to match.

24 February 1989. Roberto Duran w pts 12 Iran Barkley.
Venue: Convention Centre, Atlantic City, New Jersey, USA. **Recognition:** WBC. **Referee:** Joe Cortez.
Scorecards: 118-112, 116-112, 113-116.
Fight Summary: Seventeen years after lifting his first world title, Duran (159) became only the second man to become a champion at four different weights after winning by a very close margin. Despite being well outreached, using his experience to get to close quarters where he could inflict some damage on the champion Duran was well in the fight at the mid-point, having taken two tremendous left hooks and survived. By this time Barkley (158¼) had problems of his own as his left eye began to swell, but both men were still contesting every point with a ferocious belief. In the 11th the fight turned Duran's way when he dropped Barkley following a five-punch combination, and while he did little work in the final session two of the judges felt that he had done enough.

On 7 December, Duran was outpointed over 12 rounds by Sugar Ray Leonard at the Mirage Hotel & Casino, Las Vegas, Nevada. Although billed for the WBC super middles title held by Leonard, and made at 162lbs (six pounds below the championship limit), both men were inside 160lbs. Technically, with Duran's WBC middles title also at stake, it should have been declared vacant following the result. However, when the champion was stripped in January 1990 for failing to give a written undertaking to defend, Julian Jackson eventually moved up from the junior middleweight division to meet Herol Graham for the vacant title.

25 March 1989. Michael Nunn w co 1 Sumbu Kalambay.
Venue: Hilton Hotel, Las Vegas, Nevada, USA. **Recognition:** IBF. **Referee:** Richard Steele.
Fight Summary: Having decided to take control from the opening bell the southpaw champion immediately got down to business with the jab, but it was still quite a shock when he stepped in with a left after Kalambay (159) fell short to drop his rival heavily. Although Kalambay, who had failed to land a punch, was on his feet just after the count had ended Nunn (160) was declared the winner following just 80 seconds of action.

18 April 1989. Doug DeWitt w pts 12 Robbie Sims.
Venue: Showboat Hotel, Atlantic City, New Jersey, USA. **Recognition:** WBO. **Referee:** Joe Cortez.
Scorecards: 116-112, 115-113, 113-115.
Fight Summary: In a contest to decide the inaugural WBO title, two men who were supposed to be finished after being defeated by Sumbu Kalambay in their last fights were matched. Most of the solid blows were delivered by DeWitt (160), while the southpaw Sims (159) was always throwing punches. As game as ever, Sims was even ahead after five rounds despite being hurt in that session. The contest turned in the sixth as DeWitt got some heavy shots off, and in the seventh he almost had Sims over from a left hook. This was followed by DeWitt being badly hurt in the eighth and cut over the left eye in the ninth before finishing the fight strongly. Taking the last three sessions with a mixture of good boxing allied to solid punching, DeWitt won by a majority decision.

10 May 1989. Mike McCallum w pts 12 Herol Graham.
Venue: Royal Albert Hall, Kensington, London, England. **Recognition:** WBA. **Referee:** Enzo Montero.
Scorecards: 117-115, 115-114, 113-117.
Fight Summary: Contested for the vacant title, although Graham (159¾) made a reasonable start, landing good scoring punches before getting away unscathed, in the third round he allowed himself to caught far too often by the slower but harder punching McCallum (159). Still, having taken the initiative in the fourth, in the fifth Graham dropped McCallum with a short right hook before going on to take the next session when using his skill to the full. However, in the seventh Graham allowed himself to get caught too often again, and in the eighth he was deducted a point for throwing his man, an action that cost him dearly. Subsequently, especially after his right eye began to

close during the tenth Graham let the contest slip away by not doing enough. Even though both fighters were exhausted by the tenth, it was McCallum who did the better work.

14 August 1989. Michael Nunn w pts 12 Iran Barkley.
Venue: Lawlor Events Centre, Reno, Nevada, USA. **Recognition:** IBF. **Referee:** Carlos Padilla.
Scorecards: 116-113, 115-113, 114-114.
Fight Summary: Taking the fight to Nunn (159) throughout despite being badly cut on the lip and bleeding from the left eye early on, Barkley (160) was always in with a chance, especially when the southpaw champion decided to showboat rather than getting on with the job in hand. At times Nunn looked good, pumping in the jab and throwing blinding combinations, but lazing around too often he was hurt in the eighth, tenth and 11th rounds when Barkley got to him with solid blows. Although the 'Punch Stats' showed Nunn landing 346 punches to Barkley's 245 the decision was loudly booed by the majority of the crowd.

15 January 1990. Doug DeWitt w rtd 11 Matthew Hilton.
Venue: Convention Centre, Atlantic City, New Jersey, USA. **Recognition:** WBO. **Referee:** Randy Neumann.
Fight Summary: Starting well, winning the opening couple of rounds, Hilton (158) then had his right eye swollen shut in the third. And although he continued to go relatively well up to the beginning of the eighth the fight was now being controlled by the champion. In the ninth Hilton had a point deducted for going low but with DeWitt (160) now in complete charge, apart from one brief moment in the tenth when caught by a left-right to the jaw, he was handing out a steady beating. When Hilton's left began to close in the 11th, leaving him to fight on almost blind for the last minute of the session, it was no surprise when he was retired during the interval.

3 February 1990. Mike McCallum w pts 12 Steve Collins.
Venue: Hynes Convention Centre, Boston, Massachusetts, USA. **Recognition:** WBA. **Referee:** Bernie Soto.
Scorecards: 118-111, 117-113, 117-111.
Fight Summary: Dominating Collins (160) in the first five rounds, having opened up a cut above the Irishman's left eye in the fourth, the champion tried without success to score a kayo win in the fifth. With McCallum (159) looking tired Collins took the next two sessions as he pressured his rival, but in the eighth the Jamaican came right back, doubling up with the left from head to body to reassert himself. Although Collins was now fighting on empty, when an accidental butt cut McCallum above the right eye in the 11th he was never able to take advantage before running out a courageous loser.

14 April 1990. Michael Nunn w pts 12 Marlon Starling.
Venue: Mirage Hotel & Casino, Las Vegas, Nevada, USA. **Recognition:** IBF. **Referee:** Mills Lane.
Scorecards: 117-111, 118-110, 114-114.
Fight Summary: Much bigger than his challenger, Nunn (160) failed to take advantage of his natural assets and was happy to take no risks after initially coming to the weigh-in half a pound over the weight. Nunn even lost the opening three rounds as Starling (158) made a fast start, but once the champion got his jab working he soon piled up the points. Although Starling came again towards the end he could not hurt Nunn, who appeared to be treating the fight no differently to what he would a sparring session, the decision in his favour being met with boos and jeers.

14 April 1990. Mike McCallum w co 11 Michael Watson.
Venue: Royal Albert Hall, Kensington, London, England. **Recognition:** WBA. **Referee:** Roberto Ramirez.
Fight Summary: Although Watson (160) forced the pace for much of the fight the cagey champion, using solid blows to the head and body, was far too experienced to fight his rival's fight. It had become noticeable by the fifth that the Englishman was running out of ideas. By the eighth Watson was taking a fair amount of blows to the head as McCallum (159¾) leathered into him, but he hung on in through the pain despite being desperately tired. Into the 11th, however, with Watson now at the mercy of McCallum three solid blows sent the challenger reeling into the ropes before a crashing right to the head put him down for the full count. The finish was timed at 2.22.

29 April 1990. Nigel Benn w rsc 8 Doug DeWitt.
Venue: Caesar's Palace & Casino, Atlantic City, New Jersey, USA. **Recognition:** WBO. **Referee:** Randy Neumann.

Fight Summary: With both men setting a tremendous pace and the champion being cut over the left eye in the first round it was all systems go before Benn (158) was dropped by a left hook towards the end of the second. It was certainly all action, Benn coming back strongly in the third to have DeWitt (160) over following a big right to the jaw. The next four rounds saw some heavy punches going in, but although both men were shaken on occasion there were no knockdowns. Having held himself back somewhat, Benn struck at the start of the eighth when smashing DeWitt to the canvas with a big left hook for a 'nine' count. Although the latter was given the go-ahead he was almost out on his feet when put down again. Up at the count of 'two' DeWitt was then dropped again by a left hook, and with just 44 seconds of the round gone the fight was concluded on the 'three knockdowns in a round' ruling. Afterwards, Benn stated that despite damaging his left hand during the fight he had not let it stop him from using it.

18 August 1990. Nigel Benn w rsc 1 Iran Barkley.
Venue: Bally's Park Place Hotel, Las Vegas, Nevada, USA. **Recognition:** WBO. **Referee:** Carlos Padilla.
Fight Summary: Making his first defence, Benn (159½) retained his title under the 'three knockdowns in a round' ruling with just three seconds of the opening session remaining. Straight from the opening bell Benn charged into Barkley (160), hitting him with a tremendous right to the head before dropping him with a left hook. Back on his feet Barkley met Benn punch for punch before being put down again with a left hook and being struck while on the floor. The final blow was not considered by the referee to have been significant as Barkley took most of the 'eight' count on his feet, and although it was close to the completion of the round Benn brought the contest to an end with a powerful right to the head. Prior to the fight taking place there had been a fair amount of disquiet over the fact that Barkley had been out of action for a year following defeats at the hands of Roberto Duran and Michael Nunn, as well as having surgery for a detached retina.

18 October 1990. Michael Nunn w rsc 10 Donald Curry.
Venue: Sports Palace, Paris, France. **Recognition:** IBF. **Referee:** Denny Nelson.
Fight Summary: A double world champion at welter and junior middle, Curry (158) decided from the beginning that he would give it his best shot in the early rounds. And he was still giving the southpaw champion plenty to think about right up to the end of the sixth despite being behind on the cards. When it was clear that Curry was tiring in the seventh Nunn (159¾) dropped him for 'eight' with a good uppercut. It was generally felt that this was it, but Curry got through the next couple of rounds before Nunn, speeding up, eventually put him down following 14 unanswered blows to head and body in the tenth. With Curry on one knee but looking as though there was not much left in the tank, the referee stopped the fight on the 1.59 mark.

18 November 1990. Chris Eubank w rsc 9 Nigel Benn.
Venue: National Exhibition Centre, Birmingham, England. **Recognition:** WBO. **Referee:** Richard Steele.
Fight Summary: Reckoned to be one of the most exciting fights ever seen in a British ring, Benn (159¼) defended his title against his fellow Brit, Eubank (159½), and was shorn of his crown with five seconds of the ninth round remaining. It had been a brutal affair that saw Eubank land the better shots to win the opening two rounds before Benn came back to win the next two despite having to take some damaging punches in the process. Unfortunately for Benn, when his left eye was almost closed by the fifth he began to be picked off at distance. Even though Eubank was given a rest in the sixth after Benn had carelessly punched him in the groin he still had not shaken the effects off in the next session. In the eighth Eubank was dropped by a clubbing right to the head, but he regrouped in the ninth to take the fight to Benn whose left eye was now closed shut, landing heavily before building up a ferocious non-stop attack. With Benn on the ropes and not firing back, he was rescued by the referee in what was considered to be a perfectly timed stoppage.

24 November 1990. Julian Jackson w co 4 Herol Graham.
Venue: Torrequebrada Hotel & Casino, Benalmadena, Spain. **Recognition:** WBC. **Referee:** Joe Cortez.
Fight Summary: Looking to decide the vacant title, Britain's Graham (160) was paired against Jackson (160), a former junior middles champion with 38 inside the distance wins from 40 fights, 27 of them by clean knockouts. Making a great start, Graham had never boxed better when taking the first three rounds, closing Jackson's left eye and hurting him with solid southpaw punches, and at that stage one would have bet their house on him winning. After the doctor had taken a good look at Jackson's damaged eye during the interval the Virgin Islander came out

for the fourth, being immediately caught by a string of punches as Graham went looking for the kayo. At this stage of the fight Jackson had barely landed a blow on Graham, but when the latter moved in to finish the job leaving his chin exposed a vicious right hook smashed him to the canvas to be counted out after 1.13 of the round.

23 February 1991. Chris Eubank w tdec 10 Dan Sherry.
Venue: Conference Centre, Brighton, England. **Recognition:** WBO. **Referee:** Frank Santore Jnr.
Scorecards: 95-93, 95-92, 93-95.
Fight Summary: Sherry (160) proved to be a difficult man to catch as he went backwards for much of the time, occasionally leaping in with counters as the champion chased shadows until the middle rounds. In the opener it had looked as though the upright Canadian would not be around for long when he found himself on the floor from a left jab. Cut by the left eye in the third, it did not stop Sherry from continuously dancing around Eubank (160) scoring points. He did so well that by the ninth it seemed as though there was little in it. Having opened up a bad cut on Sherry's lower lip in that session, in the tenth Eubank butted the challenger who dropped to his knees belatedly hoping for a disqualification win. After the referee decided to deduct two points from Eubank instead of disqualifying him due to Sherry's histrionics, when the challenger was deemed not fit to continue at 2.11 of the session it went to the cards.

1 April 1991. Mike McCallum w pts 12 Sumbu Kalambay.
Venue: Louis II Stadium, Monte Carlo, Monaco. **Recognition:** WBA. **Referee:** John Coyle.
Scorecards: 116-114, 116-115, 114-115.
Fight Summary: In what was a very close contest the champion was ahead after six rounds, scoring well with solid combinations, before Kalambay (159½) picked up the pace to come back very strongly in the second half. It was probably the 11th that settled it for McCallum (159½) when he scored heavily, but Kalambay was always a threat, especially with the left hand.

McCallum forfeited WBA recognition in December when failing to sign for a defence against his mandatory challenger, Steve Collins, and then challenging James Toney for the IBF version of the title. Following that, Collins and Reggie Johnson were matched to find a successor.

18 April 1991. Chris Eubank w rsc 6 Gary Stretch.
Venue: Olympia, Kensington, London, England. **Recognition:** WBO. **Referee:** Tony Orlando.
Fight Summary: The tall southpaw challenger boxed extremely well for the opening five rounds, moving away from Eubank (160) before jumping in with solid right-lefts. All that changed in the sixth. Coming out fast, Eubank got down to work immediately, hurting Stretch (159) with a big left before the latter was deducted a point for pushing his man to the floor. Back on the attack, Eubank knew that he had Stretch going, and after dropping him twice in quick succession with a volley of blows to the head the fight was halted on the 1.16 mark when the latter was leaning on the ropes in a helpless state.

10 May 1991. James Toney w rsc 11 Michael Nunn.
Venue: John O'Donnell Stadium, Davenport, Iowa, USA. **Recognition:** IBF. **Referee:** Denny Nelson.
Fight Summary: Outboxing Toney (157) for the opening seven rounds despite having to take the occasional heavy blow, the southpaw champion began to look less than confident in the eighth when forced to fight his way off the ropes. Well behind at the start of the 11th, Toney tore into Nunn (160), blasting in big punches before the latter was dropped by a left hook. Although Nunn got up, looking as though he had received a long count, he was immediately bowled over by a right uppercut, whereupon the referee called it off with 46 seconds of the session remaining.

22 June 1991. Chris Eubank w pts 12 Michael Watson.
Venue: Exhibition Centre, Earls Court, London, England. **Recognition:** WBO. **Referee:** Frank Cappuccino.
Scorecards: 116-113, 115-113, 114-114.
Fight Summary: Although the champion appeared to be marginally ahead at the halfway stage Watson (160) came on very strong towards the end. By the final bell Watson thought he had won by a country mile, but with the heavier punches in the fight being landed by Eubank (160) that was what ultimately gained him the decision.

After Eubank relinquished his WBO version of the title in July in order to challenge for the vacant WBO super middleweight crown, Gerald McClellan and John Mugabi came together to find a new champion.

29 June 1991. James Toney w pts 12 Reggie Johnson.
Venue: Hilton Hotel, Las Vegas, Nevada, USA. **Recognition:** IBF. **Referee:** Richard Steele.
Scorecards: 114-113, 115-112, 113-114.
Fight Summary: With the aggression and extra power of Toney (159) opposed to the challenger's defensive skills and punch-picking on the back foot it was always going to be close, but in most eyes it was Johnson's fight. The only knockdown of the contest came in the opening session when a southpaw left cross to the jaw put Toney on the seat of his pants, and although Johnson (159) tried his utmost to put his rival away he was unable to do so. In a dramatic last round, in which Toney sustained a bad cut on the left eye, despite Johnson finishing strongly he went down narrowly on the cards.

14 September 1991. Julian Jackson w co 1 Dennis Milton.
Venue: Mirage Hotel & Casino, Las Vegas, Nevada, USA. **Recognition:** WBC. **Referee:** Mills Lane.
Fight Summary: Defending his title with the reputation of being the best one-punch knockout man around, Jackson (158) proved it yet again when dropping Milton (159) for the full count. It was all Jackson from the start, with Milton happy to hold and run, but once the champion found his range it was all over, a cracking short right doing the damage. Milton tried to get up before lurching down again, the finish being timed at 2.10.

12 October 1991. James Toney w rsc 4 Francesco Dell'Aquila.
Venue: Louis II Stadium, Monte Carlo, Monaco. **Recognition:** IBF. **Referee:** Frank Cappuccino.
Fight Summary: The big talking point of the fight was the fact that the IBF allowed Toney to defend his title despite him being almost half a pound over the weight. When it was clear that Toney would be unable to get the excess poundage off at the third time of asking the Italian camp agreed for the fight to go ahead. Toney was even registered by the officials as being 72.55 kilos (just inside the required 160lbs). Trying to box on the back foot and clearly outgunned, Dell'Aquila (158½) was dropped in the first round by three solid blows to the head before making it into the fourth due to Toney's lack of condition. Stepping it up during that session, Toney blasted in blows from both hands as the outclassed Italian, his right cheek badly swollen, tried to move out of the danger zone. With the end clearly in sight, when Dell'Aquila was eventually belted to the canvas, having been hit by a whole battery of shots, the referee called it off without bothering with the count.

20 November 1991. Gerald McClellan w rsc 1 John Mugabi.
Venue: Royal Albert Hall, Kensington, London, England. **Recognition:** WBO. **Referee:** Roberto Ramirez.
Fight Summary: In a battle to decide the vacant WBO title between two big punchers, it was McClellan (158½) who came out on top when dropping Mugabi (157½) three times in the opening session to enforce a stoppage win under the 'three knockdowns in a round' ruling after just 120 seconds of fighting. It was McClellan's right hand that proved to be decisive, and although Mugabi tried his utmost to fight on each time he was back on his feet he had no defence against the punch.

After McClellan relinquished the WBO version of the title in March 1993 to challenge for the WBC crown, Sumbu Kalambay and Chris Pyatt were matched to find a new champion.

13 December 1991. James Toney drew 12 Mike McCallum.
Venue: Atlantic City, New Jersey, USA. **Recognition:** IBF. **Referee:** Steve Smoger.
Scorecards: 116-112, 113-115, 114-114.
Fight Summary: Both men were soon into their rhythm, but it was the champion who struck first when decking McCallum (157¾) with a left-right combination late in the second round. Ruled as a slip, it had seemed to be a legitimate knockdown. However, it spurred on Toney (159), who began to have the better of most of the exchanges until McCallum started to get his act together by the seventh. In the ninth Toney was in some trouble from a left hook to the head following several shots to the body, but towards the end of the session he had recovered. Pressing on in the final round Toney had McCallum rubber-legged and in deep trouble before the final

bell came to the latter's aid. Many of the ringside reporters had Toney well ahead on the grounds that he had scored the most damaging blows of the fight.

8 February 1992. James Toney w pts 12 Dave Tiberi.
Venue: Taj Mahal Hotel, Atlantic City, New Jersey, USA. **Recognition:** IBF. **Referee:** Robert Palmer.
Scorecards: 115-112, 115-111, 111-117.
Fight Summary: Not given a chance, Tiberi (158½) soon made his intentions clear when taking the fight to the champion from the opening bell. Standing right in front of Toney (159¾), for the most part Tiberi, despite being cut and bruised, met him punch for punch, and in the sixth he was unlucky to be deducted a point for going low. With the eighth being the best of the fight as the men blazed away with both hands, while Toney looked to be worn out at times his better quality blows won the day. Toney had difficulty in making the weight and it showed.

15 February 1992. Julian Jackson w rsc 1 Ismael Negron.
Venue: Mirage Hotel & Casino, Las Vegas, Nevada, USA. **Recognition:** WBC. **Referee:** Mills Lane.
Fight Summary: Showing himself to be one of the hardest-hitting champions of the modern era, Jackson (159) jumped on Negron (160) right from the opening bell, smashing in heavy shots from both hands to head and body. Negron did not know what had hit him, and after being sent down heavily by a left hook to the jaw the referee stopped counting on the 50 second mark to call the fight off.

10 April 1992. Julian Jackson w rsc 5 Ron Collins.
Venue: City Bullring, Mexico City, Mexico. **Recognition:** WBC. **Referee:** Lupe Garcia.
Fight Summary: Defending his title against a former sparring partner, Jackson, who (158¾) found Collins (159½) not afraid to meet him punch for punch, was even sent slipping to the deck in the first round. Fighting in a 16-foot ring was always going to suit the champion, and by the third Collins, who had almost punched himself out, was having difficulty in avoiding the blows coming his way. After somehow getting through the fourth, come the fifth Collins was just about through for the night, the referee stopping the fight 97 seconds into the session with the latter on the floor from a solid right.

11 April 1992. James Toney w pts 12 Glenn Wolfe.
Venue: Thomas & Mack Centre, Las Vegas, Nevada, USA. **Recognition:** IBF. **Referee:** Mills Lane.
Scorecards: 117-111, 119-109, 118-110.
Fight Summary: Despite hardly getting himself out of first gear the champion was far too good for Wolfe (160), a man who had recently survived a gunshot wound that had grazed his skull. By the seventh Wolfe's left eye was closing, but Toney (160), continuing to box in short bursts, was content to let his rival last until the final bell.

22 April 1992. Reggie Johnson w pts 12 Steve Collins.
Venue: Meadowlands Arena, East Rutherford, New Jersey, USA. **Recognition:** WBA. **Referee:** Arthur Mercante.
Scorecards: 115-113, 115-114, 114-114.
Fight Summary: Contesting the vacant title, Collins (160) fell short for the second time when he was unable to overcome his clever southpaw opponent. The Irishman was fighting on equal terms until the halfway stage when Johnson (159) got his right jab going, and in the tenth his right eye was badly cut. Despite tearing into Johnson in the final two sessions, although Collins made up some of the leeway with solid blows to the head he was unable to find a finisher. Both men were deducted a point each for going low. Afterwards, Collins, who picked up another one for illegal use of the elbow, felt that the American had used his head unfairly to gain an advantage.

1 August 1992. Julian Jackson w pts 12 Thomas Tate.
Venue: Hilton Hotel, Las Vegas, Nevada, USA. **Recognition:** WBC. **Referee:** Richard Steele.
Scorecards: 117-111, 116-111, 116-111.
Fight Summary: Becoming only the third man to take the champion the distance, Tate (159) put up a good fight, almost giving as much as he took once he got his left jab working to good effect. Only in the fourth round was he in serious trouble, Jackson (159) finally putting him down after three solid blows from both hands did the damage. Although it looked as though Tate was ready to go, in the fifth he came right back to have Jackson in some trouble.

Then, in the eighth, Tate was right up against it before coming back hard, something that remained the pattern of the fight right up until the final bell.

29 August 1992. James Toney w pts 12 Mike McCallum.
Venue: Sparks Convention Centre, Reno, Nevada, USA. **Recognition:** IBF. **Referee:** Joe Cortez.
Scorecards: 118-110, 117-110, 114-114.
Fight Summary: With the champion's body punches setting the tone of the fight by the sixth McCallum (158) had begun to slow. He was still not out of it, but at this stage Toney (158¾) was landing faster, heavier shots. McCallum was right back in the mix in the eighth when keeping up the pressure and making Toney fight all the way. Despite being tired, McCallum kept up the work-rate during the last three rounds, but Toney fought back hard to maintain his lead.

Having had difficulty making the weight, Toney relinquished the IBF version of the title on becoming that body's super middleweight champion in February 1993. To fill the void the IBF matched Roy Jones, who was unbeaten in 21 contests (only one going the distance), against the USBA champion, Bernard Hopkins. After Hopkins lost his first pro fight he had then gone on to win his next 22.

27 October 1992. Reggie Johnson w pts 12 Lamar Parks.
Venue: The Summit, Houston, Texas, USA. **Recognition:** WBA. **Referee:** Jerry McKenzie.
Scorecards: 116-112, 116-113, 116-113.
Fight Summary: Making his first defence Johnson (159¼) got right down to business, sending in southpaw jabs and countering the plodding Parks (159½) with solid lefts before getting away. It was clear that Parks did not know how to deal with a tricky southpaw, but he was still in there trading punches in the latter rounds without being able to dent the clever Johnson. However, at the final bell there was only one winner.

19 January 1993. Reggie Johnson w rsc 8 Ki-Yun Song.
Venue: The Centre, Boise, Idaho, USA. **Recognition:** WBA. **Referee:** Luis Rivera.
Fight Summary: Starting as he meant to carry on the champion was soon spearing Song (159) with solid southpaw jabs before the South Korean could even find his bearings. It seemed that all Song had on offer was a wild right without the lead, his left eye being completely closed by the seventh while taking a beating as Johnson (160) went from head to body. The eighth round was the end for Song, who was rescued by the referee 40 seconds into the session after he had turned his back on Johnson following heavy body shots and a hard left flush on the jaw.

4 May 1993. Reggie Johnson w pts 12 Wayne Harris.
Venue: McNichol's Arena, Denver, Colorado, USA. **Recognition:** WBA. **Referee:** Rafael Ramos.
Scorecards: 120-108, 120-109, 120-110.
Fight Summary: Brought in as a late substitute for Jorge Castro, the tall challenger was no match for Johnson (160), who treated the fight as he would have a sparring session, prodding his rival with southpaw jabs while opening up only occasionally. Several times Harris (160) slipped off the ring apron that was far too close to the ropes and in the eighth round he actually twisted his right knee. Ordered by the doctor to continue, Harris, who had not won a round up to that point, carried on half-heartedly while Johnson failed to take advantage of the situation and did his prospects no good at all with a lethargic display that lasted through to the final bell.

8 May 1993. Gerald McClellan w rsc 5 Julian Jackson.
Venue: Thomas & Mack Centre, Las Vegas, Nevada, USA. **Recognition:** WBC. **Referee:** Mills Lane.
Fight Summary: An explosive contest between two big punchers saw Jackson (159), a man who had overcome retina operations on both eyes, lose his title to McClellan (160) when the referee stopped the fight after 2.09 of the fifth round. Both men were firing big punches from the opening bell, but the first sign of damage, a bad cut over Jackson's left eye, came from a clash of heads in the third for which McClellan had a point deducted. At the start of the fifth Jackson was slightly ahead, but after twice being dropped by solid rights and lefts to the head for counts of 'eight' and 'four' the referee had seen enough.

19 May 1993. Chris Pyatt w pts 12 Sumbu Kalambay.
Venue: Granby Halls, Leicester, England. **Recognition:** WBO. **Referee:** Ismael Fernandez.
Scorecards: 115-113, 116-114, 116-113.
Fight Summary: Contesting the title vacated by Gerald McClellan, Pyatt (158½) made a good start when winning the opening three rounds before Kalambay (160) got himself into the fight. Although throwing less than Pyatt the domiciled Italian was more accurate, and by the seventh he was right back in the fight, working from head to body and steadying his rival with solid jabs. Both men increased their momentum over the last three sessions but it was Pyatt's sheer desire, despite being extremely tired, that won the day as Kalambay failed to match the Englishman's work-rate.

22 May 1993. Roy Jones w pts 12 Bernard Hopkins.
Venue: RFK Stadium, Washington DC, USA. **Recognition:** IBF. **Referee:** Steve Smoger.
Scorecards: 116-112, 116-112, 116-112.
Fight Summary: Showing great variety and terrific hand-speed and movement, the unbeaten Jones (159½) captured the title vacated by James Toney when taking the points decision. It was not until the sixth round that Hopkins (159), who was on 22 straight, had any success, and in the eighth he began to catch Jones with some big rights to the head before the latter got back on course. The last three rounds saw Hopkins trying to step it up, but he proved to be too one-dimensional to worry Jones who took no risks at that stage of the fight.

6 August 1993. Gerald McClellan w co 1 Jay Bell.
Venue: Ruben Rodriguez Coliseum, Bayamon, Puerto Rico. **Recognition:** WBC. **Referee:** Tony Perez.
Fight Summary: The fight only lasted 30 seconds, a record for the division in modern times. Both men came out with the jab before the champion, McClellan (159½), caught the limited Bell (157½) with a tremendous left to the body after missing with a big right. It later transpired that Bell had participated in just nine fights in eight years.

18 September 1993. Chris Pyatt w co 6 Hugo Corti.
Venue: Granby Halls, Leicester, England. **Recognition:** WBO. **Referee:** Frank Cappuccino.
Fight Summary: Defending for the first time, Pyatt (158) had to overcome a huge scare towards the end of the opening session after a left to the jaw from Corti (159) had him hanging on for all he was worth. Having settled by the third round, Pyatt began to take the Argentine apart from there onwards as big rights to the head began to set the challenger up. Twice the ringside doctor had a careful look at Corti before allowing him to continue, and it came as no surprise when he was counted out at 1.58 of the sixth following a left-right to the jaw that left him seated on the canvas with nothing left.

1 October 1993. John David Jackson w pts 12 Reggie Johnson.
Venue: Obras Sanitarias Stadium, Buenos Aires, Argentina. **Recognition:** WBA. **Referee:** Oscar Coronel.
Scorecards: 115-114, 115-113, 115-113.
Fight Summary: In a battle of southpaws, Jackson (159½) dominated the early rounds as he kept the champion at arm's length with the jab before losing his way in the second half of the contest. During that period, Johnson (160) got himself right back into the frame with solid body shots that forced Jackson to get on his bike, and if he had not had a point deducted for going low in the sixth he would have retained his title.

After Jackson was stripped of the WBA version of the title in May 1994 for accepting a non-title fight without having the body's authorisation, Johnson was matched against Jorge Castro to decide the championship.

9 February 1994. Chris Pyatt w co 1 Mark Cameron.
Venue: International Hall, Brentwood, England. **Recognition:** WBO. **Referee:** Robert Gonzalez.
Fight Summary: Controlling the fight from the start the champion began to probe for openings once he realised that Cameron (158½) did not pose a threat. Towards the end of the first session Pyatt (159¼) staggered Cameron with the jab, and before the South African had time to recover a cracking right to the jaw sent him down in a heap. Although the bell to end the round sounded when the count was 'eight', the referee continued to 'ten' as Cameron struggled to make it to his feet.

4 March 1994. Gerald McClellan w rsc 1 Gilbert Baptist.
Venue: MGM Grand, Las Vegas, Nevada, USA. **Recognition:** WBC. **Referee:** Richard Steele.
Fight Summary: Coming in at short notice for the indisposed Lamar Parks, Baptist (158) was soon under pressure from the champion before being dropped in a neutral corner after taking a slamming left hook. With Baptist finished from this point, when McClellan (159) put him down twice more in quick succession the referee called a halt. The stoppage was timed at 1.37.

7 May 1994. Gerald McClellan w co 1 Julian Jackson.
Venue: MGM Grand, Las Vegas, Nevada, USA. **Recognition:** WBC. **Referee:** Joe Cortez.
Fight Summary: Having struggled to make the weight the champion tore into Jackson (160) from the first bell, catching his man with a big right hook barely 15 seconds into the fight. Although Jackson remained upright he was driven to the ropes by McClellan (160) where he was battered without let up, slipping down once before a left to the body sent him crashing to the floor to be counted out on the 1.23 mark.

McClellan vacated the WBC version of the title in January 1995 after landing a crack at super middleweight champion, Nigel Benn, which was followed by Jackson being matched against Agostino Cardamone to decide the vacancy.

11 May 1994. Steve Collins w rsc 5 Chris Pyatt.
Venue: Ponds Forge Leisure Centre, Sheffield, England. **Recognition:** WBO. **Referee:** Paul Thomas.
Fight Summary: Looking a far bigger man than the champion, with Collins (159) making a confident start he was soon getting home with right-hand counters. It was anybody's fight by the end of the fourth but it all changed in the fifth. Even though both men were getting their punches off it was Collins who landed the best one of the fight, a crunching right to the face that bowled Pyatt (159) over. After being given the mandatory 'eight' count, Pyatt was given the chance to carry on before being rescued by the referee after 2.27 of the session had elapsed when it was clear that he was taking too many punches.

When Collins relinquished the WBO version of the title in March 1995 following his victory over Chris Eubank for the WBO super middles crown, Lonnie Bradley was matched against David Mendez to find a new champion.

27 May 1994. Roy Jones w rsc 2 Thomas Tate.
Venue: MGM Grand, Las Vegas, Nevada, USA. **Recognition:** IBF. **Referee:** Richard Steele.
Fight Summary: Making his first defence, Jones (159) showed his worth when stopping the dangerous Tate (159½) after just 13 seconds of the second round. Although Tate boxed reasonably well in the opening session, despite being hurt by fast lefts and rights, as he tried to find a way in at the start of the second he was sent crashing by a long left hook. Somehow Tate managed to just about beat the count, but when his second jumped on to the ring apron the referee called it off.

Jones vacated the IBF version of the title on 18 November after beating James Toney for the IBF super middleweight crown, following which Bernard Hopkins and Segundo Mercado were matched to find a new middleweight champion.

12 August 1994. Jorge Castro w pts 12 Reggie Johnson.
Venue: Villa Lujan Defenders Football Ground, Tucuman, Argentina. **Recognition:** WBA. **Referee:** Armand Krief.
Scorecards: 116-114, 116-114, 115-116.
Fight Summary: Contesting the vacant title it was fairly even for the first ten rounds, both men having their moments. With Castro (159¾) chasing and Johnson (159¾) boxing mainly on the back foot, the latter's southpaw jab just about kept his rival at bay. However, the last two sessions saw Castro finally get to Johnson, hammering punches in from all over to take the title on a split decision.

5 November 1994. Jorge Castro w co 2 Alex Ramos.
Venue: Municipal Gym, Caleta Olivia, Argentina. **Recognition:** WBA. **Referee:** Enzo Montero.

Fight Summary: Seen as one of the worst mismatches of recent times, Ramos (159¾), who was at his peak ten years earlier and was back in the ring after a cocaine addiction, was at the mercy of the champion from the opening bell. Having been worked all over, almost being floored in the first, Ramos was dropped by a single left hook to the body and counted out in the second on the 1.31 mark. With virtually no punches coming his way, Castro (159½) had barely worked up a sweat against a man who had somehow been elevated to championship status after beating nine unknowns following a kayo defeat at the hands of Segundo Mercado.

10 December 1994. Jorge Castro w rsc 9 John David Jackson.
Venue: Baseball Stadium, Monterrey, Mexico. **Recognition:** WBA. **Referee:** Stan Christodoulou.
Fight Summary: Although Jackson (160) was badly shaken up by the champion in the opening session he got his act together in the next seven rounds, doing almost as he pleased, but could not put the Argentine on the floor. In the seventh, Castro (160) was cut over both eyes before being hammered from pillar to post in the eighth. Still Jackson could not finish the job despite hitting his man with everything at his disposal. In trouble at the start of the ninth and floundering on the ropes with the referee almost coming to his rescue, out of the blue Castro dropped the oncoming Jackson with a mighty left hook that came up from the floor. Somehow getting to his feet, Jackson was a beaten man. And after being allowed to continue he was put down twice more, which saw him stopped on the 'three knockdowns in a round' ruling with 17 seconds of the session remaining.

17 December 1994. Bernard Hopkins drew 12 Segundo Mercado.
Venue: Ruminahui Coliseum, Quito, Ecuador. **Recognition:** IBF. **Referee:** Sam Williams.
Scorecards: 114-111, 114-116, 113-113.
Fight Summary: Battling for the vacant title, and the first world championship contest in Ecuador's history, both men gave it everything before the judges decided there would have to be a rematch. Down twice, in the third and sixth rounds, but not counted on, Mercado (158) had Hopkins (157) on the floor in the fifth and seventh from solid right-hand shots to the jaw which did count. Coming into the ninth, with the high altitude taking its toll Hopkins had some work to do. And when Mercado was cut on the right eye following a clash of heads the last nine minutes were difficult for him as Hopkins began to make up the leeway. Although Hopkins finished strongly the draw was a fair result as neither man deserved to lose.

17 March 1995. Julian Jackson w rsc 2 Agostino Cardamone.
Venue: Memorial Auditorium, Worcester, Massachusetts, USA. **Recognition:** WBC. **Referee:** Marty Denkin.
Fight Summary: Going for the title vacated by Gerald McClellan, Cardamone (160) came out in confident fashion, banging in southpaw lefts and rights from head to body, and staggering Jackson (160) badly with a solid left to the jaw towards the end of the first session. With both men attacking at the start of the second again Jackson was hurt. Confident of the win Cardamone moved in to finish the job, but having missed with a left when he was caught by a cracking right to the head he was sent crashing downwards. After staggering upwards, Cardamone was rescued by the referee on the 1.50 mark when he was clearly unable to continue.

29 April 1995. Bernard Hopkins w rsc 7 Segundo Mercado.
Venue: US Air Arena, Landover, Maryland, USA. **Recognition:** IBF. **Referee:** Rudy Battle.
Fight Summary: In a return fight to decide the vacant IBF title, Hopkins (158) made it third time lucky when he stopped Mercado (160) in the seventh. The fight had begun with the taller Mercado getting away with some low blows, but by the third round Hopkins was landing solid punches that threatened a knockout. Badly dazed in the fourth, fifth and sixth, despite being battered Mercado was still there, and although taking a terrific beating in the seventh he remained upright. The fight came to an end on the 1.10 mark when it was obvious that Mercado had little left but his courage, the referee deciding he could not allow it to continue.

19 May 1995. Lonnie Bradley w rsc 12 David Mendez.
Venue: Buffalo Bill's Hotel & Casino, Reno, Nevada, USA. **Recognition:** WBO. **Referee:** Richard Steele.
Fight Summary: With the vacant title up for grabs, Bradley (160) always had things under control, boxing well behind a solid left jab and mixing up punches to head and body whenever the opportunity arose. By the eighth round, Mendez (159), both of his eyes beginning to swell, was looking as though he was ready to be taken, but still Bradley boxed in a controlled fashion. It was only in the final session that Bradley really opened up, and after

stunning Mendez with four overarm rights the referee called a halt to proceedings with 50 seconds of the fight left on the clock.

27 May 1995. Jorge Castro w rsc 12 Anthony Andrews.
Venue: Broward County Convention Centre, Fort Lauderdale, Florida, USA. **Recognition:** WBA. **Referee:** Bernie Soto.
Fight Summary: Prior to the fight it was said that Andrews (158¼) was not a worthy challenger. However, after 11 tough rounds of leather throwing, and having met Castro (159¾) punch for punch throughout he clearly deserved his chance. Not only had he taken Castro's best shots, but there was only one point between them on the cards. Coming out for the 12th both men continued to let the punches go, only this time Castro's carried more sting, and with just 46 seconds of the fight remaining the referee stopped the action with Andrews an open target and being belted along the ropes from heavy blows to the head.

15 July 1995. Lonnie Bradley w rsc 1 Dario Galindez.
Venue: Great Western Forum, Los Angeles, California, USA. **Recognition:** WBO. **Referee:** Raul Caiz.
Fight Summary: Putting his title on the line for the first time, Bradley (160) did not waste much time as he set about Galindez (159½) right from the bell. Within moments, Galindez had taken a count after being sent down and lurching around like a drunk. Although the Argentine was allowed to fight on, after a terrific right to the jaw had sent the son of Victor Galindez (the former light heavyweight champion) down for the second time the fight was stopped on the 1.54 mark.

19 August 1995. Quincy Taylor w rsc 6 Julian Jackson.
Venue: MGM Grand, Las Vegas, Nevada, USA. **Recognition:** WBC. **Referee:** Jay Nady.
Fight Summary: Taylor (159½) made a bright start to the contest with heavy southpaw lefts hurting the champion, up and down, and in the fourth round he decided to go up a gear. Having rocked Jackson (160) with solid uppercuts, towards the end of the session Taylor pulled out a tremendous left hook that sent the Virgin Islander sprawling. Making it to his feet just before the bell to end the round rang, Jackson was forced to endure a battering in the fifth before finding a terrific right that almost won the fight for him. Although stunned, Taylor remained on his feet. Then, in the sixth, Taylor went to work on the tiring Jackson, who was rescued by the referee at 2.33 when he was under pressure on the ropes and not firing back.

13 October 1995. Jorge Castro w pts 12 Reggie Johnson.
Venue: Comodoro Rivadavia Stadium, Chubut, Argentina. **Recognition:** WBA. **Referee:** John Coyle.
Scorecards: 118-113, 115-113, 112-115.
Fight Summary: Fighting for the first time since a car crash in July, it was only the lack of aggression on the part of Johnson (157¾) that saved the day for Castro (160). By the tenth, after Castro began to get into his stride he swept through the last two sessions, driving Johnson before him. The fight was too close for comfort as far as Castro was concerned, and had Johnson not been deducted a point in the sixth for butting he might have pulled it off.

19 December 1995. Shinji Takehara w pts 12 Jorge Castro.
Venue: Korakuen Hall, Tokyo, Japan. **Recognition:** WBA. **Referee:** Mitch Halpern.
Scorecards: 116-114, 118-112, 117-111.
Fight Summary: Losing for only the fifth time in 105 fights, Castro (160) was right up against it from the moment the tall Takehara (160) staggered him in the opening round with an overarm right. Although Castro tried hard to get into the fight, dropped in the third by a terrific left to the body, he was on the end of Takehara's jab for the next three sessions. Even though Castro came on strongly in the seventh and eighth, Takehara came back hard with solid combinations in the ninth before boxing his way through the remaining three sessions.

27 January 1996. Bernard Hopkins w rsc 1 Steve Frank.
Venue: Veterans Memorial Coliseum, Phoenix, Arizona, USA. **Recognition:** IBF. **Referee:** Bobby Ferrara.
Fight Summary: Making his first defence, Hopkins (159) barely raised a sweat when beating a man with a record of seven fights in the last seven years and 18 contests in all. The fight had only been underway for a few moments when Hopkins opened Frank (160) up with two solid blows before flattening him with a blasting right to the jaw.

How Frank got up at 'nine' was amazing, but after the referee had taken a good look at the stricken fighter he stopped the contest with just 24 seconds on the clock.

6 February 1996. Lonnie Bradley w rsc 2 Randy Smith.
Venue: 69th Regiment Armoury, Manhattan, NYC, New York, USA. **Recognition:** WBO. **Referee:** Samuel Viruet.
Fight Summary: Despite having 16 wins on his record from a 20-fight career Smith (158½) was not in the same league as the champion, being lucky to survive the opening round having been forced to take several heavy rights to the jaw. The second round was much of the same, and once Bradley (159½) found the range he dropped Smith for a count of 'three' after landing heavily to the body. Back on his feet, when Smith was dropped by a solid right to the jaw the referee called it off on the 2.03 mark.

16 March 1996. Bernard Hopkins w rsc 4 Joe Lipsey.
Venue: MGM Grand, Las Vegas, Nevada, USA. **Recognition:** IBF. **Referee:** Mitch Halpern.
Fight Summary: Following two well contested rounds Hopkins (160), having had his right eye damaged in the second by a southpaw left swung in by the unbeaten Lipsey (158), picked up the pace in the third when banging in several hurtful punches. The fourth round saw Hopkins pressing again, and after staggering Lipsey with a left-right a straight right put the challenger down on his side. Having seen enough, with ten seconds of the session remaining the referee stopped the fight without even picking up the count.

16 March 1996. Keith Holmes w rsc 9 Quincy Taylor.
Venue: MGM Grand, Las Vegas, Nevada, USA. **Recognition:** WBC. **Referee:** Richard Steele.
Fight Summary: Out of sorts following surgery on his left knee, Taylor (160) lost his title in his first defence when outpunched and outboxed by Holmes (159). In a battle between southpaws, it was the taller Holmes who started the better, poking in right jabs and keeping the fight at range during the opening six rounds. Although Taylor began to have more success during the next couple of sessions it did not last long, Holmes dropping him in the ninth with a right to the jaw. On getting up, after Taylor had shipped a few solid blows to the head the referee came to his rescue with 77 seconds of the round remaining.

7 May 1996. Lonnie Bradley w pts 12 Lonnie Beasley.
Venue: St John Arena, Steubenville, Ohio, USA. **Recognition:** WBO. **Referee:** Michael Ortega.
Scorecards: 120-106, 119-109, 118-109.
Fight Summary: Viewed as a poor fight, the champion was unable to finish Beasley (159) off despite dropping him in the seventh and eighth from smashing rights to the head. It was clear that Beasley was only interested in going the distance, continuing to back-pedal as Bradley (160) tried to take him out with one punch. At times Bradley gave up the chase as the fight drifted along to the final bell, having done his reputation no good at all.

24 June 1996. William Joppy w rsc 9 Shinji Takehara.
Venue: The Arena, Yokohama, Japan. **Recognition:** WBA. **Referee:** John Coyle.
Fight Summary: Defending for the first time, Takehara (160) was up against it from the opening bell, more so when Joppy (160) smashed in a terrific overarm right that dropped him. Even though Takehara had a five-inch-reach advantage it failed to help him as Joppy countered him effectively with jabs and left-rights. In the fifth Takehara was pinned on the ropes and forced to take heavy blows before fighting on more equal terms in the next two sessions. Hurt in the eighth, Takehara was eventually stopped at 2.29 of the ninth when he was unable to defend himself properly after Joppy had cornered him and was firing in heavy combinations.

16 July 1996. Bernard Hopkins w rsc 11 William Bo James.
Venue: Resorts Hotel & Casino, Atlantic City, New Jersey, USA. **Recognition:** IBF. **Referee:** Rudy Battle.
Fight Summary: Right from the start Hopkins (158¼) took the fight to his challenger, who tried hard to respond before being sent crashing in the second round by an overarm right. Several times in the first three sessions it looked as though James (158) would drop, but he bravely hung in as Hopkins chased him. Having been stunned again in the ninth James had little left, and although he got through the tenth he was pursued bitterly from corner to corner in the 11th until he was finally rescued on the 2.02 mark after slumping to the floor.

30 August 1996. Lonnie Bradley w pts 12 Simon Brown.
Venue: Municipal Stadium, Reading, Pennsylvania, USA. **Recognition:** WBO. **Referee:** Frank Cappuccino.
Scorecards: 117-111, 117-113, 117-111.
Fight Summary: With Brown (157¾) well past his best it was not too difficult a fight for the unbeaten champion and he should have done better. After being cut over the left eye in the fourth following some dangerous headwork by Brown, Bradley (159¾) was more wary, boxing mainly on the outside from thereon in. Occasionally hurt by Brown, with the latter being too slow to take advantage Bradley was eventually content to run down the clock.

19 October 1996. Keith Holmes w rsc 12 Richie Woodhall.
Venue: Showplace Arena, Upper Marlboro, Maryland, USA. **Recognition:** WBC. **Referee:** Arthur Mercante.
Fight Summary: Regardless that he had suffered surgery to his right elbow just 12 days before challenging Holmes (157) for his title, instead of pulling out Woodhall (158) decided not to withdraw, a decision he might have later regretted. Up against the southpaw champion was difficult enough, but unable to fire in straight rights Woodhall restricted his chances before a punch was thrown. Still, Woodhall was in front after six rounds due to excellent left-hand work. That was before he was hurt in the seventh by a searing uppercut and began to lose ground. With Holmes chipping away with southpaw leads and long lefts, Woodhall was eventually floored by a cracking left hook in the 12th. Although the Englishman got up at 'nine', after the champion had thrown half a dozen undefended blows the referee stopped the contest with just 28 seconds of the session remaining.

19 October 1996. William Joppy w rsc 6 Ray McElroy.
Venue: Showplace Arena, Upper Marlboro, Maryland, USA. **Recognition:** WBA. **Referee:** Ken Chevalier.
Fight Summary: Even though he showed stubborn resistance the tall McElroy (156½) offered little else in his attempt to wrest the title from Joppy (159), who won as he pleased. Several times McElroy was shaken up in the opening five rounds, and in the sixth Joppy made his move when driving the challenger to the ropes and belabouring him from head to body. At 1.41 of the session, the referee brought the fight to a close after Joppy had landed three heavy blows to the head. Even though McElroy looked to carry on it had become too one-sided and was a welcome stoppage.

4 March 1997. Lonnie Bradley drew 12 Otis Grant.
Venue: Aladdin Hotel & Casino, Las Vegas, Nevada, USA. **Recognition:** WBO. **Referee:** Richard Steele.
Scorecards: 115-113, 113-115, 114-114.
Fight Summary: In a contest between evenly matched opponents, Bradley (160) came perilously close to losing his title. He would have done so had Grant (160), a clever southpaw, upped his work-rate. Grant was always dangerous with left counters, but even after hurting Bradley in the fourth he stood back as if to admire his work. Towards the end Grant began to land more regularly with the left, but despite being shaken up a couple of times Bradley remained the busier.

19 April 1997. Bernard Hopkins w rsc 7 John David Jackson.
Venue: Memorial Auditorium, Shreveport, Louisiana, USA. **Recognition:** IBF. **Referee:** Johnny Femia.
Fight Summary: Although the champion was cautious during the opening couple of rounds he began to find Jackson (156) with overarm rights in the third before dropping his southpaw opponent with a similar blow in the fourth. By the fifth Jackson was far more tentative, but Hopkins (156½) was not able to take advantage until another big right followed by a body shot put his rival down in the sixth. The fight came to an end at 2.22 of the seventh after Hopkins had blasted away non-stop at Jackson, who was not fighting back at the time of the referee's stoppage. Afterwards, Hopkins said it was acting as Jackson's sparring partner at the start of his career that had taught him how to handle southpaws.

10 May 1997. William Joppy w pts 12 Peter Venancio.
Venue: Coconut Grove Convention Centre, Miami, Florida, USA. **Recognition:** WBA. **Referee:** Bill Connors.
Scorecards: 114-113, 115-112, 114-112.
Fight Summary: Making his second defence Joppy (159) was surprisingly set about by Venancio (159) right at the start of the contest, but after taking the next two rounds he dropped the Brazilian with a right to the head in the

fourth. Many of the rounds were close, there never being much between them. However, in the tenth Joppy dropped his man again, this time with a right to the head, only for Venancio to close the gap by winning the last two sessions on all of the cards.

28 June 1997. Lonnie Bradley w rsc 8 John Williams.
Venue: MGM Grand, Las Vegas, Nevada, USA. **Recognition:** WBO. **Referee:** Richard Steele.
Fight Summary: Despite taking 18 wins from 22 fights into the ring Williams (159½) had never fought in this kind of company before, something that showed as the champion went to work on him from the opening bell. Boxing well within himself, throwing solid jabs and classy combinations, Bradley (160) was hurting Williams almost every time he connected, the latter's left eye being badly marked in the fourth. The next three rounds saw Williams fall further and further behind, and in the eighth Bradley went for the finish. After landing several unanswered blows, a left hook dropped the man from Bradenton just as the referee had decided the stop the fight. The time of the stoppage was announced as being 45 seconds.

With Bradley indisposed due to a retina problem, Otis Grant outpointed Ryan Rhodes over 12 rounds at the Ponds Forge Leisure Centre, Sheffield, England on 13 December for the 'interim' title.

Grant was eventually recognised as the WBO champion when Bradley was forced to retire at the beginning of May 1998.

20 July 1997. Bernard Hopkins w rsc 11 Glen Johnson.
Venue: Fantasy Springs Casino Resort, Indio, California, USA. **Recognition:** IBF. **Referee:** Pat Russell.
Fight Summary: Defending his title for the fifth time Hopkins (160) at last showed that he was the best man out there, having dealt with the tough Johnson (159¾) in championship fashion. In winning every round Hopkins dominated Johnson, throwing punches from head to body while never ceasing to let the latter off the hook. Although Hopkins hurt Johnson badly in the second and fifth rounds the latter maintained a solid defence right up to the ninth when the champion was starting to grind him down. With Johnson's right eye beginning to close, following non-stop aggression from Hopkins the referee came to the challenger's rescue at 1.23 of the 11th when he was unable to fight back.

23 August 1997. Julio Cesar Green w pts 12 William Joppy.
Venue: Madison Square Garden, Manhattan, NYC, New York, USA. **Recognition:** WBA. **Referee:** Wayne Kelly.
Scorecards: 114-112, 113-112, 116-113.
Fight Summary: Shocked when he was dropped by a solid left hook from Green (159) in the second the champion came back well in the third when putting the latter down twice. However, he was unable to find a finishing blow in that session as hard as he tried. Having damaged his right hand in the third, when Joppy (160) began to box on the back foot, despite scoring well with the jab it was Green who was forcing the fight. Deducted a point in the 11th for hitting from behind did not help Joppy's cause and when Green won the final round on all three cards, after plugging away with the jab, the champion's fate was sealed.

18 November 1997. Bernard Hopkins w pts 12 Andrew Council.
Venue: Showplace Arena, Upper Marlboro, Maryland, USA. **Recognition:** IBF. **Referee:** Ken Chevalier.
Scorecards: 119-105, 118-106, 118-106.
Fight Summary: Even though he put on a worthy show, especially when attacking the body, the challenger won only one round on two of the cards as Hopkins (160) showcased his skills and gave his rival little chance of success. Even though Hopkins caught Council (160), who was cut over the left eye in the fifth, with big right hands to the head on several occasions he was unable to find a finishing blow. With Council gamely soldiering on, the final three rounds showed Hopkins at his best as he waltzed to victory. Hopkins picked up a point deduction for going low, while Council had three taken away for general misdemeanours.

5 December 1997. Keith Holmes w rsc 11 Paul Vaden.
Venue: The Amphitheatre, Pompano Beach, Florida, USA. **Recognition:** WBC. **Referee:** Brian Garry.

Fight Summary: Quickly gaining control, landing solidly with southpaw right jabs, in the fourth round the champion had the lanky Vaden over twice. Although Vaden (158) came back well in the next two sessions, once he was badly cut over the left eye in the seventh it would be just a matter of time. And when Holmes (157¼) opened up in the 11th it was all over. Beating Vaden to the punch Holmes crashed in five heavy blows from both hands, the final one sending his challenger to the boards. At that point, the referee called a halt without bothering to pick up the count. The finish was timed at 1.11.

31 January 1998. Bernard Hopkins w rsc 6 Simon Brown.
Venue: Trump Taj Mahal Casino & Hotel, Atlantic City, New Jersey, USA. **Recognition:** IBF. **Referee:** Rudy Battle.
Fight Summary: Having won the opening five rounds on all the cards the champion was looking to take Brown (160) out in the sixth. Prior to that Brown had avoided many of the wallops coming his way, but he could not avoid a tremendous right uppercut that sent him heavily to the boards. It was a miracle that Brown managed to get back on his feet in time, and when he did Hopkins (160) began whacking in punch after punch, mainly to the head, before the referee stopped the fight after 60 seconds of the session had elapsed.

31 January 1998. William Joppy w pts 12 Julio Cesar Green.
Venue: Ice Palace, Tampa, Florida, USA. **Recognition:** WBA. **Referee:** Max Parker Jnr.
Scorecards: 117-112, 117-113, 117-110.
Fight Summary: Putting his title up for the first time against the man he won it from, Green (160) was dropped by a left hook in the opening round before coming back strongly with two-fisted attacks to the body. Eventually, Joppy (159½) began to box more effectively on the outside as Green became extremely wild, and by the eighth the Dominican was clearly exasperated as he continually missed the target. By then, the tiring Green was mainly throwing arm punches while Joppy looked to make every blow count. Cut over the left eye in the tenth Green was still coming forward, but Joppy, boxing a smart fight, cruised through to the final bell.

2 May 1998. Hacine Cherifi w pts 12 Keith Holmes.
Venue: The Astroballe Sports Complex, Villeurbanne, France. **Recognition:** WBC. **Referee:** Larry O'Connell.
Scorecards: 115-112, 115-112, 115-113.
Fight Summary: The fight began with Cherifi (158¾) chasing the champion, who was happy to box on the counter with the southpaw jab. That became the general pattern as round after round Cherifi took the fight to Holmes (159½), pushing him around and firing in lefts and rights. Prior to the ninth getting underway, Holmes, having been hurt in the previous session, was admonished by his corner for not doing enough work. Then, after taking it to heart he pressured Cherifi before dropping him with a solid right hook. However, unable to finish the Frenchman off Holmes inexplicably allowed himself to be outworked for the remainder of the fight.

12 May 1998. Otis Grant w tdec 9 Ernesto Sena.
Venue: Corel Centre, Ottawa, Canada. **Recognition:** WBO. **Referee:** Mark Nelson.
Scorecards: 80-71, 80-71, 80-71.
Fight Summary: In his first defence of the title bestowed upon him following Lonnie Bradley's enforced retirement, a battle of southpaws saw Grant (159) winning the opening eight rounds against the crude Sena (159), having dropped the latter with a cracking short left to the jaw in the opener. Three times in the third Sena tripped over his own feet, and in the eighth he opened up a bad cut on Grant's left eye when accidentally butting his man. The fight went to the cards in the ninth after Grant's damaged eye worsened, the decision being a formality.

Grant relinquished the WBO version of the championship in November on moving up to light heavyweight to challenge Roy Jones for the WBA/WBC titles. The WBO then selected Bert Schenk and Freeman Barr to meet for the vacant title.

28 August 1998. Bernard Hopkins tdraw 4 Robert Allen.
Venue: Hilton Hotel, Las Vegas, Nevada, USA. **Recognition:** IBF. **Referee:** Mills Lane.
Fight Summary: Ahead on two of the cards at the end of the third round, Hopkins (159) was continually caught up in clinches as the southpaw Allen (160), the number one challenger, tried to get to close quarters. With both men repeatedly clinching, in the fourth when trying to break the two men apart the referee was unintentionally

responsible for Hopkins losing his balance and falling out of the ring. When it was clear that Hopkins could not box on, having been concussed and sustained a sprained left ankle, the referee stopped the contest with three seconds of the session remaining, the decision being marked down as a no contest (for our purposes a technical draw). Under IBF rules, the fight had to have lasted four rounds before going to the cards.

With Hopkins unavailable due to injury, Allen stopped Abdulla Ramadan in the first round of their contest at The Georgia Dome, Atlanta, Georgia on 19 September to land the vacant IBF 'interim' title. On winning, Allen made sure of being Hopkins' next challenger.

28 August 1998. William Joppy w rsc 3 Roberto Duran.
Venue: Hilton Hotel, Las Vegas, Nevada, USA. **Recognition:** WBA. **Referee:** Joe Cortez.
Fight Summary: Still fighting at the age of 47 the legendary Duran (159) failed in his final title challenge, hardly showing as Joppy (160) scored as and when he liked. Even though Joppy was unable to drop Duran, hitting him with solid blows from both hands throughout, at 2.54 of the third the referee had seen enough after the latter was being driven around the ring non-stop. It was clear that Duran was finished, but he continued to fight on until the age of 50, taking in four more contests, two of them losses.

Due to Joppy's inactivity, Julio Cesar Green and Darren Obah contested the vacant WBA 'interim' title at Madison Square Garden, Manhattan, NYC, New York on 20 February 1999, Green winning on a ninth-round stoppage to make sure of being the next challenger for the champion.

30 January 1999. Bert Schenk w co 4 Freeman Barr.
Venue: Stadium Hall, Cottbus, Germany. **Recognition:** WBO. **Referee:** Mark Nelson.
Fight Summary: Challenging for the title vacated by Otis Grant, Schenk (159) was soon landing solid southpaw shots before stepping up in the third to hurt Barr (158) with body punches. Although Barr was always in contention he seemed to be falling behind on work-rate. Then, in the fourth, Barr dropped on one knee after turning away and was counted out at 2.23 of the session. Afterwards, Barr claimed that the left hook to the head that was responsible for the finish had temporarily blinded him.

6 February 1999. Bernard Hopkins w rsc 7 Robert Allen.
Venue: Convention Centre, Washington DC, USA. **Recognition:** IBF. **Referee:** Rudy Battle.
Fight Summary: Following their four-round technical draw, Hopkins (159) wanted to put the record straight especially after Allen (159) had claimed that the champion had been capable of carrying on had he wished. This time, with Hopkins leaving nothing to chance, he was soon into his stride when throwing solid rights over the top. Clearly winning every round, despite being docked a point in the fourth for low blows, Hopkins continued to pick up the pace before knocking Allen down with a big right to the head in the sixth after good left-hand work. The end was not long in coming. With Allen cornered in the seventh, being hammered by a succession of rights to the head, the referee rescued him on the 1.18 mark.

24 April 1999. Keith Holmes w rsc 7 Hacine Cherifi.
Venue: MCI Centre, Washington DC, USA. **Recognition:** WBC. **Referee:** Frank Cappuccino.
Fight Summary: Coming back to regain the title Holmes (159) was a different man from the one who fought Cherifi (158) last time, and after he was cut over the right eye at the end of the third his whole demeanour changed. Holmes now had the bit between the teeth and was beginning to counter heavily with solid southpaw rights. Although hurt himself in the sixth, with Holmes looking to end the fight he found three or four big punches that had Cherifi wobbling in the seventh. Not letting up, when Holmes hit Cherifi with at least a dozen unanswered lefts and rights to the head the referee stopped the fight with 15 seconds of the session remaining.

22 May 1999. Bert Schenk w pts 12 Juan Ramon Medina.
Venue: Sports Palace, Budapest, Hungary. **Recognition:** WBO. **Referee:** Andre Van Grootenbruel.
Scorecards: 115-112, 117-113, 115-113.
Fight Summary: Forced to take a count in the first round, and being cut over the left eye in the second, the southpaw champion recovered well to outbox the tough Medina (157¼). Always dangerous, Medina was

continually looking to end the fight with one punch. Although the crowd booed the unanimous decision it was more in frustration that the technically superior Schenk (159) had not used his skills to open the Dominican up more.

Injured when preparing to defend the WBO title against Ryan Rhodes, Schenk was stripped to allow a title fight to take place, Jason Matthews coming in at short notice.

17 July 1999. Jason Matthews w co 2 Ryan Rhodes.
Venue: The Dome, Doncaster, England. **Recognition:** WBO. **Referee:** Mark Nelson.
Fight Summary: In a contest for the vacant title Rhodes (159¾) was a strong favourite to beat Matthews (159¾), but came unstuck after walking into a cracking right-hand counter in the opening round. Up at 'five', the switch-hitting Rhodes was forced to cover up until the end of the session before coming out for the second intent on knocking Matthews out instead of playing safe. He was soon made to pay, crashing to the floor from another right to the jaw and being counted out after just 28 seconds had elapsed. The new champion had taken the fight at just five days' notice.

24 September 1999. Keith Holmes w pts 12 Andrew Council.
Venue: MCI Centre, Washington DC, USA. **Recognition:** WBC. **Referee:** Arthur Mercante.
Scorecards: 116-110, 116-109, 117-109.
Fight Summary: Having learned from a previous meeting, the champion outboxed Council (159½) for much of the time, using an accurate southpaw jab coupled to a solid defence. Despite being occasionally caught, especially by a left hook in the second, Holmes (158½) boxed his way out of trouble, dropping Council flat on his face with a terrific right hook in the ninth. Although Council made it to his feet and lasted the round out he was hammered throughout the last three sessions, but showed a good chin to reach the final bell.

24 September 1999. William Joppy w rsc 7 Julio Cesar Green.
Venue: MCI Centre, Washington DC, USA. **Recognition:** WBA. **Referee:** Ken Chevalier.
Fight Summary: Meeting Green (159½) for the third time, with the score one apiece, the champion got down to work quickly, wobbling the Dominican with a big right in the second and cutting him over the left eye in the third. With the cut worsening round by round as Joppy (158½) played on it, when Green became desperate in the seventh the referee called the fight off as the blood flowed, the finish being timed at 1.52. According to the three judges Joppy had won all six completed rounds.

27 November 1999. Armand Krajnc w rsc 8 Jason Matthews.
Venue: Hanse Hall, Lubeck, Germany. **Recognition:** WBO. **Referee:** James Condon.
Fight Summary: Making his first defence Matthews (160) had expected to meet Bert Schenk, who was still claiming to be the champion, but when the German ruptured an Achilles tendon in his right ankle Krajnc (158¾) was drafted in. Having started brightly, Matthews was forced back and dropped after taking several left hooks. Although fighting hard he was way down on the cards at the end of the fourth. In the fifth and sixth, however, Matthews outworked Krajnc before his right eye began to suddenly swell. From there onwards Matthews was right up against it, and when Krajnc was rocking him with all manner of punches the referee called the fight off at 1.45 of the eighth.

12 December 1999. Bernard Hopkins w pts 12 Antwun Echols.
Venue: Miccosukee Indian Gaming Centre, Miami, Florida, USA. **Recognition:** IBF. **Referee:** Frank Santore Jnr.
Scorecards: 118-110, 119-109, 118-110.
Fight Summary: Defending his title for the tenth time, Hopkins (158½) lost just two rounds on the cards. However, he was badly wobbled by the tough Echols (160) on several occasions, especially when dropped in the opening round as the referee called 'break'. Although the rounds were going to Hopkins, with Echols meeting the champion punch for punch at times both men took some heavy shots without blinking. By the sixth Hopkins had begun to work the body, but back came Echols, swinging in blows from both hands to win the eighth. While looking likely to go at some stage Echols was still there come the final round. Despite being tired, both men opened up in the 12th.

At times both were on the verge of going down as the punches came in fast and furious, and while the result was a formality Hopkins stated afterwards that he had never been hit so hard in his life.

11 March 2000. Armand Krajnc w co 2 Jonathan Corn.
Venue: Hanse Hall, Lubeck, Germany. **Recognition:** WBO. **Referee:** Mark Nelson.
Fight Summary: Putting up his title for the first time, Krajnc (159¾) wasted little time in going for Corn (159¾), and by the end of the opening round it already looked as though the little known American would not be around for much longer. Picking up where he left off Krajnc was soon letting the punches go and, after chasing his man down, heavy blows to the head saw Corn almost knocked out of the ring before being counted out at 1.29 of the second.

29 April 2000. Keith Holmes w rsc 11 Robert McCracken.
Venue: The Arena, Wembley, London, England. **Recognition:** WBC. **Referee:** Alfred Asaro.
Fight Summary: Being inactive for over a year did not help the challenger's cause when trying to wrest the title from Holmes (158). Boxing off the back foot Holmes' southpaw skills were too much for the brave McCracken (159½), who was dropped by a hard left to the side of the head in the third before cuts appeared around both eyes and his left eye began to close in round five. Although McCracken tried to find a way through Holmes' defences it was not his night, and even after the American had a point deducted for holding in the tenth he came on strongly to have the Brummie stumbling and on the verge of going down. There was little action in the 11th, but when McCracken's left eye began to worsen the referee gave it a few moments before calling the fight off on the 2.24 mark.

13 May 2000. Bernard Hopkins w pts 12 Syd Vanderpool.
Venue: Conseco Fieldhouse, Indianapolis, Indiana, USA. **Recognition:** IBF. **Referee:** Bill Page.
Scorecards: 118-110, 118-109, 116-112.
Fight Summary: Coming in at late notice after the champion's original opponent, Brian Barbosa, was injured, Vanderpool (160) made a reasonable fist of it without ever looking likely to win despite taking the opening three rounds. According to *The Ring* magazine, Hopkins (158½) was strangely passive for a fighter looking to be considered among the elite and while he opened up at times, because he never went after the southpaw Canadian with a vengeance, the fight became messy. In the third, sixth and seventh rounds both men were on the floor together. Towards the end, in the 12th, Hopkins began to place his punches better, and after he had got Vanderpool up against the ropes the referee jumped between them. It looked like Hopkins was getting a stoppage win, but it turned out that the referee thought he had heard the final bell which went moments later.

20 May 2000. William Joppy w rsc 1 Rito Ruvalcaba.
Venue: Grand Casino, Tunica, Mississippi, USA. **Recognition:** WBA. **Referee:** Fred Steinwinder.
Fight Summary: Up against the WBA's mandatory challenger, Joppy (157¼) made a fast start when sending the hapless Mexican back on his heels from the first two blows of the fight. Although Ruvalcaba (155¾) remained upright it was clear that he was unlikely to be around much longer as Joppy wound up the punches, and after slamming in three big rights that catapulted him off the ropes the referee stopped the contest with 67 seconds of the first round remaining.

16 September 2000. William Joppy w pts 12 Hacine Cherifi.
Venue: MGM Grand, Las Vegas, Nevada, USA. **Recognition:** WBA. **Referee:** Joe Cortez.
Scorecards: 119-106, 118-107, 118-107.
Fight Summary: According to the reports the fight was never close, Cherifi (159) winning just one round - the fifth - and being dropped twice before going down heavily on all the cards. Right from the start it was clear that Cherifi was in for a hard night when Joppy (160) walked into him throwing solid uppercuts and combinations. Although Cherifi came through the attack and stoically resisted the champion's efforts to finish early, he was dropped in both the eighth and ninth rounds before being smashed to the floor just as the bell rang to end the ninth. Regardless of the fact that the knockdown did not count Cherifi was left badly stunned, but he somehow made it to the final bell despite taking a battering all the way. To make matters even worse for the Frenchman was a point deduction in the sixth for hitting on the break.

7 October 2000. Armand Krajnc w rsc 6 Bert Schenk.
Venue: Estrel Convention Centre, Berlin, Germany. **Recognition:** WBO. **Referee:** James Condon.
Fight Summary: Having lost his title through injury, Schenk (159½) was given the opportunity to regain it when meeting the current champion, Krajnc (159), but unfortunately for him he was eventually found wanting. Starting slowly, the southpaw Schenk lost the first two rounds before getting back into the fight when winning the third and fourth with solid counters proving effective. He was also going reasonably well in the fifth, but halfway into the session he was in trouble, and after taking a heavy right hook to the head followed by a body shot in the sixth he dropped to his knees. Back on his feet, having taken a mandatory 'eight' count, Schenk merely covered up before the referee stopped the fight on the 2.51 mark when he was not hitting back.

Further to reports that Krajnc had split from his management and renounced his WBO title during the summer of 2001, when the championship was declared vacant a match was made between the WBO junior middleweight champion, Harry Simon, and Hacine Cherifi. The contest went ahead at the Ruben Rodriguez Coliseum, Bayamon, Puerto Rico on 21 July 2001, Simon outpointing Cherifi over 12 rounds of a fight billed for the vacant title. However, when it later transpired that Krajnc had not vacated the championship, despite a letter from his lawyer to that effect, the WBO was eventually forced to accept that Simon v Cherifi was merely an 'interim' championship fight. The WBO then stated that the winner of a projected Krajnc v Paolo Roberto contest would have to defend against Simon.

1 December 2000. Bernard Hopkins w rsc 10 Antwun Echols.
Venue: Venetian Casino & Hotel, Las Vegas, Nevada, USA. **Recognition:** IBF. **Referee:** Tony Weeks.
Fight Summary: Following on from their previous dramatic encounter it was no surprise that the pair started brawling almost from the start. In the second round when the champion put Echols (160) down for at least 30 seconds from a punch to the back of the head, the referee neither counted nor deducted points before telling them to fight on. Then, in the sixth, with decisions going against him the challenger picked Hopkins (158½) up and body slammed him. Hopkins was hurt but consented to fight on, while Echols had two points taken away. After Hopkins had been pushed to the floor in the seventh he came back strongly to batter Echols through the ropes for a count, the latter being saved by the bell. Both men were throwing heavy blows from there on before Hopkins, who had lost a point for holding in the eighth, forced the referee to rescue the badly battered and tottering Echols at 1.42 of the tenth session.

2 December 2000. William Joppy w rsc 4 Jonathan Reid.
Venue: Mandalay Bay Resort & Casino, Las Vegas, Nevada, USA. **Recognition:** WBA. **Referee:** Joe Cortez.
Fight Summary: As a late substitute for Guillermo Jones and then Julio Garcia, the unbeaten Reid (160) proved no match for the champion, being totally outclassed. On the back foot from the beginning Reid got through the opening two rounds unscathed before he was blasted to the floor in the third by a salvo of punches and then saved by the bell when under another heavy attack. With it being more of the same in the fourth, when Joppy (159½) smashed Reid down with a solid left-right combination the referee immediately stopped the fight with 17 seconds of the session remaining.

14 April 2001. Bernard Hopkins w pts 12 Keith Holmes.
Venue: MSG Theatre, Manhattan, NYC, New York, USA. **Recognition:** IBF/WBC. **Referee:** Steve Smoger.
Scorecards: 119-118, 118-109, 117-110.
Fight Summary: In a contest that would unify the IBF and WBC titles, Hopkins (159) took over Holmes' WBC crown when winning virtually every round even after having a point deducted for low blows in the fifth. In that session Holmes (157½) was given about a minute's rest, but it made no difference. There were no knockdowns as such, despite Holmes, who also suffered a cut to his left eye in the fifth, going down on one knee on four occasions. Holmes was taken out of his stride throughout by Hopkins, who waged a physical battle right from the start. Although the clever southpaw, realising that he was way behind, tried to match his rival in the latter stages he was put in his place after being bombed to head and body by heavy punches.

12 May 2001. Felix Trinidad w rsc 5 William Joppy.
Venue: Madison Square Garden, Manhattan, NYC, New York, USA. **Recognition:** WBA. **Referee:** Arthur Mercante Jnr.
Fight Summary: Moving up a weight to take on Joppy (158¾) for his WBA title, the IBF and WBA junior middleweight champion made the transition without a hitch, starting well by dropping his rival with heavy left-right combinations towards the end of the first. From there onwards it was all one-way apart from in the third when Joppy made a big effort to take Trinidad (159½) out of the fight with heavy right hands. Coming straight back in the fourth Trinidad decked Joppy for the mandatory 'eight' count with a big left hook before going to work in similar vein in the fifth. Trinidad was now totally on top, ripping in blows to head and body, and after pounding away at Joppy the latter crashed to the floor from a right to the jaw. At this point the referee called the fight off on the 2.25 mark when the stricken fighter somehow got to his feet at 'four' in no condition to continue.

29 September 2001. Bernard Hopkins w rsc 12 Felix Trinidad.
Venue: Madison Square Garden, Manhattan, NYC, New York, USA. **Recognition:** IBF/WBA/WBC. **Referee:** Steve Smoger.
Fight Summary: After an opening round in which he had good look at the new WBA champion, Hopkins (157) moved up several gears to gradually take Trinidad (158½) apart prior to stopping him at 1.42 of the 12th. Hopkins was just far too good for Trinidad, whether it be boxing or fighting. Stumbling around in the 11th it was clear that Trinidad was almost finished for the night, and in the final session Hopkins opened up with both hands before sending his man down heavily with a short right to the jaw. Although Trinidad struggled up at 'nine', on seeing that he was not ready to continue the referee decided the fight was over.

Hopkins was awarded *The Ring* Championship Belt at the end of 2001. With the WBA recognising Hopkins as a 'super' champion, William Joppy took over their 'second tier' title when outpointing Howard Eastman over 12 rounds at the Mandalay Bay Resort & Casino, Las Vegas, Nevada on 17 November.

3 November 2001. Armand Krajnc w pts 12 Paolo Roberto.
Venue: Hanse Hall, Lubeck, Germany. **Recognition:** WBO. **Referee:** Joachim Jacobsen.
Scorecards: 117-111, 118-110, 118-111.
Fight Summary: Shrugging off a bad start when he was rocked by a right hook to the jaw, the champion, beginning to dictate matters, took control after the third round as Roberto (160), a hard-hitting southpaw, ran out of ideas. In the sixth Roberto was lucky to be still in the fight after a tremendous right to the head had him all over the place, but he stuck at it when surviving to the final bell as Krajnc (160) tired.

2 February 2002. Bernard Hopkins w rtd 10 Carl Daniels.
Venue: Sovereign Centre, Reading, Pennsylvania, USA. **Recognition:** IBF/WBA/WBC/The Ring. **Referee:** Frank Cappuccino.
Fight Summary: Attacking Daniels (160) from the opening bell the champion continued to march forward for ten rounds as his cute southpaw opponent stayed on the back foot for most of the time. When Hopkins (158¾) did manage to close Daniels down, the latter took what was on offer. It was only in the ninth that Daniels began to ship heavy punishment, blows to head and body sending him lurching round the ring. At the end of the tenth, which he had somehow managed to get through, Daniels made the decision not to continue knowing he had no chance of winning.

On 10 October, William Joppy, who retained the WBA 'second tier' title when stopping Naotaka Hozumi inside ten rounds at the Ryogoku Sumo Arena, Tokyo, Japan, would be Hopkins' next challenger.

6 April 2002. Harry Simon w pts 12 Armand Krajnc.
Venue: Bygningen Circus Arena, Copenhagen, Denmark. **Recognition:** WBO. **Referee:** Michael Ortega.
Scorecards: 116-112, 116-112, 116-113.
Fight Summary: The contest was fairly even during the opening few rounds, but eventually Simon (159) established a reasonable lead, his solid combination punches being effective despite not hurting the champion. A

great competitor, Krajnc (159½) was always up for it, looking as strong as when he started at the final bell. However, it was Simon who had the quality. There were no knockdowns.

With Simon failing to make a defence following injuries sustained during a car crash, Hector Velazco forced Andras Galfi to retire at the end of the seventh round to win the vacant WBO 'interim' title at the Luna Park Stadium, Buenos Aires, Argentina on 10 May 2003.

Velazco was appointed champion in early July 2003 after Simon was stripped when it was recognised that he had not fully recovered and still had legal issues to be sorted out.

29 March 2003. Bernard Hopkins w rtd 8 Morrade Hakkar.
Venue: First Union Spectrum, Philadelphia, Pennsylvania, USA. **Recognition:** IBF/WBA/WBC/The Ring. **Referee:** Frank Cappuccino.
Fight Summary: In what was a bad mismatch it was soon clear that Hakkar (159) did not belong in the same ring as the champion when sprinting around the perimeter and barely stopping to land punches. Having somehow got through five rounds, Hakkar dropped down in the sixth after taking a body shot, and with Hopkins (158½) failing to go to a neutral corner and the referee not spotting it he was probably resting on one knee for about 20 seconds. Twice in the seventh the Frenchman was on the floor without a count. In the eighth he went down again without the referee bothering to call it a knockdown. With Hopkins working the head and body when Hakkar slumped on his stool at the end of the session his corner retired him.

13 September 2003. Felix Sturm w pts 12 Hector Velazco.
Venue: Estrel Convention Centre, Berlin, Germany. **Recognition:** WBO. **Referee:** Rocky Burke.
Scorecards: 115-113, 116-112, 113-115.
Fight Summary: Putting up his title for the first time after being appointed champion, Velazco (159¼) took on Sturm (158¾) who came in as a late substitute for the injured Bert Schenk. Coming out in a southpaw stance before switch-hitting throughout, and showing much cleverness, Sturm took an early lead despite being chased all over by Velazco. With the Argentine just not getting enough punches off it was Sturm doing the better work even though he was boxing on the back foot and landing with no real snap. Whenever he had to Sturm took Velazco's best shots, being good value for the split-decision win.

13 December 2003. Bernard Hopkins w pts 12 William Joppy.
Venue: Boardwalk Hall, Atlantic City, New Jersey, USA. **Recognition:** IBF/WBA/WBC/The Ring. **Referee:** Earl Morton.
Scorecards: 119-108, 119-109, 118-109.
Fight Summary: Although Joppy (159) went the distance, winning a side-bet, despite there being no knockdowns the champion was far too good for him. Pacing himself superbly Hopkins (160) was on top in virtually every round bar the seventh when Joppy scored with a hard right uppercut, and by the eighth he was back controlling his rival from the centre of the ring. Coming out for the 11th, his left eye swelling up, Joppy gave it one final go before being forced to take a sustained beating right through to the final bell.

On 1 May 2004, at the Jai-Alai Fronton, Miami, Florida, Maselino Masoe stopped Evans Ashira inside two rounds to win the WBA 'second tier' title that had been vacated following Joppy's defeat.

20 December 2003. Felix Sturm w pts 12 Ruben Varon.
Venue: Ostsee Hall, Kiel, Germany. **Recognition:** WBO. **Referee:** Roberto Ramirez.
Scorecards: 120-108, 120-108, 118-110.
Fight Summary: Sturm (159¾), making his first defence, gave an excellent display of boxing as he outclassed Varon (158¾) from start to finish, breaking his nose and cutting him over the right eye. Although Varon started as though he meant business, landing a few solid left hooks, he was soon being contained and outboxed by the stronger Sturm who surprisingly failed to go for a stoppage win when it had looked imminent. Content to take no risks, Sturm won every round on the cards.

5 June 2004. Bernard Hopkins w pts 12 Robert Allen.
Venue: MGM Grand, Las Vegas, Nevada, USA. **Recognition:** IBF/WBA/WBC/The Ring. **Referee:** Joe Cortez.
Scorecards: 119-107, 119-107, 117-109.
Fight Summary: Clearly the superior man, the champion took on an old opponent in Allen (160), being happy to box his way to an easy points win until struck low in the fifth. While Allen was deducted a point for the infringement, Hopkins (159) upped the pace, dropping his rival with a crashing right to the head in the seventh. Although Allen was on his feet at 'six', Hopkins went after him before settling down again to box his way home against a dangerous southpaw. All the quality punches came from Hopkins, his body punching and fast lead rights making sure that he would be the man to face the winner of Oscar De La Hoya v Felix Sturm in a battle to unify the division.

5 June 2004. Oscar De La Hoya w pts 12 Felix Sturm.
Venue: MGM Grand, Las Vegas, Nevada, USA. **Recognition:** WBO. **Referee:** Vic Drakulich.
Scorecards: 115-113, 115-113, 115-113.
Fight Summary: Making his debut in the 160lbs division, De La Hoya (160) started brightly when winning four of the opening five rounds before the champion picked up his work-rate to make the contest a close-run thing. Had Sturm (160) turned southpaw earlier than the 11th he might well have won as De La Hoya found himself under a little bit of pressure, especially when being forced to take solid right uppercuts. However, the fight was really decided by the fact that De La Hoya threw punches in clusters, mixing them up from head to body, while Sturm, in the main, concentrated on single shots.

18 September 2004. Bernard Hopkins w co 9 Oscar De La Hoya.
Venue: MGM Grand, Las Vegas, Nevada, USA. **Recognition:** World/The Ring. **Referee:** Kenny Bayless.
Fight Summary: At the age of 39 Hopkins (156) put his WBA, WBC and IBF titles, as well as *The Ring* Championship Belt, up for grabs against De La Hoya (155), the WBO champion, in a match that would unify the title for the first time since 1986. In contention during the opening four rounds, having disrupted Hopkins' rhythm when snapping in four or five blows to the body before making off, De La Hoya was looking to move on. However, by round five he was running into stiff lefts. As each round came and went it was apparent that De La Hoya was having trouble getting inside Hopkins' jab. Not only that, but the latter's size and strength was also beginning to bother him. Having won the last two rounds on all the cards Hopkins began to step it up in the ninth, and following a solid left jab he stepped inside with a cracking left hook to the body that sent De La Hoya down to be counted out at 1.38 of the session. Afterwards, De La Hoya, who had never been floored by a blow to the solar plexus before, said that the punch had paralysed him.

19 February 2005. Bernard Hopkins w pts 12 Howard Eastman.
Venue: Los Angeles, California, USA. **Recognition:** World/The Ring. **Referee:** Raul Caiz Jnr.
Scorecards: 119-110, 117-111, 116-112.
Fight Summary: Unable to find the answer to the ageless champion's ability to control a fight, Eastman (159½) was beaten by a fairly substantial points margin, never really showing up. It was a case of Hopkins (159½) having just too much of everything, and although Eastman took the fight to his rival he never forced home any attack which might have left him open to the counters. With Hopkins picking his punches before moving out of range as the challenger predictably stalked him, the contest was hardly exciting. Although Eastman was never embarrassed it was a bridge too far for him.

16 July 2005. Jermain Taylor w pts 12 Bernard Hopkins.
Venue: MGM Grand, Las Vegas, Nevada, USA. **Recognition:** World/The Ring. **Referee:** Jay Nady.
Scorecards: 115-113, 115-113, 112-116.
Fight Summary: Regardless of the fact that most experts had the champion winning, and despite the ridiculous last round score from one of the judges that if corrected would have meant that Hopkins (160) retained his belts, the real problem was in the latter getting his tactics wrong and allowing Taylor (160) too much leeway. Having let Taylor build up a fair lead by the end of the eighth, when Hopkins at last realised that he had to get busy he took the last four sessions on all cards other than the one already mentioned. However, it was not enough. There were

no knockdowns, but the fight stats over 12 rounds showed that Hopkins landed 96 to Taylor's 86, while in the last four sessions the champion connected with 56 to the challenger's 23.

When Taylor relinquished the IBF title in November due to contractual problems, Arthur Abraham and Kingsley Ikeke were matched to decide a new champion.

3 December 2005. Jermain Taylor w pts 12 Bernard Hopkins.
Venue: Mandalay Bay Resort & Casino, Las Vegas, Nevada, USA. **Recognition:** WBA/WBC/WBO/The Ring. **Referee:** Jay Nady.
Scorecards: 115-113, 115-113, 115-113.
Fight Summary: As in their first contest there was nothing between them, both men showing each other too much respect, and many of the rounds were so closely contested that they could have gone either way. With neither man looking like going down, much of the action was plain boring. *Boxing News* got it right when they reported that Taylor (159), the champion, won by default, with Hopkins (160) relying on one big punch to finish it rather than busying himself.

At the Color Line Arena, Hamburg, Germany on 11 March 2006, Felix Sturm outpointed Maselino Masoe over 12 rounds to take over the Western Samoan's WBA 'second tier' title.

10 December 2005. Arthur Abraham w rsc 5 Kingsley Ikeke.
Venue: The Arena, Leipzig, Germany. **Recognition:** IBF. **Referee:** Samuel Viruet.
Fight Summary: Contesting the vacant title Abraham (159) proved too good for Ikeke (159), starting faster and getting his punches off better, especially the right over the top followed by a left hook. Although the taller Ikeke tried hard enough he could not get going. In the fifth Ikeke was caught by a heavy right-left-right combination that saw him eventually stumbling to the floor after the referee had waived it over with 84 seconds of the session remaining.

4 March 2006. Arthur Abraham w pts 12 Shannan Taylor.
Venue: EWE Arena, Oldenburg, Germany. **Recognition:** IBF. **Referee:** Wayne Kelly.
Scorecards: 120-107, 120-107, 120-106.
Fight Summary: Losing every round on all three scorecards and having a point deducted in the sixth for repeated low blows made it a bad night for the challenger, who never looked like disturbing Abraham (159¾). While Taylor (159½) kept out of serious trouble it was more to do with Abraham conserving his energy than anything else. Hurt in the fourth by body shots and again in the ninth, Taylor kept his boxing together without ever being in a position to take over.

13 May 2006. Arthur Abraham w pts 12 Kofi Jantuah.
Venue: The Stadium, Zwickau, Germany. **Recognition:** IBF. **Referee:** Robert Byrd.
Scorecards: 115-112, 117-110, 116-111.
Fight Summary: Starting slowly, Abraham (160) was forced to take some heavy shots in the early sessions before taking over from his challenger at the halfway stage, solid jabs and blows from head to body taking him to the front. Being deducted a point in the seventh for punching behind the head barely concerned Abraham as he continued banging in punches that hurt Jantuah (158¾) and forced him to hang on. Jantuah even came back to stun Abraham in the tenth with a cracking right to the jaw, but ultimately lacked the weapons required to win.

17 June 2006. Jermain Taylor drew 12 Ronald Wright.
Venue: FedEx Forum, Memphis, Tennessee, USA. **Recognition:** WBA/WBC/WBO/The Ring. **Referee:** Frank Garza.
Scorecards: 115-113, 113-115, 114-114.
Fight Summary: With his four championship belts on the line, Taylor (160) appeared lucky to retain them after his southpaw challenger cruised through the final session instead of making sure of the points. Wright (159¾) had taken the fight to Taylor from the beginning, outjabbing the latter for much of the time, but was forced to take heavy blows in return. Despite being the harder puncher, Taylor, whose left eye was almost closed at the final bell, was never able to build up momentum as Wright continually took him to the ropes and negated his power. The

Boxing News stated "Wright fought hard for 33 minutes and tamely for the last three", having thought that all he had to do to was remain on his feet.

On 15 July, Javier Castillejo stopped Felix Sturm in the tenth round to take the latter's WBA 'second tier' title at the Color Line Arena, Hamburg, Germany, prior to being handed full title status in November when the WBA decided not to recognise Taylor as their 'super' champion any longer. The WBA's decision was made after Taylor was matched against Kassim Ouma, an opponent who failed to meet their criteria.

23 September 2006. Arthur Abraham w pts 12 Edison Miranda.
Venue: Rittal Arena, Wetzlar, Germany. **Recognition:** IBF. **Referee:** Randy Neumann.
Scorecards: 114-109, 115-109, 114-109.
Fight Summary: In what was an extremely tough, close fight, Abraham (160) had to fight on with a broken jaw from the fourth, while the challenger threw his chances of winning away when being deducted five points, two in the fifth for butts, two in the seventh and one in the 11th for low blows. Had Miranda (160) not been so wild with his deliveries the title would have been his, but he lacked the control required to close the fight down. Even though Abraham looked as though he was done for on several occasions he would come back strongly to hold Miranda off. Immediately after the contest Abraham was taken to hospital to have his jaw operated on, following which he would be out of the ring for eight months.

2 December 2006. Mariano Carrera w rsc 11 Javier Castillejo.
Venue: Estrel Congress Centre, Berlin, Germany. **Recognition:** WBA. **Referee:** Guillermo Perez.
Fight Summary: Castillejo was making his first defence after the WBA had decided not to recognise Jermain Taylor any longer. Concentrating on the body, Castillejo (159½) was on the border line several times before being deducted two points, in the fourth and the tenth. Both men were taking and giving plenty throughout, but in the 11th Castillejo was badly hurt after a left hook and three-punch combination from Carrera (159½) opened him up. With Carrera banging in punches without return the referee rescued Castillejo on 2.25 mark.

The Spaniard was reinstated as champion at the end of February 2007 after a second drug sample taken from Carrera tested positive for a banned substance, the result being reclassified as a no contest.

9 December 2006. Jermain Taylor w pts 12 Kassim Ouma.
Venue: Alltel Arena, Little Rock, Arkansas, USA. **Recognition:** WBC/WBO/The Ring. **Referee:** Frank Garza.
Scorecards: 118-110, 117-111, 115-113.
Fight Summary: Defending his three championship belts Taylor (159½) was always in control of the tough Ouma (158½), who though continually trying was too small to do serious damage. Boxing a lazy fight, Taylor allowed his southpaw challenger back into it at times, especially in the remaining three sessions. Cut on the left eye in the fifth, Taylor used his five-inch reach advantage to negate rather than attack, only coming to life in the last minute of each round. In the main, while Taylor looked lethargic at times Ouma could take much credit from his performance.

28 April 2007. Felix Sturm w pts 12 Javier Castillejo.
Venue: Koenig Pilsener Arena, Oberhausen, Germany. **Recognition:** WBA. **Referee:** Raul Caiz Jnr.
Scorecards: 116-112, 116-112, 115-114.
Fight Summary: Castillejo (158¼) was making his first defence after being handed back the title when Mariano Carrera was stripped. In a return match, Sturm (159½) gained revenge for a previous defeat when moving well and countering Castillejo to good effect. It was clear that Castillejo was the harder puncher, but Sturm came back strongly from the seventh onwards to rack up the points. Although Castillejo took the last two sessions it was not enough, and had he concentrated on the body things may have been different.

19 May 2007. Jermain Taylor w pts 12 Cory Spinks.
Venue: FedEx Forum, Memphis, Tennessee, USA. **Recognition:** WBC/WBO/The Ring. **Referee:** Michael Ortega.
Scorecards: 117-111, 115-113, 111-117.

Fight Summary: Putting his three championship belts up for grabs against a crafty southpaw in Spinks (159¾), the holder of the IBF junior middleweight title, once again Taylor (159¾) was disappointing in a fight that never took off. With Spinks always moving on the back foot and ducking low when coming forward, Taylor had great difficulty in lining him up. All the harder punches of the fight came from Taylor and how one of the judges had Spinks winning nine rounds was beyond most of the observers.

26 May 2007. Arthur Abraham w rsc 3 Sebastien Demers.
Venue: JAKO Arena, Bamberg, Germany. **Recognition:** IBF. **Referee:** Ernest Sharif.
Fight Summary: Coming back after suffering a broken jaw in his last contest, Abraham (160) soon picked it up against the limited Demers (159), who had done most of his fighting in a lower division. Getting to grips with Demers in the third, Abraham hurt his man with a cluster of blows before dropping him with a solid right to the head. Although Demers made it up, once he had stumbled the referee immediately called it off, the finish coming with just three seconds of the session remaining.

30 June 2007. Felix Sturm w pts 12 Noe Tulio Gonzalez Alcoba.
Venue: Porsche Arena, Stuttgart, Germany. **Recognition:** WBA. **Referee:** Roberto Rodriguez.
Scorecards: 120-108, 118-110, 116-112.
Fight Summary: Making his first defence a successful one, Sturm (159¾) took control from the opening bell when scoring well with the jab as Gonzalez Alcoba (159½) had difficulty breaking down his rigid defence. For round after round it followed the same pattern, and even after the eighth when Gonzalez Alcoba was tired and ready to be taken Sturm let him off the hook when continuing to take no risks. It was only in the 12th that Sturm followed up his openings, but Gonzalez Alcoba survived. The third round was probably Gonzalez Alcoba's best when concentrating on the body, and his punching was solid enough to leave the right side of Sturm's face bruised and swollen by the end.

18 August 2007. Arthur Abraham w rsc 11 Khoren Gevor.
Venue: Max Schmeling Hall, Berlin, Germany. **Recognition:** IBF. **Referee:** Pete Podgorski.
Fight Summary: In a hard-fought encounter, Abraham (160) had to pull out all the stops to overcome his southpaw challenger who came to fight. It was not until the fifth that Abraham got into gear, shaking Gevor (160) up in the sixth with a left-right, and going up a gear. However, Gevor kept going despite being hurt on several occasions before coming undone in the 11th. Hurt by a big left hook in that session, Gevor was rescued by the referee at 2.41 after another heavy left hook had deposited him on the deck in a crumpled state.

29 September 2007. Kelly Pavlik w rsc 7 Jermain Taylor.
Venue: Boardwalk Hall, Atlantic City, New Jersey, USA. **Recognition:** WBC/WBO/The Ring. **Referee:** Steve Smoger.
Fight Summary: Aiming to get his hands on three championship belts, Pavlik (159½) walked into the champion from the bell only to be dropped in the second after being caught heavily on the head and follow-up blows. Somehow getting through all the punches coming his way to reach the end of the round, Pavlik came back strongly to take the next two sessions before Taylor (159) picked it up to win the fifth and sixth when utilising his boxing skills. In the seventh Pavlik showed what a powerful puncher he was when slamming in a tremendous right to the head that had Taylor staring into oblivion, and when two further heavy blows dropped the latter the referee stopped the contest immediately. The finish was timed at 2.14.

A return match made six pounds above the middleweight limit saw Pavlik outpoint Taylor over 12 rounds at the MGM Grand, Las Vegas, Nevada on 16 February 2008.

20 October 2007. Felix Sturm drew 12 Randy Griffin.
Venue: Gerry Weber Stadium, Halle, Germany. **Recognition:** WBA. **Referee:** Guillermo Perez Pineda.
Scorecards: 115-114, 114-117, 114-114.
Fight Summary: Clearly a gruelling contest, Sturm (159¾) just about held on to his title as Griffin (159½) took him all the way. Attacking throughout, throwing punches from both hands, Griffin made life difficult for Sturm. Having been taken out of his stride Sturm eventually upped his work-rate and went back to his boxing, and had he not taken the last two sessions he would have lost his title.

8 December 2007. Arthur Abraham w rsc 5 Wayne Elcock.
Venue: St Jakob Hall, Basle, Switzerland. **Recognition:** IBF. **Referee:** Wayne Kelly.
Fight Summary: Having gone well for the opening four rounds despite being knocked over in the second by a right to the head, Elcock (159) came out for the fifth with no little confidence after inducing a swelling over the champion's right eye, courtesy of solid jabs. As a known slow starter Abraham (160) had merely been biding his time, and in the fifth a cracker of a right hand sent Elcock into the ropes for a standing count. Still not recovered, Elcock was then caught by a crashing right hand followed by a left hook that saw the referee call the contest off at 1.58 of the session with the latter stunned and held up by the ropes.

29 March 2008. Arthur Abraham w co 12 Elvin Ayala.
Venue: Sparkassen Arena, Kiel, Germany. **Recognition:** IBF. **Referee:** Roberto Ramirez.
Fight Summary: After making his usual slow start the champion was back on equal terms coming into the fifth, and although knocking Ayala (159¾) down in that session the latter was soon on his feet and going well. Showing excellent defensive skills and a good jab, Ayala was making life tough for Abraham (159¾), who was clearly not at his best. Coming into the final session, Abraham, well in front, finally caught up with Ayala, and after a cluster of punches put the latter down he was counted out with just 28 seconds of the fight remaining. On review it was discovered that it was Abraham's left forearm that had administered the kayo blow.

Due to meet his mandatory challenger, Raul Marquez, on 4 October, the fight had to be postponed due to Abraham going down with flu on the morning of the contest.

5 April 2008. Felix Sturm w rsc 7 Jamie Pittman.
Venue: Castello Castle-Keeper Arena, Dusseldorf, Germany. **Recognition:** WBA. **Referee:** Russell Mora.
Fight Summary: Showing plenty of spirit the southpaw challenger gave it his best shot, throwing plenty of leather in the early sessions, but after his right eye was cut and swollen in the third things became even tougher as Sturm (158¾) picked his punches and waited for the inevitable to happen. Pittman (160) looked as though he had nothing left in the fifth after being floored by a left to the body, but he made it into the sixth only to be knocked over again. Gamely continuing, when Pittman was dropped by a right-left in the seventh the referee humanely called it off 36 seconds into the session.

7 June 2008. Kelly Pavlik w rsc 3 Gary Lockett.
Venue: Boardwalk Hall, Atlantic City, New Jersey, USA. **Recognition:** WBC/WBO/The Ring. **Referee:** Eddie Cotton.
Fight Summary: Hurt in the opening round things got worse for Lockett (159½) in the second as Pavlik (159) used his big reach advantage to bang in blows from both hands, the challenger being forced to take a knee on two occasions to limit the damage. In the third after giving it one last effort, when Lockett was dumped from a left-right to the head the referee stopped the contest at 1.40 of the session. The decision was effectively made for him when the Welshman's corner threw the towel in.

5 July 2008. Felix Sturm w pts 12 Randy Griffin.
Venue: Gerry Weber Stadium, Halle, Germany. **Recognition:** WBA. **Referee:** Guillermo Perez Pineda.
Scorecards: 116-112, 116-113, 118-110.
Fight Summary: Much improved from their earlier contest, this time round Sturm (159½) established his jab from the start to outbox the challenger in virtually all rounds other than the third, eighth, ninth and 12th. Although Griffin (159¾) never stopped trying to find a chink in Sturm's armour he was unsuccessful even if his aggression was impressive. Afterwards, Griffin was sure he had won, but had Sturm packed more power the American would never have reached the final bell.

1 November 2008. Felix Sturm w pts 12 Sebastian Sylvester.
Venue: Koenig Pilsener Arena, Oberhausen, Germany. **Recognition:** WBA. **Referee:** Guillermo Perez Pineda.
Scorecards: 118-110, 118-110, 119-109.
Fight Summary: Once again Sturm (159½) proved to be the master boxer, his left hand finding holes in the challenger's defence all night long. There was no doubting that Sylvester (159½) came to win and he fought strongly at times, but he was forced to take punches when opening up. Even though Sturm speeded up towards

the end, throwing both hands, Sylvester was still there right in front of him, always looking to unload. At the final bell, although soundly outscored it was Sylvester who got the plaudits for his game display.

8 November 2008. Arthur Abraham w rtd 6 Raul Marquez.
Venue: JAKO Arena, Bamberg, Germany. **Recognition:** IBF. **Referee:** Wayne Kelly.
Fight Summary: Boxing at his best Abraham (159¾) was too good for his southpaw challenger, who was simply not up to the task in hand. The problem for Marquez (160) was that he just could not handle Abraham's power and was continually forced to give ground as the latter bored in. Already showing wear and tear, when Marquez was cut over the right eye in the fifth things got progressively worse for the American. Despite there being no warning of what was to come, Marquez was retired at the end of the sixth when it was clear to his corner that it was his only option.

21 February 2009. Kelly Pavlik w rtd 9 Marco Antonio Rubio.
Venue: Chevrolet Centre, Youngstown, Ohio, USA. **Recognition:** WBC/WBO/The Ring. **Referee:** Frank Garza.
Fight Summary: Starting as he meant to carry on, the champion walked into Rubio (160) with a solid jab that continually pushed him back. It was only in the sixth that Rubio began to let the punches go, but that was it. The seventh saw Pavlik (159) take back command of the situation and at the end of the ninth Rubio was retired by his corner when they decided that their man had taken enough. Pavlik, who won every round, showed yet again that his long left jab was paramount to his success.

At the Race Arena, Nurburg, Germany on 11 July, Sebastian Zbik outpointed Domenico Spada over 12 rounds to win the vacant WBC 'interim' title.

14 March 2009. Arthur Abraham w pts 12 Lajuan Simon.
Venue: Ostee Hall, Kiel, Germany. **Recognition:** IBF. **Referee:** Benjy Esteves Jnr.
Scorecards: 117-110, 118-109, 117-110.
Fight Summary: Sticking with the champion all night, Simon (157¼) proved to be a tough man to dislodge, and despite being push-punched to the canvas in the third he was quickly back into the action. Not deterred, Simon continued to make a nuisance of himself, banging in left hooks when and where he could, while the poorly conditioned Abraham (159¾) looked to take time out. Despite being unable to put Simon away, the points were always with Abraham.

25 April 2009. Felix Sturm w rsc 7 Koji Sato.
Venue: Konig Sports Palace, Krefeld, Germany. **Recognition:** WBA. **Referee:** Luis Pabon.
Fight Summary: In a battle of left hands, the champion ultimately showed himself to be a cut above Sato (159¾). Although Sato threw some solid shots, Sturm (159) always appeared to be in control of the situation, especially when landing with better quality. Suffering from a rapidly swelling right eye Sato fought back hard, but in the seventh it was all over when he was driven into a corner following a terrific left hook to the body and rescued by the referee with 14 seconds of the session remaining.

27 June 2009. Arthur Abraham w rsc 10 Mahir Oral.
Venue: Max Schmeling Hall, Berlin, Germany. **Recognition:** IBF. **Referee:** Earl Brown.
Fight Summary: It was Oral (158¾) who started the better in this one, taking the opening three rounds when outboxing the champion. Having woken up in the fourth Abraham (159¾) set up Oral with some solid body shots before dropping him with a right to the head, and he repeated the knockdowns in the fifth and sixth. Strangely, when Oral was put down in the fifth the referee called it a slip. Although Oral came back well in the seventh by the tenth he was a spent force. With Abraham concentrating on the body, Oral was floored an additional three times, more from exhaustion than anything else, before the referee stopped the contest at 1.23 of the session after the towel was thrown in.

When Abraham relinquished the IBF title on 7 November in order to compete in the 'Showtime' super middleweight tournament, Sebastian Sylvester and Giovanni Lorenzo were signed up to find a new champion. Sylvester was the IBF international champion, having beaten Lajuan Simon (w pts 12 at the Max Schmeling Hall on

27 June) on the undercard of Abraham versus Oral, while Lorenzo had beaten Dionisio Miranda (w co 2 Prudential Centre, Newark, New Jersey, USA on 27 February) in an eliminating contest.

11 July 2009. Felix Sturm w pts 12 Khoren Gevor.
Venue: Nurburgring Race Track, Nurburg, Germany. **Recognition:** WBA. **Referee:** Jean-Louis Legand.
Scorecards: 115-113, 115-113, 117-111.
Fight Summary: Fighting flat out, the southpaw challenger gave Sturm (159¼) all the problems he could handle, plus some more. In a difficult contest to score all three judges plumped for Sturm, while there were many who thought Gevor (159¾) had done enough. Making the fight from the opening bell Gevor did not leave Sturm alone, realising that he had to get inside if he wanted to win. Although taken out of his stride, it was Sturm who produced the better quality before being taken to hospital suffering a haematoma to his right ear.

Gennady Golovkin won the vacant WBA 'interim' title when knocking out Milton Nunez in the opening round of their contest at the Roberto Duran Arena, Panama City, Panama on 14 August 2010, prior to being promoted to 'second tier' status on 14 October 2010.

19 September 2009. Sebastian Sylvester w pts 12 Giovanni Lorenzo.
Venue: Jahn Sports Forum, Neubrandenburg, Germany. **Recognition:** IBF. **Referee:** David Fields.
Scorecards: 116-112, 115-113, 112-116.
Fight Summary: Contested for the vacant title after Arthur Abraham decided to move up a division, it was Sylvester (159¼) who became the new champion after outscoring the tough Lorenzo (160). Right from the opening bell Sylvester made it his fight, his speed and movement leaving Lorenzo nonplussed at times. Although Lorenzo was always dangerous with solid hooks from either hand, many of which missed, Sylvester boxed with intelligence and the belief that he could make his punches count.

19 December 2009. Kelly Pavlik w rsc 5 Miguel Angel Espino.
Venue: Beeghly Centre, Youngstown, Ohio, USA. **Recognition:** WBC/WBO/The Ring. **Referee:** Steve Smoger.
Fight Summary: Despite giving his all the brave challenger did not have the tools to beat Pavlik (160), who met him with solid blows from either hand that had destruction written all over them. At the end of the opener Espino (159) was deducted a point for punching after the bell, and in second and third when the two men went head-to-head Pavlik was cut on the right eye. It hardly made any difference to Pavlik, who twice dropped Espino with right uppercuts in the fourth before going to town in the fifth. The fight ended after Espino, who had been floored for a count of 'five' by lefts and rights, continued taking a beating until the referee brought matters to a halt at 1.44 of the session on the instructions of the latter's corner.

On the same day, Sebastian Zbik successfully defended the WBC 'interim' title against Emanuele Della Rosa when winning on points over 12 rounds at the Sport & Congress Centre, Schwerin, Germany.

30 January 2010. Sebastian Sylvester w rsc 10 Billy Lyell.
Venue: Jahn Sports Forum, Neubrandenburg, Germany. **Recognition:** IBF. **Referee:** Earl Brown.
Fight Summary: Coming in at short notice for Pablo Navascues, who failed a drugs test, Lyell (156¾) put up spirited resistance against a champion who let him off the hook several times prior to the contest coming to an end in the tenth. Sylvester (159¾) started well enough, landing heavy shots from both hands in the opener and cutting Lyell's nose badly in the second, before easing off as the rounds went by. Following the eighth, which Lyell took on aggression, Sylvester picked it up in the ninth before the referee stopped the contest 36 seconds into the tenth session after the American's corner showed the towel. At the time of the stoppage, Lyell had been badly hurt by a heavy left-right and was under severe attack.

17 April 2010. Sergio Martinez w pts 12 Kelly Pavlik.
Venue: Boardwalk Hall, Atlantic City, New Jersey, USA. **Recognition:** WBC/WBO/The Ring. **Referee:** David Fields.
Scorecards: 116-111, 115-112, 115-111.
Fight Summary: Following a hand infection and weight-making difficulties, Pavlik (159½) put his three championship belts on the line against Martinez (159½), the current WBC junior middleweight champion. Using his

speed to get inside Pavlik's long reach, the southpaw challenger took the opening four rounds before coming under fire in the seventh when dropped by a short right uppercut. Pavlik had already begun the fightback in the fifth and he took the next three sessions on the cards. However, after cutting Pavlik under both eyes in the ninth Martinez poured it on to the final bell to make sure that the title went his way.

Also on 17 April, Sebastian Zbik successfully defended the WBC 'interim' title when outscoring Domenico Spada over 12 rounds at the Borderland Hall, Magdeburg, Germany.

In mid-June, Martinez was stripped of his WBO title when failing to decide within a reasonable time frame whether or not he would continue to campaign in the 160lbs weight class or remain in the junior middleweight division. Following that, Dmitry Pirog and Daniel Jacobs were signed up to contest the vacant WBO title.

Another successful defence of the WBC 'interim' title for Zbik came on 31 July when he outpointed Jorge Heiland at the O2 World Arena, Hamburg, Germany.

5 June 2010. Sebastian Sylvester drew 12 Roman Karmazin.
Venue: Jahn Sports Forum, Neubrandenburg, Germany. **Recognition:** IBF. **Referee:** Mufadel Elghazaoui.
Scorecards: 118-111, 111-117, 114-114.
Fight Summary: Showing a high work-rate the challenger gave Sylvester (159½) all the trouble he could handle when running him to a split decision draw. While Karmazin (157¾) was always working hard, banging in shots from either hand, Sylvester used a solid jab in an effort to keep him away. Having been outworked in several rounds despite landing heavily, Sylvester eventually went to the front in the final three sessions when hurting Karmazin with several heavy blows and cutting him on the left eye. Regardless of the decision, there were many who thought that Karmazin deserved better.

31 July 2010. Dmitry Pirog w rsc 5 Daniel Jacobs.
Venue: Mandalay Bay Resort & Casino, Las Vegas, Nevada, USA. **Recognition:** WBO. **Referee:** Robert Byrd.
Fight Summary: Contested for the vacant title after Sergio Martinez had been stripped of the belt, the favourite, Jacobs (159), was shockingly beaten after 57 seconds of the fifth. Although starting well enough Jacobs was rescued by the bottom rope in the second, having been caught by an overarm right and solid left to the head, and should have been counted on. That was certainly a warning that Pirog (160) was dangerous, but after ignoring it and sailing through the fourth Jacobs was smashed to the floor by another big right only a round later. After counting up to 'six', the referee called the fight off to allow Jacobs medical attention.

4 September 2010. Felix Sturm w pts 12 Giovanni Lorenzo.
Venue: Lanxess Arena, Cologne, Germany. **Recognition:** WBA. **Referee:** Luis Pabon.
Scorecards: 117-111, 117-111, 118-111.
Fight Summary: As soon as the contest was underway Lorenzo (158¼) set up an attack to take the play away from Sturm (159), but it was not long before the champion got himself into gear, his speed, movement and quality punching proving to be a match winner as early as the second round. It was soon clear that Sturm was content to outbox Lorenzo, who won three rounds at most, and as the rounds passed by solid left jabs, coupled to body shots and rights to the head softened the Dominican up. Surprisingly, Lorenzo's team even thought that their man had won, although on reflection they would have realised that aggression is not everything.

With Gennady Golovkin being promoted from 'interim' champion to 'second tier' status, Hassan N'Dam N'Jikam outpointed Avtandil Khurtsidze over 12 rounds at the Port of Versailles Sports Palace, Paris, France on 30 October to win the WBA 'interim' title.

Golovkin went on to make a successful defence of his WBA 'second tier' title on 16 December when knocking Nilson Julio Tapia out in the third round at the Daulet Sports Complex, Astana, Kazakhstan.

30 October 2010. Sebastian Sylvester w pts 12 Mahir Oral.
Venue: Stadium Hall, Rostock, Germany. **Recognition:** IBF. **Referee:** Marlon Wright.

Scorecards: 117-107, 119-106, 117-107.
Fight Summary: Having given away the opening round to Oral (159¾), the champion began to find his feet before hurting his Turkish-born opponent in the fourth with a solid straight right that shook him to his boots. Although he did not go down, Oral took so many solid shots that two of the judges marked it a 10-8 round. From thereon in it was all Sylvester (159¾), despite being badly cut over the right eye from a clash of heads. Working the body well Sylvester softened Oral up, and in the eighth, ninth and 11th he had the latter over from such punches while on his way to a convincing points win.

20 November 2010. Sergio Martinez w co 2 Paul Williams.
Venue: Boardwalk Hall, Atlantic City, New Jersey, USA. **Recognition:** WBC/The Ring. **Referee:** Earl Morton.
Fight Summary: A match-up between southpaws saw the champion come out on top when knocking out Williams (156), a former three-time title holder, at 1.10 of the second. Contested at catchweights due to both men being natural light middleweights, it was soon clear that this one would not last with the punches going in thick and fast almost from the opening bell. It was much the same in the second until Martinez (157½) found a sweeping left to the jaw that ended matters there and then.

Unable to defend against the WBC 'interim' champion, Sebastian Zbik, due to his contractual agreements with HBO, the television network, Martinez forfeited the title on 11 January 2011. Desperate not to lose Martinez completely, the WBC handed him the term 'emeritus' titleholder' while, at the same time, promoting Zbik to full championship status. Regardless of this, Martinez continued to be recognised by *The Ring* magazine as being the best man in the world at the weight.

19 February 2011. Felix Sturm w rsc 7 Ronald Hearns.
Venue: Porsche Arena, Stuttgart, Germany. **Recognition:** WBA. **Referee:** Raul Caiz Jnr.
Fight Summary: In what was his ninth defence, against Hearns (159¼), the son of the famous Thomas, Sturm (159¼) was not expected to be at risk, and that was the case as he cruised to a stoppage win in the seventh. Controlling matters most of the way, Sturm bided his time before picking it up in the sixth when hurting Hearns with solid blows just prior to the bell. Not hanging around at the start of the seventh, Sturm belted away with both hands until finding a big right hand to the head that floored Hearns. After taking a quick look at Hearns the referee called it off after 48 seconds of the session without bothering to take up the count.

On 2 April, Hassan N'Dam N'Jikam outpointed Giovanni Lorenzo over 12 rounds at the Sports Palace, Le Cannet, France to make a successful defence of his WBA 'interim' title, while on 17 June at the Roberto Duran Arena, Panama City, Panama, Gennady Golovkin stopped Kassim Ouma in the tenth round to retain his WBA 'second tier' title.

At the end of January 2012, N'Dam N'Jikam relinquished his WBA 'interim' title to put himself in line for a crack at Dmitry Pirog, the WBO champion.

12 March 2011. Sergio Martinez w rsc 8 Serhiy Dzinziruk.
Venue: Foxwoods Resort, Mashantucket, Connecticut, USA. **Recognition:** The Ring. **Referee:** Arthur Mercante Jnr.
Fight Summary: Meeting a fellow southpaw for the second time in a row, the 36-year-old holder of *The Ring* Championship Belt both started and finished strongly against Dzinziruk (158¾), whom he stopped at 1.43 of the eighth. Taking control from the start, Martinez (158¾) took the opening three sessions by dint of forceful jabs before having Dzinziruk over in the fourth when the latter touched down. He then dropped Dzinziruk in the fifth following a cracking left to the head. Although Dzinziruk came back well in the next two sessions he came unstuck in the eighth when a right to the head put him down for a count of 'five'. After being dropped twice more from another solid right and then a left hook to the head the referee came to Dzinziruk's rescue. Martinez also received a WBC diamond belt on winning.

26 March 2011. Dmitry Pirog w pts 12 Javier Maciel.
Venue: DIVS Sports Palace, Ekaterinburg, Russia. **Recognition:** WBO. **Referee:** Benjy Esteves Jnr.
Scorecards: 115-112, 117-110, 116-111.

Fight Summary: Showing a sound defence, the challenger turned out to be a tough nut for Pirog (159¼) to crack when taking him all the way. It was only when Pirog started working the body in the fourth that he began to have some joy, but back came Maciel (156¼) with some solid shots of his own, especially in the eighth. Returning the compliment, Pirog landed heavily in the ninth before dropping a point in the tenth for elbowing his opponent. All to play for in the final two sessions, it was Pirog who outgunned the Argentine to take the unanimous decision in what was generally seen as an off night for him.

7 May 2011. Daniel Geale w pts 12 Sebastian Sylvester.

Venue: Jahn Sports Forum, Neubrandenburg, Germany. **Recognition:** IBF. **Referee:** Randy Neumann.
Scorecards: 118-110, 118-112, 110-118.
Fight Summary: Making a fast start, Geale (159) moved in on Sylvester (159¾) from the opening bell in an effort to take the play away from a champion fighting on home territory. There was never much between them despite what the cards said, Geale throwing plenty of leather while Sylvester looked to pick single shots. In the seventh Geale began catching Sylvester from varying angles as he began to pick up his work-rate, but the latter stood firm and hit back. At the end of the day it was Geale who held up better to take the final three sessions and the split decision. In the wake of the verdict, Sylvester admitted that he had been outworked and had not been prepared for Geale's style of fighting.

4 June 2011. Julio Cesar Chavez Jnr w pts 12 Sebastian Zbik.

Venue: Staples Centre, Los Angeles, California, USA. **Recognition:** WBC. **Referee:** Jack Reiss.
Scorecards: 115-113, 116-112, 114-114.
Fight Summary: Defending the title he had been awarded after the WBC had placed Sergio Martinez on 'emeritus' status, Zbik (158¾) lost it at the first time of asking when dropping the majority decision to Chavez (160), the son of a famous father of the same name. Almost a stone heavier than Zbik when the fight started, due to rehydration, was clearly unfair and almost certainly gave Chavez an advantage. There were no knockdowns, but both men gave it plenty, with Zbik scoring with 391 punches to Chavez's 256 according to CompuBox. There was no doubt that Zbik proved to be a good ring technician, but most of his shots were to the head, whereas Chavez worked mainly on the body, a tactic that eventually wore the champion down. With all three judges giving Chavez the final three sessions that was where the fight was won.

25 June 2011. Felix Sturm w pts 12 Matthew Macklin.

Venue: Lanxess Arena, Cologne, Germany. **Recognition:** WBA. **Referee:** Stan Christodoulou.
Scorecards: 116-112, 116-112, 113-115.
Fight Summary: Taking the fight to Sturm (159) from the opening bell, looking to find holes in the champion's defences, Macklin (159¾) was extremely busy. By the middle stages Macklin was still going well, but his punches were beginning to lack bite as Sturm came back into the action. Although Sturm came on strongly to take the last three sessions in a grandstand finish, there were many who thought Macklin's earlier good work should have been better rewarded.

31 August 2011. Daniel Geale w pts 12 Eromosele Albert.

Venue: Derwent Entertainment Centre, Hobart, Australia. **Recognition:** IBF. **Referee:** Tony Weeks.
Scorecards: 117-111, 119-109, 116-112.
Fight Summary: Making his first defence Geale (159½) proved too good for the hardy Albert (158) who, despite coming forward for the majority of the time, was forced to take solid counters from both hands. While Albert's aggression earned him a few rounds as Geale took a break, in the main all of the good work came from the latter. By the ninth Albert was open-mouthed, having taken some hurtful blows up and down, but he gamely fought on to the final bell.

25 September 2011. Dmitry Pirog w rtd 9 Gennady Martirosyan.

Venue: Olympic Palace of Sport, Krasnodar, Russia. **Recognition:** WBO. **Referee:** Viktor Panin.
Fight Summary: Towering over his challenger, Pirog (159½) controlled the fight from the opening bell with hard lefts going in up and down, the body shots being most effective. Although Martirosyan (157¾) landed hard blows himself, he was normally the receiver. Coming into the fourth Martirosyan was already cut on the right eye, and

although fighting on gamely his corner pulled him out of the contest at the end of the ninth round after he had continued to ship punishment.

1 October 2011. Sergio Martinez w co 11 Darren Barker.
Venue: Boardwalk Hall, Atlantic City, New Jersey, USA. **Recognition:** The Ring. **Referee:** Eddie Cotton.
Fight Summary: Starting well against the holder of *The Ring* Championship Belt, Barker (159½) picked up several rounds with the jab and rights over the top before coming under pressure as the fight wore on. Having shown a certain amount of caution, Martinez (158) began stepping it up from the sixth onwards as Barker tired. By the ninth Barker was being rocked by heavy right hooks, and in the 11th he was counted out at 1.29 of the session after being floored by a solid right to the side of the head that left him on his knees. Even though he was behind on points at the finish, Barker had boxed commendably against the southpaw champion.

19 November 2011. Julio Cesar Chavez Jnr w rsc 5 Peter Manfredo.
Venue: Reliant Arena, Houston, Texas, USA. **Recognition:** WBC. **Referee:** Laurence Cole.
Fight Summary: After a slow opening round, Chavez (159¾) started the second strongly, belting in blows to head and body that put the challenger on the back foot. In spite of the pressure being exerted on him, Manfredo (159½) came back in the fourth with rights to head and body, which he repeated at the start of the fifth before being forced to take some heavy shots as Chavez hit back. With Manfredo under a relentless attack as Chavez threw everything at him the referee eventually stopped the fight at 1.52 of the session.

2 December 2011. Felix Sturm drew 12 Martin Murray.
Venue: SAP Arena, Mannheim, Germany. **Recognition:** WBA. **Referee:** Stan Christodoulou.
Scorecards: 116-112, 113-115, 114-114.
Fight Summary: In his second defence running Sturm (159¾) came close to losing his title to an Englishman as Murray (159¼) ran him close. Had Murray not lost the opening two rounds when taking his time he would have been crowned champion. From the fourth onwards Murray began to get to Sturm, especially with solid rights, and in the eighth the German was stunned by a terrific left hook. However, showing his experience Sturm hung on in to come back strongly in the final two sessions to just about scrape home on a split draw. In the final moments of the bout Sturm hammered Murray with heavy rights, but had left any chance of a stoppage win far too late.

A few days later, on 9 December, at the Ballsaal Intercontinental Hotel, Dusseldorf, Germany, Gennady Golovkin knocked out Lajuan Simon in the opening round to retain the WBA 'second tier' title.

4 February 2012. Julio Cesar Chavez Jnr w pts 12 Marco Antonio Rubio.
Venue: The Alamodome, San Antonio, Texas, USA. **Recognition:** WBC. **Referee:** Lupe Garcia.
Scorecards: 116-112, 118-110, 115-113.
Fight Summary: Once again the champion used the regulation of weighing-in a day earlier to his advantage when coming into the ring 21lbs heavier than Rubio (159). Going head-to-head with Chavez (159½) the hard-hitting Rubio matched his fellow-Mexican for pace and power for much of the contest before finding the weight discrepancy working against him towards the end. Even then Rubio hurt Chavez in the tenth and 11th, but ultimately it was the latter's body work and better conditioning that saw him walk off with the unanimous decision.

7 March 2012. Daniel Geale w pts 12 Osumanu Adama.
Venue: Derwent Entertainment Centre, Hobart, Tasmania, Australia. **Recognition:** IBF. **Referee:** Jack Reiss.
Scorecards: 118-110, 117-111, 115-113.
Fight Summary: Immediately taking control of the fight at the opening bell, the champion was soon pushing Adama (159) back with fast right hands and left hooks. Occasionally Adama caught Geale (159½) with solid shots, but the Aussie soon gained his momentum. As the pace fell off in the final few sessions, instead of trying to take Adama out Geale was happy to box conservatively with the jab in order to run the clock down. Although Adama had put up a good display and was complimented by Geale as being extremely tough, he lacked the necessary skills required to become champion.

17 March 2012. Sergio Martinez w rtd 11 Matthew Macklin.
Venue: Madison Square Garden, Manhattan, NYC, New York, USA. **Recognition:** The Ring. **Referee:** Eddie Cotton.
Fight Summary: Getting away well, the southpaw holder of *The Ring* Championship Belt caught Macklin (158) heavily several times before the latter came back with good punches of his own. In the fourth, after catching Martinez (157½) with a solid shot the Englishman was almost floored in what was becoming a tough fight. Despite being dropped in the seventh by a corking right uppercut Martinez was soon back in business, hammering away at Macklin who was rapidly tiring when coming into the ninth. By the 11th it was clear that Macklin had shot his bolt, and after being dropped twice by hard lefts he was retired by his corner at the end of the session.

13 April 2012. Felix Sturm w rtd 9 Sebastian Zbik.
Venue: Lanxess Arena, Cologne, Germany. **Recognition:** WBA. **Referee:** Raul Caiz.
Fight Summary: Although Zbik (160) went well in the opening three rounds, attacking the champion from head to body, by the fourth he was beginning to lose ground. At that point Sturm (159½) had found his jab, while his left hook was giving Zbik plenty to worry about. Still aggressive, Zbik was always a danger despite his eyes starting to swell, but by the ninth Sturm was in complete control. Looking tired, and with his vision impaired, Zbik was retired by his corner at the end of the ninth after Sturm had continued to step up the pace.

On 12 May, Gennady Golovkin stopped Makoto Fuchigami inside three rounds to retain his WBA 'second tier' title at the Terminal Ice Palace, Brovari, Ukraine.

1 May 2012. Dmitry Pirog w pts 12 Nobuhiro Ishida.
Venue: Krylatskoe Sports Complex, Moscow, Russia. **Recognition:** WBO. **Referee:** Manuel Maritxalar.
Scorecards: 119-109, 120-108, 117-111.
Fight Summary: Sticking to his game plan, the champion was soon banging out the jab and cutting up rough inside as the 35-year-old Ishida (157¾) tried to get to grips with him. Despite being cut over the right eye in the ninth, Ishida was still willing, constantly lunging in to get punches off. Even though the margin of victory for Pirog (158) was wide Ishida came to fight and was always competitive.

Hassan N'Dam N'Jikam won the vacant WBO 'interim' title when outpointing Max Bursak over 12 rounds at the Marcel Cerdan Sports Palace, Levallois-Perret, France on 4 May.

When Pirog forfeited the WBO title at the end of August after he had signed to meet Gennady Golovkin for the latter's WBA 'second tier' championship, N'Dam N'Jikam was appointed champion.

16 June 2012. Julio Cesar Chavez Jnr w rsc 7 Andy Lee.
Venue: Sun Bowl, El Paso, Texas, USA. **Recognition:** WBC. **Referee:** Laurence Cole.
Fight Summary: It was Lee (159¼) who got away the better, banging in a solid southpaw jab and countering well before the champion found his way inside in the third. From thereon in it was two-fisted fighting all the way with Lee ahead on the cards coming into the seventh. Although Chavez (159) complained of cramp prior to the seventh, once the session was underway he was all business, battering Lee around the ring until the referee rescued the latter on the 2.21 mark after a cracking right to the chin had sent him to the floor.

1 September 2012. Daniel Geale w pts 12 Felix Sturm.
Venue: Pilsner Arena, Oberhausen, Germany. **Recognition:** IBF/WBA. **Referee:** Luis Pabon.
Scorecards: 116-112, 116-112, 112-116.
Fight Summary: In a battle to unify two championship belts, the IBF champion, Geale (158¾) beat Sturm (158¾), the WBA title holder, by a split decision in a tough fight that saw the latter impressing with the jab in the early rounds before he was overhauled by the Aussie. Both men landed heavily with rights and lefts and both remained upright. By the seventh it was noticeable that Sturm was tiring as Geale stayed at close quarters working the body, and although the German came back with some quality punches he could not match his opponent's quantity.

Also on 1 September, at the Turning Stone Resort & Casino, Verona, New York, USA, Gennady Golovkin stopped Grzegorz Proksa inside five rounds to retain his WBA 'second tier' title.

At The Arena, Manchester on 24 November, England, Martin Murray stopped Jorge Navarro inside six rounds to win the vacant WBA 'interim' title.

After Geale was stripped by the WBA on 1 November for deciding to defend against Anthony Mundine instead of Golovkin, the latter was handed the title.

15 September 2012. Sergio Martinez w pts 12 Julio Cesar Chavez Jnr.
Venue: Thomas & Mack Centre, Las Vegas, Nevada, USA. **Recognition:** WBC/The Ring. **Referee:** Tony Weeks.
Scorecards: 117-110, 118-109, 118-109.
Fight Summary: Putting on a master class, despite injuring his left hand in the fourth, Martinez (159), the holder of *The Ring* Championship Belt, was just too good for the WBC champion, Chavez (158). For round after round Martinez had confused Chavez with his southpaw stance, moving him around and belting him with shots to head and body, almost without a care in the world. Prior to the final session only one judge had given Chavez a round. Unable to get near Martinez for 11 rounds, suddenly in the 12th Chavez, his left eye closed, was in with a chance after catching the Argentine with two heavy blows that left him slumped on the ropes. Following up, Chavez smashed Martinez to the floor with three hard lefts, and although the latter made it to his feet and then survived another drop which was classified as a slip he lasted out the round.

20 October 2012. Peter Quillin w pts 12 Hassan N'Dam N'Jikam.
Venue: Barclays Centre, Brooklyn, NYC, New York, USA. **Recognition:** WBO. **Referee:** Eddie Claudio.
Scorecards: 115-107, 115-107, 115-107.
Fight Summary: This was N'Dam N'Jikam's first defence of the title he was handed after Dmitry Pirog had been stripped, and he took the opening three sessions by dint of good left hand work before running into trouble in the fourth. Dropped twice by left hooks that found the mark, N'Dam N'Jikam (159) hit the floor twice more from what were called slips before coming back swinging hard. Having held up in the fifth the Cameroonian was floored twice more in the sixth, the left hook and a right doing the damage. Recovering well, N'Dam N'Jikam bravely fought it out with Quillin (159¼) during the next five sessions, only to be battered to the deck twice more by heavy lefts in the 12th prior to hearing the final bell.

19 January 2013. Gennady Golovkin w rsc 7 Gabriel Rosado.
Venue: Madison Square Garden Theatre, Manhattan, NYC, New York, USA. **Recognition:** WBA. **Referee:** Steve Smoger.
Fight Summary: Handed the title when Daniel Geale was stripped, this was Golovkin's first defence. On the back foot from the opening bell in order to negate the champion's power as best he could, Rosado (159) put on a good showing until being stopped. With Golovkin (160) coming in behind the left jab throughout to hammer in lefts and rights Rosado was gradually worn down, but not before he had landed some good punches of his own. Hurt in the sixth, the cut on his right eye bleeding badly, Rosado held out for a while before being rescued by the referee at 2.27 of the seventh after his corner threw the towel in when his vision was badly impaired.

30 January 2013. Daniel Geale w pts 12 Anthony Mundine.
Venue: Entertainment Centre, Sydney, Australia. **Recognition:** IBF. **Referee:** Robert Byrd.
Scorecards: 116-112, 117-111, 117-111.
Fight Summary: Avenging his only defeat in the paid ranks while making a successful defence of his remaining title, Geale (159¾) proved too good and too busy for the 37-year-old Mundine (158½) this time round. Working non-stop throughout, Geale pressured Mundine to such a degree that he was not able to get his best punches off, and several times he was spoken to by the referee for use of foul tactics. Winning three or four rounds at most, the former champion was beaten comprehensively.

30 March 2013. Gennady Golovkin w rsc 3 Nobuhiro Ishida.
Venue: Star Rooms, Monte Carlo, Monaco. **Recognition:** WBA. **Referee:** Stan Christodoulou.
Fight Summary: While coming to make a fight of it, Ishida (158½) ultimately played into the champion's hands. Seemingly happy to swap punches with Golovkin (159½), in the second round it was clear that this was not a wise move by Ishida when he was forced to take several heavy lefts to the head, one of which left him with a cut under

the right eye. It was more of the same in the third before Golovkin dropped Ishida with a terrific right to the jaw that left his rival hanging through the ropes with his head on the ring apron. With Ishida clearly out to the world the referee stopped the contest immediately to allow him medical treatment, the finish being timed at 2.20.

27 April 2013. Peter Quillin w rsc 7 Fernando Guerrero.
Venue: Barclays Centre, Brooklyn, NYC, New York, USA. **Recognition:** WBO. **Referee:** Harvey Dock.
Fight Summary: It did not take the champion long to show Guerrero (160) who was boss when battering his southpaw opponent to the floor twice in the second, the first knockdown coming from a heavy right to the chin before a cluster of solid shots repeated the trick. Although Guerrero landed with good left hooks himself and fought back hard, Quillin (160) was always master of the situation. Having won the sixth on all three cards, the seventh saw Guerrero finally removed from the fight when put under severe pressure from the hard-hitting Quillin. Dropped by a cracking right for the 'eight' count, when Guerrero got back into the action it was not long before the referee stopped the contest on the 1.38 mark after he had been decked for the fourth time by a left-right.

27 April 2013. Sergio Martinez w pts 12 Martin Murray.
Venue: Velez Sarsfield Sports Club, Buenos Aires, Argentina. **Recognition:** WBC/The Ring. **Referee:** Massimo Barrovecchio.
Scorecards: 115-112, 115-112, 115-112.
Fight Summary: Defending his two championship belts on home soil, Martinez (159½) rattled off the opening three rounds while Murray (159½) looked to get a foothold in the contest. From the fourth onwards it was extremely close as Murray made his move with solid left jabs and a tight defence paving the way forward. The southpaw champion was right up against it in the sixth when pushed back by heavy jabs and being cut by the left eye. In the eighth it got worse for Martinez when he was decked by a left-right, and although coming back in the ninth he was floored by a left hook in the tenth that the referee called a slip. Despite looking to go behind, Martinez finished strongly in the final two sessions to just about retain his title. There were many who thought that Murray had been unlucky after going so close.

Marco Antonio Rubio won the vacant WBC 'interim' title when knocking out Domenico Spada inside 10 rounds at the Grand Stadium, Ciudad Delicias, Chihuahua, Mexico on 5 April 2014.

29 June 2013. Gennady Golovkin w co 3 Matthew Macklin.
Venue: Foxwoods MGM Grand, Mashantucket, Connecticut, USA. **Recognition:** WBA. **Referee:** Eddie Cotton.
Fight Summary: Never in with a chance, Macklin (159) was outspeeded and outthought by the hard-hitting champion from the opening bell, lefts and rights piercing his guard as he tried to move away. Stalking Macklin throughout the second and stunning him with heavy shots, it was clear that Golovkin (159) had his man where he wanted. It was more of the same in the third, and after Golovkin smashed in a left to the short rib Macklin went down to be counted out at 1.22 of the session.

17 August 2013. Darren Barker w pts 12 Daniel Geale.
Venue: Revel Resort, Atlantic City, New Jersey, USA. **Recognition:** IBF. **Referee:** Eddie Cotton.
Scorecards: 114-113, 116-111, 113-114.
Fight Summary: Having come back from a series of bad injuries and being on the verge of retirement, Barker (159½) started well enough before having to endure time out after a low blow from the champion in the fourth and being dropped heavily by a left hook to the body in the sixth. Somehow making it to his feet and lasting out the round, Barker gradually boxed his way back into contention, pushing Geale (159½) back with solid jabs. By the ninth Barker was in full flow, and despite being cut on the left eye in the tenth he finished strongly to take the split decision.

26 October 2013. Peter Quillin w rsc 10 Gabriel Rosado.
Venue: Boardwalk Hall, Atlantic City, New Jersey, USA. **Recognition:** WBO. **Referee:** Allan Huggins.
Fight Summary: Not at his best, having left some of his ability in the gym, the champion was still too good for Rosado (160). Although knocked down in the second by a left hook Rosado came back to make a fight of it, even though he was falling behind on the cards, before being cut over the left eye in the ninth. Coming out for the tenth

it soon became clear that the cut was too bad for Rosado to carry on and, after the doctor indicated that to the referee, the contest was called off 40 seconds into the session.

2 November 2013. Gennady Golovkin w rtd 8 Curtis Stevens.
Venue: Madison Square Garden Theatre, Manhattan, NYC, New York, USA. **Recognition:** WBA. **Referee:** Harvey Dock.
Fight Summary: Although starting cautiously the champion was quick to pick it up in the second, a left hook to the head, towards the end of the round, sending Stevens (159¼) crashing. Back in action, Stevens did not do much fighting in the third before surprising Golovkin (159½) in the fourth with a heavy left-right that saw the latter backing off. From thereon in, however, it was all downhill for Stevens, who was punished without respite as Golovkin went for the finishing line. Having endured a tough session in the eighth, his right eye badly swollen and at the end of his tether, Stevens' corner wisely pulled him out of the contest during the interval.

On 21 December, at the Krylatskoye Dynamo Sports Palace, Moscow, Russia, Dmitry Chudinov stopped Juan Camilo Novoa inside six rounds. The bout was originally set for the WBA 'interim' title, but after Golovkin's request to become WBA 'super' champion was refused it became an eliminator. At the same time, Martin Murray continued as the 'interim' champion.

7 December 2013. Felix Sturm w rsc 2 Darren Barker.
Venue: Porsche Arena, Stuttgart, Germany. **Recognition:** IBF. **Referee:** Mark Nelson.
Fight Summary: Barker's reign as champion ended as suddenly as it had begun when he was forced out of the fight at 2.09 of the second round. Having been put under pressure by the Sturm (159½) left hook early in the opener, Barker (159) began to fight back before a rib problem resurfaced when he threw a right hand near the end of the session. Although trying to find his way back in the second, Barker's lack of mobility would prove his undoing. Fighting virtually on one leg Barker was easy pickings for Sturm, and after being dropped by a right hook and then taking further punishment the referee rescued him on the 2.09 mark when his corner threw the towel in.

1 February 2014. Gennady Golovkin w rsc 7 Osumanu Adama.
Venue: Room of Stars, Monaco, Monte Carlo. **Recognition:** WBA. **Referee:** Luis Pabon.
Fight Summary: Up against a challenger who had never been floored, Golovkin (159½) soon put paid to that record when forcing the Ghanaian to the floor with a solid right towards the end of the first. Despite that, Adama (159¼) came back in the second as though nothing had happened and had gradually regained his composure by the fourth even though he was forced to take heavy blows and was way down on the cards. Picking it up in the sixth, Golovkin had Adama down from a crunching left hook to the body. Up again, his right eye swollen, Adama was dropped in the seventh by a left to the jaw before the fight was called off at 1.20 of the session after he had taken another solid left hook to the chin.

The WBA stripped Martin Murray of his 'interim' title on 7 March for making no defences and appointed Dmitry Chudinov as his successor. Making his first defence, Chudinov outpointed Patrick Nielsen over 12 rounds at the Arena, Mytishchi, Russia on 1 June.

19 April 2014. Peter Quillin w pts 12 Lukas Konecny.
Venue: The Armoury, Washington DC, USA. **Recognition:** WBO. **Referee:** Kenny Chevalier.
Scorecards: 119-109, 119-109, 120-108.
Fight Summary: Even though the champion received a wide unanimous decision at the end of his contest against Konecny (158¼) he had been unable to put his rival on the floor and never looked like doing so. However, from the third onwards Quillin (159¾) was putting his punches together, especially solid lefts to the body as Konecny came on to him, but he was unable to have the latter in difficulty. Afterwards, all Quillin could say was that Konecny was one tough man who came to fight.

At the beginning of September 2014, Quillin relinquished his WBO title in order to pursue bigger opportunities at the weight.

31 May 2014. Sam Soliman w pts 12 Felix Sturm.
Venue: Konig Sports Palace, Krefeld, Germany. **Recognition:** IBF. **Referee:** Eddie Cotton.
Scorecards: 118-110, 118-110, 117-111.
Fight Summary: In a return fight between the pair, yet again Soliman (159½) proved the better man as he stayed at close quarters and gave the champion no room to get his punches off. Keeping low to make life difficult for Sturm (159), the Aussie also roughed him up, and although the latter came back hard to take the eighth and ninth he lost the last three sessions on all of the cards. It was a big disappointment for Sturm, who simply ran out of gas just when it mattered.

7 June 2014. Miguel Cotto w rtd 9 Sergio Martinez.
Venue: Madison Square Garden, Manhattan, NYC, New York, USA. **Recognition:** WBC/The Ring. **Referee:** Michael Griffin.
Fight Summary: Starting like a bomb, Cotto (155) became a four-weight world champion when Martinez (158¾), the holder of two championship belts, was retired by his corner at the end of the ninth. The fight had started badly for the southpaw champion when he was floored three times in the opening round by a mixture of solid shots, and although he somehow managed to remain upright for another seven rounds it was a nightmare. Unable to avoid hooks thrown from either hand the torment went on for Martinez for round after round. Despite trying his best to pull something out of the bag, after a heavy jab from the dominant Cotto sat Martinez down in the ninth the game was almost up.

26 July 2014. Gennady Golovkin w rsc 3 Daniel Geale.
Venue: Madison Square Garden, Manhattan, NYC, New York, USA. **Recognition:** WBA. **Referee:** Mike Ortega.
Fight Summary: Given a chance to reach the top again, Geale (159¼) was right up against it from the start after he had slipped over when trying to avoid the champion's punches coming his way, and the timekeeper had allowed the round to run to four minutes. Not only did Geale get caught up in the ropes after tripping over photographic equipment but he also returned to his corner with a cut on his right eye. Despite going down from a punch to the neck in the second as Golovkin (159¾) opened up, Geale started the third showing an excellent defence until being dropped by a right to the jaw. Although Geale made it to his feet in time the referee called the contest off with 13 seconds of the session remaining when realising the Aussie was not quite right.

Dmitry Chudinov defended his WBA 'interim' title with a three-round stoppage win over Mehdi Bouadla at the Open-Air Arena, Sevastopol, Crimea, Russia on 9 August, while Daniel Jacobs won the vacant WBA 'second tier' title when defeating Jarrod Fletcher (w rsc 5 at the Barclays Centre, Brooklyn, NYC, New York) on the same day.

When Golovkin knocked out an overweight Marco Antonio Rubio inside two rounds at the StubHub Centre, Carson, California on 18 October in a contest that was billed for the WBA title, he took over the latter's WBC 'interim' title at the same time.

8 October 2014. Jermain Taylor w pts 12 Sam Soliman.
Venue: Beau Rivage Resort & Casino, Biloxi, Mississippi, USA. **Recognition:** IBF. **Referee:** Bill Clancy.
Scorecards: 116-111, 115-109, 116-109.
Fight Summary: Having suffered a brain bleed at the hands of Arthur Abraham some five years ago, and at the age of 36, Taylor (159¾) wrested the title from the 40-year-old Soliman (160). Despite dropping rounds in the earlier stages, Taylor came back in the seventh to drop Soliman with what seemed to be a nothing jab and when he repeated the trick in the eighth it could be seen that the latter's left knee was injured. Clearly at a disadvantage, although the smaller Soliman was put down again in the ninth and 11th he managed to make it to the final bell in much pain.

The IBF stripped Taylor in February 2015 after it was reported that he had been ordered to undergo a mental health evaluation.

13 December 2014. Andy Lee w rsc 6 Matt Korobov.
Venue: The Cosmopolitan, Las Vegas, Nevada, USA. **Recognition:** WBO. **Referee:** Kenny Bayless.
Fight Summary: Following Peter Quillin's decision to hand in his belt, Lee (159¾) and Korobov (159½) came together to contest the vacant title in what was an all-southpaw battle. Having been outboxed for the opening five rounds even though he hurt Korobov in the fourth and fifth, Lee started to put the punches together with some venom in the sixth. With Korobov slowing appreciably Lee caught him with a terrific right hook, and after the latter hammered in punch after punch from both hands the referee stopped the contest at 1.10 of the session when the Russian was not fighting back.

21 February 2015. Gennady Golovkin w rsc 11 Martin Murray.
Venue: Room of Stars, Monte Carlo, Monaco. **Recognition:** WBA. **Referee:** Luis Pabon.
Fight Summary: While Murray (160) showed great courage he was ultimately no match for a champion who had both speed and power in his locker. As early as the fourth Murray was sent to his knees after taking a cracking right to the body before being put down again by a similar shot. Even though Murray fought back bravely and tried to take the fight to Golovkin (159) for several rounds he was being forced to take plenty in return. Having been dropped again by a heavy blow to the head in the tenth Murray somehow beat the count to make it into the 11th. However, 50 seconds into that session it was all over when Murray was rescued by the referee following a big right to the jaw that had left him reeling on the ropes. Golovkin's WBC 'interim' title was also on the line.

Chris Eubank Jnr stopped Dmitry Chudinov in the last round of their 12-round contest at the 02 Arena, Greenwich, London, England on 28 February to take over the latter's WBA 'interim' title.

Daniel Jacobs successfully defended his WBA 'second tier' title with a 12th-round stoppage win over Caleb Truax at the UIC Pavilion, Chicago, Illinois, USA on 24 April.

16 May 2015. Gennady Golovkin w rsc 6 Willie Monroe Jnr.
Venue: The Forum, Inglewood, California, USA. **Recognition:** WBA. **Referee:** Jack Reiss.
Fight Summary: Quickly working Monroe (160) out, Golovkin (159) had his southpaw challenger over in the second from a left hook to the side of the head before bashing him down again for a second count. Although fighting back as best he could, throwing blows to head and body Monroe surprised many by his fightback, but having survived several hard shots in the fifth his days were numbered when coming into the sixth. Banging in punch after punch the Russian finally sent Monroe to the boards again, and although the latter appeared to beat the count in the referee's eyes the official then called it off on the 45-second mark.

With Golovkin's WBC 'interim' title also on the line, even if Monroe had won he could not have claimed the title as he had failed to comply with WBC rules over the pre-fight weigh-ins.

On 1 August, at the Barclays Centre, Brooklyn, NYC, New York, USA, Daniel Jacobs stopped Sergio Mora inside two rounds in a successful defence of his WBA 'second tier' title.

Although the WBA allowed Chris Eubank Jnr's promoter to bill a fight against Tony Jeter on 24 October as a defence of his 'interim' title (w rsc 2 at the Sheffield Arena, England), they had already stripped him for inactivity in favour of Alfonso Blanco. Blanco had beaten Sergey Khomitsky (w pts 12 at the Polyhedron, Caracas, Venezuela on 10 October) in a contest that was also billed for the WBA 'interim' title.

6 June 2015. Miguel Cotto w rsc 4 Daniel Geale.
Venue: Barclays Centre, Brooklyn, NYC, New York, USA. **Recognition:** WBC/The Ring. **Referee:** Harvey Dock.
Fight Summary: With his two championship belts on the line against Geale (157), a former champion, it did not take too long for Cotto (153½) to add the Aussie to his list of victims. The opening three sessions saw both men looking for openings before Geale was shaken up by a straight right at the end of the third. Starting the fourth quickly after recognising that he had hurt Geale, Cotto soon had his challenger over from a heavy left. Just about beating the count, Geale was soon under the cosh. It was now obvious that the contest was nearly at an end, and

when Geale was floored by a right to the jaw the referee rescued him at 1.28 of the session even though he was on his feet.

20 June 2015. David Lemieux w pts 12 Hassan N'Dam N'Jikam.
Venue: Bell Centre, Montreal, Canada. **Recognition:** IBF. **Referee:** Marlon Wright.
Scorecards: 115-109, 115-109, 114-110.
Fight Summary: Contested for the title that was vacated when Jermain Taylor was stripped, Lemieux (160) provided proof of his early promise when outpointing a former champion in N'Dam N'Jikam (158½). Although it went the distance it was more down to N'Dam N'Jikam's toughness than anything else. Having been dropped by a left hook to the jaw in the second, put down twice in the fifth from heavy left hands and then a straight left counter in the seventh it was all over bar the shouting, but back came N'Dam N'Jikam with overarm rights that kept Lemieux on his toes for the rest of the contest.

17 October 2015. Gennady Golovkin w rsc 8 David Lemieux.
Venue: Madison Square Garden, Manhattan, NYC, New York, USA. **Recognition:** IBF/WBA. **Referee:** Steve Willis.
Fight Summary: Not afraid to test himself against the best it proved to be a step too far for Lemieux (159¾), the IBF champion, in his unification contest against the WBA's Golovkin (159½). In a battle of big punchers, Golovkin showed that he was the man with a plan as he held Lemieux up and unbalanced him with a solid jab right from the start. Having hurt Lemieux in the second with a left hook-right hand Golovkin merely bided his time, and in the fifth he found a left hook to the body to put the Canadian on one knee. Golovkin even hit Lemieux on the head and was lucky to get away with a caution, which was mainly due to the latter not making a meal of it. Although Lemieux staged a bit of a fightback in the sixth and seventh it was all over at 1.32 of the eighth when the referee rescued him after he had taken several heavy shots to head and body.

Golovkin also successfully defended his WBC 'interim' title in this one.

Daniel Jacobs stopped Peter Quillin inside a round at the Barclays Centre, Brooklyn, NYC, New York on 5 December to retain his WBA 'second tier' title.

21 November 2015. Saul Alvarez w pts 12 Miguel Cotto.
Venue: Mandalay Bay Hotel & Casino, Las Vegas, Nevada, USA. **Recognition:** WBC/The Ring. **Referee:** Robert Byrd.
Scorecards: 118-110, 119-109, 117-111.
Fight Summary: This one was billed for the vacant WBC title after Cotto (153½), also the holder of *The Ring* Championship Belt, refused to pay their sanctioning fee. The fight itself was much closer than the cards suggested, and although Alvarez (155) took both belts home the margin of victory appeared to flatter him. There were no knockdowns but it was a contest full of good action, the 35-year-old Cotto going with the jab and follow-up right and the two-handed Alvarez being just that bit busier. Freddie Roach, Cotto's trainer, said afterwards that he believed his man had won the fight when showing a sound defence and putting together plenty of good combinations.

19 December 2015. Billy Joe Saunders w pts 12 Andy Lee.
Venue: The Arena, Manchester, England. **Recognition:** WBO. **Referee:** Steve Gray.
Scorecards: 114-112, 115-111, 113-113.
Fight Summary: A battle between southpaws saw Lee (159¾) put his title on the line against a fellow traveller in Saunders (160), the former undefeated British, Commonwealth and European champion. Starting the sharper in what was a cagey beginning Saunders dropped Lee twice in the third from heavy right hooks when beating his man to the punch, but was never able to repeat the trick again. From thereon in Lee went back to his boxing, and although there were several bouts of hard hitting from both men the majority decision went to Saunders, who overall had been the busier of the pair.

23 April 2016. Gennady Golovkin w co 2 Dominic Wade.
Venue: Inglewood Forum, Los Angeles, California, USA. **Recognition:** IBF/WBA. **Referee:** Jack Reiss.

Fight Summary: Barely raising a sweat, the champion marched into Wade (159½) regardless of his height and reach advantages, and immediately prior to the bell to end the opening round had him over with a cracking right to the side of the head. Having beaten the count, Wade was eventually down again in the second after another right crashed into him. Getting to his feet just before the 'ten' was tolled and allowed to fight on, Wade was soon floored again after Golovkin (159) unleashed another big right. This time round Wade failed to beat the count, the finish being timed at 2.37 of the session.

Golovkin's WBC 'interim' title was also on the line in this bout.

On 9 September, Daniel Jacobs successfully defended his WBA 'second tier' belt when stopping Sergio Mora inside seven rounds at the Santander Arena, Reading, Pennsylvania, USA.

7 May 2016. Saul Alvarez w rsc 6 Amir Khan.
Venue: T-Mobile Arena, Las Vegas, Nevada, USA. **Recognition:** WBC/The Ring. **Referee:** Kenny Bayless.
Fight Summary: Stepping up two weight divisions from welter to middle to challenge Alvarez (155) for his two championship belts was just too much for Khan (155), who was eventually stopped at 2.37 of the sixth after putting on a stirring display. Taking the fight to Alvarez from the opening bell Khan took the opening two sessions with fast lefts and rights before moving out of range, and it was only in the fifth that the Mexican was able to catch up with his rival. Although Khan took a solid shot in the fifth, unfazed he was still going well in the sixth. That was until a right-hand counter sent him crashing, out to the world. Not bothering with the count the referee halted the fight immediately. It had been a gallant effort by Khan and was appreciated by all those who saw it.

When Alvarez relinquished the WBC title on 18 May, as he did not wish to be pushed around by the WBC, Gennady Golovkin, the 'interim' title holder, was appointed champion.

10 September 2016. Gennady Golovkin w rsc 5 Kell Brook.
Venue: O2 Arena, Greenwich, London, England. **Recognition:** IBF/WBA/WBC. **Referee:** Marlon Wright.
Fight Summary: Defending the full WBC title handed to him after Saul Alvarez sent back his belt along with his IBF crown, Golovkin (158¾) ultimately did what was expected of him. Moving up two weight divisions to meet the most feared puncher around the IBF welterweight champion gave it his best shot, taking the opening two sessions on the scorecards. However, by the third Golovkin was into his stride and a left hook brought about an angry swelling beneath Brook's right eye. Bravely hitting back but taking more punches at this stage, in the fifth Brook (159½) was really up against it as Golovkin unleashed punch after punch. Even when Brook's corner threw the towel in several more punches rained in prior to the referee closing matters on the 1.57 mark. Despite suffering a broken right eye socket and other lumps and bumps, Brook came out of the contest with his pride and reputation intact. The WBA did not sanction the bout as Brook was unrated, but had Golovkin lost the belt would almost certainly have been vacated.

Middleweight Boxers' Index:

(Country of birth where known/Domicile - birthplace and domicile are the same unless stated)

A

Arthur Abraham (Armenia/Germany)
Georgie Abrams (USA)
Osumanu Adama (Ghana/USA)
Young Ahearn (England/USA)
Arthur Akers (England)
Eromosele Albert (Nigeria/USA)
Kid Alberts (USA)
Josh Alexander (England)
Robert Allen (USA)
Charlie Allum (England)
Al Andrews (USA)
Anthony Andrews (Guyana)
Adrien Anneet (Belgium)
Vito Antuofermo (Italy/USA)
Fred Apostoli (USA)
Ignacio Ara (Spain)
Joey Archer (USA)
Henry Armstrong (USA)
Billy Arnold (USA)
Milt Aron (USA)
George Ashe (Russia/USA)
Evans Ashira (Kenya/Denmark)
Elvin Ayala (USA)

B

Doyle Baird (USA)
Al Baker (Belgium)
Harry Baker (USA 1892-1896)
Harry Baker (USA 1913-1921)
Alf Ball (England)
Johnny Banks (USA)
Gilbert Baptist (USA)
Brian Barbosa (USA)
Darren Barker (England)
Iran Barkley (USA)
Florrie Barnett (England)
Freeman Barr (Bahamas/USA)
Soldier Bartfield (Hungary/USA)
Carmen Barth (USA)
Charlie Bartlett (England)
Carmen Basilio (USA)
Jose Basora (Puerto Rico/USA)
Frank Battaglia (Canada)
Sam Baxter (England)
Lonnie Beasley (USA)
Jimmy Beau (USA)
Jimmy Beecham (USA)
Jay Bell (USA)

O'Neill Bell (USA)
Tommy Bell (USA)
Steve Belloise (USA)
Jimmy Belmont (USA)
Ben Bendoff (England)
Nigel Benn (England)
Leo Bens (USA)
George Benton (USA)
Nino Benvenuti (Slovenia/Italy)
Billy Berger (USA)
Swede Berglund (USA)
Georges Bernard (France)
Jupp Besselmann (Germany)
Monty Betham (Samoa/New Zealand)
Tom Bethea (USA)
Fabio Bettini (Italy/France)
Ed Binney (USA)
Whitey Black (USA)
Bandsman Blake (England)
Sam Blakelock (England)
Alfonso Blanco (Venezuela/USA)
Arthur Bobbett (England)
Tom Bogs (Denmark)
Nate Bolden (USA)
Jack Bonner (USA)
Eddie Booker (USA)
Joe Borrell (USA)
Mario Bosisio (Italy)
Mehdi Bouadla (France)
Jean-Claude Bouttier (France)
Alf Bowman (England)
Bobby Boyd (USA)
Lonnie Bradley (USA)
Pat Bradley (Ireland/USA)
Willie KO Brennan (USA)
Henry Brimm (Puerto Rico/USA)
Bennie Briscoe (USA)
Kenny Bristol (Guyana/USA)
Jack Britton (USA)
Seaman Fred Broadbent (England)
Jem Brock (England)
Kell Brook (England)
Bill Brooks (England)
Boy Brooks (Philippines)
Lou Brouillard (Canada/USA)
Ben Brown (USA)
Billy Brown (USA)
George KO Brown (Greece/USA)
Hamilton Johnny Brown (Scotland)

Peter Brown (Ireland/England)
Simon Brown (Jamaica/USA)
William Brown (England)
Jack Bryan (England)
Ted Bryant (England)
Jim Burchill (England)
Ted Burchill (England)
Dick Burge (England)
Jack Burke (Ireland/England)
Jackie Burke (USA)
Sailor Burke (USA)
Charley Burley (USA)
Alec Burns (England)
Hugh Burns (England)
Tommy Burns (Canada)
Young Johnny Burns (USA)
Max Bursak (Ukraine)
Joe Butler (USA)
George Byers (Canada/USA)

C

Norberto Cabrera (Argentina)
Rory Calhoun (USA)
Andy Callahan (USA)
Mark Cameron (South Africa)
Carmelo Candel (Algeria/France)
Tony Caponi (USA)
Frank Carbone (USA)
Agostino Cardamone (Italy)
Georges Carpentier (France)
Mariano Carrera (Argentina)
Jim Carroll (England/USA)
Joe Carter (USA)
Kid Carter (USA)
Rubin Carter (USA)
Walter Cartier (USA)
George Cashley (England)
Bobby Cassidy (USA)
Rocky Castellani (USA)
Javier Castillejo (Spain)
Jorge Castro (Argentina)
Marcel Cerdan (Algeria/France)
Robert Charron (France)
Jack Chase (USA)
Clyde Chastain (USA)
Julio Cesar Chavez Jnr (Mexico)
Bill Cheese (England)
Hacine Cherifi (France)
Nero Chink (USA)
George Chip (USA)
Joe Chip (USA)
Jose Chirino (Argentina/USA)
Henry Chmielewski (Poland/USA)

Joe Choynski (USA)
Steve Choynski (USA)
George Chrisp (England)
George Christian (USA)
Gus Christie (USA)
Dmitry Chudinov (Russia)
Larry Cisneros (USA)
Jimmy Clabby (USA)
Grant Clark (USA)
Jackie Clark (USA)
Willie Classen (USA)
Angel Clivilles (Puerto Rico)
Freddie Cochrane (USA)
Walter Coffey (USA)
Nessim Max Cohen (Morocco/France)
Johnny Colan (USA)
Mike Colbert (USA)
Nate Collins (USA)
Ron Collins (USA)
Steve Collins (Ireland)
Pat Condon (England)
Billy Conn (USA)
Bartley Connolly (USA)
Eddie Connolly (Canada)
Doc Conrad (USA)
John Conteh (England)
Arthur Cooper (England)
George Cooper (USA)
Young Corbett III (Italy/USA)
James J. Corbett (USA)
Bill Corcoran (England)
Jonathan Corn (USA)
Hugo Corro (Argentina)
Hugo Corti (Argentina)
Jack Costello (England)
Alex Costica (Romania/USA)
George Costner (USA)
Miguel Cotto (Puerto Rico)
Charley Cotton (USA)
Andrew Council (USA)
George Courtney (USA)
Jim Courtney (England)
Frank Craig (USA)
Mike Crawley (England)
Dan Creedon (New Zealand/Australia)
Arthur Cripps (Australia)
Buck Crouse (USA)
Harry Croxon (England)
Donald Curry (USA)

D

Arthur Daley (England)
Pat Daly (Ireland/England)

Tommy Danforth (USA)
Carl Daniels (USA)
Les Darcy (Australia)
Sailor Darden (USA)
Troy Darrell (Bermuda/USA)
Jackie Darthard (USA)
Laurent Dauthuille (France)
Al Bummy Davis (USA)
Bombardier Davis (England)
Charley Davis (England)
Dwight Davison (USA)
Jan De Bruin (Netherlands)
Oscar De La Hoya (USA)
Rene De Vos (Belgium)
Joey DeJohn (USA)
Jack Delaney (Canada/USA)
Cyrille Delannoit (Belgium)
Francesco Dell'Aquila (Italy)
Emanuele Della Rosa (Italy)
Sailor Demarest (USA)
Al DeMaris (USA)
Joe DeMaris (USA)
Sebastien Demers (Canada)
Nonpareil Jack Dempsey (Ireland/USA)
Jack Denning (USA)
James Desverney (USA)
Chick Devlin (Scotland/USA)
Doug DeWitt (USA)
Pascal Di Benedetto (Tunisia/France)
Al Diamond (USA)
Anthony Diamond (England)
Elio Diaz (Venezuela)
Gil Diaz (Puerto Rico/USA)
Jack Dillon (USA)
Joe DiMartino (USA)
Assane Diouf (Guinea/France)
Bill Doherty (Australia)
Jack Donoghue (England)
Billy Donovan (USA)
Matt Donovan (Trinidad/USA)
Mike Donovan (USA)
Terry Downes (England)
Anthony Downey (USA)
Bryan Downey (USA)
Harry Downie (Scotland/Australia)
Jimmy Doyle (USA)
Sid Doyle (England)
Buster Drayton (USA)
Jerry Driscoll (England)
George Duke (USA)
Vince Dundee (Italy/USA)
Juan Carlos Duran (Argentina/Italy)
Roberto Duran (Panama)

Ernie Durando (USA)
Fred Dyer (Wales)
Tom Dyer (England)
Young Dyer (England)
Serhiy Dzinziruk (Russia/Germany)

E
Howard Eastman (Guyana/England)
Harry Ebbets (USA)
Antwun Echols (USA)
Jimmy Edgar (USA)
Australian Billy Edwards (Australia/England)
Joe Egan (USA)
Sailor Einert (Germany/USA)
Wayne Elcock (England)
Andy Elms (England)
Miguel Angel Espino (USA)
Larry Estridge (St Kitts/USA)
Chris Eubank Jnr (England)
Chris Eubank (England)
Wiley Evans (USA)

F
Frank Farmer (USA)
Ted Fenton (England)
Florentino Fernandez (Cuba/USA)
Albert Finch (England)
Kevin Finnegan (England)
Henry Firpo (USA)
Tony Fisher (USA)
Young Fisher (USA)
Bob Fitzsimmons (England/USA)
Del Flanagan (USA)
Frank Fletcher (USA)
Jarrod Fletcher (Australia)
Tiger Flowers (USA)
Jack Fogarty (USA)
Vincent Forgione (Italy/USA)
Billy Fox (USA)
Steve Frank (Guyana/USA)
Bruno Frattini (Italy)
Makoto Fuchigami (Japan)
Don Fullmer (USA)
Gene Fullmer (USA)

G
Andras Galfi (Hungary)
Dario Galindez (Argentina)
Reddy Gallagher (USA)
Allentown Joe Gans (USA)
Italian Joe Gans (USA)
Panama Joe Gans (Barbados/Panama)
Ceferino Garcia (Philippines/USA)

Julio Garcia (Cuba/USA)
George Gardner (Ireland/USA)
Jimmy Gardner (Ireland/USA)
Leo Gates (USA)
Kid Gavilan (Cuba)
Daniel Geale (Australia)
Marcos Geraldo (Mexico)
Khoren Gevor (Armenia/Germany)
Ching Ghook (England)
Joey Giambra (USA)
Joey Giardello (USA)
Alex Gibbons (Virgin Islands/USA)
Mike Gibbons (USA)
Gennady Golovkin (Kazakhstan/USA)
Jo Gonzales (France)
Noe Tulio Gonzalez Alcoba (Uruguay/Argentina)
Jose Gonzalez (Puerto Rico/USA)
Bill Chesterfield Goode (England)
Jem Goode (England)
Jim Goodwin (England)
Joe Gorman (USA)
Johnny Gorman (USA)
Herol Graham (England)
Sailor Grande (Italy/USA)
Otis Grant (Jamaica/Canada)
Rocky Graziano (USA)
Wilf Greaves (Canada)
Harry Greb (USA)
George Green (USA)
Harold Green (USA)
James Green (USA)
Julio Cesar Green (Dominican Republic/USA)
Plantagenet Green (Barbados/England)
Fred Greenbank (England)
Alf Greenfield (England)
Randy Griffin (USA)
Billy Griffith (USA)
Emile Griffith (Virgin Islands/USA)
Young Griffiths (England)
Fernando Guerrero (Dominican Republic/USA)
Roy Gumbs (St Kitts/England)
Walter Gunn (England)
George Gunther (Australia/USA)

H

Marvin Hagler (USA)
Jim Haines (England)
Gene Hairston (USA)
Morrade Hakkar (France)
Jim Hall (Australia)
Loucif Hamani (Algeria/France)
Mustafa Hamsho (Syria/USA)
Jimmy Handler (Russia/USA)

Jack Hannibal (USA)
Vic Hansen (USA)
Bill Harnetty (England)
Denny Harrington (Ireland/England)
Tim Harrington (Ireland/England)
Lonnie Harris (USA)
Ronnie Harris (USA)
Sergeant Tom Harris (England)
Wayne Harris (Guyana/Canada)
Jack Harrison (England)
Jack Hart (Middleweight)
Len Harvey (England)
George Haskell (England)
Vince Hawkins (England)
Norman Hayes (USA)
Stanley Hayward (USA)
Ronald Hearns (USA)
Thomas Hearns (USA)
Gerhard Hecht (Germany)
Bill Heffernan (Scotland/South Africa)
Jorge Heiland (Argentina)
Tilly Herman (USA)
Art Hernandez (USA)
Jack Herrick (Hungary/USA)
Carl Hertz (USA)
Jack Hickey (Ireland/England)
Freddie Hicks (USA)
Jack Hicks (England)
Matthew Hilton (Canada)
Irving Hines (USA)
Billy Hirsch (USA)
Keith Holmes (USA)
Lindell Holmes (USA)
Jack Hood (England)
George Hope (England)
Bernard Hopkins (USA)
Sonny Horne (USA)
Al Hostak (USA)
Leo Houck (USA)
Jimmy Howard (USA)
Johnny Howard (USA)
Kid Hoy (USA)
Naotaka Hozumi (Japan)
Ace Hudkins (USA)
Cecil Hudson (USA)
Gustave Humery (France)
Charles Humez (France)
Bill Husbands (England)

I

Kingsley Ikeke (Nigeria/USA)
Alex Ireland (Scotland)
Nobuhiro Ishida (Japan)

J

John David Jackson (USA)
Julian Jackson (Virgin Islands/USA)
Young Jackson (USA)
Young Peter Jackson (USA)
Daniel Jacobs (USA)
Angelo Jacopucci (Italy)
KO Jaffe (USA)
Vilda Jaks (Czech Republic)
William Bo James (USA)
Jim Janey (USA)
Tony Janiro (USA)
Kofi Jantuah (Ghana/USA)
Ben Jeby (USA)
Ham Jenkins (USA)
Andrew Jeptha (South Africa/England)
Tony Jeter (USA)
Charley Johnson (USA)
Glen Johnson (Jamaica/USA)
Jack Johnson (USA)
Reggie Johnson (USA)
Bobby Jones (USA
Gorilla Jones (USA)
Guillermo Jones (Panama)
Major Jones (USA)
Ralph Tiger Jones (USA)
Roy Jones (USA)
Watson Jones (USA)
William Joppy (USA)
Charley Joseph (USA)

K

Sumbu Kalambay (DR Congo/Italy)
Ayub Kalule (Uganda/Denmark)
Russell Kane (USA)
Phil Kaplan (USA)
Roman Karmazin (Russia/USA)
Johnny Karr (USA)
Fay Keiser (USA)
Hugo Kelly (Italy/USA)
Jim Kendrick (Ireland/England)
Bill Kennedy (England)
Jackie Keough (USA)
Stanley Ketchel (USA)
Jim Keyes (USA)
Amir Khan (England)
Sergey Khomitsky (Ukraine/Belarus)
Avtandil Khurtsidze (Georgia/USA)
Alabama Kid (USA)
Cocoa Kid (Puerto Rico/USA)
Dixie Kid (USA)
Jamaica Kid (Belize/USA)
Zulu Kid (USA)

James Kinchen (USA)
Mick King (Australia)
Jack Kingsland (England)
Frank Klaus (USA)
Karl-Heinz Klein (Germany)
Johnny Klesch (USA)
Charlie Knock (England)
George Kochan (USA)
Lukas Konecny (Czech Republic)
Matt Korobov (Russia/USA)
Omar Kouidri (Algeria/France)
Armand Krajnc (Sweden)
Billy Kramer (USA)
Lucien Krawczyk (Poland/France)
Solly Krieger (USA)
Phil Krug (USA)
Dave Kurtz (USA)

L

George LaBlanche (Canada)
Jackie LaBua (USA)
Jack Lalor (Ireland/South Africa)
Jake LaMotta (USA)
Tom Lancaster (England)
Sam Langford (Canada/USA)
Walcott Langford (USA)
Willie Langford (USA)
Young Sam Langford (USA)
Pierre Langlois (France)
Steve Latzo (Austria/USA)
Walter Laurette (Lithuania/USA)
Eduardo Lausse (Argentina)
Paddy Lavin (Ireland/USA)
Gary Leach (USA)
Andy Lee (England)
Caveman Lee (USA)
Don Lee (USA)
Glen Lee (USA)
Tom Lees (Australia)
David Lemieux (Canada)
Sugar Ray Leonard (USA)
Jimmy Lester (USA)
Battling Levinsky (USA)
Harry Lewis (USA)
Ted Kid Lewis (England)
Willie Lewis (USA)
Joe Libby (USA)
Tony Licata (USA)
Joe Lipsey (USA)
Happy Littleton (USA)
Tait Littman (USA)
Cleto Locatelli (Switzerland/Italy)
Gary Lockett (Wales)

Frank Logan (Philippines/USA)
Leo Lomski (USA)
Tom Longer (England)
Giovanni Lorenzo (Dominican Republic/USA)
Tommy Loughran (USA)
David Love (USA)
Mike Lucie (USA)
Sammy Luftspring (Canada)
Billy Lyell (USA)
Bert Lytell (USA)

M

Javier Maciel (Argentina)
Marvin Mack (USA)
Matthew Macklin (England)
Jack Madden (England)
Tommy Madden (USA)
Frankie Maguire (USA)
Young Mahoney (USA)
Elijah Makathini (South Africa)
Jock Malone (USA)
Steve Mamakos (USA)
Giovanni Manca (Italy)
Peter Manfredo (USA)
Percy Manning (USA)
Frank Mantell (Germany/USA)
Kid Marcel (Algeria/France)
Carlos Marks (Trinidad)
Raul Marquez (Mexico/USA)
Lloyd Marshall (USA)
Rudy Marshall (USA)
Tito Marshall (Panama)
Harris Martin (USA)
Jack Martin (England)
Silent Martin (USA)
Tony Martin (USA)
Jimmy Martinez (USA)
Sergio Martinez (Argentina/USA)
Gennady Martirosyan (Armenia/Russia)
Jacques Marty (France)
Tony Marullo (USA)
Maselino Masoe (Samoa/New Zealand)
Jack Massey (England)
Allen Matthews (USA)
Jason Matthews (England)
Joey Maxim (USA)
Pat McAteer (England)
Mike McCallum (Jamaica/USA)
Jack McCarron (USA)
Billy McCarthy (England/Australia)
Gerald McClellan (USA)
William McClellan (USA)
Blink McCloskey (USA)

Scotty McConnell (Scotland)
Al McCoy (USA)
Charles Kid McCoy (USA)
Young Kid McCoy (USA)
Robert McCracken (England)
Ray McElroy (USA)
Packey McFarland (USA)
Jack McFarlane (England)
Hugh McGann (USA)
Eddie McGoorty (USA)
Charlie McKeever (USA)
Bill McKinnon (Canada)
Jack McVey (USA)
Pete Mead (USA)
Tom Meadows (England/Australia)
Juan Ramon Medina (Dominican Republic/Spain)
David Mendez (Mexico)
Ramon Mendez (Argentina)
Segundo Mercado (Ecuador/USA)
Doug Miller (South Africa)
Tommy Milligan (Scotland)
Dennis Milton (USA)
Holly Mims USA)
Aldo Minelli (Italy)
Alan Minter (England)
Dionisio Miranda (Colombia/USA)
Edison Miranda (Colombia/Puerto Rico)
Alf Mitchell (England)
Charlie Mitchell (England)
Young Mitchell (USA)
Tiberio Mitri (Italy)
Jack Moffat (USA)
Bob Moha (USA)
Walter Monaghan (USA)
Willie Monroe Jnr (USA)
Willie Monroe (USA)
Carlos Monzon (Argentina)
Archie Moore (USA)
Dick Moore (Ireland/USA)
Ted Moore (England)
Sergio Mora (USA)
Marcel Moreau (France)
Howard Morrow (USA)
Rocky Mosley Jnr (USA)
Denny Moyer (USA)
Peter Mueller (Germany)
John Mugabi (Uganda/USA)
Bat Mullins (England)
Anthony Mundine (Australia)
Tony Mundine (Australia)
Stockyards Tommy Murphy (USA)
Billy Murray (USA)
Martin Murray (England)

Chisanda Mutti (Zambia/Germany)

N

Hassan N'Dam N'Jikam (Cameroon/France)
Jose Napoles (Cuba/Mexico)
Ted Napper (England)
Charley Nashert (USA)
Bill Natty (England)
Jorge Navarro (Venezuela)
Pablo Navascues (Spain)
Ismael Negron (Puerto Rico/USA)
Al Neill (USA)
Ted Nelson (England)
Harry Neumier (England)
George Nichols (USA)
Patrick Nielsen (Denmark)
Juan Camilo Novoa (Colombia/USA)
Milton Nunez (Colombia)
Michael Nunn (USA)

O

Dick O'Brien (Canada/USA)
Frankie O'Brien (USA)
John O'Brien (England)
Philadelphia Jack O'Brien (USA)
Mike O'Dowd (USA)
Jimmy O'Hagan (USA)
Pat O'Keefe (England)
Tim O'Neil (USA)
Ted O'Neill (England)
Darren Obah (Australia)
Fulgencio Obelmejias (Venezuela)
Michael Olajide (England/Canada)
Carl Bobo Olson (Hawaii)
Mahir Oral (Germany)
Kassim Ouma (Uganda/USA)
Ken Overlin (USA)
Eddie Owens (USA)

P

Bobby Pacho (USA)
Eddie Palmer (USA)
Jack Palmer (England)
Garth Panter (USA)
Billy Papke (USA)
Laszlo Papp (Hungary)
Benny Kid Paret (Cuba/USA)
Curtis Parker (USA)
Lamar Parks (USA)
Kelly Pavlik (USA)
George Pearsall (USA)
Paul Pender (USA)
Harry Peppers (USA)

Dave Peters (England)
Sailor Ed Petroskey (USA)
Oddone Piazza (Italy/USA)
Jim Picton (England)
Tom Picton (England)
Dmitry Pirog (Russia)
Paul Pirrone (USA)
Jamie Pittman (Australia)
Joe Platford (England)
Dido Plumb (England)
Yolande Pompey (Trinidad/England)
Ted Pritchard (Wales/England)
Grzegorz Proksa (Poland)
Paddy Purtell (Canada/USA)
Chris Pyatt (England)

Q

Peter Quillin (USA)

R

Anton Raadik (Estonia/USA)
Abdulla Ramadan (Sudan/Canada)
Alex Ramos (USA)
Jimmy Ramos (Belize/USA)
Harry Ramsey (USA)
Eddie Ran (Latvia/USA)
Oscar Rankins (USA)
Augie Ratner (USA)
Johnny Reagan (USA)
Mickey Rees (England)
Jimmy Reeves (USA)
Frank Reiche (Germany)
Jonathan Reid (USA)
Ryan Rhodes (England)
Ted Rich (England)
Jim Richardson (Australia 1893-1903)
Jim Richardson (Hawaii/England 1889-1901)
Joe Rindone (USA)
Babe Risko (USA)
Neal Rivers (USA)
Laverne Roach (USA)
Paolo Roberto (Sweden)
Alec Roberts (England)
Dick Roberts (England)
George Roberts (England)
George Robinson (USA)
Johnny Robinson (England)
Sugar Ray Robinson (USA)
William Robinson (England)
Rudy Robles (USA)
Luis Rodriguez (CUBA/USA)
Al Rogers (USA)
Alf Rogers (England)

Raul Rojas (Cuba)
Juan Domingo Roldan (Argentina)
Edward Starlight Rollins (Guyana/Australia)
Vicente Rondon (Venezuela)
George Rooke (Ireland/USA)
Jack Root (Czech Republic/USA)
Gabriel Rosado (USA)
Dave Rosenberg (USA)
Hugh Ross (USA)
Young Al Ross (Canada)
Navy Rostan (Austria/USA)
Gustave Roth (Belgium)
Len Rowlands (USA)
Marco Antonio Rubio (Mexico)
Rito Ruvalcaba (Mexico)
Australian Jim Ryan (Australia)
Tommy Ryan (USA)

S
Bob Sage (USA)
Lee Sala (USA)
Dave Sands (Australia)
Randy Sandy (USA)
Koji Sato (Japan)
Billy Joe Saunders (England)
Milo Savage (USA)
George Say (England)
Bert Schenk (Germany)
Morrie Schlaifer (USA)
Charley Scott (USA)
Felix Scott (Bahamas/England)
Fraser Scott (USA)
Wilford Scypion (USA)
Sugar Ray Seales (Virgin Islands/USA)
Erich Seelig (Poland/USA)
Andres Antonio Selpa (Argentina)
Ernesto Sena (Argentina)
Marty Servo (USA)
Dave Shade (USA)
Reuben Shank (USA)
Joe Shaw (USA)
Johnny Shea (USA)
William Sherriff (England)
Dan Sherry (Canada)
Tony Sibson (England)
Harry Simon (Namibia)
Lajuan Simon (USA)
Robbie Sims (USA)
Bill Singleton (England)
Jimmy Slattery (USA)
Sammy Slaughter (USA)
Georgie Small (USA)
Australian Billy Smith (Australia)

Dave Smith (New Zealand/Australia)
Ed Smith (USA)
Harry Smith (Jamaica/USA)
James Tiger Smith (Wales)
Jeff Smith (USA)
Jimmy Smith (USA)
Mysterious Billy Smith (Canada/USA)
Randy Smith (USA)
Tom Smith (England)
Sam Soliman (Australia)
Ki-Yun Song (South Africa)
Billy Soose (USA)
Domenico Spada (Italy)
Cory Spinks (USA)
Bill Springhall (England)
Marlon Starling (USA)
Freddie Steele (USA)
Curtis Stevens (USA)
Jem Stewart (Scotland)
Ossie Stewart (USA)
Solomon Stewart (USA)
Jean Stock (France)
Gary Stretch (England)
Hans Stretz (Germany)
Felix Sturm (Germany)
Jim Styles (England)
Alf Suffolk (England)
Jack Twin Sullivan (USA)
Jim Sullivan (England)
Mike Twin Sullivan (USA)
Sebastian Sylvester (Germany)
Franz Szuzina (Germany)

T
Shinji Takehara (Japan)
Nilson Julio Tapia (Colombia/Slovakia)
Morris Tasco (USA)
Frank Tate (USA)
Thomas Tate (USA)
Frank Taylor (USA)
Jermain Taylor (USA)
Quincy Taylor (USA)
Shannan Taylor (Australia)
Larry Temple (USA)
Edouard Tenet (France)
Young Terry (USA)
Al Thiel (USA)
Marcel Thil (France)
Battling Thomas (USA)
Joe Thomas (USA)
Tiger Thomas (USA)
Tom Thomas (Wales)
Cyclone Johnny Thompson (USA)

Lachie Thomson (Scotland)
Joe Thorley (England)
Geoff Thorne (England)
Dave Tiberi (USA)
Dick Tiger (Nigeria)
Joe Tinsley (Canada/USA)
James Toney (USA)
Gratien Tonna (Tunisia/France)
Jose Torres (Puerto Rico)
Felix Trinidad (Puerto Rico)
Caleb Truax (USA)
Kid Tunero (Cuba)
Saverio Turiello (Italy)
Charles Turner (USA)
Earl Turner (USA)
Gil Turner (USA)
Dick Turpin (England)
Randy Turpin (England)

V

Paul Vaden (USA)
Rodrigo Valdez (Colombia)
Luc Van Dam (Netherlands)
Syd Vanderpool (Canada)
Jack Varley (England)
Ruben Varon (Spain)
Chico Varona (Cuba)
Willie Vaughn (USA)
Hector Velazco (Argentina)
Peter Venancio (Brazil)
Ernie Vigh (USA)
Robert Villemain (France)
Luis Vinales (USA)

W

Dominic Wade (USA)
Dick Wagner (USA)
Emmett Kid Wagner (USA)
Joe Walcott (Guyana/USA)
Mickey Walker (USA)
Willie Walker (USA)
Young Johnny Walker (England)
Toff Wall (England)
Jean Walzack (France)
Jean Wanes (France)
Moses Ward (USA)
Willie Warren (USA)
Michael Watson (England)

Bobby Watts (USA)
Jimmy Watts (USA)
Spider Webb (USA)
Coley Welch (USA)
Jack Welland (England)
Bermondsey Billy Wells (England)
Joe Welsh (USA)
Tommy West (Wales/USA)
Joe White (Canada/Wales)
Ted White (England)
Vearl Whitehead (USA)
Ted Whyman (England)
Howard Wiggam (USA)
Charley Doc Williams (USA)
Christy Williams (USA)
Ed Williams (Australia)
Holman Williams (USA)
Jim Williams (Wales/USA)
John Williams (USA)
Lew Williams (USA)
Paul Williams (USA)
Tiger Roy Williams (USA)
Fred Wilmott (England)
California Jackie Wilson (USA)
Charlie Wilson (England)
George Wilson (England)
Johnny Wilson (USA)
Tug Wilson (England)
Glenn Wolfe (USA)
Richie Woodhall (England)
Tom Woodley (England)
Walter Woods (USA)
Felix Wouters (Belgium)
Oliver Wright (USA)
Ronald Wright (USA)

Y

Teddy Yarosz (USA)
Tommy Yarosz (USA)
Alec Young (England)
Paddy Young (USA)

Z

Tony Zale (USA)
Sebastian Zbik (Germany)
Fritzie Zivic (USA)
Jack Zivic (USA)

Printed in Great Britain
by Amazon